PENGUIN REFERENCE

The Penguin Pocket School Dictionary

George Davidson is a former senior editor with Chambers Harrap. In addition to writing dictionaries and thesauruses, he is the author of several books on English grammar, usage, spelling and vocabulary. He lives in Edinburgh.

THE PENGUIN POCKET SCHOOL DICTIONARY

Edited by George Davidson

PENGUIN BOOKS

PENGUIN BOOKS

Published by the Penguin Group
Penguin Books Ltd, 80 Strand, London WC2R 0RL, England
Penguin Group (USA) Inc., 375 Hudson Street, New York, New York 10014, USA
Penguin Group (Canada), 90 Eglinton Avenue East, Suite 700, Toronto, Ontario, Canada M4P 2Y3
(a division of Pearson Penguin Canada Inc.)
Penguin Ireland, 25 St Stephen's Green, Dublin 2, Ireland (a division of Penguin Books Ltd)
Penguin Group (Australia), 250 Camberwell Road, Camberwell, Victoria 3124, Australia
(a division of Pearson Australia Group Pty Ltd)
Penguin Books India Pvt Ltd, 11 Community Centre, Panchsheel Park, New Delhi – 110 017, India
Penguin Group (NZ), cnr Airborne and Rosedale Roads, Albany, Auckland 1310, New Zealand
(a division of Pearson New Zealand Ltd)
Penguin Books (South Africa) (Pty) Ltd, 24 Sturdee Avenue, Rosebank 2196, South Africa

Penguin Books Ltd, Registered Offices: 80 Strand, London WC2R 0RL, England

www.penguin.com

First published 2005
1

Copyright © Penguin Books, 2005
All rights reserved

The moral right of the author has been asserted

Set in 6.5/8 pt Stone Serif
Typeset by Rowland Phototypesetting Ltd, Bury St Edmunds, Suffolk
Printed in England by Clays Ltd, St Ives plc

Except in the United States of America, this book is sold subject
to the condition that it shall not, by way of trade or otherwise, be lent,
re-sold, hired out, or otherwise circulated without the publisher's
prior consent in any form of binding or cover other than that in
which it is published and without a similar condition including this
condition being imposed on the subsequent purchaser

ISBN-13: 978-0-141-02328-1
ISBN-10: 0-141-02328-7

Contents

Acknowledgements vii

Layout of Dictionary Entries viii

The Penguin Pocket School Dictionary 1

Prefixes and Suffixes 771

Nationalities and Languages 777

Acknowledgements

PUBLISHING DIRECTOR
Nigel Wilcockson

EDITORIAL MANAGERS
Sophie Lazar, Ellie Smith

EDITOR
George Davidson

LEXICOGRAPHERS
Stephen Curtis, Alice Grandison,
Ginny Klein, Howard Sargeant

PROOFREADERS
Sandra Anderson, Stephen Curtis,
Alice Grandison

Layout of Dictionary Entries

The display below shows the main features of the dictionary entries.

headwords .... **abashed** *adjective* ashamed or embarrassed.

parts of speech .... **aboard** *preposition and adverb* on or onto a ship, aircraft, train, or vehicle.

abrasive *adjective* **1** having a rough surface used for grinding or smoothing. **2** rude or unpleasant. ~ *noun* (*plural* **abrasives**) an abrasive substance, such as sandpaper.

definitions .... **abrupt** *adjective* **1** occurring without warning; unexpected: *an abrupt change of plan.* **2** rather impolite and unfriendly: *I thought you were a bit abrupt with her.*

pronunciations .... **abstemious** /ab stee mi us/ *adjective* not
(see the notes below) allowing yourself much food, drink, or enjoyment.

inflections .... **abyss** /a bis/ *noun* (*plural* **abysses**) a
(see the notes below) very deep hole or chasm.

accost *verb* (**accosts, accosting, accosted**) to approach and speak to somebody.

airy *adjective* (**airier, airiest**) **1** spacious and full of fresh air. **2** showing lack of concern.

alternative forms or pronunciations ..... **alphabetical** *or* **alphabetic** *adjective* in
(see the notes below) the order of the letters of the alphabet.

alto /al toh *or* awl toh/ *noun* (*plural* **altos**) **1** a woman with a singing voice lower than that of a soprano. **2** a man with a singing voice higher than that of a tenor.

amoeba /a mee ba/ *noun* (*plural* **amoebas** *or* **amoebae** /a mee bee/) *Science* a single-celled organism that can change its shape.

amok *or* **amuck** ✳ **run amok** *or* **run amuck** to act wildly or be completely out of control.

as if/though in such a way that it

	Layout of Dictionary Entries
	suggested that: *It looked as if it might rain at any moment.*
examples of usage	**assure** *verb* (**assures, assuring, assured**) **1** to inform somebody that something is definitely true: *I want to assure you that your complaint will be taken seriously.*
subject, usage, and geographical labels (see the notes below)	**atoll** *noun* (*plural* **atolls**) *Geography* a coral reef surrounding a lagoon.
	atrocious *adjective* **1** extremely wicked or cruel. **2** *informal* very horrible or bad.
	attorney *noun* (*plural* **attorneys**) **1** a person who has legal authority to act for another person. **2** *N American* a lawyer.
constructions	**authority** *noun* (*plural* **authorities**) **1** the power to issue orders and expect obedience. **2** (**the authorities**) the government or law-enforcers.
	bad *adjective* (**worse, worst**) **1** poor or not acceptable in quality. **2** evil or immoral. **3** naughty or disobedient. **4** (**bad at**) unskilful or incompetent. **5** (**bad for**) harmful.
	bask *verb* (**basks, basking, basked**) **1** to lie and enjoy warmth or sunshine. **2** (**bask in**) to enjoy favour or approval.
phrases and idioms	**bat**¹ *noun* (*plural* **bats**) a specially shaped piece of wood that you hit the ball with in sports such as baseball and cricket. ~ *verb* (**bats, batting, batted**) **1** to hit a ball with a bat. **2** to take your turn to bat in sport. ✳ **off your own bat** through your own ideas and efforts.
	bated ✳ **with bated breath** in quiet nervous excitement.
derivatives (see the notes below)	**bathe** /bay*th*/ *verb* (**bathes, bathing, bathed**) **1** to go swimming. **2** to wash something gently with water or another liquid. **3** (**be bathed in**) to be filled or covered pleasantly with light. ~ *noun* (*plural* **bathes**) a swim. ▶ **bather** *noun*, **bathing** *noun*.
cross-references	**baulk** *verb* see BALK.
usage notes	*Usage Note* **between you and me**. Like other prepositions, *between* is

Layout of Dictionary Entries | x

word histories ....

> followed by the object form of the personal pronoun, not the subject form: *We divided it between us* (not *between we*). It is incorrect to say *between you and I*; the grammatically correct form is *between you and me*.
> **Word History** *Bikinis* are named after *Bikini*, an atoll in the Pacific Ocean, where atomic bombs were tested by the USA in 1946. The designer of the bikini felt that it would have an equally big impact.

Pronunciations

Pronunciations are given only where there might be uncertainty about the correct pronunciation of a word.

Pronunciations are printed between slashes: **abacus** /a ba kus/.

Syllables are separated by thin spaces, as in the example above, and the syllable with the strongest stress is printed in bold type.

The following symbols are used in the pronunciations:

Vowels

a	as in	bat	i	as in	lip
ah	as in	calm, barn	ie	as in	time, rhyme
air	as in	hair, tear	ier	as in	fire
aw	as in	law, corn	o	as in	lot
ay	as in	hay, make	oh	as in	bone, toast
e	as in	bell	oi	as in	point
ee	as in	meet, team	oo	as in	look
eer	as in	deer, near	ooh	as in	moon, chute
er	as in	her, fur	oor	as in	poor, more
ew	as in	stew, due	ow	as in	cow, round
ewr	as in	pure	u	as in	mud, ton

Consonants

b	as in	bad	k	as in	kit, can
ch	as in	chop	l	as in	long
d	as in	do	m	as in	map
f	as in	fig	n	as in	not
g	as in	green	ng	as in	singer
h	as in	hop	ngg	as in	finger
j	as in	jump	ngk	as in	stink

p	as in	pat	th	as in	that
r	as in	rose	v	as in	van
s	as in	sad, city	w	as in	wish
sh	as in	shape	y	as in	yard
t	as in	tank	z	as in	zap
th	as in	thick	zh	as in	treasure

Inflections

Inflections are given for all nouns and verbs. Where the past tense and the past participle of a verb have the same form (for example *he **walked*** and *he has **walked***), then only one form is given in the verb inflections:

walk *verb* (**walks, walking, walked**)

Where the past tense and past participle are not the same (for example, *he swam* and *he has **swum***), both forms are given:

swim *verb* (**swims, swimming, swam, swum**)

For adjectives and adverbs, inflections are shown only in cases where there is some change to the basic form when a word-ending is added; for example:

bad *adjective* (**worse, worst**)
easy *adjective* (**easier, easiest**)
feeble *adjective* (**feebler, feeblest**)
mad *adjective* (**madder, maddest**)

Where the endings *-er* and *-est* endings are simply added to the basic form of the adjective or adverb (for example *fast, faster, fastest*), no inflections are given.

Alternative forms or pronunciations

Alternative forms are generally shown with 'or':

take into account *or* **take account of** to consider something along with other factors

However, when the variation involves only one word of a phrase, the variant forms are separated by a slash:

become/get accustomed to (= **become accustomed to** *or* **get accustomed to**.)

Subject, usage, and geographical labels

The subject labels used in this dictionary are:
Art, Drama, English, Geography, History, ICT (= information and communication technology), *Maths, Music, Science*

Layout of Dictionary Entries

The usage labels used are:
> *formal, informal, literary, derogatory, offensive, humorous, dated, archaic, dialect*

The geographical labels used are:
> *Australian, N American* (= North American), *N English* (= Northern English), *New Zealand, Scottish*

Trademarks are labelled *trademark*.

When a label applies to one definition, it stands at the beginning of that definition:

> **buff** *noun* (*plural* **buffs**) **1** a pale yellowish brown colour. **2** *informal* somebody who knows a lot about a particular subject.

When a label applies to all the following definitions, it comes before the first definition number:

> **chuck¹** *verb* (**chucks, chucking, chucked**) *informal* **1** to throw something casually. **2** to get rid of something.

a or **an** *adjective* **1** known as the *indefinite article* and used before a noun to refer to one person or thing that has not been mentioned before: *Take a card, any card.* **2** every; per: *twice a day.*

aardvark /ahd vahk/ *noun* (*plural* **aardvarks**) an African animal that has a long tongue and large ears and feeds on ants and termites.

aback ∗ **be taken aback** to be surprised or shocked.

abacus /a ba kus/ *noun* (*plural* **abacuses**) a frame containing horizontal rods with beads on them, used for doing calculations.

abandon *verb* (**abandons, abandoning, abandoned**) **1** to give something up completely: *I abandoned my attempt to talk to her.* **2** to leave or desert somebody or something for some time or forever: *They abandoned the car by the side of the road.* ∗ **with (gay) abandon** in a totally carefree and uninhibited way. ➤ **abandonment** *noun*.

abase *verb* (**abases, abasing, abased**) ∗ **abase yourself** to behave very humbly: *She refused to abase herself and beg for forgiveness.*

abashed *adjective* ashamed or embarrassed.

abate *verb* (**abates, abating, abated**) to become less intense or widespread. ➤ **abatement** *noun*.

abattoir /a ba twah/ *noun* (*plural* **abattoirs**) a place where animals are killed for meat.

abbey *noun* (*plural* **abbeys**) **1** a monastery. **2** a church that was once part of a monastery.

abbot *noun* (*plural* **abbots**) a senior monk in charge of an abbey.

abbreviate *verb* (**abbreviates, abbreviating, abbreviated**) to make a word or phrase shorter.

abbreviation *noun* (*plural* **abbreviations**) a shortened form of a written word or phrase.

abdicate *verb* (**abdicates, abdicating, abdicated**) to give up the throne. ➤ **abdication** *noun*.

abdomen /ab doh min/ *noun* (*plural* **abdomens**) **1** the front part of the body between the chest and the pelvis, containing the stomach, liver, and intestines. **2** the rear part of the body of an insect. ➤ **abdominal** *adjective*.

abduct *verb* (**abducts, abducting, abducted**) to carry somebody off secretly or by force. ➤ **abduction** *noun*, **abductor** *noun*.

aberration *noun* (*plural* **aberrations**) an abnormal action or occurrence.

abet *verb* (**abets, abetting, abetted**) to help somebody to do wrong.

abeyance /a bay ans/ ∗ **in abeyance** temporarily not being used.

abhor *verb* (**abhors, abhorring, abhorred**) *formal* to hate somebody or something intensely. ➤ **abhorrence** *noun*.

abhorrent *adjective formal* very wicked; disgusting.

abide

abide *verb* (**abides, abiding, abided**) (**abide by**) to comply with a rule or decision. ✱ **cannot abide** cannot bear somebody or something.

ability *noun* (*plural* **abilities**) 1 the power to do something. 2 competence or skill.

abject *adjective* 1 wretched or miserable: *abject poverty*. 2 very humble: *an abject apology*. ➤ **abjectly** *adverb*.

ablaze *adjective and adverb* burning strongly.

able *adjective* (**abler, ablest**) 1 (**able to**) having the power, skill, or means to do something. 2 skilful or competent: *our ablest students*. ➤ **ably** *adverb*.

abnormal *adjective* not normal or average. ➤ **abnormality** *noun*, **abnormally** *adverb*.

aboard *preposition and adverb* on or onto a ship, aircraft, train, or vehicle.

abode *noun* (*plural* **abodes**) *formal* a home or residence: *of no fixed abode*.

abolish *verb* (**abolishes, abolishing, abolished**) to put an end to a custom or institution. ➤ **abolition** *noun*.

abominable *adjective* 1 disgusting or hateful. 2 *informal* disagreeable or unpleasant. ➤ **abominably** *adverb*.

Abominable Snowman *noun* (*plural* **Abominable Snowmen**) the yeti, a large hairy animal that looks similar to a human being, said to exist high in the Himalayas.

aboriginal /a bo ri ji nl/ *adjective* growing or living in a place from the earliest times. ~ *noun* (**Aboriginal**) (*plural* **Aboriginals**) an Aborigine.

Aborigine /a bo ri ji nee/ *noun* (*plural* **Aborigines**) a member of the people who have lived in Australia from the earliest times.

abort *verb* (**aborts, aborting, aborted**) 1 to remove an unborn child from its mother's womb. 2 to end an activity before the planned time because of a fault or failure.

abortion *noun* (*plural* **abortions**) 1 an operation to end a woman's pregnancy early by removing the unborn child from her womb. 2 *formal* a miscarriage.

abortive *adjective* unsuccessful.

abound *verb* (**abounds, abounding, abounded**) 1 to exist in large numbers or in great quantity. 2 (**abound in/with**) to have a large number or amount of something: *The area abounds in sites of historical interest*.

about *preposition and adverb* 1 with regard to or concerning something. 2 approximately. 3 in different parts of something: *scattered about the room*. 4 nearby: *I'm sure it's about here somewhere*. ✱ **about to** just going to do something: *I was about to sit down when I heard a knock at the door*.

above *preposition and adverb* 1 at a higher level than somebody or something. 2 more than something. 3 superior in rank to somebody. ✱ **above all** especially. **above board** honest or legal.

abrasion *noun* (*plural* **abrasions**) 1 a process of wearing or rubbing away. 2 an area of scraped skin.

abrasive *adjective* 1 having a rough surface used for grinding or smoothing. 2 rude or unpleasant. ~ *noun* (*plural* **abrasives**) an abrasive substance, such as sandpaper.

abreast *adjective and adverb* side by side and facing in the same direction: *riding three abreast*. ✱ **abreast of** up to date with trends or developments.

abridge *verb* (**abridges, abridging, abridged**) to shorten a book or other piece of writing. ➤ **abridgment** *or* **abridgement** *noun*.

abroad *adverb and adjective* in or to a foreign country.

abrupt *adjective* 1 occurring without

warning; unexpected: *an abrupt change of plan.* **2** rather impolite and unfriendly: *I thought you were a bit abrupt with her.* ➤ **abruptly** *adverb*, **abruptness** *noun*.

abscess *noun* (*plural* **abscesses**) a sore swelling filled with pus.

abscond *verb* (**absconds, absconding, absconded**) to leave secretly or hurriedly to avoid discovery or arrest.

abseil /ab sayl/ *verb* (**abseils, abseiling, abseiled**) to slide down a vertical surface on a rope secured at the top and wound round your body. ➤ **abseiling** *noun*.

absent /ab sint/ *adjective* **1** not present or attending. **2** not existing. ~ /ab sent/ *verb* (**absents, absenting, absented**) ✻ **absent yourself** to stay away. ➤ **absence** *noun*.

absentee *noun* (*plural* **absentees**) somebody who is absent. ➤ **absenteeism** *noun*.

absentminded *adjective* forgetful or inattentive because you are thinking of other things. ➤ **absentmindedly** *adverb*, **absentmindedness** *noun*.

absolute *adjective* **1** complete: *absolute nonsense.* **2** unlimited: *absolute power.* ➤ **absolutely** *adverb*.

absolution *noun* the forgiveness of sins by a priest.

absolve *verb* (**absolves, absolving, absolved**) **1** to set somebody free from an obligation or guilt. **2** to forgive a sin or sinner.

absorb *verb* (**absorbs, absorbing, absorbed**) **1** to take in a liquid or gas. **2** to learn information. **3** to make something part of an existing whole. ➤ **absorption** *noun*.

absorbent *adjective* able to absorb a liquid or gas. ➤ **absorbency** *noun*.

absorbing *adjective* very interesting; taking up all your attention.

abstain *verb* (**abstains, abstaining, abstained**) **1** to choose not to vote.

2 (**abstain from**) to choose not to do, eat, or drink something. ➤ **abstainer** *noun*, **abstention** *noun*.

abstemious /ab stee mi us/ *adjective* not allowing yourself much food, drink, or enjoyment.

abstinence *noun* making a deliberate choice not to do something enjoyable, especially not to drink alcohol. ➤ **abstinent** *adjective*.

abstract /ab strakt/ *adjective* **1** to do with theory rather than practice. **2** *Art* said about art: not representing objects or people. ~ *noun* (*plural* **abstracts**) a summary of the main points of a piece of writing. ~ /ab strakt/ *verb* (**abstracts, abstracting, abstracted**) to remove or extract something. ➤ **abstraction** *noun*.

abstracted *adjective* preoccupied or absentminded; thinking so much about one thing that you ignore or are not aware of other things.

absurd *adjective* completely ridiculous or unreasonable. ➤ **absurdity** *noun*, **absurdly** *adverb*.

abundance *noun* a very large amount.

abundant *adjective* occurring in very large amounts. ➤ **abundantly** *adverb*.

abuse /a bewz/ *verb* (**abuses, abusing, abused**) **1** to put something to a wrong or improper use: *to abuse somebody's hospitality.* **2** to insult somebody. **3** to harm or injure somebody by wrong or cruel treatment: *She had been abused as a child.* ~ /a bews/ *noun* (*plural* **abuses**) **1** improper use or treatment; misuse. **2** insults. **3** wrong or cruel treatment of a person: *child abuse.* ➤ **abuser** *noun*.

abusive *adjective* insulting: *abusive language.* ➤ **abusively** *adverb*.

abut *verb* (**abuts, abutting, abutted**) said about an area: to touch another area along a boundary.

abysmal /a biz ml/ *adjective* extremely

bad: *The play was absolutely abysmal.* ➤ **abysmally** *adverb.*

abyss /ə bis/ *noun* (*plural* **abysses**) a very deep hole or chasm.

AC *abbreviation* **1** *Science* alternating current. **2** air conditioning.

acacia /ə kay shə/ *noun* (*plural* **acacias**) a tree or shrub with white or yellow flowers.

academic *adjective* **1** to do with education at school or university. **2** of no practical relevance or real importance: *Whether they stole it or just borrowed it without permission is academic.* ~ *noun* (*plural* **academics**) a teacher or research worker at a college or university. ➤ **academically** *adverb.*

academy *noun* (*plural* **academies**) **1** a college in which special subjects or skills are taught. **2** a society of learned people organized to promote the arts or sciences.

Word History *Academy* comes from the Greek word *Akademeia*, the name of the school in Athens where the philosopher Plato taught his pupils.

accede *verb* (**accedes, acceding, acceded**) (**accede to**) to give your consent to something: *to accede to a request.* ∗ **accede to the throne** to become king or queen.

accelerate *verb* (**accelerates, accelerating, accelerated**) **1** to move faster. **2** to increase the speed of a vehicle. ➤ **acceleration** *noun.*

accelerator *noun* (*plural* **accelerators**) **1** a pedal in a motor vehicle that controls the speed of the engine. **2** *Science* a substance that speeds up a chemical reaction.

accent /ak sint/ *noun* **1** a particular way of pronouncing words: *an Irish accent.* **2** emphasis given to one particular syllable in a word. **3** a mark written above a letter to show how it should be pronounced. ~ /ak sent/ *verb* (**accents,** **accenting, accented**) to stress a vowel, syllable, or word.

accentuate /ak sen tew ayt/ *verb* (**accentuates, accentuating, accentuated**) to emphasize something. ➤ **accentuation** *noun.*

accept *verb* (**accepts, accepting, accepted**) **1** to agree to receive something offered: *to accept an award.* **2** to regard something as unavoidable or normal and not to try to change it: *to accept the situation.* **3** to recognize something as true: *I accept that they didn't mean any harm.* ➤ **acceptance** *noun.*

acceptable *adjective* good enough to be accepted. ➤ **acceptability** *noun,* **acceptably** *adverb.*

access *noun* **1** the right to go into a place or to look at something. **2** a way of getting into a place. ~ *verb* (**accesses, accessing, accessed**) to find and look at data stored on a computer.

accessible *adjective* **1** said about a place: capable of being reached or gone into. **2** in a form that can be easily understood: *Can we make the text more accessible to younger readers?* ➤ **accessibility** *noun.*

accession *noun* (*plural* **accessions**) **1** the act of becoming king or queen. **2** an item added to a library or museum.

accessory *noun* (*plural* **accessories**) **1** something extra that makes a thing more useful or attractive. **2** a person who helps somebody to commit a crime without taking part in the crime itself.

accident *noun* (*plural* **accidents**) an unpleasant or harmful event that occurs by chance. ∗ **by accident** unexpectedly and without being planned.

accidental *adjective* happening unexpectedly or by chance. ➤ **accidentally** *adverb.*

acclaim *verb* (**acclaims, acclaiming, acclaimed**) to applaud or praise somebody or something. ~ *noun* public praise or approval.

acclimatize *or* **acclimatise** *verb* (**acclimatizes, acclimatizing, acclimatized** *or* **acclimatises**, etc) to adapt to a new climate or situation. ➤ **acclimatization** *or* **acclimatisation** *noun*.

accolade *noun* (*plural* **accolades**) an award, title, or description intended to honour somebody.

accommodate *verb* (**accommodates, accommodating, accommodated**) **1** to have enough room for somebody or something. **2** to provide somebody with lodgings. **3** to do something helpful as a favour to somebody: *We always try to accommodate our customers.*

accommodating *adjective* helpful or obliging.

accommodation *noun* (*plural* **accommodations**) **1** a building or space in which somebody may live or work. **2** an arrangement or agreement that resolves differences or solves problems: *Employers are obliged to make accommodations for disabled workers.*

accompaniment /a kum pa ni mint/ *noun* (*plural* **accompaniments**) *Music* the backing music for a singer or solo player.

accompany /a kum pa ni/ *verb* (**accompanies, accompanying, accompanied**) **1** to go with somebody as their escort or companion. **2** *Music* to perform an accompaniment for a singer or musician. **3** to be present along with something else: *a bright flash accompanied by a loud bang.*

accomplice /a kum plis/ *noun* (*plural* **accomplices**) somebody who helps another person to commit a crime.

accomplish /a kum plish/ *verb* (**accomplishes, accomplishing, accomplished**) to complete a task successfully.

accomplished /a kum plisht/ *adjective* skilled: *an accomplished pianist.*

accomplishment /a kum plish mint/ *noun* (*plural* **accomplishments**) **1** the successful completion of something. **2** an achievement or ability.

accord *verb* (**accords, according, accorded**) **1** *formal* to grant something. **2** (**accord with**) to be consistent with: *This does not accord with what you said earlier.* ~ *noun* (*plural* **accords**) a treaty or agreement. * **of your own accord** on your own initiative; without being forced or asked by somebody else.

accordance * **in accordance with** doing what is asked for in instructions, etc: *in accordance with your request.*

according * **according to 1** in a way that corresponds to something: *graded according to quality.* **2** if you believe what somebody or something says: *According to Janet, the party's next Thursday.*

accordingly *adverb* **1** in an appropriate way or in the way that is to be expected: *They felt insulted and reacted accordingly.* **2** consequently.

accordion *noun* (*plural* **accordions**) a musical instrument played by squeezing the sides together and pressing keys or buttons. ➤ **accordionist** *noun*.

accost *verb* (**accosts, accosting, accosted**) to approach and speak to somebody.

account *noun* (*plural* **accounts**) **1** a description of facts or events: *Her account of the incident differs substantially from yours.* **2** a record of money received and spent: *I've been keeping an account of how much we've spent.* **3** an arrangement for keeping money in a bank or for buying goods on credit: *a savings account.* ~ *verb* (**accounts, accounting, accounted**) * **account for 1** to give a reason for:

accountable

Can you account for your absence on that day? **2** to be the explanation for: *That accounts for his absence last Monday.* **on account of** because of. **on no account** *or* **not on any account** under no circumstances: *On no account forget to turn off the gas.* **take into account** *or* **take account of** to consider something along with other factors: *We have taken into account your age and previous good behaviour.*

accountable *adjective* responsible; answerable. ➤ **accountability** *noun*.

accountant *noun* (*plural* **accountants**) a person who keeps financial accounts for a living. ➤ **accountancy** *noun*.

accoutrements /a **koo** tri mints/ *plural noun* additional items of equipment or dress.

accrue *verb* (**accrues, accruing, accrued**) **1** to increase in amount over a period of time. **2** to collect or accumulate something.

accumulate *verb* (**accumulates, accumulating, accumulated**) **1** to bring things together gradually to form a large amount or collection. **2** to increase gradually in quantity or number. ➤ **accumulation** *noun*.

accumulator *noun* (*plural* **accumulators**) a rechargeable electric battery.

accurate *adjective* **1** correct; free from mistakes. **2** reaching the intended target. ➤ **accuracy** *noun*, **accurately** *adverb*.

accusation *noun* (*plural* **accusations**) a statement saying that somebody has committed a crime or done wrong.

accuse *verb* (**accuses, accusing, accused**) to charge somebody with a fault or crime: *Are you accusing me of robbing my own children?* ➤ **accuser** *noun*.

accustom *verb* (**accustoms, accustoming, accustomed**) to make somebody or yourself used to something through experience. * **become/get accustomed to** to get used to doing

something: *I soon got accustomed to being woken at six o'clock.*

ace *noun* (*plural* **aces**) **1** a playing card marked with one spot. **2** a service in tennis that an opponent cannot return. **3** *informal* an expert or leading performer. ~ *adjective informal* excellent.

acerbic /a **ser** bik/ *adjective* speaking in an unfriendly or critical way.

ache /ayk/ *verb* (**aches, aching, ached**) to feel dull persistent pain. ~ *noun* (*plural* **aches**) a dull persistent pain.

achieve *verb* (**achieves, achieving, achieved**) to succeed in obtaining, reaching, or winning something that you want by effort: *She achieved her aim of getting to university.* ➤ **achievable** *adjective*, **achiever** *noun*.

achievement *noun* (*plural* **achievements**) something you deserve to be praised for doing.

acid *adjective* **1** sour or sharp to the taste. **2** unfriendly or uncomplimentary. ~ *noun* (*plural* **acids**) **1** *Science* a chemical compound that contains hydrogen and turns litmus paper red. **2** *informal* the drug LSD. ~ *adjective Science* having the properties of an acid: *an acid carbonate*. ➤ **acidic** *adjective*, **acidity** *noun*.

acid rain *noun Science* rain containing high levels of acid caused by pollution from burning fossil fuels.

acknowledge *verb* (**acknowledges, acknowledging, acknowledged**) **1** to admit that something is true or valid. **2** to express gratitude or appreciation for something: *Her contribution to the success of the project was never acknowledged.* **3** to confirm that you have received a letter. ➤ **acknowledgment** *or* **acknowledgement** *noun*.

acne *noun* a skin disorder characterized by red pimples.

acorn *noun* (*plural* **acorns**) the nut of

the oak tree, which is oval and has a cuplike base.

acoustic /a **kooh** stik/ *adjective* **1** to do with sound or the sense of hearing. **2** said about a musical instrument: having sound produced naturally, not electronically: *an acoustic guitar*. ➤ **acoustically** *adverb*.

acoustics *plural noun* the qualities of a room that enable sound to be heard clearly in it.

acquaint *verb* (**acquaints, acquainting, acquainted**) to make somebody familiar with something. ✶ **be acquainted with** to know somebody slightly, or to know a certain amount about a subject.

acquaintance *noun* (*plural* **acquaintances**) somebody you know slightly.

acquire *verb* (**acquires, acquiring, acquired**) to get or gain something.

acquisition *noun* (*plural* **acquisitions**) something or somebody that you have acquired.

acquisitive *adjective* fond of acquiring possessions.

acquit *verb* (**acquits, acquitting, acquitted**) to declare that somebody is not guilty of an offence. ✶ **acquit yourself well** to perform well in a difficult situation. ➤ **acquittal** *noun*.

acre *noun* (*plural* **acres**) a unit of area equal to 4840 square yards (about 4047 square metres).

acrid *adjective* unpleasantly bitter in taste or smell.

acrimonious /a kri **moh** ni us/ *adjective* characterized by personal hostility or bitterness. ➤ **acrimoniously** *adverb*.

acrobat *noun* (*plural* **acrobats**) an entertainer who performs gymnastic feats. ➤ **acrobatic** *adjective*, **acrobatically** *adverb*.

acronym /a **kroh** nim/ *noun* (*plural* **acronyms**) a word formed from the initial letters of other words, such as *Aids* from *acquired immune deficiency syndrome*.

across *adverb and preposition* **1** from one side to the other. **2** to or on the opposite side.

acrylic /a **kri** lik/ *noun* (*plural* **acrylics**) **1** *Art* a type of thick paint used in art. **2** a type of artificial fibre used in textiles.

act *noun* (*plural* **acts**) **1** a thing done, or the process of doing something. **2** a law passed by a parliament. **3** *Drama* a division of a play or opera. **4** a performance, for example by a comedian or acrobat, forming part of a show. **5** a pretence: *She's not really upset; it's just an act.* ~ *verb* (**acts, acting, acted**) **1** to take action; to do something: *The government must act quickly or the situation will get worse.* **2** to behave in a particular way: *Just act naturally.* **3** *Drama* to play a role in a play or film. **4** (**act as**) to have the function or do the job of: *Would you mind acting as my assistant?*

action *noun* (*plural* **actions**) **1** something somebody does; an act. **2** activity intended to achieve something: *We need action, not promises.* **3** combat or a battle. **4** a lawsuit: *to bring an action for libel.* ✶ **out of action** not working or functioning. **take action** to do something.

activate *verb* (**activates, activating, activated**) to cause something to start operating. ➤ **activation** *noun*.

active *adjective* **1** moving about, working, or operating. **2** characterized by energetic participation and involvement: *an active member of the society*. **3** *English* said about a verb: having as its subject the person or thing doing the action, for example 'he' in *He hit the ball*. **4** said about a volcano: liable to erupt. ➤ **actively** *adverb*.

activist *noun* (*plural* **activists**) a person who advocates vigorous social or political action. ➤ **activism** *noun*.

activity *noun* (*plural* **activities**) **1** a state in which things are happening or being done. **2** a pastime or occupation in which a person takes part: *after-school activities*.

actor *noun* (*plural* **actors**) **1** *Drama* a person who takes part in a play or film. **2** a participant in an event or situation.

actress *noun* (*plural* **actresses**) *Drama* a female actor.

actual *adjective* existing or happening in fact.

actually *adverb* really; in fact.

actuate *verb* (**actuates, actuating, actuated**) *formal* to make a device or machine operate.

acumen /a kew min/ *noun* intelligence or shrewdness.

acupuncture *noun* a type of medical treatment in which needles are inserted into parts of the body to cure disease or relieve pain. ➤ **acupuncturist** *noun*.

acute *adjective* **1** intelligent and shrewd. **2** said about a feeling or pain: strong: *acute anxiety*. **3** said about something bad: very serious: *an acute shortage of supplies*. **4** *Maths* said about an angle: measuring less than 90°. ➤ **acutely** *adverb*, **acuteness** *noun*.

acute accent *noun* (*plural* **acute accents**) a mark (´) placed over certain vowels in some languages to show how the vowels are to be pronounced, as in *cliché*.

AD *abbreviation* = (Latin) *anno Domini*, used to indicate that a date comes within the Christian era.

Usage Note **AD** and **BC**. *AD* is written before a number signifying a year, whereas *BC* is written after the number: *AD 1625; 440 BC*. Both *AD* and *BC* are written after the word 'century': *the third century AD; the seventh century BC*.

ad *noun* (*plural* **ads**) *informal* an advertisement.

adamant *adjective* refusing to change your mind. ➤ **adamantly** *adverb*.

Adam's apple *noun* (*plural* **Adam's apples**) the projection in the front of the neck, which is more prominent in men.

adapt *verb* (**adapts, adapting, adapted**) **1** to make something usable for a different purpose: *I adapted the machine so that it would run off batteries*. **2** to change to fit a new situation: *How have you adapted to your new surroundings?* ➤ **adaptability** *noun*, **adaptable** *adjective*, **adaptation** *noun*.

adapter or **adaptor** *noun* (*plural* **adapters** or **adaptors**) **1** a device for connecting two pieces of apparatus that were not intended to be joined. **2** a device for connecting several pieces of electrical equipment to a single power point.

add *verb* (**adds, adding, added**) **1** to put something with something else so as to increase or improve it: *Add some sugar to improve the taste.* **2** to say or write something else: *'And,' he added, 'it was all my own work.'* ∗ **add up 1** *Maths* to put numbers together to make a total, or to come to a total. **2** *informal* to make sense.

adder *noun* (*plural* **adders**) a poisonous snake with a dark zigzag pattern along its back.

addict /a dikt/ *noun* (*plural* **addicts**) somebody who cannot stop taking a drug. ~ /a dikt/ *verb* (**addicts, addicting, addicted**) ∗ **be addicted to** to be unable to stop taking something or doing something. ➤ **addiction** *noun*, **addictive** *adjective*.

addition *noun* (*plural* **additions**) **1** *Maths* the process of adding. **2** something or somebody added. ∗ **in addition** also; as well.

additional *adjective* added or extra. ➤ **additionally** *adverb*.

additive *noun* (*plural* **additives**) a

substance added to something in small amounts, such as a flavouring for food.

address *noun* (*plural* **addresses**) **1** a set of words and numbers showing where a person lives or a building is situated. **2** a speech delivered to an audience. ~ *verb* (**addresses, addressing, addressed**) **1** to write an address on a letter or package. **2** to speak or write directly to somebody. ➤ **addressee** *noun*.

adept *adjective* highly skilled or proficient.

adequate *adjective* sufficient or acceptable. ➤ **adequacy** *noun*, **adequately** *adverb*.

adhere *verb* (**adheres, adhering, adhered**) to stick to something.

adherent *noun* (*plural* **adherents**) a supporter of a leader or cause.

adhesive *adjective* sticky. ~ *noun* (*plural* **adhesives**) a substance that sticks things together; glue.

adjacent *adjective* near or next to something, or to one another.

adjective *noun* (*plural* **adjectives**) *English* a word that describes a person or thing, such as the words 'thin' and 'green' in the phrase *a thin green stalk*. ➤ **adjectival** *adjective*.

adjourn *verb* (**adjourns, adjourning, adjourned**) **1** to stop a meeting temporarily, intending to start it again at a later time. **2** to move to another place. ➤ **adjournment** *noun*.

adjudicate *verb* (**adjudicates, adjudicating, adjudicated**) to act as judge in a competition. ➤ **adjudication** *noun*, **adjudicator** *noun*.

adjust *verb* (**adjusts, adjusting, adjusted**) **1** to change or move something slightly so that it looks or works better or differently: *I adjusted the timer to make the heating come on earlier.* **2** to adapt yourself to new conditions: *It may take him a little time to adjust.* ➤ **adjustable** *adjective*, **adjustment** *noun*.

ad-lib *adjective* spoken or performed without preparation. ~ *verb* (**ad-libs, ad-libbing, ad-libbed**) *Drama* to say something that has not been prepared or rehearsed; to improvise. ~ *noun* (*plural* **ad-libs**) *Drama* an improvised speech, line, or performance.

administer *verb* (**administers, administering, administered**) **1** to manage or supervise something. **2** to give a medicine or punishment to somebody.

administration *noun* (*plural* **administrations**) **1** the work of running a business or country. **2** a government in power.

admirable /ad mi ra bl/ *adjective* deserving praise and respect; excellent. ➤ **admirably** *adverb*.

admiral *noun* (*plural* **admirals**) **1** the commander-in-chief of a fleet or navy. **2** a senior officer in the Royal Navy or US Navy.

admire *verb* (**admires, admiring, admired**) to think something or somebody is very good. ➤ **admiration** *noun*, **admirer** *noun*.

admissible *adjective* acceptable or permissible, especially in a law court: *admissible evidence*.

admission *noun* (*plural* **admissions**) **1** a confession that a fact or allegation is true. **2** the right to enter a place or join a group: *There's a small charge for admission.*

admit *verb* (**admits, admitting, admitted**) **1** to confess that something is true or valid: *I admit that I may have made a mistake.* **2** to allow somebody to enter a place or join a group. **3** to take somebody into a hospital for treatment.

admittance *noun* permission to enter a place.

admonish *verb* (**admonishes, admonishing, admonished**) to reprimand or

adolescent

warn somebody gently. ➤ **admonition** noun.

adolescent adjective in or to do with the period of life between childhood and adulthood. ~ noun (plural **adolescents**) an adolescent person. ➤ **adolescence** noun.

adopt verb (**adopts, adopting, adopted**) 1 to become the legal parent of somebody else's child. 2 to take something over or begin to use it. ➤ **adoption** noun.

adorable adjective lovable or charming. ➤ **adorably** adverb.

adore verb (**adores, adoring, adored**) to admire or love somebody or something greatly. ➤ **adoration** noun.

adorn verb (**adorns, adorning, adorned**) to decorate something with ornaments. ➤ **adornment** noun.

adrenalin or **adrenaline** /ə dre na lin/ noun a hormone that is produced by the body in response to stress or excitement and that increases your heart rate and energy levels.

adrift adverb and adjective 1 said about a boat: drifting without power or steering. 2 unfastened or unstuck: *The label's come adrift.*

adroit adjective clever or skilful. ➤ **adroitly** adverb.

adulation noun exaggerated love or admiration for somebody or something.

adult adjective old enough to be fully developed and mature. ~ noun (plural **adults**) an adult person. ➤ **adulthood** noun.

adultery noun sexual intercourse between a married person and somebody who is not their wife or husband. ➤ **adulterer** noun, **adulterous** adjective.

advance verb (**advances, advancing, advanced**) 1 to move forward in position or time. 2 to give money to somebody ahead of time or as a loan. ~ noun (plural **advances**) 1 a forward movement. 2 a development that shows that progress is being made. 3 money given ahead of time or as a loan. ~ adjective made, sent, or provided ahead of time. ✱ **in advance** before something happens.

advanced adjective more complex or developed.

advantage noun (plural **advantages**) 1 a favourable or helpful factor. 2 in tennis, the first point won after deuce. ✱ **take advantage of** 1 to use something to help you. 2 to exploit somebody.

advantageous /ad van tay jus/ adjective giving an advantage; favourable.

Advent noun 1 the period from the fourth Sunday before Christmas to Christmas itself. 2 (**advent**) a coming into existence; an arrival.

adventure noun (plural **adventures**) an exciting or remarkable experience. ➤ **adventurer** noun.

adventurous adjective prepared to take risks or try new experiences. ➤ **adventurously** adverb.

adverb noun (plural **adverbs**) *English* a word that goes with a verb, an adjective, or another adverb, and tells you when, where, how, or how much, such as the words 'very' and 'quickly' in *It all happened very quickly*. ➤ **adverbial** adjective.

adversary noun (plural **adversaries**) an enemy or opponent.

adverse adjective unfavourable or harmful. ➤ **adversely** adverb.

adversity noun (plural **adversities**) suffering or hardship.

advert noun (plural **adverts**) *informal* an advertisement.

advertise verb (**advertises, advertising, advertised**) 1 to try to increase sales of a product or service by saying how good it is. 2 to announce something publicly.

affirm

3 (advertise for) to try to find somebody to take a job: *The shop is advertising for an assistant manager.*
➤ **advertiser** *noun.*

advertisement /ad ver tis mint/ *noun* (*plural* **advertisements**) something published or broadcast to advertise a product or service.

advice *noun* guidance about what you should do.

advisable *adjective* sensible in the circumstances: *It's advisable to keep your money out of sight.* ➤ **advisability** *noun.*

advise *verb* (**advises, advising, advised**) **1** to give advice to somebody. **2** to recommend something. **3** *formal* to inform somebody.
➤ **adviser** *noun.*

advocate /ad voh kat/ *noun* (*plural* **advocates**) **1** somebody who openly supports a cause or proposal. **2** a lawyer representing somebody in court, especially in Scotland. ~ /ad voh kayt/ *verb* (**advocates, advocating, advocated**) to recommend a course of action.

aerate *verb* (**aerates, aerating, aerated**) to make a drink fizzy.

aerial *adjective* **1** occurring in the air or atmosphere. **2** involving aircraft. ~ *noun* (*plural* **aerials**) a metal rod designed to transmit or receive radio or television signals.

aerobatics *noun* the performance of stunts in an aircraft. ➤ **aerobatic** *adjective.*

aerobics *noun* a system of physical exercises designed to improve the heart and lungs. ➤ **aerobic** *adjective.*

aerodrome *noun* (*plural* **aerodromes**) a small airport.

aerodynamic *adjective* designed to move easily through the air.

aeroplane *noun* (*plural* **aeroplanes**) a powered aircraft with fixed wings.

aerosol *noun* (*plural* **aerosols**) a pressurized container that sprays out a liquid in fine drops.

aerospace *adjective Science* to do with flight in the earth's atmosphere and in space.

aesthetic /ees the tik/ *adjective* to do with beauty or the appreciation of beauty. ➤ **aesthetically** *adverb.*

afar *adverb* to or at a great distance.

affable *adjective* pleasant and friendly.
➤ **affability** *noun,* **affably** *adverb.*

affair *noun* (*plural* **affairs**) **1** an event or occasion. **2** (**affairs**) commercial or public business. **3** a sexual relationship between people who are not married to one another. **4** a matter causing controversy or scandal.

affect *verb* (**affects, affecting, affected**) **1** to have an effect on something or somebody. **2** to act as if you had a particular feeling or attitude: *to affect indifference.*

Usage Note **affect** *or* **effect**? Affect is a verb that means 'to influence or change': *How will this affect my chances of going to university?* Effect is usually a noun: *What effect will this have on my chances of going to university?*

---

affectation *noun* (*plural* **affectations**) an insincere or pretended display of a quality or feeling.

affected *adjective* insincere or pretentious. ➤ **affectedly** *adverb.*

affection *noun* fondness or liking.

affectionate *adjective* showing affection. ➤ **affectionately** *adverb.*

affiliate *verb* (**affiliates, affiliating, affiliated**) to make an organization a member or branch of another organization. ➤ **affiliation** *noun.*

affinity *noun* (*plural* **affinities**) **1** a natural liking for somebody or something. **2** a resemblance between related things.

affirm *verb* (**affirms, affirming,**

affirmative

affirmed) to state something positively. ➤ **affirmation** *noun*.

affirmative *adjective* stating that something is true or correct; meaning 'yes'. * **in the affirmative** saying 'yes'.

afflict *verb* (**afflicts, afflicting, afflicted**) 1 to distress somebody severely. 2 to cause serious trouble to somebody or something. ➤ **affliction** *noun*.

affluent *adjective* wealthy. ➤ **affluence** *noun*.

afford *verb* (**affords, affording, afforded**) 1 to have enough money or time for something. 2 to be able to do something without serious harm: *We can't afford to ignore the danger.* ➤ **affordable** *adjective*.

affront *noun* (*plural* **affronts**) an insult. ~ *verb* (**affronts, affronting, affronted**) to insult or offend somebody.

afield *adverb* away or at a distance.

aflame *adjective and adverb* on fire.

afloat *adjective and adverb* floating on water.

afoot *adverb and adjective* happening or about to happen.

afraid *adjective* filled with fear. * **I'm afraid that** I'm sorry to say that something is the case.

afresh *adverb* again or differently.

African *adjective* from or to do with Africa. ~ *noun* (*plural* **Africans**) a person from Africa.

Afrikaans /a fri kahns/ *noun* a language that developed from Dutch, spoken in South Africa.

aft *adverb and adjective* towards or in the rear of a ship or aircraft.

after *preposition and adverb* 1 behind in place or order. 2 later than. 3 in search or pursuit of. 4 in accordance with. 5 in imitation of.

afterlife *noun* existence after death.

aftermath *noun* the time following, or the result of, an unpleasant or disastrous event: *in the aftermath of the war.*

afternoon *noun* (*plural* **afternoons**) the time between noon or lunchtime and evening.

aftershave *noun* (*plural* **aftershaves**) a scented lotion for use on the face after shaving.

afterthought *noun* (*plural* **afterthoughts**) an idea thought of or added later.

afterwards or **afterward** *adverb* after that; subsequently.

again *adverb* 1 once more. 2 so as to be as before: *Put it back again.*

against *preposition* 1 in opposition or hostility to somebody or something. 2 in contact with somebody or something. 3 opposite to the movement or course of something: *against the tide.* 4 to protect from the effect of something: *wrapped up against the cold.*

age *noun* (*plural* **ages**) 1 the length of time a person has lived or a thing has existed. 2 a stage of life. 3 a period of past time. 4 (**ages**) *informal* a long time. ~ *verb* (**ages, ageing** or **aging, aged**) 1 to become or start to look old. 2 to make somebody or something seem old. * **come of age** to reach legal adult status.

aged *adjective* 1 /**ay** jid/ very old. 2 /ayjd/ of a specified age: *aged six years and three months.*

agency *noun* (*plural* **agencies**) 1 an establishment that does a particular type of business: *an employment agency.* 2 a department of a government: *the Environment Agency.*

agenda *noun* (*plural* **agendas**) a list of items for discussion at a meeting.

agent *noun* (*plural* **agents**) 1 a person who is authorized to act for somebody else. 2 a spy.

aggravate *verb* (**aggravates, aggravating, aggravated**) 1 to make something worse or more severe. 2 *informal* to annoy or irritate somebody. ➤ **aggravation** noun.

aggregate noun (plural **aggregates**) the whole amount resulting when several smaller amounts are combined.

aggression noun hostile or violent behaviour.

aggressive adjective **1** hostile or violent. **2** forceful or dynamic. ➤ **aggressively** adverb.

aggressor noun (plural **aggressors**) a person or country that attacks another and starts a fight.

aggrieved adjective upset about unfair treatment.

aghast adjective shocked or horrified.

agile adjective **1** able to move easily and gracefully. **2** mentally quick and resourceful. ➤ **agility** noun.

agitate verb (**agitates, agitating, agitated**) **1** to trouble or disturb somebody. **2** to shake or stir something. **3** to work to arouse public feeling about an issue. ➤ **agitation** noun, **agitator** noun.

agnostic noun (plural **agnostics**) somebody who believes it is impossible to know whether God exists. ➤ **agnostic** adjective, **agnosticism** noun.

ago adverb before now.

agog adjective full of excitement or eagerness.

agonizing or **agonising** adjective causing terrible pain or worry.

agony noun (plural **agonies**) intense physical pain or mental suffering.

agoraphobia /a gra foh bi a/ noun abnormal fear of open spaces.

agree verb (**agrees, agreeing, agreed**) **1** to have the same opinion or judgment about something: *We agree about what makes a man attractive.* **2** to be willing to do something: *They agreed to reconsider their verdict.* **3** to be the same as or correspond with something: *The two sets of figures don't agree.* **4** (**agree with**) to suit somebody's health or digestion: *Onions don't agree with me.*

agreeable adjective **1** pleasing; nice: *a very agreeable prospect.* **2** willing to agree or consent: *Would you be agreeable to letting Jamal go first?* ➤ **agreeably** adverb.

agreement noun (plural **agreements**) **1** a state where two or more people share the same opinion. **2** consent. **3** a treaty or contract.

agriculture noun farming. ➤ **agricultural** adjective.

aground adverb and adjective touching the shore or the ground below a body of water.

ahead adverb and adjective **1** in front or in a forward direction. **2** in the future.

ahoy interjection used at sea as a greeting or warning.

aid verb (**aids, aiding, aided**) to help somebody or something. ~ noun (plural **aids**) **1** help. **2** money or supplies given to a country in need. **3** something that makes doing something easier. * **in aid of** in order to help or support.

aide noun (plural **aides**) an assistant to a political leader.

Aids or **AIDS** noun a disease, caused by the HIV virus, which destroys the body's resistance to other diseases.

ailing adjective ill or in a bad state.

ailment noun (plural **ailments**) a mild illness.

aim verb (**aims, aiming, aimed**) **1** to point a weapon, camera, etc at an object or person. **2** to intend or try to do something. ~ noun (plural **aims**) **1** a clear intention or purpose. **2** the pointing of a weapon at a target.

aimless adjective without a purpose or plan. **aimlessly** adverb.

air noun (plural **airs**) **1** the mixture of invisible gases that surrounds the

airborne

earth. **2** a look or impression: *a dignified air*. **3** a tune or melody. ~ *verb* (**airs, airing, aired**) **1** to express an opinion openly. **2** to broadcast something on radio or television. **3** to expose something to fresh air or warmth. ✴ **by air** in an aircraft. **on the air** being broadcast on radio or television.

airborne *adjective* **1** carried in the air. **2** said about an aircraft: in the air after taking off.

air conditioning *noun* an apparatus for controlling the temperature in a building or vehicle. ➤ **air-conditioned** *adjective*.

aircraft *noun* (*plural* **aircraft**) an aeroplane, helicopter, or other vehicle that can fly.

airfield *noun* (*plural* **airfields**) a place where aircraft can take off and land.

air force *noun* (*plural* **air forces**) the branch of a country's armed forces that fights with aircraft.

air gun *noun* (*plural* **air guns**) a gun that propels a pellet by means of compressed air.

air hostess *noun* (*plural* **air hostesses**) a female member of the cabin crew on a passenger aircraft.

airline *noun* (*plural* **airlines**) a company that provides public air transport.

airliner *noun* (*plural* **airliners**) a large passenger aircraft.

airmail *noun* the transporting of mail by aircraft, or the mail itself. ~ *verb* (**airmails, airmailing, airmailed**) to send a letter or parcel by airmail.

airman *noun* (*plural* **airmen**) a military pilot or crew member.

airport *noun* (*plural* **airports**) a large airfield, used as a base for transporting passengers and cargo by air.

air raid *noun* (*plural* **air raids**) an attack by aircraft that drop bombs on a target.

airship *noun* (*plural* **airships**) a large gas-filled balloon with engines and steering that can carry goods or passengers.

airstrip *noun* (*plural* **airstrips**) a strip of ground where aircraft can take off and land.

airtight *adjective* not allowing air to pass through.

airway *noun* (*plural* **airways**) **1** a route along which aircraft fly. **2** *Science* the passage through which air reaches the lungs.

airworthy *adjective* said about an aircraft: fit to fly. ➤ **airworthiness** *noun*.

airy *adjective* (**airier, airiest**) **1** spacious and full of fresh air. **2** showing lack of concern. ➤ **airily** *adverb*.

aisle *noun* (*plural* **aisles**) **1** a passage between rows of seats in a church or other public building. **2** a passage between rows of shelves in a shop.

ajar *adjective and adverb* said about a door: slightly open.

akin *adjective* similar.

alabaster *noun* a type of white stone often carved into ornaments.

à la carte *adverb and adjective* providing or choosing from a menu that prices each item separately.

alacrity *noun formal* promptness or cheerful readiness.

alarm *noun* (*plural* **alarms**) **1** fear resulting from a sudden sense of danger. **2** a signal that warns or alerts you, or a device that produces a warning signal. **3** an alarm clock. ~ *verb* (**alarms, alarming, alarmed**) **1** to cause great fear or anxiety in somebody. **2** to fit something with an alarm. ➤ **alarming** *adjective*, **alarmingly** *adverb*.

alarm clock *noun* (*plural* **alarm clocks**) a clock that can be set to make a loud noise at a required time and wake somebody up.

alarmist *noun* (*plural* **alarmists**) a person who needlessly alarms other people.

alas *interjection* used to express unhappiness, pity, or disappointment.

albatross *noun* (*plural* **albatrosses** *or* **albatross**) a very large seabird with long narrow wings.

albino /al bee noh/ *noun* (*plural* **albinos**) a person or animal with very white skin and hair, and eyes with a pink pupil.

album *noun* (*plural* **albums**) **1** a blank book for holding a collection of stamps, photographs, or other flat objects. **2** a collection of musical recordings issued on a single disc.

alchemy /al ki mi/ *noun* a medieval form of chemical science concerned mainly with attempts to turn ordinary metals into gold. ➤ **alchemist** *noun*.

alcohol *noun* **1** a colourless liquid that makes people drunk and that is found in beer, wine, and other drinks. **2** drinks containing alcohol.

alcoholic *adjective* containing or caused by alcohol. ~ *noun* (*plural* **alcoholics**) somebody affected with alcoholism.

alcoholism *noun* addiction to alcoholic drink.

alcopop *noun* (*plural* **alcopops**) a soft drink to which alcohol has been added.

alcove *noun* (*plural* **alcoves**) a recess or arched opening in a wall.

ale *noun* (*plural* **ales**) a type of beer.

alert *adjective* watchful; aware. ~ *noun* (*plural* **alerts**) a period when people expect danger and are ready to deal with it. ~ *verb* (**alerts, alerting, alerted**) to warn somebody about a danger. ➤ **alertly** *adverb*, **alertness** *noun*.

A level *noun* (*plural* **A levels**) an examination taken in school or college at about the age of 18, or a qualification gained by passing this examination.

algae /al jee/ *plural noun Science* plants such as seaweed that grow in water and do not have ordinary stems, roots, and leaves.

algebra /al ji bra/ *noun Maths* a branch of mathematics in which letters and symbols represent numbers in equations and formulas. ➤ **algebraic** *adjective*.

alias /ay li as/ *adverb* otherwise called or known as. ~ *noun* (*plural* **aliases**) a false name used by a person.

alibi /a li bie/ *noun* (*plural* **alibis**) evidence to show that a person was somewhere else when a crime was committed.

alien /ay li an/ *adjective* **1** strange or foreign. **2** from another world; extraterrestrial. ~ *noun* (*plural* **aliens**) **1** somebody who is not a citizen of the country they are living in. **2** a being from another world.

alienate *verb* (**alienates, alienating, alienated**) to make somebody feel hostile or indifferent. ➤ **alienation** *noun*.

alight[1] *verb* (**alights, alighting, alighted**) **1** to get off a vehicle. **2** to descend from the air and settle.

alight[2] *adjective* on fire.

align /a lien/ *verb* (**aligns, aligning, aligned**) to bring things into a straight line. ✱ **align yourself with** to become an ally or supporter of somebody. ➤ **alignment** *noun*.

alike *adjective* very similar without being identical. ~ *adverb* in the same way; equally: *Our parents treated us both alike.*

alimentary canal *noun* (*plural* **alimentary canals**) *Science* the passage from the mouth to the anus along which food passes.

alimony *noun chiefly N American*

alive

money to help with living expenses, paid by a husband to his wife or by a wife to her husband after their separation or divorce.

alive *adjective* **1** having life; not dead. **2** lively or animated. **3** (**alive to**) aware of something: *They were alive to the danger and reacted at once.*

alkali /al ka lie/ *noun* (*plural* **alkalis**) *Science* a chemical substance that neutralizes acids and turn litmus paper blue. ➤ **alkaline** *adjective*.

all *adjective* the whole amount or quantity of. ~ *adverb* **1** wholly or altogether. **2** said about scores in games and sports: for each side: *fifteen all*. ~ *pronoun* everybody or everything. * **all but** very nearly; almost. **all in** *informal* tired out; exhausted. **all there** *informal* alert or shrewd.

Allah *noun* the Muslim name for God.

allay *verb* (**allays, allaying, allayed**) to reduce the severity of pain, fear, or suffering.

allegation /a li gay shn/ *noun* (*plural* **allegations**) a statement made without proof.

allege /a lej/ *verb* (**alleges, alleging, alleged**) to assert something without proof. ➤ **alleged** *adjective*, **allegedly** /a lej id li/ *adverb*.

allegiance /a lee jans/ *noun* (*plural* **allegiances**) loyalty to a person or cause.

allegory *noun* (*plural* **allegories**) *English* a story, poem, or picture that contains a symbolic meaning. ➤ **allegorical** *adjective*.

alleluia *interjection* see HALLELUJAH.

allergy *noun* (*plural* **allergies**) extreme sensitivity to substances that usually have no effect on the average person. ➤ **allergic** *adjective*.

alleviate /a lee vi ayt/ *verb* (**alleviates, alleviating, alleviated**) to relieve a problem or anxiety. ➤ **alleviation** *noun*.

alley *noun* (*plural* **alleys**) **1** a narrow passageway between buildings. **2** a garden walk bordered by trees or a hedge. **3** a long narrow lane for bowling or playing skittles.

alliance *noun* (*plural* **alliances**) an association between nations or groups that promise to help one another.

allied *adjective* **1** joined by an alliance. **2** closely related.

alligator *noun* (*plural* **alligators**) a large reptile related to the crocodile but with a broader head.

alliteration *noun English* the repetition of the first sounds in neighbouring words to create a special effect, as in *ripe red raspberries*. ➤ **alliterative** *adjective*.

allocate *verb* (**allocates, allocating, allocated**) **1** to give something to a person as their share. **2** to set part of something aside for a particular purpose. ➤ **allocation** *noun*.

allot *verb* (**allots, allotting, allotted**) to allocate something.

allotment *noun* (*plural* **allotments**) a small plot of land for growing flowers or vegetables.

allow *verb* (**allows, allowing, allowed**) **1** to make it possible for somebody to do something. **2** to give or reserve a suitable amount of time or money for somebody to do something: *They allow us an hour for lunch.* **3** (**allow for**) to take something into account. ➤ **allowable** *adjective*.

allowance *noun* (*plural* **allowances**) a sum of money paid to a person, usually at regular intervals. * **make allowances for** to take into account factors that excuse bad behaviour: *We have to make allowances for my father, who is extremely deaf.*

alloy *noun* (*plural* **alloys**) *Science* a mixture of metals or of a metal with a non-metal.

all right *adjective* **1** satisfactory or acceptable. **2** safe or well. **3** I agree.

all-rounder *noun* (*plural* **all-rounders**) somebody who is competent in many fields.

allude *verb* (**alludes, alluding, alluded**) (**allude to**) to refer to somebody or something indirectly, or to mention them in passing.

allure *noun* power of attraction or fascination: *the allure of life in a big city*. ➤ **alluring** *adjective*.

allusion *noun* (*plural* **allusions**) an indirect reference to somebody or something.

ally *noun* (*plural* **allies**) **1** a country that is a member of an alliance. **2** a person or group that helps or cooperates with another. ~ *verb* (**allies, allying, allied**) ✳ **ally yourself with** to become an ally of somebody.

almanac *noun* (*plural* **almanacs**) a book containing statistical information, for example about the weather or tides, published annually.

almighty *adjective* **1** having unlimited power. **2** *informal* very great or serious. ✳ **the Almighty** God.

almond /ah mond/ *noun* (*plural* **almonds**) an edible oval nut.

almost *adverb* very nearly but not exactly.

alms /ahmz/ *plural noun* money or food formerly given to help the poor.

aloft *adverb* at or to a higher place; up in the air.

alone *adjective and adverb* **1** separated from others; isolated. **2** considered by itself. **3** free from interference or help.

along *preposition* over the length of something. ~ *adverb* **1** forward; onward. **2** with you or with somebody: *Do you mind if I bring my sister along?* ✳ **all along** all the time. **along with** in addition to.

alongside *adverb and preposition* along or at the side of something.

aloof *adjective* not involved, friendly, or sympathetic. ➤ **aloofness** *noun*.

aloud *adverb* with a normal speaking voice.

alphabet *noun* (*plural* **alphabets**) a set of letters used to write a language.

alphabetical *or* **alphabetic** *adjective* in the order of the letters of the alphabet. ➤ **alphabetically** *adverb*.

alpine *adjective* found or growing in mountainous regions.

already *adverb* **1** before a particular time or the expected time. **2** previously.

Alsatian *noun* (*plural* **Alsatians**) a large dog of a wolf-like breed.

also *adverb* as well; in addition.

altar *noun* (*plural* **altars**) a table-like structure used in religious ceremonies.

alter *verb* (**alters, altering, altered**) to make somebody or something different, or to become different. ➤ **alteration** *noun*.

altercation *noun* (*plural* **altercations**) an angry discussion or quarrel.

alternate /awl ter nat/ *adjective* **1** said about two things: occurring or arranged so that one thing is always followed by the other thing: *alternate layers of brick and stone*. **2** every other; every second: *on alternate Mondays*. ~ /awl ter nayt/ *verb* (**alternates, alternating, alternated**) said about two things or people: to occur or do something one after the other. ➤ **alternately** *adverb*, **alternation** *noun*.

alternating current *noun Science* an electric current that reverses its direction at regularly recurring intervals.

alternative *adjective* **1** able to be used instead of something else. **2** different from the usual forms or kinds. ~ *noun* (*plural* **alternatives**) **1** another person or thing that could act as a replacement. **2** a choice between two or more possibilities. ➤ **alternatively** *adverb*.

although

although *conjunction* in spite of the fact or possibility that.

altimeter /al ti mee ter/ *noun* (*plural* **altimeters**) an instrument for measuring altitude.

altitude *noun* (*plural* **altitudes**) the height of an object or place above sea level.

alto /al toh *or* awl toh/ *noun* (*plural* **altos**) **1** a woman with a singing voice lower than that of a soprano. **2** a man with a singing voice higher than that of a tenor.

altogether *adverb* **1** completely; in every way. **2** with everything taken into account.

altruism *noun* unselfish concern for others. ➤ **altruist** *noun*, **altruistic** *adjective*.

aluminium *noun* Science a chemical element that is a light silver-white metal.

always *adverb* **1** at all times; continuously. **2** in all cases. **3** forever. **4** as a last resort: *You could always ask your parents to help out.*

AM *abbreviation* Assembly Member (= member of the National Assembly for Wales)

am *verb* first person singular of the present tense of BE.

a.m. *abbreviation* = (Latin) *ante meridiem* before noon.

amalgamate *verb* (**amalgamates, amalgamating, amalgamated**) to combine two or more organizations into a single one. ➤ **amalgamation** *noun*.

amass *verb* (**amasses, amassing, amassed**) to collect a large amount of something.

amateur /a ma ter/ *noun* (*plural* **amateurs**) **1** somebody who does something for pleasure and is not paid to do it. **2** somebody who does something unskilfully. ~ *adjective* **1** working as an amateur; involving amateurs: *an amateur photographer; amateur dramatics.* **2** inexpert. ➤ **amateurish** *adjective*, **amateurism** *noun*.

amaze *verb* (**amazes, amazing, amazed**) to fill somebody with wonder. ➤ **amazement** *noun*.

amazing *adjective* very surprising or wonderful. ➤ **amazingly** *adverb*.

ambassador *noun* (*plural* **ambassadors**) a diplomat sent to a foreign country as a representative of a government.

amber *noun* **1** a hard yellowish substance that is fossilized tree resin, used in jewellery. **2** a yellowish colour.

ambidextrous /am bi dek strus/ *adjective* able to use either hand with equal ease.

ambiguous *adjective* **1** able to be understood in more than one way. **2** vague; difficult to classify. ➤ **ambiguity** *noun*, **ambiguously** *adverb*.

ambition *noun* (*plural* **ambitions**) **1** a strong drive to achieve something, especially status or success. **2** something you want to achieve: *My ambition is to play for Arsenal.*

ambitious *adjective* **1** showing ambition. **2** difficult to achieve. ➤ **ambitiously** *adverb*.

ambivalent /am bi va lint/ *adjective* having mixed attitudes or feelings towards a person or thing. ➤ **ambivalence** *noun*.

amble *verb* (**ambles, ambling, ambled**) to move at a leisurely pace.

ambulance *noun* (*plural* **ambulances**) a vehicle for transporting injured or sick people to and from hospital.

ambush *verb* (**ambushes, ambushing, ambushed**) to attack somebody from a hidden position. ~ *noun* (*plural* **ambushes**) a surprise attack from a hidden position.

amen *interjection* a word used at the

end of a prayer with the meaning 'so be it'.

amenable /ameenabl/ *adjective* willing to be persuaded.

amend *verb* (**amends, amending, amended**) to make corrections to something to improve it.

amendment *noun* (*plural* **amendments**) an alteration to a document or law.

amends * **make amends** to compensate somebody for a wrong.

amenity /ameeniti *or* ameniti/ *noun* (*plural* **amenities**) something that makes a place more enjoyable or comfortable to be in.

American *adjective* from or to do with America or the USA. ~ *noun* (*plural* **Americans**) a person from America or the USA.

amethyst /amithist/ *noun* (*plural* **amethysts**) a clear purple or violet gemstone.

amiable *adjective* friendly and pleasant. ➤ **amiability** *noun*, **amiably** *adverb*.

amicable *adjective* friendly and peaceable. ➤ **amicably** *adverb*.

amid *preposition formal* in or to the middle of; among.

amiss *adverb and adjective* wrong; not as it should be.

ammonia *noun Science* a gas with a strong smell, used in making fertilizers, synthetic fibres, and explosives.

ammunition *noun* **1** bullets or shells for use in weapons. **2** points used to support an argument.

amnesia *noun* loss of memory.

amnesty *noun* (*plural* **amnesties**) a pardon granted to a large group of people who have committed offences.

amoeba /ameeba/ *noun* (*plural* **amoebas** *or* **amoebae** /ameebee/) *Science* a single-celled organism that can change its shape.

amok *or* **amuck** * **run amok** *or* **run**
amuck to act wildly or be completely out of control.

among *or* **amongst** *preposition*
1 in the middle of; surrounded by.
2 in the company of: *among friends*.
3 giving each one a share: *Divide it up among you*.

amoral /aymoral/ *adjective* not caring about moral principles or ethical judgments. ➤ **amorality** *noun*.

amorous *adjective* showing or feeling sexual love or desire. ➤ **amorously** *adverb*.

amount *noun* (*plural* **amounts**)
1 a quantity. **2** the total of two or more quantities. ~ *verb* (**amounts, amounting, amounted**) (**amount to**) **1** to add up to a total. **2** to be equivalent to something.

ampere /ampair/ *noun* (*plural* **amperes**) *Science* a unit that shows how strong an electric current is.

amphetamine /amfetameen/ *noun* (*plural* **amphetamines**) a drug used as a stimulant.

amphibian /ambian/ *noun* (*plural* **amphibians**) **1** an animal such as a frog, toad, or newt that lives in water when young and on land when fully developed. **2** a vehicle that can operate on both land and water.
➤ **amphibious** *adjective*.

amphitheatre *noun* (*plural* **amphitheatres**) a circular building without a roof and with rising tiers of seats surrounding an arena.

ample *adjective* (**ampler, amplest**)
1 enough or more than enough: *We've got ample time to get to the station*.
2 large or extensive: *an ample stomach*.
➤ **amply** *adverb*.

amplifier *noun* (*plural* **amplifiers**) an electronic device that increases sounds or electrical signals.

amplify *verb* (**amplifies, amplifying, amplified**) **1** to increase the strength of a sound or electrical signal.
2 to make a statement clearer by

amplitude

giving more details. ➤ **amplification** *noun*.

amplitude *noun* (*plural* **amplitudes**) *Science* the extent of vibration in a wave measured from the average position to a maximum.

amputate *verb* (**amputates, amputating, amputated**) to remove an arm or leg surgically. ➤ **amputation** *noun*.

amuck see AMOK.

amuse *verb* (**amuses, amusing, amused**) **1** to appeal to the sense of humour of somebody. **2** to entertain or interest somebody. ➤ **amusing** *adjective*.

amusement *noun* (*plural* **amusements**) **1** the state of being amused. **2** something enjoyable, especially a fairground entertainment.

an *adjective* used in place of *a* before words that begin with a vowel sound.

anachronism /a nak ro ni zm/ *noun* (*plural* **anachronisms**) a person or thing that seems to belong to an older time. ➤ **anachronistic** *adjective*.

anaemia /a nee mi a/ *noun Science* a condition in which a person's blood has too few red blood cells, causing a lack of energy.

anaesthetic /a nis the tik/ *noun* (*plural* **anaesthetics**) a substance that suppresses pain, so that surgery can be carried out.

anaesthetize *or* **anaesthetise** /a nees thi tiez/ (**anaesthetizes, anaesthetizing, anaesthetized** *or* **anaesthetises,** etc) *verb* to give somebody an anaesthetic. ➤ **anaesthetist** *noun*.

anagram *noun* (*plural* **anagrams**) a word or phrase made by rearranging the letters of another.

anal /ay nl/ *adjective* to do with the anus.

analgesic /a nal jee zik/ *noun* (*plural* **analgesics**) *Science* a drug that relieves pain.

analogue *or* **analog** *adjective Science* said about a clock, watch, etc: using a pointer or hands rather than having an electronic display of numbers.

analogy /a na lo ji/ *noun* (*plural* **analogies**) an explanation of something that uses a comparison with something similar.

analyse *verb* (**analyses, analysing, analysed**) to make a close examination of something, for example to find out how it is made or what it means.

analysis *noun* (*plural* **analyses**) **1** an examination of something to find out how it is made. **2** = PSYCHOANALYSIS.

analyst *noun* (*plural* **analysts**) **1** a person who analyses things. **2** a psychoanalyst.

analytical *or* **analytic** *adjective* using analysis.

anarchist *noun* (*plural* **anarchists**) somebody who believes that laws and government are unnecessary; a revolutionary. ➤ **anarchism** *noun*, **anarchistic** *adjective*.

anarchy *noun* a state of lawlessness or disorder.

anatomy *noun* (*plural* **anatomies**) **1** *Science* the scientific study of the structure of the bodies of people or animals. **2** the body structure of a person or animal. ➤ **anatomical** *adjective*.

ancestor *noun* (*plural* **ancestors**) somebody from whom a person is descended. ➤ **ancestral** *adjective*, **ancestry** *noun*.

anchor *noun* (*plural* **anchors**) a heavy hook dropped from a ship or boat to hold it in a particular place. ~ *verb* (**anchors, anchoring, anchored**) **1** to hold a ship or boat in place with an anchor. **2** to secure something firmly.

anchorage *noun* (*plural* **anchorages**) a

place where boats and ships can anchor.

anchovy *noun* (*plural* **anchovies**) a small fish with a strong taste.

ancient *adjective* **1** belonging to a remote period of history. **2** *informal* very old.

ancillary *adjective* giving assistance and support to the main workers.

and *conjunction* **1** plus; as well as. **2** *Maths* used to express the addition of numbers.

android *noun* (*plural* **androids**) in science fiction, a robot with a human shape.

anecdote *noun* (*plural* **anecdotes**) a short account of an amusing or interesting incident. ➤ **anecdotal** *adjective*.

anemone /a ne mo ni/ *noun* (*plural* **anemones**) a plant with brightly coloured flowers.

anew *adverb* again, or in a new way.

angel *noun* (*plural* **angels**) **1** a spirit, usually depicted in human form with wings, believed to serve as a messenger of God. **2** a good or loving person. ➤ **angelic** *adjective*.

anger *noun* a strong feeling of displeasure. ~ *verb* (**angers, angering, angered**) to make somebody angry.

angina /an jie na/ *noun* a disease that gives rise to severe chest pain, caused by a lack of blood to the heart.

angle *noun* (*plural* **angles**) **1** *Maths* the space formed by two lines or surfaces extending outwards from the same point or line. **2** a position from which something is observed. **3** a point of view about something. ~ *verb* (**angles, angling, angled**) **1** to place or move something in a slanting position. **2** to present information from a particular point of view.

angler *noun* (*plural* **anglers**) somebody who fishes with a rod and line.

Anglican *adjective* to do with the Church of England and related churches. ~ *noun* (*plural* **Anglicans**) a member of the Church of England or a related church. ➤ **Anglicanism** *noun*.

Anglo-Saxon *noun* (*plural* **Anglo-Saxons**) **1** a member of the Germanic peoples who conquered England in the fifth century. **2** the Old English language. ➤ **Anglo-Saxon** *adjective*.

angry *adjective* (**angrier, angriest**) feeling anger; very annoyed. ➤ **angrily** *adverb*.

anguish *noun* extreme mental distress or physical pain. ➤ **anguished** *adjective*.

angular *adjective* **1** forming an angle or having angles. **2** said about a person: lean and bony.

animal *noun* (*plural* **animals**) **1** any living creature apart from a human being or a plant. **2** a coarse, unfeeling, or cruel person.

animate *verb* (**animates, animating, animated**) **1** to make something or somebody lively and interesting. **2** to create a film using animation. ➤ **animator** *noun*.

animated *adjective* **1** lively or vivacious. **2** made using the techniques of animation. ➤ **animatedly** *adverb*.

animation *noun* **1** being lively or active. **2** the technique of filming a sequence of images or models in different positions so that they appear to be moving.

animosity *noun* a strong feeling of hostility or resentment.

aniseed *noun* the seed of a plant of the carrot family, used as a flavouring.

ankle *noun* (*plural* **ankles**) the joint between the foot and the leg.

annals *plural noun* a record of events, activities, etc, arranged year by year.

annex /a neks/ *verb* (**annexes,**

annexing, annexed) to take over another area and make it part of your own territory. ~ /a neks/ *noun* (also **annexe**) (*plural* **annexes**) **1** an extra building providing additional accommodation. **2** an addition to a document. ➤ **annexation** *noun*.

annihilate /a nie a layt/ *verb* (**annihilates, annihilating, annihilated**) to destroy something entirely. ➤ **annihilation** *noun*.

anniversary *noun* (*plural* **anniversaries**) the date on which a notable event took place in an earlier year.

annotate *verb* (**annotates, annotating, annotated**) to provide a text with notes. ➤ **annotation** *noun*.

announce *verb* (**announces, announcing, announced**) to make something known publicly. ➤ **announcement** *noun*, **announcer** *noun*.

annoy *verb* (**annoys, annoying, annoyed**) **1** to make somebody mildly angry. **2** to bother or pester somebody. ➤ **annoyance** *noun*.

annual *adjective* **1** occurring once a year. **2** covering or lasting for a period of one year. **3** said about a plant: completing its life cycle in one growing season. ~ *noun* (*plural* **annuals**) **1** a publication that appears once a year. **2** an annual plant. ➤ **annually** *adverb*.

annuity *noun* (*plural* **annuities**) an amount payable each year to a person.

annul *verb* (**annuls, annulling, annulled**) to declare something legally invalid and cancel it. ➤ **annulment** *noun*.

anode *noun* (*plural* **anodes**) *Science* the electrode by which electrons leave a device and enter an electric circuit.

anoint *verb* (**anoints, anointing, anointed**) to put oil on somebody as part of a religious ceremony.

anomaly *noun* (*plural* **anomalies**) something that is different from what is usual or expected. ➤ **anomalous** *adjective*.

anonymous /a no ni mus/ *adjective* done or produced by somebody who does not reveal his or her name.
➤ **anonymity** *noun*, **anonymously** *adverb*.

anorak *noun* (*plural* **anoraks**) a short weatherproof coat with a hood.

anorexia or **anorexia nervosa** /a no reks i a ner voh sa/ *noun* a psychological disorder that makes a person refuse to eat.

another *adjective* **1** that is a different or additional one. **2** some other.
~ *pronoun* a different or additional one.

answer *noun* (*plural* **answers**) **1** something said or written in response to a question or statement. **2** the solution to a problem. ~ *verb* (**answers, answering, answered**) **1** to give an answer to a question. **2** to act in response to a signal from something: *to answer the phone*. **3** (**answer for**) to be accountable for something. **4** (**answer to**) to have to explain your actions to somebody.

answerable *adjective* responsible to somebody for something: *You'll be answerable to me for any mistakes that occur*.

answering machine *noun* (*plural* **answering machines**) a machine that responds to telephone calls with a recorded reply and records messages spoken by callers.

ant *noun* (*plural* **ants**) a small insect that lives in large organized groups.

antagonism *noun* open hostility or antipathy.

antagonist *noun* (*plural* **antagonists**) an opponent or enemy. ➤ **antagonistic** *adjective*.

antagonize or **antagonise** *verb* (**antagonizes, antagonizing, antagonized** or **antagonises**, etc) to make somebody feel hostile towards you.

Antarctic /an tahk tik/ *adjective* to do with the South Pole or the surrounding region. ~ *noun* (**the Antarctic**) the region surrounding the South Pole.

antelope *noun* (*plural* **antelopes** or **antelope**) a fast-running mammal similar to a deer, that lives in Africa and Asia.

antenatal *adjective* to do with pregnancy.

antenna *noun* 1 (*plural* **antennae** /an te nee/) *Science* a long thin sense organ on the head of insects and crustaceans. 2 (*plural* **antennas** or **antennae**) an aerial.

anthem *noun* (*plural* **anthems**) *Music* a solemn or rousing song, often with patriotic or religious words.

anther *noun* (*plural* **anthers**) *Science* an organ at the tip of a flower's stamen that contains and releases pollen.

anthill *noun* (*plural* **anthills**) a mound of soil and leaves thrown up by ants or termites making a nest.

anthology *noun* (*plural* **anthologies**) a selection of literary or musical pieces or passages.

anthrax *noun* a serious disease of cattle and sheep that is capable of being transmitted to humans.

anthropology *noun* the scientific study of human societies and behaviour. ➤ **anthropological** *adjective*, **anthropologist** *noun*.

anti-aircraft *adjective* used against enemy aircraft: *anti-aircraft guns*.

antibiotic *noun* (*plural* **antibiotics**) *Science* a substance that kills bacteria. ➤ **antibiotic** *adjective*.

antibody *noun* (*plural* **antibodies**) *Science* a protein that is produced by the body to defend itself against a toxin, virus, etc.

anticipate *verb* (**anticipates, anticipating, anticipated**) 1 to foresee something and be ready in advance to deal with it: *I anticipated his next move.* 2 to expect or look forward to something. ➤ **anticipation** *noun*, **anticipatory** *adjective*.

anticlimax *noun* (*plural* **anticlimaxes**) an event that turns out to be much less exciting than expected.

anticlockwise *adjective and adverb* in a direction opposite to that in which the hands of a clock rotate.

antics *plural noun* foolish or funny behaviour.

antidote *noun* (*plural* **antidotes**) a remedy that counteracts the effects of poison.

antifreeze *noun* a substance added to a liquid to lower its freezing point.

antihistamine *noun* (*plural* **antihistamines**) a drug used for treating allergies.

antipathy /an ti pa thi/ *noun* a strong dislike.

antiperspirant *noun* (*plural* **antiperspirants**) a substance used to reduce perspiration.

antipodes /an ti po deez/ *plural noun* (**the Antipodes**) Australia and New Zealand.

antiquarian *adjective* old and rare, or dealing with old and rare objects.

antiquated *adjective* very old; out of date.

antique *adjective* valuable because of its age. ~ *noun* (*plural* **antiques**) an object that is valuable because it is very old.

antiquity *noun* 1 ancient times. 2 the quality of being ancient.

anti-Semitism *noun* hostility towards Jewish people. ➤ **anti-Semitic** *adjective*.

antiseptic *adjective* preventing the growth of germs that cause disease in a wound. ➤ **antiseptic** *noun*.

antisocial *adjective* 1 said about behaviour: causing annoyance to others. 2 said about a person: tending

antithesis

to avoid company; unsociable.
➤ **antisocially** adverb.

antithesis /an ti thi sis/ noun (plural **antitheses**) the direct opposite of something.

antler noun (plural **antlers**) either one of a pair of branched horns on a male deer.

antonym noun (plural **antonyms**) *English* a word that means the opposite of another word, such as *hot* and *cold* or *big* and *small*.

anus /ay nus/ noun (plural **anuses**) the opening through which solid waste matter leaves your body.

anvil noun (plural **anvils**) a heavy iron block on which metal is shaped by hammering.

anxiety noun (plural **anxieties**) an uneasy and worried feeling because of possible trouble or danger.

anxious adjective **1** uneasy in the mind because of possible trouble or danger. **2** worrying. **3** eager to do something. ➤ **anxiously** adverb.

any adjective one or some, no matter which. ~ pronoun any person or thing. ~ adverb to any extent or degree: *Don't come any closer.*

anybody pronoun any person.

anyhow adverb **1** in a haphazard manner. **2** anyway.

anyone pronoun any person.

anything pronoun any thing whatever.

anyway adverb **1** in any case; inevitably. **2** used when restarting a story, after breaking off to talk about something else. **3** nevertheless.

anywhere adverb in or to any place.

aorta /ay aw ta/ noun (plural **aortas**) *Science* the main artery carrying blood from the heart to be distributed by branch arteries throughout the body.

apart adverb **1** at a distance from something or somebody in space or time. **2** in or into two or more parts.
* **apart from** except for.

apartheid /a pah tayt *or* a pah tiet/ noun a policy of keeping different races separate and apart, formerly operating in South Africa.

apartment noun (plural **apartments**) **1** a suite of rooms for living in. **2** *N American* a flat.

apathetic adjective lacking interest; indifferent. ➤ **apathetically** adverb.

apathy noun lack of interest or enthusiasm.

ape noun (plural **apes**) a large tailless animal similar to a monkey, belonging to the group that includes gorillas, chimpanzees, orang-utans, and gibbons. ~ verb (**apes, aping, aped**) to imitate something or somebody closely but clumsily.

aperture noun (plural **apertures**) an opening or gap.

apex /ay peks/ noun (plural **apexes** or **apices** /ay pi seez/) the top or uppermost point; a tip.

aphid /ay fid/ noun (plural **aphids**) a small insect that sucks the juices of plants, such as a greenfly.

apiece adverb for each one; individually.

aplomb /a plom/ noun calm self-assurance.

apocalyptic adjective catastrophic.

apocryphal adjective said about a story: probably untrue.

apologetic adjective regretfully confessing a fault or failure. ➤ **apologetically** adverb.

apologize or **apologise** verb (**apologizes, apologizing, apologized** or **apologises**, etc) to say you are sorry for something.

apology noun (plural **apologies**) **1** a regretful admission of error or discourtesy. **2** a poor substitute: *this apology for an essay.*

apostle noun (plural **apostles**) (often **Apostle**) an early Christian teacher who preached the gospel.

apostrophe /a pos tro fi/ *noun* (*plural* **apostrophes**) *English* a punctuation mark (') used to show that letters have been missed out (as in *he won't*), or that somebody or something owns something (as in *John's book*).

appal *verb* (**appals, appalling, appalled**) to fill somebody with horror or dismay. ➤ **appalling** *adjective*, **appallingly** *adverb*.

apparatus *noun* (*plural* **apparatuses** or **apparatus**) equipment designed for a particular use.

apparel *noun formal* clothing.

apparent *adjective* **1** easily seen or understood. **2** seemingly real or true, but not necessarily so. ➤ **apparently** *adverb*.

apparition *noun* (*plural* **apparitions**) an appearance of a ghost.

appeal *noun* (*plural* **appeals**) **1** attraction. **2** an earnest plea or request. **3** a legal procedure by which a case that has been tried is brought to a higher court to be considered again. ~ *verb* (**appeals, appealing, appealed**) **1** to be attractive to somebody: *The idea of going alone doesn't really appeal to me.* **2** to make an earnest request to somebody for something. **3** to go to a higher court for a review of your case.

appealing *adjective* attractive. ➤ **appealingly** *adverb*.

appear *verb* (**appears, appearing, appeared**) **1** to become visible or present. **2** to arrive. **3** to seem.

appearance *noun* (*plural* **appearances**) **1** an act of appearing or being present. **2** the way somebody or something looks or seems: *Appearances can be deceptive.*

appease *verb* (**appeases, appeasing, appeased**) to calm somebody by agreeing to what they want. ➤ **appeasement** *noun*.

appendage *noun* (*plural* **appendages**) something added to something larger or more important.

appendicitis *noun* inflammation of the appendix.

appendix *noun* **1** (*plural* **appendixes**) a short tube that extends from the lower end of the large intestine. **2** (*plural* **appendices** /a pen di seez/) an additional section at the end of a book or other piece of writing.

appetite *noun* (*plural* **appetites**) **1** a desire to eat. **2** a strong desire or inclination.

appetizer or **appetiser** *noun* (*plural* **appetizers** or **appetisers**) food or drink that stimulates the appetite.

appetizing or **appetising** *adjective* said about food: making you want to eat it.

applaud *verb* (**applauds, applauding, applauded**) to clap or cheer somebody or something.

applause *noun* approval expressed by clapping.

apple *noun* (*plural* **apples**) a round fruit with red or green skin and crisp white flesh. ✶ **the apple of somebody's eye** a person or thing loved greatly by somebody.

appliance *noun* (*plural* **appliances**) a machine or piece of equipment.

applicable *adjective* appropriate or relevant. ➤ **applicability** *noun*.

applicant *noun* (*plural* **applicants**) a person who applies for something.

application *noun* (*plural* **applications**) **1** a formal request. **2** an act of applying. **3** a use to which something is put. **4** *ICT* a computer program that performs a particular function.

applied *adjective* said about a subject of study: put to practical use; not just theoretical.

apply *verb* (**applies, applying, applied**) **1** to put something to use. **2** to lay or spread something on a surface. **3** (**apply to**) to be relevant to something or somebody. **4** to make a formal request to somebody for something. ✱ **apply yourself** to work hard.

appoint *verb* (**appoints, appointing, appointed**) to select somebody for a job or an office.

appointment *noun* (*plural* **appointments**) **1** the act of appointing somebody. **2** a job to which somebody is appointed. **3** an arrangement for a meeting.

apposite *adjective formal* appropriate: *apposite remarks*.

appraise *verb* (**appraises, appraising, appraised**) to decide how valuable or how good something or somebody is. ➤ **appraisal** *noun*.

appreciable *adjective* large enough to notice; substantial. ➤ **appreciably** *adverb*.

appreciate *verb* (**appreciates, appreciating, appreciated**) **1** to recognize the value or importance of something or somebody. **2** to realize or be aware of something. **3** to increase in value. ➤ **appreciation** *noun*, **appreciative** *adjective*.

apprehend *verb* (**apprehends, apprehending, apprehended**) *formal* **1** to arrest a suspect. **2** to understand or perceive something.

apprehension *noun* **1** nervous anxiety or fear. **2** *formal* understanding: *I was under the apprehension that I would be given more time to pay*. **3** *formal* the arrest of a suspect.

apprehensive *adjective* nervously fearful or uneasy. ➤ **apprehensively** *adverb*.

apprentice *noun* (*plural* **apprentices**) a person who is learning a skill or trade from an employer. ➤ **apprenticeship** *noun*.

approach *verb* (**approaches, approaching, approached**) **1** to move closer to somebody or something. **2** to come near to something in quality or character. **3** to make an offer or request to somebody. **4** to begin to consider or deal with a subject. ~ *noun* (*plural* **approaches**) **1** an act of moving closer. **2** a method of doing something.

approachable *adjective* friendly and easy to talk to.

appropriate[1] /a proh pri ayt/ *verb* (**appropriates, appropriating, appropriated**) to take possession of something without permission. ➤ **appropriation** *noun*.

appropriate[2] /a proh pri at/ *adjective* suitable. ➤ **appropriately** *adverb*.

approval *noun* **1** a favourable opinion or judgment. **2** formal or official permission. ✱ **on approval** said about goods: able to be returned if unsatisfactory.

approve *verb* (**approves, approving, approved**) **1** (**approve of**) to take a favourable view of somebody or something. **2** to agree to something.

approximate /a proks i mat/ *adjective* nearly correct or exact. ~ /a proks i mayt/ *verb* (**approximates, approximating, approximated**) (**approximate to**) to come close to something in quantity or character. ➤ **approximately** *adverb*, **approximation** *noun*.

apricot /ay pri kot/ *noun* (*plural* **apricots**) an oval orange-coloured fruit with soft juicy flesh.

April *noun* the fourth month of the year.

apron *noun* (*plural* **aprons**) **1** a garment covering the front of your body and tied round your waist, used to protect your clothes. **2** *Drama* the part of a theatre stage extending in front of the curtain. **3** a paved area at an airport, used for loading and moving aircraft.

apse *noun* (*plural* **apses**) a projecting and rounded part at the end of a church.

apt *adjective* **1** likely to do something: *She's apt to forget things*. **2** suited to a purpose or occasion: *a very apt comparison*. ➢ **aptly** *adverb*, **aptness** *noun*.

aptitude *noun* (*plural* **aptitudes**) a natural ability or talent.

aqualung *noun* (*plural* **aqualungs**) an underwater breathing apparatus.

aquamarine *noun* (*plural* **aquamarines**) **1** a bluish green precious stone. **2** a pale bluish green colour.

aquarium *noun* (*plural* **aquariums** *or* **aquaria**) a glass tank filled with water for keeping fish and other sea animals.

Aquarius *noun* the eleventh sign of the zodiac (the Water Carrier).

aquatic *adjective* **1** growing or living in water. **2** taking place in or on water.

aqueduct *noun* (*plural* **aqueducts**) a bridge-like structure built to carry a canal across a valley.

Arab *noun* (*plural* **Arabs**) a member of a Semitic people living in the Middle East and North Africa. ➢ **Arab** *adjective*.

Arabian *adjective* from or having to do with Arabia, the area between the Red Sea and the Persian Gulf.

Arabic *noun* the language of the Arabs and of the Koran. ➢ **Arabic** *adjective*.

Arabic numeral *noun* (*plural* **Arabic numerals**) any of the number symbols 0, 1, 2, 3, 4, 5, 6, 7, 8, 9.

arable *adjective* said about land: suitable for crop farming.

arbiter *noun* (*plural* **arbiters**) a person who settles disputes.

arbitrary *adjective* **1** based on random personal choice or impulse rather than on a plan. **2** said about power or rule: not based on laws; tyrannical. ➢ **arbitrarily** *adverb*.

arbitrate *verb* **arbitrates, arbitrating, arbitrated**) to act as an arbitrator. ➢ **arbitration** *noun*.

arbitrator *noun* (*plural* **arbitrators**) a person chosen to settle a dispute.

arbour *noun* (*plural* **arbours**) a garden alcove formed by climbing plants or branches.

arc *noun* (*plural* **arcs**) **1** *Maths* a curve or part of the circumference of a circle. **2** a discharge of electricity across a gap in a circuit. ~ *verb* (**arcs, arcing, arced**) to form or move in an arc.

arcade *noun* (*plural* **arcades**) **1** a passageway with shops on both sides. **2** a row of arches.

arch *noun* (*plural* **arches**) **1** a curved structure, for example over an opening in a wall or supporting a bridge. **2** the inner bony structure of the foot. ~ *verb* (**arches, arching, arched**) to form or bend something into an arch.

archaeology /ah ki o lo ji/ *noun* the study of the remains of past human life and activities. ➢ **archaeological** *adjective*, **archaeologist** *noun*.

archaic /ah kay ik/ *adjective* very old; antiquated. ➢ **archaism** *noun*.

archangel /ahk ayn jil/ *noun* (*plural* **archangels**) a chief or principal angel.

archbishop *noun* (*plural* **archbishops**) a bishop of the highest rank.

archdeacon *noun* (*plural* **archdeacons**) a senior member of the clergy who has administrative duties.

archer *noun* (*plural* **archers**) a person who shoots with a bow and arrows. ➢ **archery** *noun*.

archipelago /ah ki pe la goh/ *noun* (*plural* **archipelagos** *or* **archipelagoes**) a group of scattered islands.

architect /ah ki tekt/ *noun* (*plural* **architects**) a person who designs buildings.

architecture *noun* **1** the work of designing buildings. **2** the design and structure of a building. ➢ **architectural** *adjective*.

archive /ah kiev/ *noun* (*plural* **archives**) a collection of historical documents and records.

archivist /ah ki vist/ *noun* (*plural* **archivists**) a person who organizes and looks after archives.

archway *noun* (*plural* **archways**) an arch with a passage or entrance beneath it.

Arctic /ahk tik/ *adjective* to do with the North Pole or the surrounding region. ~ *noun* (**the Arctic**) the region surrounding the North Pole.

ardent *adjective* eager or zealous. ➤ **ardently** *adverb*.

ardour *noun* **1** intense or passionate feelings. **2** great enthusiasm.

arduous *adjective* difficult or strenuous. ➤ **arduously** *adverb*.

are *verb* second person singular or plural of the present tense of BE.

area *noun* (*plural* **areas**) **1** *Maths* the extent of a surface measured in square units. **2** a piece of ground. **3** a particular space or surface. **4** a type or range of activity.

arena *noun* (*plural* **arenas**) the flat enclosed area in the centre of a stadium, where sports or entertainments take place.

aren't *contraction* **1** are not. **2** used in questions: am not.

arguable *adjective* **1** sensible, reasonable, or possible. **2** debatable or questionable; not certain. ➤ **arguably** *adverb*.

argue *verb* (**argues, arguing, argued**) **1** to disagree or quarrel. **2** to give reasons for or against something.

argument *noun* (*plural* **arguments**) **1** a quarrel or disagreement. **2** a reason or series of reasons offered as proof of something.

argumentative *adjective* tending or liking to argue.

aria /ah ri a/ *noun* (*plural* **arias**) *Music* a solo song in an opera or oratorio.

arid *adjective* *Geography* said about land: extremely dry because of a lack of rainfall. ➤ **aridity** *noun*.

Aries /air eez/ *noun* the first sign of the zodiac (the Ram).

arise *verb* (**arises, arising, arose, arisen**) **1** to come into being or to people's attention. **2** (**arise from** or **out of**) to be a result of something. **3** *formal* to stand up.

aristocracy /a ris tok ra si/ *noun* (*plural* **aristocracies**) a high social class consisting of noblemen and noblewomen.

aristocrat /a ris to krat/ *noun* (*plural* **aristocrats**) a member of an aristocracy. ➤ **aristocratic** *adjective*.

arithmetic *noun* *Maths* the branch of mathematics dealing with real numbers and calculations. ➤ **arithmetical** *adjective*.

ark *noun* (**the ark**) in the Bible and the Koran, the ship built by Noah to escape a great flood sent by God.

arm[1] *noun* (*plural* **arms**) **1** either of the human upper limbs extending from the shoulder to the hand. **2** an armrest on the side of a chair. **3** a sleeve. **4** a division of an organization.

arm[2] *verb* (**arms, arming, armed**) **1** to supply somebody with weapons. **2** to provide somebody with something that strengthens or protects them. **3** to activate the fuse of a bomb.

armada *noun* (*plural* **armadas**) a fleet of warships.

armadillo *noun* (*plural* **armadillos**) a burrowing South American mammal with a body and head encased in bony plates.

armaments *plural noun* the weapons and equipment of a nation or military force.

armchair *noun* (*plural* **armchairs**) an upholstered chair with armrests.

armed *adjective* having or using a gun.

armed forces *plural noun* (**the armed**

forces) a country's army, navy, and air force.

armistice noun (plural **armistices**) an agreement between the two sides in a war to stop fighting.

armour noun **1** a covering of metal or chain mail worn by medieval soldiers in combat. **2** a protective covering for a military ship or aircraft. **3** armoured forces and vehicles.

armoury noun (plural **armouries**) a store of weapons and military equipment.

armpit noun (plural **armpits**) the hollow under the arm at the shoulder.

armrest noun (plural **armrests**) either of the two supports for a person's arms on the side of a chair.

arms plural noun weapons, especially guns. * **up in arms** protesting strongly.

army noun (plural **armies**) **1** a large organized force for fighting on land. **2** a large crowd or group.

aroma noun (plural **aromas**) a pleasant smell. ➤ **aromatic** adjective.

aromatherapy noun the use of natural oils to promote healing and reduce tension. ➤ **aromatherapist** noun.

arose verb past tense of ARISE.

around adverb and preposition **1** nearby. **2** in various directions; to and fro. **3** approximately. **4** so as to face the opposite way. **5** so as to move in or form a circle.

arouse verb (**arouses, arousing, aroused**) **1** to stimulate a feeling or response in somebody. **2** to awaken somebody from sleep. ➤ **arousal** noun.

arrange verb (**arranges, arranging, arranged**) **1** to put things in order or into sequence. **2** to make preparations so that something can take place: *We'll have to arrange a meeting*. **3** *Music* to adapt a piece of music for different voices or instruments. ➤ **arranger** noun.

arrangement noun (plural **arrangements**) **1** something made by arranging parts together: *a flower arrangement*. **2** an informal agreement or settlement. **3** (**arrangements**) plans and preparations. **4** a musical adaptation.

array noun (plural **arrays**) **1** an imposing collection or large number of things. **2** an orderly arrangement.

arrears plural noun sums of money that should have been paid already. * **in arrears 1** behind in the payment of a debt. **2** said about rent or wages: paid at the end of each period.

arrest verb (**arrests, arresting, arrested**) **1** to take somebody and keep them in custody by legal authority. **2** to bring a process to a halt. ~ noun (plural **arrests**) the act of arresting somebody.

arresting adjective catching the attention; striking.

arrival noun (plural **arrivals**) **1** the act or time of arriving. **2** somebody or something that has arrived: *a new arrival*.

arrive verb (**arrives, arriving, arrived**) **1** to reach a destination. **2** to come. **3** to achieve success. * **arrive at** to reach a decision or conclusion by effort or thought.

arrogant adjective showing a feeling of superiority over others. ➤ **arrogance** noun, **arrogantly** adverb.

arrow noun (plural **arrows**) **1** a slender pointed shaft with feathers at the end, shot from a bow. **2** a symbol shaped like an arrow, showing direction.

arsenal noun (plural **arsenals**) a store of weapons and ammunition.

arsenic noun *Science* **1** one of the chemical elements. **2** a compound of arsenic that is a strong poison.

arson *noun* the crime of intentionally setting fire to property. ➤ **arsonist** *noun*.

art *noun* (*plural* **arts**) **1** the use of skill and creative imagination to produce things that are interesting and beautiful. **2** paintings, sculptures, and other works produced by creative imagination. **3** an activity which requires imagination as well as practical knowledge. **4** (**the arts**) subjects such as literature, art, and music.

artefact *or* **artifact** *noun* (*plural* **artefacts** *or* **artifacts**) a tool or other useful object made by human effort.

artery *noun* (*plural* **arteries**) **1** any of the vessels that carry blood from the heart to the lungs and through the body. **2** a road or other important channel of communication.

artful *adjective* cunningly or deceitfully clever. ➤ **artfully** *adverb*.

arthritis *noun* inflammation and stiffness of the joints.

artichoke *or* **globe artichoke** *noun* (*plural* **artichokes** *or* **globe artichokes**) the head of a tall thistle-like plant, used as a vegetable.

article *noun* (*plural* **articles**) **1** an object. **2** a piece of non-fictional writing in a magazine or newspaper.

articulate /ah ti kew lat/ *adjective* **1** able to express yourself clearly. **2** clearly expressed. ~ /ah ti kew layt/ *verb* (**articulates, articulating, articulated**) **1** to say words or express an idea clearly. **2** said about bones: to fit together to form a joint. ➤ **articulately** *adverb*, **articulation** *noun*.

artifact *noun* see ARTEFACT.

artificial *adjective* **1** made by humans to imitate a natural object: *an artificial limb*. **2** affected or insincere. ➤ **artificiality** *noun*, **artificially** *adverb*.

artificial intelligence *noun* ICT the ability of computers or computer programs to copy humans' ability to think, understand, and decide.

artillery *noun* **1** heavy guns used in land warfare. **2** a branch of an army that uses artillery.

artisan *noun* (*plural* **artisans**) a skilled manual worker.

artist *noun* (*plural* **artists**) **1** a person who creates paintings, sculptures, or similar artistic works. **2** a skilled performer.

artiste /ah teest/ *noun* (*plural* **artistes**) a professional entertainer.

artistic *adjective* **1** showing creative skill. **2** characteristic of art or artists. ➤ **artistically** *adverb*.

artistry *noun* artistic quality or ability.

artless *adjective* sincere or natural; free from deceit. ➤ **artlessly** *adverb*.

arty *adjective* (**artier, artiest**) showily or self-consciously artistic.

as *adverb* to the same degree; equally: *just as good*. ~ *conjunction* **1** used in comparisons: *as white as snow*. **2** because; since: *As you aren't using it, can I borrow it?* **3** in the way that: *Do as you like*. **4** while: *I'll tell you as we're going along*. ~ *preposition* in the role or function of: *to act as a replacement*.
✴ **as if/though** in such a way that it suggested that: *It looked as if it might rain at any moment*. **as well** also.

asbestos *noun* a fire-resistant mineral made of thin fibres that are harmful when breathed in by humans.

ascend *verb* (**ascends, ascending, ascended**) to move or slope upwards.

ascendancy *noun* a position of power over others.

ascent *noun* (*plural* **ascents**) **1** the act of going up. **2** a way up.

ascertain *verb* (**ascertains, ascertaining, ascertained**) to find out or learn something. ➤ **ascertainable** *adjective*.

ascetic /a se tik/ *adjective* not allowing yourself comforts or luxuries. ➤ **ascetic** *noun*, **asceticism** *noun*.

ascribe *verb* (**ascribes, ascribing,**

ascribed) to say that something is caused by something or was said by somebody: *a saying ascribed to John Lennon.* ➤ **ascription** *noun*.

asexual /ay sek sew al/ *adjective Science* having no sex organs or not involving sex.

ash[1] *noun* (*plural* **ashes**) a tall tree of the olive family with hard tough wood.

ash[2] *noun* (*plural* **ashes**) **1** the solid material left when something has been burned. **2** (**ashes**) the remains of a dead body after cremation.

ashamed *adjective* feeling shame or guilt.

ashen *adjective* extremely pale from fear or shock.

ashore *adverb* on or to the shore.

Asian *adjective* from or to do with Asia. ~ *noun* (*plural* **Asians**) a person from Asia.

Asiatic *adjective* to do with Asia.

aside *adverb* **1** to or towards the side. **2** out of the way. **3** in reserve for future use. ~ *noun* (*plural* **asides**) *Drama* an actor's remark supposedly not heard by other characters on stage but only by the audience.

ask *verb* (**asks, asking, asked**) **1** to say something that calls for an answer. **2** to speak to somebody to get them to do something or give you something. **3** to invite somebody. **4** (**ask after**) to try to find out how somebody is.

askance ✻ **look askance at** to regard with disapproval or distrust.

askew *adverb and adjective* not straight or level.

asleep *adjective* **1** in a state of sleep. **2** said about a limb: numb.

asparagus *noun* the spike-shaped shoot of a tall plant, used as a vegetable.

aspect *noun* (*plural* **aspects**) **1** a particular feature of something that is not a physical object, for example of a situation or problem: *In tackling drug abuse, we are only dealing with one aspect of the problem.* **2** the side of a building facing a particular direction, or the fact of facing in a particular direction: *The house has a southern aspect.*

aspersion ✻ **cast aspersions on** to attack the reputation of somebody.

asphalt *noun* a black substance used for surfacing roads.

asphyxiate /as k si ayt/ *verb* (**asphyxiates, asphyxiating, asphyxiated**) to make somebody unconscious, or kill them, by depriving them of oxygen. ➤ **asphyxiation** *noun*.

aspiration *noun* (*plural* **aspirations**) a strong desire or ambition.

aspire *verb* (**aspires, aspiring, aspired**) to wish to achieve a particular objective: *to aspire to be an artist.*

aspirin *noun* (*plural* **aspirin** or **aspirins**) **1** a medicine, usually in the form of a tablet, taken to relieve pain and reduce fever. **2** an aspirin tablet.

ass *noun* (*plural* **asses**) **1** a donkey. **2** a stupid or obstinate person.

assailant *noun* (*plural* **assailants**) an attacker.

assassin *noun* (*plural* **assassins**) somebody who murders a political or religious leader.

assassinate *verb* (**assassinates, assassinating, assassinated**) to murder a political or religious leader. ➤ **assassination** *noun*.

assault *noun* (*plural* **assaults**) **1** a violent attack, or the crime of attacking somebody. **2** an attempt to attack a fortified position. ~ *verb* (**assaults, assaulting, assaulted**) to make an assault on somebody.

assault course *noun* (*plural* **assault courses**) an obstacle course for training soldiers.

assemble

assemble *verb* (**assembles, assembling, assembled**) **1** to come together, or to bring people or things together, in one place. **2** to fit together the parts of a kit or product.

assembly *noun* (*plural* **assemblies**) **1** a group of people gathered together. **2** a law-making body; a parliament. **3** the fitting together of parts.

assembly line *noun* (*plural* **assembly lines**) a series of machines for assembling a product.

assent *verb* (**assents, assenting, assented**) to agree to something. ~ *noun* formal agreement or approval.

assert *verb* (**asserts, asserting, asserted**) to state something firmly. ✲ **assert yourself** to be firm and self-confident and make people listen to you.

assertion *noun* (*plural* **assertions**) a firm statement.

assertive *adjective* self-confident and firm in dealing with others. ➤ **assertively** *adverb*, **assertiveness** *noun*.

assess *verb* (**assesses, assessing, assessed**) to estimate the amount, quality, or worth of something. ➤ **assessment** *noun*, **assessor** *noun*.

asset *noun* (*plural* **assets**) **1** (**assets**) the total property of a person or company. **2** an advantage.

assign *verb* (**assigns, assigning, assigned**) **1** to allot something to somebody. **2** to appoint somebody to a particular role or task.

assignation /a sig nay shn/ *noun* (*plural* **assignations**) a secret meeting with a lover.

assignment *noun* (*plural* **assignments**) a specified task or amount of work assigned to somebody.

assimilate *verb* (**assimilates, assimilating, assimilated**) **1** to take in or absorb a substance. **2** to understand information. ➤ **assimilation** *noun*.

assist *verb* (**assists, assisting, assisted**) to help somebody or something.

assistance *noun* help or support.

assistant *noun* (*plural* **assistants**) a person whose job is to help somebody.

associate /a soh si ayt *or* a soh shi ayt/ *verb* (**associates, associating, associated**) **1** to connect somebody or something in your mind with a particular thing, quality, or feeling: *I tend to associate seaside holidays with terrible weather.* **2** (**associate with**) to mix socially with people; to be seen in somebody's company. ~ /a soh si at *or* a soh shi at/ *noun* (*plural* **associates**) a colleague, or a person who is often seen with you.

association *noun* (*plural* **associations**) **1** an organization of people who have a common interest. **2** a mental connection between ideas.

assonance /a so nans/ *noun* English repetition of the vowel sounds in two or more words as an alternative to rhyme, as in *All worms will turn.*

assorted *adjective* consisting of various kinds.

assortment *noun* (*plural* **assortments**) a mixed collection of various kinds.

assuage /a swayj/ *verb* (**assuages, assuaging, assuaged**) **1** to ease suffering or discomfort. **2** to relieve thirst or desire.

assume *verb* (**assumes, assuming, assumed**) **1** to take something as true without proof. **2** to take on a role or duty. **3** to adopt a new name or identity.

assumption *noun* (*plural* **assumptions**) **1** a fact or statement taken for granted. **2** the act of taking on a role or duty.

assurance *noun* (*plural* **assurances**) **1** a declaration that something is true. **2** confidence of mind or manner. **3** life insurance.

assure *verb* (**assures, assuring, assured**) **1** to inform somebody that something is definitely true: *I want to assure you that your complaint will be taken seriously.* **2** to make it certain that something will happen.

assured *adjective* **1** self-confident and sure of your ability. **2** certain; guaranteed. ✱ **be assured of** to be certain to get something. ➤ **assuredly** *adverb*.

asterisk *noun* (*plural* **asterisks**) the sign (*) used as a reference mark.

astern *adverb* behind or towards the rear of a ship or aircraft.

asteroid *noun* (*plural* **asteroids**) *Science* any of the small rocky planets found in a belt between Mars and Jupiter.

asthma /as ma/ *noun* an allergic condition that causes difficulty in breathing. ➤ **asthmatic** *adjective and noun*.

astonish *verb* (**astonishes, astonishing, astonished**) to make somebody feel sudden wonder or surprise. ➤ **astonishment** *noun*.

astound *verb* (**astounds, astounding, astounded**) to astonish somebody greatly.

astray *adverb* off the right path or route. ✱ **go astray 1** to get lost. **2** to make a mistake. **lead astray** to persuade somebody to do wrong.

astride *preposition* with one leg on each side of something.

astringent *adjective* causing the skin to contract. ➤ **astringency** *noun*, **astringent** *noun*.

astrology *noun* the study of the supposed influence of the planets on human affairs. ➤ **astrologer** *noun*, **astrological** *adjective*.

astronaut *noun* (*plural* **astronauts**) a person trained to travel in space.

astronomical *or* **astronomic** *adjective* **1** to do with astronomy. **2** *informal* extremely large. ➤ **astronomically** *adverb*.

astronomy *noun* the scientific study of the stars, planets, and universe. ➤ **astronomer** *noun*.

astute *adjective* shrewd and perceptive. ➤ **astutely** *adverb*, **astuteness** *noun*.

asunder *adverb literary* into parts or pieces.

asylum *noun* (*plural* **asylums**) **1** protection from arrest or danger. **2** *dated* an institution for the care of the mentally ill.

asymmetric /ay si me trik/ *or* **asymmetrical** *adjective* not symmetrical. ➤ **asymmetry** *noun*.

at *preposition* **1** indicating position in or movement towards a place. **2** indicating time. **3** indicating a rate or value. **4** indicating the object of an action: *Look at me!* **5** indicating a state: *at rest.*

ate *verb* past tense of EAT.

atheism /ay thee i zm/ *noun* the belief that there is no God. ➤ **atheist** *noun*, **atheistic** *adjective*.

athlete *noun* (*plural* **athletes**) a person who is trained or skilled in exercises and sports.

athlete's foot *noun* a form of fungal infection of the feet affecting the skin between the toes.

athletic *adjective* **1** relating to athletes or athletics. **2** vigorous or active. **3** muscular and well-proportioned. ➤ **athletically** *adverb*, **athleticism** *noun*.

athletics *noun* the sport of running and other track and field events.

Atlantic *adjective* to do with or near the Atlantic Ocean or the regions around it.

atlas *noun* (*plural* **atlases**) a book of maps or charts.

atmosphere *noun* (*plural* **atmospheres**) **1** the gas enveloping the earth or another planet. **2** a surrounding feeling or mood in a place or at an event. **3** *Science* a unit of

atoll

pressure equal to the typical pressure of the air at sea level. ➤ **atmospheric** *adjective*.

atoll *noun* (*plural* **atolls**) *Geography* a coral reef surrounding a lagoon.

atom *noun* **1** *Science* the smallest particle of an element that has all the properties of that element. **2** a tiny particle; a bit.

atom bomb or **atomic bomb** *noun* (*plural* **atom bombs** or **atomic bombs**) a very destructive bomb whose power comes from a sudden release of atomic energy in a very rapid chain reaction.

atomic *adjective* to do with atoms.

atone *verb* (**atones**, **atoning**, **atoned**) (**atone for**) to make amends for a crime or wrong.

atrocious *adjective* **1** extremely wicked or cruel. **2** *informal* very horrible or bad. ➤ **atrociously** *adverb*.

atrocity *noun* (*plural* **atrocities**) a wicked or cruel act.

attach *verb* (**attaches**, **attaching**, **attached**) **1** to join or fasten something to something else. **2** to consider something to have a certain quality, especially importance or significance.

attaché /atashay/ *noun* (*plural* **attachés**) a technical expert on the staff of an embassy.

attaché case *noun* (*plural* **attaché cases**) a slim case used for carrying papers.

attachment *noun* (*plural* **attachments**) **1** the process of attaching. **2** fondness for somebody or something. **3** *ICT* computer data sent with an email message.

attack *verb* (**attacks**, **attacking**, **attacked**) **1** to try to hurt or injure somebody. **2** to try to score against an opponent or opposing team. **3** to criticize somebody or something in a hostile way. **4** to have a harmful effect on something: *The virus attacks the nervous system.* **5** to begin to work vigorously on something: *We'll attack the garden when we've finished the house.* ~ *noun* (*plural* **attacks**) **1** an act of attacking; an assault. **2** an onset of sickness or disease: *an attack of pneumonia.* ➤ **attacker** *noun*.

attain *verb* (**attains**, **attaining**, **attained**) **1** to achieve an objective. **2** *formal* to reach a certain age. ➤ **attainable** *adjective*, **attainment** *noun*.

attempt *verb* (**attempts**, **attempting**, **attempted**) to make an effort to accomplish something. ~ *noun* (*plural* **attempts**) an effort to do something.

attend *verb* (**attends**, **attending**, **attended**) **1** to go to or be present at an event. **2** to be a servant or helper to somebody. **3** (**attend to**) to deal with a task or problem, or with somebody.

attendance *noun* (*plural* **attendances**) **1** the number of people present. **2** the number of times a person attends something. **3** the fact of being present: *Attendance at the meeting is compulsory.*

attendant *noun* (*plural* **attendants**) a servant or helper.

attention *noun* **1** a state in which your mind is concentrated on what is happening or what you are doing. **2** a position in which a soldier stands straight with both feet together. * **pay attention** to watch or listen carefully to what is going on.

attentive *adjective* **1** paying close attention. **2** concerned for the welfare of somebody else. ➤ **attentively** *adverb*.

attest *verb* (**attests**, **attesting**, **attested**) **1** to be proof of something. **2** to state that something is true.

attic *noun* (*plural* **attics**) a room or space in the roof of a building.

attire *noun formal* dress or clothing of a particular kind.

attitude *noun* (*plural* **attitudes**) **1** a way of thinking about or feeling towards something or somebody. **2** a posture. **3** *informal* a deliberately challenging manner.

attorney *noun* (*plural* **attorneys**) **1** a person who has legal authority to act for another person. **2** *N American* a lawyer.

attract *verb* (**attracts, attracting, attracted**) **1** to arouse the affection or interest of somebody. **2** to have the power to draw things towards itself. **3** to become the focus of attention.

attraction *noun* (*plural* **attractions**) **1** an attractive quality or aspect. **2** something that draws visitors or spectators. **3** the power of drawing things towards itself.

attractive *adjective* **1** good-looking or sexually interesting. **2** arousing interest or pleasure. ➤ **attractively** *adverb*, **attractiveness** *noun*.

attribute /a tri bewt/ *noun* (*plural* **attributes**) a characteristic or quality. ~ /a tri bewt/ *verb* (**attributes, attributing, attributed**) to believe that something is caused or done by something or somebody: *He attributed his success to luck.* ➤ **attributable** *adjective*, **attribution** *noun*.

attributive *adjective English* said about an adjective: standing in front of the noun it is modifying, as for example 'red' in *the red dress.* ➤ **attributively** *adverb*.

attuned *adjective* accustomed to and able to cope with or respond to something: *Our ears became attuned to the silence.*

aubergine *noun* (*plural* **aubergines**) a large purple fruit used as a vegetable.

auburn *noun* a reddish brown colour.

auction *noun* (*plural* **auctions**) a public sale in which each item is sold to the buyer offering the highest bid. ~ *verb* (**auctions, auctioning, auctioned**) to sell something at an auction. ➤ **auctioneer** *noun*.

audacious /aw **day** shus/ *adjective* **1** boldly daring. **2** insolent. ➤ **audaciously** *adverb*, **audacity** *noun*.

audible *adjective* loud enough to be heard. ➤ **audibility** *noun*, **audibly** *adverb*.

audience *noun* (*plural* **audiences**) **1** a group of listeners or spectators at a theatre or concert. **2** a formal meeting, hearing or interview.

audit *noun* (*plural* **audits**) an official examination of accounts to make sure that they are correct. ~ *verb* (**audits, auditing, audited**) to perform an audit on accounts.

audition *noun* (*plural* **auditions**) *Drama* a trial performance to assess the ability of somebody to be in a play or join an orchestra, choir, etc. ~ *verb* (**auditions, auditioning, auditioned**) *Drama* to test a performer, or to be tested, for a part.

auditorium *noun* (*plural* **auditoria** or **auditoriums**) *Drama* the part of a theatre or concert hall where the audience sits.

augment *verb* (**augments, augmenting, augmented**) to increase something. ➤ **augmentation** *noun*.

August *noun* the eighth month of the year.

august /aw **gust**/ *adjective* very dignified or grand.

aunt *noun* (*plural* **aunts**) the sister of your father or mother, or the wife of your uncle.

au pair /oh **pair**/ *noun* (*plural* **au pairs**) a young foreign person who does domestic work for a family in return for accommodation with them.

aura *noun* (*plural* **auras**) a distinctive atmosphere surrounding a person or place.

aural *adjective* to do with the ear or hearing. ➤ **aurally** *adverb*.

au revoir /oh ri **vwah**/ *interjection* goodbye.

auspices

auspices /aw spi siz/ * **under the auspices of** with the support of, or under the supervision of, a person or group.

auspicious /aw spi shus/ *adjective* likely to bring success. ➤ **auspiciously** *adverb*.

Aussie /o zi/ *noun* (*plural* **Aussies**) *informal* an Australian.

austere *adjective* **1** stern and forbidding in appearance and manner. **2** plain or simple. ➤ **austerely** *adverb*, **austerity** *noun*.

authentic *adjective* known to be genuine. ➤ **authentically** *adverb*, **authenticity** *noun*.

authenticate *verb* (**authenticates, authenticating, authenticated**) to prove or declare something to be genuine. ➤ **authentication** *noun*.

author *noun* (*plural* **authors**) **1** the writer of a book or article. **2** the inventor of something. ➤ **authorship** *noun*.

authoritarian *adjective* **1** enforcing strict discipline and obedience; **2** dictatorial. ~ *noun* (*plural* **authoritarians**) an authoritarian person.

authoritative *adjective* **1** that can be relied on to be correct: *an authoritative edition*. **2** commanding respect and obedience: *an authoritative manner*. ➤ **authoritatively** *adverb*.

authority *noun* (*plural* **authorities**) **1** the power to issue orders and expect obedience. **2** (**the authorities**) the government or law-enforcers. **3** a government organization that administers a public service. **4** an expert.

authorize *or* **authorise** *verb* (**authorizes, authorizing, authorized** *or* **authorises**, etc) to give official permission for something. ➤ **authorization** *or* **authorisation** *noun*.

autism *noun* a mental disorder marked by great difficulty in forming relationships with other people. ➤ **autistic** *adjective*.

autobiography *noun* (*plural* **autobiographies**) an account of your life that you have written yourself. ➤ **autobiographical** *adjective*.

autocrat *noun* (*plural* **autocrats**) **1** a person who rules with total power. **2** a dictatorial person. ➤ **autocratic** *adjective*, **autocratically** *adverb*.

autograph *noun* (*plural* **autographs**) a celebrity's handwritten signature given as a memento.

automate *verb* (**automates, automating, automated**) to convert a machine or system so that it operates automatically.

automatic *adjective* **1** acting or done spontaneously or unconsciously: *an automatic reaction*. **2** able to operate without human intervention: *an automatic gearbox*. **3** said about a gun: able to fire repeatedly for as long as the trigger is pressed. ~ *noun* (*plural* **automatics**) **1** a car with an automatic gearbox. **2** an automatic gun. ➤ **automatically** *adverb*.

automobile *noun* (*plural* **automobiles**) *chiefly N American* a motor car.

autonomous /aw to no mus/ *adjective* self-governing; independent. ➤ **autonomy** *noun*.

autopsy *noun* (*plural* **autopsies**) an examination of a dead body to determine the cause of death.

autumn *noun* (*plural* **autumns**) the season between summer and winter. ➤ **autumnal** *adjective*.

auxiliary *adjective* providing help or extra power. ~ *noun* (*plural* **auxiliaries**) a person, group, or device that gives extra help.

auxiliary verb *noun* (*plural* **auxiliary verbs**) *English* **1** a verb such as 'be', 'have' and 'do' that is used to form tenses, questions, etc with other verbs, as in *she is coming, she has come*, and *did she come?* **2** any of the verbs 'can', 'could', 'may', 'might', 'will', 'would', 'shall', 'should' and 'must'.

avail *verb* (**avails, availing, availed**) to help or benefit somebody. * **avail yourself of** to make use of something. **of/to no avail** useless.

available *adjective* **1** present or ready for use. **2** obtainable. ➤ **availability** *noun*.

avalanche *noun* (*plural* **avalanches**) **1** a mass of snow or ice falling rapidly down a mountain. **2** a sudden overwhelming rush.

avant-garde /a vong **gahd**/ *adjective* daringly modern or innovative.

avarice *noun* extreme desire for wealth or gain. ➤ **avaricious** *adjective*.

avenge *verb* (**avenges, avenging, avenged**) to take revenge on behalf of somebody or for a wrong. ➤ **avenger** *noun*.

avenue *noun* (*plural* **avenues**) a broad street or road, usually bordered by trees.

average *noun* (*plural* **averages**) **1** *Maths* an amount obtained by adding several figures together and dividing the total by the number of figures. **2** a level typical of a group. ~ *adjective* **1** *Maths* worked out as an average. **2** common or typical. ~ *verb* (**averages, averaging, averaged**) to amount to as an average.

averse *adjective* (**averse to**) strongly opposed to or disliking something.

Usage Note Averse or adverse? Averse means 'not liking something': *He's averse to having his picture taken.* Adverse means 'unfavourable': *adverse weather conditions.*

aversion *noun* (*plural* **aversions**) a strong dislike.

avert *verb* (**averts, averting, averted**) **1** to turn away your eyes. **2** to prevent something unwelcome from happening.

aviary *noun* (*plural* **aviaries**) an enclosure for keeping birds.

aviation *noun* the manufacture and operation of aircraft.

aviator *noun* (*plural* **aviators**) a pilot.

avid *adjective* very eager or keen. ➤ **avidly** *adverb*.

avocado *noun* (*plural* **avocados** *or* **avocadoes**) a pear-shaped fruit with green flesh.

avoid *verb* (**avoids, avoiding, avoided**) **1** to keep away from something or somebody: *Avoid the M25 during the rush hour.* **2** to prevent something bad from happening: *I changed the subject to avoid an argument.* **3** to refrain from doing something. ➤ **avoidable** *adjective*, **avoidance** *noun*.

avuncular /a vung **kew**ler/ *adjective* kindly or genial towards somebody younger.

await *verb* (**awaits, awaiting, awaited**) **1** to wait for something or somebody. **2** to be in store for something or somebody.

awake *verb* (**awakes, awaking, awoke, awoken**) to come out of sleep. ~ *adjective* not asleep.

awaken *verb* (**awakens, awakening, awakened**) **1** to wake somebody. **2** to wake up. **3** to stir up a feeling.

award *verb* (**awards, awarding, awarded**) to give somebody something intended as a reward or an honour. ~ *noun* (*plural* **awards**) **1** something given as an honour or reward. **2** the act of awarding something.

aware *adjective* knowing about or conscious of something. ➤ **awareness** *noun*.

awash *adjective* covered or flooded with water.

away *adverb* **1** at a distance: *six miles away.* **2** into a secure place: *put away in a cupboard.* **3** out of existence: *The*

awe

pain will soon pass away. **4** without interruption: *to hammer away on the keys.* ~ *adjective* said about a sports fixture: played at the opponent's ground.

awe *noun* a feeling of dread and wonder.

awesome *adjective* **1** inspiring awe. **2** *informal* impressive. ➤ **awesomely** *adverb*.

awful *adjective* extremely unpleasant. ➤ **awfully** *adverb*.

awkward *adjective* **1** difficult to use or handle. **2** clumsy. **3** causing or feeling embarrassment. ➤ **awkwardly** *adverb*.

awl *noun* (*plural* **awls**) a pointed tool for making small holes.

awning *noun* (*plural* **awnings**) a canvas cover used to protect something from the weather.

awoke *verb* past tense of AWAKE.

awoken *verb* past participle of AWAKE.

AWOL /ay wol/ *abbreviation* absent without leave.

awry /a wrie/ *adverb and adjective* out of the right position; amiss.

axe *noun* (*plural* **axes**) a tool with a large heavy blade, used for chopping. ~ *verb* (**axes, axing, axed**) to cancel or do away with something abruptly. ✶ **have an axe to grind** to have a private purpose in doing something.

axiom *noun* (*plural* **axioms**) a principle or rule generally recognized as true.

axis *noun* (*plural* **axes** /ak seez/) **1** *Science* a straight line through the centre of a rotating object. **2** *Maths* a reference line in a graph.

axle *noun* (*plural* **axles**) a shaft on which a wheel rotates.

aye *interjection archaic or dialect* yes.

azure /a zher *or* ay zher/ *noun* sky-blue.

baa verb (**baas, baaing, baaed** or **baa'd**) to make the bleat of a sheep. ➤ **baa** noun.

babble verb (**babbles, babbling, babbled**) to talk quickly and in a way that is difficult to understand. ~ noun a lot of meaningless words or sounds.

babe noun (plural **babes**) **1** literary a baby. **2** informal an attractive girl or woman.

baboon noun (plural **baboons**) a large monkey with a long face and a medium-length tail.

baby noun (plural **babies**) **1** a very young child or animal. **2** somebody who behaves in a childish way. ➤ **babyhood** noun, **babyish** adjective.

babysit verb (**babysits, babysitting, babysat**) to look after a child while the parents are out. ➤ **babysitter** noun, **babysitting** noun.

bachelor noun (plural **bachelors**) **1** a man who has not married. **2** (**Bachelor**) somebody who has a university degree of the lowest level: *Bachelor of Arts*.

bacillus /bə si lus/ noun (plural **bacilli** /bə si lie/) *Science* a rod-shaped germ that causes disease.

back noun (plural **backs**) **1** the part of your body from behind your neck down to the end of your spine. **2** the side or surface of something that is not at the front. **3** one of the players who is in a defending position in a team game such as football. ~ adverb **1** to or at the back. **2** in or into a position on your back. **3** in or into the past. **4** nearer the beginning. **5** to or in a place from which somebody or something came. **6** to or closer to the way something was before. **7** in return or reply: *Please write back.* ~ adjective at or in the back: *a back seat.* ~ verb (**backs, backing, backed**) **1** to give support to somebody or something. **2** to provide a musical accompaniment for somebody or something. **3** to drive a vehicle backwards. **4** to form or cover the back of something. **5** to place a bet on a competitor in a race. **6** (**back onto**) said about a building: to have its back against or facing something. ✱ **back and forth** backwards and forwards repeatedly. **back down** to admit that you are wrong or beaten. **back out** to decide not to do something you agreed to do. **back to front** turned so that the back is where the front should be. **back up 1** to support somebody and what they have said or done. **2** *ICT* to make a copy of data stored on a computer, to keep separately. **behind your back** without your knowledge or permission.

back-bencher noun (plural **back-benchers**) an MP who does not hold a post in the government or opposition.

backbiting noun talking about other people in a mean and spiteful way when they are not there.

backbone noun (plural **backbones**) **1** the spine of an animal. **2** the

backdate

strongest or most important part of something.

backdate *verb* (**backdates, backdating, backdated**) **1** to make a change or rule start to apply from a date in the past. **2** to put an earlier date on a document than the actual date.

backdrop *noun* (*plural* **backdrops**) **1** a painted cloth that hangs at the back of a stage. **2** a setting for an event.

backer *noun* (*plural* **backers**) somebody who gives money to support a plan or project.

backfire *verb* (**backfires, backfiring, backfired**) **1** said about a car or engine: to make a loud bang when some fuel burns in the exhaust pipe. **2** said about a plan: to fail by having the opposite effect to the one you expected.

backgammon *noun* a board game for two players, played with dice and counters.

background *noun* (*plural* **backgrounds**) **1** the scenery or area behind something. **2** the part of a painting or photograph showing what is behind the objects or people at the front. **3** the conditions that exist before something happens. **4** information that helps to explain a problem or situation. **5** somebody's experience, family, and upbringing.

backhand *noun* (*plural* **backhands**) a stroke in games such as tennis and squash made with the back of the hand turned in the direction in which you are hitting the ball. ➤ **backhand** *adjective and adverb*.

backing *noun* (*plural* **backings**) **1** financial support or aid. **2** a material used to cover or form the reverse surface of something. **3** music that is played or sung to accompany a song or singer.

backlash *noun* (*plural* **backlashes**) a strong reaction against a political or social change.

backlog *noun* (*plural* **backlogs**) a lot of things that still need to be done.

backpack *noun* (*plural* **backpacks**) a large bag with shoulder straps that you carry on your back.

backpacker *noun* (*plural* **backpackers**) somebody who travels carrying a backpack.

backside *noun* (*plural* **backsides**) *informal* the buttocks.

backstage *adjective and adverb* behind the stage in the area not seen by the audience.

backstroke *noun* a style of swimming in which you lie on your back, kick your feet, and make backward circles with your arms.

backward *adjective* **1** directed behind you: *a backward glance*. **2** not as developed as most others: *a backward country*. **3** slower at learning than most people.

backwards *adverb* **1** towards the back. **2** with the back coming or arriving first. **3** in a reverse direction or moving towards the beginning.

backwater *noun* (*plural* **backwaters**) a quiet, dull, or old-fashioned place.

bacon *noun* salted or smoked meat cut from the side or back of a pig.

bacterium /bak teer i um/ *noun* (*plural* **bacteria**) *Science* a type of microscopic organism, some of which cause disease.

bad *adjective* (**worse, worst**) **1** poor or not acceptable in quality. **2** evil or immoral. **3** naughty or disobedient. **4** (**bad at**) unskilful or incompetent. **5** (**bad for**) harmful. **6** severe. **7** unhealthy. ✱ **not bad** *informal* quite good.

bade /bad *or* bayd/ *verb archaic* past tense of BID².

badge *noun* (*plural* **badges**) a small design or symbol made of plastic, metal, or cloth that you attach to clothes, sometimes to show that you belong to a society or group.

badger¹ *noun* (*plural* **badgers**) an animal with a grey body and a black-and-white striped face.

badger² *verb* (**badgers, badgering, badgered**) to keep asking somebody for or about something in an annoying way.

badly *adverb* **1** not well; unsuccessfully. **2** unkindly; cruelly. **3** very much or severely.

badminton *noun* a game in which the players hit a shuttlecock over a net using light rackets.

baffle *verb* (**baffles, baffling, baffled**) to puzzle or confuse somebody.
➤ **baffled** *adjective*, **bafflement** *noun*, **baffling** *adjective*.

bag *noun* (*plural* **bags**) **1** a container made of soft or flexible material, used for storing or carrying things, such as a handbag or shoulder bag. **2** (**bags**) *informal* a great deal; lots. ~ *verb* (**bags, bagging, bagged**) **1** to swell out, bulge, or hang loosely. **2** to put something into a bag. **3** *informal* to get possession of something.
➤ **bagful** *noun* (*plural* **bagfuls**).

bagel /bay gl/ *noun* (*plural* **bagels**) a hard ring-shaped bread roll.

baggage *noun* suitcases and bags that people use when travelling.

baggy *adjective* (**baggier, baggiest**) loose or puffed out.

baguette /ba get/ *noun* (*plural* **baguettes**) a long thin French loaf.

bail¹ *noun* **1** money that is paid so that somebody accused of a crime can be released from the court as long as they return for their trial. **2** permission to release somebody from court when bail has been paid. ~ *verb* (**bails, bailing, bailed**) to release somebody because their bail has been paid.

bail² *noun* (*plural* **bails**) either of the two wooden pieces that rest on top of the cricket stumps to form the wicket.

bail³ *verb* (**bails, bailing, bailed**) to empty out water from a ship or boat: *We tried to bail out the water with plastic tubs.*

bail⁴ *verb* see BALE².

bailiff *noun* (*plural* **bailiffs**) **1** a law officer who brings legal documents ordering people to do something and who can legally remove their property if they owe money. **2** somebody who manages an estate or farm.

Bairam /bie rahm/ *noun* either of two Muslim festivals held every year, the Lesser Bairam and the Greater Bairam.

Baisakhi /bie sa ki/ *or* **Vaisakhi** /vie sa ki/ *noun* a Sikh festival celebrating the Sikh New Year.

bait *noun* a small amount of food that you put on a hook or in a trap to tempt an animal so that you can catch it. ~ *verb* (**baits, baiting, baited**) **1** to put bait on a hook or in a trap. **2** to tease or annoy somebody.

baize *noun* a green woollen cloth used as a covering for billiard tables.

bake *verb* (**bakes, baking, baked**) **1** to cook food in an oven. **2** to dry or harden something by heating it. **3** to become extremely hot.

baked beans *plural noun* cooked white beans in tomato sauce, sold in tins.

baker *noun* (*plural* **bakers**) somebody who bakes and sells bread and cakes.
✴ **a baker's dozen** thirteen.

bakery *noun* (*plural* **bakeries**) a shop that sells freshly baked bread and cakes, or a building in which they are baked.

baking powder *noun* a type of powder that makes cakes rise when they are baking.

balaclava /ba la klah va/ *noun* (*plural* **balaclavas**) a tight woollen hat that covers the head leaving all or part of the face uncovered.

Word History Named after *Balaclava*, a village in the Crimea, Ukraine. Soldiers in the Crimean War wore balaclavas to protect themselves from the bitter winter.

balance *noun* (*plural* **balances**) **1** a steady or stable condition achieved by spreading weight evenly on each side of a vertical axis. **2** the ability to keep yourself steady and balanced. **3** a situation in which there are contrasting elements in roughly equal amounts. **4** the difference between the amount of money you put into an account and the amount you take out. **5** the amount left over when you have used something. **6** a weighing instrument that has a balanced bar with a dish hanging from each end. ~ *verb* (**balances, balancing, balanced**) **1** to stay in or put something in a state of balance. **2** said about accounts: to have the same total amount of money going in and coming out. ➤ **balanced** *adjective*.

balcony *noun* (*plural* **balconies**) **1** a platform with a railing built out from the wall of a building. **2** an area where you can sit upstairs inside a theatre.

bald *adjective* **1** with no hair or not much hair on your head. **2** said about a tyre: with all or most of the patterned surface worn away. **3** said in a clear or blunt way. ➤ **baldly** *adverb*, **baldness** *noun*.

balding *adjective* becoming bald.

bale[1] *noun* (*plural* **bales**) a large tied bundle of hay, cloth, or paper.

bale[2] *or* **bail** *verb* (**bales, baling, baled** *or* **bails, bailing, bailed**) ✱ **bale out** *or* **bail out 1** to jump from an aircraft, using a parachute. **2** to rescue somebody from a difficult situation.

balk *or* **baulk** *verb* (**balks, balking, balked** *or* **baulks, baulking, baulked**) **1** to stop suddenly and refuse to go on: *My horse balked at the fence.* **2** to be unwilling or refuse to do something: *I balked at paying £5 for a sandwich.*

ball[1] *noun* (*plural* **balls**) **1** a solid or hollow round object that you throw, hit, or kick in various games. **2** a sphere or rounded object: *a ball of wool.* **3** (**balls**) *informal* the testicles. ✱ **the ball of your foot** the rounded part of your foot below your big toe. **on the ball** competent; alert.

ball[2] *noun* (*plural* **balls**) a large formal party at which the guests dance. ✱ **have a ball** to enjoy yourself.

ballad *noun* (*plural* **ballads**) **1** a poem or song that tells a story. **2** a slow or romantic pop song.

ballast *noun* heavy material carried in a ship to keep it steady in the water.

ballcock *noun* (*plural* **ballcocks**) *Science* a valve attached to a hollow ball that floats inside a toilet cistern and controls the amount of water coming in.

ballerina *noun* (*plural* **ballerinas**) a female ballet dancer.

ballet *noun* (*plural* **ballets**) **1** a form of artistic dancing with conventional positions and steps. **2** a performance of ballet on stage.

ballistic *adjective* **1** to do with the way bullets and similar objects move through the air. **2** *informal* violently angry.

ballistics *noun* the science concerned with the movement of objects that are fired through the air.

balloon *noun* (*plural* **balloons**) **1** a coloured rubber bag that is inflated and used as a toy or decoration. **2** a large bag-like container that floats in the atmosphere when filled with hot air or a gas lighter than air. **3** an outline containing words spoken or thought by a character in a cartoon. ~ *verb* (**balloons, ballooning, ballooned**) **1** to travel in a balloon. **2** to swell or puff out.

ballot *noun* (*plural* **ballots**) an election in which each person makes their vote secretly. ~ *verb* (**ballots, balloting, balloted**) to ask a group of people to vote about something.

ballpoint *or* **ballpoint pen** *noun* (*plural* **ballpoints** *or* **ballpoint pens**) a pen that has a tiny rotating ball as the writing point.

ballroom *noun* (*plural* **ballrooms**) a large room in which formal dances are held.

balm /bahm/ *noun* a sweet-smelling natural ointment with healing properties.

balmy *adjective* (**balmier, balmiest**) said about weather: pleasantly warm.

balsa *or* **balsa wood** /bawl sa/ *noun* a type of wood that weighs very little and is used for making models.

balustrade /ba lu strayd/ *noun* (*plural* **balustrades**) a row of upright posts with a rail across the top, at the edge of a staircase or balcony.

bamboo *noun* (*plural* **bamboos**) a tall tropical grass with thick, hard, hollow stems.

bamboozle *verb* (**bamboozles, bamboozling, bamboozled**) to confuse or puzzle somebody.

ban *verb* (**bans, banning, banned**) to forbid something, or forbid somebody from doing something, officially. ~ *noun* (*plural* **bans**) a rule or law that forbids something.

banal /ba nahl/ *adjective* not new or original; dull. ➤ **banality** *noun*.

banana *noun* (*plural* **bananas**) a long curved fruit with yellow skin and soft pale flesh.

band¹ *noun* (*plural* **bands**) **1** a narrow strip of material, sometimes with the two ends joined together to form a loop. **2** a range of radio wavelengths.

band² *verb* (**bands, banding, banded**) to join into a group in order to do something together. ~ *noun* (*plural* **bands**) **1** a group of musicians playing jazz, pop, rock, or marching music. **2** a group of people who share an interest or purpose.

bandage *noun* (*plural* **bandages**) a strip of cloth for wrapping around a wound or injury. ~ *verb* (**bandages, bandaging, bandaged**) to wrap something in a bandage.

bandit *noun* (*plural* **bandits**) a member of a band of armed robbers who attack travellers.

bandstand *noun* (*plural* **bandstands**) a covered outdoor platform where a brass band may play music.

bandwagon ✴ **jump on the bandwagon** to join in a fashionable and successful activity in order to benefit from it yourself.

bandy¹ *verb* (**bandies, bandying, bandied**) to use or mention something a lot without much thought or understanding: *There's a new term they keep bandying about at work.*

bandy² *adjective* (**bandier, bandiest**) said about somebody's legs: curving out at the knees.

bane *noun* something unpleasant, upsetting, or annoying that spoils things: *Housework is the bane of my life!*

bang¹ *verb* (**bangs, banging, banged**) **1** to hit something sharply: *I banged my elbow.* **2** to cause something to make a loud sharp or metallic noise. ~ *noun* (*plural* **bangs**) **1** a sudden loud noise. **2** a hard hit with an object.

bang² *adverb informal* exactly: *The bus arrived bang on time.*

banger *noun* (*plural* **bangers**) **1** a firework that explodes with a loud bang. **2** *informal* a sausage. **3** *informal* an old car in bad condition.

bangle

bangle *noun* (*plural* **bangles**) a rigid bracelet.

banish *verb* (**banishes, banishing, banished**) **1** to punish somebody by sending them away from a place for a long time. **2** to push an unpleasant thought out of your mind. ➤ **banishment** *noun*.

banister *noun* (*plural* **banisters**) **1** a handrail supported on upright posts at the edge of a staircase. **2** an upright post supporting a handrail.

banjo *noun* (*plural* **banjos**) a small stringed instrument with a round flat body and a long neck.

bank¹ *noun* (*plural* **banks**) **1** a mound of earth or snow. **2** a mass of cloud or fog. **3** a slope beside a lake, river, road, or railway. ~ *verb* (**banks, banking, banked**) **1** to rise in a slope or mound. **2** said about an aircraft: to tilt sideways when making a turn.

bank² *noun* (*plural* **banks**) **1** a business that issues and lends money and in which people can keep their money. **2** a store of something kept ready for use: *a blood bank*. **3** a container you put objects in for recycling: *a bottle bank*. ~ *verb* (**banks, banking, banked**) **1** to put money into a bank. **2** (**bank on/upon**) to rely on somebody or something.

bank³ *noun* (*plural* **banks**) a group, series, or row of objects arranged together: *a bank of computers*.

bank card *noun* (*plural* **bank cards**) = CASH CARD.

bank holiday *noun* (*plural* **bank holidays**) a public holiday when banks and some businesses are closed.

banknote *noun* (*plural* **banknotes**) a sum of money in the form of a paper note.

bankrupt *adjective* legally declared unable to pay debts. ~ *noun* (*plural* **bankrupts**) a bankrupt person. ~ *verb* (**bankrupts, bankrupting, bankrupted**) to make somebody bankrupt. ➤ **bankruptcy** *noun*.

banner *noun* (*plural* **banners**) a flag with a symbolic or heraldic design on it, carried or displayed during processions or ceremonies.

banquet *noun* (*plural* **banquets**) a large and elaborate meal for a special occasion.

banter *noun* light-hearted teasing or joking.

bap *noun* (*plural* **baps**) a soft round bread roll.

baptism *noun* (*plural* **baptisms**) a Christian ceremony in which somebody is sprinkled with or dipped under water and becomes a member of the Church. ➤ **baptismal** *adjective*.

Baptist *adjective* belonging to a section of the Christian Protestant Church that baptizes people as adults and not as babies. ~ *noun* (*plural* **Baptists**) a member of the Baptist Church.

baptize *or* **baptise** *verb* (**baptizes, baptizing, baptized** *or* **baptises**, etc) **1** to perform a baptism on somebody. **2** to give somebody a name at their baptism.

bar¹ *noun* (*plural* **bars**) **1** a long firm piece of hard material. **2** a counter where alcoholic drinks are served, or a room containing one. **3** a small section of written music, marked at each end by a vertical line. **4** something that stops progress or action. **5** (**the Bar**) barristers as a group, or their profession. ~ *verb* (**bars, barring, barred**) **1** to fasten a door, window, etc with a bar. **2** to shut something or somebody in or out. **3** to prevent or forbid somebody: *The judge barred him from visiting his ex-wife.* * **behind bars** in prison. ➤ **barred** *adjective*.

bar² *preposition* except for: *All the teachers bar one were women*.

barb *noun* (*plural* **barbs**) an extra spike

sticking out backwards from an arrow, etc making it difficult to remove.

barbarian /bah **bair** i an/ *noun* (*plural* **barbarians**) a cruel or uncivilized person.

barbaric /bah ba rik/ *adjective* vicious and cruel. ➤ **barbarism** *noun*.

barbecue *noun* (*plural* **barbecues**) **1** an outdoor meal at which you cook food over a charcoal fire. **2** a piece of equipment for cooking food on at a barbecue. ~ *verb* (**barbecues, barbecuing, barbecued**) to cook food on a barbecue.

barbed *adjective* **1** said about a remark: sarcastic or spiteful. **2** having a barb or barbs.

barbed wire *noun* wire with small sharp spikes along it.

barber *noun* (*plural* **barbers**) a person who cuts men's hair and beards.

barbiturate *noun* (*plural* **barbiturates**) a strong drug that affects the nervous system and makes you feel sleepy.

bar code *noun* (*plural* **bar codes**) a printed code of vertical black lines, which gives information about a product when it is read by an electronic scanner.

bard *noun* (*plural* **bards**) **1** *literary* a poet. **2** (**the Bard**) Shakespeare.

bare *adjective* (**barer, barest**) **1** not covered by clothing. **2** without any leaves or normal natural covering. **3** exposed; not concealed. **4** unfurnished or empty. **5** with nothing added. ~ *verb* (**bares, baring, bared**) to reveal or uncover something.

bareback *adverb and adjective* on the back of a horse without a saddle.

barefaced *adjective* obvious and unashamed.

barely *adverb* only just; hardly.

bargain *noun* (*plural* **bargains**) **1** something you buy more cheaply than usual. **2** an agreement between people about helping or trading with each other. ~ *verb* (**bargains, bargaining, bargained**) to negotiate about the details of a purchase or agreement. * **bargain for** to be prepared for something.

barge¹ *noun* (*plural* **barges**) a long flat-bottomed boat used on inland waterways.

barge² *verb* (**barges, barging, barged**) **1** to move clumsily or roughly: *Keep still and stop barging around!* **2** (**barge in**) to enter or interrupt rudely.

baritone *noun* (*plural* **baritones**) a male singer with a voice between bass and tenor.

barium /**bair** i um/ *noun Science* a soft silvery-white metal that is one of the chemical elements.

bark¹ *verb* (**barks, barking, barked**) to make the short loud cry of a dog. ➤ **bark** *noun*.

bark² *noun* the tough layer covering the trunk of a tree.

barley *noun* a cereal plant used in foods and for cattle feed.

barman *noun* (*plural* **barmen**) a man who serves drinks in a bar.

bar mitzvah /bah **mits** va/ *noun* (*plural* **bar mitzvahs**) a religious ceremony that takes place when a Jewish boy reaches the age of 13 and takes on adult responsibilities.

barmy *adjective* (**barmier, barmiest**) *informal* crazy or mad.

barn *noun* (*plural* **barns**) a large farm building used to store things in.

barnacle *noun* (*plural* **barnacles**) a small shellfish that fixes itself to rocks and boats.

barometer *noun* (*plural* **barometers**) an instrument that measures atmospheric pressure, used to predict changes in the weather.

baron *noun* (*plural* **barons**) a man

baroness

belonging to the lowest rank of British peers. ➤ **baronial** *adjective*, **barony** *noun*.

baroness *noun* (*plural* **baronesses**)
1 the wife or widow of a baron.
2 a woman who has the same rank as a baron.

baronet *noun* (*plural* **baronets**) a man with an inherited title that ranks below a baron and above a knight. ➤ **baronetcy** *noun*.

baroque /ba rok/ *noun Art* an ornamental style of 17th-century European art, architecture, and music. ➤ **baroque** *adjective*.

barracks *noun* (*plural* **barracks**) a group of buildings for soldiers to live in.

barrage /ba rahzh/ *noun* (*plural* **barrages**) **1** a continuous attack of heavy gunfire. **2** a continuous series of questions or complaints. ~ *verb* (**barrages, barraging, barraged**) to overwhelm somebody with questions or complaints.

barrel *noun* (*plural* **barrels**) **1** a large cylindrical container for liquids. **2** the tube of a gun, from which the bullet is fired.

barren *adjective* **1** unable to have children or offspring. **2** not fertile or productive.

barricade *noun* (*plural* **barricades**) an obstruction built quickly to block a road or entrance. ~ *verb* (**barricades, barricading, barricaded**) to block or defend something with a barricade.

barrier *noun* (*plural* **barriers**) **1** a type of fence that stops people or animals getting through. **2** something that prevents any progress or action.

barrister *noun* (*plural* **barristers**) a lawyer qualified to represent clients in higher law courts in England and Wales.

barrow¹ *noun* (*plural* **barrows**) **1** a cart with two wheels and long handles for moving it. **2** = WHEELBARROW.

barrow² *noun* (*plural* **barrows**) *History* a large mound of earth or stones over an ancient grave.

barter *verb* (**barters, bartering, bartered**) to trade by exchanging goods without using money. ~ *noun* trade by bartering.

base¹ *noun* (*plural* **bases**) **1** the lowest part of something, which supports it. **2** the fundamental part or basis of something. **3** a place from which an activity is organized or where it starts. **4** *Maths* the number on which a number system is constructed, such as 10 in the decimal system. **5** one of the four corner positions of a baseball field. **6** *Science* a chemical compound that reacts with an acid to form a salt. ~ *verb* (**bases, basing, based**)
1 (**base on/upon**) to use something as a base or basis for something else.
2 (**base in/at**) to have a particular place as a base: *The company is based in Oxford.*

base² *adjective* (**baser, basest**)
1 morally bad. **2** said about a metal: not rare or valuable.

baseball *noun* (*plural* **baseballs**) **1** an outdoor team game in which you hit a ball with a bat and run around four bases to score. **2** a ball used in this game.

baseless *adjective* not supported by any facts.

basement *noun* (*plural* **basements**) a room or part of a building below ground level.

bases¹ *noun* plural of BASE¹.

bases² *noun* plural of BASIS.

bash *informal verb* (**bashes, bashing, bashed**) to hit somebody or something hard. ~ *noun* (*plural* **bashes**)
1 a heavy blow. **2** a try: *I'd love to have a bash at skiing.* **3** a party.

bashful *adjective* self-conscious and shy. ➤ **bashfully** *adverb*.

basic *adjective* **1** forming the base of something; fundamental. **2** simple.

3 *Science* to do with a chemical base. ~ *noun* (**the basics**) fundamental facts or ideas. ➤ **basically** *adverb*.

basil *noun* a herb used in cooking.

basilica /bə'zɪlɪkə/ *noun* (*plural* **basilicas**) a type of large early-Christian church.

basin *noun* (*plural* **basins**) **1** = WASHBASIN. **2** a deep bowl used for mixing food in. **3** an area from which water drains into a river.

basis *noun* (*plural* **bases** /'beɪsiːz/) **1** the main thing that a substance is made of. **2** something that an idea or theory develops from or relies on.

bask *verb* (**basks, basking, basked**) **1** to lie and enjoy warmth or sunshine. **2** (**bask in**) to enjoy favour or approval.

basket *noun* (*plural* **baskets**) **1** a container made of woven wicker or wood. **2** an open net hung from a metal ring, used as the goal in basketball.

basketball *noun* a team game in which players score by throwing a ball through a high net fixed to a flat vertical surface.

bass[1] /bas/ *noun* (*plural* **basses** *or* **bass**) a type of edible fish.

bass[2] /beɪs/ *noun* (*plural* **basses**) *Music* **1** a man with the lowest singing voice. **2** a double bass or bass guitar. ~ *adjective Music* producing low notes or a deep sound: *a bass guitar*.

bass clef *noun* (*plural* **bass clefs**) *Music* a clef that shows that the note on the fourth line from the bottom of the staff is the F below middle C.

basset hound *noun* (*plural* **basset hounds**) a large dog with short legs, a long body, and long ears.

bassoon *noun* (*plural* **bassoons**) *Music* a large long woodwind instrument with a deep sound.

bastard *noun* (*plural* **bastards**) **1** *offensive or dated* somebody who was born when their parents were not married. **2** *informal* a very unpleasant or annoying person.

baste /beɪst/ *verb* (**bastes, basting, basted**) to pour fat and juices over meat while it is cooking.

bastion *noun* (*plural* **bastions**) an organization or group in which people still protect an old tradition or belief.

bat[1] *noun* (*plural* **bats**) a specially shaped piece of wood that you hit the ball with in sports such as baseball and cricket. ~ *verb* (**bats, batting, batted**) **1** to hit a ball with a bat. **2** to take your turn to bat in sport. ✻ **off your own bat** through your own ideas and efforts.

bat[2] *noun* (*plural* **bats**) a small mouse-like animal with wings that flies at night.

batch *noun* (*plural* **batches**) a number of things made or dealt with all at one time.

bated ✻ **with bated breath** in quiet nervous excitement.

bath *noun* (*plural* **baths**) **1** a large open container that you fill with water and lie in to wash your body. **2** an act of washing in a bath: *She's having a bath*. ~ *verb* (**baths, bathing, bathed**) to wash in a bath.

bathe /beɪð/ *verb* (**bathes, bathing, bathed**) **1** to go swimming. **2** to wash something gently with water or another liquid. **3** (**be bathed in**) to be filled or covered pleasantly with light. ~ *noun* (*plural* **bathes**) a swim. ➤ **bather** *noun*, **bathing** *noun*.

bathroom *noun* (*plural* **bathrooms**) **1** a room containing a bath, and often a shower, washbasin, and toilet. **2** *N American* a room containing a toilet.

baths *plural noun* a building containing a public swimming pool.

baton *noun* (*plural* **batons**) **1** a small stick used to conduct an orchestra.

2 a stick that is passed between the runners in a relay race.

batsman noun (plural **batsmen**) a player who bats in cricket.

battalion noun (plural **battalions**) a large organized group of soldiers made up of two or more companies.

batten noun (plural **battens**) a strip of wood or metal used to fasten or fix something. ~ verb (**battens, battening, battened**) * **batten down** to keep the hatches of a ship closed with battens.

batter¹ verb (**batters, battering, battered**) to hit somebody or something hard and repeatedly.

batter² noun (plural **batters**) a mixture of flour, egg, and milk or water, used for making pancakes or coating food.

batter³ noun (plural **batters**) a player who bats in baseball.

battered¹ adjective said about food: fried in batter.

battered² adjective **1** said about an object: old and damaged or worn. **2** said about a person: injured by being hit repeatedly.

battery noun (plural **batteries**) **1** an object that produces electric current, using connected power cells. **2** a row of similar connected things, such as lights, or cages for chickens.

battle noun (plural **battles**) **1** a major military fight. **2** a long struggle or argument. ~ verb (**battles, battling, battled**) to struggle or fight to do something.

battlefield noun (plural **battlefields**) a piece of ground where a battle is fought.

battlements plural noun walls around the top of a castle or tower, with gaps for firing through.

battleship noun (plural **battleships**) a heavily armed warship.

batty adjective (**battier, battiest**) informal crazy.

bauble noun (plural **baubles**) a cheap but decorative ornament.

baulk verb see BALK.

bawdy adjective (**bawdier, bawdiest**) referring to sex in a rude way: *a bawdy song.* ➤ **bawdiness** noun.

bawl verb (**bawls, bawling, bawled**) **1** to cry noisily. **2** to shout.

bay¹ noun (plural **bays**) a part of the coast that curves inwards.

bay² noun (plural **bays**) a small tree whose leaves are used to flavour food.

bay³ noun (plural **bays**) a special area or compartment in or on a larger structure: *a parking bay.*

bay⁴ adjective said about a horse: reddish brown.

bay⁵ verb (**bays, baying, bayed**) said about a dog: to howl or bark deeply. * **hold/keep at bay** to prevent something unpleasant from reaching or affecting you.

bayonet noun (plural **bayonets**) a blade for stabbing, attached to the end of a soldier's rifle. ~ verb (**bayonets, bayoneting, bayoneted**) to stab somebody or something with a bayonet.

bay window noun (plural **bay windows**) a window that sticks out from a house's outer wall.

bazaar noun (plural **bazaars**) **1** a market in the Middle East. **2** a sale to raise money for charity.

bazooka noun (plural **bazookas**) a weapon used to fire rockets at armoured tanks.

BBC abbreviation British Broadcasting Corporation.

BC abbreviation used after a date: before Christ.

Usage Note BC *and* AD. See note at AD.

be verb (**am, are, is; was, were; being; been**) **1** to exist or be present. **2** to occur at some time. **3** to have a specified state, function, or value. **4** used instead of *go* or *come* in the perfect tense: *I've been to New York.* **5** used with an *-ing* form to make continuous tenses: *I am listening.* **6** used with a past participle to form the passive voice: *She was asked.* ✶ **the be-all and end-all** the most important factor or part.

beach *noun* (*plural* **beaches**) an area of sand or pebbles at the edge of the sea.

beached *adjective* **1** said about a sea creature: stranded on the beach. **2** said about a boat: brought up onto the shore.

beacon *noun* (*plural* **beacons**) **1** a fire lit on top of a hill as a signal. **2** a light to guide ships or aircraft.

bead *noun* (*plural* **beads**) **1** a small piece of glass or wood threaded onto string in a necklace or bracelet. **2** a drop of liquid. ~ *verb* (**beads, beading, beaded**) to decorate or cover something with beads: *a beaded dress.*

beady *adjective* (**beadier, beadiest**) said about eyes: small, round, and attentive.

beagle *noun* (*plural* **beagles**) a medium-sized hunting dog with a smooth coat.

beak *noun* (*plural* **beaks**) the hard projecting part of a bird's mouth.

beaker *noun* (*plural* **beakers**) **1** a tall cup without a handle. **2** *Science* a cylindrical container with a flat bottom.

beam *noun* (*plural* **beams**) **1** a long piece of heavy timber used in building. **2** a bar for balancing on in gymnastics. **3** a ray or shaft of light or other radiation. **4** a broad smile. ~ *verb* (**beams, beaming, beamed**) **1** to smile broadly. **2** to send out a ray of light or other radiation.

bean *noun* (*plural* **beans**) a seed of a climbing plant, or one of its pods containing seeds, used as a vegetable.

bear[1] *noun* (*plural* **bears**) a large animal with thick fur and sharp claws.

bear[2] *verb* (**bears, bearing, bore, borne**) **1** to carry or transport something. **2** to behave in a particular way. **3** to have or show a feature: *This statement bears no relation to the truth.* **4** to give birth to a child or young. **5** to produce fruit or flowers. **6** to support the weight of something. **7** to tolerate something. **8** to pay a cost. **9** to go in a specified direction: *to bear right.* **10** (**bear on/upon**) to be relevant to something. **11** (**bear with**) to be patient with somebody. ✶ **bear in mind** to remember or consider something. ▸ **bearer** *noun.*

bearable *adjective* able to be endured; tolerable.

beard *noun* (*plural* **beards**) the hair that grows on the lower part of a man's face. ▸ **bearded** *adjective.*

bearing *noun* (*plural* **bearings**) **1** the way in which a person stands or moves. **2** a part of a machine in which another part turns or slides with little friction. **3** a compass direction, or a point in relation to another. ✶ **get your bearings** to work out where you are. **have a bearing on** to be relevant to something.

beast *noun* (*plural* **beasts**) **1** a large or wild animal. **2** *informal* a cruel or mean person.

beat *verb* (**beats, beating, beat, beaten**) **1** to hit somebody or something repeatedly. **2** said about a heart or pulse: to make repeated pumping movements. **3** to mix food vigorously. **4** to defeat an opponent in a game or sport. **5** *informal* to be better than doing something else: *TV beats housework.* **6** *informal* to baffle somebody: *It beats me why she went.* ~ *noun* (*plural* **beats**) **1** a strong repeated movement or throb. **2** steady rhythmic stress in music or poetry. **3** the area that a police officer patrols regularly. ✶ **beat about the bush** to talk without reaching the main subject. **beat up** to hurt somebody by punching or kicking them repeatedly.

beautician *noun* (*plural* **beauticians**) somebody who gives beauty treatments.

beautiful *adjective* having an appearance, sound, or feel that gives great pleasure. ➤ **beautifully** *adverb*.

beautify *verb* (**beautifies, beautifying, beautified**) to make somebody or something beautiful.

beauty *noun* (*plural* **beauties**) **1** a quality that pleases the senses. **2** *dated* a beautiful woman. **3** a classic example of something. **4** the particularly valuable or useful quality something has: *The beauty of email is its speed.*

beaver *noun* (*plural* **beavers**) an animal with brown fur, large teeth, and a broad flat tail, that builds dams across rivers. ~ *verb* (**beavers, beavering, beavered**) to work energetically: *He's still beavering away at his homework.*

because *conjunction* for the reason that; since. ✳ **because of** as a result of something or of what somebody has done: *I'm late because of you!*

beck ✳ **at your beck and call** always ready to obey you.

beckon *verb* (**beckons, beckoning, beckoned**) **1** to make a signal to somebody to come. **2** to seem appealing: *City life beckons.*

become *verb* (**becomes, becoming, became, become**) **1** to begin to be something: *He became quite ill.* **2** *formal* to suit or be suitable for somebody. **3** (**become of**) to happen to somebody or something: *What became of the bike I bought you?*

bed *noun* (*plural* **beds**) **1** a piece of furniture for sleeping on. **2** sleep. **3** a plot of ground to grow plants in. **4** the bottom of a sea or river. **5** a base or supporting surface. ✳ **go to bed with** *informal* to have sexual intercourse with somebody.

bedclothes *plural noun* the covers used on a bed.

bedding *noun* **1** bedclothes. **2** straw, wood shavings, etc for animals to sleep on.

bedlam *noun* noisy shouting and confusion, or somewhere filled with noise and confusion.

bedpan *noun* (*plural* **bedpans**) a shallow container used as a toilet by a person in bed.

bedraggled /bɪˈdræɡld/ *adjective* limp and untidy.

bedridden *adjective* forced to stay in bed because of illness or old age.

bedrock *noun* **1** a layer of solid rock under the soil. **2** the basis of something.

bedroom *noun* (*plural* **bedrooms**) a room for sleeping in.

bedsit *or* **bedsitter** *noun* (*plural* **bedsits** *or* **bedsitters**) a rented room used as both a sitting room and a bedroom.

bedspread *noun* (*plural* **bedspreads**) a decorative cover that you spread over a bed.

bedstead *noun* (*plural* **bedsteads**) the framework of a bed.

bee *noun* (*plural* **bees**) a winged insect that makes honey. ✳ **a bee in your bonnet** something you are obsessed about.

beech *noun* (*plural* **beeches**) a tree with smooth grey bark and shiny oval leaves.

beef *noun* meat from a cow, bull, or ox.

beefburger *noun* (*plural* **beefburgers**) a hamburger.

beefy *adjective* (**beefier, beefiest**) muscular or strong.

beehive *noun* (*plural* **beehives**) a box or other structure for bees to live in.

beeline ✳ **make a beeline for** to hurry straight towards something.

been *verb* past participle of BE.

beep *noun* (*plural* **beeps**) a sound made by a horn or electronic device, used as a signal or warning. ~ *verb* (**beeps, beeping, beeped**) to make a beep.

beer *noun* (*plural* **beers**) an alcoholic drink brewed from malt and hops.

beeswax *noun* a type of yellow wax produced by bees, used for polishing wood.

beet *noun* (*plural* **beets**) a plant with a swollen root, such as beetroot or sugar beet.

beetle *noun* (*plural* **beetles**) an insect with hard smooth coverings over its wings.

beetroot *noun* (*plural* **beetroots** or **beetroot**) a plant with an edible red root used as a vegetable.

befall *verb* (**befalls, befalling, befell, befallen**) *dated* to happen, or to happen to somebody.

befitting *adjective* appropriate or suitable.

before *adverb* at an earlier time. ~ *preposition* **1** earlier than somebody or something. **2** *formal* in front of somebody or something. ~ *conjunction* earlier than the time when something happens.

beforehand *adverb* earlier; before.

befriend *verb* (**befriends, befriending, befriended**) to become somebody's friend.

beg *verb* (**begs, begging, begged**) **1** to ask somebody for money, food, or help. **2** to ask for something in a desperate way.

beggar *noun* (*plural* **beggars**) **1** a person who lives by asking for money or food. **2** *informal* a specific type of person: *poor beggar*.

begin *verb* (**begins, beginning, began, begun**) **1** to start, or to start doing something. **2** to come into existence. **3** (**begin with**) to have something at the beginning.

beginner *noun* (*plural* **beginners**) somebody who is starting to learn or do something.

beginning *noun* (*plural* **beginnings**) the start.

begrudge *verb* (**begrudges, begrudging, begrudged**) to resent letting somebody, or seeing somebody, have something enjoyable.

beguile /bi giel/ *verb* (**beguiles, beguiling, beguiled**) to please or charm somebody, often deceptively. ➤ **beguiling** *adjective*.

behalf ✻ **on behalf of** in order to benefit somebody or something, or acting as their representative.

behave *verb* (**behaves, behaving, behaved**) **1** to act in a particular way. **2** to be polite and act properly.

behaviour *noun* the way in which somebody or something behaves or acts. ➤ **behavioural** *adjective*.

behead *verb* (**beheads, beheading, beheaded**) to execute somebody by cutting off their head.

beheld *verb* past tense of BEHOLD.

behind *adverb and preposition* **1** in, towards, or at the back of somebody or something. **2** in a place somebody or something has left. **3** late, or later than planned: *I'm behind with my work.* ~ *preposition* supporting, helping, or responsible for something. ~ *noun* (*plural* **behinds**) *informal* the buttocks.

behold *verb* (**beholds, beholding, beheld**) *archaic* to see or admire something or somebody. ➤ **beholder** *noun*.

beige /bayzh/ *adjective* yellowish grey or pale-brown.

being *noun* (*plural* **beings**) **1** life or existence. **2** a person or living creature.

belated *adjective* done or happening late. ➤ **belatedly** *adverb*.

belch

belch *verb* (**belches, belching, belched**) **1** to let gas out from your stomach through your mouth loudly. **2** to send out a mass of smoke or steam. ~ *noun* (*plural* **belches**) a noise or act of belching.

beleaguered *adjective* **1** experiencing constant problems and criticisms. **2** besieged by the enemy.

belfry *noun* (*plural* **belfries**) a room in a church bell tower where the bell hangs.

belief *noun* (*plural* **beliefs**) **1** something that people believe. **2** certainty about something being true or real.

believe *verb* (**believes, believing, believed**) **1** to think that something is true or that somebody is telling the truth. **2** to have a firm religious faith. **3** to think that something is real, reliable, or good: *Rachel doesn't believe in getting up early.* ➤ **believable** *adjective*, **believer** *noun*.

belittle *verb* (**belittles, belittling, belittled**) to make somebody or something seem trivial or unimportant.

bell *noun* (*plural* **bells**) **1** a hollow cup-shaped metal object that makes a ringing sound when you swing it. **2** an electrical device that rings or buzzes when you press it. **3** the sound of a bell as a signal: *Was that the lunch bell?*

belligerent /bi li ji rint/ *adjective* aggressive; wanting to fight. ➤ **belligerence** *noun*.

bellow *verb* (**bellows, bellowing, bellowed**) to shout or roar in a loud deep voice. ~ *noun* (*plural* **bellows**) a loud deep shout or roar.

bellows *plural noun* (*often treated as singular*) a device with handles and expandable sides that you use to fan a fire.

belly *noun* (*plural* **bellies**) **1** your stomach, or the front of your body below your chest. **2** the underneath surface of an animal's body.

belly flop *noun* (*plural* **belly flops**) a dive in which you hit the surface of the water with the front of your body.

belong *verb* (**belongs, belonging, belonged**) **1** (**belong to**) to be somebody's property. **2** to be in the right place or situation. **3** (**belong to**) to come from somewhere, or be a member or part of something.

belongings *plural noun* possessions.

beloved /bi lu vid/ *adjective* dearly loved.

below *preposition and adverb* **1** in, at, or to a lower place or position. **2** under; less than a particular level or rate.

belt *noun* (*plural* **belts**) **1** a leather or fabric strip worn round the waist. **2** a continuous rubber strip that carries objects along or transmits motion and power in a machine: *a conveyor belt.* **3** an area of land that has some distinctive feature: *an industrial/agricultural belt.* ~ *verb* (**belts, belting, belted**) **1** to tie something with a belt. **2** *informal* to hit somebody hard. **3** *informal* to move very quickly. ➤ **belt out** *informal* to sing something loudly.

bemused *adjective* puzzled.

bench *noun* (*plural* **benches**) **1** a long seat for two or more people. **2** a long narrow worktable. **3** (**the Bench**) the judge or magistrates in a court, or the judge's seat.

bend *verb* (**bends, bending, bent**) **1** to move something into or out of a curve or angle. **2** to stoop or lean down. **3** to change a rule slightly to suit you. ~ *noun* (*plural* **bends**) a curved part of something, such as a turn in a road. ✳ **round the bend** *informal* mad.

beneath *preposition and adverb* **1** in or to a lower position than something or somebody. **2** not suitable for or worthy of somebody.

benefactor *noun* (*plural* **benefactors**) somebody who gives financial or other aid.

beneficiary /beni shiri/ *noun* (*plural* **beneficiaries**) a person who benefits from somebody's will.

benefit *noun* (*plural* **benefits**) **1** an advantage or a helpful thing. **2** financial help provided by the state to people in need. ~ *verb* (**benefits, benefiting, benefited**) **1** to be useful or profitable to somebody. **2** to receive a benefit.

benevolent /bi nevolint/ *adjective* kind or charitable. ➤ **benevolence** *noun*.

benign *adjective* **1** gentle or mild. **2** said about a tumour: not malignant.

bent *verb* past tense of BEND. ~ *adjective* **1** not straight; curved. **2** (**bent on/upon**) determined to do something. **3** *informal* dishonest. ~ *noun* (*plural* **bents**) a special talent.

bequeath *verb* (**bequeaths, bequeathing, bequeathed**) to leave your property to somebody in a will.

bequest *noun* (*plural* **bequests**) something that you bequeath to another person.

berate *verb* (**berates, berating, berated**) to tell somebody off angrily about something they have done wrong.

bereave *verb* (**bereaves, bereaving, bereaved**) (**be bereaved**) to suffer the death of somebody you love. ➤ **bereavement** *noun*.

bereft *adjective* completely without something important: *bereft of love/hope*.

beret /be ray/ *noun* (*plural* **berets**) a round flat cloth cap.

berry *noun* (*plural* **berries**) a small soft fruit without a stone.

berserk /ber zerk/ ✱ **go berserk** to become furiously angry or violent.

berth *noun* (*plural* **berths**) **1** a place for sleeping on a ship or train. **2** a place in a harbour for a ship. ~ *verb* (**berths, berthing, berthed**) **1** said about a ship: to dock. **2** to give somebody a berth to sleep in. ✱ **give a wide berth to** to remain safely away from somebody or something.

beseech *verb* (**beseeches, beseeching, beseeched** *or* **besought**) to ask earnestly or pleadingly.

beset *verb* (**besets, besetting, beset**) *formal* to surround and attack or distress somebody.

beside *preposition* **1** by the side of something or somebody. **2** in comparison with something or somebody. **3** not relevant to something: *That's beside the point*. ✱ **beside yourself** extremely excited or worried.

besides *adverb and preposition* in addition to something or somebody.

besiege *verb* (**besieges, besieging, besieged**) **1** to surround something with armed forces. **2** to crowd round somebody or something.

besotted *adjective* extremely fond or too fond of somebody or something.

besought *verb* past tense and past participle of BESEECH.

best *adjective* **1** of the most excellent quality or type. **2** most appropriate or advisable. ~ *adverb* **1** in the best way or to the best extent. **2** as your preferred or ideal thing. ~ *noun* (**the best**) what is most excellent or desirable. ✱ **make the best of** to get some benefit from a bad situation.

bestial *adjective* brutally cruel, like a wild beast. ➤ **bestiality** *noun*.

best man *noun* (*plural* **best men**) a male friend or relative who performs special duties for the bridegroom at a wedding.

bestow *verb* (**bestow on/upon**) *formal* to give something to somebody as a gift or honour.

bestseller *noun* (*plural* **bestsellers**) a book or other product that sells in great numbers. ➤ **bestselling** *adjective*.

bet *verb* (**bets, betting, bet** *or rarely* **betted**) **1** to make an agreement with somebody in which you will lose a sum of money unless you predict the result of a future event, such as a race, correctly. **2** *informal* to guess or predict what is likely to happen. ~ *noun* (*plural* **bets**) **1** the act of betting or a sum of money that you bet. **2** an opinion or belief. **3** somebody or something that is likely to succeed.

betray *verb* (**betrays, betraying, betrayed**) **1** to give somebody or something to the enemy. **2** to be disloyal to a partner or friend. **3** to show your feelings unintentionally. ➤ **betrayal** *noun*.

betrothed *adjective dated* engaged to be married.

better *adjective* **1** of a higher quality. **2** more appropriate or advisable. **3** healthier; recovered or improving after being ill or injured. ~ *adverb* **1** in a better way. **2** to a greater degree; more. ~ *noun* (*plural* **betters**) **1** (**the better**) what is more excellent or desirable: *It was a change for the better.* **2** (**your betters**) *dated* people who are superior to you in rank or ability. ~ *verb* (**betters, bettering, bettered**) to improve on something: *These results cannot be bettered.*
✶ **better off** enjoying more money or better circumstances. **better yourself** to improve your living conditions or social status. **for better or worse** whether the result is good or bad. **get the better of** to defeat somebody. **had better** would be wise (to do something).

between *preposition and adverb* **1** in or into the space separating two places, objects, or people. **2** in the time separating two events or times. **3** involving or comparing two separate groups. **4** shared by two or more people.

Usage Note **between you and me**. Like other prepositions, *between* is followed by the object form of the personal pronoun, not the subject form: *We divided it between us* (not *between we*). It is incorrect to say *between you and I*; the grammatically correct form is *between you and me*.

beverage *noun* (*plural* **beverages**) a drink.

bewail *verb* (**bewails, bewailing, bewailed**) to express great sorrow about something.

beware *verb* (only as *imperative* or *infinitive*) to be careful of something dangerous or threatening.

bewilder *verb* (**bewilders, bewildering, bewildered**) to perplex or confuse somebody.

bewitch *verb* (**bewitches, bewitching, bewitched**) **1** to attract or charm somebody. **2** to cast a spell on somebody or something.

beyond *preposition and adverb* **1** on or to the farther side of something. **2** further or greater than something. **3** too difficult for somebody to understand or do.

Bhagavadgita /bu ga vad gee ta/ *noun* (**the Bhagavadgita**) one of the sacred books of the Hindu religion.

biannual *adjective* occurring twice a year. ➤ **biannually** *adverb*.

bias *noun* (*plural* **biases**) unfair feelings in favour of or against somebody or something.

biased *or* **biassed** *adjective* showing bias; prejudiced.

bib *noun* (*plural* **bibs**) **1** a piece of cloth or plastic worn under a young child's chin to protect its clothes while it is eating. **2** the part of an apron, etc that covers the front of your body above the waist.

Bible *noun* (**the Bible**) the sacred book of the Christian religion, consisting of the Old Testament and the New Testament.

biblical *adjective* in or to do with the Bible.

bibliography *noun* (*plural* **bibliographies**) a list of books on a particular topic or by a particular author. ➤ **bibliographical** *adjective*.

bicarbonate *noun Science* sodium bicarbonate or another acid carbonate.

bicentenary *noun* (*plural* **bicentenaries**) the celebration of a 200th anniversary.

biceps /bie seps/ *noun* (*plural* **biceps**) a large muscle at the front of the upper arm.

bicker *verb* (**bickers, bickering, bickered**) to argue in a petty way.

bicycle *noun* (*plural* **bicycles**) a two-wheeled vehicle with pedals, handlebars, and a saddle. ➤ **bicyclist** *noun*.

bid[1] *verb* (**bids, bidding, bid**) **1** to offer to pay a certain price for something at an auction. **2** to offer to do a job for a certain price. **3** (**bid for**) to attempt to do something. ~ *noun* **1** an act of bidding. **2** an offer of a price. ➤ **bidder** *noun*, **bidding** *noun*.

bid[2] *verb* (**bids, bidding, bade** /bad *or* bayd/ *or* **bid, bidden** *or* **bid**) *dated* **1** to say: *to bid farewell*. **2** to tell somebody to do something: *I bade him speak*. ➤ **bidding** *noun*.

bidet /bee day/ *noun* (*plural* **bidets**) a low basin used for washing your bottom.

biennial /bie e ni al/ *adjective* **1** occurring every two years. **2** said about a plant: living for two years.

bifocal /bie foh kl/ *adjective* said about a lens: with one part that helps you see close up and another for seeing into the distance.

big *adjective* (**bigger, biggest**) **1** large. **2** important. **3** said about a brother or sister: older or grown-up. **4** powerful.

bigamy *noun* the crime of marrying somebody when you are already married. ➤ **bigamist** *noun*, **bigamous** *adjective*.

bighead *noun* (*plural* **bigheads**) *informal* a conceited person. ➤ **big-headed** *adjective*.

bigot *noun* (*plural* **bigots**) somebody who is prejudiced and intolerant. ➤ **bigoted** *adjective*, **bigotry** *noun*.

bike *noun* (*plural* **bikes**) *informal* a bicycle or motorcycle. ~ *verb* (**bikes, biking, biked**) to ride a bicycle or motorcycle.

bikini *noun* (*plural* **bikinis**) a woman's two-piece swimsuit.

Word History Bikinis are named after *Bikini*, an atoll in the Pacific Ocean, where atomic bombs were tested by the USA in 1946. The designer of the bikini felt that it would have an equally big impact.

bilateral *adjective* having two sides or parts.

bile *noun Science* a bitter fluid produced by the liver to help digest fats.

bilingual *adjective* **1** able to use two languages fluently. **2** written in two languages: *a bilingual dictionary*.

bilious *adjective* feeling sick.

bill[1] *noun* (*plural* **bills**) **1** a list of charges for what you have bought or used. **2** a draft of a law presented to parliament for discussion. **3** a theatre or cinema poster. **4** *chiefly N American* a banknote. ~ *verb* (**bills, billing, billed**) **1** to send a bill to somebody for payment. **2** (**bill as**) to announce an entertainment to be something. ✶ **fit the bill** to be suitable.

bill[2] *noun* (*plural* **bills**) the beak of a bird.

billboard *noun* (*plural* **billboards**) a large board for advertisements.

billet *noun* (*plural* **billets**) a private home where soldiers are given board and lodging. ~ *verb* (**billets, billeting, billeted**) to provide soldiers with a billet.

billiards *noun* a game played with three balls on a cloth-covered table using a cue.

billion *noun* (*plural* **billions** *or* **billion**) **1** a thousand millions or 1,000,000,000 (10⁹). **2** *informal* (also in *plural*) a very large number: *There are billions of reasons why you can't go.* ➤ **billionth** *adjective and noun*.

billionaire *noun* (*plural* **billionaires**) somebody who has money and property worth at least a billion pounds or dollars.

billow *verb* (**billows, billowing, billowed**) to rise or swell out in large waves or swirls. ~ *noun* (*plural* **billows**) a swirling mass of flame or smoke.

billy *or* **billycan** *noun* (*plural* **billies** *or* **billycans**) a metal can with a handle and lid, used for outdoor cooking.

billy goat *noun* (*plural* **billy goats**) *informal* a male goat.

bin *noun* (*plural* **bins**) **1** a container for rubbish. **2** a large container for storage. ~ *verb* (**bins, binning, binned**) to throw something away.

binary /bie na ri/ *adjective* **1** *Maths* to do with a system of numbers that uses only the digits 0 and 1. **2** involving a choice of two alternatives, such as *on* or *off*. **3** made of two things or parts.

bind *verb* (**binds, binding, bound**) **1** to tie or fix something together, or to tie somebody or something up. **2** said about a law or duty: to force you to do something. **3** to stick together.

bindi /bin di/ *noun* (*plural* **bindis**) a mark in the middle of the forehead, worn mainly by Hindu women.

binding *noun* (*plural* **bindings**) **1** a covering that fixes the pages of a book together. **2** a thin strip of fabric used to stop edges from fraying. ~ *adjective* said about a law or agreement: that you have to obey.

binge *noun* (*plural* **binges**) *informal* a period in which you eat or drink too much. ~ *verb* (**binges, bingeing, binged**) *informal* to eat or drink too much.

bingo *noun* a game in which you cross off numbers on a card as they are randomly called out.

binoculars *plural noun* a pair of short, joined telescopes that you look through to see things in the distance.

biochemistry *noun* the scientific study of the chemical processes in living organisms. ➤ **biochemical** *adjective*.

biodegradable *adjective* capable of being broken down naturally into a harmless substance by bacteria.

biography *noun* (*plural* **biographies**) a book about a person's life. ➤ **biographer** *noun*, **biographical** *adjective*.

biological *adjective* **1** to do with biology or living organisms. **2** said about a detergent: containing an enzyme. ➤ **biologically** *adverb*.

biology *noun* the scientific study of living organisms. ➤ **biologist** *noun*.

bionic /bie o nik/ *adjective* made with electronics to imitate a living person or body part.

biopsy /bie op si/ *noun* (*plural* **biopsies**) examination of a piece of tissue from a living body for signs of disease.

bipartite *adjective* consisting of two parts or involving two groups.

biped /bie ped/ *noun* (*plural* **bipeds**) *Science* a two-footed animal.

birch *noun* (*plural* **birches**) **1** a deciduous tree with thin bark that peels. **2** (**the birch**) the punishment of being whipped with a bunch of birch twigs.

bird noun (plural **birds**) **1** an animal with feathers, a beak, and wings, that lays eggs and usually flies. **2** informal a young woman. ✷ **the birds and the bees** informal the facts about sex and sexual reproduction.

bird of prey noun (plural **birds of prey**) a bird that feeds on dead animals or on animals that it catches.

bird's-eye view noun a view from above.

Biro /bier oh/ noun (plural **Biros**) trademark a kind of ballpoint pen.

birth noun (plural **births**) **1** the event or process of a new individual coming out from the body of its parent. **2** a beginning. **3** your family origin. ✷ **give birth** said about a mother: to produce a baby.

birth control noun contraception and other ways of controlling the number of children born.

birthday noun (plural **birthdays**) an anniversary of the day somebody was born.

birthmark noun (plural **birthmarks**) a mark that is on your skin at birth.

birthright noun (plural **birthrights**) something that you are entitled to because you were born in a particular family or place.

biscuit noun (plural **biscuits**) a small flat crisp cake.

bisect /bie sekt/ verb (**bisects, bisecting, bisected**) to divide something into two parts.

bisexual adjective sexually attracted to both men and women. ~ noun (plural **bisexuals**) a bisexual person.
➤ **bisexuality** noun.

bishop noun (plural **bishops**) **1** a senior member of the Christian clergy who is in charge of a diocese. **2** a chess piece that moves diagonally across the board.

bison noun (plural **bison**) a large ox with a humped back.

bistro noun (plural **bistros**) a small bar or restaurant.

bit[1] noun (plural **bits**) **1** a small piece or amount of something. **2** a bar of metal fitted to a horse's bridle and put into its mouth. **3** a piece of a tool for drilling or boring. ✷ **a bit** informal somewhat; slightly: *It's a bit cold*. **do your bit** to do what you can for a task or cause.

bit[2] noun (plural **bits**) ICT a unit of information representing a choice between two alternatives, such as *on* and *off*.

bit[3] verb past tense of BITE.

bitch noun (plural **bitches**) **1** a female dog. **2** informal a spiteful woman. ~ verb (**bitches, bitching, bitched**) informal to make unkind or spiteful comments about somebody.

bitchy adjective (**bitchier, bitchiest**) informal malicious or spiteful.
➤ **bitchiness** noun.

bite verb (**bites, biting, bit, bitten**) **1** to seize or cut into something with your teeth. **2** said about an insect or animal: to sting somebody or something. ~ noun (plural **bites**) **1** an act of biting. **2** a wound made by biting. **3** the amount of food you eat in one bite. ✷ **bite somebody's head off** to reply angrily to somebody. **bite the dust 1** to fall dead or be killed in a fight. **2** to fail and come to an end.

biting adjective **1** said about a wind: very cold. **2** said about a remark: unkind or sarcastic.

bitter adjective **1** full of dislike, anger, or resentment. **2** caused by or causing a lot of unhappiness or regret. **3** intense or severe. **4** said about a wind: intensely cold. **5** said about a taste: sharp or sour. ➤ **bitterly** adverb, **bitterness** noun.

bitumen /bi tew min/ noun a black sticky substance used to surface roads.
➤ **bituminous** adjective.

bivouac /bi voo ak/ noun (plural

bizarre

bivouacs) a temporary camp with little or no shelter. ~ *verb* (**bivouacs, bivouacking, bivouacked**) to camp in a bivouac.

bizarre *adjective* odd or eccentric.
➤ **bizarrely** *adverb*.

blab *verb* (**blabs, blabbing, blabbed**) to reveal something secret or talk indiscreetly.

black *adjective* **1** of the darkest colour, like the sky at night. **2** relating to people with dark skin. **3** said about coffee or tea: without milk or cream. **4** hostile or disapproving: *a black look*. **5** to do with death or unpleasant things: *black humour*. ~ *noun* (plural **blacks**) **1** a black colour. **2** a black person. ~ *verb* (**blacks, blacking, blacked**) to make something black.
➤ **blackish** *adjective*, **blackness** *noun*.

black-and-blue *adjective* covered with bruises.

black-and-white *adjective* **1** said about an image: reproduced in black, white, and tones of grey. **2** viewed in a simple or extreme way.

blackberry *noun* (plural **blackberries**) a dark-purple berry made up of many small round parts, that grows on a prickly shrub.

blackbird *noun* (plural **blackbirds**) a European bird, the male of which has black feathers and an orange beak.

blackboard *noun* (plural **blackboards**) a board with a smooth dark surface for writing on with chalk.

black box *noun* (plural **black boxes**) an aircraft's flight recorder.

blackcurrant *noun* (plural **blackcurrants**) a very small, soft, sour, dark-purple fruit.

blacken *verb* (**blackens, blackening, blackened**) **1** to become black or make something black. **2** to damage somebody's reputation.

black eye *noun* (plural **black eyes**) an eye with bruising round it.

blackfly *noun* (plural **blackflies**) a small dark insect that feeds on plants.

blackhead *noun* (plural **blackheads**) a small black spot or blocked pore on the face.

black hole *noun* (plural **black holes**) *Science* an area in space with a very strong gravitational field, from which no radiation can escape.

black ice *noun* clear thin ice on a road surface.

blacklist *noun* (plural **blacklists**) a list of people or organizations who are disapproved of or excluded. ~ *verb* (**blacklists, blacklisting, blacklisted**) to put somebody or something on a blacklist.

black magic *noun* magic used to do evil.

blackmail *verb* (**blackmails, blackmailing, blackmailed**) to demand or get money from somebody by threatening to reveal secret and damaging information about them. ~ *noun* the act of blackmailing somebody.
➤ **blackmailer** *noun*.

black market *noun* (plural **black markets**) a system of buying and selling goods illegally.

blackout *noun* (plural **blackouts**) **1** a temporary loss of consciousness. **2** a sudden loss of electrical power. **3** a compulsory period of darkness as a protection from air raids.

blacksmith *noun* (plural **blacksmiths**) somebody who makes horseshoes and other iron objects.

black spot *noun* (plural **black spots**) a section of road where accidents often happen.

bladder *noun* (plural **bladders**) a bag-like organ of the body in which urine collects.

blade *noun* (plural **blades**) **1** the cutting part of a knife or other tool. **2** a long narrow leaf of grass. **3** the broad flat part of an oar, bat, propeller, etc.

blame verb (**blames, blaming, blamed**) **1** to think or say that somebody did something wrong or caused something bad to happen. **2** to criticize somebody. ~ noun **1** responsibility for doing or causing something bad. **2** disapproval or criticism. ➤ **blameless** adjective.

blanch /blahnch/ verb (**blanches, blanching, blanched**) **1** to go pale or to make somebody or something go pale. **2** to put vegetables into boiling water briefly.

blancmange /blə monj/ noun (plural **blancmanges**) a jelly-like dessert made with milk and cornflour.

bland adjective **1** dull; without any interesting features or character. **2** said about food: without much flavour. ➤ **blandly** adverb, **blandness** noun.

blank adjective **1** not marked, written on, or recorded on. **2** said about a form: not filled in. **3** showing no expression. ~ noun (plural **blanks**) **1** an empty space to be filled in on a form. **2** a gun cartridge containing powder but no bullet. ➤ **blankly** adverb, **blankness** noun.

blanket noun (plural **blankets**) **1** a large thick piece of fabric for covering a bed. **2** a thick covering or layer. ~ verb (**blankets, blanketing, blanketed**) to cover something with a thick layer. ~ adjective applying generally: *a blanket ban*.

blare verb (**blares, blaring, blared**) to make a loud harsh sound. ~ noun (plural **blares**) a loud harsh sound.

blasé /blah zay/ adjective not impressed or excited by something because you are used to it.

blaspheme /blas feem/ verb (**blasphemes, blaspheming, blasphemed**) to use a holy or sacred name without proper respect.

blasphemy /blas fi mi/ noun (plural **blasphemies**) disrespect for a holy or sacred name. ➤ **blasphemous** adjective.

blast noun (plural **blasts**) **1** a powerful explosion. **2** a strong gust of wind or rush of air. **3** a sudden loud noise. ~ verb (**blasts, blasting, blasted**) **1** to make a blast. **2** to attack or destroy something, or create a hole, with an explosive. ✱ **at full blast** at top speed or full power.

blatant /blay tənt/ adjective done without embarrassment or shame; obvious. ➤ **blatancy** noun, **blatantly** adverb.

blaze[1] noun (plural **blazes**) **1** a strongly burning flame or fire. **2** intense light. **3** a dazzling display. ~ verb (**blazes, blazing, blazed**) to burn or shine strongly.

blaze[2] noun (plural **blazes**) a broad white mark on a horse's face.

blazer noun (plural **blazers**) a jacket with outside pockets, often worn as part of a school or team uniform.

bleach verb (**bleaches, bleaching, bleached**) to make something whiter or remove its colour, chemically or naturally. ~ noun (plural **bleaches**) a strong chemical used to bleach things.

bleak adjective (**bleaker, bleakest**) **1** said about a place: cold, bare, and exposed. **2** said about a situation: not hopeful or encouraging. ➤ **bleakly** adverb, **bleakness** noun.

bleary adjective (**blearier, bleariest**) said about your eyes or eyesight: watery and blurred because you are tired. ➤ **blearily** adverb.

bleat verb (**bleats, bleating, bleated**) to make the cry of a sheep or goat. ➤ **bleat** noun.

bleed verb (**bleeds, bleeding, bled**) **1** to lose blood from your body. **2** to take or draw blood from somebody. **3** to let out liquid or gas from a system of pipes. ➤ **bleeding** noun.

bleep noun (plural **bleeps**) a short

blemish

high-pitched sound made by an electronic device. ~ *verb* (**bleeps, bleeping, bleeped**) **1** to make a bleep. **2** to call somebody to come using a bleeping device. ➤ **bleeper** *noun*.

blemish *noun* (*plural* **blemishes**) a mark, spot, or fault that spoils the way something looks. ~ *verb* (**blemishes, blemishing, blemished**) to spoil the appearance of something.

blend *verb* (**blends, blending, blended**) **1** to combine separate ingredients or elements. **2** to fit in easily without being noticeable: *The new building blends in with its surroundings.* ~ *noun* (*plural* **blends**) a mixture.

blender *noun* (*plural* **blenders**) an electrical device that mixes food or makes it into a smooth liquid.

bless *verb* (**blesses, blessing, blessed**) **1** to ask God to care for somebody or something. **2** to bring happiness or good fortune to somebody or something. **3** to make something holy.

blessed /ˈblesɪd/ *adjective* **1** holy and revered. **2** very pleasant and welcome: *a blessed relief.*

blessing *noun* (*plural* **blessings**) **1** a prayer asking God to bless somebody. **2** something good that makes you happy. **3** approval or moral support from somebody.

blew *verb* past tense of BLOW¹.

blight *noun* (*plural* **blights**) **1** a disease that makes plants wither. **2** something that has a very damaging effect. ~ *verb* (**blights, blighting, blighted**) **1** to affect a plant with blight. **2** to spoil or destroy something.

blind *adjective* **1** unable to see. **2** unable to judge or understand something rationally: *He was blind to the facts.* **3** with only one way out or opening: *a blind alley/passage.* ~ *verb* (**blinds, blinding, blinded**) **1** to make somebody or something blind. **2** to make somebody unable to see the truth about something: *Love blinded her to his faults.* ~ *noun* (*plural* **blinds**) **1** a flexible screen used to cover a window. **2** a trick to prevent somebody seeing what is really happening. ✳ **turn a blind eye** to ignore something bad. ➤ **blindly** *adverb*, **blindness** *noun*.

blind date *noun* (*plural* **blind dates**) a date between people who have never met before.

blindfold *verb* (**blindfolds, blindfolding, blindfolded**) to cover somebody's eyes with a piece of material. ~ *noun* (*plural* **blindfolds**) a piece of cloth tied around somebody's head to prevent them from seeing. ~ *adjective and adverb* wearing a blindfold.

blinding *adjective* **1** said about light: overpoweringly bright. **2** extremely obvious. ➤ **blindingly** *adverb*.

blink *verb* (**blinks, blinking, blinked**) **1** to close and open the eyes quickly or as a reflex. **2** said about a light: to go on and off intermittently. ~ *noun* (*plural* **blinks**) an act of blinking.

blinkered *adjective* **1** wearing blinkers. **2** seeing or understanding only one part of your situation.

blinkers *plural noun* two flaps designed to prevent a horse from seeing to the sides.

bliss *noun* complete happiness. ➤ **blissful** *adjective*, **blissfully** *adverb*.

blister *noun* (*plural* **blisters**) **1** a raised area of skin containing watery liquid. **2** a bubble on a painted or coated surface. ~ *verb* (**blisters, blistering, blistered**) to develop blisters.

blithe /blieth/ *adjective* **1** casual or thoughtless. **2** cheerful; happy. ➤ **blithely** *adverb*.

blitz *noun* (*plural* **blitzes**) **1** a period of intensive bombing from the air. **2** a lot of hard work or action in a short time. ~ *verb* (**blitzes, blitzing, blitzed**) **1** to attack a place in a blitz. **2** to deal with a task by having a blitz.

blizzard *noun* (*plural* **blizzards**) a severe snowstorm with a strong wind.

bloat *verb* (**bloats, bloating, bloated**) to swell up with gas or liquid. ➤ **bloated** *adjective*.

blob *noun* (*plural* **blobs**) **1** a small drop of something thick or sticky. **2** a vague shape. ➤ **blobby** *adjective*.

bloc *noun* (*plural* **blocs**) a group of nations working together for a common purpose.

block *noun* (*plural* **blocks**) **1** a large building divided into offices or flats. **2** a rectangular area of buildings enclosed by streets. **3** a solid rectangular piece of material. **4** an obstacle or blockage. ~ *verb* (**blocks, blocking, blocked**) **1** to cause an obstruction across a road or in a pipe. **2** to stop something from moving, continuing, or happening.

blockade *noun* (*plural* **blockades**) the act of surrounding a place to stop people and supplies from going in and out. ~ *verb* (**blockades, blockading, blockaded**) to put a blockade on a place.

blockage *noun* (*plural* **blockages**) something that is blocking a pipe or road.

bloke *noun* (*plural* **blokes**) *informal* a man.

blond or **blonde** *adjective* (**blonder, blondest**) **1** said about a person's hair: golden or pale-yellowish brown. **2** said about a person: having blond hair. ~ *noun* (*plural* **blonds** or **blondes**) **1** (**blond**) a man with blond hair. **2** (**blonde**) a woman with blonde hair. **3** a golden or yellowish-brown colour.

Usage Note **blond** or **blonde**? The two spellings derive from the French masculine (*blond*) and feminine (*blonde*) forms of the word. In English the form *blonde* is usually used in relation to women, whilst *blond* is used for men and in neutral contexts.

blood *noun* **1** the red liquid that flows through the arteries and veins of humans and other vertebrates. **2** family background; ancestors. ✶ **in cold blood** in a cruel and deliberate way.

bloodbath *noun* (*plural* **bloodbaths**) a massacre.

blood group *noun* (*plural* **blood groups**) any of the different types of human blood.

bloodhound *noun* (*plural* **bloodhounds**) a large hound that can track somebody or something by following their scent.

blood pressure *noun* the pressure produced by your blood as it passes through your blood vessels.

bloodshed *noun* the killing or injuring of people.

bloodshot *adjective* said about an eye: having the white part tinged with red.

blood sport *noun* (*plural* **blood sports**) a sport in which animals are hunted or killed.

bloodstream *noun* the blood circulating in your body.

bloodthirsty *adjective* (**bloodthirstier, bloodthirstiest**) **1** keen on bloodshed. **2** involving people being killed and injured.

blood vessel *noun* (*plural* **blood vessels**) any of the veins, arteries, or capillaries that your blood flows through.

bloody *adjective* (**bloodier, bloodiest**) **1** covered with blood. **2** bloodthirsty or involving a lot of bloodshed. **3** *informal* used as a swearword to express annoyance.

bloom *noun* (*plural* **blooms**) **1** a flower. **2** the time when a plant has flowers. **3** a light coating on a fruit or leaf. ~ *verb* (**blooms, blooming, bloomed**) **1** to produce flowers. **2** to

blossom

be developing in a healthy and successful way.

blossom *noun* (*plural* **blossoms**) a flower or mass of flowers on a tree or shrub. ~ *verb* (**blossoms, blossoming, blossomed**) **1** to bloom. **2** to develop or flourish.

blot *noun* (*plural* **blots**) **1** a spot of ink or other liquid. **2** a mistake or fault that spoils something. ~ *verb* (**blots, blotting, blotted**) **1** to make a spot or stain on something. **2** to dry something with absorbent material. **3** to spoil your reputation by doing something bad or wrong. ✷ **blot out 1** to cover or hide something. **2** to refuse to think about something.

blotch *noun* (*plural* **blotches**) an irregular spot or mark. ▶ **blotchy** *adjective*.

blouse *noun* (*plural* **blouses**) a piece of clothing like a shirt, for a woman or girl.

blow[1] *verb* (**blows, blowing, blew, blown**) **1** said about air or wind: to move. **2** to force air through a whistle or a musical instrument to produce a sound. **3** *informal* to waste an opportunity or money. **4** *informal* to reveal somebody's secret or disguise. ~ *noun* (*plural* **blows**) an act of blowing. ✷ **blow up 1** to shatter or destroy something or somebody, or be shattered or destroyed, in an explosion. **2** to fill something with air or gas. **3** to enlarge or exaggerate something.

blow[2] *noun* (*plural* **blows**) **1** a hard hit with somebody's hand or with a weapon. **2** a shock or very unfortunate event. ✷ **come to blows** to start fighting.

blowy *adjective* (**blowier, blowiest**) windy.

blubber *noun* the fat of whales and seals. ▶ **blubbery** *adjective*.

bludgeon *noun* (*plural* **bludgeons**) a heavy club used as a weapon. ~ *verb* (**bludgeons, bludgeoning, bludgeoned**) to hit or beat somebody with a bludgeon or anything similar.

blue *adjective* (**bluer, bluest**) **1** of the colour of a clear sky. **2** sad or depressed. **3** indecent or pornographic. **4** said about cheese: containing lines of blue or green mould. ~ *noun* (*plural* **blues**) **1** a blue colour. **2** blue clothing: *dressed in blue*. **3** (**the blues**) depression; feelings of sadness. **4** (**the blues**) a sad slow style of music first developed by black Americans. ✷ **once in a blue moon** very rarely. **out of the blue** without warning; unexpectedly: *She just turned up out of the blue*. ▶ **blueness** *noun*, **bluish** or **blueish** *adjective*.

bluebell *noun* (*plural* **bluebells**) a plant with blue bell-shaped flowers.

blueberry *noun* (*plural* **blueberries**) a very small soft dark-blue fruit.

bluebottle *noun* (*plural* **bluebottles**) a large buzzing fly with a shiny blue body.

blue-collar *adjective* said about workers: doing physical jobs rather than office jobs.

blueprint *noun* (*plural* **blueprints**) a plan of exactly how something is to be made or done.

blue whale *noun* (*plural* **blue whales**) a very large bluish grey whale.

bluff[1] *verb* (**bluffs, bluffing, bluffed**) to trick people by pretending to be stronger or more confident than you are. ~ *noun* (*plural* **bluffs**) an act or example of bluffing. ✷ **call somebody's bluff** to challenge somebody to prove or do what they have said, because you do not believe they can.

bluff[2] *noun* (*plural* **bluffs**) *Geography* a high steep bank or cliff.

blunder *noun* (*plural* **blunders**) a careless or clumsy mistake. ~ *verb* (**blunders, blundering, blundered**) **1** to make a blunder. **2** to move about in a clumsy or confused way.

blunt *adjective* **1** without a sharp edge

or point. **2** expressing yourself in a direct and straightforward way. ➤ **bluntly** adverb.

blur noun (plural **blurs**) **1** something that you cannot see clearly. **2** a smear. ~ verb (**blurs, blurring, blurred**) to become, or to make something, difficult to see or understand clearly. ➤ **blurry** adjective.

blurt verb (**blurts, blurting, blurted**) ✴ **blurt out** to say something suddenly without thinking first.

blush verb (**blushes, blushing, blushed**) to become red in the face because you are shy or embarrassed. ~ noun (plural **blushes**) a sudden reddening of the face when you blush.

blusher noun (plural **blushers**) a cream or powder for making your cheeks pinker.

bluster verb (**blusters, blustering, blustered**) to talk or act in a loud or pretentious way.

blustery adjective said about wind or rain: blowing in stormy gusts.

boa /boh a/ noun (plural **boas**) **1** a large snake that crushes its prey. **2** a long fluffy scarf made of fur or feathers.

boa constrictor noun (plural **boa constrictors**) a large American boa.

boar noun (plural **boars**) **1** a wild pig with large tusks. **2** a male pig.

board noun (plural **boards**) **1** a long thin narrow piece of timber. **2** a flat piece of some material with a special purpose: *a chess board; a bread board.* **3** a group of directors who run a company or organization. **4** daily meals provided to a lodger. ~ verb (**boards, boarding, boarded**) **1** to go onto a ship, train, aircraft, or vehicle. **2** to live in school as a boarder. ✴ **board up** to cover a door or window with boards. **on board** on or onto a ship, train, aircraft, or vehicle.

boarder noun (plural **boarders**) a boarding school pupil who lives there during the term.

board game noun (plural **board games**) a game in which you move pieces on a special board.

boarding house noun (plural **boarding houses**) a lodging house that supplies meals.

boarding school noun (plural **boarding schools**) a school at which pupils live during the term.

boardroom noun (plural **boardrooms**) a room in which a board of directors meets.

boast verb (**boasts, boasting, boasted**) **1** to praise yourself or your achievements openly. **2** to have something to be proud of: *The school boasts a fine new ICT suite.* ~ noun (plural **boasts**) a statement in which you praise yourself. ➤ **boastful** adjective, **boastfully** adverb, **boastfulness** noun.

boat noun (plural **boats**) **1** a small open craft for travelling across water. **2** a boat-shaped dish: *a gravy boat.* ✴ **in the same boat** in the same situation.

bob¹ verb (**bobs, bobbing, bobbed**) to move repeatedly up and down. ~ noun (plural **bobs**) a quick bobbing movement.

bob² noun (plural **bobs**) a short straight hairstyle for women. ~ verb (**bobs, bobbing, bobbed**) to cut hair in a bob.

bobbin noun (plural **bobbins**) a cylinder for holding thread in a machine.

bobble noun (plural **bobbles**) a small fluffy ball made from pieces of wool.

bobby noun (plural **bobbies**) *informal, dated* a police officer.

bode verb (**bodes, boding, boded**) ✴ **bode ill/well** to be a bad (or good) sign for the future.

bodice noun (plural **bodices**) the upper part of a woman's dress.

bodily adjective to do with the body.

body | 64

~ *adverb* **1** involving the whole body: *I picked him up bodily and took him outside.* **2** in physical rather than spiritual form.

body *noun* (*plural* **bodies**) **1** the physical structure of a person or animal, or the main part excluding the head, arms, and legs. **2** a corpse. **3** a star or planet, or other physical object. **4** an organized group that works together.

bodyguard *noun* (*plural* **bodyguards**) somebody whose job is to protect an important person.

bodywork *noun* the outer structure of a vehicle.

Boer /baw *or* boh er/ *noun* (*plural* **Boers**) a South African descended from the early Dutch settlers.

boffin *noun* (*plural* **boffins**) *informal* a scientist or technical expert.

bog *noun* (*plural* **bogs**) an area of wet spongy ground. ~ *verb* (**bogs, bogging, bogged**) ✲ **bog down 1** to cause a vehicle to sink into soft ground. **2** to slow somebody or something down with tasks or problems. ➤ **boggy** *adjective*.

boggle *verb* (**boggles, boggling, boggled**) (**boggle at**) *informal* to be confused or amazed by something.

bogus *adjective* not real; sham.

boil[1] *verb* (**boils, boiling, boiled**) **1** to heat a liquid until it bubbles and makes steam, or to heat a kettle or pan until the contents boil. **2** to cook food in boiling water. ~ *noun* (**the boil**) boiling point.

boil[2] *noun* (*plural* **boils**) a painful swelling containing pus.

boiler *noun* (*plural* **boilers**) a tank in which water is heated and stored.

boiling *adjective* very hot.

boiling point *noun* (*plural* **boiling points**) the temperature at which a liquid boils.

boisterous *adjective* noisy and energetic. ➤ **boisterously** *adverb*.

bold *adjective* **1** brave and adventurous. **2** cheeky. **3** strong and noticeable: *bold colours*. **4** said about printing type: darker and thicker than normal. ~ *noun* bold type. ➤ **boldly** *adverb*, **boldness** *noun*.

bollard *noun* (*plural* **bollards**) **1** a short post used to guide or keep out traffic. **2** a post for mooring a boat to.

bolshie *or* **bolshy** *adjective* (**bolshier, bolshiest**) *informal* deliberately uncooperative. ➤ **bolshiness** *noun*.

bolster *verb* (**bolsters, bolstering, bolstered**) to strengthen or support something. ~ *noun* (*plural* **bolsters**) a long pillow.

bolt *noun* (*plural* **bolts**) **1** a sliding bar for fastening a door. **2** a metal rod or pin used with a metal nut to fix things together. **3** a stroke of lightning. ~ *verb* (**bolts, bolting, bolted**) **1** to run away. **2** to lock or fasten a door with a bolt. **3** to eat food very quickly. ✲ **a bolt from the blue** something totally unexpected. **bolt upright** with a straight back. **make a bolt for** to dash towards a door, etc.

bomb *noun* (*plural* **bombs**) **1** a device that is designed to explode. **2** (**the bomb**) nuclear weapons. ~ *verb* (**bombs, bombing, bombed**) to attack a place or building with bombs.

bombard *verb* (**bombards, bombarding, bombarded**) **1** to attack a place or building with heavy gunfire or bombs. **2** to give somebody a lot of questions or information to deal with continually. ➤ **bombardment** *noun*.

bombastic /bom bas tik/ *adjective* using unnecessarily pretentious or fancy words.

bomber *noun* (*plural* **bombers**) **1** an aircraft that drops bombs. **2** a person who throws or plants bombs.

bombshell *noun* (*plural* **bombshells**) a

totally unexpected event or piece of news.

bona fide /boh na e di/ *adjective* genuine or real.

bonanza *noun* (*plural* **bonanzas**) a sudden and unexpected supply of money or success.

bond *noun* (*plural* **bonds**) **1** a strong close feeling that unites or links people. **2** something that binds or restricts you, such as an agreement that must be kept. **3** a firm connection between two surfaces that are stuck together. **4** (**bonds**) *literary* chains or ropes used to bind somebody. ~ *verb* (**bonds, bonding, bonded**) **1** to stick or fix something together. **2** to form a strong close emotional bond.

bondage *noun* slavery.

bone *noun* (*plural* **bones**) a piece of hard whitish material that forms one part of a human or animal skeleton, or this substance in general. ~ *verb* (**bones, boning, boned**) to remove the bones from fish or meat. ✳ **close to the bone** said about a remark: unpleasantly close to the truth. **have a bone to pick with** *informal* to have a complaint against somebody.
➤ **boneless** *adjective*.

bone-dry *adjective* completely dry.

bonfire *noun* (*plural* **bonfires**) a large open-air fire.

bongos or **bongoes** *plural noun* a pair of small drums that you beat with your hands.

bonkers *adjective informal* mad or crazy.

bonnet *noun* (*plural* **bonnets**) **1** a woman's or child's hat that ties under the chin. **2** the metal cover over the engine of a motor vehicle.

bonny *adjective* (**bonnier, bonniest**) *chiefly Scottish and N English dialect* pretty; attractive.

bonus /boh nus/ *noun* (*plural* **bonuses**) **1** something pleasant that is extra or unexpected. **2** an extra sum of money paid to workers or shareholders.

bony *adjective* (**bonier, boniest**) **1** like or made of bone. **2** full of bones. **3** thin; skinny.

boo *interjection* used to show disapproval, or to startle or frighten somebody. ~ *verb* (**boos, booing, booed**) to show disapproval by shouting 'boo!'

boob *noun* (*plural* **boobs**) *informal* a woman's breast.

booby trap *noun* (*plural* **booby traps**) a device that explodes when you touch or move it, hidden inside something that looks harmless.

book *noun* (*plural* **books**) **1** a set of pages in a cover, bound together down one edge and usually containing a piece of printed work. **2** (**books**) financial records or accounts. ~ *verb* (**books, booking, booked**) **1** to reserve or hire something in advance. **2** to record somebody's name in an official way when they do something illegal or wrong.

bookcase *noun* (*plural* **bookcases**) a piece of furniture with shelves for putting books on.

bookkeeper *noun* (*plural* **bookkeepers**) somebody who records the money used and spent by a business.
➤ **bookkeeping** *noun*.

booklet *noun* (*plural* **booklets**) a small book with a paper cover and not many pages.

bookmaker *noun* (*plural* **bookmakers**) a person who receives and pays bets.

bookmark *noun* (*plural* **bookmarks**) **1** a strip of card or leather for marking your place in a book. **2** *ICT* a way of recording a file or web address so that you can find it again.

bookworm *noun* (*plural* **bookworms**) *informal* somebody who enjoys reading.

boom¹ *noun* (*plural* **booms**) **1** a deep low sound. **2** a sudden major increase in economic activity. ~ *verb* (**booms, booming, boomed**) to make a deep low sound.

boom² *noun* (*plural* **booms**) **1** a pole across the bottom of a sail. **2** a pole carrying a microphone during filming.

boomerang *noun* (*plural* **boomerangs**) a bent piece of wood that returns to you when you throw it, first used by Aboriginals for hunting.

boon *noun* (*plural* **boons**) something that helps you or makes you happy.

boost *verb* (**boosts, boosting, boosted**) **1** to increase the amount or level of something. **2** to encourage somebody. ~ *noun* (*plural* **boosts**) **1** an increase in amount. **2** a support or encouragement.

boot *noun* (*plural* **boots**) **1** a shoe that goes up to your ankle or higher. **2** the luggage compartment of a car. ~ *verb* (**boots, booting, booted**) **1** to kick something or somebody roughly. **2** (**boot out**) *informal* to throw somebody out of somewhere rudely. **3** *ICT* to start up a computer. ✱ **to boot** as well.

booth *noun* (*plural* **booths**) **1** a stall or stand for selling or displaying goods. **2** a small compartment for telephoning or voting in privately.

booty *noun* valuable property that soldiers steal during a war.

booze *informal noun* alcoholic drink. ~ *verb* (**boozes, boozing, boozed**) to drink alcohol.

border *noun* (*plural* **borders**) **1** an outer part or edge. **2** a boundary of a country. **3** a narrow flower bed along the edge of a lawn. ~ *verb* (**borders, bordering, bordered**) **1** to form a border along the edge of something. **2** said about a country or region: to be next to another country or region. **3** (**border on/upon**) to be close to a particular feeling or state.

borderline *adjective* close to being in another group or level.

bore¹ *verb* (**bores, boring, bored**) to make a hole in something using a drill.

bore² *verb* (**bores, boring, bored**) to make somebody feel tired or unhappy by being dull or repetitive. ~ *noun* (*plural* **bores**) a boring or rather annoying person or situation.
➤ **bored** *adjective*.

bore³ *verb* past tense of BEAR².

boredom *noun* the state of being bored.

boring *adjective* uninteresting or repetitive.

born *adjective* **1** brought into existence by birth. **2** having a natural ability: *a born teacher*.

borne *verb* past participle of BEAR². ~ *adjective* (*combined with a noun*) carried by a specific thing: *airborne; water-borne*.

borough /bu ra/ *noun* (*plural* **boroughs**) a city area or a town that has its own local council.

borrow *verb* (**borrows, borrowing, borrowed**) to take or be given something that you will return later to the owner. ➤ **borrower** *noun*.

bosom /boo zum/ *noun* (*plural* **bosoms**) a woman's breasts.

boss *noun* (*plural* **bosses**) somebody who is in charge of other people at work. ~ *verb* (**bosses, bossing, bossed**) to give somebody orders.

bossy *adjective* (**bossier, bossiest**) always ordering people around.
➤ **bossiness** *noun*.

botany *noun* the scientific study of plant life. ➤ **botanical** *adjective*, **botanist** *noun*.

botch *verb* (**botches, botching, botched**) *informal* to do or repair something very badly.

both *adjective and pronoun* the one as well as the other of two people or things. ~ *adverb* (**both . . . and**) not only one thing or person, but also another.

bother *verb* (**bothers, bothering, bothered**) **1** to disturb, upset, or worry somebody. **2** to worry about something or take the trouble to do something. ~ *noun* fuss, effort, or difficulty. ~ *interjection* used when you are slightly annoyed about something.

bottle *noun* (*plural* **bottles**) a glass or plastic container for liquids, with a narrow neck. ~ *verb* (**bottles, bottling, bottled**) to store something in bottles.

bottle bank *noun* (*plural* **bottle banks**) a large container where people put bottles for recycling.

bottleneck *noun* (*plural* **bottlenecks**) a piece of road that gets blocked with traffic regularly.

bottom *noun* (*plural* **bottoms**) **1** the surface underneath something, which it rests on. **2** a person's buttocks. **3** the lowest part, place, or position. **4** (**bottoms**) the trousers of a two-piece outfit. ~ *adjective* at or to do with the bottom of something. ✱ **get to the bottom of** to find out the truth about something. ➤ **bottomless** *adjective*.

bough /bow/ *noun* (*plural* **boughs**) a main branch of a tree.

bought *verb* past tense and past participle of BUY.

boulder *noun* (*plural* **boulders**) a large stone or rock.

boulevard /booh li vahd/ *noun* (*plural* **boulevards**) a broad avenue.

bounce *verb* (**bounces, bouncing, bounced**) **1** to come back after hitting a surface, or to make a ball or other object do this. **2** to spring up and down when moving. **3** *informal* said about a cheque: to be returned by a bank because there is not enough money in the account to pay it.

~ *noun* (*plural* **bounces**) **1** a sudden leap or springing movement. **2** life or energy.

bouncy *adjective* (**bouncier, bounciest**) **1** tending to bounce. **2** lively or energetic.

bound¹ *verb* past tense and past participle of BIND. ~ *adjective* **1** going somewhere specific: *bound for home*. **2** certain or sure to do something: *It's bound to rain soon*. **3** (*combined with a noun*) confined to a particular place: *house-bound*. **4** (*usually combined with a noun*) legally or morally required to do something: *I'm bound to say*; *We are duty-bound to help*. **5** said about books: having a particular kind of binding: *a leather-bound volume*.

bound² *noun* (*plural* **bounds**) a leap or jump. ~ *verb* (**bounds, bounding, bounded**) **1** to leap or jump. **2** to bounce.

boundary *noun* (*plural* **boundaries**) a line that divides something or shows where its edge or limit is.

boundless *adjective* without any end or limits.

bounds *plural noun* limits or boundaries. ✱ **out of bounds** outside the area you are allowed to enter or the area a team sport must be played in.

bountiful *adjective literary* generous or plentiful.

bounty *noun* (*plural* **bounties**) **1** a financial reward for capturing a criminal. **2** *literary* generosity, or a generous gift.

bouquet /booh kay/ *noun* (*plural* **bouquets**) a bunch of flowers.

bourgeois /boor zhwah/ *adjective* belonging to or typical of middle-class people.

bout *noun* (*plural* **bouts**) **1** a short period of doing something. **2** a boxing or wrestling match. **3** an attack of an illness.

boutique /booh teek/ *noun* (*plural*

bovine

boutiques) a small shop selling fashionable clothes or gifts.

bovine /boh vien/ *adjective* affecting or to do with cattle.

bow¹ /bow/ *verb* (**bows, bowing, bowed**) **1** to bend your head or upper body when greeting somebody or showing respect. **2** (**bow to**) to accept somebody else's wishes. ~ *noun* (*plural* **bows**) a bending movement made with your head or body as a sign of respect or greeting.

bow² /boh/ *noun* (*plural* **bows**) **1** a type of knot with two loops and two free ends. **2** a flexible strip of wood with a tight cord between the two ends, used for shooting arrows. **3** a special rod used for playing a stringed instrument.

bow³ /bow/ *noun* (*plural* **bows**) the front end of a ship.

bowels /bowilz/ *plural noun* the intestines.

bowl¹ *noun* (*plural* **bowls**) **1** a round deep dish for holding or mixing food. **2** the hollow rounded part of something.

bowl² *noun* (*plural* **bowls**) **1** a heavy ball used in the game of bowls, skittles, or tenpin bowling. **2** (**bowls**) an outdoor game in which players roll bowls as close as possible to a target ball. ~ *verb* (**bowls, bowling, bowled**) **1** to roll a ball in bowls, etc. **2** to throw a ball towards a batsman in cricket. **3** (*also* **bowl out**) said about a bowler: to hit the wicket and get a batsman out in cricket. ➤ **bowler** *noun*, **bowling** *noun*.

bowlegged /boh le gid/ *adjective* with legs that curve outwards at the knees.

bow tie *noun* (*plural* **bow ties**) a short tie fastened in a bow.

bow window *noun* (*plural* **bow windows**) a curved bay window.

box *noun* (*plural* **boxes**) **1** a container with flat sides and a lid. **2** a small compartment for a group of people, for example at the theatre. **3** a rectangular space or area enclosed by straight lines. ~ *verb* (**boxes, boxing, boxed**) **1** to put something in a box. **2** to take part in boxing as a sport. ✷ **box in** to enclose or restrict somebody.

boxer *noun* (*plural* **boxers**) **1** a person who takes part in the sport of boxing. **2** a dog with short brown hair and a flat face.

boxing *noun* a sport in which two people fight with their fists, wearing thickly padded gloves.

Boxing Day *noun* 26 December, kept as a public holiday.

box office *noun* (*plural* **box offices**) the place in a cinema or theatre where tickets are sold.

boy *noun* (*plural* **boys**) a male child or young person. ➤ **boyhood** *noun*, **boyish** *adjective*.

boycott *verb* (**boycotts, boycotting, boycotted**) to refuse to deal or trade with something or somebody, as a protest or penalty. ~ *noun* (*plural* **boycotts**) an act of boycotting.

boyfriend *noun* (*plural* **boyfriends**) a regular male companion or lover.

bra *noun* (*plural* **bras**) a piece of women's underwear that supports the breasts.

brace *noun* (*plural* **braces**) **1** a device or structural part that strengthens and supports something. **2** a device that you wear on your teeth to straighten them. ~ *verb* (**braces, bracing, braced**) **1** to prepare yourself for an impact, or for something unpleasant. **2** to support something with a brace.

bracelet *noun* (*plural* **bracelets**) an ornamental band or chain worn round the wrist.

braces *plural noun* a pair of straps that you wear over your shoulders and attached to your trousers to keep them up.

bracing *adjective* refreshing or invigorating.

bracken *noun* a large fern that grows on moors.

bracket *noun* (*plural* **brackets**)
1 (**brackets**) *English, Maths* a pair of marks, such as ( ) or [ ], used to enclose a section of writing or print, or of numbers or symbols. **2** a defined group of people or things: *the highest income bracket*. **3** a support that projects horizontally from a wall. ~ *verb* (**brackets, bracketing, bracketed**) to put a word or words inside brackets. * **bracket together** to put people or things in the same category.

brag *verb* (**brags, bragging, bragged**) to boast.

Brahma *noun* one of the three main Hindu gods.

Brahmin *noun* (*plural* **Brahmins**) a member of the highest class of Hindu society, traditionally a priest.

braid *verb* (**braids, braiding, braided**) to plait hair or ribbon. ~ *noun* (*plural* **braids**) **1** a plaited strip of cord or ribbon. **2** a plait of hair.

Braille *noun* a system of printing for the blind, using patterns of raised dots.

brain *noun* (*plural* **brains**) **1** the organ inside your skull used for thinking and coordination. **2** (**brains**) intelligence.

brainchild *noun* something that a particular person invented, or a plan that they thought of.

brainwash *verb* (**brainwashes, brainwashing, brainwashed**) to make somebody believe or accept something by constantly repeating it to them.

brainwave *noun* (*plural* **brainwaves**) *informal* a sudden good idea.

brainy *adjective* (**brainier, brainiest**) *informal* intelligent.

braise *verb* (**braises, braising, braised**) to cook meat slowly by frying it briefly and then stewing it at a low heat.

brake *noun* (*plural* **brakes**) a device for slowing down or stopping a vehicle. ~ *verb* (**brakes, braking, braked**) to apply a brake on a vehicle.

bramble *noun* (*plural* **brambles**) a blackberry bush or similar prickly shrub.

bran *noun* the broken outer layer of grain that is separated from flour.

branch *noun* (*plural* **branches**)
1 a thick shoot growing from the trunk of a tree. **2** a smaller piece of road, railway line, or river that comes off the main one. **3** one part of a family, business, or organization. **4** a section of a subject that people study. ~ *verb* (**branches, branching, branched**) to grow or form branches. * **branch out** to try new activities or experiences.

brand *noun* (*plural* **brands**)
1 a product with a particular name, made by a single manufacturer. **2** a mark burnt onto the skin of a farm animal to show who owns it. ~ *verb* (**brands, branding, branded**) **1** to mark an animal with a hot iron. **2** to identify goods with a brand name. **3** to use a harsh word to describe somebody: *They branded him a liar.*

brandish *verb* (**brandishes, brandishing, brandished**) to wave a weapon in an obvious or threatening way.

brand-new *adjective* completely new and unused.

brandy *noun* (*plural* **brandies**) a strong alcoholic drink made from wine or fermented fruit juice.

brash *adjective* unpleasantly confident and direct.

brass *noun* (*plural* **brasses**) **1** a shiny yellowish metal that is an alloy of copper and zinc. **2** the brass instruments of an orchestra, such as trum-

brass band

pets and trombones. **3** a brass ornament or plate.

brass band *noun* (*plural* **brass bands**) a band consisting of brass instruments, and also drums and cymbals.

brat *noun* (*plural* **brats**) *informal* a rude or badly behaved child.

bravado /bra vah doh/ *noun* unusually confident behaviour intended to impress people.

brave *adjective* (**braver, bravest**) showing courage. ~ *verb* (**braves, braving, braved**) to face something unpleasant or dangerous with courage. ➤ **bravely** *adverb*, **bravery** *noun*.

bravo /brah voh/ *interjection* shouted by an audience to show special approval of a performance.

brawl *verb* (**brawls, brawling, brawled**) to quarrel or fight noisily. ~ *noun* (*plural* **brawls**) a noisy quarrel or fight.

brawn *noun* physical strength and muscle. ➤ **brawny** *adjective*

bray *verb* (**brays, braying, brayed**) to make the loud harsh cry of a donkey. ➤ **bray** *noun*.

brazen *adjective* without being ashamed of your bad behaviour or not trying to hide it. ➤ **brazenly** *adverb*.

brazier /bray zi er/ *noun* (*plural* **braziers**) a metal container for burning coal.

brazil nut *noun* (*plural* **brazil nuts**) a large three-sided nut with a very hard shell.

breach *noun* (*plural* **breaches**) **1** a failure to keep a law or agreement. **2** a gap made in a wall or barrier. ~ *verb* (**breaches, breaching, breached**) **1** to make a gap in a wall or barrier. **2** to break a law or agreement.

bread *noun* (*plural* **breads**) a food consisting of a baked mixture of flour and water, usually made to rise with yeast before baking.

breadcrumbs *plural noun* small fragments of bread, used in cooking.

breadth *noun* the distance across something from one side to the other.

breadwinner *noun* (*plural* **breadwinners**) the person who earns the money that supports their family.

break *verb* (**breaks, breaking, broke, broken**) **1** to separate into pieces from falling or being hit. **2** to stop working. **3** to fail to keep a promise or rule. **4** to be greater or better than something: *to break the world record*. **5** to make some news known to people. **6** said about weather: to change after a settled period. **7** said about a boy's voice: to deepen at puberty. ~ *noun* (*plural* **breaks**) **1** an act or action of breaking. **2** a place where something is broken. **3** a short rest from work. **4** a sudden dash. **5** *informal* a lucky opportunity. * **break down 1** to fail or stop working. **2** to have an emotional or physical collapse. **3** to separate something into its basic elements. **break in** to enter a building by force. **break out 1** said about something unpleasant: to start suddenly. **2** to escape from prison. **break up 1** to break into pieces. **2** to end a relationship, or to come to an end. **3** to finish doing something together and leave. ➤ **breakable** *adjective*.

breakage *noun* (*plural* **breakages**) **1** something that has been broken. **2** the action of breaking something.

breakdown *noun* (*plural* **breakdowns**) **1** a sudden failure to work properly. **2** a physical or nervous collapse. **3** the process of decomposing. **4** a detailed analysis.

breaker *noun* (*plural* **breakers**) a wave breaking into foam.

breakfast *noun* (*plural* **breakfasts**) the first meal of the day. ~ *verb* (**break-**

fasts, breakfasting, breakfasted) to eat breakfast.

break-in noun (plural **break-ins**) an act of entering a building illegally, usually by forcing open a window or door.

breakneck adjective dangerously fast.

breakthrough noun (plural **breakthroughs**) a sudden new development or discovery.

breakwater noun (plural **breakwaters**) Geography a barrier that protects a harbour or beach from the sea.

bream noun (plural **breams** or **bream**) an edible freshwater fish.

breast noun (plural **breasts**) **1** one of the two soft parts on a woman's chest that produce milk for a baby. **2** the front part of the body between the neck and the abdomen.

breastbone noun (plural **breastbones**) a flat bone down the centre of the chest to which some of the ribs are attached.

breast-feed verb (**breast-feeds, breast-feeding, breast-fed**) to feed a baby with milk from the breast.

breaststroke noun a style of swimming in which you push your arms forward then sweep them out and back, while kicking your legs out and back.

breath noun (plural **breaths**) **1** the air that goes in and out of your lungs when you breathe. **2** an act of breathing. **3** a slight movement of air. ✶ **out of breath** breathing very quickly as a result of exercise. **under your breath** in a whisper.

breathalyse or **breathalyze** verb (**breathalyses, breathalysing, breathalysed** or **breathalyzes,** etc) to test a driver's breath with a breathalyser.

breathalyser or **breathalyzer** noun (plural **breathalysers** or **breathalyzers**) a device used to test the amount of alcohol in a driver's breath.

breathe verb (**breathes, breathing, breathed**) **1** to draw air into your lungs and let it out again. **2** to say something: *I won't breathe a word*.

breather noun (plural **breathers**) informal a short break from an activity.

breathless adjective gasping for breath after hard exercise. ➤ **breathlessly** adverb.

breathtaking adjective extremely exciting or thrilling. ➤ **breathtakingly** adverb.

breeches plural noun old-fashioned knee-length trousers.

breed verb (**breeds, breeding, bred**) **1** to produce babies. **2** to produce new young plants or animals. **3** to make something develop. ~ noun a group of animals or plants of the same type. ➤ **breeder** noun, **breeding** noun.

breeze noun (plural **breezes**) a gentle wind.

breeze-block noun (plural **breeze-blocks**) a type of block used for building.

breezy adjective (**breezier, breeziest**) **1** said about weather: fresh and windy. **2** said about a person: brisk and cheerful. ➤ **breezily** adverb.

brethren noun archaic plural of BROTHER, now mainly used in religious contexts.

breve noun (plural **breves**) a musical note that lasts twice as long as a semibreve.

brevity noun shortness; the use of few words.

brew verb (**brews, brewing, brewed**) **1** to make beer. **2** to make tea. **3** (**be brewing**) to be developing. **4** (**brew up**) to think up or plot something. ➤ **brewer** noun.

brewery noun (plural **breweries**) a place where beer is brewed.

briar

briar *noun* see BRIER.

bribe *verb* (**bribes, bribing, bribed**) to try to persuade somebody to do something illegal or wrong by offering them something, such as money. ~ *noun* (*plural* **bribes**) something offered to bribe somebody. ➤ **bribery** *noun*.

bric-a-brac *noun* various small articles or ornaments.

brick *noun* (*plural* **bricks**) **1** a rectangular block of baked clay used for building. **2** a small block used as a children's toy. ~ *verb* (**bricks, bricking, bricked**) ✻ **brick up** to fill or close something with bricks.

bricklayer *noun* (*plural* **bricklayers**) somebody who lays bricks as their job.

bridal *adjective* for or to do with a bride or wedding.

bride *noun* (*plural* **brides**) a woman at the time of her wedding.

bridegroom *noun* (*plural* **bridegrooms**) a man at the time of his wedding.

bridesmaid *noun* (*plural* **bridesmaids**) a woman or girl who is a special attendant to a bride during her wedding.

bridge[1] *noun* (*plural* **bridges**) **1** a structure that goes across a river, road, railway, etc. **2** the upper bony part of the nose. **3** an enclosed platform on a ship for the captain and officers. ~ *verb* (**bridges, bridging, bridged**) to fill a gap or make a connection over or across something.

bridge[2] *noun* a card game for two pairs of players in which you try to win a certain number of tricks.

bridle *noun* (*plural* **bridles**) a set of leather straps that you put over a horse's head to control it. ~ *verb* (**bridles, bridling, bridled**) **1** to put a bridle on a horse. **2** to show hostility or resentment.

brief[1] *adjective* short. ➤ **briefly** *adverb*.

brief[2] *noun* (*plural* **briefs**) **1** a set of details and instructions about a task or legal case. **2** a barrister or solicitor who is working on a case. **3** (**briefs**) short underpants.~ *verb* (**briefs, briefing, briefed**) to give somebody instructions or information about a task or legal case.

briefcase *noun* (*plural* **briefcases**) a flat rectangular case to carry work papers in.

briefing *noun* (*plural* **briefings**) a meeting for giving somebody instructions or information.

brier or **briar** *noun* (*plural* **briers** or **briars**) a thorny or prickly plant.

brigade *noun* (*plural* **brigades**) **1** a large section of an army. **2** *informal* a group of people who do something together or all share a particular opinion.

brigadier *noun* (*plural* **brigadiers**) an officer who ranks below a major general in the British Army.

bright *adjective* **1** giving off a lot of light; shining. **2** lively and cheerful. **3** quick to learn. ➤ **brightly** *adverb*, **brightness** *noun*.

brighten *verb* (**brightens, brightening, brightened**) to become brighter or to make something or somebody brighter.

brilliant *adjective* **1** very bright or bold. **2** extremely clever. **3** *informal* very good. ➤ **brilliance** *noun*, **brilliantly** *adverb*.

brim *noun* (*plural* **brims**) the edge or rim of a container or a hat. ~ *verb* (**brims, brimming, brimmed**) to be full to the brim.

brimful /brim fool/ *adjective* full to the brim.

brine *noun* salty water.

bring *verb* (**brings, bringing, brought**) **1** to take or carry somebody or something to a place. **2** to cause something to happen or to come.

bring about to cause something to happen. **bring on** to cause a feeling or symptom. **bring out 1** to publish or produce something. **2** to emphasize something. **bring up 1** to educate and look after a child. **2** to introduce a subject to consider.

brink noun (plural **brinks**) **1** the edge of a cliff or water. **2** the point at which something is about to happen.

brisk adjective energetic and fast. ➤ **briskly** adverb.

bristle noun (plural **bristles**) a short stiff hair. ~ verb (**bristles, bristling, bristled**) said about hair or fur: to rise and stand up stiffly. ➤ **bristly** adjective.

brittle adjective (**brittler, brittlest**) hard and easily broken.

broach verb (**broaches, broaching, broached**) to introduce a subject for discussion.

broad adjective **1** large from side to side; wide. **2** general, not dealing with details. **3** said about an accent: very noticeable. ➤ **broadly** adverb.

broad bean noun (plural **broad beans**) a large flat green bean.

broadcast verb (**broadcasts, broadcasting, broadcast**) **1** to transmit a television or radio programme. **2** to tell a lot of people about something. ~ noun (plural **broadcasts**) a radio or television programme. ➤ **broadcaster** noun.

broaden verb (**broadens, broadening, broadened**) to make something broad or broader, or to become broader.

broad-minded adjective tolerant of other people's views or behaviour.

broadsheet noun (plural **broadsheets**) a newspaper printed on large folded sheets.

brocade /bro kayd/ noun (plural **brocades**) a heavy fabric woven with raised patterns.

broccoli noun a vegetable with a green or purplish flower head.

brochure /broh sher/ noun (plural **brochures**) a thin book containing information about products or holidays you can buy.

brogue[1] /brohg/ noun (plural **brogues**) a strong shoe with decorative holes punched into the leather.

brogue[2] /brohg/ noun (plural **brogues**) a dialect or regional accent.

broke[1] verb past tense of BREAK.

broke[2] adjective informal having no money.

broken verb past participle of BREAK.

broken-down adjective old, broken, and needing repair.

brokenhearted adjective extremely sad or grieving deeply.

broken home noun (plural **broken homes**) a family in which the parents have separated.

broker noun (plural **brokers**) somebody who buys and sells shares or other goods for other people as their job.

bronchial /brong ki al/ adjective Science to do with the tubes leading from the windpipe to the lungs.

bronchitis /brong kie tis/ noun an illness in which your bronchial tubes are inflamed and you cough badly.

bronze noun (plural **bronzes**) **1** a yellowish brown metal that is an alloy of copper and tin. **2** a sculpture made of bronze. **3** a yellowish brown colour.

Bronze Age noun (**the Bronze Age**) History the period in which bronze and copper tools and weapons were common, between the Stone Age and the Iron Age.

bronze medal noun (plural **bronze medals**) a medal made of bronze, awarded for coming third in a competition.

brooch /brohch/ noun (plural

brood

brooches) an ornament with a pin at the back for fixing it onto clothing.

brood *noun* (*plural* **broods**) a group of young birds hatched at one time. ~ *verb* (**broods, brooding, brooded**) **1** said about a bird: to sit on eggs to hatch them. **2** to worry about something for a long time.

broody *adjective* (**broodier, broodiest**) **1** said about a hen: ready to hatch eggs. **2** *informal* said about a woman: keen to have a baby. **3** worried and unhappy. ➤ **broodily** *adverb*.

brook *noun* (*plural* **brooks**) a small stream.

broom *noun* (*plural* **brooms**) **1** a long-handled brush for sweeping. **2** a shrub with yellow flowers.

broomstick *noun* (*plural* **broomsticks**) a brush made of twigs on a long thin handle, used by witches to fly through the air in children's stories.

broth *noun* (*plural* **broths**) a type of thin soup or stock.

brothel *noun* (*plural* **brothels**) a building in which prostitutes work.

brother *noun* **1** (*plural* **brothers**) a man or boy with the same parents as another person. **2** (*plural* **brothers** or *sometimes* **brethren**) a man belonging to a religious group or trade union. ➤ **brotherly** *adjective*.

brotherhood *noun* (*plural* **brotherhoods**) **1** an organization for men. **2** fellowship or friendship between human beings.

brother-in-law *noun* (*plural* **brothers-in-law**) **1** the brother of your husband or wife. **2** your sister's husband.

brought *verb* past tense and past participle of BRING.

brow *noun* (*plural* **brows**) **1** the forehead. **2** an eyebrow. **3** the highest point of a hill.

brown *adjective* **1** of the colour of dead leaves, bark, or soil. **2** with a dark or tanned complexion. ~ *noun* (*plural* **browns**) a brown colour. ~ *verb* (**browns, browning, browned**) to go brown, or to make something brown, during cooking. ➤ **brownish** *adjective*, **brownness** *noun*.

brownie *noun* (*plural* **brownies**) **1** (**Brownie**) a girl in the junior section of the Guide Association. **2** a square piece of rich chocolate cake.

browse *verb* (**browses, browsing, browsed**) **1** to look casually through a book or a collection of things. **2** *ICT* to look through information on the Internet. ~ *noun* (*plural* **browses**) a period of browsing.

browser *noun* (*plural* **browsers**) **1** *ICT* a computer program for viewing information on the Internet. **2** somebody who is browsing.

bruise *noun* (*plural* **bruises**) a dark or discoloured area on the skin caused by an injury. ~ *verb* (**bruises, bruising, bruised**) to give somebody a bruise or bruises, or to develop bruises.

brunch *noun* (*plural* **brunches**) a meal eaten in the late morning, combining breakfast and lunch.

brunette /brooh net/ *noun* (*plural* **brunettes**) a girl or woman with dark-brown hair.

brunt *noun* the main force of an attack or a blow.

brush[1] *noun* (*plural* **brushes**) **1** an object with bristles or wires set into a handle, used to tidy your hair or for painting or cleaning. **2** an act of brushing. **3** a quick light touch. **4** the bushy tail of a fox. ~ *verb* (**brushes, brushing, brushed**) **1** to clean or tidy something with a brush. **2** to touch something lightly when passing it. ✶ **brush up** to revise a subject or skill: *I must brush up on my French.*

brush[2] *noun* rough vegetation, or land covered with it.

brush³ *noun* (*plural* **brushes**) a short unfriendly meeting or fight.

brusque /broosk/ *adjective* blunt or abrupt in the way you behave or speak. ➤ **brusquely** *adverb*.

Brussels sprout *noun* (*plural* **Brussels sprouts**) a type of green vegetable like a very small cabbage.

brutal *adjective* **1** cruel and violent. **2** harsh or severe. ➤ **brutality** *noun*, **brutally** *adverb*.

brute *noun* (*plural* **brutes**) **1** a cruel and violent person. **2** a large animal. ~ *adjective* purely physical: *brute force*. ➤ **brutish** *adjective*.

bubble *noun* (*plural* **bubbles**) **1** a small amount of gas inside something liquid or solid. **2** a thin transparent film of liquid containing air or gas. ~ *verb* (**bubbles, bubbling, bubbled**) to form or produce bubbles.

bubble gum *noun* chewing gum that you can blow into a bubble.

bubbly *adjective* (**bubblier, bubbliest**) full of bubbles. ~ *noun informal* champagne.

buck¹ *noun* (*plural* **bucks**) a male deer or rabbit.

buck² *verb* (**bucks, bucking, bucked**) said about a horse: to spring into the air with its back curved.

buck³ *noun* (*plural* **bucks**) *informal* a dollar.

bucket *noun* (*plural* **buckets**) an open container with a handle, used to carry liquids. ➤ **bucketful** *noun* (*plural* **bucketfuls**).

buckle *noun* (*plural* **buckles**) a blunt pin fixed to a hard rim, used to fasten a belt or strap. ~ *verb* (**buckles, buckling, buckled**) **1** to fasten something with a buckle. **2** to bend or collapse under a weight.

bud *noun* (*plural* **buds**) a small growth that will develop into a flower, leaf, or shoot. ~ *verb* (**buds, budding, budded**) to grow buds.

Buddhism /boo diz m/ *noun* a religion based on the teaching of Gautama Buddha. ➤ **Buddhist** *noun and adjective*.

budding *adjective* starting to develop into a person with a special skill: *a budding scientist*.

budge *verb* (**budges, budging, budged**) to move, or to move something, by any amount: *The donkey wouldn't budge*; *The key is stuck and I can't budge it*.

budgerigar *noun* (*plural* **budgerigars**) a type of small colourful bird with a long tail that is often kept as a pet and can be trained to talk.

budget *noun* (*plural* **budgets**) **1** a statement of money received and spent over a set period. **2** the amount of money you allocate for a particular purpose. **3** (**the Budget**) an official statement of the government's financial position and plans. ~ *verb* (**budgets, budgeting, budgeted**) to decide how to allocate and use the money you have available. ➤ **budgetary** *adjective*.

budgie *noun* (*plural* **budgies**) *informal* a budgerigar.

buff *noun* (*plural* **buffs**) **1** a pale-yellowish brown colour. **2** *informal* somebody who knows a lot about a particular subject. ~ *verb* (**buffs, buffing, buffed**) to polish something with a soft cloth.

buffalo *noun* (*plural* **buffaloes** or **buffalo**) a large cow-like animal with horns, such as the American bison or the African ox.

buffer *noun* (*plural* **buffers**) **1** a device to absorb the shock of impact, fixed at the end of a train or railway track. **2** *ICT* a temporary storage area in a computer.

buffet¹ /boo fay/ *noun* (*plural* **buffets**) **1** a meal set out on a table so that people can serve themselves.

buffet

2 a counter where food and drink is sold.

buffet² /buˈfit/ *verb* (**buffets, buffeting, buffeted**) to beat or hit against something or somebody repeatedly.

bug *noun* (*plural* **bugs**) **1** a tiny insect. **2** *informal* a germ or virus, or an illness caused by one. **3** *ICT* a fault in a computer program. **4** a secret listening device. ~ *verb* (**bugs, bugging, bugged**) **1** *informal* to annoy somebody. **2** to put a secret listening device in an object or room.

buggy *noun* (*plural* **buggies**) **1** a foldable pushchair. **2** a light one-horse carriage.

bugle /bewgl/ *noun* (*plural* **bugles**) a brass instrument like a small trumpet. ➤ **bugler** *noun*.

build *verb* (**builds, building, built**) **1** to make something by putting materials together. **2** to develop or increase gradually, or make something do this: *The tension is building; He built up his business slowly.* ~ *noun* (*plural* **builds**) the shape and size of a person or animal. ➤ **builder** *noun*.

building *noun* (*plural* **buildings**) **1** a permanent structure with walls and a roof. **2** the business of building structures.

built *verb* past tense and past participle of BUILD. ~ *adjective* with a particular size or structure: *a heavily built man*.

built-in *adjective* not separate but forming part of something's main structure: *a built-in cupboard*.

built-up *adjective* filled with houses and other buildings: *a built-up area*.

bulb *noun* (*plural* **bulbs**) **1** a thick rounded part from which the stem and roots of a plant grow. **2** (*also* **light bulb**) a hollow rounded glass object that produces light when electricity passes through it.

bulbous *adjective* round like a bulb.

bulge *noun* (*plural* **bulges**) a swelling sticking out from a flat surface. ~ *verb* (**bulges, bulging, bulged**) to swell outwards in a curved shape.

bulimia /booˈlimiə/ *noun* an illness in which you overeat and then starve yourself or make yourself vomit. ➤ **bulimic** *adjective and noun*.

bulk *noun* **1** the volume or size of something. **2** a large or heavy mass. **3** (**the bulk of**) most of something. * **in bulk** in large amounts.

bulky *adjective* (**bulkier, bulkiest**) awkwardly large.

bull *noun* (*plural* **bulls**) an adult male of various large animals, such as cattle, elephants, and whales.

bulldog *noun* (*plural* **bulldogs**) a dog with a short neck and wide head.

bulldoze *verb* (**bulldozes, bulldozing, bulldozed**) to clear or knock down something with a bulldozer.

bulldozer *noun* (*plural* **bulldozers**) a heavy vehicle with a broad blade across the front, for clearing ground.

bullet *noun* (*plural* **bullets**) **1** a small metal object that is fired from a gun. **2** *ICT* a large printed dot.

bulletin *noun* (*plural* **bulletins**) **1** a short news item or broadcast. **2** a small journal published regularly.

bullion *noun* bars of gold or silver.

bullock *noun* (*plural* **bullocks**) a young castrated bull.

bull's-eye *noun* (*plural* **bull's-eyes**) the centre of a target, or a shot that hits it.

bully *verb* (**bullies, bullying bullied**) to frighten or hurt other people regularly and deliberately. ~ *noun* (*plural* **bullies**) somebody who bullies people weaker than themselves.

bulrush *noun* (*plural* **bulrushes**) a grass-like plant that grows in wet areas.

bum *noun* (*plural* **bums**) *informal* the buttocks.

bumble *verb* (**bumbles, bumbling,**

bumbled) to speak or behave in a clumsy or confused way: *He was bumbling about, knocking things over.*

bumblebee *noun* (*plural* **bumblebees**) a round fat bee with a loud hum.

bump *verb* (**bumps, bumping, bumped**) **1** to hit or knock against something. **2** to move in a series of bumps: *bumping along the road.* ~ *noun* (*plural* **bumps**) **1** a knock or jolt. **2** a swelling or lump. ✱ **bump into** to meet somebody unexpectedly. **bump off** *informal* to murder somebody.

bumper[1] *noun* (*plural* **bumpers**) a bar fixed along the end of a motor vehicle to absorb the shock if it bumps into something.

bumper[2] *adjective* unusually large: *a bumper crop*.

bumptious /**bump**shus/ *adjective* unpleasantly self-confident and bossy.

bumpy *adjective* (**bumpier, bumpiest**) **1** covered with bumps. **2** with lots of jolts: *a bumpy ride*.

bun *noun* (*plural* **buns**) **1** a small cake or bread roll. **2** a tight knot of hair at the back of the head.

bunch *noun* (*plural* **bunches**) **1** a group of things that are tied or held together. **2** *informal* a group of people. ~ *verb* (**bunches, bunching, bunched**) to form into a bunch or form something into bunches: *Bunch up so that we can all sit down.*

bundle *noun* (*plural* **bundles**) a collection of things held loosely together. ~ *verb* (**bundles, bundling, bundled**) **1** to form something into a bundle or package. **2** *informal* to hurry or push somebody or something in a rough or undignified way: *She bundled me out of the house.*

bung *verb* (**bungs, bunging, bunged**) **1** to block or close: *Leaves are bunging up the drain.* **2** *informal* to throw or put something somewhere roughly. ~ *noun* (*plural* **bungs**) a stopper used to block a hole in a barrel.

bungalow *noun* (*plural* **bungalows**) a house with rooms all on one floor.

bungle *verb* (**bungles, bungling, bungled**) to do something badly or clumsily. ➤ **bungler** *noun*.

bunion *noun* (*plural* **bunions**) a painful swelling on the big toe.

bunk[1] *noun* (*plural* **bunks**) a narrow built-in bed on a boat or train, or one of a set of bunk beds.

bunk[2] *verb* (**bunks, bunking, bunked**) (**bunk off**) *informal* to play truant from school. ✱ **do a bunk** *informal* to escape or run away.

bunk beds *plural noun* two beds fixed one on top of the other.

bunker *noun* (*plural* **bunkers**) **1** a large container or cupboard for storing fuel: *a coal bunker.* **2** an underground shelter for protection against bombs. **3** a dip filled with sand on a golf course.

bunny *noun* (*plural* **bunnies**) *informal* a rabbit.

Bunsen burner *noun* (*plural* **Bunsen burners**) *Science* a gas burner used in laboratories.

bunting *noun* flags and streamers used as outdoor decorations.

buoy /boi/ *noun* (*plural* **buoys**) a floating object that is tied in position to guide boats.

buoyant /**boi**ant/ *adjective* **1** able to float. **2** cheerful. ➤ **buoyancy** *noun*.

burble *verb* (**burbles, burbling, burbled**) to make a soft bubbling or murmuring sound. ➤ **burble** *noun*.

burden *noun* (*plural* **burdens**) **1** a heavy load or object to carry. **2** a tiring or worrying responsibility. ~ *verb* (**burdens, burdening, burdened**) to put a strain or burden on somebody or something. ➤ **burdensome** *adjective*.

bureau /**bew**roh/ *noun* (*plural* **bureaus** or **bureaux** /**bew**rohz/) **1** a public

bureaucracy

office or department. **2** a writing desk with a sloping top.

bureaucracy /bew ro kra si/ *noun* (*plural* **bureaucracies**) lots of fixed rules, procedures, and different levels of authority, or a large organization or government with this. ➤ **bureaucratic** *adjective*.

bureaucrat /bew roh krat/ *noun* (*plural* **bureaucrats**) a government official who works in a bureaucracy.

burgeoning /ber jo ning/ *adjective* growing rapidly.

burger *noun* (*plural* **burgers**) a hamburger.

burglar *noun* (*plural* **burglars**) somebody who gets into a building and steals things. ➤ **burglary** *noun*.

burgle *verb* (**burgles, burgling, burgled**) to steal from a building: *Our house was burgled*.

burial /be ri al/ *noun* (*plural* **burials**) the burying of a dead body.

burly *adjective* (**burlier, burliest**) with a strong, broad, heavily built body.

burn *verb* (**burns, burning, burned** or **burnt**) **1** to be used or to use something as fuel to produce fire. **2** to damage something or somebody with fire, heat, or chemicals, or to be damaged in this way. **3** said about a fire: to produce heat, light, or flames. ~ *noun* (*plural* **burns**) an injury caused by burning. ➤ **burner** *noun*, **burning** *adjective*.

burp *verb* (**burps, burping, burped**) to let gas out from your stomach through your mouth loudly. ~ *noun* (*plural* **burps**) a noise or act of burping.

burrow *noun* (*plural* **burrows**) a hole or small tunnel in the ground made by a small animal. ~ *verb* (**burrows, burrowing, burrowed**) **1** to make a burrow by tunnelling. **2** to dig into or under something to cover yourself or to search for something.

bursary *noun* (*plural* **bursaries**) a grant of money awarded to a student.

burst *verb* (**bursts, bursting, burst**) **1** to break open or into pieces suddenly and violently. **2** (**burst out/into**) to start doing something suddenly and loudly: *to burst out laughing/crying; to burst into tears/song*. **3** (**burst with**) to be extremely full of something: *bursting with pride*. ~ *noun* (*plural* **bursts**) **1** a sudden or brief period of something. **2** an explosion or breaking open, when something bursts.

bury /be ri/ *verb* (**buries, burying, buried**) **1** to place or hide something in the ground. **2** to cover something completely. **3** (**bury in**) to concentrate all your attention on something.

bus *noun* (*plural* **buses**) a large motor vehicle that carries passengers.

bush *noun* (*plural* **bushes**) **1** a shrub with a woody stem. **2** (**the bush**) large wild areas of Africa or Australia.

bushy *adjective* (**bushier, bushiest**) **1** growing thickly. **2** covered with bushes.

business /biz nis/ *noun* (*plural* **businesses**) **1** the work of buying and selling or producing things, or a company that does this. **2** somebody's regular work. **3** a situation or subject. **4** a subject that concerns you.

businesslike *adjective* efficient.

businessman or **businesswoman** *noun* (*plural* **businessmen** or **businesswomen**) a person who works in business.

busk *verb* (**busks, busking, busked**) to play music in the street to collect money. ➤ **busker** *noun*.

bust[1] *noun* (*plural* **busts**) **1** a woman's breasts. **2** a sculpture of somebody's head, neck, and shoulders.

bust[2] *informal verb* (**busts, busting, busted** or **bust**) to break something. ~ *adjective* broken. ✷ **go bust** to go bankrupt.

bustle verb (**bustles, bustling, bustled**) **1** to hurry about busily. **2** to be full of people and activity. ~ noun noisy and energetic activity.

busy /biˈzi/ adjective (**busier, busiest**) **1** fully occupied with things to do. **2** full of activity. ~ verb (**busies, busying, busied**) to keep yourself busy. ➤ **busily** adverb, **busyness** noun.

busybody noun (plural **busybodies**) somebody who interferes in things that are not to do with them.

but conjunction used between two words or two parts of a sentence that express different or contrasting information: *poor but happy*. ~ preposition except; other than: *all but one*.

butcher noun (plural **butchers**) **1** somebody who sells meat or who kills animals for their meat. **2** somebody who kills people brutally. ~ verb (**butchers, butchering, butchered**) **1** to kill and prepare an animal to use its meat. **2** to kill people brutally. **3** to spoil or ruin something. ➤ **butchery** noun.

butler noun (plural **butlers**) a male servant in charge of a house and any other servants working there.

butt[1] verb (**butts, butting, butted**) to hit or push something or somebody like a goat or ram, with the head or horns. * **butt in** to interrupt rudely.

butt[2] noun (plural **butts**) **1** the thicker end of a tool or weapon. **2** the unsmoked end of a cigar or cigarette.

butt[3] noun (plural **butts**) an object or person that people make fun of or insult.

butt[4] noun (plural **butts**) a large barrel.

butter noun a pale-yellow substance made from milk, often spread on bread. ~ verb (**butters, buttering, buttered**) to spread butter on something. * **butter up** informal to charm somebody by flattering them.

buttercup noun (plural **buttercups**) a small yellow wild flower.

butterfingers noun (plural **butterfingers**) informal somebody who tends to drop things.

butterfly noun (plural **butterflies**) **1** an insect with large, brightly coloured wings. **2** a style of swimming in which you swing both arms out of the water together and then push them back. **3** (**butterflies**) informal an uncomfortable nervous feeling.

butterscotch noun hard toffee with a buttery taste.

buttery adjective like or containing butter.

buttock noun (plural **buttocks**) one of the two fleshy parts of your body between your back and your legs; the parts you sit on.

button noun (plural **buttons**) **1** a small round object that you push through a buttonhole on a piece of clothing to fasten it. **2** a knob that you press on a machine to make it do something. ~ verb (**buttons, buttoning, buttoned**) to do up a piece of clothing with buttons: *I buttoned up my cardigan*.

buttonhole[1] noun (plural **buttonholes**) **1** a small slit in a piece of clothing, for pushing a button through. **2** a flower that you wear on your lapel.

buttonhole[2] verb (**buttonholes, buttonholing, buttonholed**) to approach somebody and talk to them in a way that stops them getting away.

buttress noun (plural **buttresses**) a structure built against a wall or building to support it. ~ verb (**buttresses, buttressing, buttressed**) to strengthen and support something with a buttress.

buy verb (**buys, buying, bought**) to pay for something so that you own it. ~ noun (plural **buys**) something you buy: *a good buy*. ➤ **buyer** noun.

buzz *verb* (**buzzes, buzzing, buzzed**) to make a long or continuous vibrating sound. ~ *noun* (*plural* **buzzes**) **1** a buzzing sound, such as a signal made by a buzzer. **2** *informal* a telephone call. **3** *informal* a thrill.

buzzard *noun* (*plural* **buzzards**) a large bird of prey with broad wings.

buzzer *noun* (*plural* **buzzers**) an electrical device that makes a buzzing sound as a signal.

by *preposition* **1** through the action of somebody or something. **2** near to somebody or something. **3** during: *by night*. **4** before a particular time. **5** using a particular method. ~ *adverb* past.

bye *interjection informal* = GOODBYE.

by-election *noun* (*plural* **by-elections**) an election that is held to fill a single vacancy in parliament or a local council, not to elect a completely new government or council.

bygone *adjective* belonging to an earlier time.

by-law *noun* (*plural* **by-laws**) a law passed by a local authority and which only applies in that area.

bypass *noun* (*plural* **bypasses**) **1** a road built to take traffic round a town centre. **2** *Science* an operation to take the blood around a blocked or damaged area of the body. ~ *verb* (**bypasses, bypassing, bypassed**) **1** to go round something using a bypass. **2** to avoid something.

bystander *noun* (*plural* **bystanders**) somebody who is not involved in a situation or event but who is there.

byte *noun* (*plural* **bytes**) *ICT* a unit for measuring information stored on a computer.

byway *noun* (*plural* **byways**) a minor road.

C *abbreviation* Celsius or centigrade: *34°C*.

cab *noun* (*plural* **cabs**) **1** a taxi. **2** a compartment for the driver of a train, bus, or large vehicle.

cabaret /ka ba ray/ *noun* (*plural* **cabarets**) a series of acts, for example by singers, dancers, and comedians, providing entertainment at a nightclub.

cabbage *noun* (*plural* **cabbages**) a plant with a head of closely packed leaves, used as a vegetable.

cabin *noun* (*plural* **cabins**) **1** a private room or compartment on a ship. **2** the passenger compartment in an aircraft. **3** a small simple wooden house.

cabinet *noun* (*plural* **cabinets**) **1** a cupboard with doors and shelves for storing or displaying articles. **2** (*often* **Cabinet**) a committee consisting of the prime minister and the senior government ministers.

cabin crew *noun* (*plural* **cabin crews**) the members of the crew of a passenger aircraft who look after the passengers.

cable *noun* (*plural* **cables**) **1** a strong thick rope of fibre or metal. **2** a set of electrical wires surrounded by a sheath. **3** = CABLE TELEVISION.

cable car *noun* (*plural* **cable cars**) a cabin hanging from a moving cable, used to transport passengers up and down a mountain.

cable television *noun* a television system in which viewers pay to receive programmes along a cable rather than through an aerial or satellite dish.

cacao /ka kah oh/ *noun* (*plural* **cacaos**) a South American tree whose seeds are used in making cocoa and chocolate.

cache /kash/ *noun* (*plural* **caches**) a hidden store of food or weapons.

cachet /ka shay/ *noun* prestige that comes from being considered high-class or using high-class things: *A Rolls-Royce has a definite cachet*.

cackle *verb* (**cackles, cackling, cackled**) **1** to make the squawking cry of a hen. **2** to talk or laugh noisily. ➤ **cackle** *noun*.

cacophony /ka ko fo ni/ *noun* (*plural* **cacophonies**) a loud and unpleasant combination of sounds. ➤ **cacophonous** *adjective*.

cactus *noun* (*plural* **cacti** /kak tie/ *or* **cactuses**) a plant with a fleshy stem and scales or spines instead of leaves.

cad *noun* (*plural* **cads**) *dated* a dishonourable man. ➤ **caddish** *adjective*.

cadaverous /ka da vi rus/ *adjective* unhealthily pale or thin.

caddie *or* **caddy** *noun* (*plural* **caddies**) somebody who carries a golfer's clubs and gives the golfer advice.

caddy[1] *noun* (*plural* **caddies**) a small container for tea.

caddy[2] *noun* see CADDIE.

cadence /kay dins/ *noun* (*plural* **cadences**) **1** the natural rhythmic up-and-down movement of the voice

cadenza

in speaking. **2** *Music* a sequence of chords that brings a passage of music to a satisfying close.

cadenza /kə den zə/ *noun* (*plural* **cadenzas**) *Music* an elaborate solo passage in a concerto.

cadet *noun* (*plural* **cadets**) **1** a trainee officer in the armed forces or the police force. **2** a young person receiving basic military training.

cadge *verb* (**cadges, cadging, cadged**) *informal* to get something simply by asking somebody to give it to you: *He cadged a fiver from his brother.*

cadmium *noun* *Science* a bluish white metallic element used in batteries.

Caesarean or **Caesarean section** /si zair i ən/ *noun* (*plural* **Caesareans** or **Caesarean sections**) an operation for delivering a baby by cutting through the wall of the mother's abdomen.

café /ka fay/ *noun* (*plural* **cafés**) a small restaurant serving light meals and drinks.

cafeteria /ka fi teer i ə/ *noun* (*plural* **cafeterias**) a self-service restaurant.

caffeine /ka feen/ *noun* a stimulant occurring naturally in tea and coffee.

caftan *noun* see KAFTAN.

cage *noun* (*plural* **cages**) an enclosure with bars for keeping or carrying animals. ~ *verb* (**cages, caging, caged**) to put or keep an animal in a cage.

cagey or **cagy** *adjective* (**cagier, cagiest**) *informal* hesitant about speaking or committing yourself. ➤ **cagily** *adverb*, **caginess** *noun*.

cagoule or **kagoul** /kə goohl/ *noun* (*plural* **cagoules** or **kagouls**) a lightweight waterproof jacket with a hood.

cagy *adjective* see CAGEY.

cahoots ✱ **in cahoots** *informal* working together secretly.

caiman *noun* see CAYMAN.

cairn *noun* (*plural* **cairns**) a pile of stones built as a memorial or landmark.

cajole *verb* (**cajoles, cajoling, cajoled**) to persuade somebody with flattery or deception. ➤ **cajolery** *noun*.

cake *noun* (*plural* **cakes**) **1** a sweet baked food usually made from a mixture of flour, sugar, fat, and eggs. **2** a flat round mass of something, such as food or soap.

caked *adjective* covered with a thick layer of something: *caked with grease*.

calamine *noun* a pink powder used in soothing or cooling lotions.

calamity *noun* (*plural* **calamities**) an extremely serious and damaging event; a disaster. ➤ **calamitous** *adjective*.

calcium *noun* *Science* a chemical element found in teeth and bones.

calculate *verb* (**calculates, calculating, calculated**) *Maths* to work something out using mathematical processes: *I'm trying to calculate how much money we'll need.* ➤ **calculable** *adjective*, **calculation** *noun*.

calculated *adjective* planned to accomplish a purpose; intentional: *a remark calculated to upset a lot of people; a calculated insult.*

calculating *adjective* making sure that you get what you want; scheming.

calculator *noun* (*plural* **calculators**) an electronic device for making mathematical calculations.

calculus *noun* *Maths* a branch of mathematics dealing with rates of change.

calendar *noun* (*plural* **calendars**) **1** a chart or table showing the days of the year. **2** a system for fixing the length and divisions of the year: *the Gregorian calendar.* **3** a list of events in the order of the dates on which they happen: *the festival calendar.*

calf[1] *noun* (*plural* **calves** or **calfs**) **1** a young cow or bull. **2** the young of

calf² *noun* (*plural* **calves**) the fleshy part at the back of the leg below the knee.

calibrate *verb* (**calibrates, calibrating, calibrated**) to mark in the divisions of the scale on a gauge or thermometer. ➤ **calibration** *noun*.

calibre /ka li ber/ *noun* (*plural* **calibres**) **1** the diameter of a gun barrel or bullet. **2** level of quality or ability.

call *verb* (**calls, calling, called**) **1** to shout loudly. **2** to shout to somebody to attract their attention. **3** said about a bird or animal: to make its characteristic sound. **4** to telephone somebody. **5** to ask or order somebody to come. **6** to use a name or description for somebody or something. **7** to make a short visit. **8** to stop at a particular place. ~ *noun* (*plural* **calls**) **1** an act of calling with the voice. **2** the cry of a bird or animal. **3** a request or command to come. **4** need or justification: *There's no call for you to get upset.* **5** a short visit. **6** an act of telephoning. ✻ **call for 1** to come to collect somebody. **2** to need or demand something: *This calls for immediate action.* **call off** to cancel an event. **call on 1** to pay a visit to somebody. **2** to require somebody to do something: *You may be called on to be a witness.* ➤ **caller** *noun*.

calligraphy /ka li gra fi/ *noun* the art of producing decorative handwriting. ➤ **calligrapher** *noun*.

calling *noun* (*plural* **callings**) a profession or occupation.

calliper *noun* (*plural* **callipers**) **1** (**callipers**) a measuring instrument with two hinged arms. **2** a support for the human leg.

callous *adjective* cruelly insensitive. ➤ **callously** *adverb*, **callousness** *noun*.

callow *adjective* immature and lacking experience.

callus *noun* (*plural* **calluses**) a hard thickened area on skin or bark.

calm *adjective* **1** free from anger, nervousness, or excitement. **2** quiet or still; not windy or rough. ~ *noun* a calm state, especially when there is no wind and the sea is smooth. ~ *verb* (**calms, calming, calmed**) (*also* **calm down**) to become calm, or to make somebody calm. ➤ **calmly** *adverb*, **calmness** *noun*.

calorie *noun* (*plural* **calories**) **1** *Science* a unit for measuring energy in the form of heat. **2** a unit for measuring the energy-producing value of food. ➤ **calorific** *adjective*.

calves *noun* plural of CALF¹ and CALF².

calypso *noun* (*plural* **calypsos**) *Music* a West Indian song with improvised lyrics on a topical subject.

calyx /kay liks/ *noun* (*plural* **calyxes** *or* **calyces** /kay li seez/) *Science* the outer leafy part of a flower surrounding the bud.

camaraderie /ka ma rah di ri/ *noun* a spirit of good humour and trust among friends.

camber *noun* (*plural* **cambers**) a slightly curved shape given to a road surface so that water will drain off it.

camcorder *noun* (*plural* **camcorders**) a video camera with a built-in video recorder.

came *verb* past tense of COME.

camel *noun* (*plural* **camels**) an animal with a long neck and either one or two humps on its back, used for riding in desert regions.

camellia /ka mee li a/ *noun* (*plural* **camellias**) a shrub with glossy leaves and bright flowers.

cameo /ka mi oh/ *noun* (*plural* **cameos**) **1** a precious stone with a raised design of a head in profile carved on it. **2** *Drama* a small role in a play or film played by a well-known actor.

camera *noun* (*plural* **cameras**) a device

camomile

for taking photographs or moving pictures.

camomile *noun* a strong-scented plant with leaves and flowers that are used in herbal remedies.

camouflage /ka mo flahzh/ *noun* **1** the technique of disguising things so that they blend in with their surroundings. **2** clothing and other coverings used for this purpose. **3** animal markings and colouring that match the animals' natural surroundings. ~ *verb* (**camouflages, camouflaging, camouflaged**) to conceal or disguise something with camouflage.

camp *noun* (*plural* **camps**) **1** an area where tents or other temporary shelters are erected. **2** a place with accommodation and other facilities for troops, holidaymakers, prisoners, etc. **3** the supporters of a political party or cause. ~ *verb* (**camps, camping, camped**) **1** to set up a camp. **2** to live temporarily in a tent or other outdoor accommodation. ➤ **camper** *noun*, **camping** *noun*.

campaign *noun* (*plural* **campaigns**) **1** a series of organized actions for achieving a particular result: *an election campaign*. **2** a series of military operations in a particular area. ~ *verb* (**campaigns, campaigning, campaigned**) to take part in a campaign. ➤ **campaigner** *noun*.

camphor *noun* a chemical compound used for rubbing on the skin to relieve aches or as an insect repellent.

campus *noun* (*plural* **campuses**) the grounds and buildings of a university.

can[1] *verb* (**can, could**) **1** to be able to. **2** to have permission to. **3** to have a certain tendency: *It can be cold at night*.

can[2] *noun* (*plural* **cans**) a cylindrical metal container for food or drink. ~ *verb* (**cans, canning, canned**) to preserve food or drink in a can.

canal *noun* (*plural* **canals**) **1** an artificial river made to carry ships or boats. **2** a channel used for drainage or irrigation. **3** a tubular passage in the body of an animal or plant.

canary *noun* (*plural* **canaries**) a small bird with yellow feathers that sings very sweetly.

cancan *noun* (*plural* **cancans**) an energetic dance with high kicks.

cancel *verb* (**cancels, cancelling, cancelled**) **1** to decide that something that was previously arranged will not take place: *The outing was cancelled because of bad weather.* **2** to stop an order for something or the delivery of something: *I cancelled my subscription to the magazine.* **3** to mark a ticket or postage stamp to show that it has been used. ✱ **cancel out** to have the opposite effect to something else, so that the situation remains the same: *Our losses this year will cancel out the profit we made last year.* ➤ **cancellation** *noun*.

cancer *noun* **1** a serious medical condition caused when abnormal cells multiply in part of the body. **2** an abnormal and harmful growth in the body caused by cancer. **3** (**Cancer**) the fourth sign of the zodiac (the Crab). ➤ **cancerous** *adjective*.

candelabrum /kan di lah brum/ *noun* (*plural* **candelabra**) a branched candlestick or lamp with several lights.

candid *adjective* frank or sincere. ➤ **candidly** *adverb*.

candidate *noun* (*plural* **candidates**) **1** somebody who applies for a job or award. **2** somebody who is taking an examination. ➤ **candidacy** *noun*.

candied *adjective* said about fruit: preserved with a thick coating of sugar.

candle *noun* (*plural* **candles**) a cylindrical length of wax with a wick that is burned to give light.

candlestick *noun* (*plural* **candlesticks**) a holder for a candle.

candour *noun* sincerity or frankness.

candy *noun* (*plural* **candies**) N American a sweet or sweets.

candy floss *noun* a light fluffy mass of spun sugar, wound round a stick.

cane *noun* (*plural* **canes**) **1** a hollow stem of some reeds and grasses. **2** a length of cane used as a walking stick or for beating somebody. ~ *verb* (**canes, caning, caned**) to beat somebody with a cane. ➤ **caning** *noun*.

canine /kay nien/ *adjective* to do with dogs or the dog family. ~ *noun* (*plural* **canines**) a pointed tooth near the front of the mouth.

canister *noun* (*plural* **canisters**) a small round container for storage.

cannabis *noun* the dried leaves of hemp plants, used as a drug.

cannelloni /ka ni **loh** ni/ *plural noun* tubes of pasta served with a filling of meat, vegetables, or cheese.

cannibal *noun* (*plural* **cannibals**) a human being who eats human flesh. ➤ **cannibalism** *noun*, **cannibalistic** *adjective*.

cannon *noun* (*plural* **cannons** or **cannon**) **1** *History* a large gun on a carriage that fired solid metal balls. **2** an automatic gun for firing shells, mounted in an aircraft or tank. ~ *verb* (**cannons, cannoning, cannoned**) (**cannon into**) to bump into something hard.

cannonball *noun* (*plural* **cannonballs**) *History* a metal ball for firing from a cannon.

cannot *contraction* can not.

canny *adjective* (**cannier, canniest**) cautious and clever. ➤ **cannily** *adverb*.

canoe *noun* (*plural* **canoes**) a long light narrow boat with pointed ends, propelled with a paddle. ~ *verb* (**canoes, canoeing, canoed**) to travel in a canoe. ➤ **canoeist** *noun*.

canon *noun* (*plural* **canons**) **1** an accepted rule or principle. **2** a member of the clergy attached to a cathedral. **3** *Music* a composition in which a tune is repeated by several voices or instruments entering one after the other and overlapping.

canonize or **canonise** *verb* (**canonizes, canonizing, canonized** or **canonises**, etc) to state officially that a dead person is a saint. ➤ **canonization** or **canonisation** *noun*.

canoodle *verb* (**canoodles, canoodling, canoodled**) *informal* to kiss and cuddle.

canopy *noun* (*plural* **canopies**) **1** a cloth covering hung over a bed or throne. **2** an ornamental roof-like structure. **3** the part of a parachute that spreads open. **4** the spreading leafy branches at the top of a forest.

cant[1] *noun* insincere or hypocritical talk.

cant[2] *verb* (**cants, canting, canted**) to tilt or slope.

can't *contraction* can not.

cantankerous *adjective* bad-tempered or quarrelsome.

canteen *noun* (*plural* **canteens**) **1** a restaurant in a school or factory. **2** a box for holding cutlery. **3** a small flask used by soldiers or campers to carry water.

canter *noun* (*plural* **canters**) **1** a running pace for a horse that is smoother and slower than a gallop. **2** a ride or run at a canter. ~ *verb* (**canters, cantering, cantered**) to move or ride at a canter.

cantilever *noun* (*plural* **cantilevers**) a projecting beam supported at only one end. ➤ **cantilevered** *adjective*.

canton *noun* (*plural* **cantons**) *Geography* one of the administrative areas into which Switzerland is divided.

canvas *noun* (*plural* **canvases**) **1** a strong closely woven cloth used especially for making sails and tents. **2** *Art* a cloth surface for painting on in

canvass

oils. **3** the floor of a boxing or wrestling ring.

canvass *verb* (**canvasses, canvassing, canvassed**) to visit voters to ask them to vote for you or your party or to find out their opinions. ➤ **canvasser** *noun*.

canyon *noun* (*plural* **canyons**) *Geography* a deep valley or gorge.

cap *noun* (*plural* **caps**) **1** a soft close-fitting hat with a peak and no brim. **2** a special cap awarded to a member of an international sports team. **3** a cover or lid for a container. **4** a small explosive charge in a strip of paper, which bangs when fired in a toy pistol. ~ *verb* (**caps, capping, capped**) **1** to cover something with a cap. **2** to select a player for an international team. **3** to follow something with a better example: *She capped my story about a dog with one about three cats.*

capability *noun* (*plural* **capabilities**) the ability to do something.

capacious /ka **pay** shus/ *adjective* able to hold a great deal; roomy.

capacity *noun* (*plural* **capacities**) **1** the maximum amount that can be contained or produced. **2** the power or ability to do something. **3** a position or role that somebody has: *in my capacity as treasurer of the society.*

cape¹ *noun* (*plural* **capes**) a short cloak.

cape² *noun* (*plural* **capes**) *Geography* an area of land jutting out into the sea.

caper¹ *verb* (**capers, capering, capered**) to leap about playfully. ~ *noun* (*plural* **capers**) **1** a playful or carefree leap. **2** an adventure or prank.

caper² *noun* (*plural* **capers**) the flower bud or berry of a shrub, pickled and used as a seasoning.

capillary /ka **pi** la ri/ *noun* (*plural* **capillaries**) *Science* a thin blood vessel connecting small arteries with veins. ~ *adjective* **1** said about a tube or passage: very narrow. **2** *Science* to do with a type of pressure that causes liquids to move along narrow tubes: *capillary action.*

capital *noun* (*plural* **capitals**) **1** the city where a country's government is based. **2** wealth or goods used by a business to produce further wealth or goods. **3** an amount of money that a person has saved or invested to produce interest. **4** a capital letter. **5** the top part of a pillar or column.

capitalism *noun* an economic system based on private ownership of property and businesses that are run to make a profit. ➤ **capitalist** *noun and adjective*.

capitalize *or* **capitalise** *verb* (**capitalizes, capitalizing, capitalized** *or* **capitalises**, etc) **1** to write or print something in capitals or with an initial capital letter. **2** (**capitalize on**) to use an advantage that you already have to improve your situation further. ➤ **capitalization** *or* **capitalisation** *noun*.

capital letter *noun* (*plural* **capital letters**) a letter used to begin a sentence or a proper name, for example *A, B, C* as opposed to *a, b, c*.

capital punishment *noun* the punishing of a crime by death.

capitulate *verb* (**capitulates, capitulating, capitulated**) to surrender or cease resisting. ➤ **capitulation** *noun*.

cappuccino /ka poo **chee** noh/ *noun* (*plural* **cappuccinos**) frothy coffee made with steamed milk.

caprice /ka **prees**/ *noun* (*plural* **caprices**) a sudden unexpected change of mind.

capricious *adjective* liable to sudden and unpredictable changes of mind or mood. ➤ **capriciously** *adverb*.

Capricorn *noun* the tenth sign of the zodiac (the Goat).

capsize *verb* (**capsizes, capsizing, capsized**) said about a boat: to overturn in the water.

capstan noun (plural **capstans**) a rotating cylinder or shaft on which rope or cable is wound.

capsule noun (plural **capsules**) **1** a hollow shell enclosing a dose of a medicine. **2** a compartment in a spacecraft that contains the crew and controls, and which can be detached from the rest of the craft.

captain noun (plural **captains**) **1** the person in command of a ship or civil aircraft. **2** the leader of a sports team. **3** a naval officer ranking below a commodore. **4** an army officer ranking below a major. ~ verb (**captains, captaining, captained**) to be captain of a team. ➤ **captaincy** noun.

caption noun (plural **captions**) a title, comment, or description printed above or below a picture or cartoon.

captivate verb (**captivates, captivating, captivated**) to fascinate somebody or charm them irresistibly. ➤ **captivating** adjective.

captive adjective imprisoned or unable to escape. ~ noun (plural **captives**) somebody who has been taken prisoner. ➤ **captivity** noun.

captor noun (plural **captors**) somebody who takes a person prisoner.

capture noun **1** the act of gaining control or possession of somebody or something. **2** *ICT* the storing of data on a computer. ~ verb (**captures, capturing, captured**) **1** to take somebody prisoner. **2** to represent or preserve an idea or impression in words or pictures. **3** *ICT* to store data in a computer.

car noun (plural **cars**) **1** a motor vehicle designed for carrying a small number of people. **2** a railway carriage.

carafe /ka raf/ noun (plural **carafes**) a glass bottle with an open top, used for serving wine.

caramel noun (plural **caramels**) **1** sugar heated to a brown colour and used as a colouring and flavouring. **2** a chewy soft toffee.

carapace /ka ra pays/ noun (plural **carapaces**) *Science* a hard case on the back of a turtle, crab, etc.

carat noun (plural **carats**) **1** a unit of weight used for precious stones. **2** a unit showing the purity of gold.

caravan noun (plural **caravans**) **1** a vehicle designed to be towed and for living in when parked. **2** a group of travellers on a journey through a desert.

caraway noun the seeds of an aromatic plant, used in cookery.

carbohydrate noun (plural **carbohydrates**) *Science* a compound of carbon, hydrogen, and oxygen that is found in many types of food and provides energy.

carbon noun (plural **carbons**) **1** *Science* a chemical element occurring naturally as diamond and graphite, and forming part of all living things. **2** a carbon copy. **3** = CARBON PAPER.

carbon copy noun (plural **carbon copies**) **1** a copy made with carbon paper. **2** an exact replica of something.

carbon dioxide noun *Science* a gas breathed out by humans and animals or formed by the burning of organic substances, and absorbed by plants.

carbon paper noun a type of thin paper coated with dark pigment, placed between two sheets of paper so that what is written on the top sheet is copied onto the bottom sheet

carbuncle noun (plural **carbuncles**) **1** a painful inflammation of the skin. **2** a red gemstone.

carburettor noun (plural **carburettors**) a device for mixing the fuel with air in an internal-combustion engine.

carcass noun (plural **carcasses**) the dead body of a slaughtered animal.

carcinogen /kah si no jin/ noun (plural

carcinogens) a substance that causes cancer. ➤ **carcinogenic** *adjective*.

card *noun* (*plural* **cards**) **1** thin cardboard or stiff paper. **2** a piece of card that you can write on either to send a message or to record information. **3** a postcard. **4** a playing card. **5** (**cards**) a game played with playing cards. **6** a rectangular piece of plastic, issued by a bank or credit card company, used to withdraw cash or make payments. * **on the cards** possible or likely.

cardboard *noun* a stiff material made from paper pulp.

cardiac *adjective* to do with the heart.

cardigan *noun* (*plural* **cardigans**) a knitted jacket with buttons down the front.

cardinal *noun* (*plural* **cardinals**) in the Roman Catholic Church, a high-ranking bishop who takes part in the election of a new pope.

cardinal number *noun* (*plural* **cardinal numbers**) *Maths* a number such as one, two, or three, used in counting.

cardinal point *noun* (*plural* **cardinal points**) any one of the four main points of the compass, north, south, east, or west.

cardiology *noun* the branch of medicine concerned with the heart and its diseases. ➤ **cardiologist** *noun*.

care *noun* (*plural* **cares**) **1** close attention to what you are doing: *She chose her outfit with care.* **2** concern for and protective treatment of somebody or something: *care of the elderly.* **3** supervision of or responsibility for somebody or something: *I left the packages in Martin's care.* **4** legal responsibility for children by a local authority. **5** anxiety, or a cause for anxiety: *He seemed not to have a care in the world.* ~ *verb* (**cares, caring, cared**) **1** to be concerned about or be interested in something or somebody: *I don't care whether we go or not.* **2** to wish or like to do something: *Would you care to step inside?* * **care for 1** to look after somebody or something. **2** to have a liking or love for something or somebody: *I don't really care for shepherd's pie.* **care of** on letters or parcels: at the address of somebody other than the addressee. **take care 1** to be cautious so that you do not harm yourself. **2** to make sure that you do something: *I took care not to let anyone see me leaving the house.* **take care of** to deal with or look after somebody or something.

career *noun* (*plural* **careers**) **1** a person's working life and the various jobs they do. **2** a person's progress in one particular occupation. ~ *verb* (**careers, careering, careered**) to move swiftly in an uncontrolled way.

carefree *adjective* free from anxiety or responsibility.

careful *adjective* **1** cautious; not taking risks. **2** marked by concentration and thoroughness: *careful attention to detail.* ➤ **carefully** *adverb*.

careless *adjective* **1** not taking enough care. **2** indifferent or unconcerned. ➤ **carelessly** *adverb*, **carelessness** *noun*.

carer *noun* (*plural* **carers**) a person who looks after somebody who is ill, elderly, or disabled.

caress *noun* (*plural* **caresses**) a gentle or loving touch. ~ *verb* (**caresses, caressing, caressed**) to touch somebody or something lightly and lovingly.

caretaker *noun* (*plural* **caretakers**) a person who looks after a school or other public building.

cargo *noun* (*plural* **cargoes** *or* **cargos**) goods carried by a ship, aircraft, or vehicle.

Caribbean *adjective* from or to do with the Caribbean Sea and its islands.

caribou /ka ri booh/ *noun* (*plural*

caribou) a large North American deer with broad branching antlers.

caricature *noun* (*plural* **caricatures**) a picture or description that comically exaggerates the appearance or main features of a person or thing.

caries /kair eez/ *noun* (*plural* **caries**) decay of a tooth or bone.

carmine /kah min/ *noun* a rich crimson or scarlet colour.

carnage *noun* the killing of a lot of people.

carnal *adjective* to do with the body rather than the soul, or to do with sex.

carnation *noun* (*plural* **carnations**) a plant with fragrant red, pink, or white flowers on long stems.

carnival *noun* (*plural* **carnivals**) a festival with music, dancing, and processions.

carnivore *noun* (*plural* **carnivores**) a meat-eating animal. ➤ **carnivorous** *adjective*.

carol *noun* (*plural* **carols**) *Music* a Christmas song or hymn.

carousel /ka ro sel/ *noun* (*plural* **carousels**) 1 a merry-go-round. 2 a rotating platform for baggage at an airport.

carp[1] *noun* (*plural* **carp**) a large edible freshwater fish.

carp[2] *verb* (**carps, carping, carped**) to complain or find fault.

carpel *noun* (*plural* **carpels**) *Science* the female reproductive organ of a flowering plant.

carpenter *noun* (*plural* **carpenters**) a person who builds with wood. ➤ **carpentry** *noun*.

carpet *noun* (*plural* **carpets**) 1 a floor covering made of a heavy woven material. 2 a thick layer. ~ *verb* (**carpets, carpeting, carpeted**) 1 to cover a floor or room with a carpet. 2 to cover an area with a thick layer of something.

carport *noun* (*plural* **carports**) an open-sided shelter for a car.

carriage *noun* (*plural* **carriages**) 1 a vehicle that carries passengers and forms part of a train. 2 a horse-drawn passenger vehicle. 3 a movable part of a machine that supports another part. 4 the carrying or conveying of goods.

carriageway *noun* (*plural* **carriageways**) the part of a road used by vehicles.

carrier *noun* (*plural* **carriers**) 1 a company or organization that transports goods or people. 2 a bag with handles for carrying shopping. 3 a person or animal that can transmit a disease while being immune to it themselves.

carrion *noun* dead and decomposing flesh.

carrot *noun* (*plural* **carrots**) a long orange root eaten as a vegetable.

carry *verb* (**carries, carrying, carried**) 1 to hold and transport somebody or something from one place to another. 2 to have something with you: *I never carry much money.* 3 to support the weight of something. 4 to bear blame or responsibility. 5 said about sounds: to be audible at a distance. * **be carried** said of a motion in a debate: to be approved by the majority of the people voting. **be/get carried away** to lose self-control. **carry off** to perform something successfully. **carry on 1** to continue doing something. 2 to conduct or manage a business, etc. 3 *informal* to behave in a rowdy manner. 4 *informal* to complain. **carry out** to perform a task.

cart *noun* (*plural* **carts**) an open vehicle, usually pulled by an animal, used for transporting loads. ~ *verb* (**carts, carting, carted**) 1 to transport something in a cart. 2 *informal* to carry something heavy with difficulty.

carte blanche /kaht blahnsh/ *noun* freedom to take whatever action you think is necessary.

carthorse *noun* (*plural* **carthorses**) a

cartilage

strong horse used for pulling heavy loads.

cartilage /kah ti lij/ *noun Science* a firm but elastic type of tissue that is found around the joints in the body and forms structures such as the external ear and the larynx. ➤ **cartilaginous** *adjective*.

cartography *noun Geography* the science of drawing maps and charts. ➤ **cartographer** *noun*, **cartographic** *adjective*.

carton *noun* (*plural* **cartons**) a container made of cardboard or plastic.

cartoon *noun* (*plural* **cartoons**) **1** an amusing drawing in a newspaper or magazine. **2** a series of drawings telling a story. **3** an animated film made from a sequence of drawings.

cartridge *noun* (*plural* **cartridges**) **1** a tube containing a bullet and explosive, for firing from a gun. **2** a case that fits inside a device and holds material used by that device, for example ink for a pen or film for a camera.

cartwheel *noun* (*plural* **cartwheels**) **1** a sideways handspring with arms and legs extended. **2** a wheel of a cart.

carve *verb* (**carves, carving, carving**) **1** to cut and shape wood or stone with a cutting tool. **2** to cut meat into pieces or slices. ➤ **carver** *noun*.

carving *noun* (*plural* **carvings**) an object carved from wood, stone, etc.

cascade *noun* (*plural* **cascades**) a small waterfall, or a series of small waterfalls. ~ *verb* (**cascades, cascading, cascaded**) to flow or pour in large amounts: *All the coins cascaded out of her purse onto the floor*.

case¹ *noun* (*plural* **cases**) **1** a situation or set of circumstances: *In that case we would cancel the contract immediately*. **2** an instance or example of something: *a case of measles*. **3** an investigation into a crime, carried out by the police. **4** a matter tried in a court of law. **5** the evidence or arguments supporting an idea or proposal: *She made out a convincing case for extending the recycling scheme*. **6** *English* in the grammar of some languages, any of two or more different forms of a noun, adjective, or pronoun (for example, *I* and *me, they* and *them*) that indicate the grammatical relationships between words in sentences. ✳ **be the case** to be what is actually happening: *If that is the case, then we shall have to make other arrangements*. **in case** for use if something happens: *Take an umbrella in case it rains*.

case² *noun* (*plural* **cases**) **1** a box for holding something: *a packing case*. **2** an outer covering. **3** a suitcase.

casement *noun* (*plural* **casements**) a window that opens on hinges at the side.

cash *noun* **1** money in notes and coins. **2** money paid at the time of purchase. ~ *verb* (**cashes, cashing, cashed**) to obtain, or pay, cash for a cheque, etc.

cashew *noun* (*plural* **cashews**) the edible kidney-shaped nut of a tropical American tree.

cash card *noun* (*plural* **cash cards**) a plastic card, issued by a bank, with which you can get money from a cash dispenser.

cash dispenser *noun* (*plural* **cash dispensers**) a machine that enables people to withdraw money in the form of cash from their bank account using a card.

cashier *noun* (*plural* **cashiers**) **1** somebody who takes money for purchases in a shop. **2** somebody who pays out or takes in money in a bank.

cashmere *noun* fine wool from the inner coat of the Kashmir goat.

cash register *noun* (*plural* **cash registers**) a machine used in a shop to record the amount of a sale and hold the money received.

casing noun (plural **casings**) an outer cover or shell.

casino noun (plural **casinos**) a building or room used for gambling.

cask noun (plural **casks**) a large barrel for holding liquids.

casket noun (plural **caskets**) a small chest or box for jewels.

cassava /ka sah va/ noun the edible starchy root of a tropical plant, used as food.

casserole noun (plural **casseroles**) **1** a heatproof covered dish for cooking food in an oven. **2** a stew cooked in a casserole.

cassette noun (plural **cassettes**) a sealed case containing magnetic tape or film for inserting into a player or camera.

cassock noun (plural **cassocks**) an ankle-length garment worn by Christian clergy and choristers.

cast verb (**casts, casting, cast**) **1** to throw something with force. **2** to direct your eyes or mind to something: *Cast your mind back to last year*. **3** to make a vote. **4** *Drama* to choose people to play the parts in a play or film. **5** to shape metal, plastic, etc in a mould. **6** to throw out a line and bait with a fishing rod. ~ noun (plural **casts**) **1** *Drama* the performers in a play or film. **2** a shape made by pouring metal, plastic, or plaster into a mould. * **cast off** to untie a boat from its moorings.

castanets plural noun *Music* a pair of small wooden or plastic shells clicked together in the hand by flamenco dancers.

castaway noun (plural **castaways**) a person who is drifting on the sea or has landed on a deserted shore after a shipwreck.

caste /kahst/ noun (plural **castes**) one of the four classes into which society is divided in Hinduism.

caster sugar or **castor sugar** noun white sugar in fine grains used in baking, etc.

castigate verb (**castigates, castigating, castigated**) *formal* to punish or reprimand somebody severely. ➤ **castigation** noun.

casting vote noun a deciding vote made by the person chairing a meeting in the event of a tie.

cast iron noun a hard alloy of iron and carbon cast in a mould.

castle noun (plural **castles**) **1** a large fortified building or set of buildings. **2** = ROOK[3].

cast-off noun (plural **cast-offs**) something that a person no longer wants.

castor noun (plural **castors**) a small swivelling wheel on the base of a piece of furniture.

castor oil noun oil obtained from the seeds of a tropical plant and used as a laxative.

castor sugar noun see CASTER SUGAR.

castrate verb (**castrates, castrating, castrated**) to remove the testicles of a male. ➤ **castration** noun.

casual adjective **1** lacking seriousness or commitment; offhand: *a casual attitude*. **2** occurring by chance; unplanned. **3** said about workers: employed for irregular periods. **4** said about clothes: designed for informal wear. ➤ **casually** adverb.

casualty noun (plural **casualties**) **1** a person killed or injured in combat or in an accident. **2** the department of a hospital that deals with accidents and emergencies.

cat noun (plural **cats**) **1** a small furry animal kept as a pet. **2** a wild animal of the same family as the domestic cat, such as a lion or cheetah. * **let the cat out of the bag** to reveal a secret accidentally.

cataclysm /ka ta kli zm/ noun (plural **cataclysms**) a terrible violent and

catacomb

destructive event. ➤ **cataclysmic** *adjective*.

catacomb /ka ta koohm/ *noun* (*plural* **catacombs**) an underground cemetery.

catalogue *noun* (*plural* **catalogues**) 1 a list of items arranged in order. 2 a brochure or magazine showing items for sale. ~ *verb* (**catalogues, cataloguing, catalogued**) to list things in a catalogue.

catalyst /ka ta list/ *noun* (*plural* **catalysts**) 1 *Science* a substance that increases the rate of a chemical reaction but itself remains unchanged. 2 somebody or something that causes a change to take place. ➤ **catalytic** *adjective*.

catalytic converter *noun* (*plural* **catalytic converters**) a device in a motor vehicle that reduces the polluting substances in exhaust fumes.

catamaran *noun* (*plural* **catamarans**) a sailing boat with twin hulls side by side.

catapult *noun* (*plural* **catapults**) 1 a Y-shaped stick with a piece of elastic material fixed between the two prongs, used for shooting small stones. 2 *History* a military weapon used for hurling missiles. ~ *verb* (**catapults, catapulting, catapulted**) to move somebody or something, or put them in a different situation, suddenly and unexpectedly: *Her role in that film catapulted her to stardom.*

cataract *noun* (*plural* **cataracts**) 1 a large steep waterfall. 2 a clouding of the lens of the eye, causing blurred vision.

catarrh /ka tah/ *noun* inflammation in the nose and throat, causing an excess of mucus.

catastrophe /ka ta stro fi/ *noun* (*plural* **catastrophes**) a sudden momentous or tragic event. ➤ **catastrophic** *adjective*, **catastrophically** *adverb*.

catcall *noun* (*plural* **catcalls**) a loud or shrill cry expressing disapproval.

catch *verb* (**catches, catching, caught**) 1 to grasp and keep hold of a moving object such as a ball. 2 to capture or seize a person or animal, especially after pursuing them or by using a trap. 3 said about a container: to take in and retain: *a bucket to catch the drips.* 4 to unexpectedly discover somebody doing something: *We caught them kissing.* 5 to cause somebody or something to become entangled, fastened, or stuck: *I caught my sleeve on a nail.* 6 to hit or strike somebody or something: *He caught his elbow on the edge of the table.* 7 to become infected with a disease. 8 to attract somebody's attention. 9 to get something momentarily or quickly: *to catch a glimpse of somebody.* 10 to be in time for: *to catch a bus.* 11 to hear or understand something: *I'm afraid I didn't quite catch your name.* ~ *noun* (*plural* **catches**) 1 an act of catching a ball, etc. 2 the total quantity of fish caught at one time. 3 a device for fastening a door or window. 4 a concealed difficulty or snag. ✱ **catch fire** to start to burn. **catch on** *informal* 1 to become popular. 2 to understand. **catch out** to detect somebody making a mistake or doing wrong. **catch sight of** to see something or somebody suddenly or momentarily. **catch up** 1 to succeed in reaching somebody who is ahead of you. 2 to complete remaining or overdue work.

catching *adjective* said about a disease: infectious.

catchment area *noun* (*plural* **catchment areas**) 1 the area from which a river, lake, reservoir, etc gets its water. 2 the area from which a school takes its pupils or a hospital takes its patients.

catchphrase *noun* (*plural* **catch-**

phrases) a well-known phrase associated with a particular person or group.

catchy *adjective* (**catchier, catchiest**) said about a tune: easy to remember.

catechism /ka ti ki zm/ *noun* a summary of religious teaching in the form of questions and answers.

categorical *adjective* absolute and unqualified. ➤ **categorically** *adverb*.

categorize *or* **categorise** *verb* (**categorizes, categorizing, categorized** *or* **categorises,** etc) to put something or somebody into a category; to classify them. ➤ **categorization** *or* **categorisation** *noun*.

category *noun* (*plural* **categories**) a division or group of people or things within a system of classification.

cater *verb* (**caters, catering, catered**) **1** to provide and serve a supply of prepared food. **2** (**cater for/to**) to supply what is needed or wanted by somebody. ➤ **caterer** *noun*, **catering** *noun*.

caterpillar *noun* (*plural* **caterpillars**) the worm-like larva of a butterfly or moth.

cathedral *noun* (*plural* **cathedrals**) the main church of a district governed by a bishop or archbishop.

Catherine wheel *noun* (*plural* **Catherine wheels**) a firework in the form of a flat coil that spins when lit.

catheter /ka thi ter/ *noun* (*plural* **catheters**) a flexible tube inserted into a hollow body part to draw off fluid.

cathode *noun* (*plural* **cathodes**) *Science* the electrode by which electrons leave an external circuit and enter a device.

cathode-ray tube *noun* (*plural* **cathode-ray tubes**) *Science* a vacuum tube in which a beam of electrons is projected onto a screen, for example to produce a television picture.

catholic *adjective* **1** including everything, or covering a broad range of different things: *catholic tastes*.

2 (**Catholic**) Roman Catholic.
➤ **Catholic** *noun*, **Catholicism** *noun*.

catkin *noun* (*plural* **catkins**) a spike of flowers hanging from a tree such as a willow or hazel.

catnap *noun* (*plural* **catnaps**) a brief period of sleep during the day.

Catseye *noun* (*plural* **Catseyes**) *trademark* a small reflecting stud set in the road to mark the middle or edge of the carriageway.

catsuit *noun* (*plural* **catsuits**) a tightly fitting one-piece garment combining top and trousers.

cattery *noun* (*plural* **catteries**) a place for the breeding or care of cats.

cattle *plural noun* cows and oxen.

catty *adjective* (**cattier, cattiest**) spiteful or malicious. ➤ **cattily** *adverb*.

catwalk *noun* (*plural* **catwalks**) a narrow stage extending into the audience at a fashion show.

Caucasian *adjective* belonging to the white race of humans. ➤ **Caucasian** *noun*.

caucus *noun* (*plural* **caucuses**) a meeting of political party members to decide on party policy.

caught *verb* past tense of CATCH.

cauldron *noun* (*plural* **cauldrons**) a large metal cooking pot.

cauliflower *noun* (*plural* **cauliflowers**) a vegetable of the cabbage family with a white flower head.

cause *noun* (*plural* **causes**) **1** somebody or something that is responsible for making something happen. **2** a reason or motive. **3** a principle or aim worth defending or supporting. ~ *verb* (**causes, causing, caused**) to be the cause of something; to make something happen.

causeway *noun* (*plural* **causeways**) a raised road or path across wet ground.

caustic *adjective* **1** capable of destroying or eating away by chemical action. **2** sarcastic or cutting.

cauterize *or* **cauterise** *verb* (**cauterizes, cauterizing, cauterized** *or* **cauterises,** etc) to burn a wound with a hot iron to stop bleeding or destroy infection.

caution *noun* (*plural* **cautions**) **1** careful action or planning intended to minimize risk. **2** an official warning given to somebody who has committed a minor offence. ~ *verb* (**cautions, cautioning, cautioned**) **1** to warn somebody. **2** to give a legal caution to somebody.

cautionary *adjective* serving as a warning: *a cautionary tale.*

cautious *adjective* careful or prudent. ➤ **cautiously** *adverb*, **cautiousness** *noun*.

cavalcade *noun* (*plural* **cavalcades**) a procession of people on horseback or in vehicles.

Cavalier *noun* (*plural* **Cavaliers**) *History* a supporter of King Charles I in the English Civil War.

cavalier *adjective* casual and arrogant in attitude.

cavalry *noun History* the troops of an army who fought on horseback. ➤ **cavalryman** *noun*.

cave *noun* (*plural* **caves**) a natural hollow chamber underground or in the side of a hill or cliff. ~ *verb* (**caves, caving, caved**) ✶ **cave in 1** to fall in or collapse. **2** to stop resisting or arguing.

caveat /ka vi at/ *noun* (*plural* **caveats**) *formal* a warning.

cavern *noun* (*plural* **caverns**) a large underground chamber or cave. ➤ **cavernous** *adjective*.

caviar *or* **caviare** /ka vi ah/ *noun* the salted roe of a sturgeon or other large fish, used as food.

cavil *verb* (**cavils, cavilling, cavilled**) to raise trivial objections. ➤ **cavil** *noun*.

cavity *noun* (*plural* **cavities**) **1** a hollowed-out space. **2** an area of decay in a tooth.

cavort *verb* (**cavorts, cavorting, cavorted**) to prance or leap about.

caw *verb* (**caws, cawing, cawed**) to utter the harsh cry of the crow. ➤ **caw** *noun*.

cayenne *noun* a hot-tasting red pepper made from dried chillies.

cayman *or* **caiman** *noun* (*plural* **caymans** *or* **caimans** *or* **cayman** *or* **caiman**) a North American reptile closely related to the alligators.

CBE *abbreviation* Commander of the Order of the British Empire.

cc *abbreviation* **1** carbon copy. **2** cubic centimetre.

CCTV *abbreviation* closed-circuit television.

CD *noun* (*plural* **CDs**) = COMPACT DISC.

CD-ROM *noun* (*plural* **CD-ROMs**) a compact disc on which large amounts of data can be stored for use by a computer.

cease *verb* (**ceases, ceasing, ceased**) to stop, or to bring something to an end.

cease-fire *noun* (*plural* **cease-fires**) an agreement to stop fighting.

ceaseless *adjective* continuing without stopping. ➤ **ceaselessly** *adverb*.

cedar *noun* (*plural* **cedars**) a tall evergreen tree of the pine family.

cede *verb* (**cedes, ceding, ceded**) to give up territory or power to somebody else.

cedilla /si di la/ *noun* (*plural* **cedillas**) a little hook put under the letter *c* to show that it is pronounced /s/, as in *façade*.

ceiling *noun* (*plural* **ceilings**) **1** the overhead inside surface of a room. **2** an upper limit on prices, expenditure, etc.

celebrate *verb* (**celebrates, celebrating, celebrated**) **1** to mark an occasion with special activities. **2** to perform a religious ceremony: *to celebrate the Eucharist*. ➤ **celebration** *noun*, **celebratory** *adjective*.

celebrated *adjective* famous.

celebrity *noun* (*plural* **celebrities**) 1 a famous person. 2 the state of being famous.

celestial *adjective* to do with heaven or the sky.

celibate *adjective* abstaining from sexual relations. ➤ **celibacy** *noun*.

cell *noun* (*plural* **cells**) 1 a small room in a prison, convent, or monastery. 2 *Science* the smallest unit of living matter. 3 a compartment of a honeycomb. 4 a small and sometimes subversive group within a larger organization. 5 a device for generating electricity by chemical action.

cellar *noun* (*plural* **cellars**) 1 an underground room used for storage. 2 a stock of wine.

cello /che loh/ *noun* (*plural* **cellos**) *Music* a large stringed musical instrument of the violin family that is held upright between the player's knees. ➤ **cellist** *noun*.

Cellophane *noun trademark* thin transparent material for wrapping.

cellular *adjective* 1 to do with or consisting of cells. 2 said about a phone or radio system: based on small areas each of which has its own transmitter.

cellulite *noun* body fat that produces a dimpled effect on the skin.

celluloid *noun* photographic film made of transparent plastic.

cellulose *noun Science* a carbohydrate from plants, used to make paper, rayon, paint, and Cellophane.

Celsius /sel si us/ *adjective Science* measured by a scale of temperature on which water freezes at 0° and boils at 100°: *60° Celsius*.

Celt *or* **Kelt** /kelt/ *noun* (*plural* **Celts** *or* **Kelts**) *History* a member of a people living in Britain and Europe from before the time of the Roman Empire. ➤ **Celtic** *or* **Keltic** *adjective*.

cement *noun* 1 a powder containing lime and clay, used to bind together the ingredients in mortar and concrete. 2 concrete or mortar. 3 a substance used for sticking objects together. ~ *verb* (**cements, cementing, cemented**) 1 to join or fix things with cement. 2 to make an alliance or relationship firm and strong.

cemetery *noun* (*plural* **cemeteries**) a burial ground.

cenotaph *noun* (*plural* **cenotaphs**) a monument in honour of members of the armed forces killed in war.

censor *noun* (*plural* **censors**) an official who examines publications and films and removes parts that are unacceptable or offensive. ~ *verb* (**censors, censoring, censored**) to remove unacceptable parts from a publication or film. ➤ **censorship** *noun*.

Usage Note Do not confuse *censor* and *censure*.

censorious /sen saw ri us/ *adjective* severely critical.

censure *noun* strong disapproval or condemnation. ~ *verb* (**censures, censuring, censured**) to express strong disapproval of somebody or something.

Usage Note Do not confuse *censure* and *censor*.

census *noun* (*plural* **censuses**) an official counting of the population.

cent *noun* (*plural* **cents**) a unit of money worth 100th of the dollar or other unit of currency.

centaur /sen taw/ *noun* (*plural* **centaurs**) a mythological creature with the head, arms, and upper body of a man, and the lower body and legs of a horse.

centenarian /sen ti nair i an/ *noun* (*plural* **centenarians**) somebody who is at least 100 years old.

centenary /sen **tee** na ri/ *noun* (*plural* **centenaries**) a 100th anniversary.

centigrade *adjective* = CELSIUS.

centimetre *noun* (*plural* **centimetres**) a metric unit of length equal to 100th of a metre (about 0.4 of an inch).

centipede *noun* (*plural* **centipedes**) a small long animal with a flattened segmented body and many legs.

central *adjective* **1** at or near the centre. **2** most important. **3** having overall control. ➤ **centrally** *adverb*.

central heating *noun* a heating system in which heat is produced in a central source, usually a boiler, and carried in pipes around a building.

centralize *or* **centralise** *verb* (**centralizes, centralizing, centralized** *or* **centralises**, etc) to bring something under the control of a central authority. ➤ **centralization** *or* **centralisation** *noun*.

centre *noun* (*plural* **centres**) **1** the middle point or part of something. **2** a building in which a particular activity is concentrated: *a sports centre*. **3** the part of a town or city where most of the shops, banks, offices, etc are situated. **4** a focus of attention or activity. ~ *verb* (**centres, centring, centred**) **1** (**centre on/round/around**) to have something as a centre; to focus on something. **2** to place or fix something in a centre.

centre of gravity *noun* (*plural* **centres of gravity**) the point in an object around which its weight is evenly distributed.

centrepiece *noun* (*plural* **centrepieces**) the most important or outstanding item.

centrifugal force /sen tri **few** gl/ *noun Science* a force that appears to drive an object moving on a circular path away from the centre.

centurion *noun* (*plural* **centurions**) *History* an officer commanding a force of 100 men in the ancient Roman army.

century *noun* (*plural* **centuries**) **1** a period of 100 years. **2** a score of 100 runs made by a cricketer in one innings. **3** *History* a unit of 100 men in the ancient Roman army.

ceramic *adjective Art* made from clay by firing at high temperatures.

ceramics *noun Art* the process of making ceramic articles.

cereal *noun* (*plural* **cereals**) **1** a plant that produces grain suitable for food. **2** a breakfast food made from grain.

cerebral /**se** ri bral/ *adjective* **1** to do with the brain. **2** intellectual, or appealing to the intellect.

cerebral palsy /se ri bral **pawl** zi/ *noun* a disability involving speech disturbance and lack of muscular coordination.

ceremonial *adjective* to do with or used in ceremonies. ➤ **ceremonially** *adverb*.

ceremonious *adjective* very formal and polite. ➤ **ceremoniously** *adverb*.

ceremony *noun* (*plural* **ceremonies**) **1** a formal action or series of actions carried out to show that an event is serious and important: *a wedding ceremony*. **2** formal politeness.

cerise /si **reez** *or* si **rees**/ *noun* a light purplish red colour.

certain *adjective* **1** convinced in your mind: *Are you certain you saw her there?* **2** established beyond doubt or question: *She was there, that's certain.* **3** definitely going to happen, etc; inevitable: *certain death.* **4** noticeable, but difficult to describe exactly: *The house has a certain charm.* **5** some: *There are certain aspects of the case that are very unusual.* ✽ **for certain** without doubt.

certainly *adverb* **1** undoubtedly; definitely. **2** yes; of course.

certainty *noun* (*plural* **certainties**) **1** something that is certain. **2** somebody or something that cannot fail. **3** the state of being certain.

certificate *noun* (*plural* **certificates**) a document officially stating something, for example that a person was born at a particular time and place.

certify *verb* (**certifies, certifying, certified**) **1** to confirm something officially in writing. **2** to declare somebody officially to be insane. ➤ **certification** *noun*.

certitude *noun* the state of being or feeling certain.

cervix *noun* (*plural* **cervixes**) *Science* the narrow outer end of the uterus. ➤ **cervical** *adjective*.

cessation *noun formal* a stop or ending.

cesspool *or* **cesspit** *noun* (*plural* **cesspools** *or* **cesspits**) an underground basin for sewage.

cf. *abbreviation* compare.

CFC *abbreviation Science* chlorofluorocarbon, a gas formerly used in aerosols and refrigerators and thought to harm the ozone layer.

chador *noun* (*plural* **chadors**) a cloth worn round the head and top part of the body by some Muslim women.

chafe *verb* (**chafes, chafing, chafed**) **1** to make part of the body sore by rubbing. **2** to feel irritation or discontent.

chaff *noun* husks separated from the seed in threshing grain.

chaffinch *noun* (*plural* **chaffinches**) a finch with a pinkish breast and white wing bars.

chagrin /sha grin/ *noun* a very unhappy feeling caused by humiliation, disappointment, or failure.

chain *noun* (*plural* **chains**) **1** a length of connected metal rings. **2** a series of linked or connected things: *a chain of mountains*. **3** a group of shops or hotels with the same owner. ~ *verb* (**chains, chaining, chained**) to fasten something or somebody, or prevent them from moving, with a chain.

chain mail *noun History* flexible armour made of linked metal rings.

chain reaction *noun* (*plural* **chain reactions**) **1** a series of related events, each one of which sets off the next. **2** *Science* a chemical or nuclear reaction yielding energy that causes further reactions.

chain saw *noun* (*plural* **chain saws**) a saw which cuts by means of a continuous revolving chain with teeth, powered by a motor.

chair *noun* (*plural* **chairs**) **1** a seat for one person, with legs, a back, and sometimes arms. **2** a job as professor at a university. **3** the chairperson at a meeting. ~ *verb* (**chairs, chairing, chaired**) to act as chairperson at a meeting.

chair lift *noun* (*plural* **chair lifts**) a ski lift with seats for passengers.

chairman *or* **chairwoman** *noun* (*plural* **chairmen** *or* **chairwomen**) somebody who is in charge of a meeting or of a board of directors. ➤ **chairmanship** *noun*.

chairperson *noun* (*plural* **chairpersons**) a person who is in charge of a meeting.

chaise longue /shayz long/ *noun* (*plural* **chaises longues** /shayz long/) a low sofa with a partial backrest and only one armrest.

chalet /sha lay/ *noun* (*plural* **chalets**) **1** a wooden house with a steep roof and overhanging eaves, common in Switzerland. **2** a cabin at a holiday camp.

chalice *noun* (*plural* **chalices**) a large drinking cup or goblet.

chalk *noun* (*plural* **chalks**) **1** a soft

white limestone. **2** a piece of chalk-like material used for writing and drawing. ➤ **chalky** *adjective*.

challenge *verb* (**challenges, challenging, challenged**) **1** to invite somebody to fight or compete with you. **2** to say that something is untrue or incorrect. **3** to test the ability of somebody. ~ *noun* **1** an invitation to fight or compete. **2** an objection. **3** a task that is demanding or stimulating. ➤ **challenger** *noun*, **challenging** *adjective*.

chamber *noun* (*plural* **chambers**) **1** an enclosed space. **2** a group of people who make laws or administer the law. **3** the part of a gun that holds the charge or cartridge. **4** *archaic* a bedroom.

chamberlain /chaym ber lin/ *noun* (*plural* **chamberlains**) the chief official of a royal or noble household.

chambermaid *noun* (*plural* **chambermaids**) a woman who cleans and tidies bedrooms in a hotel.

chamber music *noun* Music classical music written for a small group of instruments.

chameleon /ka mee li on/ *noun* (*plural* **chameleons**) a small lizard that can change the colour of its skin to match its surroundings.

chamois *noun* (*plural* **chamois**) **1** /sham wah/ a small European antelope. **2** /sha mi/ a soft leather made from the skin of the chamois or sheep.

champ¹ *verb* (**champs, champing, champed**) to munch noisily.
✱ **champing at the bit** very impatient.

champ² *noun* (*plural* **champs**) *informal* a champion in a sport or game.

champagne /sham payn/ *noun* a fizzy white wine from the northeastern region of France.

champion *noun* (*plural* **champions**) **1** the winner of a series of competitive events. **2** an active supporter of a person or cause. ~ *verb* (**champions, championing, championed**) to be a supporter of or fighter for something or somebody.

championship *noun* (*plural* **championships**) **1** a contest to find a champion. **2** the position or title of champion.

chance *noun* (*plural* **chances**) **1** a factor that makes events happen unpredictably. **2** an event without an observable cause. **3** an opportunity: *This is your last chance to enter the competition.* ~ *adjective* happening by chance. ~ *verb* (**chances, chancing, chanced**) **1** to happen by chance to do something: *I chanced to look up at that very moment.* **2** (**chance on/upon**) to find something by chance. ✱ **by chance** without planning or intention.
chance it to take a risk and do something. **take a chance** *or* **take chances** to do something risky.

chancel *noun* (*plural* **chancels**) the part of a church near the altar.

chancellor *noun* (*plural* **chancellors**) **1** the chief minister in some European countries. **2** the head of a British university.

Chancellor of the Exchequer *noun* (*plural* **Chancellors of the Exchequer**) the British government minister in charge of public finances.

chancy *adjective* (**chancier, chanciest**) uncertain or risky.

chandelier /shan di leer/ *noun* (*plural* **chandeliers**) an ornamental light fitting with many branches, which hangs from a ceiling.

chandler *noun* (*plural* **chandlers**) a dealer in supplies for ships and boats.

change *verb* (**changes, changing, changed**) **1** to make something different, or to become different. **2** to replace one thing with another. **3** to convert something into something else. **4** to give money of one currency in exchange for an equivalent amount in another currency: *to change pounds* into euros. **5** to put on fresh clothes. ~ *noun* (*plural* **changes**) **1** a process of becoming different. **2** something different: *a change from our advertised programme*. **3** an alternative set of clothes. **4** money returned when a payment exceeds the amount due. **5** coins of low value.

changeable *adjective* **1** likely to vary: *changeable weather*. **2** capable of being altered.

change-over *noun* (*plural* **change-overs**) a conversion to a different system or function.

channel *noun* (*plural* **channels**) **1** a narrow region of sea between two areas of land. **2** a hollowed-out path along which a stream of water runs. **3** the part of a river or harbour that ships can sail in. **4** a path for communication or information. **5** a band of frequencies for radio or television broadcasting. ~ *verb* (**channels, channelling, channelled**) **1** to send water, etc through a channel. **2** to direct something towards a particular purpose: *He should channel his energy into more constructive activities*.

chant *verb* (**chants, chanting, chanted**) to sing or recite something in a repeated rhythm or tune. ~ *noun* (*plural* **chants**) **1** a repetitive type of singing used in some religious services or ceremonies. **2** a rhythmic set of words repeated again and again.

Chanukah *noun* see HANUKKAH.

chaos /kay os/ *noun* a state of utter confusion. ➤ **chaotic** *adjective*, **chaotically** *adverb*.

chap *noun* (*plural* **chaps**) *informal* a man or fellow.

chapati or **chapatti** /cha pah ti/ *noun* (*plural* **chapatis** or **chapattis**) in Indian cookery, a flat round piece of bread made without yeast.

chapel *noun* (*plural* **chapels**) **1** a small church. **2** a separate area of a church with its own altar.

chaperon or **chaperone** /sha pi rohn/ *noun* (*plural* **chaperons** or **chaperones**) an older woman who accompanies an unmarried younger woman on social occasions.

chaplain *noun* (*plural* **chaplains**) a member of the clergy attached to a branch of the armed forces or an institution such as a prison, hospital, or university. ➤ **chaplaincy** *noun*.

chapped *adjective* said about the skin: cracked and sore from being exposed to the wind or cold.

chapter *noun* (*plural* **chapters**) **1** a section of a book. **2** the clergy attached to a cathedral.

char[1] *verb* (**chars, charring, charred**) to burn something slightly.

char[2] *noun* (*plural* **chars**) *informal* a woman employed to do cleaning work in a private house.

character *noun* (*plural* **characters**) **1** the qualities that distinguish a particular person or thing from others. **2** a person portrayed in a novel, film, or play. **3** *informal* an interesting or eccentric person. **4** a person's good reputation. **5** determination or moral strength. **6** a letter or other symbol used in writing or printing.

characteristic *adjective* typical of a particular person or thing. ~ *noun* (*plural* **characteristics**) a quality that is typical of an individual or of a certain type of person or thing. ➤ **characteristically** *adverb*.

characterize or **characterise** *verb* (**characterizes, characterizing, characterized** or **characterises**, etc) **1** to be typical of somebody or something. **2** to describe the character or quality of somebody or something: *How would you characterize him?* ➤ **characterization** or **characterisation** *noun*.

charade

charade /sha rahd/ *noun* (*plural* **charades**) **1** (**charades**) a game in which a word or phrase is acted out for other players to guess. **2** a ridiculous pretence.

charcoal *noun* **1** a material made by partly burning wood and used, for example, as fuel for barbecues. **2** *Art* this material used in pencil form for drawing. **3** a dark grey colour.

charge *verb* (**charges, charging, charged**) **1** to ask a certain amount as the price for something: *He charges £50 per hour*. **2** to ask for payment from somebody: *We won't charge you for the phone call*. **3** to accuse somebody of having committed an offence. **4** (**charge with**) to entrust somebody with a task or responsibility. **5** to rush forward in attack. **6** to load or fill. **7** (*also* **charge up**) to store electrical energy in a battery. ~ *noun* (*plural* **charges**) **1** a price asked or paid for something. **2** a formal accusation. **3** somebody or something that has been entrusted or committed to a person's care. **4** a rush forwards in attack. **5** a quantity of explosive used for example in blasting or to fire a gun or cannon. **6** a quantity of electricity held by a battery. ∗ **in charge** in control or command. ➤ **chargeable** *adjective*.

charger *noun* (*plural* **chargers**) **1** a device used to charge a battery. **2** a horse ridden in battle or parades.

chariot *noun* (*plural* **chariots**) *History* a two-wheeled horse-drawn vehicle used in ancient warfare and racing. ➤ **charioteer** *noun*.

charisma /ka riz ma/ *noun* a special kind of charm that inspires loyalty and enthusiasm in other people. ➤ **charismatic** *adjective*.

charitable *adjective* **1** devoted to helping people who are poor, sick, in trouble, etc. **2** merciful or kind in judging others. ➤ **charitably** *adverb*.

charity *noun* (*plural* **charities**) **1** generosity and helpfulness shown to those in need. **2** an institution set up to help people in need. **3** money or other help given to people in need.

charlatan /shah la tan/ *noun* (*plural* **charlatans**) somebody who pretends to have special knowledge or ability.

charm *noun* (*plural* **charms**) **1** an ability to attract and delight people. **2** a particularly pleasing or attractive quality or feature. **3** an action or words believed to have magic power. **4** a small ornament worn on a bracelet or chain. ~ *verb* (**charms, charming, charmed**) **1** to use attractive qualities and obliging manners to delight people. **2** to gain something or influence somebody by the use of personal charm. **3** to put a magic spell on somebody or something. ➤ **charmer** *noun*.

charming *adjective* extremely pleasing or delightful. ➤ **charmingly** *adverb*.

chart *noun* (*plural* **charts**) **1** a map used for sea or air navigation. **2** information in the form of a table or graph. **3** (**the charts**) a weekly list of the best-selling recorded pop music. ~ *verb* (**charts, charting, charted**) to outline the course or progress of somebody or something.

charter *noun* (*plural* **charters**) **1** a document that defines the rights of a city, an educational or professional institution, or a company. **2** a lease of a ship or aircraft for a particular use or group: *charter flights*.

chartered *adjective* officially qualified for membership of a professional institution: *a chartered accountant*.

chary *adjective* (**charier, chariest**) cautious and wary. ➤ **charily** *adverb*.

chase *verb* (**chases, chasing, chased**) to follow somebody rapidly in order to catch up with them. ➤ **chase** *noun*.

chasm /ka zm/ *noun* a deep cleft in the earth.

chassis /sha si/ *noun* (*plural* **chassis** /sha siz/) **1** the framework supporting the body of a vehicle. **2** a frame supporting a piece of equipment.

chaste *adjective* **1** not having sexual intercourse at all, or not outside marriage. **2** pure in thought and behaviour. ➤ **chastity** *noun*.

chasten /chay sn/ *verb* (**chastens, chastening, chastened**) to make somebody feel sorry or humble about things they have done wrong.

chastise *verb* (**chastise, chastising, chastised**) to punish somebody, especially by beating them. ➤ **chastisement** *noun*.

chat *verb* (**chats, chatting, chatted**) to talk informally. ~ *noun* (*plural* **chats**) an informal conversation.
✽ **chat up** *informal* to talk to somebody in a flirtatious way.

château /sha toh/ *noun* (*plural* **châteaus** *or* **châteaux** /sha tohz/) a large country house or castle in France.

chattel *noun* (*plural* **chattels**) *archaic* an item of personal property.

chatter *verb* (**chatters, chattering, chattered**) **1** to talk a lot, especially about trivial things. **2** said about teeth: to click together repeatedly from cold. ➤ **chatter** *noun*.

chatterbox *noun* (*plural* **chatterboxes**) *informal* somebody who likes to chatter.

chauffeur /shoh fer/ *noun* (*plural* **chauffeurs**) a person employed to drive somebody in a private car.

chauvinism /shoh vi ni zm/ *noun* unjustified belief in the superiority of your own country, sex, cause, etc.
➤ **chauvinist** *noun and adjective*, **chauvinistic** *adjective*.

cheap *adjective* **1** low in price. **2** charging low prices. **3** of poor quality. **4** unworthy or despicable.
➤ **cheaply** *adverb*.

cheapen *verb* (**cheapens, cheapening, cheapened**) to reduce the value or quality of something.

cheapskate *noun* (*plural* **cheapskates**) *informal* a miserly or stingy person.

cheat *verb* (**cheats, cheating, cheated**) **1** to use dishonest and illegal methods to try to win a game or competition. **2** to deceive or swindle somebody. **3** to deprive somebody of something by deceit or fraud. **4** (**cheat on**) to be sexually unfaithful to somebody. ~ *noun* (*plural* **cheats**) **1** somebody who cheats. **2** a trick or fraud.

check *noun* (*plural* **checks**) **1** a test of the accuracy, state, or quality of something. **2** somebody or something that restrains something or slows something down. **3** in chess, exposure of a king to direct attack. **4** a pattern of squares of alternating colours. **5** *N American* a bill in a restaurant. ~ *verb* (**checks, checking, checked**) **1** to test or inspect something to make sure that it is satisfactory or accurate. **2** to slow something down or bring it to a stop. ✽ **check in** to arrive and register at a hotel or airport. **check out 1** to leave a hotel. **2** to get information about something. **check up on** to make inquiries about. ➤ **checkable** *adjective*.

checkmate *noun* in chess, the act of winning a game by putting an opponent's king in a position where it is impossible to get out of check.

checkout *noun* (*plural* **checkouts**) **1** a cash desk at a supermarket or large shop. **2** the act of checking out of a hotel etc.

checkup *noun* (*plural* **checkups**) a routine medical or dental examination.

Cheddar *noun* a type of hard cheese.

cheek *noun* (*plural* **cheeks**) **1** the side of the face below the eye. **2** rudeness or lack of respect. **3** *informal* a buttock.

cheekbone *noun* (*plural* **cheekbones**) the bone just below the eye.

cheeky *adjective* (**cheekier, cheekiest**) rude or disrespectful; impudent. ➤ **cheekily** *adverb*.

cheep *verb* (**cheeps, cheeping, cheeped**) said of a young bird: to make a faint shrill sound. ➤ **cheep** *noun*.

cheer *noun* (*plural* **cheers**) **1** a shout of joy, congratulation, or encouragement. **2** happiness or gaiety. ~ *verb* (**cheers, cheering, cheered**) to shout with pleasure or in applause. ✱ **cheer up** to become, or to make somebody, happier or more hopeful.

cheerful *adjective* **1** happy. **2** making you feel happy, for example by being bright and colourful. ➤ **cheerfully** *adverb*, **cheerfulness** *noun*.

cheerless *adjective* gloomy or miserable.

cheers *interjection* used as a drinking toast, an informal farewell, or an expression of thanks.

cheery *adjective* (**cheerier, cheeriest**) cheerful and optimistic. ➤ **cheerily** *adverb*.

cheese *noun* (*plural* **cheeses**) a food made from processed milk curds.

cheesecake *noun* (*plural* **cheesecakes**) a dessert with a filling of cream cheese on a biscuit or pastry base.

cheesy *adjective* (**cheesier, cheesiest**) **1** like cheese. **2** *informal* poor in quality and taste.

cheetah *noun* (*plural* **cheetahs**) a long-legged spotted African cat that can run very fast.

chef /shef/ *noun* (*plural* **chefs**) a cook in a restaurant or hotel.

chemical *adjective* used in or produced by chemistry. ~ *noun* (*plural* **chemicals**) a substance produced by chemistry. ➤ **chemically** *adverb*.

chemist *noun* (*plural* **chemists**) **1** a person who makes and sells medicines. **2** a shop where medicines and other articles, such as cosmetics and films, are sold. **3** *Science* somebody who studies chemistry.

chemistry *noun* **1** a science that deals with the nature and composition of substances and the changes they undergo. **2** a natural attraction between people.

chemotherapy /kee moh the ra pi/ *noun* the use of chemical substances in the treatment of cancer.

cheque *noun* (*plural* **cheques**) a written order for a bank to pay money to a named person or account.

chequered *adjective* patterned with squares of alternating colours.

cherish *verb* (**cherishes, cherishing, cherished**) **1** to feel or show affection for somebody. **2** to look after somebody or something with care and affection.

cherry *noun* (*plural* **cherries**) **1** a smooth red or blackish fruit with sweet flesh and a hard stone. **2** a bright red colour.

cherub *noun* **1** (*plural* **cherubim**) a type of angel. **2** (*plural* **cherubs**) a chubby child with wings in painting and sculpture. **3** (*plural* **cherubs**) a sweet, beautiful, or well-behaved little child. ➤ **cherubic** *adjective*.

chess *noun* a board game for two players who have sixteen pieces each and who each try to put the opponent's king into checkmate.

chest *noun* (*plural* **chests**) **1** a storage box with a lid. **2** the part of the body enclosed by the ribs and breastbone. **3** the front of the body from the neck to the waist. ✱ **get something off your chest** to admit or confess something.

chestnut *noun* (*plural* **chestnuts**) **1** an edible nut with shiny brown skin. **2** a tree that produces chestnuts. **3** a reddish brown colour. **4** *informal* an often repeated joke or story.

chest of drawers noun (plural **chests of drawers**) a piece of furniture with a set of drawers in it.

chesty adjective (**chestier, chestiest**) suffering from catarrh.

chevron /shev ron/ noun (plural **chevrons**) a V-shaped stripe.

chew verb (**chews, chewing, chewed**) to grind or gnaw something with your teeth. ✱ **chew over** to consider something at length.

chewing gum noun a flavoured and sweetened stretchy substance for chewing.

chewy adjective (**chewier, chewiest**) tough and difficult to chew.

chic /sheek/ adjective (**chicer, chicest**) elegant and fashionable.

chicane /shi kayn/ noun (plural **chicanes**) a series of tight turns in a motor-racing track.

chick noun (plural **chicks**) 1 a newly hatched chicken or bird. 2 informal a young woman.

chicken noun (plural **chickens**) 1 a bird that is kept on farms to lay eggs and provide meat. 2 informal a coward. ~ adjective informal scared or cowardly. ~ verb (**chickens, chickening, chickened**) ✱ **chicken out** informal to refuse to do something because you are frightened.

chickenpox noun an infectious disease marked by a rash of small blisters.

chickpea noun (plural **chickpeas**) a yellow seed of an Asian plant, used as a vegetable.

chicory noun a plant with edible thick roots and leaves used in salads.

chide verb (**chides, chiding, chided** or **chid, chided** or **chidden**) to scold somebody.

chief noun (plural **chiefs**) the head of an organization or group of people. ~ adjective most important; main. ➤ **chiefly** adverb.

chieftain noun (plural **chieftains**) the leader of a tribe or clan.

chiffon /shi fon/ noun a thin silky fabric.

chihuahua /chi wah wah/ noun (plural **chihuahuas**) a very small dog with a round head and large ears.

chilblain noun (plural **chilblains**) a sore spot on the feet or hands, caused by exposure to cold.

child noun (plural **children**) 1 a young person aged between a baby and a youth. 2 a son or daughter. ➤ **childhood** noun.

childbirth noun the process of giving birth to a child.

childish adjective 1 to do with children or childhood. 2 silly or immature. ➤ **childishly** adverb.

childless adjective having no children.

childlike adjective innocent and trusting like a child.

childminder noun (plural **childminders**) a person who looks after other people's children.

chill verb (**chills, chilling, chilled**) 1 to make somebody or something cold. 2 to frighten or horrify somebody. 3 (also **chill out**) informal to relax. ~ noun (plural **chills**) 1 an unpleasant sensation of coldness. 2 a feverish cold. ~ adjective unpleasantly cold.

chilli noun (plural **chillies**) the pod of a hot pepper used as a flavouring or spice.

chilly adjective (**chillier, chilliest**) 1 unpleasantly cold. 2 unfriendly.

chime noun (plural **chimes**) Music the sound made by a set of bells, each of which is tuned to a different note. ~ verb (**chimes, chiming, chimed**) to make a musical ringing sound.

chimney noun (plural **chimneys**) a vertical structure for carrying smoke from a fireplace or furnace to a point above a roof.

chimney breast noun (plural **chimney**

chimney pot

breasts) part of a wall that sticks out into a room because it encloses a chimney.

chimney pot noun (plural **chimney pots**) an outlet pipe at the top of a chimney.

chimpanzee noun (plural **chimpanzees**) a medium-sized African ape with dark brown or black fur.

chin noun (plural **chins**) the lower portion of the face below the mouth. * **keep your chin up** to remain cheerful.

china noun items such as cups and plates made from fine white clay.

chinchilla noun (plural **chinchillas**) a small South American rodent with soft pearly-grey fur.

chink¹ noun (plural **chinks**) a narrow opening, slit, or crack.

chink² verb (**chinks, chinking, chinked**) to make a sharp ringing sound. ➤ **chink** noun.

chintz noun a printed fabric made from shiny cotton.

chip noun (plural **chips**) **1** a small piece broken or flaked off a hard substance. **2** a damaged place left after a chip is removed. **3** a strip of potato fried in deep fat. **4** N American a potato crisp. **5** a counter used in gambling games. **6** an integrated circuit or microchip. ~ verb (**chips, chipping, chipped**) **1** to cut or break a small piece off something. **2** to kick or hit a ball in a short high arc. **3** to cut potatoes into chips. * **chip in** informal to contribute to a conversation or to a sum of money. **a chip off the old block** a person who is like one or other of their parents. **have had your chips** informal to be doomed or dead.

chipboard noun a board made from compressed wood chips.

chipmunk noun (plural **chipmunks**) a small striped American squirrel.

chipolata /chi po lah ta/ noun (plural **chipolatas**) a small sausage.

chipper adjective informal cheerful and bright.

chiropody /ki ro po di/ noun the care and treatment of the feet. ➤ **chiropodist** noun.

chirp verb (**chirps, chirping, chirped**) said about a small bird or insect: to make a short shrill sound. ➤ **chirp** noun.

chirpy adjective (**chirpier, chirpiest**) informal lively and cheerful. ➤ **chirpily** adverb.

chisel noun (plural **chisels**) a tool that has a blade with a cutting edge at one end, used in shaping wood, stone, or metal. ~ verb (**chisels, chiselling, chiselled**) to shape something with a chisel.

chivalrous /shi val rus/ adjective **1** courteous and considerate to women. **2** honourable or generous. ➤ **chivalrously** adverb, **chivalry** noun.

chives plural noun the long thin leaves of a plant of the onion family used to flavour and garnish food.

chivvy or **chivy** verb (**chivvies, chivvying, chivvied** or **chivies,** etc) informal to try to make somebody move or work faster.

chlorinate /klaw ri nayt/ verb (**chlorinates, chlorinating, chlorinated**) to treat water with chlorine to kill algae or bacteria. ➤ **chlorination** noun.

chlorine /klaw reen/ noun Science a chemical element that is a pungent greenish yellow gas.

chloroform /klo ro fawm/ noun a liquid that gives off a vapour that makes people unconscious.

chlorophyll /klo ro fil/ noun Science the green colouring matter of plants that enables them to absorb sunlight.

chock noun (plural **chocks**) a wedge placed under a wheel or door to prevent it from moving.

chock-a-block *adjective and adverb* crowded or tightly packed.

chocolate *noun* (*plural* **chocolates**) **1** a sweet food prepared from ground roasted cacao seeds. **2** a sweet made or coated with chocolate. **3** a drink made by mixing chocolate with hot water or milk. **4** a dark brown colour.

choice *noun* (*plural* **choices**) **1** the act of choosing. **2** the power of choosing: *I had no choice, I had to go.* **3** somebody or something chosen: *My first choice would be a trip to New York.* **4** a number or variety of things to choose from. ~ *adjective* **1** of high quality. **2** selected with care.

choir *noun* (*plural* **choirs**) **1** an organized group of singers. **2** the part of a church between the sanctuary and the nave.

choirboy or **choirgirl** *noun* (*plural* **choirboys** or **choirgirls**) a boy or girl singer in a church choir.

choke *verb* (**chokes, choking, choked**) **1** to stop somebody breathing by pressing on or blocking their windpipe. **2** to become unable to breathe. **3** to block a pipe, road, or passageway. ~ *noun* (*plural* **chokes**) a valve in a petrol engine for controlling the mixture of fuel and air.

cholera /ko li ra/ *noun* a very infectious disease that causes severe disorders of the stomach and intestines.

cholesterol /ko les ti rol/ *noun* a substance present in animal and plant cells and thought to contribute to heart disease.

chomp *verb* (**chomps, chomping, chomped**) to bite or chew something noisily.

choose *verb* (**chooses, choosing, chose, chosen**) **1** to decide on and take somebody or something from several alternatives offered. **2** to decide to do something.

choosy *adjective* (**choosier, choosiest**) very concerned to get exactly what you want, and therefore careful in making choices.

chop *verb* (**chops, chopping, chopped**) **1** (**chop off/down**) to remove or fell something by a blow or repeated blows with a sharp instrument. **2** (*also* **chop up**) to cut something into pieces. **3** to strike something or somebody with a short sharp blow. ~ *noun* (*plural* **chops**) **1** a forceful blow or cutting stroke. **2** a small cut of meat often including part of a rib. ✽ **chop and change** to keep changing your mind or plans. **get the chop** *informal* to be dismissed or cancelled.

chopper *noun* (*plural* **choppers**) **1** an axe with a short handle. **2** *informal* a helicopter.

choppy *adjective* (**choppier, choppiest**) said about the sea: rough with small waves.

chopsticks *plural noun* two thin sticks used in oriental countries for eating food.

chop suey *noun* (*plural* **chop sueys**) a Chinese-style dish of shredded meat or chicken with bean sprouts and other vegetables.

choral /kaw ral/ *adjective* Music intended for singing by a choir.

chord *noun* (*plural* **chords**) Music a combination of notes sounded together.

chore *noun* (*plural* **chores**) a routine or tedious task.

choreograph /ko ri o grahf/ *verb* (**choreographs, choreographing, choreographed**) to arrange the steps and dances for a ballet or show. ➤ **choreographer** *noun*, **choreography** *noun*.

chorister /ko ris ter/ *noun* (*plural* **choristers**) a singer in a choir; a choirboy or choirgirl.

chortle *verb* (**chortles, chortling, chortled**) to laugh or chuckle. ➤ **chortle** *noun*.

chorus noun (plural **choruses**) 1 *Music* an organized group of singers who sing the choral parts of music, opera, or musicals. 2 *Music* a composition sung by a chorus. 3 *Music* a section of a song or hymn repeated at intervals. 4 something said by a number of people at the same time: *There was a chorus of denials from the girls.* ~ verb (**choruses, chorusing, chorused**) to say or sing something together.

chose verb past tense of CHOOSE.

chosen verb past participle of CHOOSE.

chow mein /chow mayn/ noun (plural **chow meins**) a Chinese-style dish of fried noodles usually mixed with shredded meat and vegetables.

Christ noun a title given by Christians to Jesus.

christen verb (**christens, christening, christened**) 1 to give a name to a baby at baptism. 2 to give a name to something. 3 *informal* to use something for the first time.

Christianity noun the religion based on the life, death, and teachings of Jesus Christ as told in the New Testament. ➤ **Christian** noun and adjective.

Christian name noun (plural **Christian names**) a name given to a person at their baptism; a first name.

Christmas noun a festival of the Christian Church commemorating the birth of Jesus Christ, held on 25 December.

chromatic /kroh ma tik/ adjective 1 to do with colour. 2 *Music* said about a musical scale: based entirely on semitones.

chrome /krohm/ noun a plating of chromium.

chromium /kroh mi um/ noun *Science* a chemical element, a bluish white metal used in alloys.

chromosome /kroh mo sohm/ noun (plural **chromosomes**) *Science* a tiny rod-shaped structure found in the nucleus of a cell, which contains the genes of an animal or plant.

chronic /kro nik/ adjective said about an illness or difficulty: lasting for a long time and difficult to cure. ➤ **chronically** adverb.

chronicle /kro ni kl/ noun (plural **chronicles**) an account of events arranged in the order in which they happened.

chronological /kro no lo ji kl/ adjective arranged in the order in which things happen over a period of time. ➤ **chronologically** adverb.

chronology /kro no lo ji/ noun a system of dating past events in chronological order.

chronometer /kro no mi ter/ noun (plural **chronometers**) an instrument for measuring time very accurately.

chrysalis /kri sa lis/ noun (plural **chrysalises**) *Science* the casing in which a caterpillar wraps itself while it changes into a butterfly or moth.

chrysanthemum /kri san thi mum/ noun (plural **chrysanthemums**) a garden plant with brightly coloured flowers.

chubby adjective (**chubbier, chubbiest**) round and plump. ➤ **chubbiness** noun.

chuck[1] verb (**chucks, chucking, chucked**) *informal* 1 to throw something casually. 2 to get rid of something.

chuck[2] noun (plural **chucks**) a device for holding a drill or bit in a tool.

chuckle verb (**chuckles, chuckling, chuckled**) to laugh quietly. ➤ **chuckle** noun.

chuff verb (**chuffs, chuffing, chuffed**) to make the sound of a steam engine.

chuffed adjective *informal* very pleased.

chug verb (**chugs, chugging, chugged**) to move with a repeated heavy sound.

chum noun (plural **chums**) *informal, dated* a friend or mate.

chump *noun* (*plural* **chumps**) *informal* a foolish person.

chunk *noun* (*plural* **chunks**) a thick or solid lump. ➤ **chunky** *adjective*.

church *noun* (*plural* **churches**) **1** a building for Christian worship. **2** (**the Church**) all Christians considered as a group. **3** a Christian denomination: *the Church of Scotland*.

churchyard *noun* (*plural* **churchyards**) an enclosed piece of ground surrounding a church.

churlish *adjective* uncooperative and unfriendly. ➤ **churlishly** *adverb*.

churn *noun* (*plural* **churns**) **1** a container in which milk or cream is stirred and shaken to make butter. **2** a large metal container for transporting milk. ~ *verb* (**churns, churning, churned**) **1** to stir milk or cream to make butter. **2** to be stirred up violently. ✶ **churn out** to produce something in large quantities.

chute /shoot/ *noun* (*plural* **chutes**) **1** an inclined channel down which things pass to a lower level. **2** a slide into a swimming pool.

chutney *noun* (*plural* **chutneys**) a spicy mixture of fruits, vegetables, sugar, vinegar, and spices.

CIA *abbreviation* N American Central Intelligence Agency.

CID *abbreviation* Criminal Investigation Department.

cider *noun* (*plural* **ciders**) an alcoholic drink made of fermented apple juice.

cigar *noun* (*plural* **cigars**) a roll of tobacco leaves for smoking.

cigarette *noun* (*plural* **cigarettes**) a cylinder of cut tobacco rolled in paper for smoking.

cinder *noun* (*plural* **cinders**) a piece of partly burned coal or wood.

cinema *noun* (*plural* **cinemas**) **1** a theatre where films are shown. **2** the film industry. ➤ **cinematic** *adjective*.

cinnamon *noun* a spice obtained from the dried bark of an Asian tree.

cipher /sie fer/ *noun* (*plural* **ciphers**) **1** a code. **2** a key to a code.

circa /ser ka/ *preposition* approximately; around: *circa 1662*.

circle *noun* (*plural* **circles**) **1** a shape in the form of a closed curved line, every point of which is the same distance from the centre. **2** a balcony or tier of seats in a theatre. **3** a group of people who are friends or who share a common interest. ~ *verb* (**circles, circling, circled**) **1** to move in a circle. **2** to enclose in a circle.

circuit /ser kit/ *noun* (*plural* **circuits**) **1** a track, route, or journey that goes round in a circle. **2** a system of electrical components connected so as to allow a current to pass through them.

circuitous /ser kew i tus/ *adjective* indirect in route or method; not by the quickest, straightest, or shortest way.

circular *adjective* having the form of a circle, or moving in a circle. ~ *noun* (*plural* **circulars**) a letter or leaflet intended for distribution to a large number of people.

circulate *verb* (**circulates, circulating, circulated**) **1** to follow a course that returns to its starting point: *Blood circulates through the body*. **2** to flow freely through or around something. **3** to send a letter or document to a number of different people. **4** to go from group to group at a social gathering.

circulation *noun* **1** the movement of blood through the vessels of the body driven by the pumping action of the heart. **2** the passing of things from one person to another. **3** the number of copies of a publication sold over a given period.

circumcise *verb* /ser kum siez/ (**circumcises, circumcising, circumcised**) to cut off the foreskin of a male or the clitoris of a female. ➤ **circumcision** noun.

circumference /ser kum fi rins/ noun (plural **circumferences**) *Maths* the line marking the outer edge of a circle or the distance around that line.

circumflex /ser kum fleks/ noun (plural **circumflexes**) a mark (^) written above a letter in some languages to show that a vowel has a particular sound, as in *table d'hôte*.

circumlocution noun the use of an unnecessarily large number of words to express an idea.

circumnavigate verb (**circumnavigates, circumnavigating, circumnavigated**) to travel by sea or air all the way round the earth. ➤ **circumnavigation** noun.

circumscribe verb (**circumscribes, circumscribing, circumscribed**) to restrict the range or activity of something or somebody.

circumspect adjective cautious. ➤ **circumspection** noun.

circumstance noun (plural **circumstances**) **1** a fact or detail relating to an event or story. **2** (**circumstances**) the situation you find yourself in, especially your financial situation.
✱ **in/under the circumstances** considering the situation.

circumstantial /ser kum stan shl/ adjective said about evidence: not directly proving something, but suggesting that it is very probable that it happened: *circumstantial evidence*. ➤ **circumstantially** adverb.

circumvent verb (**circumvents, circumventing, circumvented**) to find a way round a difficulty. ➤ **circumvention** noun.

circus noun (plural **circuses**) a group of performers, including acrobats, animal trainers, and clowns, who entertain people, usually in a large tent.

cistern noun (plural **cisterns**) **1** a water tank for a toilet. **2** a tank at the top of a house or building.

citadel noun (plural **citadels**) a fortress in a city.

cite verb (**cites, citing, cited**) to quote something or somebody in order to support what you are saying. ➤ **citation** noun.

citizen noun (plural **citizens**) **1** a person who belongs to a state: *a British citizen*. **2** an inhabitant of a city or town.

citizenship noun **1** the fact of being a member of a state: *British citizenship*. **2** the duties and responsibilities of a citizen of a country.

citrus /sit rus/ noun (plural **citruses**) a juicy fruit with thick peel such as an orange, lemon, lime, or grapefruit.

city noun (plural **cities**) **1** a large town, especially one that has been created by charter and has a cathedral. **2** (**the City**) the financial and commercial area of London.

civic adjective to do with a city or citizenship.

civil adjective **1** courteous and polite. **2** involving the general public as opposed to the armed forces or clergy. **3** to do with private rights rather than criminal offences: *civil law*. ➤ **civilly** adverb.

civil engineer noun (plural **civil engineers**) an engineer who designs large-scale public works such as roads and bridges. ➤ **civil engineering** noun.

civilian noun (plural **civilians**) somebody who is not a member of the armed forces or the police. ➤ **civilian** adjective.

civility noun politeness.

civilization or **civilisation** noun (plural **civilizations** or **civilisations**) **1** a high level of cultural and technological development in a society. **2** the lifestyle and culture characteristic of a particular time or place. **3** *informal* a place that offers the comforts of the modern world: *After a week in the wilderness, it was good to get back to civilization.*

civilize *or* **civilise** *verb* (**civilizes, civilizing, civilized** *or* **civilises,** etc) **1** to bring people to a state of civilization. **2** to teach somebody to be polite and refined. ➤ **civilized** *or* **civilised** *adjective.*

civil liberties *plural noun* a person's rights in relation to the state.

civil rights *plural noun* the rights of citizens, especially as regards equal treatment regardless of race or other differences.

civil servant *noun* (*plural* **civil servants**) a member of a civil service.

civil service *noun* the people who do administrative work for government departments.

civil war *noun* (*plural* **civil wars**) a war between citizens of the same country.

clad *adjective* clothed or covered in something: *clad in armour.*

claim *verb* (**claims, claiming, claimed**) **1** to ask for something that you think you have a right to: *to claim a reward.* **2** to take something that you are the rightful owner of. **3** to state something without being able to prove it: *She claims that she's been cheated.* ~ *noun* (*plural* **claims**) **1** a statement that has not been proved. **2** a demand for something that you have a right to, for example under an insurance policy. ➤ **claimant** *noun.*

clairvoyance /klair**voi**ans/ *noun* the ability to see things, such as what will happen in the future, that are hidden from most people. ➤ **clairvoyant** *adjective and noun.*

clam *noun* (*plural* **clams**) a large shellfish with a tightly closed hinged shell.

clamber *verb* (**clambers, clambering,** **clambered**) to climb awkwardly or with difficulty.

clammy *adjective* (**clammier, clammiest**) **1** unpleasantly damp and clinging. **2** said about the weather: humid.

clamour *noun* **1** noisy shouting. **2** a loud confused noise. **3** insistent demands for or protests against something. ~ *verb* (**clamours, clamouring, clamoured**) (**clamour for**) to demand something loudly and insistently. ➤ **clamorous** *adjective.*

clamp *noun* (*plural* **clamps**) **1** a device that holds two or more things firmly together. **2** a device placed round the wheel of an illegally parked vehicle to prevent it from being moved. ~ *verb* (**clamps, clamping, clamped**) to hold or fasten something with a clamp. ✶ **clamp down on** to take strict measures to stop people doing something.

clan *noun* (*plural* **clans**) especially in Scotland or among people of Scottish origin, a group consisting of people who have the same family name. ➤ **clansman** *noun,* **clanswoman** *noun.*

clandestine /klan**des**tin *or* klan**des**tien/ *adjective* held or done in secret. ➤ **clandestinely** *adverb.*

clang *verb* (**clangs, clanging, clanged**) to make a loud ringing metallic sound. ➤ **clang** *noun.*

clank *verb* (**clanks, clanking, clanked**) to make a sharp metallic sound. ➤ **clank** *noun.*

clap *verb* (**claps, clapping, clapped**) **1** to strike your hands together repeatedly in applause. **2** to hit somebody with the flat of the hand in a friendly way. **3** to put somebody forcefully or suddenly in a certain place or condition: *He was clapped in irons.* ~ *noun* (*plural* **claps**) **1** the act or sound of clapping hands. **2** a loud sound of thunder. **3** a friendly slap.

clapper noun (plural **clappers**) the tongue of a bell.

claret noun (plural **clarets**) a red wine from the Bordeaux region of France.

clarify verb (**clarifies, clarifying, clarified**) to make something easier to understand. ➤ **clarification** noun.

clarinet noun (plural **clarinets**) Music a woodwind instrument with a single reed, a flared end, and holes stopped by keys. ➤ **clarinettist** noun.

clarity noun the quality or state of being clear.

clash noun (plural **clashes**) 1 a noisy metallic sound, such as the sound made by cymbals hitting one another. 2 a conflict or quarrel. 3 a situation where two incompatible colours are put together. 4 a situation where two events happen at the same time. ~ verb (**clashes, clashing, clashed**) 1 to make a clash. 2 to come into conflict with one another. 3 said about colours: to look unpleasant when put together. 4 said about events: to happen at the same time so you cannot go to both.

clasp noun (plural **clasps**) 1 a device for holding objects or parts together. 2 a tight hold on something. ~ verb (**clasps, clasping, clasped**) 1 to fasten something with a clasp. 2 to enclose and hold somebody or something in your arms. 3 to seize something with your hand.

class noun (plural **classes**) 1 a group of students who are taught together. 2 a lesson at a school or college. 3 a distinct group of things sharing common characteristics. 4 a group in society who have the same economic or social status: *the working class*. 5 a level of quality, achievement, or service. 6 *informal* high quality; elegance: *That girl really has class!* ~ verb (**classes, classing, classed**) to classify or grade people or things.

classic adjective 1 setting a standard of excellence: *classic recordings*. 2 in a simple elegant style that will not go out of date. 3 being a typical example of some particular thing or occurrence: *a classic case of first-night nerves*. ~ noun (plural **classics**) 1 a work of lasting excellence. 2 (**Classics**) the study of Greek and Latin literature, history, and philosophy.

classical adjective 1 *History* to do with the ancient Greek and Roman world. 2 *Music* belonging to the European tradition of serious music as opposed to popular music, folk music, or jazz. ➤ **classically** adjective.

classification noun (plural **classifications**) 1 the systematic arrangement of things in defined groups. 2 a class or category.

classified adjective 1 said about information or documents: not revealed to the general public for reasons of security. 2 said about newspaper or magazine advertisements: organized according to their subjects.

classify verb (**classifies, classifying, classified**) 1 to arrange things in classes. 2 to place something or somebody in a category.

classroom noun (plural **classrooms**) a room in a school where classes are held.

classy adjective (**classier, classiest**) *informal* elegant and stylish.

clatter verb (**clatters, clattering, clattered**) to make a loud rattling or banging noise. ➤ **clatter** noun.

clause noun (plural **clauses**) 1 *English* a group of words containing a subject and verb and forming part of a sentence. 2 a separate item or condition in a contract.

claustrophobia /klaw stro foh bi a/ noun abnormal fear of being in confined spaces. ➤ **claustrophobic** adjective.

clavicle noun (plural **clavicles**) *Science* the collarbone.

claw noun (plural **claws**) a sharp curved

nail on an animal's toe. ~ *verb* (**claws, clawing, clawed**) to scratch or dig something with the claws or fingernails.

clay *noun* **1** *Art* an earthy material, soft when moist but hard when fired, used for making bricks and pottery. **2** thick and clinging earth or mud. ➤ **clayey** *adjective*.

clean *adjective* **1** free from dirt. **2** free from contamination or disease. **3** not obscene. **4** unused or unmarked. **5** having no record of wrongdoing or offences. **6** said about an action: smooth and effective. ~ *verb* (**cleans, cleaning, cleaned**) to make something clean. ~ *noun* an act of cleaning. ~ *adverb* all the way; completely: *The bullet went clean through his arm.*
✱ **clean out 1** to clean the inside of something thoroughly. **2** *informal* to take away everything that is in something or everything somebody has. ➤ **cleaner** *noun*, **cleanly** *adverb*.

cleanliness /klen li nis/ *noun* care in keeping things or yourself clean.

cleanse /klenz/ *verb* (**cleanses, cleansing, cleansed**) to clean or purify something thoroughly. ➤ **cleanser** *noun*.

clear *adjective* **1** easy to understand. **2** easy to see or hear. **3** transparent. **4** said about the air or sky: free from cloud, mist, or dust. **5** free from obstructions or interruptions. ~ *adverb* **1** clearly. **2** all the way. ~ *verb* (**clears, clearing, cleared**) **1** to free something from obstructions or unwanted things. **2** to remove all the people from an area or building. **3** to remove or dispose of something. **4** to go over an obstacle without touching it. **5** in football, to kick the ball away from the goal. **6** to declare somebody to be not guilty or not to blame.
✱ **clear away 1** to put things back into storage after use. **2** to remove used plates and cutlery after a meal. **clear of** not touching; away from. **clear off** *informal* to go away. **clear something with somebody** to obtain permission or approval for something from somebody. **clear up 1** to remove dirt or mess. **2** to tidy a room or area by removing unwanted things. **3** to provide a solution for a problem or mystery. **4** said about an illness: to be cured or get better. **5** said about the weather: to become fine again. **in the clear** free of suspicion or danger. ➤ **clearly** *adverb*.

clearance *noun* **1** the removal of obstructions or unwanted things. **2** clear space allowing one thing to pass another. **3** official authorization.

clearing *noun* (*plural* **clearings**) an area of land cleared of wood and undergrowth.

cleavage *noun* the hollow space between a woman's breasts.

cleaver *noun* (*plural* **cleavers**) a butcher's chopping implement with a large heavy blade.

clef *noun* (*plural* **clefs**) *Music* a sign placed on a stave to indicate the pitch of the notes following it: *the treble clef.*

cleft *noun* (*plural* **clefts**) a space or opening made when something splits.

cleft palate *noun* (*plural* **cleft palates**) a split in the roof of the mouth.

clematis *noun* (*plural* **clematises**) a climbing plant with white, pink, or purple flowers.

clemency *noun* mercy or leniency shown to an offender.

clementine /kle min tien *or* kle min teen/ *noun* (*plural* **clementines**) a small citrus fruit with bright orange skin.

clench *verb* (**clenches, clenching, clenched**) to close your fists or teeth tightly.

clergy *noun* the priests or ministers of a Christian Church.

clergyman *or* **clergywoman** *noun*

clerical

(*plural* **clergymen** or **clergywomen**) an ordained priest or minister.

clerical *adjective* **1** involving or doing routine office work such as typing and filing. **2** to do with the clergy.

clerk /klahk/ *noun* (*plural* **clerks**) a person who keeps records or accounts or does general office work.

clever *adjective* **1** mentally quick and intelligent. **2** showing skill or intelligence. ➤ **cleverly** *adverb*, **cleverness** *noun*.

cliché /klee shay/ *noun* (*plural* **clichés**) an idea or expression that has been used so often that it seems boring and almost meaningless. ➤ **clichéd** *adjective*.

click *noun* (*plural* **clicks**) **1** a light sharp sound made by hard parts locking into one another. **2** *ICT* an action of pressing and releasing a mouse button. ~ *verb* (**clicks, clicking, clicked**) **1** to produce, or make something produce, a click. **2** *ICT* to press and release a button on a mouse. **3** (**click on**) *ICT* to move the cursor onto an icon, etc and press the mouse button. **4** *informal* to become friendly or successful.

client *noun* (*plural* **clients**) somebody who uses the services of a professional person or organization.

clientele /klie in tel/ *noun* the clients of a business, shop, etc.

cliff *noun* (*plural* **cliffs**) a steep high face of rock on a mountain or the coast.

cliffhanger *noun* (*plural* **cliffhangers**) an ending to an episode in a story that leaves the reader or viewer in suspense.

climate *noun* (*plural* **climates**) *Geography* the average weather conditions in a particular area over a long period. ➤ **climatic** *adjective*.

climax *noun* (*plural* **climaxes**) the most important or exciting point in something, usually occurring near the end. ➤ **climactic** *adjective*.

climb *verb* (**climbs, climbing, climbed**) **1** to go up to or down from a higher position, often using your hands and feet to hold on to something. **2** said about an aircraft: to go gradually upwards. **3** to slope upwards. **4** to get into or out of a confined space with effort. * **climb down** to change your opinion, policy, etc because a lot of people have protested against it. ➤ **climb** *noun*.

climbing frame *noun* (*plural* **climbing frames**) a framework of bars for children to climb on.

clinch *verb* (**clinches, clinching, clinched**) to settle something finally: *to clinch a deal*. ~ *noun* (*plural* **clinches**) a tight hold or embrace.

cling *verb* (**clings, clinging, clung**) (**cling to**) **1** to hold on tightly to something or somebody. **2** to stick to something. **3** to remain convinced of something.

clingfilm *noun* thin transparent plastic used to wrap food and keep it fresh.

clinic *noun* (*plural* **clinics**) a place where medical treatment or advice is given.

clinical *adjective* **1** to do with the medical treatment of patients. **2** analytic or emotionally detached. ➤ **clinically** *adverb*.

clink *verb* (**clinks, clinking, clinked**) to make a light sharp sound. ➤ **clink** *noun*.

clip[1] *noun* (*plural* **clips**) a device, often with a spring, that grips or holds things. ~ *verb* (**clips, clipping, clipped**) to clasp or fasten something with a clip.

clip[2] *verb* (**clips, clipping, clipped**) **1** to cut hair or wool with shears or scissors. **2** to cut off the end or outer part of something. **3** to hit something or somebody with a quick hard blow. ~ *noun* (*plural* **clips**) **1** a sharp blow.

2 a short excerpt from a film or broadcast.

clipboard *noun* (*plural* **clipboards**) a small writing board with a spring clip for holding papers.

clipper *noun* (*plural* **clippers**) **1** (**clippers**) an implement for trimming hair or nails. **2** a fast sailing ship.

clipping *noun* (*plural* **clippings**) **1** a piece cut or trimmed from something. **2** an extract cut from a newspaper or magazine.

clique /kleek/ *noun* (*plural* **cliques**) a small group of people with a shared interest who discourage other people from joining them. ➤ **cliquey** *adjective*.

clitoris /kli to ris/ *noun* (*plural* **clitorises**) a small area at the front of a woman's vulva that is very sensitive.

cloak *noun* (*plural* **cloaks**) **1** a long sleeveless outer garment that hangs loosely. **2** something that conceals. ~ *verb* (**cloaks, cloaking, cloaked**) to cover or hide something.

cloak-and-dagger *adjective* involving melodramatic intrigue and secrecy.

cloakroom *noun* (*plural* **cloakrooms**) **1** a room in which clothing or bags may be left. **2** a room with a toilet.

clobber[1] *noun informal* clothing or equipment.

clobber[2] *verb* (**clobbers, clobbering, clobbered**) *informal* to hit somebody hard.

cloche /klosh/ *noun* (*plural* **cloches**) a cover put over outdoor plants, for example to protect them from frost.

clock *noun* (*plural* **clocks**) **1** a device for indicating or measuring time. **2** *informal* a speedometer or other metering device. ~ *verb* (**clocks, clocking, clocked**) to time somebody or something with a stopwatch or electric timing device. ✽ **clock in/on** to record the time of arriving at work.

clock off/out to record the time of leaving work. **clock up** *informal* to achieve a time, speed, score, etc. **round the clock** all day and night.

clockwise *adverb and adjective* in the direction in which the hands of a clock move.

clockwork *noun* a mechanism powered by a coiled spring. ✽ **like clockwork** smoothly and with no problems.

clod *noun* (*plural* **clods**) a lump of earth or clay.

clog[1] *noun* (*plural* **clogs**) a shoe with a thick wooden sole.

clog[2] *verb* (**clogs, clogging, clogged**) to block something.

cloister *noun* (*plural* **cloisters**) a covered path along the wall of a courtyard in a church, monastery, college, etc.

clone *noun* (*plural* **clones**) **1** an animal or plant produced from the cells of another and identical to it. **2** *informal* an exact copy of something. ~ *verb* (**clones, cloning, cloned**) to make a clone of something.

close[1] /klohs/ *adjective* (**closer, closest**) **1** near in space, time, or relationship. **2** said about a connection: strong. **3** said about a resemblance: showing only small variations. **4** having little space in between; dense. **5** said about a game or contest: with very little difference between the competitors' skill or results. **6** very careful and concentrated. **7** said about the weather: hot and stuffy. ~ *adverb* (**closer, closest**) in a close position or manner. ~ *noun* (*plural* **closes**) **1** a road closed at one end. **2** the area around a cathedral. ✽ **close on** almost. ➤ **closely** *adverb*.

close[2] /klohz/ *verb* (**closes, closing, closed**) **1** to shut or cover something. **2** to prevent people or vehicles going into a road or entrance. **3** to end. **4** (*also* **close down**) said about a business, etc: to stop its operations

close call

permanently. **5** said about a shop: to stop trading for the day. ~ *noun* (*plural* **closes**) the end or conclusion of something. ✶ **close in** to come closer to and surround a place or person.

close call *noun* (*plural* **close calls**) a narrow escape.

closed-circuit television *noun* a television system where the signal is transmitted by wire to a limited number of receivers and which is usually used for surveillance in a building or area.

closed shop *noun* (*plural* **closed shops**) an establishment which employs only union members.

close-knit *adjective* said about a community or family: whose members are very friendly and supportive to one another.

close season *noun* (*plural* **close seasons**) a period during which fishing or hunting is not allowed, or a sport is not played.

close shave *noun* (*plural* **close shaves**) *informal* a narrow escape.

closet *noun* (*plural* **closets**) **1** a small or private room. **2** *chiefly N American* a cupboard. ✶ **be closeted with** to be in a small private place talking to somebody.

close-up *noun* (*plural* **close-ups**) a photograph or film sequence taken at close range.

closure /kloh *zher*/ *noun* (*plural* **closures**) **1** the act of closing. **2** a device that closes or seals a container.

clot *noun* (*plural* **clots**) **1** a small solid mass produced when blood or cream coagulates. **2** *informal* a foolish person. ~ *verb* (**clots, clotting, clotted**) to form clots.

cloth *noun* (*plural* **cloths**) **1** a fabric made by weaving or knitting fibres. **2** a piece of cloth used for a particular purpose.

clothe *verb* (**clothes, clothing, clothed**) **1** to put clothing on somebody. **2** to cover something.

clothes *plural noun* articles made of cloth or other material worn to cover the body.

clothing *noun* clothes.

clotted cream *noun* a thick cream made by heating and cooling whole milk.

cloud *noun* (*plural* **clouds**) **1** a mass of water particles high up in the air. **2** a mass of smoke or dust in the air. ~ *verb* (**clouds, clouding, clouded**) **1** (**cloud over/up**) said about the sky or weather: to become cloudy. **2** to make something blurred or unclear.

cloudburst *noun* (*plural* **cloudbursts**) a sudden heavy fall of rain.

cloudy *adjective* (**cloudier, cloudiest**) **1** covered with or full of clouds. **2** not clear or transparent.

clout *noun* (*plural* **clouts**) *informal* **1** a heavy blow. **2** power or influence. ~ *verb* (**clouts, clouting, clouted**) *informal* to hit somebody or something hard.

clove[1] *noun* (*plural* **cloves**) one of the segments that make up a bulb of garlic.

clove[2] *noun* (*plural* **cloves**) the dried bud of a tropical tree, used as a spice.

cloven hoof *noun* (*plural* **cloven hooves** or **hoofs**) the divided hoof of a sheep, cow, etc.

clover *noun* a plant with leaves that consist of three leaflets. ✶ **in clover** in luxury.

clown *noun* (*plural* **clowns**) **1** a comic entertainer in a circus. **2** a person who jokes and fools about. ➤ **clownish** *adjective*. ~ *verb* (**clowns, clowning, clowned**) ✶ **clown about/around** to behave in a comic or silly way.

cloying *adjective* too sweet or sentimental. ➤ **cloyingly** *adverb*.

club *noun* (*plural* **clubs**) **1** an association of people who enjoy a common interest or activity. **2** a building where members can stay, eat, or socialize. **3** a place where people dance to recorded music. **4** a thick heavy stick used as a weapon. **5** a stick used to hit the ball in golf. **6** (**clubs**) the suit in a pack of playing cards that is marked with black figures in the shape of a clover leaf. ~ *verb* (**clubs, clubbing, clubbed**) **1** to hit somebody with a club. **2** *informal* to visit clubs. ✱ **club together** to share a cost or expense.

cluck *verb* (**clucks, clucking, clucked**) to make the sound of a hen. ➤ **cluck** *noun*.

clue *noun* **1** something that provides evidence to solve a problem or mystery. **2** a phrase from which you work out the answer to part of a crossword puzzle. ✱ **not have a clue 1** to know nothing. **2** to be incompetent.

clued-up *adjective informal* well-informed.

clueless *adjective informal* completely ignorant or incompetent.

clump *noun* (*plural* **clumps**) **1** a group of trees or bushes growing close together. **2** a compact mass or cluster. **3** a heavy tramping sound. ~ *verb* (**clumps, clumping, clumped**) **1** to form clumps. **2** to tread clumsily and noisily.

clumsy *adjective* (**clumsier, clumsiest**) **1** awkward and ungraceful in movement. **2** lacking tact or subtlety. ➤ **clumsily** *adverb*, **clumsiness** *noun*.

clung *verb* past tense and past participle of CLING.

clunk *verb* (**clunks, clunking, clunked**) to make the dull sound of one heavy object striking another. ➤ **clunk** *noun*.

cluster *noun* (*plural* **clusters**) a compact group of similar things or people. ~ *verb* (**clusters, clustering, clustered**) to form a cluster.

clutch¹ *verb* (**clutches, clutching, clutched**) to grasp something or somebody or hold them tightly. ~ *noun* (*plural* **clutches**) **1** a tight grasp. **2** a device that connects and disconnects the engine and the wheels in a vehicle. ✱ **in somebody's clutches** held or controlled by somebody.

clutch² *noun* (*plural* **clutches**) a number of eggs laid at one time, or a brood of chicks hatched from them.

clutter *verb* (**clutters, cluttering, cluttered**) to fill or cover an area untidily with scattered things. ~ *noun* an untidy scattering of things.

cm *abbreviation* centimetre or centimetres.

Co. *abbreviation* company.

coach *noun* (*plural* **coaches**) **1** a comfortable single-deck bus used for long-distance travel. **2** a railway carriage. **3** a large, four-wheeled, horse-drawn carriage. **4** somebody who gives training in a sport. **5** a person who gives private lessons in a subject. ~ *verb* (**coaches, coaching, coached**) **1** to train somebody in a sport. **2** to give private lessons to somebody.

coagulate /koh a gew layt/ *verb* (**coagulates, coagulating, coagulated**) said about a liquid: to become thicker and more solid. ➤ **coagulation** *noun*.

coal *noun* a black solid mineral used as a fuel.

coalesce /koh a les/ *verb* (**coalesces, coalescing, coalesced**) to fuse into a whole. ➤ **coalescence** *noun*.

coalfield *noun* (*plural* **coalfields**) a region in which deposits of coal occur.

coalition /koh a li shn/ *noun* (*plural* **coalitions**) a temporary alliance of political parties.

coalmine *noun* (*plural* **coalmines**) a mine that produces coal.

coarse *adjective* (**coarser, coarsest**) **1** rough in texture. **2** composed of large particles: *coarse sand*. **3** rude or

unrefined in manners or language.
➤ **coarsely** *adverb*, **coarseness** *noun*.

coast *noun* (*plural* **coasts**) **1** the edge of land where it reaches the sea. **2** the land near a shore. ~ *verb* (**coasts, coasting, coasted**) to move downhill or along without using power. ∗ **the coast is clear** there is no danger. ➤ **coastal** *adjective*.

coaster *noun* (*plural* **coasters**) **1** a small mat for resting glasses or mugs on. **2** a ship that sails from port to port along a coast.

coastguard *noun* (*plural* **coastguards**) an official or organization that keeps guard over coastal waters.

coat *noun* (*plural* **coats**) **1** a full-length outer garment with sleeves. **2** the hair or fur of an animal. **3** a layer of paint or another liquid covering. ~ *verb* (**coats, coating, coated**) to cover or spread something with a layer of something else.

coat of arms *noun* (*plural* **coats of arms**) a design on a shield that is the symbol of a particular family, city, or institution.

coax *verb* (**coaxes, coaxing, coaxed**) to try gently to persuade somebody.

cob *noun* (*plural* **cobs**) **1** a male swan. **2** the core on which sweet corn grows. **3** a small rounded loaf.

cobalt /koh bawlt/ *noun* *Science* a chemical element, a silver-white metal used in alloys.

cobble[1] *verb* (**cobbles, cobbling, cobbled**) to repair or make shoes. ∗ **cobble together** to make or assemble something roughly or hastily. ➤ **cobbler** *noun*.

cobble[2] *noun* (*plural* **cobbles**) a small rounded stone used for paving a street. ➤ **cobbled** *adjective*.

cobra /koh bra/ *noun* (*plural* **cobras**) a poisonous Asian and African snake with grooved fangs.

cobweb *noun* (*plural* **cobwebs**) a spider's web.

cocaine *noun* an addictive drug obtained from the leaves of the coca plant.

coccyx /kok siks/ *noun* (*plural* **coccyxes**) *Science* a small triangular bone at the base of the spinal column.

cochineal *noun* a red dye used as a colouring agent for food.

cochlea /kok li a/ *noun* (*plural* **cochleae** /kok li ee/) *Science* a coiled part of the inner ear, filled with liquid.

cock *noun* (*plural* **cocks**) **1** a male bird, especially a male chicken. **2** the hammer of a firearm. ~ *verb* (**cocks, cocking, cocked**) **1** to turn upward or to one side: *The bird cocked its head.* **2** to draw back and set the hammer of a gun for firing.

cockade *noun* (*plural* **cockades**) a rosette or knot of ribbon worn on the hat as a badge.

cockatoo *noun* (*plural* **cockatoos**) a large parrot with a crest and white plumage.

cockerel *noun* (*plural* **cockerels**) a young male chicken.

cocker spaniel *noun* (*plural* **cocker spaniels**) a small spaniel with long ears and a silky coat.

cockle *noun* (*plural* **cockles**) an edible shellfish with a ribbed shell.

cockney *noun* (*plural* **cockneys**) **1** a person who comes from the East End of London. **2** the dialect or accent of East London. ➤ **cockney** *adjective*.

cockpit *noun* (*plural* **cockpits**) a space in the fuselage of an aircraft or spacecraft for the pilot and crew.

cockroach *noun* (*plural* **cockroaches**) an insect that looks like a beetle with a flattened body and long antennae and lives in dirty places.

cocksure *adjective* *informal* arrogantly self-confident.

cocktail *noun* (*plural* **cocktails**)

1 a mixed alcoholic drink. **2** a mixture of different things.

cocky *adjective* (**cockier, cockiest**) *informal* self-confident in an arrogant or cheeky way.

cocoa /**koh** koh/ *noun* (*plural* **cocoas**) a drink made from roasted and powdered cacao seeds.

coconut *noun* (*plural* **coconuts**) the large oval fruit of a tropical palm, with a hard hairy husk, thick edible white flesh, and sweet milk.

cocoon *noun* (*plural* **cocoons**) **1** a silk envelope which an insect larva forms about itself when going through the pupa stage. **2** a protective covering like a cocoon. ~ *verb* (**cocoons, cocooning, cocooned**) to wrap something or somebody up for protection.

cod *noun* (*plural* **cod**) a large grey sea fish used for food.

coda *noun* (*plural* **codas**) *Music* a separate concluding section to a piece of music.

coddle *verb* (**coddles, coddling, coddled**) **1** to cook eggs slowly in liquid. **2** to treat a person or animal with excessive care.

code *noun* (*plural* **codes**) **1** a system of letters, numbers, or symbols used to represent and replace the normal ones for secrecy. **2** *ICT* a system of numbers and symbols for conveying instructions to a computer. **3** a set of laws, rules, or principles. ~ *verb* (**codes, coding, coded**) to put a message into the form of a code. ➤ **coded** *adjective*.

codicil /**koh** di sil/ *noun* (*plural* **codicils**) a clause added to a will to modify an existing part.

codify *verb* (**codifies, codifying, codified**) to organize laws or rules in a systematic form. ➤ **codification** *noun*.

co-education *noun* the education of students of both sexes at the same school. ➤ **co-educational** *adjective*.

coefficient *noun* (*plural* **coefficients**) *Maths* a number placed before the variable factor in an algebraic expression to show that the expression is multiplied by that number.

coerce /koh **ers**/ *verb* (**coerces, coercing, coerced**) to compel somebody to do something. ➤ **coercion** *noun*.

coexist *verb* (**coexists, coexisting, coexisted**) **1** to exist together or at the same time. **2** to live together harmoniously. ➤ **coexistence** *noun*.

coffee *noun* (*plural* **coffees**) **1** a drink made from the roasted seeds (called beans) of a tropical shrub. **2** the roasted and ground coffee beans from which the drink is made.

coffee table *noun* (*plural* **coffee tables**) a low table placed in a living room.

coffer *noun* (*plural* **coffers**) a chest or box for valuables.

coffin *noun* (*plural* **coffins**) a box or chest for the burial or cremation of a corpse.

cog *noun* (*plural* **cogs**) **1** a tooth on the rim of a wheel or gear. **2** a toothed wheel that engages with others to transmit motion.

cogent /**koh** jint/ *adjective* said about an argument: clear and convincing. ➤ **cogency** *noun*, **cogently** *adverb*.

cogitate /**ko** ji tayt/ *verb* (**cogitates, cogitating, cogitated**) to think carefully about something. ➤ **cogitation** *noun*.

cognac /**kon** yak/ *noun* brandy from the Cognac region of France.

cohabit *verb* (**cohabits, cohabiting, cohabited**) to live together as husband and wife although not married. ➤ **cohabitation** *noun*.

cohere *verb* (**coheres, cohering, cohered**) to hold together firmly. ➤ **cohesion** *noun*, **cohesive** *adjective*.

coherent /koh **heer** int/ *adjective* **1** able to speak clearly and understandably.

cohort

2 said about a statement, essay, etc: logical and consistent. ➤ **coherence** noun, **coherently** adverb.

cohort noun (plural **cohorts**) **1** History a division of a Roman legion. **2** a group of individuals sharing certain characteristics.

coiffure noun (plural **coiffures**) a hairstyle. ➤ **coiffured** adjective.

coil verb (**coils, coiling, coiled**) **1** to wind a rope, etc into rings or spirals. **2** to move in a circular or winding course. ~ noun (plural **coils**) a length of rope, etc gathered into loops.

coin noun (plural **coins**) a small disc of metal used as money. ~ verb (**coins, coining, coined**) **1** to make coins. **2** to invent a new word or phrase.

coinage noun (plural **coinages**) **1** the coins in use in a particular country. **2** a new word or phrase.

coincide /koh in sied/ verb (**coincides, coinciding, coincided**) **1** said about two events: to occur at the same time or place. **2** to be the same: *Our views on this issue coincide.*

coincidence /koh in si dins/ noun (plural **coincidences**) the chance occurrence of two or more events at the same time or place. ➤ **coincidental** adjective, **coincidentally** adverb.

coke noun a solid fuel produced by heating coal.

colander /ko lan der *or* ku lan der/ noun (plural **colanders**) a perforated bowl for washing or draining food.

cold adjective **1** having a low temperature. **2** said about a person or their behaviour: unfriendly and unemotional. **3** dead or unconscious: *He was out cold.* **4** unprepared. ~ noun (plural **colds**) **1** a condition of low temperature. **2** cold weather. **3** an infection characterized by a runny nose and sneezing. ✳ **get cold feet** to become too nervous to do something. **give somebody the cold shoulder** to refuse to be friendly to somebody. **in cold blood** deliberately. ➤ **coldly** adverb, **coldness** noun.

cold-blooded adjective **1** done or acting without feeling; ruthless. **2** said about animals: having a body temperature roughly the same as that of the environment.

Cold War noun (**the Cold War**) History the period between 1945 and 1989 when the Western and Communist alliances were enemies but no actual fighting took place between them.

coleslaw noun a salad of chopped raw cabbage and carrots mixed with mayonnaise.

colic noun pain in the intestines caused by wind. ➤ **colicky** adjective.

collaborate verb (**collaborates, collaborating, collaborated**) **1** to work together on a common project. **2** to cooperate with an enemy. ➤ **collaboration** noun, **collaborative** adjective, **collaborator** noun.

collage /ko lazh/ noun (plural **collages**) *Art* a composition made of pieces of different materials fixed to a surface.

collapse verb (**collapses, collapsing, collapsed**) **1** to fall down or break completely. **2** to fail suddenly and completely. **3** to suffer a breakdown through exhaustion or disease. **4** to fold down into a more compact shape. ~ noun (plural **collapses**) **1** an instance of collapsing. **2** a sudden failure or breakdown. ➤ **collapsible** adjective.

collar noun (plural **collars**) **1** a band of fabric round the neckline of a garment. **2** a band fitted round the neck of a pet animal. ~ verb (**collars, collaring, collared**) *informal* to catch or arrest somebody.

collarbone noun (plural **collarbones**) a bone in the shoulder linking the shoulder blade and breastbone.

collate verb (**collates, collating, collated**) to collect and compare information.

collateral *adjective* secondary or less important. ~ *noun* property pledged by a borrower to secure a loan.

colleague *noun* (*plural* **colleagues**) a fellow worker.

collect *verb* (**collects, collecting, collected**) **1** to bring things or people together. **2** to obtain money from a number of sources. **3** to come together in a group or mass. **4** to fetch something or somebody from a place. **5** to regain control of your thoughts. **6** to assemble a collection of something, such as stamps or coins, as a hobby. ➤ **collectable** *adjective*, **collector** *noun*.

collected *adjective* **1** calm and composed. **2** assembled from a number of sources: *the collected poems of Walter de la Mare.*

collection *noun* (*plural* **collections**) **1** the act of collecting. **2** a group of objects gathered for study or exhibition. **3** an organized effort to collect money from people, for example during a church service or for a charity.

collective *adjective* made or held in common by a group of individuals: *our collective judgment.* ➤ **collectively** *adverb*.

collective noun *noun* (*plural* **collective nouns**) *English* a noun that refers to a number of individuals considered as a group, for example 'herd' or 'pack'.

college *noun* (*plural* **colleges**) **1** an institution that provides education for people who have left school. **2** an independent part of a university: *King's College is part of Cambridge University.* ➤ **collegiate** *adjective*.

collide *verb* (**collides, colliding, collided**) to hit one another while moving. ➤ **collision** *noun*.

collie *noun* (*plural* **collies**) a large dog with a pointed nose and long hair.

colliery *noun* (*plural* **collieries**) a coal-mine and its associated buildings.

colloquial /ko loh kwi al/ *adjective* English in the style of ordinary informal speech; conversational. ➤ **colloquially** *adverb*.

collude *verb* (**colludes, colluding, colluded**) to cooperate with somebody secretly. ➤ **collusion** *noun*.

collywobbles *plural noun informal* **1** discomfort in the stomach. **2** a nervous or anxious feeling.

cologne /ko lohn/ *noun* scented toilet water.

colon¹ *noun* (*plural* **colons**) *Science* the lower end of the large intestine. ➤ **colonic** *adjective*.

colon² *noun* (*plural* **colons**) *English* a punctuation mark (:) used to introduce a quotation, a list of items, or an explanation of the words it follows.

colonel /ker nil/ *noun* (*plural* **colonels**) an officer in the army in command of a regiment.

colonial *adjective* to do with a colony.

colonialism *noun* the policy of establishing colonies to acquire control over other countries. ➤ **colonialist** *noun and adjective*.

colonize *or* **colonise** *verb* (**colonizes, colonizing, colonized**) **1** to establish a colony in a place. **2** said about plants and animals: to begin to live and breed in a new area or environment. ➤ **colonization** *or* **colonisation** *noun*.

colonnade *noun* (*plural* **colonnades**) a row of columns supporting a roof.

colony *noun* (*plural* **colonies**) **1** a group of settlers living in a new territory that is controlled by the state that the settlers come from. **2** the territory settled or controlled in this way. **3** a group of people or animals living close together.

coloration *or* **colouration** *noun* colouring.

colossal *adjective* very large or great. ➤ **colossally** *adverb*.

colossus

colossus *noun* (*plural* **colossuses** *or* **colossi** /ko lo sie/) **1** a statue of gigantic size. **2** a person or thing of great size or importance.

colour *noun* (*plural* **colours**) **1** a visual sensation of things being red, blue, yellow, etc, caused by the wavelength of light. **2** a hue or shade, such as red or blue. **3** a substance that gives colour when applied to an object. **4** the skin colour characteristic of a particular race. **5** (*often* **colours**) the flag of a ship or regiment. **6** vitality or interest. ~ *verb* (**colours, colouring, coloured**) **1** to give colour to something. **2** to influence or affect somebody's opinion or judgment. **3** to blush.

colouration *noun* see COLORATION.

colour-blind *adjective* unable to distinguish certain colours. ➤ **colour blindness** *noun*.

coloured *adjective* **1** having colour. **2** *offensive* having a brown or black skin.

colourful *adjective* **1** having striking colours. **2** full of variety or interest. ➤ **colourfully** *adverb*.

colouring *noun* (*plural* **colourings**) **1** the application or combination of colours. **2** the effect produced by colours. **3** complexion.

colourless *adjective* **1** lacking colour. **2** dull or uninteresting.

colt *noun* (*plural* **colts**) a young male horse.

column *noun* (*plural* **columns**) **1** a round pillar. **2** a long narrow formation of soldiers, vehicles, etc in rows. **3** a vertical section of printing on a page. **4** a regular feature in a newspaper or magazine. ➤ **columnist** *noun*.

coma /koh ma/ *noun* (*plural* **comas**) a state of prolonged deep unconsciousness. ➤ **comatose** *adjective*.

comb *noun* (*plural* **combs**) **1** a flat object with teeth, used for arranging or holding your hair. **2** a toothed device used to separate and arrange textile fibres. **3** a fleshy crest on the head of a cock. **4** a honeycomb. ~ *verb* (**combs, combing, combed**) **1** to smooth or arrange your hair with a comb. **2** to search an area thoroughly.

combat *noun* (*plural* **combats**) **1** a fight or contest. **2** active fighting in a war. ~ *verb* (**combats, combating, combated**) to act to prevent something bad or unwelcome: *strategies to combat inflation*.

combatant *noun* (*plural* **combatants**) a person or state engaged in combat.

combative *adjective* eager to fight.

combination *noun* (*plural* **combinations**) **1** the act of combining things. **2** a collection of people or things that have been combined. **3** the sequence of letters or numbers that will open a combination lock.

combination lock *noun* (*plural* **combination locks**) a lock operated by entering a specific combination of letters or numbers.

combine /kom bien/ *verb* (**combines, combining, combined**) **1** to unite or mix. **2** to act together. ~ /kom bien/ *noun* a combination of people or organizations for commercial activities.

combine harvester *noun* (*plural* **combine harvesters**) a harvesting machine that cuts, threshes, and cleans grain while moving over a field.

combustible *adjective* able to catch fire easily.

combustion *noun* **1** the act of burning. **2** *Science* the chemical process in which substances combine with oxygen from the air to produce light and heat.

come *verb* (**comes, coming, came, come**) **1** to move from a place in a direction towards the speaker. **2** to arrive: *They're coming at 7.30*. **3** to happen: *No harm will come to you*. **4** to

move into a certain state: *The screws have come loose.* **5** to reach a certain position or limit: *to come to an end.* **6** to be available in a specified form: *The product comes in three sizes.*
✻ **come across** to meet or find something by chance. **come by** to manage to get something. **come clean** *informal* to admit everything. **come down 1** to decrease in amount or price. **2** said about an aircraft: to land or crash. **come of** to result from something. **come off** to work or succeed. **come on 1** to make progress. **2** to hurry up. **come out 1** to be published or made public. **2** to declare yourself in favour of or opposed to something. **3** to declare yourself to be homosexual. **come out with** to say something unexpected. **come to 1** to recover consciousness. **2** to reach a total. **come to pass** to happen. **come up** to arise or occur. **come up with** to think of an idea or solution.

comeback *noun* (*plural* **comebacks**) a return to former success or popularity.

comedian *noun* (*plural* **comedians**) an entertainer who aims at making people laugh.

comedown *noun informal* **1** a loss of rank or dignity. **2** a disappointment.

comedy *noun* (*plural* **comedies**) *Drama* a light and amusing kind of play, film, etc.

comely /kum li/ *adjective* (**comelier, comeliest**) attractive.

comestibles *plural noun formal* food.

comet *noun* (*plural* **comets**) an object moving through space consisting of an icy nucleus surrounded by a trailing cloud of gas and dust.

comfort *noun* (*plural* **comforts**) **1** conditions in which your body can feel relaxed. **2** consolation or encouragement in time of trouble or worry. ~ *verb* (**comforts, comforting, comforted**) to cheer somebody up or console them. ➤ **comforter** *noun*.

comfortable *adjective* **1** providing or feeling physical comfort. **2** said about a win or success: achieved with ease. **3** free from stress or tension. ➤ **comfortably** *adverb*.

comfy *adjective* (**comfier, comfiest**) *informal* comfortable.

comic *adjective* funny. ~ *noun* (*plural* **comics**) **1** a comedian. **2** a magazine containing strip cartoons.

comical *adjective* funny. ➤ **comically** *adverb*.

comma *noun* (*plural* **commas**) *English* a punctuation mark (,) used to separate parts of a sentence or list.

command *verb* (**commands, commanding, commanded**) **1** to give an order to somebody. **2** to be in charge of a military force. **3** to ask for and receive something: *to command respect.* ~ *noun* (*plural* **commands**) **1** an order to somebody to do something. **2** a position as leader with the authority to give orders: *took command of the regiment.* **3** the ability to use or control something effectively: *her poor command of the language.* **4** *ICT* an instruction that makes a computer perform a function. ➤ **commander** *noun.*

commandant /ko man dant/ *noun* (*plural* **commandants**) a commanding officer.

commandeer /ko man deer/ *verb* (**commandeers, commandeering, commandeered**) to take something with or without the owner's consent for military purposes or for your own use.

commander-in-chief *noun* (*plural* **commanders-in-chief**) an officer in overall command of the armed forces of a country.

commandment *noun* (*plural* **commandments**) a rule or law, for example one of the Ten Commandments.

commando *noun* (*plural* **commandos**) a soldier trained to carry out raids.

commemorate *verb* (**commemorates, commemorating, commemorated**) to remember and honour an event or a person from the past with a ceremony. ➤ **commemoration** *noun*, **commemorative** *adjective*.

commence *verb* (**commences, commencing, commenced**) to start or begin something. ➤ **commencement** *noun*.

commend *verb* (**commends, commending, commended**) 1 to praise somebody or something. 2 to entrust a person or thing to somebody for care or preservation. ➤ **commendation** *noun*.

commendable *adjective* deserving praise; admirable. ➤ **commendably** *adverb*.

comment *noun* (*plural* **comments**) 1 a remark expressing an opinion or attitude. 2 discussion of a topical issue. ~ *verb* (**comments, commenting, commented**) to make a comment on something.

commentary *noun* (*plural* **commentaries**) 1 a description of an event as it happens, especially for radio or television. 2 a series of explanations or interpretations of a book, play, etc.

commentate *verb* (**commentates, commentating, commentated**) to give a commentary on an event. ➤ **commentator** *noun*.

commerce *noun* the buying and selling of goods.

commercial *adjective* 1 to do with commerce. 2 likely to be profitable. 3 supported by advertising: *commercial television*. ~ *noun* (*plural* **commercials**) a television or radio advertisement. ➤ **commercially** *adverb*.

commercialism *noun* the attitude that doing business and making a profit are the most important considerations in anything.

commercialized *or* **commercialised** *adjective* organized so as to benefit businesses who want to make a profit.

commiserate *verb* (**commiserates, commiserating, commiserated**) to express sympathy. ➤ **commiseration** *noun*.

commission *noun* (*plural* **commissions**) 1 an authorization or command to perform a task. 2 a group of people who are authorized to perform a duty or investigate something. 3 a fee that is a percentage of the amount of money that an agent or employee has made for their employer. 4 an appointment as an officer in the armed services. ~ *verb* (**commissions, commissioning, commissioned**) to instruct somebody to perform a task or function. ✱ **out of commission** out of use or working order. ➤ **commissioner** *noun*.

commissionaire /ko mi sho nair/ *noun* (*plural* **commissionaires**) a uniformed attendant at a hotel, theatre, etc.

commit *verb* (**commits, committing, committed**) 1 to carry out a crime. 2 to entrust something or somebody to somebody's care. 3 to place somebody in a prison or psychiatric hospital. ✱ **commit yourself** to state definitely that you will do something or that you believe something. ➤ **committed** *adjective*.

commitment *noun* (*plural* **commitments**) 1 an agreement or promise to do something. 2 an engagement or obligation: *I can't see you this afternoon, I have too many other commitments*. 3 loyalty to a system of thought or action.

committal *noun* (*plural* **committals**) 1 the sending of somebody to prison or a psychiatric hospital, or for trial. 2 the burial of a body.

committee *noun* (*plural* **committees**) a group of people elected or appointed to make decisions or discuss and investigate matters on behalf of an organization.

commodious *adjective formal* comfortable or spacious.

commodity *noun* (*plural* **commodities**) **1** something that can be bought and sold. **2** something useful or valuable.

commodore *noun* (*plural* **commodores**) a senior captain in a merchant shipping line or navy.

common *adjective* **1** occurring or appearing frequently: *a common sight.* **2** belonging to or shared by two or more individuals: *a common interest.* **3** affecting the community at large; public: *for the common good.* **4** not having special status or privileges: *the common people.* **5** lacking refinement; vulgar. ~ *noun* (*plural* **commons**) an area of land available for the general public to use. ✻ **common or garden** ordinary or everyday. **in common 1** shared together. **2** used jointly. ➤ **commonly** *adverb*.

commoner *noun* (*plural* **commoners**) somebody who is not royal or noble.

Common Market *noun* (**the Common Market**) the economic association that became the European Union.

common noun *noun* (*plural* **common nouns**) *English* a noun that is the name of a general class or type of person or thing rather than of one particular person or thing, for example *boy* as opposed to *Tom*, or *city* as opposed to *London*.

commonplace *adjective* ordinary or unremarkable. ~ *noun* (*plural* **commonplaces**) an obvious or unoriginal saying.

common room *noun* (*plural* **common rooms**) a room in a school or college that staff or students can use when they are not working.

common sense *noun* sound practical judgment based on ordinary experience. ➤ **commonsensical** *adjective*.

Commonwealth *noun* (**the Commonwealth**) an association consisting of the United Kingdom and states that were formerly British colonies.

commotion *noun* **1** a noisy disturbance. **2** noisy activity.

communal *adjective* shared or used in common by members of a group or community. ➤ **communally** *adverb*.

commune /ko **mewn**/ *noun* (*plural* **communes**) a community of individuals or families who share their possessions. ~ /ko **mewn**/ *verb* (**communes, communing, communed**) (**commune with**) to have a private conversation with somebody or receive feelings and influences from something: *communing with nature.*

communicable *adjective* said about a disease: able to be transmitted to other people.

communicant *noun* (*plural* **communicants**) a full member of a church who is entitled to take part in Communion.

communicate *verb* (**communicates, communicating, communicated**) **1** to pass on or share information about something. **2** said about rooms: to lead from one to another through a connecting door. ➤ **communicator** *noun*.

communication *noun* (*plural* **communications**) **1** the exchange of knowledge or information. **2** a verbal or written message. **3** (**communications**) the systems that enable people to communicate, e.g. roads and railways or telephones and radios.

communicative *adjective* talkative.

communion *noun* **1** a close relationship. **2** (**Communion**) the religious service in Christian churches in which bread and wine are shared.

communiqué /ko **mew**ni kay/ *noun*

(*plural* **communiqués**) an official announcement.

communism *noun* **1** a political theory or system advocating abolition of private property. **2** (**Communism**) a political and economic system based on Marxist socialism, formerly followed in the Soviet Union and its allies. ➤ **communist** *noun and adjective*.

community *noun* (*plural* **communities**) a group of people living in a particular area or sharing the same religion, ethnic origins, profession, etc.

community service *noun* work done by offenders for the benefit of the community, as an alternative to a prison sentence.

commute *verb* (**commutes, commuting, commuted**) **1** to use a form of transport to travel regularly between home and work. **2** to reduce a severe punishment to a less severe one: *The death sentence was commuted to life imprisonment.* ➤ **commuter** *noun*.

compact[1] /kom pakt/ *adjective* **1** consisting of parts or material closely packed or joined. **2** efficiently occupying a small space or container. ~ /kom pakt/ *noun* (*plural* **compacts**) a small case for face powder. ~ /kom pakt/ *verb* (**compacts, compacting, compacted**) to press loose material together to make it firm.

compact[2] /kom pakt/ *noun* (*plural* **compacts**) an agreement or contract.

compact disc *noun* (*plural* **compact discs**) a small disc on which sound or information is stored in digital form.

companion *noun* (*plural* **companions**) **1** a person who accompanies or spends time with somebody. **2** something belonging to a pair or set of matching things. **3** a handbook on a subject: *a crossword companion*. ➤ **companionship** *noun*.

companionable *adjective* friendly and sociable.

company *noun* (*plural* **companies**) **1** a business organization. **2** having other people with you: *She likes company.* **3** visitors or guests. **4** a unit of soldiers. **5** an organization of musical or dramatic performers.

comparable *adjective* **1** able to be compared. **2** approximately equivalent; similar. ➤ **comparably** *adverb*.

comparative *adjective* **1** considered in comparison to something else: *In this group of old friends, Paula was a comparative stranger.* **2** *English* said about an adjective or adverb: expressing a greater degree or amount, for example *smaller* or *sooner*. ➤ **comparative** *noun*, **comparatively** *adverb*.

compare *verb* (**compares, comparing, compared**) to examine a number of things or people in order to discover resemblances or differences. ✱ **cannot compare with** is nothing like as good as something else. **compare notes** to exchange information or opinions. **compare to** to say that somebody or something is like somebody or something else: *I've never been compared to Einstein before.* **compare to/with** to say how one thing or person is like or unlike another: *How does life at university compare with life at home?*

comparison *noun* (*plural* **comparisons**) the comparing of one thing or person to or with another.

compartment *noun* (*plural* **compartments**) **1** any of the parts into which an enclosed space is divided. **2** a separate division or section.

compass *noun* (*plural* **compasses**) **1** an instrument with a needle that points to magnetic north, used to find directions. **2** (*also* **compasses**) an instrument for drawing circles, consisting of two arms joined at one end by a handle round which they pivot.

compassion *noun* sympathetic concern for the hardships of others. ➤ **compassionate** *adjective*, **compassionately** *adverb*.

compatible *adjective* **1** able to exist or live together in harmony. **2** said about equipment: able to be used together. ➤ **compatibility** *noun*.

compatriot /kom pa tri ot/ *noun* (*plural* **compatriots**) a person from the same country as you.

compel *verb* (**compels, compelling, compelled**) **1** to force somebody to do something.

compelling *adjective* very powerful, convincing, or absorbing. ➤ **compellingly** *adverb*.

compendium *noun* (*plural* **compendiums** *or* **compendia**) **1** a book that gathers together a lot of information on a subject. **2** a collection of games and puzzles.

compensate *verb* (**compensates, compensating, compensated**) (**compensate for**) **1** to give somebody money, etc to repay them for damage, loss, or injury that they have suffered. **2** to cancel out something bad: *Her good behaviour yesterday can't compensate for her bad behaviour last Saturday.* ➤ **compensation** *noun*, **compensatory** *adjective*.

compere /kom pair/ *noun* (*plural* **comperes**) the presenter of a radio or television programme or a variety show.

compete *verb* (**competes, competing, competed**) **1** to try to do as well as or better than others, or to be able to do so: *We'll have to cut our costs if we are to compete with the Koreans.* **2** to take part in a competition.

competent *adjective* showing an ability to carry out a task properly. ➤ **competence** *noun*, **competently** *adverb*.

competition *noun* (*plural* **competitions**) **1** the process of competing. **2** an organized test of people's skills, performance, etc to find out who is best. **3** the people or organizations you are competing with.

competitive *adjective* **1** involving competition. **2** liking to compete. **3** at least as good as those offered by rivals: *a competitive price.* ➤ **competitively** *adverb*.

competitor *noun* (*plural* **competitors**) **1** a person or thing that competes with others. **2** a person who takes part in a race or competition.

compile *verb* (**compiles, compiling, compiled**) to put together a book or collection from various materials. ➤ **compilation** *noun*.

complacent *adjective* uncritically satisfied that there is no need to change the way you do things. ➤ **complacency** *noun*, **complacently** *adverb*.

complain *verb* (**complains, complaining, complained**) **1** to express feelings of discontent or dissatisfaction. **2** to say that you have a pain or symptom.

complaint *noun* (*plural* **complaints**) **1** an expression of discontent. **2** a minor illness.

complement /kom pli mint/ *noun* (*plural* **complements**) **1** something that makes something else complete or adds extra features. **2** the total number of staff or passengers required. **3** *English* in grammar, a word or expression that follows a verb such as 'be' or 'become' and gives information about the subject of the sentence, for example 'red' in the sentence *The roof is red.* ~ /kom pli ment/ *verb* (**complements, complementing, complemented**) to add to something or go well with it: *a scarf that complements the rest of the outfit.*

Usage Note Do not confuse **complement** and **compliment**.

complementary *adjective* **1** that completes or goes well with something. **2** said about medicine: not based on conventional science.

complete *adjective* **1** having all its necessary parts; whole or entire. **2** fully carried out; thorough. **3** total or absolute: *a complete fiasco*. ~ *verb* (**completes, completing, completed**) **1** to bring something to an end; to finish doing something. **2** to make something whole or perfect. **3** to fill in a form. ➤ **completely** *adverb*, **completion** *noun*.

complex *adjective* **1** composed of two or more parts. **2** hard to analyse or solve. ~ *noun* (*plural* **complexes**) **1** a set of buildings forming a unit. **2** a group of repressed feelings that have a bad effect on somebody's personality and behaviour. ➤ **complexity** *noun*.

complexion *noun* (*plural* **complexions**) the appearance of the skin of a person's face.

compliance *noun* willingness to obey the wishes of others. ➤ **compliant** *adjective*.

complicate *verb* (**complicates, complicating, complicated**) to make something complex or difficult.

complicated *adjective* **1** difficult to analyse, understand, or explain. **2** consisting of several parts intricately combined.

complication *noun* (*plural* **complications**) **1** the act of complicating something. **2** a factor that occurs unexpectedly and affects a situation. **3** a secondary illness developing while another illness is being treated.

complicity *noun* participation in a wrongful act.

compliment /kom pli mint/ *noun* (*plural* **compliments**) **1** words or an action to express your admiration. **2** (**compliments**) best wishes; regards. ~ /kom pli ment/ *verb* (**compliments,** **complimenting, complimented**) to pay a compliment to somebody: *She complimented me on my performance.*

Usage Note Do not confuse **compliment** and **complement**.

complimentary *adjective* **1** expressing or containing a compliment. **2** given free of charge.

comply *verb* (**complies, complying complied**) (**comply with**) **1** to obey a rule or act in accordance with somebody's wishes. **2** to meet a certain standard.

component *noun* (*plural* **components**) a part, especially of a machine. ~ *adjective* said about a part: helping to make up a whole.

compose *verb* (**composes, composing, composed**) **1** to combine together to form something. **2** to create a work of art, especially a piece of music or poem. **3** to calm or settle yourself. ✱ **be composed of** to be made up of various things or people.

composed *adjective* calm.

composer *noun* (*plural* **composers**) *Music* a person who writes music.

composite /kom po zit/ *adjective* made up of separate parts or constituents.

composition *noun* (*plural* **compositions**) **1** a piece of writing or music. **2** the act of composing works of art. **3** the various elements or ingredients that make up something.

compos mentis /kom pos men tis/ *adjective* of sound mind; sane.

compost *noun* decayed organic matter used as a fertilizer.

composure *noun* calmness of mind or behaviour.

compound[1] /kom pownd/ *noun* (*plural* **compounds**) something formed by combining different elements or parts. ~ *adjective* made by combining separate elements or parts. ~ /kom pownd/ *verb* (**compounds,**

compounding, compounded) 1 to combine things. **2** to make something bad worse.

compound² /kom pownd/ *noun* (*plural* **compounds**) an enclosed area containing a group of buildings.

comprehend *verb* (**comprehends, comprehending, comprehended**) to understand something. **2** *formal* to include a range of things.

comprehensible *adjective* understandable.

comprehension *noun* (*plural* **comprehensions**) **1** the process of or capacity for understanding. **2** an exercise testing student's understanding of a passage.

comprehensive *adjective* **1** including everything involved in something. **2** said about education or schools: teaching children of all levels of ability together. ~ *noun* (*plural* **comprehensives**) a comprehensive school. ➤ **comprehensively** *adverb*.

compress /kom pres/ *verb* (**compresses, compressing, compressed**) **1** to press or squeeze something together. **2** to force something into a smaller space.
~ /kom pres/ *noun* a pad pressed on to a part of the body to ease the pain and swelling of a bruise. ➤ **compression** *noun*, **compressor** *noun*.

comprise *verb* (**comprises, comprising, comprised**) to be made up of a specified number or amount of people or things: *The family comprises two adults and three children.*

Usage Note Do not use *of* with *comprise*. It is wrong to say that something *is comprised of* something. Instead say it *consists of* or *is composed of* something.

compromise /kom pro miez/ *noun* (*plural* **compromises**) a settlement reached by each side giving way on some points. ~ *verb* (**compromises, compromising, compromised**) **1** to reach an agreement by each side giving way on some points. **2** to expose somebody to suspicion or danger. **3** to go against your principles in order to achieve or gain something.

compulsion *noun* (*plural* **compulsions**) **1** compelling somebody or being compelled to do something. **2** an irresistible desire to do something.

compulsive *adjective* unable to stop doing something: *a compulsive liar.*
➤ **compulsively** *adverb*.

compulsory *adjective* that has to be done by a law or rule.

compunction *noun* anxiety arising from a feeling of compassion or guilt: *He had no compunction about fiddling his tax return.*

compute *verb* (**computes, computing, computed**) to calculate a quantity or number.

computer *noun* (*plural* **computers**) *ICT* an electronic device that can store, retrieve, and process data following instructions given by a user or a program.

computerize *or* **computerise** *verb* (**computerizes, computerizing, computerized** *or* **computerises**, etc) *ICT* to carry out an operation or process by means of a computer.

comrade *noun* (*plural* **comrades**) **1** a friend or associate. **2** a member of the same organization. ➤ **comradeship** *noun*.

con *noun* (*plural* **cons**) *informal* a confidence trick. ~ *verb* (**cons, conning, conned**) *informal* to cheat or deceive somebody.

concave *adjective* rounded inwards like the inside of a bowl.

conceal *verb* (**conceals, concealing, concealed**) **1** to hide something or somebody. **2** to keep something secret. ➤ **concealment** *noun*.

concede *verb* (**concedes, conceding,**

conceded) **1** to admit that something is true or accurate. **2** to grant a right or privilege to somebody. **3** to allow a goal or point to be scored against you. **4** to admit defeat.

conceit *noun* an excessively high opinion of yourself. ➤ **conceited** *adjective*.

conceivable *adjective* able to be imagined or believed. ➤ **conceivably** *adverb*.

conceive *verb* (**conceives, conceiving, conceived**) **1** to become pregnant. **2** to visualize or imagine something.

concentrate *verb* (**concentrates, concentrating, concentrated**) **1** to focus your mind or attention on something. **2** to gather things or people together in one place. **3** to remove water from a solution to make it stronger.

concentration *noun* (*plural* **concentrations**) **1** attention totally focused on something. **2** *Science* the amount of a substance in a mixture or a solution.

concentration camp *noun* (*plural* **concentration camps**) a camp where political prisoners are confined.

concept *noun* (*plural* **concepts**) a thought or idea.

conception *noun* (*plural* **conceptions**) **1** the process of conceiving a baby; the beginning of pregnancy. **2** a general idea or concept.

concern *verb* (**concerns, concerning, concerned**) **1** to be about something or somebody. **2** to involve or have an influence on something or somebody. **3** to be a cause of trouble or distress to somebody. ~ *noun* (*plural* **concerns**) **1** something that relates to or involves somebody. **2** anxiety or a cause of anxiety. **3** a business organization.

concerned *adjective* anxious or troubled.

concerning *preposition* about; relating to.

concert *noun* (*plural* **concerts**) *Music* a public performance of music.

concerted /kon ser tid/ *adjective* planned or done together: *a concerted effort*.

concertina *noun* (*plural* **concertinas**) *Music* a small musical instrument played by squeezing like an accordion.

concerto /kon cher toh/ *noun* (*plural* **concertos**) *Music* a piece of music for an orchestra and one or more soloists.

concession *noun* (*plural* **concessions**) **1** the act of conceding something. **2** something that you allow or grant to somebody. **3** a reduction in price for people in certain categories.

conciliate *verb* (**conciliates, conciliating, conciliated**) to act in a friendly way towards somebody to stop them from being angry or hostile. ➤ **conciliation** *noun*, **conciliatory** *adjective*.

concise *adjective* brief and clear, with a minimum of detail. ➤ **concisely** *adverb*, **concision** *noun*.

conclave *noun* (*plural* **conclaves**) a private meeting or assembly.

conclude *verb* (**concludes, concluding, concluded**) **1** to come to an end, or bring something to an end. **2** to arrive at an opinion by reasoning: *I concluded that they were right after all*.

conclusion *noun* **1** an end or ending. **2** a final summing up of an argument or essay. **3** a judgment arrived at by reasoning.

conclusive *adjective* putting an end to debate or question; decisive. ➤ **conclusively** *adverb*.

concoct *verb* (**concocts, concocting, concocted**) **1** to prepare something from various ingredients. **2** to invent a story or excuse. ➤ **concoction** *noun*.

concord *noun* a state of agreement or harmony.

concourse *noun* (*plural* **concourses**) a

large open space in a building or where roads or paths meet.

concrete *adjective* **1** real. **2** specific or particular. ~ *noun* a building material made by mixing cement, sand, and gravel with water. ~ *verb* (**concretes, concreting, concreted**) to cover an area with concrete.

concur *verb* (**concurs, concurring, concurred**) to agree with somebody.

concurrent *adjective* occurring at the same time. ➤ **concurrence** *noun*, **concurrently** *adverb*.

concussion *noun* temporary unconsciousness caused by a blow to the head. ➤ **concussed** *adjective*.

condemn *verb* (**condemns, condemning, condemned**) **1** to declare a person or an action to be utterly wrong or bad. **2** to sentence somebody to a punishment, especially death. **3** to cause somebody to suffer something unpleasant. **4** to declare a building unfit for use. ➤ **condemnation** *noun*.

condensation *noun* **1** droplets of water formed on a cold surface when water vapour in the air cools and becomes liquid. **2** *Science* the process of changing from a vapour or gas to a liquid.

condense *verb* (**condenses, condensing, condensed**) **1** to express something in fewer words. **2** *Science* to change from a vapour or gas to a liquid.

condensed milk *noun* milk thickened by evaporation and sweetened.

condescend *verb* (**condescends, condescending, condescended**) **1** to act towards a person in a way that suggests that you are superior to them. **2** to agree to do something that is normally beneath your dignity: *He even condescended to help with the washing-up.* ➤ **condescending** *adjective*, **condescension** *noun*.

condiment *noun* (*plural* **condiments**) a flavouring for food, such as pepper or mustard.

condition *noun* (*plural* **conditions**) **1** the state of something with regard to its appearance or fitness for use: *in good condition*. **2** a defective state of health: *a heart condition*. **3** (**conditions**) the surroundings and circumstances in which somebody lives, works, etc: *Conditions in the prison were very bad.* **4** something that must exist or must be done in order to allow something else to exist or be done. ~ *verb* (**conditions, conditioning, conditioned**) **1** to train a person or animal to act in a particular way. **2** to put something into a proper or desired state. ✴ **on condition that** providing that.

conditional *adjective* **1** subject to a condition: *conditional acceptance*. **2** *English* in grammar, expressing something that must happen to enable something else to happen, often using the word 'if'. ➤ **conditionally** *adverb*.

conditioner *noun* (*plural* **conditioners**) a substance applied to hair or fabric to improve its condition.

condolences /kon doh lin siz/ *plural noun* expressions of sympathy, especially after somebody has died.

condom *noun* (*plural* **condoms**) a sheath worn over the penis during sexual intercourse to prevent conception or the transmission of disease.

condone *verb* (**condones, condoning, condoned**) to pardon or overlook an offence.

condor *noun* (*plural* **condors**) a large South American vulture.

conducive *adjective* (**conducive to**) likely to cause something.

conduct /kon dukt/ *noun* **1** personal behaviour. **2** the way in which something is carried out. ~ /kon dukt/ *verb* (**conducts, conducting, conducted**) **1** to guide or escort somebody somewhere. **2** to carry on or direct an

conductor

operation. **3** to be able to transmit heat, light, or electricity. **4** *Music* to direct the performance of a musical work. ✳ **conduct yourself** to act or behave.

conductor *noun* (*plural* **conductors**) **1** a person who directs a group of musicians. **2** a substance capable of transmitting electricity or heat. **3** somebody who collects fares on a bus.

conduit *noun* (*plural* **conduits**) **1** a channel for conveying fluid. **2** a tube protecting electric wires or cables.

cone *noun* (*plural* **cones**) **1** *Maths* a solid shape that tapers evenly to a point from a circular base. **2** a cone-shaped wafer for holding ice cream. **3** the hard fruit of a pine or fir tree.

confectionery *noun* sweets and chocolate.

confederation or **confederacy** *noun* (*plural* **confederations** or **confederacies**) an alliance of independent states.

confer *verb* (**confers, conferring, conferred**) **1** to bestow an honour or award on somebody. **2** to hold a discussion or consultation with somebody.

conference *noun* (*plural* **conferences**) a formal meeting for discussions.

confess *verb* (**confesses, confessing, confessed**) to admit that you have done wrong.

confession *noun* **1** an admission of a wrongdoing. **2** an admission of your sins to a priest.

confessional *noun* (*plural* **confessionals**) a cubicle in a church where a priest hears confessions.

confessor *noun* (*plural* **confessors**) a priest who hears confessions and gives absolution.

confetti *noun* small pieces of coloured paper for throwing over the bride and groom at a wedding.

confidant or **confidante** *noun* (*plural* **confidants** or **confidantes**) a friend that you can confide in.

confide *verb* (**confides, confiding, confided**) (**confide in**) to tell secrets and other private matters to somebody.

confidence *noun* (*plural* **confidences**) **1** strong trust in something or somebody. **2** a feeling that your own abilities are sufficient to enable you to do something successfully. **3** a secret. ✳ **in confidence** as private or secret information.

confidence trick *noun* (*plural* **confidence tricks**) a swindle performed by getting somebody to trust you.

confident *adjective* **1** showing confidence. **2** convinced; certain. ➤ **confidently** *adverb*.

confidential *adjective* intended to be kept secret. ➤ **confidentiality** *noun*, **confidentially** *adverb*.

configuration *noun* (*plural* **configurations**) an arrangement of parts relative one to another.

confine *verb* (**confines, confining, confined**) **1** to keep something within certain limits. **2** to keep somebody shut up in a place. **3** said about an illness or injury: to keep somebody in bed or a wheelchair.

confined *adjective* said about a space: cramped or enclosed.

confinement *noun* **1** a state of being confined. **2** the time when a woman is about to give birth.

confirm *verb* (**confirms, confirming, confirmed**) **1** to establish that a report, suspicion, etc is correct. **2** to be evidence or proof of something. **3** to say definitely that you want an arrangement or booking to be made. **4** to make a person a full member of a Christian church. ➤ **confirmation** *noun*.

confiscate verb (**confiscates, confiscating, confiscated**) to use your authority to take something away from somebody. ➤ **confiscation** noun.

conflagration noun (plural **conflagrations**) a large and disastrous fire.

conflict /ˈkonflikt/ noun (plural **conflicts**) **1** war or fighting. **2** a sharp disagreement or clash. ~ /kənˈflikt/ verb (**conflicts, conflicting, conflicted**) to be incompatible with or in opposition to each other.

confluence noun (plural **confluences**) the meeting of two rivers or streams.

conform verb (**conforms, conforming, conformed**) **1** to behave in a way that accords with generally accepted rules and practices. **2** to correspond to a certain standard or pattern: *All our equipment conforms with official safety standards.* ➤ **conformist** noun and adjective, **conformity** noun.

confound verb (**confounds, confounding, confounded**) **1** to surprise or puzzle somebody. **2** to prove an argument or prediction wrong.

confront verb (**confronts, confronting, confronted**) **1** said about a problem, situation, etc: to have to be dealt with by somebody. **2** to face up to a problem or an opponent. **3** to present somebody with unwelcome facts.

confrontation noun (plural **confrontations**) a situation in which people or groups meet face to face in a hostile way. ➤ **confrontational** adjective.

confuse verb (**confuses, confusing, confused**) **1** to make somebody feel that they do not clearly know what is happening. **2** to mistake one person or thing for another. ➤ **confused** adjective, **confusing** adjective, **confusion** noun.

conga noun (plural **congas**) a dance performed by a group in single file.

congeal verb (**congeals, congealing, congealed**) to become solid during cooking or freezing.

congenial adjective pleasant and suited to your tastes.

congenital adjective said about a disease or abnormality: existing from birth.

congested adjective **1** crowded with people or traffic. **2** said about the lungs or nose: blocked by mucus. ➤ **congestion** noun.

conglomerate noun (plural **conglomerates**) a large business organization formed when one company acquires several other companies.

congratulate verb (**congratulates, congratulating, congratulated**) to tell somebody that you are pleased about their success or good fortune. ➤ **congratulation** noun, **congratulatory** adjective.

congregate verb (**congregates, congregating, congregated**) to gather together.

congregation noun (plural **congregations**) an assembly of people for a religious service.

congress noun (plural **congresses**) **1** a conference. **2** (**Congress**) the supreme law-making body of the USA and some other countries. ➤ **congressional** adjective.

congruent adjective *Maths* said about triangles: identical in size and shape.

conical adjective having the shape of a cone.

conifer noun (plural **conifers**) a tree that bears cones, for example the fir or the pine. ➤ **coniferous** adjective.

conjecture noun (plural **conjectures**) a conclusion or opinion based on incomplete evidence. ➤ **conjectural** adjective. ~ verb (**conjectures, conjecturing, conjectured**) to guess.

conjugal /ˈkonjoohgəl/ adjective to do with marriage or married people.

conjugate /kon jooh gayt/ *verb* (**conjugates, conjugating, conjugated**) *English* to give the different forms of a verb. ➤ **conjugation** *noun*.

conjunction *noun English* in grammar, a word that links words or clauses, such as 'and', 'or', 'but', 'if', and 'when'. ✱ **in conjunction with** acting or occurring together with somebody or something.

conjunctivitis *noun* inflammation of the lining of the eyelid.

conjure *verb* (**conjures, conjuring, conjured**) to perform tricks that appear to use magic. ✱ **conjure up** to bring ideas or images into people's minds. ➤ **conjurer** *or* **conjuror** *noun*.

conk *verb* (**conks, conking, conked**) ✱ **conk out** *informal* said about a machine: to break down.

conker *noun* (*plural* **conkers**) the hard shiny brown nut of the horse chestnut tree.

connect *verb* (**connects, connecting, connected**) **1** to link things together. **2** to think of things as having something in common. **3** to link two callers by telephone. ➤ **connective** *adjective*, **connector** *noun*.

connection *noun* (*plural* **connections**) **1** something that connects; a link. **2** a relationship or association. **3** a train, bus, plane, etc that you transfer to in order to continue a journey. **4** somebody you know socially or through your work.

connive *verb* (**connives, conniving, connived**) (**connive at**) to ignore or secretly support a wrong action. ➤ **connivance** *noun*.

connoisseur /ko no ser/ *noun* (*plural* **connoisseurs**) an expert judge in matters of taste: *a connoisseur of fine wines*.

connotation *noun* (*plural* **connotations**) *English* something suggested by a word as distinct from its direct meaning.

conquer *verb* (**conquers, conquering, conquered**) **1** to defeat and gain control over a country or its people. **2** to overcome a bad feeling or a weakness. ➤ **conqueror** *noun*.

conquest *noun* (*plural* **conquests**) **1** the act of conquering. **2** a conquered territory. **3** a person who has been won over by love or sexual attraction.

conscience /kon shins/ *noun* (*plural* **consciences**) the part of your mind that judges your actions and tells you if you have done wrong.

conscientious /kon shi en shus/ *adjective* very careful to do your work properly or keep your promises. ➤ **conscientiously** *adverb*.

conscious *adjective* **1** aware of and able to respond to your surroundings. **2** aware of something. **3** said about an action: deliberate. ➤ **consciously** *adverb*, **consciousness** *noun*.

conscript /kon skript/ *noun* (*plural* **conscripts**) a person who has been called for military service. ~ /kon skript/ *verb* (**conscripts, conscripting, conscripted**) to make somebody do military service. ➤ **conscription** *noun*.

consecrate *verb* (**consecrates, consecrating, consecrated**) to make something sacred by a solemn ceremony. ➤ **consecration** *noun*.

consecutive *adjective* following one another in order without gaps. ➤ **consecutively** *adverb*.

consensus *noun* a situation where most people agree about something.

consent *verb* (**consents, consenting, consented**) to say that you are willing to do something or will allow somebody to something. ~ *noun* approval or permission.

consequence *noun* (*plural* **consequences**) **1** a result or effect. **2** importance or relevance: *It's of no consequence.*

consequent *adjective* following as a result or effect. ➤ **consequently** *adjective*.

conservation *noun* the preservation and protection of the environment and natural resources. ➤ **conservationist** *noun*.

conservative *adjective* **1** holding traditional views and tending to resist change. **2** (**Conservative**) belonging to a political party associated with support of private enterprise and freedom from government control. **3** moderate or cautious: *a conservative estimate*. ➤ **conservative** *noun*, **conservatism** *noun*, **conservatively** *adverb*.

conservatory *noun* (*plural* **conservatories**) a room with a glass roof and large windows, built on to a house.

conserve *verb* (**conserves, conserving, conserved**) to look after something and avoid spoiling it or wasting it.

consider *verb* (**considers, considering, considered**) **1** to think about something carefully. **2** to judge or think to be something: *I consider it a first-class opportunity*. **3** to show concern for somebody or their feelings.

considerable *adjective* quite large. ➤ **considerably** *adverb*.

considerate *adjective* showing concern for others. ➤ **considerately** *adverb*.

consideration *noun* **1** careful thought. **2** a factor taken into account in making a decision. **3** concern for others.

considering *preposition and adverb* taking something into account. ~ *conjunction* in view of the fact that (something is the case).

consign *verb* (**consigns, consigning, consigned**) to put something in or send something to a place.

consignment *noun* (*plural* **consignments**) a batch of goods for delivery.

consist *verb* (**consists, consisting, consisted**) **1** (**consist of**) to be made up of various things or people. **2** (**consist in**) to be or derive from something: *True happiness consists in doing good*.

consistency *noun* (*plural* **consistencies**) **1** the thickness or firmness of a substance. **2** the quality of being consistent.

consistent *adjective* **1** not varying over a period of time. **2** logical and coherent. **3** (**consistent with**) in agreement with something; not contradicting it. ➤ **consistently** *adverb*.

consolation *noun* (*plural* **consolations**) **1** comfort received by somebody who has suffered loss or disappointment. **2** something that affords comfort.

consolation prize *noun* (*plural* **consolation prizes**) a prize given to a competitor who fails to win a main prize.

console[1] /kon sohl/ *verb* (**consoles, consoling, consoled**) to comfort somebody in grief or disappointment. ➤ **consolable** *adjective*.

console[2] /kon sohl/ *noun* (*plural* **consoles**) **1** a panel or switchboard housing a set of controls. **2** an electronic device for playing computerized video games.

consolidate *verb* (**consolidates, consolidating, consolidated**) **1** to strengthen something or make it more stable. **2** to combine several separate elements into one unit. ➤ **consolidation** *noun*.

consonant *noun* (*plural* **consonants**) a speech sound such as /p/, /f/, or /m/, that is formed by totally or slightly blocking the flow of air through your mouth, or a letter that represents such a sound.

consort /kon sawt/ *noun* (*plural* **consorts**) **1** the husband or wife of a reigning monarch. **2** *Music* a group of musicians performing together. ~ /kon sawt/ *verb* (**consorts, consorting, consorted**) *formal* (**consort with**) to keep regular company with somebody.

consortium *noun* (*plural* **consortia** or **consortiums**) a group of businesses acting together.

conspicuous *adjective* easily seen; very noticeable. ➤ **conspicuously** *adverb*.

conspiracy *noun* (*plural* **conspiracies**) a secret plot to do wrong.

conspire *verb* (**conspires, conspiring, conspired**) 1 to plot secretly to do wrong. 2 said about events or circumstances: to seem to be acting together to produce undesirable results. ➤ **conspirator** *noun*, **conspiratorial** *adjective*.

constable *noun* (*plural* **constables**) a police officer of the lowest rank.

constabulary *noun* (*plural* **constabularies**) a local police force.

constant *adjective* 1 faithful. 2 never changing. 3 continually present or recurring; regular. ~ *noun* (*plural* **constants**) 1 *Maths, Science* a number that has a fixed value. 2 something that is always present or does not change. ➤ **constancy** *noun*, **constantly** *adverb*.

constellation *noun* (*plural* **constellations**) a group of stars forming a pattern in the night sky.

consternation *noun* a state of confusion and dismay.

constipation *noun* difficulty in emptying the bowels because of compacted faeces. ➤ **constipated** *adjective*.

constituency *noun* (*plural* **constituencies**) a district represented by a Member of Parliament, or the voters who live there.

constituent *noun* (*plural* **constituents**) 1 an essential part; a component. 2 a voter in a constituency.

constitute *verb* (**constitutes, constituting, constituted**) to be, form, or amount to something: *to constitute a danger to society*.

constitution *noun* (*plural* **constitutions**) 1 a set of basic laws governing how a nation or organization is run and the rights and duties of its citizens or members. 2 the act of establishing or setting up. 3 a person's level of physical healthiness. ➤ **constitutional** *adjective*.

constrain *verb* (**constrain, constraining, constrained**) 1 to force somebody to do something. 2 to restrict something or somebody.

constraint *noun* (*plural* **constraints**) a restriction.

constrict *verb* (**constricts, constricting, constricted**) 1 to make a passage or opening narrower. 2 to compress or squeeze something. ➤ **constriction** *noun*.

construct *verb* (**constructs, constructing, constructed**) to make something from various parts; to build something.

construction *noun* (*plural* **constructions**) 1 the process of constructing. 2 a building or other structure. 3 a particular interpretation. 4 *English* a group of words that perform a particular grammatical function.

constructive *adjective* said about a criticism, suggestion, etc: positive and helpful. ➤ **constructively** *adverb*.

construe *verb* (**construes, construed, construing**) to interpret something in a certain way.

consul *noun* (*plural* **consuls**) 1 an official appointed by a government to look after the interests of its citizens in a foreign country. 2 *History* either of the two elected chief magistrates of the Roman republic. ➤ **consular** *adjective*.

consulate noun (plural **consulates**) the building where a consul works.

consult verb (**consults, consulting, consulted**) 1 to seek the advice or opinion of somebody, especially a professional person. 2 to look in a reference book to find information. ➤ **consultation** noun, **consultative** adjective.

consultant noun (plural **consultants**) 1 an expert who gives professional advice or services. 2 a senior hospital doctor.

consume verb (**consumes, consuming, consumed**) 1 to eat or drink food or drink. 2 to use up a fuel or other resource. 3 said about fire: to destroy something completely. 4 said about an emotion: to obsess somebody.

consumer noun (plural **consumers**) somebody who uses goods or services.

consumerism noun the idea that it is good for a country's economy if people buy a lot of things. ➤ **consumerist** noun and adjective.

consummate /kon su mat or kon sew mat/ adjective extremely skilled; of the highest standard: *consummate musicianship.* ~ /kon sew mayt/ verb 1 to make a marriage complete by sexual intercourse. 2 to make something complete and perfect. ➤ **consummately** adverb, **consummation** noun.

consumption noun 1 the process of consuming. 2 an amount consumed. 3 *dated* tuberculosis of the lungs.

contact noun (plural **contacts**) 1 the action of physically touching. 2 meeting or communication with somebody. 3 a useful business acquaintance or relationship. 4 an electrical connection or junction. ~ verb (**contacts, contacting, contacted**) to communicate with somebody or something. ➤ **contactable** adjective.

contact lens noun (plural **contact lenses**) a thin lens placed over the eye to correct a sight defect.

contagion noun the transmission of a disease by physical contact.

contagious adjective 1 said about a disease: communicable by contact. 2 said about a person: suffering from a contagious disease. 3 said about a mood or attitude: tending to spread from one person to another: *Her laughter was contagious.*

contain verb (**contains, containing, contained**) 1 to have or hold something within itself. 2 to comprise or include various things. 3 to keep something within limits: *to contain the spread of the infection.* ➤ **containment** noun.

container noun (plural **containers**) 1 a box, tin, etc that contains things. 2 a large metal case for transporting goods by ship.

contaminate verb (**contaminates, contaminating, contaminated**) to make something impure or unfit for use. ➤ **contamination** noun.

contemplate verb (**contemplates, contemplating, contemplated**) 1 to look at something or somebody attentively. 2 to consider something as a course of action: *She contemplated selling her house and moving abroad.*

contemporary adjective 1 happening or existing in the same period of time. 2 modern or fashionable. ~ noun (plural **contemporaries**) a person living at the same time as another.

contempt noun a feeling that somebody or something is bad or worthless.

contemptible adjective deserving contempt. ➤ **contemptibly** adverb.

contemptuous adjective showing or expressing contempt. ➤ **contemptuously** adverb.

contend verb (**contend, contending, contended**) 1 to struggle or compete. 2 to assert something. 3 (**contend**

content

with) to try to overcome difficulties. ➤ **contender** *noun*.

content¹ /kon tent/ *adjective* happy or satisfied. ~ *verb* (**contents, contenting, contented**) to make somebody feel happy or satisfied. ~ *noun* a state of happy satisfaction. ✶ **to your heart's content** as much as you want. ➤ **contentment** *noun*.

content² /kon tent/ *noun* (*plural* **contents**) **1** (**contents**) the things that are contained in something. **2** (**contents**) the topics dealt with in a book and usually listed at the front of it. **3** the amount of a specified material contained in something: *fat content*.

contented *adjective* satisfied or happy. ➤ **contentedly** *adverb*.

contention *noun* (*plural* **contentions**) **1** strong disagreement or rivalry. **2** an assertion made during a discussion or debate. ✶ **in contention** trying to win something.

contentious *adjective* likely to cause disagreement or controversy. ➤ **contentiously** *adverb*.

contest /kon test/ *noun* (*plural* **contests**) **1** a struggle for superiority or victory. **2** a competition or competitive event. ~ /kon test/ *verb* (**contests, contesting, contested**) **1** to stand as a candidate in an election. **2** to argue that a claim or decision is wrong.

contestant *noun* (*plural* **contestants**) a participant in a contest.

context *noun* (*plural* **contexts**) **1** the parts surrounding a word or passage that clarify its meaning. **2** the conditions in which something exists or occurs. ➤ **contextual** *adjective*.

contiguous *adjective* touching another thing or each other.

continent *noun* (*plural* **continents**) **1** one of the seven large divisions of land on the earth; Europe, Asia, Africa, North and South America, Australia, or Antarctica. **2** (**the Continent**) Europe regarded from the British Isles. ➤ **continental** *adjective*.

continental breakfast *noun* (*plural* **continental breakfasts**) a light breakfast of rolls and coffee.

contingency *noun* (*plural* **contingencies**) an event that may occur but cannot be definitely predicted.

contingent *adjective* (**contingent on/upon**) *formal* dependent on something. ~ *noun* (*plural* **contingents**) a group of people forming part of a larger body.

continual *adjective* happening again and again: *continual interruptions*. ➤ **continually** *adverb*.

Usage Note **continual** or **continuous**? Something *continuous* continues without any interruptions; something *continual* happens many times but with intervals in between.

continuation *noun* (*plural* **continuations**) **1** the process of continuing something. **2** something that continues or adds to something.

continue *verb* (**continues, continuing, continued**) **1** to carry on doing something. **2** to restart an activity after an interruption. **3** to remain or last. **4** to say something further.

continuous *adjective* continuing without interruption; unbroken: *a continuous humming*. ➤ **continuity** *noun*, **continuously** *adverb*.

Usage Note **continuous** or **continual**? See note at **continual**.

contort *verb* (**contorts, contorting, contorted**) to twist something out of shape. ➤ **contorted** *adjective*, **contortion** *noun*.

contortionist *noun* (*plural* **contortionists**) a performer who twists their body into strange positions.

contour *noun* (*plural* **contours**) **1** an

outline. **2** *Geography* a line on a map connecting points of equal height.

contraband *noun* goods that have been brought into a country illegally.

contraception *noun* the use of contraceptives to prevent pregnancy.

contraceptive *noun* (*plural* **contraceptives**) a device or drug that aims at preventing a woman becoming pregnant. ➤ **contraceptive** *adjective*.

contract /kon trakt/ *noun* (*plural* **contracts**) **1** a legally binding agreement. **2** *informal* an arrangement for the murder of somebody by a hired killer. ~ /kon trakt/ *verb* **1** to reduce something to a smaller size. **2** to shorten a word by omitting letters. **3** to sign a contract agreeing to do something. **4** to catch a disease. ➤ **contractual** *adjective*.

contraction *noun* (*plural* **contractions**) **1** the process of contracting. **2** a tightening of the muscles of the womb during childbirth. **3** a shortening of a word.

contractor *noun* (*plural* **contractors**) a person, especially a builder, who contracts to do work.

contradict *verb* (**contradicts, contradicting, contradicted**) **1** to state that somebody is wrong in what they are saying or that something is incorrect or untrue. **2** to state or show the opposite of something.

contradiction *noun* (*plural* **contradictions**) **1** the act of contradicting. **2** a statement containing ideas that are incompatible with each other. ➤ **contradictory** *adjective*.

contraflow *noun* (*plural* **contraflows**) a temporary two-way system on one carriageway of a motorway while the other is closed off.

contralto *noun* (*plural* **contraltos**) *Music* a female singer with the lowest singing voice.

contraption *noun* (*plural* **contraptions**) a strange or complicated device or gadget.

contrariwise /kon trair i wiez/ *adverb* in an opposite direction or way.

contrary *adjective* **1** /kon tra ri/ opposite in nature, meaning, or direction. **2** /kon trair i/ stubbornly opposing the wishes of other people. ✷ **on the contrary** just the opposite.

contrast /kon trahst/ *noun* (*plural* **contrasts**) **1** comparison of similar objects to show the ways in which they are different. **2** a person or thing with which another may be contrasted. **3** the degree of difference between the lightest and darkest parts of a photograph or television picture. ~ /kon trahst/ *verb* (**contrasts, contrasting, contrasted**) **1** to compare two things in order to show their differences. **2** (**contrast with**) to be different from something.

contravene *verb* (**contravenes, contravening, contravened**) to break a law. ➤ **contravention** *noun*.

contretemps /kon tri tong/ *noun* (*plural* **contretemps**) a minor disagreement or quarrel.

contribute *verb* (**contributes, contributing, contributed**) **1** to give something towards a common cause. **2** to help bring about a result. **3** to write something for a publication such as a magazine. ➤ **contribution** *noun*, **contributor** *noun*, **contributory** *adjective*.

contrite *adjective* sorry for doing wrong. ➤ **contritely** *adverb*, **contrition** *noun*.

contrivance *noun* (*plural* **contrivances**) an ingenious device or a plan.

contrive *verb* (**contrives, contriving, contrived**) **1** to devise or plan something ingenious. **2** to manage to do something.

contrived *adjective* said about art, language, etc: unnatural; produced by too great an attempt to be clever.

control *verb* (**controls, controlling, controlled**) **1** to be in charge of something or somebody and make them do what you want. **2** to operate and direct a machine or vehicle. **3** to restrain yourself or your emotions. ~ *noun* (*plural* **controls**) **1** the power to control something or somebody, or the act of controlling. **2** (**controls**) the levers, wheels, switches, etc used to operate a vehicle or machine. ✻ **in control** having control or command. **out of control** unable to be controlled. ➤ **controller** *noun*.

control tower *noun* (*plural* **control towers**) a tall airport building from which movements of aircraft are controlled.

controversial *adjective* likely to cause arguments. ➤ **controversially** *adverb*.

controversy /kon tro ver si *or* kon tro ver si/ *noun* (*plural* **controversies**) **1** debate or disagreement. **2** a dispute over a specific issue.

contusion *noun* (*plural* **contusions**) *formal* a bruise.

conundrum *noun* (*plural* **conundrums**) **1** a riddle. **2** an intricate and difficult problem.

conurbation *noun* (*plural* **conurbations**) a large urban area, formed when the suburbs of two or more towns merge.

convalesce *verb* (**convalesces, convalescing, convalesced**) to recover gradually after illness or injury. ➤ **convalescence** *noun*, **convalescent** *adjective and noun*.

convection *noun* Science the transfer of heat by the movement of a heated gas or liquid.

convene *verb* (**convenes, convening, convened**) to assemble, or to call people together, for a meeting. ➤ **convener** or **convenor** *noun*.

convenience *noun* (*plural* **conveniences**) **1** ease of use or access. **2** personal comfort or advantage. **3** a useful appliance or service. **4** a public toilet.

convenient *adjective* **1** suited to personal comfort or easy use. **2** nearby; easily accessible. ➤ **conveniently** *adverb*.

convent *noun* (*plural* **convents**) a community of nuns.

convention *noun* (*plural* **conventions**) **1** a generally accepted way of doing things. **2** an agreement between states. **3** an assembly or conference.

conventional *adjective* **1** generally accepted or practised. **2** lacking originality or individuality. **3** said about warfare: not using nuclear weapons. ➤ **conventionally** *adverb*.

converge *verb* (**converges, converging, converged**) to move from different directions towards a common point. ➤ **convergence** *noun*, **convergent** *adjective*.

conversant *adjective* (**conversant with**) familiar with facts, principles, etc.

conversation *noun* (*plural* **conversations**) **1** a situation where two or more people talk to one another. **2** talking with other people. ➤ **conversational** *adjective*.

converse[1] /kon vers/ *verb* (**converses, conversing, conversed**) to have a conversation.

converse[2] /kon vers/ *adjective* opposite. ~ *noun* a situation, fact, etc that is the opposite of something else. ➤ **conversely** *adverb*.

conversion *noun* (*plural* **conversions**) **1** the process of converting, or something converted. **2** the adoption of a different religious faith, political allegiance, etc. **3** in rugby, a successful kick at goal after a try.

convert /kon vert/ *verb* (**converts, converting, converted**) **1** to change something from one form or function to another. **2** to persuade somebody to follow a principle, religious belief, etc. **3** in rugby, to complete a try by successfully kicking a goal. ~ /kon vert/ *noun* (*plural* **converts**) a person who has been persuaded to adopt a new belief.

convertible *adjective* **1** capable of being converted. **2** said about a car: having a top that can be lowered. ➤ **convertible** *noun*.

convex *adjective* rounded outwards like the outside of a bowl.

convey *verb* (**conveys, conveying, conveyed**) **1** to take or carry somebody or something from one place to another. **2** to communicate a feeling or idea.

conveyance *noun* (*plural* **conveyances**) **1** the conveying of something. **2** a means of transport.

conveyor belt *noun* (*plural* **conveyor belts**) a moving belt carrying objects from one part of a building to another.

convict /kon vikt/ *verb* to prove and declare somebody to be guilty of a crime. ~ /**kon** vikt/ *noun* (*plural* **convicts**) a person who has been convicted of a crime and imprisoned.

conviction *noun* (*plural* **convictions**) **1** a strongly held belief. **2** the state of being convinced. **3** the process of convicting somebody of a crime, or the fact of having been convicted of a crime: *She has several convictions for theft.*

convince *verb* (**convinces, convincing, convinced**) **1** to make somebody believe or accept something. **2** to persuade somebody to follow a course of action. ➤ **convincing** *adjective*, **convincingly** *adverb*.

convivial *adjective* sociable or friendly. ➤ **conviviality** *noun*.

convoluted *adjective* complex and difficult to understand. ➤ **convolution** *noun*.

convoy *noun* (*plural* **convoys**) a group of ships or vehicles travelling together.

convulse *verb* (**convulses, convulsing, convulsed**) to cause a person to shake with rage, laughter, etc. ➤ **convulsive** *adjective*.

convulsion *noun* (*plural* **convulsions**) **1** a jerking movement of the body caused by a violent contraction of the muscles. **2** a violent disturbance. **3** (**convulsions**) uncontrollable fits of laughter.

coo *verb* (**coos, cooing, cooed**) **1** to make the low soft cry of a dove or pigeon. **2** to talk lovingly or appreciatively. ➤ **coo** *noun*.

cook *verb* (**cooks, cooking, cooked**) **1** to prepare food for eating by heating it. **2** said about food: to be cooked by heating. ~ *noun* (*plural* **cooks**) a person who cooks food. ✻ **cook up** *informal* to invent a story or plan. ➤ **cooking** *noun*.

cooker *noun* (*plural* **cookers**) **1** an appliance for cooking food, with an oven, hot plates, and a grill. **2** *informal* an apple suitable only for cooking.

cookery *noun* the art or practice of cooking.

cookie *noun* (*plural* **cookies**) **1** ICT data downloaded from an Internet website to identify a user on future visits. **2** N American a sweet biscuit.

cool *adjective* **1** moderately cold. **2** unfriendly or lacking enthusiasm. **3** calm and self-controlled. **4** *informal* very good. ~ *verb* (**cools, cooling, cooled**) to become cool or to make something cool. ➤ **coolly** *adverb*, **coolness** *noun*.

coop *noun* (*plural* **coops**) a small enclosure for poultry. ~ *verb* (**coops, cooping, cooped**) ✻ **coop up** to confine a person or animal in a small space.

co-op *noun* (*plural* **co-ops**) *informal* a cooperative.

cooperate *or* **co-operate** *verb*

cooperative

(**cooperates, cooperating, cooperated** or **co-operates,** etc) **1** to act or work together for a common purpose. **2** to do or agree to what is asked. ➤ **cooperation** noun.

cooperative or **co-operative** adjective **1** showing a willingness to work with others. **2** said about an organization: owned by and operated for the benefit its members. ~ noun (plural **cooperatives**) a cooperative organization or business. ➤ **cooperatively** adverb.

co-opt verb (**co-opts, co-opting, co-opted**) said about a committee or other body: to ask somebody to become a member. ➤ **co-option** noun.

coordinate or **co-ordinate** /koh aw di nayt/ verb (**coordinates, coordinating, coordinated** or **co-ordinates,** etc) to make arrangements to enable different people or things to work together effectively. ~ /koh aw di nat/ noun (plural **coordinates**) Maths a number used to specify the location of a point on a line or surface, or in space. ➤ **coordinator** noun.

coot noun (plural **coots**) a water bird with dark plumage and a white bill.

cop noun (plural **cops**) informal a police officer. ~ verb (**cops, copping, copped**) ✱ **cop it** informal to be in serious trouble.

cope verb (**copes, coping, coped**) to deal effectively with something difficult or awkward.

copier noun (plural **copiers**) a machine for making copies of documents.

co-pilot noun (plural **co-pilots**) a second pilot in an aircraft.

coping noun (plural **copings**) a sloping row of bricks or stones on the top of a wall.

copious adjective abundant or plentiful. ➤ **copiously** adverb.

copper noun (plural **coppers**) **1** Science a reddish metal that is one of the chemical elements. **2** a reddish brown colour. **3** a coin made of copper or bronze. **4** informal a police officer.

copperplate noun a style of fine handwriting with lines of contrasting thickness.

coppice noun (plural **coppices**) a woodland area in which the trees are regularly cut back to promote growth.

copse noun (plural **copses**) a small area of trees.

copulate verb (**copulates, copulating, copulated**) to have sexual intercourse. ➤ **copulation** noun.

copy noun (plural **copies**) **1** something made to imitate or be identical to something else. **2** a single specimen of a book, CD, etc. **3** written material ready to be printed and published. ~ verb (**copies, copying, copied**) **1** to make a copy of something. **2** to imitate or model yourself on somebody.

copycat noun (plural **copycats**) informal somebody who copies somebody else.

copyright noun the right to publish or perform a literary, musical, or artistic work for a fixed period.

coracle noun (plural **coracles**) a small round boat made of waterproof material over a wicker frame.

coral noun (plural **corals**) **1** a hard substance consisting of the skeletons of small sea animals, usually forming large underwater structures. **2** a reddish pink colour.

cor anglais /kawr ong glay/ noun (plural **cors anglais** /kawr ong glay or kawrz ong glay/) Music a woodwind instrument of the oboe family.

corbel noun (plural **corbels**) a projection from a wall which supports a weight.

cord noun (plural **cords**) **1** a length of several strands of thread or yarn woven or twisted together. **2** an electric flex. **3** corduroy. **4** (**cords**) trousers made of corduroy. ➤ **cordless** *adjective*.

cordial *adjective* **1** warm and friendly. **2** sincerely or deeply felt: *a cordial dislike of cats.* ~ *noun* (*plural* **cordials**) a non-alcoholic sweetened fruit drink. ➤ **cordiality** *noun*, **cordially** *adverb*.

cordon *noun* (*plural* **cordons**) a line of troops or police, preventing access to an area. ~ *verb* (**cordons, cordoning, cordoned**) ✱ **cordon off** to form a cordon round an area.

cordon bleu /kawdong bler/ *adjective* said about cookery: of the highest standard.

corduroy *noun* a cotton fabric with lengthways ribs.

core *noun* (*plural* **cores**) **1** the central part of some fruits. **2** the essential or central part of something.

corgi *noun* (*plural* **corgis**) a dog with short legs and a fox-like head.

coriander *noun* a plant of the carrot family with leaves and seeds used in cooking.

cork *noun* (*plural* **corks**) **1** the tough outer tissue of a type of oak tree. **2** a cork stopper for a bottle. ~ *verb* (**corks, corking, corked**) to close a bottle with a cork.

corkscrew *noun* (*plural* **corkscrews**) a tool for removing corks from bottles. ~ *verb* (**corkscrews, corkscrewing, corkscrewed**) to move or twist in a spiral.

corm *noun* (*plural* **corms**) *Science* a thick underground base of some plants.

cormorant *noun* (*plural* **cormorants**) a dark-coloured seabird with a long neck and hooked beak.

corn[1] *noun* **1** the seeds of a cereal crop. **2** *N American, Australian, New Zealand* maize.

corn[2] *noun* (*plural* **corns**) a painful hardening of the skin on the top of a toe.

cornea /kawnia/ *noun* (*plural* **corneas**) the transparent covering of the iris and pupil of the eye.

corned beef *noun* tinned beef preserved with brine.

corner *noun* (*plural* **corners**) **1** an angle where converging lines, edges, or sides meet. **2** a place where two streets or roads meet. **3** in football, a free kick from a corner of the pitch. **4** the part of a boxing or wrestling ring in which a fighter rests between rounds. **5** a private or remote place. ~ *verb* (**corners, cornering, cornered**) **1** to drive a person or animal into a place from which they cannot escape. **2** to go round a corner in a road.

cornerstone *noun* (*plural* **cornerstones**) **1** a block of stone forming the base of a corner of a building. **2** the most basic part of something.

cornet *noun* (*plural* **cornets**) **1** *Music* a brass instrument that looks like a short trumpet. **2** an ice cream cone.

cornflakes *plural noun* toasted flakes of maize eaten as a breakfast cereal.

cornflour *noun* flour made from maize.

cornflower *noun* (*plural* **cornflowers**) a plant with narrow leaves and blue, purple, or white flowers.

cornice *noun* (*plural* **cornices**) an ornamental band of plaster between the wall and ceiling of a room.

corny *adjective* (**cornier, corniest**) *informal* **1** sentimental. **2** overused and unoriginal.

corollary /koʀolari/ *noun* (*plural* **corollaries**) something that naturally follows or accompanies something else.

corona /koʀohna/ *noun* (*plural* **coronas** or **coronae** /koʀohnee/) *Science* a coloured circle of light seen round the sun, the moon, or a star.

coronary /koʀonari/ *adjective* to do with the arteries and veins that supply the heart with blood. ~ *noun* (*also* **coronary thrombosis**) (*plural* **coronaries** *or* **coronary thromboses**) a blockage in an artery of the heart.

coronation *noun* (*plural* **coronations**) the ceremony of crowning a sovereign.

coroner *noun* (*plural* **coroners**) an official who enquires into the cause of a sudden or suspicious death.

coronet *noun* (*plural* **coronets**) a small crown.

corporal[1] *noun* (*plural* **corporals**) a non-commissioned army officer ranking below sergeant.

corporal[2] *adjective* to do with the body.

corporal punishment *noun* physical punishment such as caning.

corporate *adjective* 1 to do with companies or businesses. 2 involving a group of individuals.

corporation *noun* (*plural* **corporations**) 1 a group of people, especially a business organization, legally authorized to act as a single person. 2 a town or city council.

corps /kaw/ *noun* (*plural* **corps** /kawz/) 1 a large army unit. 2 a group of people engaged in a specific activity: *the diplomatic corps*.

corpse *noun* (*plural* **corpses**) a dead body.

corpulent *adjective* fat; obese. ➤ **corpulence** *noun*.

corpuscle *noun* (*plural* **corpuscles**) a blood cell.

corral /ko rahl/ *noun* (*plural* **corrals**) *N American* an enclosure for livestock.

correct *adjective* 1 true or right. 2 conforming to an accepted standard of behaviour. ~ *verb* (**corrects, correcting, corrected**) 1 to make or set something right. 2 to alter something so as to remove an error or imperfection. 3 to point out or punish somebody's faults. ➤ **correction** *noun*, **corrective** *adjective*, **correctly** *adverb*, **correctness** *noun*.

correlate *verb* (**correlates, correlating, correlated**) to bring things together to compare them and show their relationship to one another. ➤ **correlation** *noun*.

correspond *verb* (**corresponds, corresponding, corresponded**) 1 to match or be compatible with something. 2 to be equivalent or similar to something. 3 to communicate by exchanging letters.

correspondence *noun* (*plural* **correspondences**) 1 letters, or communication by letter. 2 agreement or similarity.

correspondent *noun* (*plural* **correspondents**) 1 a person who communicates by letter. 2 a newspaper or broadcasting journalist who reports on a particular subject.

corridor *noun* (*plural* **corridors**) a passage with doors leading into rooms.

corroborate *verb* (**corroborates, corroborating, corroborated**) to support a claim or an opinion with evidence from another source. ➤ **corroboration** *noun*, **corroborative** *adjective*.

corrode *verb* (**corrodes, corroding, corroded**) to wear away metal by chemical action. ➤ **corrosion** *noun*.

corrosive *adjective* 1 causing corrosion. 2 harmful or destructive.

corrugated *adjective* folded into ridges and grooves. ➤ **corrugation** *noun*.

corrupt *adjective* 1 open to bribery or other improper conduct. 2 in a morally state. 3 *ICT* said about computer data: damaged and unusable. ~ *verb* (**corrupts, corrupting, corrupted**) to make somebody or something corrupt. ➤ **corruptible** *adjective*, **corruption** *noun*, **corruptly** *adverb*.

corset *noun* (*plural* **corsets**) a

supporting undergarment for the middle part of a woman's body.

cortège or **cortege** /kawtezh/ *noun* (*plural* **cortèges** or **corteges**) a funeral procession.

cosh *noun* (*plural* **coshes**) a short heavy stick used as a weapon.

cosine /kohsien/ *noun* (*plural* **cosines**) *Maths* the ratio in a right-angled triangle between the length of the side adjacent to a particular angle and the length of the hypotenuse.

cosmetic *noun* (*plural* **cosmetics**) a substance designed to be applied to the skin or hair to improve its appearance. ~ *adjective* **1** intended to make you look more beautiful. **2** affecting or improving something on the surface without really changing it. ➤ **cosmetically** *adverb*.

cosmic *adjective* relating to the universe.

cosmonaut *noun* (*plural* **cosmonauts**) a Russian astronaut.

cosmopolitan *adjective* composed of people or things from many parts of the world.

cosmos *noun* the universe.

Cossack *noun* (*plural* **Cossacks**) a member of a people of southern Russia and Ukraine famous for their skilful horse-riding. ➤ **Cossack** *adjective*.

cosset *verb* (**cossets, cosseting, cosseted**) to treat a person or animal in an excessively protective way.

cost *noun* (*plural* **costs**) **1** the price paid or charged for something. **2** the effort or sacrifice made to achieve something. **3** the loss or penalty incurred in gaining something. **4** (**costs**) legal expenses. ~ *verb* (**costs, costing, cost**) **1** to have a price of a specified amount. **2** to cause somebody to suffer or lose something: *The attempt cost him his life.* **3** (*past tense and past participle* **costed**) to estimate or set the cost of something. ✱ **at all costs** regardless of the price or difficulties.

co-star *noun* (*plural* **co-stars**) a leading performer who appears with another leading performer in a film or play.

cost-effective *adjective* economically worthwhile.

costly *adjective* (**costlier, costliest**) **1** expensive or valuable. **2** achieved with considerable sacrifice.

costume *noun* (*plural* **costumes**) a set of clothing belonging to a specific time, place, or character.

cosy *adjective* (**cosier, cosiest**) providing warmth and comfort; snug. ~ *noun* (*plural* **cosies**) a cover for a teapot or boiled egg, to keep it hot. ➤ **cosily** *adverb*, **cosiness** *noun*.

cot *noun* (*plural* **cots**) a small bed for a baby or young child, with high sides of vertical bars.

cot death *noun* (*plural* **cot deaths**) the unexplained death of a baby while asleep.

cottage *noun* (*plural* **cottages**) a small house in the country.

cottage cheese *noun* a soft white cheese made from the curds of skimmed milk.

cotton *noun* (*plural* **cottons**) **1** a soft white fibrous substance surrounding the seeds of a tropical plant. **2** yarn or fabric made of cotton.

cotton wool *noun* fluffy soft material in balls or pads, used for cleaning the skin.

couch *noun* (*plural* **couches**) a long upholstered piece of furniture for sitting or lying on. ~ *verb* (**couches, couching, couched**) to phrase something in a particular way: *The letter was couched in hostile terms.*

couch potato *noun* (**couch potatoes**) *informal* somebody who watches a lot of television.

cougar /koohger/ *noun* (*plural* **cougars**) *N American* a puma.

cough verb (**coughs, coughing, coughed**) to send out air from the lungs with a loud sharp noise. ~ noun (plural **coughs**) **1** an act or sound of coughing. **2** a condition marked by repeated or frequent coughing.

cough mixture noun (plural **cough mixtures**) a liquid medicine used to relieve coughing.

could verb past tense of CAN[1].

couldn't contraction could not.

council noun (plural **councils**) **1** a group of people elected or appointed to administer something or make laws. **2** a local authority administering a city, county, or district. ➤ **councillor** noun.

Usage Note Do not confuse **council** and **counsel**.

council house noun (plural **council houses**) a house rented to tenants by a local council.

counsel noun (plural **counsels**) **1** formal or personal advice. **2** (plural **counsel**) a barrister or other lawyer engaged in a court case. ~ verb (**counsels, counselling, counselled**) **1** to advise somebody. **2** to give somebody help with psychological or personal problems. ➤ **counselling** noun, **counsellor** noun.

Usage Note Do not confuse **counsel** and **council**.

count[1] verb (**counts, counting, counted**) **1** to find the total number of something. **2** to name the numbers in order. **3** to include something or somebody when calculating: *There will be seven of us, counting you.* **4** to think of somebody or something as having a particular quality or function. **5** to have value or importance. ~ noun (plural **counts**) **1** the act of counting. **2** a total obtained by counting. **3** in law, a charge being considered when somebody is tried in a court. ✻ **count on** to rely on somebody or something. **out for the count 1** in boxing, knocked down and unable to rise again during a count of ten. **2** *informal* unconscious or deeply asleep.

count[2] noun (plural **counts**) a European nobleman equal in rank to a British earl.

countdown noun (plural **countdowns**) a continuous count from a higher number to zero showing the time remaining before an event.

countenance noun (plural **countenances**) a person's face as an indication of mood or character. ~ verb (**countenances, countenancing, countenanced**) to allow or approve something.

counter[1] noun (plural **counters**) **1** a level surface over which goods are sold or food is served. **2** a small disc used in counting or in board games. **3** a person or machine that counts.

counter[2] verb (**counters, countering, countered**) **1** to counteract something. **2** to defend yourself or retaliate against an attack. ✻ **counter to** in the opposite direction to somebody or something.

counteract verb (**counteracts, counteracting, counteracted**) to lessen or neutralize the bad effects of something. ➤ **counteractive** adjective.

counterattack or **counter-attack** verb (**counterattacks, counter-attacking, counterattacked** or **counter-attacks**, etc) to make an attack in response to an attack on you. ➤ **counterattack** noun.

counterbalance verb (**counterbalances, counterbalancing, counterbalanced**) to balance something with an equal weight or force. ➤ **counterbalance** noun.

counterespionage or **counter-espionage** noun activities intended to stop enemy espionage.

counterfeit *adjective* made in imitation of something with intent to deceive or defraud. ~ *noun* (*plural* **counterfeits**) a forgery. ~ *verb* (**counterfeits, counterfeiting, counterfeited**) to imitate or copy something fraudulently.

counterfoil *noun* (*plural* **counterfoils**) the part of a cheque, ticket, etc that is kept as a record or receipt.

counterintelligence or **counter-intelligence** *noun* activity designed to block an enemy's sources of information.

countermand *verb* (**countermands, countermanding, countermanded**) to cancel a command by a contrary order.

counterpane *noun* (*plural* **counterpanes**) a bedspread.

counterpart *noun* (*plural* **counterparts**) a person or thing with the same function or characteristics as another.

counterpoint *noun* Music the combination of two or more independent melodies in a single passage.

counterproductive *adjective* having effects opposite to those intended.

countersign *verb* (**countersigns, countersigning, countersigned**) to add a signature to a document as a witness to another signature. ➤ **countersignature** *noun*.

countertenor *noun* (*plural* **countertenors**) Music a male singer with a voice higher than tenor.

countess *noun* (*plural* **countesses**) 1 the wife or widow of an earl or count. 2 a woman who has the same rank as an earl or count.

countless *adjective* too many to be counted; innumerable.

countrified *adjective* in the style or manner of people who live in the country.

country *noun* (*plural* **countries**) 1 a political state or nation or its territory or people. 2 areas of fields and woods as opposed to towns and cities.

countryman or **countrywoman** *noun* (*plural* **countrymen** or **countrywomen**) 1 somebody who lives in the country rather than in a town. 2 a citizen of the same country as yourself.

countryside *noun* (**the countryside**) country areas as opposed to cities and towns.

county *noun* (*plural* **counties**) one of the areas into which Britain and some other countries are divided for administrative purposes.

coup /kooh/ or **coup d'état** /kooh day **tah**/ *noun* (*plural* **coups** /koohz/ or **coups d'état** /kooh day **tah**/) a sudden seizure of power by a group within a country.

couple *noun* (*plural* **couples**) 1 two things considered together; a pair. 2 two people who are married, living together, or have a steady relationship. 3 *informal* a small number; a few. ~ *verb* (**couples, coupling, coupled**) to link or fasten two or more things together.

couplet *noun* (*plural* **couplets**) English two lines of verse that follow one another and rhyme.

coupon *noun* (*plural* **coupons**) 1 a voucher. 2 a part of a printed advertisement that can be cut out, filled in, and sent off, for example to enter a competition.

courage *noun* mental or moral strength to confront danger, suffering, or difficulty. ➤ **courageous** *adjective*, **courageously** *adverb*.

courgette /kaw **zhet**/ *noun* (*plural* **courgettes**) a small marrow used as a vegetable.

courier *noun* (*plural* **couriers**) 1 a person who collects and delivers parcels and documents. 2 a person employed to assist tourists abroad.

course noun (plural **courses**) **1** the route which something, especially a ship or aircraft, is taking or intends to take. **2** a plan of action. **3** a series of lessons or lectures relating to a subject. **4** a part of a meal served at one time. **5** a medical treatment administered over a period. **6** an area of land marked out for a sport such as golf or racing. * **in the course of** during. **of course 1** yes, certainly. **2** without doubt. **3** as you would expect; naturally.

court noun (plural **courts**) **1** an official assembly of people authorized to conduct legal trials. **2** (also **court of law** or **law court**) a place in which a trial is held. **3** a space marked off for playing tennis or other ball games. **4** a courtyard. **5** the family and attendants of a king or queen. ~ verb (**courts, courting, courted**) **1** to try to win the love or support of somebody. **2** to act in a way that risks a bad result: *to court disaster*.

court card noun (plural **court cards**) a king, queen, or jack in a pack of cards.

courteous adjective showing respect and consideration; polite. ➤ **courteously** adverb, **courtesy** noun.

courtier noun (plural **courtiers**) an attendant or companion to a king or queen.

courtly adjective (**courtlier, courtliest**) elegant and refined.

court-martial noun (plural **courts-martial** or **court-martials**) **1** a court that tries members of the armed forces. **2** a trial by a military court. ~ verb (**court-martials, court-martialling, court-martialled**) to try somebody by court-martial.

courtship noun **1** a period of courting somebody. **2** the rituals of animals who are getting ready to mate.

courtyard noun (plural **courtyards**) a yard surrounded by walls or buildings.

cousin noun (plural **cousins**) a child of your uncle or aunt.

cove noun (plural **coves**) a small sheltered bay.

coven /ku vin/ noun (plural **covens**) a group or gathering of witches.

covenant /ku vi nant/ noun (plural **covenants**) a formal agreement or contract.

cover verb (**covers, covering, covered**) **1** to place or spread something over a thing to conceal or protect it. **2** to lie or be spread over something. **3** to hide something from sight. **4** to travel a specified distance. **5** said about an amount of money: to be enough to pay for something. **6** to include something or take it into account. **7** to report news about an event. **8** to provide protection against a risk by insurance. **9** to protect somebody by being in a position to fire at an attacker. ~ noun (plural **covers**) **1** something put over an object to conceal or protect it. **2** a jacket for a book. **3** shelter or protection from the weather, an attack, etc. **4** a pretext or disguise. **5** protection under an insurance policy. * **cover for** to act as a substitute for somebody. **cover up** to try to prevent people from finding out about a mistake or crime.
➤ **covering** noun.

coverage noun **1** an area or amount covered. **2** the amount of time or space devoted to reporting an event.

coverlet noun (plural **coverlets**) a bedspread.

covert[1] /koh vert *or* ku vət/ adjective done in secret. ➤ **covertly** adverb.

covert[2] /ku vət/ noun (plural **coverts**) a thicket providing cover for game.

cover-up noun (plural **cover-ups**) an attempt to conceal an error or a crime.

cover version noun (plural **cover versions**) a new version of a pop song previously recorded by another performer.

covet /ku vit/ *verb* (**covets, coveting, coveted**) to long to have something that belongs to somebody else. ➤ **covetous** *adjective*.

cow[1] *noun* (*plural* **cows**) **1** the mature female animal of domestic cattle. **2** a mature female of some other large animals. **3** *informal* an unpleasant woman. ✳ **till the cows come home** forever.

cow[2] *verb* (**cows, cowing, cowed**) to make somebody feel afraid by threats.

coward *noun* (*plural* **cowards**) somebody who lacks courage or resolve. ➤ **cowardice** *noun*, **cowardly** *adjective*.

cowboy *noun* (*plural* **cowboys**) **1** a man on horseback who herds cattle in North America. **2** *informal* an incompetent or dishonest workman.

cower *verb* (**cowers, cowering, cowered**) to crouch down or shrink away in fear.

cowl *noun* (*plural* **cowls**) **1** a monk's hood. **2** a chimney covering designed to improve ventilation.

cowslip *noun* (*plural* **cowslips**) a wild plant of the primrose family with yellow flowers.

cox *noun* (*plural* **coxes**) a person who steers a racing boat and directs the rowers.

coxswain /kok sn/ *noun* (*plural* **coxswains**) **1** = cox. **2** a sailor who commands a ship's boat.

coy *adjective* pretending to be shy or modest. ➤ **coyly** *adverb*.

coyote /koi oh ti/ *noun* (*plural* **coyotes** or **coyote**) a wolf-like wild dog of North America.

crab *noun* (*plural* **crabs**) a sea creature with a broad flat shell and pincers at the front.

crab apple *noun* (*plural* **crab apples**) a small sour wild apple.

crack *verb* (**cracks, cracking, cracked**) **1** to make a sudden sharp noise. **2** to break or split without coming apart. **3** to tell a joke. **4** to work out a code or mystery. **5** said about the voice: to change tone suddenly, for example because of emotion. **6** to collapse emotionally under stress. ~ *noun* (*plural* **cracks**) **1** a sudden sharp loud noise. **2** a narrow opening where something has split or broken. **3** a sharp resounding blow. **4** *informal* a witty remark. **5** *informal* an attempt at something. **6** (*also* **crack cocaine**) *informal* a strong and addictive variety of cocaine. ~ *adjective informal* very able or skilled: *a crack shot*. ✳ **crack down on** *informal* to deal harshly with something.

cracker *noun* (*plural* **crackers**) **1** a paper tube that makes a cracking noise when pulled apart and that usually contains a toy, a joke, and a paper hat. **2** a thin savoury biscuit.

crackers *adjective informal* mad or eccentric.

crackle *verb* (**crackles, crackling, crackled**) to make a series of small cracking noises. ➤ **crackle** *noun*, **crackly** *adjective*.

crackling *noun* the crisp skin of roast pork.

crackpot *noun* (*plural* **crackpots**) *informal* a crazy or eccentric person.

cradle *noun* (*plural* **cradles**) **1** a baby's bed or cot on rockers. **2** a supporting framework of wood or metal. ~ *verb* (**cradles, cradling, cradled**) to hold something or somebody protectively.

craft *noun* **1** (*plural* **crafts**) an activity or trade requiring manual or artistic skill. **2** (*plural* **craft**) a boat, ship, aircraft, or spacecraft. **3** skill in deception.

craftsman *or* **craftswoman** *noun* (*plural* **craftsmen** *or* **craftswomen**) a man or woman who practises a skilled craft. ➤ **craftsmanship** *noun*.

crafty *adjective* (**craftier, craftiest**)

cleverly able to deceive people; cunning. ➤ **craftily** *adverb*, **craftiness** *noun*.

crag *noun* (*plural* **crags**) a steep rugged rock or cliff. ➤ **craggy** *adjective*.

cram *verb* (**crams, cramming, crammed**) **1** to pack things into a container until it is completely full. **2** to thrust something forcefully into something. **3** to study intensively for an examination.

cramp *noun* (*plural* **cramps**) a pain caused when a muscle contracts suddenly. ~ *verb* (**cramps, cramping, cramped**) to give somebody or something too little room to move easily.

cramped *adjective* too small or crowded for comfort.

cranberry *noun* (*plural* **cranberries**) a sour red berry used in sauces and jellies.

crane *noun* (*plural* **cranes**) **1** a machine with a swinging arm, used for raising heavy weights. **2** a tall wading bird. ~ *verb* (**cranes, craning, craned**) to stretch your neck in order to see better.

crane fly *noun* (*plural* **crane flies**) a fly with a long thin body and long legs.

cranium *noun* (*plural* **craniums** *or* **crania**) the part of the skull that encloses the brain. ➤ **cranial** *adjective*.

crank *noun* (*plural* **cranks**) **1** a part of an axle or shaft bent at right angles to convert back-and-forth motion into circular motion. **2** an eccentric person.

cranny *noun* (*plural* **crannies**) a small crack or slit.

crash *verb* (**crashes, crashing, crashed**) **1** to hit something and make a loud smashing noise. **2** to damage a vehicle or aircraft in a collision or accident. **3** said about a vehicle or aircraft: to collide with something or hit the ground and be damaged. **4** *ICT* said about a computer system: to fail. **5** (*also* **crash out**) *informal* to go to sleep. ~ *noun* (*plural* **crashes**) **1** a loud smashing noise. **2** a violent collision. **3** a sudden decline or failure. ~ *adjective* designed to achieve a rapid result: *a crash diet*.

crash helmet *noun* (*plural* **crash helmets**) a padded helmet worn to protect the head.

crash-land *verb* (**crash-lands, crash-landing, crash-landed**) said about an aircraft: to land roughly in an emergency. ➤ **crash-landing** *noun*.

crass *adjective* **1** insensitive and stupid. **2** complete; gross. ➤ **crassly** *adverb*.

crate *noun* (*plural* **crates**) **1** a wooden framework or box for holding or transporting goods. **2** *informal* an old dilapidated vehicle. ~ *verb* (**crates, crating, crated**) to pack objects in a crate.

crater *noun* (*plural* **craters**) a bowl-shaped depression in the ground caused by an impact or explosion or forming the mouth of a volcano.

cravat /krə vat/ *noun* (*plural* **cravats**) a decorative band like a wide tie, worn round the neck by men.

crave *verb* (**craves, craving, craved**) **1** to have a strong desire for something. **2** *formal* to ask for something. ➤ **craving** *noun*.

craven *adjective* cowardly. ➤ **cravenly** *adverb*.

crawl *verb* (**crawls, crawling, crawled**) **1** to move slowly on hands and knees. **2** to proceed slowly or laboriously. **3** to be swarming with creeping or unwelcome things. ~ *noun* **1** a crawling movement. **2** a very slow speed. **3** a style of swimming with overarm movements and up-and-down kicking of the legs.

crayfish *noun* (*plural* **crayfish** *or* **crayfishes**) a freshwater crustacean like a small lobster.

crayon *noun* (*plural* **crayons**) a stick of coloured chalk or wax used for drawing.

craze *noun* (*plural* **crazes**) a short-lived fashion; a fad.

crazed *adjective* mad.

crazy *adjective* (**crazier, craziest**) *informal* **1** insane or eccentric. **2** foolish or impractical. **3** very fond of or enthusiastic about something. ➤ **crazily** *adverb*, **craziness** *noun*.

crazy paving *noun* a paved surface made up of irregularly shaped flat stones.

creak *verb* (**creaks, creaking, creaked**) to make a grating or squeaking noise. ➤ **creak** *noun*, **creaky** *adjective*.

cream *noun* (*plural* **creams**) **1** the thick yellowish part of milk which forms a surface layer when milk is allowed to stand. **2** a food prepared with or resembling cream. **3** a thick liquid cosmetic applied to the skin. **4** a pale yellowish white colour. ~ *verb* (**creams, creaming, creamed**) to beat butter and sugar to the consistency of cream. ✱ **the cream of** the best part of something or the best members of a group. **cream off** to take the best part of something. ➤ **creamy** *adjective*.

creamery *noun* (*plural* **creameries**) a place where butter and cheese are made.

crease *noun* (*plural* **creases**) **1** a ridge or line made in fabric, paper, etc by crushing or folding. **2** a line marked on a cricket pitch near a wicket. ~ *verb* (**creases, creasing, creased**) **1** to make creases in cloth or paper. **2** to become creased.

create *verb* (**creates, creating, created**) **1** to bring something into existence. **2** to produce or cause something. **3** *informal* to make a loud fuss.

creation *noun* (*plural* **creations**) **1** something created. **2** the world. **3** (**the Creation**) the act of making the universe.

creative *adjective* showing the ability to create; imaginative. ➤ **creatively** *adverb*, **creativity** *noun*.

creator *noun* (*plural* **creators**) **1** a person who creates something. **2** (**the Creator**) God.

creature *noun* (*plural* **creatures**) a living being, especially a non-human one.

crèche /kresh/ *noun* (*plural* **crèches**) a place where young children are looked after, for example while their parents are at work.

credence /kree dins/ *noun* belief.

credentials *plural noun* letters or other documents that prove your identity or status.

credible *adjective* able to be believed; likely or reasonable. ➤ **credibility** *noun*, **credibly** *adverb*.

credit *noun* (*plural* **credits**) **1** a source of honour or pride: *a credit to his parents*. **2** acknowledgment or approval: *Give credit where credit is due*. **3** the amount of money that a person has available in a bank account. **4** an amount of money made available to a person by a bank, which usually has to be repaid with interest. **6** time given for payment for goods or services. **7** an entry in an account recording money received. **8** (**credits**) a list of the people who have contributed, shown at the beginning or end of a film or television programme. ~ *verb* (**credits, crediting, credited**) **1** to believe something. **2** to place an amount of money in an account. **3** (**credit with**) to recognize somebody as having a characteristic or as having done something: *Credit me with some intelligence!*

creditable *adjective* deserving praise even if not successful. ➤ **creditably** *adverb*.

credit card *noun* (*plural* **credit cards**) a card allowing the holder to obtain goods and services and pay for them later.

creditor *noun* (*plural* **creditors**) a person to whom a debt is owed.

credulous *adjective* too ready to believe things. ➤ **credulity** *noun*, **credulously** *adverb*.

creed *noun* (*plural* **creeds**) a set or statement of beliefs, especially religious beliefs.

creek *noun* (*plural* **creeks**) 1 a small narrow inlet of a lake or sea. 2 *N American* a stream or brook. ✱ **up the creek** *informal* in bad trouble.

creep *verb* (**creeps, creeping, crept**) 1 to move along with your body close to the ground. 2 to go very slowly. 3 to move cautiously or quietly. ~ *noun* (*plural* **creeps**) 1 a creeping movement. 2 *informal* an unpleasant person. ✱ **give you the creeps** *informal* to unnerve or disgust you.

creeper *noun* (*plural* **creepers**) a plant that grows over a surface.

creepy *adjective* (**creepier, creepiest**) *informal* slightly sinister or unpleasant.

cremate *verb* (**cremates, cremating, cremated**) to reduce a dead body to ashes by burning. ➤ **cremation** *noun*.

crematorium *noun* (*plural* **crematoriums** *or* **crematoria**) a place where dead bodies are cremated.

crème de la crème /krem di la krem/ *noun* (**the crème de la crème**) the very best of a group.

creosote *noun* a brownish oily liquid used as a wood preservative.

crepe *or* **crêpe** /krayp/ *noun* (*plural* **crepes** *or* **crêpes**) 1 a light crinkled fabric. 2 a thin pancake.

crept *verb* past tense and past participle of CREEP.

crescendo /kri shen doh/ *noun* (*plural* **crescendos**) *Music* a gradual increase in volume.

crescent *noun* (*plural* **crescents**) 1 a narrow rounded shape coming to a point at each end. 2 a curved street.

cress *noun* a plant with mildly pungent leaves, used in salads.

crest *noun* (*plural* **crests**) 1 a tuft or projection on the head of a bird or animal. 2 a symbol of a family or organization above the shield in a coat of arms. 3 the top of a wave, roof, or mountain. ➤ **crested** *adjective*.

crestfallen *adjective* disheartened or dejected.

cretin *noun* (*plural* **cretins**) a very foolish person. ➤ **cretinous** *adjective*.

crevasse /kri vas/ *noun* (*plural* **crevasses**) a deep wide crack in a glacier.

crevice *noun* (*plural* **crevices**) a narrow opening resulting from a split or crack.

crew[1] *noun* (*plural* **crews**) 1 the people who work on a ship or boat, excluding the captain and officers. 2 the people who work on an aircraft or train. 3 a number of people working together.

crew[2] *verb* past tense of CROW.

crew cut *noun* (*plural* **crew cuts**) a short bristly haircut.

crew neck *noun* (*plural* **crew necks**) a round neckline on a knitted pullover.

crib *noun* (*plural* **cribs**) 1 *chiefly N American* a child's cot. 2 a cattle stall. 3 a manger or rack for animal fodder. 4 a translation of a text, used as an aid by students. 5 = CRIBBAGE. ~ *verb* (**cribs, cribbing, cribbed**) to copy somebody else's work dishonestly.

cribbage *noun* a card game for two to four players.

crick *noun* a painful stiff feeling in the muscles of the neck or back.

cricket[1] *noun* a team game played with a bat and ball on a large field with two wickets near its centre. ➤ **cricketer** *noun*.

cricket[2] *noun* (*plural* **crickets**) a leaping insect noted for its chirping sound.

cried *verb* past tense and past participle of CRY.

crime *noun* (*plural* **crimes**) **1** an action that violates a law. **2** activity that is against the law. **3** *informal* something deplorable or disgraceful.

criminal *adjective* **1** relating to or guilty of a crime. **2** *informal* disgraceful. ~ *noun* (*plural* **criminals**) a person who has committed a crime. ➤ **criminality** *noun*, **criminally** *adverb*.

criminology *noun* the study of crime, criminals, and methods of punishment.

crimp *verb* (**crimps, crimping, crimped**) **1** to make hair wavy or curly. **2** to pinch or press material together to seal or join it.

crimson *noun* a deep purplish red colour.

cringe *verb* (**cringes, cringing, cringed**) **1** to curl up your body or shrink back in fear. **2** to feel acute embarrassment.

crinkle *verb* (**crinkles, crinkling, crinkled**) to form small wrinkles in something. ➤ **crinkly** *adjective*.

crinoline /kri no lin/ *noun* (*plural* **crinolines**) *History* a full skirt or a petticoat with hoops, formerly worn by women.

cripple *noun* (*plural* **cripples**) *offensive* a lame or partly disabled person. ~ *verb* (**cripples, crippling, crippled**) **1** to make somebody lame or partially disabled. **2** to damage something so severely that it can no longer operate or proceed.

crisis *noun* (*plural* **crises**) a time of acute difficulty or danger.

crisp *adjective* **1** brittle or easily crumbled. **2** desirably firm and fresh. **3** decisive or sharp in manner. **4** said about the weather: cold and fresh. ~ *noun* (*plural* **crisps**) a thin slice of fried potato. ➤ **crisply** *adverb*.

crisscross *adjective* marked with a pattern or network of intersecting lines. ~ *verb* (**crisscrosses, crisscrossing, crisscrossed**) **1** to pass back and forth across an area. **2** to mark something with intersecting lines.

criterion *noun* (*plural* **criteria** or **criterions**) a standard on which a judgment may be based.

Usage Note **criterion** and **criteria**. *Criteria* is the plural form of *criterion*. A phrase such as *this criteria* is incorrect.

critic *noun* (*plural* **critics**) **1** a person who evaluates works of art, literature, or music. **2** a person who tends to judge harshly.

critical *adjective* **1** inclined to criticize severely. **2** to do with criticism or critics. **3** involving careful evaluation. **4** crucial or decisive. ➤ **critically** *adverb*.

criticism *noun* (*plural* **criticisms**) **1** the act of criticizing or disapproving. **2** a critical observation or remark. **3** a detailed or reasoned assessment of something.

criticize *or* **criticise** *verb* (**criticizes, criticizing, criticized** *or* **criticises,** etc) **1** to find fault with somebody or something. **2** to evaluate a literary or artistic work.

croak *verb* (**croaks, croaking, croaked**) **1** to give the cry of a frog or crow. **2** to speak in a hoarse voice. ➤ **croak** *noun*.

crochet /kroh shay/ *noun* the art of making things by pulling wool or thread into a pattern of loops using a hooked needle.

crock[1] *noun* (*plural* **crocks**) *informal* **1** an elderly infirm person. **2** an old broken-down vehicle.

crock[2] *noun* (*plural* **crocks**) a thick earthenware pot or jar.

crockery *noun* earthenware or china dishes.

crocodile *noun* (*plural* **crocodiles**)

crocodile tears

1 a large reptile with a thick skin, long jaws, and a long body with a tail. **2** a line of schoolchildren walking in pairs.

crocodile tears *plural noun* insincere sorrow.

crocus *noun* (*plural* **crocuses**) a small plant that produces a single brightly coloured flower in spring.

croft *noun* (*plural* **crofts**) a small farm in Scotland. ➤ **crofter** *noun*.

croissant /krwah song/ *noun* (*plural* **croissants**) a flaky crescent-shaped roll.

crone *noun* (*plural* **crones**) an ugly old woman.

crook *noun* (*plural* **crooks**) **1** an implement with a bent or hooked shape. **2** a shepherd's staff. **3** *informal* a criminal. ~ *verb* (**crooks, crooking, crooked**) to bend or curve something.

crooked /kroo kid/ *adjective* **1** having a crook or curve; bent. **2** *informal* not morally straightforward; dishonest.

croon *verb* (**croons, crooning, crooned**) to sing in a low or soft voice. ➤ **crooner** *noun*.

crop *noun* (*plural* **crops**) **1** a plant grown and harvested for food. **2** a short riding whip. **3** a short haircut. **4** a pouch in a bird's throat in which food is stored and prepared for digestion. ~ *verb* (**crops, cropping, cropped**) **1** to trim something or cut it short. **2** said about an animal: to graze on grass, etc. ✱ **crop up** *informal* to happen or appear unexpectedly.

cropper ✱ **come a cropper** *informal* to fall or fail dramatically.

croquet /kroh kay/ *noun* a game in which wooden balls are knocked with mallets through a series of hoops.

crosier or **crozier** /kroh zi er/ *noun* (*plural* **crosiers** or **croziers**) a bishop's staff like a shepherd's crook.

cross *noun* (*plural* **crosses**) **1** a figure formed by two intersecting lines (+ or x). **2** *History* a cross-shaped upright stake used for executions. **3** (**the Cross**) the cross on which Jesus was crucified. **4** a cross-bred animal or plant. **5** a person or thing that combines characteristics of two different types: *a cross between a screwdriver and a knife.* **6** the act of crossing the ball in football. ~ *verb* (**crosses, crossing, crossed**) **1** to go across or from one side to the other of something. **2** to pass one another simultaneously in opposite directions. **3** (**cross off/out/through**) to cancel an item by drawing a line across it. **4** to finish off a letter *t* or *f* with the horizontal bar. **5** to move your arms, fingers, or legs so that one is resting on the other. **6** to crossbreed animals of two breeds. **7** to kick or pass the ball across the field in football. ~ *adjective* angry or annoyed. ✱ **at cross purposes** misunderstanding each other or having different intentions. ➤ **crossly** *adverb*.

crossbar *noun* (*plural* **crossbars**) **1** a bar between the uprights of a football goal. **2** a bar extending from the handlebars of a bicycle to the saddle.

crossbow *noun* (*plural* **crossbows**) a mechanical bow used to shoot a type of short blunt arrow.

crossbreed *verb* (**crossbreeds, crossbreeding, crossbred**) to produce an animal or plant by mixing two breeds. ➤ **crossbreed** *noun*.

cross-check *verb* (**cross-checks, cross-checking, cross-checked**) to check information by referring to more than one source.

cross-country *adjective and adverb* over countryside rather than by roads.

cross-examine *verb* (**cross-examines, cross-examining, cross-examined**) to question a witness who is giving evidence for the other side in a law case. ➤ **cross-examination** *noun*.

cross-eyed *adjective* having one or both eyes squinting inwards.

crossfire *noun* firing from two or more points in crossing directions.

cross-hatch *verb* (**cross-hatches, cross-hatching, cross-hatched**) *Art* to shade in an area of a picture with crossed parallel lines.

crossing *noun* (*plural* **crossings**) **1** part of a road marked for pedestrians to cross. **2** a place where roads or railway lines cross. **3** a journey across a stretch of water.

cross-legged *adverb and adjective* with ankles crossed and knees bent outwards.

crossover *noun* (*plural* **crossovers**) music that combines two different styles.

cross-question *verb* (**cross-questions, cross-questioning, cross-questioned**) to cross-examine somebody or question them intensively.

cross-reference *noun* (*plural* **cross-references**) a reference from one part of a book to another, for additional information.

crossroads *noun* (*plural* **crossroads**) a place where two or more roads cross.

cross-section *noun* (*plural* **cross-sections**) **1** a surface made by cutting across something at right angles to its length. **2** a representative sample of a group.

crosswise or **crossways** *adverb* so as to cross something; across.

crossword *noun* (*plural* **crosswords**) a puzzle in which words are entered horizontally and vertically in a pattern of numbered squares as answers to clues.

crotch *noun* (*plural* **crotches**) **1** the angle of the body between the inner thighs. **2** a fork in a tree.

crotchet *noun* (*plural* **crotchets**) *Music* a musical note with the time value of one beat.

crotchety *adjective informal* bad-tempered.

crouch *verb* (**crouches, crouching, crouched**) to lower the body by bending your knees and sloping your upper body forward. ➤ **crouch** *noun*.

croup /kroop/ *noun* a children's disease causing rasping breathing.

croupier /krooh pi er/ *noun* (*plural* **croupiers**) a person who runs the gaming tables in a casino.

crow *noun* (*plural* **crows**) a large black bird with a loud cry. ~ *verb* (**crows, crowing, crowed** or **crew, crowed**) **1** to make the shrill cry of a cock. **2** to boast about a success or gloat over somebody else's failure. ✲ **as the crow flies** in a direct line across country.

crowbar *noun* (*plural* **crowbars**) an iron or steel bar with a flattened end, used as a lever.

crowd *noun* (*plural* **crowds**) a large number of people gathered together. ~ *verb* (**crowds, crowding, crowded**) **1** to gather in large numbers. **2** to fill a place with people.

crown *noun* (*plural* **crowns**) **1** a round metal headdress worn by a royal ruler. **2** (**the Crown**) the king or queen as head of state. **3** the topmost part of something. **4** an artificial substitute for the top part of a tooth. ~ *verb* (**crowns, crowning, crowned**) **1** to place a crown on the head of somebody, especially at a ceremony to make them king or queen. **2** to form the top of something. **3** to be the conclusion or climax of something. **4** to put a crown on a tooth. **5** *informal* to hit somebody on the head.

crow's-feet *plural noun* the wrinkles round the outer corners of the eyes.

crow's nest *noun* (*plural* **crow's nests**) a high lookout platform on a ship's mast.

crozier *noun* see CROSIER.

crucial *adjective* very important or significant. ➤ **crucially** *adverb*.

crucible *noun* (*plural* **crucibles**) a container in which substances can be melted and mixed at a high temperature.

crucifix *noun* (*plural* **crucifixes**) a representation of Jesus on the cross.

crucify *verb* (**crucifies, crucifying, crucified**) **1** to execute somebody by fastening them to a cross. **2** *informal* to criticize somebody ruthlessly. ➤ **crucifixion** *noun*.

crude *adjective* **1** in a natural unprocessed state: *crude oil*. **2** coarse or vulgar. **3** rough or inexpert. ➤ **crudely** *adverb*, **crudity** *noun*.

cruel *adjective* (**crueller, cruellest**) **1** liking to inflict pain or suffering; pitiless. **2** painful. ➤ **cruelly** *adverb*, **cruelty** *noun*.

cruet *noun* (*plural* **cruets**) a set of small containers on a stand for holding salt, pepper, etc.

cruise *verb* (**cruises, cruising, cruised**) **1** to travel by sea for pleasure. **2** said about a vehicle: to travel at a steady speed.

cruise *noun* (*plural* **cruises**) a sea voyage for pleasure.

cruiser *noun* (*plural* **cruisers**) **1** a yacht or motor boat with passenger accommodation. **2** a large fast warship.

crumb *noun* (*plural* **crumbs**) **1** a small fragment of bread, cake, biscuit, or cheese. **2** a small amount.

crumble *verb* (**crumbles, crumbling, crumbled**) to break into small pieces. ~ *noun* (*plural* **crumbles**) a dessert of stewed fruit with a crumbly topping. ➤ **crumbly** *adjective*.

crumpet *noun* (*plural* **crumpets**) a small round unsweetened cake that is often eaten toasted.

crumple *verb* (**crumples, crumpling, crumpled**) **1** to crush a material so that it becomes creased or wrinkled. **2** to collapse.

crunch *verb* (**crunches, crunching, crunched**) to chew or bite something with a noisy crushing sound. ~ *noun* (*plural* **crunches**) **1** a crunching sound or action. **2** (**the crunch**) *informal* the decisive situation or moment.

crusade *noun* (*plural* **crusades**) **1** (**the Crusades**) *History* a series of medieval Christian military expeditions to win the Holy Land from the Muslims. **2** a campaign, especially to reform something. ➤ **crusader** *noun*, **crusading** *adjective*.

crush *verb* (**crushes, crushing, crushed**) **1** to deform or flatten something by pressing it. **2** to reduce a substance to particles by pounding or grinding. **3** to defeat somebody heavily. ~ *noun* (*plural* **crushes**) **1** a crowd of people in a small space. **2** a soft fruit drink. ✷ **have a crush on** *informal* to feel very attracted to somebody.

crust *noun* (*plural* **crusts**) **1** the hardened surface of a loaf of bread. **2** the pastry cover of a pie. **3** a hard or brittle surface layer. **4** the outer rocky layer of the earth.

crustacean *noun* (*plural* **crustaceans**) a sea creature with a hard shell, such as a lobster or crab.

crusty *adjective* (**crustier, crustiest**) **1** having a hard well-baked crust. **2** bad-tempered.

crutch *noun* (*plural* **crutches**) a long stick of wood or metal used to support an injured person in walking.

cry *verb* (**cries, crying, cried**) **1** to shed tears. **2** to call loudly. **3** said about a bird or animal: to utter its call. ~ *noun* (*plural* **cries**) **1** a spell of shedding tears. **2** a loud call or shout. **3** the call of an animal or bird. ✷ **cry off** to decide not to go ahead with an arrangement. **cry out for** to require a certain response or treatment urgently.

crypt *noun* (*plural* **crypts**) an underground chamber beneath a church.

cryptic *adjective* **1** mysterious or secret. **2** obscure in meaning. ➤ **cryptically** *adverb*.

crystal *noun* (*plural* **crystals**) **1** a piece of a natural solid material with symmetrical faces. **2** a clear transparent mineral, especially colourless quartz. **3** a fine clear glass. ➤ **crystalline** *adjective*.

crystallize *or* **crystallise** *verb* (**crystallizes, crystallizing, crystallized** *or* **crystallises,** etc) **1** to form crystals. **2** to give a thought a definite form. **3** to coat or preserve fruit with sugar.

cub *noun* (*plural* **cubs**) **1** a young fox, bear, lion, or other meat-eating mammal. **2** (**Cub** *or* **Cub Scout**) a member of the junior branch of the Scout Association.

cubbyhole *noun* (*plural* **cubbyholes**) a small room or enclosed space.

cube *noun* (*plural* **cubes**) *Maths* **1** a three-dimensional shape with six equal square faces. **2** the result of multiplying a number by itself twice. ~ *verb* (**cubes, cubing, cubed**) **1** to multiply (a number) by itself twice: *Four cubed is sixty-four.* **2** to cut food into small cubes.

cube root *noun* (*plural* **cube roots**) *Maths* the number that produces a given number when cubed: *The cube root of sixty-four is four.*

cubic *adjective* **1** having the shape of a cube. **2** three-dimensional. **3** used with a unit of length: indicating a volume equal to that of a cube whose edges are of the specified unit: *a cubic foot.*

cubicle *noun* (*plural* **cubicles**) a small partitioned space or compartment.

cuckoo *noun* (*plural* **cuckoos**) a greyish brown bird that lays its eggs in the nests of other birds.

cucumber *noun* (*plural* **cucumbers**) a long green fruit eaten raw in salads.

cud *noun* partly digested food brought back into the mouth by a cow to be chewed again.

cuddle *verb* (**cuddles, cuddling, cuddled**) to hold somebody or something in your arms and hug them. ➤ **cuddle** *noun*.

cuddly *adjective* (**cuddlier, cuddliest**) attractively soft and plump.

cudgel *noun* (*plural* **cudgels**) a short heavy club.

cue[1] *noun* (*plural* **cues**) **1** *Drama* a signal to a performer to begin a speech or action. **2** a signal or hint prompting action. * **on cue** at exactly the right time.

cue[2] *noun* (*plural* **cues**) a long rod for striking the ball in billiards, snooker, or pool.

cuff[1] *noun* (*plural* **cuffs**) a fold or band at the end of a sleeve which encircles the wrist. * **off the cuff** without preparation.

cuff[2] *verb* (**cuffs, cuffing, cuffed**) to strike somebody with the palm of the hand. ➤ **cuff** *noun*.

cuff link *noun* (*plural* **cuff links**) a fastener for a shirt cuff.

cuisine /kwi zeen/ *noun* a particular way of preparing or cooking food, especially one that is typical of country or area: *French cuisine.*

cul-de-sac *noun* (*plural* **cul-de-sacs** *or* **culs-de-sac di sac** /kul di sac/) a street or path that is closed at one end.

culinary *adjective* to do with cookery.

cull *verb* (**culls, culling, culled**) **1** to reduce a population of animals by selective killing. **2** to select a number of people or things from a range of sources. ➤ **cull** *noun*.

culminate *verb* (**culminates, culminating, culminated**) to reach the

culpable

highest or decisive point. ➤ **culmination** *noun*.

culpable *adjective* deserving blame; guilty. ➤ **culpability** *noun*, **culpably** *adverb*.

culprit *noun* (*plural* **culprits**) a person who is guilty of an offence or wrong.

> **Word History** Culprit comes from a French phrase used in English law courts after the Norman Conquest. If a prisoner pleaded 'not guilty', the prosecuting lawyer would say that he *was* guilty (*culpable* in Old French) and that the prosecution was ready (*prit* in Old French) to prove it. This was written in the court records as *cul. prit.* The two words came to be written as a single word *culprit*, and changed in meaning to refer to somebody accused of or guilty of wrongdoing.

cult *noun* (*plural* **cults**) **1** a system of religious beliefs and ritual, or its followers. **2** a religion regarded as unorthodox. **3** great devotion among a group to a particular person, idea, or thing.

cultivate *verb* (**cultivates, cultivating, cultivated**) **1** to use land for the growing of crops. **2** to grow a plant or crop on a large scale. **3** to improve or refine your mind. ➤ **cultivated** *adjective*, **cultivation** *noun*.

cultural *adjective* **1** to do with the arts and education. **2** to do with a society's culture and traditions. ➤ **culturally** *adverb*.

culture *noun* (*plural* **cultures**) **1** intellectual and artistic knowledge and good taste. **2** the customary beliefs and traditions of a people or group. **3** the growing of living cells, viruses, etc for experimental purposes.

cultured *adjective* well educated; appreciating the arts.

culvert *noun* (*plural* **culverts**) a small passage taking water under a road or railway.

cumbersome *adjective* heavy and difficult to carry or manage.

cumin /ku min/ *noun* the seeds of a plant, used as a spice.

cumulative *adjective* increasing by successive additions. ➤ **cumulatively** *adverb*.

cunning *adjective* **1** clever in a deceitful way; crafty. **2** ingenious. ~ *noun* craftiness. ➤ **cunningly** *adverb*.

cup *noun* (*plural* **cups**) **1** a small bowl-shaped drinking vessel with a handle. **2** an ornamental metal cup with two handles awarded as a prize in a sports competition. **3** something like a cup in shape. ~ *verb* (**cups, cupping, cupped**) to curve your hands into the shape of a cup round something. ➤ **cupful** (*plural* **cupfuls**) *noun*.

cupboard /ku bud/ *noun* (*plural* **cupboards**) a piece of furniture with a door, used for storage.

Cupid *noun* the Roman god of sexual love, pictured as a naked boy with wings, holding a bow and arrow.

cupidity *noun* excessive desire for wealth or possessions.

cupola /kew po la/ *noun* (*plural* **cupolas**) a small domed structure built on top of a roof.

cur *noun* (*plural* **curs**) a mongrel or low-quality dog.

curate *noun* (*plural* **curates**) an assistant to a priest in a parish.

curative *adjective* used to cure disease.

curator *noun* (*plural* **curators**) a person in charge of a museum or gallery.

curb *noun* (*plural* **curbs**) a check or restraint. ~ *verb* (**curbs, curbing, curbed**) to restrain or control something.

curd *noun* (*plural* **curds**) the thick part of coagulated milk used as food or made into cheese.

curdle *verb* (**curdles, curdling,**

curdled) to separate into solid curds or lumps and liquid.

cure *noun* (*plural* **cures**) **1** a drug or treatment that gives relief or recovery from an illness. **2** relief or recovery from an illness. **3** something that puts right a wrong or difficulty. ~ *verb* (**cures, curing, cured**) **1** to restore somebody to health. **2** to bring about recovery from an illness or other disorder. **3** to put right a harmful or troublesome situation. **4** to free somebody from something objectionable or harmful. **5** to preserve meat or fish by salting, drying, or smoking it. ➤ **curable** *adjective*.

curfew *noun* (*plural* **curfews**) a regulation requiring people to be indoors by a stated time.

curio *noun* (*plural* **curios**) an object that is considered unusual or rare.

curiosity *noun* (*plural* **curiosities**) **1** desire to know about something or somebody. **2** inquisitiveness. **3** a strange, interesting, or rare object.

curious *adjective* **1** eager to learn and find things out. **2** inquisitive. **3** strange or unusual. ➤ **curiously** *adverb*.

curl *verb* (**curls, curling, curled**) **1** to form hair into waves or coils. **2** to move or grow in curves or spirals. ~ *noun* (*plural* **curls**) **1** a curled lock of hair. **2** something with a spiral or coiled form.

curler *noun* (*plural* **curlers**) a small roller on which hair is wound for curling.

curlew *noun* (*plural* **curlews** or **curlew**) a wading bird with long legs and a long curved bill.

curling *noun* a team game in which players slide heavy flat stones over ice towards a marked circle.

curmudgeon /ker mu jon/ *noun* (*plural* **curmudgeons**) a bad-tempered old man. ➤ **curmudgeonly** *adjective*.

currant *noun* (*plural* **currants**) a small seedless dried grape used in cooking.

Usage Note Do not confuse this word with **current**.

currency *noun* (*plural* **currencies**) **1** a system of money used in a country. **2** the state of being in general use.

current *adjective* **1** occurring now or belonging to the present time. **2** generally accepted or used. ~ *noun* (*plural* **currents**) **1** a stream of water, air, etc that moves in a certain direction. **2** a flow of electricity. ➤ **currently** *adverb*.

Usage Note Do not confuse this word with **currant**.

curriculum *noun* (*plural* **curricula** or **curriculums**) the courses offered by an educational institution. ➤ **curricular** *adjective*.

curriculum vitae /vee tie/ *noun* (*plural* **curricula vitae**) a summary of a person's career and qualifications.

curry[1] *verb* (**curries, currying, curried**) ✶ **curry favour** to seek approval by flattering or being attentive to somebody.

curry[2] *noun* (*plural* **curries**) a dish of Indian origin, seasoned with hot spices and sauces.

curse *noun* (*plural* **curses**) **1** an appeal to a supernatural power to cause harm or injury to somebody. **2** a swearword or offensive expression. **3** a cause of misfortune. ~ *verb* (**curses, cursing, cursed**) **1** to wish harm to somebody with a curse. **2** to swear or use offensive language.

cursor *noun* (*plural* **cursors**) *ICT* a movable pointer on a computer screen, indicating the position where an input will take effect.

cursory *adjective* rapid and superficial. ➤ **cursorily** *adverb*.

curt

curt *adjective* rude or brusque. ➤ **curtly** *adverb*.

curtail *verb* (**curtails, curtailing, curtailed**) to limit something or cut it short. ➤ **curtailment** *noun*.

curtain *noun* (*plural* **curtains**) a piece of fabric hung at a window or at the front of a theatre stage, forming a screen when pulled across.

curtsy *noun* (*plural* **curtsies**) a woman's or girl's gesture of respect made by bending the knees with one leg behind the other. ~ *verb* (**curtsies, curtsying, curtsied**) to make a curtsy.

curvature *noun* **1** curved shape. **2** an abnormal curving of the spine.

curve *verb* (**curves, curving, curved**) to bend gradually from a straight line or course. ~ *noun* (*plural* **curves**) a curving line or surface.

cushion *noun* (*plural* **cushions**) a soft pillow or padded bag used for sitting or leaning on. ~ *verb* (**cushions, cushioning, cushioned**) **1** to protect something against force or shock. **2** to reduce the effects of something unpleasant.

cushy *adjective* (**cushier, cushiest**) *informal* easy or effortless.

cusp *noun* a pointed projection like the horn of a crescent moon. ✱ **on the cusp** between one state and another.

custard *noun* a thick sweetened sauce made with milk and eggs or milk and flavoured cornflour.

custodial *adjective* said about a sentence: involving imprisonment.

custodian *noun* (*plural* **custodians**) a person who guards and protects something.

custody *noun* **1** care or guardianship. **2** imprisonment or detention.

custom *noun* (*plural* **customs**) **1** an established or socially accepted practice. **2** (**customs**) taxes imposed on imports or exports, or the officials who collect them. **3** the customers who use a business.

customary *adjective* usual. ➤ **customarily** *adverb*.

custom-built *adjective* built exactly as a customer wants it.

customer *noun* (*plural* **customers**) **1** a person who buys a commodity or service. **2** an individual with a specified unfavourable quality: *an awkward customer*.

customize *or* **customise** *verb* (**customizes, customizing, customized** *or* **customises,** etc) to build or adjust something to somebody's personal requirements.

cut *verb* (**cuts, cutting, cut**) **1** to make an opening in something with a sharp object. **2** to shorten, divide, or detach something by cutting. **3** to make or shape something by cutting. **4** to reduce the amount of something: *to cut spending*. **5** to shorten or edit a text. **6** to break or interrupt a flow or supply, etc. **7** to cross or intersect a line. **8** to divide a pack of cards into two parts. **9** to ignore somebody deliberately or spitefully. **10** to switch off an engine or machine. **11** to stop filming or recording. ~ *noun* (*plural* **cuts**) **1** an opening or wound made with a sharp instrument. **2** a reduction or economy. **3** the style in which the hair or a piece of clothing is cut. **4** *informal* a share. ✱ **a cut above** superior to somebody or something. **cut both ways** to have advantages and disadvantages. **cut corners** to do something cheaply or quickly by making risky economies. **cut down 1** to make a tree fall by cutting through it. **2** to reduce or restrict an activity, expenditure, etc. **cut off 1** to remove something by cutting. **2** to stop the supply of something. **3** to stop somebody's supply of water, gas, or electricity. **4** to block access to a place. **5** to disconnect somebody during a telephone call. **cut out 1** to make by cutting from a larger piece. **2** to stop doing something. **3** said about an engine: to stop operating.

cut-and-dried *adjective* completely decided and unalterable.

cutback *noun* (*plural* **cutbacks**) a reduction or decrease.

cute *adjective* (**cuter, cutest**) **1** *informal* appealingly attractive or pretty. **2** shrewd; clever. ➤ **cutely** *adverb*.

cut glass *noun* glass with patterns cut into its surface.

cuticle /kew ti kl/ *noun* (*plural* **cuticles**) dead skin round the base and sides of a fingernail or toenail.

cutlass *noun* (*plural* **cutlasses**) *History* a short curved sword used by sailors.

cutlery *noun* knives, forks, and spoons.

cutlet *noun* (*plural* **cutlets**) **1** a small slice of meat. **2** a fried cake of minced meat or vegetables.

cutout *noun* (*plural* **cutouts**) **1** something cut out from a larger piece. **2** a device that stops the flow of an electric current or the operation of a machine.

cutter *noun* (*plural* **cutters**) **1** a person or implement that cuts. **2** a light fast boat.

cutting *noun* (*plural* **cuttings**) **1** a piece cut from a newspaper or magazine. **2** a piece cut from a plant for growing into a new plant. **3** a passage dug through high ground for a railway, road, etc. ~ *adjective* **1** said about a remark: likely to hurt or offend. **2** said about wind: piercingly cold. ✳ **the cutting edge** the most advanced or ambitious stage of an activity.

cuttlefish *noun* (*plural* **cuttlefish**) a sea creature like an octopus, with ten arms.

CV *abbreviation* curriculum vitae.

cwt *abbreviation* hundredweight.

cyanide *noun* an extremely poisonous chemical.

cybernetics *noun* the branch of science that studies and compares communications in organic systems, such as the nervous system of humans, and in machines, such as computers. ➤ **cybernetic** *adjective*.

cyberspace *noun* everywhere that communication between computers takes place.

cycle *noun* (*plural* **cycles**) **1** a series of related events happening in a set order. **2** a bicycle. ~ *verb* (**cycles, cycling, cycled**) to ride a bicycle.

cyclone *noun* (*plural* **cyclones**) **1** a system of winds rotating around a centre of low atmospheric pressure and often bringing rain. **2** a violent storm. ➤ **cyclonic** *adjective*.

cygnet /sig nit/ *noun* (*plural* **cygnets**) a young swan.

cylinder *noun* (*plural* **cylinders**) **1** a shape with circular ends and parallel sides. **2** the chamber in a steam or internal-combustion engine in which a piston works.

cymbal *noun* (*plural* **cymbals**) *Music* a percussion instrument consisting of a brass plate that is struck with a stick or against another cymbal.

cynic /si nik/ *noun* (*plural* **cynics**) a person who believes that people's actions are always motivated by selfish interests. ➤ **cynical** *adjective*, **cynically** *adverb*, **cynicism** *noun*.

cypress /sie pris/ *noun* (*plural* **cypresses**) an evergreen tree with overlapping leaves resembling scales.

cyst /sist/ *noun* (*plural* **cysts**) an abnormal swelling containing watery liquid or gas.

czar *noun* see TSAR.

dab verb (**dabs, dabbing, dabbed**) **1** to touch something lightly and repeatedly. **2** to apply a liquid or powder with light strokes. ~ *noun* (*plural* **dabs**) **1** a small amount of something soft or moist. **2** a gentle touch or stroke.

dabble verb (**dabbles, dabbling, dabbled**) **1** to move your fingers or toes about in water. **2** to have a casual involvement or interest in something: *She dabbles in art*.

dab hand noun (*plural* **dab hands**) *informal* a person who is good at something.

dachshund /dak sund/ noun (*plural* **dachshunds**) a small dog with a long body, short legs, and long drooping ears.

dad or **daddy** noun (*plural* **dads** or **daddies**) *informal* your father.

daddy longlegs noun (*plural* **daddy longlegs**) a crane fly.

daffodil noun (*plural* **daffodils**) a plant with a yellow flower with a long trumpet-shaped centre.

daft adjective *informal* silly or foolish.

dagger noun (*plural* **daggers**) a short knife used as a weapon.

dahlia /day li a/ noun (*plural* **dahlias**) a plant with large, brightly coloured flowers.

Dáil /doil *or* dahl/ noun (**the Dáil**) (also **Dáil Éireann** /air an/) the lower house of parliament in the Republic of Ireland.

daily adjective and adverb occurring every day. ~ *noun* (*plural* **dailies**) *informal* a newspaper published daily from Monday to Saturday.

dainty adjective (**daintier, daintiest**) small, delicate, and beautiful.
➤ **daintily** adverb.

dairy noun (*plural* **dairies**) **1** a place where milk is processed and butter or cheese is made. **2** (*used before a noun*) involving milk, butter, or cheese.

dais /day is/ noun (*plural* **daises**) a raised platform that you stand on to make a speech.

daisy noun (*plural* **daisies**) a plant with small flowers that have yellow centres and thin white petals.

dale noun (*plural* **dales**) a valley.

Dalmatian noun (*plural* **Dalmatians**) a large short-haired dog with a white coat with black or brown spots.

dam noun (*plural* **dams**) a barrier built across a river to hold back and store the water. ~ *verb* (**dams, damming, dammed**) to build a dam across a river.

damage noun **1** loss or harm resulting from injury. **2** (**damages**) money that a court orders one person or organization to pay to another. ~ *verb* (**damages, damaging, damaged**) **1** to cause damage to something. **2** to become damaged. ➤ **damaging** *adjective*.

dame noun (*plural* **dames**) **1** (**Dame**) the title of a woman who has been given an honour equivalent to a knighthood. **2** in a pantomime, the part of a comic old woman played by a man. **3** N American, informal a woman.

damn /dam/ verb (**damns, damning, damned**) to say that something or somebody is very bad or worthless. ~ interjection used to express annoyance.

damnation /dam **nay** shn/ noun the punishment of being sent to hell.

damned adjective informal used to describe something that is annoying you.

damp adjective slightly wet. ~ noun moisture in the air or in the walls of buildings.

dampen verb (**dampens, dampening, dampened**) **1** to make something damp. **2** to make something less strong or intense.

damper noun (plural **dampers**) **1** Music a device that stops the vibration of a piano string. **2** a valve that controls the flow of air in a furnace. ✶ **put a damper on** to spoil something that should be enjoyable.

damp squib noun (plural **damp squibs**) something that is far less impressive or enjoyable than you expected it to be.

damson noun (plural **damsons**) a small purple fruit similar to a plum.

dance verb (**dances, dancing, danced**) to move your body in time to music. ~ noun (plural **dances**) **1** a series of movements performed in time to music. **2** a social event with dancing. **3** a piece of music for dancing to. ➤ **dancer** noun.

dandelion noun (plural **dandelions**) a common weed with yellow flowers and seeds that form a fluffy ball.

dandruff noun dead skin that comes off your scalp in small white flakes.

danger noun (plural **dangers**) **1** a situation in which you might be injured or hurt, or might lose some-thing. **2** something that causes you to be in such a situation: *the dangers of working in a mine.* **3** the possibility that something unpleasant will happen: *There's a danger we'll be late.*

dangerous adjective able to do harm or cause injury. ➤ **dangerously** adverb.

dangle verb (**dangles, dangling, dangled**) **1** to hang or swing loosely. **2** to offer something enticing: *The manager dangled promotion in front of her.* ➤ **dangly** adjective.

dank adjective unpleasantly moist or wet.

dapper adjective said about a man: dressed neatly and smartly.

dappled adjective marked with light and dark patches of colour

dare verb (**dares, daring, dared**) **1** to have enough courage to do something: *He didn't dare disagree.* **2** to challenge somebody to do something: *They dared him to jump the stream.* ~ noun (plural **dares**) a challenge to do something difficult or dangerous. ✶ **I dare say/daresay** it is likely or probable.

daredevil noun (plural **daredevils**) somebody who does dangerous things without thinking or caring about the risks.

daring adjective brave enough to try doing difficult or dangerous things. ~ noun the brave attitude of somebody who is willing to try difficult or dangerous things. ➤ **daringly** adverb.

dark adjective **1** with little or no light. **2** said about a colour: not light or pale. **3** said about somebody's hair or complexion: not fair. **4** secret or mysterious: *dark plans.* **5** sinister or evil: *dark deeds.* **6** dismal or sad: *Those were dark times for us.* ~ noun **1** the absence of light; darkness. **2** night or nightfall. ✶ **in the dark** not knowing something. ➤ **darkly** adverb, **darkness** noun.

Dark Ages plural noun (**the Dark**

darken

Ages) *History* the period of European history from the end of the Roman Empire in AD 476 to about AD 1000, thought of as a time when there was no culture or learning.

darken *verb* (**darkens, darkening, darkened**) **1** to become, or make something, dark or darker. **2** to become unhappy or angry: *Her mood darkened.*

dark horse *noun* (*plural* **dark horses**) somebody or something that people know little about.

darkroom *noun* (*plural* **darkrooms**) a room with special low light, for processing photographs.

darling *noun* (*plural* **darlings**) **1** an affectionate word you use when you are speaking to somebody you like or love. **2** a dearly loved person. ~ *adjective* **1** dearly loved: *my darling son.* **2** charming: *a darling little cottage.*

darn *verb* (**darns, darning, darned**) to mend knitted material by stitching up holes. ~ *noun* (*plural* **darns**) a darned area of a garment.

dart *noun* (*plural* **darts**) **1** an object like a small arrow, used as a weapon or in the game of darts. **2** a tapering fold put in a garment to shape it. **3** (**darts**) an indoor game in which darts are thrown at a round board marked in numbered sections. ~ *verb* (**darts, darting, darted**) to move suddenly or rapidly.

dash *verb* (**dashes, dashing, dashed**) **1** to move with speed or haste. **2** to throw something with great force. **3** to destroy hopes or plans. ~ *noun* (*plural* **dashes**) **1** *English* a punctuation mark (–) used to indicate a break or a missing word. **2** a quick or hurried movement. **3** *chiefly N American* a sprint. **4** a small amount of a substance. **5** = DASHBOARD.

dashboard *noun* (*plural* **dashboards**) in a vehicle, the panel where the dials and controls are.

dashing *adjective* dressed in a smart and stylish way.

data *plural noun* **1** *ICT* the information stored and processed by a computer. **2** facts or information generally.

Usage Note Data is, strictly speaking, a plural noun with the singular form *datum*, but it is increasingly used as a singular noun like *information* or *news*: *The data is currently being processed.*

database *noun* (*plural* **databases**) *ICT* a large collection of information stored in a computer.

date[1] *noun* (*plural* **dates**) **1** a particular day of the month or year, identified by a number. **2** the time at which an event occurred or will occur. **3** *informal* a romantic or social engagement, or the person you go to meet. **4** a single show or concert in a series. ~ *verb* (**dates, dating, dated**) **1** to find out the date of something. **2** to mark something with a date. **3** *informal* to go out with somebody on romantic dates. **4** to belong to a specified time in the past: *coins dating from Anglo-Saxon times.* **5** to become old-fashioned: *a style that will soon date.* ✽ **to date** up to now.

date[2] *noun* (*plural* **dates**) a small brown oval fruit with a sweet taste, eaten fresh or dried.

dated *adjective* no longer modern or fashionable.

datum *noun* see usage note at DATA.

daub *verb* (**daubs, daubing, daubed**) to put a soft thick substance on a surface in a rough or careless way

daughter *noun* (*plural* **daughters**) **1** a female child. **2** a female descendant.

daughter-in-law *noun* (*plural* **daughters-in-law**) the wife of a son.

daunt *verb* (**daunts, daunting, daunted**) to dishearten somebody by seeming very difficult to do or achieve.

daunting *adjective* seeming so difficult to do or achieve that you are disheartened.

dawdle *verb* (**dawdles, dawdling, dawdled**) to move slowly or in a lazy way.

dawn *noun* (*plural* **dawns**) **1** the first appearance of light in the morning. **2** the first appearance or beginning of something. ~ *verb* (**dawns, dawning, dawned**) **1** said about the day: to begin to grow light. **2** (**dawn on**) to be realized or begin to be understood: *The truth finally dawned on him.*

day *noun* (*plural* **days**) **1** a period of 24 hours beginning at midnight. **2** the period of daylight between sunrise and sunset. **3** the hours spent daily at work or school. **4** (*also in plural*) a particular time or period in the past: *in my grandmother's day; in the days of horse-drawn carriages.* * **these days** at the present time.

daybreak *noun* dawn.

daydream *noun* (*plural* **daydreams**) pleasant thoughts you have while you are awake. ~ *verb* (**daydreams, daydreaming, daydreamed**) to have a daydream.

daylight *noun* **1** the light of the sun during the day. **2** dawn.

daylight robbery *noun informal* unfairly high prices or charges.

day-to-day *adjective* happening often as part of ordinary life.

daze *noun* a state of confusion or shock. ➤ **dazed** *adjective.*

dazzle *verb* (**dazzles, dazzling, dazzled**) **1** to blind somebody temporarily with a sudden bright light. **2** to impress somebody very much. ~ *noun* sudden blinding brightness. ➤ **dazzling** *adjective.*

DC *abbreviation* **1** *Science* direct current. **2** District of Columbia (US postal abbreviation).

deacon *noun* (*plural* **deacons**) **1** in some Christian churches, an ordained minister who ranks below a priest. **2** a lay minister or official in various Protestant churches.

dead *adjective* **1** no longer alive. **2** said about a body part: numb. **3** said about equipment: no longer working: *The engine was dead.* **4** no longer used, active, or relevant: *a dead language.* **5** *informal* lacking in activity or interest: *The campus is dead at weekends.* **6** *informal* complete or absolute: *a dead certainty.* ~ *adverb* **1** absolutely or exactly: *The horse stopped dead.* **2** *informal* very. ~ *noun* the time when something is most intense: *the dead of winter.*

deaden *verb* (**deadens, deadening, deadened**) **1** to make a sound quieter. **2** to make pain less intense. **3** to numb a part of the body.

dead end *noun* (*plural* **dead ends**) **1** a street or passage without an exit. **2** a situation in which no progress can be made.

dead heat *noun* (*plural* **dead heats**) a race or contest where two or more competitors finish level.

deadline *noun* (*plural* **deadlines**) a date or time before which something must be completed.

Word History From a line marked round the edge of Andersonville prison during the American Civil War. Guards were instructed to shoot any prisoner who stepped over the line.

---

deadlock *noun* (*plural* **deadlocks**) a situation in which no progress can be made because of serious disagreements. ➤ **deadlocked** *adjective.*

deadly *adjective* (**deadlier, deadliest**) **1** able to cause death. **2** with no mistakes at all: *deadly accuracy.* ~ *adverb* absolutely: *deadly accurate.*

deadpan *adjective and adverb* showing no feelings.

dead ringer *noun* (*plural* **dead**

deaf *adjective* **1** partially or completely unable to hear. **2** (**deaf to**) unwilling to listen to something that somebody says. ➤ **deafness** *noun*.

deafen *verb* (**deafens, deafening, deafened**) to be so loud as to make somebody temporarily unable to hear.

deafening *adjective* extremely loud.

deal *verb* (**deals, dealing, dealt** /delt/) **1** to give out cards to players in a card game. **2** (**deal out**) to give or share something out. **3** (**deal in**) to buy and sell things: *The company deals in recycled waste.* **4** *informal* to buy and sell drugs illegally. ~ *noun* (*plural* **deals**) **1** an agreement. **2** a particular kind of treatment: *a raw deal*. **3** the process of giving out cards in a card game. ✱ **deal with 1** to take action with regard to something: *I'll deal with my letters tomorrow.* **2** to cope with something: *He can't deal with screaming children.* **3** to have business relations with somebody: *We deal with several Japanese companies.* **4** to be concerned with a theme or subject: *Chapter 1 deals with health problems.* **a good/great deal 1** a lot: *a great deal of money.* **2** considerably: *I feel a good deal better today.*

dealer *noun* (*plural* **dealers**) **1** a person who deals in goods or services. **2** a person who sells illegal drugs. **3** the player who deals the cards in a card game.

dealings *plural noun* business or personal relationships.

dean *noun* (*plural* **deans**) **1** a senior priest in some churches where there are several priests. **2** in some universities, the head of a college or department.

dear *adjective* **1** much loved: *my dear friend.* **2** a polite way of addressing somebody in a letter. **3** expensive. ~ *noun* (*plural* **dears**) **1** an affectionate word you use when you are speaking to somebody. **2** a lovable person.

dearly *adverb* **1** very much: *I would dearly like to help.* **2** in a way that involves great loss: *We paid dearly for our mistake.*

dearth /derth/ *noun* a lack of something.

death *noun* (*plural* **deaths**) **1** the end of life, or the state of being dead. **2** an instance of dying: *deaths caused by smoking.*

deathly *adjective and adverb* (**deathlier, deathliest**) reminding you of death; as if somebody was dead: *Her face was deathly pale.*

death penalty *noun* (**the death penalty**) the punishment of being killed for committing a serious crime.

debase *verb* (**debases, debasing, debased**) to lower the status, quality, or value of something. ➤ **debasement** *noun*.

debatable *adjective* about which people have different opinions.

debate *noun* (*plural* **debates**) **1** a formal discussion in which opposing speakers say why they believe something. **2** an argument or controversy. ~ *verb* (**debates, debating, debated**) **1** to discuss a question by stating opposing arguments. **2** to consider something from different viewpoints.

debilitating *adjective* making you feel very weak.

debit *noun* (*plural* **debits**) **1** an entry in an account showing that money is owed. **2** a sum of money taken out of a bank account. ~ *verb* (**debits, debiting, debited**) **1** to record an amount as a debit. **2** said about a bank: to take a sum of money from a customer's bank account.

debit card *noun* (*plural* **debit cards**) a bank card that allows you to pay for things, with the payment being taken from your bank account straight away.

debris /de bree/ *noun* scattered remains or rubbish left after something has been broken.

debt /det/ *noun* **1** money that somebody owes. **2** the state of owing money or thanks.

debtor *noun* (*plural* **debtors**) somebody who owes a debt.

debut /day bew/ *noun* (*plural* **debuts**) a first public appearance.

debutante /de bew tahnt/ *noun* (*plural* **debutantes**) a young upper-class woman who has just started going to important social events.

decade *noun* (*plural* **decades**) a period of ten years.

decadent /de ka dint/ *adjective* **1** having or involving low moral standards. **2** choosing to do or have something enjoyable that you might sometimes deny yourself. ➤ **decadence** *noun*.

decaffeinated /dee ka fi nay tid/ *adjective* said about coffee: having had most of its caffeine removed.

decagon /de ka gon/ *noun* (*plural* **decagons**) *Maths* a flat shape with ten angles and ten straight sides.

decanter /di kan ter/ *noun* (*plural* **decanters**) an ornamental glass bottle into which wine, whisky, or brandy is poured for serving.

decapitate /di ka pi tayt/ *verb* (**decapitates, decapitating, decapitated**) to cut off somebody's head. ➤ **decapitation** *noun*.

decathlon /di kath lon/ *noun* (*plural* **decathlons**) an athletics contest in which each competitor takes part in ten events. ➤ **decathlete** *noun*.

decay *verb* (**decays, decaying, decayed**) **1** to rot or decompose. **2** to become less good or less strong. ~ *noun* **1** the state or process of decaying: *a society in decay*. **2** decayed parts: *tooth decay*.

deceased *noun* (*plural* **deceased**) (**the deceased**) *formal* a person who has recently died. ~ *adjective formal* recently dead.

deceit *noun* behaviour that deliberately makes somebody believe something that is false.

deceitful *adjective* tending to deceive people. ➤ **deceitfully** *adverb*.

deceive *verb* (**deceives, deceiving, deceived**) to deliberately make somebody believe something that is false.

decelerate /dee se li rayt/ *verb* (**decelerates, decelerating, decelerated**) to slow down. ➤ **deceleration** *noun*.

December *noun* the twelfth month of the year.

decency *noun* behaviour that follows normal rules about fairness, honesty, and politeness.

decent /dee snt/ *adjective* **1** following normal rules about fair, honest, and polite behaviour. **2** good enough, if not outstanding: *decent food*. **3** *informal* kind: *It was decent of you to help*. ➤ **decently** *adverb*.

deception *noun* (*plural* **deceptions**) **1** the act of deceiving somebody, or the state of being deceived. **2** an occasion when somebody is deceived: *a cruel deception*.

deceptive *adjective* tending to make people believe something that is not true, or not realize something that is true.

deceptively *adverb* **1** in a way that disguises the reality; misleadingly: *Her voice was deceptively calm*. **2** despite how something appears: *deceptively spacious*.

decibel *noun* (*plural* **decibels**) *Science* a unit for measuring the intensity of sounds.

decide *verb* (**decides, deciding, decided**) **1** to make a definite choice or come to a firm conclusion. **2** to influence somebody to make a choice: *What decided you?* **3** to settle the outcome of something: *the goal that decided the match.*

decided *adjective* **1** definite: *a decided advantage.* **2** unhesitating; firm: *a woman of decided opinions.* ➤ **decidedly** *adverb.*

decider *noun* (*plural* **deciders**) a final point or additional contest that decides who wins a competition.

deciduous /di si dew us/ *adjective* said about a tree: with leaves that fall off in winter.

decimal /de si ml/ *adjective* Maths based on the number ten, and divided into units that are tenths, hundredths, etc of one another. ~ *noun* (*plural* **decimals**) (*also* **decimal fraction**) Maths a fraction that is expressed by a dot followed by figures for the number of tenths, hundredths, etc.

decimal place *noun* (*plural* **decimal places**) Maths the position of a figure to the right of a decimal point.

decimal point *noun* (*plural* **decimal points**) Maths the dot placed between a whole number and a decimal fraction.

decimate *verb* (**decimates, decimating, decimated**) **1** to kill a large number of people or animals from among a group or population. **2** to destroy a large part of something. ➤ **decimation** *noun.*

decipher /di sie fer/ *verb* (**deciphers, deciphering, deciphered**) to make out the meaning of something that is difficult to understand.

decision *noun* (*plural* **decisions**) **1** a choice or conclusion that you reach after considering various alternatives. **2** quickness and firmness when deciding something: *a man of decision.*

decisive *adjective* **1** of crucial importance in settling the outcome of something: *the decisive battle.* **2** tending to make firm decisions quickly. ➤ **decisively** *adverb*, **decisiveness** *noun.*

deck[1] *noun* (*plural* **decks**) **1** the open platform on a ship, which you can walk on. **2** one of several floors on a large ship. **3** one of the two floors on a double-decker bus. **4** the upper operating surface of a record player. **5** a wooden platform that extends from a house into the garden. **6** *N American* a pack of playing cards. **7** (**the deck**) *informal* the ground or floor.

deck[2] *verb* (**decks, decking, decked**) **1** to decorate a place: *The hall was decked with flags.* **2** to dress somebody in specified clothes: *rich women decked out in furs.*

deck chair *noun* (*plural* **deck chairs**) a folding chair made of canvas stretched over a wooden frame.

decking *noun* material used to make a deck in a garden.

declaration *noun* (*plural* **declarations**) a formal or official statement.

declare *verb* (**declares, declaring, declared**) **1** to state something formally or officially. **2** to tell tax officials about money you have earned, or tell customs officials about goods you have brought into a country. **3** said about a cricket captain or team: to end the team's innings before all the batsmen are out.

decline *verb* (**declines, declining, declined**) **1** to become gradually smaller, less strong, or less good. **2** to refuse something politely. ~ *noun* **1** a gradual reduction or change for the worse. **2** the period when something is approaching its end.

decode *verb* (**decodes, decoding, decoded**) to convert a coded message into ordinary language. ➤ **decoder** *noun.*

decompose *verb* (**decomposes, decomposing, decomposed**) **1** to decay or rot. **2** *Science* to split into separate components, elements, atoms, etc. ➤ **decomposition** *noun.*

decor or **décor** /day kaw/ noun the style in which a room is decorated and furnished.

decorate verb (**decorates, decorating, decorated**) 1 to give something a more attractive appearance by adding colour or pretty objects: *a hat decorated with feathers*. 2 to put paint or wallpaper on the walls of a room. 3 to award a medal or honour to somebody.

decoration noun (plural **decorations**) 1 the act or process of decorating. 2 an ornament. 3 a medal or honour.

decorative adjective making a room or object look attractive. ➤ **decoratively** adverb.

decorator noun (plural **decorators**) somebody whose job is painting and wallpapering rooms.

decorum /di kaw rum/ noun behaviour that follows rules about politeness and good taste.

decoy noun (plural **decoys**) 1 something used to lure a person or animal into a trap. 2 somebody or something used to divert the attention of an enemy.

decrease /di krees/ verb (**decreases, decreasing, decreased**) to become, or make something become, gradually less in size, number, or intensity. ~ /dee krees/ noun (plural **decreases**) 1 the amount by which something decreases. 2 the process of decreasing.

decree noun (plural **decrees**) an official or legal order. ~ verb (**decrees, decreeing, decreed**) to order something officially or legally.

dedicate verb (**dedicates, dedicating, dedicated**) 1 to give a lot of time or effort to achieving something. 2 to say formally that you have produced something such as a book or song for a particular person.

dedicated adjective 1 working hard to achieve something. 2 kept and used only for a particular purpose.

dedication noun (plural **dedications**) 1 commitment to achieving a particular goal. 2 words used to dedicate something such as a book or song to somebody.

deduce verb (**deduces, deducing, deduced**) to establish a fact or the truth by reasoning and considering the information available.

deduct verb (**deducts, deducting, deducted**) to subtract an amount from a total. ➤ **deductible** adjective.

deduction noun (plural **deductions**) 1 an amount that is deducted from a total. 2 a conclusion that you reach after reasoning and considering the information available.

deed noun (plural **deeds**) 1 something that somebody does: *evil deeds*. 2 a legal document.

deem verb (**deems, deeming, deemed**) *formal* to have a particular opinion or judgment about something or somebody.

deep adjective 1 extending far downwards, inwards, or back from a surface or area: *a deep valley*. 2 used for stating how far something extends in a downward direction: *a well 20 metres deep*. 3 said about a colour: rich and dark. 4 said about a sound: having a low pitch. 5 intellectually demanding or difficult to understand: *This poem is too deep for me*. 6 capable of serious thought: *a deep thinker*. 7 intense or extreme: *a deep sleep*. 8 in sport, near or towards the outer limits of the playing area. ➤ **deeply** adverb.

deepen verb (**deepens, deepening, deepened**) to become deeper, or make something deeper.

deep-fry verb (**deep-fries, deep-frying, deep-fried**) to fry food by completely immersing it in hot oil.

deer noun (plural **deer**) a large mammal with hoofs and often with antlers.

deface verb (**defaces, defacing,**

default

defaced) to spoil the appearance of something.

default /dɪˈfawlt/ *noun* **1** something that happens or is selected automatically unless you deliberately choose something else. **2** failure to do something required by law, for example failure to pay debts or appear in court. ~ *verb* (**defaults, defaulting, defaulted**) to fail to do something that you are obliged to do, for example to fail to pay a bill. * **by default** because there was no alternative or because nothing was done to change a situation.

defeat *verb* (**defeats, defeating, defeated**) **1** to win a victory over somebody. **2** to frustrate somebody who is trying to achieve or solve something. ~ *noun* (*plural* **defeats**) **1** failure to win. **2** a contest or battle that you lose.

defeatism *noun* the attitude of somebody who expects defeat or accepts defeat too early. ➤ **defeatist** *noun and adjective*.

defecate *verb* (**defecates, defecating, defecated**) to get rid of solid waste from your bowels through your anus. ➤ **defecation** *noun*.

defect /ˈdeefekt/ *noun* (*plural* **defects**) a fault or shortcoming. ~ /dɪˈfekt/ *verb* (**defects, defecting, defected**) to leave your country, organization, or political party and join an enemy or rival. ➤ **defection** *noun*, **defector** *noun*.

defective *adjective* faulty.

defence *noun* (*plural* **defences**) **1** the act of defending something. **2** a means of defending something. **3** an argument that supports or justifies something. **4** a defendant's case in court. **5** the lawyers representing a defendant in a court. **6** in sport, defending players or moves. ➤ **defenceless** *adjective*.

defend *verb* (**defends, defending,**

168

defended) **1** to protect somebody or something from attack. **2** to attempt to hold on to a military position, a sporting title, or a parliamentary or local council seat that others are trying to gain. **3** to argue in support of something or somebody that is being opposed or criticized. **4** in sport, to attempt to prevent an opponent from scoring. **5** to act as the legal representative of an accused person in court. ➤ **defender** *noun*.

defendant *noun* (*plural* **defendants**) a person or organization accused of something in a court case.

defensible *adjective* capable of being defended in an argument or war.

defensive *adjective* **1** designed to defend or protect something or somebody. **2** sensitive to criticism and eager to justify your own actions or views. * **on the defensive** in the position of having to defend yourself against attack or criticism. ➤ **defensively** *adverb*, **defensiveness** *noun*.

defer[1] *verb* (**defers, deferring, deferred**) to postpone an action or decision. ➤ **deferment** *noun*, **deferral** *noun*.

defer[2] *verb* (**defers, deferring, deferred**) (**defer to**) to acknowledge somebody's superiority and do as they say or accept their opinion.

deference /ˈdefrɪns/ *noun* the respect that you give to somebody who is superior to you.

deferential /defɪˈrenshl/ *adjective* showing respect for somebody who is superior. ➤ **deferentially** *adverb*.

defiance *noun* bold resistance or disobedience.

defiant *adjective* boldly resisting or disobeying somebody. ➤ **defiantly** *adverb*.

deficient *adjective* **1** lacking in some necessary quality or element. **2** not as good as it should be. ➤ **deficiency** *noun*.

deficit /ˈdefisit/ *noun* (*plural* **deficits**) the amount by which the total money spent is greater than the total money earned.

define *verb* (**defines, defining, defined**) **1** to explain the meaning of a word or phrase. **2** to explain or decide the precise nature or limits of something: *Your task was clearly defined.* **3** to show the outline of something clearly. ➤ **definable** *adjective*.

definite *adjective* **1** about which there can be no misunderstanding: *She gave me a definite answer.* **2** clearly apparent: *We had a definite advantage.* ➤ **definitely** *adverb*.

definite article *noun* (*plural* **definite articles**) *English* the word *the*.

definition *noun* (*plural* **definitions**) **1** a statement of what a word or phrase means. **2** the distinctness of an outline, shape, or detail.

definitive /diˈnitiv/ *adjective* **1** deciding something firmly and finally: *a definitive answer.* **2** giving the best information available: *the definitive guide to wine.* ➤ **definitively** *adverb*.

deflate *verb* (**deflates, deflating, deflated**) **1** to release air or gas from something such as a balloon or tyre. **2** to cause somebody to lose all their self-confidence, self-importance, or enthusiasm.

deflation *noun* **1** a reduction in the amount of money and credit available in an economy, and a resulting decline in economic activity and price levels. **2** the act of letting the air or gas out of something such as a balloon or tyre. ➤ **deflationary** *adjective*.

deflect *verb* (**deflects, deflecting, deflected**) **1** to make something that is moving change its direction slightly. **2** to make somebody change their mind. ➤ **deflection** *noun*.

deforestation *noun* the practice of cutting down the trees in an area.

deformed *adjective* having an abnormal shape or appearance.

deformity *noun* (*plural* **deformities**) **1** the state of being deformed. **2** a physical blemish or disfigurement.

defraud *verb* (**defrauds, defrauding, defrauded**) to cheat somebody out of something.

defrost *verb* (**defrosts, defrosting, defrosted**) **1** to thaw out frozen food. **2** to get rid of the ice in a refrigerator or freezer.

deft *adjective* done quickly, easily and with great skill. ➤ **deftly** *adverb*, **deftness** *noun*.

defunct *adjective* no longer existing or in use.

defuse *verb* (**defuses, defusing, defused**) **1** to make a bomb or mine safe by removing the fuse. **2** to make a situation less dangerous or tense.

defy *verb* (**defies, defying, defied**) **1** to openly refuse to obey a person or rule. **2** to challenge somebody to do something you consider impossible.

degenerate /deeˈjenirayt/ *verb* (**degenerates, degenerating, degenerated**) to sink to a very bad state. ~ /deeˈjenirət/ *adjective* having sunk to a very bad state. ~ *noun* a morally corrupt person. ➤ **degeneracy** *noun*, **degeneration** *noun*, **degenerative** *adjective*.

degradation /ˌdegrəˈdayshn/ *noun* the state of being very poor and unhappy.

degrade *verb* (**degrades, degrading, degraded**) **1** to cause somebody to lose their self-respect or the respect of others. **2** *Science* in chemistry, to cause a substance to decompose or disintegrate. ➤ **degrading** *adjective*.

degree *noun* (*plural* **degrees**) **1** the extent of something: *a high degree of risk.* **2** *Science* a unit for measuring temperature. **3** *Maths, Geography* a

dehydrated

unit for measuring angles and for measuring longitude and latitude on a map. **4** a qualification that you get after completing a course of study at a university, or the course of study itself.

dehydrated *adjective* weak or ill because you have not drunk enough water.

deign /dayn/ *verb* (**deigns, deigning, deigned**) to do something that you normally refuse to do because you think it is beneath you: *He finally deigned to speak to me.*

deity /day i ti *or* dee i ti/ *noun* (*plural* **deities**) a god or goddess.

déjà vu /day zhah vooh/ *noun* the feeling that you are remembering scenes and events when, in fact, you are experiencing them for the first time.

dejected *adjective* having lost all hope or enthusiasm. ➤ **dejection** *noun*.

delay *noun* (*plural* **delays**) the time during which something is prevented from happening. ~ *verb* (**delays, delaying, delayed**) **1** to put something off to a later time. **2** to detain or hinder somebody for a time. **3** to fail to act or move immediately: *Don't delay!*

delectable *adjective* delightful or delicious. ➤ **delectably** *adverb*.

delegate /de li gat/ *noun* (*plural* **delegates**) a person appointed to represent somebody else, for example at a conference. ~ /de li gayt/ *verb* (**delegates, delegating, delegated**) **1** to give somebody a duty or responsibility. **2** to appoint somebody as your representative.

delegation *noun* (*plural* **delegations**) **1** a group of people appointed to represent others. **2** the act of delegating a duty or responsibility to somebody.

delete *verb* (**deletes, deleting, deleted**) to cross out or get rid of something written or printed. ➤ **deletion** *noun*.

deli /de li/ *noun* (*plural* **delis**) *informal* a delicatessen.

deliberate /di li bi rat/ *adjective* **1** done with a definite purpose in mind; intentional. **2** slow or unhurried: *deliberate movements.* ~ /di li bi rayt/ *verb* (**deliberates, deliberating, deliberated**) to think about or discuss something carefully before reaching a decision. ➤ **deliberately** *adverb*.

deliberation *noun* (*plural* **deliberations**) careful and serious thought or discussion.

delicacy *noun* (*plural* **delicacies**) **1** a delicious food that is considered rare or luxurious. **2** a fragile or dainty quality.

delicate *adjective* **1** easily damaged. **2** gently pleasing to the senses: *a delicate shade of blue*. **3** requiring tact or careful treatment: *a delicate situation*. **4** weak or ill: *still feeling delicate*. ➤ **delicately** *adverb*.

delicatessen /de li ka te sn/ *noun* (*plural* **delicatessens**) a shop where high-class, often imported, foods are sold.

delicious *adjective* **1** having a very pleasant taste. **2** delightful. ➤ **deliciously** *adverb*.

delight *verb* (**delights, delighting, delighted**) **1** (**delight in**) to take great pleasure in something: *He delights in teasing her.* **2** to give somebody great enjoyment. ~ *noun* (*plural* **delights**) **1** great pleasure or satisfaction. **2** something that gives great pleasure or satisfaction.

delighted *adjective* extremely pleased. ➤ **delightedly** *adverb*.

delightful *adjective* extremely pleasing; charming. ➤ **delightfully** *adverb*.

delinquent *noun* (*plural* **delinquents**) somebody who has behaved in an anti-social or criminal way. ~ *adjective* guilty of wrongdoing. ➤ **delinquency** *noun*.

delirious *adjective* **1** suffering from delirium. **2** wildly happy. ➤ **deliriously** *adverb*.

delirium *noun* **1** confused behaviour or speech caused by a fever or other illness. **2** great excitement or happiness.

deliver *verb* (**delivers, delivering, delivered**) **1** to bring or take something to a specified place or person. **2** to give a speech or verdict. **3** to assist in the birth of a baby. **4** *informal* to produce the promised, desired, or expected results.

delivery *noun* (*plural* **deliveries**) **1** the act of delivering something. **2** an item or items delivered at one time. **3** the act of giving birth. **4** an instance of bowling the ball in cricket.

dell *noun* (*plural* **dells**) a small secluded hollow or valley.

delphinium *noun* (*plural* **delphiniums**) a plant with tall spikes of blue or purple flowers.

delta *noun* (*plural* **deltas**) a wide triangular area at the mouth of a river that has divided into several branches.

delude *verb* (**deludes, deluding, deluded**) to mislead or deceive somebody.

deluge /deˈlewj/ *noun* (*plural* **deluges**) **1** a great flood. **2** a sudden very heavy fall of rain. **3** an overwhelming amount or number: *a deluge of applications*. ~ *verb* (**deluges, deluging, deluged**) to overwhelm somebody.

delusion *noun* (*plural* **delusions**) a false belief or impression.

de luxe /diˈluks/ *adjective* of very high quality.

delve *verb* (**delves, delving, delved**) **1** to make a careful search for information. **2** to reach inside something and search about in.

demagogue /ˈdeməgog/ *noun* (*plural* **demagogues**) a political leader who makes use of popular prejudices to gain power.

demand *noun* (*plural* **demands**) **1** a claim or forceful request. **2** (**demands**) requirements: *Studying makes great demands on my time.* **3** the desire of consumers to buy a product. ~ *verb* (**demands, demanding, demanded**) **1** to ask for something in an authoritative or forceful way: *The king has demanded it.* **2** to call for something urgently or insistently: *Workers are demanding higher wages.* **3** to require something: *a task that demands your full attention.* ✴ **in demand** sought after; popular. **on demand** whenever people ask for it.

demanding *adjective* **1** needing much effort or skill. **2** difficult to please.

demean *verb* (**demeans, demeaning, demeaned**) to cause somebody to lose their dignity or other people's respect.

demeanour *noun* behaviour towards others, or outward manner.

demented *adjective* insane.

dementia /diˈmenshiə/ *noun* a severe mental disorder with symptoms that include memory failure and personality changes.

demigod *noun* (*plural* **demigods**) a mythological being, greater than a human but with less power than a god.

demise /diˈmiez/ *noun* **1** *formal* death. **2** the end of something, such as an industry.

demo *noun* (*plural* **demos**) *informal* **1** a political demonstration. **2** a version of a musical recording or computer game used for demonstration purposes.

democracy /diˈmokrəsi/ *noun* (*plural* **democracies**) **1** a form of government in which people choose political leaders by voting. **2** a state governed in this way.

democrat /ˈdeməkrat/ *noun* (*plural*

democrats) 1 somebody who supports the notion of democracy. 2 (**Democrat**) a member of the Democratic Party of the USA.

democratic *adjective* 1 practising or favouring democracy. 2 (*often* **Democratic**) to do with the Democratic Party of the USA, which is associated with policies of social reform and internationalism. ➤ **democratically** *adverb*.

demographic /de mo gra fik/ *adjective* *Geography* to do with the size of, or changes in, human population.

demolish *verb* (**demolishes, demolishing, demolished**) 1 to destroy a building by knocking it down. 2 to defeat an opponent or argument convincingly. 3 *informal* to devour food. ➤ **demolition** *noun*.

demon *noun* (*plural* **demons**) 1 an evil supernatural being. 2 (*often used before a noun*) a very forceful, skilled, or enthusiastic person: *a demon with a paintbrush; a demon cook.* ➤ **demonic** *adjective*.

demonstrate *verb* (**demonstrates, demonstrating, demonstrated**) 1 to show that something is true. 2 to show how something is done by doing it. 3 to take part in a political demonstration. ➤ **demonstrator** *noun*.

demonstration *noun* (*plural* **demonstrations**) 1 an instance of showing how to do something by doing it yourself. 2 a procession or mass meeting organized to allow people to express their grievances or political views.

demonstrative /di mon stra tiv/ *adjective* tending to show feelings of affection or love openly. ➤ **demonstratively** *adverb*.

demoralize *or* **demoralise** *verb* (**demoralizes, demoralizing, demoralized** *or* **demoralises**, etc) to weaken somebody's confidence.

➤ **demoralizing** *or* **demoralising** *adjective*.

demote *verb* (**demotes, demoting, demoted**) to reduce somebody to a lower grade or rank. ➤ **demotion** *noun*.

demure *adjective* behaving in a quiet modest way. ➤ **demurely** *adverb*.

den *noun* (*plural* **dens**) 1 the lair of a wild animal. 2 a centre of secret or unlawful activity. 3 a comfortable secluded room.

denial *noun* (*plural* **denials**) 1 a statement saying that what somebody says is false. 2 a refusal to do what somebody asks.

denigrate *verb* (**denigrates, denigrating, denigrated**) to make negative or critical statements about somebody or something, usually unjustly. ➤ **denigration** *noun*.

denim *noun* (*plural* **denims**) 1 a thick cotton fabric used for jeans. 2 (**denims**) denim jeans.

denomination *noun* (*plural* **denominations**) 1 a distinctive group within a religion. 2 a value shown on a coin or stamp.

denominator *noun* (*plural* **denominators**) *Maths* the part of a vulgar fraction below the line, indicating how many parts the numerator is divided into.

denote *verb* (**denotes, denoting, denoted**) 1 to be a sign or symbol of something: *Red denotes danger.* 2 to indicate something: *A swollen belly denotes starvation.*

denounce *verb* (**denounces, denouncing, denounced**) 1 to criticize somebody or something severely and publicly. 2 to inform against somebody.

dense *adjective* (**denser, densest**) 1 with parts or particles crowding together: *dense fog; a dense forest.* 2 *informal* stupid. ➤ **densely** *adverb*.

density noun (plural **densities**) **1** the state of being dense. **2** *Science* the mass of a substance per unit of volume. **3** the degree to which something is crowded or full.

dent noun (plural **dents**) a depression made by a blow or pressure. ~ verb (**dents, denting, dented**) **1** to make a dent in something. **2** to affect something adversely.

dental adjective to do with the teeth or dentistry.

dentine /den teen/ noun the material a tooth is made of.

dentist noun (plural **dentists**) somebody who treats people's teeth.
▸ **dentistry** noun.

dentures plural noun a set of false teeth.

denunciation noun (plural **denunciations**) the act of criticizing somebody or something severely and publicly.

deny verb (**denies, denying, denied**) **1** to state that something is untrue or invalid. **2** to refuse to give or allow somebody something.

deodorant noun (plural **deodorants**) a substance that stops or covers up body odour.

depart verb (**departs, departing, departed**) **1** to leave. **2** (**depart from**) to do something different from what is usual or was prearranged.

department noun (plural **departments**) **1** a major division of a government, institution, or business.
2 *informal* an area of responsibility: *The housework isn't my department.*
▸ **departmental** adjective.

department store noun (plural **department stores**) a large shop that sells different types of goods.

departure noun (plural **departures**) **1** the act of departing. **2** something that is different from what is usual or was prearranged.

depend verb (**depends, depending, depended**) (**depend on/upon**)
1 to be determined by something: *My future depends on this interview.*
2 to rely on somebody: *We're all depending on you.*

dependable adjective reliable or trustworthy.

dependant noun (plural **dependants**) a person who relies on another person for financial support.

Usage Note **dependant** or **dependent**? *Dependent* is an adjective and *dependant* is a noun meaning 'a dependent person'.

dependence noun the fact of needing somebody or something else in order to live.

dependency noun (plural **dependencies**) **1** a country that is under the control of another nation. **2** = DEPENDENCE.

dependent adjective **1** relying on somebody for financial support.
2 determined by something: *Success is dependent on hard work.* **3** having a need for something, such as a drug.

Usage Note **dependent** or **dependant**? See note at **dependant**.

depict verb (**depicts, depicting, depicted**) to represent somebody or something in a picture or film. ▸ **depiction** noun.

deplete verb (**depletes, depleting, depleted**) to reduce the size or quantity of something. ▸ **depletion** noun.

deplorable adjective extremely bad.
▸ **deplorably** adverb.

deplore verb (**deplores, deploring, deplored**) to disapprove of something very strongly.

deploy verb (**deploys, deploying, deployed**) **1** to organize troops or weapons so that they are ready to use.
2 to make use of something: *He*

deport

deployed all his powers of persuasion. ➤ **deployment** noun.

deport verb (**deports, deporting, deported**) to send somebody out of a country, for example because they have entered illegally. ➤ **deportation** noun.

deportment noun the way a person stands, sits, or walks.

depose verb (**deposes, deposing, deposed**) to remove somebody from a position of authority.

deposit verb (**deposits, depositing, deposited**) 1 to put money in a bank account. 2 to put something somewhere for safekeeping. ~ noun (**deposits**) 1 money paid into a bank account. 2 money given as a down payment. 3 a substance left somewhere by a natural process.

depot /de poh/ noun (plural **depots**) a place for storing goods.

depraved adjective behaving in an offensively immoral way.

depravity noun offensively immoral behaviour.

depreciate verb (**depreciates, depreciating, depreciated**) to lessen in value. ➤ **depreciation** noun.

depress verb (**depresses, depressing, depressed**) 1 to make somebody very sad or dispirited. 2 to make something less strong or active. 3 to push something down: *This key depresses the lever.*

depressed adjective 1 very sad or dispirited. 2 suffering from depression. 3 suffering from economic depression.

depression noun (plural **depressions**) 1 a mental disorder with symptoms of inactivity, difficulty in thinking and concentration, and deep sadness. 2 a deeply unhappy mood. 3 a period of low economic activity and rising levels of unemployment. 4 an area of low atmospheric pressure that usually brings bad weather.

deprivation noun (plural **deprivations**) hardship caused by lack of basic necessities such as food or shelter.

deprive verb (**deprives, depriving, deprived**) to prevent somebody from making use of or benefiting from something.

deprived adjective lacking the necessities of life.

dept abbreviation department.

depth noun (plural **depths**) 1 the distance from the top to the bottom of something, or from front to back. 2 a part that is far from the outside or surface of something: *the depths of the forest.* 3 an intense state of emotion: *in the depths of despair.* ✽ **out of your depth** 1 in water that is deeper than your height. 2 faced with a situation that you cannot deal with.

deputation noun (plural **deputations**) a small group of people chosen to represent the members of a larger group.

deputize or **deputise** verb (**deputizes, deputizing, deputized** or **deputises**, etc) to act as a deputy for somebody.

deputy noun (plural **deputies**) a person appointed as a substitute for another.

derail verb (**derails, derailing, derailed**) 1 to cause a train to leave the rails. 2 to throw a process off course. ➤ **derailment** noun.

deranged adjective mad.

derby /dah bi/ noun (plural **derbies**) 1 (**the Derby**) a flat race for three-year-old horses held annually at Epsom. 2 a sporting match against a major local rival.

derelict adjective abandoned and in disrepair.

deride verb (**derides, deriding, derided**) to mock or scorn something or somebody.

derision noun scorn or ridicule.

derisive /di rie ziv/ *adjective* mocking or scornful. ➤ **derisively** *adverb*.

derisory /di rie zo ri/ *adjective* ridiculously and unfairly small and inadequate.

derivation *noun* (*plural* **derivations**) 1 the formation of a word from another word or root. 2 the origin of something.

derivative /di ri va tiv/ *adjective* based on something else and not original. ~ *noun* (*plural* **derivatives**) 1 *English* a word formed from another word, such as 'goodness' from 'good'. 2 a substance produced from another substance.

derive *verb* (**derives, deriving, derived**) 1 to get something: *She derives a lot of pleasure from reading.* 2 to come from something or somewhere: *The tradition derives from India.*

dermatitis /der ma tie tis/ *noun* a serious disease of the skin.

dermatology *noun* the branch of medicine dealing with the skin and skin diseases. ➤ **dermatological** *adjective*, **dermatologist** *noun*.

derogatory /di ro ga to ri/ *adjective* expressing a low opinion of something or somebody.

derrick *noun* 1 a type of crane. 2 a framework over an oil well for supporting drilling machinery.

dervish *noun* (*plural* **dervishes**) a member of a Muslim religious order known especially for its energetic dances.

descant *noun* (*plural* **descants**) an additional melody sung or played above the main tune.

descend *verb* (**descends, descending, descended**) 1 to go to a lower level. 2 to slope or extend downwards. 3 (**be descended from**) to have a particular family or group as ancestors. 4 (**descend on/upon**) to arrive somewhere in large numbers.

descendant *noun* (*plural* **descendants**) somebody descended from a particular ancestor.

descent *noun* (*plural* **descents**) 1 movement to a lower level. 2 family origins: *of French descent.*

describe *verb* (**describes, describing, described**) 1 to give an account of something or somebody in words. 2 *Maths* to draw the shape or outline of something.

description *noun* (*plural* **descriptions**) 1 an account in words. 2 a type: *people of every description.*

descriptive *adjective* describing something or somebody vividly. ➤ **descriptively** *adverb*.

desecrate /de si krayt/ *verb* (**desecrates, desecrating, desecrated**) to treat something sacred with a lack of respect, for example by damaging it deliberately. ➤ **desecration** *noun*.

desert[1] /de zert/ *noun* (*plural* **deserts**) *Geography* a barren region where very little grows.

Usage Note **desert** or **dessert**? The noun *desert* has the stress on the first syllable; the verb *desert* has the stress on the second. Do not confuse these with *dessert* (sweet course), which has the stress on the second syllable.

---

desert[2] /di zert/ *verb* (**deserts, deserting, deserted**) 1 to abandon somebody when you should stay and help or protect them. 2 to leave a military post or unit without permission. ➤ **deserter** *noun*, **desertion** *noun*.

deserted *adjective* empty of people.

deserts /di zerts/ *plural noun* a reward or, more often, punishment that you deserve: *She got her just deserts.*

deserve *verb* (**deserves, deserving, deserved**) to be worthy of a reward, punishment, or particular type of treatment. ➤ **deservedly** *adverb*.

deserving *adjective* worthy of being helped or supported.

desiccated /de si kay tid/ *adjective* with all the moisture removed: *desiccated coconut*.

design *verb* (**designs, designing, designed**) **1** to draw the plans for something that is to be made or built. **2** to intend something for a specific purpose: *The comment was designed to be an apology*. ~ *noun* (*plural* **designs**) **1** a drawing showing how something is to be made or built. **2** a decorative pattern. **3** the style of something.

designate /de zig nayt/ *verb* (**designates, designating, designated**) **1** to give something a name that describes its status or function. **2** to give somebody a particular position or duty.

designation *noun* (*plural* **designations**) a name or title.

designer *noun* (*plural* **designers**) **1** somebody who designs manufactured objects. **2** (*used before a noun*) made by a well-known fashion designer: *designer jeans*.

desirable *adjective* **1** worth having or doing. **2** sexually attractive. ➤ **desirability** *noun*.

desire *verb* (**desires, desiring, desired**) to want something very much. ~ *noun* (*plural* **desires**) **1** something that you want very much. **2** strong sexual feelings.

desist /di zist/ *verb* (**desists, desisting, desisted**) *formal* to stop doing something.

desk *noun* (*plural* **desks**) **1** a table designed for writing or working at. **2** a counter where a service is available: *the information desk*.

desktop *noun* (*plural* **desktops**) **1** the working surface of a desk. **2** *ICT* the main screen displayed by a computer's operating system, from which programs can be opened. ~ *adjective* *ICT* small enough to be used on a desk: *desktop computers*.

desolate /de so lat/ *adjective* **1** barren, lifeless, or uninhabited. **2** extremely unhappy. ➤ **desolation** *noun*.

despair *noun* complete loss of hope. ~ *verb* (**despairs, despairing, despaired**) to lose all hope. ➤ **despairing** *adjective*.

despatch *verb and noun* see DISPATCH.

desperate *adjective* **1** wanting something very much: *I was desperate for a chance to talk to her*. **2** extremely dangerous or difficult: *a desperate situation*. **3** willing to do anything to get something or escape from the situation you are in. ➤ **desperately** *adjective*, **desperation** *noun*.

despicable /di spi ka bl/ *adjective* deserving to be hated. ➤ **despicably** *adverb*.

despise *verb* (**despises, despising, despised**) to hate something or somebody.

despite *preposition* in spite of something.

despondent *adjective* extremely discouraged or dejected. ➤ **despondency** *noun*, **despondently** *adverb*.

despot *noun* a cruel ruler with absolute power. ➤ **despotic** *adjective*, **despotism** *noun*.

dessert /di zert/ *noun* (*plural* **desserts**) a sweet dish served at the end of a meal.

Usage Note **dessert** or **desert**? See note at **desert**[1].

dessertspoon *noun* (*plural* **dessertspoons**) a spoon that is bigger than a teaspoon and smaller than a tablespoon.

destination *noun* (*plural* **destinations**) a place that a person is travelling to or that a parcel is being sent to.

destined *adjective* **1** certain to happen, as if decided by fate: *She was destined* *to marry him. We seemed destined for failure.* **2** going to a place: *ships destined for Spain.*

destiny *noun* (*plural* **destinies**) **1** the power that some people believe decides what happens. **2** the things that will happen or have happened to somebody.

destitute *adjective* extremely poor. ➤ **destitution** *noun.*

destroy *verb* (**destroys, destroying, destroyed**) **1** to demolish or ruin something. **2** to kill an animal humanely.

destruction *noun* the act of destroying something.

destructive *adjective* **1** demolishing, ruining, or ending something. **2** said about criticism: pointing out faults without offering ideas for improvement. ➤ **destructively** *adverb.*

desultory /de sul to ri/ *adjective* going aimlessly from one subject or activity to another.

detach *verb* (**detaches, detaching, detached**) to separate something from a larger object or group. ➤ **detachable** *adjective.*

detached *adjective* **1** not connected to something else. **2** said about a person: not emotionally involved.

detachment *noun* (*plural* **detachments**) **1** the feeling of not being emotionally involved. **2** a small group of soldiers on a special mission.

detail *noun* (*plural* **details**) **1** an individual part or fact. **2** such small parts or facts collectively: *We admired the detail in the painting.* ✱ **in detail** item by item; thoroughly.

detailed *adjective* including many details.

detain *verb* (**detains, detaining, detained**) **1** to delay somebody. **2** to put somebody in prison.

detainee *noun* (*plural* **detainees**) a person held in prison for political reasons.

detect *verb* (**detects, detecting, detected**) to notice or discover something. ➤ **detectable** *adjective.*

detection *noun* the investigation of a crime.

detective *noun* (*plural* **detectives**) a police officer who investigates crimes.

detention *noun* **1** the act of holding somebody in prison: *detention without trial.* **2** a period during which a pupil is kept in school after normal hours as a punishment.

deter *verb* (**deters, deterring, deterred**) to discourage somebody from doing something. ➤ **deterrence** *noun.*

detergent *noun* (*plural* **detergents**) a chemical substance used for cleaning.

deteriorate *verb* (**deteriorates, deteriorating, deteriorated**) to become worse. ➤ **deterioration** *noun.*

determination *noun* **1** firmness in your decisions and intentions. **2** the act of determining something.

determine *verb* (**determines, determining, determined**) **1** to influence what happens or how something happens. **2** to work something out. **3** to decide something.

determined *adjective* firm in your decisions or intentions. ➤ **determinedly** *adverb.*

determiner *noun* (*plural* **determiners**) *English* a word, such as 'this', 'my' and 'his', that comes before a noun and any descriptive adjective relating to that noun.

deterrent *noun* (*plural* **deterrents**) something that discourages somebody from doing something.

detest *verb* (**detests, detesting, detested**) to hate something or somebody. ➤ **detestable** *adjective.*

detonate *verb* (**detonates, detonating, detonated**) **1** to cause a bomb

detour

or missile to explode. **2** said about a bomb or missile: to explode. ➤ **detonation** *noun*, **detonator** *noun*.

detour *noun* (*plural* **detours**) an alternative route that is longer than the normal or planned route.

detract *verb* (**detracts, detracting, detracted**) (**detract from**) to make something less attractive, valuable, or interesting.

detriment /de tri mint/ *noun* a bad effect; harm.

detrimental /de tri men tl/ *adjective* having a bad effect.

deuce /dews/ *noun* in tennis, a score of 40 to each player or team, when either of them must win the next two points to win the game.

devalue *verb* (**devalues, devaluing, devalued**) **1** to make something less valuable or worthwhile. **2** to reduce the value of a country's currency. ➤ **devaluation** *noun*.

devastate *verb* (**devastates, devastating, devastated**) to cause great damage to a place. ➤ **devastation** *noun*.

devastated *adjective* extremely upset.

devastating *adjective* **1** causing great destruction. **2** extremely upsetting. ➤ **devastatingly** *adverb*.

develop *verb* (**develops, developing, developed**) **1** to change and become something more advanced or severe: *a child developing into an adult*. **2** to start to exist: *A relationship soon developed*. **3** to start to suffer from an illness. **4** to make photographs from film using chemicals. **5** to acquire something gradually: *He developed a taste for computer games*. **6** to build on land.

developing country *noun* (*plural* **developing countries**) *Geography* a country that has not yet developed industry and manufacturing.

development *noun* (*plural* **developments**) **1** something which changes a situation. **2** an area of new building. **3** an innovation or new product. **4** the act of developing. ➤ **developmental** *adjective*.

deviant *adjective* different from what people accept as normal or morally right: *deviant behaviour*. ~ *noun* (*plural* **deviants**) a person whose behaviour is unacceptably different. ➤ **deviance** *noun*.

deviate *verb* (**deviates, deviating, deviated**) to do something that is different from what was planned or agreed, or from what is normal or expected.

device *noun* (*plural* **devices**) a piece of equipment designed for a special purpose. ✻ **leave somebody to their own devices** to leave somebody to do as they please.

devil *noun* (*plural* **devils**) **1** (**the Devil**) the supreme spirit of evil in Jewish, Christian, and Muslim belief. **2** an evil spirit. **3** *informal* a person: *You're a lucky devil*.

devious *adjective* dishonest in a clever way. ➤ **deviously** *adverb*, **deviousness** *noun*.

devise *verb* (**devises, devising, devised**) to invent something such as a system or scheme.

devoid *adjective* totally lacking in something.

devolution *noun* the transfer of power from central government to regional or local councils.

devolve *verb* (**devolves, devolving, devolved**) to transfer power from central government to regional or local councils.

devote *verb* (**devotes, devoting, devoted**) to spend time or effort on something.

devoted *adjective* loving or loyal. ➤ **devotedly** *adverb*.

devotee /de vo tee/ *noun* (*plural* **devotees**) an enthusiast.

devotion *noun* great love, affection, or dedication.

devour *verb* (**devours, devouring, devoured**) **1** to eat food hungrily or greedily. **2** to take something in eagerly: *She devours books.*

devout *adjective* following religious rules sincerely. ➤ **devoutly** *adverb*.

dew *noun* moisture that forms on cool surfaces at night.

dexterity *noun* skill in using your hands.

diabetes /die a **bee** teez/ *noun* the condition of having too much sugar in your blood because your body does not produce enough insulin to process the sugar.

diabetic /die a **be** tik/ *adjective* suffering from diabetes. ~ *noun* (*plural* **diabetics**) a person who suffers from diabetes.

diabolical *adjective informal* very bad; appalling. ➤ **diabolically** *adverb*.

diagnose *verb* (**diagnoses, diagnosing, diagnosed**) to recognize a disease or problem and say what it is. ➤ **diagnostic** *adjective*.

diagnosis *noun* (*plural* **diagnoses**) a judgment about what an illness is or what the cause of a problem is.

diagonal *adjective* said about a line: straight and slanting. ~ *noun* (*plural* **diagonals**) a diagonal line. ➤ **diagonally** *adverb*.

diagram *noun* (*plural* **diagrams**) a drawing that illustrates facts or shows the arrangement of the parts of something.

dial *noun* (*plural* **dials**) **1** the face of a clock or similar device with a pointer on it. **2** a device that you turn to control something. ~ *verb* (**dials, dialling, dialled**) to select a telephone number.

dialect *noun* (*plural* **dialects**) a variety of a language used by people from a particular region or in a particular social or ethnic group.

dialogue *noun* (*plural* **dialogues**) **1** conversation between characters in a book, play, or film. **2** any conversation or discussion.

dialysis /die a **li** sis/ *noun* treatment for kidney diseases that involves passing a person's blood through a machine to remove impurities.

diameter *noun* (*plural* **diameters**) *Maths* a straight line that goes through the centre of a circle or sphere, or the length of this line.

diametrically *adverb* completely.

diamond *noun* (*plural* **diamonds**) **1** a very hard, clear precious stone that is a form of carbon. **2** *Maths* a square or rhombus that rests on one of its angles. **3** (**diamonds**) the suit in a pack of playing cards that is marked with red diamond-shaped figures.

diamond wedding *noun* (*plural* **diamond weddings**) a sixtieth wedding anniversary.

diaphragm /die a fram/ *noun* (*plural* **diaphragms**) the layer of muscle that separates your chest from your abdomen.

diarist *noun* (*plural* **diarists**) somebody who writes a diary.

diarrhoea /die a **ree** a/ *noun* an illness that makes the solid waste in your body very runny and makes you go to the toilet a lot.

diary *noun* (*plural* **diaries**) a book for keeping a daily record of appointments or for writing personal experiences or feelings.

diatribe *noun* (*plural* **diatribes**) a long angry complaint or criticism.

dice *noun* (*plural* **dice**) a small cube marked with spots that represent numbers, used in games. ~ *verb* (**dices, dicing, diced**) to cut food into small cubes.

dicey *adjective* (**dicier, diciest**) *informal* risky.

dictate *verb* (**dictates, dictating, dictated**) **1** to say words for somebody else to write down. **2** to give orders in an overbearing way. **3** to decide or control what happens. ➤ **dictation** *noun*.

dictator *noun* (*plural* **dictators**) an evil ruler with absolute power. ➤ **dictatorial** *adjective*.

dictatorship *noun* (*plural* **dictatorships**) a state ruled by a dictator.

diction *noun* how clearly somebody pronounces words when they speak.

dictionary *noun* (*plural* **dictionaries**) a book that gives the meanings of words or gives their equivalents in a foreign language.

did past tense of DO.

didn't *contraction* did not.

die[1] *verb* (**dies, dying, died**) **1** to stop living. **2** to stop existing. **3** to become weaker or fainter. **4** to want something very much: *I'm dying for a drink. We were dying to speak to him.* ✽ **die away** to become weaker or fainter, then disappear. **die down** to become quieter or less intense. **die off** to die one by one. **die out 1** to become extinct. **2** to cease to exist or be done. **to die for** *informal* excellent or desirable.

die[2] *noun* **1** (*plural* **dice**) = DICE. **2** (*plural* **dies**) a tool for pressing something into shape or stamping a design on something.

diesel /deezl/ *noun* (*plural* **diesels**) **1** a heavy mineral oil used as fuel. **2** a vehicle that uses this fuel.

diet *noun* (*plural* **diets**) **1** the eating of less food or particular foods in order to lose weight or become healthier, or the foods eaten: *on a diet; a vegetarian diet.* **2** the food that a person or animal usually eats. **3** (*used before a noun*) said about food and drinks: low in calories or fat content. ~ *verb* (**diets, dieting, dieted**) to eat less food or particular foods in order to lose weight or become healthier.

dietary /dieitari/ *adjective* to do with food or special diets.

dietician *or* **dietitian** *noun* (*plural* **dieticians** *or* **dietitians**) somebody who gives advice on healthy eating or special diets.

differ *verb* (**differs, differing, differed**) **1** to be different. **2** to disagree.

difference *noun* (*plural* **differences**) **1** a way in which people or things are different. **2** a disagreement or dispute. **3** a remainder left after you subtract one number from another. **4** a significant effect on a situation: *Complaining will make no difference.*

different *adjective* **1** not like something or somebody else. **2** distinct and separate: *We visited different places.* **3** other: *I'd like a different knife – this one's dirty.* **4** *informal* unusual or special: *That haircut's a bit different.* ➤ **differently** *adverb*.

Usage Note **different from/to/than**. The preferred combination is *different from*. British English also accepts *different to*. *Different than* is acceptable only in American English.

differentiate *verb* (**differentiates, differentiating, differentiated**) **1** to see the difference between things. **2** to be a fact or feature that makes things different. ➤ **differentiation** *noun*.

difficult *adjective* **1** hard to do, make, or understand. **2** said about a person: hard to deal with, manage, or please.

difficulty *noun* (*plural* **difficulties**) **1** the state of being difficult. **2** a cause of trouble or embarrassment.

diffident *adjective* lacking in self-confidence; shy. ➤ **diffidence** *noun*, **diffidently** *adverb*.

diffraction *noun* Science the fact that a

beam of light splits into bands as it goes through a narrow gap or hits an obstacle.

diffuse /di**fews**/ *adjective* scattered over a wide area. ~ /di**fewz**/ *verb* (**diffuses, diffusing, diffused**) **1** to spread out. **2** *Science* said about atomic particles: to spread throughout a substance. ➤ **diffusion** *noun*.

dig *verb* (**digs, digging, dug**) **1** to turn over, loosen, or remove soil. **2** to search for something. **3** to poke or prod somebody. ~ *noun* (*plural* **digs**) **1** a poke or prod. **2** *informal* an unkind remark. **3** a place where archaeologists are digging up objects from the past. ✶ **dig out 1** to search for and find something. **2** to remove something from soil by digging. **dig up 1** to discover something by searching. **2** to remove something from soil by digging. **dig your heels in** *informal* to refuse to change your mind. ➤ **digger** *noun*.

digest /die**jest**/ *verb* (**digests, digesting, digested**) **1** to convert food into a form the body can use. **2** to take information into your mind and understand it. ➤ **digestible** *adjective*.

digestion *noun* the process of digesting food.

digestive *adjective* to do with digestion.

digit *noun* (*plural* **digits**) **1** *Maths* any of the numbers from 0 to 9. **2** *formal* a finger or toe.

digital *adjective* **1** *ICT* using data stored or transmitted in the form of numbers of the type that computers use: *digital photography*. **2** *Science* said of a clock, watch, etc: presenting information in the form of numbers rather than by a pointer and a dial. ➤ **digitally** *adverb*.

dignified *adjective* showing or having dignity.

dignitary *noun* (*plural* **dignitaries**) an important person.

dignity *noun* calm and self-controlled behaviour that people admire.

digress *verb* (**digresses, digressing, digressed**) to go off the main subject when you are writing or speaking. ➤ **digression** *noun*.

dike *noun* see DYKE.

dilapidated *adjective* in very bad condition through neglect.

dilate /die**layt**/ *verb* (**dilates, dilating, dilated**) to become wider or wider open. ➤ **dilated** *adjective*, **dilation** *noun*.

dilatory /di**la**to ri/ *adjective* slow to take action.

dilemma *noun* (*plural* **dilemmas**) a situation involving a choice between two unpleasant alternatives.

diligent *adjective* hard-working and conscientious. ➤ **diligence** *noun*, **diligently** *adverb*.

dill *noun* a herb with thin feathery leaves.

dilute /die**looht** *or* di**looht**/ *verb* (**dilutes, diluting, diluted**) **1** to make a liquid thinner or weaker by adding more of another liquid. **2** to make something less powerful or effective by adding other elements. ~ *adjective* weak; diluted. ➤ **dilution** *noun*.

dim *adjective* (**dimmer, dimmest**) **1** not bright or brightly lit. **2** seen or remembered only vaguely: *a dim memory*. **3** *informal* unintelligent. ~ *verb* (**dims, dimming, dimmed**) to become dim, or make something dim. ✶ **take a dim view of** to disapprove of something. ➤ **dimly** *adverb*.

dimension /die**men**shn *or* di**men**shn/ *noun* (*plural* **dimensions**) **1** a measurement of the length, breadth, or height of an object. **2** (**dimensions**) the extent of something: *a problem of enormous* *dimensions.* **3** an aspect of something: *the political dimension of the decision.*

diminish *verb* (**diminishes, diminishing, diminished**) to become smaller in size or intensity, or reduce the size or intensity of something.

diminutive *adjective* small. ~ *noun* (*plural* **diminutives**) *English* **1** a word-forming element such as 'mini' or a suffix such as '-ette' that indicates a smaller-sized version of something. **2** a word formed in this way, such as *miniskirt* or *kitchenette*.

dimple *noun* (*plural* **dimples**) a slight indentation in somebody's cheek or chin. ➤ **dimpled** *adjective*.

din *noun* a loud unpleasant noise.

dine *verb* (**dines, dining, dined**) *formal* to have a meal, especially dinner.

diner *noun* (*plural* **diners**) **1** somebody who is dining. **2** *N American* a small restaurant.

dinghy /ding gi/ *noun* (*plural* **dinghies**) **1** a small open sailing boat. **2** a small inflatable rubber boat.

dingo *noun* (*plural* **dingoes** *or* **dingos**) an Australian wild dog.

dingy /din ji/ *adjective* (**dingier, dingiest**) dirty and in bad condition.

dinner *noun* (*plural* **dinners**) **1** the meal that you eat in the evening. **2** a formal evening meal. **3** *informal* lunch.

dinosaur *noun* (*plural* **dinosaurs**) **1** a large reptile of a type that existed from 245 to 65 million years ago. **2** a person or organization that is outdated and reluctant to change.

dint ✱ **by dint of** by means of.

diocese /die o sis/ *noun* (*plural* **dioceses** /die o seez/) the group of churches and congregations that a bishop is in charge of. ➤ **diocesan** *adjective*.

dioxide *noun* (*plural* **dioxides**) *Science* an oxide containing two atoms of oxygen for every one atom of another element.

dip *verb* (**dips, dipping, dipped**) **1** to plunge something in a liquid. **2** to decrease temporarily and by a small amount. **3** to lower something and then raise it again. ~ *noun* (*plural* **dips**) **1** a soft mixture into which food is dipped before being eaten. **2** a short swim. **3** a short drop: *a dip in sales.* **4** a short drop in the level of the ground. ✱ **dip into 1** to use some of your money or supplies. **2** to read something superficially.

diphthong /dif thong/ *noun* (*plural* **diphthongs**) *English* a sound that combines two vowels in one syllable, such as /oy/ in *toy*.

diploma *noun* (*plural* **diplomas**) a certificate that you get for completing a course of study.

diplomacy *noun* **1** political negotiations between countries or groups. **2** skill in dealing with people sensitively.

diplomat *noun* (*plural* **diplomats**) a person whose job is conducting political negotiations with other countries.

diplomatic *adjective* **1** good at dealing with people sensitively. **2** to do with political negotiations between countries or groups. ➤ **diplomatically** *adverb*.

dire *adjective* **1** desperately urgent: *people in dire need of food and medicine.* **2** *informal* extremely bad.

direct *adjective* **1** going in a straight line or by the shortest route. **2** operating with no other person or group intervening: *We have direct control over company policy.* **3** dealing with people frankly. **4** exact: *the direct opposite.* ~ *verb* (**directs, directing, directed**) **1** to control something. **2** to decide how a film, play, or broadcast is performed and how it will look.

direct **3** to tell or show somebody how to get somewhere.

direct current noun Science an electric current that flows in one direction only.

direction noun (plural **directions**) **1** the line or course that something moves along. **2** the side that somebody or something faces. **3** guidance or control. **4** (**directions**) instructions on how to do something or get to a place. ➤ **directional** adjective.

directive noun (plural **directives**) an official order.

directly adverb **1** in a direct manner. **2** immediately or very soon.

direct object noun (plural **direct objects**) English the noun or pronoun in a sentence that the action of the verb applies to. In the sentence *Sue gave me the book*, 'the book' is the direct object and 'me' is the indirect object.

director noun (plural **directors**) **1** a member of the group that manages a company or organization. **2** the person who decides how a film, play, or broadcast is performed and how it will look. ➤ **directorial** adjective, **directorship** noun.

directory noun (plural **directories**) **1** an alphabetical list of things such as names, addresses, or telephone numbers. **2** *ICT* a large computer file that contains several other files.

direct speech noun English the words that somebody actually says, repeated in writing, usually enclosed in quotation marks.

dirge noun (plural **dirges**) a slow sad piece of music.

dirt noun **1** any unpleasant substance that spoils or marks something. **2** soil. **3** *informal* scandalous gossip. ✶ **treat somebody like dirt** *informal* to treat somebody very badly.

dirty adjective (**dirtier, dirtiest**) **1** not clean or pure. **2** unfair or dishonest: *dirty tactics*. **3** describing or showing sex in an offensive way: *dirty books*. **4** showing resentment or disgust: *a dirty look*. ~ verb (**dirties, dirtying, dirtied**) to make something dirty.

disability noun (plural **disabilities**) a physical or mental condition that affects how somebody lives.

disable verb (**disables, disabling, disabled**) to make a machine or device incapable of operating.

disabled adjective having a physical or mental condition that affects how you live.

disadvantage noun (plural **disadvantages**) something that makes your situation or chances not as good as somebody else's. ➤ **disadvantaged** adjective.

disagree verb (**disagrees, disagreeing, disagreed**) **1** to have a different opinion. **2** (**disagree with**) to disapprove of something: *I disagree with the policy*. **3** (**disagree with**) to have a bad effect on you when you eat it or experience it: *Hot weather disagrees with me*. ➤ **disagreement** noun.

disagreeable adjective unpleasant.

disappear verb (**disappears, disappearing, disappeared**) **1** to stop being visible. **2** to stop existing. **3** *informal* to leave. ➤ **disappearance** noun.

disappoint verb (**disappoints, disappointing, disappointed**) to be less successful or impressive than you expected and so make you feel sad or annoyed. ➤ **disappointed** adjective, **disappointing** adjective.

disappointment noun (plural **disappointments**) **1** a sad or annoyed feeling you get when something is less successful or impressive than you expected. **2** somebody or something that disappoints you.

disapprove verb (**disapproves, disapproving, disapproved**) to think that something should not happen or

disarm

should not be allowed. ➤ **disapproval** *noun*, **disapproving** *adjective*.

disarm *verb* (**disarms, disarming, disarmed**) **1** to get rid of your weapons. **2** to make a bomb or missile harmless by removing a fuse or warhead. **3** to make somebody stop being angry or suspicious. ➤ **disarming** *adjective*.

disarmament *noun* the giving up of weapons.

disarray *noun* lack of order.

disassemble *verb* (**disassembles, disassembling, disassembled**) to take something to pieces.

disaster *noun* (*plural* **disasters**) **1** something that causes great harm or destruction. **2** *informal* a great failure. ➤ **disastrous** *adjective*, **disastrously** *adverb*.

disband *verb* (**disbands, disbanding, disbanded**) said about a group: to break up.

disbelief *noun* the attitude of not believing that something is true.

disc *noun* (*plural* **discs**) **1** a thin flat circular object. **2** a thin plate of cartilage between vertebrae in your spine. **3** a CD, DVD, or vinyl record.

Usage Note **disc** or **disk**? *Disc* is the correct spelling in British English, except in the context of computers where *disk* is preferred.

discard *verb* (**discards, discarding, discarded**) to get rid of something that is no longer useful or that you no long want.

discern /di sern/ *verb* (**discerns, discerning, discerned**) to notice something. ➤ **discernible** *adjective*.

discerning *adjective* able to judge the quality of things well. ➤ **discernment** *noun*.

discharge /dis chahj/ *verb* **1** to send or pour out a liquid or gas. **2** to allow somebody to leave hospital. **3** to dismiss somebody from their job.

~ /dis chahj/ *noun* (*plural* **discharges**) a substance that is released, especially a substance produced by your body.

disciple /di sie pl/ *noun* (*plural* **disciples**) **1** any of Jesus's twelve original followers. **2** a person who learns from a teacher or instructor.

disciplinary /di si pli na ri/ *adjective* done as a punishment.

discipline /di si plin/ *noun* (*plural* **disciplines**) **1** the enforcing of rules in order to achieve good behaviour among people. **2** a subject of study. ~ *verb* (**disciplines, disciplining, disciplined**) **1** to punish somebody in order to maintain good behaviour within a group. **2** to control your own behaviour in order to maintain the standards you set for yourself. ➤ **disciplined** *adjective*.

disc jockey or **DJ** *noun* (*plural* **disc jockeys** or **DJs**) a person who plays recorded music on a radio programme, in a club, or at a party.

disclose *verb* (**discloses, disclosing, disclosed**) **1** to make information known. **2** to allow people to see something. ➤ **disclosure** *noun*.

disco *noun* (*plural* **discos**) **1** a club where people dance to pop music. **2** a party with dancing to pop music. **3** a type of dance music popular in the 1970s.

discoloured *adjective* changed to an unhealthy or unpleasant colour. ➤ **discoloration** or **discolouration** *noun*.

discomfort *noun* **1** slight pain. **2** embarrassment.

disconcert /dis kon sert/ *verb* (**disconcerts, disconcerting, disconcerted**) to make somebody lose their calmness or confidence.

disconnect *verb* (**disconnects, disconnecting, disconnected**) **1** to separate things so that they are no longer connected. **2** to cut off somebody's gas, electricity, or water supply, or their telephone service. ➤ **disconnection** noun.

discontented adjective unhappy or dissatisfied. ➤ **discontent** noun.

discontinue verb (**discontinues, discontinuing, discontinued**) **1** to stop producing or manufacturing something. **2** to stop doing something. ➤ **discontinuation** noun.

discord noun (plural **discords**) **1** disagreement or conflict. **2** Music an unpleasant combination of musical sounds.

discount /dis kownt/ noun (plural **discounts**) a reduction in the price of something. ~ /dis kownt/ verb (**discounts, discounting, discounted**) to disregard something.

discourage verb (**discourages, discouraging, discouraged**) **1** to make somebody less confident or less willing. **2** to advise somebody not to do something that they want to do. ➤ **discouragement** noun, **discouraging** adjective.

discourse noun (plural **discourses**) **1** conversation. **2** a formal speech or piece of writing.

discover verb (**discovers, discovering, discovered**) **1** to be the first to see, find, or know about something. **2** to find something out. **3** to find something by searching or by chance.

discovery noun (plural **discoveries**) **1** something that somebody discovers. **2** the act of discovering something.

discredit verb (**discredits, discrediting, discredited**) **1** to damage somebody's reputation. **2** to make people believe that something is not good or worthwhile. ~ noun loss of reputation.

discreet adjective good at keeping secrets and behaving sensitively. ➤ **discreetly** adverb.

Usage Note Do not confuse **discreet** and **discrete**.

discrepancy noun (plural **discrepancies**) a difference between things that you expect to be the same.

discrete adjective separate from each other. ➤ **discretely** adverb.

Usage Note Do not confuse **discrete** and **discreet**.

discretion /dis kre shn/ noun **1** discreet behaviour. **2** the freedom to make decisions based on your own judgment.

discretionary /dis kre sho na ri/ adjective which you make a decision about based on your own judgment.

discriminate verb (**discriminates, discriminating, discriminated**) **1** (**discriminate against/in favour of**) to give somebody different treatment because of their race, sex, age, religion, etc. **2** (**discriminate between**) to understand the differences between similar things.

discrimination noun **1** different treatment given to somebody because of their race, sex, age, religion, etc. **2** good judgment or taste.

discriminatory adjective representing unfairly different treatment.

discus noun (plural **discuses**) **1** a solid disc thrown in athletic contests. **2** the contest itself.

discuss verb (**discusses, discussing, discussed**) **1** to talk about something in order to make decisions. **2** to talk or write about the different aspects of something.

discussion noun (plural **discussions**) **1** a conversation or debate. **2** a piece of writing in which you consider the different aspects of something.

disdain noun the feeling that you have for something that does not deserve your approval or attention.

disease noun (plural **diseases**) an unhealthy physical or mental condition. ➤ **diseased** adjective.

disembark verb (**disembarks,**

disembarking, disembarked) to get off a ship or plane. ➤ **disembarkation** noun.

disembodied adjective 1 existing apart from a person's body: *a disembodied spirit*. 2 coming from a place that you cannot see: *a disembodied voice*.

disenchanted adjective no longer thinking that something is good. ➤ **disenchantment** noun.

disfigured adjective having a face that has been badly damaged by disease or in an accident. ➤ **disfigurement** noun.

disgrace noun 1 the state of no longer being respected by people. 2 somebody or something that makes you feel ashamed. ~ verb (**disgraces, disgracing, disgraced**) to make people lose respect for something or somebody.

disgraceful adjective so bad that it makes people annoyed or ashamed. ➤ **disgracefully** adverb.

disgruntled adjective dissatisfied and annoyed.

disguise verb (**disguises, disguising, disguised**) 1 to make a person or thing look or seem different in order to fool people. 2 to hide your true feelings. ~ noun (plural **disguises**) 1 a costume or other means of concealing your identity. 2 the state of being disguised: *in disguise*.

disgust noun a strong feeling of disapproving of or disliking something. ~ verb (**disgusts, disgusting, disgusted**) to make somebody feel disgust. ➤ **disgusted** adjective, **disgusting** adjective.

dish noun (plural **dishes**) 1 a shallow container for holding or serving food. 2 (**dishes**) the crockery and cutlery used in preparing and serving a meal. 3 a type of food prepared in a particular way. ~ verb (**dishes, dishing, dished**) * **dish out** 1 to serve food. 2 *informal* to give advice or criticism freely. **dish up** 1 to serve food. 2 *informal* to present facts or information.

disheartened adjective no longer enthusiastic, hopeful, or confident. ➤ **disheartening** adjective.

dishevelled /di she vild/ adjective with untidy clothes and hair.

dishonest adjective not honest, truthful, or sincere. ➤ **dishonesty** noun.

dishwasher noun (plural **dishwashers**) an electrical machine that washes dishes.

disillusioned adjective disappointed because you have learned the unpleasant truth about somebody or something.

disincentive noun (plural **disincentives**) something that makes you not want to do or have something.

disinfectant noun (plural **disinfectants**) a substance that kills germs in the home and in wounds.

disingenuous /dis in je new us/ adjective insincere.

disintegrate verb (**disintegrates, disintegrating, disintegrated**) to break up into small pieces.

disinterested adjective able to make fair decisions because you are not personally involved.

Usage Note **disinterested** or **uninterested**? *Disinterested* means 'not biased'; *uninterested* means 'not interested'.

disjointed adjective having sections or elements that do not seem to belong together; incoherent.

disk noun (plural **disks**) *ICT* a device that computer data is stored on, either inside the computer or separate from it.

Usage Note **disk** or **disc**? See the note at **disc**.

dislike verb (**dislikes, disliking, disliked**) to not like something or somebody. ~ *noun* (*plural* **dislikes**) **1** a feeling of not liking something or somebody. **2** something that you dislike.

dislocate *verb* (**dislocates, dislocating, dislocated**) to force a bone out of its normal position in a joint.

dislodge *verb* (**dislodges, dislodging, dislodged**) to force something out of the place it is stuck or fixed in.

disloyal *adjective* not loyal. ➤ **disloyalty** *noun*.

dismal *adjective* making you feel sad or depressed. ➤ **dismally** *adverb*.

dismantle *verb* (**dismantles, dismantling, dismantled**) to take something to pieces.

dismay *noun* the sad and worried feeling you have when you feel something is not good or right. ~ *verb* (**dismays, dismaying, dismayed**) to cause somebody to feel dismay.

dismember *verb* (**dismembers, dismembering, dismembered**) to cut or tear a body to pieces. ➤ **dismemberment** *noun*.

dismiss *verb* (**dismisses, dismissing, dismissed**) **1** to decide not to consider or accept something such as a suggestion. **2** to order somebody to leave. **3** to force somebody to leave their job. **4** in cricket, to bowl out a batsman or side. ➤ **dismissal** *noun*.

dismissive *adjective* showing that you think something is not worth considering at all. ➤ **dismissively** *adverb*.

disobedient *adjective* refusing or failing to obey somebody. ➤ **disobedience** *noun*.

disobey *verb* (**disobeys, disobeying, disobeyed**) to refuse or fail to obey a person or an order.

disorder *noun* (*plural* **disorders**) **1** lack of order or tidiness. **2** an illness. ➤ **disordered** *adjective*.

disorderly *adjective* **1** untidy. **2** violent or disruptive.

disorganized *adjective* **1** badly organized. **2** doing things in an unmethodical way.

disorientated *adjective* confused and not at ease because you are not in your normal place, situation, or mental state. ➤ **disorientation** *noun*.

disown *verb* (**disowns, disowning, disowned**) to say that you no longer have any connection with somebody or something because you disapprove of them.

disparage *verb* (**disparages, disparaging, disparaged**) to speak about something or somebody in a way that shows you have no respect for them. ➤ **disparaging** *adjective*.

disparate /ˈdɪspərət/ *adjective* quite separate and distinct.

disparity *noun* (*plural* **disparities**) a difference between things, especially things that you expect to be the same: *a disparity between the two sets of figures*.

dispatch *or* **despatch** *verb* (**dispatches, dispatching, dispatched** *or* **despatches**, etc) **1** to send something such as a letter somewhere. **2** to send somebody somewhere to carry out a task. ~ *noun* (*plural* **dispatches**) an official message or report.

dispel *verb* (**dispels, dispelling, dispelled**) to get rid of unpleasant feelings such as fear or doubt.

dispensary *noun* (*plural* **dispensaries**) a part of a hospital or chemist's shop where medicines and supplies are given out.

dispense *verb* (**dispenses, dispensing, dispensed**) **1** to prepare and give out medicines. **2** to give out something, such as advice. **3** (**dispense with**) to get rid of something or do without it.

disperse *verb* (**disperses, dispersing, dispersed**) **1** to spread out over a

dispirited

wide area. **2** said about a crowd: to break up and leave in different directions. ➤ **dispersal** *noun*, **dispersion** *noun*.

dispirited *adjective* no longer enthusiastic, hopeful, or confident. ➤ **dispiriting** *adjective*.

displace *verb* (**displaces, displacing, displaced**) **1** to take the place of something or somebody. **2** to force something out of its usual place.

displaced *adjective* forced to leave your own country.

displacement *noun* **1** *Science* the volume or weight of water displaced by an object floating in it. **2** the fact of being displaced.

display *verb* (**displays, displaying, displayed**) **1** to set something out for people to see. **2** *ICT* to show information on a screen. **3** to demonstrate a quality in what you do or how you behave. ~ *noun* (*plural* **displays**) **1** *ICT* a screen on which information is shown. **2** an exhibition or performance.

displease *verb* (**displeases, displeasing, displeased**) to annoy somebody.

displeasure *noun* disapproval or annoyance.

disposable *adjective* designed to be used once and then thrown away.

disposal *noun* the act of getting rid of something. * **at your disposal** available for you to use.

dispose *verb* (**disposes, disposing, disposed**) (**dispose of**) to get rid of something unwanted.

disposed *adjective* **1** willing to do something: *I'm not disposed to grant your request.* **2** having a particular attitude to somebody or something: *She seemed kindly disposed to us.*

disposition *noun* (*plural* **dispositions**) a person's temperament.

disproportionate *adjective* **1** too big or too small and odd-looking. **2** too extreme or severe in the circumstances. ➤ **disproportionately** *adverb*.

disprove *verb* (**disproves, disproving, disproved**) to prove that a statement is false.

dispute *noun* (*plural* **disputes**) a quarrel or disagreement. ~ *verb* (**disputes, disputing, disputed**) to argue that a statement, claim, etc is not valid.

disqualify *verb* (**disqualifies, disqualifying, disqualified**) to decide officially that somebody is not allowed to do something. ➤ **disqualification** *noun*.

disquiet *noun* anxiety or worry. ➤ **disquieting** *adjective*.

disregard *verb* (**disregards, disregarding, disregarded**) to ignore something. ~ *noun* failure to pay proper attention or show proper respect for something.

disrepair *noun* the bad condition of something that has been neglected.

disrepute *noun* lack of good reputation or respectability.

disrespect *noun* lack of respect or politeness. ➤ **disrespectful** *adjective*.

disrupt *verb* (**disrupts, disrupting, disrupted**) to interrupt something or prevent it from happening or working normally. ➤ **disruption** *noun*, **disruptive** *adjective*.

dissatisfied *adjective* feeling that something is not good enough.

dissect *verb* (**dissects, dissecting, dissected**) **1** to cut an animal or plant into pieces for scientific examination. **2** to analyse or examine something in great detail. ➤ **dissection** *noun*.

dissent *noun* strong disagreement with official rules, or behaviour that breaks those rules. ~ *verb* (**dissents, dissenting, dissented**) **1** to express an opinion that is contrary to official rules or policies. **2** in sport, to show angry disagreement with a referee's decision. ➤ **dissenter** noun.

dissertation noun (plural **dissertations**) a long essay written as part of a university degree course.

disservice * **do somebody a disservice** to do something that is harmful or not helpful to somebody: *They did him a disservice by postponing the trial.*

dissident noun (plural **dissidents**) a person who publicly opposes their government's policies. ~ *adjective* publicly opposed to official policy. ➤ **dissidence** noun.

dissimilar adjective unlike each other.

dissipate verb (**dissipates, dissipating, dissipated**) **1** to scatter things. **2** to waste money, energy, time, etc.

dissociate verb (**dissociates, dissociating, dissociated**) to separate two ideas in your mind. * **dissociate yourself** to say that you have no connection with somebody or something.

dissolution noun **1** the breaking up of a parliament before a general election. **2** the ending of a marriage or partnership.

dissolve verb (**dissolves, dissolving, dissolved**) **1** to mix a solid substance into a liquid, or to become mixed into a liquid. **2** to break up a parliament before a general election. **3** to end a marriage or partnership.

dissuade verb (**dissuades, dissuading, dissuaded**) to persuade somebody not to do something. ➤ **dissuasion** noun.

distance noun (plural **distances**) **1** the space between two points or places, or the length of this space. **2** an area that is far away: *in the distance.* ~ *verb* (**distances, distancing, distanced**) (**distance yourself**) to avoid getting involved. * **keep your distance** to avoid getting involved.

distant adjective **1** far away in space or time. **2** not closely related. **3** not friendly. ➤ **distantly** adverb.

distaste noun dislike and disapproval.

distasteful adjective unpleasant and slightly offensive.

distil verb (**distils, distilling, distilled**) **1** to purify a liquid by heating it until it evaporates and then cooling it again. **2** to make whisky or other spirits by this method. ➤ **distillation** noun, **distiller** noun.

distillery noun (plural **distilleries**) a factory where whisky or other spirits are distilled.

distinct adjective **1** clearly different or separate. **2** easy to see or notice; clear. ➤ **distinctly** adverb.

distinction noun (plural **distinctions**) **1** a difference between things that are similar but not the same. **2** outstanding merit or special talent. **3** the highest level of excellence in passing an exam.

distinguish verb (**distinguishes, distinguishing, distinguished**) **1** (**distinguish between/from**) to recognize the difference between two or more things: *distinguish right from wrong.* **2** to be able to see or hear something: *I could distinguish a woman's voice.* **3** to be a special feature that allows you to identify something: *A black band on its head distinguishes this bird from similar birds.* * **distinguish yourself** to do something impressive or admirable. ➤ **distinguishable** adjective.

distinguished adjective **1** excellent. **2** having a dignified manner or appearance.

distort verb (**distorts, distorting, distorted**) **1** to twist something out of shape. **2** to change something so that it is not longer true or accurate, in order to mislead people. ➤ **distortion** noun.

distract verb (**distracts, distracting, distracted**) to take somebody's atten-

distraction

tion away from what they are doing. ➤ **distracting** *adjective*, **distracted** *adjective*.

distraction *noun* (*plural* **distractions**) something that distracts your attention.

distraught /di'strawt/ *adjective* extremely worried or upset; frantic.

distress *noun* **1** great mental or physical pain. **2** a dangerous situation that you must escape from immediately. ~ *verb* (**distresses, distressing, distressed**) to cause somebody great mental or physical pain. ➤ **distressing** *adjective*.

distribute *verb* (**distributes, distributing, distributed**) **1** to hand things out to people. **2** to share things out among several people. ➤ **distribution** *noun*.

distributor *noun* (*plural* **distributors**) **1** a company that delivers goods to shops. **2** the part of an engine that sends electricity to the spark plugs.

district *noun* (*plural* **districts**) an area of a town or region.

distrust *noun* suspicion or lack of trust. ~ *verb* (**distrusts, distrusting, distrusted**) to consider somebody to be untrustworthy or unreliable. ➤ **distrustful** *adjective*.

disturb *verb* (**disturbs, disturbing, disturbed**) **1** to interrupt somebody or something. **2** to worry or upset somebody. **3** to move things out of position.

disturbance *noun* (*plural* **disturbances**) **1** an interruption. **2** an outbreak of rowdy behaviour.

disturbed *adjective* emotionally or mentally unstable.

disturbing *adjective* worrying or upsetting.

disuse *noun* the state of no longer being used. ➤ **disused** *adjective*.

ditch *noun* (*plural* **ditches**) a long narrow hole dug in the ground, for example to allow water to flow away. ~ *verb* (**ditches, ditching, ditched**) **1** said about a pilot or aircraft: to land on water in an emergency. **2** *informal* to get rid of something or somebody.

dither *verb* (**dithers, dithering, dithered**) to behave nervously or indecisively.

ditto *noun* **1** used to avoid repeating a word: the same. **2** a mark (,, or ") that indicates that the word directly above is to be repeated.

ditty *noun* (*plural* **ditties**) a short simple song.

diva /'deeva/ *noun* (*plural* **divas**) a female opera singer who sings leading parts.

Divali *noun* see DIWALI.

dive *verb* (**dives, diving, dived**) **1** to jump into water headfirst. **2** to swim underwater using breathing equipment. **3** said about a submarine or sea creature: to go below the surface of water. **4** said about a bird or an aircraft: to drop steeply through the air. **5** to move quickly downwards or under cover. ~ *noun* (*plural* **dives**) **1** a headlong jump into water. **2** a steep descent by an aircraft.

diver *noun* (*plural* **divers**) a person who dives as a competitive sport or who works or explores underwater.

diverge *verb* (**diverges, diverging, diverged**) **1** said about opinions, paths, etc: to separate and move away in different directions. **2** to be different from each other. ➤ **divergence** *noun*, **divergent** *adjective*.

diverse *adjective* made up of different types; varied.

diversify *verb* (**diversifies, diversifying, diversified**) **1** to make something more varied. **2** said about a company: to start being involved in other additional types of business. ➤ **diversification** *noun*.

diversion *noun* (*plural* **diversions**) **1** a temporary route for traffic when the usual route is closed. **2** a welcome chance to stop doing something or do something different. ➤ **diversionary** *adjective*.

diversity *noun* the fact that something contains or consists of many different types.

divert *verb* (**diverts, diverting, diverted**) to change the direction that something is going in.

divide *verb* (**divides, dividing, divided**) **1** to separate, or become separated, into parts, branches, or groups. **2** to share something between people. **3** *Maths* to find out how many times a larger number contains a smaller one. **4** to cause people to disagree. ~ *noun* (*plural* **divides**) a major difference that separates people or groups.

dividend *noun* (*plural* **dividends**) **1** a part of a company's profits that is paid to shareholders. **2** *Maths* a number that is divided by another. ✱ **pay dividends** to bring benefits.

dividers *plural noun* a measuring instrument consisting of two arms joined at one end and with a sharp point at the other end.

divine *adjective* **1** from, or to do with, a god. **2** *informal* extremely good or pleasant. ~ *verb* (**divines, divining, divined**) **1** *formal* to discover something by guessing or using supernatural powers. **2** to find water or minerals underground using a special rod that twitches. ➤ **divinely** *adverb*.

divinity *noun* (*plural* **divinities**) **1** the state of being a god. **2** a god. **3** the study of religion.

divisible *adjective* *Maths* said about a number: capable of being divided by another number without a remainder.

division *noun* (*plural* **divisions**) **1** the act of dividing something into parts. **2** any of the parts into which something is divided: *head of the company's sales division*. **3** *Maths* the process of dividing one number by another. **4** in sport, a part of a league consisting of teams that play each other. **5** disagreement that leads to a splitting up. ➤ **divisional** *adjective*.

division sign *noun Maths* the mathematical symbol (÷) used to indicate division.

divisive /di**vie**siv/ *adjective* tending to cause disagreements that split a group up.

divisor /di**vie**zer/ *noun* (*plural* **divisors**) *Maths* a number that another number is divided by.

divorce *noun* (*plural* **divorces**) the legal ending of a marriage. ~ *verb* (**divorces, divorcing, divorced**) **1** to legally end a marriage to somebody. **2** to treat things as separate. ➤ **divorced** *adjective*.

divorcee /di**vaw**see/ *or* /di**vaw**see/ *noun* (*plural* **divorcees**) a divorced person.

divulge *verb* (**divulges, divulging, divulged**) to reveal secret information.

Diwali /di**wah**li/ *or* **Divali** /di**vah**li/ *noun* the Hindu and Sikh Festival of Lights, celebrated in October or November at the end of the monsoon.

DIY *noun* = do-it-yourself, repair and building work that people do in their own homes.

dizzy *adjective* (**dizzier, dizziest**) experiencing a whirling sensation in your head that makes you lose your balance. **2** *informal* foolish or silly. ➤ **dizziness** *noun*.

DJ *noun* see DISC JOCKEY.

DNA *noun* = deoxyribonucleic acid /dee ok si rie boh new **klee** ik **a** sid/, the material in the nuclei of cells that makes up genes.

do *verb* (**does, doing, did, done**) **1** to perform an action or activity: *Anya did a cartwheel*. **2** to make or provide something: *Who's doing the cooking?* **3** to have a particular effect:

docile

A rest will do you good. **4** to work at something: *Sanjay is doing French at university.* **5** to be adequate: *There's no wire – will string do?* ~ *auxiliary verb* **1** used to form questions and negative statements: *Do you like fish? We don't go to school at the weekend.* **2** used for emphasis: *I do hope you can come.* **3** used as a substitute for a verb already mentioned: *I am learning more than I did last year.* ~ *noun* (*plural* **dos** *or* **do's**) *informal* a party. ✳ **do away with** *informal* to get rid of something. **do up 1** to wrap or fasten something. **2** *informal* to repair or refurbish something. **do without** to manage in spite of not having something. **to do with** concerned with something or somebody.

docile *adjective* easily controlled.
➤ **docility** *noun*.

dock[1] *noun* (*plural* **docks**) an enclosed area of water in a port, where a ship can be unloaded or repaired. ~ *verb* (**docks, docking, docked**) **1** said about a ship: to go into a dock. **2** said about a spacecraft: to join another spacecraft in space.

dock[2] *noun* (*plural* **docks**) the enclosure where the accused person stands in a court.

dock[3] *verb* (**docks, docking, docked**) **1** to cut an animal's tail short. **2** to deduct an amount from wages or a score.

dock[4] *noun* (*plural* **docks**) a weed with broad leaves used to treat nettle stings.

docker *noun* (*plural* **dockers**) a person whose job is loading and unloading ships.

dockyard *noun* (*plural* **dockyards**) a place where ships are built or repaired.

doctor *noun* (*plural* **doctors**) **1** a person qualified to treat people who are ill. **2** somebody who holds the highest academic degree. ~ *verb* (**doctors, doctoring, doctored**) to change something for a dishonest purpose.

doctorate *noun* (*plural* **doctorates**) the highest academic degree.

doctrine /dok´trin/ *noun* (*plural* **doctrines**) a set of principles, religious beliefs, or political policies.
➤ **doctrinal** *adjective*.

document /do´kew mint/ *noun* (*plural* **documents**) **1** a piece of paper, or a brochure or book, that gives official information or acts as a record. **2** ICT a single computer file that you create or can change. ~ *verb* /do kew ment´/ (**documents, documenting, documented**) to record an event in detail.

documentary *noun* (*plural* **documentaries**) a film or television programme that shows real events. ~ *adjective* consisting of documents: *documentary evidence.*

documentation *noun* official documents.

dodge *verb* (**dodges, dodging, dodged**) **1** to move your body suddenly in order to avoid something. **2** to avoid doing something or dealing with it.

dodgy *adjective* (**dodgier, dodgiest**) *informal* **1** dishonest. **2** risky or dangerous. **3** liable to collapse or break down.

dodo *noun* (*plural* **dodoes** *or* **dodos**) a large extinct flightless bird that formerly lived on the island of Mauritius.

doe *noun* (*plural* **does**) **1** an adult female fallow deer. **2** the adult female of various mammals, such as the rabbit.

does /duz/ *verb* third person singular present tense of DO.

doesn't *contraction* does not.

dog *noun* (*plural* **dogs**) **1** a four-legged meat-eating mammal kept as a pet, for hunting, or to work. **2** any member of the dog family, such as a wolf, jackal, or fox. **3** (*sometimes used before a noun*) a male dog or fox: *a dog fox*. ~ *verb* (**dogs, dogging, dogged**) **1** to follow somebody closely. **2** said about something unwanted: to regularly cause problems for somebody: *dogged by ill health*.

dog collar *noun* (*plural* **dog collars**) *informal* a priest's collar.

dog-eared *adjective* said about a book: read so often that the pages have creased corners.

dogged /dogid/ *adjective* stubbornly determined. ➤ **doggedly** *adverb*.

dogma *noun* (*plural* **dogmas**) a set of principles that members of a religion or political party must follow.

dogmatic *adjective* stating beliefs or opinions in a firm way that shows you expect other people to accept them. ➤ **dogmatically** *adverb*.

doldrums ✳ **in the doldrums 1** fed up. **2** said about an economy, business, etc: in which there is very little activity.

dole *noun informal* money paid by the government to people who are unemployed. ~ *verb* (**doles, doling, doled**) ✳ **dole out** to give something or hand something out.

doll *noun* (*plural* **dolls**) a child's toy in the form of a person.

dollar *noun* (*plural* **dollars**) the basic unit of money in the USA, Canada, Australia, and various other countries.

dollop *noun* (*plural* **dollops**) a soft shapeless lump of food.

dolphin *noun* (*plural* **dolphins**) a sea animal like a small whale with a long snout.

domain *noun* (*plural* **domains**) **1** an area that somebody controls or has influence over. **2** a subject or activity. **3** *ICT* the part of a website address or email address that identifies a server on the Internet, which, in an email address, is the part that comes after the @ symbol.

dome *noun* (*plural* **domes**) a roof in the shape of a hemisphere.

domestic *adjective* **1** to do with homes or families. **2** to do with your own country; not foreign or international. **3** said about an animal: bred and trained to live or work with people; not wild. ➤ **domestically** *adverb*.

domesticated *adjective* said about an animal: bred and trained to live or work with people; not wild. ➤ **domestication** *noun*.

domesticity *noun* home or family life.

domicile *noun* (*plural* **domiciles**) *formal* a home.

dominant *adjective* better, more important, or more powerful than all others. ➤ **dominance** *noun*.

dominate *verb* (**dominates, dominating, dominated**) **1** to be better, more important, or more powerful than all others. **2** to be so big that you cannot avoid seeing it from all parts of a place. ➤ **domination** *noun*.

domineer *verb* (**domineers, domineering, domineered**) (**domineer over**) to bully people and try to control them. ➤ **domineering** *adjective*.

dominion *noun* (*plural* **dominions**) **1** the power to rule. **2** a place ruled or controlled by somebody.

domino *noun* (*plural* **dominoes** or **dominos**) **1** a flat block with sets of dots on one of its sides, used in the game of dominoes. **2** (**dominoes**) a game in which dominoes with a matching number of dots are laid end to end.

don¹ *noun* (*plural* **dons**) a teacher at Oxford or Cambridge University.

don² *verb* (**dons, donning, donned**) to put on a piece of clothing.

donate *verb* (**donates, donating, donated**) **1** to give money to a

done | 194

charity or other organization. **2** to give blood, semen, or organs for use in the medical treatment of other people. ➤ **donation** *noun*.

done *verb* past participle of DO. ~ *adjective* **1** completed. **2** said about food: cooked sufficiently.

donkey *noun* (*plural* **donkeys**) an animal like a small horse with long ears.

donor *noun* (*plural* **donors**) a person who donates something.

don't *contraction* do not.

doodle *verb* (**doodles, doodling, doodled**) to draw shapes in a bored or aimless way. ~ *noun* (*plural* **doodles**) an aimless scribble or sketch.

doom *noun* something very unpleasant such as death or destruction that cannot be avoided.

doomed *adjective* **1** certain to fail or be ruined. **2** certain to die.

doomsday *noun* the end of the world.

door *noun* (*plural* **doors**) a hinged or sliding panel closing the entrance to a building, room, or vehicle. ✱ **out of doors** in or into the open air.

doorstep *noun* (*plural* **doorsteps**) a step in front of an outside door.

dope *noun* informal marijuana, opium, or a similar illegal drug. ~ *verb* informal (**dopes, doping, doped**) **1** to give a racehorse or greyhound a drug to make it run faster or slower. **2** to secretly put a drug in somebody's food or drink.

dormant *adjective* **1** asleep during hibernation. **2** not active or growing at the moment.

dormitory *noun* (*plural* **dormitories**) a large room with beds for several people, for example in a boarding school.

dormouse *noun* (*plural* **dormice**) a small animal that looks like a fat mouse with a long bushy tail.

dorsal fin *noun* the fin on the back of a fish, whale, or dolphin.

dose *noun* (*plural* **doses**) a measured quantity of medicine taken at one time.

dossier /do si er *or* do si ay/ *noun* (*plural* **dossiers**) a file of papers containing a detailed report or information.

dot *noun* (*plural* **dots**) a small round spot or mark. ~ *verb* (**dots, dotting, dotted**) ✱ **be dotted with** said about an area or a surface: to have things in many parts: *a field dotted with poppies*. **on the dot** exactly; precisely. **the year dot** *informal* a very long time ago.

dotcom *noun* (*plural* **dotcoms**) a company that operates exclusively or mainly on the Internet.

dote *verb* (**dotes, doting, doted**) (**dote on/upon**) to show a lot of affection or love for somebody. ➤ **doting** *adjective*.

double *adjective* **1** consisting of two similar parts: *double doors*. **2** of twice the usual size or quantity: *a double portion*. **3** designed for two people: *a double bed*. ~ *verb* (**doubles, doubling, doubled**) **1** to become twice as large or great, or make something twice as large or great. **2** to fold something in two. **3** (**double as**) to have a second use: *The stool doubles as a bedside table*. ~ *noun* (*plural* **doubles**) **1** somebody who looks exactly like another person. **2** (**doubles**) in tennis, badminton, and table tennis, a match with two players on each side.
~ *adverb* twice as much: *We'll pay you double*. ✱ **double back** to return the way you came. **double up/over** to bend over in pain or laughter.
➤ **doubly** *adverb*.

double bass /du bl bays/ *noun* (*plural* **double basses**) *Music* the largest instrument of the violin family, which you play standing up.

double bed *noun* (*plural* **double beds**) a bed for two people.

double-cross *verb* (**double-crosses, double-crossing, double-crossed**) to betray somebody that you are pretending to help or support.

double-decker *noun* (*plural* **double-deckers**) a bus with two floors.

double entendre /dooh bl on **ton** drer/ *noun* (*plural* **double entendres** /dooh bl on **ton** drer/) a phrase that has two meanings, a literal meaning and a rude meaning.

double glazing *noun* windows that have two panes of glass separated by an air space.

double standard *noun* (*plural* **double standards**) a moral principle that you apply strictly to other people but not to yourself.

doubt *verb* (**doubts, doubting, doubted**) 1 to think that something is probably not true: *The police doubted her story.* 2 to think that something is unlikely: *I doubt if she'll accept our invitation.* ~ *noun* (*plural* **doubts**) 1 uncertainty. 2 the feeling that something is probably not true. ✱ **no doubt** certainly; probably.

doubtful *adjective* 1 unlikely to be true or possible. 2 thinking that something is probably not true. ➤ **doubtfully** *adverb*.

doubtless *adverb* certainly.

dough /doh/ *noun* 1 a stiff mixture of flour and liquid used to make bread or pastry. 2 *informal* money.

doughnut *noun* (*plural* **doughnuts**) a sweet, ring-shaped cake of deep-fried dough.

dour /door/ *adjective* grumpy and unfriendly.

dove /duv/ *noun* (*plural* **doves**) a bird that looks like a small pigeon.

dovetail *noun* (*plural* **dovetails**) a joint in which a wedge-shaped peg on one piece of wood fits into a wedge-shaped slot on another piece.

dowager /dow a jer/ *noun* (*plural* **dowagers**) a widow who has inherited property or a title from her husband.

dowdy *adjective* (**dowdier, dowdiest**) wearing shabby or plain and old-fashioned clothes.

dowel *noun* (*plural* **dowels**) a wooden pin used to hold parts together.

down[1] *adverb and preposition* 1 in a lower place or to a lower position. 2 to a lower amount or figure. ~ *adjective* 1 very unhappy. 2 said about a computer system: temporarily out of action. ✱ **down to** the responsibility of the person named.

down[2] *noun* fine soft feathers or hairs.

downcast *adjective* 1 depressed or disappointed. 2 said about eyes: looking down.

downfall *noun* 1 a sudden loss of power or status. 2 the thing that causes somebody to be unsuccessful.

downgrade *verb* (**downgrades, downgrading, downgraded**) 1 to move somebody to a less important position or job. 2 to change the status of something to show that you think it is less important or valuable than before.

downhill *adverb and adjective* towards the bottom of a hill. ✱ **go downhill** to become worse.

download *verb* (**downloads, downloading, downloaded**) *ICT* to transfer programs or data from an Internet site to your computer, or from one computer to another. ~ *noun* (*plural* **downloads**) *ICT* a program or file that is available to download from the Internet.

down payment *noun* (*plural* **down payments**) a first payment of part of the cost of something.

downpour *noun* (*plural* **downpours**) a heavy fall of rain.

downright

downright *adverb* absolutely: *downright careless*. ~ *adjective* absolute: *downright lies*.

downs *plural noun* a series of high rounded hills.

Down's syndrome *noun* a medical disorder that causes learning difficulties and physical characteristics that include a broad face and rather flat facial features.

downstairs *adverb and adjective* on or to a lower floor.

downstream *adverb and adjective* in the direction that a stream or river is flowing.

down-to-earth *adjective* practical and realistic.

downward *adjective* moving to a lower place or level: *a downward spiral*.

downwards *adverb* to a lower place or level.

downwind *adverb and adjective* in or to a position where the wind is blowing something, such as smoke or a smell, towards you.

dowry *noun* (*plural* **dowries**) the money or property that a woman's family gives to her husband when she gets married.

doze *verb* (**dozes, dozing, dozed**) to sleep lightly. ~ *noun* (*plural* **dozes**) a short light sleep.

dozen /duzn/ *noun* (*plural* **dozens** or **dozen**) **1** a group of twelve things or people. **2** (**dozens**) an indefinitely large number.

drab *adjective* (**drabber, drabbest**) **1** uninteresting. **2** dull in colour.

draconian /dra koh ni an/ *adjective* said about laws or actions: extremely severe.

> **Word History** Draconian comes from *Draco*, who was a lawmaker in ancient Athens and whose laws were extremely harsh.

draft *noun* (*plural* **drafts**) **1** a first rough version of something such as a letter or design. **2** a written order to a bank to pay money to somebody. ~ *verb* (**drafts, drafting, drafted**) **1** to produce a draft of a letter, design, etc. **2** to select somebody for a particular job or purpose.

drag *verb* (**drags, dragged, dragging**) **1** to pull something along slowly or with difficulty. **2** to trail along a surface: *His coat was dragging on the ground*. **3** ICT to move an icon or piece of text across a computer screen using the mouse. **4** to search a river or lake with a large net or hook. ~ *noun* **1** *Science* the force that slows down an object moving through air or water. **2** women's clothing worn by a man for a performance. **3** *informal* a boring experience.

dragon *noun* (*plural* **dragons**) a mythical monster usually represented as a fire-breathing reptile with wings.

dragonfly *noun* (*plural* **dragonflies**) an insect with a long thin body and two pairs of large delicate wings.

dragoon *verb* (**dragoons, dragooning, dragooned**) to force somebody to do something. ~ *noun* (*plural* **dragoons**) a soldier who belongs to a cavalry unit.

drain *noun* (*plural* **drains**) **1** a pipe or channel that carries water or other liquid away. **2** something that uses up energy or resources. ~ *verb* (**drains, draining, drained**) **1** to draw liquid off gradually: *Nurses drained the wound*. **2** said about liquid: to flow away. **3** to use up a lot of energy or resources. **4** to empty a glass by drinking the contents. ✷ **down the drain** *informal* wasted.

drainage *noun* **1** how well water drains away from a surface: *The pitch has very good drainage*. **2** a system of drains.

drake *noun* (*plural* **drakes**) a male duck.

drama *noun* (*plural* **dramas**) **1** *Drama* a play. **2** *Drama* plays in general.

3 a situation full of excitement or emotion.

dramatic *adjective* **1** extreme, impressive, or exciting. **2** *Drama* to do with acting or plays. ➤ **dramatically** *adverb*.

dramatics *noun Drama* the study or practice of acting and stage management.

dramatist *noun* (*plural* **dramatists**) *Drama* somebody who writes plays.

dramatize or **dramatise** *verb* (**dramatizes, dramatizing, dramatized** or **dramatises,** etc) **1** *Drama* to turn something such as a book or a real event into a play or film. **2** to react to or describe something as if it were much more serious or exciting than it really is. ➤ **dramatization** or **dramatisation** *noun*.

drank *verb* past tense of DRINK.

drape *verb* (**drapes, draping, draped**) **1** to put a cloth or anything similar loosely over something. **2** to put your arm on or around something casually or heavily.

drastic *adjective* having a major and often sudden effect on something. ➤ **drastically** *adverb*.

draught *noun* (*plural* **draughts**) **1** an unpleasant current of cold air in a room. **2** the depth of water that a ship needs to float in. **3** (**draughts**) a board game for two players each of whom moves twelve disc-shaped pieces across a chessboard. ~ *adjective* said about beer: served from the barrel, not in bottles or cans.

draughtsman or **draughtswoman** *noun* (*plural* **draughtsmen** or **draughtswomen**) a person who draws technical plans and sketches.

draughty *adjective* (**draughtier, draughtiest**) with unpleasant currents of cold air blowing through it.

draw *verb* (**draws, drawing, drew, drawn**) **1** to produce a picture, diagram, etc by making lines on a surface. **2** to pull something somewhere. **3** to pull curtains to an open or closed position. **4** to attract a crowd of people. **5** to take money out of a bank account. **6** to take something such as water or power from a source. **7** to have equal scores at the end of a game. **8** to come or go somewhere steadily: *The train was drawing out of the station.* **9** (**draw on/upon**) to use a resource: *The players have years of experience they can draw on.* ~ *noun* (*plural* **draws**) **1** an act of choosing something at random, such as the winning numbers in a lottery or the contestants in a sports competition. **2** a contest that ends with the scores even. ✻ **draw up 1** to prepare a document or proposal. **2** to come to a halt.

drawback *noun* (*plural* **drawbacks**) a fact or feature that makes something less useful or desirable.

drawbridge *noun* (*plural* **drawbridges**) a bridge that can be raised or let down.

drawer *noun* (*plural* **drawers**) an open-topped storage box that slides out of a piece of furniture.

drawing *noun* (*plural* **drawings**) a picture of something in lines made with a pencil, pen, or crayon.

drawing pin *noun* (*plural* **drawing pins**) a pin with a broad flat head used to fasten paper to a surface.

drawing room *noun* (*plural* **drawing rooms**) in former times, a living room or lounge.

drawl *verb* (**drawls, drawling, drawled**) to speak slowly or lazily with long vowels. ~ *noun* a drawling way of speaking.

drawn *verb* past participle of DRAW. ~ *adjective* **1** looking worried, tired, or ill. **2** said about a game: ending with both sides having the same score.

dread *verb* (**dreads, dreading, dreaded**) to be very worried and

dreadful

frightened about something that might or will happen. ~ *noun* great worry and fear.

dreadful *adjective* **1** extremely unpleasant or shocking. **2** very bad. ➤ **dreadfully** *adverb*.

dreadlocks *plural noun* hair worn in long, tightly curled plaits, especially by male Rastafarians.

dream *noun* (*plural* **dreams**) **1** a series of things that you imagine you experience during sleep. **2** a great ambition or desire. **3** (*used before a noun*) perfect: *our dream team*. ~ *verb* (**dreams, dreaming, dreamed** *or* **dreamt** /dremt/) **1** to imagine you experience things during sleep. **2** to have a great ambition or desire. **3** to think that something is possible or likely: *I never dreamt she'd say yes.* **4** to consider doing something: *I wouldn't dream of hurting him.* ✶ **dream up** *informal* to devise or invent something: *Who dreamt up this stupid system?* ➤ **dreamer** *noun*.

dreamy *adjective* (**dreamier, dreamiest**) **1** tending to daydream a lot. **2** like in a dream.

dreary *adjective* (**drearier, dreariest**) dull and depressing. ➤ **drearily** *adverb*, **dreariness** *noun*.

dregs *plural noun* a small amount of liquid left at the bottom of a container, often containing sediment.

drench *verb* (**drenches, drenching, drenched**) to make something or somebody thoroughly wet.

dress *verb* (**dresses, dressing, dressed**) **1** to put clothes on yourself or somebody else. **2** to wear particular clothes: *We're not dressed for cold weather.* **3** to put a dressing on a wound. ~ *noun* (*plural* **dresses**) **1** a woman's garment consisting of a top and skirt combined. **2** clothing. ✶ **dress up** to dress in smart clothes or in a particular costume.

dresser *noun* (*plural* **dressers**) a sideboard with a high back with open shelves for holding dishes.

dressing *noun* (*plural* **dressings**) **1** a cold sauce for salads. **2** a bandage or other material used to cover a wound.

dressing gown *noun* (*plural* **dressing gowns**) a loose robe worn over nightclothes.

dress rehearsal *noun* (*plural* **dress rehearsals**) *Drama* a full rehearsal of a play, using all the costumes and props that will be used in a performance.

drew *verb* past tense of DRAW.

dribble *verb* (**dribbles, dribbling, dribbled**) **1** to let saliva trickle from your mouth. **2** said about liquid: to fall or flow in drops or in a thin stream. **3** in football, hockey, basketball, etc, to move a ball along using slight taps or bounces. ~ *noun* (*plural* **dribbles**) **1** a small trickling flow of liquid. **2** saliva trickling from your mouth.

dried *verb* past tense and past participle of DRY.

drier[1] *or* **dryer** *noun* (*plural* **driers** *or* **dryers**) a machine or device for drying something.

drier[2] *adjective* comparative form of DRY.

drift *verb* (**drifts, drifting, drifted**) **1** to be carried along by a current of water or air. **2** to move from place to place or from job to job in an aimless way. ~ *noun* (*plural* **drifts**) **1** a mass of snow or leaves piled up by wind. **2** a general underlying meaning.

drifter *noun* (*plural* **drifters**) somebody who travels about aimlessly.

driftwood *noun* wood floating on water or washed onto a beach.

drill *noun* (*plural* **drills**) **1** a tool for making a hole in a solid substance. **2** training that involves exercises that are repeated regularly, or an exercise of this kind. ~ *verb* (**drills, drilling,**

drilled) **1** to make a hole with a drill. **2** to fix something in somebody's mind by repeating it.

drily or **dryly** adverb in a matter-of-fact, serious, or ironic way.

drink verb (**drinks, drinking, drank, drunk**) **1** to swallow a liquid. **2** to drink alcohol. ~ noun (plural **drinks**) **1** an amount of liquid for drinking. **2** alcoholic drink. ▶ **drinkable** adjective, **drinker** noun.

drip verb (**drips, dripping, dripped**) to fall in drops, or let liquid fall in drops. ~ noun (plural **drips**) **1** a drop of liquid. **2** a device that sends a slow flow of liquid drugs or nutrients into a patient's blood.

dripping noun solidified fat from roasted meat.

drive verb (**drives, driving, drove, driven**) **1** to control a vehicle and direct where it goes. **2** to transport somebody or something in a vehicle. **3** to put something somewhere using strong physical force. **4** to make somebody take action of a particular kind: *What drove him to kill her?* ~ noun (plural **drives**) **1** a journey in a car. **2** a private road leading to a building. **3** determination in pursuing a goal. ▶ **driver** noun.

drivel noun nonsense.

drizzle noun very light rain.

droll adjective amusing.

dromedary /dromidari/ noun (plural **dromedaries**) a one-humped camel.

drone verb (**drones, droning, droned**) **1** to make a deep murmuring or buzzing sound. **2** to talk boringly and for a long time. ~ noun (plural **drones**) **1** a male bee whose only function is to mate with the queen. **2** a droning sound.

drool verb (**drools, drooling, drooled**) **1** to let saliva trickle from your mouth. **2** (**drool over**) to show your enthusiasm or desire for something in a very obvious way.

droop verb (**droops, drooping, drooped**) to hang down because of a lack of strength or firmness. ▶ **droopy** adjective.

drop noun (plural **drops**) **1** a round or pear-shaped mass of falling liquid. **2** a very small quantity, especially of liquid. **3** a fall, decrease, or decline. **4** a small round sweet. **5** the distance from something high down to the ground. ~ verb (plural **drops, dropping, dropped**) **1** to fall to the ground, or let something fall to the ground. **2** to become weaker or less. **3** to abandon an idea, accusation, friendship, etc. **4** to leave a player out of a team. **5** to set a passenger down somewhere: *I'll drop you by the post office.* ✴ **drop off 1** to fall asleep, especially unintentionally. **2** to become less. **drop out** to withdraw from an activity or a course of study.

droplet noun (plural **droplets**) a small drop of liquid.

droppings plural noun animal excrement.

drought /drowt/ noun (plural **droughts**) a long period with little or no rainfall.

drove[1] noun (plural **droves**) **1** a herd of animals moving together. **2** (**droves**) large numbers of people or things.

drove[2] verb past tense of DRIVE.

drown verb (**drowns, drowning, drowned**) to die from being underwater and unable to breathe, or to kill somebody by forcing them underwater. ✴ **drown out** to be so loud as to make another sound impossible to hear.

drowsy adjective (**drowsier, drowsiest**) sleepy. ▶ **drowsily** adverb, **drowsiness** noun.

drudgery noun hard boring work.

drug noun (plural **drugs**) **1** a substance used to treat or prevent disease. **2** a substance that people take illegally

druid

for its stimulating effect or because they are addicted to it. ~ *verb* (**drugs, drugging, drugged**) to give a drug to a person or animal in order to make them unconscious.

druid or **Druid** *noun* (*plural* **druids** or **Druids**) a member of an ancient Celtic order of priests.

drum *noun* (*plural* **drums**) **1** a hollow cylindrical percussion instrument that you play by hitting it with sticks or with your hands. **2** a cylindrical container or mechanical part. ~ *verb* (**drums, drumming, drummed**) **1** to play a drum. **2** to make a continuous tapping or throbbing sound. **3** (**drum into**) to repeat something as a way of making somebody learn it.

drumstick *noun* (*plural* **drumsticks**) **1** a stick used for playing a drum. **2** the lower portion of a cooked chicken leg.

drunk *verb* past participle of DRINK. ~ *adjective* under the influence of alcohol. ~ *noun* (*plural* **drunks**) a person who is regularly drunk.

drunken *adjective* **1** under the influence of alcohol. **2** caused by drinking too much alcohol: *a drunken stupor*.

dry *adjective* (**drier** or **dryer**, **driest** or **dryest**) **1** not wet or no longer wet. **2** said about wine, etc: not sweet. **3** uninteresting. **4** expressed in a matter-of-fact, serious, or ironic way. ~ *verb* (**dries, drying, dried**) **1** to make something dry, or to become dry. **2** to preserve something, for example food or a flower, by removing its moisture. ➤ **dryness** *noun*.

dry-clean *verb* (**dry-cleans, dry-cleaning, dry-cleaned**) to clean clothes with chemicals rather than with water. ➤ **dry-cleaner** *noun*, **dry-cleaning** *noun*.

dryer *noun* see DRIER1 and **DRY**.

dryly *adv* see DRILY.

dual *adjective* **1** consisting of two parts or elements. **2** having two different aspects or characteristics. ➤ **duality** *noun*.

dual carriageway *noun* (*plural* **dual carriageways**) a road that has traffic travelling in two or more lanes in each direction.

dub[1] *verb* (**dubs, dubbing, dubbed**) to call something or somebody by an unofficial name or nickname.

dub[2] *verb* (**dubs, dubbing, dubbed**) **1** to give a film or television programme a soundtrack in a different language. **2** to add in sound effects, music, etc to a film or television programme. ➤ **dubbing** *noun*.

dubious *adjective* **1** not certain that something is true or likely. **2** probably not safe, reliable, or honestly obtained. ➤ **dubiously** *adverb*.

duchess *noun* (*plural* **duchesses**) **1** the wife or widow of a duke. **2** a woman who has the same rank as a duke.

duchy *noun* (*plural* **duchies**) an area or country ruled by a duke or duchess.

duck[1] *noun* (*plural* **ducks** or **duck**) **1** a swimming bird with a short neck, short legs, webbed feet, and a broad flat beak. **2** a female duck.

duck[2] *verb* (**ducks, ducking, ducked**) **1** to lower your head or body suddenly to avoid being seen or hit. **2** to push somebody under water for a moment. **3** to evade a duty, question, responsibility, etc.

duck[3] *noun* (*plural* **ducks**) a score of zero, especially in cricket.

duckling *noun* (*plural* **ducklings**) a young duck.

duct *noun* (*plural* **ducts**) **1** a pipe or channel that carries air, power lines, telephone cables, etc. **2** a tube in your body that carries a liquid of some kind.

ductile *adjective* said about a metal:

capable of being pulled or hammered into different shapes.

dud *noun* (*plural* **duds**) *informal* something that does not work properly. ~ *adjective informal* faulty.

due *adjective* **1** owed as a debt. **2** expected to arrive or occur. **3** proper or appropriate: *with due care and attention*. ~ *adverb* directly or exactly: *due south*. * **due to 1** caused by: *The delay was due to bad weather*. **2** because of: *Due to circumstances beyond our control, the train has been delayed*. **give somebody their due** to give somebody the credit they deserve. **in due course** at some time in the future.

duel *noun* (*plural* **duels**) **1** a formal fight with weapons fought between two people to settle a quarrel. **2** a conflict between evenly matched people, ideas, or forces. ~ *verb* (**duels, duelling, duelled**) to fight a duel.

dues *plural noun* charges or fees.

duet *noun* (*plural* **duets**) *Music* a piece of music sung or played by two people together.

dug *verb* past tense and past participle of DIG.

dugout *noun* (*plural* **dugouts**) **1** a shelter at the side of a sports ground where coaches and substitutes sit. **2** a shelter for soldiers, dug in the ground. **3** a boat made by hollowing out a log.

duke *noun* (*plural* **dukes**) a man who has the highest rank in the British aristocracy. ➤ **dukedom** *noun*.

dulcet /dul sit/ *adjective* said about sounds: pleasant.

dull *adjective* **1** boring. **2** cloudy. **3** lacking brightness: *dull colours*. **4** unintelligent. ➤ **dullness** *noun*, **dully** *adverb*.

duly *adverb* at the appropriate time, or in the appropriate way.

dumb *adjective* **1** lacking the ability to speak. **2** unwilling or temporarily unable to speak. **3** *informal* stupid. ~ *verb* (**dumbs, dumbing, dumbed**) * **dumb down** *informal* to make something so easy to understand that it stops being interesting or challenging. ➤ **dumbly** *adverb*.

dumbfounded *adjective* too surprised or impressed to speak.

dumbstruck *adjective* too surprised or impressed to speak.

dummy *noun* (*plural* **dummies**) **1** an imitation of something used for demonstration purposes. **2** a model of a person used for displaying clothes. **3** a rubber teat for babies to suck. **4** *informal* a stupid person.

dump *verb* (**dumps, dumping, dumped**) **1** to leave something unwanted somewhere. **2** to drop something carelessly or heavily. **3** to get rid of something or somebody in a sudden, often cruel way. ~ *noun* (*plural* **dumps**) **1** a place where rubbish is left. **2** *informal* a place you find boring or unattractive.

dumpling *noun* (*plural* **dumplings**) a small lump of cooked dough, often served in a stew.

dumps * **down in the dumps** *informal* feeling miserable.

dunce *noun* (*plural* **dunces**) a stupid person or a slow learner.

Word History Dunce comes from *Dunses*, the name given to the followers of John *Duns* Scotus, a 13th-century Scottish philosopher. Dunses were thought to be rather dull, unimaginative people.

dune *noun* (*plural* **dunes**) a small hill of sand piled up by the wind.

dung *noun* the excrement of an animal.

dungarees *plural noun* a one-piece garment consisting of trousers and a bib with shoulder straps.

dungeon *noun* (*plural* **dungeons**) a dark underground prison.

dunk *verb* (**dunks, dunking, dunked**)

duo *noun* (*plural* **duos**) two people performing together.

dupe *verb* (**dupes, duping, duped**) to cheat or deceive somebody. ~ *noun* (*plural* **dupes**) somebody who is easily deceived or cheated.

duplicate /dewplikət/ *adjective* being a copy of another thing: *a duplicate key*. ~ *noun* (*plural* **duplicates**) a copy of something. ~ /dewplikayt/ *verb* (**duplicates, duplicating, duplicated**) to make an exact copy of something. ➤ **duplication** *noun*.

duplicity *noun* deceitful behaviour. ➤ **duplicitous** *adjective*.

durable *adjective* able to be used for a long time without wearing out. ➤ **durability** *noun*.

duration *noun* the time during which something exists or lasts.

duress /dewres/ *noun* the situation of being forced to do something: *under duress*.

during *preposition* **1** throughout a period of time. **2** at some point in a period of time.

dusk *noun* the time when it is getting dark, before night.

dust *noun* **1** fine particles of dirt on household surfaces. **2** fine particles of any solid: *gold dust*. **3** an act of dusting something. ~ *verb* (**dusts, dusting, dusted**) to wipe dust off household surfaces. ✻ **dust down/off** to prepare to use something again after not using it for a long time.

dustbin *noun* (*plural* **dustbins**) a large container for household waste.

duster *noun* (*plural* **dusters**) a cloth for wiping dust off household surfaces.

dustman *noun* (*plural* **dustmen**) somebody employed to remove household waste.

dusty *adjective* (**dustier, dustiest**) covered in dust.

dutiful *adjective* doing what you feel you ought to do or what you know people expect you to do. ➤ **dutifully** *adverb*.

duty *noun* (*plural* **duties**) **1** something that you feel you ought to do or that you know people expect you to do. **2** something that you must do as part of your job. **3** a tax on imports and on the transfer of property. ✻ **on/off duty** currently doing (or not doing) your usual work.

duty-free *adjective* said about something you buy: on which you do not have to pay duty.

duvet /doohvay/ *noun* (*plural* **duvets**) a thick quilt used in place of an upper sheet and blankets.

DVD *noun* (*plural* **DVDs**) = digital versatile disc, a disc with a large capacity for storing audio, video, or other information.

dwarf *noun* (*plural* **dwarfs** *or* **dwarves**) **1** a person whose body is abnormally small. **2** in stories, a small human-like creature with magical powers. ~ *adjective* smaller than normal size. ~ *verb* (**dwarfs, dwarfing, dwarfed**) to be much bigger than something and make it seem small or unimportant by comparison.

dwell *verb* (**dwells, dwelling, dwelt** *or* **dwelled**) **1** *formal* to live somewhere. **2** (**dwell on/upon**) to think, write, or speak about something a lot.

dwelling *noun* (*plural* **dwellings**) *formal* a house, flat, or other place where somebody lives.

dwindle *verb* (**dwindles, dwindling, dwindled**) to become steadily smaller or weaker.

dye *noun* (*plural* **dyes**) a liquid used to colour something. ~ *verb* (**dyes, dyed, dyeing**) to change the colour of something using a dye.

dying *verb* present participle of DIE.

dyke *or* **dike** *noun* (*plural* **dykes** *or* **dikes**) **1** a bank of soil built to keep back water and prevent flooding. **2** a ditch.

dynamic /die na mik/ *adjective* **1** said about a person: very energetic and enthusiastic. **2** *Science* to do with physical force or energy in motion. **3** *Music* to do with variations in the loudness of a note. ➤ **dynamically** *adverb*.

dynamics *noun Science* the branch of mechanics that deals with forces and their relation to motion. ~ *plural noun Music* variations in the loudness of a note.

dynamism *noun* energy and enthusiasm.

dynamite *noun* a type of explosive.

dynamo *noun* (*plural* **dynamos**) a machine that converts movement into electricity.

dynasty /di nas ti/ *noun* (*plural* **dynasties**) *History* a series of rulers from the same family who rule a country one after the other for a long time. ➤ **dynastic** *adjective*.

dysentery /dis sn tri/ *noun* an infection of the intestines that causes severe diarrhoea.

dyslexia /dis lek si a/ *noun* difficulties with reading, writing and spelling, caused by a mild brain disorder. ➤ **dyslexic** *adjective and noun*.

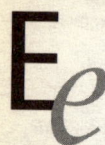

E *abbreviation* East or Eastern.

each *adjective and pronoun* every member of a group considered separately.

eager *adjective* keen to do something. ➤ **eagerly** *adverb*, **eagerness** *noun*.

eagle *noun* (*plural* **eagles**) a large strong bird of prey.

eagle-eyed *adjective* having very good eyesight.

ear[1] *noun* (*plural* **ears**) the part of your body that you hear with.

ear[2] *noun* (*plural* **ears**) the top part of a stalk of corn, where the seed is.

eardrum *noun* (*plural* **eardrums**) a membrane in your ear that vibrates when sound waves reach it.

earl *noun* (*plural* **earls**) a British nobleman who ranks below a marquis and above a viscount.

earlobe *noun* (*plural* **earlobes**) the soft part at the bottom of your ear.

early *adjective and adverb* (**earlier, earliest**) **1** before the usual or expected time. **2** near the beginning of a period of time: *in early January*.

earmark *verb* (**earmarks, earmarking, earmarked**) to set something aside for a specific use.

earn *verb* (**earns, earning, earned**) **1** to receive money in return for work that you have done. **2** to deserve a reward because of your behaviour, help, etc.

earnest *adjective* determined and serious. ✽ **in earnest** seriously or wholeheartedly. ➤ **earnestly** *adverb*.

earnings *plural noun* money that you receive for work that you have done.

earphones *plural noun* a device that you wear on your ears to listen to a personal CD player or radio.

earplug *noun* (*plural* **earplugs**) something you put in your ear to protect it against loud noise, water, etc.

earring *noun* (*plural* **earrings**) a piece of jewellery that you wear on your earlobe.

earshot *noun* the range within which something can be heard: *out of earshot*.

earth *noun* (*plural* **earths**) **1** (*often* **Earth**) the planet on which we live. **2** solid ground or soil. **3** an electrical connection to the ground, used to carry current safely from a circuit if there is a fault. **4** a hole in the ground where a fox or badger lives. ~ *verb* (**earths, earthing, earthed**) to connect a piece of electrical equipment to the ground.

earthenware *noun* pottery made of clay baked at a low temperature.

earthly *adjective* to do with human life on earth. ✽ **no earthly reason** no reason at all.

earthquake *noun* (*plural* **earthquakes**) a sudden violent shaking of the ground caused by pressures in the earth's crust.

earthworm *noun* (*plural* **earthworms**) a common worm that lives in the soil.

earthy *adjective* (**earthier, earthiest**)

1 like earth or soil. **2** said about a person or humour: coarse or vulgar.

earwig noun (plural **earwigs**) a small slender insect with pincers at the end of its body.

Word History People used to believe that earwigs crawled into your ears.

---

ease noun lack of difficulty, pain, or anxiety: *He won the race with ease.* ~ verb (**eases, easing, eased**) **1** to make somebody's pain or suffering less severe. **2** to move somewhere gently or carefully. * **ease off** said about pain or activity: to become less.

easel noun (plural **easels**) *Art* a frame for supporting an artist's canvas.

easily adverb **1** without difficulty. **2** by far: *She is easily the best.*

east noun **1** the direction of the sunrise. **2** regions or countries lying towards the east. ~ adjective and adverb **1** at or towards the east. **2** said about the wind: blowing from the east.

Easter noun a Christian festival held on a Sunday between 21 March and 25 April to celebrate Jesus's resurrection.

easterly adjective and adverb **1** in an eastern position or direction. **2** said about a wind: blowing from the east.

eastern adjective in or towards the east.

eastward adjective and adverb towards the east; in a direction going east. ➤ **eastwards** adverb.

easy adjective (**easier, easiest**) **1** causing little difficulty. **2** causing little pain or anxiety: *an easy life.* * **take it easy** to relax or rest.

easygoing adjective relaxed and tolerant.

eat verb (**eats, eating, ate, eaten**) **1** to put food in your mouth and swallow it. **2** to have a meal: *We normally eat at seven.* * **eat away at** or **eat up** to use something up gradually. ➤ **eatable** adjective.

eau de cologne /oh di ko lohn/ noun a kind of light perfume.

eaves plural noun the edges of a roof that hang over the top of the walls.

eavesdrop verb (**eavesdrops, eavesdropping, eavesdropped**) to listen secretly to what people are saying in private.

ebb verb (**ebbs, ebbing, ebbed**) said about the tide: to flow out towards the sea. * **at a low ebb** in a weak state or at a low level: *Her confidence was at a low ebb.* **ebb away** to become gradually less.

ebony noun **1** hard dark wood from a tropical tree. **2** deep black.

ebullient /i bu li ant/ adjective lively and enthusiastic. ➤ **ebullience** noun.

eccentric /ik sen trik/ adjective unusual, unconventional, and amusingly odd. ➤ **eccentrically** adverb, **eccentricity** noun.

ecclesiastical /i klee zi as ti kl/ adjective to do with the Christian church.

echelon /e shi lon/ noun (plural **echelons**) a level or grade of authority or seniority in an organization.

echo /e koh/ noun (plural **echoes**) the repetition of a sound caused by the reflection of sound waves. ~ verb (**echoes, echoing, echoed**) **1** to produce an echo. **2** to repeat or imitate what somebody says.

éclair /i klair/ noun (plural **éclairs**) a long narrow pastry cake filled with cream and topped with chocolate icing.

eclipse noun (plural **eclipses**) the total or partial blocking from view of the sun or the moon by the moon or the earth coming in between. ~ verb (**eclipses, eclipsing, eclipsed**) to do better than somebody or something else: *He has eclipsed his father's success.*

eco-friendly *adjective* not harmful to the environment.

ecology *noun* the scientific study of how living things relate to each other and to their environment. ➤ **ecological** *adjective*, **ecologically** *adverb*, **ecologist** *noun*.

economic /eeko no mik *or* e ko no mik/ *adjective* **1** to do with economics or an economy. **2** making a profit.

economical /eeko no mi kl *or* e ko no mi kl/ *adjective* not wasting money. ➤ **economically** *adverb*.

economics /eeko no miks *or* e ko no miks/ *noun* the study of how goods and services are produced, distributed, paid for, and used. ➤ **economist** *noun*.

economy *noun* (*plural* **economies**) **1** the system used in a country to produce and sell goods and services and create wealth. **2** efficient use of money, time, or effort. **3** a saving: *We had to make economies*.

ecosystem *noun* (*plural* **ecosystems**) *Science* the plants and animals in an area and the environment they exist in.

ecstasy *noun* (*plural* **ecstasies**) **1** a feeling of great happiness. **2** (**Ecstasy**) an illegal drug that can make people very happy or excited. ➤ **ecstatic** *adjective*, **ecstatically** *adverb*.

eczema /ek si ma/ *noun* a skin disease that causes itching and blisters.

eddy *noun* (*plural* **eddies**) a swirling current of water or air.

edge *noun* (*plural* **edges**) **1** the line where an object or area ends. **2** the cutting side of a blade. ~ *verb* (**edges, edging, edged**) **1** to provide something with an edge: *a card edged in silver*. **2** to move somewhere gradually or cautiously. ✴ **on edge** anxious or nervous.

edgy *adjective* (**edgier, edgiest**) tense or anxious. ➤ **edginess** *noun*.

edible *adjective* fit to be eaten as food.

edict /ee dikt/ *noun* (*plural* **edicts**) an official public decree or command.

edifice /e di fis/ *noun* (*plural* **edifices**) a large building.

edit *verb* (**edits, editing, edited**) **1** to shorten or improve a piece of writing. **2** to put together a film or recording by cutting out, adding, and rearranging parts. **3** to be the editor of a newspaper, magazine, or book.

edition *noun* (*plural* **editions**) **1** the form in which a book or magazine is published: *a leather-bound edition*. **2** a number of copies of a newspaper, magazine, or book published at one time. **3** a particular instalment of a radio or television series.

editor *noun* (*plural* **editors**) **1** a person who is in overall charge of the content of a newspaper, magazine, or book, or of a radio or television programme. **2** a person who edits a piece of writing or a film or recording.

editorial *adjective* to do with editing. ~ *noun* (*plural* **editorials**) a newspaper or magazine column giving the opinions of the editor. ➤ **editorially** *adverb*.

educate *verb* (**educates, educating, educated**) to teach or instruct somebody.

educated *adjective* having had a good education.

education *noun* the process of being taught or instructed and the knowledge resulting from this. ➤ **educational** *adjective*, **educationally** *adverb*.

Edwardian *adjective* dating from the reign of King Edward VII (1901–1910).

eel *noun* (*plural* **eels**) a long thin fish that looks like a snake.

eerie *or* **eery** *adjective* (**eerier, eeriest**) frighteningly strange or gloomy. ➤ **eerily** *adverb*.

effect *noun* (*plural* **effects**) **1** the result

of what somebody does or of something that happens: *the effects of the flood*. **2** the kind of impression that something or somebody creates: *His voice had a calming effect*. ✶ **take effect** to begin to apply: *This law will take effect from next year*.

Usage Note **effect** or **affect**? See note at **affect**.

effective *adjective* producing the desired result. ➤ **effectively** *adverb*.

effeminate *adjective* said about a man: having qualities or behaviour considered more typical of a woman.

efficient *adjective* working well without wasting much time, money, or effort. ➤ **efficiency** *noun*, **efficiently** *adverb*.

effigy /**e**fi ji/ *noun* (*plural* **effigies**) a model of a person, especially somebody you hate.

effort *noun* (*plural* **efforts**) **1** the use of physical or mental power. **2** a serious attempt to do something.

effortless *adjective* done easily and without strain. ➤ **effortlessly** *adverb*.

e.g. *abbreviation* = (Latin) *exempli gratia* for example.

egalitarian /i ga li**tair**i an/ *adjective* believing in equality for all human beings.

egg¹ *noun* (*plural* **eggs**) **1** a round or oval object with a hard or soft casing, produced by a female bird, fish, or reptile, from which a baby creature may develop. **2** = OVUM. **3** the egg of a hen, duck, goose, or other bird, used as food.

egg² *verb* (**eggs, egging, egged**) ✶ **egg on** to encourage somebody to do something wrong or something daring: *The other boys egged him on to steal a bar of chocolate*.

eggplant *noun* (*plural* **eggplants**) *chiefly N American* = AUBERGINE.

ego /**ee**goh/ *noun* (*plural* **egos**) **1** your sense of your own worth. **2** too high an opinion of your own worth.

egocentric *adjective* thinking too much about what you want; selfish.

egotism *noun* too high an opinion of your own importance. ➤ **egotist** *noun*, **egotistic** *adjective*.

Eid /eed/ *noun* either of two Muslim festivals held every year – Eid-ul-Fitr, which marks the end of the fast of Ramadan, and Eid-ul-Adha, which marks the end of the annual pilgrimage to Mecca.

eight *adjective and noun* (*plural* **eights**) **1** the number 8. **2** the crew of eight on a racing boat. ➤ **eighth** *adjective and noun*.

eighteen *adjective and noun* (*plural* **eighteens**) the number 18. ➤ **eighteenth** *adjective and noun*.

eighty *adjective and noun* (*plural* **eighties**) **1** the number 80. **2** (**the eighties**) the numbers 80 to 89. ➤ **eightieth** *adjective and noun*.

eisteddfod /ie**steth**vod/ *noun* (*plural* **eisteddfods**) a Welsh festival of music and poetry.

either *adjective* both of the two: *on either side of the path*. ~ *adjective and pronoun* one or the other of two: *Take either road. Either will do*. ~ *conjunction* used before the first of two alternatives: *either milk or orange juice*.

ejaculate *verb* (**ejaculates, ejaculating, ejaculated**) **1** said about a man: to have semen come out of his penis. **2** *formal* to say something suddenly and with force. ➤ **ejaculation** *noun*.

eject *verb* (**ejects, ejecting, ejected**) to throw somebody or something out, using physical force. ➤ **ejection** *noun*.

eke *verb* (**ekes, eking, eked**) ✶ **eke out** to make a supply of something last longer by using a little at a time.

elaborate /i**la**bo rat/ *adjective* complicated and very detailed. ~ /i**la**bo rayt/

elapse

verb (**elaborates, elaborating, elaborated**) to give more information about something: *Could you elaborate on that statement?* ➤ **elaborately** *adverb*, **elaboration** *noun*.

elapse *verb* (**elapses, elapsing, elapsed**) said about a period of time: to pass by.

elastic *adjective* **1** said about a material: able to return to its former shape after being stretched or squashed. **2** flexible or adaptable. ~ *noun* a material containing rubber that is easily stretched. ➤ **elasticated** *adjective*, **elasticity** *noun*.

elated *adjective* feeling great joy. ➤ **elation** *noun*.

elbow *noun* (*plural* **elbows**) the joint in the middle of your arm where it bends. ~ *verb* (**elbows, elbowing, elbowed**) to shove somebody with your elbow: *She elbowed me aside.*

elder[1] *adjective* older: *their elder son.* ~ *noun* (*plural* **elders**) **1** somebody who is older than you: *your elders.* **2** a member of a tribe or other group who has authority because of age and experience. **3** an official in certain Christian churches.

elder[2] *noun* (*plural* **elders**) a shrub or small tree with white flowers and black or red berries.

elderly *adjective* rather old.

eldest *adjective* oldest: *my eldest sister.*

elect *verb* (**elects, electing, elected**) **1** to select somebody by vote for an position. **2** *formal* to choose to do something. ~ *adjective* selected for a position but not yet in that position: *the President elect.* ➤ **elector** *noun*.

election *noun* (*plural* **elections**) **1** an occasion when people vote to elect somebody to a position of authority. **2** the act of electing somebody or being elected. ➤ **electoral** *adjective*.

electorate *noun* the people who can vote in an election.

electric *adjective* **1** to do with or operated by electricity. **2** said about an atmosphere: exciting or thrilling.

electrical *adjective* to do with or producing electricity. ➤ **electrically** *adverb*.

electric chair *noun* an electrified chair that is used to kill criminals by an electric shock.

electrician *noun* (*plural* **electricians**) a person who installs or repairs electrical equipment.

electricity *noun Science* a form of energy that passes along wires and is used to give light and to provide power for machines.

electric shock *noun* (*plural* **electric shocks**) a sudden sharp pain caused by electricity passing through your body if you touch something that is connected to an electrical supply.

electrified *adjective* operated by electricity.

electrifying *adjective* exciting or thrilling.

electrocute *verb* (**electrocutes, electrocuting, electrocuted**) to kill somebody by an electric shock. ➤ **electrocution** *noun*.

electrode *noun* (*plural* **electrodes**) *Science* an electrical conductor that makes contact with a non-metallic part of a circuit, such as the acid in a car battery.

electron *noun* (*plural* **electrons**) *Science* a tiny particle, smaller than an atom, that has a negative electrical charge.

electronic *adjective ICT* **1** to do with transistors or microchips, in which a flow of electrons is controlled by a voltage. **2** to do with computers or other electronic systems. ➤ **electronically** *adverb*.

electronic mail *noun ICT* = EMAIL.

electronics *noun* the scientific study of electronic devices. ~ *plural noun* the circuits and devices of a piece of electronic equipment.

elegant *adjective* graceful, refined, and stylish. ➤ **elegance** *noun*, **elegantly** *adverb*.

elegy /**el**i ji/ *noun* (*plural* **elegies**) *English* a song or poem expressing sorrow for a dead person.

element *noun* (*plural* **elements**) **1** *Science* a substance consisting of atoms of only one kind. **2** any of the parts that make up the whole of something. **3** a group of a particular type within a larger group: *the criminal element*. **4** a small quantity of something: *an element of doubt*. **5** the part of an electric kettle that contains the heating wire. **6** (**the elements**) the weather, especially bad weather.

elementary *adjective* basic or simple.

elephant *noun* (*plural* **elephants** *or* **elephant**) a very large animal with a long trunk and two ivory tusks, found in Africa and South Asia.

elevate *verb* (**elevates, elevating, elevated**) **1** to lift something up. **2** to raise somebody to a higher rank or position.

elevation *noun* **1** height above sea level. **2** the act of elevating somebody or something.

elevator *noun* (*plural* **elevators**) *chiefly N American* = LIFT (definition 1).

eleven *adjective and noun* (*plural* **elevens**) **1** the number 11. **2** a cricket, football, or hockey team. ➤ **eleventh** *adjective and noun*.

elf *noun* (*plural* **elves**) a small mischievous fairy.

elicit /i**lis**it/ *verb* (**elicits, eliciting, elicited**) to draw out a response from somebody.

eligible /**el**i ji bl/ *adjective* qualified to do or receive something: *eligible for membership*. ➤ **eligibility** *noun*.

eliminate *verb* (**eliminates, eliminating, eliminated**) **1** to get rid of somebody or something completely. **2** to remove a competitor or a team from a competition by defeating them. ➤ **elimination** *noun*.

elite *or* **élite** /i li**leet**/ *noun* (*plural* **elites** *or* **élites**) a group considered to be intellectually, professionally, or socially superior to others.

Elizabethan /i li za **bee** thn/ *adjective* to do with the reign of Queen Elizabeth I of England (1558–1603).

elk *noun* (*plural* **elks** *or* **elk**) a very large deer of Europe and Asia.

ellipse *noun* (*plural* **ellipses**) a shape that looks like a flattened circle.

elm *noun* (*plural* **elms**) a large tree with jagged leaves.

elocution *noun* the study of how to speak clearly.

elongate *verb* (**elongates, elongating, elongated**) to make something longer. ➤ **elongated** *adjective*.

elope *verb* (**elopes, eloping, eloped**) said about a couple: to run away secretly to get married.

eloquent *adjective* able to express yourself cleverly in words. ➤ **eloquence** *noun*, **eloquently** *adverb*.

else *adverb* different from the person or thing already mentioned: *somebody else*. ✶ **or else** otherwise.

elsewhere *adverb* in or to another place.

elude *verb* (**eludes, eluding, eluded**) **1** to avoid somebody. **2** to be forgotten by somebody: *Her name eludes me*.

elusive *adjective* difficult to find or to remember.

elves *noun plural of* ELF.

emaciated *adjective* extremely thin or weak because of lack of food. ➤ **emaciation** *noun*.

email *noun* (*plural* **emails**) *ICT* **1** a system for sending messages from one computer to another through a modem and telephone line.

emancipate

2 a message sent in this way. ~ *verb* (**emails, emailing, emailed**) *ICT* to send a message to somebody by email.

emancipate *verb* (**emancipates, emancipating, emancipated**) to free somebody from slavery or from social or legal restrictions. ➤ **emancipation** *noun*.

embankment *noun* (*plural* **embankments**) an area of sloping ground on either side of a road or railway.

embargo *noun* (*plural* **embargoes**) a government ban on trading with a particular country.

embark *verb* (**embarks, embarking, embarked**) **1** to go on board a ship or aircraft. **2** to begin something: *I embarked on my new career.*

embarrass *verb* (**embarrasses, embarrassing, embarrassed**) to make somebody feel awkward and self-conscious. ➤ **embarrassed** *adjective*, **embarrassing** *adjective*, **embarrassment** *noun*.

embassy *noun* (*plural* **embassies**) the official home or offices of an ambassador.

embed *or* **imbed** *verb* (**embeds, embedding, embedded** *or* **imbeds**, etc) to fix something firmly somewhere: *seashells embedded in the rock.*

embellish *verb* (**embellishes, embellishing, embellished**) to decorate something.

ember *noun* (*plural* **embers**) a piece of coal or wood that is still burning in a dying fire.

embittered *adjective* having become bitter or resentful because of something that has happened.

emblazon /im blay zn/ *verb* (**emblazons, emblazoning, emblazoned**) to decorate something with a design.

emblem *noun* (*plural* **emblems**) a design or symbol that represents something: *The thistle is the national emblem of Scotland.*

embody *verb* (**embodies, embodying, embodied**) to represent an idea or quality: *She embodies kindness.* ➤ **embodiment** *noun*.

emboss *verb* (**embosses, embossing, embossed**) to carve a raised design on a surface.

embrace *verb* (**embraces, embracing, embraced**) **1** to hold somebody in your arms as a sign of affection. **2** to take up a belief or opportunity enthusiastically. ➤ **embrace** *noun*.

embroider *verb* (**embroiders, embroidering, embroidered**) to sew a design onto a piece of cloth or item of clothing.

embroidery *noun* (*plural* **embroideries**) **1** the art of embroidering. **2** an embroidered design.

embroil *verb* (**embroils, embroiling, embroiled**) to involve somebody in an argument.

embryo /em bri oh/ *noun* (*plural* **embryos**) an unborn baby or animal in the early stages of growth in its mother's womb. ➤ **embryonic** *adjective*.

emerald *noun* (*plural* **emeralds**) **1** a bright green gemstone. **2** a bright green colour.

emerge *verb* (**emerges, emerging, emerged**) **1** to come out into view. **2** said about a fact: to become known. ➤ **emergence** *noun*, **emergent** *adjective*.

emergency *noun* (*plural* **emergencies**) a potentially dangerous occurrence that requires immediate action.

emery board *noun* (*plural* **emery boards**) a strip of cardboard with a rough coating on one side, which is used to smooth your nails.

emigrant *noun* (*plural* **emigrants**) a person who emigrates.

emigrate *verb* (**emigrates, emigrating, emigrated**) to leave your country to live permanently in another country.

emigration *noun* the act of emigrating, sometimes by large numbers of people during particular periods of history.

eminent *adjective* known and respected by a lot of people: *an eminent brain surgeon.* ➤ **eminence** *noun*, **eminently** *adverb*.

emir /e meer/ *noun* (*plural* **emirs**) a ruler of a Muslim state.

emission *noun* (*plural* **emissions**) something emitted, such as fumes or radiation.

emit *verb* (**emits, emitting, emitted**) to give out light, smoke, or radiation. **2** to make (a sound).

emoticon /i moh ti kon/ *noun* (*plural* **emoticons**) *ICT* a symbol used in email messages to suggest an emotion such as happiness or anger.

emotion *noun* (*plural* **emotions**) a strong feeling such as anger, fear, or joy.

emotional *adjective* **1** to do with the emotions. **2** feeling or showing emotion. ➤ **emotionally** *adverb*.

emotive *adjective* said about a subject: arousing emotion.

empathize or **empathise** *verb* (**empathizes, empathizing, empathized** or **empathises**, etc) to understand and share the feelings of another person: *I empathize with you in your grief.*

empathy *noun* the ability to understand and share the feelings of another person.

emperor *noun* (*plural* **emperors**) the ruler of an empire.

emphasis *noun* (*plural* **emphases**) special importance given to something, especially in speaking or writing.

emphasize or **emphasise** *verb* (**emphasizes, emphasizing, emphasized** or **emphasises**, etc) to give emphasis to something.

emphatic *adjective* spoken with or marked by emphasis. ➤ **emphatically** *adverb*.

empire *noun* (*plural* **empires**) **1** a large group of countries under the authority of a single ruler. **2** a large group of companies owned by the same person.

employ *verb* (**employs, employing, employed**) **1** to pay somebody in return for their work. **2** to use something for a specific purpose.

employee *noun* (*plural* **employees**) a person who is employed to work for wages or a salary.

employer *noun* (*plural* **employers**) a person or company that employs people.

employment *noun* **1** the act of employing somebody. **2** paid work.

empower *verb* (**empowers, empowering, empowered**) **1** to give authority or power to. **2** to give somebody the confidence to act on their own initiative. ➤ **empowerment** *noun*.

empress *noun* (*plural* **empresses**) **1** the wife or widow of an emperor. **2** a woman who has the rank of emperor.

empty *adjective* (**emptier, emptiest**) **1** containing nothing or nobody. **2** without meaning or sincerity: *empty words.* ~ *verb* (**empties, emptying, emptied**) **1** to remove the contents of something. **2** to become empty. ➤ **emptiness** *noun*.

emu /ee mew/ *noun* (*plural* **emus**) an Australian bird that cannot fly, related to but smaller than the ostrich.

emulate /e mew layt/ *verb* (**emulates, emulating, emulated**) to copy somebody that you admire. ➤ **emulation** *noun*.

emulsion *noun* a type of water-based paint used on walls and ceilings.

enable *verb* (**enables, enabling, enabled**) to give somebody the means or opportunity to do something.

enact *verb* (**enacts, enacting, enacted**) **1** to make a bill law. **2** to perform a role or a scene. ➤ **enactment** *noun*.

enamel *noun* **1** a glassy protective coating on the surface of metal, glass, or pottery. **2** a white substance that forms a hard layer on your teeth. **3** a paint that dries with a glossy appearance. ~ *verb* (**enamels, enamelling, enamelled**) to cover or decorate an object with enamel. ➤ **enamelled** *adjective*.

enamoured /i na merd/ *adjective* fond of a person or thing.

encapsulate *verb* (**encapsulates, encapsulating, encapsulated**) to express an idea in a few words.

encase *verb* (**encases, encasing, encased**) to enclose something in a case.

enchant *verb* (**enchants, enchanting, enchanted**) **1** to cast a spell on somebody. **2** to attract and delight somebody. ➤ **enchanted** *adjective*, **enchanting** *adjective*.

encircle *verb* (**encircles, encircling, encircled**) to form a circle round somebody or something.

enclave /en klayv/ *noun* (*plural* **enclaves**) an area within a country that belongs to another country.

enclose *verb* (**encloses, enclosing, enclosed**) **1** to include something in an envelope along with a letter. **2** to surround a place completely.

enclosure *noun* (*plural* **enclosures**) **1** an area of ground with a fence round it. **2** something enclosed with a letter.

encompass *verb* (**encompasses, encompassing, encompassed**) to include a number of things.

encore /ong kaw/ *noun* (*plural* **encores**) an additional performance at the request of the audience.

encounter *verb* (**encounters, encountering, encountered**) to meet or be faced with somebody or something. ➤ **encounter** *noun*.

encourage *verb* (**encourages, encouraging, encouraged**) **1** to give somebody confidence or hope. **2** to give support or approval to a process or action. ➤ **encouragement** *noun*, **encouraging** *adjective*.

encroach *verb* (**encroaches, encroaching, encroached**) to intrude gradually on somebody's possessions or rights. ➤ **encroachment** *noun*.

encrust *verb* (**encrusts, encrusting, encrusted**) to cover something with a hard or decorative layer.

encyclopaedia or **encyclopedia** *noun* (*plural* **encyclopaedias** or **encyclopedias**) a book containing general information on a wide range of subjects.

encyclopaedic or **encyclopedic** *adjective* wide and detailed: *an encyclopaedic knowledge of butterflies*.

end *noun* (*plural* **ends**) **1** the point at which something stops or is completed. **2** the last part of something. **3** either of the parts farthest from the middle of something long. **4** a goal or purpose: *a means to an end*. ~ *verb* (**ends, ending, ended**) to come to an end or bring something to an end.

endanger *verb* (**endangers, endangering, endangered**) to put somebody or something in danger.

endangered *adjective* said about a species: at risk of becoming extinct.

endear *verb* (**endears, endearing, endeared**) to make somebody become fond of you. ➤ **endearing** *adjective*.

endeavour /in de ver/ *verb* (**endeavours, endeavouring, endeavoured**)

ending noun (plural **endings**) the last part of something such as a story, book, or film.

endless adjective being or seeming to be without end. ➤ **endlessly** adverb.

endorse or **indorse** verb (**endorses, endorsing, endorsed** or **indorses**, etc) **1** to express support for somebody or something publicly. **2** to sign the back of a cheque to authorize payment. ➤ **endorsement** noun.

endow verb (**endows, endowing, endowed**) to provide somebody with an ability or quality: *She was not endowed with much intelligence.*

endurance noun the ability to put up with difficulties.

endure verb (**endures, enduring, endured**) **1** to put up with difficulties. **2** to last for a long time.

enemy noun (plural **enemies**) a person who is opposed to somebody else.

energetic adjective having a lot of energy. ➤ **energetically** adverb.

energy noun **1** the natural strength and vitality that you need to keep you active. **2** sources of power, such as electricity.

enforce verb (**enforces, enforcing, enforced**) to force people to obey a rule or law. ➤ **enforceable** adjective, **enforcement** noun.

engage verb (**engages, engaging, engaged**) **1** to hold somebody's attention. **2** to participate in an activity.

engaged adjective **1** occupied or in use. **2** having agreed to marry somebody.

engagement noun (plural **engagements**) **1** an agreement to marry somebody. **2** an appointment to meet somebody.

engine noun (plural **engines**) **1** a machine that converts energy into mechanical force and motion. **2** a railway locomotive.

engineer noun (plural **engineers**) a person who is trained in engineering. ~ verb (**engineers, engineering, engineered**) to go to great lengths to arrange for something to happen.

engineering noun the study of the design and construction of machines or of bridges and roads.

engrave verb (**engraves, engraving, engraved**) to cut a design or lettering on metal or stone. ➤ **engraver** noun, **engraving** noun.

engross verb (**engrosses, engrossing, engrossed**) to completely occupy somebody's attention: *She was engrossed in the film.*

engulf verb (**engulfs, engulfing, engulfed**) to flow over and completely cover something.

enhance verb (**enhances, enhancing, enhanced**) to improve the value or appearance of something. ➤ **enhancement** noun.

enigma noun (plural **enigmas**) somebody or something that is hard to understand. ➤ **enigmatic** adjective, **enigmatically** adverb.

enjoy verb (**enjoys, enjoying, enjoyed**) **1** to take pleasure in something. **2** to have the benefit of something. ✱ **enjoy oneself** to have fun. ➤ **enjoyment** noun.

enjoyable adjective giving pleasure.

enlarge verb (**enlarges, enlarging, enlarged**) **1** to become larger or make something larger. **2** to say more about something: *Could you enlarge on that last statement?*

enlargement noun (plural **enlargements**) **1** a larger version of a photograph. **2** the act of enlarging something.

enlighten verb (**enlightens, enlightening, enlightened**) to give somebody knowledge or information. ➤ **enlightenment** noun.

enlist verb (**enlists, enlisting,**

enliven

enlisted) 1 to join the army, navy, or air force. **2** to persuade somebody to help you with something: *I enlisted Ahmed to help with the gardening.*

enliven /in lie vn/ *verb* (**enlivens, enlivening, enlivened**) to make something more lively or interesting.

en masse /on mas/ *adverb* all together.

enmity *noun* a feeling or state of hatred or hostility.

enormity *noun* (*plural* **enormities**) **1** the state of being enormous. **2** great wickedness, or a terribly wicked act.

enormous *adjective* extremely large.
➤ **enormously** *adverb*.

enough *adjective* sufficient in amount, number, or degree. ~ *adverb* **1** to a sufficient degree. **2** fairly: *The film was amusing enough.* ~ *pronoun* a sufficient amount or number.

enquire *or* **inquire** *verb* (**enquires, enquiring, enquired** *or* **inquires**, etc) to ask about something.

Usage Note **enquire** *or* **inquire**? *Enquire* is the commoner British English spelling; *inquire* is generally used in American English.

enquiry *or* **inquiry** *noun* (*plural* **enquiries** *or* **inquiries**) **1** a request for information. **2** an investigation into something: *a government inquiry.*

enrage *verb* (**enrages, enraging, enraged**) to make somebody very angry.

enrich *verb* (**enriches, enriching, enriched**) to improve the quality of something. ➤ **enrichment** *noun*.

enrol *verb* (**enrols, enrolling, enrolled**) to register somewhere as a member or student. ➤ **enrolment** *noun*.

en route /on rooht/ *adverb and adjective* along the way.

ensconced *adjective* settled comfortably.

ensemble /on som bl/ *noun* (*plural* **ensembles**) **1** a group that works together as a whole. **2** a complete outfit of matching garments. **3** a group of actors, musicians, etc who perform together.

ensign *noun* (*plural* **ensigns**) a flag flown by a ship.

ensue *verb* (**ensues, ensuing, ensued**) to take place as a result of something that has already happened.

ensure *verb* (**ensures, ensuring, ensured**) to make sure.

Usage Note Do not confuse *ensure* with *insure*. To *insure* something means to take out insurance on it: *The house is insured for £1 million.*

entangle *verb* (**entangles, entangling, entangled**) to involve somebody in a difficult situation.

enter *verb* (**enters, entering, entered**) **1** to go into a place. **2** to write a piece of information in a diary, an account, or a computer file. **3** to become a member of a profession: *to enter politics.* **4** to take part in a competition.

enterprise *noun* (*plural* **enterprises**) **1** a project. **2** a business organization.

enterprising *adjective* bold and imaginative.

entertain *verb* (**entertains, entertaining, entertained**) **1** to amuse people. **2** to give people food in your home.

entertainment *noun* something that you watch or do for fun.

enthral /in thrawl/ *verb* (**enthrals, enthralling, enthralled**) to hold somebody's attention.

enthusiasm *noun* keen interest.
➤ **enthusiast** *noun*.

enthusiastic *adjective* extremely interested in something. ➤ **enthusiastically** *adverb*.

entice *verb* (**entices, enticing,**

enticed) to tempt somebody to do something.

entire *adjective* having no element or part left out. ➤ **entirely** *adverb*.

entirety /in tier i ti/ *noun* the whole of something. * **in its entirety** with nothing left out.

entitle *verb* (**entitles, entitling, entitled**) to give somebody the right to do or have something. ➤ **entitlement** *noun*.

entourage /on too rahzh/ *noun* (*plural* **entourages**) a group of people who accompany an important person.

entrails *plural noun* the intestines.

entrance¹ /en trans/ *noun* (*plural* **entrances**) **1** *Drama* the act of entering a place or appearing on stage. **2** a door or gate.

entrance² /in trahns/ *verb* (**entrances, entrancing, entranced**) to fill somebody with delight; to fascinate them. ➤ **entrancing** *adjective*.

entrant *noun* (*plural* **entrants**) somebody who enters a contest or a profession.

entreat *verb* (**entreats, entreating, entreated**) to plead with somebody to do something.

entrenched *adjective* said about a belief or a custom: so firmly established that it is difficult to change.

entrust *verb* (**entrusts, entrusting, entrusted**) to give somebody the responsibility of looking after somebody or something.

entry *noun* (*plural* **entries**) **1** the act of entering a place. **2** a door or gate. **3** a record made in a diary, account book, computer file, etc.

E number *noun* (*plural* **E numbers**) a number with the letter *E* in front of it, used to indicate an artificial substance that is added to food to improve the colour or taste or to make it stay fresh longer.

envelop /in ve lop/ *verb* (**envelops, enveloping, enveloped**) to cover or surround something completely.

envelope /en vi lohp/ *noun* (*plural* **envelopes**) a flat container for a letter, made of folded and gummed paper.

enviable *adjective* causing people to feel envy.

envious *adjective* feeling envy. ➤ **enviously** *adverb*.

environment *noun* (*plural* **environments**) **1** the conditions and surroundings in which you live. **2** (**the environment**) the natural surroundings, and the plant and animal life, among which people live. ➤ **environmental** *adjective*, **environmentally** *adverb*.

environmentalism *noun* concern for the protection of the natural environment. ➤ **environmentalist** *noun and adjective*.

envisage *verb* (**envisages, envisaging, envisaged**) **1** to have a mental picture of something. **2** to consider something as a future possibility: *I don't envisage any problems.*

envoy *noun* (*plural* **envoys**) an official representative of one country's government in another country.

envy *noun* a desire to have what somebody else has. ~ *verb* (**envies, envying, envied**) to feel envy for what somebody else has.

enzyme *noun* (*plural* **enzymes**) a protein produced by living cells in the body.

ephemeral /i fe mi ral/ *adjective* lasting a very short time.

epic *noun* (*plural* **epics**) a long story or film about heroic deeds. ~ *adjective* great in size or scope.

epidemic *noun* (*plural* **epidemics**) **1** an outbreak of a disease affecting a lot of people in an area. **2** a sudden rapid spread of something undesirable.

epigram *noun* (*plural* **epigrams**) a short witty remark.

epilepsy *noun* a brain condition that causes fits and loss of consciousness. ➤ **epileptic** *noun and adjective*.

episode *noun* (*plural* **episodes**) **1** a significant event. **2** an instalment of a radio or television serial.

epistle /i pi sl/ *noun* (*plural* **epistles**) *formal* a letter.

epitaph *noun* (*plural* **epitaphs**) an inscription on a gravestone or monument.

epithet *noun* (*plural* **epithets**) a word or phrase describing somebody, often one that is used as part of their name, as for example 'the Great' in *Pope Gregory the Great*.

epitome /i pi to mi/ *noun* a typical example of something: *the very epitome of a pop star*.

epoch /ee pok/ *noun* (*plural* **epochs**) a period in history.

equal *adjective* **1** of the same quantity, size, or value as another person or thing. **2** (**equal to**) capable of performing a task. ~ *noun* (*plural* **equals**) a person or thing that is equal to another. ~ *verb* (**equals, equalling, equalled**) to be equal to somebody or something. ➤ **equality** *noun*, **equally** *adverb*.

equalize or **equalise** (**equalizes, equalizing, equalized** or **equalises**, etc) *verb* to bring the scores level in a football or rugby match. ➤ **equalizer** or **equaliser** *noun*.

equate *verb* (**equates, equating, equated**) (**equate with**) to treat people or things as equal or the same.

equation *noun* (*plural* **equations**) **1** *Maths* a statement of the equality of two mathematical expressions. **2** *Science* an expression representing a chemical reaction by means of chemical symbols. **3** the act of equating.

equator *noun* (**the equator**) *Geography* the imaginary circle round the middle of the earth. ➤ **equatorial** *adjective*.

equestrian *adjective* to do with horses.

equilateral *adjective* *Maths* said about a triangle: having all its sides of equal length.

equilibrium *noun* (*plural* **equilibria**) a state of balance.

equine /e kwien/ *adjective* to do with horses.

equinox *noun* (*plural* **equinoxes**) either of the two times each year, around 21 March and 23 September, when day and night are of equal length.

equip *verb* (**equips, equipping, equipped**) to provide somebody with the tools and supplies needed for a particular purpose.

equipment *noun* the tools and supplies needed for a particular purpose.

equitable *adjective* fair and just.

equity *noun* fairness and justice.

equivalent *adjective* equal in effect, amount, or value. ~ *noun* (*plural* **equivalents**) a person or thing that is equivalent to another. ➤ **equivalence** *noun*.

era /eer a/ *noun* (*plural* **eras**) a period in history.

eradicate *verb* (**eradicates, eradicating, eradicated**) to destroy or do away with something. ➤ **eradication** *noun*.

erase *verb* (**erases, erasing, erased**) **1** to rub out something written. **2** to remove something recorded from a tape.

eraser *noun* (*plural* **erasers**) a piece of rubber or a felt pad used to erase pencil or chalk.

erect *adjective* upright and straight. ~ *verb* (**erects, erecting, erected**) to build something.

erection *noun* (*plural* **erections**) **1** something that has been erected, especially a building. **2** the act of erecting something.

ermine /ˈer min/ *noun* white fur from a stoat's winter coat.

erode *verb* (**erodes, eroding, eroded**) to wear something away gradually.

erosion *noun Geography* the process of eroding, especially of land by the action of wind or water.

erotic *adjective* to do with sexual desire. ➤ **erotically** *adverb*.

err *verb* (**errs, erring, erred**) to make a mistake.

errand *noun* (*plural* **errands**) a short trip to do a job for somebody.

erratic *adjective* inconsistent or unpredictable. ➤ **erratically** *adverb*.

erroneous *adjective* incorrect. ➤ **erroneously** *adverb*.

error *noun* (*plural* **errors**) a mistake or inaccuracy.

erudite /ˈe roo diet/ *adjective* having a great deal of knowledge.

erupt *verb* (**erupts, erupting, erupted**) **1** said about a volcano: to throw out lava, steam, and ash violently. **2** said about a row: to become suddenly active or violent.

escalate *verb* (**escalates, escalating, escalated**) to increase in amount, intensity, or seriousness. ➤ **escalation** *noun*.

escalator *noun* (*plural* **escalators**) a moving staircase.

escapade *noun* (*plural* **escapades**) a reckless and mischievous adventure.

escape *verb* (**escapes, escaping, escaped**) **1** to get out of or away from a place. **2** to avoid danger. **3** not to be noticed or remembered by somebody: *The name escapes me.* ➤ **escape** *noun*, **escapee** *noun*.

escapism *noun* entertainment that takes your mind off unpleasant realities. ➤ **escapist** *adjective*.

escort /ˈe skawt/ *noun* (*plural* **escorts**) one or more people or vehicles that accompany somebody somewhere, for protection or company. ~ /i ˈskawt/ *verb* (**escorts, escorting, escorted**) to accompany somebody somewhere.

Eskimo *noun* (*plural* **Eskimos** or **Eskimo**) a member of a people who live in Greenland, northern Canada, Alaska, and eastern Siberia.

especially *adverb* in particular.

espionage /ˈe spi o nahzh/ *noun* the use of spies to obtain information.

espouse *verb* (**espouses, espousing, espoused**) to begin to support a cause, belief, etc.

espresso *noun* (*plural* **espressos**) coffee brewed by forcing steam through finely ground coffee beans.

Esq. *abbreviation* Esquire, used after a man's name as a title instead of 'Mr'.

essay *noun* (*plural* **essays**) a short piece of prose writing on a specific topic.

essence *noun* (*plural* **essences**) **1** the most important qualities of a person or thing, which make them what they are. **2** a concentrated liquid obtained from a plant, used to make perfume or flavouring.

essential *adjective* extremely important or necessary. ➤ **essential** *noun*, **essentially** *adverb*.

establish *verb* (**establishes, establishing, established**) **1** to set up a business or a relationship on a firm basis. **2** to prove the truth of something.

establishment *noun* (*plural* **establishments**) **1** the act of establishing something. **2** a business organization. **3** (**the Establishment**) the group of people who have influence in the running of a country.

estate *noun* (*plural* **estates**) **1** a house on a large area of land that is privately owned. **2** an area where a lot of similar houses or a lot of businesses are situated. **3** all the possessions left by somebody who has died.

estate agent

estate agent noun (plural **estate agents**) a person who sells land and houses for clients.

esteem verb (**esteems, esteeming, esteemed**) to admire and respect somebody. ~ *noun* admiration and respect.

estimate /e sti mat/ *noun* (plural **estimates**) **1** *Maths* a rough calculation. **2** a statement from a company of the expected cost of a job. **3** an opinion or judgment. ~ /e sti mayt/ *verb* (**estimates, estimating, estimated**) **1** to make an estimate of something. **2** to conclude or guess something. ➤ **estimation** *noun*.

estranged *adjective* **1** no longer living with your husband or wife. **2** no longer in touch with your family.

estuary *noun* (plural **estuaries**) *Geography* the point where a river flows into the sea.

etc. or **etc** *abbreviation* = ET CETERA.

et cetera = (Latin) and other similar things.

etch *verb* (**etches, etching, etched**) to engrave a picture on metal or glass using acid. ✶ **etched on your memory** very clear in your mind and unlikely to be forgotten.

etching *noun* (plural **etchings**) a picture produced by etching.

eternal *adjective* lasting for ever or for a long time. ➤ **eternally** *adverb*.

eternity *noun* **1** time that goes on forever. **2** *informal* a very long time.

ether /ee ther/ *noun* *Science* a liquid that burns easily and is used as a solvent.

ethereal /i theer i al/ *adjective* delicate and light.

ethics *plural noun* a set of moral principles or values by which a person lives. ~ *noun* the study of the nature of moral principles and judgments.

ethical *adjective* morally right. ➤ **ethically** *adverb*.

ethnic *adjective* **1** to do with the things, such as race, culture, or language, that a group of people have in common. **2** belonging to a particular race or culture, especially a non-Western one. ➤ **ethnically** *adverb*.

ethos /ee thos/ *noun* the guiding beliefs by which a person or group lives.

etiquette /e ti kit/ *noun* the accepted standards of proper behaviour.

etymology /e ti mo lo ji/ *noun* (plural **etymologies**) **1** the origin of a word. **2** the study of the origin and development of words.

EU *abbreviation* European Union.

eucalyptus /ew ka lip tus/ *noun* (plural **eucalyptuses** or **eucalypti** /ew ka l ip tie/) an Australian evergreen tree.

Eucharist /ew ka rist/ *noun* the Christian ceremony in which bread and wine are consumed to commemorate the Last Supper.

eulogy /ew lo ji/ *noun* (plural **eulogies**) a speech praising somebody at their funeral.

eunuch /ew nuk/ *noun* (plural **eunuchs**) a man who has been castrated.

euphemism *noun* (plural **euphemisms**) a mild word used in place of an offensive one. ➤ **euphemistic** *adjective*, **euphemistically** *adverb*.

euphoria *noun* an intense feeling of joy. ➤ **euphoric** *adjective*.

euro *noun* (plural **euros**) the unit of money used by most countries in the European Union.

European *adjective* from or to do with Europe. ~ *noun* (plural **Europeans**) a person from Europe.

euthanasia /ew tha nay zi a/ *noun* the painless killing of somebody who is incurably ill in order to end their suffering.

evacuate *verb* (**evacuates, evacu-**

ating, evacuated) to remove people from a dangerous place. ➤ **evacuation** noun, **evacuee** noun.

evade verb (**evades, evading, evaded**) **1** to avoid somebody or something by skill or deception. **2** to avoid answering a question.

evaluate verb (**evaluates, evaluating, evaluated**) to work out the amount or the worth of something.

evaluation noun (plural **evaluations**) **1** the act of evaluating something. **2** the process of testing a design to judge how well it will work.

evangelical adjective said about a Christian: belonging to a Protestant group that emphasizes salvation through faith, personal conversion, and the authority of the Bible.

evangelist noun (plural **evangelists**) a person who preaches the Christian gospel, trying to convert people.

evangelize or **evangelise** verb (**evangelizes, evangelizing, evangelized** or **evangelises**, etc) to preach the Christian gospel, trying to convert people.

evaporate verb (**evaporates, evaporating, evaporated**) *Science* to change gradually from a liquid to a gas. ➤ **evaporation** noun.

evasion noun (plural **evasions**) the act of avoiding something or somebody.

evasive adjective trying to avoid something.

eve noun (plural **eves**) the evening or day before a special day: *Christmas Eve.*

even adjective **1** flat or level. **2** without any variation. **3** said about a score: equal. **4** *Maths* said about a number: able to be divided exactly by two. ~ adverb used to emphasize something: *even better than last time.* ~ verb (**evens, evening, evened**) (*often* **even up**) to become even or make something even. ✻ **even if/though** in spite of the possibility (or fact) that. **even so** in spite of that. **get even with somebody** to take revenge on somebody. ➤ **evenly** adverb.

evening noun (plural **evenings**) the part of the day between afternoon and night.

event noun (plural **events**) **1** a happening or occurrence, especially an important one. **2** any of the contests in a sporting programme. ✻ **in the event of/that** if the specified thing should happen.

eventful adjective full of important or exciting occurrences.

eventual adjective taking place at an unspecified later time. ➤ **eventually** adverb.

eventuality noun (plural **eventualities**) a possible happening.

ever adverb **1** at any time. **2** always: *an ever-growing need.* **3** used for emphasis: *Why ever not?*

evergreen adjective said about a tree: having leaves that remain green throughout the year.

everlasting adjective lasting forever.

every adjective **1** all of a group, without exception. **2** each or all possible: *She was given every chance.* **3** once in each: *every 5000 miles.* ✻ **every other** each alternate.

everybody pronoun every person.

everyday adjective routine or ordinary.

everyone pronoun every person.

everything pronoun **1** all that exists. **2** something of the greatest importance.

everywhere adverb in, at, or to every place.

evict verb (**evicts, evicting, evicted**) to force a tenant to leave a rented home. ➤ **eviction** noun.

evidence noun something that gives reason for believing something, especially information used by a court to arrive at the truth.

evident *adjective* clear or obvious.
➤ **evidently** *adverb*.

evil *adjective* **1** sinful or wicked.
2 disagreeable or offensive: *an evil smell*. ~ *noun* (*plural* **evils**)
1 wickedness or sin. **2** something that is harmful or morally wrong.

evoke *verb* (**evokes, evoking, evoked**) to cause somebody to have a particular memory or emotion.
➤ **evocative** *adjective*.

evolution *noun* **1** the process by which species of animals and plants have gradually developed, over a long period of time, from species that previously existed. **2** any gradual process of change and development.
➤ **evolutionary** *adjective*.

evolve (**evolves, evolving, evolved**)
1 to develop gradually. **2** said about a species: to develop by evolution.

ewe *noun* (*plural* **ewes**) a female sheep.

exacerbate /ig za ser bayt/ *verb* (**exacerbates, exacerbating, exacerbated**) to make a bad situation worse.
➤ **exacerbation** *noun*.

exact *adjective* **1** precise or accurate.
2 marked by thorough consideration of all details. ~ *verb* (**exacts, exacting, exacted**) to demand and obtain money from somebody by force or threats.

exacting *adjective* requiring careful attention and accuracy.

exactly *adverb* accurately or precisely.
✱ **not exactly** not at all: *He is not exactly a genius*.

exaggerate *verb* (**exaggerates, exaggerating, exaggerated**) **1** to say that something is greater, better, worse, etc than it is. **2** to make something more obvious than usual: *He exaggerated his limp*. ➤ **exaggeration** *noun*.

exalt *verb* (**exalts, exalting, exalted**) to raise somebody to a high rank or status.

exam *noun* (*plural* **exams**) an examination at school, college, or university.

examination *noun* (*plural* **examinations**) **1** a close inspection.
2 an exercise designed to test knowledge or skill.

examine *verb* (**examines, examining, examined**) **1** to inspect something closely. **2** said about a doctor: to investigate the health of a patient. **3** to test the knowledge or skill of a pupil or student. ➤ **examiner** *noun*.

example *noun* (*plural* **examples**)
1 something that is typical of the group or type to which it belongs.
2 somebody or something that may other people may copy: *She is a good example to her younger sister*.

exasperate *verb* (**exasperates, exasperating, exasperated**) to irritate somebody intensely. ➤ **exasperating** *adjective*, **exasperation** *noun*.

excavate *verb* (**excavates, excavating, excavated**) to dig out and remove soil or earth. ➤ **excavation** *noun*.

exceed *verb* (**exceeds, exceeding, exceeded**) **1** to be greater than somebody or something. **2** to go beyond the limits of something.

exceedingly *adverb* very or extremely.

excel *verb* (**excels, excelling, excelled**) (**excel at/in**) to be extremely good at something: *Shereen excels in maths*.

Excellency *noun* (*plural* **Excellencies**) a title for certain important church and government officials: *Your Excellency*.

excellent *adjective* outstandingly good.
➤ **excellence** *noun*.

except *preposition* excluding. ✱ **except for** with the exception of.

exception *noun* (*plural* **exceptions**) somebody or something that is left out, especially a case to which a rule does not apply.

exceptional *adjective* **1** unusual.

2 outstanding or superior. ➤ **exceptionally** adverb.

excerpt noun (plural **excerpts**) a short piece quoted or shown from a book, film, etc.

excess noun (plural **excesses**) **1** an amount that is more than is needed or wanted. **2** unacceptable extreme behaviour. ~ adjective more than is allowed: *excess baggage*. ✶ **in excess of** more than.

excessive adjective more than is needed or wanted. ➤ **excessively** adverb.

exchange noun (plural **exchanges**) **1** the act of giving one thing in return for another. **2** the conversion of one currency into another. **3** a place for trading in stocks and shares. ~ verb (**exchanges, exchanging, exchanged**) to give something in return for something else.

exchequer noun (**the Exchequer**) in the UK, the government department in charge of the country's money.

excise noun a tax charged on the manufacture or sale of goods within a country.

excitable adjective easily excited. ➤ **excitability** noun.

excite verb (**excites, exciting, excited**) **1** to cause somebody to feel thrilled or nervous. **2** to provoke a response. ➤ **excited** adjective, **excitement** noun, **exciting** adjective.

exclaim verb (**exclaims, exclaiming, exclaimed**) to shout something out.

exclamation noun (plural **exclamations**) a word or remark cried out suddenly.

exclamation mark noun (plural **exclamation marks**) *English* the punctuation mark (!), used after an exclamation.

exclude verb (**excludes, excluding, excluded**) **1** not to include somebody or something. **2** to prevent somebody from taking part. **3** to shut somebody out. ➤ **exclusion** noun.

exclusive adjective **1** limited to a one person or group: *an exclusive interview*. **2** limited to rich or privileged people: *an exclusive polo club*. ~ noun (plural **exclusives**) an interview or article published by only one newspaper or broadcast by only one television channel or radio station. ➤ **exclusively** adverb.

excrement /ek skri mint/ noun waste matter from the bowels.

excrete verb (**excretes, excreting, excreted**) to discharge waste matter from the bowels. ➤ **excretion** noun, **excretory** adjective.

excruciating adjective causing great pain. ➤ **excruciatingly** adverb.

excursion noun (plural **excursions**) a short pleasure trip.

excuse /ik skewz/ verb (**excuses, excusing, excused**) **1** to be an acceptable reason for some wrongdoing. **2** to forgive somebody. **3** to allow somebody to leave. **4** to free somebody from having to perform a duty. ~ /ik skews/ noun (plural **excuses**) a reason given to explain or justify some wrongdoing.

execute verb (**executes, executing, executed**) **1** to put a plan or an order into action. **2** to put somebody to death as a punishment for a serious crime. **3** *ICT* to run a computer program or file. ➤ **execution** noun, **executioner** noun.

executive /ig ze kew tiv/ adjective to do with making and carrying out important decisions. ~ noun (plural **executives**) a person or group that controls an organization.

executor /ig ze kew ter/ noun (plural **executors**) a person appointed to carry out the instructions in another person's will.

exemplary adjective **1** excellent or

exemplify

outstanding. **2** said about a punishment: serving as a warning.

exemplify *verb* (**exemplifies, exemplifying, exemplified**) **1** to be a good example of something. **2** to give an example of something.

exempt *adjective* excused from a duty or requirement. ~ *verb* (**exempts, exempting, exempted**) to excuse somebody from a duty or requirement. ➤ **exemption** *noun*.

exercise *noun* (*plural* **exercises**) **1** physical exertion in order to keep fit. **2** an activity practised in order to develop a skill. ~ *verb* (**exercises, exercising, exercised**) **1** to engage in physical exertion in order to keep fit. **2** to take advantage of a right.

exert *verb* (**exerts, exerting, exerted**) to use strength or authority in dealing with a situation. ✽ **exert yourself** to make an effort. ➤ **exertion** *noun*.

exhale *verb* (**exhales, exhaling, exhaled**) to breathe out.

exhaust *verb* (**exhausts, exhausting, exhausted**) **1** to tire somebody out. **2** to use up a supply of something. **3** to deal with a subject so fully that there is no more to say about it. ~ *noun* (*plural* **exhausts**) **1** a pipe through which used gases come out of a vehicle's engine. **2** the gases that come out of the engine.

exhaustion *noun* extreme tiredness.

exhaustive *adjective* dealing with every aspect of a subject. ➤ **exhaustively** *adverb*.

exhibit *verb* (**exhibits, exhibiting, exhibited**) **1** to show a work of art publicly. **2** to show a feeling or a symptom outwardly. ~ *noun* (*plural* **exhibits**) something exhibited in a gallery or museum. ➤ **exhibitor** *noun*.

exhibition *noun* (*plural* **exhibitions**) *Art* a public showing of works of art. ✽ **make an exhibition of yourself** to behave foolishly in public.

exhilarating /ig zi la ray ting/ *adjective* making you feel very happy and excited. ➤ **exhilaration** *noun*.

exile *noun* (*plural* **exiles**) **1** the state of being banished from your country or home. **2** a person who is sent into exile. ~ *verb* (**exiles, exiling, exiled**) to send somebody into exile.

exist *verb* (**exists, existing, existed**) to live or to be real.

existence *noun* **1** the state of existing. **2** a manner of living.

exit *verb* (**exits, exiting, exited**) **1** *Drama* used as a stage direction to tell a particular character to leave the stage. **2** to leave a place. ~ *noun* (*plural* **exits**) **1** a way out of a place. **2** the act of going out or going off stage.

exodus *noun* the departure of a lot of people at the same time.

exotic *adjective* **1** said about a plant: brought in from another country. **2** excitingly different or unusual.

expand *verb* (**expands, expanding, expanded**) **1** to become larger or make something larger. **2** to speak or write more fully on something: *I asked him to expand on his suggestion.* ➤ **expansion** *noun*, **expansive** *adjective*.

expanse *noun* (*plural* **expanses**) a wide area of something.

expatriate *noun* (*plural* **expatriates**) a person who lives outside the country where they were born.

expect *verb* (**expects, expecting, expected**) **1** to consider an event probable or certain. **2** to consider respect, obedience, etc to be your right. **3** to be waiting for the arrival of somebody or something. ✽ **be expecting** *informal* to be pregnant

expectant *adjective* **1** waiting for something to happen. **2** said about a woman: pregnant. ➤ **expectancy** *noun*, **expectantly** *adverb*.

expectation *noun* (*plural* **expec-**

tations) 1 the state of expecting something. **2** something that you expect.

expedient *adjective* convenient but not necessarily right or ethical. ~ *noun* (*plural* **expedients**) an action that is convenient but not necessarily right. ➤ **expediency** *noun*.

expedition *noun* (*plural* **expeditions**) a journey made for a specific purpose, such as for exploration. ➤ **expeditionary** *adjective*.

expel *verb* (**expels, expelling, expelled**) **1** to force something out of a container. **2** to force somebody to leave a school or group.

expend *verb* (**expends, expending, expended**) to spend time or attention on dealing with somebody or something.

expendable *adjective* able to be got rid of in order to achieve an aim.

expenditure *noun* the amount of money spent.

expense *noun* (*plural* **expenses**) the amount that something costs.

expensive *adjective* costing a great deal of money. ➤ **expensively** *adverb*.

experience *noun* (*plural* **experiences**) **1** something that has happened to you. **2** all the things that you have done, for example at work. ~ *verb* (**experiences, experiencing, experienced**) to have something happen to you.

experiment /ik spe ri mint/ *noun* (*plural* **experiments**) a test carried out to make a discovery or to prove something. ~ *verb* /ik spe ri ment/ (**experiments, experimenting, experimented**) to try something out to see if it works. ➤ **experimental** *adjective*, **experimentally** *adverb*, **experimentation** *noun*.

expert *adjective* showing special skill or knowledge in a particular subject. ~ *noun* (*plural* **experts**) a person who has special skill or knowledge in a particular subject. ➤ **expertly** *adverb*.

expertise /ek sper teez/ *noun* skill in or knowledge of a particular subject.

expire *verb* (**expires, expiring, expired**) to come to an end: *My membership has expired.* ➤ **expiry** *noun*.

explain *verb* (**explains, explaining, explained**) to make something clear or understandable by giving details. ➤ **explanation** *noun*, **explanatory** *adjective*.

explicit *adjective* clear and open: *explicit instructions.* ➤ **explicitly** *adverb*.

explode *verb* (**explodes, exploding, exploded**) **1** to burst suddenly and violently with a loud noise, often causing a lot of damage. **2** said about a person: to become suddenly angry or emotional.

exploit /ek sploit/ *noun* (*plural* **exploits**) a notable or heroic action. ~ /ik sploit/ *verb* (**exploits, exploiting, exploited**) **1** to use or develop resources or materials fully. **2** to take unfair advantage of somebody. ➤ **exploitation** *noun*.

explore *verb* (**explores, exploring, explored**) **1** to travel through an unfamiliar place in order to learn about it. **2** to consider an idea carefully. ➤ **exploration** *noun*, **exploratory** *adjective*, **explorer** *noun*.

explosion *noun* (*plural* **explosions**) an instance of exploding.

explosive *adjective* **1** capable of exploding. **2** said about a situation: threatening to cause serious trouble. ~ *noun* (*plural* **explosives**) an explosive substance

exponent *noun* (*plural* **exponents**) **1** somebody who puts forward an idea or theory. **2** somebody who is very skilled at something.

export /ik spawt/ *verb* (**exports, exporting, exported**) to send goods to another country in order to sell them. ~ /ek spawt/ *noun* (*plural*

exports) something that is exported. ➤ **exporter** noun.

expose verb (**exposes, exposing, exposed**) **1** to uncover or display something. **2** to lay somebody open to attack or danger. **3** to bring something shameful to public notice.

exposure noun **1** the fact of being exposed to something harmful. **2** the physical damage caused by being exposed to very cold weather.

express verb (**expresses, expressing, expressed**) to show your thoughts or feelings in words or by other means. ~ adjective very fast and direct. ~ noun (plural **expresses**) an express train.

expression noun (plural **expressions**) **1** *English* the act or a means of expressing your thoughts or feelings. **2** a word or phrase. **3** a look on somebody's face that shows their feelings.

expressive adjective showing your feelings clearly.

expulsion noun (plural **expulsions**) the act of expelling something or somebody.

exquisite /ik skwi zit/ adjective extremely beautiful and delicate.

extend verb (**extends, extending, extended**) **1** to make something longer. **2** to continue over a particular distance, area, or length of time. **3** to hold out your hand or arm.

extension noun (plural **extensions**) **1** the act of extending something. **2** an extra room or rooms added to a building. **3** an extra telephone connected to the main line.

extensive adjective **1** extending over a large area. **2** covering a wide range of things. ➤ **extensively** adverb.

extent noun (plural **extents**) **1** the size or the scope of something. **2** the degree to which something applies.

exterior adjective on the outside ~ noun (plural **exteriors**) **1** the outside of something. **2** an outward appearance.

exterminate verb (**exterminates, exterminating, exterminated**) to kill or destroy animals or people. ➤ **extermination** noun.

external adjective on or intended for the outside. ➤ **externally** adverb.

extinct adjective **1** said about a species: no longer existing. **2** said about a volcano: no longer active. ➤ **extinction** noun.

extinguish verb (**extinguishes, extinguishing, extinguished**) to put out a fire or a light. ➤ **extinguisher** noun.

extortionate adjective extremely expensive. ➤ **extortionately** adverb.

extra adjective more than is usual or necessary. ~ noun (plural **extras**) **1** something extra, such as an additional charge. **2** somebody hired to act in a group scene in a film or play.

extract /ik strakt/ verb (**extracts, extracting, extracted**) **1** to pull something out from inside something. **2** to obtain information from somebody with effort. ~ /ek strakt/ noun (plural **extracts**) a short passage taken from a book or film.

extraction noun **1** the act of extracting something. **2** ancestry or origin: *She is of Greek extraction.*

extraordinary /ik straw di na ri/ adjective highly unusual or remarkable. ➤ **extraordinarily** adverb.

extravagant adjective **1** spending or costing a lot of money. **2** lacking in moderation. ➤ **extravagance** noun, **extravagantly** adverb.

extravaganza noun (plural **extravaganzas**) a spectacular show.

extreme adjective **1** existing to a very high degree. **2** exceedingly severe or drastic. **3** situated at the farthest possible point from a centre. ~ noun (*plural* **extremes**) **1** something situated at one end or the other of a range. **2** a very pronounced or extreme degree. ➤ **extremely** *adverb*.

extremist *noun* (*plural* **extremists**) a person who holds extreme views.

extremity /ik stre mi ti/ *noun* (*plural* **extremities**) **1** the furthest part of something. **2** (**the extremities**) the hands and feet.

extricate *verb* (**extricates, extricating, extricated**) to remove yourself or somebody else from a difficult situation.

extrovert *noun* (*plural* **extroverts**) an outgoing person. ➤ **extrovert** *adjective*.

exuberant /ig zew bi rant/ *adjective* cheerful and enthusiastic. ➤ **exuberance** *noun*, **exuberantly** *adverb*.

exude *verb* (**exudes, exuding, exuded**) to display a large degree of a particular quality or feeling.

eye *noun* (*plural* **eyes**) **1** an organ of sight. **2** the hole through the head of a needle. ~ *verb* (**eyes, eyeing** or **eying, eyed**) to look at somebody or something closely.

eyeball *noun* (*plural* **eyeballs**) the ball-shaped part of the eye.

eyebrow *noun* (*plural* **eyebrows**) the line of hair that grows on the ridge above the eye.

eyelash *noun* (*plural* **eyelashes**) the fringe of hair edging the eyelid or a single hair of this fringe.

eyelid *noun* (*plural* **eyelids**) a fold of skin and muscle that can be closed over the eyeball.

eyesight *noun* the ability to see.

eyesore *noun* (*plural* **eyesores**) something that is ugly.

eyewitness *noun* (*plural* **eyewitnesses**) a person who sees an event take place.

eyrie /eer i/ *noun* (*plural* **eyries**) the nest of a bird of prey.

Ff

F *abbreviation* Fahrenheit: *47°F*.

FA *abbreviation* Football Association.

fable *noun* (*plural* **fables**) **1** a short story intended to convey a moral. **2** a legendary story of supernatural happenings.

fabled *adjective* famous or legendary.

fabric *noun* (*plural* **fabrics**) **1** a material made by weaving or knitting; cloth. **2** the floor, walls, and roof of a building. **3** the basic structure of an organization or society.

fabricate *verb* (**fabricates, fabricating, fabricated**) **1** to invent evidence or a story in order to deceive people. **2** to manufacture a product from various parts. ➤ **fabrication** *noun*.

fabulous *adjective* **1** incredible or extraordinary. **2** *informal* excellent. **3** mentioned in or based on fable. ➤ **fabulously** *adverb*.

facade or **façade** /fa sahd/ *noun* (*plural* **facades** or **façades**) **1** the front of a building. **2** a false display of a feeling or quality: *He hid his emotion behind a facade of unconcern*.

face *noun* (*plural* **faces**) **1** the front part of the human head from the chin to the forehead. **2** a facial expression, especially an ugly or complaining one: *to pull a face*. **3** *Maths* a surface of a solid geometrical shape: *How many faces has a cube?* **4** the side of a mountain or cliff. ~ *verb* (**faces, facing, faced**) **1** to have the face or front turned in a specific direction: *facing north*. **2** to have to deal with, or to be unable to avoid, a situation or problem: *They were facing certain death*. **3** (*also* **face up to**) to show firmness and not try to avoid something or somebody that threatens you: *You've got to face up to your problems*. **4** to cover the front or surface of an object with a different material: *a building faced with marble*. ✳ **on the face of it** at first sight; apparently.

faceless *adjective* who hide their identity and show no feelings: *faceless bureaucrats*.

face-lift *noun* (*plural* **face-lifts**) **1** an operation to remove wrinkles or sagging skin from the face. **2** a renovation or overhaul.

face-saving *adjective* done to preserve your dignity or reputation.

facet /fa sit/ *noun* (*plural* **facets**) **1** any of the flat surfaces of a cut gem. **2** an aspect of something.

facetious /fa see shus/ *adjective* inappropriately humorous. ➤ **facetiously** *adverb*.

facial *adjective* on or to do with the face: *facial hair*. ~ *noun* (*plural* **facials**) a beauty treatment for the face. ➤ **facially** *adverb*.

facilitate /fa si li tayt/ *verb* (**facilitates, facilitating, facilitated**) to make a task or procedure easier. ➤ **facilitation** *noun*.

facility *noun* (*plural* **facilities**) **1** a building or piece of equipment designed to provide a particular service. **2** an ability to do something easily.

facing *noun* (*plural* **facings**) **1** a lining at the edge of a garment, for stiffening or decorating it. **2** an ornamental or protective layer on a wall.

facsimile /fak si mi li/ *noun* (*plural* **facsimiles**) **1** an exact copy of something. **2** = FAX.

fact *noun* (*plural* **facts**) **1** a piece of information that is undoubtedly true. **2** reality or truth. ✱ **the facts of life** information about sex and how babies are born. **in fact** in reality; actually.

faction *noun* (*plural* **factions**) a minority group within a political party.

factor *noun* (*plural* **factors**)
1 a condition, force, or fact that contributes to a result. **2** *Maths* one of two or more numbers that can be multiplied together to produce a given number.

factory *noun* (*plural* **factories**) a building containing machinery that is used to produce goods.

factual *adjective* restricted to or based on fact. ➤ **factually** *adverb*.

faculty *noun* (*plural* **faculties**)
1 a natural ability or function of the body or mind, such as hearing or understanding. **2** a group of related departments in a university.

fad *noun* (*plural* **fads**) **1** a short-lived fashion; a craze. **2** a fussy personal liking for or dislike of something. ➤ **faddy** *adjective*.

fade *verb* (**fades, fading, faded**) **1** to disappear gradually: *The light was fading.* **2** to lose freshness or colour.

faeces /fee seez/ *plural noun* the solid brown waste that comes out of your body through your anus. ➤ **faecal** *adjective*.

fag *noun* (*plural* **fags**) *informal* **1** a tiring or boring task. **2** a cigarette. ✱ **fagged out** *informal* very tired.

fair

faggot *noun* (*plural* **faggots**) **1** a fried mass of minced meat and herbs. **2** a bundle of sticks used as fuel.

Fahrenheit /fa rin hiet/ *adjective Science* measured by a scale of temperature on which water freezes at 32° and boils at 212°: *76° Fahrenheit*.

fail *verb* (**fails, failing, failed**) **1** to be unsuccessful when you try to do something. **2** not to do something: *The vehicle failed to stop.* **3** to stop functioning: *The brakes failed.* **4** to be unable to reach the required standard in an examination. **5** to judge somebody or something to have failed a test or examination: *She failed me for not stopping at a red light.* **6** to let somebody down. ✱ **without fail** whatever the circumstances.

failing *noun* (*plural* **failings**) a defect in somebody's character.

failure *noun* (*plural* **failures**) **1** lack of success. **2** an unsuccessful person or thing. **3** not doing something expected of you: *failure to inform the police.* **4** a breakdown of normal functioning: *heart failure.*

faint *adjective* **1** not easy to see or hear. **2** slight: *a faint chance.* **3** on the point of losing consciousness: *to feel faint.* ~ *verb* (**faints, fainting, fainted**) to lose consciousness briefly. ~ *noun* a brief loss of consciousness. ➤ **faintly** *adverb*.

faint-hearted *adjective* lacking courage or determination.

fair[1] *adjective* **1** honest and just. **2** allowed by the rules: *a fair tackle*. **3** said about somebody's hair or complexion: light in colour. **4** moderately good or large: *a fair size*. **5** said about the weather: fine and dry. ➤ **fairness** *noun*.

fair[2] *noun* (*plural* **fairs**) **1** an outdoor event with sideshows and amusements. **2** an exhibition for promoting products of a particular type.

fairground noun (plural **fairgrounds**) an area where an outdoor fair is held.

fairly adverb **1** honestly and justly, or in a proper or legal manner. **2** to a moderate degree; quite: *fairly well*.

fair trade noun trade that supports producers in developing countries.

fairway noun (plural **fairways**) the mown part of a golf course between a tee and a green.

fairy noun (plural **fairies**) a small mythical being in human form with magical powers.

fairy godmother noun (plural **fairy godmothers**) a woman who helps you generously when you least expect it, especially in fairy stories.

fairy story or **fairy tale** noun (plural **fairy stories** or **fairy tales**)
1 a children's story about magical or imaginary people and places.
2 a made-up account or excuse.

faith noun (plural **faiths**) **1** confidence or belief. **2** a system of religious beliefs: *the Christian faith*.

faithful adjective **1** loyal or steadfast: *a faithful friend*. **2** true to the facts; accurate: *a faithful account*. **3** not having sex with anyone except your partner. ➤ **faithfully** adverb.

faithless adjective disloyal or untrustworthy.

fake adjective not genuine. ~ noun (plural **fakes**) a person or thing that is not genuine. ~ verb (**fakes, faking, faked**) to pretend to have an illness or emotion.

falcon /fawl kon/ noun (plural **falcons**) a hawk with long pointed wings.

fall verb (**falls, falling, fell, fallen**)
1 to descend by the force of gravity. **2** to collapse to the ground. **3** to hang down. **4** said about a place during a war: to be surrendered or captured. **5** said about a government: to stop being in power. **6** to become less in number or value. **7** to become: *to fall ill*. **8** to occur at a specified time: *Her birthday falls on a Wednesday this year.* ~ noun (plural **falls**) **1** an act of dropping down from a height.
2 N American autumn. **3** (**falls**) a steep waterfall. **4** a decrease in quantity or value. **5** a loss of power or position: *the fall of the government*. **6** the fact of being conquered or captured: *the fall of Constantinople*. ✻ **fall back** to retreat. **fall back on** to use something in an emergency. **fall behind** to fail to keep up. **fall for** *informal* **1** to fall in love with somebody. **2** to be deceived by a trick, etc. **fall off** to become less or weaker gradually. **fall out** to have a disagreement. **fall over yourself** *informal* to make great efforts to do something. **fall short** to fail to achieve a goal or target. **fall through** to fail; not to be carried out.

fallacy /fa la si/ noun (plural **fallacies**) a mistaken idea. ➤ **fallacious** adjective.

fallback noun (plural **fallbacks**) an alternative option if the main one fails.

fallible /fa li bl/ adjective capable of being wrong. ➤ **fallibility** noun.

Fallopian tube /fa loh pi an tewb/ noun (plural **Fallopian tubes**) either of the two tubes bringing eggs from the ovaries to the uterus in female mammals.

fallout noun **1** radioactive particles resulting from a nuclear explosion. **2** unfavourable results or effects.

fallow adjective said about land: not sown with seed after ploughing.

false adjective **1** untrue or incorrect. **2** intended to look real, but artificial: *false teeth*. **3** disloyal or treacherous. ➤ **falsely** adverb, **falsity** noun.

false alarm noun (plural **false alarms**) a warning about a danger that does not actually exist.

falsehood noun (plural **falsehoods**) **1** an untrue statement; a lie. **2** lying.

falsetto *noun* (*plural* **falsettos**) an unnaturally high-pitched male voice.

falsify *verb* (**falsifies, falsifying, falsified**) to change information in order to deceive people. ➤ **falsification** *noun*.

falter *verb* (**falters, faltering, faltered**) **1** to hesitate as you try to move or to do or say something. **2** to lose strength or effectiveness.

fame *noun* the state of being famous.

famed *adjective* famous.

familiar *adjective* **1** common or well-known: *a familiar sight*. **2** close or intimate: *a familiar friend*. **3** (**familiar with**) having knowledge of something. ➤ **familiarity** *noun*.

familiarize *or* **familiarise** *verb* (**familiarizes, familiarizing, familiarized** *or* **familiarises**, etc) to make somebody, or yourself, familiar with something. ➤ **familiarization** *or* **familiarisation** *noun*.

family *noun* (*plural* **families**) **1** a group consisting of parents and their children. **2** the children of a parent or parents. **3** a group of people related to one another by descent or marriage. **4** *Science* a group of related animals or plants.

family planning *noun* using contraception to control the number of children born in a family.

family tree *noun* (*plural* **family trees**) a diagram showing a family's history and relationships.

famine *noun* (*plural* **famines**) an extreme scarcity of food.

famished *adjective informal* very hungry.

famous *adjective* very well-known.

famously *adverb informal* very well.

fan[1] *noun* (*plural* **fans**) **1** a device with rotating blades for producing a current of air. **2** a folding semicircular device that is waved to and fro to cool the face. ~ *verb* (**fans, fanning, fanned**) to cause a current of air to blow on somebody or something. ✽ **fan out** to move outwards from a central point, gradually getting farther and farther apart.

fan[2] *noun* (*plural* **fans**) a supporter or admirer of a sport, a team, a celebrity, etc.

fanatic *noun* (*plural* **fanatics**) a person who is excessively enthusiastic about a religion, cause, or activity. ➤ **fanatical** *adjective*, **fanatically** *adverb*, **fanaticism** *noun*.

fanciful *adjective* imaginary or unrealistic.

fancy *noun* (*plural* **fancies**) **1** a liking for something or somebody: *He took a fancy to her*. **2** the imagination. ~ *verb* (**fancies, fancying, fancied**) **1** to feel a liking or desire for something or somebody. **2** to consider somebody or something likely to do well. **3** to believe or imagine something. ~ *adjective* (**fancier, fanciest**) highly decorated. ✽ **fancy yourself** *informal* to have a high opinion of your own worth and ability. ➤ **fanciable** *adjective*.

fancy dress *noun* an unusual or amusing costume worn by a person at a party.

fanfare *noun* (*plural* **fanfares**) a short piece of music played on loud instruments such as trumpets to introduce somebody or something.

fang *noun* (*plural* **fangs**) **1** a long tooth by which an animal seizes and holds its prey. **2** a tooth of a venomous snake.

fanlight *noun* (*plural* **fanlights**) a semicircular window over a door.

fantasize *or* **fantasise** *verb* (**fantasizes, fantasizing, fantasized** *or* **fantasises**, etc) to form pictures in your mind about something you would like to happen.

fantastic *adjective* **1** *informal* wonderful; excellent. **2** unreal or

fantasy

imaginary: *fantastic tales of adventures in outer space.* **3** forming very strange and elaborate shapes: *fantastic decorations.* ➤ **fantastically** *adverb.*

fantasy *noun* (*plural* **fantasies**) **1** a mental image or daydream. **2** books or other works with strange characters and settings, often in imaginary worlds.

far *adverb* (**farther** *or* **further**, **farthest** *or* **furthest**) **1** to, at, or from a large distance away in space or time: *Have you come far?* **2** very much: *far better.* ~ *adjective* (**farther** *or* **further**, **farthest** *or* **furthest**) a long way away in space or time. ✱ **as/so far as** to the extent that. **by far** by a considerable amount. **a far cry from** totally different to something. **go far** to be successful in life. **go too far** to behave in a way that has become unacceptable. **so far** up to the present.

Usage Note **farther** *or* **further**? See usage not at **farther**.

faraway *adjective* **1** situated a great distance away; remote. **2** dreamy or absentminded: *a faraway look.*

farce *noun* (*plural* **farces**) **1** a comedy based on an improbable plot. **2** a ridiculous or nonsensical situation. ➤ **farcical** *adjective,* **farcically** *adverb.*

fare *noun* (*plural* **fares**) **1** the price charged to travel on public transport. **2** a paying passenger. **3** food provided for a meal. ~ *verb* (**fares, faring, fared**) to get along in an activity; to do: *The team has fared better since the new coach arrived.*

Far East *noun* (**the Far East**) Japan, North and South Korea, China, and the countries to the south of China, and often also including Malaysia, Singapore, Indonesia, and the Philippines. ➤ **Far Eastern** *adjective.*

farewell *interjection* archaic goodbye.

~ *noun* (*plural* **farewells**) an act of saying goodbye.

farfetched *adjective* exaggerated and hard to believe.

farm *noun* (*plural* **farms**) **1** an area of land used for growing crops or raising animals. **2** a farmhouse. ~ *verb* (**farms, farming, farmed**) **1** to produce crops or livestock as food for people. **2** to manage and cultivate an area of land as a farm. ➤ **farming** *noun.*

farmer *noun* (*plural* **farmers**) somebody who owns or runs a farm.

farmhouse *noun* (*plural* **farmhouses**) a house on a farm.

farrier *noun* (*plural* **farriers**) a blacksmith who shoes horses.

farther *adverb and adjective* at or to a greater distance.

Usage Note **farther** *or* **further**? When you are talking about physical distances, *farther* and *further* are equally correct: *Denmark lies farther (or further) north than Ireland.* If you want to want to talk about time or the amount of something, use *further: of no further use; closed until further notice.* If in doubt, use *further.*

farthest *adverb and adjective* to or at the greatest distance in space or time.

fascia /**fay**shə/ *noun* (*plural* **fascias**) **1** a nameplate over the front of a shop. **2** the dashboard of a motor vehicle.

fascinate /**fa**sinayt/ *verb* (**fascinates, fascinating, fascinated**) to arouse a very strong interest or curiosity in somebody. ➤ **fascinating** *adjective,* **fascination** *noun.*

fascism /**fa**shizm/ *noun* an extreme right-wing political system, based on nationalism and belief in strict control by a centralized government under a dictatorial leader. ➤ **fascist** *noun and adjective.*

fashion *noun* (*plural* **fashions**) **1** a style of dress or way of doing something that is adopted by most people now, or that was popular in a particular period. **2** a manner or way: *They lined up in an orderly fashion.* ~ *verb* (**fashions, fashioning, fashioned**) to shape or make something. ✱ **in fashion** fashionable. **out of fashion** unfashionable.

fashionable *adjective* worn or done by most people. ➤ **fashionably** *adverb*.

fast[1] *adjective* **1** moving or able to move at a high speed. **2** done in only a short time. **3** said about a clock or watch: showing a time later than the actual time. **4** firmly fixed or attached. ~ *adverb* **1** quickly. **2** firmly; so that it cannot move: *stuck fast*. **3** sound or deeply: *fast asleep*.

fast[2] *verb* (**fasts, fasting, fasted**) to go without food or drink for a time. ➤ **fast** *noun*.

fasten *verb* (**fastens, fastening, fastened**) to attach or secure something.

fastener *or* **fastening** *noun* (*plural* **fasteners** *or* **fastenings**) a device used to fasten a piece of clothing.

fast food *noun* hot food that can be cooked and served quickly.

fastidious *adjective* difficult to satisfy or please; choosy. ➤ **fastidiously** *adverb*.

fat *noun* (*plural* **fats**) **1** body tissue consisting of greasy or oily substances that store energy. **2** the greasy white parts in meat. **3** a greasy or oily substance such as butter or margarine, used in cooking. ~ *adjective* (**fatter, fattest**) **1** having a thick rounded body; overweight. **2** containing a large amount of fat. **3** large or thick: *a fat wad of notes*. ✱ **fat chance** *informal* no chance at all. ➤ **fatness** *noun*.

fatal *adjective* **1** causing death: *a fatal accident.* **2** bringing ruin: *a fatal mistake.* ➤ **fatally** *adverb*.

fatalism *noun* the belief that all events are controlled by fate and human beings can do nothing to change them. ➤ **fatalist** *noun*, **fatalistic** *adjective*.

fatality /fəˈtaliti/ *noun* (*plural* **fatalities**) a death resulting from an accident or disaster.

fate *noun* (*plural* **fates**) **1** a power beyond human control that is believed to decide what happens in the world. **2** what happens to a particular person, especially what happens to a person in the end. ✱ **be fated** to be certain to experience, do, or become something.

fateful *adjective* having very important and often unpleasant consequences: *a fateful decision.*

father *noun* (*plural* **fathers**) **1** a male parent. **2** a priest. **3** somebody who originates something. ~ *verb* (**fathers, fathering, fathered**) to be the father of a child. ➤ **fatherhood** *noun*, **fatherly** *adjective*.

father-in-law *noun* (*plural* **fathers-in-law**) the father of your husband or wife.

fathom *noun* (*plural* **fathoms**) a unit of length for measuring the depth of water, equal to 6 feet (about 1.83 metres). ~ *verb* (**fathoms, fathoming, fathomed**) (*also* **fathom out**) to consider and begin to understand something: *I can't fathom out her motives.*

fatigue *noun* tiredness. ~ *verb* (**fatigues, fatiguing, fatigued**) to make somebody feel tired.

fatten *verb* (**fattens, fattening, fattened**) to make a person or animal fatter.

fatty *adjective* (**fattier, fattiest**) **1** containing large amounts of fat. **2** oily; greasy. ➤ **fattiness** *noun*.

fatuous *adjective* foolish and useless. ➤ **fatuity** *noun*, **fatuously** *adverb*.

fault *noun* (*plural* **faults**) **1** something that is wrong or imperfect in something or somebody; a defect: *There's a*

faultless

fault in the electrical system. **2** responsibility for wrongdoing or failure: *It's not her fault.* **3** a crack in the rock layers under the Earth's crust that causes earthquakes. ~ *verb* (**faults, faulting, faulted**) to find a fault in something or somebody: *I can't fault her work.* ✶ **at fault** responsible for doing something wrong. **cannot fault** can find nothing wrong with somebody or something.

faultless *adjective* perfect. ➤ **faultlessly** *adverb*.

faulty *adjective* (**faultier, faultiest**) having a fault or defect.

fauna *noun* the animal life of a region or period.

favour *noun* (*plural* **favours**) **1** approval or liking. **2** an act of kindness. ~ *verb* (**favours, favouring, favoured**) to show a greater liking for one thing or person than for another. ✶ **be in favour of** to support or approve of something. **in somebody's favour** to the advantage of somebody.

favourable *adjective* **1** showing approval. **2** that helps or benefits you: *a favourable wind.* **3** successful. ➤ **favourably** *adverb*.

favourite *noun* (*plural* **favourites**) **1** a person or thing that you like more than others. **2** the competitor thought most likely to win. ~ *adjective* preferred to all the others.

favouritism *noun* unfairly selecting one person or some people for much better treatment than the others.

fawn *noun* (*plural* **fawns**) **1** a young deer. **2** a light-brown colour. ~ *verb* (**fawns, fawning, fawned**) (**fawn on**) to show exaggerated respect for and approval of somebody.

fax *noun* (*plural* **faxes**) **1** a copy of a document that is scanned and sent electronically over a telephone line. **2** a machine for sending and receiving faxes. ~ *verb* (**faxes, faxing, faxed**) to send a fax to somebody.

FBI *abbreviation* N American Federal Bureau of Investigation.

FC *abbreviation* Football Club.

fear *noun* (*plural* **fears**) an unpleasant emotion caused by awareness of danger. ~ *verb* (**fears, fearing, feared**) **1** to be afraid of something or somebody. **2** to be worried that something might happen: *to fear the worst.*

fearful *adjective* **1** afraid. **2** frightening. **3** *informal* extremely bad or great. ➤ **fearfully** *adverb*.

fearless *adjective* not or never feeling fear; very brave.

fearsome *adjective* awesome or frightening. ➤ **fearsomely** *adverb*.

feasible *adjective* **1** capable of being done or carried out. **2** *informal* reasonable or likely. ➤ **feasibility** *noun*.

feast *noun* (*plural* **feasts**) **1** a grand or elaborate meal. **2** a religious festival. ~ *verb* (**feasts, feasting, feasted**) ✶ **feast your eyes on** to look appreciatively at something or somebody.

feat *noun* (*plural* **feats**) an act of skill or courage.

feather *noun* (*plural* **feathers**) any of the light horny growths that cover a bird's body. ➤ **feathery** *adjective*.

feature *noun* (*plural* **features**) **1** an important or distinctive part or characteristic of something. **2** a part of the face. **3** (**features**) the face. **4** the main film in a cinema programme. **5** an important article or story in a newspaper or magazine. ~ *verb* (**features, featuring, featured**) **1** to give special importance to something. **2** to have something as a characteristic. **3** (**feature in**) to play an important part in something.

February /fe broo a ri *or* fe bew ri/ *noun* the second month of the year.

fed *verb* past tense and past participle of FEED.

federal *adjective* said about a system of government: in which separate states have self-government in local matters, but send representatives to a central government that takes decisions affecting the country as a whole.

federation *noun* (*plural* **federations**) a group of states or organizations combined under a federal system.

fee *noun* (*plural* **fees**) a sum of money paid to somebody, for example for admission to a place or for a professional service.

feeble *adjective* (**feebler, feeblest**) lacking in strength or authority; weak. ➤ **feebly** *adverb*.

feed *verb* (**feeds, feeding, fed**) **1** to give food to a person or animal. **2** to provide enough food for a certain number of people. **3** said about a baby or animal: to eat. **4** to supply material to a machine: *Paper is automatically fed into the copier.* ~ *noun* (*plural* **feeds**) **1** an act of eating. **2** food for animals. ➤ **feeder** *noun*.

feedback *noun* **1** information given to somebody who made or wrote something to tell them what was good or bad about it. **2** an unpleasant noise caused when part of the output signal is fed back to a microphone.

feel *verb* (**feels, feeling, felt**) **1** to handle or touch something to examine or explore it. **2** to give a particular sensation when touched: *Your hands feel very cold.* **3** to experience an emotion or physical sensation: *I didn't feel at all frightened.* **4** to be affected by something: *He's feeling the effects of having been up all night.* **5** to believe or think: *I feel you ought to try again.* ~ *noun* the way that something feels when you touch it: *the feel of velvet.* ✲ **feel for** to have sympathy or pity for somebody. **feel like** to have a wish for something. **feel up to** to be well or fit enough to do something.

feeler *noun* (*plural* **feelers**) **1** an animal's feeling organ.
2 (**feelers**) cautious attempts to find out what other people think.

feeling *noun* (*plural* **feelings**) **1** an emotional state or reaction: *a feeling of joy.* **2** an opinion or belief that comes from inside you rather than from evidence: *I have a feeling we're going to be lucky this time.* **3** the ability to feel sensations or emotions: *He's lost all feeling in his right arm.*

feet *noun* plural of FOOT.

feign /fayn/ *verb* (**feigns, feigning, feigned**) to pretend something.

feint *noun* (*plural* **feints**) a mock blow or attack made to confuse or mislead somebody.

felicitations *plural noun formal* congratulations.

felicity *noun formal* **1** great happiness. **2** effectiveness in the use of something, such as language for artistic purposes.

feline /**fee**lien/ *adjective* **1** to do with cats or the cat family. **2** resembling a cat. ~ *noun* (*plural* **felines**) a member of the cat family.

fell[1] *verb* past tense of FALL.

fell[2] *verb* (**fells, felling, felled**) **1** to cut down a tree **2** to knock somebody down.

fell[3] *noun* (*plural* **fells**) a rugged stretch of high moorland, especially in northern England.

fellow *noun* (*plural* **fellows**) **1** *informal* a man or a boy. **2** a senior member of a scientific or medical association or a college. ~ *adjective* belonging to the same group: *fellow travellers.*

fellowship *noun* (*plural* **fellowships**) **1** friendly relations between people. **2** a group of people with similar interests; an association.

felt[1] *noun* a cloth made by compressing wool or fur.

felt[2] *verb* past tense and past participle of FEEL.

female *adjective* **1** belonging to the sex

feminine

that bears children or produces eggs or fruit. **2** consisting of, or typical of, women. ~ *noun* (*plural* **females**) a female animal, person, or plant.

feminine *adjective* **1** female. **2** characteristic of women. **3** in some languages, belonging to or having to do with a class of words that refer mainly to females. ➤ **femininity** *noun*.

feminism *noun* support for women's rights and interests. ➤ **feminist** *noun and adjective*.

femur /fee mer/ *noun* (*plural* **femurs** or **femora** /fe mo ra/) *Science* the thighbone.

fen *noun* (*plural* **fens**) an area of low marshy or flooded land.

fence *noun* (*plural* **fences**) **1** a barrier of wire or boards enclosing an area. **2** an upright obstacle to be jumped by a horse. **3** *informal* a person who buys stolen goods from thieves and resells them. ~ *verb* (**fences, fencing, fenced**) **1** (**fence in**) to enclose an area with a fence. **2** (**fence off**) to separate an area with a fence. **3** to fight with long narrow swords, especially as a sport. ✶ **sit on the fence** to remain undecided or uncommitted. ➤ **fencer** *noun*, **fencing** *noun*.

fend *verb* (**fends, fending, fended**) ✶ **fend for yourself** to get or do the things that you need to take care of yourself. **fend off** to stop something from hitting you or affecting you.

fender *noun* (*plural* **fenders**) **1** a cushion of rope or wood hung over the side of a ship to absorb impacts. **2** a low metal guard to prevent coal spilling from a fire.

feng shui /fung shway *or* feng shooh i/ *noun* a Chinese system of rules for positioning and arranging objects, such as furniture in a room, so as to benefit from the flow of energy in the environment.

feral *adjective* said about an animal: not or no longer domesticated: *feral cats*.

ferment /fer ment/ *verb* (**ferments, fermenting, fermented**) to go through a chemical change as a result of the effects of bacteria and produce alcohol. ~ /fer ment/ *noun* a state of unrest or upheaval. ➤ **fermentation** *noun*.

fern *noun* (*plural* **ferns**) a flowerless plant with feathery green leaves called fronds.

ferocious *adjective* extremely fierce or violent. ➤ **ferociously** *adverb*, **ferocity** *noun*.

ferret *noun* (*plural* **ferrets**) a small fierce animal with a long thin body, used for hunting rabbits. ~ *verb* (**ferrets, ferreting, ferreted**) **1** (**ferret about/around**) *informal* to search for something. **2** to hunt with ferrets.

ferris wheel *noun* (*plural* **ferris wheels**) a fairground amusement consisting of a large upright revolving wheel with seats round the rim.

ferry *noun* (*plural* **ferries**) a boat or ship that carries passengers and vehicles across water. ~ *verb* (**ferries, ferrying, ferried**) **1** to transport somebody or something by boat or ship across water. **2** to transport somebody by car from one place to another.

fertile *adjective* **1** said about land or soil: capable of growing crops. **2** said about the mind: imaginative or inventive. **3** said about a person or animal: capable of having children or young. ➤ **fertility** *noun*.

fertilize *or* **fertilise** *verb* (**fertilizes, fertilizing, fertilized** *or* **fertilises**, etc) **1** to make an egg able to develop into a new individual by combining it with a male cell. **2** to apply a fertilizer to soil. ➤ **fertilization** *or* **fertilisation** *noun*.

fertilizer *or* **fertiliser** *noun* (*plural* **ferti-**

lizers or **fertilisers**) a substance used to make soil more fertile.

fervent *adjective* showing deep emotion. ➤ **fervently** *adverb*.

fervour *noun* passionate intensity of feeling.

fester *verb* (**festers, festering, festered**) 1 said about a wound: to generate pus. 2 said about a bad feeling or situation: to become worse.

festival *noun* (*plural* **festivals**) 1 a time marked by special celebration. 2 a programme of cultural events or entertainment. 3 a religious feast.

festive *adjective* 1 suitable for a feast or festival. 2 joyous or merry.

festivity *noun* (*plural* **festivities**) a party or celebration.

festoon *verb* (**festoons, festooning, festooned**) to cover something with a lot of decorations, such as ribbons, paper chains, or garlands of flowers.

fetch *verb* (**fetches, fetching, fetched**) 1 to go to a place, collect something or somebody, and bring them back. 2 to be sold for a specified price: *It might fetch £2000 at auction.*

fetching *adjective* attractive or becoming.

fete *or* **fête** /fayt/ *noun* (*plural* **fetes** *or* **fêtes**) an outdoor bazaar or other event held to raise money. ~ *verb* (**fetes, feting, feted** *or* **fêtes,** etc) to honour or celebrate somebody or something.

fetid *adjective* see FOETID.

fetish *noun* (*plural* **fetishes**) 1 an object believed to have magical power. 2 an object or part of the body that excites a person sexually.

fetlock *noun* (*plural* **fetlocks**) a projecting part with a tuft of hair on it on the back of a horse's leg above the hoof.

fetter *noun* (*plural* **fetters**) a shackle put around a prisoner's feet. ~ *verb* (**fetters, fettering, fettered**) 1 to put a fetter on somebody. 2 to restrict or restrain somebody.

fettle *noun* a state of physical or mental fitness.

feud /fewd/ *noun* (*plural* **feuds**) a quarrel or state of hostility or hatred between people that lasts for a very long time.

feudalism /fewˈdə li zm/ *noun* the medieval social system in which ordinary people were given land to farm by a lord and had to work or fight for him in return.

fever *noun* (*plural* **fevers**) 1 a rise of body temperature above the normal. 2 a state of intense emotion or activity. ➤ **fevered** *adjective*, **feverish** *adjective*, **feverishly** *adverb*.

few *adjective* 1 only a small number of people, things, etc. 2 (**a few**) some but not many. ~ *plural noun* not many. ✻ **few and far between** scarce. **quite a few** *or* **a good few** a fairly large number of; several.

Usage Note **fewer** *or* **less**? *Fewer* means 'a smaller number of'. It should be used with plural nouns: *fewer books; fewer people*. *Less* means 'a smaller amount of'. It should be used with singular nouns: *less work, less sugar*.

fez *noun* (*plural* **fezzes**) a red brimless hat with a flat top, worn by men in some Muslim countries.

fiancé /fiˈon say/ *noun* (*plural* **fiancés**) the man to whom a woman is engaged to be married.

fiancée /fiˈon say/ *noun* (*plural* **fiancées**) the woman to whom a man is engaged to be married.

fiasco *noun* (*plural* **fiascos**) a complete and humiliating failure.

fib *informal noun* (*plural* **fibs**) a trivial or childish lie. ~ *verb* (**fibs, fibbing, fibbed**) to tell a fib. ➤ **fibber** *noun*.

fibre *noun* (*plural* **fibres**) 1 a thin natural or manufactured thread, for example of wool, cotton, or glass.

fibreglass

2 material made of fibres. **3** the part of food that helps digestion. ➤ **fibrous** *adjective*.

fibreglass *noun* a tough material made from glass fibres.

fibre optics *noun Science* the use of glass or plastic fibres to transmit information as light signals.

fibula /ˈbewlə/ *noun* (*plural* **fibulae** /ˈbewlee/ *or* **fibulas**) *Science* the outer of the two bones between the knee and ankle.

fickle *adjective* always changing your mind about who or what you like.

fiction *noun* (*plural* **fictions**) **1** writings describing imaginary people and events. **2** something untrue or invented. ➤ **fictional** *adjective*.

fictitious *adjective* invented or unreal.

fiddle *informal noun* (*plural* **fiddles**) **1** a violin. **2** a dishonest way of making money. ~ *verb* (**fiddles, fiddling, fiddled**) **1** to move your hands or fingers restlessly. **2** (**fiddle with**) to keep touching, moving, or interfering with something. **3** to falsify accounts. ➤ **fiddler** *noun*.

fiddly *adjective* (**fiddlier, fiddliest**) *informal* awkward to use.

fidelity /fiˈdeliti/ *noun* **1** being faithful; loyalty. **2** accuracy when you are copying, reproducing, or translating something.

fidget *verb* (**fidgets, fidgeting, fidgeted**) to move your body about restlessly or nervously. ~ *noun* (*plural* **fidgets**) somebody who fidgets. ➤ **fidgety** *adjective*.

field *noun* (*plural* **fields**) **1** an enclosed area of land used for growing crops or feeding animals. **2** a large expanse of ice. **3** an outdoor area marked for a game or sport. **4** an area of activity or knowledge. ~ *verb* (**fields, fielding, fielded**) **1** to stop the ball struck by the batsman in cricket and pick it up. **2** to deal with a question by giving an answer. **3** to put a team in to play in a match. ➤ **fielder** *noun*.

field event *noun* (*plural* **field events**) an athletics event that does not involve racing round a track, for example the high jump or discus.

field marshal *noun* (*plural* **field marshals**) an officer of the highest rank in the British army.

field trip *noun* (*plural* **field trips**) a visit made by students, for example to a farm or museum, so that they can actually see the things they are learning about.

fiend *noun* (*plural* **fiends**) **1** a demon. **2** a person of great wickedness or cruelty. **3** *informal* somebody who is very enthusiastic about a particular activity.

fiendish *adjective* **1** extremely cruel or wicked. **2** *informal* extremely difficult or complex. ➤ **fiendishly** *adverb*.

fierce *adjective* (**fiercer, fiercest**) **1** showing anger and hostility: *a fierce glare*. **2** likely to attack you: *a fierce animal*. **3** extremely intense or severe: *fierce heat*. ➤ **fiercely** *adverb*, **fierceness** *noun*.

fiery *adjective* (**fierier, fieriest**) **1** consisting of or looking like fire, or very hot. **2** passionate. **3** easily angered.

fife *noun* (*plural* **fifes**) a small flute used in military bands.

fifteen *adjective and noun* (*plural* **fifteens**) **1** the number 15. **2** a rugby team. ➤ **fifteenth** *adjective and noun*.

fifth *adjective and noun* see FIVE.

fifty *adjective and noun* (*plural* **fifties**) **1** the number 50. **2** (**the fifties**) the numbers 50 to 59. ➤ **fiftieth** *adjective and noun*.

fifty-fifty *adjective* equally likely to be either good or bad, successful or unsuccessful, etc: *a fifty-fifty chance*. ~ *adverb* so that two people or groups take or pay equal shares: *We'll go fifty-fifty on the bill.*

fig *noun* (*plural* **figs**) a fleshy fruit with many seeds.

fight *verb* (**fights, fighting, fought**) **1** to take part in a battle or physical combat against somebody. **2** to argue. **3** to struggle to achieve or prevent something: *to fight for your rights; to fight injustice.* ~ *noun* (*plural* **fights**) **1** an act or spell of fighting. **2** a heated argument. **3** a struggle to achieve or prevent something.

fighter *noun* (*plural* **fighters**) **1** somebody or something that fights; a boxer. **2** a fast military aircraft.

figment * **a figment of your imagination** something that you have imagined and that does not really exist.

figurative *adjective* English using figures of speech; not literal. ➤ **figuratively** *adverb*.

figure *noun* (*plural* **figures**) **1** a symbol representing a number. **2** an amount given as a number: *I can't give you an exact figure, but I think it was about £300.* **3** a person's, especially a woman's, bodily shape. **4** a person not clearly seen or not recognized: *A figure emerged from the doorway.* **5** an important or well-known person. **6** a diagram or illustration in a text. ~ *verb* (**figures, figuring, figured**) *chiefly N American, informal* to think something. * **figure in** to play an important part in something. **figure out** to work something out.

figurehead *noun* (*plural* **figureheads**) **1** an ornamental carved figure on a ship's bow. **2** a leader who has no real power.

figure of speech *noun* (*plural* **figures of speech**) English a form of expression, used for special effect, in which some words do not have their usual literal meaning.

filament *noun* (*plural* **filaments**) **1** a thin thread. **2** a thin wire in an electric light bulb, that glows when an electric current passes through it.

filch *verb* (**filches, filching, filched**) *informal* to steal something.

file[1] *noun* (*plural* **files**) **1** a box or folder for keeping papers in order. **2** a collection of letters and documents on a subject. **3** *ICT* a collection of data stored under one name in a computer. ~ *verb* (**files, filing, filed**) to store or organize papers in files.

file[2] *noun* (*plural* **files**) a row of people, animals, or things arranged one behind the other. ~ *verb* (**files, filing, filed**) to walk or move one behind the other: *We all filed into the hall.*

file[3] *noun* (*plural* **files**) a steel tool with a rough surface for shaping or smoothing. ~ *verb* (**files, filing, filed**) to shape or smooth something with a file.

filial / li al/ *adjective* to do with a son or daughter's relationship to a parent.

fill *verb* (**fills, filling, filled**) **1** to become full, or to make something full. **2** to plug a hole or gap. **3** to spread through or occupy the whole of something or somebody: *The room was suddenly filled with light.* **4** to appoint somebody to an office or post. * **eat your fill** to eat as much as you want. **fill in 1** (*also* **fill out**) to complete a form. **2** to give somebody information: *Fill me in on what's been happening.* **3** to act as a temporary substitute: *I'm filling in for her while she's on holiday.*

filler *noun* (*plural* **fillers**) a substance used to fill holes or increase the bulk of something.

fillet *noun* (*plural* **fillets**) **1** a fleshy boneless piece of meat. **2** a long slice of fish with the bones removed. ~ *verb* (**fillets, filleting, filleted**) to remove the bones from a fish.

filling *noun* (*plural* **fillings**) **1** something used to fill a hole, for example in a tooth. **2** the food put

fillip

inside a sandwich, pie, or cake. ~ *adjective* said about food: that soon makes you feel full.

fillip *noun* (*plural* **fillips**) a boost or stimulus.

filly *noun* (*plural* **fillies**) a young female horse.

film *noun* (*plural* **films**) **1** a roll or strip of plastic coated with a light-sensitive material, used for taking photographs or moving pictures. **2** a story, documentary, etc, recorded on film for showing in cinemas or on television. **3** a thin layer or covering: *a film of grease*. ~ *verb* (**films, filming, filmed**) **1** to take moving pictures of somebody or something. **2** to make a film of a book or story.

filmy *adjective* (**filmier, filmiest**) **1** very thin and light. **2** covered with a mist or film.

filter *noun* (*plural* **filters**) **1** a substance or device that allows liquid or gas to pass through but catches any solid material. **2** a traffic light that allows vehicles to turn either left or right while the main flow is stopped. ~ *verb* (**filters, filtering, filtered**) **1** to put gas or liquid through a filter. **2** (**filter out**) to remove solid material with a filter. **3** said about information: to become known gradually: *News was starting to filter through from the war zone*. **4** to move gradually in small groups: *The audience filtered back into the hall*. **5** said about traffic: to turn left or right from the main flow.

filth *noun* **1** dirt or refuse. **2** obscene or pornographic material.

filthy *adjective* (**filthier, filthiest**) **1** extremely or offensively dirty. **2** obscene or pornographic. * **filthy rich** extremely wealthy.

fin *noun* (*plural* **fins**) **1** a flattened part projecting from the body of a fish or whale, used to propel it through the water. **2** a flattened projecting part attached to an aircraft or rocket to keep it stable in the air.

final *adjective* **1** last; occurring at the end: *a final attempt*. **2** that ends the discussion or argument and will not be changed: *Is that your final answer?* ~ *noun* (*plural* **finals**) the last game in a sport or competition, which determines the overall winner. ➤ **finally** *adverb*, **finality** *noun*.

finale /fi nah li/ *noun* (*plural* **finales**) the last part or item in a piece of music or other entertainment.

finalist *noun* (*plural* **finalists**) a contestant or team taking part in the final round of a competition.

finalize *or* **finalise** *verb* (**finalizes, finalizing, finalized** *or* **finalises,** etc) to put something into a final or finished form: *to finalize the arrangements for the meeting*.

finance *noun* (*plural* **finances**) **1** the use and management of large amounts of money. **2** a supply of money for a project. **3** (**finances**) the money somebody has available. ~ *verb* (**finances, financing, financed**) to provide money for a project or activity.

financial *adjective* to do with money or finance. ➤ **financially** *adverb*.

financier *noun* (*plural* **financiers**) a person who manages large-scale finance or investment.

finch *noun* (*plural* **finches**) a songbird with a short conical beak.

find *verb* (**finds, finding, found**) **1** to come upon or encounter something or somebody accidentally or by searching. **2** to obtain something, such as money or time, for a purpose. **3** to discover or realize what a person or thing is like: *I found her absolutely charming*. **4** said about a jury or judge: to give a decision in a trial: *They found him not guilty*. ~ *noun* (*plural* **finds**) a valuable object or talented person that you discover. * **find fault with** to criticize somebody or something. **find out 1** to learn or discover something by investigation: *I'd like to find out more about him.* **2** to detect a person doing wrong: *He would never lie, because he'd be found out.* **find your feet** to gain confidence with experience.

finding *noun* (*plural* **findings**) something decided and made known at the end of an investigation or enquiry.

fine[1] *adjective* (**finer, finest**) **1** superior in quality. **2** satisfactory or acceptable. **3** said about weather: dry and sunny. **4** said about a person: in good health and happy. **5** consisting of relatively small particles. ✱ **cut it fine** to act at the last possible moment. ➤ **finely** *adverb*.

fine[2] *noun* (*plural* **fines**) a sum of money payable as punishment for an offence. ~ *verb* (**fines, fining, fined**) to punish somebody with a fine.

fine print *noun* small print in which parts of some legal documents are printed.

finery *noun* elaborate or special clothes or jewellery.

finesse /fi nes/ *noun* skilful and subtle handling of a situation.

fine-tune *verb* (**fine-tunes, fine-tuning, fine-tuned**) to make small adjustments to something to make it work as well as possible.

finger *noun* (*plural* **fingers**) **1** one of the four long narrow parts at the end of your hand. **2** something that is like a finger in being long and narrow. ~ *verb* (**fingers, fingering, fingered**) to touch or handle something. ✱ **keep your fingers crossed** to hope for the best. **not lift a finger** to make no effort to help. **put your finger on** to identify a problem or cause.

fingernail *noun* (*plural* **fingernails**) the thin horny plate on the upper surface at the tip of a finger.

fingerprint *noun* (*plural* **fingerprints**) an ink impression of the lines on the fingertip, taken for purposes of identification.

finicky *adjective* **1** very hard to please; fussy. **2** requiring delicate attention to detail.

finish *verb* (**finishes, finishing, finished**) **1** to reach the end of something. **2** to bring something to an end. **3** to stop doing something. **4** (*also* **finish off/up**) to eat, drink, use, or dispose of all of something. **5** to end a competition in a specified place or order: *to finish third.* ~ *noun* (*plural* **finishes**) **1** the end or final stage. **2** the place where a race ends. **3** the final treatment or coating of a surface. ✱ **finish up** to reach a specified place or state. **finish with 1** to have no further need of something. **2** to break off relations with somebody. ➤ **finisher** *noun*.

finite /ˈeɪniet/ *adjective* having limits to its size or extent.

fiord *noun* see FJORD.

fir *noun* (*plural* **firs**) an evergreen tree with small, flat, needle-shaped leaves.

fire *noun* (*plural* **fires**) **1** the flames, heat, and light produced when something burns. **2** a mass of burning fuel. **3** a destructive process of burning a building, forest, etc. **4** a small domestic heater using gas or electricity. **5** intense energy or emotion. **6** the shooting of guns. ~ *verb* (**fires, firing, fired**) **1** to shoot a bullet from a gun. **2** to direct questions or commands in quick succession at somebody. **3** to dismiss an employee. **4** to bake pottery, ceramics, or bricks in a kiln. **5** to inspire somebody or fill them with enthusiasm. ✱ **catch fire** to begin to burn. **on fire** burning. **open/cease fire** to begin (or stop) shooting a weapon. **set fire to** *or* **set on fire** to start something burning. **under fire 1** being shot at. **2** being harshly criticized.

firearm *noun* (*plural* **firearms**) a pistol or rifle.

fire brigade *noun* (*plural* **fire brigades**) an organization for controlling and putting out fires.

fire drill *noun* (*plural* **fire drills**) a practice of the action to be taken if a fire starts.

fire engine *noun* (*plural* **fire engines**) a vehicle that carries firefighting equipment and firefighters.

fire escape *noun* (*plural* **fire escapes**) a staircase or other means of escape from a burning building.

fire extinguisher *noun* (*plural* **fire extinguishers**) an apparatus for putting out fires with chemicals.

firefighter *noun* (*plural* **firefighters**) a person trained to put out fires. ▸ **firefighting** *noun*.

firefly *noun* (*plural* **fireflies**) a night-flying beetle that produces a bright intermittent light.

fireman *noun* (*plural* **firemen**) a male firefighter.

fireplace *noun* (*plural* **fireplaces**) an opening at the base of a chimney in a room to hold a fire.

fire station *noun* (*plural* **fire stations**) a building where fire engines are kept and firefighters are on duty.

firewood *noun* wood used for fuel.

firework *noun* (*plural* **fireworks**) a device containing explosive material that goes off with dramatic light and sound effects.

firing squad *noun* (*plural* **firing squads**) a detachment of soldiers who shoot a person who has been condemned to death.

firm¹ *adjective* **1** solidly or securely fixed. **2** not giving way to pressure; solid and compact. **3** said about an opinion or principle: unchanging and steadfast. **4** said about a decision or arrangement: settled or definite. **5** resolute in dealing with people or situations. ▸ **firmly** *adverb*, **firmness** *noun*.

firm² *noun* (*plural* **firms**) a business organization.

firmament *noun* (**the firmament**) *literary* the sky.

first *adjective* **1** before anybody or anything else. **2** in the top or winning place. **3** most important. ~ *adverb* before anybody or anything else. ~ *noun* **1** (*plural* **first**) a person or thing that is first: *They were the first to reach the moon.* **2** (*plural* **firsts**) a thing that has never happened before. ✳ **at first** to start with; initially. **first thing** early in the morning. ▸ **firstly** *adverb*.

first aid *noun* emergency treatment given to an ill or injured person. ▸ **first-aider** *noun*.

first-class *adjective* **1** offering the best kind of service: *first-class travel.* **2** excellent.

first-hand *adjective* coming directly from the original source or personal experience. ✳ **at first hand** directly.

first lady *noun* (*plural* **first ladies**) the wife of a US president.

first name *noun* (*plural* **first names**) a personal or Christian name.

first person *noun* *English* in grammar, the term used to refer to the speaker or speakers, represented by the pronouns *I* or *we*.

first-rate *adjective* of the best class or quality; excellent.

firth *noun* (*plural* **firths**) a sea inlet or estuary.

fiscal *adjective* to do with public finances and taxation.

fish *noun* (*plural* **fishes** *or* **fish**) **1** an animal that lives in water and that has a long scaly body, fins, and gills. **2** the flesh of a fish used as food. ~ *verb* (**fishes, fishing, fished**) **1** to try to catch fish. **2** to feel about trying to find something.

fisherman *noun* (*plural* **fishermen**) a

person who catches fish as a living or for sport.

fishery *noun* (*plural* **fisheries**) an area for catching fish and other sea animals.

fishing rod *noun* (*plural* **fishing rods**) a rod with a reel, used with a line and hook for catching fish.

fishmonger *noun* (*plural* **fishmongers**) a person who sells fish for food.

fishy *adjective* (**fishier, fishiest**) **1** tasting or smelling like fish. **2** *informal* causing doubt or suspicion.

fissile *adjective* **1** *Science* said about an atom or element: capable of undergoing nuclear fission. **2** said about rock: easily split.

fission *noun* **1** the act of splitting or breaking up into parts. **2** *Science* the splitting of an atomic nucleus with the release of large amounts of energy.

fissure / sher/ *noun* (*plural* **fissures**) a long narrow opening, especially in rock.

fist *noun* (*plural* **fists**) the hand clenched with the fingers and thumb folded into the palm. ➤ **fistful** *noun* (*plural* **fistfuls**).

fit[1] *adjective* (**fitter, fittest**) **1** in a suitable state for something or to do something. **2** strong and healthy. ~ *verb* (**fits, fitting, fitted**) **1** to be the right size or shape for something or somebody. **2** to install a device or component, or to supply somebody or something with a piece of equipment. **3** to match or correspond to something: *She doesn't fit the description*. **4** to make somebody or something suitable for something. ~ *noun* the manner in which something fits. ➤ **fitness** *noun*.

fit[2] *noun* (*plural* **fits**) **1** a sudden violent attack of a disease accompanied by convulsions or unconsciousness. **2** an outburst of coughing, sneezing, laughing, etc. ✱ **by/in fits and starts** in an impulsive or irregular manner.

fitful *adjective* happening in irregular bursts. ➤ **fitfully** *adverb*.

fitment *noun* (*plural* **fitments**) a fixed piece of equipment or furniture.

fitted *adjective* made to fit a space or shape closely: *a fitted kitchen*. ✱ **fitted for/to** suitable or qualified for something.

fitting *adjective* appropriate to a situation. ~ *noun* (*plural* **fittings**) **1** an act of trying on clothes which are being made or altered. **2** (**fittings**) items in a property, such as carpets and curtains, that the owner is entitled to remove if the property is sold. ➤ **fittingly** *adverb*.

five *noun* (*plural* **fives**) the number 5. ➤ **fifth** *adjective and noun*, **fifthly** *adverb*.

fiver *noun* (*plural* **fivers**) *informal* a five-pound note.

fix *verb* (**fixes, fixing, fixed**) **1** to position and attach something firmly. **2** to make something firm, stable, or permanent: *I'm trying to fix the rules in my mind*. **3** to decide on something, for example a date or price. **4** to arrange something or make it possible. **5** to repair something, or put something right. ~ *noun* (*plural* **fixes**) *informal* **1** a difficult or embarrassing situation. **2** a dose of a narcotic drug. ✱ **fix up 1** to organize or arrange something. **2** *informal* to provide somebody with something. ➤ **fixer** *noun*.

fixated ✱ **be fixated on** to be obsessed with something.

fixation *noun* (*plural* **fixations**) an obsession.

fixative *noun* (*plural* **fixatives**) a substance used to hold something in place or to make it permanent.

fixture *noun* (*plural* **fixtures**) **1** a piece of equipment or furniture that is fixed in position. **2** (**fixtures**) items in a property, such as plumbing, cupboards, worktops, etc, that the

fizz *verb* (**fizzes, fizzing, fizzed**) **1** to make a hissing or sputtering sound. **2** said about a liquid: to produce bubbles of gas.

fizzle *verb* (**fizzles, fizzling, fizzled**) to make a weak fizzing sound. * **fizzle out** *informal* to fail or end feebly or disappointingly.

fizzy *adjective* (**fizzier, fizziest**) said about a drink: having bubbles of gas in it.

fjord or **fiord** /fyawd/ *noun* (*plural* **fjords** or **fiords**) a narrow inlet of the sea, especially in Norway.

flab *noun informal* soft loose body tissue.

flabbergasted *adjective informal* shocked or astonished.

flabby *adjective* (**flabbier, flabbiest**) soft, loose, and wobbly. ➤ **flabbiness** *noun*.

flaccid /ak sid or a sid/ *adjective* soft or limp. ➤ **flaccidity** *noun*.

flag[1] *noun* (*plural* **flags**) a piece of fabric with a distinctive colour and design, used as the symbol of a nation or as a signalling device. ~ *verb* (**flags, flagging, flagged**) **1** to mark something for attention. **2** to become tired and lose energy. * **flag down** to signal to a driver or vehicle to stop.

flag[2] or **flagstone** *noun* (*plural* **flags** or **flagstones**) a slab of stone used for paving.

flagon *noun* (*plural* **flagons**) a large squat jug or bottle for holding cider, wine, etc.

flagpole or **flagstaff** *noun* (*plural* **flagpoles** or **flagstaffs**) a tall pole on which to hoist a flag.

flagrant /ay grant/ *adjective* very obvious and shocking: *a flagrant breach of the rules.* ➤ **flagrantly** *adverb*.

flagship *noun* (*plural* **flagships**) **1** the ship that carries the commander of a fleet. **2** something considered the best thing produced by an organization.

flail *noun* (*plural* **flails**) a short swinging stick attached to a handle, used for threshing grain. ~ *verb* (**flails, flailing, flailed**) to wave your arms and legs violently.

flair *noun* **1** a natural ability or talent for something. **2** style and originality.

flak *noun* **1** the fire from anti-aircraft guns. **2** *informal* heavy criticism.

flake *noun* (*plural* **flakes**) a small loose piece of something, especially a thin flat piece. ~ *verb* (**flakes, flaking, flaked**) * **flake off** to come away in flakes. ➤ **flaky** *adj*.

flamboyant *adjective* lively, showy, and colourful. ➤ **flamboyance** *noun*, **flamboyantly** *adverb*.

flame *noun* (*plural* **flames**) **1** a bright mass of burning gas coming from something that is on fire. **2** a brilliant reddish orange colour. **3** *informal* a former lover: *an old flame.* ~ *verb* (**flames, flaming, flamed**) **1** to burn strongly. **2** to go bright red.

flamenco *noun* (*plural* **flamencos**) a lively style of Spanish guitar music accompanied by singing and dancing.

flamingo *noun* (*plural* **flamingos** or **flamingoes**) a wading bird with long legs, curved beak, and rosy-white and pink plumage.

flammable *adjective* easily set on fire.

flan *noun* (*plural* **flans**) an open-topped pastry case baked with a sweet or savoury filling.

flank *noun* (*plural* **flanks**) the side of something, especially of a person, an animal, or a formation of troops. ~ *verb* (**flanks, flanking, flanked**) to be positioned at the side of somebody.

flannel *noun* (*plural* **flannels**) **1** a soft woollen fabric with a slightly hairy surface. **2** a small square of towelling used for washing yourself.

flap *noun* (*plural* **flaps**) **1** a flexible or hinged piece that hangs loose or covers an opening. **2** a movable surface on the wing of an aircraft for controlling its upward or downward movement. **3** *informal* a state of excitement or panic. ~ *verb* (**flaps, flapping, flapped**) **1** to move up and down or from side to side, creating a noise. **2** said about a bird or bat: to move its wings in flight. **3** *informal* to be agitated or in a panic.

flapjack *noun* (*plural* **flapjacks**) **1** a soft biscuit made with oats and syrup. **2** *N American* a pancake.

flare *verb* (**flares, flaring, flared**) **1** to shine or blaze with a sudden flame. **2** to get wider at one end. ~ *noun* (*plural* **flares**) **1** a sudden glaring light or flame. **2** a device producing a very bright light, used as a signal. **3** a gradual widening at one end. **4** (**flares**) flared trousers. ✳ **flare up 1** to become suddenly angry. **2** said about violence or conflict: to break out.

flash *verb* (**flashes, flashing, flashed**) **1** to shine briefly with a bright light. **2** to move past at high speed. **3** to direct a smile or look at somebody briefly. ~ *noun* (*plural* **flashes**) **1** a sudden burst of light. **2** a sudden experience in which you realize or learn something: *a flash of inspiration*. **3** a camera attachment that produces a flash of light for photography in dark conditions. ✳ **a flash in the pan** something that seems promising but does not last. **in a flash** very quickly.

flashback *noun* (*plural* **flashbacks**) **1** a scene in a book, play, or film that shows events earlier than the time of the main action. **2** a sudden memory of a past event.

flash flood *noun* (*plural* **flash floods**) a sudden local flood caused by heavy rainfall.

flashlight *noun* (*plural* **flashlights**) a powerful electric torch.

flashy *adjective* (**flashier, flashiest**) tastelessly showy.

flask *noun* (*plural* **flasks**) **1** a glass container with a narrow neck. **2** = VACUUM FLASK.

flat *adjective* (**flatter, flattest**) **1** horizontal, not sloping: *a flat roof*. **2** smooth, without raised or hollow areas. **3** having a broad surface and little thickness. **4** clear and unmistakable: *a flat refusal*. **5** said about a charge: fixed: *a flat rate*. **6** dull or monotonous. **7** said about a drink: no longer fizzy. **8** said about a tyre: lacking air; deflated. **9** said about a battery: no longer able to produce electric current. **10** *Music* said about a note: lowered a semitone in pitch. **11** *Music* singing or playing lower than intended or specified by the music. ~ *adverb* (**flatter, flattest**) **1** so as to be level or spread out: *Lay it down flat*. **2** *informal* completely, utterly: *flat broke*. **3** *informal* precisely: *in two minutes flat*. **4** *Music* lower than specified by the notes. ~ *noun* (*plural* **flats**) **1** a set of rooms within a larger building that are used as a dwelling. **2** *Music* a musical note one semitone lower than a specified or unaltered note. **3** *Music* the symbol (♭) that indicates such a note. **4** *informal* a flat tyre. ✳ **fall flat** to fail to achieve the intended effect. **flat out** as hard or fast as possible.

flat feet *plural noun* a condition in which the arches of the insteps are flattened so that the soles rest entirely on the ground.

flatfish *noun* (*plural* **flatfishes** or **flatfish**) a sea fish with a flattened body and both eyes on its upper surface.

flatmate *noun* (*plural* **flatmates**)

flat race

somebody who shares a flat with another person.

flat race *noun* (*plural* **flat races**) a race for horses on a course without jumps. ➤ **flat racing** *noun*.

flatten *verb* (**flattens, flattening, flattened**) (*also* **flatten out**) **1** to become flat or flatter, or to make something flat or flatter. **2** to press yourself flat against a surface. **3** to knock something or somebody down to the ground.

flatter *verb* (**flatters, flattering, flattered**) **1** to praise somebody insincerely because you want their support or help. **2** to make somebody seem better or more attractive than they deserve. ➤ **flatterer** *noun*.

flattery *noun* insincere or excessive praise.

flaunt *verb* (**flaunts, flaunting, flaunted**) to show something off openly, especially so as to shock other people or make them feel envious: *If you've got it, flaunt it!*

Usage Note **flaunt** *or* **flout**? Do not confuse **flaunt** with **flout**, which means 'to disregard something': *to flout the rules.*

flautist *noun* (*plural* **flautists**) a person who plays the flute.

flavour *noun* (*plural* **flavours**) the particular taste of a substance in the mouth. ~ *verb* (**flavours, flavouring, flavoured**) to give or add flavour to something. ✻ **flavour of the month** a person or thing that is currently fashionable or in favour. ➤ **flavoured** *adjective*, **flavouring** *noun*, **flavourless** *adjective*.

flaw *noun* (*plural* **flaws**) a blemish, imperfection, or hidden defect. ➤ **flawless** *adjective*. ➤ **flawed** *adjective*.

flax *noun* a plant cultivated for its strong woody fibre, used to make linen, and its seeds.

flaxen *adjective* said about hair: pale-yellow.

flay *verb* (**flays, flaying, flayed**) **1** to strip the skin off an animal. **2** to whip somebody savagely.

flea *noun* (*plural* **fleas**) a wingless jumping insect that feeds on the blood of animals.

fleck *noun* (*plural* **flecks**) **1** a small spot of colour or light. **2** a grain or particle. ~ *verb* (**flecks, flecking, flecked**) to cover with small spots or marks.

fledged *adjective* said about a young bird: having wing feathers developed enough for it to fly.

fledgling *or* **fledgeling** *noun* (*plural* **fledglings** *or* **fledgelings**) a young bird that has just begun to fly.

flee *verb* (**flees, fleeing, fled**) to run away from danger or harm.

fleece *noun* (*plural* **fleeces**) **1** a sheep's coat of wool. **2** a jacket made of a soft warm synthetic fabric. ~ *verb* (**fleeces, fleecing, fleeced**) *informal* to overcharge or swindle somebody. ➤ **fleecy** *adjective*.

fleet[1] *noun* (*plural* **fleets**) **1** a number of warships under a single command. **2** a group of vehicles, ships, or aircraft operating together or owned by one company.

fleet[2] *adjective* quick and nimble.

fleeting *adjective* lasting only a very short time: *a fleeting glimpse*. ➤ **fleetingly** *adverb*.

flesh *noun* **1** the soft parts of the body. **2** the edible pulpy part of a plant or fruit. **3** the physical body and life of humans, as opposed to their soul and spiritual life. ✻ **in the flesh** in person.

fleshy *adjective* (**fleshier, fleshiest**) **1** plump. **2** made up of pulp and juice.

flew *verb* past tense of FLY.

flex *verb* (**flexes, flexing, flexed**) **1** to bend a limb or joint. **2** to tense a muscle. **3** to bend and revert to an original position or shape. ~ *noun* (*plural* **flexes**) an electrical cable used to connect an appliance to a socket.

flexible *adjective* **1** capable of being bent. **2** adaptable. ➤ **flexibility** *noun*, **flexibly** *adverb*.

flick *noun* (*plural* **flicks**) **1** a quick sharp movement with your hand. **2** *informal* a cinema film. ~ *verb* (**flicks, flicking, flicked**) **1** to move something with a flick. **2** (**flick through**) to look at or read the pages of something quickly.

flicker *verb* (**flickers, flickering, flickered**) **1** to burn or shine unsteadily. **2** to move irregularly or unsteadily. ~ *noun* (*plural* **flickers**) **1** a brief unsteady light or movement. **2** a momentary feeling or sensation: *a flicker of interest*.

flick knife *noun* (*plural* **flick knives**) a knife with a blade that springs out from the handle when a button is pressed.

flier *noun* see FLYER.

flight *noun* (*plural* **flights**) **1** the act of flying. **2** a journey made in an aircraft or spacecraft. **3** the path of a ball or other object moving through the air. **4** escape from danger or captivity. **5** a series of stairs leading from one floor to the next. ✶ **flight of fancy** an imaginative idea.

flight deck *noun* (*plural* **flight decks**) **1** the cockpit of a passenger aircraft. **2** the deck of an aircraft carrier.

flight recorder *noun* (*plural* **flight recorders**) a device fitted to an aircraft that records details of its flight.

flighty *adjective* (**flightier, flightiest**) irresponsible or flirtatious.

flimsy *adjective* (**flimsier, flimsiest**) **1** weak and insubstantial. **2** thin and light. **3** unconvincing: *a flimsy excuse*. ➤ **flimsily** *adverb*.

flinch *verb* (**flinches, flinching, flinched**) to make a nervous shrinking movement in response to fear or pain.

fling *verb* (**flings, flinging, flung**) **1** to throw something with force. **2** to put something somewhere carelessly. ~ *noun* (*plural* **flings**) **1** a brief period of enjoyment. **2** *informal* a brief sexual relationship. **3** a vigorous Scottish dance.

flint *noun* (*plural* **flints**) **1** a hard stone with a smooth bluish black surface. **2** a piece of metal used to produce a spark in a cigarette lighter.

flip *verb* (**flips, flipping, flipped**) **1** to turn something over with a quick neat movement. **2** to propel something with a flick of the fingers. **3** *informal* to lose your self-control. **4** (**flip through**) to read through something quickly or casually. ~ *noun* (*plural* **flips**) **1** a flipping movement or action. **2** a somersault.

flip-flop *noun* (*plural* **flip-flops**) a light sandal with two diagonal straps that meet and are fixed between the big toe and the second toe.

flippant *adjective* not showing proper respect or seriousness. ➤ **flippancy** *noun*, **flippantly** *adverb*.

flipper *noun* (*plural* **flippers**) **1** the broad flat limb of a seal or turtle, used for swimming. **2** a flat rubber paddle worn on each foot for underwater swimming.

flip side *noun* (*plural* **flip sides**) *informal* **1** the less important side of a pop record. **2** the other, usually less pleasant, side of a person or situation.

flirt *verb* (**flirts, flirting, flirted**) to act as if you are sexually attracted to somebody without wishing to start a relationship with them. ~ *noun* (*plural* **flirts**) a person who likes to flirt. ✶ **flirt with 1** to show a casual interest in something. **2** to risk danger deliberately for excitement. ➤ **flirtation** *noun*, **flirtatious** *adjective*.

flit *verb* (**flits, flitting, flitted**) to move or fly lightly and quickly.

flitter *verb* (**flitters, flittering,**

float

flittered) to move about in a random or agitated way.

float *verb* (**floats, floating, floated**) **1** to rest on the surface of a fluid without sinking. **2** to drift gently on a liquid on or through the air. **3** to offer the shares of a company for sale for the first time on the stock market. ~ *noun* (*plural* **floats**) **1** something that floats, especially if used as a marker or support. **2** the platform of a lorry carrying an exhibit in a parade. **3** an electrically powered delivery vehicle. **4** a sum of money available for giving change at a stall or in a shop.

floating voter *noun* (*plural* **floating voters**) a person who has not yet decided which party they will vote for in an election.

flock *noun* (*plural* **flocks**) a group of birds or mammals. ~ *verb* (**flocks, flocking, flocked**) to move in a crowd: *People came flocking in to see the exhibition.*

floe *noun* (*plural* **floes**) *Geography* a sheet of floating ice.

Usage Note Do not confuse *floe* and *flow*.

flog *verb* (**flogs, flogging, flogged**) **1** to beat somebody with a stick or whip. **2** *informal* to sell something. ➤ **flogging** *noun*.

flood *noun* (*plural* **floods**) **1** an overflow of water onto dry land. **2** the flowing in of water associated with a rising tide. **3** an overwhelming quantity of something. ~ *verb* (**floods, flooding, flooded**) **1** to cover and submerge an area. **2** said about an area: to become submerged under water that has overflowed. **3** said about a river: to rise and overflow its banks. **4** to arrive in overwhelming quantities: *Complaints have been flooding in.*

floodlight *noun* (*plural* **floodlights**) a powerful lamp used for lighting a theatre stage or a sports ground. ~ *verb* (**floodlights, floodlighting, floodlit**) to light a place with floodlights.

floor *noun* (*plural* **floors**) **1** the lower surface of a room or passage. **2** a storey of a building. ~ *verb* (**floors, flooring, floored**) **1** to fit a room with a floor. **2** to knock somebody to the floor or ground. **3** to confuse or disconcert somebody.

floorboard *noun* (*plural* **floorboards**) a long plank forming part of a wooden floor.

flop *verb* (**flops, flopping, flopped**) **1** to swing or hang loosely and heavily. **2** to sit or lie down in a heavy or clumsy manner. **3** *informal* to fail completely. ~ *noun* (*plural* **flops**) *informal* a complete failure.

floppy *adjective* (**floppier, floppiest**) limp and hanging loosely. ~ *noun* (*plural* **floppies**) *ICT* a floppy disk.

floppy disk *noun* (*plural* **floppy disks**) *ICT* a flexible disk in a plastic case used for storing small amounts of data.

flora *noun* the plant life of a region or period.

floral *adjective* to do with or made up of flowers.

florist *noun* (*plural* **florists**) a person or shop that sells cut flowers.

floss *noun* **1** soft silk or cotton thread used in embroidery. **2** soft thread for cleaning between the teeth. ~ *verb* (**flosses, flossing, flossed**) to clean your teeth with dental floss.

flotation *noun* (*plural* **flotations**) **1** the act of floating. **2** the launching of a company on the stock market by offering shares for the first time.

flotilla /flo ti la/ *noun* (*plural* **flotillas**) a small fleet of ships or boats.

flotsam *noun* floating wreckage of a

ship or its cargo. ✻ **flotsam and jetsam** odds and ends.

flounce verb (**flounces, flouncing, flounced**) to move in an exaggerated manner, especially to show that you are annoyed. ~ noun (plural **flounces**) a wide strip of fabric attached to the hem of a skirt or dress.

flounder[1] noun (plural **flounders** or **flounder**) a small flatfish that lives in the sea.

flounder[2] verb (**flounders, floundering, floundered**) 1 to stagger about in soft mud or water. 2 to seem confused and unable to cope when trying to do or say something.

flour noun finely ground grain, especially wheat, used in cooking. ➤ **floury** adjective.

flourish /ˈflʌrɪʃ/ verb (**flourishes, flourishing, flourished**) 1 to grow or develop well. 2 to achieve success; to prosper. 3 to wave something with dramatic gestures. ~ noun (plural **flourishes**) a showy or dramatic gesture.

flout verb (**flouts, flouting, flouted**) to disregard a rule or order.

Usage Note **flout** or **flaunt**? See note at **flaunt**.

flow verb (**flows, flowing, flowed**) 1 to move or pour steadily and continuously. 2 to hang down or stream out gracefully. ~ noun (plural **flows**) a continuous flowing or stream.

Usage Note Do not confuse *flow* with *floe*, a sheet of floating ice.

flow chart noun (plural **flow charts**) a diagram showing the stages of a procedure or system.

flower noun (plural **flowers**) the part of a plant that has bright petals and from which the seeds or fruit develop. ~ verb (**flowers, flowering, flowered**) 1 to produce flowers. 2 to develop and flourish.

flowerpot noun (plural **flowerpots**) a container for growing plants, usually shaped like a small bucket and made of pottery or plastic.

flowery adjective 1 patterned with flowers. 2 said about language: full of elaborate expressions.

flown verb past participle of FLY.

flu noun influenza.

fluctuate verb (**fluctuates, fluctuating, fluctuated**) to rise and fall or change unpredictably. ➤ **fluctuation** noun.

flue noun (plural **flues**) a channel in a chimney for flame and smoke to escape.

fluent adjective able to speak, write, or read without difficulty. ➤ **fluency** noun, **fluently** adverb.

fluff noun (plural **fluffs**) 1 small loose bits of waste material gathered in clumps. 2 soft light fur or hair. 3 *informal* a blunder in speaking or performing. ~ verb (**fluffs, fluffing, fluffed**) 1 (**fluff out/up**) to make something softer and plumper. 2 *informal* to do or say something badly.

fluffy adjective (**fluffier, fluffiest**) like fluff; light and soft or airy.

fluid adjective 1 capable of flowing. 2 said about plans: not yet definite. ~ noun (plural **fluids**) 1 a substance that flows; a liquid or gas. 2 a liquid in the body of an animal or plant. ➤ **fluidity** noun, **fluidly** adverb.

fluke noun (plural **flukes**) a lucky success that happens by chance. ➤ **fluky** adjective.

flume noun (plural **flumes**) a water chute at an amusement park or swimming pool.

flummox verb (**flummoxes, flummoxing, flummoxed**) to bewilder or confuse somebody.

flung *verb* past tense of FLING.

fluorescent /flaw re snt/ *adjective Science* producing a bright light by emitting radiation. ➤ **fluorescence** *noun*.

fluoridate /aw ri dayt/ *verb* (**fluoridates, fluoridating, fluoridated**) to add fluoride to water. ➤ **fluoridation** *noun*.

fluoride /oo o ried/ *noun Science* a chemical compound added to toothpaste or drinking water to reduce tooth decay.

flurry *noun* (*plural* **flurries**) **1** a gust of wind. **2** a small mass of snow, rain, or leaves blown about by a light wind. **3** a state of nervous excitement. **4** a short burst of activity.

flush[1] *noun* (*plural* **flushes**) **1** a red colour in the cheeks. **2** a sudden flow of water. **3** in poker, a hand of playing cards all of the same suit. ~ *verb* (**flushes, flushing, flushed**) **1** to glow brightly with a rosy colour. **2** to blush. **3** to clean or dispose of something with a stream of liquid.

flush[2] *adjective* **1** level with a surface. **2** arranged edge to edge so as to fit snugly. **3** *informal* having plenty of money.

fluster *verb* (**flusters, flustering, flustered**) to make somebody agitated or confused. ➤ **flustered** *adjective*.

flute *noun* (*plural* **flutes**) *Music* a high-pitched woodwind instrument that consists of a cylindrical tube with finger holes, held horizontally when played.

flutter *verb* (**flutters, fluttering, fluttered**) **1** to flap the wings rapidly. **2** to move with quick wavering or flapping motions. ~ *noun* (*plural* **flutters**) **1** a state of nervous confusion or excitement. **2** *informal* a small bet. ➤ **fluttery** *adjective*.

flux ✷ **in flux** continually changing.

fly *verb* (**flies, flying, flew, flown**) **1** to move through the air by means of wings. **2** to float or wave in the air. **3** to operate an aircraft or spacecraft in flight. **4** to travel in an aircraft. **5** to move, pass, or leave quickly. ~ *noun* (*plural* **flies**) **1** a flying insect with two thin wings. **2** an artificial fly attached to a hook as bait for fish. **3** (**flies**) an opening in the front of a pair of trousers, closed with buttons or a zip and covered by a fold of cloth. ✷ **fly at** to attack somebody suddenly. **fly off the handle** *informal* to become suddenly angry. **a fly on the wall** a hidden observer. **with flying colours** with great success or distinction.

flyer or **flier** *noun* (*plural* **flyers** or **fliers**) **1** a person or thing that flies or moves very fast. **2** a passenger on an aircraft. **3** a small leaflet or handbill.

flying saucer *noun* (*plural* **flying saucers**) a round flying object supposed to come from outer space.

flying squad *noun* (*plural* **flying squads**) a police unit ready to act swiftly in an emergency.

flying start *noun* a successful beginning giving an advantage over other competitors.

flyleaf *noun* (*plural* **flyleaves**) a blank page at the beginning or end of a book, fastened to the cover.

flyover *noun* (*plural* **flyovers**) a bridge carrying one road or railway line over another at a crossing.

flypaper *noun* (*plural* **flypapers**) a strip of sticky paper hung up to attract and kill flies.

flypast *noun* (*plural* **flypasts**) a ceremonial flight by aircraft over a gathering of people.

fly sheet *noun* (*plural* **fly sheets**) a protective sheet covering a tent or its entrance.

flywheel *noun* (*plural* **flywheels**) a heavy wheel that revolves to make a machine or engine run smoothly.

foal *noun* (*plural* **foals**) a young horse.

~ *verb* (**foals, foaling, foaled**) to give birth to a foal.

foam *noun* **1** a light frothy mass of fine bubbles formed on the surface of a liquid. **2** a rubber or plastic material filled with small holes by the introduction of gas bubbles. ~ *verb* (**foams, foaming, foamed**) to produce or form foam. ➤ **foamy** *adjective*.

fob[1] *noun* (*plural* **fobs**) **1** a tab on a key ring. **2** a short chain attached to a watch carried in a pocket.

fob[2] *verb* (**fobs, fobbing, fobbed**) ✷ **fob off** to make somebody go away by giving them something else instead of what they really wanted: *Don't let them fob you off with any more excuses.*

focal *adjective* to do with a focus.

focus *noun* (*plural* **focuses** *or* **foci** /foh sie/) **1** a point at which rays of light come together. **2** the point at which an object must be placed to produce a sharp image in a lens or mirror. **3** a centre of activity or attention. ~ *verb* (**focuses, focusing, focused** *or* **focusses**, etc) **1** to adjust a camera or telescope to obtain a sharp image. **2** to become able to see clearly. **3** to concentrate one's thoughts or attention on something. ✷ **in** *or* **out of focus** said about an image: having (or lacking) a sharp outline.

focus group *noun* (*plural* **focus groups**) a group of people gathered together to discuss a new product or policy.

fodder *noun* food for cattle.

foe *noun* (*plural* **foes**) *literary* an enemy or adversary.

foetid *or* **fetid** /fe tid/ *adjective* having an unpleasant smell; stinking.

foetus /fee tus/ *noun* (*plural* **foetuses**) an unborn human baby or young of a mammal. ➤ **foetal** *adjective*.

fog *noun* (*plural* **fogs**) a thick mist. ~ *verb* (**fogs, fogging, fogged**) to cover something, or be covered, with condensation so that it is difficult to see through. ➤ **foggy** *adjective*.

fogey *or* **fogy** *noun* (*plural* **fogeys** *or* **fogies**) a person with old-fashioned ideas.

foghorn *noun* (*plural* **foghorns**) a deep horn sounded in a fog to give warning to ships.

foible *noun* (*plural* **foibles**) a minor weakness or shortcoming.

foil[1] *noun* (*plural* **foils**) **1** metal in thin sheets. **2** a person or thing that serves as a contrast to another.

foil[2] *verb* (**foils, foiling, foiled**) to prevent somebody from carrying out an action, especially a wicked act.

foil[3] *noun* (*plural* **foils**) a light fencing sword with a blunted tip.

foist *verb* (**foists, foisting, foisted**) (**foist on**) to force somebody to accept something or somebody that they do not want: *The job was foisted on me by the manager.*

fold[1] *verb* (**folds, folding, folded**) **1** to lay one part of something over another part, for example to reduce its length. **2** to clasp your arms together. **3** to stir a food ingredient into a mixture gently. **4** *informal* said about a business: to stop operating. ~ *noun* (*plural* **folds**) **1** a part folded over. **2** a line or crease made by folding.

fold[2] *noun* (*plural* **folds**) an enclosure for sheep.

folder *noun* (*plural* **folders**) a folded cover or envelope for holding loose papers.

foliage *noun* the leaves of a plant or plants.

folk *noun* **1** (*also* **folks**) *informal* people in general. **2** = FOLK MUSIC.

folk dance *noun* (*plural* **folk dances**) a traditional dance of a people or region.

folklore *noun* the traditional customs and stories of a people or region.

folk music *noun* the traditional music and songs of a people or region.

folk song *noun* (*plural* **folk songs**) a traditional song of a people or region. ➤ **folksinger** *noun*.

follow *verb* (**follows, following, followed**) **1** to go or come after somebody or something. **2** to go after somebody or something to observe them or watch their movements. **3** to accept somebody as a guide or leader. **4** to obey rules or instructions. **5** to take place as a result of something. **6** to support a football team, etc. **7** to understand the meaning of something you hear or read. ✱ **follow suit** to do as somebody else has done. ➤ **follower** *noun*.

following *adjective* **1** that comes next. **2** now to be mentioned. ~ *noun* (*plural* **followings**) a group of supporters. ~ *preposition* after.

folly *noun* (*plural* **follies**) **1** a lack of good sense or prudence. **2** a foolish act or idea. **3** a fanciful building built for scenic effect.

foment *verb* (**foments, fomenting, fomented**) to cause people to start trouble, rebellion, etc.

fond *adjective* **1** (**fond of**) having an affection or liking for somebody or something. **2** affectionate; loving. **3** foolish; naïve: *fond hopes*. ➤ **fondly** *adverb*, **fondness** *noun*.

fondle *verb* (**fondles, fondling, fondled**) to touch or caress tenderly and lovingly or erotically.

font¹ *noun* (*plural* **fonts**) a special basin in a church for the water used in baptism.

font² *noun* (*plural* **fonts**) *ICT* a complete set of letters and symbols for printing in one style.

food *noun* (*plural* **foods**) material taken into the body of a living organism to provide energy and sustain life. ✱ **food for thought** something that needs thinking about.

food chain *noun* (*plural* **food chains**) a sequence of organisms each of which eats the one below it in the sequence.

foodstuff *noun* (*plural* **foodstuffs**) a substance used as food.

fool *noun* (*plural* **fools**) **1** a person lacking in sense or understanding. **2** a jester. **3** a cold dessert made from fruit and whipped cream. ~ *verb* (**fools, fooling, fooled**) **1** to trick or deceive somebody. **2** to say or do something as a joke. ✱ **act/play the fool** to misbehave. **fool about/around** to behave in a silly or irresponsible way. **a fool's paradise** a state of happiness that is based on not understanding the real situation. **make a fool of yourself** to behave in an embarrassing way.

foolhardy *adjective* foolishly bold or rash. ➤ **foolhardiness** *noun*.

foolish *adjective* unwise; silly. ➤ **foolishly** *adverb*, **foolishness** *noun*.

foolproof *adjective* extremely simple or reliable.

foot *noun* (*plural* **feet**) **1** the end part of the leg, on which an animal or person stands. **2** (*plural also* **foot**) a unit of length equal to 12 inches (30.5 centimetres). **3** the lowest part; the bottom. **4** the basic unit of verse, consisting of a group of syllables. ✱ **have/keep your feet on the ground** to remain sensible and practical. **not put a foot wrong** to make no mistakes at all. **on/by foot** walking or running, as opposed to using transport. **put your foot down** to take a firm stand. **put your foot in it** to make an embarrassing mistake.

footage *noun* a length of cinema or television film.

foot-and-mouth disease *noun* a disease of cattle, sheep, pigs, and goats, with ulcers in the mouth, round the hoofs, and on the udders.

football *noun* (*plural* **footballs**) **1** a team game that involves kicking a

football noun. **2** the inflated round or oval ball used in a game of football. ➤ **footballer** noun.

footbridge noun (plural **footbridges**) a bridge for pedestrians.

footfall noun (plural **footfalls**) the sound of a footstep.

foothill noun (plural **foothills**) a hill at the foot of a mountain.

foothold noun (plural **footholds**) **1** a place where your foot can be placed securely while climbing. **2** an established position from which you can progress.

footing noun **1** a secure grip with your feet on the ground: *He lost his footing and fell down.* **2** a person's position or status in a relationship with others or with regard to a situation: *We had similar jobs, so we started out on an equal footing.*

footlights plural noun Drama a row of lights set across the front of a stage floor.

footman noun (plural **footmen**) a servant in livery who receives and attends to visitors.

footnote noun (plural **footnotes**) an extra note or comment placed at the bottom of a printed page.

footpath noun (plural **footpaths**) a path or pavement for people on foot.

footprint noun (plural **footprints**) a mark made on the ground by a foot or shoe.

footsore adjective having sore feet from walking.

footstep noun (plural **footsteps**) a step or pace taken in walking.

footstool noun (plural **footstools**) a low stool used to support the feet when sitting.

for preposition **1** used to indicate purpose or reason: *for love.* **2** used to indicate direction or intention: *to head for home.* **3** used to indicate length of time or distance: *for two hours.* **4** used to indicate cost or payment: *work for nothing.* **5** in favour of: *Are you for the plan or against it?* **6** considering: *tall for her age.* **7** with respect to: *a stickler for detail.* ~ *conjunction* because.

fora noun a plural of FORUM.

forage noun **1** food for animals, such as hay or straw. **2** a search. ~ *verb* (**forages, foraging, foraged**) to search for something, especially food.

foray noun (plural **forays**) **1** a sudden raid into an enemy's territory. **2** a brief attempt to do something new: *a brief foray into the world of orienteering.*

forbade or **forbad** verb past tense of FORBID.

forbear verb (**forbears, forbearing, forbore, forborne**) to hold oneself back from doing something.

forbearance noun patience or self-restraint.

forbid verb (**forbids, forbidding, forbade** /faw bad/ or **forbad, forbidden**) to refuse to allow somebody to do something.

forbidding adjective looking threatening or unfriendly.

forbore verb past tense of FORBEAR.

forborne verb past participle of FORBEAR.

force noun (plural **forces**) **1** Science strength or energy used to move something. **2** violence or compulsion used to achieve something. **3** an organized group of soldiers, police, or workers. **4** (**the forces**) the armed services of a nation. ~ *verb* (**forces, forcing, forced**) **1** to make somebody do something whether they want to or not. **2** to break open a door or lock. * **in force 1** said about a law or rule: valid and needing to be obeyed. **2** in large numbers.

forceful adjective powerful or effective. ➤ **forcefully** adverb.

forceps *noun* (*plural* **forceps**) a pair of large pincers used in surgery.

forcible *adjective* **1** carried out by force: *forcible entry*. **2** powerful; forceful. ➤ **forcibly** *adverb*.

ford *noun* (*plural* **fords**) a shallow part of a river or stream that can be crossed in a vehicle or on foot. ~ *verb* (**fords, fording, forded**) to cross a river or stream at a ford. ➤ **fordable** *adjective*.

fore *adjective and adverb* situated in or towards the front. * **to the fore** in a prominent position.

forearm[1] /fawr ahm/ *noun* (*plural* **forearms**) the human arm between the elbow and the wrist.

forearm[2] /fawr ahm/ *verb* (**forearms, forearming, forearmed**) to prepare somebody to deal with an attack or danger.

forebear *noun* (*plural* **forebears**) an ancestor.

foreboding *noun* (*plural* **forebodings**) a feeling that something bad is about to happen.

forecast *verb* (**forecast, forecasting, forecast** or **forecasted**) to say that something is going to happen in the future. ~ *noun* (*plural* **forecasts**) a prediction of a future happening or condition. ➤ **forecaster** *noun*.

forecastle /fohk sl/ *noun* (*plural* **forecastles**) an area below the deck at the front end of a ship.

forecourt *noun* (*plural* **forecourts**) an open area in front of a building, especially a petrol station.

forefather *noun* (*plural* **forefathers**) an ancestor.

forefinger *noun* (*plural* **forefingers**) the finger next to the thumb.

forefoot *noun* (*plural* **forefeet**) either of the front feet of a four-footed animal.

forefront *noun* the foremost part or place.

forego *verb* see FORGO.

foregoing *adjective* going before; immediately preceding. ~ *verb* see FORGO.

foregone *verb* see FORGO.

foregone conclusion *noun* (*plural* **foregone conclusions**) something that is certain to happen: *It was a foregone conclusion that she would win.*

foreground *noun* **1** the part of a picture or view nearest to the viewer. **2** a prominent position.

forehand *noun* (*plural* **forehands**) a stroke in games such as tennis and squash made with the palm of the hand turned in the direction in which you are hitting the ball. ➤ **forehand** *adjective and adverb*.

forehead /faw hed *or* fo rid/ *noun* (*plural* **foreheads**) the part of the face above the eyes.

foreign *adjective* **1** born in or belonging to a country other than your own. **2** relating to other nations. * **foreign to** not characteristic of somebody or something.

foreigner *noun* (*plural* **foreigners**) a person from a foreign country.

foreleg *noun* (*plural* **forelegs**) either of the front legs of an animal.

foreman *noun* (*plural* **foremen**) **1** a worker who supervises other workers. **2** the chairman and spokesman of a jury.

foremost *adjective* most important or best known.

forename *noun* (*plural* **forenames**) a name that comes before a surname.

forensic /fo ren sik/ *adjective* to do with the scientific investigation of crime: *forensic medicine*.

forerunner *noun* (*plural* **forerunners**) a person or thing that is an earlier example or version of something that came later.

foresee *verb* (**foresees, foreseeing, foresaw, foreseen**) to imagine a development or event happening before it happens. ➤ **foreseeable** *adjective*.

foreshadow *verb* (**foreshadows, foreshadowing, foreshadowed**) to be an early sign of something that happens later.

foreshore *noun* the part of a seashore between the high-tide and low-tide marks.

foreshorten *verb* (**foreshortens, foreshortening, foreshortened**) *Art* to shorten a detail in a drawing or painting so as to create an illusion of depth.

foresight *noun* the ability to foresee and prepare yourself for future events.

foreskin *noun* (*plural* **foreskins**) the fold of skin that covers the tip of the penis.

forest *noun* (*plural* **forests**) a dense growth of trees covering a large area of land.

forestall *verb* (**forestalls, forestalling, forestalled**) to prevent something from happening by taking action in advance.

forestry *noun* the scientific management of trees and forests. ➤ **forester** *noun*.

foretaste *noun* (*plural* **foretastes**) an advance indication or experience of something: *The snow on Thursday was just a foretaste of the blizzards to come.*

foretell *verb* (**foretells, foretelling, foretold**) to predict something.

forethought *noun* careful consideration of what is likely to happen or be needed.

forever *adverb* **1** (*also* **for ever**) for all future time; indefinitely. **2** persistently; constantly: *She's forever getting in my way.*

forewarn *verb* (**forewarns, forewarning, forewarned**) to warn somebody in advance.

forewent *verb* see FORGO.

foreword *noun* (*plural* **forewords**) a preface to a book written by somebody other than the author of the text.

forfeit /fawfit/ *noun* (*plural* **forfeits**) something taken away as a penalty. ~ *verb* (**forfeits, forfeiting, forfeited**) to lose the right to something as a penalty. ➤ **forfeiture** *noun*.

forgave *verb* past tense of FORGIVE.

forge[1] *noun* (*plural* **forges**) an open furnace or workshop where metal is heated and worked. ~ *verb* (**forges, forging, forged**) **1** to shape metal by heating and hammering it. **2** to make a copy of a signature, document, or banknote, in order to make people believe it is the real thing. ➤ **forger** *noun*, **forgery** *noun*.

forge[2] *verb* (**forges, forging, forged**) to move forwards powerfully. * **forge ahead** to make rapid progress.

forget *verb* (**forgets, forgetting, forgot, forgotten**) **1** to be unable to remember something. **2** to disregard or give no attention to something. * **forget yourself** to act unsuitably or unworthily. ➤ **forgettable** *adjective*.

forgetful *adjective* likely to forget. ➤ **forgetfully** *adverb*, **forgetfulness** *noun*.

forgive *verb* (**forgives, forgiving, forgave, forgiven**) to stop feeling angry about something or resentful towards somebody. ➤ **forgivable** *adjective*, **forgiveness** *noun*.

forgo *or* **forego** *verb* (**forgoes, forgoing, forwent, forgone** *or* **foregoes**, etc) to do without or give up something desirable.

forgot *verb* past tense of FORGET.

forgotten *verb* past participle of FORGET.

fork *noun* (*plural* **forks**) **1** an implement with two or more prongs for eating or serving food. **2** a similar larger tool for digging or carrying something. **3** a place where a road or river divides into two, or either of these divisions. ~ *verb* (**forks, forking, forked**) **1** to divide into two or more branches. **2** to go down one of the branches of a fork in a road. **3** to pick up or dig something with a fork. * **fork out** *informal* to make a payment or contribution.

forklift truck *noun* (*plural* **forklift trucks**) a vehicle for lifting heavy loads by means of two horizontal prongs at the front.

forlorn *adjective* **1** sad and lonely. **2** nearly hopeless: *a forlorn attempt.* ➤ **forlornly** *adverb*.

form *noun* (*plural* **forms**) **1** the shape and structure of something. **2** a kind or variety of something. **3** a document with blank spaces for inserting information. **4** a bench. **5** a school class or year group. **6** a state in which a sportsperson is able to perform well: *He's been off form lately.* ~ *verb* (**forms, forming, formed**) **1** to create something. **2** to come into existence; to take shape. **3** to make up or constitute something.

formal *adjective* **1** characterized by dignity and the following of correct procedures: *a formal dinner.* **2** suitable for an important or ceremonial occasion: *formal dress.* **3** very polite, dignified, and serious: *He seemed friendly, but rather formal.* ➤ **formally** *adverb*.

formality *noun* (*plural* **formalities**) **1** formal behaviour. **2** something of little real significance but required by rule or custom: *You'll need to show us your passport, but that's just a formality.*

format *noun* (*plural* **formats**) **1** the general method of organizing or presenting something. **2** the shape, size, and general make-up of a book. **3** *ICT* the way in which data is organized or stored. ~ *verb* (**formats, formatting, formatted**) **1** to arrange something in a particular format. **2** *ICT* to prepare a disk to receive data.

formation *noun* (*plural* **formations**) **1** the act of forming something. **2** a group of people or things arranged in a special way.

formative *adjective* having a significant influence on growth or development.

former *adjective* **1** occurring in the past: *in former times.* **2** who or which used to be: *the former prime minister.* * **the former** the first of two things previously mentioned or understood: *If I was offered more money or more free time, I'd choose the former.*

formerly *adverb* at an earlier time; previously.

formidable *adjective* **1** difficult or challenging: *a formidable task.* **2** said about a person: causing fear or respect. ➤ **formidably** *adverb*.

formula *noun* (*plural* **formulas** or **formulae** /faw mew lee/) **1** *Maths* a mathematical rule or principle expressed in symbols. **2** *Science* a symbolic expression of the chemical composition of a substance: *The chemical formula for sulphuric acid is H_2SO_4.* **3** a fixed form of words for use in a ceremony or ritual. **4** a recipe or method for making or achieving something.

formulate *verb* (**formulates, formulating, formulated**) **1** to put an idea into words. **2** to devise or develop a plan. ➤ **formulation** *noun*.

fornication *noun formal* sexual relations with a person you are not married to.

forsake *verb* (**forsakes, forsaking, forsook, forsaken**) to abandon somebody or something.

fort *noun* (*plural* **forts**) a strongly fortified building.

forte /faw tay/ *noun* the thing that a person is best at. ~ *adjective and adverb Music* said about a piece of music: to be performed loudly.

forth *adverb formal* **1** onwards in time,

place, or order. **2** out; into view. * **and so forth** and so on.

forthcoming *adjective* **1** about to occur or appear. **2** made available: *New funds will be forthcoming next year.* **3** willing to give information.

forthright *adjective* saying exactly what you think.

forthwith *adverb* immediately.

fortify *verb* (**fortifies, fortifying, fortified**) **1** to strengthen a place against attack. **2** to give strength or endurance to somebody. ➤ **fortification** *noun*.

fortissimo *adjective and adverb Music* said about a piece of music: to be performed very loudly.

fortitude *noun* courage or endurance in the face of difficulty.

fortnight *noun* (*plural* **fortnights**) a period of two weeks.

fortnightly *adjective and adverb* occurring or appearing once a fortnight.

fortress *noun* (*plural* **fortresses**) a large fortified building or town.

fortuitous *adjective* occurring by chance. ➤ **fortuitously** *adverb*.

Usage Note Do not confuse *fortuitous* and *fortunate*

fortunate *adjective* **1** unexpectedly bringing good luck. **2** lucky. ➤ **fortunately** *adverb*.

fortune *noun* (*plural* **fortunes**) **1** a large quantity of money or possessions. **2** luck or chance seen as a force affecting human affairs. **3** your future destiny: *to tell somebody's fortune*.

forty *adjective and noun* (*plural* **forties**) **1** the number 40. **2** (**the forties**) the numbers 40 to 49. ➤ **fortieth** *adjective and noun*.

forum *noun* (*plural* **forums** or **fora**) **1** a meeting place or gathering for exchanging opinions. **2** the marketplace or central square of an ancient Roman city, where public business was dealt with.

forward *adjective* **1** directed or turned towards the front. **2** cheeky or assertive. ~ *adverb* **1** forwards. **2** into the future. **3** into a prominent position or open view. ~ *noun* (*plural* **forwards**) an attacking player in games such as football and hockey. ~ *verb* (**forwards, forwarding, forwarded**) to send a letter or goods on to a further destination.

forwards *adverb* towards what is ahead or in front.

forwent *verb* past tense of FORGO.

fossil *noun* (*plural* **fossils**) **1** the remains of an animal or plant of a past geological age preserved in rock. **2** an outdated person or thing.

fossil fuel *noun* (*plural* **fossil fuels**) a fuel, for example coal, that is derived from the remains of living things.

fossilize *or* **fossilise** *verb* (**fossilizes, fossilizing, fossilized** *or* **fossilises**, etc) to become, or turn something into, a fossil.

foster *verb* (**fosters, fostering, fostered**) **1** to promote the growth or development of something. **2** to give parental care to a child who is not your own. ~ *adjective* providing or receiving care by fostering: *foster mother; foster child*.

fought *verb* past tense of FIGHT.

foul *adjective* **1** that smells or tastes very bad. **2** particularly unpleasant or disagreeable: *foul weather*. **3** obscene or abusive: *foul language*. **4** breaking the rules of a game or sport. **5** polluted. ~ *noun* (*plural* **fouls**) a breaking of the rules in a game or sport. ~ *verb* (**fouls, fouling, fouled**) **1** to make something dirty; to pollute something. **2** in sport, to commit a foul against somebody. **3** to obstruct or block something. **4** to become entangled or collide with something.

foulmouthed *adjective* using coarse or abusive language.

foul play *noun* **1** murder or violence. **2** play that breaks the rules in a game or sport.

found[1] *verb* past tense of FIND.

found[2] *verb* (**founds, founding, founded**) to establish an institution or organization: *The college was founded in 1473.* ✻ **be founded on** to be based on something.

foundation *noun* (*plural* **foundations**) **1** the solid bottom structure on which a building rests. **2** the basis or principle underlying something. **3** a reason or justification. **4** the act of establishing something. **5** a cream or lotion applied to the face as a base for other make-up.

founder[1] *noun* (*plural* **founders**) a person who establishes an institution or organization.

founder[2] *verb* (**founders, foundering, foundered**) **1** said about a ship: to sink. **2** said about a plan or project: to fail.

foundling *noun* (*plural* **foundlings**) an infant abandoned by unknown parents and discovered and looked after by other people.

foundry *noun* (*plural* **foundries**) a place for making things from metal.

fountain *noun* (*plural* **fountains**) an ornamental structure that sends a jet of water into the air.

fountain pen *noun* (*plural* **fountain pens**) a pen with a nib and a small container for holding ink.

four *noun* (*plural* **fours**) **1** the number 4. **2** a shot in cricket that crosses the boundary after having hit the ground and scores four runs. ✻ **on all fours** on your hands and knees. ➤ **fourth** *adjective and noun,* **fourthly** *adverb*.

four-poster *noun* (*plural* **four-posters**) a large bed with corner posts supporting curtains or a canopy.

foursome *noun* (*plural* **foursomes**) a group of four people or things.

fourteen *adjective and noun* (*plural* **fourteens**) the number 14. ➤ **fourteenth** *adjective and noun*.

fowl *noun* (*plural* **fowls** or **fowl**) a domestic bird such as a chicken, turkey, or duck.

fox *noun* (*plural* **foxes**) an animal of the dog family with a pointed muzzle and a long bushy tail. ~ *verb* (**foxes, foxing, foxed**) to outwit or baffle somebody.

foxglove *noun* (*plural* **foxgloves**) a tall plant with white or purple tubular flowers.

foxhound *noun* (*plural* **foxhounds**) a hound bred to hunt foxes.

foyer /foi ay/ *noun* (*plural* **foyers**) an entrance hall or lobby in a theatre or large building.

fracas *noun* (*plural* **fracas**) a noisy quarrel or brawl.

fraction *noun* (*plural* **fractions**) **1** a number that is not a whole number, and is usually less than one, for example ¾ or 0.75. **2** a small portion or amount. ➤ **fractional** *adjective,* **fractionally** *adverb*.

fractious *adjective* irritable and hard to control.

fracture *noun* (*plural* **fractures**) a break in something, especially in a bone. ~ *verb* (**fractures, fracturing, fractured**) to break, or to break something.

fragile *adjective* easily broken or shattered. ➤ **fragility** *noun*.

fragment /frag mint/ *noun* (*plural* **fragments**) a part that is incomplete or broken off something larger. ~ /frag ment/ *verb* (**fragments, fragmenting, fragmented**) to break something into small pieces, or to fall to pieces. ➤ **fragmentary** *adjective,* **fragmentation** *noun*.

fragrance *noun* (*plural* **fragrances**)

1 a sweet or pleasant smell.
2 a perfume or aftershave.

fragrant *adjective* smelling sweet or pleasant.

frail *adjective* **1** weak and delicate. **2** easily broken.

frailty *noun* (*plural* **frailties**) **1** being frail. **2** a moral or physical weakness.

frame *noun* (*plural* **frames**)
1 a structure that gives shape or strength to a building, opening, vehicle, etc. **2** a rigid structure round a painting or photograph. **3** the physical structure of the human body. **4** (**frames**) the outer structure holding the lenses of a pair of glasses. **5** a single picture on a length of film. ~ *verb* (**frames, framing, framed**) **1** to put a frame round a picture or photograph. **2** to plan, shape, or construct something. **3** *informal* to make up evidence against an innocent person.

frame of mind *noun* (*plural* **frames of mind**) a particular mental or emotional state.

framework *noun* (*plural* **frameworks**) **1** a supporting frame or structure. **2** a basic plan for an essay, etc.

franc *noun* (*plural* **francs**) the basic unit of money in Switzerland, and formerly in France, Belgium, and Luxembourg (until replaced by the euro in 2002).

franchise *noun* (*plural* **franchises**) **1** (**the franchise**) the right to vote. **2** a right to sell goods or services on behalf of a company within a particular area.

frank *adjective* honest and straightforward in saying what you think or showing your feelings. ~ *verb* (**franks, franking, franked**) to mark a piece of mail with an official stamp showing that postal charges have been paid. ➤ **frankly** *adverb*, **frankness** *noun*.

frankfurter *noun* (*plural* **frankfurters**) a sausage made from beef and pork, used in hot dogs.

frankincense *noun* a type of fragrant gum that is burned as incense.

frantic *adjective* **1** emotionally out of control. **2** marked by fast and nervous activity. ➤ **frantically** *adverb*.

fraternal *adjective* brotherly. ➤ **fraternally** *adverb*.

fraternity *noun* (*plural* **fraternities**) **1** a group of people organized for a common purpose or interest. **2** a club for male students in some US universities. **3** brotherly feeling.

fraternize *or* **fraternise** *verb* (**fraternizes, fraternizing, fraternized** *or* **fraternises**, etc) to be on friendly terms with somebody. ➤ **fraternization** *or* **fraternisation** *noun*.

fraud *noun* (*plural* **frauds**) **1** the crime of deceiving people in order to make money for yourself. **2** an act of deception; a trick. **3** a person who is not what they pretend to be.

fraudster *noun* (*plural* **fraudsters**) somebody who commits a fraud.

fraudulent *adjective* involving fraud. ➤ **fraudulently** *adverb*.

fraught *adjective* very anxious and tense. ✻ **fraught with** filled with something unpleasant: *an enterprise fraught with danger*.

fray[1] *verb* (**frays, fraying, frayed**) **1** said about fabric or rope: to become worn at the edges. **2** said about a person's temper or nerves: to show strain.

fray[2] ✻ **the fray** a situation in which people are fighting, arguing, or competing with one another: *Two more candidates now decided to enter the fray.*

freak *noun* (*plural* **freaks**) **1** a person, animal, or plant with a physical abnormality. **2** a very unusual and unforeseeable event. **3** *informal* an obsessive enthusiast: *a sci-fi freak*. ~ *verb*

freckle | 258

(**freaks**, **freaking**, **freaked**) * **freak out** *informal* to behave irrationally or wildly. ➤ **freakish** *adjective*.

freckle *noun* (*plural* **freckles**) a small brown spot on the skin. ➤ **freckled** *adjective*, **freckly** *adjective*.

free *adjective* (**freer**, **freest**) **1** not under the control of another person. **2** not tied up or in prison. **3** not affected by something unpleasant: *free from pain*. **4** having no obligations or commitments: *I'm free this evening*. **5** not obstructed or restricted; clear. **6** not being used or occupied. **7** not costing or charging anything. **8** generous: *She's very free with her compliments*. ~ *verb* (**frees**, **freeing**, **freed**) **1** to set somebody or something free. **2** (**free up**) to make something available. ➤ **freely** *adverb*.

freebie *noun* (*plural* **freebies**) *informal* a gift or service offered free.

freedom *noun* (*plural* **freedoms**) **1** the state of being free. **2** the right to speak or act as you wish.

free enterprise *noun* an economic system that relies on private business operating competitively for profit.

free fall *noun* downward motion caused and controlled solely by gravity.

free-for-all *noun* (*plural* **free-for-alls**) a disorganized contest or situation in which anyone may take part.

freehand *adjective and adverb* drawn or written by hand without the aid of instruments.

freehold *noun* (*plural* **freeholds**) ownership of land or property with an unconditional right to sell it. ➤ **freeholder** *noun*.

free kick *noun* (*plural* **free kicks**) in football or rugby, an unhindered kick awarded after a breach of the rules by the other side.

freelance *noun* (*plural* **freelances**) a self-employed person who works for several companies. ➤ **freelance** *adjective and adverb*.

Freemason *noun* (*plural* **Freemasons**) a man who belongs to a men's secret society whose members offer each other support and friendship. ➤ **Freemasonry** *noun*.

free-range *adjective* **1** said about farm animals: reared in the open air and allowed to move about. **2** said about eggs: produced by free-range hens.

freesia *noun* (*plural* **freesias**) a plant with sweet-scented red, white, yellow, or purple flowers.

freestanding *adjective* standing alone; not supported by something else.

freethinker *noun* (*plural* **freethinkers**) a person who rejects or questions accepted opinions, especially about religion.

free trade *noun* trade based on the unrestricted international exchange of goods.

freewheel *verb* (**freewheels**, **freewheeling**, **freewheeled**) to ride along on a bicycle without using the pedals.

free will *noun* the ability to make your own moral choices.

freeze *verb* (**freezes**, **freezing**, **froze**, **frozen**) **1** said about a liquid: to turn solid from cold. **2** to convert a liquid to a solid by cold. **3** to become very cold. **4** to preserve food by maintaining it at a temperature below 0° Celsius. **5** to remain absolutely still. **6** not to allow something to change: *to freeze prices*. ~ *noun* (*plural* **freezes**) **1** a period of freezing cold weather. **2** an act of not allowing something to change: *a wage freeze*.

freezer *noun* (*plural* **freezers**) an insulated cabinet or room for freezing and storing food.

freezing *adjective* **1** *informal* very cold. **2** below 0° Celsius.

freight *noun* **1** goods transported

freighter *noun* (*plural* **freighters**) a ship or aircraft used chiefly to carry freight.

French fries *plural noun chiefly N American* chips.

French horn *noun* (*plural* **French horns**) *Music* a brass instrument with a coiled tube that flares out at the end.

French windows *plural noun* a pair of glass doors opening out from a house.

frenetic *adjective* frenzied or frantic. ➤ **frenetically** *adverb*.

frenzy *noun* (*plural* **frenzies**) a state of extreme agitation or excitement. ➤ **frenzied** *adjective*.

frequency *noun* (*plural* **frequencies**) **1** the rate at which something occurs over a period of time. **2** the state of happening often. **3** *Science* the number of complete oscillations per second of an electromagnetic wave.

frequent /free kwint/ *adjective* often repeated or occurring. ~ /free**kwent**/ *verb* (**frequents, frequenting, frequented**) to visit a place often or habitually. ➤ **frequently** *adverb*.

fresco *noun* (*plural* **frescoes** or **frescos**) *Art* a painting done by applying watercolours to plaster before it is dry.

fresh *adjective* **1** new or different. **2** newly come or arrived; inexperienced. **3** said about food: newly picked or made, not stale or preserved. **4** said about water: not salty. **5** said about air or weather: cool and invigorating. ➤ **freshly** *adverb*, **freshness** *noun*.

freshen *verb* (**freshens, freshening, freshened**) **1** to become, or to make something, fresh or fresher. **2** said about a wind: to increase in strength. ✶ **freshen up** to wash and tidy yourself.

fret[1] *verb* (**frets, fretting, fretted**) to be anxious and agitated. ➤ **fretful** *adjective*, **fretfully** *adverb*.

fret[2] *noun* (*plural* **frets**) *Music* each of a series of ridges fixed across the fingerboard of a guitar or other stringed instrument.

fretsaw *noun* (*plural* **fretsaws**) a saw consisting of a narrow blade held in a frame, which is used for cutting patterns in thin wood.

fretwork *noun* ornamental designs cut in thin wood.

friar *noun* (*plural* **friars**) a monk who does not stay in a monastery but goes out to do religious work among people in their communities.

friary *noun* (*plural* **friaries**) a building where friars live.

friction *noun* **1** the rubbing of one object against another. **2** disagreement between people.

Friday *noun* (*plural* **Fridays**) the sixth day of the week; the day of the week following Thursday.

fridge *noun* (*plural* **fridges**) a refrigerator.

fried *verb* past tense and past participle of FRY[1].

friend *noun* (*plural* **friends**) **1** a person you know and like. **2** somebody who supports a cause or institution. **3** (**Friend**) a Quaker. ✶ **make friends** to become friendly. ➤ **friendless** *adjective*, **friendship** *noun*.

friendly *adjective* (**friendlier, friendliest**) **1** like a friend; kind. **2** adapted to the needs of a particular kind of people: *user-friendly*. ~ *noun* (*plural* **friendlies**) a match not played as part of a competition. ➤ **friendliness** *noun*.

fries *plural noun chiefly N American* chips. ~ *verb* third person singular present tense of FRY[1].

frieze /freez/ *noun* (*plural* **friezes**) a sculptured or painted band on a wall or building.

frigate noun (plural **frigates**) a small warship.

fright noun (plural **frights**) 1 fear caused by sudden danger or shock. 2 informal something ugly or shocking.

frighten verb (**frightens, frightening, frightened**) 1 to make somebody afraid. 2 to force somebody into doing something by frightening them. ➤ **frightened** adjective, **frightening** adjective.

frightful adjective 1 causing fear or shock. 2 informal unpleasant or difficult. ➤ **frightfully** adverb.

frigid adjective 1 intensely cold. 2 unenthusiastic or unfriendly. ➤ **frigidity** noun.

frill noun (plural **frills**) 1 a gathered or pleated edging on clothing. 2 something decorative but not essential; a luxury. ➤ **frilly** adjective.

fringe noun (plural **fringes**) 1 an ornamental border of threads or tassels on a curtain or clothing. 2 a border or edge. 3 hair that falls over your forehead. ~ verb (**fringes, fringing, fringed**) 1 to decorate something with a fringe. 2 to be positioned along the edge of something: *a pond fringed with trees*.

fringe benefit noun (plural **fringe benefits**) an extra benefit received by an employee in addition to wages.

frisbee noun (plural **frisbees**) trademark a plastic disc thrown through the air from person to person for exercise or amusement.

frisk verb (**frisks, frisking, frisked**) 1 to leap or dance playfully. 2 informal to search a person by running your hands over their clothing.

frisky adjective (**friskier, friskiest**) lively and energetic.

fritter[1] noun (plural **fritters**) a piece of food fried in batter.

fritter[2] verb (**fritters, frittering, frittered**) ✱ **fritter away** to waste money or time gradually.

frivolous adjective 1 lacking value or purpose. 2 said about a person: unconcerned and carefree. ➤ **frivolity** noun, **frivolously** adverb.

frizz noun hair in a mass of tight curls.

frock noun (plural **frocks**) dated a woman's or girl's dress.

frog noun (plural **frogs**) a small jumping amphibious animal with a smooth skin and webbed feet. ✱ **have a frog in one's throat** to be hoarse.

frogman noun (plural **frogmen**) a diver equipped with a rubber suit, flippers, and an air supply for spending a long time underwater.

frogspawn noun a mass of frogs' eggs.

frolic verb (**frolics, frolicking, frolicked**) to play and run about happily. ~ noun (plural **frolics**) a light-hearted game. ➤ **frolicsome** adjective.

from preposition 1 used to indicate a starting point for a journey, process, or measurements: *from 1 to 10*. 2 used to indicate separation or removal: *far from home*. 3 used to indicate a source or cause: *suffering from the cold*.

frond noun (plural **fronds**) a leaf of a palm or fern.

front noun (plural **fronts**) 1 the part or surface of something that usually faces forward. 2 an area where fighting is taking place during a war. 3 a political coalition. 4 in weather forecasting, the edge of a mass of warm or cold air where it meets another mass. 5 something that masks a person's true identity or purpose. 6 a road or paved area next to the beach at a seaside resort. ~ adjective situated at the front. ✱ **in front of 1** directly ahead of somebody or something. 2 in the presence of somebody.

frontage noun (plural **frontages**) 1 the front of a building. 2 the land between the front of a building and the street.

front bench *noun* (*plural* **front benches**) a bench in the House of Commons on which party leaders sit. ➤ **front-bencher** *noun*.

frontier *noun* (*plural* **frontiers**) **1** a border between two countries. **2** a region at the edge of settled territory.

frontispiece *noun* (*plural* **frontispieces**) an illustration facing the title page of a book or magazine.

front line *noun* (*plural* **front lines**) an army's position nearest the enemy.

front-runner *noun* (*plural* **front-runners**) the leading contestant in a competition.

frost *noun* (*plural* **frosts**) **1** a covering of ice crystals formed on a cold surface when the temperature falls below freezing. **2** a period of freezing weather. ~ *verb* (**frosts, frosting, frosted**) to cover an object with frost.

frostbite *noun* damage to the body caused by partial freezing.

frosted *adjective* **1** covered with frost. **2** said about glass: having a roughened surface that is difficult to see through.

frosty *adjective* (**frostier, frostiest**) **1** marked by frost; freezing. **2** unfriendly. ➤ **frostily** *adverb*.

froth *noun* a mass of bubbles formed on or in a liquid. ➤ **frothy** *adjective*.

frown *verb* (**frowns, frowning, frowned**) **1** to wrinkle your forehead as a sign of anger, worry, or concentration. **2** (**frown on**) to disapprove of something. ~ *noun* (*plural* **frowns**) a frowning expression.

froze *verb* past tense of FREEZE.

frozen *verb* past participle of FREEZE.

frugal /froo gl/ *adjective* **1** economical in the use of resources. **2** small in quantity and costing little money: *a frugal meal.* ➤ **frugality** *noun*, **frugally** *adverb*.

fruit *noun* (*plural* **fruits**) **1** the part of a plant that contains a seed, especially one that has edible pulp. **2** edible fruits: *fruit and vegetables.* **3** a beneficial effect or consequence of an action. ➤ **fruity** *adjective*.

fruitful *adjective* having beneficial results; profitable. ➤ **fruitfully** *adverb*.

fruition *noun* the realization or fulfilment of a project.

fruitless *adjective* useless or unsuccessful. ➤ **fruitlessly** *adverb*.

fruit machine *noun* (*plural* **fruit machines**) a coin-operated gambling machine.

frustrate *verb* (**frustrates, frustrating, frustrated**) **1** to prevent somebody from carrying out a plan, or prevent a plan from being carried out. **2** to make somebody feel annoyed or helpless. ➤ **frustrating** *adjective*, **frustration** *noun*.

fry[1] *verb* (**fries, frying, fried**) **1** to cook food in hot oil or fat over direct heat. **2** *informal* to feel very hot in the sun. ➤ **fryer** *noun*.

fry[2] *plural noun* recently hatched fish.

frying pan *noun* (*plural* **frying pans**) a shallow pan with a long handle, used for frying food. ✽ **out of the frying pan into the fire** free of one difficulty only to encounter a worse one.

ft *abbreviation* foot or feet.

fuchsia /few sha/ *noun* (*plural* **fuchsias**) a shrub with deep-red or purple hanging flowers.

fuddled *adjective* confused and dazed.

fuddy-duddy *noun* (*plural* **fuddy-duddies**) *informal* a person who is old-fashioned and pompous.

fudge *noun* (*plural* **fudges**) **1** a soft creamy sweet made of sugar, milk, and butter. **2** a statement or decision that is deliberately vague.

fuel *noun* (*plural* **fuels**) a material used to produce heat or power when it is burned. ~ *verb* (**fuels, fuelling,**

further education

bring something closer to completion. ➤ **furtherance** *noun*.

Usage Note **further** or **farther**? See note at **farther**.

further education *noun* education for people who have left school.

furthermore *adverb* in addition; moreover.

furthest *adverb and adjective* to or at the greatest distance in space, time, or degree.

Usage Note **furthest** or **farthest**? See note at **farther**.

furtive *adjective* not wanting to be seen or found out. ➤ **furtively** *adverb*.

fury *noun* (*plural* **furies**) **1** intense or violent rage. **2** a violent or stormy state.

furze *noun* = GORSE.

fuse *noun* (*plural* **fuses**) **1** a device that sets off a bomb or an explosive, often a length of material that you set light to. **2** a device that interrupts an electrical circuit when the current exceeds a safe level. ~ *verb* (**fuses, fusing, fused**) **1** to blend two substances by melting them together. **2** to combine two or more things to form a whole, or to become combined. **3** to cause an electrical circuit to fail by activating a fuse: *When you turn the washing machine on, it fuses the lights.*

fuselage /few zi lahzh/ *noun* (*plural* **fuselages**) the central body of an aircraft.

fusillade /few zi layd/ *noun* (*plural* **fusillades**) a number of shots fired simultaneously or in rapid succession.

fusion *noun* **1** the process of joining things to form a whole. **2** *Science* a process in which light atomic nuclei unite to form heavier nuclei, resulting in the release of large quantities of energy.

fuss *noun* **1** needless or useless bustle or excitement. **2** an objection or protest. ~ *verb* (**fusses, fussing, fussed**) **1** to pay too much attention to small details. **2** to become unnecessarily agitated or upset. ✱ **make a fuss of** to treat somebody very kindly and affectionately.

fusspot *noun* (*plural* **fusspots**) *informal* a person who fusses a lot.

fussy *adjective* (**fussier, fussiest**) **1** showing too much concern over details. **2** choosy and very hard to please. **3** having too much detail in its decoration. ➤ **fussily** *adverb*, **fussiness** *noun*.

fusty *adjective* (**fustier, fustiest**) **1** stale or smelling of damp. **2** old-fashioned.

futile *adjective* ineffective or pointless. ➤ **futilely** *adverb*, **futility** *noun*.

futon *noun* (*plural* **futons**) a padded quilt laid down to serve as a bed.

future *noun* **1** (**the future**) time that is to come. **2** a likelihood of success: *I'm not sure you have a future in this business.* **3** *English* in grammar, the verb tense that expresses action or state in the future. ~ *adjective* **1** that is to be. **2** *English* to do with the future tense. ✱ **in future** from now on.

futuristic *adjective* having very advanced design or technology and seeming to belong to the future rather than the present. ➤ **futuristically** *adverb*.

fuzz *noun* **1** fine light hairs or fibres. **2** (**the fuzz**) *informal* the police.

fuzzy *adjective* (**fuzzier, fuzziest**) **1** covered in fuzz. **2** blurred or indistinct. ➤ **fuzziness** *noun*.

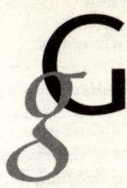

g *abbreviation* gram or grams.

gabble *verb* (**gabbles, gabbling, gabbled**) to talk rapidly or unintelligibly. ➤ **gabble** *noun*.

gaberdine *or* **gabardine** /ga ber deen/ *noun* a hard-wearing fabric used for making waterproof coats.

gable *noun* (*plural* **gables**) the triangular section of wall between two slopes of a pitched roof.

gad *verb* (**gads, gadding, gadded**) ✳ **gad about/around** to go from place to place in search of pleasure.

gadget *noun* (*plural* **gadgets**) a usually small and often novel tool or device. ➤ **gadgetry** *noun*.

Gaelic /gay lik *or* ga lik/ *noun* the Celtic languages of Ireland, the Isle of Man, and Scotland, or any one of them.

gaff *noun* (*plural* **gaffs**) a pole with a hook for landing heavy fish.

gaffe *noun* (*plural* **gaffes**) an embarrassing mistake.

gaffer *noun* (*plural* **gaffers**) *informal* a boss or foreman.

gag *noun* (*plural* **gags**) **1** something put over a person's mouth to stop them speaking. **2** a joke. ~ *verb* (**gags, gagging, gagged**) **1** to put a gag over the mouth of somebody. **2** to prevent somebody from saying what they want to. **3** to choke as if you are about to be sick.

gaga *adjective informal* **1** senile. **2** slightly mad.

gaggle *noun* (*plural* **gaggles**) a flock of geese.

gaiety *noun* cheerfulness or merriment.

gaily *adverb* **1** cheerfully or merrily. **2** with bright colours. **3** without thinking.

gain *verb* (**gains, gaining, gained**) **1** to get possession of, win, or acquire something. **2** to arrive at a place: *gain the harbour*. **3** to increase in speed, weight, etc. **4** to benefit or profit from something. **5** said about a watch or clock: to start to show a time ahead of the real time. **6** (**gain on**) to start catching up with somebody you are chasing. ~ *noun* (*plural* **gains**) **1** something acquired or won. **2** a profit. **3** an increase.

gainful *adjective* producing an income; useful or profitable: *gainful employment*. ➤ **gainfully** *adverb*.

gait *noun* (*plural* **gaits**) a way of walking.

gaiters *plural noun* cloth or leather leggings worn by men.

gal. *abbreviation* gallon or gallons.

gala /gah la/ *noun* (*plural* **galas**) **1** a public celebration or entertainment. **2** a special sports meeting.

galaxy *noun* (*plural* **galaxies**) **1** a large star system. **2** (**the Galaxy**) the Milky Way. ➤ **galactic** *adjective*.

gale *noun* (*plural* **gales**) a strong wind.

gall[1] *noun* **1** the boldness to do something offensive without embarrassment. **2** hatred or bitterness.

gall[2] *noun* (*plural* **galls**) a sore area on your skin that is caused by rubbing.

gallant

gallant *adjective* **1** courteous, honourable, and brave. **2** polite and attentive to women. ➤ **gallantly** *adverb*, **gallantry** *noun*.

gall bladder *noun* (*plural* **gall bladders**) a small bag-like organ, attached to the liver, in which bile is stored.

galleon *noun* (*plural* **galleons**) a large sailing ship with several decks, used for war or commerce.

gallery *noun* (*plural* **galleries**) **1** a room or building used for exhibitions of works of art. **2** a large balcony on an inside wall of a church or hall. **3** the highest seating area in a theatre. **4** a long and narrow room or passage.

galley *noun* (*plural* **galleys**) **1** a large single-decked ship propelled by oars. **2** a narrow kitchen, especially on a ship or aircraft.

galling *adjective* extremely irritating.

gallivant *verb* (**gallivants, gallivanting, gallivanted**) to roam about looking for enjoyment.

gallon *noun* (*plural* **gallons**) a unit used to measure liquids, equal to eight pints (4.546 litres).

gallop *noun* (*plural* **gallops**) **1** the fastest running speed of a horse. **2** a ride or run at a gallop. ~ *verb* (**gallops, galloping, galloped**) **1** to go or ride at a gallop. **2** to read, talk, move, or do something at great speed.

gallows *noun* (*plural* **gallows** or **gallowses**) a structure for hanging criminals.

gallstone *noun* (*plural* **gallstones**) a stone-like solid mass formed in the gall bladder or bile ducts.

galore *adjective* in great numbers: *bargains galore*.

galoshes *plural noun* rubber shoes worn over ordinary shoes.

galvanize or **galvanise** *verb* (**galvanizes, galvanizing, galvanized** or **galvanises**, etc) **1** to stimulate or shock somebody into action. **2** to coat iron or steel with zinc to protect it from rust. ➤ **galvanized** or **galvanised** *adjective*.

gambit *noun* (*plural* **gambits**) **1** a move or remark that is intended to gain an advantage in some situation. **2** a set of opening moves in chess.

gamble *verb* (**gambles, gambling, gambled**) **1** to play a game of chance for money. **2** to take a risk with something in the hope of gaining an advantage. ~ *noun* (*plural* **gambles**) something involving an element of risk. ➤ **gambler** *noun*, **gambling** *noun*.

gambol *verb* (**gambols, gambolling, gambolled**) to jump about in a playful way.

game *noun* (*plural* **games**) **1** an organized activity or competition that children or adults engage in for fun. **2** a sports match or similar contest. **3** one part of a larger contest, especially a tennis match. **4** (**games**) an organized event with contests in various types of sport. **5** (**games**) a lesson or period at school devoted to sports. **6** animals that are hunted, especially wild mammals, birds, and fish. ~ *adjective* ready to take risks or try something new. ✻ **give the game away** to reveal a secret. ➤ **gamely** *adverb*.

gamekeeper *noun* (*plural* **gamekeepers**) somebody who breeds and protects game animals or birds on a private estate.

game of chance *noun* (*plural* **games of chance**) a game in which the result cannot be predicted but depends on where a ball happens to stop, which card happens to be dealt, etc.

gamete /ga meet/ *noun* (*plural* **gametes**) *Science* a cell capable of fusing with a cell of the other sex to begin the development of a new organism.

gaming *noun* gambling.

gammon *noun* ham that has been smoked or cured.

gamut /gamut/ *noun* an entire range or series. ✱ **run the gamut** to go through the whole range of something.

gander *noun* (*plural* **ganders**) an adult male goose.

gang *noun* (*plural* **gangs**) **1** a group of criminals. **2** a group of people working together, for example as labourers. **3** a group of people who regularly spend time together. ~ *verb* (**gangs, ganging, ganged**) ✱ **gang up on** to form a group to attack somebody.

gangling *adjective* tall, thin, and awkward.

gangplank *noun* (*plural* **gangplanks**) = GANGWAY.

gangrene /gang green/ *noun* the decay of soft tissues in an area of the body due to a loss of blood supply. ➤ **gangrenous** *adjective*.

gangster *noun* (*plural* **gangsters**) a member of a criminal gang.

gangway *noun* (*plural* **gangways**) **1** a narrow passage, for example between sections of seats in a theatre. **2** a movable bridge used to board a ship from a quay or another ship

gannet *noun* (*plural* **gannets**) a large white fish-eating seabird.

gantry *noun* (*plural* **gantries**) a raised framework extending across something and on which something, such as a railway signal or a travelling crane, is mounted.

gaol *noun and verb* see JAIL.

gap *noun* (*plural* **gaps**) **1** a break in a wall or hedge. **2** an empty space between two objects. **3** an interval. **4** a large difference: *the gap between the wealthiest and the poorest*.

gape *verb* (**gapes, gaping, gaped**) **1** to open or part widely. **2** to gaze at something with your mouth open in surprise or wonder. ➤ **gaping** *adjective*.

gap year *noun* (*plural* **gap years**) a year's break between leaving school and starting college or university.

garage *noun* (*plural* **garages**) **1** a building where motor vehicles are kept. **2** a place where motor vehicles can be repaired or supplied with fuel. ~ *verb* (**garages, garaging, garaged**) to keep or put a car in a garage.

garb *noun* a style of clothing; dress. ~ *verb* (**garbs, garbing, garbed**) *literary* to dress somebody in something.

garbage *noun chiefly N American* **1** rubbish or waste. **2** nonsense.

garble *verb* (**garbles, garbling, garbled**) to make mistakes in a message when writing it down or transmitting it, so that it becomes unintelligible.

garden *noun* (*plural* **gardens**) **1** an area of ground, usually beside a house, where vegetables and flowers are grown. **2** (*also* **gardens**) a public park. ~ *verb* (**gardens, gardening, gardened**) to do work in a garden. ✱ **lead somebody up the garden path** to mislead or deceive somebody. ➤ **gardener** *noun*, **gardening** *noun*.

gargle *verb* (**gargles, gargling, gargled**) to wash out the back of your throat by blowing air up from your lungs through liquid held in your mouth. ~ *noun* (*plural* **gargles**) **1** a liquid used in gargling. **2** an act or the sound of gargling.

gargoyle *noun* (*plural* **gargoyles**) a rainwater spout in the form of a grotesque human or animal figure projecting from a roof gutter.

garish /gairish/ *adjective* excessively or unpleasantly brightly coloured. ➤ **garishly** *adverb*.

garland *noun* (*plural* **garlands**) a wreath of flowers or leaves worn as an

garlic

ornament or trophy. ~ *verb* (**garlands, garlanding, garlanded**) to hang a garland on somebody or something.

garlic *noun* the strong-smelling bulb of a plant of the lily family, used as a flavouring in cookery.

garment *noun* (*plural* **garments**) an article of clothing.

garner *verb* (**garners, garnering, garnered**) to collect evidence or information.

garnet *noun* (*plural* **garnets**) a deep red gemstone.

garnish *verb* (**garnishes, garnishing, garnished**) to decorate something especially a dish of food. ~ *noun* (*plural* **garnishes**) a decorative addition to a dish of food.

garret *noun* (*plural* **garrets**) a small room just under the roof of a house.

garrison *noun* (*plural* **garrisons**) a force of troops stationed in a town or fortress to defend it. ~ *verb* (**garrisons, garrisoning, garrisoned**) to station troops in a place.

garrotte /ga rot/ *noun* (*plural* **garrottes**) a wire or cord used for strangling somebody. ~ *verb* (**garrottes, garrotting, garrotted**) to kill somebody with a garrotte.

garrulous /ga ru lus/ *adjective* excessively talkative. ➤ **garrulity** *noun*.

garter *noun* (*plural* **garters**) a band worn to hold up a stocking or sock.

gas *noun* (*plural* **gases**) **1** *Science* a substance, such as air, oxygen, or hydrogen, that is neither liquid nor solid and tends to expand indefinitely. **2** a gas or mixture of gases used as a fuel or anaesthetic. **3** *N American, informal* petrol. ~ *verb* (**gasses, gassing, gassed**) **1** to poison or kill a person or animal with gas. **2** *informal* to talk idly. ➤ **gaseous** *adjective*.

gas chamber *noun* (*plural* **gas chambers**) a room in which prisoners are executed or animals killed by poison gas.

gash *noun* (*plural* **gashes**) a deep long cut. ~ *verb* (**gashes, gashing, gashed**) to injure or damage somebody or something with a deep long cut.

gas mask *noun* (*plural* **gas masks**) a mask with a chemical air filter, used as a protection against harmful gases.

gasoline *noun* N American petrol.

gasometer /ga so mi ter/ *noun* (*plural* **gasometers**) a large cylindrical building that is a storage container for gas.

gasp *verb* (**gasps, gasping, gasped**) **1** to breathe in suddenly and loudly, for example with shock. **2** to breathe with difficulty. **3** to say something while gasping. ~ *noun* (*plural* **gasps**) a sudden loud intake of breath.

gassy *adjective* (**gassier, gassiest**) fizzy.

gastric *adjective* to do with the stomach.

gastronomy *noun* the art or science of good eating. ➤ **gastronomic** *adjective*.

gastropod *noun* (*plural* **gastropods**) *Science* an animal such as a snail or slug that has a single large flattened foot.

gasworks *noun* (*plural* **gasworks**) a place where gas is manufactured.

gate *noun* (*plural* **gates**) **1** a hinged frame that closes an opening in a wall or fence. **2** an exit from an airport building to the airfield. **3** a barrier in a canal lock or at a level crossing. **4** the number of spectators at a sporting event.

gateau /ga toh/ *noun* (*plural* **gateaux** /ga tohz/ or **gateaus**) a rich cream cake.

gate-crash *verb* (**gate-crashes, gate-crashing, gate-crashed**) to attend a party without an invitation. ➤ **gatecrasher** noun.

gatepost noun (plural **gateposts**) the post on which a gate is hung or against which it closes.

gateway noun (plural **gateways**) **1** an opening for a gate. **2** a point at which you enter something or can begin to progress towards something: *the gateway to success in business*.

gather verb (**gathers, gathering, gathered**) **1** to bring things together in one place. **2** to come together to form a group or mass. **3** to pick flowers or harvest crops. **4** to prepare yourself for an effort. **5** to pull fabric together to create small tucks. **6** to reach a conclusion from what you have heard or been told: *I gather you've had a hard time*. * **gather speed** to go faster.

gathering noun (plural **gatherings**) an assembly or meeting.

gauche /gohsh/ adjective lacking social experience or grace.

gaudy adjective (**gaudier, gaudiest**) excessively and tastelessly colourful or ornamented. ➤ **gaudily** adverb.

gauge /gayj/ noun (plural **gauges**) **1** an instrument that measures or tests something and indicates the result on a dial, etc: *a fuel gauge*. **2** a measurement of thickness, for example of thin metal or plastic sheets, or of diameter, for example of wire. **3** the distance between the rails of a railway. ~ verb (**gauges, gauging, gauged**) **1** to estimate or judge the size or capacity of something. **2** to measure something with a gauge.

gaunt adjective looking thin and as if you have suffered a lot.

gauntlet[1] noun (plural **gauntlets**) **1** a strong protective glove with a wide part above the wrist. **2** a glove formerly worn with medieval armour.

* **throw down the gauntlet** to issue a challenge.

gauntlet[2] * **run the gauntlet** to have to suffer criticism or a testing experience in order to achieve something.

gauze noun **1** a thin, often transparent, fabric. **2** a fine mesh of metal or plastic. ➤ **gauzy** adjective.

gave verb past tense of GIVE.

gavel /gavil/ noun (plural **gavels**) a small hammer used by a chairman or judge to get people's attention or by an auctioneer to announce that something is sold.

gawky adjective (**gawkier, gawkiest**) awkward and lanky.

gawp verb (**gawps, gawping, gawped**) informal to gape or stare stupidly.

gay adjective **1** homosexual. **2** to do with homosexuals. **3** bright or attractive. **4** happy and carefree. ~ noun (plural **gays**) a homosexual, especially a homosexual man.

gaze verb (**gazes, gazing, gazed**) to look steadily at somebody or something. ~ noun (plural **gazes**) a fixed intent look.

gazelle noun (plural **gazelles** or **gazelle**) a small graceful antelope.

gazette noun (plural **gazettes**) a newspaper or journal, especially a journal containing official announcements.

gazetteer /gazɪteer/ noun (plural **gazetteers**) a dictionary of place names.

GB abbreviation **1** (also **Gb**) gigabyte or gigabytes. **2** Great Britain.

GBH abbreviation grievous bodily harm.

GCSE noun (plural **GCSEs**) = *General Certificate of Secondary Education*, an examination taken in school or college at about the age of 15 or 16, or a qualification gained by passing this examination.

gear noun (plural **gears**) **1** a set of interlocking cogwheels that is part of the

gearbox

system transmitting power from the engine of a vehicle to its wheels. **2** a setting of the transmission system that makes the vehicle go in a particular direction or at a particular speed: *second gear*. **3** equipment. **4** *informal* clothing. ~ *verb* (**gears, gearing, geared**) (**gear to**) to adjust something to meet the needs of something else: *geared to the needs of young people*. ✶ **gear up** to make somebody ready or equipped to do something.

gearbox *noun* (*plural* **gearboxes**) a set of vehicle gears or the protective casing enclosing them.

geek *noun* (*plural* **geeks**) *informal* **1** somebody unfashionable or socially awkward. **2** somebody obsessively interested in computers and technology.

geese *noun* plural of GOOSE.

geezer *noun* (*plural* **geezers**) *informal* a man.

Geiger counter /gie ger kown ter/ *noun* (*plural* **Geiger counters**) an instrument for detecting and measuring radioactivity.

geisha /gay sha/ *noun* (*plural* **geishas** *or* **geisha**) a Japanese woman trained to provide entertaining and light-hearted company for men.

gel *noun* (*plural* **gels**) a jelly-like substance. ~ *verb* (**gels, gelling, gelled**) **1** said about a liquid: to set. **2** said about an idea, plan, etc: to become definite. **3** said about a group of people: to get on well together. **4** to put gel on your hair.

gelatin /je la tin/ *or* **gelatine** /je la teen/ *noun* a jelly-like material obtained from animal tissues by boiling, used in food, for example to set jellies, and in photography.

geld /geld/ *verb* (**gelds, gelding, gelded**) to castrate a male animal.

gelding *noun* (*plural* **geldings**) a castrated male horse.

gelignite /je lig niet/ *noun* a type of dynamite.

gem *noun* (*plural* **gems**) **1** a precious stone. **2** somebody or something excellent.

Gemini *noun* the third sign of the zodiac (the Twins).

gemstone *noun* (*plural* **gemstones**) a precious stone used for example in jewellery.

gendarme /zhong dahm/ *noun* (*plural* **gendarmes**) a member of an armed police force, especially in France.

gender *noun* (*plural* **genders**) **1** *English* in some languages, any of two or more grammatical classes of nouns, such as masculine, feminine, or neuter. **2** the state of being male or female, especially as regards cultural and social differences. **3** the members of one or other sex.

gene *noun* (*plural* **genes**) a unit of DNA that is carried on a chromosome and controls the way in which characteristics are passed from parents to children.

genealogy /jee ni a lo ji/ *noun* (*plural* **genealogies**) **1** a description of the way in which a person or family is descended from their ancestors. **2** the study of family histories. ➤ **genealogical** *adjective*, **genealogist** *noun*.

genera *noun* plural of GENUS.

general *adjective* **1** involving most members of a class, kind, or group. **2** concerned with the main aspects of something rather than particular details. **3** ranking above others with the same title: *the general manager*. ~ *noun* (*plural* **generals**) **1** a commander of an army. **2** an officer in the British army ranking below a field marshal. ✶ **in general** usually; for the most part.

general anaesthetic *noun* (*plural* **general anaesthetics**) an anaesthetic that causes loss of consciousness and lack of sensation over the whole body.

general election *noun* (*plural* **general elections**) an election in which candidates are elected in all constituencies of a nation.

generality *noun* (*plural* **generalities**) a statement that applies to most cases, but which may be rather vague and without specific details or examples.

generalize *or* **generalise** *verb* (**generalizes, generalizing, generalized** *or* **generalises,** etc) to make statements that apply to most cases, but that may not be relevant to a particular situation and may be rather vague. ➤ **generalization** *or* **generalisation** *noun*.

generally *adverb* **1** without regard to specific cases. **2** usually; as a rule.

general practitioner *noun* (*plural* **general practitioners**) a medical doctor who treats all types of disease. ➤ **general practice** *noun*.

generate *verb* (**generates, generating, generated**) to create or be the cause of something.

generation *noun* (*plural* **generations**) **1** all the people born and living at the same time. **2** a group forming a single stage in the development of a family. **3** a period of about 30 years, equal to the average time between the birth of parents and the birth of their children. **4** production or creation.

generator *noun* (*plural* **generators**) a machine for producing electrical energy.

generic /ji ne rik/ *adjective* characteristic of a whole group or class. ➤ **generically** *adverb*.

generous *adjective* **1** giving money, help, etc freely. **2** large: *a generous helping*. ➤ **generosity** *noun*, **generously** *adverb*.

genesis /je ni sis/ *noun* the origin or coming into being of something.

genetic *adjective* Science **1** to do with genetics. **2** to do with genes. ➤ **genetically** *adverb*.

genetically modified *adjective* Science said about food: containing an ingredient that has had its genetic structure altered, for example to make it grow better.

genetics *noun* Science the branch of biology that deals with the ways in which characteristics are passed from parents to children. ➤ **geneticist** *noun*.

genial *adjective* cheerfully good-tempered. ➤ **geniality** *noun*, **genially** *adverb*.

genie *noun* (*plural* **genies**) a spirit in Arabian folklore who can be summoned to grant wishes.

genital *adjective* to do with the reproductive organs. ~ *noun* (**genitals**) the external reproductive and sexual organs.

genius *noun* (*plural* **geniuses**) **1** a person of a very high intelligence or skill. **2** extraordinary intellectual power.

genocide *noun* the deliberate murder of all the members of a racial or cultural group. ➤ **genocidal** *adjective*.

genre /*zho*n ra/ *noun* Art, Music, English a general category to which many artistic works belong.

gent *noun* (*plural* **gents**) *informal* a gentleman.

genteel *adjective* showing, or trying to show, upper-class refinement or manners. ➤ **gentility** *noun*.

gentile *noun* (*plural* **gentiles**) (*often* **Gentile**) a non-Jewish person. ➤ **gentile** *adjective*.

gentle *adjective* (**gentler, gentlest**) **1** said about a person: kind and mild; not harsh or violent. **2** soft or delicate. **3** said about a breeze: moderate. **4** said about a slope: not steep. ➤ **gentleness** *noun*, **gently** *adverb*.

gentleman *noun* (*plural* **gentlemen**) **1** a man who is courteous and honourable. **2** a man belonging to the gentry

gentry

or nobility. **3** in polite or formal use: a man. ➤ **gentlemanly** *adjective*.

gentry *noun* the class of land-owning people next below the nobility.

genuflect /je new flekt/ *verb* (**genuflects, genuflecting, genuflected**) to go down on one knee briefly, as a gesture of respect to sacred objects. ➤ **genuflection** *noun*.

genuine *adjective* **1** actually what it is claimed to be. **2** sincere. ➤ **genuinely** *adverb*.

genus /jee nus/ *noun* (*plural* **genera** /je ni ra/) *Science* a class of living things made up of related species.

geography *noun* the science that deals with the earth, its physical features, and the distribution of plant, animal, and human life over its surface.
➤ **geographer** *noun*, **geographic** *adjective*, **geographical** *adjective*, **geographically** *adverb*.

geology *noun* the science that deals with the structure and history of the earth, especially as recorded in rocks. ➤ **geological** *adjective*, **geologically** *adverb*, **geologist** *noun*.

geometric *adjective* **1** relating to geometry. **2** using patterns formed with straight and curved lines. ➤ **geometrical** *adjective*, **geometrically** *adverb*.

geometry *noun Maths* a branch of mathematics that deals with points, lines, angles, surfaces, and solids.

Georgian *adjective* dating from the reigns of the first four King Georges of Britain (1714–1830).

geranium *noun* (*plural* **geraniums**) a garden plant with red, pink, or white flowers.

gerbil *noun* (*plural* **gerbils**) a burrowing desert rodent with long hind legs.

geriatric *adjective* **1** to do with very elderly people. **2** *informal* aged or decrepit. ~ *noun* (*plural* **geriatrics**) an elderly person.

germ *noun* (*plural* **germs**)
1 a micro-organism, especially one that causes disease. **2** a small mass of cells capable of developing into an organism. **3** the very early state from which something develops: *the germ of an idea*.

Germanic *adjective* to do with a family of languages including English, German, Dutch, Danish, Swedish, and Norwegian, or with the people who speak these languages.

German measles *noun* = RUBELLA.

German shepherd *noun* (*plural* **German shepherds**) = ALSATIAN.

germicide *noun* (*plural* **germicides**) a substance that kills germs. ➤ **germicidal** *adjective*.

germinate *verb* (**germinates, germinating, germinated**) to begin to grow; to sprout. ➤ **germination** *noun*.

gerrymander *verb* (**gerrymanders, gerrymandering, gerrymandered**) to deliberately divide an area into voting districts in such a way as to give your political party an advantage over its opponents.

Word History *Gerrymander* is a combination of the surname of Elbridge *Gerry*, the governor of the US state of Massachusetts in the early 19th century, and *salamander*, an animal that looks like a lizard. When the voting districts in Massachusetts were rearranged by Governor Gerry's party to give themselves an advantage in elections, they formed a shape that some people thought was rather like a salamander. His opponents called it a 'gerrymander'.

---

gerund *noun* (*plural* **gerunds**) *English* a noun ending in *-ing* that is formed from a verb, such as 'singing' in *He likes singing*.

Gestapo /gi stah poh/ *noun History* the secret police in Nazi Germany.

gestation /je stay shn/ *noun Science* the

process of development of an unborn child or animal in the womb.

gesticulate /je sti kew layt/ *verb* (**gesticulates, gesticulating, gesticulated**) to make expressive gestures, especially when speaking.
➤ **gesticulation** *noun*.

gesture /jes cher/ *noun* (*plural* **gestures**) **1** a movement of your body or your arms or legs that expresses something, such as a feeling or an order. **2** something said or done as a sign of what you feel: *Sending a thank-you card would be a nice gesture.*
~ *verb* (**gestures, gesturing, gestured**) to make a gesture: *They gestured to us to get out of the way.*

get *verb* (**gets, getting, got**) **1** to gain possession of something; to obtain or receive something. **2** to fetch something. **3** to capture something or somebody. **4** to succeed in achieving something. **5** to be affected by an illness: *get the measles.* **6** to cause something or somebody to come into a certain condition: *I must get my shoes mended.* **7** to persuade, ask, or force somebody to do something: *Get him to phone me back.* **8** to become: *to get drunk.* **9** to travel by a form of public transport: *get the bus.* **10** *informal* to hear or understand something said. **11** *informal* to punish or harm somebody. ✱ **get at 1** to reach something or somebody. **2** *informal* to criticize or tease somebody. **get away** to escape. **get away with** to avoid punishment or blame for something. **get by** to manage with difficulty or on limited resources. **get down to** to start to give attention to an activity. **get off** to escape punishment. **get on 1** to be on friendly terms. **2** to succeed. **get over 1** to overcome a difficulty.
2 to recover from an illness or unpleasant experience. **get round to** to eventually make a start on a task, etc. **get through to 1** to make yourself understood by somebody.
2 to make contact by telephone with somebody. **get up** to rise from a sitting or lying position, or from your bed. **get up to** *informal* to be involved in something wrong, mischievous, etc. **get your own back** to take revenge on somebody. **have got to** must.

getaway *noun* (*plural* **getaways**) a departure or escape.

get-together *noun* (*plural* **get-togethers**) an informal social gathering or meeting.

get-up *noun* (*plural* **get-ups**) *informal* an outfit or costume.

geyser /gee zer/ *noun* (*plural* **geysers**) a spring that throws out jets of hot water and steam.

ghastly *adjective* (**ghastlier, ghastliest**) **1** terrifyingly horrible.
2 *informal* intensely unpleasant or objectionable. **3** pale and ill.
➤ **ghastliness** *noun*.

gherkin *noun* (*plural* **gherkins**) a small pickled cucumber.

ghetto *noun* (*plural* **ghettos** *or* **ghettoes**) **1** an area of a city in which a minority group live. **2** part of a city in which Jews formerly lived.

ghetto blaster *noun* (*plural* **ghetto blasters**) *informal* a large portable radio.

ghost *noun* (*plural* **ghosts**) the soul of a dead person seen by a living person.
➤ **ghostly** *adjective*.

ghost town *noun* (*plural* **ghost towns**) a town that was once busy and prosperous but is now deserted.

ghoul /goohl/ *noun* (*plural* **ghouls**)
1 an evil spirit or ghost. **2** a person with a morbid interest in fatal accidents, disasters, etc. ➤ **ghoulish** *adjective*.

giant *noun* (*plural* **giants**)
1 a legendary being, like a human in shape, but very tall and very strong.
2 an extraordinarily large person,

gibber /ji ber/ *verb* (**gibbers, gibbering, gibbered**) to make rapid and incomprehensible sounds, usually because you are frightened.

gibberish *noun* unintelligible or meaningless language.

gibbet /ji bit/ *noun* (*plural* **gibbets**) **1** a gallows. **2** an upright post with an arm, used formerly for displaying the bodies of executed criminals as a warning.

gibbon *noun* (*plural* **gibbons**) a small tailless ape from Southeast Asia with long arms to help it swing through the trees.

gibe *noun and verb* see JIBE.

giblets /jib lits/ *plural noun* the heart, liver, neck, and other edible internal organs of a chicken or other bird.

giddy *adjective* (**giddier, giddiest**) **1** feeling unsteady, as if everything is whirling round. **2** light-hearted and frivolous. ➤ **giddiness** *noun*.

gift *noun* (*plural* **gifts**) **1** something freely given by one person to another; a present or donation. **2** a natural talent.

gifted *adjective* having great natural ability or intelligence.

gig *noun* (*plural* **gigs**) *informal* a live performance by a singer, rock group, etc.

gigabyte *noun* (*plural* **gigabytes**) *ICT* a quantity of data equal to one thousand million bytes.

gigantic *adjective* unusually great; enormous.

giggle *verb* (**giggles, giggling, giggled**) to laugh in a silly or nervous manner. ~ *noun* (*plural* **giggles**) **1** an act of giggling. **2** *informal* something amusing. ➤ **giggly** *adjective*.

gild *verb* (**gilds, gilding, gilded**) to cover something with a thin covering of gold.

gill /jil/ *noun* (*plural* **gills**) a measure of liquid equal to a quarter of a pint (0.142 of a litre).

gills /gilz/ *plural noun* Science the organs that a fish has for taking in oxygen from water.

gilt *noun* gold leaf or gold paint laid on a surface. ~ *adjective* covered with gold or gilt.

gimlet /gim lit/ *noun* (*plural* **gimlets**) a T-shaped pointed tool for boring small holes in wood.

gimmick *noun* (*plural* **gimmicks**) a scheme or object intended to gain attention or publicity. ➤ **gimmickry** *noun*, **gimmicky** *adjective*.

gin[1] *noun* (*plural* **gins**) an alcoholic drink flavoured with juniper berries.

gin[2] *noun* (*plural* **gins**) **1** a machine for separating cotton fibre from seeds and waste material. **2** a snare for catching animals.

ginger *noun* **1** the root of a tropical plant, which has a strong hot taste and is dried and ground to make a spice. **2** a reddish or yellowish brown colour. ~ *verb* (**gingers, gingering, gingered**) ✳ **ginger up** to make something or somebody more lively.

ginger ale *noun* (*plural* **ginger ales**) a sweet fizzy non-alcoholic drink flavoured with ginger.

ginger beer *noun* (*plural* **ginger beers**) a weak fizzy alcoholic drink, made by fermenting ginger and syrup.

gingerbread *noun* a thick cake made with treacle and flavoured with ginger.

gingerly *adverb* very cautiously or carefully.

gingham /ging am/ *noun* a light cotton fabric with a checked pattern.

gipsy *noun* see GYPSY.

giraffe *noun* (*plural* **giraffes** or **giraffe**) a large African animal with long legs and a very long neck.

girder *noun* (*plural* **girders**) a strong horizontal metal beam.

girdle *noun* (*plural* **girdles**) **1** a belt or cord encircling the waist. **2** a woman's tightly fitting undergarment that extends from the waist to below the hips.

girl *noun* (*plural* **girls**) **1** a female child. **2** a young woman. **3** a girlfriend. ➤ **girlish** *adjective*.

girlfriend *noun* (*plural* **girlfriends**) **1** a regular female companion with whom somebody is romantically or sexually involved. **2** a female friend.

giro /jier oh/ *noun* (*plural* **giros**) **1** a computerized system for transferring money from one bank or post office account to another. **2** *informal* a giro cheque or payment, especially for a social security benefit.

girth *noun* (*plural* **girths**) **1** a measurement round something, such as a tree trunk or somebody's waist. **2** a strap that passes under the body of a horse to fasten a saddle on its back.

gist /jist/ *noun* (**the gist**) the main point of something said or written.

give *verb* (**gives, giving, gave, given**) **1** to pass or transfer something to another person so that they can own or use it. **2** to offer advice, a promise, a reason, etc. **3** to provide or organize something: *to give a party*. **4** to cause somebody to experience or suffer something: *You gave me a fright*. **5** to utter a sound. **6** to collapse or bend under pressure. ~ *noun* the capacity to bend to pressure. ✽ **give away 1** to make a present of something. **2** to reveal a secret. **give in** to yield or surrender. **give out 1** to distribute something. **2** said about a supply: to come to an end. **give up 1** to abandon an activity and admit that you have failed. **2** to discontinue a habit. **give way 1** to allow somebody to pass or go first. **2** to collapse under pressure. ➤ **giver** *noun*.

giveaway *noun* (*plural* **giveaways**) **1** an unintentional revelation. **2** something given free or at a reduced price.

given *verb* past participle of GIVE. ~ *adjective* fixed; specified. ~ *preposition* in view of. ✽ **given to** having a tendency to do something: *given to exaggeration*.

gizmo or **gismo** /giz moh/ *noun* (*plural* **gizmos** or **gismos**) *informal* a gadget.

gizzard /gi zad/ *noun* (*plural* **gizzards**) a part of the digestive system of birds, with thick muscular walls for breaking up and grinding food.

glacé /gla say/ *adjective* said about fruit: coated with a sugar glaze; candied.

glacial /glay shl/ *adjective* **1** *Geography* to do with glaciers. **2** extremely cold.

glaciation /glay si ay shn/ *noun* *Geography* the process of forming ice or glaciers.

glacier /gla si er/ *noun* (*plural* **glaciers**) *Geography* a large mass of ice moving slowly down a slope.

glad *adjective* (**gladder, gladdest**) **1** pleased or delighted. **2** causing happiness. **3** (**glad of**) grateful for something; pleased to have something. ➤ **gladly** *adverb*, **gladness** *noun*.

gladden *verb* (**gladdens, gladdening, gladdened**) to make somebody glad.

glade *noun* (*plural* **glades**) an open space in a wood or forest.

gladiator *noun* (*plural* **gladiators**) *History* a man trained to fight in a public arena in ancient Rome or other Roman towns. ➤ **gladiatorial** *adjective*.

glamorize or **glamorise** *verb* (**glamorizes, glamorizing, glamorized** or **glamorises**, etc) to make something seem more attractive, romantic, or

glamour

exciting than it really is. ➤ **glamorization** *or* **glamorisation** *noun*.

glamour *noun* a romantic and exciting attractiveness. ➤ **glamorous** *adjective*.

glance *verb* (**glances, glancing, glanced**) to take a quick look at something. ~ *noun* (*plural* **glances**) a quick look. * **glance off** to strike a surface at an angle and bounce off it also at an angle.

gland *noun* (*plural* **glands**) *Science* an organ of the body that secretes chemical substances. ➤ **glandular** *adjective*.

glare *verb* (**glares, glaring, glared**) **1** to stare angrily or fiercely at somebody. **2** to shine with a harsh light. ~ *noun* (*plural* **glares**) **1** an angry or fierce stare. **2** a harsh uncomfortably bright light.

glaring *adjective* very obvious: *a glaring error.*

glass *noun* (*plural* **glasses**) **1** a hard brittle substance you can see through, used for example in windows. **2** a glass container that you drink out of. **3** a mirror. **4** a barometer. **5** (**glasses**) a pair of glass lenses in a frame, worn in front of your eyes to correct defects of vision or for protection. ➤ **glassy** *adjective*.

glass fibre *noun* = FIBREGLASS.

glaze *verb* (**glazes, glazing, glazed**) **1** to fit glass into a window frame or door. **2** to coat food or pottery with a glaze. ~ *noun* (*plural* **glazes**) a liquid coating applied to pottery or food, which hardens to give a glossy finish. ➤ **glazing** *noun*.

glazier /glay zi er/ *noun* (*plural* **glaziers**) a person who fits glass into windows and doors.

gleam *noun* (*plural* **gleams**) **1** a shine from reflected light or a weak flash of light. **2** a brief or faint indication of emotion, etc. ~ *verb* (**gleams, gleaming, gleamed**) to shine, especially with reflected light.

glean *verb* (**gleans, gleaning, gleaned**) **1** to gather grain left behind by reapers. **2** to gather information bit by bit.

glee *noun* a feeling of joy or delight. ➤ **gleeful** *adjective*, **gleefully** *adverb*.

glen *noun* (*plural* **glens**) *Geography* a narrow valley, especially in Scotland or Ireland.

glib *adjective* (**glibber, glibbest**) clever in speaking or writing, but often superficial or dishonest. ➤ **glibly** *adverb*.

glide *verb* (**glides, gliding, glided**) **1** to move in a smooth, continuous, and effortless manner. **2** said about an aircraft: to fly without the use of engines. ➤ **glide** *noun*.

glider *noun* (*plural* **gliders**) a light aircraft without an engine.

glimmer *verb* (**glimmers, glimmering, glimmered**) to shine faintly or unsteadily. ~ *noun* (*plural* **glimmers**) **1** a feeble or unsteady light. **2** a small sign or amount.

glimpse *verb* (**glimpses, glimpsing, glimpsed**) to see something or somebody briefly or partially. ~ *noun* (*plural* **glimpses**) a brief look or partial view.

glint *verb* (**glints, glinting, glinted**) to shine with tiny bright flashes. ~ *noun* (*plural* **glints**) a tiny bright flash of reflected light.

glisten *verb* (**glistens, glistening, glistened**) to shine like a wet or oily surface.

glitch *noun* (*plural* **glitches**) *informal* a temporary breakdown or setback.

glitter *verb* (**glitters, glittering, glittered**) to shine by reflection in bright flashes. ~ *noun* **1** bright shimmering reflected light. **2** small sparkling particles used for ornamentation. ➤ **glittery** *adjective*.

glitz *noun informal* superficial glamour.

gloaming *noun* (**the gloaming**) *literary* twilight or dusk.

gloat verb (**gloats, gloating, gloated**) to talk about something, especially your own achievements or another person's misfortunes, with great satisfaction. ➤ **gloating** adjective.

global adjective **1** involving the entire world. **2** general; comprehensive. ➤ **globally** adverb.

global warming noun Science an increase in the average temperature of the earth's atmosphere, believed to be caused by the greenhouse effect.

globe noun (plural **globes**) **1** a sphere with a map on it representing the earth. **2** (**the globe**) the world; the earth. **3** something spherical or rounded, such as a glass bowl or light.

globe artichoke noun see ARTICHOKE.

globetrotter noun (plural **globetrotters**) informal somebody who travels widely. ➤ **globetrotting** noun and adjective.

globule /glo bewl/ noun (plural **globules**) a tiny ball or drop, especially of liquid. ➤ **globular** adjective.

gloom noun **1** partial or total darkness. **2** a sad or depressed state.

gloomy adjective (**gloomier, gloomiest**) **1** dismally or depressingly dark. **2** feeling or causing sadness. ➤ **gloomily** adverb.

glorify verb (**glorifies, glorifying, glorified**) **1** to make something appear admirable or splendid. **2** to give praise to God. ➤ **glorification** noun.

glorious adjective **1** deserving honour and praise. **2** very beautiful, splendid, or excellent. ➤ **gloriously** adverb.

glory noun (plural **glories**) **1** honour or fame won for a special achievement. **2** praise and thanksgiving offered to God. **3** something that is splendid or magnificent. ~ verb (**glories, glorying, gloried**) (**glory in**) informal to take great pride or pleasure in something.

gloss[1] noun **1** a shiny quality on a surface. **2** something that gives this: *lip gloss*. **3** a deceptively attractive outer appearance. **4** paint that gives a shiny finish. ~ verb (**glosses, glossing, glossed**) (**gloss over**) to try to hide something undesirable by not saying much about it.

gloss[2] noun (plural **glosses**) a brief explanation or translation of a difficult word or expression. ~ verb (**glosses, glossing, glossed**) to supply a gloss for a word, text, etc.

glossary noun (plural **glossaries**) a list of terms used in a particular text or a specialized field, with their meanings.

glossy adjective (**glossier, glossiest**) shiny and smooth.

glove noun (plural **gloves**) **1** a close-fitting covering for the hand with separate sections for each of the fingers and the thumb. **2** a padded covering for the fist worn by a boxer.

glow verb (**glows, glowing, glowed**) **1** to shine with a steady light. **2** said about the complexion: to have a strong healthy colour. **3** to show great pleasure or satisfaction. ~ noun **1** a steady light. **2** a satisfying feeling, for example of pride.

glower /glow er/ verb (**glowers, glowering, glowered**) to stare at somebody in an angry or threatening way. ➤ **glower** noun.

glowing adjective highly appreciative; containing lots of praise.

glow-worm noun (plural **glow-worms**) a type of beetle that emits light from its abdomen.

glucose noun Science a simple natural sugar that is the usual form in which carbohydrate is absorbed and used in the body.

glue noun (plural **glues**) a substance used for sticking things together. ~ verb (**glues, glueing** or **gluing, glued**) to stick something tightly to something with glue. * **be glued to**

glum *adjective* (**glummer, glummest**) sad; downcast. ➤ **glumly** *adverb*.

glut *noun* (*plural* **gluts**) an excessive supply of something.

gluten /glooh tn/ *noun* a protein substance in wheat flour that gives dough its sticky properties.

glutinous /glooh ti nus/ *adjective* thick and sticky.

glutton *noun* (*plural* **gluttons**) somebody who habitually eats and drinks too much. ✱ **glutton for punishment** somebody who is keen to take on difficult or unpleasant tasks. ➤ **gluttonous** *adjective*, **gluttony** *noun*.

glycerin /gli si rin/ *or* **glycerine** /gli si reen *or* gli si rin/ *noun* a sweet syrupy fluid obtained from fats and used in medicines.

GM *abbreviation* genetically modified.

gm *abbreviation* gram or grams.

GMT *abbreviation* Greenwich Mean Time.

gnarled /nahld/ *adjective* **1** said about a tree: covered with knots or lumps. **2** said about hands, etc: rough and twisted, especially with age.

gnash /nash/ *verb* (**gnashes, gnashing, gnashed**) to grind your teeth together.

gnat /nat/ *noun* (*plural* **gnats**) a small two-winged fly that bites.

gnaw /naw/ *verb* (**gnaws, gnawing, gnawed**) **1** to bite or chew on something hard, such as a bone, and nibble bits of it away. **2** to cause continuous pain or anxiety.

gnome /nohm/ *noun* (*plural* **gnomes**) in folklore, a dwarf who lives under the ground and guards treasure.

gnu /noo/ *noun* (*plural* **gnus** *or* **gnu**) a large African antelope with a head like an ox and a short mane.

GNVQ *noun* (*plural* **GNVQs**) = *General National Vocational Qualification*, a qualification given for gaining skills of use in a particular job.

go *verb* (**goes, going, went, gone**) **1** to move; to travel. **2** to leave. **3** to extend from one point to another. **4** to make an expedition for a specified activity: *to go fishing*. **5** (**go to**) to attend an institution regularly: *go to school*. **6** to arrive at a specified state or condition: *to go mad; to go to sleep*. **7** to be used up. **8** to disappear. **9** to function, especially in the proper way: *I've managed to get the clock going again*. **10** to be compatible or harmonize with something. **11** to be capable of passing through or into something, or of being contained in something: *Those boxes won't all go in the car*. **12** to belong: *The knives go in that drawer*. **13** to make a sound: *to go pop*. ~ *noun* (*plural* **goes**) **1** a turn in an activity, such as a game. **2** an attempt; a try. **3** energy; vigour. ✱ **be going to** to be about to or intending to do something: *Is it going to rain?* **go ahead 1** to begin. **2** to continue or proceed. **go along with** to agree to or cooperate with somebody or something. **go back on** to fail to keep a promise. **go down 1** to decrease. **2** to sink. **3** to be received in a certain way: *The best man's speech went down well with the guests*. **go for 1** to try to gain something. **2** to choose something. **3** to attack somebody. **go in for 1** to engage in an activity. **2** to compete in a test or race. **go into 1** said about a number: to be contained in another number. **2** to investigate or explain something in depth. **go off 1** said about a bomb or firework: to explode. **2** said about food: to begin to decay. **3** *informal* to stop liking somebody or something. **go on 1** to continue. **2** to take place.

go out 1 to go to social events, entertainments, etc. **2** to spend time regularly with somebody in a romantic relationship. **3** to be extinguished. **go over** to examine, inspect, or check something. **go through 1** to examine, study, or discuss something. **2** to experience something difficult or unpleasant. **go without** to be deprived of something. **leave/let go of** to stop holding something or somebody. **on the go** *informal* constantly or restlessly active.

goad *noun* (*plural* **goads**) a pointed rod used to urge on an animal. ~ *verb* (**goads, goading, goaded**) to nag or annoy somebody until you make them do something.

go-ahead *adjective* energetic and ambitious. ~ *noun* (**the go-ahead**) permission to do something.

goal *noun* (*plural* **goals**) **1** in sport, a framework with a net into which players must put the ball in order to score. **2** an instance of scoring in football, etc. **3** an aim or objective. **4** the destination of a journey. ➤ **goalless** *adjective*.

goalkeeper *noun* (*plural* **goalkeepers**) a player who defends the goal in football, hockey, lacrosse, etc.

goalpost *noun* (*plural* **goalposts**) a vertical post forming part of the goal in football, rugby, etc. ✱ **move the goalposts** to change the rules or conditions that apply to something.

goat *noun* (*plural* **goats**) an animal with horns that curve backwards and a straight thick coat.

gobble *verb* (**gobbles, gobbling, gobbled**) **1** to eat something greedily or noisily. **2** to make the sound of a turkey. ➤ **gobbler** *noun*.

gobbledygook or **gobbledegook** *noun* speech or writing that is pompous and difficult to understand.

go-between *noun* (*plural* **go-betweens**) somebody who carries messages or conducts negotiations between other people or groups.

goblet *noun* (*plural* **goblets**) a drinking cup or glass with a rounded bowl, a foot, and a stem.

goblin *noun* (*plural* **goblins**) an ugly and mischievous elf.

gobsmacked *adjective informal* surprised and shocked.

go-cart *noun* see GO-KART.

god *noun* (*plural* **gods**) **1** (**God**) the being worshipped as creator and ruler of the universe. **2** a being with supernatural powers who is worshipped.

godchild *noun* (*plural* **godchildren**) somebody for whom another person becomes godparent. ➤ **goddaughter** *noun*, **godson** *noun*.

goddess *noun* (*plural* **goddesses**) a female god.

godforsaken *adjective* remote; desolate.

godhead *noun* **1** divine nature. **2** (**the Godhead**) God.

godless *adjective* **1** atheistic. **2** wicked.

godly *adjective* (**godlier, godliest**) pious; devout.

godparent *noun* (*plural* **godparents**) somebody who takes responsibility for the religious education of another person at baptism. ➤ **godfather** *noun*, **godmother** *noun*.

godsend *noun* something needed that comes at just the right time.

goggle *verb* (**goggles, goggling, goggled**) to stare at somebody or something with wide eyes.

goggles *plural noun* protective glasses with a flexible, snugly fitting frame.

going *adjective* **1** living; existing: *the best novelist going*. **2** available; to be had: *Are there any jobs going?* **3** current: *the going rate*. ✱ **be hard/heavy going** to be difficult. **be slow going** to take a long time.

goings-on *plural noun* **1** actions or events. **2** suspicious activities.

go-kart or **go-cart** noun (plural **go-karts** or **go-carts**) a small racing car used in karting.

gold noun **1** Science, Art a chemical element that exists as a precious yellow metal used in jewellery. **2** gold coins. **3** a deep metallic yellow colour.

golden adjective **1** consisting of gold. **2** coloured gold. **3** prosperous, happy, and successful: *golden days*. **4** very favourable: *a golden opportunity*. **5** marking a fiftieth anniversary: *golden jubilee*.

golden eagle noun (plural **golden eagles**) a large eagle with brownish yellow tips on its head and neck feathers.

golden wedding noun (plural **golden weddings**) a fiftieth wedding anniversary.

goldfish noun (plural **goldfishes** or **goldfish**) a small reddish orange fish that is kept in aquariums and ponds.

gold leaf noun gold beaten into very thin sheets.

gold medal noun (plural **gold medals**) a medal made of gold, awarded for coming first in a competition.

goldsmith noun (plural **goldsmiths**) somebody who makes articles of gold.

golf noun a game in which players use clubs with long thin handles and hard heads to attempt to hit a small ball into each of the holes on a golf course. ➤ **golfer** noun.

golf course noun (plural **golf courses**) an area of land laid out for playing golf.

gondola noun (plural **gondolas**) a long narrow flat-bottomed boat used on the canals of Venice.

gondolier /gon do leer/ noun (plural **gondoliers**) somebody who rows a gondola.

gone verb past participle of GO. ~ adjective **1** past; ended. **2** used up. ~ adverb later or older than: *It's gone three o'clock*.

gong noun (plural **gongs**) a metal disc that produces a deep ringing tone when struck.

goo noun informal a sticky substance.

good adjective (**better, best**) **1** favourable or desirable: *good news*. **2** of a high standard: *good work*. **3** agreeable; pleasant: *Have a good time*. **4** (**good for**) beneficial to your health or character: *Vegetables are good for you*. **5** morally admirable; virtuous. **6** well-behaved. **7** (**good of**) kind; benevolent: *It was good of you to come*. **8** (**good at**) competent; skilful: *good at woodwork*. **9** suitable; fit: *a good opportunity to set the record straight*. **10** thorough; full: *a good clear-out*. ~ noun **1** benefit; advantage: *It's for your own good*. **2** (**goods**) things that can be bought or sold; merchandise. **3** (**goods**) freight. ✶ **for good** forever; permanently. **make good 1** to be successful in life. **2** to repair damage.

goodbye interjection a word used when leaving somebody or when ending a telephone conversation.

Good Friday noun the Friday before Easter Sunday, observed in the Christian church as the anniversary of the crucifixion of Jesus.

good-looking adjective attractive.

good-natured adjective kind, cheerful, and cooperative.

goodwill noun a kindly feeling of approval and support.

goody noun (plural **goodies**) informal **1** something particularly attractive or desirable. **2** a good person or hero, especially in a film or book.

goody-goody noun (plural **goody-goodies**) informal somebody who is so well behaved that they seem insincere or they irritate you.

gooey adjective (**gooier, gooiest**) soft and sticky.

goose *noun* (*plural* **geese**) **1** a large water bird with a long neck and webbed feet. **2** the female of such a bird.

gooseberry /gooz bri/ *noun* (*plural* **gooseberries**) a small round edible green or yellow fruit with soft prickly skin.

goose pimples *or* **goosebumps** *plural noun* small bumps on the skin caused by cold or fear.

gore¹ *noun* thick or clotted blood, especially when shed as a result of violence.

gore² *verb* (**gores, goring, gored**) said about a bull, etc: to wound somebody with a horn or tusk.

gorge¹ *noun* (*plural* **gorges**) *Geography* a narrow steep-walled valley.

gorge² *verb* (**gorges, gorging, gorged**) to eat hungrily or greedily.

gorgeous *adjective* **1** splendidly beautiful. **2** *informal* very pleasant.

gorilla *noun* (*plural* **gorillas**) a large ape found in the forests of western Africa.

gormless *adjective informal* slow to act or understand; stupid.

gorse *noun* an evergreen shrub with yellow flowers and green spines.

gory *adjective* (**gorier, goriest**) **1** full of violence and bloodshed. **2** covered with blood.

gosling /goz ling/ *noun* (*plural* **goslings**) a young goose.

gospel *noun* (*plural* **gospels**) **1** (**the Gospel**) the teachings of Jesus Christ. **2** (**Gospel**) any of the four books of the New Testament that tell the story of Jesus. **3** something so authoritative that it cannot be questioned. **4** (*also* **gospel music**) a type of religious music rooted in black American culture.

gossamer *noun* **1** a film of cobwebs floating in the air. **2** a very light and delicate material.

gossip *noun* (*plural* **gossips**) **1** a chat. **2** talk or sensational rumours about other people. **3** somebody who habitually gossips. ~ *verb* (**gossips, gossiping, gossiped**) to engage in casual conversation or spread gossip. ➤ **gossipy** *adjective*.

Word History *Gossip* comes from the Old English word *godsibb*, meaning a godparent. Because of the close relationship between a child's parents and godparents, the word came to mean 'somebody you chat to or share news with', and from that gradually developed the idea of being a 'gossip'.

got *verb* past tense and past participle of GET.

Gothic *noun Art* a style of architecture of the 12th to the 16th centuries characterized by pointed arches. ➤ **Gothic** *adjective*.

gouge /gowj/ *verb* (**gouges, gouging, gouged**) to make an uneven hole or groove in a surface. ✷ **gouge out** to force something out roughly or violently.

goulash /gooh lash/ *noun* a meat stew, originally from Hungary, highly seasoned with paprika.

gourd *noun* (*plural* **gourds**) a rounded fruit of a climbing plant, which has a hard rind and is used to make containers.

gourmet /goor may *or* gaw may/ *noun* somebody who is very knowledgeable about food and drink.

gout *noun* a disease that results in painful inflammation of the joints, especially of the big toe.

govern *verb* (**governs, governing, governed**) **1** to be in control of a state or organization. **2** to be a deciding influence on something.

governess *noun* (*plural* **governesses**) a woman who teaches a child or children in a private household.

government *noun* (*plural* **governments**) **1** the group of people who govern a country. **2** the act of governing. ➤ **governmental** *adjective*.

governor *noun* (*plural* **governors**) **1** a ruler or elected head of a political unit such as a state of the USA. **2** the person in charge of a prison. **3** a member of a group that controls a school.

gown *noun* (*plural* **gowns**) **1** a loose robe worn by a judges, lawyers, university teachers, and students on official occasions. **2** a woman's dress, especially an elegant or formal one. **3** a protective outer garment worn in an operating theatre.

GP *noun* (*plural* **GPs**) = GENERAL PRACTITIONER.

grab *verb* (**grabs, grabbing, grabbed**) **1** to take hold of somebody or something hastily or roughly. **2** to take advantage of something eagerly. **3** *informal* to impress somebody: *It doesn't really grab me.* ~ *noun* an attempt to grab somebody or something. ✳ **up for grabs** *informal* available for anyone to take or win.

grace *noun* **1** an easy and flowing quality in movement. **2** approval; favour. **3** assistance or salvation given by God to human beings. **4** a short prayer at a meal giving thanks. **5** (**Her/His/Your Grace**) used as a title for a duke, duchess, or archbishop. ~ *verb* (**graces, gracing, graced**) to confer honour on somebody with your presence.

graceful *adjective* showing grace or elegance. ➤ **gracefully** *adverb*.

gracious *adjective* marked by kindness and courtesy. ➤ **graciously** *adverb*.

grade *noun* (*plural* **grades**) **1** a position in a scale of ranks or qualities. **2** a mark indicating at the quality of a person's work at school. ~ *verb* (**grades, grading, graded**) **1** to sort things according to their quality. **2** to mark a student's work. ✳ **make the grade** to succeed.

gradient *noun* (*plural* **gradients**) **1** the steepness of a slope. **2** a sloping road or railway.

gradual *adjective* happening little by little, usually over a long period. ➤ **gradually** *adverb*.

graduate /gra dew at/ *noun* (*plural* **graduates**) a person who has a degree from a university or college. ~ /gra dew ayt/ *verb* (**graduates, graduating, graduated**) **1** to mark an instrument or container with degrees of measurement. **2** to receive an academic degree. **3** (**graduate to**) to move up to a higher stage of proficiency or prestige. ➤ **graduation** *noun*.

graffiti /gra fee tee/ *plural noun* unauthorized drawings or writing on a wall in a public place.

Usage Note Graffiti is a plural noun, but it is often used with a singular verb.

graft[1] *verb* (**grafts, grafting, grafted**) **1** to fix a cutting from a plant into another growing plant so that the cutting grows from that other plant. **2** to attach or add something onto something else. **3** to implant living tissue into a person's body by a surgical operation. ~ *noun* (*plural* **grafts**) **1** a grafted plant cutting. **2** a piece of living tissue implanted in a person's body, or the operation to implant it: *a skin graft*.

graft[2] *informal verb* (**grafts, grafting, grafted**) to work hard. ~ *noun* hard work.

grain *noun* (*plural* **grains**) **1** cereals or similar food plants. **2** the edible seeds of cereal plants. **3** a small hard particle, for example of sand or salt. **4** a very small amount: *a grain of truth*. **5** the arrangement of the fibres in wood. ➤ **grainy** *adjective*.

gram *noun* (*plural* **grams**) *Science* a unit of weight equal to one thousandth of a kilogram (about 0.04 of an ounce).

grammar *noun* (*plural* **grammars**) *English* **1** the study of the functions of words and their relations in sentences. **2** a grammar textbook.

grammar school *noun* (*plural* **grammar schools**) a selective secondary school providing an academic type of education.

grammatical *adjective English* **1** to do with grammar. **2** conforming to the rules of grammar. ➤ **grammatically** *adverb*.

gramophone *noun* (*plural* **gramophones**) *dated* a record player.

gran *noun* (*plural* **grans**) *informal* your grandmother.

granary *noun* (*plural* **granaries**) a storehouse for grain.

granary bread *noun* brown bread containing malted wheat grains.

grand *adjective* **1** large and striking. **2** magnificent or richly decorated. **3** extremely dignified and proud. **4** having more importance than others; principal. **5** *informal* very good; wonderful. ~ *noun* (*plural* **grand**) *informal* a thousand pounds or dollars. ➤ **grandly** *adverb*.

grandad or **granddad** *noun* (*plural* **grandads** or **granddads**) *informal* your grandfather.

grandchild *noun* (*plural* **grandchildren**) a child of your son or daughter. ➤ **granddaughter** *noun*, **grandson** *noun*.

grandeur *noun* impressiveness and beauty.

grandfather *noun* (*plural* **grandfathers**) the father of your father or mother.

grandfather clock *noun* (*plural* **grandfather clocks**) a tall clock standing on the floor.

grandiose /gran dee ohz/ *adjective* on a large scale and intended to impress people.

grandma *noun* (*plural* **grandmas**) *informal* your grandmother.

grandmother *noun* (*plural* **grandmothers**) the mother of your father or mother.

grandpa *noun* (*plural* **grandpas**) *informal* your grandfather.

grandparent *noun* (*plural* **grandparents**) a parent of your father or mother.

grand piano *noun* (*plural* **grand pianos**) a large piano with a horizontal frame and strings.

grandstand *noun* (*plural* **grandstands**) the main stand at a racecourse or stadium, giving the best view.

grand total *noun* (*plural* **grand totals**) the final amount after several items have been added together.

grange *noun* (*plural* **granges**) a large country house, often with many outbuildings.

granite /gra nit/ *noun* a very hard grey rock.

granny *noun* (*plural* **grannies**) *informal* your grandmother.

granny knot *noun* (*plural* **granny knots**) a reef knot tied the wrong way and therefore not secure.

grant *verb* (**grants, granting, granted**) **1** to agree to carry out a wish or request. **2** to formally give or transfer something, such as a title or property. **3** to be willing to admit that something is true: *I grant you it was a rather rash decision.* ~ *noun* (*plural* **grants**) **1** an amount of money for a particular purpose. **2** the act of granting. ✶ **take for granted 1** to assume something to be true or certain to occur. **2** to become so used to somebody or something that you do not value them enough.

Granth

Granth *noun* see GURU GRANTH SAHIB.

granulated *adjective* formed into granules. ➤ **granulation** *noun*.

granule *noun* (*plural* **granules**) a small hard particle. ➤ **granular** *adjective*.

grape *noun* (*plural* **grapes**) a juicy green or purple berry that grows in clusters on a grapevine, eaten as a fruit or fermented to produce wine.

grapefruit *noun* (*plural* **grapefruit**) a large round citrus fruit with a yellow skin and a rather acid pulp.

grapevine *noun* (*plural* **grapevines**) **1** a vine on which grapes grow. **2** (**the grapevine**) *informal* an unofficial means of circulating information or gossip.

graph *noun* (*plural* **graphs**) *Maths* a diagram showing how quantities are related, usually by means of a line joining points plotted relative to a vertical and a horizontal axis.

graphic *adjective* **1** (*also* **graphical**) *Art* to do with drawing or pictures. **2** said about a description: clear and vivid. ➤ **graphically** *adverb*.

graphic design *noun Art* the art of combining words and illustrations in printed texts.

graphics *plural noun* **1** designs, for example advertising posters, containing both letters and pictures. **2** *ICT* pictures produced on or by a computer.

graphite *noun* a soft black form of carbon used in lead pencils and in lightweight sports equipment.

graph paper *noun Maths* paper printed with small squares, for drawing graphs and diagrams.

grapple *verb* (**grapples, grappling, grappled**) (**grapple with**) **1** to wrestle with somebody. **2** to struggle to deal with something.

grasp *verb* (**grasps, grasping, grasped**) **1** to take hold of something or somebody eagerly or firmly. **2** to succeed in understanding something. ~ *noun* **1** a firm hold. **2** the ability to reach or attain something. **3** understanding of something.

grasping *adjective* eager for possessions; greedy.

grass *noun* (*plural* **grasses**) **1** vegetation in the form of low spreading plants with slender green leaves. **2** an area covered in growing grass. **3** a species of grass. **4** *informal* a police informer. ~ *verb* (**grasses, grassing, grassed**) to cover an area with grass. ✷ **grass on/up** *informal* to inform on somebody to the police. ➤ **grassy** *adjective*.

grasshopper *noun* (*plural* **grasshoppers**) a jumping insect with long hind legs that produce a chirping noise when rubbed together.

grass roots *plural noun* the ordinary members of society or an organization as opposed to the leadership.

grate[1] *noun* (*plural* **grates**) a frame of metal bars that holds the fuel in a fireplace or furnace.

grate[2] *verb* (**grates, grating, grated**) **1** to reduce a hard food to small particles by rubbing it on something rough. **2** to rub or rasp noisily. ➤ **grater** *noun*.

grateful *adjective* feeling or expressing thanks. ➤ **gratefully** *adverb*.

gratify *verb* (**gratifies, gratifying, gratified**) **1** to give pleasure or satisfaction to somebody. **2** to satisfy a desire. ➤ **gratification** *noun*.

grating[1] *noun* (*plural* **gratings**) a framework of parallel bars, for example covering a window.

grating[2] *adjective* said about sounds: annoyingly harsh.

gratis /gra tis/ *adverb and adjective* without charge; free.

gratitude *noun* being grateful; thankfulness.

gratuitous /gra tew i tus/ *adjective* done

for its own sake, not required by the situation: *gratuitous violence*. ➤ **gratuitously** *adverb*.

gratuity *noun* (*plural* **gratuities**) a small sum of money given in return for a service; a tip.

grave¹ *noun* (*plural* **graves**) a pit dug for the burial of a body.

grave² *adjective* (**graver, gravest**) **1** serious; important. **2** causing concern. **3** solemn and dignified. ➤ **gravely** *adverb*.

grave accent /grahv/ *noun* (*plural* **grave accents**) a mark (ˋ) placed over a vowel in some languages to show that it is pronounced in a particular way, as for example in *crème de la crème*.

gravel *noun* loose fragments of rock or small stones, used to surface roads and paths. ➤ **gravelled** *adjective*.

gravestone *noun* (*plural* **gravestones**) a stone placed over or at one end of a grave, usually with the name of the dead person carved on it.

graveyard *noun* (*plural* **graveyards**) an area of ground used for burials.

gravitate *verb* (**gravitates, gravitating, gravitated**) to move gradually and steadily.

gravitation *noun Science* movement caused by gravity. ➤ **gravitational** *adjective*.

gravity *noun* **1** *Science* the force that attracts objects towards the earth, or towards any body that has mass. **2** dignity or solemnity of bearing. **3** seriousness.

gravy *noun* a hot brown sauce made from the fat and juices of cooked meat.

graze¹ *verb* (**grazes, grazing, grazed**) said about animals: to feed on growing grass and other green plants.

graze² *verb* (**grazes, grazing, grazed**) to scrape or scratch your skin. ~ *noun* (*plural* **grazes**) a minor wound on your skin, made by scraping it against a rough surface.

grease /grees/ *noun* **1** a thick oily substance used as a lubricant. **2** animal fat used or produced in cooking. ~ /grees *or* greez/ *verb* (**greases, greasing, greased**) to smear or lubricate something with grease.

greasepaint *noun Drama* theatrical make-up.

greasy *adjective* (**greasier, greasiest**) **1** smeared with or containing grease. **2** oily in texture. **3** insincerely polite.

great *adjective* **1** larger than normal in size, number, or degree. **2** very important; momentous. **3** very gifted and famous. **4** (*in compound nouns*) one stage further away in family relationship: *My great-aunt Mary is my mother's aunt*. **5** *informal* wonderful, excellent, or very enjoyable. ➤ **greatly** *adverb*, **greatness** *noun*.

Great Britain *noun* the large island divided into England, Scotland, and Wales.

Great Dane *noun* (*plural* **Great Danes**) a very large, long-legged dog with a smooth coat.

grebe *noun* (*plural* **grebes**) a diving bird similar to a duck.

greed *noun* **1** excessive desire for food. **2** excessive desire for possessions.

greedy *adjective* (**greedier, greediest**) having an excessive desire for something, especially food. ➤ **greedily** *adverb*.

green *adjective* **1** of the colour of grass and leaves. **2** covered by grass or other vegetation. **3** said about a person: inexperienced or naive. **4** beneficial to the natural environment. **5** (*often* **Green**) concerned about environmental issues. ~ *noun* (*plural* **greens**) **1** a green colour. **2** (**greens**) green vegetables. **3** an area of grass for public use. **4** a smooth area of grass prepared for a special purpose,

green belt

especially bowling or putting. **5** (*often* **Green**) a supporter of an environmentalist party or group. ➤ **greenish** *adjective*, **greenness** *noun*.

green belt *noun* (*plural* **green belts**) an area of countryside surrounding a town or city that people are not usually allowed to build on.

greenery *noun* green leaves or plants.

greenfly *noun* (*plural* **greenflies** *or* **greenfly**) a small green insect that is destructive to plants.

greengage *noun* (*plural* **greengages**) a small greenish plum.

greengrocer *noun* (*plural* **greengrocers**) somebody who sells fresh vegetables and fruit.

greenhouse *noun* (*plural* **greenhouses**) a building with walls and roof of glass where plants are grown.

greenhouse effect *noun* (**the greenhouse effect**) the warming of the atmosphere that occurs when heat from the sun, reflected from the earth, cannot escape because of a build-up of carbon dioxide and other substances in the air.

greenhouse gas *noun* (*plural* **greenhouses gases**) a gas such as carbon dioxide or methane that contributes to the greenhouse effect.

Greenwich Mean Time /grenich/ *noun* time as measured at longitude 0°, which passes through Greenwich in southeast London, used as the basis for calculating time in all other regions of the world.

greet *verb* (**greets, greeting, greeted**) **1** to say something to somebody when they arrive or when you meet them. **2** to react to something in a specified manner: *The announcement was greeted with cheers*.

greeting *noun* (*plural* **greetings**) a phrase or gesture expressing welcome or recognition.

gregarious /grigairius/ *adjective* **1** said about a person: liking to be with other people; sociable. **2** said about animals: living in groups, flocks, or herds.

gremlin *noun* (*plural* **gremlins**) an imaginary creature said to cause machinery or equipment to go wrong.

grenade *noun* (*plural* **grenades**) a small bomb that is thrown by hand or fired from a launcher.

grew *verb* past tense of GROW.

grey *adjective* **1** of a colour between black and white, like that of ash or a rain cloud. **2** dull. ~ *noun* (*plural* **greys**) a grey colour. ➤ **greyish** *adjective*, **greyness** *noun*.

grey area *noun* (*plural* **grey areas**) a subject or situation that is difficult to categorize.

greyhound *noun* (*plural* **greyhounds**) a tall slender dog with a smooth coat, used for racing.

grid *noun* (*plural* **grids**) **1** a framework of metal bars that are arranged side by side or across one another.
2 a network of evenly spaced horizontal and vertical lines, for example for locating points on a map.
3 a network of cables for the distribution of electricity.

griddle *noun* (*plural* **griddles**) a flat metal plate on which food is cooked by dry heat.

gridlock *noun* (*plural* **gridlocks**) a severe traffic jam affecting a whole area. ➤ **gridlocked** *adjective*.

grief *noun* **1** deep sadness, especially caused by the death of somebody. **2** *informal* trouble. ✽ **come to grief** to end badly; to fail.

grievance *noun* (*plural* **grievances**) a cause for dissatisfaction or complaint.

grieve *verb* (**grieves, grieving, grieved**) **1** to feel or express grief. **2** to cause to suffer grief; distress.

grievous /greevus/ *adjective* **1** causing

severe pain or sorrow. **2** very serious. ➤ **grievously** *adverb*.

Usage Note Notice that there is no *i* after the *v*. This word should *not* be pronounced /**gree**vi us/.

grievous bodily harm *noun* serious physical harm done to a person in a criminal attack.

griffin *or* **griffon** *or* **gryphon** *noun* (*plural* **griffins** *or* **griffons** *or* **gryphons**) a mythical animal with the head and wings of an eagle and the body and tail of a lion.

grill *noun* (*plural* **grills**) **1** a set of parallel metal bars on which food is cooked. **2** an apparatus on a cooker under which food is cooked or browned. **3** a dish of grilled food. **4** = GRILLE. ~ *verb* (**grills, grilling, grilled**) **1** to cook food on or under a grill. **2** *informal* to subject somebody to intense questioning.

grille *noun* (*plural* **grilles**) a grating forming a barrier or screen.

grim *adjective* (**grimmer, grimmest**) **1** severe and unwelcoming. **2** unpleasant; nasty. ➤ **grimly** *adverb*.

grimace /gri**mays** *or* gri**mas**/ *noun* (*plural* **grimaces**) an expression of disgust, anger, or pain, that distorts the features of your face. ~ *verb* (**grimaces, grimacing, grimaced**) to make a grimace.

grime *noun* dirt, especially when sticking to a surface. ➤ **grimy** *adjective*.

grin *verb* (**grins, grinning, grinned**) to smile broadly, showing your teeth. ✶ **grin and bear it** to put up with an unpleasant experience without complaining. ➤ **grin** *noun*.

grind *verb* (**grinds, grinding, ground**) **1** to reduce a substance to powder or small fragments by crushing. **2** to polish, sharpen, or wear down something by rubbing it against a rough surface. ~ *noun* dreary monotonous work or routine. ✶ **grind to a halt** to come to a stop suddenly or noisily. **grind your teeth** to rub your teeth together, for example as a sign of anger. ➤ **grinder** *noun*.

grindstone *noun* (*plural* **grindstones**) a revolving stone or abrasive disc used for grinding, polishing, or sharpening objects.

grip *verb* (**grips, gripping, gripped**) **1** to seize or hold something firmly. **2** to attract and hold the interest of somebody. **3** said about an emotion: to take control of somebody: *gripped by fear*. ~ *noun* (*plural* **grips**) **1** a strong grasp. **2** control or power. **3** a part by which something is grasped. **4** a travelling bag. ✶ **come/get to grips with** to set about dealing with something. **get a grip** to start to deal with something effectively. **lose your grip** to be unable to deal with things effectively any longer.

gripe *noun* (*plural* **gripes**) **1** (**gripes**) a stabbing pain in the stomach or abdomen. **2** *informal* a grievance or complaint, especially a trivial one. ~ *verb* (**gripes, griping, griped**) *informal* to complain persistently.

gripping *adjective* very exciting and absorbing.

grisly *adjective* (**grislier, grisliest**) causing horror, fear, or disgust. ➤ **grisliness** *noun*.

grist *noun* grain for grinding. ✶ **grist to the mill** something that can be put to use or profit.

gristle *noun* tough matter in cooked meat. ➤ **gristly** *adjective*.

grit *noun* **1** small hard particles of stone or sand. **2** *informal* determination. ~ *verb* (**grits, gritting, gritted**) **1** to cover a road surface with grit. **2** to clench your teeth as a sign of determination. ➤ **gritty** *adjective*.

grizzle *verb* (**grizzles, grizzling, grizzled**) *informal* said about a child: to cry quietly and fretfully.

grizzled *adjective* said about hair: streaked with grey.

grizzly or **grizzly bear** *noun* (*plural* **grizzlies** or **grizzly bears**) a very large bear that has brownish fur streaked with white.

groan *verb* (**groans, groaning, groaned**) 1 to utter a deep moan. 2 to creak under a heavy weight. ➤ **groan** *noun*.

grocer *noun* (*plural* **grocers**) a shop-keeper who sells basic foodstuffs and household supplies.

groceries *plural noun* the food and other goods sold by a grocer.

groggy *adjective* (**groggier, groggiest**) weak and dazed.

groin *noun* the area of the body between the lower abdomen and the inner part of the thigh.

groom *noun* (*plural* **grooms**) 1 somebody who takes care of horses. 2 a bridegroom. ~ *verb* (**grooms, grooming, groomed**) 1 to clean and care for a horse, dog, etc, especially by brushing its coat. 2 to make yourself neat or attractive. 3 to get somebody ready for a specific role by giving them the skills and experience they need.

groove *noun* (*plural* **grooves**) 1 a long narrow channel cut into wood, stone, etc. 2 the continuous spiral track on a gramophone record.

grope *verb* (**gropes, groping, groped**) to search about blindly for something, especially with your hands.

gross¹ /grohs/ *adjective* 1 extremely noticeable; flagrant. 2 coarse or vulgar. 3 excessively overweight. 4 *informal* disgustingly unpleasant; repulsive. 5 being an overall total before any deductions, for example for taxes, are made: *gross income*.
➤ **grossly** *adverb*, **grossness** *noun*.

gross² /grohs/ *noun* (*plural* **gross**) a group of twelve dozen (144) things.

grotesque *adjective* 1 amusingly or repellently ugly in appearance. 2 absurdly unsuitable or out of place.
➤ **grotesquely** *adverb*.

grotto *noun* (*plural* **grottoes** or **grottos**) a small natural or artificial cave.

grotty *adjective* (**grottier, grottiest**) *informal* 1 dirty. 2 unpleasant. 3 unwell.

ground¹ *noun* (*plural* **grounds**) 1 the solid surface of the earth. 2 soil or earth. 3 an area of land used for a particular purpose: *a cricket ground*. 4 (**grounds**) the area around a large building. 5 (*also* **grounds**) a reason for belief, action, or argument. ~ *verb* (**grounds, grounding, grounded**) 1 to forbid a pilot or aircraft to fly. 2 *informal* to forbid a child to go out, as a punishment. ✽ **be grounded in/on** to be based on something. **gain ground** to become more widely accepted. **get off the ground** to get something started.

ground² *verb* past tense and participle of GRIND.

ground-breaking *adjective* introducing entirely new methods; pioneering.

ground control *noun* the equipment and operators that control aircraft from the ground.

ground floor *noun* the floor of a house on a level with the ground.

grounding *noun* basic training in a subject.

groundless *adjective* for which there is no reason; unjustified.

ground rule *noun* (*plural* **ground rules**) a basic rule.

groundsheet *noun* (*plural* **groundsheets**) a waterproof sheet placed on the ground in a tent.

groundsman *noun* (*plural* **groundsmen**) somebody who looks after a playing field.

groundwork *noun* work done to provide a basis for later work.

group *noun* (*plural* **groups**) **1** a number of people or things gathered together or forming a single unit. **2** *Music* a small band of musicians, especially playing pop music. ~ *verb* (**groups, grouping, grouped**) to form things or people into a group, or to combine in a group.

grouse[1] *noun* (*plural* **grouse**) a game bird with a plump body.

grouse[2] *verb* (**grouses, grousing, groused**) *informal* to complain. ➤ **grouse** *noun*.

grove *noun* (*plural* **groves**) a small wood or group of trees.

grovel /grovil *or* gruvil/ *verb* (**grovels, grovelling, grovelled**) **1** to lie or creep on the ground, especially to show humility. **2** to act in a very humble and apologetic way in order to earn forgiveness or favour.

grow *verb* (**grows, growing, grew, grown**) **1** said about an organism: to increase in size and develop to maturity. **2** to increase or expand. **3** to become something gradually: *She grew tired of listening to his excuses.* **4** to cultivate a plant, fruit, or vegetables. **5** (**grow on**) to become gradually more pleasing to somebody. ✻ **grow out of** to become too big or too mature for something. **grow up** said about a person: to become older or more mature. ➤ **grower** *noun*.

growl *verb* (**growls, growling, growled**) **1** to utter a deep sound in the throat that expresses hostility. **2** to speak in an angry or hostile way. ➤ **growl** *noun*.

grown-up *adjective* fully mature; adult. ~ *noun* (*plural* **grown-ups**) an adult.

growth *noun* (*plural* **growths**) **1** the process of growing. **2** an increase or expansion. **3** something that grows or has grown. **4** a tumour.

grub[1] *verb* (**grubs, grubbing, grubbed**) to dig in the ground. ✻ **grub up** to dig something up or out.

grub[2] *noun* (*plural* **grubs**) **1** a worm-like larva of an insect. **2** *informal* food.

grubby *adjective* (**grubbier, grubbiest**) **1** dirty; grimy. **2** disreputable or sordid.

grudge *verb* (**grudges, grudging, grudged**) to feel resentful towards somebody who has something you envy. ~ *noun* (*plural* **grudges**) ✻ **have a grudge against somebody** *or* **bear somebody a grudge** to feel bitter or hostile towards somebody for something they have done to you in the past.

grudging *adjective* offered or given only unwillingly. ➤ **grudgingly** *adverb*.

gruelling *adjective* extremely tiring or demanding.

gruesome *adjective* horrible or repulsive.

gruff *adjective* said about somebody's voice: deep and harsh. ➤ **gruffly** *adverb*.

grumble *verb* (**grumbles, grumbling, grumbled**) to mutter discontentedly or in complaint. ➤ **grumble** *noun*.

grumpy *adjective* (**grumpier, grumpiest**) cross; bad-tempered. ➤ **grumpily** *adverb*.

grunt *verb* (**grunts, grunting, grunted**) **1** to make the sound of a pig. **2** to make a similar sound to express, for example, reluctant agreement. ➤ **grunt** *noun*.

gryphon *noun* see GRIFFIN.

guarantee *noun* (*plural* **guarantees**) **1** a written promise, given by the manufacturer or seller of something, that they will repair or replace it if it is defective. **2** something that makes it certain that something will happen: *There's no guarantee the weather will be*

guard

fine. ~ *verb* (**guarantees, guaranteeing, guaranteed**) **1** to provide a guarantee for a product, work, etc. **2** to give a promise relating to something, or make it certain that something will happen: *I can't guarantee he will be there.* ➤ **guarantor** *noun*.

guard *verb* (**guards, guarding, guarded**) **1** to protect somebody from danger. **2** to watch over somebody so as to prevent them escaping. **3** (**guard against**) to attempt to prevent something by taking precautions. ~ *noun* (*plural* **guards**) **1** the duty or task of guarding somebody or something. **2** a person or group that guards somebody or something. **3** a device or cover, for example fitted on a machine, to prevent injury. **4** the person in charge of the carriages, passengers, etc in a railway train. ✶ **on/off your guard** ready (or not ready) to deal with a threat.

guardian *noun* (*plural* **guardians**) **1** somebody who guards or protects something. **2** somebody entrusted by law with the care of a child whose parents cannot look after him or her. ➤ **guardianship** *noun*.

guerrilla *or* **guerilla** /gi ri la/ *noun* (*plural* **guerrillas** *or* **guerillas**) a member of a small unofficial fighting force which engages in sabotage and raids and ambushes regular troops.

guess *verb* (**guesses, guessing, guessed**) **1** to estimate or judge something using your own resources when you do not have accurate knowledge or information to help you. **2** to arrive at a correct conclusion about something by guessing: *He guessed the answer.* ~ *noun* (*plural* **guesses**) an opinion or estimate arrived at by guessing.

guesswork *noun* the act of guessing, or a judgment based on a guess.

guest *noun* (*plural* **guests**) **1** a person invited to stay in another person's home or given a meal or entertainment at another person's expense. **2** a person who pays to stay at a hotel, etc. **3** somebody who is present or takes part in a show, etc by invitation.

guesthouse *noun* (*plural* **guesthouses**) a private house used to accommodate paying guests.

guffaw *verb* (**guffaws, guffawing, guffawed**) to laugh loudly or boisterously. ➤ **guffaw** *noun*.

guidance *noun* advice or instructions on how to do something.

guide *noun* (*plural* **guides**) **1** somebody who leads, directs, or advises others. **2** a book providing information about a place, activity, etc. **3** something that helps you to carry out an action correctly. **4** (**Guide**) a member of a worldwide movement for girls that aims to form character and teach good citizenship. ~ *verb* (**guides, guiding, guided**) **1** to lead or direct somebody along a route or to a place. **2** to control and direct the movement of a missile, etc. **3** to give advice or instructions to somebody regarding their behaviour or actions.

guidebook *noun* (*plural* **guidebooks**) a book of information for travellers.

guide dog *noun* (*plural* **guide dogs**) a dog trained to lead a blind person.

guideline *noun* (*plural* **guidelines**) a recommendation about how something should be done.

guild /gild/ *noun* (*plural* **guilds**) **1** an association of people with similar interests. **2** *History* a medieval association of merchants or craftsmen.

guile /giel/ *noun* deceitful cunning.

guillotine /gi lo teen/ *noun* (*plural* **guillotines**) **1** a machine for beheading people, with a heavy blade that slides down between grooved posts. **2** a machine with a long blade for cutting paper or metal. ~ *verb* (**guillotines, guillotining, guillotined**) to cut off somebody's head with a guillotine.

Word History The *guillotine* is named after Joseph *Guillotin*, a French doctor at the time of the French Revolution in the late 18th century. He did not invent the machine but advocated its use as a method of execution, both so that execution would be as painless as possible and also so that all people, whether noble or not, would be executed in the same way.

guilt *noun* **1** the fact of having committed a crime. **2** a feeling of being at fault or to blame. ➤ **guiltless** *adjective*.

guilty *adjective* (**guiltier**, **guiltiest**) **1** responsible for an offence or wrongdoing. **2** found to have committed a crime by a judge or jury after a trial. **3** feeling or showing guilt. ➤ **guiltily** *adverb*.

guinea /gɪni/ *noun* (*plural* **guineas**) a former British gold coin worth 21 shillings (£1.05).

guinea pig *noun* (*plural* **guinea pigs**) **1** a tailless South American rodent often kept as a pet. **2** somebody or something used as a subject of research or experimentation.

guise /giez/ *noun* (*plural* **guises**) outward appearance; disguise. ✶ **in the guise of** pretending to be something.

guitar *noun* (*plural* **guitars**) *Music* a stringed musical instrument played by plucking. ➤ **guitarist** *noun*.

gulf *noun* (*plural* **gulfs**) **1** a large area of sea partially surrounded by land. **2** a deep chasm. **3** a very great difference, for example between the attitudes or opinions of different people.

gull *noun* (*plural* **gulls**) a seabird with long wings, webbed feet, and mainly white and either grey or black plumage.

gullet *noun* (*plural* **gullets**) the oesophagus or throat.

gullible *adjective* easily tricked or deceived. ➤ **gullibility** *noun*.

gully *noun* (*plural* **gullies**) **1** a trench worn in the earth by running water. **2** a deep gutter or drain.

gulp *verb* (**gulps**, **gulping**, **gulped**) **1** (**gulp down**) to swallow something hurriedly or greedily. **2** to make a sudden swallowing movement as if surprised or nervous. ~ *noun* (*plural* **gulps**) **1** a swallowing sound or action. **2** the amount swallowed in a gulp.

gum[1] *noun* (*plural* **gums**) the part of the mouth that holds your teeth.

gum[2] *noun* **1** a plant substance that is sticky when moist but hardens on drying. **2** a soft glue used especially for sticking paper. **3** *informal* = CHEWING GUM. ~ *verb* (**gums**, **gumming**, **gummed**) to stick something with gum. ➤ **gummy** *adjective*.

gumboot *noun* (*plural* **gumboots**) a long waterproof rubber boot.

gumdrop *noun* (*plural* **gumdrops**) a hard jelly-like sweet.

gumption *noun* the intelligence and courage to take action; initiative.

gum tree *noun* (*plural* **gum trees**) a tree that produces gum, especially a eucalyptus tree.

gun *noun* (*plural* **guns**) **1** a weapon that fires a bullet or shell through a metal tube. **2** a device that releases a controlled amount of something, such as grease or glue. ~ *verb* (**guns**, **gunning**, **gunned**) ✶ **be gunning for** to be intent on criticizing or punishing somebody. **gun down** to kill somebody by shooting them. **jump the gun** to move or act before the proper time. **stick to your guns** to refuse to change your intentions or opinions in spite of opposition.

gunge *noun informal* an unpleasant, dirty, or sticky substance.

gunk *noun informal* = GUNGE.

gunman *noun* (*plural* **gunmen**) a criminal armed with a gun.

gunner *noun* (*plural* **gunners**) a soldier who operates a large gun.

gunnery *noun* the science of the effective use of guns.

gunpoint ✷ **at gunpoint** while threatening somebody, or being threatened, with a gun.

gunpowder *noun* an explosive mixture of potassium nitrate, charcoal, and sulphur.

gunship *noun* (*plural* **gunships**) a heavily armed helicopter.

gunwale /gu nl/ *noun* the upper edge of a ship's or boat's side.

gurdwara /ger dwah ra/ *noun* (*plural* **gurdwaras**) a Sikh place of worship.

gurgle *verb* (**gurgles, gurgling, gurgled**) to make a low-pitched bubbling sound. ➢ **gurgle** *noun*.

guru /goo rooh/ *noun* (*plural* **gurus**) **1** a Hindu or Sikh religious teacher and spiritual guide. **2** *informal* an expert in a subject.

Guru Granth Sahib /goo rooh grunt sah hib/ *noun* (**the Guru Granth Sahib**) the main holy book of the Sikh religion.

gush *verb* (**gushes, gushing, gushed**) **1** to flow out, or send out liquid, in large quantities. **2** to speak very sentimentally or enthusiastically about something. ➢ **gush** *noun*, **gushing** *adjective*.

gust *noun* (*plural* **gusts**) **1** a sudden brief rush of wind. **2** a sudden outburst. ~ *verb* (**gusts, gusting, gusted**) to blow in gusts. ➢ **gusty** *adjective*.

gusto *noun* enthusiastic enjoyment or vitality.

gut *noun* **1** (*also* **guts**) the belly or abdomen. **2** the intestine. **3** (*used before a noun*) to do with a person's emotions or instinct: *a gut feeling*.

4 (**guts**) *informal* the inner essential parts. **5** (**guts**) *informal* courage or determination. ~ *verb* (**guts, gutting, gutted**) **1** to remove the intestines of an animal. **2** to destroy the inside of a building.

gutsy *adjective* (**gutsier, gutsiest**) *informal* courageous.

gutted *adjective informal* deeply disappointed.

gutter[1] *noun* (*plural* **gutters**) a trough just below the eaves of a roof or at the side of a street to carry off water.

gutter[2] *verb* (**gutters, guttering, guttered**) said about a candle: to burn with a flickering or feeble flame.

guttural /gu ta ral/ *adjective* said about a sound: pronounced in the throat, often sounding rough or harsh.

guy[1] *noun* (*plural* **guys**) **1** *informal* a man. **2** (**guys**) *informal* people of either sex. **3** a humorous effigy of Guy Fawkes, who attempted to blow up the Houses of Parliament in 1605, burned in Britain on 5 November.

guy[2] *noun* (*plural* **guys**) a rope used to secure a tent.

guzzle *verb* (**guzzles, guzzling, guzzled**) to eat or drink something greedily.

gym *noun* (*plural* **gyms**) **1** = GYMNASIUM. **2** = GYMNASTICS.

gymkhana *noun* (*plural* **gymkhanas**) a local sporting event featuring competitions and displays of horse riding.

gymnasium *noun* (*plural* **gymnasiums** *or* **gymnasia**) a large room or separate building used for indoor sports and gymnastics.

gymnast *noun* (*plural* **gymnasts**) somebody trained in gymnastics.

gymnastics *noun* physical exercises to develop bodily strength and coordination. ➢ **gymnastic** *adjective*.

gynaecology /gie ni ko lo ji/ *noun* a branch of medicine that deals with illnesses that affect women, especially disorders of the female reproductive system. ➤ **gynaecological** *adjective*, **gynaecologist** *noun*.

gypsy *or* **gipsy** *noun* (*plural* **gypsies** *or* **gipsies**) a member of a people of Indian origin who travel from place to place living in caravans.

Word History *Gypsy* is a shortened form of 'Egyptian'. When gypsies first came to Europe, they claimed to be from a country called 'Little Egypt'.

gyrate /jie rayt/ *verb* (**gyrates, gyrating, gyrated**) to spin round and round. ➤ **gyration** *noun*.

gyroscope /jier o skohp/ *noun* (*plural* **gyroscopes**) a device used in navigational equipment, which remains level while a ship or plane rocks or turns because it has a heavy wheel revolving inside it.

haberdashery /ha ber da shi ri/ *noun* small items and equipment used for sewing and dressmaking, such as thread, buttons, pins, and needles.

habit *noun* (*plural* **habits**) **1** something you do regularly. **2** an addiction to a drug. **3** a long dress-like garment worn by a monk or nun. ➤ **habitual** *adjective*, **habitually** *adverb*.

habitat *noun* (*plural* **habitats**) the place where a plant or animal naturally grows or lives.

hack *verb* (**hacks, hacking, hacked**) **1** to cut something by hitting it roughly many times. **2** *ICT* to get into and use somebody's computer system illegally. ➤ **hacker** *noun*.

hackles *plural noun* the hairs on the neck and back of an animal which rise when it is angry.

hackneyed *adjective* said about a phrase: overused and unoriginal.

hacksaw *noun* (*plural* **hacksaws**) a saw with very small teeth, used to cut metal.

had *verb* past tense and past participle of HAVE.

haddock *noun* (*plural* **haddock**) a sea fish used for food.

hadn't *contraction* had not.

haemoglobin /hee mo gloh bin/ *noun Science* a substance in red blood cells that carries oxygen around the body.

haemophilia /hee mo li a/ *noun* an illness in which your blood does not clot properly if you bleed. ➤ **haemophiliac** *noun and adjective*.

haemorrhage /he mo rij/ *noun* (*plural* **haemorrhages**) serious bleeding, usually inside your body. ~ *verb* (**haemorrhages, haemorrhaging, haemorrhaged**) to have a haemorrhage.

haemorrhoids /he mo roydz/ *plural noun* swollen veins round the anus that often bleed.

hag *noun* (*plural* **hags**) an ugly or unpleasant old woman.

haggard /ha gad/ *adjective* looking thin and ill or tired.

haggis *noun* (*plural* **haggis** or **haggises**) a Scottish food consisting of the minced liver, kidney, etc, of a sheep or calf, plus oatmeal and seasonings, traditionally cooked in a bag made from the animal's stomach.

haggle *verb* (**haggles, haggling, haggled**) to argue about a price or an arrangement.

hail[1] *noun* **1** small balls of ice or compacted snow falling from the sky. **2** a large number of things coming at once. ~ *verb* (**hails, hailing, hailed**) to fall as hail.

hail[2] *verb* (**hails, hailing, hailed**) **1** to greet or call out to somebody. **2** to announce something approvingly: *He was hailed a hero*. **3** to signal for a taxi.

hailstone *noun* (*plural* **hailstones**) a small ball of hail.

hair *noun* (*plural* **hairs**) **1** a thin threadlike strand growing from the skin of an animal, person, or plant.

2 all of the hairs covering somebody's head or an animal's body. ➤ **hairless** *adjective*.

haircut *noun* (*plural* **haircuts**) an occasion of getting your hair cut, or the style it is cut in.

hairdo *noun* (*plural* **hairdos**) *informal* a hairstyle.

hairdresser *noun* (*plural* **hairdressers**) somebody who cuts and styles people's hair. ➤ **hairdressing** *noun*.

hairdryer *or* **hairdrier** *noun* (*plural* **hairdryers** *or* **hairdriers**) an electrical device for drying hair.

hairpin *noun* (*plural* **hairpins**) a narrow U-shaped piece of wire for holding hair in place.

hairpin bend *noun* (*plural* **hairpin bends**) a sharp U-shaped bend in a road.

hair-raising *adjective* very frightening.

hairspray *noun* (*plural* **hairsprays**) a substance that you spray on your hair to keep it in place.

hairstyle *noun* (*plural* **hairstyles**) the way in which your hair is cut or arranged.

hairy *adjective* (**hairier, hairiest**) covered with hair. **2** *informal* dangerous or frightening.

hajj *noun* (**the hajj**) the journey to Mecca which Muslims make as a religious duty.

hake *noun* (*plural* **hake**) a large sea fish used for food.

halal /ha lahl/ *adjective* said about meat: prepared in the way Islamic law requires.

halcyon /hal si on/ *adjective* wonderfully peaceful and happy.

Word History The *halcyon* was a mythical bird. People in ancient times believed that it made a nest that floated on the sea and that it could put a spell on the waves in order to keep the sea calm.

hale *adjective* said about a person: strong and healthy.

half *noun* (*plural* **halves**) one of the two equal parts you can divide something into. ~ *adjective* consisting of half of an entire object or amount. ~ *adverb* not completely but partly, or up to a half: *half dead with cold*; *half full*. ✱ **half past** thirty minutes past an hour.

half-baked *adjective* badly thought out or planned.

half board *noun* the arrangement of having your breakfast and evening meal at your hotel, but not lunch.

half brother *noun* (*plural* **half brothers**) a brother who is the son of one of your parents, but not both.

half-dozen *or* **half a dozen** *noun* six.

halfhearted *adjective* not showing much effort or enthusiasm. ➤ **halfheartedly** *adverb*.

halfpenny /hayp ni/ *noun* (*plural* **halfpennies**) an old British coin worth half an old penny.

half sister *noun* (*plural* **half sisters**) a sister who is the daughter of one of your parents, but not both.

half term *noun* (*plural* **half terms**) a short holiday halfway through a school term.

halftime *noun* a break between the two halves of a game.

halfway *adjective and adverb* in the centre between two points.

halibut *noun* (*plural* **halibut**) a large flatfish used for food.

hall *noun* (*plural* **halls**) **1** a room or passage at the entrance of a building. **2** a large room for public gatherings. **3** a large country house.

hallelujah /ha li looh ya/ *or* **alleluia** /a li looh ya/ *interjection* expressing praise or joy.

hallmark *noun* (*plural* **hallmarks**) **1** an official mark stamped on good-quality gold and silver objects. **2** a special characteristic.

hallo *interjection* = HELLO.

hallowed *adjective* holy, or greatly respected.

Halloween *or* **Hallowe'en** *noun* 31 October, when traditionally many people dress up as ghosts and witches.

> **Word History** Halloween is the day before the Christian festival of All Saints' Day (1 November). *All Hallows* is an old name for All Saints' Day and *een* is a shortened form of *even*, meaning 'evening' or 'eve', as in Christmas Eve.

hallucinate *verb* (**hallucinates, hallucinating, hallucinated**) to have a hallucination.

hallucination /ha looh si **nay** shn/ *noun* (*plural* **hallucinations**) something that you think you see although it is not really there. ➤ **hallucinatory** *adjective*.

halo *noun* (*plural* **haloes** *or* **halos**) a circle of light around the head of a holy person, especially in pictures, or around the sun or moon.

halt *verb* (**halts, halting, halted**) to stop or bring something to a stop. ~ *noun* a stop or interruption. ✻ **call a halt** to demand a stop to an activity.

halter *noun* (*plural* **halters**) a rope or strap used to tie up or lead an animal.

halve *verb* (**halves, halving, halved**) **1** to divide something into two equal parts. **2** to reduce an amount by half.

ham[1] *noun* (*plural* **hams**) meat from a pig's upper back leg, cured with salt.

ham[2] *noun* (*plural* **hams**) **1** a bad actor who exaggerates when performing. **2** an amateur radio operator.

hamburger *noun* (*plural* **hamburgers**) mince made into a flat round cake, often served in a bread roll when cooked.

hamlet *noun* (*plural* **hamlets**) a small village.

hammer *noun* (*plural* **hammers**) a tool with a heavy metal head on a handle, used to knock in nails, or a similar solid object for hitting something with. ~ *verb* (**hammers, hammering, hammered**) **1** to hit something or knock something in with a hammer or something else. **2** (**hammer into**) to repeat something to somebody until they remember it. **3** *informal* to defeat somebody badly. ✻ **hammer away** to keep working hard at something, or keep repeating something.

hammock *noun* (*plural* **hammocks**) a hanging bed made from a piece of net or canvas tied to something at each end.

hamper[1] *verb* (**hampers, hampering, hampered**) to prevent something or somebody from moving or getting on properly.

hamper[2] *noun* (*plural* **hampers**) a large rectangular basket with a lid, usually made of wicker.

hamster *noun* (*plural* **hamsters**) a small furry animal often kept as a pet.

hamstring *noun* (*plural* **hamstrings**) a tendon at the back of the knee, attached to your thigh muscles.

hand *noun* (*plural* **hands**) **1** the part of your body at the end of your arm, with fingers on it. **2** a pointer on a clock or dial. **3** a unit of length used for measuring a horse's height. **4** a round of applause: *Give them a big hand.* **5** one player's cards in a card game. **6** a worker paid to do physical work. ~ *verb* (**hands, handing, handed**) to give or pass something to somebody. ✻ **at hand** near. **by hand 1** with your hands, rather than with machinery. **2** in person rather than by post. **give/lend a hand** to help. **hand down** to pass something on to somebody younger to keep. **hand out** to give something out to a group of people. **hand over** to pass something officially to somebody else. **in hand** being done. **off hand** without checking or investigating. **on hand** ready to use or help. **out of hand** out of control. **to hand** available and ready to use.

handbag *noun* (*plural* **handbags**) a woman's bag for keeping money and small personal items in.

handbook *noun* (*plural* **handbooks**) a book of information about how to do or use something.

hand brake *noun* (*plural* **hand brakes**) a brake you apply with your hand when a vehicle has stopped, to prevent it moving.

handcuff *verb* (**handcuffs, handcuffing, handcuffed**) to put handcuffs on somebody.

handcuffs *plural noun* a pair of joined metal rings for locking round a prisoner's wrists.

handful *noun* (*plural* **handfuls**) **1** an amount that you can hold in your hand. **2** a small number of things. **3** *informal* somebody who is difficult to control.

hand grenade *noun* (*plural* **hand grenades**) a small bomb that is thrown by hand.

handicap *noun* (*plural* **handicaps**) **1** a disadvantage that makes a task more difficult. **2** an advantage or disadvantage given to contestants to even out everyone's chances of winning. ~ *verb* (**handicaps, handicapping, handicapped**) to make it more difficult for somebody to do something. ➤ **handicapped** *adjective*.

handicraft *noun* (*plural* **handicrafts**) an activity which involves making something with your hands, or something you make in this way.

handiwork *noun* somebody's own work or actions.

handkerchief *noun* (*plural* **handkerchiefs**) a small piece of cloth used for blowing your nose.

handle *noun* (*plural* **handles**) the part of something that you are meant to hold on to with your hand. ~ *verb* (**handles, handling, handled**) **1** to touch or feel something with your hands. **2** to deal with or manage somebody or something. **3** to buy, sell, or distribute goods. ➤ **handler** *noun*.

handlebar *noun* or **handlebars** *plural noun* a bar across the front of a bicycle or motorcycle for steering it with.

handmade *adjective* made by hand rather than by machine.

handout *noun* (*plural* **handouts**) **1** a free item of food, clothing, or money given to somebody who needs it. **2** a free sheet of information.

hand-picked *adjective* carefully chosen.

handset *noun* (*plural* **handsets**) **1** the part of a telephone that you lift up to your mouth and ear. **2** a remote control for an electronic item such as a television.

handshake *noun* (*plural* **handshakes**) an act of shaking somebody's hand.

handsome *adjective* **1** said about a man: attractive or good-looking. **2** large or generous: *a handsome reward*. ➤ **handsomely** *adverb*.

handspring *noun* (*plural* **handsprings**) a gymnastic movement in which your body turns over in a circle, landing first on your hands and then on your feet.

handstand *noun* (*plural* **handstands**) an act of balancing upside down on your hands with your legs in the air.

handwriting *noun* **1** writing done with a pen or pencil. **2** a person's particular style of writing. ➤ **handwritten** *adjective*.

handy *adjective* (**handier, handiest**) **1** convenient or useful. **2** clever in practical ways. ➤ **handily** *adverb*.

handyman *noun* (*plural* **handymen**) a

man who repairs things and does various jobs.

hang *verb* (**hangs, handing, hung**) **1** to fix something at the top so that the lower part is free, or to be fixed in this way. **2** (*past tense and past participle* **hanged**) to suspend somebody by their neck until they are dead. **3** to paste wallpaper to a wall. ~ *noun* the way in which something hangs. ✴ **get the hang of** *informal* to learn how to do or use something. **hang about/around** to wait somewhere, doing nothing or for no particular reason. **hang on 1** to keep holding onto something. **2** *informal* to wait for a short time. **hang over** said about something coming in the future: to make somebody feel worried or frightened: *I've still got my French exam hanging over me.* **hang up** to end a telephone conversation.

hangar *noun* (*plural* **hangars**) a large shed for aircraft.

hanger *noun* (*plural* **hangers**) an object in the shape of a curve or a triangle with a hook at the top, for hanging clothes on.

hang-glider *noun* (*plural* **hang-gliders**) a glider controlled by somebody hanging in a harness underneath it. ➤ **hang-gliding** *noun*.

hangman *noun* (*plural* **hangmen**) an executioner who hangs condemned prisoners.

hangnail *noun* (*plural* **hangnails**) a piece of loose hard skin at the edge of a fingernail.

hangover *noun* (*plural* **hangovers**) the unpleasant way you feel after drinking too much alcohol.

hang-up *noun* (*plural* **hang-ups**) *informal* something you constantly feel embarrassed about or afraid of.

hanker *verb* (**hankers, hankering, hankered**) to want something for a long time: *She's always hankered after a pet rabbit.* ➤ **hankering** *noun*.

hankie *or* **hanky** *noun* (*plural* **hankies**) *informal* a handkerchief.

Hanukkah *or* **Chanukah** /hah nu ka/ *noun* a Jewish festival in December, lasting for eight days.

haphazard /hap ha zad/ *adjective* without any method or order. ➤ **haphazardly** *adverb*.

hapless *adjective literary* unlucky or unfortunate.

happen *verb* (**happens, happening, happened**) **1** to take place or occur. ✴ **happen on** *literary* to meet somebody or find something by chance. **happen to** to do something or occur by chance.

happening *noun* (*plural* **happenings**) something that happens; an event.

happy *adjective* (**happier, happiest**) **1** pleased or contented. **2** lucky or fortunate: *a happy coincidence*. **3** willing: *I'd be happy to help.* ➤ **happily** *adverb*, **happiness** *noun*.

happy-go-lucky *adjective* cheerful and carefree.

harangue /ha rang/ *noun* (*plural* **harangues**) a long, fierce, written or spoken criticism. ~ *verb* (**harangues, haranguing, harangued**) to criticize somebody directly, fiercely, and at great length.

harass /ha ras/ *verb* (**harasses, harassing, harassed**) to constantly annoy or worry somebody. ➤ **harassed** *adjective*, **harassment** *noun*.

harbour *noun* (*plural* **harbours**) a port where boats can anchor. ~ *verb* (**harbours, harbouring, harboured**) **1** to have or keep thoughts or feelings in your mind. **2** to provide a bad person or thing with somewhere to stay.

hard *adjective* **1** solid and firm. **2** difficult to understand or explain. **3** needing energy or stamina to do. **4** harsh, severe, or violent. **5** definite. **6** said about an alcoholic drink: strong. **7** said about a drug: addictive and harmful. ~ *adverb* **1** with great effort, energy, or force. **2** firmly or tightly. ✶ **hard done by** unfairly treated. ✶ **hard going** difficult. ➤ **hardness** *noun*.

hardback *noun* (*plural* **hardbacks**) a book with hard covers that do not bend.

hardboard *noun* board made from compressed shredded wood.

hard-boiled *adjective* said about an egg: boiled until the yolk is solid.

hard copy *noun* ICT a paper copy of data held on computer.

hard disk or **hard drive** *noun* (*plural* **hard disks** or **hard drives**) ICT a rigid disk that remains inside a computer and can hold a large amount of data.

harden *verb* (**hardens, hardening, hardened**) to become or make something hard or harder.

hard feelings *plural noun* feelings of resentment.

hardhearted *adjective* uncaring.

hardly *adverb* **1** only just; barely: *I hardly knew what to say.* **2** not at all: *I'm hardly surprised.*

hardship *noun* (*plural* **hardships**) a problem or state of suffering or poverty.

hard shoulder *noun* a strip at the edge of a motorway for driving on or stopping on in an emergency.

hard up *adjective informal* poor.

hardware *noun* **1** tools and equipment used in the house or garden. **2** ICT the solid parts of a computer system, rather than the programs it uses.

hard-wearing *adjective* strong enough to stand a lot of use.

hardwood *noun* (*plural* **hardwoods**) strong hard wood from a tree that grows slowly, such as oak.

hardy *adjective* (**hardier, hardiest**) tough; able to cope with difficult conditions. ➤ **hardiness** *noun*.

hare *noun* (*plural* **hares**) an animal like a rabbit but larger and with longer ears and back legs. ~ *verb* (**hares, haring, hared**) *informal* to run fast.

harem /hah reem *or* hair im/ *noun* (*plural* **harems**) a group of women living in a Muslim household, or their separate living area.

haricot /ha ri koh/ *noun* (*plural* **haricots**) a type of white bean eaten cooked, mainly in the form of baked beans.

hark *verb* (**harks, harking, harked**) *literary or archaic* **1** to listen. **2** (**hark back**) to refer or go back to an earlier subject or time.

harm *noun* damage or injury. ~ *verb* (**harms, harming, harmed**) to damage or injure somebody or something, or have a bad effect on them. ➤ **harmful** *adjective*, **harmfully** *adverb*.

harmless *adjective* not likely to cause harm. ➤ **harmlessly** *adverb*.

harmonic *adjective* to do with, or using, musical harmony.

harmonica *noun* (*plural* **harmonicas**) a small rectangular musical instrument that you blow and suck to produce different notes.

harmonious /hah moh ni us/ *adjective* **1** arranged so that the different parts sound or look pleasing together. **2** peaceful and friendly. ➤ **harmoniously** *adverb*.

harmonize or **harmonise** *verb* (**harmonizes, harmonizing, harmonized** or **harmonises,** etc) to make something harmonious. ➤ **harmonization** or **harmonisation** *noun*.

harmony *noun* (*plural* **harmonies**) **1** *Music* a pleasant combination of notes in a chord, or the way a composer combines notes or chords. **2** peaceful or friendly agreement.

harness *noun* (*plural* **harnesses**) a set of straps used to attach an animal such as a horse or ox to something it is pulling, or to attach a person to a

harp

parachute, rope, etc: *a safety harness*. ~ *verb* (**harnesses, harnessing, harnessed**) **1** to put a harness on an animal or person. **2** to make use of a natural source of energy.

harp *noun* (*plural* **harps**) a large triangular musical instrument with strings that you pluck. ~ *verb* (**harps, harping, harped**) (**harp on**) to keep talking about something in a boring way. ➤ **harpist** *noun*.

harpoon *noun* (*plural* **harpoons**) a spear with a hook on it, used to catch whales. ~ *verb* (**harpoons, harpooning, harpooned**) to stick a harpoon into something.

harpsichord *noun* (*plural* **harpsichords**) a keyboard instrument with strings that are plucked when its keys are pressed.

harrowing *adjective* very upsetting and difficult to experience.

harsh *adjective* unusually severe, unpleasant, unkind, or difficult. ➤ **harshly** *adverb*.

harvest *noun* (*plural* **harvests**) the time when farmers gather in their crops, or the crop itself. ~ *verb* (**harvests, harvesting, harvested**) to gather in a crop, or to collect a natural product in a similar way. ➤ **harvester** *noun*.

has *verb* third person singular of the present tense of HAVE.

has-been *noun* (*plural* **has-beens**) *informal* somebody or something that is no longer important.

hash¹ *noun* (*plural* **hashes**) reheated chopped meat and vegetables.
✽ **make a hash of something** *informal* to do something badly.

hash² *noun* (*plural* **hashes**) *ICT* the symbol #.

hash³ or **hashish** *noun* cannabis.

hasn't *contraction* has not.

hassle *noun* (*plural* **hassles**) *informal* a difficult, worrying, or annoying situation, or problems from other people hassling you. ~ *verb* (**hassles, hassling, hassled**) *informal* to worry or annoy somebody by continually wanting or asking for things.

haste *noun* doing things fast or too fast.

hasten /hay sn/ *verb* (**hastens, hastening, hastened**) to hurry or act quickly, or to make something happen more quickly.

hasty *adjective* (**hastier, hastiest**) too quickly, or hurried. ➤ **hastily** *adverb*.

hat *noun* (*plural* **hats**) a piece of clothing you wear on your head.

hatch¹ *noun* (*plural* **hatches**) a small door or opening.

hatch² *verb* (**hatches, hatching, hatched**) **1** to come out of an egg or pupa. **2** said about an egg: to open and let out a baby bird or creature. **3** to keep an egg warm until it hatches. **4** to think up a plan.

hatch³ *verb* (**hatches, hatching, hatched**) *Art* to shade or fill an area with close parallel lines. ➤ **hatching** *noun*.

hatchback *noun* (*plural* **hatchbacks**) a car with a large door at the back which you lift to open.

hatchet *noun* (*plural* **hatchets**) a small axe.

hate *verb* (**hates, hating, hated**) to dislike somebody or something very much. ~ *noun* (*plural* **hates**) **1** very strong dislike. **2** *informal* something you hate.

hatred *noun* very strong dislike; hate.

hat trick *noun* (*plural* **hat tricks**) three wins or successes in a row.

haughty /haw ti/ *adjective* (**haughtier, haughtiest**) proud or arrogant. ➤ **haughtily** *adverb*, **haughtiness** *noun*.

haul *verb* (**hauls, hauling, hauled**) to pull or drag something with effort. ~ *noun* (*plural* **hauls**) a quantity of

something caught or stolen at once.
✷ **a long haul** a long and difficult process.

haulage *noun* the act or commercial business of transporting goods in lorries, etc.

haunch *noun* (*plural* **haunches**) **1** (**haunches**) your thighs, hips, and buttocks, or the similar part of an animal. **2** a joint of meat from the back half of an animal's side.

haunt *verb* (**haunts, haunting, haunted**) **1** said about a ghost: to be present in a place regularly. **2** to visit a place often. **3** said about a thought: to keep coming into your mind and disturbing you. ~ *noun* (*plural* **haunts**) a place you often visit. ➤ **haunted** *adjective*.

haunting *adjective* **1** constantly coming back into your mind or memory. **2** said about music: sad and beautiful. ➤ **hauntingly** *adverb*.

have *verb* (**has, having, had**) **1** to own, hold, or possess something. **2** to experience or be affected by something: *to have doubts/fun/a headache*. **3** to eat or drink: *Let's have lunch*. **4** to accommodate or be host to somebody: *to have guests*. **5** to arrange or organize something: *I'm having a party*. ~ *auxiliary verb* used to form the perfect tenses of verbs: *They have gone; She had eaten it*. ✷ **have on 1** to be wearing. **2** to have an event planned. **3** *informal* to trick or tease somebody. **have to** to be obliged to; must.

haven *noun* (*plural* **havens**) a safe place.

haven't *contraction* have not.

havoc *noun* widespread destruction, or confusion and disorder. ✷ **play havoc with** to confuse and disorganize something totally.

hawk[1] *noun* (*plural* **hawks**) a bird of prey with short rounded wings.

hawk[2] *verb* (**hawks, hawking, hawked**) to sell goods to people in the street. ➤ **hawker** *noun*.

hawthorn *noun* (*plural* **hawthorns**) a shrub with white or pink flowers and red berries.

hay *noun* dry mown grass that is used to feed animals.

hay fever *noun* an allergy to pollen that makes your nose and eyes itchy and runny.

haystack *noun* (*plural* **haystacks**) a large pile of stacked hay.

haywire *adjective* *informal* out of control.

hazard *noun* (*plural* **hazards**) a risk, danger, or obstacle. ~ *verb* (**hazards, hazarding, hazarded**) to put somebody or something in danger.
✷ **hazard a guess** to make a guess.
➤ **hazardous** *adjective*.

haze *noun* **1** a light mist or cloud.
2 vagueness or confusion.

hazel *noun* (*plural* **hazels**) **1** a small tree that produces nuts in autumn and catkins in spring. **2** a yellowish brown colour. ➤ **hazelnut** *noun*.

hazy *adjective* (**hazier, haziest**) **1** misty or cloudy. **2** vague. ➤ **hazily** *adverb*.

he *pronoun* used to refer to a male person or animal mentioned earlier, or to a person in general.

head *noun* (*plural* **heads**) **1** the part at the top of your body containing your brain, mouth, nose, and ears, or a similar part of an animal, bird, fish, or insect. **2** your mind or intelligence.
3 (**heads**) the side of a coin showing the head of a monarch or president.
4 the upper or higher end of something, or the most important end, or the growing or flowering end: *sitting at the head of the table*; *He chopped the heads off the daffodils*. **5** a director or leader. **6** a teacher in charge of a school. **7** a person: *£25 a head*. ~ *adjective* principal or chief. ~ *verb* (**heads, heading, headed**) **1** to lead some-

headache

thing or be at the head or top of something. **2** to hit a ball with your head. **3** to move in a specific direction: *The plane headed north; He's heading for the door.* ✳ **come to a head** to reach a crisis. **a head start** an advantage at the beginning of a contest. **keep your head** to stay calm and sensible. **lose your head** to panic or behave irrationally.

headache *noun* (*plural* **headaches**) **1** a pain in your head. **2** *informal* a problem or worry.

headdress *noun* (*plural* **headdresses**) a decorative or ceremonial covering for the head.

header *noun* (*plural* **headers**) **1** a shot or pass in football made with the head. **2** *informal* a headfirst fall.

headfirst *adverb and adjective* with your head going first.

headgear *noun* clothing for the head.

heading *noun* (*plural* **headings**) a title at the top of a letter, chapter, etc.

headland *noun* (*plural* **headlands**) *Geography* a piece of high land that juts out into the sea.

headlight *or* **headlamp** *noun* (*plural* **headlights** *or* **headlamps**) a main light at the front of a motor vehicle.

headline *noun* (*plural* **headlines**) **1** a title printed in large type above a newspaper story or article. **2** (**the headlines**) a short report of the main news on television or radio.

headlong *adverb and adjective* **1** = HEADFIRST. **2** without waiting or thinking; fast and uncontrolled.

headmaster *or* **headmistress** *noun* (*plural* **headmasters** *or* **headmistresses**) the head teacher of a school.

head-on *adverb and adjective* **1** with the front hitting first. **2** with directly opposite opinions.

headphones *plural noun* a pair of earphones that you wear on your head.

headquarters *noun* (*plural* **headquarters**) a place from which a business or activity is directed.

headset *noun* (*plural* **headsets**) a set of earphones and a microphone that you wear on your head.

headstone *noun* (*plural* **headstones**) a memorial stone placed at the top end of a grave.

headstrong *adjective* determined to do what you want to do and unwilling to listen to advice.

head teacher *noun* (*plural* **head teachers**) the teacher in charge of a school.

headway ✳ **make headway** to make progress or move forward.

headwind *noun* (*plural* **headwinds**) a wind blowing in the opposite direction to the way you are travelling.

heady *adjective* (**headier, headiest**) exciting or exhilarating.

heal *verb* (**heals, healing, healed**) to make somebody or something healthy again, or to become healthy again after an illness or injury.

health *noun* the condition of your body or mind: *Smoking is bad for your health.*

health food *noun* natural foods that are thought to be good for your health.

healthy *adjective* (**healthier, healthiest**) **1** physically fit and well. **2** good for your health. **3** successful, strong, or in good condition.
➤ **healthily** *adverb*.

heap *noun* (*plural* **heaps**) **1** a pile of things. **2** (**heaps**) *informal* a large quantity. ~ *verb* (**heaps, heaping, heaped**) **1** to put something in a heap or to form a heap: *Rubbish was heaped up everywhere.* **2** to load something or somebody, or to give somebody a large amount of something: *Her plate* was heaped with food; *We heaped her with praise.*

hear *verb* (**hears, hearing, heard**) **1** to be aware of sounds by using your ears. **2** to know or find out about something by hearing it: *I just heard about the accident; Haven't you heard of Napoleon?* **3** to consider a case legally in court. **4** (**hear from**) to get a letter, telephone call, etc from somebody.

hearing *noun* (*plural* **hearings**) **1** the ability to hear. **2** an opportunity to be heard. **3** a trial or formal meeting in court.

hearing aid *noun* (*plural* **hearing aids**) a device that you wear in your ear to help you hear better.

hearsay *noun* something you hear about from another person.

hearse /hers/ *noun* (*plural* **hearses**) a large car used for taking a coffin to a funeral.

heart *noun* (*plural* **hearts**) **1** the organ that pumps blood around your body. **2** the most important part or the centre of something. **3** your deepest feelings. **4** (**hearts**) a suit in a pack of cards, marked with red hearts. **4** love or compassion. **5** courage or confidence. ✶ **by heart** from memory.

heartache *noun* (*plural* **heartaches**) unhappiness.

heart attack *noun* (*plural* **heart attacks**) a sudden failure of the heart to work properly.

heartbreak *noun* intense grief. ➤ **heartbreaking** *adjective*.

heartbroken *adjective* extremely sad.

heartburn *noun* a burning pain in the chest caused by indigestion.

hearten *verb* (**heartens, heartening, heartened**) to cheer or encourage somebody. ➤ **heartening** *adjective*.

heart failure *noun* the sudden failure of the heart to continue working properly.

heartfelt *adjective* deeply felt; sincere.

hearth /hahth/ *noun* (*plural* **hearths**) the area in front of a fireplace.

heartless *adjective* unfeeling or cruel. ➤ **heartlessly** *adverb*.

heart-rending *adjective* extremely sad.

heart-throb *noun* (*plural* **heart-throbs**) *informal* somebody people find very attractive.

heart-to-heart *noun* (*plural* **heart-to-hearts**) a private honest talk about your feelings.

hearty *adjective* (**heartier, heartiest**) **1** vigorous or enthusiastic. **2** strong and healthy. **4** said about a meal: large and filling. ➤ **heartily** *adverb*.

heat *noun* (*plural* **heats**) **1** the state of being hot, or the form of energy that causes this. **2** passion or strong feeling. **3** an early round of a contest. ~ *verb* (**heats, heating, heated**) **1** (*often* **heat up**) to get hot or make something hot: *I'll heat this up in the oven.* **2** (**heat up**) to get or make something more exciting or intense. ✶ **on heat** said about a female animal: ready for mating.

heater *noun* (*plural* **heaters**) a device for heating air or water.

heath *noun* (*plural* **heaths**) a flat area of land covered with heather, gorse, etc.

heathen *noun* (*plural* **heathens**) *archaic* somebody who does not believe in any of the main religions.

heather *noun* (*plural* **heathers**) a plant with pink, white, or purple flowers, often found on moors.

heating *noun* a system of pipes, etc used to heat a building.

heatstroke *noun* an illness caused by staying for too long in strong heat.

heat wave *noun* (*plural* **heat waves**) a long period of unusually hot weather.

heave *verb* (**heaves, heaving, heaved**) **1** to lift, pull, or throw something with great effort. **2** to rise and fall rhythmically. **3** to vomit or nearly

heaven

vomit. ~ *noun* (*plural* **heaves**) an act of heaving. ✱ **heave a sigh** to sigh loudly.

heaven *noun* (*plural* **heavens**) **1** the place where God lives and good people go when they die, according to some religions. **2** (**the heavens**) *literary* the sky. **3** *informal* a totally enjoyable place or experience.

heavenly *adjective* **1** to do with heaven or the sky. **2** *informal* delightful.

heavy *adjective* (**heavier**, **heaviest**) **1** weighing a lot; difficult to carry, move, or lift. **2** large, thick, or solid. **3** falling with force; powerful: *heavy footsteps*. **4** unusually large in size, strength, or number: *heavy traffic*. **5** loud and rhythmic. **6** needing a lot of effort or commitment; serious: *a heavy responsibility*. ✱ **a heavy heart** great sadness. ➤ **heavily** *adverb*, **heaviness** *noun*.

heavy-duty *adjective* strongly made to stand a lot of use.

heavyweight *noun* (*plural* **heavyweights**) **1** a boxer or wrestler in the heaviest weight category. **2** *informal* an important or influential person.

Hebrew /hee brooh/ *noun* the language of the ancient Jewish people, or the modern form of it.

heckle *verb* (**heckles**, **heckling**, **heckled**) to interrupt somebody during a speech or performance with shouts or insults. ➤ **heckler** *noun*.

hectare /hek tair/ *noun* (*plural* **hectares**) 10,000 square metres (2.471 acres).

hectic *adjective* extremely busy. ➤ **hectically** *adverb*.

he'd *contraction* he had or he would.

hedge *noun* (*plural* **hedges**) a thick row of shrubs or bushes used as a boundary or fence. ~ *verb* (**hedges**, **hedging**, **hedged**) **1** to surround or protect something with a hedge. **2** to avoid saying anything definite. ✱ **hedge your bets** to avoid making the wrong choice by choosing two or more options.

hedgehog *noun* (*plural* **hedgehogs**) a small wild animal that is covered in spines.

hedgerow *noun* (*plural* **hedgerows**) a hedge along the edge of a field.

heed *verb* (**heeds**, **heeding**, **heeded**) *formal* to pay close attention to a warning or advice. ~ *noun* careful attention: *They paid no heed to what I said*.

heel *noun* (*plural* **heels**) **1** the back of your foot below your ankle. **2** the part of a shoe or sock that covers your heel. ~ *verb* (**heels**, **heeling**, **heeled**) **1** to put a new heel on a shoe. **2** to hit a ball with your heel.

hefty *adjective* (**heftier**, **heftiest**) large, heavy, or powerful.

Hegira *or* **Hejira** /he ji ra/ *noun* (**the Hegira** *or* **the Hejira**) the event in AD 622 which marks the beginning of the Muslim era, when Muhammad left Mecca and escaped to Medina.

heifer /he fer/ *noun* (*plural* **heifers**) a young cow.

height /hiet/ *noun* (*plural* **heights**) **1** the distance from the top to the bottom of something; how high something is. **2** a high place. **3** the time or point when something is most intense or successful: *at the height of the tourist season*. **4** the best or worst example of something: *the height of fashion/stupidity*.

heighten *verb* (**heightens**, **heightening**, **heightened**) to become or make something higher, greater, or more intense.

heinous /hay nus *or* hee nus/ *adjective* very wicked; monstrous.

heir /air/ *noun* (*plural* **heirs**) somebody who inherits something or receives a title or position after somebody else.

heiress *noun* (*plural* **heiresses**) a female heir.

heirloom *noun* (*plural* **heirlooms**) a valuable object handed down within a family from one generation to another.

Hejira *noun* see HEGIRA.

held *verb* past tense and past participle of HOLD.

helicopter *noun* (*plural* **helicopters**) an aircraft with a set of long blades on top which rotate horizontally.

helium /hee li um/ *noun* Science a chemical element that is a gas that is lighter than air and is used for inflating balloons.

helix /hee liks/ *noun* (*plural* **helices** /he li seez/ *or* **helixes**) Maths a spiral.

hell *noun* **1** a place where people who have led bad lives are punished after death, according to some religions. **2** *informal* an extremely bad place or experience. ✶ **for the hell of it** *informal* just for fun.

he'll *contraction* he shall or he will.

hellish *adjective informal* extremely difficult or unpleasant. ➤ **hellishly** *adverb*.

hello *or* **hallo** *interjection* used as a greeting, or sometimes to express surprise or attract attention.

helm *noun* (*plural* **helms**) **1** a tiller or wheel for steering a ship. **2** (**the helm**) the position of control or leadership.

helmet *noun* (*plural* **helmets**) a hard hat that protects your head.

help *verb* (**helps, helping, helped**) **1** to give somebody assistance or support. **2** to be useful to somebody or something, or to make a situation better or easier. ~ *noun* **1** aid or assistance. **2** somebody who helps you: *Peter's a great help.* ✶ **can/can't help** can (or cannot) stop yourself from doing something or prevent something happening. **help yourself 1** to take something without permission or dishonestly. **2** to serve yourself with food or drink. **no help for** no way of avoiding something. ➤ **helper** *noun*.

helpful *adjective* **1** ready to help. **2** useful. ➤ **helpfully** *adverb*.

helping *noun* (*plural* **helpings**) a serving of food.

helpless *adjective* **1** without any protection or support. **2** unable to do anything. ➤ **helplessly** *adverb*, **helplessness** *noun*.

hem *noun* (*plural* **hems**) the edge of a piece of clothing or cloth that is turned back on itself and stitched down.

hemisphere *noun* (*plural* **hemispheres**) **1** a half sphere. **2** the northern or southern half of the earth.

hemp *noun* the Asian plant that cannabis is obtained from, or its fibre which is used to make rope and fabrics.

hen *noun* (*plural* **hens**) **1** a female chicken. **2** any female bird.

hence *adverb* **1** for this reason. **2** from now on: *six weeks hence*.

henceforth *adverb* from this time on.

henchman *noun* (*plural* **henchmen**) a follower or supporter, especially one who does unpleasant jobs for you.

Word History Henchman comes from the Old English word *hengestman*, which means 'a groom, a man who looks after horses'. In the 19th century, the Scottish writer Sir Walter Scott used the word *henchman* in his books to refer to the chief attendant of a Highland chief. The word then came to mean the follower of any important person, and especially one who does bad or dishonest things.

---

henna *noun* a reddish brown dye obtained from the leaves of a tropical shrub.

hepatitis /he pa tie tis/ *noun* inflammation of the liver.

heptagon *noun* (*plural* **heptagons**)

Maths a flat figure with seven angles and seven sides. ➤ **heptagonal** *adjective*.

her *pronoun and adjective* used to refer to a female person or animal, or to something that belongs or relates to a female.

herald *noun* (*plural* **heralds**) **1** *archaic* an official messenger. **2** a person or event which is a sign that something is coming. ~ *verb* (**heralds, heralding, heralded**) to be a sign that something is coming.

heraldry *noun* the system of designing and using coats of arms. ➤ **heraldic** *adjective*.

herb *noun* (*plural* **herbs**) a plant used to flavour food or in medicine.

herbivore *noun* (*plural* **herbivores**) an animal that eats plants. ➤ **herbivorous** *adjective*.

herd *noun* (*plural* **herds**) a group of the same kind of animal that live or are kept together. ~ *verb* (**herds, herding, herded**) to gather, keep, or move animals or people in a group.

here *adverb* in, at, or to this place or position. ✷ **here and there** in various places. **neither here nor there** not important.

hereafter *adverb formal* after this time or point; from now on.

hereby *adverb formal* by these words, or by this method: *I hereby declare you the winner*.

hereditary *adjective* passed from a parent to a child, either from body to body or as a legal right: *a hereditary disease; a hereditary title*.

heredity /hi re di ti/ *noun* the process of passing on characteristics, in the genes, from one generation to the next.

herein /heer in/ *adverb formal* in this document.

heresy /he ri si/ *noun* (*plural* **heresies**) an idea or belief that disagrees with one that is accepted as true, especially in religion.

heretic /he ri tik/ *noun* (*plural* **heretics**) a person who believes in or spreads a heresy. ➤ **heretical** *adjective*.

heritage *noun* the valuable things that earlier generations have given to us.

hermit *noun* (*plural* **hermits**) somebody who lives apart from other people, usually for religious reasons.

hernia *noun* (*plural* **hernias**) a section of intestine that pushes through a weak area in the enclosing muscle wall.

hero *noun* (*plural* **heroes**) **1** somebody who is admired for their special courage or achievements. **2** the main male character in a book, play, or film.

heroic /hi roh ik/ *adjective* very impressive or brave. ➤ **heroically** *adverb*.

heroin /he roh in/ *noun* a very addictive and powerful drug made from morphine.

heroine /he roh in/ *noun* (*plural* **heroines**) **1** a woman admired for her special courage or achievements. **2** the main female character in a book, play, or film.

heroism /he roh i zm/ *noun* great courage.

heron *noun* (*plural* **herons** or **heron**) a large grey bird with a long neck and long legs that catches fish and frogs in rivers and ponds.

herpes /her peez/ *noun* a virus that affects the skin, causing blisters.

herring *noun* (*plural* **herrings** or **herring**) a slim silver sea fish eaten as food.

herringbone *noun* a pattern made up of alternating rows of slanted parallel lines.

hers *pronoun* belonging to or associated with a particular female.

Usage Note Notice that there is no apostrophe in *hers*.

herself *pronoun* **1** used to refer back to a female subject of a clause or sentence: *She burnt herself.* **2** used to emphasize 'she' or a female noun: *The Queen herself told me.* ✱ **by herself** alone.

hertz *noun* (*plural* **hertz**) *Science* a unit of frequency used for measuring sound and radio waves.

he's *contraction* he is or he has.

hesitant *adjective* unsure; hesitating. ➤ **hesitancy** *noun*, **hesitantly** *adverb*.

hesitate *verb* (**hesitates, hesitating, hesitated**) to pause because you are unsure or undecided about something, or because you do not want to do it. ➤ **hesitation** *noun*.

hessian *noun* a coarse fabric used to make sacks.

heterosexual *adjective* sexually attracted to people of the opposite sex. ~ *noun* (*plural* **heterosexuals**) a heterosexual person. ➤ **heterosexuality** *noun*.

hew *verb* (**hews, hewing, hewed, hewed** *or* **hewn**) to chop wood with a heavy blade or axe.

hexagon *noun* (*plural* **hexagons**) *Maths* a flat figure with six angles and six sides. ➤ **hexagonal** *adjective*.

heyday *noun* the most successful or energetic period of your life.

hiatus /hie ay tus/ *noun* (*plural* **hiatuses**) an unexpected break or gap.

hibernate /hie ber nayt/ *verb* (**hibernates, hibernating, hibernated**) said about an animal: to spend the winter in a state of deep sleep. ➤ **hibernation** *noun*.

hiccup *noun* (*plural* **hiccups**) **1** a sudden, sharp, uncontrollable sound from the back of your throat, caused by the muscle contracting suddenly. **2** a short problem or delay. ~ *verb* (**hiccups, hiccupping, hiccupped**) to make the sound of a hiccup or repeated hiccups.

hide¹ *verb* (**hides, hiding, hid, hidden**) **1** to put something where it cannot be seen, or to get into a place where you cannot be seen. **2** to keep something secret.

hide² *noun* (*plural* **hides**) the skin of an animal.

hide-and-seek *noun* a children's game in which some of the players hide and one or more of the others look for them.

hideous /hi di us/ *adjective* **1** extremely ugly. **2** very unpleasant. ➤ **hideously** *adverb*.

hideout *noun* (*plural* **hideouts**) a hiding place.

hierarchy /hier ah ki/ *noun* (*plural* **hierarchies**) a system in which people or things are positioned at different levels by their importance or status. ➤ **hierarchical** *adjective*.

hieroglyphics /hier o gli fiks/ *plural noun* pictures or symbols used to represent words or sounds in a system of writing.

hi-fi /hie fie/ *noun* (*plural* **hi-fis**) *informal* a set of equipment that reproduces the sound of recorded music accurately.

higgledy-piggledy *adverb and adjective* in an untidy and confused mess.

high *adjective* **1** extending up a long way or to a specific height. **2** situated a long way above ground or sea level. **3** more or greater than average. **4** important in terms of rank or status. **5** near the top of the musical scale. **6** powerful: *a high wind; high explosives.* **7** *informal* in an excited state caused by drugs or alcohol. ~ *adverb* at or to a high place, level, or pitch. ~ *noun* (*plural* **highs**) **1** a high point or level. **2** *informal* a state of extreme happiness. **3** a region of high atmospheric pressure. ✱ **high time** a time when something should already have happened. **on high** in or to a high place.

highbrow *adjective* intellectual and cultured.

high court *noun* (*plural* **high courts**) a very important law court.

higher education *noun* education above secondary-school level, at college or university.

high jump *noun* (**the high jump**) a sports event in which you jump over a high bar.

highlands *plural noun* high, hilly land or mountains.

Highlander *noun* (*plural* **Highlanders**) a person from the north of Scotland.

highlight *verb* (**highlights, highlighting, highlighted**) to draw attention to a particular thing. ~ *noun* (*plural* **highlights**) **1** a special event or detail. **2** *Art* a light area in a painting or photograph. **3** (**highlights**) lighter streaks in your hair.

highly *adverb* **1** extremely. **2** in an approving way: *They think highly of you.*

highly-strung *adjective* nervous or sensitive.

Highness *noun* (*plural* **Highnesses**) (**Your/Her/His Highness**) a title used by people in the royal family.

high-rise *adjective* said about a building: with many storeys.

high school *noun* (*plural* **high schools**) a secondary school.

high-spirited *adjective* lively.

high technology *noun* advanced technological machinery and methods. ➤ **high-tech** *adjective*.

high tide *noun* the time when the sea reaches its highest level.

highway *noun* (*plural* **highways**) a public road or main road.

highwayman *noun* (*plural* **highwaymen**) in the past, a robber on horseback who stole from travellers on the road.

hijack *verb* (**hijacks, hijacking, hijacked**) to seize control of a vehicle or aircraft during a journey. ➤ **hijacker** *noun*.

hike *noun* (*plural* **hikes**) a long walk in the country. ~ *verb* (**hikes, hiking, hiked**) to go on a hike. ➤ **hiker** *noun*.

hilarious *adjective* extremely funny. ➤ **hilariously** *adverb*, **hilarity** *noun*.

hill *noun* (*plural* **hills**) a rounded area of high land, lower than a mountain. ✷ **over the hill** *informal* old and past your best. ➤ **hilly** *adjective*.

hillock *noun* (*plural* **hillocks**) a small hill.

hilt *noun* (*plural* **hilts**) the handle of a sword, dagger, or knife.

him *pronoun* used to refer to a male person or animal.

himself *pronoun* used **1** used to refer back to a male subject of a clause or sentence: *He hurt himself.* **2** used to emphasize 'he' or a male noun: *He himself didn't go.* ✷ **by himself** alone.

hind¹ /hiend/ *adjective* placed at the back or behind.

hind² /hiend/ *noun* (*plural* **hinds**) a female deer.

hinder /hin der/ *verb* (**hinders, hindering, hindered**) to obstruct or delay something or somebody.

Hindi *noun* one of the main languages of northern India.

hindquarters *plural noun* the back legs and rear part of a four-legged animal.

hindrance *noun* (*plural* **hindrances**) an obstacle or delay.

hindsight *noun* looking at and understanding a situation after it has happened.

Hinduism *noun* an Indian religion that includes belief in reincarnation and the worship of many gods. ➤ **Hindu** *adjective and noun*.

hinge *noun* (*plural* **hinges**) a device fixed to the edge of a door, window, or lid so that it can swing open and shut. ~ *verb* (**hinges, hingeing** or **hinging, hinged**) **1** to attach something with a hinge. **2 (hinge on)** to depend on something.

hint *noun* (*plural* **hints**) **1** a suggestion or piece of advice. **2** a slight or subtle sign: *There was a hint of anger in her voice.* ~ *verb* (**hints, hinting, hinted**) to say or suggest something in a way that is not obvious: *What are you hinting at?*

hip *noun* (*plural* **hips**) the part on each side of your body between the top of your thigh and your waist.

hippie *noun* (*plural* **hippies**) somebody who lives and dresses unconventionally, and rejects the aims and values of modern society.

hippo *noun* (*plural* **hippos** *or* **hippo**) *informal* = HIPPOPOTAMUS.

hippopotamus *noun* (*plural* **hippopotamuses** *or* **hippopotami** /hi poh **po** ta mie/) a large African animal with a large head and mouth, thick skin, and short legs, living beside and in water.

hire *verb* (**hires, hiring, hired**) **1** to pay money to use something for a time. **2 (hire out)** to lend something to somebody in return for payment. *noun* being hired or hiring something, or the payment given for this: *Bikes for hire.*

hirsute /her sewt/ *adjective formal* hairy.

his *pronoun and adjective* used to refer to a male person or animal, or to something that belongs or relates to him.

hiss *verb* (**hisses, hissing, hissed**) to make a sharp sound like a long /s/. ~ *noun* (*plural* **hisses**) a hissing sound.

histogram *noun* (*plural* **histograms**) *Maths* a diagram with a series of rectangles whose height and width represent different variables.

historian *noun* (*plural* **historians**) somebody who studies or writes about history.

historic *adjective* famous or important in history: *a historic victory.*

historical *adjective* **1** to do with history. **2** that really happened or existed in the past: *a historical battle.*
➤ **historically** *adverb.*

Usage Note Do not confuse *historic* and *historical*. *Historic* means not just that it happened in history, but that it was important.

history *noun* (*plural* **histories**) **1** past events, or the study of them **2** a written record of past events. **3** a person's past life or experience.

hit *verb* (**hits, hitting, hit**) **1** to strike somebody or something with your hand or an object. **2** to knock a ball, etc away from you. **3** to reach a target. **4** to affect somebody or something badly. ~ *noun* (*plural* **hits**) **1** a shot or blow that meets its target. **2** a popular or successful person or thing. **3** *ICT* a successful match when you search a database. **4** *ICT* a specific occasion when somebody visits a site on the Internet. ✷ **hit it off** *informal* to enjoy each other's company. **hit the roof** *informal* to become extremely angry.

hit-and-run *adjective* said about a road accident: involving a driver who does not stop after hitting somebody or something.

hitch *verb* (**hitches, hitching, hitched**) **1** to fasten something with a knot. **2** to pull something up with a jerk. **3** *informal* to get a free lift in a passing vehicle. ~ *noun* (*plural* **hitches**) **1** a short problem or delay. **2** an act of hitching.

hitchhike *verb* (**hitchhikes, hitchhiking, hitchhiked**) to travel by getting free lifts in passing vehicles.
➤ **hitchhiker** *noun.*

hi-tech *adjective* another spelling of HIGH-TECH.

hither *adverb archaic* to or towards this place.

hitherto *adverb* until now.

HIV *abbreviation* = human immuno-deficiency virus, the virus that causes Aids.

hive *noun* (*plural* **hives**) 1 a beehive. 2 a busy place: *a hive of industry*.

hoard *noun* (*plural* **hoards**) a store of money, food, or other useful things for the future. ~ *verb* (**hoards, hoarding, hoarded**) to store up a hoard of something. ➤ **hoarder** *noun*.

Usage Note Do not confuse this word with *horde*, which means 'a large number of people', as in *hordes of visitors*.

hoarding *noun* (*plural* **hoardings**) a large board for displaying advertisements on.

hoarse *adjective* (**hoarser, hoarsest**) said about a voice: rough or harsh. ➤ **hoarsely** *adverb*.

hoax *noun* (*plural* **hoaxes**) a trick or practical joke. ~ *verb* (**hoaxes, hoaxing, hoaxed**) to deceive or trick somebody. ➤ **hoaxer** *noun*.

hob *noun* (*plural* **hobs**) the top surface of a cooker, for heating pans on.

hobble *verb* (**hobbles, hobbling, hobbled**) to walk awkwardly or painfully.

hobby *noun* (*plural* **hobbies**) an activity that you enjoy doing in your spare time.

hock¹ *noun* (*plural* **hocks**) the middle, angled joint of an animal's hind leg.

hock² *verb* (**hocks, hocking, hocked**) *informal* to pawn something. ✳ **in hock 1** having been pawned. **2** in debt.

hockey *noun* a team game in which the players hit a small hard ball with long sticks with curved ends.

hoe *noun* (*plural* **hoes**) a gardening tool with a long handle and a small flat blade. ~ *verb* (**hoes, hoeing, hoed**) to remove weeds or break up soil with a hoe.

hog *noun* (*plural* **hogs**) 1 a castrated male pig. 2 *informal* a greedy person. ~ *verb* (**hogs, hogging, hogged**) *informal* to take more of something than is fair, or to keep it or use it for too long. ✳ **go the whole hog** *informal* to do something thoroughly.

hoist *verb* (**hoists, hoisting, hoisted**) to lift something or somebody using ropes or a machine. ~ *noun* (*plural* **hoists**) a piece of equipment for hoisting something.

hold *verb* (**holds, holding, held**) 1 to have or support something in your hands or arms. 2 said about a container: to contain or be able to contain something. 3 to stay, or to keep something or somebody, in a particular situation or position. 4 to occupy a position or job. 5 to believe something. 6 to organize a meeting, party, etc. 7 to take part in a conversation. ~ *noun* (*plural* **holds**) 1 a way of holding something or somebody. 2 something you hold on to for support. 3 control. 4 the cargo compartment of a ship or aircraft. ✳ **hold forth** to speak for a long time. **hold on** to wait. **hold on to** to keep or grip something. **hold out** 1 to continue despite difficulties. 2 to last. **hold something against somebody** to refuse to forgive somebody for something. **hold up** 1 to delay a person or activity. 2 to rob somebody or something at gunpoint. **on hold** postponed or waiting for a time. **take hold** 1 to grasp something. 2 to take effect. ➤ **holder** *noun*.

holdall *noun* (*plural* **holdalls**) a large bag for clothes and belongings.

holdup *noun* (*plural* **holdups**) 1 an armed robbery. 2 a delay.

hole *noun* (*plural* **holes**) 1 a gap, opening, or hollow in something. 3 a small round space in the ground which you hit the ball into in golf, or the part of the golf course leading to this. **4** *informal* an awkward or unpleasant situation. ~ *verb* (**holes, holing, holed**) **1** to make a hole in something. **2** in golf, to hit the ball into the hole.

holiday *noun* (*plural* **holidays**) a day or a longer period of time when you do not do your normal work. ~ *verb* (**holidays, holidaying, holidayed**) to take or spend a holiday.

holidaymaker *noun* (*plural* **holidaymakers**) somebody on holiday away from home.

holiness *noun* **1** being holy. **2** (**His/Your Holiness**) a title for the Pope and some other religious leaders.

hollow *adjective* **1** curving inwards from the surface. **2** with a hole inside. **3** said about a sound: echoing. **4** not genuine or sincere: *hollow promises*. ~ *verb* (**hollows, hollowing, hollowed**) to make something hollow: *Hollow out the pumpkin with a spoon*. ~ *noun* (*plural* **hollows**) **1** a small valley. **2** a space or cavity.

holly *noun* a shrub with shiny green spiky leaves and red berries.

holocaust /ho lo kawst/ *noun* (*plural* **holocausts**) **1** a time of great destruction or many deaths. **2** (**the Holocaust**) the murder of European Jews by the Nazis during World War II.

hologram /ho lo gram/ *noun* (*plural* **holograms**) a photograph that gives the effect of a three-dimensional image. ➤ **holographic** *adjective*.

holster *noun* (*plural* **holsters**) a holder for a pistol, worn on a belt.

holy *adjective* (**holier, holiest**) **1** given or belonging to God; sacred. **2** spiritually pure.

Holy Land *noun* (**the Holy Land**) the area occupied by modern Israel and Palestine.

Holy Spirit *noun* (**the Holy Spirit**) in the Christian religion, the spirit of God.

homage /ho mij/ *noun* public honour or respect shown to somebody.

home *noun* (*plural* **homes**) **1** the place where you live or where you come from. **2** a place where elderly, ill, or disabled people live and receive care. ~ *adverb* to or at your home. ~ *adjective* **1** to do with your home or your own country. **2** in the place where something is based or situated. ~ *verb* (**homes, homing, homed**) said about a bird or animal: to return home by instinct. ✱ **at home** relaxed and comfortable. **bring home to** to make somebody realize something. **home in on** to move towards or concentrate on something.

homeland *noun* (*plural* **homelands**) the country that you come from.

homely *adjective* (**homelier, homeliest**) **1** ordinary, simple, and comfortably familiar. **2** kind and sympathetic. ➤ **homeliness** *noun*.

homeopathy /hoh mee o pa thi/ *noun* a way of treating diseases with tiny doses of substances that produce symptoms similar to those of the diseases you are treating. ➤ **homeopathic** *adjective*.

home page *noun* (*plural* **home pages**) *ICT* the page of a website that you access first, showing general information.

homesick *adjective* missing your home while you are away. ➤ **homesickness** *noun*.

homestead *noun* (*plural* **homesteads**) a house with land attached to it.

homework *noun* **1** school work that a pupil is given to do at home. **2** reading or research done in advance.

homicide /ho mi sied/ *noun* (*plural* **homicides**) murder. ➤ **homicidal** *adjective*.

homogeneous /ho moh jee ni us/ *adjective* of the same kind.

homograph /ho mo grahf/ *noun* (*plural*

homonym

homographs) *English* a word that has the same spelling as another word but a different pronunciation and meaning, such as the noun *lead* (= the metal) and the verb *lead* (= 'to guide or be in front').

homonym /ho mo nim/ *noun* (*plural* **homonyms**) *English* a word that has the same spelling and pronunciation as another word but a different meaning and origin, such as the noun *bear* (= the animal) and the verb *bear* (= 'to carry').

homophobia *noun* fear or dislike of homosexuality and homosexuals. ➤ **homophobic** *adjective*.

homophone *noun* (*plural* **homophones**) *English* a word that is pronounced like another word but has a different meaning, origin, or spelling, such as *to*, *too*, and *two*.

homo sapiens /hoh moh sa pi enz/ *noun* the human species; human beings.

homosexual *adjective* having a sexual preference for members of the same sex. ~ *noun* (*plural* **homosexuals**) a homosexual person.
➤ **homosexuality** *noun*.

honest *adjective* truthful, sincere, and trustworthy. ➤ **honestly** *adverb*, **honesty** *noun*.

honey *noun* a sweet sticky golden substance made by bees and used as a food.

honeycomb *noun* (*plural* **honeycombs**) a mass of six-sided wax cells which bees build to contain their eggs and store honey in.

honeymoon *noun* (*plural* **honeymoons**) a holiday which a married couple take immediately after their wedding.

honeysuckle *noun* a climbing shrub with sweet-smelling flowers.

honk *verb* (**honks, honking, honked**) **1** to sound a car horn. **2** to make the cry of a goose. ➤ **honk** *noun*.

honorary *adjective* **1** awarded to somebody as an honour. **2** unpaid: *the honorary secretary of the association.*

honour *noun* (*plural* **honours**) **1** public recognition or fame for your good reputation or achievements. **2** a privilege. **3** an award for achievement or excellence. **4** a sense of morality and justice. **5** (**Honours**) the highest standard in a degree course or examination. **6** (**Your/His/Her Honour**) a title for a judge in court.
~ *verb* (**honours, honouring, honoured**) **1** to show great respect to somebody, or to give them something which shows respect. **2** to carry out a duty or promise. ✻ **in honour of** as a mark of respect for somebody or something.

honourable *adjective* **1** honest, decent, and fair. **2** worthy of respect. **3** (**the Honourable**) used as a title for the children of some members of the nobility. **4** used in Parliament when one MP is talking to or about another MP: *My honourable friend is mistaken.*

hood *noun* (*plural* **hoods**) **1** a covering, usually attached to the back of a coat or jacket, that you can pull up over your head and neck. **2** a cover or canopy. ➤ **hooded** *adjective*.

hoodwink *verb* (**hoodwinks, hoodwinking, hoodwinked**) to deceive or trick somebody.

hoof *noun* (*plural* **hooves** *or* **hoofs**) the hard horny part on the foot of a horse, cow, etc. ➤ **hoofed** *adjective*.

hook *noun* (*plural* **hooks**) **1** a curved piece of metal or plastic for hanging things on or attaching things to. **2** a punch in boxing delivered in a short circular movement. ~ *verb* (**hooks, hooking, hooked**) to attach or catch something with a hook. ✻ **be hooked** *informal* to be addicted or fascinated. **be let off the hook** *informal* to be allowed to escape or avoid something difficult or unpleasant. **by hook or by crook** in any way you can.

hooligan *noun* (*plural* **hooligans**) a violent young person who damages property and behaves badly. ➤ **hooliganism** *noun*.

hoop *noun* (*plural* **hoops**) **1** a circular strip of metal, wood, etc. **2** a small arch which you hit the balls through in croquet.

hooray *interjection* = HURRAY.

hoot *verb* (**hoots, hooting, hooted**) **1** said about an owl: to call out. **2** to sound the horn of a vehicle. **3** to laugh loudly or scornfully. ~ *noun* (*plural* **hoots**) **1** a hooting sound. **2** *informal* something very funny.

Hoover *noun* (*plural* **Hoovers**) *trademark* a vacuum cleaner. ~ *verb* (**hoovers, hoovering, hoovered**) to clean a carpet with a vacuum cleaner.

hooves *noun* plural of HOOF.

hop *verb* (**hops, hopping, hopped**) **1** to jump repeatedly on one foot. **2** said about birds and other animals: to jump with both feet, with a quick springy movement. **3** to go somewhere or get into something quickly: *I'll hop on a bus.* ~ *noun* (*plural* **hops**) **1** a hopping movement. **2** a short journey by air. * **catch on the hop** *informal* to find somebody unprepared.

hope *verb* (**hopes, hoping, hoped**) **1** to want or expect something to be true or to happen. ~ *noun* (*plural* **hopes**) **1** the feeling that what you want to happen can happen, or a chance that it may happen. **2** (**hopes**) the things you want to happen. **3** somebody or something you are depending on. * **hope for the best** to hope that things will work out as you want them to.

hopeful *adjective* feeling hope or giving you hope. ~ *noun* (*plural* **hopefuls**) somebody who hopes to be successful.

hopefully *adverb* **1** in a hopeful manner. **2** *informal* I hope.

Usage Note Some people disapprove of using *hopefully* to mean 'I hope', as in *Hopefully, I'll be home before dark*. It is therefore better not to use it in this way in formal written English.

hopeless *adjective* **1** having no chance of succeeding or of being solved successfully. **2** incompetent or useless. ➤ **hopelessly** *adverb*, **hopelessness** *noun*.

hops *plural noun* a type of small dried flowers used to give a bitter taste to beer.

hopscotch *noun* a game which children play by hopping on a set of squares drawn on the ground.

horde *noun* (*plural* **hordes**) a large disorganized group of people.

Usage Note Do not confuse this word with *hoard*, which means 'a supply of something', as in *a hoard of money*.

horizon *noun* (*plural* **horizons**) **1** the line in the distance where the land and the sky appear to meet. **2** (**horizons**) the things you understand, know, or have experienced.

horizontal *adjective* parallel to the earth's surface; flat. ➤ **horizontally** *adverb*.

hormone *noun* (*plural* **hormones**) *Science* a substance produced in the body that affects the way your body grows and develops. ➤ **hormonal** *adjective*.

horn *noun* (*plural* **horns**) **1** a piece of bony material that animals such as cattle and goats grow on their heads. **2** *Music* a brass instrument shaped like a coiled tube with a wide end. **3** a device in a vehicle that makes a loud noise to warn others. ➤ **horned** *adjective*, **horny** *adjective*.

hornet noun (plural **hornets**) a large wasp.

horoscope noun (plural **horoscopes**) a forecast of your future, based on where the planets and stars were when you were born.

horrendous adjective dreadful or horrible. ➤ **horrendously** adverb.

horrible adjective **1** extremely unpleasant. **2** horrifying. ➤ **horribly** adverb.

horrid adjective very nasty and unpleasant.

horrific adjective causing horror; horrifying. ➤ **horrifically** adverb.

horrify verb (**horrifies, horrifying, horrified**) to make somebody extremely frightened or shocked. ➤ **horrifying** adjective.

horror noun **1** intense fear. **2** shock or disgust.

horse noun (plural **horses**) **1** a large four-footed animal which people use for riding and to pull vehicles. **2** a wooden block that you vault over in gymnastics.

horseback ✱ **on horseback** riding on a horse or horses.

horsebox noun (plural **horseboxes**) a lorry or trailer for transporting horses.

horse chestnut noun (plural **horse chestnuts**) **1** a large tree with large leaves divided into five parts. **2** a shiny brown nut from this tree, with a prickly outer case; a conker.

horseman noun (plural **horsemen**) a man who rides a horse. ➤ **horsemanship** noun.

horsepower noun Science a unit of power equal to about 746 watts.

horseradish noun a plant with a hot-tasting root used to make a sauce.

horseshoe noun (plural **horseshoes**) a U-shaped metal shoe for horses.

horsewoman noun (plural **horsewomen**) a woman who rides a horse.

horticulture noun the science of growing fruit, vegetables, and flowers. ➤ **horticultural** adjective.

hose noun (plural **hoses**) a flexible tube for water or another liquid or gas to pass through. ~ verb (**hoses, hosing, hosed**) to spray or water something with a hose: *I hosed the car down to get the mud off.*

hosepipe noun (plural **hosepipes**) a long piece of hose.

hosiery /hoh zi ə ri/ noun socks, stockings, and tights.

hospice noun (plural **hospices**) a home where dying patients are cared for.

hospitable adjective welcoming; pleasant and friendly to visitors. ➤ **hospitably** adverb.

hospital noun (plural **hospitals**) a place where sick or injured people receive medical care.

hospitality noun friendly treatment of visitors.

Host noun (**the Host**) the bread that is made holy in the Christian service of Mass or Communion.

host[1] noun (plural **hosts**) **1** somebody who organizes and invites guests to a social event. **2** somebody who introduces the guests on a radio or television programme. **3** Science an animal or plant which has a parasite or smaller organism living on or in it. ~ verb (**hosts, hosting, hosted**) to be the host at a party, etc.

host[2] noun (plural **hosts**) **1** a very large number. **2** archaic an army.

hostage noun (plural **hostages**) somebody who is held prisoner to make another person do something.

hostel noun (plural **hostels**) a building with rooms for a particular group of people to stay in: *a student/youth hostel.*

hostess noun (plural **hostesses**) a female host.

hostile adjective **1** aggressive and

unfriendly. **2** from or to do with an enemy. ➤ **hostility** *noun*.

hot *adjective* (**hotter, hottest**) **1** having a high temperature. **2** uncomfortable because of heat. **3** spicy. **4** *informal* new and exciting or popular. **5** *informal* stolen. **6** (**hot on**) strict about something. **7** (**hot on**) knowledgeable about something. ~ *verb* (**hots, hotting, hotted**) *informal* ✶ **hot up** to become more exciting.

hot-blooded *adjective* excitable or passionate.

hot cross bun *noun* (*plural* **hot cross buns**) a spicy fruit bun with a cross on top.

hot dog *noun* (*plural* **hot dogs**) a hot sausage served in a bread roll.

hotel *noun* (*plural* **hotels**) a building with rooms you can pay to sleep in and which also provides you with food.

hothouse *noun* (*plural* **hothouses**) a heated greenhouse.

hotly *adverb* keenly or passionately.

hot-water bottle *noun* (*plural* **hot-water bottles**) a rubber container that you fill with hot water and use to warm a bed.

hound *noun* (*plural* **hounds**) a hunting dog. ~ *verb* (**hounds, hounding, hounded**) to follow somebody around continually, asking or wanting things.

hour *noun* (*plural* **hours**) **1** a period of 60 minutes. **2** a particular time of day. **3** (**hours**) the set period for a specific activity: *visiting hours*.

hourly *adjective and adverb* at or during every hour.

house /hows/ *noun* (*plural* **houses** /howziz/) **1** a building for people to live in. **2** a building, organization, or section with a particular purpose: *an opera house; a publishing house*. **3** the area where the audience sits in a theatre or cinema. **4** a section of Parliament: *the House of Commons*. **5** *History* an important or ancient family: *the House of Tudor*. ~ /howz/ *verb* (**houses, housing, housed**) to store or find a place for something. ✶ **on the house** provided free by the management.

houseboat *noun* (*plural* **houseboats**) a boat on a canal, used as a home.

household *noun* (*plural* **households**) a house or flat and all the people who live in it. ~ *adjective* to do with life in a house or flat: *household expenses*.

household name *noun* (*plural* **household names**) something or somebody everyone has heard of.

housekeeper *noun* (*plural* **housekeepers**) somebody who is paid to cook, clean, and manage a house. ➤ **housekeeping** *noun*.

House of Commons *noun* (**the House of Commons**) the section of Parliament consisting of elected MPs.

House of Lords *noun* (**the House of Lords**) the section of Parliament consisting of some members of the nobility, some bishops and archbishops, and some senior judges.

house-proud *adjective* liking your home to look very clean, tidy, and nice.

housewife *noun* (*plural* **housewives**) a woman who runs her family's home.

housework *noun* the work involved in running a home.

housing *noun* houses or accommodation generally.

hovel /hovil/ *noun* (*plural* **hovels**) a small, very dirty house or room.

hover /hover/ *verb* (**hovers, hovering, hovered**) **1** to stay in one place in the air. **2** to wait around uncertainly or nervously.

hovercraft *noun* (*plural* **hovercraft**) a vehicle that travels over water and land by blowing air from underneath to lift it.

how *adverb* **1** in what way or by what

however

method. **2** in what condition. **3** by what amount. **4** used to emphasize something or show surprise: *How odd!*

however *adverb* **1** nevertheless; even so. **2** in whatever way. **3** no matter how.

howl *verb* (**howls, howling, howled**) **1** to make a long, loud cry or wailing sound. **2** to cry loudly. ➤ **howl** *noun*.

HTML *abbreviation* ICT = hypertext markup language, a system used to write text to display on the Internet.

hub *noun* (*plural* **hubs**) **1** the central part of a wheel or propeller. **2** a centre of activity.

hubbub *noun* noisy confusion or uproar.

huddle *verb* (**huddles, huddling, huddled**) **1** to gather in a tight group: *We huddled together to keep warm.* **2** to curl up or crouch. ~ *noun* (*plural* **huddles**) a tight group.

hue *noun* (*plural* **hues**) a colour or shade.

hue and cry *noun* a loud public outcry.

huff *verb* (**huffs, huffing, huffed**) to make loud puffing noises or pointless threats. ~ *noun* (*plural* **huffs**) a loud puffing noise or breath. ✴ **in a huff** sulky and offended. ➤ **huffy** *adjective*.

hug *verb* (**hugs, hugging, hugged**) **1** to hold somebody tightly in your arms. **2** to keep close to something. ~ *noun* (*plural* **hugs**) an act of hugging.

huge *adjective* (**huger, hugest**) very large. ➤ **hugely** *adverb*.

hulk *noun* (*plural* **hulks**) **1** the bare main structure of a disused ship. **2** a very big and awkward person or thing.

hulking *adjective informal* very big.

hull *noun* (*plural* **hulls**) the main body of a ship.

hullabaloo *noun* (*plural* **hullabaloos**) *informal* a loud confused noise.

hum *verb* (**hums, humming, hummed**) **1** to make a long /m/ sound or a low buzz like a flying insect. **2** to sing with your lips closed. ~ *noun* (*plural* **hums**) a humming sound.

human *adjective* to do with or belonging to people. ~ *noun* (*plural* **humans**) a man, woman, or child. ➤ **humanly** *adverb*.

humane *adjective* kind and compassionate. ➤ **humanely** *adverb*.

humanism *noun* the belief that human beings are good and valuable in their own right and do not need religion. ➤ **humanist** *noun and adjective*, **humanistic** *adjective*.

humanitarian *adjective* concerned with helping and comforting people. ~ *noun* (*plural* **humanitarians**) a humanitarian person.

humanity *noun* (*plural* **humanities**) **1** human beings as a group. **2** the quality of being human or humane. **3** (**humanities**) subjects to do with human culture, such as literature and history, as opposed to science.

human rights *plural noun* the basic rights that all human beings are entitled to.

humble *adjective* (**humbler, humblest**) **1** modest; not considering yourself special or important. **2** low in rank or status. ~ *verb* (**humbles, humbling, humbled**) to make somebody feel humble. ➤ **humbly** *adverb*.

humbug *noun* (*plural* **humbugs**) **1** a hard, stripy, peppermint-flavoured sweet. **2** a lot of lies or nonsense.

humdrum *adjective* ordinary or dull.

humid *adjective* said about air or the climate: warm and moist. ➤ **humidity** *noun*.

humiliate *verb* (**humiliates, humiliating, humiliated**) to make somebody feel foolish or ashamed. ➤ **humiliation** *noun*.

humility *noun* the quality of being humble.

hummingbird *noun* (*plural* **hummingbirds**) a tiny colourful bird that beats its wings so fast they make a humming sound.

humorous *adjective* funny. ➤ **humorously** *adverb*.

humour *noun* (*plural* **humours**) **1** a comic or amusing quality. **2** a mood or state of mind. ~ *verb* (**humours, humouring, humoured**) to please somebody by doing or allowing what they want. ➤ **humourless** *adjective*.

hump *noun* (*plural* **humps**) **1** a rounded lump on the back of an animal or person. **2** a mound. ~ *verb* (**humps, humping, humped**) to carry something heavy, with difficulty. ➤ **humped** *adjective*.

humus /hew mus/ *noun* Science partly decomposed plant or animal material that makes soil fertile.

hunch[1] *verb* (**hunches, hunching, hunched**) to sit or stand with your back curved, or to bend your shoulders forward.

hunch[2] *noun* (*plural* **hunches**) an instinctive feeling that you know something.

hunchback *noun* (*plural* **hunchbacks**) *offensive* a person with a humped back.

hundred *noun* (*plural* **hundreds** *or* **hundred**) **1** the number 100. **2** *informal* (*also in plural*) a large number: *We caught hundreds of fish.* ➤ **hundredth** *adjective and noun*.

hung *verb* past tense and past participle of HANG.

hunger *noun* **1** the feeling you have when you need food. **2** a longing for something. ~ *verb* (**hungers, hungering, hungered**) **1** to feel or suffer hunger. **2** (**hunger for/after**) to long for something.

hunger strike *noun* (*plural* **hunger strikes**) refusal to eat, as an act of protest.

hungry *adjective* (**hungrier, hungriest**) feeling hunger. ➤ **hungrily** *adverb*.

hunk *noun* (*plural* **hunks**) a large piece of something.

hunt *verb* (**hunts, hunting, hunted**) **1** to chase and kill an animal for food or enjoyment. **2** (**hunt for**) to try to find something. ~ *noun* (*plural* **hunts**) **1** an act of hunting. **2** a group of riders and hounds that hunt. ➤ **hunter** *noun*, **hunting** *noun*, **huntsman** *noun*.

hurdle *noun* (*plural* **hurdles**) **1** a light barrier which athletes jump over in a race. **2** a difficulty or problem you have to overcome. ➤ **hurdler** *noun*.

hurl *verb* (**hurls, hurling, hurled**) **1** to throw something forcefully. **2** to shout insults at somebody.

hurrah *interjection* = HURRAY.

hurray /hu ray/, **hurrah** /hu rah/, *or* **hooray** /hu ray/ *interjection* used to express joy, approval, or encouragement.

hurricane *noun* (*plural* **hurricanes**) a storm with extremely strong winds.

hurry *verb* (**hurries, hurrying, hurried**) to move or act quickly, or to make somebody or something go faster: *Hurry up or you'll miss the bus.* ~ *noun* rush. ✲ **in a hurry 1** needing to hurry. **2** quickly. ➤ **hurried** *adjective*, **hurriedly** *adverb*.

hurt *verb* (**hurts, hurting, hurt**) **1** to injure somebody or something or cause them pain. **2** to be painful. **3** to offend or upset somebody. ~ *adjective* **1** injured. **2** upset or offended. ~ *noun* emotional pain.

hurtful *adjective* unkind. ➤ **hurtfully** *adverb*.

hurtle *verb* (**hurtles, hurtling,**

husband

hurtled) to move very fast or dangerously fast.

husband *noun* (*plural* **husbands**) the man a woman is married to.

husbandry *noun* **1** farming. **2** careful or economical management.

hush *verb* (**hushes, hushing, hushed**) to become quiet or make somebody or something quiet. ~ *noun* silence or quietness. * **hush up** to keep something secret. ➤ **hushed** *adjective*.

husk *noun* (*plural* **husks**) the dry outer covering of a seed or fruit.

husky[1] *adjective* (**huskier, huskiest**) said of a voice: hoarse and rough. ➤ **huskily** *adverb*.

husky[2] *noun* (*plural* **huskies**) a powerful dog used to pull sledges over snow.

hustings *plural noun* the speeches and campaigning in a political election.

hustle *verb* (**hustles, hustling, hustled**) to push somebody to make them go somewhere or do something: *They hustled her out of the door.*

hut *noun* (*plural* **huts**) a small simple shelter or house.

hutch *noun* (*plural* **hutches**) a pen or cage for a small animal.

hyacinth /hie a sinth/ *noun* (*plural* **hyacinths**) a plant with a spike of blue, pink, or white flowers.

hybrid *noun* (*plural* **hybrids**)
1 an animal or plant bred from two different breeds or varieties.
2 something that is a combination of different things.

hydrangea /hie drayn ja/ *noun* (*plural* **hydrangeas**) a shrub with large clusters of white, pink, or pale blue flowers.

hydrant *noun* (*plural* **hydrants**) a pipe you can attach a hose to to get water from the water main.

hydraulic /hie draw lik/ *adjective* worked by the pressure of water or liquid being forced through pipes, etc.
➤ **hydraulically** *adverb*.

hydroelectric *adjective* to do with producing electricity using water power. ➤ **hydroelectricity** *noun*.

hydrogen *noun Science* a flammable gas that is the simplest and lightest of the chemical elements.

hyena /hie ee na/ *noun* (*plural* **hyenas**) a dog-like wild animal with a loud shrieking call.

hygiene /hie jeen/ *noun* clean conditions and habits that help people avoid germs and disease.
➤ **hygienic** *adjective*, **hygienically** *adverb*.

hymn /him/ *noun* (*plural* **hymns**) a song of praise to God.

hype *noun informal* exaggerated advertising or publicity. * **be hyped up** to be very excited or nervous.

hyperactive *adjective* abnormally active; unable to relax or stay still.
➤ **hyperactivity** *noun*.

hyperbole /hie per bo li/ *noun English* deliberate exaggeration for special effect, as in *It took me years to get here*.

hyperlink *noun* (*plural* **hyperlinks**) *ICT* a link that you click on to get to another page on the Internet, or to another part of a document, etc.

hypersensitive *adjective* abnormally sensitive. ➤ **hypersensitivity** *noun*.

hypertension *noun Science* abnormally high blood pressure.

hypertext *noun ICT* a type of computer document containing hyperlinks.

hyphen *noun* (*plural* **hyphens**) a punctuation mark (-) used to join two words or to split a word at the end of a line.

hyphenate *verb* (**hyphenates, hyphenating, hyphenated**) to join or split words with a hyphen. ➤ **hyphenation** *noun*.

hypnosis /hip noh sis/ *noun* the state of

being hypnotized. ➤ **hypnotic** *adjective*, **hypnotically** *adverb*.

hypnotism /hip no ti zm/ *noun* the use of hypnosis. ➤ **hypnotist** *noun*.

hypnotize *or* **hypnotise** *verb* (**hypnotizes, hypnotizing, hypnotized** *or* **hypnotises**, etc) **1** to put somebody into a sleep-like state in which you can influence their thoughts and behaviour. **2** to fascinate somebody.

hypochondria /hie poh kon dri a/ *noun* unnecessary anxiety about your health.

Word History Hypochondria comes from an ancient Greek word *hypochondrios*, meaning 'to do with the parts of your body below your ribs'. People used to think that this was where sad and anxious feelings came from.

hypochondriac *noun* (*plural* **hypochondriacs**) somebody who worries too much about their health.

hypocrisy /hi po kri si/ *noun* the behaviour of a hypocrite.

hypocrite /hi poh krit/ *noun* (*plural* **hypocrites**) somebody who pretends to have better standards of behaviour or qualities than they actually have. ➤ **hypocritical** *adjective*.

hypodermic /hie poh der mik/ *adjective* said about a syringe or needle: used to inject drugs beneath the skin. ~ *noun* (*plural* **hypodermics**) a hypodermic syringe.

hypotenuse /hie po ti newz/ *noun* (*plural* **hypotenuses**) *Maths* the longest side of a right-angled triangle, opposite the right angle.

hypothermia /hie poh ther mi a/ *noun Science* a condition in which your body temperature is dangerously low.

hypothesis /hie po thi sis/ *noun* (*plural* **hypotheses**) a theory or suggestion used to explain an event or situation, without definite proof.

hypothetical /hie po the ti kl/ *adjective* only possible or theoretical, not real or proved. ➤ **hypothetically** *adverb*.

hysterectomy /his ti rek to mi/ *noun* (*plural* **hysterectomies**) an operation to remove a woman's womb.

hysteria /his teer i a/ *noun* extreme uncontrolled distress or excitement.

hysterical /his te ri kl/ *adjective* **1** to do with, or in a state of, hysteria. **2** *informal* extremely funny.

hysterics *plural noun* **1** a fit of hysteria. **2** *informal* uncontrollable laughter or crying.

I *pronoun* the word used by a speaker or writer to refer to himself or herself.

ice *noun* (*plural* **ices**) **1** frozen water. **2** an ice cream. ~ *verb* (**ices, icing, iced**) **1** to cover a cake with icing. **2** to chill a drink with ice. ✶ **ice over** **and ice up** to become covered with ice: *The river iced over; The car was iced up this morning.*

ice age *noun* (*plural* **ice ages**) (*often* **Ice Age**) *History* a period when much of the earth's surface was covered in ice.

iceberg *noun* (*plural* **icebergs**) a large mass of ice floating in the sea.

ice cap *noun* (*plural* **ice caps**) *Geography* a permanent covering of ice over the North Pole and the South Pole.

ice cream *noun* (*plural* **ice creams**) a sweet frozen food made from milk, cream, or custard.

ice hockey *noun* a game like hockey played on an ice rink by two teams of six players.

ice lolly *noun* see LOLLY.

ice rink *noun* (*plural* **ice rinks**) an ice-covered floor for skating.

ice skate *noun* (*plural* **ice skates**) a shoe made for skating on ice, with a metal blade attached to the sole.

ice-skate *verb* (**ice-skates, ice-skating, ice-skated**) to glide on ice wearing ice skates.

icicle /ie si kl/ *noun* (*plural* **icicles**) a pointed piece of ice that hangs down from a surface, formed when dripping water freezes.

icing *noun* a sweet coating for cakes and biscuits, made from icing sugar mixed with water or butter.

icing sugar *noun* sugar in the form of a fine powder.

icon /ie kon/ *noun* (*plural* **icons**) **1** in Christianity, a small painting of Jesus, Mary, or a saint. **2** *ICT* a symbol on a computer screen providing access to a program or window.

icy *adjective* (**icier, iciest**) **1** covered with or full of ice. **2** intensely cold.

idea *noun* (*plural* **ideas**) **1** a thought or image in your mind. **2** an opinion or belief. ✶ **have no idea** not to know at all: *I have no idea why she left.*

ideal *noun* (*plural* **ideals**) **1** a standard of excellence that people try to achieve. **2** a person or thing that is regarded as perfect. ~ *adjective* perfect. ➤ **ideally** *adverb*.

idealism *noun* the practice of trying to live according to your ideals. ➤ **idealist** *noun*, **idealistic** *adjective*.

idealize *or* **idealise** *verb* (**idealizes, idealizing, idealized** *or* **idealises**, etc) to consider somebody or something as perfect, usually without justification.

identical *adjective* **1** the very same; exactly alike. **2** said about twins or triplets: having developed from the same egg and therefore very similar in appearance. ➤ **identically** *adverb*.

identification *noun* **1** the act of identifying somebody or something. **2** proof of your identity.

illegitimate

identify *verb* (**identifies, identifying, identified**) **1** to recognize somebody or something, or say who they are or what it is: *She identified her stolen ring.* **2** to understand or share somebody else's feelings: *I can identify with you in your disappointment.* ➤ **identifiable** *adjective*.

identity *noun* (*plural* **identities**) the individual characteristics that make somebody or something who or what they are.

ideology /ie di o lo ji/ *noun* (*plural* **ideologies**) the set of political beliefs held by a person or group. ➤ **ideological** *adjective*.

idiocy /i di o si/ *noun* foolishness.

idiom *noun* (*plural* **idioms**) *English* an expression that has a meaning that cannot be understood from the meanings of each of the separate words, such as *in hot water* which means 'in serious trouble'.

idiosyncrasy /i di oh **sing** kra si/ *noun* (*plural* **idiosyncrasies**) a way of thinking or behaving that is typical of a particular person. ➤ **idiosyncratic** *adjective*.

idiot *noun* (*plural* **idiots**) a silly or foolish person.

idiotic *adjective* extremely foolish. ➤ **idiotically** *adverb*.

idle *adjective* (**idler, idlest**) lazy or not occupied. ➤ **idleness** *noun*, **idly** *adverb*.

idol /ie dl/ *noun* (*plural* **idols**) **1** an image of a god that some people worship. **2** a famous person who has a large number of enthusiastic admirers: *a pop idol*.

idolize *or* **idolise** *verb* (**idolizes, idolizing, idolized** *or* **idolises**, etc) to admire somebody to an extreme degree.

idyll /i dl/ *noun* (*plural* **idylls**) a time or place of peace and happiness. ➤ **idyllic** *adjective*.

i.e. *abbreviation* = (Latin) *id est* that is to say.

if *conjunction* **1** supposing or on condition that: *If you go, I'll go too.* **2** whether: *I don't know if I should tell you.*

igloo *noun* (*plural* **igloos**) a dome-shaped house made of snow blocks, where an Eskimo lives.

igneous *adjective* said about rocks: formed from melted rock from the earth's core.

ignite *verb* (**ignites, igniting, ignited**) to set fire to something, or to catch fire.

ignition *noun* a device in a car's engine that ignites the fuel.

ignominious /ig noh **mi** ni us/ *adjective* causing disgrace or humiliation. ➤ **ignominiously** *adverb*.

ignominy /ig **noh** mi ni/ *noun* deep disgrace or humiliation.

ignoramus /ig noh **ray** mus/ *noun* (*plural* **ignoramuses**) an ignorant or stupid person.

ignorant *adjective* **1** having a general lack of knowledge or education. **2** not knowing something: *ignorant of the facts.* ➤ **ignorance** *noun*, **ignorantly** *adverb*.

ignore *verb* (**ignores, ignoring, ignored**) to take no notice of somebody or something.

iguana /i **gwah** na/ *noun* (*plural* **iguanas**) a large tropical American lizard.

ill *adjective* (**worse, worst**) **1** not in good health. **2** causing discomfort or inconvenience: *ill effects.* ✻ **ill at ease** uneasy or uncomfortable.

illegal *adjective* against the law. ➤ **illegality** *noun*, **illegally** *adverb*.

illegible /i le ji bl/ *adjective* said about writing: not clear enough to read. ➤ **illegibility** *noun*.

illegitimate /i li ji ti mat/ *adjective* said about a child: born to parents who are

ill-fated

not married to each other. ➤ **illegitimacy** noun.

ill-fated adjective bound to fail: an ill-fated business venture.

illicit /i lis it/ adjective not permitted by law or custom.

illiterate /i li ti rat/ adjective unable to read or write. ➤ **illiteracy** noun.

illness noun (plural **illnesses**) **1** the condition of being unwell. **2** a disease.

illogical adjective said about an argument: not making sense. ➤ **illogicality** noun, **illogically** adverb.

illuminate verb (**illuminates, illuminating, illuminated**) to light up a building or a sign.

illumination noun (plural **illuminations**) **1** the act of lighting up a place. **2** (**illuminations**) decorative lighting on a building or street.

illusion noun (plural **illusions**) **1** a false impression or belief. **2** Art something that deceives the eye by appearing to be what it is not: The artist has created an illusion of depth. **3** a magic trick designed to deceive the eye.

illusory /i looh so ri/ adjective seeming to be real but actually false.

illustrate verb (**illustrates, illustrating, illustrated**) **1** to provide a story, book, or magazine with pictures. **2** to explain something by using examples. ➤ **illustrator** noun.

illustration noun (plural **illustrations**) **1** a picture illustrating a story, book, or magazine. **2** an example that explains something.

illustrious adjective admired and well-known.

ill will noun unfriendly feeling towards somebody.

image noun (plural **images**) **1** a picture or statue of somebody or something. **2** a picture in your mind of somebody or something that is not actually present. **3** the idea that people have what a famous person is like.

imagery /i mi ji ri/ noun English the use of words to describe something in a way that creates a clear mental picture of it.

imaginary adjective not real; existing only in your imagination.

imagination noun the ability to form pictures in your mind and to have new and interesting ideas.

imaginative adjective having a good imagination. ➤ **imaginatively** adverb.

imagine verb (**imagines, imagining, imagined**) **1** to form a picture of something in your mind. **2** to suppose or think: I imagine you must be hungry.

imam /i mahm/ noun (plural **imams**) the person who leads the prayers in a mosque.

imbalance noun a lack of proportion or balance.

imbecile /im bi seel/ noun (plural **imbeciles**) informal a fool or idiot.

imitate verb (**imitates, imitating, imitated**) **1** to try to be like somebody by doing what they do. **2** to mimic somebody for comical effect. ➤ **imitator** noun.

imitation noun (plural **imitations**) **1** the act of imitating somebody. **2** a copy of something. ~ adjective artificial: imitation leather.

immaculate /i ma kew lat/ adjective **1** spotlessly clean and very tidy. **2** having no flaws or errors. ➤ **immaculately** adverb.

immaterial adjective unimportant or not relevant.

immature adjective **1** not yet fully grown or fully developed. **2** lacking the wisdom and good sense associated with being an adult. ➤ **immaturity** noun.

immediate adjective **1** occurring at once or about to occur. **2** closest in space, time, or relationship: our immediate neighbours.

immediately *adverb* **1** at once. **2** directly: *immediately after lunch*.

immemorial ✳ **from time immemorial** for longer than anybody can remember.

immense *adjective* very large or very great. ➤ **immensely** *adverb*, **immensity** *noun*.

immerse *verb* (**immerses, immersing, immersed**) to plunge something completely into a liquid. ✳ **immerse yourself in** to give all your attention to something. ➤ **immersion** *noun*.

immersion heater *noun* (*plural* **immersion heaters**) an electric water-heater inside a hot-water storage tank.

immigrant *noun* (*plural* **immigrants**) a person who immigrates.

immigrate *verb* (**immigrates, immigrating, immigrated**) to come from the country where you were born to live permanently in another country. ➤ **immigration** *noun*.

imminent *adjective* about to happen. ➤ **imminence** *noun*, **imminently** *adverb*.

immobile *adjective* not moving. ➤ **immobility** *noun*.

immoral *adjective* not living by accepted moral standards. ➤ **immorality** *noun*.

immortal *adjective* **1** living for ever. **2** remembered or remaining well-known for a very long time: *the immortal words of Charles Dickens*. ➤ **immortality** *noun*.

immovable *or* **immoveable** *adjective* not able to be moved or persuaded.

immune *adjective* **1** unable to catch a disease: *immune to measles*. **2** not affected by something: *immune to criticism*. ➤ **immunity** *noun*.

immune system *noun* (*plural* **immune systems**) all the cells and tissues in your body that protect it from infection.

imp *noun* (*plural* **imps**) a mischievous creature like a fairy. ➤ **impish** *adjective*.

impact *noun* (*plural* **impacts**) **1** a collision between one person or thing and another. **2** a powerful effect or impression.

impair *verb* (**impairs, impairing, impaired**) to damage or spoil something. ➤ **impairment** *noun*.

impale *verb* (**impales, impaling, impaled**) to pierce something or somebody with a pointed object.

impart *verb* (**imparts, imparting, imparted**) to give some information to somebody.

impartial *adjective* not showing any favouritism. ➤ **impartiality** *noun*, **impartially** *adverb*.

impasse /am pahs/ *noun* a point where no further progress can be made.

impassive *adjective* showing no emotion.

impasto /im **pas** toh/ *noun* Art the process of applying paint so thickly that it stands out from the canvas.

impatient *adjective* **1** likely to become angry quickly. **2** anxious to do something. ➤ **impatience** *noun*, **impatiently** *adverb*.

impeccable *adjective* having no faults or blemishes. ➤ **impeccably** *adverb*.

impede *verb* (**impedes, impeding, impeded**) to hinder the progress of somebody or something.

impediment /im pe di mint/ *noun* (*plural* **impediments**) **1** something that hinders progress. **2** a speech problem such as a stammer or lisp.

impel *verb* (**impels, impelling, impelled**) to make somebody feel the need to do something: *I felt impelled to complain*.

impending *adjective* about to happen.

impenetrable *adjective* difficult to get through: *an impenetrable forest*.

imperative *adjective* very urgent or

imperfect

important. ~ *noun* (*plural* **imperatives**) *English* the form of a verb used to express a command, such as the verb 'stop' in *Stop that at once!*

imperfect *adjective* having faults. ~ *noun* (*plural* **imperfects**) a verb tense used to express something that happened repeatedly, or over a period of time, in the past. ➤ **imperfection** *noun*, **imperfectly** *adverb*.

imperial /im peer i al/ *adjective* **1** to do with an empire, emperor, or empress. **2** belonging to a system of weights and measures such as the pound and the pint.

imperialism *noun History* a system of government in which one powerful country takes control over other countries. ➤ **imperialist** *noun and adjective*.

imperious *adjective* proud and domineering.

impersonal *adjective* not influenced by or involving personal feelings. ➤ **impersonally** *adverb*.

impersonate *verb* (**impersonates, impersonating, impersonated**) to pretend to be somebody, either for entertainment or to deceive somebody else. ➤ **impersonation** *noun*, **impersonator** *noun*.

impertinent *adjective* rude; insolent. ➤ **impertinence** *noun*, **impertinently** *adverb*.

impetuous *adjective* acting quickly and without planning properly. ➤ **impetuously** *adverb*.

impetus /im pi tus/ *noun* **1** an influence that makes something progress more quickly. **2** *Science* the energy possessed by a moving object.

impinge *verb* (**impinges, impinging, impinged**) to have an impact on somebody.

implacable /im pla ka bl/ *adjective* determined and unwilling to change your mind. ➤ **implacably** *adverb*.

implant /im plahnt/ *verb* (**implants, implanting, implanted**) to insert something, such as artificial tissue or a hormone, into a person's body. ~ /im plahnt/ *noun* (*plural* **implants**) something implanted in a person's body.

implausible *adjective* not likely to be true.

implement /im pli mint/ *noun* (*plural* **implements**) a tool. ~ /im pli ment/ *verb* (**implements, implementing, implemented**) to put plans into effect. ➤ **implementation** *noun*.

implicate *verb* (**implicates, implicating, implicated**) to show that a person is involved in some wrongdoing.

implication *noun* (*plural* **implications**) **1** a possible result or effect. **2** something implied.

implicit /im pli sit/ *adjective* **1** implied rather than directly stated. **2** absolute and unquestioning: *I have an implicit belief in his honesty*. ➤ **implicitly** *adverb*.

implore *verb* (**implores, imploring, implored**) to beg somebody to do something.

imply *verb* (**implies, implying, implied**) to hint at something without saying it directly.

Usage Note **imply** or **infer**? To *imply* something is to suggest it by what you say without stating it directly: *She implied that I was untrustworthy*. To *infer* something is to work it out from what somebody says, even though they have not directly said as much: *I inferred from her remark that she thought me untrustworthy*.

impolite *adjective* not polite; not having good manners.

import /im pawt/ *verb* (**imports, importing, imported**) to bring in goods from a foreign country. ~ /im pawt/ *noun* (*plural* **imports**) a product that is imported from a foreign country. ➤ **importer** *noun*.

important *adjective* having great significance or influence, or high rank. ➤ **importance** *noun*, **importantly** *adverb*.

impose *verb* (**imposes, imposing, imposed**) **1** to force a rule or a tax on people. **2** to cause inconvenience to somebody: *I didn't want to impose on him by asking for help.* ➤ **imposition** *noun*.

imposing *adjective* large and impressive.

impossible *adjective* not possible; that could not exist or happen. ➤ **impossibility** *noun*, **impossibly** *adverb*.

impostor or **imposter** *noun* (*plural* **impostors** or **imposters**) a person who pretends to be somebody else in order to deceive people.

impotent /im poh tint/ *adjective* lacking in strength or power. ➤ **impotence** *noun*.

impound *verb* (**impounds, impounding, impounded**) said about the police or another official: to take away something belonging to somebody as evidence of wrongdoing.

impoverished *adjective* very poor.

impracticable *adjective* incapable of being carried out.

impractical *adjective* **1** said about a person: not good at doing practical tasks. **2** said about an idea or plan: unrealistic.

Usage Note **impracticable** or **impractical**? If something is *impracticable*, you simply cannot do it; it's impossible. Something that is *impractical* could in theory be done, but there is some reason why it would be difficult to do.

---

impregnable /im preg na bl/ *adjective* said about a building: too strongly protected to be captured or broken into.

impregnate /im preg nayt/ *verb* (**impregnates, impregnating, impregnated**) to spread a substance through something: *paper hankies impregnated with perfume.*

impresario /im pri sah ri oh/ *noun* (*plural* **impresarios**) a person who organizes and finances shows or concerts.

impress *verb* (**impresses, impressing, impressed**) **1** to make a good impression on somebody. **2** to fix an idea or thought firmly in somebody's mind: *They impressed on their children to be careful when crossing the road.*

impression *noun* (*plural* **impressions**) **1** an influence or effect that somebody or something has on you, especially a favourable one. **2** an imitation of somebody as a form of entertainment.

impressionable *adjective* easily influenced.

impressionism *noun* Art a style of painting in which the artist reproduces the effect of the subject rather than a realistic representation of it.

impressionist *noun* (*plural* **impressionists**) **1** a painter working in the style of impressionism. **2** an entertainer who does impressions.

impressive *adjective* large enough or good enough to arouse admiration. ➤ **impressively** *adverb*.

imprint /im print/ *noun* (*plural* **imprints**) **1** a mark made by pressing on a surface. **2** a strong impression: *Her sharp wit left an imprint on my mind.* ~ /im print/ *verb* (**imprints, imprinting, imprinted**) to fix something firmly in your mind or memory: *That holiday is for ever imprinted on my memory.*

imprison *verb* (**imprisons, imprisoning, imprisoned**) to put somebody in prison. ➤ **imprisonment** *noun*.

improbable *adjective* unlikely to be true or to happen. ➤ **improbably** *adverb*.

impromptu /im promp tew/ *adjective*

improper

and adverb made or done on the spur of the moment.

improper *adjective* not decent, appropriate, or correct. ➤ **improperly** *adverb*.

improper fraction *noun* (*plural* **improper fractions**) *Maths* a fraction in which the number above the line is greater than the number below the line.

improve *verb* (**improves, improving, improved**) to make something better or become better. ➤ **improvement** *noun*.

improvise *verb* (**improvises, improvising, improvised**) **1** to make or provide something using whatever is available. **2** to perform music, poetry, or drama, making it up as you do so. ➤ **improvisation** *noun*.

impudent /im pew dint/ *adjective* showing disrespect. ➤ **impudence** *noun*, **impudently** *adverb*.

impulse *noun* (*plural* **impulses**) a sudden strong desire to do something.

impulsive *adjective* acting on the basis of a sudden desire to do something. ➤ **impulsively** *adverb*.

impure *adjective* not pure, as a result of contamination.

impurity *noun* (*plural* **impurities**) **1** the state of being impure. **2** something that makes something else impure.

in *preposition and adverb* used to indicate location, time, or condition: *Come in!*; *in five minutes*; *in pain*.

in. *abbreviation* inch or inches.

inability *noun* lack of sufficient power, skill, or intelligence to do something.

inaccessible *adjective* difficult or impossible to reach.

inaccurate *adjective* faulty or incorrect.

inactive *adjective* not moving or not functioning. ➤ **inactivity** *noun*.

inadequate *adjective* **1** not of the required quantity or quality. **2** unable to cope with people or situations.

➤ **inadequacy** *noun*, **inadequately** *adverb*.

inadvertent *adjective* unintentional. ➤ **inadvertently** *adverb*.

inane *adjective* senseless or unintelligent. ➤ **inanely** *adverb*, **inanity** *noun*.

inanimate *adjective* not alive.

inappropriate *adjective* not appropriate or suitable. ➤ **inappropriately** *adverb*.

inarticulate *adjective* unable to express yourself clearly.

inaudible *adjective* too quiet to be heard. ➤ **inaudibly** *adverb*.

inaugurate /i naw gew rayt/ *verb* (**inaugurates, inaugurating, inaugurated**) **1** to open a new building or leader with a ceremony. **2** to introduce a new system or project. ➤ **inaugural** *adjective*, **inauguration** *noun*.

inborn *adjective* said about a quality or ability: natural; not learned.

incandescent /in kan de snt/ *adjective* glowing white with intense heat. ➤ **incandescence** *noun*.

incapable *adjective* lacking the ability to do something.

incarcerate /in kah si rayt/ *verb* (**incarcerates, incarcerating, incarcerated**) to imprison somebody. ➤ **incarceration** *noun*.

Incarnation *noun* (**the Incarnation**) in Christian belief, the appearance of Christ as God in human form.

incendiary /in sen di a ri/ *adjective* said about a bomb: designed to start fires.

incense[1] /in sens/ *noun* a substance that produces a sweet smell when it burns.

incense[2] /in sens/ *verb* (**incenses, incensing, incensed**) to make somebody extremely angry.

incentive /in sen tiv/ *noun* (*plural* **incentives**) something that makes a person want to do something.

inception /in sep shn/ *noun* the beginning of a process.

incessant /in se snt/ *adjective*

continuing without interruption. ➤ **incessantly** *adverb*.

incest /in sest/ *noun* sexual intercourse between people who are closely related. ➤ **incestuous** *adjective*.

inch *noun* (*plural* **inches**) a unit of length equal to one twelfth of a foot (about 2.54 centimetres). ~ *verb* (**inches, inching, inched**) to move somewhere gradually.

incident *noun* (*plural* **incidents**) something that happens.

incidental *adjective* happening as a minor consequence of something.

incidentally *adverb* by the way.

incinerate /in si ni rayt/ *verb* (**incinerates, incinerating, incinerated**) to burn something to ashes. ➤ **incineration** *noun*.

incinerator *noun* (*plural* **incinerators**) a furnace or container for burning rubbish.

incipient /in si pi int/ *adjective* just beginning to develop.

incision /in si zhn/ *noun* (*plural* **incisions**) a cut, especially one made by a surgeon during an operation.

incisive /in sie siv/ *adjective* showing sharp intelligence.

incite /in siet/ *verb* (**incites, inciting, incited**) to encourage people to behave violently or unlawfully. ➤ **incitement** *noun*.

inclination *noun* **1** a natural tendency or urge to do something. **2** a liking for something.

incline /in klien/ *verb* (**inclines, inclining, inclined**) to influence somebody to a do or think something. ~ /in klien/ *noun* (*plural* **inclines**) a slope. ✱ **inclined to** having a tendency to do or be something.

include *verb* (**includes, including, included**) to take in or contain as a part of a larger whole.

including *preposition* with the inclusion of.

inclusion *noun* the act of including something or somebody.

inclusive *adjective* including everything or the specified things.

incognito /in kog nee toh/ *adverb and adjective* in disguise or under a false name.

incoherent /in koh heer int/ *adjective* too confused and muddled to be clearly understood. ➤ **incoherence** *noun*, **incoherently** *adverb*.

income *noun* (*plural* **incomes**) money that is paid in return for work.

income tax *noun* a tax on what a person earns.

incoming *adjective* **1** coming in: *incoming calls*. **2** about to take on a position: *the incoming governor*.

incomparable /in kom pa ra bl/ *adjective* too good to be compared with anything or anybody else.

incompatible /in kom pa ta bl/ *adjective* unable to live or exist together because of being too different.

incompetent *adjective* lacking the ability or experience needed to do something. ➤ **incompetence** *noun*.

incomplete *adjective* not complete.

incomprehensible /in kom pri hen sa bl/ *adjective* impossible to understand.

inconceivable *adjective* impossible to imagine or believe.

inconclusive *adjective* leading to no definite result.

incongruous /in kong groo us/ *adjective* seeming out of place in a particular situation. ➤ **incongruously** *adverb*.

inconsiderate *adjective* not caring about other people's feelings or wishes.

inconsistent *adjective* behaving differently at different times. ➤ **inconsistency** *noun*.

inconspicuous /in kon spi kew us/ *adjective* not easily noticeable. ➤ **inconspicuously** *adverb*.

incontinent

incontinent *adjective* unable to control your bladder or bowels. ➤ **incontinence** *noun*.

inconvenience *noun* the fact of being difficult or troublesome. ~ *verb* (**inconveniences, inconveniencing, inconvenienced**) to cause inconvenience to somebody. ➤ **inconvenient** *adjective*.

incorporate *verb* (**incorporates, incorporating, incorporated**) to make something a part of a larger thing. ➤ **incorporation** *noun*.

incorrect *adjective* inaccurate, wrong, or improper. ➤ **incorrectly** *adverb*.

increase /in krees/ *verb* (**increases, increasing, increased**) to become or make something greater in size, number, or degree. ~ /in krees/ *noun* (*plural* **increases**) an amount by which something increases. ➤ **increasing** *adjective*, **increasingly** *adverb*.

incredible *adjective* **1** too improbable to be believed. **2** *informal* excellent or outstanding. ➤ **incredibly** *adverb*.

incredulous *adjective* unwilling to believe something. ➤ **incredulously** *adverb*, **incredulity** *noun*.

increment /in kri mint/ *noun* (*plural* **increments**) an increase, especially one of a series of regular salary increases. ➤ **incremental** *adjective*.

incriminate *verb* (**incriminates, incriminating, incriminated**) to suggest that somebody is guilty of a crime.

incubate /in kew bayt/ *verb* (**incubates, incubating, incubated**) said about a bird: to sit on eggs to hatch them by the warmth of its body. ➤ **incubation** *noun*.

incubator *noun* (*plural* **incubators**) a hospital apparatus in which a weak or sick baby is kept warm.

incumbent *noun* (*plural* **incumbents**) the person who currently holds a particular job or position. ~ *adjective* imposed as a duty on somebody: *It is incumbent on us to look after those less fortunate than ourselves.*

incur *verb* (**incurs, incurring, incurred**) to cause something unpleasant to happen to yourself.

incurable /in kewr a bl/ *adjective* not able to be cured. ➤ **incurably** *adverb*.

indebted /in de tid/ *adjective* **1** owing gratitude to somebody. **2** owing money.

indecent *adjective* improper or morally offensive. ➤ **indecency** *noun*, **indecently** *adverb*.

indecisive *adjective* incapable of making quick decisions.

indeed *adverb* **1** used for emphasis: *It has been very cold indeed.* **2** used to introduce additional information: actually: *It's not far to the station – indeed, it's within walking distance.*

indefinite *adjective* **1** vague or unsettled. **2** lasting for an unspecified length of time. ➤ **indefinitely** *adverb*.

indefinite article *noun* English the word *a* or *an*.

indelible /in de la bl/ *adjective* said about a mark or ink: incapable of being removed.

indent *verb* (**indents, indenting, indented**) **1** to set a line of text in from the margin. **2** to notch the edge of something.

indentation *noun* (*plural* **indentations**) **1** a notch cut in the edge of something. **2** a dent or depression.

independent *adjective* **1** not connected with something else: *an independent review.* **2** not depending on other people. **3** said about a country: not governed by another country. ➤ **independence** *noun*, **independently** *adverb*.

in-depth *adjective* extremely detailed and thorough.

indestructible *adjective* impossible to destroy.

index *noun* (*plural* **indexes**) **1** an alphabetical list of names or

topics mentioned in a book.
2 a catalogue of the books in a library.

index finger *noun* = FOREFINGER.

Indian summer *noun* (*plural* **Indian summers**) a period of warm weather in late autumn.

indicate *verb* (**indicates, indicating, indicated**) **1** to point to or point out something. **2** to be a sign of something. **3** to say or suggest something: *He indicated that he wanted to leave.* **4** to signal that you intend to turn left or right when driving. ➤ **indication** *noun*.

indicative /in di ka tiv/ *adjective* being a sign of something. ~ *noun English* the form of a verb used to express a statement, for example the verb 'live' in *I live in Glasgow*.

indicator *noun* (*plural* **indicators**) **1** a device that shows a measurement or level, or gives information about something. **2** a flashing light on a vehicle, used to show that the driver intends to turn left or right.

indict /in diet/ *verb* (**indicts, indicting, indicted**) to charge somebody with a serious crime. ➤ **indictment** *noun*.

indifferent *adjective* **1** of rather poor quality. **2** not interested in or affected by something: *indifferent to cricket/pain.* ➤ **indifference** *noun*, **indifferently** *adverb*.

indigenous /in di ji nus/ *adjective* coming originally from a particular place: *indigenous to China*.

indigestion *noun* pain or discomfort caused by difficulty in digesting food.

indignant *adjective* filled with indignation. ➤ **indignantly** *adverb*.

indignation *noun* anger aroused by something unjust.

indignity *noun* (*plural* **indignities**) something that makes you feel embarrassed or ashamed.

indigo *noun* a dark greyish-blue colour.

indirect *adjective* **1** not going straight to a place or to the point. **2** not being a direct cause or result of something. ➤ **indirectly** *adverb*.

indirect speech *noun English* the reported form of what somebody has said, as in *Abeer said she would come*.

indiscriminate /in dis kri mi nat/ *adjective* showing a lack of care in making choices. ➤ **indiscriminately** *adverb*.

indispensable *adjective* impossible to do without.

indisposed *adjective* slightly ill.

indistinct *adjective* not clearly seen or heard. ➤ **indistinctly** *adverb*.

individual *adjective* **1** to do with a single person or thing. **2** having unusual characteristics. ~ *noun* (*plural* **individuals**) **1** a particular person or thing. **2** a person who has unusual characteristics. ➤ **individually** *adverb*.

individuality *noun* the quality of having unusual characteristics.

indoctrinate *verb* (**indoctrinates, indoctrinating, indoctrinated**) to teach somebody to accept a view without questioning it. ➤ **indoctrination** *noun*.

indomitable *adjective* impossible to subdue.

indoor *adjective* done or situated inside a building.

indoors *adverb* inside or into a building.

indorse *verb* see ENDORSE.

induce *verb* (**induces, inducing, induced**) **1** to persuade somebody to do something. **2** to cause a particular state: *The announcement induced panic in the crowd.*

inducement *noun* (*plural* **inducements**) something offered to encourage somebody to do something.

indulge *verb* (**indulges, indulging, indulged**) **1** to allow yourself to do or have something pleasurable: *I indulged*

indulgence

in a bar of chocolate. **2** to allow somebody to do or have whatever they want.

indulgence *noun* (*plural* **indulgences**) **1** the act of indulging yourself of somebody else. **2** something enjoyable that you indulge in.

indulgent *adjective* showing indulgence. ➤ **indulgently** *adverb*.

industrial *adjective* to do with industry. ➤ **industrially** *adverb*.

industrial action *noun* a form of protest, such as a strike, by a group of workers.

industrialist *noun* (*plural* **industrialists**) a person who owns or runs a factory or an industrial company.

Industrial Revolution *noun* (**the Industrial Revolution**) *History* the large-scale introduction of machinery in factories in Britain in the late 18th and early 19th centuries.

industrious *adjective* hard-working.

industry *noun* (*plural* **industries**) **1** the processing of raw materials and the production of goods in factories. **2** a particular branch of this: *the steel industry.*

inedible *adjective* not fit to be eaten.

inefficient *adjective* not working in a capable or economical way. ➤ **inefficiency** *noun*, **inefficiently** *adverb*.

inept *adjective* incompetent or clumsy. ➤ **ineptitude** *noun*.

inequality *noun* the state of being unequal.

inert *adjective* not moving or unable to move.

inertia /i ner sha/ *noun* the state of being inactive or lazy.

inevitable *adjective* bound to happen. ➤ **inevitability** *noun*, **inevitably** *adverb*.

inexcusable *adjective* too bad to be excused.

inexhaustible *adjective* said about a supply of something: incapable of being used up.

inexorable /i nek so ra bl/ *adjective* impossible to halt: *the inexorable rise in house prices.* ➤ **inexorably** *adverb*.

inexpensive *adjective* low in price.

inexperience *noun* lack of experience. ➤ **inexperienced** *adjective*.

inexplicable /i nik spli ka bl/ *adjective* incapable of being explained. ➤ **inexplicably** *adverb*.

inextricable /i nik stri ka bl/ *adjective* that cannot be separated from one another. ➤ **inextricably** *adverb*.

infallible *adjective* incapable of being wrong. ➤ **infallibility** *noun*.

infamous /in fa mus/ *adjective* having a bad reputation for something bad.

infant *noun* (*plural* **infants**) **1** a very young child. **2** a schoolchild between the ages of five and seven. ➤ **infancy** *noun*.

infantile *adjective* childish or immature.

infantry *noun* soldiers trained and equipped to fight on foot.

infatuated /in fa tew ay tid/ *adjective* having strong but temporary feelings of love for somebody. ➤ **infatuation** *noun*.

infect *verb* (**infects, infecting, infected**) to pass on a disease to somebody.

infection *noun* (*plural* **infections**) **1** an infectious disease. **2** the act of infecting somebody.

infectious *adjective* **1** said about a disease: able to be passed on from one person to another. **2** said about laughter or enthusiasm: spreading from one person to the others in a group. ➤ **infectiously** *adverb*.

infer *verb* (**infers, inferring, inferred**) to deduce something from the evidence that you have. ➤ **inference** noun.

Usage Note **infer** or **imply**? See note at **imply**.

inferior *adjective* of low or lower rank, quality, or importance. ~ *noun* (*plural* **inferiors**) a person who is lower in rank, position, or ability than another.

infernal *adjective informal* dreadful or unpleasant: *Stop that infernal racket!*

inferno *noun* (*plural* **infernos**) a raging fire.

infertile *adjective* **1** unable to have children. **2** said about land: not suitable for growing crops in. ➤ **infertility** *noun*.

infest *verb* (**infests, infesting, infested**) said about insects or animals: to spread throughout a place causing damage or disease. ➤ **infestation** *noun*.

infidelity *noun* unfaithfulness, especially to your husband or wife.

infighting *noun* disagreement among members of a group or organization.

infiltrate *verb* (**infiltrates, infiltrating, infiltrated**) to enter an organization secretly, often to spy on it. ➤ **infiltration** *noun*, **infiltrator** *noun*.

infinite /in fi nit/ *adjective* having no limits to its size or extent. ➤ **infinitely** *adverb*.

infinitive *noun* (*plural* **infinitives**) *English* the basic form of a verb, often preceded by *to* (for example 'go' in *I must go* or 'to go' in *I want to go*).

infinity *noun* unlimited time, space, or number.

infirm *adjective* physically weak from age.

infirmary *noun* (*plural* **infirmaries**) a hospital.

inflamed *adjective* said about a part of your body: red, swollen, and painful, as a result of injury or infection.

inflammable *adjective* easily set on fire.

inflammation *noun* redness, swelling, and pain in a part of your body as a result of injury or infection.

inflammatory /in a ma to ri/ *adjective* tending to make people angry.

inflate *verb* (**inflates, inflating, inflated**) to make a balloon or tyre swell by filling it with air or gas. ➤ **inflatable** *adjective*.

inflation *noun* a continuing rise in prices. ➤ **inflationary** *adjective*.

inflection *or* **inflexion** *noun* (*plural* **inflections** *or* **inflexions**) *English* a change in the form of a word, for example to show the plural of a noun (as in *horses* or *feet*) or the past tense of a verb (as in *walked* or *came*).

inflexible *adjective* unwilling or unable to change.

inflict *verb* (**inflicts, inflicting, inflicted**) to impose something unpleasant or painful on somebody.

influence *noun* (*plural* **influences**) **1** the power to produce an effect on somebody or something. **2** somebody or something with influence. ~ *verb* (**influences, influencing, influenced**) to affect a person or thing so that they do something. ✱ **under the influence** *informal* drunk.

influential *adjective* having influence over people or things.

influenza *noun* a disease that causes fever, aches and pains, and a runny or blocked nose.

influx /in fluks/ *noun* an arrival of people or things in large numbers.

inform *verb* (**informs, informing, informed**) **1** to pass on information to somebody. **2** to give the police information about a criminal or crime. ➤ **informant** *noun*.

informal *adjective* casual and without formality. ➤ **informality** *noun*, **informally** *adverb*.

information

information *noun* facts you obtain by investigation or study or from teachers.

information technology *noun* ICT the use of computers and telecommunications to store, gather, and send information.

informative *adjective* conveying information.

informer *noun* (*plural* **informers**) somebody who gives information to the police about a criminal or crime.

infrared *adjective* Science said about light or radiation: outside the range of colours that humans can see, between red light and microwaves, and generally experienced as heat.

infrastructure *noun* (*plural* **infrastructures**) Geography things that are needed for a country to have a strong economy, such as roads and railways, power supplies, factories, and schools.

infrequent *adjective* not frequent.

infringe *verb* (**infringes, infringing, infringed**) **1** to do something that interferes with somebody's rights or privileges. **2** to break a law or an agreement. ➤ **infringement** *noun*.

infuriate *verb* (**infuriates, infuriating, infuriated**) to make somebody furious. ➤ **infuriating** *adjective*.

infuse *verb* (**infuses, infusing, infused**) **1** to steep tea or herbs in liquid so as to draw out the flavour. **2** to fill somebody with joy or excitement. ➤ **infusion** *noun*.

ingenious /in jee ni us/ *adjective* original, resourceful, and clever. ➤ **ingeniously** *adverb*, **ingenuity** *noun*.

ingot /ing got/ *noun* (*plural* **ingots**) a block of gold.

ingrained *adjective* said about habits, dirt, or stains: deeply implanted and hard to remove.

ingredient *noun* (*plural* **ingredients**) one of the parts that make up a mixture, especially one of the foodstuffs used to make a recipe.

inhabit *verb* (**inhabits, inhabiting, inhabited**) to live in a place.

inhabitant *noun* (*plural* **inhabitants**) a person who lives in a particular place.

inhale *verb* (**inhales, inhaling, inhaled**) to breathe in.

inhaler *noun* (*plural* **inhalers**) a device used for inhaling a medication, for example to relieve asthma.

inherent /in he rint/ *adjective* forming an essential part of something. ➤ **inherently** *adverb*.

inherit *verb* (**inherits, inheriting, inherited**) **1** to be left money or property by somebody when they die. **2** to have a characteristic that is passed on to you by your father or mother. ➤ **inheritance** *noun*, **inheritor** *noun*.

inhibit *verb* (**inhibits, inhibiting, inhibited**) to discourage somebody from behaving freely or spontaneously. ➤ **inhibited** *adjective*.

inhibition *noun* (*plural* **inhibitions**) a feeling of embarrassment that discourages you from behaving freely or spontaneously.

inhospitable *adjective* not friendly or welcoming.

inhuman *adjective* **1** extremely cruel. **2** not human.

inhumane /in[hi]hew mayn/ *adjective* completely lacking in kindness or compassion. ➤ **inhumanity** *noun*.

inimitable /i ni mi ta bl/ *adjective* so good that no others can match it.

initial *adjective* existing or placed at the beginning. ~ *noun* (*plural* **initials**) the first letter of a name. ~ *verb* (**initials, initialling, initialled**) to authorize something by putting your initials on it. ➤ **initially** *adverb*.

initiate /i ni shi ayt/ *verb* (**initiates, initiating, initiated**) **1** to start something: *She initiated the conversation.*

2 to introduce somebody to a new activity or into an organization. ➤ **initiation** noun.

initiative /inishativ/ noun (plural **initiatives**) **1** the ability to act without being told what to do. **2** a new plan or programme of action.

inject verb (**injects, injecting, injected**) **1** to insert medicine into a person's body using a syringe. **2** to introduce something into a situation: *I tried to inject some humour into my speech.* ➤ **injection** noun.

injunction noun (plural **injunctions**) a court order forbidding somebody from doing something.

injure verb (**injures, injuring, injured**) to hurt somebody.

injury noun (plural **injuries**) a hurt caused to somebody's body, or to their feelings.

injustice noun **1** unfairness. **2** an unjust act: *You did me an injustice when you accused me of lying.*

ink noun (plural **inks**) a coloured liquid used for writing and printing.

inkling noun a slight knowledge or vague idea: *I had an inkling that he was unhappy.*

inlaid adjective set into a surface for decoration.

inland adjective and adverb in or towards the middle of a country.

Inland Revenue noun (**the Inland Revenue**) the government department responsible for collecting taxes.

in-laws plural noun *informal* the members of your husband's or wife's family.

inlet noun (plural **inlets**) *Geography* a long narrow bay in the coastline.

inmate noun (plural **inmates**) somebody who is living in a prison or hospital.

inn noun (plural **inns**) a pub or hotel.

innards /inadz/ plural noun *informal* **1** the intestines. **2** the inside parts of a machine.

innate /inayt/ adjective said about a quality or ability: that somebody has from the time of their birth: *an innate sense of rhythm.*

inner adjective situated inside something or near its centre.

innermost adjective most secret and private: *my innermost feelings.*

innings noun (plural **innings**) a part of a cricket match during which one side bats and the other bowls.

innocent adjective **1** not guilty of a crime or other wrongdoing. **2** not intending any harm. ➤ **innocence** noun, **innocently** adverb.

innocuous /inokewus/ adjective having no harmful effects.

innovation noun a change that introduces a new idea or way of doing things. ➤ **innovative** adjective.

innuendo /inewendoh/ noun (plural **innuendos** or **innuendoes**) a comment worded in such a way as to suggest something rude or nasty without actually saying it.

innumerable adjective too many to be counted.

inoculate verb (**inoculates, inoculating, inoculated**) to make somebody immune to a disease by putting a tiny amount of the germs into their body, for example by injection. ➤ **inoculation** noun.

inpatient noun (plural **inpatients**) a patient who stays in hospital for a time while having treatment.

input noun **1** *ICT* the energy, material, or data supplied to a machine or system. **2** the work, suggestions, or advice that somebody contributes to a project. ~ verb (**inputs, inputting, input** or **inputted**) *ICT* to put data into a computer.

inquest noun (plural **inquests**) **1** an enquiry, usually by a coroner, into the cause of a death. **2** an investigation, especially into something that has failed.

inquire *verb* see ENQUIRE.

Usage Note **inquire** or **enquire**? See note at **enquire**.

inquiry *noun* see ENQUIRY.

inquisition *noun* (*plural* **inquisitions**) a very harsh investigation.

inquisitive /in kwi zi tiv/ *adjective* eager for knowledge, especially about what other people are doing. ➤ **inquisitively** *adverb*.

inroads * **make inroads into** to begin to affect or achieve something: *There's a lot of work to be done, but we're beginning to make inroads into it.*

ins and outs *plural noun* details: *I don't need to know all the ins and outs of your trip.*

insane *adjective* **1** dated, offensive suffering from a mental illness. **2** utterly absurd. ➤ **insanely** *adverb*, **insanity** *noun*.

insatiable /in say sha bl/ *adjective* unable to be satisfied. ➤ **insatiably** *adverb*.

inscribe *verb* (**inscribes, inscribing, inscribed**) to write, engrave, or print words on a hard surface.

inscription *noun* (*plural* **inscriptions**) written or engraved words, for example on a statue or a coin.

inscrutable /in skrooh ta bl/ *adjective* said about a person: hard to figure out. ➤ **inscrutably** *adverb*.

insect *noun* (*plural* **insects**) *Science* a small animal with six legs, such as a fly or a beetle.

insecticide *noun* (*plural* **insecticides**) a substance that kills insects.

insecure *adjective* **1** lacking in self-confidence. **2** not firmly fixed or supported. ➤ **insecurity** *noun*.

insensitive *adjective* unsympathetic to the needs or feelings of others. ➤ **insensitivity** *noun*.

inseparable /in se pa ra bl/ *adjective* said about two people: almost always together.

insert *verb* (**inserts, inserting, inserted**) to put something into another thing. ➤ **insertion** *noun*.

inshore *adjective and adverb* at sea but near the shore.

inside *noun* (*plural* **insides**) **1** an inner surface. **2** an interior or internal part. **3** (**insides**) the stomach or the intestines. ~ *adjective* **1** on or towards the inside. **2** carried out by somebody within an organization: *an inside job*. ~ *adverb and preposition* **1** in or into the interior of a place. **2** in less than a particular period of time. * **inside out** with the inner surface on the outside.

insider *noun* (*plural* **insiders**) somebody who belongs to a group and knows private information.

insidious /in si di us/ *adjective* acting gradually but with very harmful consequences. ➤ **insidiously** *adverb*.

insight *noun* the ability to know and understand the true nature of something or somebody.

insignia /in sig ni a/ *noun* the badge of an organization.

insignificant *adjective* too unimportant or too small to be worth consideration. ➤ **insignificance** *noun*.

insincere *adjective* not expressing feelings or opinions honestly. ➤ **insincerely** *adverb*, **insincerity** *noun*.

insinuate *verb* (**insinuates, insinuating, insinuated**) to hint at something unpleasant. ➤ **insinuation** *noun*.

insipid *adjective* **1** lacking flavour. **2** with no interesting qualities.

insist *verb* (**insists, insisting, insisted**) to demand something forcefully, accepting no refusal: *He insisted on* having a window seat. ➤ **insistence** noun, **insistent** adjective.

insolent /in soh lint/ adjective disrespectful and rude. ➤ **insolence** noun, **insolently** adverb.

insoluble /in sol ewbl/ adjective **1** Science that does not dissolve. **2** impossible to solve.

insolvent adjective unable to pay your debts. ➤ **insolvency** noun.

insomnia noun inability to sleep. ➤ **insomniac** noun.

inspect verb (**inspects, inspecting, inspected**) to examine something closely. ➤ **inspection** noun.

inspector noun (plural **inspectors**) **1** somebody who inspects things. **2** a police officer immediately above a sergeant in rank.

inspire verb (**inspires, inspiring, inspired**) **1** Drama to fill somebody with creative energy: *The death of her child inspired her to write some beautiful poetry.* **2** to cause somebody to feel a particular emotion: *His success inspired envy in his colleagues.* ➤ **inspiration** noun.

instability noun lack of stability.

install verb (**installs, installing, installed**) **1** to place a machine in position for use. **2** to establish somebody in a specified place or position. ➤ **installation** noun.

instalment noun (plural **instalments**) **1** any of the parts that an amount of money you owe is divided into for repayment. **2** any of several parts of a publication or broadcast presented at intervals.

instance noun (plural **instances**) an example or occurrence of something. * **for instance** as an example.

instant noun (plural **instants**) a very brief period of time; a moment. ~ adjective immediate.

instantaneous /in stan tay ni us/ adjective occurring or acting instantly. ➤ **instantaneously** adverb.

instead adverb as a substitute or alternative.

instep noun (plural **insteps**) the arched middle part of the foot.

instigate verb (**instigates, instigating, instigated**) to bring about a course of action. ➤ **instigation** noun.

instil verb (**instils, instilling, instilled**) to cause information to become firmly fixed in somebody's mind over time.

instinct noun (plural **instincts**) a way of acting or thinking that is inborn, not learned. ➤ **instinctive** adjective, **instinctively** adverb.

institute noun (plural **institutes**) a place or organization for research or education. ~ verb (**institutes, instituting, instituted**) to start a rule or procedure.

institution noun (plural **institutions**) **1** an established organization, such as a university or hospital. **2** an established practice. ➤ **institutional** adjective.

instruct verb (**instructs, instructing, instructed**) **1** to teach somebody: *He instructs the children in karate.* **2** to order somebody to do something. ➤ **instruction** noun, **instructive** adjective, **instructor** noun.

instrument noun (plural **instruments**) **1** an implement, tool, or device used for delicate work or measurement. **2** Music a device used to produce music.

instrumental adjective **1** playing an active part in something: *He was instrumental in ending the war.* **2** Music performed on musical instruments with no singing. ~ noun (plural **instrumentals**) Music a musical performance or recording with instruments but no singing.

instrumentalist noun (plural **instrumentalists**) Music a person who plays a musical instrument.

insufficient *adjective* not enough.

insular /in sew lar/ *adjective* not mixing with other people.

insulate *verb* (**insulates, insulating, insulated**) to cover something with protective material so as to prevent loss of electricity, heat, or sound. ➤ **insulation** *noun*, **insulator** *noun*.

insulin /in sew lin/ *noun* a substance that controls the amount of sugar in the blood.

insult /in sult/ *verb* (**insults, insulting, insulted**) to make an unkind or rude remark about somebody. ~ /in sult/ *noun* (*plural* **insults**) an unkind or rude remark made about somebody.

insurance *noun* 1 an arrangement by which a person makes regular payments to a company who will pay them back some money if something unpleasant (such as an accident or a fire) happens. 2 the business of providing insurance.

insure *verb* (**insures, insuring, insured**) to arrange insurance for yourself or your property.

intact *adjective* not harmed or damaged.

intake *noun* the amount of something that you take in, such as food or drink.

integer /in ti jer/ *noun* (*plural* **integers**) *Maths* a whole number.

integral /in ti gral/ *adjective* essential: *an integral part of the business*.

integrate *verb* (**integrates, integrating, integrated**) 1 to blend separate elements of something together to form a whole thing. 2 to become part of a group.

integrated circuit *noun* (*plural* **integrated circuits**) an electronic circuit in or on a tiny piece of material such as silicon that acts as a semiconductor.

integrity *noun* the quality of being honest and living according to your moral principles.

intellect *noun* the ability to think intelligently.

intellectual *adjective* using or requiring the intellect for understanding. ~ *noun* (*plural* **intellectuals**) an intelligent person who thinks a lot about serious subjects. ➤ **intellectually** *adverb*.

intelligence *noun* the ability to learn, understand, and think. ➤ **intelligent** *adjective*, **intelligently** *adverb*.

intelligentsia /in te li jent si a/ *plural noun* intellectuals considered as a group.

intelligible *adjective* capable of being understood.

intend *verb* (**intends, intending, intended**) 1 to have something in mind as a purpose. 2 to plan for something to have a specified use.

intense *adjective* 1 occurring to a great degree. 2 feeling or expressing deep emotion. ➤ **intensely** *adverb*, **intensity** *noun*.

intensify *verb* (**intensifies, intensifying, intensified**) to become, or make something, more intense.

intensive *adjective* very thorough and concentrated within a short time.

intent *noun* (*plural* **intents**) an intention. ~ *adjective* determined to do something: *She was intent on going to Cuba*. ✳ **to all intents and purposes** in every important respect. ➤ **intently** *adverb*.

intention *noun* (*plural* **intentions**) what somebody intends to do; an aim.

intentional *adjective* deliberate. ➤ **intentionally** *adverb*.

interact *verb* (**interacts, interacting, interacted**) to produce an effect on each other. ➤ **interaction** *noun*.

interactive *adjective* *ICT* to do with the exchange of information between a computer and user while a program is being run.

intercept /in ter sept/ *verb* (**intercepts,**

intercepting, intercepted) to stop something or somebody reaching the place they are going to.

interchange *noun* (*plural* **interchanges**) **1** a junction of two or more roads at different levels. **2** the act of putting each of two things in the place of the other. ➤ **interchangeable** *adjective*.

intercom *noun* (*plural* **intercoms**) a device, resembling a telephone, for communicating with other people in the same building.

intercourse *noun* = SEXUAL INTERCOURSE.

interest *noun* (*plural* **interests**) **1** an inclination to learn about or be involved in something. **2** a subject or activity that you are want to learn about or be involved in. **3** a quality in a thing that makes you interested in it. **4** a charge for money that you have borrowed, usually a percentage of the amount borrowed. **5** (**interests**) benefit or advantage: *It would be in your best interests to follow this advice.* ~ *verb* (**interests, interesting, interested**) to engage the attention or arouse the interest of somebody. ➤ **interested** *adjective*, **interesting** *adjective*, **interestingly** *adverb*.

interface *noun* (*plural* **interfaces**) **1** the point where two systems meet and act on each other. **2** *ICT* a piece of computer hardware or software that allows a user to communicate with a computer.

interfere *verb* (**interferes, interfering, interfered**) **1** to be a hindrance to something: *His constant chatting interferes with my concentration.* **2** to take a part in matters that do not concern you: *She keeps interfering in my private life.* ➤ **interference** *noun*.

interim /in ti rim/ *adjective* temporary: *the interim president.*

interior *adjective* lying or occurring inside something. ~ *noun* (*plural* **interiors**) the inner part of something.

interjection *noun* (*plural* **interjections**) an expression of surprise, anger, or pleasure.

interlocking *adjective* fitting together.

interlude *noun* (*plural* **interludes**) a break between parts of a play or other performance.

intermarry *verb* (**intermarries, intermarrying, intermarried**) to become connected by marriage with another group.

intermediary /in ter mee di a ri/ *noun* (*plural* **intermediaries**) a go-between.

intermediate /in ter mee di at/ *adjective* **1** existing or occurring between two extremes. **2** involving a level of skill or knowledge greater than that of a beginner, but not yet advanced.

interminable /in ter mi na bl/ *adjective* lasting a long time. ➤ **interminably** *adverb*.

intermission *noun* (*plural* **intermissions**) **1** a break between the acts of a play or other performance. **2** a pause or respite.

intermittent *adjective* occurring at irregular intervals. ➤ **intermittently** *adverb*.

intern /in tern/ *verb* (**interns, interning, interned**) to lock somebody up in prison or a concentration camp. ➤ **internment** *noun*.

internal *adjective* existing or situated inside something or somebody. ➤ **internally** *adverb*.

internal-combustion engine *noun* an engine in which the combustion that creates the energy for the engine takes place within the engine and not in a separate furnace.

international *adjective* *Geography* to do with two or more countries. ~ *noun* (*plural* **internationals**) **1** a sporting or other contest between two national teams. **2** a player who has taken part in such a contest. ➤ **internationally** adverb.

Internet noun ICT (**the Internet**) the worldwide computer network for the exchange of information via telephone lines and satellite links.

interplay noun the effect that two or more things have on each other.

interpret verb (**interprets, interpreting, interpreted**) 1 to understand or explain the meaning of something. 2 to translate somebody's words from one language into another. ➤ **interpretation** noun, **interpreter** noun.

interrogate verb (**interrogates, interrogating, interrogated**) to question somebody thoroughly or harshly. ➤ **interrogation** noun, **interrogator** noun.

interrogative /in ti ro ga tiv/ noun (plural **interrogatives**) English a word, such as *who* or *why*, used in asking questions.

interrupt verb (**interrupts, interrupting, interrupted**) 1 to break the flow of a speaker or speech. 2 to break the continuity of something. ➤ **interruption** noun.

intersect verb (**intersects, intersecting, intersected**) 1 to divide a line or area by passing through or across it. 2 said about lines or roads: to meet and cross at a point. ➤ **intersection** noun.

interspersed adjective scattered throughout something: *a serious speech interspersed with jokes*.

interval noun (plural **intervals**) 1 an intervening space, for example a time between events or states. 2 *Music* the difference in pitch between two notes. 3 a break in the presentation of a play, concert, etc.

intervene verb (**intervenes, intervening, intervened**) 1 to come between two things. 2 to settle a dispute between two other people or groups. ➤ **intervening** adjective, **intervention** noun.

interview noun (plural **interviews**) 1 a meeting at which an employer gets to know somebody who has applied for a job in order to decide whether they are suitable. 2 a meeting at which a journalist or a radio or television presenter asks somebody questions, often about themselves. ~ verb (**interviews, interviewing, interviewed**) to hold an interview with somebody. ➤ **interviewee** noun, **interviewer** noun.

intestine /in tes tin/ noun (plural **intestines**) a tube in your body through which food passes from your stomach to your bowels. ➤ **intestinal** adjective.

intimate /in ti mat/ adjective 1 marked by a warm friendship. 2 cosy and privacy: *an intimate dinner*. 3 of a very personal or private nature: *intimate details of their relationship*. 4 said about knowledge: very thorough and detailed. ~ /in ti mayt/ verb (**intimates, intimating, intimated**) to hint at or imply something. ➤ **intimacy** noun, **intimately** adverb, **intimation** noun.

intimidate /in ti mi dayt/ verb (**intimidates, intimidating, intimidated**) to frighten or threaten somebody. ➤ **intimidation** noun.

into preposition 1 so as to be in or inside. 2 used in division: *Divide 35 into 70*. 3 *informal* involved with or keen on: *I am not into football*.

intolerable adjective too bad or unpleasant to put up with. ➤ **intolerably** adverb.

intolerant adjective unwilling to accept other people's views or lifestyles. ➤ **intolerance** noun.

intonation noun the rise and fall of your voice when you speak.

intoxicate verb (**intoxicates, intoxicating, intoxicated**) 1 said about alcohol or drugs: to make somebody feel very relaxed or excited and confused, so that they are not in full control of their behaviour. **2** to make somebody feel very excited and happy. ➤ **intoxicated** *adjective*, **intoxicating** *adjective*, **intoxication** *noun*.

intractable *adjective* stubborn and awkward.

intransitive *adjective* English said about a verb: not having a direct object.

intravenous /in tra **vee** nus/ *adjective* into or through a vein. ➤ **intravenously** *adverb*.

intrepid /in **tre** pid/ *adjective* fearless and bold. ➤ **intrepidity** *noun*.

intricate /**in** tri kit/ *adjective* very detailed and complex. ➤ **intricacy** *noun*, **intricately** *adverb*.

intrigue /in **treeg**/ *verb* (**intrigues, intriguing, intrigued**) to arouse somebody's interest or curiosity: *I am intrigued by her quiet manner.* ~ /in treeg/ *noun* (*plural* **intrigues**) **1** a secret scheme or plot. **2** the use of scheming or underhand plots to try to achieve your goal. ➤ **intriguing** *adjective*, **intriguingly** *adverb*.

intrinsic *adjective* to do with the basic nature of something or somebody: *his intrinsic goodness.* ➤ **intrinsically** *adverb*.

introduce *verb* (**introduces, introducing, introduced**) **1** to bring something into use or to somebody's attention for the first time. **2** to present yourself or somebody else to a person that you or they do not know. **3** to make some remarks to the audience about a performer or a show before the performance begins. ➤ **introductory** *adjective*.

introduction *noun* (*plural* **introductions**) **1** the act of introducing somebody or something. **2** a part of a book that comes before the main part.

introvert *noun* (*plural* **introverts**) a shy person who spends a lot of time thinking about their own feelings and concerns. ➤ **introvert** *adjective*, **introverted** *adjective*.

intrude *verb* (**intrudes, intruding, intruded**) to put yourself into a situation or a place where you are not invited or not welcome: *I don't want to intrude on your family party.* ➤ **intruder** *noun*, **intrusion** *noun*, **intrusive** *adjective*.

intuition /in tew **i** shn/ *noun* the feeling that you know something without consciously having learned it: *My intuition told me that something was wrong.* ➤ **intuitive** *adjective*, **intuitively** *adverb*.

inundate /**i** nun dayt/ *verb* (**inundates, inundating, inundated**) to give or send somebody a large number of things such as demands, offers, or letters: *We have been inundated with requests for this song.*

invade *verb* (**invades, invading, invaded**) **1** to enter a country in order to attack it. **2** to intrude on somebody's privacy. ➤ **invader** *noun*.

invalid[1] /**in** va lid/ *noun* (*plural* **invalids**) a person who is unwell or disabled.

invalid[2] /in **va** lid/ *adjective* **1** not legal or valid: *Your documents are invalid.* **2** said about an argument: not logically correct.

invalidate /in **va** li dayt/ *verb* (**invalidates, invalidating, invalidated**) to make something invalid. ➤ **invalidation** *noun*.

invalidity /in va li **di** ti/ *noun* **1** the fact of being an invalid. **2** the fact of not being valid.

invaluable *adjective* very useful: *Thank you for your invaluable advice.*

invariably /in **vair** i ab li/ *adverb* always.

invasion *noun* (*plural* **invasions**) **1** *History* the act of entering a country in order to attack it. **2** the act of intruding on somebody's privacy.

invective *noun* abusive or insulting language.

invent *verb* (**invents, inventing, invented**) **1** to think of or produce a device or machine for the first time. **2** to think up a story, in order to deceive somebody. ➤ **inventor** *noun*.

invention *noun* (*plural* **inventions**) **1** something that has been invented. **2** the act of inventing something.

inventive *adjective* creative and original in your thinking.

inventory /ˈin ven to ri/ *noun* (*plural* **inventories**) a detailed list of the contents of a building or stock in a warehouse.

inverse /ˈin vers/ *adjective* opposite in order, direction, or effect. ➤ **inversely** *adverb*.

invert *verb* (**inverts, inverting, inverted**) to turn something inside out or upside down. ➤ **inversion** *noun*.

invertebrate /in ˈver ti brat/ *noun* (*plural* **invertebrates**) an animal without a backbone, such as an insect or a worm.

inverted comma *noun* = QUOTATION MARK.

invest *verb* (**invests, investing, invested**) **1** to put money into a bank account or a business deal in the hope of making a profit: *They have invested a lot of money in property.* **2** to devote time or effort to something: *We have invested a lot of time in this project.* **3** *informal* to buy something: *I'm going to invest in a winter coat.* ➤ **investor** *noun*.

investigate *verb* (**investigates, investigating, investigated**) **1** to make a thorough examination or study of something. **2** to conduct an official enquiry into a crime. ➤ **investigation** *noun*, **investigative** *adjective*, **investigator** *noun*.

investment *noun* (*plural* **investments**) **1** something that is bought in the hope that it will become useful or profitable in the future. **2** the act of investing something.

inveterate /in ˈve ti rat/ *adjective* being so by habit and unlikely to change: *an inveterate liar.*

invigilate /in ˈvi ji layt/ *verb* (**invigilates, invigilating, invigilated**) to supervise students sitting an examination. ➤ **invigilator** *noun*.

invigorate /in ˈvi go rayt/ *verb* (**invigorates, invigorating, invigorated**) to make somebody feel more lively and energetic. ➤ **invigorating** *adjective*.

invincible /in ˈvin sa bl/ *adjective* incapable of being defeated. ➤ **invincibility** *noun*.

invisible *adjective* unable to be seen, either by nature or because of concealment. ➤ **invisibility** *noun*, **invisibly** *adverb*.

invitation *noun* (*plural* **invitations**) a request for somebody to attend an event.

invite /in ˈviet/ *verb* (**invites, inviting, invited**) **1** to ask somebody to attend an event. **2** to ask somebody formally to do something: *I was invited to review his new book.* ~ /ˈin viet/ *noun* (*plural* **invites**) *informal* an invitation.

inviting *adjective* attractive or tempting. ➤ **invitingly** *adverb*.

invoice *noun* (*plural* **invoices**) a list of goods or services provided, together with a note of the sum of money that is owed.

invoke *verb* (**invokes, invoking, invoked**) **1** to appeal to an authority for help. **2** to arouse a particular feeling or memory in somebody.

involuntary *adjective* **1** said of a movement or sound: made unintentionally and unable to be controlled. **2** done against your will. ➤ **involuntarily** *adverb*.

involve *verb* (**involves, involving, involved**) **1** to cause somebody to

take part in something: *I was involved in planning the party.* **2** to require something as a necessary part: *Gardening involves getting your hands dirty.*
➤ **involvement** *noun*.

involved *adjective* **1** very complex. **2** taking part in something. **3** emotionally connected with somebody or something.

invulnerable /in vul ni ra bl/ *adjective* incapable of being injured or harmed.
➤ **invulnerability** *noun*.

inward *adjective* said about thoughts or feelings: private and personal.
➤ **inwardly** *adverb*.

inwards *adverb* **1** towards the inside of something. **2** towards the mind or the feelings.

iodine /ie o deen/ *noun* **1** *Science* a blackish grey non-metallic chemical element. **2** a solution of iodine in alcohol, used as an antiseptic.

ion /ie on/ *noun* (*plural* **ions**) an atom that has a positive or negative electric charge.

iota /ie oh ta/ *noun* a tiny amount; a bit: *not one iota.*

IOU *noun* (*plural* **IOUs**) a written acknowledgment of a debt.

IQ *abbreviation* = *intelligence quotient*, a measure of a person's intelligence.

irascible /i ra sa bl/ *adjective* easily made angry.

irate /ie rayt/ *adjective* extremely angry.

ire *noun literary* anger.

iris /ier is/ *noun* (*plural* **irises**) **1** the round coloured part of the eye. **2** a plant with long straight leaves and large bluish flowers.

irk *verb* (**irks, irking, irked**) to irritate or annoy somebody.

irksome *adjective* troublesome or annoying.

iron *noun* (*plural* **irons**) **1** *Science* a chemical element that exists as a heavy, dark grey, magnetic metal. **2** a metal device with a flat heated base, used to smooth the wrinkles out of clothing. **3** (**irons**) iron devices and chains intended to keep a prisoner from escaping. ~ *verb* (**irons, ironing, ironed**) to smooth a garment with a heated iron.

Iron Age *noun* (**the Iron Age**) *History* the period, dating from before 1000 BC, when people started using iron for making tools and weapons.

Iron Curtain *noun* (**the Iron Curtain**) *History* the political barrier that formerly separated the Communist and non-Communist countries in Europe.

ironmonger /ieon mung ger/ *noun* (*plural* **ironmongers**) a shopkeeper who sells hardware.

irony /ier o ni/ *noun* (*plural* **ironies**) **1** the humorous use of words to express a meaning opposite to their literal meaning. **2** the contrast between the actual results of a particular course of action and what would have been expected. ➤ **ironic** *adjective*, **ironically** *adverb*.

irrational /i ra sho nl/ *adjective* not according to reason; illogical. ➤ **irrationality** *noun*, **irrationally** *adverb*.

irregular *adjective* **1** occurring unpredictably. **2** not balanced or even. **3** against rules or customs. ➤ **irregularity** *noun*.

irrelevant *adjective* not relevant; not applicable. ➤ **irrelevance** *noun*.

irreparable /i re pa ra bl/ *adjective* not able to be repaired or put right. ➤ **irreparably** *adverb*.

irrepressible *adjective* impossible to restrain or control.

irreproachable *adjective* beyond criticism or blame.

irresistible *adjective* too attractive or powerful to resist. ➤ **irresistibly** *adverb*.

irrespective ✶ **irrespective of** regardless of: *Everyone is invited, irrespective of their beliefs.*

irresponsible *adjective* showing no concern for the consequences of your actions. ➤ **irresponsibly** *adverb*.

irreverence *noun* lack of respect. ➤ **irreverent** *adjective*, **irreverently** *adverb*.

irreversible *adjective* unable to be changed back into a previous state.

irrigate *verb* (**irrigates, irrigating, irrigated**) to supply land with water by means of water channels. ➤ **irrigation** *noun*.

irritable *adjective* easily angered or annoyed. ➤ **irritability** *noun*, **irritably** *adverb*.

irritant *noun* (*plural* **irritants**) something that irritates.

irritate *verb* (**irritates, irritating, irritated**) 1 to make somebody impatient or angry. 2 to cause a part of the body to become sore or itchy. ➤ **irritating** *adjective*, **irritatingly** *adverb*, **irritation** *noun*.

is *verb* third person singular present tense of BE.

Islam /iz lahm/ *noun* the religious faith of Muslims, including belief in Allah as the one God and in Muhammad as his prophet. ➤ **Islamic** *adjective*.

island /ie land/ *noun* (*plural* **islands**) an area of land surrounded by water. ➤ **islander** *noun*.

isle *noun* (*plural* **isles**) an island.

isolate *verb* (**isolates, isolating, isolated**) 1 to set yourself or somebody else apart from others. 2 *Science* to separate a substance out from a mixture of substances. ➤ **isolation** *noun*.

isolated *adjective* 1 cut off from others; lonely. 2 single or exceptional: *an isolated example of carelessness.*

isosceles /ie so si leez/ *adjective Maths* said about a triangle: having two equal sides.

issue /i shooh/ *noun* (*plural* **issues**) 1 a matter or topic that is being disputed. 2 any of a series of newspapers or magazines published regularly: *Have you seen this week's issue of Rap Up?* 3 the act of issuing something. ~ *verb* (**issues, issuing, issued**) 1 to send a newspaper or magazine out for sale. 2 to give a statement out officially. 3 to go, come, or flow out. ✶ **take issue with** to disagree or argue with a person or something they have said.

isthmus /is mus/ *noun* (*plural* **isthmuses**) *Geography* a narrow strip of land connecting two larger land areas.

IT *abbreviation* information technology.

it *pronoun* 1 that thing, animal, or situation. 2 used as the subject of a verb in expressions describing time, weather, a state of affairs, etc: *It's ten o'clock; It's raining; How's it going?*

italic *noun* (*plural* **italics**) a printed character that slants upwards to the right, like the labels *noun* and *adjective* in this dictionary. ~ *adjective* printed in italic.

itch *noun* (*plural* **itches**) an irritating sensation in the skin that makes you want to scratch. ~ *verb* (**itches, itching, itched**) 1 to have or cause an itch. 2 *informal* to have a restless desire to do something: *I am itching to cut her fringe.*

item *noun* (*plural* **items**) 1 a separate piece of news or information. 2 a separate article in a series. 3 *informal* two people in a romantic relationship.

itinerary /ie ti ni ra ri/ *noun* (*plural* **itineraries**) the planned route of a journey, including a list of stops on the way.

its *adjective* used to refer to a thing,

animal, or situation: *The eagle was flapping its wings; The plan has its merits.*

Usage Note its *or* **it's**? Do not confuse *its*, the possessive form of *it* with an apostrophe and *it's*, a shortened form of *it is* or *it has*.

it's *contraction* **1** it is. **2** it has.

itself *pronoun* **1** used to refer to a thing, animal, or situation that is the subject of the sentence: *The cat hurt itself.* **2** used for emphasis when referring to a thing, animal, or situation: *The play itself was very good but the acting was poor.* ✶ **by itself** alone.

ITV *abbreviation* Independent Television.

ivory /ie vo ri/ *noun* (*plural* **ivories**) **1** the hard creamy-white substance of which elephants' tusks are made. **2** a creamy-white colour.

ivy *noun* a common climbing plant with evergreen leaves.

jab *verb* (**jabs, jabbing, jabbed**) to pierce something or poke somebody sharply. ~ *noun* (*plural* **jabs**) **1** a sharp piercing or poking movement. **2** *informal* an injection.

jabber *verb* (**jabbers, jabbering, jabbered**) to talk rapidly and without making sense.

jack *noun* (*plural* **jacks**) **1** a device for lifting a vehicle in order to change a tyre. **2** a playing card that ranks above a ten and below a queen. **3** a small target ball in the game of bowls. ~ *verb* (**jacks, jacking, jacked**) ✳ **jack up** to lift a vehicle with a jack.

jackal *noun* (*plural* **jackals**) a type of wild dog.

jackass *noun* (*plural* **jackasses**) **1** a male ass. **2** a stupid person.

jackdaw *noun* (*plural* **jackdaws**) a black and grey bird of the crow family.

jacket *noun* (*plural* **jackets**) **1** a short coat. **2** a cover that protects or insulates something.

jackpot *noun* (*plural* **jackpots**) the largest prize in a lottery or on a fruit machine.

Jacobean /ja ko bee an/ *adjective History* to do with the reign of James I of England (1603–25).

Jacobite /**ja** koh biet/ *noun* (*plural* **Jacobites**) *History* a supporter of James II of England or of the Stuarts after James abdicated in 1688.

Jacuzzi /ja **kooh** zi/ *noun* (*plural* **Jacuzzis**) *trademark* a large bath with underwater jets that massage the body.

jade *noun* a hard green mineral used in jewellery.

jaded *adjective* bored by something that you have done or had too often.

jagged *adjective* with sharp irregular points or edges.

jaguar *noun* (*plural* **jaguars**) a large wild animal of the cat family, similar to a leopard.

jail or **gaol** *noun* (*plural* **jails** or **gaols**) a prison. ~ *verb* (**jails, jailing, jailed** or **gaols**, etc) to put somebody in jail.

Jainism /**jie** ni zm/ *noun* an Indian religion founded by Mahavira, with some similarities to Hinduism and Buddhism and an emphasis on asceticism and not harming any living creatures. ➤ **Jain** *noun and adjective*.

jam *noun* (*plural* **jams**) **1** a thick soft sweet food made by boiling fruit and sugar. **2** a crowd or mass that blocks progress. **3** *informal* an awkward situation. ~ *verb* (**jams, jamming, jammed**) **1** to pack things or people tightly into a space. **2** to push something somewhere with force. **3** to cause something to become stuck somewhere, often painfully. **4** to prevent a radio signal from being heard by sending out interfering signals. **5** *informal* to play in an informal session with other musicians.

jamboree /jam bo **ree**/ *noun* (*plural* **jamborees**) a large party or informal gathering.

jangle *verb* (**jangles, jangling, jangled**) **1** to make a harsh ringing noise, or cause something to make this noise. **2** said about your nerves: to be tense. ➤ **jangly** *adjective*.

janitor *noun* (*plural* **janitors**) somebody who looks after a large building.

January *noun* the first month of the year.

jar[1] *noun* (*plural* **jars**) a glass container.

jar[2] *verb* (**jars, jarring, jarred**) **1** to hit something suddenly and forcefully so that it shakes. **2** to be irritatingly unpleasant.

jargon *noun* the words and expressions used by people in a particular group or involved in a particular activity.

jasmine /jaz min/ *noun* a climbing plant with fragrant yellow or white flowers.

jaundice *noun* abnormal yellowing of the skin.

jaundiced *adjective* believing that people are generally not honest or good, or that things are generally not worthwhile.

jaunt *noun* (*plural* **jaunts**) a short journey for pleasure.

jaunty *adjective* (**jauntier, jauntiest**) showing that you feel happy or confident. ➤ **jauntily** *adverb*.

javelin *noun* (*plural* **javelins**) a spear thrown in an athletics event.

jaw *noun* (*plural* **jaws**) **1** each of the two bones that form the framework of your mouth. **2** (**jaws**) the grabbing or crushing parts of a machine.

jay *noun* (*plural* **jays**) a noisy bird of the crow family, with light pinkish brown plumage.

jaywalking *noun* crossing a street without taking care or watching out for traffic.

jazz *noun* music in which brass, woodwind, and percussion instruments feature prominently, often containing improvised passages. ~ *verb* (**jazzes, jazzing, jazzed**) ✷ **jazz up** *informal* to make something more lively or interesting.

jazzy *adjective* (**jazzier, jazziest**) *informal* bright, colourful, or flamboyant. ➤ **jazzily** *adverb*.

jealous *adjective* **1** envious of something good that somebody else has. **2** angry because you suspect your boyfriend or girlfriend likes somebody else. **3** careful to protect what is yours. ➤ **jealously** *adverb*, **jealousy** *noun*.

jeans *plural noun* casual trousers made of denim.

jeep *noun* (*plural* **jeeps**) *trademark* a four-wheel drive car built for rough roads.

jeer *verb* (**jeers, jeering, jeered**) to laugh or shout in a mocking way. ~ *noun* (*plural* **jeers**) a mocking remark.

Jehovah *noun* a Hebrew name for God.

jelly *noun* (*plural* **jellies**) **1** a soft fruit-flavoured dessert. **2** any thick, sticky, semi-liquid substance.

jellyfish *noun* (*plural* **jellyfishes** *or* **jellyfish**) a small sea animal with a soft round transparent body and stinging tentacles.

jeopardize *or* **jeopardise** /je pa diez/ *verb* (**jeopardizes, jeopardizing, jeopardized** *or* **jeopardises**, etc) to put something at risk of being lost or damaged.

jeopardy /je pa di/ *noun* risk of being lost or damaged.

jerk *verb* (**jerks, jerking, jerked**) to move with a short sudden movement, or make something move in this way. ~ *noun* (*plural* **jerks**) **1** a short sudden movement. **2** *chiefly N American, informal* a stupid or irritating person.

jerkin *noun* (*plural* **jerkins**) a close-fitting sleeveless jacket.

jerky *adjective* (**jerkier, jerkiest**) said about movements: short and sudden. ➤ **jerkily** *adverb*.

jersey *noun* (*plural* **jerseys**) **1** a knitted

garment with sleeves. **2** a shirt worn by a footballer or other sports player. **3** a type of knitted fabric used for clothing.

jest *noun* (*plural* **jests**) a joke. ~ *verb* (**jests, jesting, jested**) to make a joke. ✳ **in jest** as a joke.

jester *noun* (*plural* **jesters**) in the past, a clown whose job was entertaining people in a royal household.

Jesuit /jezewit/ *noun* (*plural* **Jesuits**) a member of a Roman Catholic order of monks and priests called the Society of Jesus.

jet¹ *noun* (*plural* **jets**) **1** a stream of liquid or gas forced out under pressure from a nozzle. **2** an aircraft powered by jet engines. ~ *verb* (**jets, jetted, jetting**) to travel by jet aircraft.

jet² *noun* **1** a hard black mineral used in jewellery. **2** (**jet black**) an intense black colour.

jet engine *noun* (*plural* **jet engines**) an aircraft engine in which hot gases are forced backwards to produce forward motion.

jet lag *noun* changes in your body's normal rhythms that occur after a long flight from one time zone to another. ➤ **jet-lagged** *adjective*.

jetsam *noun* objects thrown overboard from a ship and washed up on shore. ✳ **flotsam and jetsam** see FLOTSAM.

jettison *verb* (**jettisons, jettisoning, jettisoned**) **1** to get rid of something you no longer want. **2** to throw objects overboard to make a ship or aircraft lighter.

jetty *noun* (*plural* **jetties**) a small pier where small boats can stop.

Jew *noun* (*plural* **Jews**) **1** a member of the ethnic group whose ancestors were the Semitic people of ancient Israel. **2** a person whose religion is Judaism. ➤ **Jewish** *adjective*.

jewel *noun* (*plural* **jewels**) a precious stone used in jewellery. ➤ **jewelled** *adjective*.

jeweller *noun* (*plural* **jewellers**) a person who makes or sells jewellery.

jewellery *noun* ornaments that people wear, such as rings and necklaces.

jib *noun* (*plural* **jibs**) **1** a triangular sail at the front of a ship. **2** the arm of a crane.

jibe or **gibe** *noun* (*plural* **jibes** or **gibes**) a mocking or insulting remark. ~ *verb* (**jibes, jibing, jibed** or **gibes**, etc) to make jibes.

jig *noun* (*plural* **jigs**) **1** a fast folk dance. **2** the part of a machine that holds a piece of wood or metal that is being cut or shaped. ~ *verb* (**jigs, jigging, jigged**) to move up and down in a rapid and jerky fashion.

jiggle *verb* (**jiggles, jiggling, jiggled**) *informal* to move with quick short jerks. ➤ **jiggly** *adjective*.

jigsaw *noun* (*plural* **jigsaws**) **1** a puzzle consisting of small irregularly cut pieces of wood or card that you fit together to form a picture. **2** a power-driven saw that can cut irregular shapes.

jihad /jihad/ *noun* (*plural* **jihads**) a war that a Muslim group fights against people they regard as enemies of the Islamic religion.

jilt *verb* (**jilts, jilting, jilted**) to end a relationship with a boyfriend or girlfriend suddenly and in an unkind way.

jingle *noun* (*plural* **jingles**) **1** a short song or tune designed to be easy to remember, used especially to advertise something on radio or television. **2** a light clinking or tinkling sound. ~ *verb* (**jingles, jingling, jingled**) to make a light clinking or tinkling sound. ➤ **jingly** *adjective*.

jingoism *noun* the annoying or offensive attitude of somebody who believes their country is better than all others. ➤ **jingoistic** *adjective*.

jinx noun (plural **jinxes**) informal somebody or something that brings bad luck. ~ verb (**jinxes, jinxing, jinxed**) to bring bad luck to somebody or something.

jitters plural noun (**the jitters**) a feeling of being very nervous. ➤ **jittery** adjective.

job noun (plural **jobs**) 1 regular paid employment. 2 a piece of work. 3 a task or duty: *It's my job to see that no one gets hurt.* ✷ **just the job** exactly what is needed. ➤ **jobless** adjective.

job centre noun (plural **job centres**) a government office where unemployed people can get information about jobs.

jockey noun (plural **jockeys**) a rider in a horse race. ~ verb (**jockeys, jockeying, jockeyed**) ✷ **jockey for position** to try to get an advantage over other people you are competing with for something.

jocular adjective joking. ➤ **jocularity** noun, **jocularly** adverb.

jodhpurs /jod perz/ plural noun trousers that are baggy at the top and tight below the knee, worn for riding horses.

jog verb (**jogs, jogging, jogged**) 1 to run at a slow steady pace. 2 to knock something gently, especially by accident. ~ noun (plural **jogs**) 1 a run at a slow steady pace. 2 a fairly slow running pace.

join verb (**joins, joining, joined**) 1 to put things together to form a unit, or to come together to form a unit. 2 to become a member or employee of a club, organization, etc. 3 to go somewhere to be with somebody: *I'll join you later.* ~ noun (plural **joins**) a place where two parts are joined. ✷ **join forces** to form an alliance or combine efforts. **join up** 1 to become a member of the armed forces. 2 to come together.

joiner noun (plural **joiners**) somebody who makes and repairs the wooden parts of buildings and other large structures. ➤ **joinery** noun.

joint noun (plural **joints**) 1 a place where two parts join. 2 a part of your body where two or more bones are joined. 3 a large piece of meat for roasting. 4 informal a place of entertainment such as a pub or café. 5 informal a cannabis cigarette. ~ *adjective* shared or carried out by two or more people: *joint responsibility; a joint effort.* ~ verb (**joints, jointing, jointed**) to cut a piece of meat containing bones into parts by cutting it at the joints.

joist noun (plural **joists**) a wooden or metal beam that supports a floor or ceiling.

joke noun (plural **jokes**) 1 a short funny story that you tell to make people laugh. 2 a trick that you play for fun. 3 something or somebody that is ridiculously unsuitable or inadequate. ~ verb (**jokes, joking, joked**) to tease somebody by saying something that is not true. ➤ **jokey** or **joky** adjective.

joker noun (plural **jokers**) 1 a playing card with a picture of a jester on it, which, in some games, can have any value you want. 2 somebody who often tells jokes or teases people.

jolly adjective (**jollier, jolliest**) 1 cheerful and good-humoured. 2 lively and amusing. ~ *adverb* informal very. ~ verb (**jollies, jollying, jollied**) ✷ **jolly along** to encourage somebody cheerfully. ➤ **jolliness** noun.

jolt verb (**jolts, jolting, jolted**) 1 to knock something and cause it to move or shake. 2 to give somebody a nasty shock. ~ noun (plural **jolts**) 1 a knock that moves or shakes something. 2 a nasty shock.

jostle verb (**jostles, jostling, jostled**) to shove somebody roughly.

jot *verb* (**jots, jotting, jotted**) ✳ **jot down** to write something down briefly or hurriedly.

jotter *noun* (*plural* **jotters**) a small notebook or pad.

joule /joohl/ *noun* (*plural* **joules**) *Science* a unit used in measuring work or energy.

journal *noun* (*plural* **journals**) **1** a periodical that deals with a particular subject. **2** a daily diary.

journalist *noun* (*plural* **journalists**) a person who writes news for a newspaper or prepares news reports for radio or television programmes. ➤ **journalism** *noun*, **journalistic** *adjective*.

journey *noun* (*plural* **journeys**) an occasion when you travel from one place to another. ~ *verb* (**journeys, journeying, journeyed**) to travel.

joust *noun* (*plural* **jousts**) a medieval competition on horseback between knights armed with lances. ~ *verb* (**jousts, jousting, jousted**) **1** to fight in a joust. **2** to be involved in a contest or argument with somebody.

jovial *adjective* good-humoured and cheerful. ➤ **joviality** *noun*, **jovially** *adverb*.

joy *noun* (*plural* **joys**) **1** a feeling of great happiness or pleasure. **2** something that gives you great pleasure. **3** *informal* success or satisfaction: *We had no joy at the first shop.* ➤ **joyless** *adjective*.

joyful *adjective* causing or feeling joy. ➤ **joyfully** *adverb*.

joyous *adjective* *literary* joyful. ➤ **joyously** *adverb*.

joyriding *noun* the crime of driving around recklessly in a stolen car. ➤ **joyrider** *noun*.

joystick *noun* (*plural* **joysticks**) **1** a lever used to control an aircraft. **2** a lever for controlling a computer game or other piece of software.

JP *abbreviation* Justice of the Peace.

jubilant *adjective* filled with or expressing great joy or triumph. ➤ **jubilantly** *adverb*.

jubilation *noun* feelings of great joy or triumph, or behaviour that expresses such feelings.

jubilee *noun* (*plural* **jubilees**) a special anniversary of a major event.

Judaism *noun* the religion of Jewish people, involving a belief in one God and obedience to the laws set down in the Torah. ➤ **Judaic** *adjective*.

judder *verb* (**judders, juddering, juddered**) to vibrate jerkily. ~ *noun* (*plural* **judders**) a sharp vibrating movement.

judge *noun* (*plural* **judges**) **1** a public official who is in charge of trials in a law court. **2** somebody appointed to decide the winner of a competition or contest. ~ *verb* (**judges, judging, judged**) **1** to form an opinion about something or somebody. **2** to decide the result of a competition.

judgment *or* **judgement** *noun* (*plural* **judgments** *or* **judgements**) **1** the ability to form good opinions or making sensible decisions. **2** an opinion. **3** a formal decision by a court or judge.

judgmental *or* **judgemental** *adjective* tending to make moral judgments about other people.

judicial *adjective* to do with judges or courts of law, or carried out by them. ➤ **judicially** *adverb*.

judiciary *noun* (*plural* **judiciaries**) the judges in a country.

judicious *adjective* sensible. ➤ **judiciously** *adverb*.

judo *noun* a martial art that involves throwing your opponent.

jug *noun* (*plural* **jugs**) a container for holding and pouring liquids, with a handle and a lip.

juggernaut *noun* (*plural* **juggernauts**) a large articulated lorry.

> *Word History* **Juggernaut** comes from the Hindi word *Jagannath*, a name for the Hindu god Krishna that means 'lord of the world'. It is said that worshippers of Krishna would sometimes throw themselves under the wheels of a heavy chariot carrying his idol and be crushed to death.

juggle *verb* (**juggles, juggling, juggled**) **1** to keep several objects moving in the air at the same time by alternately throwing them up and catching them. **2** to deal with several activities at the same time. ➤ **juggler** *noun*.

jugular *noun* (*plural* **jugulars**) any of the large veins at the side of your neck.

juice *noun* (*plural* **juices**) **1** the liquid contained in a fruit or vegetable. **2** a drink made from fruit juice. **3** (**juices**) the natural fluids in your body.

juicy *adjective* (**juicier, juiciest**) **1** full of juice; succulent. **2** *informal* interesting because of scandalous or sexual details: *Give me all the juicy details*.

jukebox *noun* (*plural* **jukeboxes**) a coin-operated machine that plays pop music.

July *noun* the seventh month of the year.

jumble *verb* (**jumbles, jumbling, jumbled**) to mix things up in a confused or untidy way. ~ *noun* **1** a confused or untidy mass of things mixed together. **2** articles for a jumble sale.

jumble sale *noun* (*plural* **jumble sales**) a sale of secondhand articles to raise money for charity.

jumbo *noun* (*plural* **jumbos**) = JUMBO JET. ~ *adjective* of larger-than-usual size.

jumbo jet *noun* (*plural* **jumbo jets**) a large passenger jet aircraft.

jump *verb* (**jumps, jumping, jumped**) **1** to spring into the air using your feet and legs. **2** to get over an obstacle by jumping. **3** to move quickly and with energy: *We jumped into the car*. **4** to move suddenly from shock or surprise: *You made me jump*. **5** to increase suddenly and sharply: *Prices jumped following the news*. **6** (**jump on**) to make a sudden verbal or physical attack on somebody. ~ *noun* (*plural* **jumps**) **1** an act of springing into the air; a leap. **2** an obstacle to be jumped over. **3** a sudden sharp increase. ✷ **jump at** to accept an opportunity eagerly.

jumper *noun* (*plural* **jumpers**) a knitted garment that covers your upper body; a sweater.

jumpy *adjective* (**jumpier, jumpiest**) nervous.

junction *noun* (*plural* **junctions**) a place where roads or railway lines meet.

juncture *noun* (*plural* **junctures**) *formal* a particular point in time or in a process.

June *noun* the sixth month of the year.

jungle *noun* (*plural* **jungles**) a tropical area with trees and other plants growing together thickly.

junior *adjective* **1** made up of younger pupils, players, etc. **2** of a fairly low status or rank. ~ *noun* (*plural* **juniors**) **1** a member of a junior school, sports team, etc. **2** somebody of a fairly low status or rank. **3** a person who is younger than another by a stated amount: *He is three years her junior*.

juniper *noun* (*plural* **junipers**) an evergreen shrub with small purple berries.

junk[1] *noun* **1** things that people have thrown away. **2** something useless or worthless. ~ *verb* (**junks, junking, junked**) *informal* to get rid of something worthless.

junk² *noun* (*plural* **junks**) a flat-bottomed sailing ship in the Far East.

junk food *noun* unhealthy processed food.

junkie *or* **junky** *noun* (*plural* **junkies**) *informal* a drug addict.

junk mail *noun* unwanted advertising material that you receive by post.

jurisdiction *noun* the authority to make legal decisions.

juror *noun* (*plural* **jurors**) a member of a jury.

jury *noun* (*plural* **juries**) a group of people in a court of law who decide whether the accused person is guilty or innocent.

just *adverb* **1** exactly or precisely: *It's just three o'clock.* **2** immediately or very soon: *I'm just coming.* **3** only a very short time ago: *I've just done it.* **4** by a very small margin: *We were just too late.* **4** only or simply: *just a small present.* ~ *adjective* fair, suitable, or deserved. ➤ **justly** *adverb*.

justice *noun* (*plural* **justices**) **1** fairness in a decision or outcome. **2** the quality of being fair, suitable, or deserved. **3** the business of a court of law. **3** a judge or magistrate.

justice of the peace *noun* (*plural* **justices of the peace**) a magistrate who judges minor cases.

justifiable *adjective* able to be justified. ➤ **justifiably** *adverb*.

justify *verb* (**justifies, justifying, justified**) **1** to show that something is right or reasonable. **2** *ICT* to make a piece of text flush with both left and right margins. ➤ **justification** *noun*.

jut *verb* (**juts, jutting, jutted**) ✶ **jut out** to extend past the edge or line of something; to stick out.

jute *noun* the fibre of an Indian plant, used for making rope or sacking.

juvenile *adjective* **1** childish. **2** to do with young people. ~ *noun* (*plural* **juveniles**) a young person.

juxtapose *verb* (**juxtaposes, juxtaposing, juxtaposed**) to place different things next to each other, or consider different things together. ➤ **juxtaposition** *noun*.

kaftan or **caftan** noun (plural **kaftans** or **caftans**) a long loose garment worn by men in Arab countries.

kagoul noun see CAGOULE.

kale noun a cabbage with curled leaves.

kaleidoscope /ka lie do skohp/ noun (plural **kaleidoscopes**) **1** a tube with mirrors inside that create different patterns as you look down the tube and twist its end. **2** a continually changing pattern. ➤ **kaleidoscopic** adjective.

kamikaze /ka mi kah zi/ noun in World War II, a Japanese pilot who was willing to die by deliberately crashing his aircraft full of explosives on a target.

Word History Kamikaze means 'divine wind'. The word was first applied to a wind that destroyed the Mongol fleet that attacked Japan in 1281.

kangaroo noun (plural **kangaroos**) an Australian animal that hops on its powerful hind legs and has a long thick tail and a pouch.

kaolin /kay oh lin/ noun fine white clay used in ceramics and medicine.

kaput adjective informal broken or useless.

karaoke /ka ri oh ki/ noun singing with a backing of recorded music from a machine.

karate /ka rah ti/ noun a martial art in which people fight using their hands and feet.

karma noun in Hinduism and Buddhism, a spiritual force that is created by a person's actions and that influences their destiny.

karting noun racing in go-karts.

kayak /kie ak/ noun (plural **kayaks**) a canoe made of a frame covered with a water-resistant material with a small opening for the canoeist to sit in.

KB or **Kb** abbreviation ICT kilobyte or kilobytes.

kebab noun (plural **kebabs**) cubes of meat or vegetables grilled on a skewer.

keel noun (plural **keels**) a projecting structure running along the bottom of a ship that improves its stability. ~ verb (**keels, keeling, keeled**) ✱ **keel over 1** said about a ship: to capsize. **2** said about a person or object: to fall over. **on an even keel** steady.

keen[1] adjective **1** enthusiastic and eager. **2** said about a blade: sharp. **3** said about a feeling: intense. **4** said about the mind or senses: strongly aware of things. **5** (**keen on**) fond of somebody or something. ➤ **keenly** adverb, **keenness** noun.

keen[2] verb (**keens, keening, keened**) to wail loudly for the dead.

keep verb (**keeps, keeping, kept**) **1** to retain possession or control of something. **2** to remain, or make somebody or something remain, in a specified place or condition: *Keep quiet*. **3** to continue to do something, or do something again and again: *Keep*

keeper

going; *She keeps annoying me.* **4** to store something: *Where do you keep the butter?* **5** to record something in a book or on paper: *Keep a note of what is said.* **6** to provide somebody with money, food, and other things they need to live. **7** to obey a law or carry out a promise, etc. **8** to delay or detain somebody. **9** not to reveal a secret. **10** said about food: to remain in good condition. ~ *noun* (*plural* **keeps**) **1** the fortified tower of a castle. **2** money and other things you need to live. ✱ **for keeps** permanently. **keep up 1** to go or work as fast as somebody else. **2** to continue to do something: *Keep up the good work.*

keeper *noun* (*plural* **keepers**) **1** somebody who protects, guards, or imprisons another person. **2** somebody who looks after animals in a zoo. **3** = GOALKEEPER *or* WICKET-KEEPER.

keeping *noun* custody or care. ✱ **in keeping with** suiting or going well with something.

keepsake *noun* (*plural* **keepsakes**) something kept to remind you of the person who gave it.

keg *noun* (*plural* **kegs**) a small barrel.

kelp *noun* a type of seaweed with large brown fronds.

Kelt *noun* see CELT.

kelvin *noun* (*plural* **kelvins**) *Science* a unit for measuring temperature.

kennel *noun* (*plural* **kennels**) **1** a shelter for a dog. **2** (**kennels**) a place where dogs can be left while their owners are away.

kept *verb* past tense of KEEP.

kerb *noun* (*plural* **kerbs**) a stone edging to a pavement or path. ▸ **kerbstone** *noun.*

kernel *noun* (*plural* **kernels**) **1** the inner soft part of a seed, fruit stone, or nut. **2** a central or essential part of something.

kerosene *or* **kerosine** *noun* = PARAFFIN.

kestrel *noun* (*plural* **kestrels**) a small falcon that hovers in the air.

ketchup *noun* a sauce made from tomatoes, vinegar, and seasonings.

kettle *noun* (*plural* **kettles**) a container with a lid, handle, and spout, used for boiling water.

kettledrum *noun* (*plural* **kettledrums**) a large bowl-shaped drum.

key *noun* (*plural* **keys**) **1** a metal instrument used to open or close a lock. **2** a device used to wind up something, such as a clock. **3** *ICT* a small button on a computer or typewriter keyboard. **4** *Music* a lever on an instrument that is pressed to produce a note. **5** *Music* a system of seven notes based on their relationship to the first and lowest note: *the key of A minor.* **6** something that gives an explanation or solution to a mystery or puzzle. **7** a list of words or phrases explaining symbols. ~ *verb* (**keys, keying, keyed**) *ICT* to enter data by typing on a keyboard. ~ *adjective* very important. ✱ **be keyed up** to be tense or excited.

keyboard *noun* (*plural* **keyboards**) **1** a set of keys on a piano, computer, typewriter, etc. **2** *Music* an electronic musical instrument with keys.

keyhole *noun* (*plural* **keyholes**) a hole in a lock into which the key is put.

keyhole surgery *noun* surgery performed through a very small cut in the patient's body.

keynote *noun* (*plural* **keynotes**) **1** the main idea or subject of a speech or conference. **2** *Music* the base note of a scale.

keypad *noun* (*plural* **keypads**) a small keyboard or set of buttons for operating a portable electronic device.

keystone *noun* (*plural* **keystones**) the central stone at the top of an arch that holds all the others together.

kg *abbreviation* kilogram or kilograms.

khaki *noun* **1** a dull yellowish brown colour. **2** cloth of this colour used for military uniforms.

kibbutz /ki boots/ *noun* (*plural* **kibbutzim** /ki boo tseem/ *or* **kibbutzes**) a farm in Israel run as a cooperative.

kick *verb* (**kicks, kicking, kicked**) **1** to strike something or somebody hard with your foot. **2** to strike out with your foot or feet. **3** *informal* to free yourself of a habit. ~ *noun* (*plural* **kicks**) **1** an act of kicking. **2** a pleasurable experience or feeling: *I get a kick out of dancing.* **3** *informal* an interest or fad: *a health food kick.* ✶ **kick off 1** in ball games, to start or resume play. **2** *informal* to start doing something. **kick out** *informal* to make somebody leave a place or a job. **kick the bucket** *informal* to die. **kick yourself** to blame yourself afterwards for making a silly mistake.

kickboxing *noun* a martial art in which people fight using gloved hands and bare feet. ➤ **kickboxer** *noun*.

kickoff *noun* (*plural* **kickoffs**) the start of a football game.

kid *noun* (*plural* **kids**) **1** a young goat. **2** *informal* a child or young person. ~ *verb* (**kids, kidding, kidded**) *informal* to deceive or tease somebody playfully.

kidnap *verb* (**kidnaps, kidnapping, kidnapped**) to capture and detain a person by force, usually to get a ransom. ➤ **kidnap** *noun*, **kidnapper** *noun*.

kidney *noun* (*plural* **kidneys**) **1** one of a pair of organs in the body that filter the blood and remove waste that is excreted as urine. **2** the kidney of an animal eaten as food.

kidney bean *noun* (*plural* **kidney beans**) a dark red kidney-shaped bean.

kidney machine *noun* (*plural* **kidney machines**) a machine that purifies the blood when the kidneys do not function properly.

kill *verb* (**kills, killing, killed**) **1** to make a person or animal die. **2** to put an end to something. **3** to pass time, especially while waiting for something. **4** *informal* to switch off an engine or lights. **5** *informal* to cause somebody pain, or exhaust them. ~ *noun* (*plural* **kills**) **1** an act of killing. **2** something killed as game or prey. ➤ **killer** *noun*.

killer whale *noun* (*plural* **killer whales**) a meat-eating black-and-white whale.

killing *noun* (*plural* **killings**) an act of causing death. ✶ **make a killing** *informal* to make a huge profit.

killjoy *noun* (*plural* **killjoys**) somebody who spoils the pleasure of other people.

kiln *noun* (*plural* **kilns**) an oven for burning, hardening, or drying a substance, especially for firing clay.

kilo /kee loh/ *noun* (*plural* **kilos**) a kilogram.

kilobyte *noun* (*plural* **kilobytes**) *ICT* a unit of memory or information equal to 1024 bytes.

kilogram *noun* (*plural* **kilograms**) the basic metric unit of mass equal to the weight of one litre of water (about 2.205 pounds).

kilometre /ki loh mee ter *or* ki lo mi ter/ *noun* (*plural* **kilometres**) a unit of length equal to 1000 metres (about 0.62 of a mile).

kilowatt *noun* (*plural* **kilowatts**) 1000 watts.

kilt *noun* (*plural* **kilts**) a tartan pleated skirt that was part of the traditional dress of men in the Scottish Highlands, now worn by many Scotsmen and men of Scottish descent.

kimono /ki moh noh/ *noun* (*plural* **kimonos**) a loose Japanese robe with wide sleeves.

kin *plural noun* your relatives. ➤ **kinsman** *noun*, **kinswoman** *noun*.

kind[1] *noun* (*plural* **kinds**) a group of people or things with common features; a type or sort. ✱ **in kind 1** in the same way. **2** in goods or services as distinct from money. **kind of** *informal* **1** somewhat; rather: *It's kind of difficult to explain.* **2** so to speak: *You have to kind of twist it.*

Usage Note It is incorrect to say *these kind of things*. Say either *this kind of thing* or *these kinds of things*.

kind[2] *adjective* considerate, helpful, or generous. ➤ **kindly** *adverb*, **kindness** *noun*.

kindergarten /kin der gah tn/ *noun* (*plural* **kindergartens**) a school for very young children.

kindle *verb* (**kindles, kindling, kindled**) **1** to cause a fire to start burning. **2** to arouse an emotion.

kindling *noun* small sticks for lighting a fire.

kindly *adjective* (**kindlier, kindliest**) sympathetic or generous. ➤ **kindliness** *noun*.

kindred *plural noun* your relatives. ~ *adjective* **1** similar in nature or character. **2** related.

kindred spirit *noun* (*plural* **kindred spirits**) somebody with similar interests or opinions to yours.

kinetic /ki ne tik/ *adjective* Science to do with motion. ➤ **kinetically** *adverb*.

king *noun* (*plural* **kings**) **1** a man who is the royal ruler of a state. **2** the most important, famous, or skilful man in a particular field of activity. **3** in chess, the principal piece on each side, which the opposing side tries to trap. **4** a playing card with a picture of a king on it. ➤ **kingly** *adjective*, **kingship** *noun*.

kingdom *noun* (*plural* **kingdoms**) **1** a country ruled by a king or queen. **2** *Science* any of the major divisions into which natural objects are classified: *the animal kingdom*.

kingfisher *noun* (*plural* **kingfishers**) a fish-eating bird with bright blue feathers.

king-size *or* **king-sized** *adjective* larger than the standard size.

kink *noun* (*plural* **kinks**) **1** a short twist or curl. **2** a peculiar characteristic or eccentricity.

kinky *adjective* (**kinkier, kinkiest**) **1** twisted or curled. **2** *informal* sexually unusual.

kinship *noun* **1** blood relationship. **2** similarity.

kiosk /kee osk/ *noun* (*plural* **kiosks**) **1** a small stall or stand for the sale of newspapers, cigarettes, and sweets. **2** a public telephone box.

kip *noun informal* a short sleep. ~ *verb* (**kips, kipping, kipped**) *informal* to sleep.

kipper *noun* (*plural* **kippers**) a herring that has been split open, salted, and smoked.

kiss *verb* (**kisses, kissing, kissed**) **1** to touch somebody or something with your lips as a mark of affection or greeting. **2** to touch something gently or lightly. ➤ **kiss** *noun*.

kiss of life *noun* (**the kiss of life**) helping a person who has stopped breathing to start breathing again by blowing air from your mouth into their mouth and lungs.

kit *noun* (*plural* **kits**) **1** a set of clothes or equipment for a particular activity. **2** a set of parts that you put together to make something. ~ *verb* (**kits, kitting, kitted**) ✱ **kit out** to provide somebody with suitable clothes or equipment.

kitbag *noun* (*plural* **kitbags**) a large cylindrical shoulder bag used by soldiers to carry their possessions.

kitchen *noun* (*plural* **kitchens**) a room where food is prepared and cooked.

kitchenette noun (plural **kitchenettes**) a small kitchen.

kite noun (plural **kites**) 1 a light frame covered with thin material that is flown in the air at the end of a long string. 2 a hawk with a forked tail.

kith * **kith and kin** your friends and relatives.

kitten noun (plural **kittens**) a young cat.

kitty noun (plural **kitties**) 1 a jointly held fund of money. 2 a sum of money that can be won in a card game.

kiwi /kee wee/ noun (plural **kiwis**) 1 a flightless bird found in New Zealand. 2 (**Kiwi**) informal a person from New Zealand.

kiwi fruit noun (plural **kiwi fruits** or **kiwi fruit**) a fruit with brown hairy skin, green flesh, and black seeds.

kleptomania noun an irresistible desire to steal things. ➤ **kleptomaniac** noun.

km abbreviation kilometre or kilometres.

knack noun a special skill needed to do something.

knacker noun (plural **knackers**) somebody who buys and slaughters worn-out horses and other animals. ~ verb (**knacker, knackering, knackered**) informal to exhaust somebody.

knapsack noun (plural **knapsacks**) a small rucksack for carrying supplies or belongings.

knave noun (plural **knaves**) 1 archaic a dishonest man. 2 a jack in a pack of playing cards.

knead verb (**kneads, kneading, kneaded**) to press and stretch something soft, especially dough, with your hands.

knee noun (plural **knees**) the joint where your leg bends.

kneecap noun (plural **kneecaps**) a thick flat bone that protects the front of the knee joint.

knee-deep adjective sunk in something up to your knees.

knee-jerk adjective done without thinking; automatic: *a knee-jerk reaction.*

kneel verb (**kneels, kneeling, knelt** or **kneeled**) to be in a position where your knees are on the ground and the rest of your body is upright.

knell noun the sound of a bell rung slowly to show that somebody has died.

knew verb past tense of KNOW.

knickerbockers plural noun short baggy trousers gathered at the knee.

knickers plural noun women's or girls' underpants.

knick-knack noun (plural **knick-knacks**) informal a small ornament that is not very valuable.

knife noun (plural **knives**) a cutting tool consisting of a blade fixed in a handle. ~ verb (**knifes, knifing, knifed**) to stab somebody with a knife.

knight noun (plural **knights**) 1 *History* in medieval times, a man of high social rank serving a king or lord as a soldier on horseback. 2 a man given the title 'Sir' as an honour by the king or queen. 3 in chess, either of two pieces of each colour in the shape of a horse's head. ~ verb (**knights, knighting, knighted**) to make somebody a knight. ➤ **knighthood** noun.

knit verb (**knits, knitting, knitted** or **knit**) 1 to make something by working yarn into a series of interlocking loops using needles or a machine. 2 to link or join people or things together. 3 to contract your brow into wrinkles.

knitwear noun knitted clothing.

knob noun (plural **knobs**) 1 a small rounded handle on a door, drawer,

knobble *noun* (*plural* **knobbles**) a small knob or lump. ➤ **knobbly** *adjective*.

knock *verb* (**knocks, knocking, knocked**) **1** to hit a surface sharply with your knuckles or a hard object. **2** to bang on a door to be let in. **3** to drive in, make, or remove something by hitting it. **4** to collide with something. **5** *informal* to find fault with something. ~ *noun* (*plural* **knocks**) **1** a sharp blow or collision. **2** the sound of knocking. ✱ **knock off 1** to stop work. **2** to produce something hurriedly. **3** to deduct an amount. **4** *informal* to steal something. **knock out 1** to make somebody unconscious. **2** to eliminate a team or contestant from a competition. **3** *informal* to impress somebody greatly.

knocker *noun* (*plural* **knockers**) a metal object attached to a door by a hinge, for knocking on the door to let somebody know you are there.

knockout *noun* (*plural* **knockouts**) **1** in boxing, a blow that knocks an opponent down and ends the match. **2** a competition with rounds in which the losing competitors are eliminated. **3** *informal* a very impressive person or thing.

knoll /nohl/ *noun* (*plural* **knolls**) a small hill or mound.

knot *noun* (*plural* **knots**) **1** a fastening made by looping string, thread, etc round itself and pulling it tight. **2** a tangled mass of hair or wool. **3** a lump or swelling in body tissue. **4** a hard dark spot in timber where a branch was attached to the tree trunk. **5** a cluster of people or things. **6** a unit of speed equal to one nautical mile per hour. ~ *verb* (**knots, knotting, knotted**) **1** to tie something in or with a knot. **2** to tangle hair or wool. ✱ **tie in knots** to confuse or bewilder somebody. **tie the knot** to get married.

knotty *adjective* (**knottier, knottiest**) **1** full of knots. **2** complicated or difficult.

know *verb* (**knows, knowing, knew, known**) **1** to be aware of or have information about something. **2** to be convinced or certain of something. **3** to recognize or identify somebody or something. **4** to be acquainted or familiar with somebody or something. ✱ **be known as** to be called something. **in the know** having information that only a small number of people share.

know-all *noun* (*plural* **know-alls**) somebody who thinks they know everything.

know-how *noun* expertise in a particular field.

knowing *adjective* **1** suggesting knowledge of a secret. **2** shrewd. **3** deliberate or conscious. ➤ **knowingly** *adverb*.

knowledge /no lij/ *noun* **1** information or understanding acquired through learning or experience. **2** the total of known facts about a subject.

knowledgeable *adjective* well-informed. ➤ **knowledgeably** *adverb*.

known *verb* past participle of KNOW.

knuckle *noun* (*plural* **knuckles**) a joint between the hand and the fingers or between the bones of the fingers. ~ *verb* (**knuckles, knuckling, knuckled**) ✱ **knuckle down** to start to work hard. **knuckle under** to give in or submit.

koala /koh ah la/ *noun* (*plural* **koalas**) a small bear-like Australian mammal that lives in trees, with large ears and grey fur.

Koran *or* **Qur'an** /kaw rahn *or* ko rahn/ *noun* (**the Koran** *or* **the Qur'an**) the sacred book of Islam, believed by

Muslims to contain revelations made to the prophet Muhammad by Allah.

kosher /**koh**sher/ *adjective* **1** said about food: prepared according to Jewish law. **2** *informal* proper or legitimate.

Kremlin *noun* (**the Kremlin**) a large palace and fortress in Moscow where the Russian government is based.

krill *plural noun* small sea animals that resemble shrimps and are the chief food of whales and other sea creatures.

krypton *noun Science* a colourless gas that is one of the chemical elements and is used in fluorescent lights.

kudos /**kew**dos/ *noun* prestige resulting from having achieved something special.

kung fu /kung **fooh**/ *noun* a Chinese martial art resembling karate.

kW *abbreviation* kilowatt or kilowatts.

L

L *abbreviation* learner driver.

l *abbreviation* litre or litres.

lab *noun* (*plural* **labs**) *informal* a laboratory.

label *noun* (*plural* **labels**) **1** a piece of paper or cloth attached to something to give information about it. **2** a brand name, especially of a fashion or record company. **3** a descriptive or identifying word or phrase. ~ *verb* (**labels, labelling, labelled**) **1** to fasten a label to something. **2** to describe or categorize somebody or something.

laboratory *noun* (*plural* **laboratories**) *Science* a place equipped for carrying out scientific experiments.

laborious *adjective* requiring a lot of time or effort. ➤ **laboriously** *adverb*.

labour *noun* (*plural* **labours**) **1** work or a task, especially hard work or work done for wages. **2** workers as a group. **3** the period during childbirth when the muscles contract strongly to push the baby out of the womb. ~ *verb* (**labours, labouring, laboured**) **1** to work hard. **2** to struggle to do something difficult. **3** to move with difficulty. **4** to take too long or go into too much detail, for example in making a point or telling a joke.

laboured *adjective* done clumsily with too much effort or in too much detail.

labourer *noun* (*plural* **labourers**) a person who does unskilled manual work, especially outdoors.

Labour Party *noun* (**the Labour Party**) in Britain, a political party founded to represent working people and based on socialist principles.

Labrador *noun* (*plural* **Labradors**) a large black or gold-coloured dog with a smooth coat.

laburnum /la ber num/ *noun* (*plural* **laburnums**) a shrub or tree with bright yellow poisonous flowers that hang in clusters.

labyrinth /la bi rinth/ *noun* (*plural* **labyrinths**) a place that is a network of complicated passageways. ➤ **labyrinthine** *adjective*.

lace *noun* (*plural* **laces**) **1** a light decorative fabric made by looping fine thread in a symmetrical pattern with many holes in it. **2** a cord or string used for drawing together two edges, for example on shoes or clothing.
~ *verb* (**laces, lacing, laced**)
1 to fasten a shoe, etc with a lace.
2 to twine your fingers together.
3 to add a small quantity of a stronger ingredient, especially an alcoholic drink, to a drink or dish.

lacerate /la si rayt/ *verb* (**lacerates, lacerating, lacerated**) to tear or cut skin or flesh roughly. ➤ **laceration** *noun*.

lack *verb* (**lacks, lacking, lacked**) not to have something. ~ *noun* an absence or shortage of something. ✽ **be lacking in** to have too little of something.

lackadaisical *adjective* **1** lacking enthusiasm or commitment. **2** casual or negligent.

lackey *noun* (*plural* **lackeys**)

1 a servant, especially a footman in uniform. **2** a person who is somebody else's humble and willing servant.

lacklustre *adjective* lacking in vitality or enthusiasm; uninspired.

laconic /la ko nik/ *adjective* using few words. ➤ **laconically** *adverb*.

lacquer *noun* (*plural* **lacquers**) **1** a clear or coloured varnish for wood. **2** a substance sprayed on hair to fix it in place.

lacrosse *noun* an outdoor team game played with a long-handled sticks with a net pouch for throwing and catching the ball.

lacy *adjective* (**lacier, laciest**) **1** like lace; delicate and full of holes. **2** made of or trimmed with lace.

lad *noun* (*plural* **lads**) *informal* a boy or young man.

ladder *noun* (*plural* **ladders**) **1** a structure for climbing up, consisting of two long vertical pieces joined by horizontal steps. **2** a vertical line in tights or stockings caused by stitches coming undone. ~ *verb* (**ladders, laddering, laddered**) to cause a ladder to develop in stockings or tights.

laddie *noun* (*plural* **laddies**) *informal* a boy.

laden /lay dn/ *adjective* carrying a heavy load.

ladle *noun* (*plural* **ladles**) a long-handled spoon with a deep bowl. ~ *verb* (**ladles, ladling, ladled**) to serve out a liquid with a ladle.

lady *noun* (*plural* **ladies**) **1** a woman of refinement or high social position. **2** in polite or formal use, a woman. **3** (**Lady**) a title given to a peeress or to the wife of a knight or peer.

ladybird *noun* (*plural* **ladybirds**) a small beetle that has red wing cases with black spots.

lady-in-waiting *noun* (*plural* **ladies-in-waiting**) a woman of high social position who is an attendant to a queen or princess.

ladylike *adjective* befitting a lady; refined and dignified.

Ladyship *noun* (**Her/Your Ladyship**) a title used when talking about or to a lady who is a member of the nobility or the wife of a knight.

lag¹ *verb* (**lags, lagging, lagged**) (*often* **lag behind**) to go slower than others and fall behind. ~ *noun* a delay between two events.

lag² *verb* (**lags, lagging, lagged**) to cover pipes, etc with insulating material so that they do not lose heat. ➤ **lagging** *noun*.

lager /lah ger/ *noun* (*plural* **lagers**) a type of light beer.

lagoon *noun* (*plural* **lagoons**) a shallow pool of salt water separated from the sea by a sand bank, reef, etc.

laid *verb* past tense and past participle of LAY¹. ✶ **laid back** *informal* relaxed or casual.

lain *verb* past participle of LIE¹.

lair *noun* (*plural* **lairs**) the place where a wild animal rests or lives.

laissez-faire /le say fair/ *noun* a doctrine opposing government interference in economic affairs.

laity *noun* (**the laity**) lay people.

lake *noun* (*plural* **lakes**) a large inland area of water.

lama /lah ma/ *noun* (*plural* **lamas**) a Tibetan or Mongolian Buddhist monk.

lamb *noun* (*plural* **lambs**) **1** a young sheep. **2** meat from a lamb.

lame *adjective* (**lamer, lamest**) **1** having a disabled leg or foot and unable to walk properly. **2** said about a story or excuse: weak and unconvincing. ➤ **lamely** *adverb*, **lameness** *noun*.

lament *noun* (*plural* **laments**) **1** an expression of grief. **2** a song or poem expressing grief. ~ *verb* (**laments, lamenting, lamented**) to

lamentable

express grief or regret for something, especially a person's death. ➤ **lamentation** noun.

lamentable adjective **1** very bad or inadequate. **2** regrettable. ➤ **lamentably** adverb.

laminate verb (**laminates, laminating, laminated**) **1** to cover something with a thin sheet of metal, plastic, etc. **2** to make something by bonding several layers of material together. ➤ **laminated** adjective, **lamination** noun.

lamp noun (plural **lamps**) a device using electricity, oil, or gas to give out light.

lamppost noun (plural **lampposts**) a tall post carrying a street light.

lance[1] noun (plural **lances**) History a long spear, used by cavalry soldiers or by knights.

lance[2] verb (**lances, lancing, lanced**) to open a boil with a sharp instrument.

lance corporal noun (plural **lance corporals**) a non-commissioned officer of the lowest rank in the British army.

lancet noun (plural **lancets**) a sharp-pointed, two-edged surgical instrument used to make small incisions.

land noun (plural **lands**) **1** the solid part of the earth's surface, as distinct from seas, lakes, rivers, etc. **2** ground owned as property or attached to a building. **3** (**the land**) ground used for agriculture. **4** a country or state. ~ verb (**lands, landing, landed**) **1** to bring an aircraft down onto the ground from the air. **2** said about an aircraft, bird, person jumping etc: to come down onto a surface. **3** to put people or goods on shore, or to go ashore, from a ship. **4** informal to gain or obtain a job, etc. **5** to catch and bring in a fish. **6** informal to cause a blow to hit somebody: *to land a punch*. ✴ **land in** or **land up in** informal to end up, or put somebody, in a (usually undesirable) place or situation. **land with** informal to burden somebody with something they do not want.

landed adjective owning land.

landfill noun (plural **landfills**) **1** a site where rubbish is disposed of by being buried in a pit. **2** rubbish disposed of in this way.

landing noun (plural **landings**) **1** the act of coming or bringing to land. **2** a level space at the top of a flight of stairs.

landing gear noun the part of an aircraft that includes the wheels.

landlady noun (plural **landladies**) **1** a woman who owns and rents out land, buildings, or accommodation. **2** a woman who keeps a guesthouse or pub.

landlocked adjective Geography said about a country: with no access to the sea; completely enclosed by land.

landlord noun (plural **landlords**) **1** a person, usually a man, who owns and rents out land, buildings, or accommodation. **2** a person, usually a man, who keeps a guesthouse or pub.

landlubber noun (plural **landlubbers**) informal a person who knows nothing about the sea or seamanship.

landmark noun (plural **landmarks**) **1** an object that is easily seen and can be used to identify an area. **2** a very important event in the history or development of something.

landmine noun (plural **landmines**) an explosive mine hidden just below the surface of the ground.

landscape noun (plural **landscapes**) **1** Geography an expanse of natural inland scenery. **2** Art a picture, drawing, etc of a landscape.

landslide noun (plural **landslides**) **1** a movement of a mass of rock, earth, etc down a slope.

2 an overwhelming victory in an election.

lane *noun* (*plural* **lanes**) **1** a narrow passageway or road. **2** a strip of road for a single line of vehicles. **3** a marked-out course for a competitor in a running or swimming race.

language *noun* (*plural* **languages**) **1** a system of sounds, gestures, or signs used to communicate ideas or feelings. **2** the words, grammar, and sounds used for communication in a particular community. **3** *ICT* a system of signs and symbols used in programming a computer.

languid /lang gwid/ *adjective* **1** without energy; moving slowly or lazily. **2** weak or drooping from fatigue.
➤ **languidly** *adverb*.

languish *verb* (**languishes, languishing, languished**) **1** to be or become feeble. **2** to suffer hardship or neglect: *She languished in prison for two years.*

languor /lang ger/ *noun* a feeling of weariness or drowsiness.
➤ **languorous** *adjective*.

lank *adjective* said about hair: straight and limp.

lanky *adjective* (**lankier, lankiest**) tall, thin, and ungraceful.

lanolin *or* **lanoline** *noun* grease extracted from wool for use in ointments and cosmetics.

lantern *noun* (*plural* **lanterns**) a light in a portable case with transparent windows.

lanyard *noun* (*plural* **lanyards**) a cord worn round your neck to hold something, such as a whistle.

lap[1] *noun* (*plural* **laps**) the front part of the thighs of a seated person. ✻ **in the lap of luxury** in great comfort and wealth.

lap[2] *noun* (*plural* **laps**) **1** one circuit round a course or track. **2** one stage of a journey. ~ *verb* (**laps, lapping, lapped**) to overtake another contestant in a race and be ahead of them by one full circuit of the track.

lap[3] *verb* (**laps, lapping, lapped**) **1** said about an animal: to take in liquid with its tongue. **2** said about water: to splash against something in little waves. ✻ **lap up** to take in something such as information or praise eagerly or uncritically.

lapel *noun* (*plural* **lapels**) a fold at the top of the front edge of a coat or jacket.

Lapp *noun* (*plural* **Lapps**) a member of a nomadic people who live in Lapland, in northern Scandinavia.

lapse *noun* (*plural* **lapses**) **1** a slight error, for example of memory or in manners. **2** a decline in standards. **3** the passing of a period of time: *after a lapse of several years.* ~ *verb* (**lapses, lapsing, lapsed**) **1** said about a right, etc: to become invalid, especially because it has not been exercised. **2** (**lapse into**) to pass gradually into a particular condition, way of behaving, etc.

laptop *noun* (*plural* **laptops**) a portable computer with a flat screen that folds down.

larceny *noun dated* theft of personal property.

larch *noun* (*plural* **larches**) a tree of the pine family with short deciduous needles.

lard *noun* soft white solid fat from a pig, used in cooking.

larder *noun* (*plural* **larders**) a room or cupboard where food is stored.

large *adjective* (**larger, largest**) bigger than average in size, quantity, extent, etc. ✻ **at large 1** moving about freely; not imprisoned or under arrest. **2** as a whole: *among the population at large.*

largely *adverb* to a great extent; mostly.

largesse

largesse /lah jes/ *noun* **1** generosity. **2** something, such as money, given generously.

lark¹ *noun* (*plural* **larks**) a brown singing bird, especially a skylark.

lark² *noun* (*plural* **larks**) *informal* a mischievous trick or light-hearted adventure. ~ *verb* (**larks, larking, larked**) *informal* * **lark about/around** to have fun in a playful or mischievous way.

larva *noun* (*plural* **larvae** /lah vee/) *Science* the immature, often worm-like, form of an insect when it hatches from its egg.

laryngitis /la rin jie tis/ *noun* inflammation of the larynx which causes a sore throat.

larynx /la ringks/ *noun* (*plural* **larynxes** or **larynges** /la rin jeez/) the upper part of the throat, containing the vocal cords.

lasagne /la zan ya/ *noun* **1** pasta in the form of broad flat sheets. **2** a baked dish with layers of minced meat or vegetables, lasagne, and cheese sauce.

laser *noun* (*plural* **lasers**) a device that generates an intense narrow beam of light.

lash¹ *verb* (**lashes, lashing, lashed**) **1** to strike somebody or something with a whip. **2** said about the wind, rain, or sea: to beat hard against something. **3** said about an animal: to flick its tail quickly or sharply. ~ *noun* (*plural* **lashes**) **1** a blow with a whip. **2** the flexible part of a whip. **3** = EYELASH. * **lash out 1** to strike at somebody suddenly and violently. **2** *informal* to spend lots of money.

lash² (**lashes, lashing, lashed**) *verb* to tie or fasten something with a cord, rope, etc.

lashings *plural noun informal* a very large quantity of something.

lass or **lassie** *noun* (*plural* **lasses** or **lassies**) a girl or young woman.

lasso *noun* (*plural* **lassos** or **lassoes**) a rope with a sliding noose at the end, used especially in North America for catching horses and cattle. ~ *verb* (**lassoes** or **lassos, lassoing, lassoed**) to catch an animal with a lasso.

last¹ *adjective* **1** following all the rest in time, place, or order: *in last place*. **2** being the only remaining one: *Anyone want the last sausage?* **3** being the one before the present: *last year*. **4** (**the last**) least suitable or likely: *She's the last person you would think of asking.* ~ *adverb* **1** on the most recent occasion: *When did we last meet?* **2** after all others. **3** in conclusion. ~ *noun* (*plural* **last**) somebody or something that is last: *They were the last to arrive.* * **at last** or **at long last** after a long time or much delay. **the last of** the remaining part, amount, etc of something. **on your last legs** on the verge of failure, exhaustion, etc.
➤ **lastly** *adverb*.

last² *verb* (**lasts, lasting, lasted**) **1** to go on for a specified time. **2** to remain in good condition. **3** to be enough for the needs of somebody during a particular length of time: *Their supplies will last them a week.*

last³ *noun* (*plural* **lasts**) a shoemaker's model of a foot, used to hold a shoe that is being made or repaired.

lasting *adjective* permanent; not soon finished or destroyed.

Last Supper *noun* (**the Last Supper**) the last meal that Jesus and his disciples had together before he was crucified.

latch¹ *noun* (*plural* **latches**) **1** a device for fastening a gate or door, with a bar that lifts up to open it and drops into a notch to hold it shut. **2** a type of door lock that can only be opened from outside with a key. ~ *verb* (**latches, latching, latched**) to fasten a door with a latch. * **latch onto**

1 to notice or realize something. **2** to join up with somebody.

late *adjective* **1** occurring after the expected time. **2** happening far on in a particular period. **3** far on in the day or night. **4** (**the late**) who has recently died. **5** very recent. ~ *adverb* **1** after the usual or proper time. **2** at or near the end of a period of time or a process. **3** far on in the day or night. ✶ **of late** recently. ➤ **lateness** *noun*.

lately *adverb* recently.

latent /**lay**tnt/ *adjective* present but not yet visible or active. ➤ **latency** *noun*.

later *adverb* **1** afterwards. **2** at some time in the future.

lateral *adjective* situated on or coming from the side. ➤ **laterally** *adverb*.

lateral thinking *noun* thinking that concentrates on unexpected or unconventional aspects of a problem in order to find a fresh approach to solving it.

latest *adjective* most recent; most up-to-date. ✶ **at the latest** no later than a specified time. **the latest** the most recent news.

latex /**lay**teks/ *noun* (*plural* **latexes**) a milky white fluid from various plants that is the source of rubber and chewing gum.

lath /lath/ *noun* (*plural* **laths**) a thin narrow strip of wood.

lathe /lay*th*/ *noun* (*plural* **lathes**) a machine for shaping wood or metal by rotating it against a cutting tool.

lather *noun* foam or froth. ~ *verb* (**lathers, lathering, lathered**) **1** to form a lather. **2** to cover something with a lather.

Latin *noun* the language of ancient Rome and the Roman Empire. ➤ **Latin** *adjective*.

Latin America *noun* Geography the parts of the American continent where Spanish or Portuguese is spoken. ➤ **Latin American** *adjective*.

latitude *noun* (*plural* **latitudes**) **1** Geography the distance of a place north or south of the equator, measured in degrees. **2** freedom of action or choice.

latrine /lat**reen**/ *noun* (*plural* **latrines**) a small pit used as a toilet, especially in a military camp or barracks.

latte /**lah**tay *or* **la**tay/ *noun* (*plural* **lattes**) a drink made by mixing espresso coffee and hot milk.

latter *adjective* near the end; later: *the latter stages of a process*. ✶ **the latter** the second of two things mentioned: *Given the choice of ham or beef, I'd prefer the latter*.

latterly *adverb* recently.

lattice *noun* (*plural* **lattices**) a framework of crossed wooden or metal strips with open spaces between.

laudable *adjective* worthy of praise; commendable.

laugh *verb* (**laughs, laughing, laughed**) **1** to make sounds expressing amusement. **2** (**laugh at**) to make fun of somebody or something. ~ *noun* (*plural* **laughs**) an act of laughing. ✶ **a laugh** *informal* a bit of fun.

laughable *adjective* ridiculous. ➤ **laughably** *adverb*.

laughing stock *noun* (*plural* **laughing stocks**) somebody or something that is thought ridiculous.

laughter *noun* the act or sound of laughing.

launch *verb* (**launches, launching, launched**) **1** to set a boat or ship afloat. **2** to send a rocket up into the air. **3** to start something, or set somebody on a course or career. **4** to introduce a new product onto the market. **5** to throw yourself forward. **6** (**launch into**) to begin to do something energetically. ~ *noun* (*plural*

launch pad

launches) 1 an act of launching something. **2** a large motorboat. ➤ **launcher** noun.

launch pad noun (plural **launch pads**) a platform from which a rocket can be launched.

launder verb (**launders, laundering, laundered**) **1** to wash and iron dirty clothes, etc. **2** informal to pass stolen money through a bank or legal business to disguise its origins.

launderette noun (plural **launderettes**) a self-service laundry with coin-operated machines.

laundry noun (plural **laundries**) **1** clothes and linen that have been, or are going to be, washed. **2** a place where sheets, clothes, etc are washed and ironed.

laurel noun (plural **laurels**) an evergreen tree or shrub that has smooth shiny leaves.

lava /lahva/ noun molten rock flowing from a volcano, or this same rock after it has cooled and solidified.

lavatory noun (plural **lavatories**) a toilet.

lavender noun **1** a shrub with narrow sweet-smelling leaves and spikes of lilac or purple flowers. **2** a pale purple colour.

lavish adjective **1** given in very large quantities or splendid style. **2** giving or spending generously. ~ verb (**lavishes, lavishing, lavished**) to spend or give something in large quantities. ➤ **lavishly** adverb.

law noun (plural **laws**) **1** a rule governing people's behaviour, enforced by the authorities within a community. **2** (**the law**) all these rules considered together. **3** (**the law**) informal the police. **4** Science a general statement of scientific fact. * **lay down the law** to give orders or express opinions forcefully.

law-abiding adjective said about a person: obeying the law.

law court noun (plural **law courts**) a place in which a trial is held.

lawful adjective allowed by law; rightful or legal. ➤ **lawfully** adverb.

lawless adjective **1** not having laws. **2** showing no respect for the law. ➤ **lawlessness** noun.

lawn noun (plural **lawns**) an area of ground covered with mown grass.

lawn mower noun (plural **lawn mowers**) a machine for cutting grass on lawns.

lawsuit noun (plural **lawsuits**) a case in a court of law that concerns a dispute between individuals, not a crime.

lawyer noun (plural **lawyers**) a person qualified to give advice on legal matters and represent people in court.

lax adjective not strict or conscientious; negligent. ➤ **laxity** noun.

laxative noun (plural **laxatives**) a medicine that relaxes the bowels to relieve constipation.

lay[1] verb (**lays, laying, laid**) **1** to put something down on or spread it over a surface. **2** to make something ready for use: *to lay the table*. **3** to make a charge or accusation. **4** to place the blame, emphasis, etc on somebody or something. **5** said about a bird: to produce an egg. * **lay down** to make or state a rule or law. **lay into** informal to attack or criticize somebody fiercely. **lay off 1** to stop employing a worker because of a shortage of work. **2** informal to give up: *Lay off the beer*. **lay out** verb **1** to arrange something according to a plan. **2** informal to make somebody unconscious. **3** informal to spend an amount of money. **lay to rest 1** to dispel a fear or anxiety. **2** to bury somebody in a grave.

lay[2] verb past tense of LIE[1].

lay[3] adjective **1** not belonging to the clergy. **2** not having expert or professional knowledge.

lay⁴ *noun* (*plural* **lays**) a simple poem intended to be sung.

layabout *noun* (*plural* **layabouts**) a lazy, idle person.

lay-by *noun* (*plural* **lay-bys**) an area at the side of a road where vehicles can stop without obstructing traffic.

layer *noun* (*plural* **layers**) a single thickness of some substance lying over or under another.

layman *noun* (*plural* **laymen**) a layperson.

layout *noun* (*plural* **layouts**) the plan or arrangement of something, such as rooms in a building or material to be printed.

layperson *noun* (*plural* **laypeople**) **1** somebody who is not a member of the clergy. **2** somebody without special or professional knowledge.

laze *verb* (**lazes, lazing, lazed**) to act or rest lazily.

lazy *adjective* (**lazier, laziest**) **1** unwilling to work or be active. **2** not energetic or vigorous. ➤ **lazily** *adverb*, **laziness** *noun*.

lb *abbreviation* pound or pounds.

lbw *abbreviation* in cricket, leg before wicket.

lea *noun* (*plural* **leas**) *literary* a meadow.

leach *verb* (**leaches, leaching, leached**) to dissolve a substance from soil, etc, or to be dissolved, in a liquid passing through it.

lead¹ /leed/ *verb* (**leads, leading, led**) **1** to guide a person or an animal somewhere, especially by going in front. **2** to go or be at the head of a procession or column of people. **3** to be first or ahead in a race, etc. **4** to be in command of a group or organization. **5** to carry on a specified kind of life. **6** to influence somebody to do or believe something. ~ *noun* (*plural* **leads**) **1** a position at the front or ahead. **2** guidance or example. **3** an indication or clue. **4** *Drama* a principal performer or role. **5** a line or strap for restraining a dog. **6** an insulated wire that conducts an electric current.

lead² /led/ *noun* **1** *Science* a heavy, soft, bluish white metal that is one of the chemical elements. **2** a thin stick of graphite in a pencil.

leaden /ledn/ *adjective* **1** heavy and slow. **2** sluggish or dull. **3** dull grey. ➤ **leadenly** *adverb*.

leader *noun* (*plural* **leaders**) **1** somebody or something that guides, is in front, or is beating all the others. **2** somebody who is in command. **3** = LEADING ARTICLE. ➤ **leadership** *noun*.

leading *adjective* coming or ranking first; foremost.

leading article *noun* (*plural* **leading articles**) an article in a newspaper that gives the opinion of the editor or publishers.

leaf *noun* (*plural* **leaves**) **1** a flat, green part of a plant that grows out from the stem or branches. **2** a sheet of paper, especially in a book, with a page on each side. **3** a part of a table that slides or is hinged. **4** gold or silver in very thin sheets. ~ *verb* (**leafs, leafing, leafed**) (**leaf through**) to turn over the pages of (a book, magazine, etc) quickly while just glancing at the contents. ✳ **take a leaf out of somebody's book** to copy somebody's behaviour. **turn over a new leaf** to change to a better way of behaving. ➤ **leafy** *adjective*.

leaflet *noun* (*plural* **leaflets**) **1** a single sheet of paper or small pamphlet containing advertisements or information. **2** a small leaf.

league¹ *noun* (*plural* **leagues**) **1** an alliance of nations, groups, or people. **2** an association of sports clubs that organizes a competition between the clubs. ✳ **in league** allied or conspiring together.

league² *noun* (*plural* **leagues**) an old

unit of distance equal to about 3 miles (5 kilometres).

leak *verb* (**leaks, leaking, leaked**) **1** said about a liquid, gas, etc: to get in or out through a crack or hole. **2** said about a container: to let something get in or out in this way. **3** (**leak out**) said about information: to become known despite efforts to keep it secret. **4** to give out secret information. ~ *noun* (*plural* **leaks**) **1** a crack or hole through which something leaks. **2** information that leaks out.
➤ **leakage** *noun*, **leaky** *adjective*.

lean[1] *verb* (**leans, leaning, leaned** *or* **leant**) **1** to be in a sloping position. **2** to rest for support against something. *✱ **lean on 1** to rely on somebody for support. **2** *informal* to put pressure on somebody to do something.

lean[2] *adjective* **1** said about a person or animal: thin. **2** said about meat: containing little or no fat.

leaning *noun* (*plural* **leanings**) a tendency, or a fondness for something.

leap *verb* (**leaps, leaping, leaped** *or* **leapt**) **1** to jump in or through the air, or over something. **2** to move suddenly from one state, topic, etc to another. ~ *noun* (*plural* **leaps**) a jump. *✱ **by/in leaps and bounds** very rapidly. **leap at** to seize an opportunity, offer, etc eagerly.

leapfrog *noun* a game in which one player bends down and another leaps over them with legs apart.

leap year *noun* (*plural* **leap years**) a year with an extra day added, occurring every fourth year.

learn *verb* (**learns, learning, learned** *or* **learnt**) **1** to gain knowledge of or skill in a subject. **2** to memorize something. **3** to become able to do something. **4** to find out about something.
➤ **learner** *noun*.

learned /lernid/ *adjective* having a lot of knowledge through study.

learning *noun* knowledge or skills acquired by study.

learnt *verb* past tense and past participle of LEARN.

lease *noun* (*plural* **leases**) a contract that allows somebody to use another person's land or property for a stated period by paying rent. ~ *verb* (**leases, leasing, leased**) to allow somebody to use something, or to have the use of something, in return for rent. *✱ **a new lease of life** a renewed period of healthy activity or usefulness.

leash *noun* (*plural* **leashes**) a lead for a dog.

least *adjective and adverb* smallest, or to the smallest degree or extent. *✱ **at least 1** as a minimum. **2** if nothing else. **3** anyway. **least of all** especially not.

leather *noun* tanned animal skin used in clothing, upholstery, etc.
➤ **leathery** *adjective*.

leave[1] *verb* (**leaves, leaving, left**) **1** to go away from a place, person, etc. **2** to desert or abandon something. **3** to stop belonging to an organization, institution, etc. **4** to allow something or somebody to remain in a specified place or condition: *She left her notes at home.* **5** to allow to somebody to continue doing something without interference. **6** to put something where it can be collected or dealt with. **7** to give something to somebody in a will. **8** to have a quantity as a remainder: *Ten from twelve leaves two.* *✱ **leave alone/be** *informal* to refrain from interfering with, annoying, or disturbing somebody. **leave off** to stop doing something. **leave out** to fail to include something or somebody.

leave[2] *noun* **1** a period of time when you are allowed to be absent from employment. **2** *formal* permission. *✱ **take your leave** to say goodbye.

leaves *noun* plural of LEAF.

lecher *noun* (*plural* **lechers**) a lecherous man.

lecherous *adjective* showing excessive or offensive sexual desire. ➤ **lechery** *noun*.

lectern *noun* (*plural* **lecterns**) a tall stand with a sloping top that holds an open book, papers, etc from which a person can read aloud.

lecture *noun* (*plural* **lectures**) 1 a talk on an educational subject given to a class or an audience. 2 a lengthy reprimand. ~ *verb* (**lectures, lecturing, lectured**) 1 to give a lecture.
2 to reprimand somebody severely.

led *verb* past tense of LEAD¹.

ledge *noun* (*plural* **ledges**) a narrow horizontal surface projecting from a wall or rock face.

ledger *noun* (*plural* **ledgers**) a book recording financial accounts.

lee *noun* the side of a ship that is sheltered from the wind.

leech *noun* (*plural* **leeches**) a bloodsucking worm that lives in fresh water.

leek *noun* (*plural* **leeks**) a plant with a white cylindrical stalk and bulb, used as a vegetable.

leer *verb* (**leers, leering, leered**) to look at somebody in a lecherous way. ➤ **leer** *noun*.

leeward *adjective and adverb* in the direction towards which the wind is blowing.

leeway *noun* 1 free space in which to move. 2 flexibility in arrangements or in demands made on people.

left¹ *adjective and adverb* on or towards the side of somebody or something that is nearer the west when the front faces north. ~ *noun* 1 the part, direction, etc on the left side. 2 (**the left**) in politics, people with socialist or radical views.

left² *verb* past tense of LEAVE¹.

left-handed *adjective* usually using the left hand to write with or hold things.

leftovers *plural noun* things, especially food, left unused or uneaten.

leg *noun* (*plural* **legs**) 1 a long thin part of a person's or animal's body on which they stand and walk.
2 an upright pole serving as a support for a chair, table, etc. 3 one stage of a trip or race. 4 one round of a competition, or one of two or more events constituting a round. * **not have a leg to stand on** to have nothing to justify your arguments or actions.

legacy *noun* (*plural* **legacies**) 1 a sum of money or piece of property received under a will. 2 something remaining from the past.

legal *adjective* 1 to do with the law.
2 permitted by law. ➤ **legally** *adverb*.

legal aid *noun* money to pay for legal advice for those who cannot afford it.

legalize *or* **legalise** *verb* (**legalizes, legalizing, legalized** *or* **legalises**, etc) to make something legal. ➤ **legalization** *or* **legalisation** *noun*.

legend *noun* (*plural* **legends**)
1 a popular story that has come down to us from the past but is not necessarily true. 2 a very famous person or thing. ➤ **legendary** *adjective*.

leggings *plural noun* 1 close-fitting stretchy trousers worn by women or children. 2 close-fitting protective garments for the legs.

legible *adjective* able to be read or deciphered. ➤ **legibility** *noun*, **legibly** *adverb*.

legion *noun* (*plural* **legions**) 1 *History* the principal unit of the ancient Roman army, comprising 3000–6000 soldiers. 2 an association of former soldiers: *the British Legion*.

legionary *noun* (*plural* **legionaries**) *History* a soldier in the Roman army.

legislate *verb* (**legislates, legislating,**

legislation

legislated) to make laws. ➤ **legislator** noun.

legislation noun formal laws.

legislative /lejis la tiv/ adjective having the power to make laws.

legislature /lejis lay cher/ noun (plural **legislatures**) a body of people, such as a parliament, with the power to make laws.

legitimate adjective **1** in accordance with law, or accepted rules and standards. **2** genuine. **3** said about a child: born to parents who are married to each other. **4** reasonable or logical. ➤ **legitimacy** noun, **legitimately** adverb.

leisure noun time free from work or duties. ✶ **at leisure** free; not working. **at your leisure 1** without hurrying. **2** at your convenience.

leisurely adjective unhurried; relaxed.

lemming noun (plural **lemmings**) a small furry Arctic rodent with a short tail, which sometimes migrates in large numbers resulting in the death of many through drowning in the sea.

lemon noun (plural **lemons**) **1** a yellow citrus fruit with a thick rind and acid flesh. **2** a pale yellow colour.

lemonade noun (plural **lemonades**) a fizzy soft drink, flavoured with lemon.

lend verb (**lends, lending, lent**) **1** to give something to somebody for a time on condition that they return it. **2** to give money to somebody on condition that they repay it, usually with interest. **3** to add or contribute something. ✶ **lend a hand** to help. **lend itself to** to be suitable for something. ➤ **lender** noun.

length noun (plural **lengths**) **1** a measurement of how long something is from end to end. **2** the extent of something from beginning to end. **3** the amount of time something lasts. **4** the fact of being long. **5** a piece of something long and narrow: *a length of rope*. ✶ **at length 1** for a long time.
2 at last; eventually. **go to great/any lengths** to make a great effort (or use any means possible) to achieve something.

lengthen verb (**lengthens, lengthening, lengthened**) to become longer, or make something longer.

lengthways or **lengthwise** adverb and adjective from end to end; in the direction of its length.

lengthy adjective (**lengthier, lengthiest**) long. ➤ **lengthily** adverb.

lenient adjective merciful or tolerant. ➤ **leniency** noun.

lens noun (plural **lenses**) **1** a piece of transparent material with a curved surface, used to form an image by focusing rays of light, for example in a camera or microscope. **2** a transparent part of the eye that focuses light rays on the retina.

Lent noun the period of time that includes the 40 weekdays before Easter Saturday, observed by many Christians as a time of penitence and fasting.

lent verb past tense and past participle of LEND.

lentil noun (plural **lentils**) a small fairly flat seed used as a vegetable.

Leo noun the fifth sign of the zodiac (the Lion).

leopard /leperd/ noun (plural **leopards**) a big cat of South Asia and Africa that has a tawny coat with black spots. ➤ **leopardess** noun.

leotard /lee oh tahd/ noun (plural **leotards**) a close-fitting stretchy one-piece garment worn for dance, gymnastics, etc.

leper noun (plural **lepers**) a person suffering from leprosy.

leprechaun /lepri kawn/ noun (plural **leprechauns**) a mischievous elf in Irish folklore.

leprosy noun a contagious disease

affecting the skin that can cause wasting of muscles and disfigurement.

lesbian noun (plural **lesbians**) a homosexual woman. ▶ **lesbian** adjective, **lesbianism** noun.

less adjective and adverb smaller or not so much. ~ preposition minus. ~ noun a smaller amount.

Usage Note **fewer** or **less**? See the usage note at FEWER.

lessen verb (**lessens, lessening, lessened**) to become less, or to make something less.

lesser adjective and adverb less in size, quality, or importance.

lesson noun (plural **lessons**) **1** a period of teaching or learning. **2** an instructive or warning example. **3** something learned by study or experience. **4** a passage from the Bible read during a church service.

lest conjunction **1** to avoid the possibility of something happening. **2** used after an expression of fear, anxiety, etc: that: *He was anxious lest he should appear ignorant.*

let[1] verb (**lets, letting, let**) **1** to allow somebody to do something. **2** used to introduce a request or suggestion: *Let's go now.* **3** to rent or lease a house or flat to somebody. ✷ **let alone** and definitely not: *He was too worried to think clearly, let alone sleep.* **let down** verb **1** to fail to support or assist somebody. **2** to disappoint somebody by not keeping a promise, appointment, etc. **3** to deflate a tyre, etc. **let go 1** to stop holding. **2** to release somebody captured. **let off 1** to excuse somebody from punishment or a responsibility. **2** to cause a bomb or firework to explode. **let up** to become less intense.

let[2] noun (plural **lets**) a serve or shot in tennis, squash, etc that does not count and must be replayed.

lethal /**lee**thal/ adjective capable of causing death. ▶ **lethally** adverb.

lethargic /li**thah**jik/ adjective slow moving, usually through lack of energy or interest. ▶ **lethargically** adverb, **lethargy** noun.

let's contraction let us.

letter noun (plural **letters**) **1** a written symbol representing a speech sound. **2** a written or printed message sent through the post. ✷ **to the letter** precisely or literally.

letter box noun (plural **letter boxes**) **1** a hole in a door to receive material delivered by post. **2** = POSTBOX (sense 1).

lettering noun the letters used in an inscription.

lettuce noun (plural **lettuces**) a vegetable with edible leaves eaten raw in salads.

leukaemia /loo**kee**mia/ noun a type of cancer that causes an abnormal increase in white blood cells in the body.

level adjective **1** having no part higher than another. **2** at the same height. **3** equal in amount, position, or importance. ~ noun (plural **levels**) **1** a horizontal surface or state: *Make sure the keyboard is on the level.* **2** the height that something is above the ground: *at eye level.* **3** a layer in a vertical structure, for example a floor in a building. **4** a position in a scale or rank: *at intermediate level.* ~ verb (**levels, levelling, levelled**) **1** (*also* **level off**) to make a line or surface horizontal. **2** to aim a weapon. **3** to aim or direct criticism, an accusation, etc at somebody. **4** to equalize a score, etc. **5** to knock something flat or destroy it completely. ✷ **a level playing field** a situation in which nobody has an unfair advantage. **level with** *informal* to deal frankly and openly with somebody. **on the level**

level crossing

informal honest; genuine. ➤ **levelly** *adverb*.

level crossing *noun* (*plural* **level crossings**) a place where a railway crosses a road on the same level.

levelheaded *adjective* calm and sensible.

lever *noun* (*plural* **levers**) 1 a bar used for prising up or dislodging something. 2 a projecting rod that operates a mechanism. ~ *verb* (**levers, levering, levered**) to raise or move something with a lever.

leverage *noun* 1 the force exerted when using a lever. 2 power or influence.

leveret /ˈlevərit/ *noun* (*plural* **leverets**) a young hare.

levitate *verb* (**levitates, levitating, levitated**) to rise or float in the air. ➤ **levitation** *noun*.

levity *noun* lack of seriousness when dealing with a serious subject.

levy *noun* (*plural* **levies**) an amount of money collected as a tax. ~ *verb* (**levies, levying, levied**) to impose a tax, etc by legal authority.

lewd *adjective* indecent or sexually suggestive.

lexicography /leksiˈkɒɡrəfi/ *noun* the work of compiling dictionaries. ➤ **lexicographer** *noun*.

liability *noun* (*plural* **liabilities**) 1 the fact of being liable. 2 a debt. 3 a hindrance or drawback.

liable *adjective* 1 legally responsible for something. 2 (**liable to**) likely to do something.

liaise /liːˈeɪz/ *verb* (**liaises, liaising, liaised**) (**liaise with**) to establish contact and cooperate with somebody.

liaison /liːˈeɪzn/ *noun* (*plural* **liaisons**) 1 communication and cooperation. 2 an illicit sexual relationship.

liar *noun* (*plural* **liars**) a person who tells lies.

libel /ˈlaɪbl/ *noun* (*plural* **libels**) 1 the act of writing something about somebody that is untrue and damages their reputation. 2 a false statement that damages somebody's reputation. ~ *verb* (**libels, libelling, libelled**) to publish a libel about somebody. ➤ **libellous** *adjective*.

liberal *adjective* 1 broad-minded or tolerant. 2 in politics, advocating individual rights and freedom and moderate reform. 3 generous. 4 ample. ➤ **liberal** *noun*, **liberalism** *noun*, **liberality** *noun*, **liberally** *adverb*.

Liberal Democrat *noun* (*plural* **Liberal Democrats**) a member of the Liberal Democratic Party, which supports individual rights and moderate reforms.

liberalize *or* **liberalise** *verb* (**liberalizes, liberalizing, liberalized** *or* **liberalises**, etc) to make a law, etc less strict or restrictive. ➤ **liberalization** *or* **liberalisation** *noun*.

liberate *verb* (**liberates, liberating, liberated**) 1 to set somebody free. 2 to free somebody from social conventions. ➤ **liberated** *adjective*, **liberation** *noun*, **liberator** *noun*.

liberty *noun* (*plural* **liberties**) freedom. ✱ **take liberties** 1 to show disrespect. 2 to disregard the need for strict accuracy.

Libra *noun* the seventh sign of the zodiac (the Scales).

librarian *noun* (*plural* **librarians**) a person who manages or works in a library.

library *noun* (*plural* **libraries**) 1 a room or building in which books, magazines, etc are kept for reference or for borrowing by the public. 2 a person's collection of books.

lice *noun* plural of LOUSE.

licence *noun* (*plural* **licences**) 1 an official document showing that the holder is authorized to do something. **2** freedom of action. **3** immoral behaviour.

license *verb* (**licenses, licensing, licensed**) to give official permission to somebody to do something or for something to take place.

licensee *noun* (*plural* **licensees**) the holder of a licence, especially to sell alcoholic drink.

licentious *adjective* immoral, especially as regards sexual behaviour.

lichen /lie kin/ *noun* (*plural* **lichens**) a plant that grows in flat greyish, greenish, or yellowish patches on rocks and tree trunks.

lick *verb* (**licks, licking, licked**) **1** to pass your tongue over something. **2** said about flames, etc: to touch something lightly. **3** *informal* to defeat somebody, especially decisively. ~ *noun* (*plural* **licks**) **1** an act of licking. **2** *informal* a small amount. ✴ **at a lick** *informal* at a fast speed.

lid *noun* (*plural* **lids**) **1** a hinged or detachable cover for a container. **2** = EYELID.

lie[1] *verb* (**lies, lying, lay, lain**) **1** to rest in a horizontal position. **2** (*often* **lie down**) to get into a horizontal position. **3** to be in a specified state or condition: *The machinery was lying idle.* **4** to be located: *The village lies about 10 miles east of Delhi.* ✴ **lie low** to stay in hiding or avoid notice.

lie[2] *noun* (*plural* **lies**) a statement that is not true, especially one deliberately intended to deceive somebody. ~ *verb* (**lies, lied, lying**) to make an untrue statement or statements.

lie detector *noun* (*plural* **lie detectors**) an instrument that can detect whether a person is lying or telling the truth through, for example, a change in their pulse rate.

lieu /lew/ ✴ **in lieu of** instead of.

lieutenant /lef te nant/ *noun* (*plural* **lieutenants**) **1** a deputy or representative. **2** a junior officer in the army or navy.

life *noun* (*plural* **lives**) **1** the quality or state of being alive. **2** the period from the birth to the death of an individual. **3** a way or manner of living. **4** living creatures: *forest life.* **5** the period of usefulness of a machine, etc. **6** vitality or excitement. **7** *informal* a sentence of life imprisonment.

life assurance *noun* = LIFE INSURANCE.

lifebelt *noun* (*plural* **lifebelts**) a ring of light material for keeping a person afloat.

lifeblood *noun* a factor that enables something to keep existing or working: *Efficient communication is the lifeblood of business.*

lifeboat *noun* (*plural* **lifeboats**) **1** a shore-based boat for saving lives at sea. **2** a boat carried by a ship for use in an emergency.

lifeguard *noun* (*plural* **lifeguards**) an person employed to look after the safety of other people at a swimming pool or beach.

life insurance *noun* insurance that will pay a specified sum if the insured person dies or at the end of a fixed period.

life jacket *noun* (*plural* **life jackets**) an inflatable jacket designed to keep a person afloat.

lifeless *adjective* **1** dead. **2** unconscious. **3** having no living beings. **4** dull.

lifelike *adjective* accurately showing what somebody looks like.

lifeline *noun* (*plural* **lifelines**) **1** a rope used to pull a person to safety from water. **2** something vital for the somebody or something's survival.

lifelong *adjective* lasting or continuing throughout a person's life.

life raft *noun* (*plural* **life rafts**) an inflatable raft for use in an emergency at sea.

life span *noun* (*plural* **life spans**)

lifestyle

1 length of life. **2** the length of time something works or remains usable.

lifestyle *noun* (*plural* **lifestyles**) the way of life of a person or group.

lifetime *noun* (*plural* **lifetimes**) the time during which a living being exists or a thing remains useful.

lift *verb* (**lifts, lifting, lifted**) **1** to raise something to a higher position. **2** to pick something or somebody up in order to move them. **3** to put an end to a ban. ~ *noun* (*plural* **lifts**) **1** a device for transporting people or objects from one level to another, especially in a building. **2** a free ride as a passenger in a motor vehicle. **3** a feeling of encouragement. **4** *Science* the upward force acting on a wing that enables an aircraft to fly.

ligament *noun* (*plural* **ligaments**) a tough band of tissue connecting two or more bones.

ligature *noun* (*plural* **ligatures**) a thread used in surgery to tie something.

light[1] *noun* (*plural* **lights**) **1** natural radiation that causes the brightness that allows you to see things. **2** a source of light, such as a lamp or a candle. **3** = DAYLIGHT. **4** a flame to light a cigarette. **5** (**lights**) = TRAFFIC LIGHTS. ~ *adjective* **1** having plenty of light; bright. **2** pale in colour. ~ *verb* (**lights, lighting, lit** *or* **lighted**) **1** to provide light in a room, etc. **2** to catch fire. **3** to set fire to something. ✱ **bring to light** to reveal something. **come to light** to be revealed. **in the light of** taking something into account. **light on/upon** to find something by chance. **light up 1** to fill a space or make an object visible with light. **2** to make somebody or something more lively or cheerful. **3** to start smoking a cigarette, pipe, etc. ➤ **lightness** *noun*.

light[2] *adjective* **1** not heavy, or not heavy enough. **2** occurring in small quantities: *light rain*. **3** gentle or soft. **4** requiring little effort. **5** graceful or nimble. **6** cheerful. **7** intended chiefly to entertain: *light reading*. ➤ **lightly** *adverb*, **lightness** *noun*.

light bulb *noun* see BULB.

lighten[1] *verb* (**lightens, lightening, lightened**) to make a colour, hair, etc paler.

lighten[2] *verb* (**lightens, lightening, lightened**) to become lighter or to make something lighter or less burdensome. ✱ **lighten up** to become less serious.

lighter *noun* (*plural* **lighters**) a device for lighting a cigarette, cigar, etc.

light fitting *noun* (*plural* **light fittings**) the often ornamental device that holds a light bulb and provides light in a room.

light-headed *adjective* faint or dizzy.

light-hearted *adjective* **1** free from care or worry. **2** playful or amusing.

lighthouse *noun* (*plural* **lighthouses**) a tall narrow building equipped with a powerful light to warn or guide ships.

lighting *noun* **1** the apparatus providing a supply of light. **2** the arrangement of lights to produce a particular effect.

lightning *noun* the flash produced when electricity travels between two clouds or between a cloud and the earth. ~ *adjective* very quick, short, or sudden.

lightning conductor *noun* (*plural* **lightning conductors**) a metal rod fixed to the highest point of a building to carry lightning safely to the ground.

lightweight *noun* (*plural* **lightweights**) **1** a weight in boxing between welterweight and featherweight. **2** *informal* somebody of little ability or importance. ➤ **lightweight** *adjective*.

light-year *noun* (*plural* **light-years**)

Science the distance that light travels in one year, approximately 9460 thousand million kilometres (about 5878 thousand million miles).

likable *or* **likeable** *adjective* pleasant or agreeable.

like¹ *preposition* **1** similar to. **2** typical of: *Isn't that just like James!* **3** in the manner of. **4** such as; for example. ~ *noun* (*plural* **likes**) somebody or something that is similar. ~ *adjective* similar in appearance, character, or quantity. * **the like** similar things.

like² *verb* (**likes, liking, liked**) **1** to consider something or somebody pleasant or acceptable. **2** to wish or choose to have, be, or do something. ~ *noun* (*plural* **likes**) a liking or preference.

likeable *adjective* see LIKABLE.

likelihood *noun* probability.

likely *adjective* (**likelier, likeliest**) **1** probable. **2** promising. **3** (**likely to**) expected or probably going to do something.

liken *verb* (**likens, likening, likened**) (**liken to**) to say that a person or thing is similar to another.

likeness *noun* (*plural* **likenesses**) **1** resemblance. **2** a portrait.

likewise *adverb* **1** moreover; in addition. **2** similarly.

liking *noun* a taste or fondness for somebody or something.

lilac *noun* (*plural* **lilacs**) **1** a shrub with large clusters of white or pale purple flowers. **2** a pale pinkish purple colour.

lilt *noun* a rhythmic rise and fall in music or speech. ▶ **lilting** *adjective*.

lily *noun* (*plural* **lilies**) a plant that grows from bulbs and has colourful trumpet-shaped flowers.

lily-livered *adjective* cowardly.

limb *noun* **1** the leg or arm of a human being. **2** a large branch of a tree. * **out on a limb** supporting or suggesting something that does not have other people's support.

limber *verb* (**limbers, limbering, limbered**) * **limber up** to prepare for physical action by gentle exercise.

limbo¹ * **in limbo** in a situation in which you have no control over what happens to you and you just have to wait.

limbo² *noun* (*plural* **limbos**) an acrobatic West Indian dance that involves bending backwards to pass under a horizontal pole.

lime¹ *noun* a white substance, calcium oxide, used in building and in fertilizers.

lime² *noun* (*plural* **limes**) a tree with heart-shaped leaves and clusters of yellow flowers.

lime³ *noun* (*plural* **limes**) **1** a small green citrus fruit with acid juicy pulp. **2** a bright greenish yellow colour.

limelight *noun* (**the limelight**) the centre of attention.

limerick *noun* (*plural* **limericks**) a humorous verse form of five lines.

Word History Limerick is a city in Ireland. The name of this type of poem is said to come from the chorus 'Will you come up to Limerick' that was added between the verses of improvised songs at parties in Victorian times.

limestone *noun* rock consisting mainly of the chemical calcium carbonate ($CaCO_3$).

limit *noun* (*plural* **limits**) **1** the end or boundary of something. **2** the maximum or minimum amount or number allowed. ~ *verb* (**limits, limiting, limited**) to allow only a certain amount of something, or allow somebody to have only a certain amount of something. ▶ **limitless** *adjective*.

limitation *noun* (*plural* **limitations**) **1** a restriction. **2** a defect or weak point.

limited *adjective* having a limit on size or amount; not a lot: *with limited success*.

limited company *noun* (*plural* **limited companies**) a company in which individual shareholders are responsible for only a limited portion of the company's debts.

limo *noun* (*plural* **limos**) *informal* = LIMOUSINE.

limousine /li ma zeen/ *noun* (*plural* **limousines**) a large luxurious car.

limp¹ *verb* (**limps, limping, limped**) **1** to walk with an uneven step, usually because of an injured leg. **2** to proceed slowly or with difficulty. ➤ **limp** *noun*.

limp² *adjective* **1** lacking firmness and stiffness. **2** lacking energy. ➤ **limply** *adverb*.

limpet *noun* (*plural* **limpets**) a shellfish that clings very tightly to rocks.

limpid *adjective* transparent or clear.

linchpin *or* **lynchpin** *noun* (*plural* **linchpins** *or* **lynchpins**) **1** a pin inserted through the end of an axle to hold a wheel in place. **2** somebody or something regarded as vital.

line¹ *noun* (*plural* **lines**) **1** a long narrow mark across a surface. **2** a wrinkle, especially on your face. **3** a boundary, border, or outline. **4** a row or queue. **5** a horizontal row of written or printed characters. **6** (**lines**) *Drama* all of the text making up a particular role in a play. **7** a thread, string, cord, or rope. **8** a wire or cable carrying electric power or a telecommunications signal. **9** a telephone connection. **10** a railway track or route. **11** a particular type of product or service. **12** a field of activity or business. ~ *verb* (**lines, lining, lined**) **1** to form a line along a route, etc. **2** to mark or cover something with lines. ✱ **draw the line** to set a limit to what is acceptable. **in line for** likely to get something. **in line with** conforming to something. **line up 1** to arrange people or things in a line, or to form a line. **2** to assemble or organize people or things in readiness for something. **on the line** at risk.

line² *verb* (**lines, lining, lined**) to cover the inner surface of something, especially a piece of clothing.

lineage /li ni ij/ *noun* all the descendants of one ancestor.

linear /li ni ar/ *adjective* **1** arranged in a straight line. **2** consisting of lines.

linen *noun* **1** cloth made from flax. **2** household articles, such as sheets and tablecloths, that were formerly always made of linen.

liner¹ *noun* (*plural* **liners**) a large passenger ship.

liner² *noun* (*plural* **liners**) something used to line a container: *a bin/drawer liner*.

linesman *noun* (*plural* **linesmen**) in sport, an official who assists the referee or umpire in determining if a ball or player is out of the playing area.

line-up *noun* (*plural* **line-ups**) a group of people or items assembled for a particular purpose.

linger *verb* (**lingers, lingering, lingered**) **1** to delay going or be reluctant to leave. **2** to be slow in disappearing. ➤ **lingering** *adjective*.

lingerie /lan zhi ree/ *noun* women's underwear and nightclothes.

lingo *noun* (*plural* **lingoes** *or* **lingos**) *informal* **1** a foreign language. **2** the special vocabulary of a particular subject; jargon.

linguist *noun* (*plural* **linguists**) somebody who studies language or is good at languages.

linguistic *adjective* to do with language or linguistics. ➤ **linguistically** *adverb*.

linguistics *noun* the scientific study of language.

liniment *noun* a medicinal liquid rubbed on the skin to relieve pain.

lining *noun* (*plural* **linings**) a layer of a different material used to cover the inside of something, such as an item of clothing.

link *noun* (*plural* **links**) **1** a single ring of a chain. **2** a connection or relationship between people or things. **3** a system that enables people, machines, etc to communicate. ~ *verb* (**links, linking, linked**) **1** (*often* **link up**) to join or connect things or people, or to become connected. **2** to suggest that people or things are associated. ➤ **linkage** *noun*.

links *plural noun* a golf course, especially along a seashore.

lino /lie noh/ *noun informal* = LINOLEUM.

linoleum /li noh li um/ *noun* a type of hard, usually patterned, floor covering.

linseed *noun* the seed of flax that produces an oil used in making paints, varnishes, linoleum, etc.

lint *noun* a soft absorbent material used chiefly for covering wounds.

lintel *noun* (*plural* **lintels**) a horizontal support above an opening, especially a door.

lion *noun* (*plural* **lions**) a large meat-eating African animal of the cat family with a tawny body and, in males, a dark shaggy mane. ➤ **lioness** *noun*.

lip *noun* (*plural* **lips**) **1** either of the two fleshy folds that surround the mouth. **2** the edge of a hollow container or cavity. **3** a pointed part on the edge of a jug or container to make pouring easier.

lip-read *verb* (**lip-reads, lip-reading, lip-read**) to understand what somebody is saying by watching their lips move rather than hearing them.

lipstick *noun* (*plural* **lipsticks**) a stick of waxy cosmetic for colouring the lips.

liquefy *verb* (**liquefies, liquefying, liquefied**) to become liquid or make something liquid. ➤ **liquefaction** *noun*.

liqueur /li kewr/ *noun* (*plural* **liqueurs**) a strong and usually sweet alcoholic drink.

liquid *adjective* **1** flowing freely like water. **2** *said about assets*: consisting of cash, or easy to convert into cash. ~ *noun* (*plural* **liquids**) a liquid substance.

liquidate *verb* (**liquidates, liquidating, liquidated**) **1** to settle a debt. **2** to close down a business and use its assets to pay off its debts. **3** *informal* to kill somebody. ➤ **liquidation** *noun*.

liquidize *or* **liquidise** *verb* (**liquidizes, liquidizing, liquidized** *or* **liquidises**, etc) to mash fruit or vegetables into a liquid. ➤ **liquidizer** *or* **liquidiser** *noun*.

liquor /li ker/ *noun* **1** alcoholic drink. **2** a liquid produced by cooking food or in which food has been cooked.

liquorice /li ko ris/ *noun* an extract from the dried black root of a plant of the pea family, used in sweets.

lisp *noun* a speech defect in which the sound /s/ is replaced by /th/. ~ *verb* (**lisps, lisping, lisped**) to speak with a lisp.

list[1] *noun* (*plural* **lists**) a series of words or numbers arranged in order usually down a page. ~ *verb* (**lists, listing, listed**) **1** to make a list of something. **2** to include something or somebody on a list.

list[2] *verb* (**lists, listing, listed**) *said about a ship*: to lean to one side.

listed *adjective* *said about a building*: protected because it is historically or architecturally important.

listen *verb* (**listens, listening, listened**) **1** to pay attention to sound.

listless

2 to hear and give thoughtful consideration to somebody or something. ➤ **listener** noun.

listless adjective showing lack of energy and indifference. ➤ **listlessly** adverb.

lit verb past tense and past participle of LIGHT¹.

litany noun (plural **litanies**) **1** a prayer consisting of a series of petitions by the leader, each followed by a response from the congregation. **2** a long list of complaints, etc.

literacy noun **1** the ability to read and write. **2** knowledge of a particular subject: *computer literacy*.

literal adjective **1** basic, factual, or straightforward: *The literal meaning of the word 'cold' is 'having a low temperature'*. **2** said about a translation: exact, word for word.

literally adverb **1** in the literal sense. **2** *informal* used for emphasis: *She was literally tearing her hair out*.

literary adjective *English* **1** to do with literature. **2** said about words: most likely to be found in serious works of literature.

literate adjective **1** able to read and write. **2** possessing knowledge in a particular field of activity: *computer literate*.

literature noun **1** *English* writings in prose or verse, especially those having artistic value. **2** all the writings on a particular subject. **3** printed matter such as leaflets or circulars.

lithe adjective supple and athletic.

litigation noun the use of the courts or lawsuits to settle issues.

litmus noun *Science* a colouring matter that turns red in acid solutions and blue in alkaline solutions.

litmus paper noun *Science* paper coloured with litmus, used as an indicator of whether a substance is acid or alkaline.

litre noun (plural **litres**) a unit for measuring liquids, equal to 1000 cubic centimetres (about 1.75 pints).

litter noun (plural **litters**) **1** scattered rubbish, especially in a public place. **2** an untidy accumulation of things. **3** a group of animal babies born at one birth. **4** absorbent material for a cat to urinate and defecate on. **5** *History* a portable couch or a stretcher for carrying people. ~ verb (**litters, littering, littered**) to scatter litter or other things over an area.

little adjective **1** small in size or short in extent. **2** said about a person: young or younger. **3** not much. ~ adverb (**less, least**) **1** not much: *little-known facts*. **2** hardly or not at all: *little better than before*. ~ noun not much: *There's little we can do*. ✻ **a little 1** to a small extent or degree. **2** a small amount or portion. **3** a short time or distance.

liturgy noun (plural **liturgies**) a form of public worship in which the same words are used every time. ➤ **liturgical** adjective.

live¹ /liv/ verb (**lives, living, lived**) **1** to be alive. **2** to remain alive. **3** to have a home. **4** to have a particular way of life, aim in life, etc. **5** to earn a living: *He lives by walking people's dogs for them*. ✻ **live down** to overcome the shame or embarrassment caused by a mistake or offence. **live it up** *informal* to celebrate lavishly. **live off** to rely on somebody or something for the things you need to live. **live on** to use something as food. **live together** to share a home and have a sexual relationship without being married. **live up to** to achieve an expected standard.

live² /liev/ adjective **1** having life. **2** connected to a source of electric power. **3** unexploded or unfired. **4** broadcast as it happens.

livelihood noun (plural **livelihoods**)

something, especially a job, that provides a person with the means to support themselves.

lively *adjective* (**livelier, liveliest**) **1** active and energetic. **2** full of life, movement, or excitement. ➤ **liveliness** *noun*.

liven /lievn/ *verb* (**livens, livening, livened**) ✳ **liven up** to become more lively, or to make somebody or something more lively.

liver /liver/ *noun* (*plural* **livers**) **1** a large organ in the body that helps to digest food and purify the blood. **2** the liver of an animal eaten as food.

livery *noun* (*plural* **liveries**) **1** a distinctive uniform worn by servants, employees, officials, etc. **2** a distinctive colour scheme, e.g. on a vehicle, to show that it belongs to an organization. ➤ **liveried** *adjective*.

Word History The word *livery* is related to *delivery*. The word originally meant the giving of food and clothing to servants, and then came to mean the actual food and clothes themselves. From there, the word changed in meaning again to denote the special uniform worn by a particular person's servants.

lives *noun* plural of LIFE.

livestock *noun* farm animals.

live wire *noun* (*plural* **live wires**) *informal* a very dynamic or lively person.

livid *adjective* **1** *informal* very angry. **2** discoloured by bruising.

living *adjective* **1** alive. **2** still in use, especially still spoken: *a living language*. ~ *noun* (*plural* **livings**) the money you need to pay for food and the other things you need: *earn a living*.

living room *noun* (*plural* **living rooms**) a room in a home used for everyday activities.

lizard *noun* (*plural* **lizards**) a usually small four-legged reptile with a long body and tail.

llama /lah ma/ *noun* (*plural* **llamas**) a South American mammal with a woolly fleece.

load *noun* (*plural* **loads**) **1** an amount, especially a large or heavy one, that is carried or supported. **2** a burden of responsibility, anxiety, etc. **3** *informal* (*also* **loads**) a large quantity; a lot. ~ *verb* (**loads, loading, loaded**) **1** to put a load in or on a vehicle, ship, etc. **2** to put ammunition into a gun. **3** to insert a film, tape, program, etc into a piece of equipment.

loaf[1] *noun* (*plural* **loaves**) a shaped mass of baked bread.

loaf[2] *verb* (**loafs, loafing, loafed**) to spend time being lazy. ➤ **loafer** *noun*.

loam *noun* rich crumbly soil.

loan *noun* (*plural* **loans**) **1** something lent, especially money on which you have to pay interest. **2** the act of lending. ~ *verb* (**loans, loaning, loaned**) to lend somebody something. ✳ **on loan** being temporarily used by a borrower.

loath *or* **loth** /lohth/ *adjective* (**loath to**) unwilling to do something; reluctant.

loathe /lohth/ *verb* (**loathes, loathing, loathed**) to dislike something or somebody intensely. ➤ **loathing** *noun*.

Usage Note Do not confuse the verb *loathe* and the adjective *loath*.

loathsome /lohthsum/ *adjective* hateful or disgusting.

loaves *noun* plural of LOAF[1].

lob *verb* (**lobs, lobbing, lobbed**) to throw or hit a ball, etc in a high curve through the air. ➤ **lob** *noun*.

lobby *noun* (*plural* **lobbies**) **1** a porch or entrance hall. **2** a room next to a debating chamber where Members of Parliament go to vote or where they meet members of the public. **3** a group of people engaged in

lobe

lobbying. ~ *verb* (**lobbies, lobbying, lobbied**) to try to influence the opinion of members of a parliament or council on a particular issue. ➢ **lobbyist** *noun*.

lobe *noun* (*plural* **lobes**) 1 a flat, curved, projecting part, such as the lower part of the ear. 2 a rounded section of an organ of the body, especially the brain.

lobster *noun* (*plural* **lobsters** or **lobster**) a large ten-legged shellfish with a pair of large claws.

local *adjective* 1 to do with a particular place; not general or widespread. 2 serving the needs of a particular area: *a local newspaper*. ~ *noun* (*plural* **locals**) 1 a local person or thing. 2 *informal* the neighbourhood pub. ➢ **locally** *adverb*.

local anaesthetic *noun* (*plural* **local anaesthetics**) an anaesthetic affecting only a part of the body.

locality *noun* (*plural* **localities**) a particular area or neighbourhood.

localize or **localise** *verb* (**localizes, localizing, localized** or **localises,** etc) to restrict something to a particular place. ➢ **localization** or **localisation** *noun*.

locate *verb* (**locates, locating, located**) to find the position of something. ✶ **be located** to be sited or situated.

location *noun* (*plural* **locations**) 1 a particular place or position. 2 a place outside a studio where a broadcast or film is made. 3 the act of locating.

loch /lokh/ *noun* (*plural* **lochs**) a lake in Scotland.

loci *noun* plural of LOCUS.

lock[1] *noun* (*plural* **locks**) 1 a fastening that can be opened only by using a special key, code, etc. 2 an enclosed section of a river or canal with gates at each end, in which the water level can be raised or lowered to allow boats to pass through. 3 in wrestling, etc, a tight hold on a part of your opponent's body. ~ *verb* (**locks, locking, locked**) 1 to shut or fasten a door, window, box, etc with a lock. 2 to put something in a secure place and lock a door, lid, etc so that people cannot get at it. 3 to become fixed or jammed. ✶ **lock, stock, and barrel** wholly or completely. **lock up** *verb* 1 to lock all the doors of a building. 2 to put somebody in prison. ➢ **lockable** *adjective*.

lock[2] *noun* (*plural* **locks**) 1 a curl or tuft of hair. 2 (**locks**) *literary* somebody's hair.

locker *noun* (*plural* **lockers**) 1 a cupboard or compartment that can be locked. 2 a storage compartment on a boat or ship.

locket *noun* (*plural* **lockets**) a small gold or silver case with space for a memento, usually worn on a chain round your neck.

locksmith *noun* (*plural* **locksmiths**) somebody who makes or mends locks.

locomotive *noun* (*plural* **locomotives**) a railway engine.

locum /loh kum/ *noun* (*plural* **locums**) *informal* a doctor or member of the clergy acting as a temporary replacement for another.

locus /loh kus/ *noun* (*plural* **loci** /loh sie or loh kie/) *Maths* a set of points whose positions are determined by a stated condition.

locust *noun* (*plural* **locusts**) a large grasshopper that travels in huge swarms through tropical areas, eating all the vegetation.

lodge *noun* (*plural* **lodges**) 1 a house lived in during a particular season, for example the hunting season. 2 a small house at the gates or in the grounds of a country estate. 3 a porter's room at the entrance to a college, block of flats, etc. 4 a beaver's or otter's den. ~ *verb* (**lodges, lodging, lodged**)

1 to live temporarily as a lodger. **2** to fix something, or become fixed, firmly in place. **3** to make a complaint to an authority.

lodger *noun* (*plural* **lodgers**) somebody who occupies a rented room in somebody else's house.

lodgings *plural noun* a rented room or rooms, usually in a private house.

loft *noun* (*plural* **lofts**) **1** an attic. **2** an upper floor in a barn or warehouse used for storage. **3** a shed or coop for pigeons. ~ *verb* (**lofts, lofting, lofted**) to propel a ball, etc high up into the air.

lofty *adjective* (**loftier, loftiest**) **1** impressively high. **2** showing high ideals or moral principles. **3** haughty. ➤ **loftily** *adverb*.

log *noun* (*plural* **logs**) **1** a piece of unshaped timber ready for sawing or use as firewood. **2** the full record of a ship's voyage or an aircraft's flight. ~ *verb* (**logs, logging, logged**) **1** to enter a piece of information in a log. **2** to cut down trees for timber. ✴ **log off/out** to end a session at a computer terminal. **log on/in** to begin a session at a computer terminal. ➤ **logger** *noun*.

logarithm *noun* (*plural* **logarithms**) *Maths* the number that shows the power to which a base must be raised to make a particular number; on the base 10, the logarithm of 1000 is 3, since $1000 = 10 \times 10 \times 10 = 10^3$.

logbook *noun* (*plural* **logbooks**) **1** a book recording the details of a ship's voyage or an aircraft's flight. **2** an official document recording details of a motor vehicle and its ownership.

loggerheads ✴ **at loggerheads** quarrelling or completely disagreeing.

logic *noun* **1** a science that deals with the principles of reasoning. **2** a rational and orderly connection between ideas. **3** *ICT* the principles by which circuit elements are connected in a computer. ➤ **logician** *noun*.

logical *adjective* **1** using or based on sound reasoning. **2** to be expected under the circumstances. ➤ **logically** *adverb*.

logistics *noun* the planning and organizing of a large and complex operation. ➤ **logistic** *adjective*.

logo /loh goh/ *noun* (*plural* **logos**) an identifying symbol used by a company.

loin *noun* (*plural* **loins**) **1** the part of the body between the hip bone and the lower ribs. **2** (**loins**) the genitals.

loincloth *noun* (*plural* **loincloths**) a cloth worn round the hips and covering the genitals.

loiter *verb* (**loiters, loitering, loitered**) **1** to remain in an area for no obvious reason. **2** to dawdle. ➤ **loiterer** *noun*.

loll *verb* (**lolls, lolling, lolled**) **1** to lie or move in a lazy manner. **2** to hang down loosely.

lollipop *noun* (*plural* **lollipops**) a large round sweet made of boiled sugar on the end of a stick.

lolly *noun* (*plural* **lollies**) **1** = LOLLIPOP. **2** (*also* **ice lolly**) a flavoured piece of ice or ice cream on a stick. **3** *informal* money.

lone *adjective* **1** single or sole. **2** isolated.

lonely *adjective* (**lonelier, loneliest**) **1** sad from being alone or without friends. **2** cut off from others; solitary. **3** not often visited by people. ➤ **loneliness** *noun*.

loner *noun* (*plural* **loners**) a person who prefers to be alone.

long¹ *adjective* **1** extending for a considerable or specified distance or time: *a long way*; *a long wait*; *The pole was about two metres long*. **2** containing a large number or a specified number of items: *a long list*; *The*

long

song is about forty verses long. ~ *adverb* **1** for a long time. **2** throughout a specified period: *all night long*. **3** far in the past: *long ago*. ✶ **before long** soon. **be long** *informal* to take a long time. **in the long run** considered over a long period of time. **no longer** in the past but not now. **so/as long as** providing that. **so long** *informal* goodbye.

long² *verb* (**longs, longing, longed**) to feel a strong desire for something or to do something.

longevity /lon jevi ti *or* long jevi ti/ *noun* great length of life.

long face *noun* (*plural* **long faces**) a sad expression.

longhand *noun* handwriting.

longing *noun* (*plural* **longings**) a strong desire, especially for something difficult to attain. ➤ **longing** *adjective*, **longingly** *adverb*.

longitude *noun* (*plural* **longitudes**) *Geography* the distance, measured in degrees, of a place east or west of the Greenwich meridian.

Usage Note Notice that this word is *longitude*, not *longtitude*, which is a common error.

longitudinal *adjective* **1** extending lengthways. **2** to do with longitude. ➤ **longitudinally** *adverb*.

long jump *noun* (**the long jump**) an athletic event consisting of a jump for distance from a running start.

long-range *adjective* **1** involving, or designed to go, long distances. **2** involving a long period of time.

longship *noun* (*plural* **longships**) *History* a long open Viking warship propelled by oars and a sail.

long shot *noun* (*plural* **long shots**) something that has little chance of success.

long-sighted *adjective* unable to see clearly things that are close to your eyes.

long-suffering *adjective* patiently putting up with pain, difficulty, or provocation.

longways *adverb* = LENGTHWAYS.

long-winded *adjective* tediously long in speaking or writing.

loo *noun* (*plural* **loos**) *informal* = TOILET.

loofah *noun* (*plural* **loofahs**) the dried seed pod of a plant, used as a bath sponge.

look *verb* (**looks, looking, looked**) **1** to direct your eyes in a specified direction. **2** to appear or seem. **3** to be facing in a particular direction. ~ *noun* (*plural* **looks**) **1** an act of looking; a glance. **2** (**looks**) physical appearance. **3** the general appearance of somebody or something. **4** a style or fashion. ✶ **look after** to take care of somebody. **look back** to think about the past. **look down on** to regard somebody or something as inferior. **look for** to try to find somebody or something. **look into** to investigate something. **look out** to remain alert in case of trouble. **look up 1** to improve in prospects. **2** to search for something in, for example, a reference book. **3** *informal* to visit or make contact with somebody. **look up to** to have great respect for somebody.

lookalike *noun* (*plural* **lookalikes**) somebody or something that looks like somebody or something else.

looking glass *noun* (*plural* **looking glasses**) a mirror.

lookout *noun* (*plural* **lookouts**) **1** a place or structure from which you can keep watch. **2** somebody who is keeping watch. **3** a careful watch. **4** *informal* a person's own concern or responsibility: *If she made the wrong decision, that's her lookout*.

loom¹ *noun* (*plural* **looms**) a machine for weaving thread into cloth.

loom² *verb* (**looms, looming, loomed**) **1** to appear suddenly as a large, indistinct, and often threatening shape. **2** to be about to happen.

loony *adjective* (**loonier, looniest**) *informal* crazy or foolish.

loop *noun* (*plural* **loops**) **1** a shape formed when a line is drawn in an elongated circle and its ends are crossed. **2** a manoeuvre in which an aircraft flies up and down again in a circle. ~ *verb* (**loops, looping, looped**) to form or move in a loop.

loophole *noun* (*plural* **loopholes**) **1** something that is missing from or unclear in a law or rule and that enables you to avoid doing what the law or rule says or intends. **2** a small opening in a wall through which you can fire a gun, bow, etc.

loose[1] *adjective* **1** not fastened tightly or attached securely. **2** not tight-fitting: *loose clothes*. **3** not tied up or confined. **4** not kept together in a bundle, container, etc. **5** not dense or compact. **6** not tightly stretched. **7** not precise or exact. ~ *verb* (**looses, loosing, loosed**) **1** to release somebody or something. **2** to unfasten or detach something. * **on the loose** free, especially having escaped. ➤ **loosely** *adverb*, **looseness** *noun*.

Usage Note **loose** *or* **lose**? Do not confuse **loose** (pronounced /loohs/) and the verb **lose** (pronounced /loohz/).

loose end *noun* (*plural* **loose ends**) an incomplete or unexplained detail. * **at a loose end** bored or unoccupied.

loose-leaf *adjective* said about an album or book: bound so that individual leaves can be detached or inserted.

loosen *verb* (**loosens, loosening, loosened**) to become, or to make something, loose or looser. * **loosen up 1** to become more relaxed. **2** to warm up your muscles before exercising.

loot *noun* **1** goods taken as plunder in a war or illegally. **2** *informal* money. ~ *verb* (**loots, looting, looted**) to steal goods from a place during a war or riot. ➤ **looter** *noun*.

lop *verb* (**lops, lopping, lopped**) to cut off branches or twigs from a tree. * **lop off** to remove something unnecessary or undesirable.

lope *verb* (**lopes, loping, loped**) to move in an easy, bounding run. ➤ **lope** *noun*.

lop-eared *adjective* said about an animal: with ears that droop.

lopsided *adjective* with one side heavier or lower than the other.

Lord *noun* **1** God. **2** Jesus Christ. **3** (**the Lords**) the House of Lords. * **my Lord** used as a form of address to judges, bishops, and noblemen.

lord *noun* (*plural* **lords**) **1** a nobleman. **2** a ruler or leader.

lordly *adjective* (**lordlier, lordliest**) **1** dignified or noble. **2** disdainful and arrogant. ➤ **lordliness** *noun*.

Lord Mayor *noun* (*plural* **Lord Mayors**) the mayor of the City of London and some other large British cities.

Lord Provost *noun* (*plural* **Lord Provosts**) the provost of certain Scottish cities.

Lordship *noun* (**His/Your Lordship**) a title used when talking about or to a bishop, a High Court judge, or a nobleman.

lore *noun* traditional knowledge or beliefs.

lorry *noun* (*plural* **lorries**) a large motor vehicle for carrying loads by road.

lose *verb* (**loses, losing, lost**) **1** to realize that you do not have something and be unable to find it. **2** to cease to have, or have less of, something: *to lose weight*. **3** to suffer loss through the death of somebody: *She lost her husband last year*. **4** to be defeated in a contest. **5** to make less money from something than you spent on it. **6** said about a watch or clock: to start to show a time behind the real time. * **lose it** *informal* to lose control of yourself. **lose your way** to be unable to find the correct direction to go in. ➤ **loser** *noun*.

Usage Note **lose** or **loose**? Do not confuse *lose* (pronounced /loohz/) and *loose* (pronounced /loohs/).

loss *noun* (*plural* **losses**) **1** the act of losing something. **2** the harm or sadness resulting from loss. **3** a person, thing, or amount lost. **4** an amount by which costs exceed income. * **at a loss 1** uncertain or puzzled. **2** not making enough money to cover your costs.

lost *verb* past tense of LOSE. ~ *adjective* **1** unable to find the correct way to somewhere. **2** bewildered or helpless. **3** killed or destroyed. * **be lost for words** to be unable to think what to say. **be lost on** not to be noticed or appreciated by somebody. **get lost** *informal* to go away. **lost in** rapt or absorbed by something.

lost cause *noun* (*plural* **lost causes**) something that has no chance of success.

lot *noun* (*plural* **lots**) **1** (**a lot** *or* **lots**) *informal* a large amount or number. **2** (**the lot**) the whole amount or number. **3** *informal* a number of associated people or things. **4** an item offered for sale in an auction. * **a lot 1** *informal* much or considerably. **2** *informal* often. **draw lots** to decide something by asking people to choose something at random, for example a slip of paper from among several slips.

loth *adjective* see LOATH.

lotion *noun* (*plural* **lotions**) a medicinal or cosmetic liquid for use on the skin.

lottery *noun* (*plural* **lotteries**) a way of raising money by selling tickets with numbers on them, some of which, chosen at random, entitle the holder to a prize.

lotus *noun* (*plural* **lotuses**) a large tropical water lily.

loud *adjective* **1** producing a high volume of sound. **2** tastelessly bright in colour. ➤ **loudly** *adverb*, **loudness** *noun*.

loudspeaker *noun* (*plural* **loudspeakers**) a device that converts electrical energy into sound.

lounge *verb* (**lounges, lounging, lounged**) to sit, lie, or stand in a lazy or relaxed way. ~ *noun* (*plural* **lounges**) **1** a sitting room in a private house. **2** a room in a public building providing comfortable seating.

lounge suit *noun* (*plural* **lounge suits**) a man's suit for wear during the day.

lour /lowr/ *verb* (**lours, louring, loured**) **1** to scowl or look sullen. **2** said about the sky or weather: to become dark and threatening.

louse *noun* (*plural* **lice**) **1** a small wingless insect that is a parasite on animals, fish, or plants. **2** (*plural* **louses**) *informal* a contemptible person.

lousy *adjective* (**lousier, lousiest**) *informal* very bad, unpleasant, useless, etc.

lout *noun* (*plural* **louts**) a rough badmannered man or boy. ➤ **loutish** *adjective*.

lovable *or* **loveable** *adjective* charming and able to inspire affection.

love *noun* (*plural* **loves**) **1** a strong feeling of attachment, tenderness, and protectiveness for another person. **2** attraction based on sexual desire. **3** strong interest in and enjoyment of something. **4** a person or thing that you love. **5** a score of zero in tennis, squash, etc. ~ *verb* (**loves, loving, loved**) to feel love for somebody or something. * **make love** to have sexual intercourse. ➤ **loveless** *adjec-*

tive, **lover** noun, **loving** adjective, **lovingly** adverb.

love affair noun (plural **love affairs**) a sexual or romantic relationship between people.

lovely adjective (**lovelier, loveliest**) 1 delightfully beautiful. 2 very pleasing; fine. ➤ **loveliness** noun.

low¹ adjective 1 not high or tall. 2 of less than the usual degree, size, amount, or value: *low prices*. 3 considered comparatively unimportant. 4 said about sound: soft or deep. 5 weak or depressed. 6 morally bad. ~ adverb in or to a low position. ~ noun (plural **lows**) 1 a low point or level. 2 a region of low atmospheric pressure.

low² verb (**lows, lowing, lowed**) to make the deep sound of a cow; moo.

lower¹ /loor/ verb (**lowers, lowering, lowered**) 1 to move something down or allow it to descend. 2 to reduce something in height, value, amount, pitch, etc.

lower² /lowr/ verb (**lowers, lowering, lowered**) = LOUR.

lower case noun small letters, for example a, b, c rather than A, B, C. ➤ **lower-case** adjective.

low-key adjective made to seem not very important; restrained.

lowland noun 1 (also *lowlands*) low or level country. 2 (**the Lowlands**) the part of Scotland lying south and east of the Highlands. ➤ **lowlander** noun.

lowly adjective (**lowlier, lowliest**) low-ranking; humble. ➤ **lowliness** noun.

low tide noun the time when the sea reaches its lowest level.

loyal adjective faithfully supporting a person, country, or cause. ➤ **loyally** adverb, **loyalty** noun.

loyalist noun (plural **loyalists**) 1 somebody who is loyal to a government or sovereign, especially during a revolt. 2 (**Loyalist**) in Northern Ireland, a supporter of continued union with the United Kingdom.

lozenge noun (plural **lozenges**) 1 a small medicated sweet. 2 a diamond or rhombus.

LP noun (plural **LPs**) a long-playing gramophone record.

LSD noun = *lysergic acid diethylamide*/lie ser jik **a** sid die **e** thil a mied/, an illegal drug with a powerful mind-altering effect.

Ltd abbreviation Limited.

lubricant noun (plural **lubricants**) a substance, such as grease or oil, used to reduce friction and wear between surfaces.

lubricate verb (**lubricates, lubricating, lubricated**) to apply a greasy substance to something to reduce friction and wear between its surfaces. ➤ **lubrication** noun.

lucid adjective 1 able to be clearly understood. 2 able to think clearly; sane. ➤ **lucidity** noun, **lucidly** adverb.

luck noun 1 whatever good or bad events happen to a person by chance. 2 good fortune. ✱ **try your luck** to attempt to do something that may or may not succeed.

luckless adjective unlucky or unfortunate.

lucky adjective (**luckier, luckiest**) having, resulting from, or bringing good luck.

lucrative /looh kra tiv/ adjective profitable.

ludicrous adjective absurd. ➤ **ludicrously** adverb.

ludo noun a board game played with counters and dice.

lug¹ verb (**lugs, lugging, lugged**) to drag or carry something with great effort.

lug² noun (plural **lugs**) 1 something, such as a handle, that sticks out like an ear. 2 *humorous* an ear.

luggage *noun* cases, bags, etc containing a traveller's belongings.

lugubrious /loo gooh bri us/ *adjective* very sad or gloomy, or sad and gloomy in an exaggerated way.

lukewarm *adjective* **1** moderately warm; tepid. **2** lacking enthusiasm.

lull *verb* (**lulls, lulling, lulled**) **1** to calm somebody with soothing sounds, rocking movements, etc. **2** to fool somebody into thinking they are safe. ~ *noun* (*plural* **lulls**) a temporary pause in activity.

lullaby *noun* (*plural* **lullabies**) a song used to lull children to sleep.

lumbago /lum bay goh/ *noun* pain in the lower back.

lumbar *adjective* to do with the lower back.

lumber[1] *verb* (**lumbers, lumbering, lumbered**) to move heavily or clumsily.

lumber[2] *noun* **1** surplus or disused articles. **2** *N American* timber or logs. ~ *verb* (**lumbers, lumbering, lumbered**) *informal* to burden somebody with something unwanted.

lumberjack *noun* (*plural* **lumberjacks**) a person who cuts down and saws up trees.

luminescence *noun* *Science* light produced at low temperatures, for example by chemical action. ➤ **luminescent** *adjective*.

luminous *adjective* emitting light; bright. ➤ **luminosity** *noun*.

lump *noun* (*plural* **lumps**) **1** a compact mass of indefinite size and shape. **2** an abnormal swelling. ~ *verb* (**lumps, lumping, lumped**) to group things together, often disregarding their differences. ✱ **lump it** *informal* to put up with something. ➤ **lumpy** *adjective*.

lump sum *noun* (*plural* **lump sums**) a sum of money given in a single payment.

lunacy *noun* **1** foolishness. **2** insanity.

lunar *adjective* to do with the moon.

lunar month *noun* (*plural* **lunar months**) the period of time, averaging 29½ days, between two new moons.

lunatic *noun* (*plural* **lunatics**) **1** a mentally ill person. **2** a foolish or foolhardy person.

lunch *noun* (*plural* **lunches**) a midday meal. ~ *verb* (**lunches, lunching, lunched**) to eat lunch.

luncheon *noun* (*plural* **luncheons**) **1** *formal* = LUNCH. **2** a formal lunch.

lung *noun* (*plural* **lungs**) either of the pair of organs in the chest that are used for breathing.

lunge *verb* (**lunges, lunging, lunged**) to make a sudden forward movement or thrust. ➤ **lunge** *noun*.

lurch[1] *verb* (**lurches, lurching, lurched**) to move in an abrupt, uncontrolled, and jerky way. ➤ **lurch** *noun*.

lurch[2] ✱ **in the lurch** in a difficult and vulnerable position.

lure *noun* (*plural* **lures**) **1** something used to entice an animal into a trap. **2** the power to appeal or attract. ~ *verb* (**lures, luring, lured**) to attract a person or animal with something that promises pleasure, food, or gain.

lurid *adjective* **1** unnaturally or unattractively bright in colour. **2** sensational or shocking. ➤ **luridly** *adverb*.

lurk *verb* (**lurks, lurking, lurked**) **1** to lie hidden in wait. **2** to be present but undetected.

luscious *adjective* having a delicious taste or smell.

lush *adjective* growing thickly.

lust *noun* (*plural* **lusts**) **1** strong sexual desire. **2** a craving. ~ *verb* (**lusts, lusting, lusted**) (**lust for/after**) to have an intense especially sexual desire for somebody or something. ➤ **lustful** *adjective*.

lustre *noun* a glow of reflected light; a sheen. ➤ **lustrous** *adjective*.

lusty *adjective* (**lustier, lustiest**) full of vitality; healthy and vigorous. ➤ **lustily** *adverb*.

lute *noun* (*plural* **lutes**) *Music* a stringed instrument with a large pear-shaped body and long neck.

luxuriant *adjective* growing and spreading strongly. ➤ **luxuriance** *noun*, **luxuriantly** *adverb*.

luxuriate *verb* (**luxuriates, luxuriating, luxuriated**) to enjoy the pleasure of something wholeheartedly.

luxurious *adjective* extremely comfortable and usually expensive and elegant. ➤ **luxuriously** *adverb*.

luxury *noun* (*plural* **luxuries**) **1** great comfort based on the use of expensive items. **2** something desirable or expensive but not essential.

Lycra /lie kra/ *noun trademark* a man-made stretchy yarn used chiefly in tight-fitting sportswear and swimwear.

lying *verb* present participle of LIE¹ and LIE².

lymph *noun* a pale body fluid containing white blood cells.

lynch *verb* (**lynches, lynching, lynched**) to put somebody to death illegally by mob action.

lynchpin *noun* see LINCHPIN.

lynx *noun* (*plural* **lynxes** *or* **lynx**) a wildcat with a short tail, mottled coat, and tufted ears.

lyre *noun* (*plural* **lyres**) *Music* a U-shaped stringed instrument like a harp, used by the ancient Greeks.

lyric *noun* (*plural* **lyrics**) **1** (**lyrics**) the words of a popular song. **2** a lyric poem. ~ *adjective English* said about poetry: expressing direct personal emotion.

lyrical *adjective* **1** having a beautiful, song-like quality. **2** lyric. ✱ **wax lyrical** to talk with great admiration or enthusiasm about something. ➤ **lyrically** *adverb*, **lyricism** *noun*.

m *abbreviation* **1** metre or metres. **2** mile or miles.

ma'am /mam *or* mahm/ *noun* madam.

macabre /ma kah bra/ *adjective* to do with or describing the unpleasant aspects of death.

macaroni *noun* pasta in the shape of thin hollow tubes.

macaroon *noun* (*plural* **macaroons**) a biscuit made with ground almonds or coconut.

macaw *noun* (*plural* **macaws**) a large brightly coloured parrot from South and Central America.

mace[1] *noun* (*plural* **maces**) a large ornamental stick carried during ceremonies as a symbol of authority.

mace[2] *noun* a spice made from the shell of a nutmeg.

Mach /mak *or* mahk/ *noun* (*also* **Mach number**) used as a unit of speed relative to the speed of sound; Mach 1 is the speed of sound, Mach 2 is twice as fast as that, Mach 3 three times as fast, and so on.

Word History Mach numbers are named after Ernst *Mach*, an Austrian scientist.

machete /ma she ti/ *noun* (*plural* **machetes**) a large heavy knife used in tropical regions as a cutting tool and weapon.

machine *noun* (*plural* **machines**) a mechanical apparatus designed to perform a task. ~ *verb* (**machines, machining, machined**) to make or shape something with a machine.

machine gun *noun* (*plural* **machine guns**) a gun that fires a continuous stream of bullets.

machine-readable *adjective* ICT in a form that can be processed by a computer.

machinery *noun* **1** machines. **2** the moving parts of a machine. **3** the organization that controls an activity or process.

machismo /ma kiz moh *or* ma chiz moh/ *noun* behaviour intended to show a man's physical strength or toughness.

macho /ma choh/ *adjective* **1** intended as a show of physical strength or toughness. **2** tending to behave in an aggressively masculine way.

mackerel *noun* (*plural* **mackerels** *or* **mackerel**) an edible striped fish from the North Atlantic.

mackintosh *or* **macintosh** *noun* (*plural* **mackintoshes** *or* **macintoshes**) a raincoat.

macrobiotic /ma kroh bie o tik/ *adjective* said about a diet: consisting mainly of whole grains and raw or lightly cooked vegetables.

mad *adjective* (**madder, maddest**) **1** insane. **2** utterly foolish. **3** (**mad at**) very angry. **4** (**mad about/on**) obsessively enthusiastic. ✴ **like mad** *informal* very hard, fast, loud, etc. ➤ **madness** *noun*.

madam *noun* a polite way of addressing a lady, such as a female customer.

mad cow disease *noun informal* = bovine spongiform encephalopa-

thy/boh vien spun ji fawm in se fa lo pa thi/, a disease of cattle that affects the brain and spine.

maddening *adjective* annoying or frustrating.

made *verb* past tense and past participle of MAKE.

made-up *adjective* **1** wearing make-up. **2** fictional or invented.

madly *adverb* **1** very fast and with a lot of energy. **2** very: *madly in love*.

madrigal *noun* (*plural* **madrigals**) **1** *Music* a song for several voices, sung without music. **2** *English* a short medieval love poem.

maestro /mie stroh/ *noun* (*plural* **maestros** *or* **maestri** /mie stree/) *Music* a very talented conductor or classical musician.

Mafia *noun* (**the Mafia**) a secret international criminal organization that originated in Sicily.

magazine *noun* (*plural* **magazines**) **1** a publication that contains a lot of articles, photographs, and illustrations. **2** a holder for the bullets in an automatic gun. **3** a storeroom for weapons and ammunition.

Word History The word *magazine* comes from Arabic *makhzan*, which means 'a storehouse'. In the 17th century, the word was used in book titles to suggest a store of information, and from there it developed its modern meaning.

magenta /ma jen ta/ *noun* a deep purplish red colour.

maggot *noun* (*plural* **maggots**) the soft-bodied larva of a fly. ➤ **maggoty** *adjective*.

magic *noun* **1** illusions performed to entertain people. **2** the use of supernatural powers. ~ *adjective* **1** to do with illusions: *magic tricks*. **2** *informal* very good or exciting. ➤ **magical** *adjective*, **magically** *adverb*.

magician *noun* (*plural* **magicians**) **1** an entertainer who creates illusions. **2** a wizard.

magistrate *noun* (*plural* **magistrates**) a local law officer who judges minor cases and holds preliminary hearings. ➤ **magistracy** *noun*.

magma *noun* molten rock from beneath the earth's surface.

magnanimous *adjective* generous and mature enough to forgive people in situations where others might be bitter and petty. ➤ **magnanimity** *noun*, **magnanimously** *adverb*.

magnate *noun* (*plural* **magnates**) a rich and powerful business person.

magnesium *noun* *Science* a light silver-white metallic element which burns with a bright white light.

magnet *noun* (*plural* **magnets**) *Science* a piece of iron or steel that has the power to attract iron objects towards itself.

magnetic *adjective* *Science* **1** having the power to attract iron objects. **2** to do with magnets. ➤ **magnetically** *adverb*.

magnetic field *noun* (*plural* **magnetic fields**) *Science* the area around a magnetic object within which its magnetism has an effect.

magnetic north *noun* *Geography* the northerly direction in the earth's magnetic field; it is not quite the same as the geographical north.

magnetism *noun* *Science* a magnet's power to attract iron objects towards itself.

magnetize *or* **magnetise** *verb* (**magnetizes, magnetizing, magnetized** *or* **magnetises,** etc) *Science* to make a piece of iron or steel magnetic. ➤ **magnetization** *or* **magnetisation** *noun*.

magnification *noun* (*plural* **magnifications**) **1** the amount by which something is magnified. **2** the process of magnifying something.

magnificent *adjective* **1** strikingly beautiful or impressive. **2** exceptionally good. ➤ **magnificence** *noun*, **magnificently** *adverb*.

magnify *verb* (**magnifies, magnifying, magnified**) **1** to make something appear bigger using a lens or system of lenses. **2** to make something seem more important or extreme.

magnifying glass *noun* (*plural* **magnifying glasses**) a single lens, often with a handle, for magnifying things.

magnitude *noun* **1** size or extent. **2** importance or significance.

magnolia *noun* (*plural* **magnolias**) **1** a small tree with large white, yellow, pink, or purple flowers. **2** a pale creamy white colour.

magpie *noun* (*plural* **magpies**) a large, long-tailed, black and white bird of the crow family.

mahogany /ma ho ga ni/ *noun* **1** a reddish brown hardwood. **2** a reddish brown colour.

maid *noun* (*plural* **maids**) **1** a woman who cleans the rooms in a hotel. **2** a female servant.

maiden *noun* (*plural* **maidens**) *archaic* a young unmarried woman. ~ *adjective* first ever: *a maiden voyage*.

maiden name *noun* (*plural* **maiden names**) the surname that a woman had before she was married and started to use her husband's surname.

mail[1] *noun* (*plural* **mails**) **1** letters and parcels sent by post. **2** the postal system. **3** *ICT* email or an email message. ~ *verb* (**mails, mailing, mailed**) **1** to send something by post. **2** *ICT* to contact somebody by email.

mail[2] *noun* armour made of small interlocking metal rings.

mail order *noun* a system of ordering goods and receiving them by post.

maim *verb* (**maims, maiming, maimed**) to cause somebody a severe and permanent injury.

main *adjective* biggest or most important. ~ *noun* (*plural* **mains**) **1** a large pipe carrying gas or water, or a large cable carrying electricity. **2** (**the mains**) the pipes or cables that supply water, gas, or electricity to an area.

mainframe *noun* (*plural* **mainframes**) *ICT* a large computer that has several workstations connected to it.

main clause *noun* see PRINCIPAL CLAUSE.

mainland *noun* *Geography* the largest land area of a continent or country, as opposed to its islands.

mainly *adverb* mostly; chiefly.

mainstay *noun* the person or thing most responsible for making something successful.

mainstream *noun* the opinions, styles, and activities of most people in society.

maintain *verb* (**maintains, maintaining, maintained**) **1** to keep something in good or working order. **2** to keep something at its present level. **3** to give somebody the money and things they need to live. **4** to keep stating that something is true when other people are doubting it or disagreeing.

maintenance *noun* **1** work you do to keep something in good condition or working order. **2** money that somebody gives to a husband, wife, or child that they no longer live with, to help pay for the things they need to live.

maize *noun* a tall cereal plant with seeds that are called sweet corn.

majestic *adjective* very grand or beautiful. ➤ **majestically** *adverb*.

majesty *noun* (*plural* **majesties**) **1** impressive grandeur or beauty. **2** (**Her/His/Your Majesty**) a title used in referring to or speaking to a king or queen.

major *adjective* **1** very large, important, or severe. **2** *Music* said about a musical scale: with semitones between the third and fourth and the seventh and eighth notes. ~ *noun* (*plural* **majors**) an army officer of the rank immediately above a captain.

majority *noun* (*plural* **majorities**) **1** the group forming more than half the total of a number of things or people. **2** in an election, the difference between the number of votes cast for the winning party and the number cast for its nearest rival or all its rivals together.

make *verb* (**makes, making, made**) **1** to produce something or cause something to exist. **2** to do something: *Let's make a start.* **3** to put something or somebody into a particular state: *You've made me very happy.* **4** (**make into**) to change something or somebody so that they become something different: *They made the dining room into an office.* **5** to have a particular function: *This box makes a good seat.* **6** to force somebody to do something: *They made me do it.* **7** to earn money as income: *How much does she make a year?* **8** to achieve or reach something: *The story made the national papers.* **9** (**make for/towards**) to move in a particular direction: *He made for the door.* ~ *noun* (*plural* **makes**) a manufacturer or brand. ✴ **make away/off with** to take or steal something. **make do** to manage with limited resources. **make out 1** to manage with difficulty to see, hear, or understand something. **2** to claim or pretend something: *He made out that he hadn't seen me.* **make up 1** to invent a story or excuse. **2** to form something: *Girls make up two-thirds of the class.* **3** to make friends again after an argument. **4** (**make up for**) to compensate for a disadvantage or loss. ➤ **maker** *noun*.

make-believe *noun* imagination or fantasy.

makeover *noun* (*plural* **makeovers**) **1** work done to repair or renovate something. **2** a change of personal appearance that usually includes changes in make-up, hairstyle, and clothes.

makeshift *adjective* done or built inadequately using the only things that are available.

make-up *noun* **1** cosmetics for the face. **2** the way in which the parts of something are put together.

maladjusted *adjective* unable to behave normally or cope with normal life.

malaise /ma layz/ *noun* a vague feeling of being unhappy or nervous.

malaria *noun* a disease caused by mosquito bites, with attacks of chills and fever.

male *adjective* **1** belonging to the sex that fertilizes a female to produce babies or fruit. **2** consisting of, or typical of, men. ~ *noun* (*plural* **males**) a male animal, person, or plant.

male chauvinist /mayl shoh vi nist/ *noun* (*plural* **male chauvinists**) a man who believes that men are always better than women.

malevolent /ma le vo lint/ *adjective* intending to harm other people.
➤ **malevolence** *noun*, **malevolently** *adverb*.

malfunction *verb* (**malfunctions, malfunctioning, malfunctioned**) to break down or fail to work normally.
➤ **malfunction** *noun*.

malice *noun* the desire to harm other people.

malicious *adjective* wanting to, or intended to, harm other people.
➤ **maliciously** *adverb*.

malign /ma lien/ *verb* (**maligns, maligning, maligned**) to say nasty things about somebody. ~ *adjective* having a harmful effect. ➤ **malignity** *noun*.

malignancy *noun* (*plural* **malig-**

malignant | 390

nancies) 1 a malignant tumour. 2 harmful effects or qualities.

malignant *adjective* 1 harmful. 2 said about a tumour: consisting of cancer cells and likely to cause death if not treated.

malinger *verb* (**malingers, malingering, malingered**) to pretend to be ill or injured to avoid work. ➤ **malingerer** *noun*.

mall *noun* (*plural* **malls**) a large indoor shopping centre.

mallard *noun* (*plural* **mallards**) a large wild duck, the male of which has a shiny green head.

malleable /ma li a bl/ *adjective* 1 said about metal: able to be hammered or rolled into shape. 2 said about a person: easily influenced or persuaded. ➤ **malleability** *noun*.

mallet *noun* (*plural* **mallets**) a hammer with a large wooden head.

malnourished *adjective* suffering from malnutrition.

malnutrition *noun* ill health caused by lack of food.

malpractice *noun* serious mistakes made by a professional person who does not do their job with skill or care.

malt *noun* softened and roasted grain used in brewing and distilling. ➤ **malted** *adjective*.

mammal *noun* (*plural* **mammals**) a warm-blooded animal which has live babies that are fed by the mother with milk from her own body. ➤ **mammalian** *adjective*.

mammoth *adjective* huge. ~ *noun* (*plural* **mammoths**) an extinct animal like a huge hairy elephant with very long tusks.

man *noun* (*plural* **men**) 1 an adult human male. 2 the human race: *environmental damage caused by man.* 3 a piece used in a board game. ~ *verb* (**mans, manning, manned**) to be the person or people operating or running something.

manacles *plural noun* handcuffs or shackles.

manage *verb* (**manages, managing, managed**) 1 to succeed in achieving something difficult. 2 to control a business, team, or other group of people. 3 to look after the career of a sports player, entertainer, etc. ➤ **manageable** *adjective*.

management *noun* 1 the activity of managing a business, team, or other group of people. 2 the people who manage a business, etc.

manager *noun* (*plural* **managers**) 1 a person who manages a business, team, or other group of people. 2 a person who manages the career of a sports player, entertainer, etc. ➤ **managerial** *adjective*.

manageress *noun* (*plural* **manageresses**) a woman who manages a shop.

Usage Note In business, sport, etc, a woman who manages a business, team, etc is always referred to as a *manager*, never a manageress.

mandarin *noun* (*plural* **mandarins**) 1 a small orange with a loose skin. 2 (**Mandarin**) the official standard dialect of the Chinese language.

mandate *noun* (*plural* **mandates**) 1 the right to govern a country, given to the winning party in an election. 2 an official instruction, for example to a bank.

mandatory /man da to ri/ *adjective* which somebody must do; compulsory.

mandir /mun deer/ *noun* (*plural* **mandirs**) a Hindu or Jain temple.

mandolin *noun* (*plural* **mandolins**) a musical instrument like a small guitar, with a rounded body and four pairs of strings.

mane *noun* (*plural* **manes**) a growth of

thick hair on the neck of a horse, male lion, etc.

manganese *noun Science* a greyish white brittle metallic element.

manger *noun* (*plural* **mangers**) an animal's feeding trough or box.

mangle *verb* (**mangles, mangling, mangled**) to damage something severely by tearing, twisting, or crushing it. ~ *noun* (*plural* **mangles**) a machine with rollers for squeezing water from laundry.

mango *noun* (*plural* **mangoes** or **mangos**) a yellowish red tropical fruit with juicy orange flesh.

mangrove *noun* (*plural* **mangroves**) a tropical tree or bush with thick roots that are partly above ground.

mangy or **mangey** /mayn ji/ *adjective* (**mangier, mangiest**) **1** said about an animal: suffering from mange, a skin disease. **2** badly worn or shabby. ➤ **manginess** *noun*.

manhole *noun* (*plural* **manholes**) a covered vertical hole that leads down to a sewer or some other underground system of pipes or passages.

mania *noun* (*plural* **manias**) **1** a great enthusiasm for something. **2** a mental illness that causes very excited and disorganized behaviour.

maniac /may ni ak/ *noun* (*plural* **maniacs**) **1** a mentally ill person suffering from mania. **2** a person with a great enthusiasm for something.

manic /ma nik/ *adjective* **1** behaving in a very excited or nervous way. **2** suffering from mania. ➤ **manically** *adverb*.

manicure *noun* (*plural* **manicures**) a beauty treatment for the fingernails and hands.

manifest *verb* (**manifests, manifesting, manifested**) to show something: *How does the disease manifest itself?* ~ *adjective* easy to notice; obvious. ➤ **manifestly** *adverb*.

manslaughter

manifestation *noun* (*plural* **manifestations**) evidence that something exists.

manifesto *noun* (*plural* **manifestos** or **manifestoes**) a printed statement of a political party's policies, published before an election.

manipulate *verb* (**manipulates, manipulating, manipulated**) **1** to control something or somebody using clever methods that people are not aware of. **2** to handle something skilfully. ➤ **manipulation** *noun*, **manipulative** *adjective*, **manipulator** *noun*.

mankind *noun* the human race.

manly *adjective* (**manlier, manliest**) having qualities such as courage and physical strength that people think of as typically masculine. ➤ **manliness** *noun*.

manner *noun* (*plural* **manners**) **1** a way of doing something. **2** a person's usual way of behaving. **3** (**manners** or **good manners**) polite behaviour. **4** (**bad manners**) impolite behaviour.

mannerism *noun* (*plural* **mannerisms**) a gesture, expression, or way of speaking that is typical of a particular person.

manoeuvre /ma noo ver/ *verb* (**manoeuvres, manoeuvring, manoeuvred**) **1** to guide something carefully into position. **2** to use clever tactics to achieve something. ~ *noun* (*plural* **manoeuvres**) **1** something clever that somebody does in order to achieve something. **2** a movement that requires skill and control. ➤ **manoeuvrable** *adjective*.

manor *noun* (*plural* **manors**) a large country house with an estate. ➤ **manorial** *adjective*.

manpower *noun* workers.

mansion *noun* (*plural* **mansions**) a large impressive house.

manslaughter *noun* the crime of killing somebody accidentally.

mantelpiece *or* **mantlepiece** *noun* (*plural* **mantelpieces** *or* **mantlepieces**) a shelf above a fireplace.

mantle *noun* (*plural* **mantles**) **1** a cloak. **2** *literary* a layer that covers something: *The fields were covered by a mantle of snow.* **3** a role that one person takes over from another: *The eldest girl took on the mantle of mother to her younger sisters.* **4** *Geography* the part of the earth that lies between the crust and the central core.

mantra *noun* (*plural* **mantras**) a word or sound that people who are meditating repeat to help their concentration.

manual *adjective* **1** said about work: involving the use of your hands and often also a lot of physical effort. **2** said about a worker: doing manual work. **3** done by hand rather than automatically or by machine. ~ *noun* (*plural* **manuals**) a book of instructions or information. ➤ **manually** *adverb*.

manufacture *verb* (**manufactures, manufacturing, manufactured**) to make products using machines in a factory. ~ *noun* the activity of making products on a large scale using machinery. ➤ **manufacturer** *noun*.

manure *noun* animal dung used to fertilize soil.

manuscript *noun* (*plural* **manuscripts**) a version of a book that the author produces, before it is published.

Manx *adjective* from or to do with the Isle of Man.

many *adjective* (**more, most**) in large numbers: *Many people disagreed.* ~ *pronoun* a large number of people or things: *Many preferred not to vote.* ~ *noun* (**the many**) *literary* the great majority of people.

Maori /mow ri/ *noun* (*plural* **Maoris** *or* **Maori**) **1** a member of the original people of New Zealand. **2** the language of this people.

map *noun* (*plural* **maps**) **1** a diagram of part of the earth's surface, showing features such as towns, roads, and rivers. **2** a diagram of the layout of anything: *a map of the London underground.* ~ *verb* (**maps, mapping, mapped**) ✴ **map out** to plan something in detail.

maple *noun* (*plural* **maples**) a tree with broad leaves that have five pointed sections.

mar *verb* (**mars, marring, marred**) to spoil something.

marathon *noun* (*plural* **marathons**) **1** a race run over 26 miles 385 yards (42.2 kilometres). **2** a long or strenuous activity.

Word History The *marathon* is named after *Marathon* in Greece, the site of a battle between the Greeks and the Persians in 490 BC. The race commemorates the feat of a Greek soldier who, according to an ancient Greek story, ran from Marathon to Athens (a distance of about 25 or 26 miles) after the battle to tell the Athenians that the Greeks had won.

---

marauding *adjective* going around destroying property or attacking people. ➤ **marauder** *noun*.

marble *noun* (*plural* **marbles**) **1** a hard mottled stone that can be polished very smooth. **2** a small glass ball used in children's games. **3** (**marbles**) the children's game of hitting marbles against each other.

March *noun* the third month of the year.

march *verb* (**marches, marching, marched**) **1** to walk in a formal military style at a regular pace. **2** to walk in a purposeful way: *She marched up to him to complain.* **3** to walk in a procession organized as a demonstration of support or protest: *students marching on parliament.* ~ *noun* (*plural* **marches**) a procession organized as a

marketing

demonstration of support or protest. ➤ **marcher** noun.

marchioness /mah sho nes/ noun (plural **marchionesses**) **1** the wife or widow of a marquis. **2** a woman who has the same rank as a marquis.

mare noun (plural **mares**) a female horse.

margarine noun a spreadable substance like butter, made from vegetable oils.

margin noun (plural **margins**) **1** the blank parts of a page around the main area of text. **2** the edge of an area. **3** the difference between one amount and another.

marginal adjective **1** very small or slight: *a marginal improvement.* **2** printed or written in the margin. ➤ **marginally** adverb.

marginalize or **marginalise** verb (**marginalizes, marginalizing, marginalized** or **marginalises**, etc) to treat something or somebody as unimportant. ➤ **marginalization** or **marginalisation** noun.

marigold noun (plural **marigolds**) a garden plant with yellow, orange, or red flowers.

marijuana /ma ri wah na/ noun a mild form of cannabis.

marina noun (plural **marinas**) a harbour for yachts and small boats.

marinade noun (plural **marinades**) a mixture that you soak food in before cooking it to give it more flavour.

marinate verb (**marinates, marinating, marinated**) to soak food in a marinade.

marine adjective to do with the sea. ~ noun (plural **marines**) a soldier trained to fight at sea as well as on land.

marital adjective to do with marriage or the relations between a husband and wife.

maritime adjective to do with the sea and ships.

marjoram /mah jo ram/ noun **1** a herb with small leaves and pink flowers, related to oregano. **2** = OREGANO.

mark noun (plural **marks**) **1** a stain, scratch, or other fault that spoils the way something looks. **2** a line or notch that records the position of something. **3** a number or letter indicating how good a student's work is. **4** a gesture or symbol: *a mark of respect.* ~ verb (**marks, marking, marked**) **1** to record the position of something with a mark. **2** to read a student's work and indicate how good it is. **3** in a team game, to stay close to an opponent to prevent them from getting or passing the ball. **4** to be a sign of something or be when something takes place: *This year marks their 50th anniversary.* ✷ **mark time 1** to move your feet up and down in a marching rhythm but without moving forward. **2** to fail to make progress or do anything productive. **quick off the mark** reacting promptly. **wide of the mark** not accurate or relevant.

marked adjective noticeable. ➤ **markedly** adverb.

marker noun (plural **markers**) **1** a felt-tip pen with a broad tip. **2** in a team game, a player who marks an opponent.

market noun (plural **markets**) **1** a hall or area with stalls selling various goods. **2** a place where goods or animals are bought and sold. **3** trade in or demand for goods of a particular type: *a buoyant property market; the market in organic fruit.* ~ verb (**markets, marketing, marketed**) to promote or offer something for people to buy. ✷ **on the market** available to buy. ➤ **marketable** adjective.

marketing noun the promotion and

market research

advertising of goods or services for sale.

market research *noun* information collected about what goods and services people like and dislike.

marksman *noun* (*plural* **marksmen**) a person trained to shoot a gun very accurately. ➤ **marksmanship** *noun*.

marmalade *noun* jam made from oranges or other citrus fruit.

maroon *noun* a dark brownish red colour.

marooned *adjective* left in a remote place that is impossible to escape from without help.

marquee /mah kee/ *noun* (*plural* **marquees**) a large tent used for outdoor parties and other events.

marquis *or* **marquess** /mah kwis/ *noun* (*plural* **marquises** *or* **marquesses**) a nobleman who ranks below a duke and above an earl.

marriage *noun* (*plural* **marriages**) **1** the state of being husband and wife, or the relationship between a husband and wife. **2** a wedding.

married *adjective* having a husband or a wife.

marrow *noun* (*plural* **marrows**) **1** a large green cylindrical vegetable. **2** a soft tissue inside bones, in which blood cells are produced.

marry *verb* (**marries, marrying, married**) **1** to become somebody's husband or wife. **2** to be the priest or official who joins people in marriage.

marsh *noun* (*plural* **marshes**) an area of land that is always soft and wet. ➤ **marshy** *adjective*.

marshal *noun* (*plural* **marshals**) an official who helps to control the crowd at a public event. ~ *verb* (**marshals, marshalling, marshalled**) to put people or things into organized groups.

marshmallow *noun* (*plural* **marshmallows**) **1** a light spongy sweet that is usually white or pink. **2** a pink-flowered plant that grows in marshes.

marsupial /mah sooh pi al/ *noun* (*plural* **marsupials**) a mammal that carries its babies in a pouch on its abdomen.

martial *adjective* to do with war.

martial art *noun* (*plural* **martial arts**) a fighting sport that developed in the Far East, such as karate or tae kwon do.

martial law *noun* a situation in which soldiers police the streets and enforce strict laws.

Martian *adjective* to do with the planet Mars. ~ *noun* (*plural* **Martians**) a supposed inhabitant of Mars.

martinet /mah ti net/ *noun* (*plural* **martinets**) a very strict boss or leader.

Word History The word *martinet* comes from the name of Jean *Martinet*, an officer in the French army in the 17th century who introduced a very strict training regime.

martyr /mah ter/ *noun* (*plural* **martyrs**) a person who is killed because they refuse to give up their religious beliefs. ~ *verb* (**martyrs, martyring, martyred**) to kill somebody because they refuse to give up their religious beliefs. ➤ **martyrdom** *noun*.

marvel *verb* (**marvels, marvelling, marvelled**) (**marvel at**) to be extremely impressed by or surprised at something. ~ *noun* (*plural* **marvels**) something or somebody that is amazingly impressive.

marvellous *adjective* extremely good. ➤ **marvellously** *adverb*.

Marxism *noun* History the principles and policies of the 19th-century political thinker Karl Marx, on which communism is based. ➤ **Marxist** *noun and adjective*.

marzipan *noun* a paste made from

ground almonds, sugar, and egg whites, used to cover cakes and chocolates.

mascara /mas kah ra/ *noun* a cosmetic that makes eyelashes darker and thicker.

mascot *noun* (*plural* **mascots**) a person, animal, or object that people believe brings good luck.

masculine *adjective* **1** to do with men or typical of men. **2** in some languages, belonging to or having to do with a class of words that refer mainly to males. ➤ **masculinity** *noun*.

mash *verb* (**mashes, mashing, mashed**) to crush something to a soft pulpy state. ~ *noun informal* mashed potatoes.

mask *noun* (*plural* **masks**) a covering for the face that you wear for fun, for protection, or as a disguise. ~ *verb* (**masks, masking, masked**) to disguise or conceal something. ➤ **masked** *adjective*.

masochism /ma soh ki zm/ *noun* the enjoyment of physical pain or suffering. ➤ **masochist** *noun*, **masochistic** *adjective*.

mason *noun* (*plural* **masons**) **1** a skilled worker who builds things with stone. **2** (**Mason**) = FREEMASON.

Masonic *adjective* to do with Freemasons.

masonry *noun* the stone parts of a building.

masquerade /mas ki rayd or mah ski rayd/ *verb* (**masquerades, masquerading, masqueraded**) to pretend to be something that you are not: *masquerading as a doctor*.

mass[1] *noun* (*plural* **masses**) **1** a large amount of something: *a mass of information*. **2** an irregular lump of something. **3** *Science* in physics, the amount of material in an object, measured as its resistance to changes in its speed or position. **4** *informal* (**masses**) a large quantity or amount: *We've got masses of time left.* **5** (**the masses**) ordinary people. ~ *adjective* involving a lot of people: *a mass protest*. ~ *verb* (**masses, massing, massed**) to gather into a single group.

mass[2] or **Mass** *noun* (*plural* **masses** or **Masses**) a Roman Catholic service in which people eat bread or wafers, and the priest also drinks wine, to remember Jesus Christ's death.

massacre *verb* (**massacres, massacring, massacred**) to kill a large number of people violently and cruelly. ~ *noun* (*plural* **massacres**) the brutal killing of large numbers of people.

massage /ma sahzh/ *noun* (*plural* **massages**) the action of rubbing a person's body to relieve aches and give relaxation. ~ *verb* (**massages, massaging, massaged**) to give somebody a massage.

massive *adjective* extremely large. ➤ **massively** *adverb*.

mass-produce *verb* (**mass-produces, mass-producing, mass-produced**) to produce goods in large quantities in factories. ➤ **mass-produced** *adjective*, **mass-production** *noun*.

mast *noun* (*plural* **masts**) a tall pole that supports the sails on a ship.

master *noun* (*plural* **masters**) **1** a man with great skill in a particular activity. **2** a man who owns an animal. **3** the head of a college in some universities. **4** (**Master**) somebody who has a university degree of the level next above a Bachelor's degree: *Master of Science*. ~ *verb* (**masters, mastering, mastered**) **1** to become very skilled in something. **2** to get control of something.

masterful *adjective* **1** tending to take control of situations and dominate people. **2** done with great skill. ➤ **masterfully** *adverb*.

masterly *adjective* extremely clever or skilful.

mastermind *noun* (*plural* **masterminds**) a person who plans and runs a complex project. ~ *verb* (**masterminds, masterminding, masterminded**) to plan and run a complex project.

masterpiece *noun* (*plural* **masterpieces**) an excellent painting, book, film, or other artistic work.

mastery *noun* **1** complete control or authority. **2** great skill or knowledge in a subject.

masturbate (**masturbates, masturbating, masturbated**) *verb* to stroke your own or somebody else's genitals for sexual pleasure. ➤ **masturbation** *noun*.

mat *noun* (*plural* **mats**) **1** a piece of thick fabric used as a floor covering. **2** a flat piece of material used to protect a table from heat, moisture, etc.

matador *noun* (*plural* **matadors**) in a bullfight, the main bullfighter, who eventually kills the bull.

match¹ *noun* (*plural* **matches**) **1** a contest between teams or players. **2** one thing that goes well with another. ~ *verb* (**matches, matching, matched**) **1** to be equal to another person or thing. **2** to go well with something else.

match² *noun* (*plural* **matches**) a short thin stick tipped with a mixture that makes a flame when you rub it against a rough surface.

mate¹ *noun* (*plural* **mates**) **1** a friend. **2** an animal that is breeding with another. **3** an officer on a merchant ship who ranks below a captain. ~ *verb* (**mates, mating, mated**) said about animals: to come together to breed.

mate² *noun* in chess, checkmate.

material *noun* (*plural* **materials**) **1** the substance or substances that something is made of. **2** fabric. **3** (**materials**) things that you use for doing or making something. ~ *adjective* **1** important or measurable: *no material difference between them.* **2** concerned with physical rather than spiritual things: *material wealth.* ➤ **materially** *adverb*.

materialism *noun* the attitude of somebody who thinks that the most important things in life are money and possessions. ➤ **materialist** *noun and adjective*, **materialistic** *adjective*.

materialize *or* **materialise** *verb* (**materializes, materializing, materialized** *or* **materialises**, etc) to happen or start to exist.

maternal *adjective* to do with mothers or typical of a mother. ➤ **maternally** *adverb*.

maternity *adjective* to do with having babies: *maternity clothes.*

matey *or* **maty** *adjective* (**matier, matiest**) *informal* friendly.

mathematics *noun* the science that deals with numbers and their use in making calculations and taking measurements. ➤ **mathematical** *adjective*, **mathematically** *adverb*, **mathematician** *noun*.

maths *noun* = MATHEMATICS.

matinée /ma ti nay/ *noun* (*plural* **matinées**) an afternoon performance in a theatre or cinema.

matrimony *noun* marriage. ➤ **matrimonial** *adjective*.

matrix /**may** triks/ *noun* (*plural* **matrices** /**may** tri seez/ *or* **matrixes**) **1** *Science* a substance or environment in which something develops. **2** *Maths* a set of numbers arranged in a square and used to make calculations.

matron *noun* (*plural* **matrons**) a senior nurse in charge of all the nurses in a hospital.

matt *or* **matte** *adjective* not glossy or shiny; dull.

matted *adjective* said about threads, hair, etc: tangled.

matter *noun* (*plural* **matters**) **1** a fact, situation, or subject that you are dealing with or are concerned about. **2** a type of object or substance: *waste matter; reading matter.* **3** *Science* the substance that anything consists of. ~ *verb* (**matters, mattering, mattered**) to be important or relevant. ✱ **no matter 1** that is of no importance. **2** regardless of a certain thing: *We can't win now, no matter how many goals we score.* **what's the matter?** what is wrong?; why are you upset or angry?

matter-of-fact *adjective* not at all upset, excited, or impressed, which is unusual in the circumstances.

mattress *noun* (*plural* **mattresses**) a thick padded case that you lie on in bed.

mature *adjective* **1** showing the good sense and reasonable behaviour that you expect from adults or sensible young people. **2** fully grown: *mature plants.* ~ *verb* (**matures, maturing, matured**) to become mature. ➤ **maturely** *adverb*.

maturity *noun* **1** a mature state. **2** sensible and reasonable behaviour or attitudes.

maty *adjective* see MATEY.

maudlin *adjective* sentimental in a way that seems silly.

maul *verb* (**mauls, mauling, mauled**) **1** said about an animal: to attack somebody and cause them serious injury. **2** to damage something by handling it roughly.

mausoleum *noun* (*plural* **mausoleums**) a large elaborate tomb.

mauve /mohv/ *noun* a pinkish purple colour.

maverick /ma vi rik/ *noun* (*plural* **mavericks**) somebody who does what they want to do or what they think is right, and does not care if they break rules or if other people disapprove.

Word History Samuel *Maverick* was a 19th-century American rancher who refused to brand his cattle. Unbranded cattle were known as *mavericks*, and the word then came to be used for people who do as they please.

maxim *noun* (*plural* **maxims**) a short saying that expresses a general truth about life.

maximize or **maximise** *verb* (**maximizes, maximizing, maximized** or **maximises**, etc) to make something as good or large as possible. ➤ **maximization** or **maximisation** *noun*.

maximum *noun* (*plural* **maximums**) the greatest amount or number that is possible or that has ever been recorded. ~ *adjective* greatest in amount or number.

May *noun* the fifth month of the year.

may[1] *verb* (**may, might**) **1** expressing permission: *You may go now; May I have another biscuit?* **2** expressing possibility: *They may have left already.* **3** expressing a wish or hope: *Long may it continue.*

may[2] *noun* hawthorn bushes or hawthorn blossom.

maybe *adverb* perhaps.

Mayday *noun* (*plural* **Maydays**) an international radio distress signal.

Word History *Mayday* represents the sound of French *m'aider* in the phrase *venez m'aider* 'come and help me'.

mayhem *noun* a state of great confusion or disorder.

mayonnaise *noun* a thick dressing made with egg yolks, vegetable oil, and vinegar or lemon juice.

mayor *noun* (*plural* **mayors**) the head of the local council in a city or borough. ➤ **mayoral** *adjective*.

mayoress *noun* (*plural* **mayoresses**)

maze

1 the wife of a mayor. **2** a woman who is a mayor.

maze *noun* (*plural* **mazes**) **1** a complex network of paths that are difficult to find your way through, designed for amusement. **2** any complex system that is frustratingly difficult to make progress in.

Mb *abbreviation* ICT megabyte or megabytes.

MBE *abbreviation* Member of the Order of the British Empire.

MD *abbreviation* **1** Doctor of Medicine. **2** Managing Director.

ME *abbreviation* = *myalgic encephalomyelitis* /mie al jik in se fa loh mie i lie tis/, an illness that causes extreme tiredness and aching joints.

me *pronoun* used by somebody to refer to himself or herself; the object form of 'I'.

meadow *noun* (*plural* **meadows**) a field with grass growing in it.

meagre *adjective* available or supplied only in very small quantities. ➤ **meagreness** *noun*.

meal[1] *noun* (*plural* **meals**) **1** an amount of food that you eat at one sitting. **2** an occasion when people eat a meal.

meal[2] *noun* the ground seeds of a cereal plant.

mealy-mouthed *adjective* too dishonest or shy to speak plainly or directly.

mean[1] *verb* (**means, meaning, meant** /ment/) **1** to intend something: *I didn't mean to upset you.* **2** to have a particular meaning: *What does this word mean?* **3** to indicate something: *What does a red flag mean?* **4** to have a particular importance: *Your apology means a lot to me.* **5** to be a cause of something: *Failing your exams means you won't get into university.*

mean[2] *adjective* **1** not generous. **2** unpleasant and spiteful: *That was a mean thing to say.* **3** *informal* excellent or impressive: *I make a mean lasagne.* ➤ **meanly** *adjective*, **meanness** *noun*.

mean[3] *noun* (*plural* **means**) Maths an average of a set of numbers. ~ *adjective* Maths average.

meander /mee an der/ *verb* (**meanders, meandering, meandered**) said about a river or road: to have a lot of bends.

meaning *noun* (*plural* **meanings**) **1** what a word refers to or is intended to convey. **2** sense or significance: *the meaning of life.*

meaningful *adjective* **1** having a special meaning: *a meaningful glance.* **2** worthwhile: *Do something meaningful with your life.* ➤ **meaningfully** *adverb*.

meaningless *adjective* having no meaning or purpose. ➤ **meaninglessly** *adverb*.

means *plural noun* **1** a method. **2** money or other resources. ✴ **by all means** of course; certainly. **by means of** with the help or use of. **by no means** not at all; in no way.

means test *noun* (*plural* **means tests**) an examination of somebody's finances to see whether they are eligible to receive government benefits of some kind.

meant *verb* past tense and past participle of MEAN1.

meantime ✴ **in the meantime** = MEANWHILE.

meanwhile *adverb* **1** during the time between two events. **2** during the same period.

measles *noun* an infectious disease that causes a red rash and high fever.

measly *adjective* (**measlier, measliest**) *informal* inadequate or ungenerously small.

measure *verb* (**measures, measuring, measured**) **1** to find out the size, amount, or degree of something. **2** to have a particular measurement. **3** (**measure out**) to take or give something in measured amounts. ~ *noun* (*plural* **measures**) **1** something that you do or plan to do in order to achieve something. **2** a unit of measurement. **3** a device used for measuring. ➤ **measurable** *adjective*, **measurably** *adverb*.

measured *adjective* **1** slow and regular: *a measured pace*. **2** carefully thought out: *a measured reply*.

measurement *noun* (*plural* **measurements**) **1** a figure or amount that is the result of measuring. **2** the act of measuring something.

meat *noun* animal flesh used as food.

mecca *noun* a place that attracts a particular group of people: *a mecca for tourists*.

Word History Mecca is a city in Saudi Arabia that is a holy place of pilgrimage for Muslims.

mechanic *noun* (*plural* **mechanics**) **1** a skilled worker who repairs or maintains machinery. **2** (**mechanics**) *Science* the branch of science that deals with energy and forces and their effect on movement. **3** (**mechanics**) the working parts of something.

mechanical *adjective* **1** to do with machines or done by machines. **2** done without thinking or without emotion: *a mechanical response*. ➤ **mechanically** *adverb*.

mechanism *noun* (*plural* **mechanisms**) **1** a set of moving parts in a machine. **2** a process designed to achieve a result.

mechanized *or* **mechanised** *adjective* done by machines, not by hand. ➤ **mechanization** *or* **mechanisation** *noun*.

medal *noun* (*plural* **medals**) a stamped metal disc given as an award or made to commemorate a person or event.

medallion *noun* (*plural* **medallions**) a pendant in the shape of a medal.

medallist *noun* (*plural* **medallists**) a person who has been awarded a medal for achievement in sport.

meddle *verb* (**meddles, meddling, meddled**) **1** to interfere in other people's affairs. **2** to touch something and spoil or damage it. ➤ **meddler** *noun*.

media *plural noun* **1** newspapers, radio, and television as a source of news and information for the public. **2** the plural of MEDIUM.

Usage Note The word *media* is plural, and should be followed by a plural verb: *The media have shown little interest in this event.*

mediaeval *adjective* see MEDIEVAL.

median *noun* (*plural* **medians**) *Maths* **1** a number that is in the middle of a range of numbers. **2** a straight line from one angle of a triangle to the middle of the opposite side. ~ *adjective* positioned in the middle.

mediate *verb* (**mediates, mediating, mediated**) to try to settle a dispute. ➤ **mediation** *noun*, **mediator** *noun*.

medical *adjective* to do with doctors or the treatment they give. ~ *noun* (*plural* **medicals**) a thorough examination by a doctor. ➤ **medically** *adverb*.

medication *noun* medicines.

medicinal *adjective* used to treat illnesses. ➤ **medicinally** *adverb*.

medicine *noun* (*plural* **medicines**) **1** a substance used to treat illnesses. **2** the work that doctors do. **3** the study of illnesses and their treatment.

medieval *or* **mediaeval** *adjective* *History* in or to do with the Middle Ages, the period of European history from about 1000 to 1500.

mediocre /mee di oh ker/ *adjective* of ordinary or average quality; not good or excellent.

meditate *verb* (**meditates, meditating, meditated**) **1** to fix your mind on one thing or on nothing, as a religious or spiritual exercise.

Mediterranean

2 to think about something very carefully. ➤ **meditation** *noun*, **meditative** *adjective*.

Mediterranean *adjective* of the Mediterranean Sea or the region around it.

medium *noun* (*plural* **media** *or* **mediums**) **1** a means of communication: *the medium of radio*. **2** a way in which an artist expresses ideas: *the medium of sculpture*. **3** (*plural* **mediums**) a person who claims to communicate with the spirits of dead people. ~ *adjective* of middle size; intermediate.

medley *noun* (*plural* **medleys**) **1** a varied mixture of things. **2** a song or piece of music made up of parts of other songs or pieces.

meek *adjective* quiet, shy, and obedient. ➤ **meekly** *adverb*.

meet *verb* (**meets, meeting, met**) **1** to come together with somebody as arranged: *We'll meet at the hotel.* **2** to come together with somebody by accident: *Guess who I met in town?* **3** to become acquainted with somebody: *Have you met my brother?* **4** (**meet with**) to experience something: *We met with a few problems.* **5** (**meet with**) to react to something: *My suggestion was met with silence.* **6** to satisfy a requirement: *Would this room meet your needs?*

meeting *noun* (*plural* **meetings**) **1** a gathering of people for formal discussion or business. **2** a coming together of two or more people.

megabyte *noun* (*plural* **megabytes**) *ICT* a unit of computer storage equal to one million bytes.

megahertz *noun* (*plural* **megahertz**) *ICT* a unit of computer speed equal to one million hertz.

megalomaniac /me ga loh **may** ni ak/ *noun* (*plural* **megalomaniacs**) somebody who wants to get control over as many people or things as they can. ➤ **megalomania** *noun*.

melancholy /**me** lan ko li/ *adjective* **1** depressed or dejected. **2** expressing or causing sadness. ➤ **melancholy** *noun*.

melee /**me** lay/ *noun* (*plural* **melees**) a confused fight or struggle involving a lot of people.

mellow *adjective* **1** rich and soft in colour or taste. **2** relaxed or relaxing. ~ *verb* (**mellows, mellowing, mellowed**) to become relaxed and gentle as you get older.

melodic *adjective* **1** *Music* to do with a melody. **2** melodious. ➤ **melodically** *adverb*.

melodious *adjective* having a pleasant sound or tune.

melodrama *noun* (*plural* **melodramas**) **1** *Drama* a film or play with an exciting plot and exaggerated emotions. **2** sensational or dramatic behaviour. ➤ **melodramatic** *adjective*, **melodramatically** *adverb*.

melody *noun* (*plural* **melodies**) *Music* **1** the basic tune in a song or piece of music. **2** a simple tune.

melon *noun* (*plural* **melons**) a large round fruit with sweet juicy flesh.

melt *verb* (**melts, melting, melted**) to change from a solid to a liquid state when heated, or to cause something to change in this way by heating it. ✱ **melt away** to disappear gradually.

melting pot *noun* a place where people of different races, religions, or cultures live together and influence each other.

member *noun* (*plural* **members**) **1** an individual person or thing that is part of a group or organization. **2** *archaic* a limb or other part of the body. ➤ **membership** *noun*.

member of parliament *noun* (*plural* **members of parliament**) somebody who has been elected to represent people in a parliament.

membrane *noun* (*plural* **membranes**)

a thin layer of tissue that covers, lines, or connects organs or cells in animals and plants. ➤ **membranous** *adjective*.

memento *noun* (*plural* **mementos** or **mementoes**) something that you keep as a reminder of the past.

memo *noun* (*plural* **memos**) *informal* a brief note sent from one person to another in an organization.

memoirs *plural noun* a book that somebody writes about their life; an autobiography.

memorabilia *plural noun* objects that are interesting or valuable because they are connected with people or events in the past.

memorable *adjective* **1** worth remembering; notable. **2** easy to remember. ➤ **memorably** *adverb*.

memorandum *noun* (*plural* **memorandums** or **memoranda**) *formal* a memo.

memorial *noun* (*plural* **memorials**) a monument that commemorates a person or event. ➤ **memorial** *adjective*.

memorize or **memorise** *verb* (**memorizes, memorizing, memorized** or **memorises**, etc) to make a particular effort to learn or remember something in detail.

memory *noun* (*plural* **memories**) **1** the ability to remember facts and experiences. **2** something that you remember. **3** *ICT* a computer's capacity for storing data.

men *noun* plural of MAN.

menace *noun* (*plural* **menaces**) **1** a threatening or dangerous person or thing. **2** a threatening atmosphere or tone. ~ *verb* (**menaces, menacing, menaced**) to threaten somebody. ➤ **menacing** *adjective*.

menagerie /mi na ji ri/ *noun* (*plural* **menageries**) a small collection of wild animals.

mend *verb* (**mends, mending, mended**) to put something damaged back into good condition; to repair something.

menial *adjective* said about work: boring and involving little skill.

meningitis *noun* a serious disease that causes inflammation of the brain and spinal cord.

menopause *noun* (**the menopause**) the time of life when a woman stops menstruating. ➤ **menopausal** *adjective*.

menorah /mi naw ra/ *noun* (*plural* **menorahs**) a candelabrum with seven branches, a symbol of Judaism.

menstrual *adjective* to do with menstruation.

menstruate *verb* (**menstruates, menstruating, menstruated**) said about a woman: to lose blood naturally from the womb when not pregnant, which happens for a few days every month. ➤ **menstruation** *noun*.

mental *adjective* **1** to do with your mind. **2** *informal* mad. ➤ **mentally** *adverb*.

mentality *noun* (*plural* **mentalities**) a way of thinking.

mention *verb* (**mentions, mentioning, mentioned**) to refer to something or somebody briefly. ~ *noun* (*plural* **mentions**) a brief reference to something or somebody.

mentor *noun* (*plural* **mentors**) a senior person who gives somebody help and advice, for example in a new job.

menu *noun* (*plural* **menus**) **1** a list of the dishes available in a restaurant. **2** *ICT* a list of available programs, functions, commands, etc displayed on a computer screen.

meow *verb* see MIAOW.

MEP *abbreviation* Member of the European Parliament.

mercantile *adjective* relating to merchants or trading.

mercenary *adjective* interested only in

merchandise

money, or doing something only for the money. ~ *noun* (*plural* **mercenaries**) a soldier who is hired to fight for a foreign country.

merchandise *noun* goods for sale.

merchant *noun* (*plural* **merchants**) somebody who buys and sells goods of a particular type.

merchant navy *noun* (*plural* **merchant navies**) a country's commercial ships, as opposed to warships.

merciful *adjective* **1** showing mercy. **2** giving relief from suffering: *a merciful death*. ➤ **mercifully** *adverb*.

merciless *adjective* showing no mercy; pitiless. ➤ **mercilessly** *adverb*.

mercury *noun* Science a heavy silver-white liquid metallic element used in thermometers and barometers.

mercy *noun* (*plural* **mercies**) **1** a generous and forgiving attitude towards an enemy or somebody who has broken rules or behaved badly. **2** a fortunate circumstance. ✽ **at the mercy of** wholly in the power of another person.

mere *adjective* **1** used for emphasizing how small or slight something is: *a mere 1% increase*. **2** used for saying that you are referring only to one particular thing, not to something else bigger, more impressive, etc: *He blushes at the mere mention of her name*.

merely *adverb* only; simply.

merge *verb* (**merges, merging, merged**) to combine to form a single thing or substance.

merger *noun* (*plural* **mergers**) a combining of two businesses to form one.

meridian *noun* (*plural* **meridians**) Geography a line on a map or globe that runs from north to south.

meringue /mɪˈrang/ *noun* (*plural* **meringues**) a crisp sweet dessert that is a baked mixture of egg whites and sugar.

merit *noun* (*plural* **merits**) **1** worth or excellence. **2** a good aspect or quality. ~ *verb* (**merits, merited, meriting**) to be worthy of something.

mermaid *noun* (*plural* **mermaids**) a mythical sea creature with a woman's head and upper body and a fish's tail.

merry *adjective* (**merrier, merriest**) happy and lively. ➤ **merrily** *adverb*.

merry-go-round *noun* (*plural* **merry-go-rounds**) a revolving fairground machine with model horses or vehicles that people ride on.

mesh *noun* (*plural* **meshes**) **1** the threads that make up a net: *wire mesh*. **2** the size of the spaces in a net: *a 3-inch mesh*.

mesmerize *or* **mesmerise** *verb* (**mesmerizes, mesmerizing, mesmerized** *or* **mesmerises,** etc) to completely fascinate somebody.

mess *noun* (*plural* **messes**) **1** an untidy or dirty state. **2** a state of confusion or disorder. **3** a place where members of the armed forces eat their meals. ~ *verb* (**messes, messing, messed**) ✽ **mess about/around** to behave in a lazy or stupid way. **mess up 1** to spoil something. **2** to make something untidy or dirty. **mess with** to touch something and spoil or damage it.

message *noun* (*plural* **messages**) **1** a written or spoken communication. **2** the main idea expressed in a poem, painting, film, etc.

messenger *noun* (*plural* **messengers**) a person who delivers a message.

Messiah /mɪˈsiːə/ *noun* (**the Messiah**) **1** in Christianity, a title given to Jesus. **2** in Judaism, the saviour that Jewish people believe will come into the world in the future.

Messrs /ˈmesərz/ *noun* plural of MR.

messy *adjective* (**messier, messiest**) **1** untidy or dirty. **2** unpleasant to deal with: *a messy divorce*. ➤ **messily** *adverb*, **messiness** *noun*.

met *verb* past tense and past participle of MEET.

metabolism /mɪˈtæbəlɪzm/ *noun* the processes in your body that convert food into energy. ➤ **metabolic** *adjective*.

metal *noun* (*plural* **metals**) a hard substance such as iron, steel, or copper, that can be melted and is a good conductor of electricity and heat.

metallic *adjective* **1** containing metal or like metal. **2** said about a sound: sharp and ringing.

metamorphic *adjective Geography* said about rock: formed by changes in underground heat and pressure.

metamorphosis *noun* (*plural* **metamorphoses**) *Science* a natural change in the form of an insect or amphibian, such as the change from a tadpole to a frog.

metaphor *noun* (*plural* **metaphors**) *English* a word or phrase that describes one thing by saying that it is another thing, as, for example, when a brave person is referred to as a *lion*. ➤ **metaphorical** *adjective*, **metaphorically** *adverb*.

meteor *noun* (*plural* **meteors**) a piece of rock from space that falls into the earth's atmosphere and glows as it falls.

meteoric *adjective* rapid and very successful: *her meteoric rise to stardom*.

meteorite *noun* (*plural* **meteorites**) a piece of rock from space that has landed on the surface of the earth.

meteorology *noun* the scientific study of weather. ➤ **meteorological** *adjective*, **meteorologist** *noun*.

meter *noun* (*plural* **meters**) a device for measuring and recording something, often the amount of something used.

methane *noun* a flammable gas that is produced naturally when plants decay and is used as a fuel.

method *noun* (*plural* **methods**)
1 a way of doing something.
2 an organized way of doing things in general.

methodical *adjective* done in a very organized way; systematic.
➤ **methodically** *adverb*.

Methodism *noun* a Protestant branch of the Christian church, established in the 18th century. ➤ **Methodist** *noun and adjective*.

meths *noun informal* = METHYLATED SPIRITS.

methylated spirits *or* **methylated spirit** *noun* a form of alcohol used as a fuel, mixed with another chemical (methanol) to make it unfit for drinking.

meticulous *adjective* taking great care to get every detail right, or done with great attention to detail. ➤ **meticulously** *adverb*.

metre[1] *noun* (*plural* **metres**) *Maths* the basic metric unit of length, equal to 100 centimetres (39.37 inches).

metre[2] *noun* (*plural* **metres**) *English* the rhythm of poetry.

metric *adjective* using the metric system of weights and measures.

metric system *noun* (**the metric system**) a decimal system of weights and measures based on the metre, the litre, and the kilogram.

metro *noun* (*plural* **metros**) an underground railway system in a city.

metropolis *noun* (*plural* **metropolises**) a capital city or other big city.

metropolitan *adjective* to do with a big city or a large urban area.

mettle *noun* strength of character.
✱ **on your mettle** ready to do your best.

mew *verb* SEE MIAOW.

mg *abbreviation Science* milligram or milligrams.

MHz *abbreviation ICT* megahertz.

miaow or **meow** or **mew** *verb* (**miaows, miaowing, miaowed** or **meows,** etc or **mews,** etc) said about a cat: to make its usual high-pitched sound. ➤ **miaow** or **meow** or **mew** *noun*.

mice *noun* plural of MOUSE.

microbe *noun* (*plural* **microbes**) a micro-organism, especially a bacterium that causes disease.

microchip *noun* (*plural* **microchips**) *ICT* a small thin piece of silicon with tiny electronic circuits on it, used in computers.

micro-organism *noun Science* (*plural* **micro-organisms**) a bacterium or other microscopic organism.

microphone *noun* (*plural* **microphones**) a device that you speak into to record or transmit your voice or make it louder for public speaking.

microprocessor *noun* (*plural* **microprocessors**) *ICT* a computer's central processing unit, which usually consists of a set of microchips.

microscope *noun* (*plural* **microscopes**) a piece of equipment that magnifies tiny objects so you can see them clearly and study them.

microscopic *adjective* extremely small; so small that you need a microscope to see it. ➤ **microscopically** *adverb*.

microwave *noun* (*plural* **microwaves**) **1** *Science* a radiation wave that has a very short wavelength. **2** an electric oven in which food is heated by means of microwaves. ~ *verb* (**microwaves, microwaving, microwaved**) to cook or heat food in a microwave oven.

midday *noun* twelve o'clock in the middle of the day, or the time around the middle of the day.

middle *adjective* **1** having an equal number of things on either side; central: *the middle table*. **2** intermediate in size, rank, or quality: *a middle-sized packet*. ~ *noun* (*plural* **middles**) **1** a middle point or position: *You stand in the middle*. **2** *informal* your waist or abdomen.

middle-aged *adjective* between the ages of about 40 to 60. ➤ **middle age** *noun*.

Middle Ages *plural noun* (**the Middle Ages**) *History* the period of European history from about 1000 to 1500.

middle class *noun* (**the middle class**) the social class consisting of people who work in professional jobs and are usually well educated. ➤ **middle-class** *adjective*.

Middle East *noun* (**the Middle East**) the countries of southwest Asia and northern Africa, including Libya, Egypt, Lebanon, Syria, Israel, Jordan, the states of the Arabian Peninsula, Iran, and Iraq. ➤ **Middle Eastern** *adjective*.

Middle English *noun English* the form of the English language that was used in the period 1150 to 1500.

middleman *noun* (*plural* **middlemen**) somebody who buys goods or services from a company and sells them to a consumer.

middle school *noun* (*plural* **middle schools**) a school for pupils aged from 8 or 9 to 12 or 13.

middling *adjective* of only average quality.

midge *noun* (*plural* **midges**) a very small fly that bites people.

midget *noun* (*plural* **midgets**) **1** a very small person. **2** (*used before a noun*) smaller than usual.

Midlands *plural noun* (**the Midlands**) the central region of England.

midnight *noun* twelve o'clock at night.

midriff *noun* (*plural* **midriffs**) the middle part of your body; your abdomen.

midst ✱ **in somebody's midst** among

a group of people: *We have an informer in our midst.* **in the midst of** in the middle of an event or period of time: *I arrived in the midst of the celebrations.*

midsummer *noun* the period around the middle of summer.

midway *adverb and adjective* halfway.

midwife *noun* (*plural* **midwives**) a nurse who cares for a woman who is having a baby. ➤ **midwifery** *noun*.

midwinter *noun* the period around the middle of winter.

might[1] *verb* **1** past tense of MAY[1]: *I asked if I might open a window.* **2** used to express a polite question: *Might I make a suggestion?*

might[2] *noun* great power or strength.

mightily *adverb* very.

mightn't *contraction* might not.

mighty *adjective* (**mightier, mightiest**) very powerful or strong. ➤ **mightiness** *noun*.

migraine /mie grayn *or* mee grayn/ *noun* (*plural* **migraines**) a severe headache that causes nausea and problems with vision.

migrant *noun* (*plural* **migrants**) **1** an animal that migrates. **2** a person who moves regularly to find seasonal work. ➤ **migrant** *adjective*.

migrate *verb* (**migrates, migrating, migrated**) **1** said about an animal: to go from one region to another in order to feed or breed. **2** said about a person: to move from one country or region to another looking for seasonal work. ➤ **migration** *noun*, **migratory** *adjective*.

mike *noun* (*plural* **mikes**) *informal* a microphone.

mild *adjective* **1** not severe: *a mild case of flu.* **2** not strong in flavour or effect: *mild cheddar; mild painkillers.* **3** not strongly felt or expressed: *mild surprise.* **4** said about the weather: quite warm. ➤ **mildly** *adverb*, **mildness** *noun*.

mildew *noun* a white fungus that grows on things in warm damp conditions. ➤ **mildewed** *adjective*.

mile *noun* (*plural* **miles**) **1** a unit of distance equal to 1760 yards (about 1.61 kilometres). **2** (**miles**) *informal* a very long distance: *The school is miles away.* ~ *adverb* (**miles**) *informal* very much: *That's miles better.*

mileage *noun* (*plural* **mileages**) **1** the distance you travel, in miles. **2** *informal* an advantage or benefit: *He gets a lot of mileage out of being team captain.*

milestone *noun* (*plural* **milestones**) **1** an important event or stage in your life or in a process. **2** a stone that has the distance to a place marked on it, placed at the side of a road.

militant *adjective* tending or willing to take firm action to achieve things, especially political changes. ➤ **militancy** *noun*, **militant** *noun*, **militantly** *adverb*.

militarism *noun* the belief that your country needs powerful armed forces and that armed forces should be used to solve political problems. ➤ **militarist** *noun*, **militaristic** *adjective*.

military *adjective* to do with armed forces and war. ~ *noun* (**the military**) a country's armed forces. ➤ **militarily** *adverb*.

militia /mi li sha/ *noun* (*plural* **militias**) a group of people who fight like an army but are not professional soldiers. ➤ **militiaman** *noun*.

milk *noun* **1** a white liquid produced by female mammals to feed their young. **2** the milk of cows, goats, etc used as food for humans. **3** the juice of a plant or a coconut. ~ *verb* (**milks, milking, milked**) **1** to take milk from an animal. **2** to get full advantage from a situation or person.

milkman *noun* (*plural* **milkmen**) a man who delivers milk to people's houses.

milkshake *noun* (*plural* **milkshakes**) a

cold drink made from milk whisked with a flavouring syrup.

milk tooth *noun* (*plural* **milk teeth**) any of a child's first set of teeth, which fall out as the child grows up.

milky *adjective* (**milkier, milkiest**) **1** containing milk. **2** like milk in colour or consistency. ➤ **milkiness** *noun*.

Milky Way *noun* (**the Milky Way**) the galaxy that the earth is part of, which can be seen as a broad band of faint light stretching across the sky.

mill *noun* (*plural* **mills**) **1** a machine or building for grinding grain into flour. **2** a device for grinding coffee beans or peppercorns. **3** a building with machinery for manufacturing a substance: *a woollen mill*. ~ *verb* (**mills, milling, milled**) **1** to grind something in a mill. **2** (**mill about/around**) said about a group or crowd: to move around in an aimless or confused way.

millennium *noun* (*plural* **millennia** *or* **millenniums**) **1** a period of a thousand years. **2** the date on which one period of a thousand years ends and another begins. ➤ **millennial** *adjective*.

miller *noun* (*plural* **millers**) a person who owns or works a grain mill.

millet *noun* a cereal plant with very small round seeds.

milligram *noun* (*plural* **milligrams**) a unit of weight equal to one thousandth of a gram (0.0353 of an ounce)

millilitre *noun* (*plural* **millilitres**) a unit of volume equal to one thousandth of a litre (0.002 of a pint).

millimetre *noun* (*plural* **millimetres**) a unit of length equal to one thousandth of a metre (about 0.039 of an inch).

million *noun* (*plural* **millions** *or* **million**) **1** the number 1,000,000 (10^6). **2** *informal* (*also in plural*) a very large number: *There were millions of people at the party.* ➤ **millionth** *adjective and noun*.

millionaire *noun* (*plural* **millionaires**) somebody who has money and property worth at least a million pounds or dollars.

millstone *noun* (*plural* **millstones**) **1** an awkward problem or important responsibility that causes you a lot of difficulty. **2** each of a pair of circular stones in a mill that grind grain to make flour.

mime *noun* (*plural* **mimes**) **1** the art of portraying a character or telling a story using gestures and body movements only, with no words. **2** a performance of mime, or a person who performs mime. ~ *verb* (**mimes, miming, mimed**) **1** to act something out using mime. **2** to pretend to sing or play a musical instrument while a recording is being played.

mimic *verb* (**mimics, mimicking, mimicked**) to imitate a person or their mannerisms, usually in order to make fun of them or make people laugh. ~ *noun* (*plural* **mimics**) somebody who mimics other people.

minaret *noun* (*plural* **minarets**) a tall thin tower on a mosque, from which Muslims are called to prayer.

mince *noun* meat that has been shredded into small pieces using a machine. ~ *verb* (**minces, mincing, minced**) **1** to shred meat into very small pieces. **2** to walk with short steps in an affected way. ✻ **not mince your words** to speak frankly. ➤ **mincer** *noun*.

mincemeat *noun* a sweet mixture of dried fruit, suet, and spices, used as a pie filling.

mind *noun* (*plural* **minds**) **1** your ability to think and reason: *She has a brilliant mind.* **2** your memories and thoughts: *I can't get that image out of my mind.* **3** an opinion: *He knows his own mind.* ~ *verb* (**minds, minding,**

minded) 1 to object to something or be annoyed about it: *I don't mind the noise; Do you mind if I don't come?* **2** to look after something or somebody: *Who's minding the baby?* **3** to be careful about something: *Mind you don't fall.* ✱ **bear/keep in mind** to think of or remember something when you are making a decision. **change your mind** to alter a decision or opinion. **I wouldn't mind** used to say that you would like to have or do something: *I wouldn't mind a cup of tea.* **on your mind** occupying your thoughts or worrying you.

mindful *adjective* keeping something in mind; aware of something.

mindless *adjective* **1** done for no reason and without thinking or caring about the consequences: *mindless violence.* **2** extremely boring: *a mindless task.* ➤ **mindlessly** *adverb.*

mine¹ *pronoun* the one or ones belonging to the person speaking or writing.

mine² *noun* (*plural* **mines**) **1** an area where coal or other minerals are dug out of the ground. **2** an explosive device, placed in the ground or sea, that explodes when something touches it. ~ *verb* (**mines, mining, mined**) **1** to get coal or other minerals by digging them out of the ground. **2** to put explosive mines in an area of land or sea.

minefield *noun* (*plural* **minefields**) **1** an area where explosive mines have been laid. **2** a situation full of awkward problems or hidden dangers.

miner *noun* (*plural* **miners**) a person who works in a mine.

mineral /mi ni rəl/ *noun* (*plural* **minerals**) **1** a useful substance that exists naturally in the earth, such as coal, stone, or petroleum. **2** a naturally occurring chemical substance in food that keeps you healthy: *vitamins and minerals.*

mineral water *noun* water that comes from a natural spring, or water that has been made fizzy with carbon dioxide.

minestrone /mi ni stroh ni/ *noun* a thick Italian soup containing vegetables and pasta.

mingle *verb* (**mingles, mingling, mingled**) **1** to become mixed together. **2** to move among a group of people and talk briefly to several of them.

mini *adjective* small of its kind; miniature.

miniature *adjective* much smaller than the usual size. ~ *noun* (*plural* **miniatures**) **1** an object or copy that is much smaller than the usual size. **2** a tiny portrait painted on ivory or metal. ➤ **miniaturist** *noun.*

minibus *noun* (*plural* **minibuses**) a small bus for about ten passengers.

MiniDisc *noun* (*plural* **MiniDiscs**) *trademark* a small CD for recording sound or computer information.

minim *noun* (*plural* **minims**) *Music* a musical note with the time value of two crotchets or half a semibreve.

minimal *adjective* very little, or as little as possible. ➤ **minimally** *adverb.*

minimize *or* **minimise** *verb* (**minimizes, minimizing, minimized** *or* **minimises**, etc) **1** to keep something at as low a level or extent as possible. **2** to describe something as much less important or serious than it really is.

minimum *noun* (*plural* **minimums**) the least possible quantity or value. ~ *adjective* least in amount or number.

minister *noun* (*plural* **ministers**) **1** a head of a government department. **2** a priest in a Protestant Christian church. ~ *verb* (**ministers, ministering, ministered**) (**minister to**) to give somebody assistance or care; to look after somebody. ➤ **ministerial** *adjective.*

ministry *noun* (*plural* **ministries**) **1** a government department headed by a minister. **2** the position or profession of a Protestant minister.

mink *noun* (*plural* **minks** *or* **mink**) a small mammal with a thick coat of soft fur.

minnow *noun* (*plural* **minnows** *or* **minnow**) a small dark-coloured freshwater fish.

minor *adjective* **1** not serious or dangerous: *minor injuries*. **2** small in importance or size: *minor changes*. **3** *Music* said about a musical scale: with semitones between the second and third, fifth and sixth, and sometimes seventh and eighth notes.
~ *noun* (*plural* **minors**) a person who is not old enough to be considered legally an adult.

minority *noun* (*plural* **minorities**) **1** the smaller of two groups of people that form a larger group. **2** a group of people in a society who belong to a different race, religion, or ethnic group to most people in that society.

minstrel *noun* (*plural* **minstrels**) a medieval singer, poet, or musician.

mint¹ *noun* (*plural* **mints**) **1** a plant with leaves that have a strong taste and smell, used as a flavouring. **2** a sweet flavoured with peppermint.
➤ **minty** *adjective*.

Word History Mint comes from Latin *mentha*. The plant was perhaps named after a beautiful Greek nymph *Minthe*, who according to legend was turned into a plant by the jealous wife of the god Pluto.

mint² *noun* (*plural* **mints**) **1** a place where coins or medals are made. **2** *informal* a large sum of money.
~ *verb* (**mints, minting, minted**) to make coins or medals by stamping metal. ✳ **in mint condition** new and in perfect condition.

Word History Mint comes from the Latin word *moneta*. The name *Moneta* (which means 'the one who gives warnings') was given to the Roman goddess Juno. The Romans made their coins in the temple of Juno Moneta, and so the word *moneta* came to mean 'a coin' or 'a mint'. The word *money* also comes from *moneta*.

minus *preposition* **1** reduced or subtracted by. **2** *informal* without: *I'm minus my phone today*. ~ *adjective* less than zero; negative. ~ *noun* (*plural* **minuses**) (*also* **minus sign**) the symbol (–) used to show subtraction or a negative quantity.

minuscule *adjective* very small.

Usage Note Notice that the spelling is *minu*scule, not *mini*scule which is a common error.

minute¹ /mi nit/ *noun* (*plural* **minutes**) **1** a unit of time equal to one sixtieth of an hour. **2** a unit for measuring angles, equal to one sixtieth of a degree. **3** *informal* a short space of time. **4** (**minutes**) the official record of what is said at a meeting.

minute² /mie newt/ *adjective* extremely small. ➤ **minutely** *adverb*.

minutiae /mie new shi ee/ *plural noun* very small details.

miracle *noun* (*plural* **miracles**) **1** an amazing supernatural happening that people believe is the work of God. **2** something amazingly fortunate that you are very pleased about.

miraculous *adjective* **1** amazing and supernatural and believed to be the work of God. **2** amazingly fortunate or excellent. ➤ **miraculously** *adverb*.

mirage /mi rahj/ *noun* (*plural* **mirages**) an optical illusion that appears as a pool of water or as the reflection of distant objects, caused by the reflection of rays of light by a layer of hot air.

mire *noun* (*plural* **mires**) **1** a swamp. **2** a very unpleasant situation that is difficult to escape from. ➤ **miry** *adjective*.

mirror *noun* (*plural* **mirrors**) a glass surface coated with a silvery substance, designed to reflect things. ~ *verb* (**mirrors, mirroring, mirrored**) to be the same as something else in a different place or situation.

mirth *noun* cheerful amusement. ➤ **mirthful** *adjective*.

misbehave *verb* (**misbehaves, misbehaving, misbehaved**) to behave badly. ➤ **misbehaviour** *noun*.

miscarriage *noun* (*plural* **miscarriages**) an occasion when a pregnant woman's womb abnormally forces the baby out when it is too small to survive, causing it to die. ✱ **miscarriage of justice** an occasion when a court of law makes a wrong decision, which means that justice is not done.

miscellaneous /mi si lay ni us/ *adjective* consisting of things of many different kinds.

mischief *noun* bad behaviour that annoys people or causes minor problems.

mischievous *adjective* causing mischief. ➤ **mischievously** *adverb*.

Usage Note Notice the spelling. This word does *not* end in -ious.

misconception *noun* (*plural* **misconceptions**) a wrong idea about something.

misconduct *noun* bad behaviour by somebody in a professional job or important position.

misdemeanour *noun* (*plural* **misdemeanours**) something bad that is not serious enough to be regarded as a crime.

miser *noun* (*plural* **misers**) a mean person who avoids spending money.

miserable *adjective* **1** extremely unhappy. **2** causing great discomfort or unhappiness: *miserable living conditions*. **3** depressingly inadequate: *The wages are miserable*. ➤ **miserably** *adverb*.

misery *noun* (*plural* **miseries**) **1** great unhappiness or discomfort. **2** *informal* a grumpy person.

misfire *verb* (**misfires, misfiring, misfired**) to fail to have the intended effect: *The joke misfired*.

misfit *noun* (*plural* **misfits**) a person who does not get on with others or is out of place in a particular situation.

misfortune *noun* (*plural* **misfortunes**) **1** bad luck. **2** an unfortunate incident or event.

misgiving *noun* (*plural* **misgivings**) a feeling of doubt or suspicion.

misguided *adjective* believing things that are not true.

mishap *noun* (*plural* **mishaps**) an unfortunate accident.

misinterpret *verb* (**misinterprets, misinterpreting, misinterpreted**) to understand something wrongly. ➤ **misinterpretation** *noun*.

misjudge *verb* (**misjudges, misjudging, misjudged**) to have a wrong opinion, especially an unfairly bad opinion, about something or somebody. ➤ **misjudgment** or **misjudgement** *noun*.

mislay *verb* (**mislays, mislaying, mislaid**) to lose something because you cannot remember where you put it.

mislead *verb* (**misleads, misleading, misled**) to make somebody believe something that is not true, whether intentionally or unintentionally. ➤ **misleading** *adjective*.

misnomer *noun* (*plural* **misnomers**) an unsuitable name for something or somebody.

misogynist /mi so ji nist/ *noun* (*plural* **misogynists**) a man who dislikes women. ➤ **mysogynistic** *adjective*, **mysogyny** *noun*.

misplace *verb* (**misplaces, misplacing, misplaced**) to put something in the wrong place.

misplaced *adjective* said about a feeling: inappropriate, usually because the person or thing it is directed at does not deserve it: *misplaced enthusiasm*.

misprint *noun* (*plural* **misprints**) a printing error.

misrepresent *verb* (**misrepresents, misrepresenting, misrepresented**) to give people a false impression of something. ➤ **misrepresentation** *noun*.

Miss *noun* **1** a title used for a girl or unmarried woman. **2** used as a term of address to a female schoolteacher.

miss *verb* (**misses, missing, missed**) **1** to fail to hit or catch something: *I swung the bat but missed the ball.* **2** to be sad because somebody is not with you or because you no longer have something: *He misses his sister.* **3** to fail to notice or see something: *You can't miss the statue – it's huge; I missed the first episode.* **4** (**miss out**) to leave something or somebody out. **5** to notice that something is no longer there: *I didn't miss my watch for several hours.* **6** to be too late to catch a bus, train, etc. ✳ **miss out on** to fail to experience something. ~ *noun* (*plural* **misses**) a failure to hit, catch, or achieve something.

missile *noun* (*plural* **missiles**) **1** an explosive weapon that propels itself through the air. **2** an object that somebody throws or fires.

missing *adjective* **1** absent or lost. **2** not confirmed as alive or dead.

mission *noun* (*plural* **missions**) **1** a specific task that a group of people are sent somewhere to carry out. **2** a group of people sent on a mission. **3** a journey made for military or scientific purposes. **4** a group of people who have gone to a foreign country to spread their religious faith.

missionary *noun* (*plural* **missionaries**) a member of a religious mission.

mist *noun* water in the form of tiny particles in the air or on a surface.

mistake *noun* (*plural* **mistakes**) **1** something wrong that you do or say. **2** a misunderstanding of something. ~ *verb* (**mistakes, mistaking, mistook, mistaken**) **1** to confuse one person or thing with another. **2** to misunderstand something.

mistaken *adjective* **1** based on wrong thinking; incorrect. **2** said about a person: believing something that is not true. ➤ **mistakenly** *adverb*.

Mister *noun* = MR.

mistletoe *noun* a shrub with thick leaves and waxy white berries that grows as a parasite on trees.

mistreat *verb* (**mistreats, mistreating, mistreated**) to treat a person or animal badly. ➤ **mistreatment** *noun*.

mistress *noun* (*plural* **mistresses**) **1** a woman who owns a dog or other pet. **2** a woman with whom a married man has a sexual relationship outside marriage.

mistrust *verb* (**mistrusts, mistrusting, mistrusted**) to have no trust in somebody or something. ~ *noun* a lack of trust. ➤ **mistrustful** *adjective*.

misty *adjective* (**mistier, mistiest**) **1** covered with mist or hidden by mist. **2** said about eyes: full of tears.

misunderstand *verb* (**misunderstands, misunderstanding, misunderstood**) to fail to understand something or somebody correctly. ➤ **misunderstanding** *noun*.

misuse /mis ewz/ *verb* (**misuses, misusing, misused**) to use something for a wrong or dishonest purpose.

~ /mis**ews**/ *noun* the use of something for a wrong or dishonest purpose.

mite *noun* (*plural* **mites**) **1** a tiny animal that is related to spiders and ticks. **2** a small child or animal that you feel pity for.

mitigate *verb* (**mitigates, mitigating, mitigated**) to make something less severe or intense. ➤ **mitigating** *adjective*, **mitigation** *noun*.

mitre /mie**ter**/ *noun* (*plural* **mitres**) **1** a tall pointed hat that a bishop wears. **2** a joint that forms a corner, made by joining two pieces of wood that have been cut at angles.

mitten *noun* (*plural* **mittens**) a glove that has one section for all four fingers and another for the thumb.

mix *verb* (**mixes, mixing, mixed**) **1** to combine things to form a single substance or unit. **2** to control the balance of various sounds during a musical recording. ~ *noun* (*plural* **mixes**) a mixture or combination. ✻ **mix up 1** to mistake one person or thing for another. **2** to make things untidy or disordered. **be/get mixed up in** to be involved in something unpleasant or criminal.

mixed *adjective* **1** combining things of different types: *a box of mixed biscuits*. **2** involving people of different sexes or races: *mixed classes*. **3** with some good parts and some bad parts: *The weather was a bit mixed*.

mixer *noun* (*plural* **mixers**) a device or machine for mixing substances.

mixture *noun* (*plural* **mixtures**) a combination or blend that you make by mixing things.

mix-up *noun* (*plural* **mix-ups**) *informal* an occasion when one thing is mistaken for another, or when the wrong thing is done.

ml *abbreviation* **1** mile or miles. **2** millilitre or millilitres.

mm *abbreviation* millimetre or millimetres.

mnemonic /ni mo nik/ *noun* (*plural* **mnemonics**) a word or rhyme that helps you to remember something.

moan *verb* (**moans, moaning, moaned**) **1** to make a long low sound because you are in pain or you are very upset. **2** *informal* to grumble. ~ *noun* (*plural* **moans**) **1** a long low sound of pain or grief. **2** *informal* a minor complaint.

moat *noun* (*plural* **moats**) a deep trench filled with water, round a castle or other fortified place.

mob *noun* (*plural* **mobs**) a large crowd of angry or violent people. ~ *verb* (**mobs, mobbing, mobbed**) to crowd round somebody and jostle them.

mobile *adjective* **1** designed to be moved or carried around. **2** said about a library, shop, etc: set up in a vehicle and travelling from place to place. ~ *noun* (*plural* **mobiles**) **1** a small portable phone that works using a cellular radio system. **2** a decoration with hanging parts that move when a baby plays with them or when the wind blows them. ➤ **mobility** *noun*.

mobilize *or* **mobilise** *verb* (**mobilizes, mobilizing, mobilized** *or* **mobilise**, etc) to get people together and get them ready to take action of some kind. ➤ **mobilization** *or* **mobilisation** *noun*.

moccasin *noun* (*plural* **moccasins**) a soft leather shoe.

mock *verb* (**mocks, mocking, mocked**) to say unkind things about somebody, or copy their behaviour in an unkind way, in order to make them look ridiculous. ~ *adjective* not real or honest: *a mock battle; mock sympathy*. ~ *noun* (*plural* **mocks**) a school examination used as practice.

mockery *noun* unkind things you say or do to make somebody look ridiculous. ✻ **make a mockery of something** to make something look foolish or pointless.

mode *noun* (*plural* **modes**) **1** a setting on a machine, or one of a series of functions that a machine performs. **2** a way of doing something.

model *noun* (*plural* **models**) **1** a small-scale replica of something. **2** a person who displays clothes by wearing them. **3** a person who poses for an artist or photographer. **4** a version of a manufactured product. ~ *verb* (**models, modelling, modelled**) **1** to design or produce something to be similar to something else. **2** to display clothes by wearing them.

modem *noun* (*plural* **modems**) *ICT* a device that connects a computer to a telephone line.

moderate /mo di rat/ *adjective* **1** average in quality, amount, or extent. **2** in favour of small or gradual political changes. ~ *noun* (*plural* **moderates**) a person who is in favour of small or gradual political changes. ~ /mo di rayt/ *verb* (**moderates, moderating, moderated**) to make something less extreme or violent. ➤ **moderately** *adverb*.

moderation *noun* behaviour that avoids extremes.

modern *adjective* **1** to do with the present time or the recent past. **2** involving the latest techniques or ideas. ➤ **modernity** *noun*.

modernize *or* **modernise** *verb* (**modernizes, modernizing, modernized** *or* **modernises,** etc) to make something modern. ➤ **modernization** *or* **modernisation** *noun*.

modest *adjective* **1** tending not to boast about your abilities or achievements. **2** fairly small in size or amount. ➤ **modestly** *adverb*, **modesty** *noun*.

modification *noun* (*plural* **modifications**) a small change that improves something.

modifier *noun* (*plural* **modifiers**) *English* a word that gives information about another word, for example 'horror' in *horror film*.

modify *verb* (**modifies, modifying, modified**) to make small changes in order to improve something.

modular *adjective* made up of separate parts.

module *noun* (*plural* **modules**) **1** a part of a course of study that deals with a specific topic. **2** any of several units that join together to make something.

mohair *noun* very soft wool made from the hair of the Angora goat.

moist *adjective* slightly wet; damp.

moisten *verb* (**moistens, moistening, moistened**) to make something moist.

moisture *noun* liquid in the form of tiny droplets.

molar *noun* (*plural* **molars**) any of the large square teeth at the back of your mouth.

mole[1] *noun* (*plural* **moles**) **1** a small furry burrowing mammal with tiny eyes. **2** a person in an organization who gives information to a rival or enemy; a spy.

mole[2] *noun* (*plural* **moles**) a dark raised spot on the skin.

mole[3] *noun* (*plural* **moles**) *Science* a unit used for measuring the amount of a substance, equal to the amount of the substance that contains the same number of atoms, molecules, etc as there are atoms in 12g of carbon.

molecule /mo li kewl/ *noun* (*plural* **molecules**) *Science* the smallest unit of a chemical compound, consisting of two or more atoms.

molehill *noun* (*plural* **molehills**) a small pile of soil thrown up by a burrowing mole.

molest *verb* (**molests, molesting, molested**) to touch somebody in a sexual way that they do not like or want. ➤ **molestation** *noun*, **molester** *noun*.

mollify *verb* (**mollifies, mollifying, mollified**) to make somebody less angry or hostile. ➤ **mollification** *noun*.

mollusc *noun* (*plural* **molluscs**) an animal such as a snail or squid that has a soft body and no spine.

molten *adjective* in a liquid state after being heated.

moment *noun* (*plural* **moments**) **1** a very short time. **2** a specific point in time: *The moment I saw him, I knew he'd lost the match.*

momentarily *adverb* for a short time only.

momentary *adjective* lasting a short time only.

momentous *adjective* having a great effect on what happens in the future.

momentum *noun* **1** *Science* the force that makes a moving object continue to move. **2** the fact that something is making more progress or becoming more successful.

monarch *noun* (*plural* **monarchs**) a king, queen, or other royal ruler. ➤ **monarchical** *adjective*.

monarchy *noun* (*plural* **monarchies**) **1** a country that has a monarch as head of state. **2** a country's royal family.

monastery *noun* (*plural* **monasteries**) a community of monks or the buildings they live and work in.

monastic *adjective* **1** to do with monks or nuns. **2** as simple or harsh as life in a monastery. ➤ **monasticism** *noun*.

Monday *noun* (*plural* **Mondays**) the first working day of the week, the day that follows Sunday.

monetary /mu ni ta ri/ *adjective* to do with money.

money *noun* **1** coins or paper currency used to pay for things. **2** wealth.

Word History The word *money* comes from Latin *moneta*. See MINT².

Mongol *noun* (*plural* **Mongols**) a member of certain peoples of Mongolia, northern China, and central Asia.

mongoose *noun* (*plural* **mongooses**) a furry African and Asian mammal that looks like a weasel and often attacks snakes.

mongrel /mung gril/ *noun* (*plural* **mongrels**) a dog whose parents were of different breeds.

monitor *noun* (*plural* **monitors**) **1** a pupil given the job of helping a teacher. **2** a person or machine that keeps a check on something. **3** *ICT* a screen on which computer information is displayed. ~ *verb* (**monitors, monitoring, monitored**) to keep a check on something.

monk *noun* (*plural* **monks**) a male member of a religious community living a simple life that follows strict rules.

monkey *noun* (*plural* **monkeys**) **1** a long-tailed furry animal that lives in trees in tropical countries. **2** *informal* a mischievous child.

monochrome *adjective* said about photographs or other images: reproduced in shades of black and white, or of a single colour. ➤ **monochromatic** *adjective*.

monocle *noun* (*plural* **monocles**) a single lens worn to correct eyesight in one eye only.

monogamy *noun* the practice of being married to one person at any time. ➤ **monogamous** *adjective*.

monogram *noun* (*plural* **monograms**) a design that consists of the interwoven initials of a name. ➤ **monogrammed** *adjective*.

monologue *noun* (*plural* **monologues**)

monopolize

Drama a long speech by an actor who is alone on the stage or screen.

monopolize *or* **monopolise** *verb* (**monopolizes, monopolizing, monopolized** *or* **monopolises**, etc) to use or keep something all for yourself, so that other people get none of it.

monopoly *noun* (*plural* **monopolies**) an industry or market that a single company controls because it is the only company that sells a particular thing.

monorail *noun* (*plural* **monorails**) a railway with trains that run on a single rail, often overhead.

monosyllabic *adjective* **1** *English* consisting of one syllable. **2** said about a person: not saying much. ➤ **monosyllable** *noun*.

monotone *noun* a tone of voice that is boring or depressing because it does not change.

monotonous *adjective* boring because it is always the same. ➤ **monotonously** *adverb*, **monotony** *noun*.

monoxide *noun* (*plural* **monoxides**) *Science* a chemical compound that contains one atom of oxygen.

monsoon *noun* (*plural* **monsoons**) **1** a season of very heavy rain in the summer in southeast Asia. **2** the wind that brings this rain.

monster *noun* (*plural* **monsters**) **1** a terrifying imaginary creature. **2** an exceptionally large thing of its kind. **3** an extremely cruel person.

monstrosity *noun* (*plural* **monstrosities**) a very big thing that is unpleasant to look at.

monstrous *adjective* **1** extremely big. **2** extremely unfair; outrageous. ➤ **monstrously** *adverb*, **monstrousness** *noun*.

montage /mon tah*zh*/ *noun* (*plural* **montages**) *Art* a picture made by combining or overlapping several separate pictures.

month *noun* (*plural* **months**) **1** each of the twelve named periods into which the year is divided. **2** a period of four weeks. **3** the interval between a date in one month and the same date in the following month.

monthly *adjective and adverb* occurring once every month.

monument *noun* (*plural* **monuments**) a large sculpture or other structure built to commemorate a person or event.

monumental *adjective* **1** very big in size or effect. **2** in the form of a monument. ➤ **monumentally** *adverb*.

moo *verb* (**moos, mooing, mooed**) to make the long low noise of a cow. ➤ **moo** *noun*.

mood *noun* (*plural* **moods**) **1** the way you are feeling: *a confident mood*. **2** a bout of bad temper: *He's been in a mood all day*.

moody *adjective* (**moodier, moodiest**) **1** not happy or hopeful. **2** tending to change your mood frequently; temperamental. ➤ **moodily** *adverb*, **moodiness** *noun*.

moon *noun* (*plural* **moons**) **1** (**the moon** *or* **the Moon**) a natural satellite that is the size of a small planet and goes round the earth. **2** a natural satellite of any planet.

moonlight *noun* light from the sun that is reflected by the moon at night. ➤ **moonlit** *adjective*.

moonlighting *noun* working secretly in a second job that you have not told the tax office about. ➤ **moonlighter** *noun*.

moor[1] *noun* (*plural* **moors**) an area of high open land where only small plants such as heather grow.

moor[2] *verb* (**moors, mooring, moored**) to tie a boat to the land when it is not being sailed.

mooring *noun* (*plural* **moorings**) a place where a boat is tied to the land.

moorland *noun* = MOOR¹.

moose *noun* (*plural* **moose**) a large North American deer related to the elk.

moot *verb* (**moots, mooting, mooted**) to suggest something so that people will discuss it. * **a moot point** something that people have different opinions about.

mop *noun* (*plural* **mops**) **1** an object for washing floors, consisting of a long handle with a head of absorbent strings or other material. **2** a mass of untidy hair. ~ *verb* (**mops, mopping, mopped**) **1** to clean a floor with a mop. **2** to soak up liquid with something absorbent.

mope *verb* (**mopes, moping, moped**) to behave in a sad or bored way. ➤ **mopy** *adjective*.

moped /moh ped/ *noun* (*plural* **mopeds**) a motorcycle with a very small engine.

moral *adjective* **1** to do with principles of right and wrong in human behaviour: *moral issues*. **2** tending to behave in an honest and fair way. ~ *noun* (*plural* **morals**) **1** (**morals**) standards of honest or fair behaviour. **2** a truth about life or behaviour that you learn from a story or experience. ➤ **morally** *adverb*.

morale /mo rahl/ *noun* the degree of enthusiasm and confidence that people in a group are feeling.

morality *noun* how honest or fair somebody's behaviour is.

morbid *adjective* showing an unnatural interest in death or other unpleasant things. ➤ **morbidly** *adverb*.

more *adjective* **1** greater in amount, number, or degree: *We need more chairs than that.* **2** additional: *Would you like more juice?* ~ *adverb* **1** as an additional amount: *There's not much more to do.* **2** to a greater degree, extent, or amount: *I'm more sad than angry.* **3** again: *once more.* **4** used with an adjective or adverb to form the comparative: *The film was more interesting than I imagined.* ~ *pronoun* **1** a greater amount or number: *There are only five people here. I expected more.* **2** an additional amount or number: *There are some sausages left – would you like more?* * **more or less** approximately.

moreover *adverb* in addition to what has been said.

morgue /mawg/ *noun* (*plural* **morgues**) a room or building in which dead bodies are kept before being buried or cremated.

Mormon *noun* (*plural* **Mormons**) a member of the Church of Jesus Christ of Latter-Day Saints, established in the USA in 1830. ➤ **Mormonism** *noun*.

morning *noun* (*plural* **mornings**) **1** the part of the day from when you wake up to lunchtime. **2** the part of the day from midnight to midday.

moron *noun* (*plural* **morons**) *informal* a stupid person. ➤ **moronic** *adjective*.

morose *adjective* depressed and bad-tempered. ➤ **morosely** *adverb*.

morphine *noun* a strong painkilling drug made from opium.

Morse or **Morse code** *noun* a signalling code in which letters are represented by combinations of short and long sounds or flashes of light.

morsel *noun* (*plural* **morsels**) a small piece of food.

mortal *adjective* **1** certain to die at some time in the future. **2** said about an injury: so severe that it causes death. ~ *noun* (*plural* **mortals**) a human being. ➤ **mortally** *adverb*.

mortality *noun* **1** the fact that people are certain to die at some time in the future. **2** the number of deaths: *a high mortality rate*.

mortar *noun* (*plural* **mortars**)

mortgage

1 a mixture of cement, lime, sand, and water used to join bricks.
2 a small artillery gun that fires shells over short distances.

mortgage *noun* (*plural* **mortgages**) a loan used to buy a house or other property. ~ *verb* (**mortgages, mortgaging, mortgaged**) to use your house or other property as security for a loan.

mortified *adjective* deeply ashamed or embarrassed. ➤ **mortifying** *adjective*.

mortise or **mortice** /maw tis/ *noun* (*plural* **mortises** or **mortices**) a specially shaped cavity cut into a piece of wood, into which a matching piece called a tenon is fitted to form a joint.

mortuary *noun* (*plural* **mortuaries**) a room or building in which dead bodies are kept before being buried or cremated.

mosaic *noun* (*plural* **mosaics**) a pattern or picture made from small pieces of glass or stone.

Moslem *noun* see MUSLIM.

mosque /mosk/ *noun* (*plural* **mosques**) a place of worship for Muslims.

mosquito /mo skee toh/ *noun* (*plural* **mosquitoes** or **mosquitos**) a small fly that sucks the blood of animals and humans and can transmit diseases in this way.

moss *noun* a plant that grows as a spongy green mass in grass, on stones, etc. ➤ **mossy** *adjective*.

most *adjective* greatest in amount, number, or degree: *Most people agreed with me.* ~ *adverb* **1** (*often* **the most**) to the greatest degree or extent: *The thing I like most about Spain is the hot weather.* **2** (*often* **the most**) used with an adjective or adverb to form the superlative: *He's the most annoying boy I know; Adam writes the most neatly.* **3** very: *Thank you for a most informative talk.* ~ *pronoun* the greatest amount or number: *Some people stayed but most left early.*

mostly *adverb* **1** mainly: *The soil is mostly sand.* **2** in most cases; usually: *In the evenings, we mostly watch TV.*

MOT *noun* (*plural* **MOTs**) a compulsory annual test of a vehicle to check that it is safe to drive and that is does not produce too much pollution.

motel *noun* (*plural* **motels**) a roadside hotel for motorists.

moth *noun* (*plural* **moths**) a flying insect that looks like a butterfly and is active at night.

mother *noun* (*plural* **mothers**) **1** a female parent. **2** a woman who brings up a child but is not the child's biological parent. ~ *verb* (**mothers, mothering, mothered**) to give somebody too much loving care and protection. ➤ **motherhood** *noun*.

mother-in-law *noun* (*plural* **mothers-in-law**) the mother of somebody's husband or wife.

motif /moh teef/ *noun* (*plural* **motifs**) a design or pattern.

motion *noun* (*plural* **motions**) **1** a way in which a person or thing moves. **2** a gesture: *He made a beckoning motion with his hand.* **3** a formal suggestion made for discussion at a meeting. ~ *verb* (**motions, motioning, motioned**) to make a gesture to show somebody where to go. ➤ **motionless** *adjective*.

motivate *verb* (**motivates, motivating, motivated**) **1** to influence somebody: *What motivated her to steal?* **2** to make somebody feel enthusiastic and determined to do well: *You need a teacher who can motivate young people.* ➤ **motivator** *noun*.

motivation *noun* (*plural* **motivations**) **1** something that influences somebody; a motive. **2** enthusiasm and determination to do well. ➤ **motivational** *adjective*.

motive *noun* (*plural* **motives**) a need or

desire that causes somebody to do something.

motley *adjective* made up of things or people of different types.

motor *noun* (*plural* **motors**)
1 a machine that produces movement. **2** (*used before a noun*) to do with cars or other vehicles: *the motor trade*.

motor bike *noun* (*plural* **motor bikes**) *informal* a motorcycle.

motorboat *or* **motor boat** *noun* (*plural* **motorboats** *or* **motor boats**) a small boat with an engine.

motorcade *noun* (*plural* **motorcades**) a procession of cars that includes the car that an important person is travelling in.

motorcycle *noun* (*plural* **motorcycles**) a two-wheeled motor vehicle.
➤ **motorcyclist** *noun*.

motorist *noun* (*plural* **motorists**) somebody who drives a car.

motorway *noun* (*plural* **motorways**) a major road designed for high-speed traffic, with separate carriageways that each have several lanes.

mottled *adjective* marked with spots or patches of a different colour.

motto *noun* (*plural* **mottoes** *or* **mottos**) a short phrase that expresses an organization's principles or beliefs.

mould[1] *noun* (*plural* **moulds**) a shaped container that you pour something liquid into so that it will take that shape when it becomes solid: *Pour the jelly into the mould and let it cool.*
~ *verb* **1** to shape something.
2 to influence how something or somebody develops.

mould[2] *noun* a growth of small fungi that forms on damp surfaces and decaying things.

moult *verb* (**moults, moulting, moulted**) said about birds or animals: to shed hair, feathers, or skin naturally.

mount[1] *verb* (**mounts, mounting,** **mounted**) **1** to go up something.
2 to get on a horse or bicycle in order to ride it. **3** to increase in amount or degree. **4** to organize an activity.
5 to fix a picture to a backing in order to display it. ~ *noun* (*plural* **mounts**)
1 a backing that a picture is fixed to for display. **2** a horse for riding.

mount[2] *noun* (*plural* **mounts**) a hill or mountain.

mountain *noun* (*plural* **mountains**)
1 a very large and very tall hill. **2** (*also in plural*) a vast amount or quantity: *a mountain of homework*.

mountaineer *noun* (*plural* **mountaineers**) a person who climbs mountains.
➤ **mountaineering** *noun*.

mountainous *adjective* containing many mountains.

mourn *verb* (**mourns, mourning, mourned**) **1** to feel or express great sadness because somebody has died.
2 to feel sad because something no longer exists or you no longer have it.
➤ **mourner** *noun*.

mournful *adjective* expressing great sadness. ➤ **mournfully** *adverb*.

mourning *noun* **1** great sadness that you feel because somebody has died.
2 black clothes worn by people who are mourning.

mouse *noun* (*plural* **mice**) **1** a small rodent with a pointed nose and a long thin tail. **2** (*plural also* **mouses**) *ICT* in computing, a small device that you move by hand to control the cursor on a VDU screen and carry out commands by clicking buttons.
3 a shy person.

mousse *noun* (*plural* **mousses**)
1 a sweet or savoury dish made with whipped egg whites. **2** a frothy cosmetic that holds hair in position.

moustache *noun* (*plural* **moustaches**) a band of hair growing above a man's upper lip.

mouth /mowth/ *noun* (*plural* **mouths** /mowthz/) **1** the opening on your face

mouthpiece | 418

that contains your teeth and tongue. **2** an opening or entrance: *the mouth of the cave*. **3** the place where a river enters a sea or lake. ~ /mow*th*/ *verb* (**mouths, mouthing, mouthed**) to form a word with your lips but without making a sound.

mouthpiece *noun* (*plural* **mouthpieces**) **1** a part of a musical instrument or a telephone that you put into or next to your mouth. **2** somebody who speaks on behalf of a person or organization.

movable *or* **moveable** *adjective* capable of being moved.

move *verb* (**moves, moving, moved**) **1** to go in a particular direction. **2** to change position, or put something in a different position: *I saw her lips move; Who's moved my keys?* **3** to change your home or place of work. **4** to affect somebody emotionally: *a film that can't fail to move you*. ~ *noun* (*plural* **moves**) **1** an act of moving; a movement. **2** a step taken to achieve something: *a wise move*. **3** a change of home or work. **4** the act of moving a piece in a game. * **get a move on** to hurry up. **move on** to change to a new location, job, etc. **move out** to leave your home. ➤ **mover** *noun*.

movement *noun* (*plural* **movements**) **1** the act or process of moving. **2** a particular way of moving. **3** (**movements**) a person's activities during a specified time. **4** an organization set up to achieve a particular objective. **5** *Music* a section of a long piece of classical music.

movie *noun* (*plural* **movies**) a cinema film.

moving *adjective* causing people to feel strong emotions. ➤ **movingly** *adverb*.

mow *verb* (**mows, mowing, mowed, mowed** *or* **mown**) to trim grass. * **mow down** to kill large numbers of people suddenly and violently. ➤ **mower** *noun*.

MP *abbreviation* Member of Parliament.

Mr *noun* a title used before a man's name.

Mrs *noun* a title used before a married woman's name.

MS *abbreviation* multiple sclerosis.

Ms *noun* a title used before the name of a woman, whether married or not.

MSP *abbreviation* Member of the Scottish Parliament.

Mt *abbreviation* Mount.

much *adjective and pronoun* **1** a large amount or extent. **2** used in questions about amount or extent: *How much do you want?* ~ *adverb* to a great degree or extent: *not much different*.

muck *noun* **1** dirt or any unpleasant substance. **2** manure. ~ *verb* (**mucks, mucking, mucked**) * **muck about/ around** *informal* to waste time or act in a silly way. **2** (**muck about/ around with**) to interfere with or spoil something. **muck up** *informal* to spoil something. ➤ **mucky** *adjective*.

mucous /mewkus/ *adjective* to do with mucus, or covered with mucus.

mucus /mewkus/ *noun* a thick slimy substance that lines your nose, throat, and similar parts of the body.

mud *noun* soft wet or sticky earth.

muddle *verb* (**muddles, muddling, muddled**) to get things confused or out of order. ~ *noun* a state of confusion. ➤ **muddled** *adjective*.

muddy *adjective* (**muddier, muddiest**) covered with mud.

muesli /moohzli *or* mewzli/ *noun* a breakfast food consisting of oats, dried fruit, and nuts.

muezzin /mooh e zin/ *noun* (*plural* **muezzins**) a mosque official who calls Muslims to prayer.

muffin *noun* (*plural* **muffins**) **1** a round flat bun that you eat toasted and buttered. **2** a small round cake.

muffled *adjective* said about a sound: partially blocked by something and therefore not clearly heard.

mug[1] *noun* (*plural* **mugs**) **1** a large drinking cup with a handle. **2** *informal* somebody's face or mouth. **3** *informal* a foolish or gullible person.

mug[2] *verb* (**mugs, mugging, mugged**) to attack and rob somebody in a public place. ➤ **mugger** *noun*.

muggy *adjective* (**muggier, muggiest**) said about the weather: unpleasantly warm and airless; close.

mule *noun* (*plural* **mules**) an animal that is the child of a female horse and a male donkey.

mull *verb* (**mulls, mulling, mulled**)
✻ **mull over** to think about something carefully for a long time.

mullah /mu la *or* moo la/ *noun* (*plural* **mullahs**) a Muslim teacher of, or expert in, Islamic law.

mullet *noun* (*plural* **mullets** *or* **mullet**) any of various types of edible fish.

multicoloured *adjective* having many colours.

multicultural *adjective* made up of people from several different cultures. ➤ **multiculturalism** *noun*.

multilateral *adjective* involving people from several groups or countries. ➤ **multilaterally** *adverb*.

multilingual *adjective* using or speaking several languages.

multimedia *adjective* ICT said of a computer system: capable of producing sounds and images and of processing data from a number of sources, for example CDs and DVDs.

multimillionaire *noun* (*plural* **multimillionaires**) a person with money and property of a value that amounts to several million pounds or dollars.

multinational *noun* (*plural* **multinationals**) a very large company that operates in several countries.

multiple *adjective* having several parts or types. ~ *noun* (*plural* **multiples**) *Maths* a number that can be divided exactly by another number; for example, eight is a multiple of two.

multiple-choice *adjective* said about an examination question: giving several choices from which the correct answer has to be chosen.

multiple sclerosis /mul ti pl skli roh sis/ *noun* a serious illness that causes gradual paralysis in several parts of the body, resulting from the hardening of tissue in the nerves of the brain and spinal cord.

multiplex *noun* (*plural* **multiplexes**) a cinema with several auditoriums.

multiplication *noun* *Maths* the process of multiplying.

multiplication sign *noun* (*plural* **multiplication signs**) *Maths* the symbol (x) used to show that quantities are to be multiplied together.

multiplication table *noun* (*plural* **multiplication tables**) *Maths* a list of the results of multiplying a number by various other numbers.

multiplicity *noun* a great number or variety.

multiply /mul ti plie/ *verb* (**multiplies, multiplying, multiplied**) **1** to increase in number. **2** *Maths* to add a number to itself a specified number of times to produce a larger number.

multiracial *adjective* involving people from several racial groups.

multitude *noun* a very large number or crowd.

mum *noun* (*plural* **mums**) *informal* your mother.

mumble *verb* (**mumbles, mumbling, mumbled**) to say something quietly or not clearly. ➤ **mumble** *noun*.

mummy[1] *noun* (*plural* **mummies**) *informal* your mother.

mummy[2] *noun* (*plural* **mummies**) a dead body embalmed and wrapped for

mumps *noun* a disease that causes the glands in the sides of the face to become very swollen.

munch *verb* (**munches, munching, munched**) to eat something slowly and noisily.

mundane *adjective* ordinary and unexciting.

municipal *adjective* to do with a town or district, or to do with a local council.

munitions *plural noun* military weapons, ammunition, and equipment.

mural *noun* (*plural* **murals**) *Art* a picture painted directly onto a wall.

murder *noun* (*plural* **murders**) the crime of intentionally killing a person. ~ *verb* (**murders, murdering, murdered**) to kill somebody unlawfully and intentionally. ➤ **murderer** *noun*.

murderous *adjective* intentionally causing death: *a murderous attack*.

murky *adjective* (**murkier, murkiest**) **1** dark and rather frightening. **2** said about water: cloudy or dirty.

murmur *noun* (*plural* **murmurs**) a sound that you can only just hear. ~ *verb* (**murmurs, murmuring, murmured**) to say something in a very soft voice.

muscle /mu sil/ *noun* (*plural* **muscles**) **1** a mass of tissue in your body that contracts and relaxes to make something, such as your arm or leg, move. **2** physical strength. ➤ **muscly** *adjective*.

muscular *adjective* **1** having well-developed muscles. **2** affecting your muscles.

muse *verb* (**muses, musing, mused**) **1** to think about something. **2** to say something thoughtfully.

museum *noun* (*plural* **museums**) a place where objects of historical or cultural interest are displayed.

mush *noun* a soft mass of a semiliquid substance. ➤ **mushy** *adjective*.

mushroom *noun* (*plural* **mushrooms**) a fungus with a short stem and a dome-shaped cap. ~ *verb* (**mushrooms, mushrooming, mushroomed**) to grow rapidly.

music *noun* **1** the sounds of voices and instruments that have rhythm, melody, or harmony. **2** the art of playing or writing music. **3** written or printed symbols that represent musical notes.

musical *adjective* **1** to do with music or musicians. **2** having the pleasant harmonious qualities of music. ~ *noun* (*plural* **musicals**) a film or play with songs and dances in it. ➤ **musically** *adverb*.

musician *noun* (*plural* **musicians**) somebody who plays music. ➤ **musicianship** *noun*.

musk *noun* a strong-smelling substance obtained from deer and used in perfume. ➤ **musky** *adjective*.

musket *noun* (*plural* **muskets**) a gun with a long barrel, used by soldiers in the past.

Muslim /mooz lim/ *or* **Moslem** /moz lim/ *noun* (*plural* **Muslims** *or* **Moslems**) a person whose religion is Islam. ➤ **Muslim** *or* **Moslem** *adjective*.

muslin *noun* a type of thin cotton fabric.

mussel *noun* (*plural* **mussels**) a type of shellfish with a bluish black shell that is round at one end and pointed at the other.

must *verb* **1** to have to do something: *You must stop at a red light.* **2** to be necessary: *The essay must be all your own work.* **3** to be probable: *They must have left by now.* ~ *noun* (*plural* **musts**) something that is essential.

mustard *noun* **1** a strong-tasting

yellow or brown paste made from the seeds of a plant of the cabbage family. **2** a brownish yellow colour.

muster *verb* (**musters, mustering, mustered**) **1** to force yourself to have a particular strong feeling or quality in order to deal with a situation: *as much determination as I could muster*. **2** to gather, or gather people together, for a purpose.

mustn't *contraction* must not.

musty *adjective* (**mustier, mustiest**) tasting or smelling of damp and decay.

mutant *noun* (*plural* **mutants**) an animal or organism that has developed in an unusual way and has a strange appearance.

mutate *verb* (**mutates, mutating, mutated**) to develop in an unusual way that results in a strange appearance.

mutation *noun* (*plural* **mutations**) **1** unusual physical development that results in a strange appearance. **2** an animal or organism that has developed in this way; a mutant.

mute *adjective* **1** saying nothing. **2** unable to speak. **3** said about an emotion: felt but not expressed: *mute sympathy*. ➤ **mutely** *adverb*.

muted *adjective* **1** said about a colour or sound: soft. **2** said about a response: unenthusiastic.

mutilate *verb* (**mutilates, mutilating, mutilated**) **1** to injure somebody severely. **2** to spoil or damage something badly. ➤ **mutilation** *noun*.

mutiny *noun* (*plural* **mutinies**) an organized revolt against people in authority. ~ *verb* (**mutinies, mutinying, mutinied**) to take part in a mutiny; to rebel.

mutter *verb* (**mutters, muttering, muttered**) **1** to say something under your breath. **2** to complain quietly; to grumble.

mutton *noun* meat from a sheep.

mutual *adjective* **1** felt by each of two people towards the other: *mutual respect*. **2** shared by two people: *a mutual interest*. ➤ **mutually** *adverb*.

muzzle *noun* (*plural* **muzzles**) **1** the jaws and nose of an animal. **2** a covering for the mouth of an animal. **3** the end of a gun barrel. ~ *verb* (**muzzles, muzzling, muzzled**) **1** to put a muzzle on an animal. **2** to prevent somebody from telling the truth or speaking openly.

my *adjective* belonging to the person speaking or writing.

mynah or **myna** or **mina** *noun* (*plural* **mynahs** or **mynas** or **minas**) an Asian bird that can imitate sounds of human speech.

myriad /miriad/ *adjective* very many; countless. ~ *noun* (*plural* **myriads**) a very large number of things.

myrrh /mer/ *noun* the fragrant resin of various African and Asian trees, used in perfumes and incense.

myself *pronoun* **1** used for saying that the person who does something is also the person who is affected by it: *I cut myself with that knife*. **2** used for emphasizing that you are referring to you: *I myself prefer hot chocolate*. ✱ **by myself** alone.

mysterious *adjective* difficult to understand or explain. ➤ **mysteriously** *adverb*.

mystery *noun* (*plural* **mysteries**) **1** something that is not easy to understand or explain. **2** somebody that you know very little about. **3** a book that deals with the investigation of a mysterious crime.

mystic *noun* (*plural* **mystics**) a person who spends a lot of time meditating or thinking about religious problems and ideas. ~ *adjective* = MYSTICAL.

mystical *adjective* **1** having a meaning that only people with special religious knowledge or experience can under-

mysticism

stand. **2** strange and mysterious. ➤ **mystically** *adverb*.

mysticism *noun* religious meditation or deep religious thought designed to give you direct knowledge of God.

mystify *verb* (**mystifies, mystifying, mystified**) to be impossible for you to understand or explain. ➤ **mystifying** *adjective*.

mystique /mi steek/ *noun* a special quality or importance that surrounds a person or thing.

myth *noun* (*plural* **myths**)
1 a traditional story involving gods and heroes that embodies popular beliefs or explains a natural phenomenon. **2** something false that many people believe to be true.

mythical *adjective* **1** to do with myths. **2** invented or imagined, not real or true.

mythology *noun* a collection of myths. ➤ **mythological** *adjective*.

N *abbreviation* North or Northern.

nab *verb* (**nabs, nabbing, nabbed**) *informal* to arrest somebody.

naff *adjective informal* not fashionable or stylish.

nag[1] *noun* (*plural* **nags**) a horse, especially one that is old or of poor quality.

nag[2] *verb* (**nags, nagging, nagged**) **1** to scold somebody continually, or keep on asking them to do something. **2** to be a continual source of annoyance or discomfort to somebody. ➤ **nag** *noun*, **nagging** *adjective*.

nail *noun* (*plural* **nails**) **1** a thin spike with a flat head, designed to be hammered into something. **2** a horny sheath protecting the upper end of each finger and toe. ~ *verb* (**nails, nailing, nailed**) **1** to fasten something with nails. **2** *informal* to detect or arrest a criminal, etc. ✶ **hit the nail on the head** to describe or explain something exactly.

nail-biting *adjective informal* causing tension and excitement.

naive or **naïve** /nie eev/ *adjective* showing a lack of knowledge about society and how people usually behave. ➤ **naively** or **naïvely** *adverb*, **naivety** or **naïvety** *noun*.

naked *adjective* **1** having no clothes on. **2** not covered or enclosed. **3** said about a feeling: shown openly; not disguised. ✶ **the naked eye** eyesight unaided by a magnifying glass, telescope, etc. ➤ **nakedness** *noun*.

name *noun* (*plural* **names**) **1** a word or phrase by which a person, place, or thing is known and referred to. **2** a famous or important person. **3** a person's reputation. ~ *verb* (**names, naming, named**) **1** to give a name to somebody or something. **2** to identify or mention somebody by name. **3** to appoint somebody to a position. **4** to specify a sum, date, etc. ✶ **call somebody names** to insult somebody. **in name only** officially, but not in reality. **name after** to give somebody or something the same name as somebody or something else.

nameless *adjective* **1** without a name. **2** not named, for example to avoid embarrassment.

namely *adverb* that is to say.

namesake *noun* (*plural* **namesakes**) somebody or something with the same name as the person or thing in question.

nan *noun* (*plural* **nans**) *informal* your grandmother.

nanny or **nannie** *noun* (*plural* **nannies**) a woman employed to look after children in their own home.

nanny goat *noun* (*plural* **nanny goats**) *informal* a female goat.

nap[1] *verb* (**naps, napping, napped**) to take a short sleep, especially during the day. ~ *noun* (*plural* **naps**) a short sleep. ✶ **catch somebody napping** to catch somebody unprepared.

nap[2] *noun* a hairy or downy surface on a woven fabric.

napalm /nay pahm/ *noun* petrol in jelly

nape

form, used in incendiary bombs and flamethrowers.

nape *noun* (*plural* **napes**) the back of the neck.

napkin *noun* (*plural* **napkins**)
1 a square piece of cloth or paper, used to wipe your lips or fingers and protect your clothes during a meal. **2** *formal* a baby's nappy.

nappy *noun* (*plural* **nappies**) a shaped pad of absorbent material or a square piece of towelling worn by babies to absorb their urine and faeces.

narcissism *noun* abnormal interest in yourself or your appearance. ➤ **narcissistic** *adjective*.

narcissus *noun* (*plural* **narcissi** /nah si sie/ *or* **narcissuses**) a daffodil with pale outer petals and an orange or bright yellow centre.

narcotic *noun* (*plural* **narcotics**)
1 a drug that causes drowsiness or unconsciousness. **2** an illegal or addictive drug that affects behaviour. ➤ **narcotic** *adjective*.

narrate *verb* (**narrates, narrating, narrated**) to tell a story or give a spoken account of something. ➤ **narration** *noun*, **narrator** *noun*.

narrative *noun* (*plural* **narratives**) something narrated; a story.

narrow *adjective* **1** small in width, especially in comparison with height or length. **2** limited in size or scope. **3** only just sufficient or successful: *a narrow majority; a narrow escape*. ~ *verb* (**narrows, narrowing, narrowed**)
1 to become narrower. **2** (*often* **narrow down**) to restrict the scope of, for example, research or an enquiry. ➤ **narrowly** *adverb*, **narrowness** *noun*.

narrow-minded *adjective* unwilling to accept new ways of thinking or tolerate other people's behaviour and views. ➤ **narrow-mindedness** *noun*.

NASA *abbreviation* N *American* National Aeronautics and Space Administration.

nasal /nay zl/ *adjective* **1** to do with the nose. **2** said about somebody's speech: with sounds produced through the nose. ➤ **nasally** *adverb*.

nasturtium /na ster shum/ *noun* (*plural* **nasturtiums**) a common garden plant with circular leaves and bright orange, red, or yellow flowers.

nasty *adjective* (**nastier, nastiest**)
1 unpleasant or disgusting. **2** said about people: spiteful, bad-tempered, or vicious. **3** harmful or dangerous. ➤ **nastily** *adverb*, **nastiness** *noun*.

natal /nay tl/ *adjective* to do with birth.

nation *noun* (*plural* **nations**)
1 a community of people who share the same origins, traditions, and language. **2** a people with its own territory and government; a country.

national *adjective* relating or belonging to a nation. ~ *noun* (*plural* **nationals**) a citizen of a specified nation: *French nationals*. ➤ **nationally** *adverb*.

national anthem *noun* (*plural* **national anthems**) a patriotic song officially adopted by a nation for use on ceremonial occasions.

national curriculum *noun* (**the national curriculum**) a set of subjects that must be taught in state schools in England and Wales.

National Insurance *noun* a compulsory scheme that insures citizens against sickness, retirement, and unemployment.

nationalism *noun* **1** devotion, or excessive devotion, to your nation. **2** the desire for political independence for your nation. ➤ **nationalist** *noun and adjective*, **nationalistic** *adjective*.

nationality *noun* (*plural* **nationalities**) the fact of belonging to a particular nation.

nationalize *or* **nationalise** *verb* (**nationalizes, nationalizing,**

nationalized or **nationalises**, etc) to transfer control of an industry to the state government. ➤ **nationalization** or **nationalisation** noun.

national park noun (plural **national parks**) an area of countryside, where the landscape and wildlife are protected by the government, that the public can visit.

national service noun a period of compulsory service in your country's armed forces.

nationwide adjective and adverb throughout the whole country.

native adjective **1** where you were born: *my native city*. **2** belonging to a particular place by birth. **3** said about an animal, plant etc: living or growing naturally in a particular region: *native to Antarctica*. **4** that you were born with; innate: *native intelligence*. ~ noun (plural **natives**) **1** a person born or reared in a particular place: *a native of Glasgow*. **2** dated, offensive an original inhabitant of a country colonized by Europeans.

Native American noun (plural **Native Americans**) a member of one of the peoples who inhabited North, South, or Central America before the arrival of European settlers.

nativity noun (**the Nativity**) the birth of Jesus.

NATO or **Nato** abbreviation North Atlantic Treaty Organization.

natter verb (**natters, nattering, nattered**) informal to chatter or gossip. ➤ **natter** noun.

natty adjective (**nattier, nattiest**) informal neat and stylish.

natural adjective **1** existing in nature, or produced by nature without human intervention. **2** normal; to be expected: *It's natural to feel upset.* **3** that you were born with: *a natural talent for languages.* **4** not affected or forced; easy and relaxed. **5** Music said about a note: neither sharp nor flat.

~ noun (plural **naturals**) **1** informal a person with natural skills, talents, or abilities. **2** Music a natural note, or a sign () indicating that a note is not sharp or flat. ➤ **naturally** adverb.

natural gas noun gas occurring naturally underground and used chiefly as a fuel.

natural history noun the study of plants and animals.

naturalist noun (plural **naturalists**) a person who studies animals and plants.

naturalize or **naturalise** verb (**naturalizes, naturalizing, naturalized** or **naturalises**, etc) **1** to make a foreigner a citizen of a country. **2** to establish a plant or animal in an area where it is not native.

natural selection noun Science a natural process of evolution that results in the survival of organisms best adapted to their environment.

nature noun (plural **natures**) **1** the physical world of landscape, plants, and animals, as distinct from human creations. **2** the essential character of a person or thing. **3** a kind or class of thing.

nature reserve noun (plural **nature reserves**) an officially protected area where there are interesting plants or animals.

nature trail noun (plural **nature trails**) a walk, for example in a nature reserve, that enables you to see interesting plants or animals.

naturism noun = NUDISM. ➤ **naturist** adjective and noun.

naughty adjective (**naughtier, naughtiest**) **1** said about a child: badly behaved; disobedient. **2** slightly rude or improper. ➤ **naughtiness** noun.

nausea /naw zi a/ noun a sick feeling in your stomach and an urge to vomit.

nauseate /naw zi ayt/ verb (**nauseates,**

nauseous

nauseating, nauseated) to make somebody feel sick. ➤ **nauseating** *adjective*, **nauseatingly** *adverb*.

nauseous /naw zi us/ *adjective* **1** feeling sick. **2** disgusting.

nautical *adjective* to do with sailors, sailing, or ships.

nautical mile *noun* (*plural* **nautical miles**) a unit for measuring distances travelled by ships and aircraft, equal to 1852 metres (about 6076.17 feet).

naval *adjective* to do with a navy.

nave *noun* (*plural* **naves**) the long central part of a church.

navel *noun* (*plural* **navels**) the depression in the middle of the abdomen marking the point where the umbilical cord was attached.

navigable *adjective* **1** suitable for ships to pass along. **2** *ICT* said about a website: containing hyperlinks for access to other information.

navigate *verb* (**navigates, navigating, navigated**) **1** to plan the course or route a ship, aircraft, or car. **2** *ICT* to explore the Internet using hyperlinks. ➤ **navigation** *noun*, **navigational** *adjective*, **navigator** *noun*.

navvy *noun* (*plural* **navvies**) an unskilled labourer.

navy *noun* (*plural* **navies**) **1** the branch of a country's armed services made up of warships and their crews. **2** = NAVY BLUE.

navy blue *noun* a deep dark blue colour.

nay *adverb* archaic no.

Nazi /nah tsi/ *noun* (*plural* **Nazis**) a member of the National Socialist German Workers' Party, which controlled Germany from 1933 to 1945. ➤ **Nazi** *adjective*, **Nazism** *noun*.

NB *abbreviation* = (Latin) *nota bene* note well.

NCO *noun* (*plural* **NCOs**) = NON-COMMISSIONED OFFICER.

NE *abbreviation* **1** northeast. **2** northeastern.

Neanderthal /nee an der tahl/ *noun* (*plural* **Neanderthals**) an extinct species of human being that inhabited Europe between 120,000 and 35,000 years ago.

near *adverb* **1** at or to only a short distance away. **2** almost: *with near-disastrous results.* ~ *preposition* a short distance or time from something. ~ *adjective* **1** close in place or time. **2** almost but not quite a particular thing: *a near disaster.* **3** closely related. ~ *verb* (**nears, nearing, neared**) to approach a place or point. ➤ **nearness** *noun*.

nearby *adverb and adjective* close to where you are.

nearly *adverb* almost but not quite.

nearside *noun* the side of a vehicle nearest the kerb.

nearsighted *adjective* able to see near things more clearly than distant ones.

neat *adjective* **1** tidy or orderly. **2** skilfully done. **3** said about an alcoholic drink: without anything added. **4** *N American, informal* excellent. ➤ **neatly** *adverb*, **neatness** *noun*.

neaten *verb* (**neatens, neatening, neatened**) to make something neat.

nebula *noun* (*plural* **nebulas** or **nebulae** /ne bew lee/) an immense cloud of gas or dust in space, visible as a bright patch in the night sky.

nebulous *adjective* said about ideas, etc: indistinct or vague.

necessarily *adverb* as a necessary result; inevitably.

necessary *adjective* **1** essential; indispensable. **2** inevitable; inescapable. ~ *noun* (*plural* **necessaries**) an indispensable item.

necessitate *verb* (**necessitates, necessitating, necessitated**) to make something necessary or unavoidable.

necessity *noun* (*plural* **necessities**) **1** the fact of being necessary: *She reminded us of the necessity of constant vigilance.* **2** pressing need or desire. **3** something indispensable.

neck *noun* (*plural* **necks**) **1** the part of a person or animal that connects the head with the body. **2** the part of a piece of clothing that fits around the neck. **3** a narrow extension on the end of something, such as a bottle. * **neck and neck** equal with one another in a race. **up to your neck in** deeply involved in something, such as business or trouble.

necklace *noun* (*plural* **necklaces**) a string of jewels, beads, etc worn round the neck as an ornament.

neckline *noun* (*plural* **necklines**) the upper edge of a garment that forms the opening for the neck and head.

nectar *noun* **1** a sweet liquid secreted by plants and made into honey by bees. **2** in ancient Greek and Roman mythology, the drink of the gods.

nectarine *noun* (*plural* **nectarines**) a type of peach with a smooth skin.

née *or* **nee** /nay/ *adjective* used to state a married woman's maiden name: *Mary Thomson, née Wilkinson.*

need *verb* (**needs, needing, needed**) **1** to have to have something or somebody in order to function, be complete, be happy, etc. **2** to be in a position where it is essential to do something: *We need to discuss this urgently.* **3** (*third person singular present tense* **need**) to be compelled or obliged to do something: *She need not decide straight away.* ~ *noun* (*plural* **needs**) **1** something you require. **2** a very strong feeling that you have to have or do something. **3** poverty; deprivation. * **there's no need to** it is not necessary to do something.

needle *noun* (*plural* **needles**) **1** a small, thin, pointed tool with a hole at one end for thread, used in sewing. **2** a thin rod used in crocheting or knitting. **3** the thin, hollow, pointed part of a hypodermic syringe. **4** an indicator on a dial or compass. **5** a stylus for playing records. **6** a needle-shaped leaf on a conifer. ~ *verb* (**needles, needling, needled**) *informal* to annoy somebody.

needless *adjective* not needed; unnecessary. * **needless to say** of course. ➤ **needlessly** *adverb*.

needlework *noun* sewing or embroidery.

needn't *contraction* need not.

needy *adjective* (**needier, neediest**) poor; deprived. ➤ **neediness** *noun*.

ne'er *adverb literary* never.

nefarious /nɪfairiəs/ *adjective formal* highly suspect or criminal.

negate *verb* (**negates, negating, negated**) **1** to make something ineffective or invalid. **2** to say that something is not the case. ➤ **negation** *noun*.

negative *adjective* **1** expressing 'no' or 'not'. **2** indicating the absence of something: *a negative test result*. **3** having an unfavourable or discouraging attitude. **4** *Maths* said about a number: less than zero. **5** *Science* having lower electric potential so that current flows towards it from the external circuit. ~ *noun* (*plural* **negatives**) **1** *English* in grammar, a word such as *no, not*, or *never*, or a statement that says that something is not the case. **2** a photographic image in which the light and dark parts are reversed. ➤ **negatively** *adverb*, **negativity** *noun*.

neglect *verb* (**neglects, neglecting, neglected**) **1** to fail to give a person, animal, or thing proper care and attention. **2** to fail to do something required of you: *He neglected to check whether the machine was switched off.* ~ *noun* **1** lack of proper care and

negligence

attention. **2** the act of neglecting something. ➤ **neglectful** *adjective*.

negligence *noun* **1** carelessness or forgetfulness. **2** in law, the offence of failing to take appropriate care, resulting in damage or harm. ➤ **negligent** *adjective*.

negligible *adjective* too slight or insignificant to be worth considering.

negotiable *adjective* capable of being changed or dealt with by discussion.

negotiate *verb* (**negotiates, negotiating, negotiated**) **1** to discuss a problem with other people in order to come to an agreement about it. **2** to achieve a settlement, etc by discussion. **3** to succeed in passing an obstacle. ➤ **negotiator** *noun*, **negotiation** *noun*.

Negro *noun* (*plural* **Negroes**) *offensive* a black person. ➤ **Negro** *adjective*.

neigh *verb* (**neighs, neighing, neighed**) to make the characteristic sound of a horse. ➤ **neigh** *noun*.

neighbour *noun* (*plural* **neighbours**) a person who lives next door to you, or very close to you.

neighbourhood *noun* (*plural* **neighbourhoods**) **1** the area surrounding your own home. **2** a particular area of a town.

neighbouring *adjective* situated next to or near a place.

neighbourly *adjective* kind, friendly, and helpful, as a good neighbour should be.

neither /nie*th*er *or* nee*th*er/ *adjective and pronoun* not the one or the other of two. ~ *conjunction* used before the first of two or more alternatives that are part of the same negative statement: *Neither Janet nor her sister is coming.* ~ *adverb* similarly not; also not: *'I can't understand it.' 'Neither can I'.*

neon *noun* *Science* a chemical element that is a gas that glows when electricity passes through it, used in fluorescent signs and lighting.

nephew *noun* (*plural* **nephews**) the son of your brother or sister.

nepotism *noun* favouritism shown to a relative.

Word History *Nepotism* comes from the Latin word *nepos*, meaning 'grandson' or 'nephew'. The word was first used to refer to the privileges and profitable positions given by some medieval popes to their 'nephews' (who were often actually their illegitimate sons).

nerd *or* **nurd** *noun* (*plural* **nerds** *or* **nurds**) *informal* a person who is obsessed with a technical subject, especially computing, and is often boring about it.

nerve *noun* (*plural* **nerves**) **1** a thread-like band of tissue that transmits sensations and messages to and from the brain. **2** courage and self-discipline. **3** *informal* cheek; audacity. **4** (**nerves**) feelings of nervousness or anxiety. ✱ **get on somebody's nerves** to annoy somebody.

nerve-racking *or* **nerve-wracking** *adjective* causing great tension and anxiety.

nervous *adjective* **1** to do with the nerves. **2** anxious or apprehensive. ➤ **nervously** *adverb*, **nervousness** *noun*.

nervous breakdown *noun* (*plural* **nervous breakdowns**) a state of depression and severe tiredness that prevents somebody from coping with their responsibilities.

nervous system *noun* (*plural* **nervous systems**) the brain, spinal cord, and nerves together forming a system for transmitting impulses to muscles, glands, etc.

nervy *adjective* (**nervier, nerviest**) suffering from nervousness or anxiety.

nest *noun* (*plural* **nests**) **1** a structure

built by a bird to lay eggs in and shelter its young. **2** a structure where other creatures, such as insects or mice, breed or shelter. **3** a set of things that fit one inside the other: *a nest of tables*. ~ *verb* (**nests, nesting, nested**) **1** said about birds, etc: to build or occupy a nest. **2** to fit a set of tables, etc one inside the other.

nest egg *noun* (*plural* **nest eggs**) an amount of money saved up.

nestle *verb* (**nestles, nestling, nestled**) to settle snugly or comfortably.

nestling *noun* (*plural* **nestlings**) a young bird that has not left the nest.

net[1] *noun* (*plural* **nets**) **1** a fabric made of threads, cords, etc, twisted or knotted together to leave square spaces in between. **2** a device made of net for catching fish, birds, or insects. **3** in tennis, badminton, etc, a net barrier that divides the court in half. **4** in football, hockey, etc, a goal. **5** (**the Net**) the Internet.

net[2] *adjective* **1** remaining after all deductions, for example for taxes. **2** excluding the weight of the packaging or container.

netball *noun* a game played between teams of seven players who try to score goals by tossing a ball through a high horizontal ring on a post.

nether *adjective formal* lower or under.

nettle *noun* (*plural* **nettles**) a plant with jagged leaves covered with stinging hairs. ✱ **grasp the nettle** to tackle a problem boldly.

network *noun* (*plural* **networks**) **1** a structure or pattern consisting of crisscrossing horizontal and vertical lines. **2** a system of linked railways, roads, etc. **3** a group of broadcasting stations presenting the same programmes. **4** *ICT* a set of computers or terminals linked to one another. **5** a group of people who maintain contact with each other and exchange information.

neural /new ral/ *adjective* to do with nerves or the nervous system.

neuralgia /new ral ja/ *noun* pain felt along a nerve, especially in your head or face.

neurology /new ro lo ji/ *noun* the study of the nervous system and diseases of the nerves. ➤ **neurological** *adjective*, **neurologist** *noun*.

neuron /new ron/ or **neurone** /new rohn/ *noun* (*plural* **neurons** or **neurones**) a specialized type of cell that transmits impulses through the nervous system.

neurosis /new roh sis/ *noun* (*plural* **neuroses**) a nervous disorder in which phobias, anxiety, and obsessions make normal life difficult.

neurotic /new ro tik/ *adjective* **1** caused by a neurosis. **2** said about a person: very sensitive or obsessive about something. ➤ **neurotic** *noun*, **neurotically** *adverb*.

neuter *adjective* **1** *English* said about nouns, etc: neither masculine nor feminine. **2** lacking sexual or reproductive organs. ~ *verb* (**neuters, neutering, neutered**) to remove the sex organs of an animal.

neutral *adjective* **1** said about a country or a person: not engaged on either side of a war, dispute, etc. **2** impartial or unbiased. **3** having no special or unusual characteristics. **4** coloured in a shade of beige or grey. **5** *Science* said about a chemical substance: neither acid nor alkaline. **6** *Science* said about an electric wire: neither positive nor negative; going to earth. ~ *noun* (*plural* **neutrals**) **1** a neutral person or state. **2** the gear position in a vehicle in which no gear is engaged. ➤ **neutrality** *noun*.

neutralize or **neutralise** *verb* (**neutralizes, neutralizing, neutralized** or **neutralises,** etc) to

neutron

counteract something by having the opposite effect. ➤ **neutralization** or **neutralisation** noun.

neutron noun (plural **neutrons**) Science a tiny particle with no electric charge, found in the nucleus of an atom.

never adverb **1** not ever; at no time. **2** used emphatically to mean 'not': *You're never going out in those old clothes, are you?*

nevermore adverb literary never again.

nevertheless adverb in spite of that; however.

new adjective **1** recently bought, made, built, invented, etc. **2** fresh; unfamiliar. **3** doing something for the first time. **4** replacing the previous one. ➤ **newness** noun.

newborn adjective just born.

newcomer noun (plural **newcomers**) **1** a recent arrival. **2** a beginner.

newfangled adjective modern and unnecessarily complicated or gimmicky.

newly adverb lately; recently.

newlywed noun (plural **newlyweds**) a recently married person.

new moon noun the phase of the moon when it first appears as a thin crescent.

news noun **1** information about something that has recently happened. **2** (**the news**) a broadcast report of recent events.

newsagent noun (plural **newsagents**) a person who sells newspapers and magazines.

newsflash noun (plural **newsflashes**) a brief broadcast that interrupts a programme to report an important item of news.

newsletter noun (plural **newsletters**) a publication containing news sent to members of a group, association, etc.

newspaper noun (plural **newspapers**) a daily or weekly publication containing news reports and articles.

newsworthy adjective interesting enough to be worth reporting.

newt noun (plural **newts**) a small amphibious animal with a long slender body and tail and short legs.

New Testament noun (**the New Testament**) the second part of the Christian Bible, containing the Gospels, Epistles, etc.

New World noun (**the New World**) North and South America.

New Year noun **1** the first day or days of a year. **2** the festive period around 31 December and 1 January.

next adjective **1** immediately beside something. **2** following straight after something in place, time, or order. ~ adverb **1** in the time, place, or position immediately following. **2** on the following occasion.

Usage Note When referring to days of the week, *next* usually refers to a day in the *following* week; so, for example, speaking on Monday 1st, 'next Wednesday' usually means Wednesday 10th, not Wednesday 3rd.

next door adverb and adjective in or to the next building, room, etc.

next of kin noun (plural **next of kin**) the person most closely related to you.

NHS abbreviation National Health Service.

nib noun (plural **nibs**) the pointed end of a pen, from which the ink flows.

nibble verb (**nibbles, nibbling, nibbled**) **1** to bite something cautiously or gently. **2** to eat or chew something in small bites. ➤ **nibble** noun.

nice adjective (**nicer, nicest**) **1** pleasant or agreeable. **2** said about a person: kind, considerate, or helpful. **3** subtle: *a nice distinction*. ➤ **nicely** adverb, **niceness** noun.

nicety /nie si ti/ noun (plural **niceties**) a subtle point or distinction.

niche /neesh or nich/ noun (plural

niches) **1** a recess in a wall. **2** a place or activity for which a person is best suited.

nick *noun* (*plural* **nicks**) **1** a small cut or notch. **2** (**the nick**) *informal* a prison or police station. ~ *verb* (**nicks, nicking, nicked**) **1** to make a nick in something. **2** *informal* to steal something. **3** *informal* to arrest somebody. ✻ **in good/bad nick** *informal* in good (or bad) condition. **in the nick of time** just before it would be too late.

nickel *noun* (*plural* **nickels**) **1** *Science* a chemical element that is a silver-white metal, used in coins and in alloys. **2** a US coin worth five cents.

nickname *noun* (*plural* **nicknames**) an informal or humorous name used in place of a proper name.

nicotine *noun* a poisonous chemical that occurs in tobacco.

niece *noun* (*plural* **nieces**) the daughter of your brother or sister.

nifty *adjective* (**niftier, niftiest**) *informal* **1** very good or effective. **2** quick or deft.

niggardly *adjective* grudgingly mean; miserly.

niggle *verb* (**niggles, niggling, niggled**) **1** to cause somebody slight but continual discomfort or anxiety. **2** to find fault constantly in a petty way. ➤ **niggle** *noun*.

nigh *adverb, adjective, and preposition archaic* near.

night *noun* (*plural* **nights**) **1** the period of darkness from dusk to dawn. **2** an evening characterized by a specified activity: *a karaoke night*.

nightcap *noun* (*plural* **nightcaps**) **1** formerly, a cloth cap worn in bed. **2** a drink taken at bedtime.

nightclub *noun* (*plural* **nightclubs**) a place of entertainment open at night, usually with a bar and a cabaret or disco.

nightdress *noun* (*plural* **nightdresses**) a woman's or girl's loose garment for sleeping in.

nightfall *noun* dusk.

nightie *or* **nighty** *noun* (*plural* **nighties**) *informal* a nightdress.

nightingale *noun* (*plural* **nightingales**) a small bird that sings very sweetly and is usually heard at night.

nightlife *noun* late-evening entertainment or social life.

nightly *adjective and adverb* happening every night.

nightmare *noun* (*plural* **nightmares**) **1** a frightening or distressing dream. **2** a very unpleasant or terrifying experience or situation. ➤ **nightmarish** *adjective*.

nil *noun* nothing; zero.

nimble *adjective* quick and light in movement. ➤ **nimbly** *adverb*.

nine *adjective and noun* (*plural* **nines**) the number 9. ➤ **ninth** *adjective and noun*.

nineteen *adjective and noun* (*plural* **nineteens**) the number 19. ➤ **nineteenth** *adjective and noun*.

ninety *adjective and noun* (*plural* **nineties**) **1** the number 90. **2** (**the nineties**) the numbers 90 to 99. ➤ **ninetieth** *adjective and noun*.

nip *verb* (**nips, nipping, nipped**) **1** to bite, squeeze, or pinch somebody sharply. **2** *informal* to go quickly or briefly. ~ *noun* (*plural* **nips**) **1** a sharp chill in the air. **2** a sharp squeeze, pinch, or bite. **3** a small drink of whisky, brandy, etc. ✻ **nip something in the bud** to stop something from growing or developing while it is still at an early stage.

nipper *noun* (*plural* **nippers**) **1** (**nippers**) pincers or pliers. **2** *informal* a child.

nipple *noun* (*plural* **nipples**) the small projecting part on a breast, from which milk is sucked.

nippy *adjective* (**nippier, nippiest**)

1 nimble and lively. **2** said about the weather: chilly.

nirvana /neer vah na/ *noun* in Hinduism and Buddhism, a final state of bliss and freedom from being reborn.

nit *noun* (*plural* **nits**) the egg of a louse.

nit-picking *noun* petty and often unjustified criticism.

nitrogen /nie troh jin/ *noun Science* a chemical element that is a gas that makes up about 78% of the atmosphere.

nitty-gritty *noun informal* (**the nitty-gritty**) the important basic details or realities.

no *interjection* used in answers expressing disagreement, denial, or refusal. ~ *adverb* not in any respect or degree: *no better than before.* ~ *adjective* **1** not any: *no smoking.* **2** not a: *He's no expert.* ~ *noun* (*plural* **noes** or **nos**) a negative reply or vote. * **no way** *informal* certainly not!

no. *abbreviation* number.

nobility *noun* (*plural* **nobilities**) **1** the quality of being noble. **2** the class of people who have aristocratic rank and titles.

noble *adjective* **1** having a title such as duke, earl, etc. **2** having or showing a good and generous character or high ideals. **3** imposing; stately. ~ *noun* (*plural* **nobles**) a person of noble rank or birth. ➤ **nobleman** *noun*, **noblewoman** *noun*, **nobly** *adverb*.

nobody *pronoun* no person. ~ *noun* (*plural* **nobodies**) a person of no importance.

nocturnal *adjective* occurring or active at night.

nocturne /nok tern/ *noun* (*plural* **nocturnes**) *Music, Art* a work of art dealing with evening or night, especially a dreamy composition for the piano.

nod *verb* (**nods, nodding, nodded**)
1 to make one or more short down-and-up movements with your head, especially as a sign of agreement or as a greeting. **2** to become drowsy or sleepy. ~ *noun* (*plural* **nods**) an act of nodding. **nod off** to fall asleep, especially unintentionally while in a sitting position.

node *noun* (*plural* **nodes**) *Science* the point where a leaf is attached to a stem.

nodule *noun* (*plural* **nodules**) any small hard rounded mass, for example of cells in the body.

noise *noun* (*plural* **noises**) **1** loud, confused, or unpleasant sounds. **2** a sound, especially if sudden or harsh. ➤ **noiseless** *adjective*, **noisy** *adjective*, **noisily** *adverb*, **noisiness** *noun*.

nomad *noun* (*plural* **nomads**) a member of a people that wander from place to place, for example to find grazing for their animals. ➤ **nomadic** *adjective*.

nom de plume /nom di ploohm/ *noun* (*plural* **noms de plume** /nom di ploohm/) a pseudonym under which an author writes.

nominal *adjective* **1** in name only, not actually: *The president is the nominal ruler, but the real power is held by the generals.* **2** said about a sum of money: very small. ➤ **nominally** *adverb*.

nominate *verb* (**nominates, nominating, nominated**) to recommend somebody for an appointment, award, etc. ➤ **nomination** *noun*, **nominee** *noun*.

nonagenarian *noun* (*plural* **nonagenarians**) a person between 90 and 99 years old.

nonchalant /non sha lant/ *adjective* giving the impression of being completely unconcerned or indifferent. ➤ **nonchalance** *noun*, **nonchalantly** *adverb*.

non-commissioned officer *noun* (*plural* **non-commissioned officers**) an officer in the armed forces who does not hold a commission, for example a sergeant, corporal, or lance corporal.

non-committal *adjective* giving no clear indication of attitude or feeling.

nonconformist *noun* (*plural* **nonconformists**) **1** a person who does not think or behave in the way that most people do. **2** (**Nonconformist**) a member of a Protestant church that was formed by separating from the Church of England. ➤ **Nonconformism** *noun*, **nonconformist** *adjective*, **nonconformity** *noun*.

nondescript *adjective* lacking distinctive or interesting qualities; dull.

none *pronoun* **1** not any. **2** *literary* nobody. ~ *adverb* not in the least; not at all: *They were none the worse for their adventure.*

nonentity *noun* (*plural* **nonentities**) somebody of little importance or interest.

nonetheless *or* **none the less** *adverb* nevertheless.

non-event *noun* (*plural* **non-events**) an event that turns out to be much duller or less important than expected.

non-existent *adjective* **1** not real. **2** totally absent.

non-fiction *noun* written works that are based on fact and deal with real people or events.

non-flammable *adjective* difficult or impossible to set alight.

non-metallic *adjective* not a metal.

no-nonsense *adjective* serious, businesslike, or straightforward.

nonplussed *adjective* puzzled or disconcerted.

nonsense *noun* **1** meaningless words or language. **2** frivolous or insolent behaviour. ➤ **nonsensical** *adjective*.

non-starter *noun* (*plural* **non-starters**) **1** somebody or something that is sure to fail. **2** a competitor, racehorse, etc that fails to take part in a race.

non-stop *adjective* **1** continuous. **2** said about a journey: with no intermediate stops. ➤ **non-stop** *adverb*.

noodles *plural noun* narrow flat ribbons of pasta made with egg.

nook *noun* (*plural* **nooks**) a small secluded place; a corner or recess. ✱ **every nook and cranny** everywhere possible.

noon *noun* twelve o'clock in the day; midday.

no one *or* **no-one** *pronoun* nobody.

noose *noun* (*plural* **nooses**) a loop with a running knot that tightens as the rope is pulled.

nor *adverb and conjugation* and not; neither.

Nordic *adjective* characteristic of Scandinavia, Finland, and Iceland and their peoples.

norm *noun* (*plural* **norms**) **1** (**the norm**) the average or usual level or situation. **2** a standard or model.

normal *adjective* **1** usual or typical. **2** natural and healthy. ➤ **normality** *noun*, **normally** *adverb*.

Norman *noun* (*plural* **Normans**) *History* a member of a people from Normandy in northern France, who conquered England in 1066. ➤ **Norman** *adjective*.

north *noun* **1** the direction in which a compass needle normally points. **2** regions or areas lying towards the north. ~ *adjective and adverb* **1** at or towards the north. **2** said about the wind: blowing from the north.

northeast *noun* **1** the direction midway between north and east. **2** regions or areas lying towards the northeast. ~ *adjective and adverb* **1** at or towards the northeast. **2** said about the wind: blowing from the northeast. ➤ **northeasterly** *adjective*, **northeastern** *adjective*.

northerly *adjective and adverb* **1** in a

northern northern position or direction. **2** said about the wind: blowing from the north.

northern *adjective* in or towards the north.

northerner *noun* (*plural* **northerners**) a person from the northern part of a country.

northward *adjective and adverb* towards the north; in a direction going north. ➤ **northwards** *adverb*.

northwest *noun* **1** the direction midway between north and west. **2** regions or areas lying towards the northwest. ~ *adjective and adverb* **1** at or towards the northwest. **2** said about the wind: blowing from the northwest. ➤ **northwesterly** *adjective*, **northwestern** *adjective*.

nose *noun* (*plural* **noses**) **1** the projecting part of the face above the mouth, used for breathing and smelling. **2** the front end of a vehicle. ~ *verb* (**noses, nosing, nosed**) **1** said about an animal: to push its nose into or against something. **2** said about a vehicle or driver: to move slowly forward. ✴ **keep your nose clean** *informal* to stay out of trouble. **keep your nose out of** *informal* not to interfere in somebody else's business. **look down your nose at** *informal* to show disdain for somebody or something. **nose about/around** to pry. **nose to tail** said about vehicles: in a long slowly-moving queue. **turn your nose up at** *informal* to refuse something disdainfully.

nose bag *noun* (*plural* **nose bags**) a bag for feeding a horse or other animal that covers its muzzle.

nosebleed *noun* (*plural* **nosebleeds**) an attack of bleeding from the nose.

nose dive *noun* (*plural* **nose dives**) **1** a downward nose-first plunge of an aircraft. **2** a sudden dramatic drop.

nosey *adjective* see NOSY.

nosh *noun* *informal* food; a meal.

nostalgia /no stal ja/ *noun* a wistful longing for the past. ➤ **nostalgic** *adjective*.

nostril *noun* (*plural* **nostrils**) either of the two external openings of the nose.

nosy *or* **nosey** *adjective* (**nosier, nosiest**) *informal* inquisitive; prying.

not *adverb* used to change the meaning of a word by denying that something is the case.

notable *adjective* worthy of notice; remarkable or distinguished. ~ *noun* (*plural* **notables**) an important or famous person. ➤ **notably** *adverb*.

notation *noun* a system of marks, signs, or symbols used in mathematics, music, choreography, etc.

notch *noun* (*plural* **notches**) **1** a V-shaped cut. **2** a degree or point on a scale. ~ *verb* (**notches, notching, notched**) to make a notch in something. ✴ **notch up** to score or achieve a success.

note *noun* (*plural* **notes**) **1** a short written record. **2** a brief comment or explanation. **3** a short informal letter. **4** a piece of paper money. **5** *Music* a sound with a definite pitch and length, or a written symbol for such a sound. **6** a feeling or element of something: *The discussions ended on an optimistic note.* ~ *verb* (**notes, noting, noted**) **1** to pay attention to something. **2** (*often* **note down**) to record information in writing. ✴ **of note 1** distinguished. **2** significant. **take note** to pay attention.

notebook *noun* (*plural* **notebooks**) **1** a book for notes. **2** *ICT* a small portable computer.

noted *adjective* well-known; famous.

notepaper *noun* paper for letter-writing.

noteworthy *adjective* worthy of attention.

nothing *pronoun and noun* (*plural* **nothings**) **1** not anything. **2** a thing of no importance. **3** the symbol o. * **for nothing 1** without pay or without paying. **2** to no purpose; without achieving anything. **nothing but** only.

notice *noun* (*plural* **notices**)
1 a placard or poster displaying information. **2** attention or observation: *It must have escaped my notice.* **3** advance warning. **4** formal notification of your intention to end an agreement, for example that you intend to leave your job or property you are renting. ~ *verb* (**notices, noticing, noticed**) to become aware of something or somebody. * **at short notice** with little or no warning. **take no notice of** to pay no attention to something.

noticeable *adjective* able to be seen or detected. ➤ **noticeably** *adverb*.

notice board *noun* (*plural* **notice boards**) a board on which notices may be displayed.

notify *verb* (**notifies, notifying, notified**) to let somebody know about something, especially officially. ➤ **notification** *noun*.

notion *noun* (*plural* **notions**)
1 a concept. **2** an idea or belief, especially a foolish or unlikely one.

notorious *adjective* well-known for something bad. ➤ **notoriety** *noun*, **notoriously** *adverb*.

notwithstanding *preposition* in spite of.

nougat /nooh gah/ *noun* (*plural* **nougats**) a sweet consisting of nuts or fruit pieces in a sugar paste.

nought *noun and pronoun* (*plural* **noughts**) **1** the symbol o; zero.
2 nothing.

noun *noun* (*plural* **nouns**) *English* a word that is the name of a person, thing, animal, quality, or state.

nourish *verb* (**nourishes, nourishing, nourished**) to provide a person, animal, or plant with the substances needed for healthy growth and development. ➤ **nourishing** *adjective*, **nourishment** *noun*.

novel[1] *noun* (*plural* **novels**) *English* an invented prose story of book length.

novel[2] *adjective* new and unlike anything previously known.

novelist *noun* (*plural* **novelists**) *English* a writer of novels.

novelty *noun* (*plural* **novelties**)
1 something new and unusual. **2** the quality of being novel. **3** a small ornament or toy.

November *noun* the eleventh month of the year.

novice *noun* (*plural* **novices**) **1** a person who is new or inexperienced in a job, etc; a beginner. **2** a person training to be a monk or nun.

now *adverb* **1** at the present time.
2 immediately. **3** in the light of recent developments. ~ *conjunction* (*often* **now that**) as a result of the fact that; since. * **now and again/then** occasionally.

nowadays *adverb* in these modern times.

nowhere *adverb and pronoun* not anywhere.

noxious *adjective* harmful to living things.

nozzle *noun* (*plural* **nozzles**) a projecting outlet for liquid or gas.

nuance /new ans/ *noun* (*plural* **nuances**) a subtle but noticeable variation in colour, meaning, or tone.

nub *noun* (**the nub**) the crucial element in a situation.

nubile /new biel/ *adjective* said about a girl: young and sexually attractive.

nuclear *adjective* **1** to do with a nucleus. **2** using the energy released when atomic nuclei are split or fused.

nucleus *noun* (*plural* **nuclei** /new k lee ie/ *or* **nucleuses**) **1** the central and main part of something, especially a group. **2** *Science* a specialized structure within a cell containing the chromo-

nude

somes. **3** *Science* the central part of an atom.

nude *adjective* not wearing clothes; naked. ~ *noun* (*plural* **nudes**) a painting or sculpture of a naked human figure. ➤ **nudity** *noun*.

nudge *verb* (**nudges, nudging, nudged**) **1** to poke somebody gently with your elbow, especially to draw their attention to something. **2** to push or move something gently in a certain direction. ➤ **nudge** *noun*.

nudism *noun* the practice of going naked as much as possible. ➤ **nudist** *noun*.

nugget *noun* (*plural* **nuggets**) a solid lump of a precious metal in its natural state.

nuisance *noun* (*plural* **nuisances**) an annoying person or thing.

null ✱ **null and void** having no force in law; invalid.

nullify *verb* (**nullifies, nullifying, nullified**) **1** to make something null and void. **2** to cancel something out. ➤ **nullification** *noun*.

numb *adjective* **1** not feeling anything, especially as a result of cold or an anaesthetic. **2** unable to feel emotion or react. ~ *verb* (**numbs, numbing, numbed**) **1** to make a person or a body part numb. **2** to reduce the sharpness of a pain. ➤ **numbly** *adverb*, **numbness** *noun*.

number *noun* (*plural* **numbers**)
1 a word, numeral, or other symbol used in counting or calculating.
2 a numeral or set of digits used to identify something. **3** a quantity or total. **4** (**a number of**) several.
5 a single issue of a periodical.
6 a song or a piece of pop or jazz music. ~ *verb* (**numbers, numbering, numbered**) **1** to amount to a total.
2 to give numbers to things in a series.
✱ **number among** to be included in, or regard a person or thing as being included in, a certain group. ➤ **numberless** *adjective*.

numberplate *noun* (*plural* **numberplates**) a rectangular plate on a vehicle showing its registration number.

numeral *noun* (*plural* **numerals**) a symbol that represents a number or zero.

numerate *adjective* able to use numbers for calculating. ➤ **numeracy** *noun*.

numerator *noun* (*plural* **numerators**) *Maths* the part of a fraction that is above the line.

numerical *adjective* to do with, or expressed in, numbers. ➤ **numerically** *adverb*.

numerous *adjective* many.

nun *noun* (*plural* **nuns**) a female member of a religious community who makes vows of chastity, poverty, and obedience.

nunnery *noun* (*plural* **nunneries**) a convent of nuns.

nuptial *adjective* to do with marriage.

nuptials *plural noun literary* a wedding.

nurd *noun* see NERD.

nurse *noun* (*plural* **nurses**) a person trained to care for the sick or injured. ~ *verb* **1** to look after a sick person. **2** to breastfeed a baby. **3** to hold or handle something carefully. **4** to have a feeling in your mind.

nursemaid *noun* (*plural* **nursemaids**) a girl or woman employed to look after children.

nursery *noun* (*plural* **nurseries**)
1 a children's bedroom or playroom.
2 a place where plants, trees, etc are grown for sale or transplanting.

nursery rhyme *noun* (*plural* **nursery rhymes**) a short traditional story in rhyme for children.

nursery school *noun* (*plural* **nursery schools**) a school for children aged usually from three to five.

nursing home *noun* (*plural* **nursing homes**) a small hospital or home, where care is provided for people who are old or ill.

nurture *verb* (**nurtures, nurturing, nurtured**) **1** to provide a person or plant with food, care, and the means for growth and development. **2** to encourage and develop an interest, talent, etc. ➤ **nurture** *noun*.

nut *noun* (*plural* **nuts**) **1** a dry fruit or seed consisting of a hard rind or shell and an often edible kernel. **2** a kernel of such a fruit. **3** a small metal block with a threaded central hole, which can be screwed onto a bolt. **4** *informal* a person's head. **5** *informal* an insane or eccentric person. ➤ **nutty** *adjective*.

nutcrackers *plural noun* a tool for cracking nuts or their shells.

nutmeg *noun* (*plural* **nutmegs**) the hard seed of an Indonesian tree, used as a spice.

nutrient /new tree int/ *noun* (*plural* **nutrients**) something that provides nourishment.

nutrition /new tri shn/ *noun* the process of taking in and using food.
➤ **nutritional** *adjective*, **nutritionist** *noun*.

nutritious /new tri shus/ *adjective* nourishing.

nuts *adjective informal* crazy; mad.

nutshell *noun* (*plural* **nutshells**) the hard outside covering of a nut. ✽ **in a nutshell** in very few words.

nuzzle *verb* (**nuzzles, nuzzling, nuzzled**) to rub your nose or face against something or somebody affectionately.

NVQ *abbreviation* National Vocational Qualification.

NW *abbreviation* **1** northwest. **2** northwestern.

nylon *noun* **1** a strong light man-made material, used especially in textiles and plastics. **2** (**nylons**) stockings made of nylon.

nymph *noun* (*plural* **nymphs**) **1** a female spirit in classical mythology. **2** *Science* an immature insect, especially the larva of a dragonfly.

oaf *noun* (*plural* **oafs**) a clumsy or rude person. ➤ **oafish** *adjective*.

oak *noun* (*plural* **oaks**) a tree with a tough hard wood, which produces acorns.

OAP *noun* (*plural* **OAPs**) = OLD AGE PENSIONER.

oar *noun* (*plural* **oars**) a long wooden pole with a broad blade at one end, used for rowing a boat. ➤ **oarsman** *noun*, **oarswoman** *noun*.

oasis /oh **ay** sis/ *noun* (*plural* **oases** /oh **ay** seez/) a fertile area with a source of water in a desert.

oath *noun* (*plural* **oaths**) **1** a form of words by which a person solemnly swears to do something, especially to tell the truth. **2** a swearword. ✶ **on/under oath** committed by a solemn promise to tell the truth.

oatmeal *noun* ground oats.

oats *plural noun* a cereal plant producing grain used to make porridge, etc and to feed livestock.

OBE *abbreviation* Officer of the Order of the British Empire.

obedient *adjective* willingly carrying out the commands of another person. ➤ **obedience** *noun*, **obediently** *adverb*.

obelisk *noun* (*plural* **obelisks**) a four-sided pillar that tapers towards the top.

obese /oh **bees**/ *adjective* very overweight. ➤ **obesity** *noun*.

obey *verb* (**obeys, obeying, obeyed**) to do what another person, the law, an order, etc commands you to do.

obituary *noun* (*plural* **obituaries**) a short biography of a person who has recently died that is printed in a newspaper, etc.

object /**ob** jikt/ *noun* (*plural* **objects**) **1** something that can be seen and touched. **2** something that is being considered or examined. **3** something or somebody that arouses an emotion or provokes a reaction. **4** a goal or purpose. **5** a noun following a preposition or representing the person or thing affected by the action of a verb, such as 'them' in *underneath them* and *we beat them*. ~ /ob **jekt**/ *verb* (**objects, objecting, objected**) to express dislike, disapproval, or opposition to something. ➤ **objector** *noun*.

objection *noun* (*plural* **objections**) a feeling or statement of dislike, disapproval, or opposition.

objectionable *adjective* unpleasant or offensive.

objective *adjective* **1** dealing with facts and not affected by personal feelings or prejudices. **2** existing outside the mind in the real world. ~ *noun* (*plural* **objectives**) a goal or aim. ➤ **objectively** *adverb*, **objectivity** *noun*.

objet d'art /ob **zhay** dah/ *noun* (*plural* **objets d'art** /ob **zhay** dah/) an article with artistic value.

obligation *noun* (*plural* **obligations**) **1** something a person is bound to do; a duty. **2** a state of owing somebody something in return for a service or favour they have done you.

obligatory /o bli ga to ri/ *adjective* compulsory; that has to be done.

oblige *verb* (**obliges, obliging, obliged**) **1** to compel somebody to do something. **2** to do a favour for somebody. * **obliged to** grateful or indebted to somebody.

obliging *adjective* eager to help. ➤ **obligingly** *adverb*.

oblique /o bleek/ *adjective* **1** sloping. **2** not straightforward or explicit; indirect: *She made some oblique references to her previous books.* ➤ **obliquely** *adverb*.

obliterate *verb* (**obliterates, obliterating, obliterated**) **1** to destroy all trace of something. **2** to make something illegible. ➤ **obliteration** *noun*.

oblivion *noun* **1** the state of being oblivious. **2** the state of being forgotten or no longer existing.

oblivious *adjective* (**oblivious of/to**) completely unaware of something.

oblong *noun* (*plural* **oblongs**) a rectangle with two longer parallel sides and two shorter ones. ➤ **oblong** *adjective*.

obnoxious *adjective* highly offensive or unpleasant.

oboe *noun* (*plural* **oboes**) *Music* a woodwind instrument with a double reed. ➤ **oboist** *noun*.

obscene /ob seen/ *adjective* **1** offending against accepted standards of sexual decency. **2** morally objectionable or indefensible. ➤ **obscenely** *adverb*, **obscenity** *noun*.

obscure *adjective* **1** hard to understand. **2** not well known. **3** difficult to see or identify. ~ *verb* (**obscures, obscuring, obscured**) **1** to prevent something or somebody from being seen, identified, or discovered. **2** to make something unclear. ➤ **obscurely** *adverb*, **obscurity** *noun*.

obsequious /ob see kwi us/ *adjective* excessively respectful and eager to serve or admire somebody; fawning. ➤ **obsequiously** *adverb*, **obsequiousness** *noun*.

observance *noun* compliance with a custom, rule, or law.

observant *adjective* **1** quick to notice. **2** paying close attention; watchful.

observation *noun* (*plural* **observations**) **1** the act of observing, especially watching something or somebody to gather information. **2** a piece of information obtained by observing. **3** a remark or comment.

observatory *noun* (*plural* **observatories**) a building containing equipment for observing the stars, weather, etc.

observe *verb* (**observes, observing, observed**) **1** to see or take note of somebody or something. **2** to keep a close watch on somebody or something. **3** to obey a law, the speed limit, etc. **4** to celebrate or carry out something in the traditional way. **5** to remark or comment. ➤ **observable** *adjective*, **observer** *noun*.

obsess *verb* (**obsesses, obsessing, obsessed**) to occupy somebody's mind intensely or excessively. ➤ **obsessed** *adjective*.

obsession *noun* (*plural* **obsessions**) **1** a persistent and usually excessive preoccupation with something or somebody. **2** something that occupies somebody's mind intensely or excessively. ➤ **obsessive** *adjective*, **obsessively** *adverb*.

obsolescent /ob so le sint/ *adjective* becoming obsolete.

obsolete *adjective* **1** no longer in use. **2** outmoded; old-fashioned.

obstacle *noun* (*plural* **obstacles**) something that hinders you or obstructs you.

obstetrics *noun* a branch of medicine dealing with the treatment of women during childbirth. ➤ **obstetric** *adjective*, **obstetrician** *noun*.

obstinate *adjective* **1** clinging stubbornly to an opinion, decision, or course of action. **2** not easily cured or removed. ➤ **obstinacy** *noun*, **obstinately** *adverb*.

obstreperous /ob stre pi rus/ *adjective* noisy and badly behaved.

obstruct *verb* (**obstructs, obstructing, obstructed**) **1** to block or close something with an obstacle. **2** to prevent somebody from making progress.

obstruction *noun* (*plural* **obstructions**) **1** something that obstructs. **2** the act of deliberately hindering or delaying somebody or something. ➤ **obstructive** *adjective*.

obtain *verb* (**obtains, obtaining, obtained**) to gain or be given something. ➤ **obtainable** *adjective*.

obtrusive *adjective* irritatingly noticeable. ➤ **obtrusively** *adverb*.

obtuse *adjective* **1** lacking sensitivity or mental alertness. **2** *Maths* said about an angle: greater than 90° but less than 180°.

obverse *noun* the side of a coin, medal, etc that shows the principal design and lettering.

obvious *adjective* **1** very easily perceived by the senses or understanding; clear. **2** lacking subtlety. ➤ **obviously** *adverb*.

occasion *noun* (*plural* **occasions**) **1** a time at which something happens. **2** a suitable opportunity. **3** *formal* a reason: *There was no occasion for you to speak to me like that.* **4** a special event or ceremony. ~ *verb* (**occasions, occasioning, occasioned**) *formal* to cause something. ✱ **on occasion** from time to time.

occasional *adjective* **1** happening not very often or not regularly. **2** acting in a specified capacity from time to time. ➤ **occasionally** *adverb*.

occult /o kult *or* o kult/ *noun* (**the occult**) **1** happenings in which supernatural forces are involved. **2** secret knowledge of the supernatural. ➤ **occult** *adjective*.

occupant *noun* (*plural* **occupants**) somebody who is living or staying in a particular building, room, etc. ➤ **occupancy** *noun*.

occupation *noun* (*plural* **occupations**) **1** a job or profession. **2** an activity or pastime. **3** the act of taking possession or control of a place, especially by a foreign military force.

occupational *adjective* to do with or resulting from a particular job or profession.

occupational therapy *noun* creative activity intended to help somebody who is ill or injured to recover.

occupy *verb* (**occupies, occupying, occupied**) **1** to live in or use a building. **2** to fill up an amount of space or time. **3** said about troops or demonstrators: to go into and take control of a place. **4** to be what somebody is thinking about or working on. ➤ **occupier** *noun*.

occur *verb* (**occurs, occurring, occurred**) **1** to happen. **2** to be found; to exist. ✱ **occur to** to come into somebody's mind.

occurrence *noun* (*plural* **occurrences**) **1** something that happens; an event. **2** the act of occurring.

ocean *noun* (*plural* **oceans**) *Geography* one of the large expanses of salt water that divide the continents on the earth's surface. ➤ **oceanic** *adjective*.

ocelot /o si lot/ *noun* (*plural* **ocelots**) a medium-sized wildcat from Central and South America with a dotted and striped coat.

o'clock *adverb* used in specifying the hour of the day when telling the time.

octagon *noun* (*plural* **octagons**) *Maths* a flat figure with eight angles and eight sides. ➤ **octagonal** *adjective*.

octave *noun* (*plural* **octaves**) *Music* an

interval of eight notes between a note and another note with the same name lying above or below it.

octet *noun* (*plural* **octets**) *Music* a group of eight instruments, voices, or performers, or a piece of music for such a group.

October *noun* the tenth month of the year.

octogenarian *noun* (*plural* **octogenarians**) a person between 80 and 89 years old.

octopus *noun* (*plural* **octopuses**) a sea creature with eight arms equipped with suckers.

ocular /o kew ler/ *adjective* to do with the eye.

oculist /o kew list/ *noun* (*plural* **oculists**) a person who treats diseases of the eyes or makes glasses.

odd *adjective* **1** different from the usual; strange. **2** left over when others are paired or grouped. **3** not matching. **4** *Maths* said about a number: not able to be divided by two without leaving a remainder. **5** occasional; spare: *at odd moments*. **6** approximately the specified number: *300-odd pages*. ✱ **odd man out** somebody or something that differs from all the others in a group. ➤ **oddly** *adverb*, **oddness** *noun*.

oddity *noun* (*plural* **oddities**) **1** an odd person, thing, or event. **2** strangeness.

oddments *plural noun* things left over; remnants.

odds *plural noun* **1** the ratio between the amount paid if you win a bet and the amount you bet, so that, at odds of 5 to 1, you win £5 if you bet £1. **2** (**the odds**) the probability of something happening. ✱ **at odds (with)** disagreeing or in conflict with somebody or something.

odds and ends *plural noun* various small items or remnants.

odds-on *adjective* **1** having a better than even chance of winning. **2** likely to succeed, happen, etc.

ode *noun* (*plural* **odes**) *English* a poem of medium length, often addressed to a particular person or thing or celebrating an event.

odious *adjective* hateful; horrible.

odour *noun* (*plural* **odours**) a scent or smell. ➤ **odorous** *adjective*, **odourless** *adjective*.

odyssey /o di see/ *noun* (*plural* **odysseys**) a long and wandering journey or quest.

oesophagus /ee so fa gus/ *noun* (*plural* **oesophagi** /ee so fa gie/) the tube leading from the back of the mouth to the stomach.

oestrogen /ee stro jin/ *noun* a hormone that stimulates the development of female sex characteristics.

of *preposition* **1** belonging or related to: *the leg of the chair*. **2** composed or made from: *a crown of gold*. **3** containing: *a cup of tea*. **4** from among: *one of us*. **5** possessing or characterized by: *a woman of courage*. **6** concerned with; about: *the story of the three bears*.

of course *adverb* **1** as might be expected. **2** used to express agreement or permission.

off *adverb* **1** so as not to be in contact or attached. **2** away in space or ahead in time: *far off*. **3** away from a course or direction. **4** into or in a state of where it is not operating or suspension: *switched off*. **5** away from work. ~ *preposition* **1** used to indicate separation or distance from: *off the ground*. **2** lying or turning aside from: *off the road*. **3** so as to become detached from. **4** not occupied in. **5** no longer interested in or using. ~ *adjective* **1** started on a journey or race. **2** cancelled. **3** no longer fresh; beginning to decay. **4** provided: *How are you off for socks?*

offal *noun* the inner organs of an

offbeat

animal used as food, including the heart, brains, tongue, liver, kidney, and intestines.

offbeat *adjective informal* unusual or unconventional.

off chance *noun* a remote possibility. * **on the off chance** just in case.

off-colour *adjective* unwell.

offcut *noun* (*plural* **offcuts**) a piece of fabric, wood, etc left after the required amount has been cut.

offence *noun* (*plural* **offences**) **1** an act that breaks a law, rule, etc; a crime. **2** a feeling of displeasure or resentment.

offend *verb* (**offends, offending, offended**) **1** to hurt or insult somebody. **2** to cause to somebody feel indignation or disgust. **3** to commit a crime. ➤ **offender** *noun*.

offensive *adjective* **1** causing indignation, outrage, or disgust. **2** designed for attack. ~ *noun* (*plural* **offensives**) a large-scale military attack. ➤ **offensively** *adverb*.

offer *verb* (**offers, offering, offered**) **1** to present something to somebody for them to accept, reject, or consider. **2** to make something available; to provide something. **3** to declare your willingness to do something. ~ *noun* (*plural* **offers**) **1** an expression of willingness to do or give something. **2** a sum that a buyer is willing to pay. **3** an article on sale at a reduced price. * **on offer 1** available. **2** for sale at a reduced price.

offering *noun* (*plural* **offerings**) something offered, especially a sacrifice or donation.

offhand *adjective* **1** rude or unfriendly. **2** casual. ~ *adverb* without thinking about it or getting more information: *I can't tell you offhand how many there are.*

office *noun* (*plural* **offices**) **1** a room in which administrative or clerical work is done. **2** a building where the business of an organization is carried out. **3** a position giving authority or having special responsibilities. **4** a government department. * **in** *or* **out of office** in (or not in) power as the government or a member of the government.

officer *noun* (*plural* **officers**) **1** somebody who has a position of authority in the armed forces. **2** a member of a police force. **3** somebody who holds a position with special duties or responsibilities, for example in a government or business.

official *adjective* **1** authorized or done by people in authority. **2** used or done as part of your job. **3** formal or ceremonial. ~ *noun* (*plural* **officials**) somebody who holds a position of authority, especially in national or local government. ➤ **officially** *adverb*.

officiate *verb* (**officiates, officiating, officiated**) to be in charge at a ceremony.

officious *adjective* tending to interfere in other people's affairs; bossy.

offing * **in the offing** likely to happen in the near future.

off-licence *noun* (*plural* **off-licences**) a shop that sells alcoholic drinks to be drunk somewhere else.

off-line *adverb and adjective ICT* not connected to the Internet.

off-putting *adjective informal* disagreeable, or causing you to lose your concentration.

offset *verb* (**offsets, offsetting, offset**) to balance or compensate for something: *Many companies offset their losses in one country with profits made in another country.*

offshoot *noun* (*plural* **offshoots**) something that develops out of something else.

offshore *adjective and adverb* **1** going away from the shore. **2** at a distance from the shore. **3** located or operating abroad.

offside *adverb and adjective* in a position ahead of other players where the rules forbid you to play the ball.

off side *noun* the side of a vehicle farthest from the kerb.

offspring *noun* (*plural* **offspring**) a person's child or an animal's baby.

offstage *adverb and adjective* not visible to the audience in a theatre.

often *adverb* **1** at many times. **2** in many cases.

ogle /oh gl/ *verb* (**ogles, ogling, ogled**) to stare at somebody in a way that shows you have a sexual interest in them.

ogre /oh ger/ *noun* (*plural* **ogres**) **1** a hideous giant in folklore. **2** a very fierce person.

ohm *noun* (*plural* **ohms**) *Science* a unit of electrical resistance.

oil *noun* (*plural* **oils**) **1** a smooth greasy liquid substance, obtained from plants or animals, that does not dissolve in water. **2** = PETROLEUM. **3** a substance made from petroleum, used for fuel, lubrication, etc. **4** = OIL PAINT. ~ *verb* (**oils, oiling, oiled**) to put oil on something, especially to make it run more smoothly.

oilfield *noun* (*plural* **oilfields**) an area where there are large amounts of oil under the ground.

oil paint *noun* (*plural* **oil paints**) artist's paint made of coloured material mixed with oil. ➤ **oil painting** *noun*.

oilskin *noun* (*plural* **oilskins**) **1** cloth treated with oil to make it waterproof. **2** a piece of clothing made of oilskin.

oily *adjective* (**oilier, oiliest**) **1** resembling or covered with oil. **2** too eager to please or flatter people. ➤ **oiliness** *noun*.

ointment *noun* (*plural* **ointments**) an oily cream used to heal or soothe the skin.

OK *or* **okay** *interjection* an expression of agreement or permission. ~ *adjective* **1** quite good, but not outstanding. **2** permissible; acceptable. **3** unharmed or in good health. ~ *adverb* quite well; adequately or satisfactorily. ~ *verb* (**OK's, OK'd, OK'ing** *or* **okays, okayed, okaying**) to give permission or approval for something.

Word History OK probably comes from the initial letters of the humorous 19th-century American spelling 'oll korrect' for *all correct*.

old *adjective* **1** having lived or existed for many years. **2** having lived or existed for a specified period of time: *twenty years old*. **3** dating from the past. **4** of long standing: *an old friend*. **5** former: *my old boss*.

old age *noun* the final stage of the normal life span.

old age pensioner *noun* (*plural* **old age pensioners**) a person who has retired from work and receives a pension.

olden *adjective literary* of a bygone era.

Old English *noun English* the earliest form of the English language, in use from 650 to 1150; Anglo-Saxon.

old-fashioned *adjective* no longer used or fashionable; outdated.

old hand *noun* (*plural* **old hands**) somebody with a lot of experience: *an old hand at hanging wallpaper*.

old maid *noun* (*plural* **old maids**) an elderly unmarried woman.

old master *noun* (*plural* **old masters**) *Art* **1** a distinguished European painter of the 16th to early 18th centuries. **2** a painting produced by an old master.

Old Testament *noun* (**the Old Testament**) the collection of writings forming the Jewish Scriptures and the first part of the Christian Bible.

old wives' tale *noun* (*plural* **old wives' tales**) a traditional superstitious notion.

Old World *noun* (**the Old World**) Europe, Asia, and Africa.

olfactory *adjective* to do with the sense of smell.

oligarchy /o li gah ki/ *noun* (*plural* **oligarchies**) **1** a state or organization in which a small group exercises control. **2** a small governing group. ➤ **oligarch** *noun*, **oligarchic** *adjective*.

olive *noun* (*plural* **olives**) **1** a small green or black fruit with a stone, used as a food and a source of oil. **2** the evergreen tree that bears this fruit. **3** (*also* **olive green**) a greyish green colour.

olive branch *noun* an offer to make peace.

Word History The notion of an olive branch as a symbol of peace comes from the Bible story in which Noah sends out a dove from the Ark. The dove returns with an olive branch in its beak, a sign that the flood has gone down and God is at peace with people once again.

Olympic Games *plural noun* (**the Olympic Games**) **1** (*also* **the Olympics**) an international sports meeting held once every four years in a different host country. **2** *History* an ancient Greek festival held every four years with athletic, literary, and musical contests.

ombudsman *noun* (*plural* **ombudsmen**) an official who investigates complaints against government or public bodies.

omelette *noun* (*plural* **omelettes**) a dish consisting of beaten eggs cooked in a shallow pan until solid.

omen *noun* (*plural* **omens**) an event believed to be a sign of something, especially something bad, that will happen in the future.

ominous *adjective* suggesting that disaster or evil will happen. ➤ **ominously** *adverb*.

omission *noun* (*plural* **omissions**) **1** the act of omitting. **2** something omitted. **3** failure to do something.

omit *verb* (**omits, omitting, omitted**) **1** to leave something out or not mention something. **2** to fail to do something.

omnibus *noun* (*plural* **omnibuses**) **1** a book containing reprints of a number of works originally published separately. **2** a television or radio programme containing of two or more episodes of a series, originally broadcast separately. **3** *formal, dated* a bus.

omnipotent /om ni po tint/ *adjective* having unlimited or very great power. ➤ **omnipotence** *noun*.

omniscient /om ni si int/ *adjective* knowing everything. ➤ **omniscience** *noun*.

omnivorous /om ni vo rus/ *adjective* feeding on all types of food. ➤ **omnivore** *noun*.

on *preposition* **1** in contact with something below; supported from below by something. **2** attached or fastened to something. **3** carried by somebody. **4** positioned at or towards: *on the left*. **5** with regard to; concerning. **6** belonging to a team, etc. **7** paid for by: *Dinner's on me*. **8** in the specified state, process, manner, etc: *on fire*. **9** using as transport. **10** regularly taking a drug. **11** indicating a time, especially a day of the week, when something happens. ~ *adverb* **1** being worn: *What did she have on?* **2** ahead or forwards in space or time: *further on*. **3** with the specified part forward: *head on*. **4** without interruption: *talked on and on*. **5** in or into operation: *switched on*. ~ *adjective* **1** taking place. **2** performing or broadcasting. **3** operating. **4** *informal* possible or practicable: *That's not on*.

once *adverb* **1** one time and no more.

2 at some indefinite time in the past; formerly. ~ *conjunction* as soon as. ✱ **at once 1** immediately. **2** simultaneously. **once again/more 1** now again as before: *Once again we find ourselves in difficulties.* **2** for one more time. **once in a while** occasionally. **once or twice** a few times.

oncoming *adjective* approaching from the front.

one *adjective* **1** single. **2** particular but unspecified: *early one morning.* **3** the same. **4** united. ~ *pronoun* **1** anybody at all: *One often hears such stories.* **2** I or we: *One does one's best.* **3** (*plural* **ones**) used to refer to a noun or noun phrase previously mentioned or understood: *a grey shirt and two red ones.* ~ *noun* (*plural* **ones**) the number 1. ✱ **one or two** a few.

one-liner *noun* (*plural* **one-liners**) a short funny remark.

one-off *adjective* occurring only once; unique. ➤ **one-off** *noun*.

onerous /oh ni rus/ *adjective* requiring a lot of effort; difficult to manage. ➤ **onerousness** *noun*.

oneself *pronoun* **1** used as the object of a verb when *one* is the subject and the action of the verb affects the subject: *One could kick oneself sometimes.* **2** used to emphasize 'one': *One could not oneself have written a book like this.* ✱ **by oneself** alone.

ongoing *adjective* **1** actually in progress. **2** growing or developing.

onion *noun* (*plural* **onions**) a strong-tasting edible bulb that is used as a vegetable.

on-line *adverb and adjective* connected to the Internet.

onlooker *noun* (*plural* **onlookers**) a person who watches something happen without being involved in it.

only *adjective* **1** alone of its kind; sole. **2** without a brother or sister: *an only child.* ~ *adverb* **1** nothing more than; merely. **2** solely or exclusively. ~ *conjunction informal* **1** but or however: *I want a car like that, only red rather than blue.* **2** if it were not for the fact that: *I would come, only I've got to finish this essay.*

onomatopoeia /o noh ma toh **pee** a/ *noun English* the use of words intended to imitate the sound of something, such as *buzz* or *moo*. ➤ **onomatopoeic** *adjective*.

onset *noun* a time or point at which something begins.

onshore *adjective and adverb* **1** towards the shore. **2** on or near the shore.

onside *adverb and adjective* in a position permitted by the rules of the game; not offside.

onslaught /on slawt/ *noun* (*plural* **onslaughts**) a fierce attack.

onstage *adjective and adverb* on or onto the stage; in view of the audience.

onto or **on to** *preposition* to a position on something. ✱ **be onto somebody** *informal* to know about somebody or know what they are doing.

onus /oh nus/ ✱ **the onus is on you** it is your duty or responsibility to do something.

onward *adjective* directed or moving forwards. ~ *adverb* = ONWARDS.

onwards *adverb* towards a point ahead in space or time.

onyx /o niks/ *noun* a gemstone with layers of different colours.

ooze *verb* (**oozes, oozing, oozed**) said about a liquid: to flow or come out of something slowly.

opacity *noun* the state of being opaque.

opal *noun* (*plural* **opals**) a milky-coloured gemstone that seems to have other colours shimmering inside it.

opaque /oh **payk**/ *adjective* **1** not able to be seen through. **2** hard to understand.

open *adjective* **1** allowing people or

things to pass through; not shut or locked. **2** not fastened or sealed. **3** not covered or protected. **4** not enclosed or built on: *open fields*. **5** spread out or unfolded. **6** ready for business. **7** not disguised, concealed, or kept secret. **8** not finally decided or settled: *an open question*. **9** candid or frank. **10** not prejudiced: *an open mind*. **11** not restricted to particular people. ~ *verb* (**opens, opening, opened**) **1** to become open, or to make something open. **2** to unfold or spread out. **3** to start operating for business. **4** to begin. **5** to perform a ceremony to declare a building, an exhibition, a fete, etc to be ready for business or visitors. ✶ **in the open 1** (*also* **in the open air**) outdoors. **2** no longer secret, or not in secret. **open to 1** willing to receive and consider. **2** likely to be subjected to something bad, such as criticism. ➤ **opener** *noun*, **openly** *adverb*, **openness** *noun*.

opencast *adjective* said about a mine or mining: in which a mineral is reached by digging away the earth that covers it rather than by tunnelling into the ground.

opening *noun* (*plural* **openings**) **1** a space through which something can pass; a gap. **2** a beginning or first part. **3** a ceremony indicating that a building, exhibition, fete, etc can now be visited by the public. **4** *Drama* a first performance. **5** a job opportunity; a vacancy. ~ *adjective* coming at or marking the beginning of something.

open-minded *adjective* willing to consider new arguments or ideas; not prejudiced. ➤ **open-mindedness** *noun*.

opera[1] *noun* (*plural* **operas**) *Music* a drama in which all or most of the words are set to music and sung. ➤ **operatic** *adjective*.

opera[2] *noun* a plural of OPUS.

operate *verb* (**operates, operating, operated**) **1** said about a machine: to work. **2** to direct the work done by a machine. **3** to carry out trade, business, or a military action. **4** to perform surgery on somebody.

operating system *noun* (*plural* **operating systems**) *ICT* the software that controls of the basic running of a computer.

operation *noun* (*plural* **operations**) **1** the act of operating. **2** a planned action or series of actions carried out by, for example, military forces. **3** a surgical procedure carried out on a living body with special instruments. **4** *ICT* a single step performed by a computer in executing a program. **5** a business organization. ✶ **in operation** working; in force. ➤ **operational** *adjective*.

operative *adjective* **1** in force or operation. **2** significant or relevant. **3** to do with surgical operations. ~ *noun* (*plural* **operatives**) a worker.

operator *noun* (*plural* **operators**) **1** somebody who operates a machine. **2** somebody who works a telephone switchboard.

operetta *noun* (*plural* **operettas**) *Music* a less formal or serious form of opera, usually on a romantic or humorous theme, in which some of the words are spoken, not sung.

ophthalmic /of**thal**mik/ *adjective* to do with the eyes and diseases of the eyes. ➤ **ophthalmology** *noun*, **ophthalmologist** *noun*.

opinion *noun* (*plural* **opinions**) **1** a view or judgment about a particular matter. **2** a belief that is not supported by definite knowledge.

opinionated *adjective* having strong opinions and always ready to express them.

opinion poll *noun* (*plural* **opinion polls**) a survey in which a selected number of people are questioned to find out what public opinion is on some matter.

opium *noun* an addictive drug from the juice of poppy seeds.

opponent *noun* (*plural* **opponents**) **1** somebody whom you are playing or competing against. **2** somebody who opposes a plan or proposal.

opportune *adjective* **1** suitable for a particular occurrence or action. **2** occurring at an appropriate time. ➤ **opportunely** *adverb*.

opportunist *noun* (*plural* **opportunists**) somebody who takes advantage of opportunities with little regard for principles. ➤ **opportunism** *noun*, **opportunistic** *adjective*.

opportunity *noun* (*plural* **opportunities**) **1** a situation that enables you to do something. **2** a chance to improve your situation.

oppose *verb* (**opposes, opposing, opposed**) **1** to fight or argue against somebody or something. **2** to contrast something with something else. ✶ **as opposed to** in contrast to. ➤ **opposing** *adjective*.

opposite *adjective* **1** positioned at a distance from and facing somebody or something else, often on the other side of something: *on opposite sides of the road*. **2** totally different; contrary: *going in opposite directions*. ~ *preposition* **1** across from and usually facing something or somebody. **2** *Drama* acting in the same play or film as somebody. ~ *adverb* on or to an opposite side. ~ *noun* (*plural* **opposites**) something that is totally different from or the reverse of something.

opposition *noun* **1** hostility or resistance: *opposition to the new road*. **2** a group of people opposing something. **3** (**the Opposition**) the main political party opposing the party in power.

oppress *verb* (**oppresses, oppressing, oppressed**) **1** to treat people in a harsh or authoritarian manner. **2** to make somebody feel weighed down with worry. ➤ **oppression** *noun*, **oppressor** *noun*.

oppressive *adjective* **1** unreasonably harsh or severe. **2** causing a person to feel weighed down or trapped. **3** said about the weather: very hot and windless; close. ➤ **oppressively** *adverb*.

opt *verb* (**opts, opting, opted**) to make a choice to do something. ✶ **opt out** to choose not to take part in something.

optic *adjective* to do with eyesight or the eyes.

optical *adjective* to do with optics, vision, or light.

optical illusion *noun* (*plural* **optical illusions**) something that makes observers believe they are seeing something that they are not actually seeing.

optician *noun* (*plural* **opticians**) somebody who examines eyes and prescribes glasses or contact lenses to cure eye defects.

optics *noun Science* the science concerned with the nature, properties, and uses of light.

optimal *adjective* most satisfactory. ➤ **optimally** *adverb*.

optimism *noun* a tendency to see the good side of situations and to be hopeful about the future. ➤ **optimist** *noun*, **optimistic** *adjective*, **optimistically** *adverb*.

optimum *adjective* most favourable; best. ~ *noun* (*plural* **optima** *or* **optimums**) the most favourable or best condition.

option *noun* (*plural* **options**) **1** an alternative course of action; a choice. **2** the right to choose.

optional *adjective* available as a choice; not compulsory. ➤ **optionally** *adverb*.

opulent *adjective* rich or luxurious. ➤ **opulence** *noun*, **opulently** *adverb*.

opus *noun* (*plural* **opera** or **opuses**) *Music* a composition or set of compositions, usually given a number.

or *conjunction* used to join two or more alternatives.

oracle *noun* (*plural* **oracles**) *History* a priest or priestess of ancient Greece or Rome who gave answers, which were thought to come from a god, to questions about the future.

oral *adjective* **1** involving speech rather than writing. **2** to do with the mouth. ~ *noun* (*plural* **orals**) an examination in which you give spoken answers. ➤ **orally** *adverb*.

orange *noun* (*plural* **oranges**) **1** a round citrus fruit with a reddish yellow rind and sweet juicy edible pulp. **2** a colour between red and yellow, the usual colour of the rind of an orange.

orangeade *noun* (*plural* **orangeades**) a fizzy soft drink flavoured with oranges.

orang-utan or **orang-utang** *noun* (*plural* **orang-utans** or **orang-utangs**) an ape with orange-brown skin and hair and very long arms.

orator *noun* (*plural* **orators**) a skilled public speaker.

oratorio *noun* (*plural* **oratorios**) *Music* a large-scale choral work usually with an orchestral accompaniment and based on a religious subject.

oratory *noun* **1** the art of public speaking. **2** impressive or eloquent speech. ➤ **oratorical** *adjective*.

orb *noun* (*plural* **orbs**) **1** a golden globe with a cross on top, symbolizing royal power. **2** a spherical object.

orbit *noun* (*plural* **orbits**) **1** *Science* a regular path followed by a planet, moon, spacecraft, or satellite around an object in space. **2** an area within which somebody is active or has influence. ~ *verb* (**orbits, orbiting, orbited**) to revolve in an orbit round something.

orchard *noun* (*plural* **orchards**) an area in which fruit trees are planted.

orchestra *noun* (*plural* **orchestras**) *Music* a large group of musicians playing together. ➤ **orchestral** *adjective*.

orchestrate *verb* (**orchestrates, orchestrating, orchestrated**) **1** *Music* to arrange a piece for an orchestra. **2** to arrange something cleverly to achieve the result you want. ➤ **orchestration** *noun*.

orchid *noun* (*plural* **orchids**) a plant that has colourful flowers with an enlarged lip-like middle petal.

ordain *verb* (**ordains, ordaining, ordained**) **1** to make somebody a priest, minister, or elder. **2** to order something by a decree or law.

ordeal *noun* (*plural* **ordeals**) a very unpleasant or testing experience.

order *noun* (*plural* **orders**) **1** a command. **2** a request for goods to be supplied, food to be served, etc. **3** correct or tidy arrangement of things. **4** an arrangement of objects, people, etc in a particular sequence: *in numerical order*. **5** a proper or working condition. **6** the rule of law or proper authority. **7** *Science* a category or kind, especially a classification of living things ranking above a family. **8** a religious community living under a specific rule. ~ *verb* (**orders, ordering, ordered**) **1** to put things in order; to arrange them. **2** to give a command to somebody. **3** to place an order for goods, food, etc. ✱ **in/of the order of** approximately. **out of order 1** not in the correct sequence. **2** not in working condition. **3** *informal* not acceptable or appropriate.

orderly[1] *adjective* **1** arranged or carried out in a neat and methodical way. **2** well behaved or peaceful. ➤ **orderliness** *noun*.

orderly[2] *noun* (*plural* **orderlies**) **1** a soldier who assists an officer by, for example, carrying messages. **2** a hospital attendant.

ordinal number *noun* (*plural* **ordinal numbers**) *Maths* a number, such as 'first', 'second', or 'third', showing the place somebody or something has in a series.

ordinary *adjective* routine or usual; not special. * **out of the ordinary** unusual. ➤ **ordinarily** *adverb*, **ordinariness** *noun*.

ordination *noun* (*plural* **ordinations**) the act of ordaining somebody as a priest, minister, or elder.

ordnance *noun* **1** military supplies. **2** heavy artillery.

ore *noun* (*plural* **ores**) rock containing metal or other valuable substances.

oregano /o ri **gah** noh/ *noun* a bushy plant with leaves used as a herb in cooking.

organ *noun* (*plural* **organs**) **1** *Music* an instrument with a keyboard and sets of pipes played by compressed air, or an electronic keyboard instrument producing a similar sound. **2** *Science* a specialized body part that performs a specific function, for example the heart or a leaf. ➤ **organist** *noun*.

organic *adjective* **1** to do with living organisms. **2** said about food, farming, etc: produced or carried out without using chemical fertilizers, pesticides, etc. **3** to do with an organ of the body. ➤ **organically** *adverb*.

organism *noun* (*plural* **organisms**) *Science* an individual member of a biological species; a living creature.

organization *or* **organisation** *noun* (*plural* **organizations** *or* **organisations**) **1** an organized group of people doing something together, for example a business or a political party. **2** the act of organizing. **3** the state of being planned or happening in an orderly manner. ➤ **organizational** *or* **organisational** *adjective*.

organize *or* **organise** *verb* (**organizes, organizing, organized** *or* **organises, etc**) **1** to arrange things or people in an orderly way or so that they can work together. **2** to plan and make preparations for an event. ➤ **organizer** *or* **organiser** *noun*.

orgasm *noun* (*plural* **orgasms**) the point of greatest pleasure and excitement in sexual activity. ➤ **orgasmic** *adjective*.

orgy *noun* (*plural* **orgies**) **1** a wild party with a lot of drinking and sex. **2** an excessive indulgence in something. ➤ **orgiastic** *adjective*.

Orient *noun* (**the Orient**) *dated* the countries of eastern Asia.

orient *verb* (**orients, orienting, oriented**) = ORIENTATE.

oriental *adjective* from or to do with the Orient.

orientate *verb* (**orientates, orientating, orientated**) **1** to position something in relation to the points of the compass. **2** to adjust something to a particular environment or situation. * **orientate yourself** to find out your position when in unfamiliar surroundings, or get to know all the details of a new situation. ➤ **orientation** *noun*.

orienteering *noun* a sport in which contestants have to cross unfamiliar country on foot using a map and compass.

orifice *noun* (*plural* **orifices**) *formal* an opening.

origami /o ri **gah** mi/ *noun* the Japanese art of folding paper into complex shapes.

origin *noun* (*plural* **origins**) **1** a source or starting-point. **2** a person's family background.

original *adjective* **1** first or earliest. **2** not copied from or imitating something else. **3** inventive or creative. ~ *noun* (*plural* **originals**) something from which a copy, reproduction, or translation is made. ➤ **originally** *adverb*.

originate *verb* (**originates, originating, originated**) **1** to come from a source or place. **2** to bring something into existence. ➤ **origination** *noun*, **originator** *noun*.

ornament /**aw** na mint/ *noun* (*plural* **ornaments**) **1** a small decorative object. **2** decoration. ~ /**aw** na ment/ *verb* (**ornaments, ornamenting, ornamented**) to decorate something. ➤ **ornamentation** *noun*.

ornate *adjective* elaborately or excessively decorated. ➤ **ornately** *adverb*.

ornithology *noun* the scientific study of birds. ➤ **ornithological** *adjective*, **ornithologist** *noun*.

orphan *noun* (*plural* **orphans**) a child whose parents are dead.

orphanage *noun* (*plural* **orphanages**) a place where orphans are taken care of.

orthodox *adjective* **1** keeping to official doctrine or practice. **2** conventional or normal. **3** (**Orthodox**) to do with any of the Eastern Christian churches, for example in Greece or Russia. ➤ **orthodoxy** *noun*.

orthopaedics /aw thoh **pee** diks/ *noun* a branch of medicine that treats problems and deformities in bones and muscles. ➤ **orthopaedic** *adjective*.

Oscar *noun* (*plural* **Oscars**) a small gold statue awarded for outstanding achievement in the cinema.

oscillate *verb* (**oscillates, oscillating, oscillated**) **1** to swing backward and forward like a pendulum. **2** to vary between opposing beliefs or feelings. **3** *Science* to have regular changes from a maximum point to a minimum point and back to maximum again. ➤ **oscillation** *noun*.

osmosis *noun Science* a process in which a liquid passes through a membrane into a more concentrated solution.

ostensible *adjective* seeming to be, or given as, the cause or motive for something, but not necessarily the true one: *the ostensible reason for her visit*. ➤ **ostensibly** *adverb*.

ostentatious *adjective* designed to impress or attract attention. ➤ **ostentation** *noun*, **ostentatiously** *adverb*.

osteopath /o stee oh path/ *noun* (*plural* **osteopaths**) a person who treats diseases by manipulating bones or other parts of the body. ➤ **osteopathy** *noun*.

osteoporosis /o stee oh paw roh sis/ *noun* a disease that causes a person's bones to become thin, brittle, and porous.

ostracize or **ostracise** *verb* (**ostracizes, ostracizing, ostracized** or **ostracises,** etc) to exclude somebody from a group and have nothing to do with them. ➤ **ostracism** *noun*.

ostrich *noun* (*plural* **ostriches**) a large African bird with a long neck and long legs but with wings so small that it cannot fly.

other *adjective* **1** not the same; different. **2** additional or further. **3** second; alternate: *every other Tuesday*. **4** far or opposite: *the other side of the road*. **5** recently past: *the other day*. ~ *pronoun and noun* (*plural* **others**) **1** the remaining or opposite one. **2** a different or additional one.

otherwise *adverb* **1** in different circumstances. **2** in other respects. **3** in a different way. **4** if not; or else.

otter *noun* (*plural* **otters**) a fish-eating animal with a long furry body and webbed feet.

ought *verb* **1** used to express moral obligation: *We ought to pay our debts*. **2** used to express what is advisable or recommended: *You ought to wear a safety helmet*. **3** used to express probability or expectation: *They ought to have arrived by now.*

> *Usage Note* The correct negative form of *ought* in standard English is *ought not*. The form *didn't ought* is not standard English.

oughtn't *contraction* ought not.

ounce *noun* (*plural* **ounces**) **1** a unit of weight equal to one sixteenth of a pound (about 28.35 grams). **2** the least amount: *There's not an ounce of truth in what he said.*

our *adjective* belonging to or associated with us.

ours *pronoun* the one or ones that belong to us.

ourselves *pronoun* **1** used as the object of a verb when *we* is the subject and the action of the verb affects the subject. **2** used to emphasize 'we' or 'us': *We ourselves prefer football to cricket.* ✳ **by ourselves** alone.

oust *verb* (**ousts, ousting, ousted**) to remove somebody from a position of authority.

out *adverb* **1** away from the inside or centre. **2** away from a place, especially away from your home or business. **3** clearly in or into view or public knowledge. **4** inaccurate. **5** no longer in fashion. **6** to the fullest extent; completely. **7** so as to be eliminated, especially from a game. **8** in or into a state of unconsciousness. ~ *adjective* **1** directed outwards. **2** not permissible or possible. **3** in cricket, baseball, etc, not allowed to continue batting. **4** said about a ball, shot, etc: landing outside the playing area. **5** *informal* open about your homosexuality. ✳ **be out of** not to have any of something left or in stock.

out-and-out *adjective* complete; utter.

outback *noun* (**the outback**) remote rural areas in Australia.

outboard motor *noun* (*plural* **outboard motors**) a motor, with a propeller and rudder attached, fitted to the stern of a small boat.

outbreak *noun* (*plural* **outbreaks**) a sudden or violent occurrence of something.

outbuilding *noun* (*plural* **outbuildings**) a smaller building separate from but belonging to a main building.

outburst *noun* (*plural* **outbursts**) a violent expression of a feeling.

outcast *noun* (*plural* **outcasts**) a person who is rejected by society.

outclass *verb* (**outclasses, outclassing, outclassed**) to be far better than somebody or something else.

outcome *noun* (*plural* **outcomes**) a result.

outcrop *noun* (*plural* **outcrops**) *Geography* the part of a rock formation that appears at the surface of the ground.

outcry *noun* (*plural* **outcries**) an expression of anger or disapproval by a lot of people.

outdated *adjective* old-fashioned or obsolete.

outdo *verb* (**outdoes, outdoing, outdid, outdone**) to do better than somebody.

outdoor *adjective* situated, done, or used outdoors.

outdoors *adverb* in or into the open air. ~ *noun* (**the outdoors**) a place or the whole area outside buildings; the open air.

outer *adjective* **1** external. **2** situated farther out. ➤ **outermost** *adjective*.

outer space *noun* space outside the earth's atmosphere.

outfit *noun* (*plural* **outfits**) **1** a set of clothes worn together. **2** *informal* a group that works as a team. ~ *verb* (**outfits, outfitting, outfitted**) to provide somebody with an outfit. ➤ **outfitter** *noun*.

outgoing *adjective* **1** about to give up a

outgoings *plural noun* money spent.

outgrow *verb* (**outgrows, outgrowing, outgrew, outgrown**) 1 to grow too large for clothes, etc. 2 to lose a habit as you grow older.

outhouse *noun* (*plural* **outhouses**) = OUTBUILDING.

outing *noun* (*plural* **outings**) a short pleasure trip.

outlandish *adjective* very unusual; bizarre.

outlast *verb* (**outlasts, outlasting, outlasted**) to last longer than something.

outlaw *noun* (*plural* **outlaws**) *History* a person who has committed a crime and is being hunted by the authorities. ~ *verb* (**outlaws, outlawing, outlawed**) to make something illegal.

outlay *noun* (*plural* **outlays**) expenditure or a payment.

outlet *noun* (*plural* **outlets**) 1 an opening through which a liquid or gas comes out. 2 a means of expressing an emotion, talent, etc. 3 a shop through which a product is sold.

outline *noun* (*plural* **outlines**) 1 a line around the outer edge of something, indicating its shape. 2 a plan or summary giving the main points of, for example, a book or an essay. ~ *verb* (**outlines, outlining, outlined**) 1 to draw a line around the edge of something. 2 to state or explain the main points of something.

outlive *verb* (**outlives, outliving, outlived**) to live longer than somebody.

outlook *noun* (*plural* **outlooks**) 1 a view from a particular place. 2 an attitude or point of view. 3 a prospect for the future.

outlying *adjective* far away from a central or main point.

outmanoeuvre *verb* (**outmanoeuvres, outmanoeuvring, outmanoeuvred**) to defeat somebody by using cleverer tactics.

outmoded *adjective* no longer in fashion.

outnumber *verb* (**outnumbers, outnumbering, outnumbered**) to be greater in number than another group.

out of bounds *adverb* outside the allowed boundaries.

out of date *adjective* 1 old-fashioned or obsolete. 2 no longer valid or usable.

out of doors *adverb* outside.

outpatient *noun* (*plural* **outpatients**) a patient who visits a hospital for treatment but does not stay there overnight.

outpost *noun* (*plural* **outposts**) a settlement far away from the areas of the country where most people live.

output *noun* (*plural* **outputs**) 1 the amount produced by somebody or something. 2 the process of producing. 3 power or energy produced by a machine or system. 4 *ICT* the data produced by a computer.

outrage *noun* (*plural* **outrages**) 1 fierce anger caused by injury or insult. 2 a shockingly violent, criminal, or immoral act. ~ *verb* (**outrages, outraging, outraged**) to arouse intense anger in somebody.

Word History The word *outrage* is not related to *rage*. *Outrage* is derived from the French verb *outrer*, which means 'to act in an unacceptably extreme way'.

---

outrageous *adjective* shocking or offensive. ➤ **outrageously** *adverb*.

outrider *noun* (*plural* **outriders**) a person mounted on a horse or motorcycle escorting a carriage or car.

outrigger *noun* (*plural* **outriggers**) a framework, often with a float attached, fixed to the side of a boat.

outright *adverb* **1** completely; altogether: *banned outright*. **2** instantaneously; on the spot: *killed outright*. **3** directly and openly: *I told him outright not to be such a fool*. ~ *adjective* utter; complete.

outset *noun* (**the outset**) the beginning or start.

outshine *verb* (**outshines, outshining, outshone**) to outdo or surpass somebody.

outside *noun* (*plural* **outsides**) **1** the outer side or surface of something. **2** the outward appearance of something or somebody. **3** the part surrounding or beyond the boundaries of something. ~ *adjective* **1** on or near the outside. **2** coming from outside or elsewhere. **3** maximum. **4** barely possible; remote: *an outside chance*. ~ *adverb* **1** on or to the outside. **2** outdoors. ~ *preposition* **1** on or to the outside of. **2** beyond the limits of. ✴ **at the outside** at the most.

outsider *noun* (*plural* **outsiders**) **1** somebody who does not belong to a particular group. **2** a competitor who has only a remote chance of winning.

outsize *adjective* exceptionally large.

outskirts *plural noun* the parts of a town that are farthest from the centre.

outsmart *verb* (**outsmarts, outsmarting, outsmarted**) to get the better of somebody by being cleverer than them.

outspoken *adjective* saying exactly what you think; frank.

outstanding *adjective* **1** extremely good; excellent. **2** unpaid. ➤ **outstandingly** *adverb*.

outstrip *verb* (**outstrips, outstripping, outstripped**) **1** to go faster or farther than somebody. **2** to do better than somebody.

out-take *noun* (*plural* **out-takes**) a section of film, recording, etc that is cut out during editing.

outvote *verb* (**outvotes, outvoting, outvoted**) to defeat somebody by getting more votes than they do.

outward *adjective* **1** situated on or directed towards the outside. **2** going away from a place. **3** relating to external appearances. ~ *adverb* = OUTWARDS. ➤ **outwardly** *adverb*.

outwards *adverb* towards the outside; away from the centre.

outweigh *verb* (**outweighs, outweighing, outweighed**) to be more valuable or important than something else.

outwit *verb* (**outwits, outwitting, outwitted**) to outsmart somebody.

ova *noun* plural of OVUM.

oval *adjective* having the shape of an egg or ellipse. ➤ **oval** *noun*.

ovary *noun* (*plural* **ovaries**) **1** a female reproductive organ that produces eggs and female sex hormones. **2** the base of the female reproductive organ of a flowering plant. ➤ **ovarian** *adjective*.

ovation *noun* (*plural* **ovations**) a long period of enthusiastic applause.

oven *noun* (*plural* **ovens**) an enclosed space that can be heated, especially one used in a kitchen for cooking food.

over *preposition* **1** higher than. **2** vertically above but not touching. **3** across. **4** so as to cover. **5** used to indicate authority, power, or preference. **6** more than. **7** during: *over lunch*. ~ *adverb* **1** across a barrier or intervening space. **2** to a particular place. **3** downwards from an upright position. **4** so as to be reversed or upside down: *turned over*. **5** in excess; remaining. **6** so as to cover the whole surface. **7** at an end. ~ *noun* (*plural* **overs**) in cricket, a series of six balls bowled by one bowler. ✴ **over and above** besides; in addition to.

overact *verb* (**overacts, overacting, overacted**) *Drama* to speak and gesture in an exaggerated way.

overall *noun* (*plural* **overalls**) **1** (**overalls**) a piece of protective clothing consisting of a trousers and a jacket combined. **2** a loose protective coat worn over other clothing. ~ *adjective and adverb* including or considering everything.

overarm *adjective and adverb* with the hand and arm lifted above shoulder level and brought down.

overawe *verb* (**overawes, overawing, overawed**) to make somebody nervous with respect or fear.

overbalance *verb* (**overbalances, overbalancing, overbalanced**) **1** to lose your balance and fall. **2** to cause something to overbalance.

overbearing *adjective* trying to dominate everybody.

overboard *adverb* over the side of a ship or boat into the water.

overcast *adjective* said of the sky: cloudy.

overcharge *verb* (**overcharges, overcharging, overcharged**) to charge a customer too much.

overcoat *noun* (*plural* **overcoats**) a warm coat for wearing outdoors over other clothing.

overcome *verb* (**overcomes, overcoming, overcame, overcome**) **1** to deal with a problem, handicap, etc successfully. **2** to overpower or overwhelm somebody.

overcrowded *adjective* containing too many people or things for the available space.

overdo *verb* (**overdoes, overdoing, overdid, overdone**) **1** to do or use too much of something. **2** to cook food too much. * **overdo it** to exhaust yourself, especially through overwork.

overdose *noun* (*plural* **overdoses**) a dangerously excessive dose of a drug.

overdraft *noun* (*plural* **overdrafts**) **1** permission from a bank to take more money out of your account than you have in it. **2** the amount by which an account is overdrawn.

overdrawn *adjective* owing money to a bank.

overdrive *noun* a special gear in a motor vehicle higher than top gear. * **go into** *or* **be in overdrive** to be extremely active.

overdue *adjective* not paid or not arriving at the proper time.

overestimate *verb* (**overestimates, overestimating, overestimated**) to judge something to be bigger than it actually is. **2** to overrate somebody or something. ➤ **overestimate** *noun*.

overflow *verb* (**overflows, overflowing, overflowed**) **1** to flow over or beyond a brim or edge. **2** to be too many, large, etc to be contained in something. **3** to be filled with an emotion. ~ *noun* (*plural* **overflows**) **1** an amount of people, things, etc that cannot be contained in something. **2** an outlet for surplus liquid.

overgrown *adjective* covered with weeds or plants that have not been controlled.

overhang *verb* (**overhangs, overhanging, overhung**) to stick out over or beyond something. ➤ **overhang** *noun*.

overhaul *verb* (**overhauls, overhauling, overhauled**) **1** to examine something, such as a machine, thoroughly and make any necessary repairs. **2** to overtake somebody or something. ➤ **overhaul** *noun*.

overhead *adverb and adjective* above your head.

overheads *plural noun* business expenses that are not connected with making a product, for example rent, insurance, and heating.

overhear verb (**overhears, overhearing, overheard**) to hear what somebody says without that person knowing.

overhung verb past participle of OVERHANG.

overjoyed adjective extremely pleased.

overlaid verb past tense and past participle of OVERLAY.

overland adverb and adjective by land rather than sea or air.

overlap verb (**overlaps, overlapping, overlapped**) **1** to extend over and cover a part of something. **2** to happen partly at the same time. **3** to have some things in common. ~ noun (plural **overlaps**) a part or amount that overlaps.

overlay verb (**overlays, overlaying, overlaid**) to cover or decorate a surface with something laid over it. ➤ **overlay** noun.

overleaf adverb on the other side of the page.

overload verb (**overloads, overloading, overloaded**) to put too big or heavy a load on something. ➤ **overload** noun.

overlook verb (**overlooks, overlooking, overlooked**) **1** to fail to notice somebody or something. **2** to ignore or excuse a bad action or mistake. **3** to provide a view of something from above.

overly adverb excessively.

overnight adverb and adjective **1** during or throughout the night. **2** for a single night. **3** happening suddenly.

overpower verb (**overpowers, overpowering, overpowered**) **1** to defeat somebody by being stronger than they are. **2** to be so strong or intense as to make somebody feel weak, faint, or very emotional. ➤ **overpowering** adjective.

overqualified adjective having more education, training, or experience than a job needs.

overran verb past tense of OVERRUN.

overrate verb (**overrates, overrating, overrated**) to consider something or somebody to be better than they actually are.

overreach verb (**overreaches, overreaching, overreached**) ✻ **overreach yourself** to fail by trying to do or gain too much.

overreact verb (**overreacts, overreacting, overreacted**) to react to something with more violent action or more intense feeling than is appropriate. ➤ **overreaction** noun.

override verb (**overrides, overriding, overrode, overridden**) **1** to be more important than something. **2** to overrule a decision made by somebody else. **3** to take over control from the mechanism that usually controls a machine.

overrule verb (**overrules, overruling, overruled**) to use your superior authority to disallow a decision, judgment, or objection made by somebody.

overrun verb (**overruns, overrunning, overran, overrun**) **1** to invade and occupy a place in large numbers. **2** to go on beyond the time at which it is supposed to stop.

overseas adverb and adjective beyond or across the sea; abroad; foreign.

oversee verb (**oversees, overseeing, oversaw, overseen**) to supervise a task, operation, etc. ➤ **overseer** noun.

overshadow verb (**overshadows, overshadowing, overshadowed**) **1** to cast a shadow over something. **2** to be more important than something or somebody. **3** to make an occasion less happy than it should have been.

oversight noun (plural **oversights**) an accidental omission or error.

oversleep verb (**oversleeps, over-**

overspend

sleeping, overslept) to sleep beyond the time when you intended to wake.

overspend *verb* (**overspends, overspending, overspent**) to spend too much money.

overspill *noun* the movement of people from towns into less crowded areas, such as new towns.

overstate *verb* (**overstates, overstating, overstated**) to state something too strongly; to exaggerate something. ➤ **overstatement** *noun*.

overstep *verb* (**oversteps, overstepping, overstepped**) to go beyond a limit. * **overstep the mark** to go beyond what is acceptable.

overstretch *verb* (**overstretches, overstretching, overstretched**) to make too many demands on time or resources.

oversubscribed *adjective* having more applicants than there are e.g. places or shares available.

overt *adjective* not concealed or disguised. ➤ **overtly** *adverb*.

overtake *verb* (**overtakes, overtaking, overtook, overtaken**) 1 to catch up with something or somebody and move past them. 2 to do better than somebody. 3 to happen to somebody suddenly.

overthrow *verb* (**overthrows, overthrowing, overthrew, overthrown**) to remove somebody from power.
~ *noun* (*plural* **overthrows**) 1 removal from power. 2 in cricket, a run scored when a fielder returns the ball inaccurately.

overtime *noun* extra time worked in addition to a standard working day or week.

overtone *noun* (*plural* **overtones**) a quality or meaning suggested by something but not directly expressed.

overtook *verb* past tense of OVERTAKE.

overture *noun* (*plural* **overtures**) *Music* the orchestral introduction to an opera, oratorio, or musical show.
* **make overtures to** to approach somebody in a friendly way with a view starting negotiations or reaching an agreement.

overturn *verb* (**overturns, overturning, overturned**) 1 to turn, or turn something, upside down. 2 to cancel or reverse e.g. a decision.

overweight *adjective* too fat or too heavy.

overwhelm *verb* (**overwhelms, overwhelming, overwhelmed**) 1 to defeat somebody by greatly superior force or numbers. 2 to make somebody feel intense emotion. ➤ **overwhelming** *adjective*.

overwork *verb* (**overworks, overworking, overworked**) 1 to work, or make somebody work, too hard or too long. 2 to use something too much or too often. ➤ **overwork** *noun*.

overwrought *adjective* extremely excited or agitated.

oviparous /oh vi pa rus/ *adjective* *Science* said about an animal: producing eggs that hatch outside the mother's body.

ovulate *verb* (**ovulates, ovulating, ovulated**) to produce eggs from an ovary. ➤ **ovulation** *noun*.

ovum *noun* (*plural* **ova**) a female reproductive cell in animals that, when fertilized, can develop into a new individual.

owe *verb* (**owes, owing, owed**) 1 to have to pay money to somebody for something. 2 to be obliged to give an explanation, respect, etc to somebody. 3 to have something thanks to something or somebody else: *He owes his success to luck.*

owing *adjective* unpaid; due. * **owing to** because of.

owl *noun* (*plural* **owls**) a bird of prey that has large eyes and a short hooked beak and that mostly hunts at night.

own¹ *adjective* belonging to or done by yourself or itself. ~ *pronoun* one or ones belonging to yourself or itself. ✶ **on your own 1** alone. **2** without assistance or control.

own² *verb* (**owns, owning, owned**) to possess something. ✶ **own up** to confess to a fault or wrongdoing.

owner *noun* (*plural* **owners**) the person who owns something. ➤ **ownership** *noun*.

ox *noun* (*plural* **oxen**) a large cow-like animal used especially for pulling carts.

oxide *noun* (*plural* **oxides**) *Science* a compound of oxygen with a chemical element or radical.

oxidize or **oxidise** *verb* (**oxidizes, oxidizing, oxidized** or **oxidises**, etc) *Science* to combine with oxygen. ➤ **oxidization** or **oxidisation** *noun*.

oxtail *noun* (*plural* **oxtails**) the tail of an ox, used especially in making soup.

oxygen *noun Science* a chemical element that occurs as a colourless odourless gas forming about 21% of the atmosphere and essential for the life of most organisms.

oxymoron *noun* (*plural* **oxymora**) *English* a surprising combination of words with opposite meanings, for example *cruel kindness*.

oyster *noun* (*plural* **oysters**) an edible sea animal with a rough irregular hinged shell.

oz *abbreviation* ounce or ounces.

ozone /oh zohn/ *noun* **1** a poisonous form of oxygen with three atoms in each molecule. **2** *informal* pure and refreshing air.

ozone layer *noun* (**the ozone layer**) a layer very high up in the atmosphere that has a high ozone content and protects the earth by absorbing ultraviolet radiation from the sun.

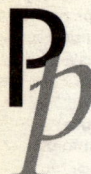

pace *noun* (*plural* **paces**) **1** the speed at which something travels or develops. **2** a step that you take in walking. ~ *verb* (**paces, pacing, paced**) **1** to walk up and down anxiously. **2** (**pace off/out**) to measure a distance by counting the number of the steps it takes to walk it. * **keep pace with** to progress at the same speed as something. **put somebody through their paces** to test somebody by making them demonstrate their abilities.

pacemaker *noun* (*plural* **pacemakers**) **1** an electronic device implanted in somebody's heart to control their heartbeat. **2** a runner whose role in a race is to set a good pace to help a teammate win the race and perhaps break a record.

Pacific *adjective* to do with the Pacific Ocean or the regions around it.

pacifism *noun* opposition to war and violence as means of settling disputes. ➤ **pacifist** *noun and adjective*.

pacify *verb* (**pacifies, pacifying, pacified**) to calm somebody who is angry or anxious.

pack *noun* (*plural* **packs**) **1** a light paper or cardboard container for goods. **2** a rucksack. **3** a set of playing cards. **4** a group of dogs working together, or a group of wolves hunting together. **5** an organized group of Cub Scouts or Brownie Guides. ~ *verb* (**packs, packing, packed**) **1** to put your clothes and other possessions in a case or bag ready for travelling. **2** (*also* **pack up**) to place things in a container so that they can be transported or stored. **3** said about a large number of people: to fill a place. * **pack off** *informal* to send somebody away abruptly or uncaringly. **pack up** *informal* to break down. ➤ **packer** *noun*.

package *noun* (*plural* **packages**) **1** a number of things wrapped up together. **2** a group of proposals, terms, or services offered together.

packaging *noun* materials used to wrap objects.

packed *adjective* completely full, especially of people.

packet *noun* (*plural* **packets**) **1** a paper or cardboard container. **2** a parcel. **3** *informal* a large sum of money.

pact *noun* (*plural* **pacts**) an agreement or treaty.

pad *noun* (*plural* **pads**) **1** a thick piece of soft or absorbent material. **2** an object that you wear to protect a part of your body from impact. **3** any of the parts of an animal's paw that make contact with the ground when it walks. **4** a number of sheets of paper fastened together at one edge. **5** a flat surface for a helicopter to land on or for launching a rocket. ~ *verb* (**pads, padding, padded**) **1** to protect something with a pad. **2** to make something look bigger or fatter by adding stuffing. **3** to make a speech or piece of writing longer by adding meaningless sections. **4** to walk with soft steps.

padding *noun* material packed round something to make it bigger or thicker, or to protect it from impact.

paddle *noun* (*plural* **paddles**) a small oar with a wide blade, used to move a boat through water. ~ *verb* (**paddles, paddling, paddled**) **1** to move a boat through water with a paddle. **2** to walk in shallow water. ➤ **paddler** *noun*.

paddock *noun* (*plural* **paddocks**) **1** a small enclosed field for horses. **2** an area where racehorses are paraded before a race.

paddy or **paddyfield** *noun* (*plural* **paddies** or **paddyfields**) a field of wet ground for growing rice.

padlock *noun* (*plural* **padlocks**) a detachable lock with a metal ring that goes through a loop and is secured. ~ *verb* (**padlocks, padlocking, padlocked**) to lock something using a padlock.

padre /pah dray/ *noun* (*plural* **padres**) a priest or minister in the armed forces.

paediatrics /pee di a triks/ *noun* the branch of medicine that deals with diseases that children have. ➤ **paediatric** *adjective*, **paediatrician** *noun*.

paella /pie e la/ *noun* a Spanish dish of rice, meat, seafood, and vegetables.

pagan *adjective* to do with religious beliefs that do not belong to the main religions of the world, especially beliefs that existed before the main religions were established. ~ *noun* (*plural* **pagans**) a follower of a pagan religion. ➤ **paganism** *noun*.

page[1] *noun* (*plural* **pages**) **1** a single leaf of a book, or a single side of a leaf. **2** a section of a computer document or website that corresponds in size to a printed page.

page[2] *noun* (*plural* **pages**) **1** a boy who walks behind the bride at a wedding. **2** formerly, a boy being trained for the rank of knight.

page[3] *verb* (**pages, paging, paged**) to call somebody by sending a message to their pager.

pageant /pa jant/ *noun* (*plural* **pageants**) **1** a play in which a historical event is re-enacted. **2** a procession of people in colourful costumes.

pageantry *noun* colourful costumes and impressive ceremonies.

pager *noun* (*plural* **pagers**) a small electronic device that beeps or displays a message to say that somebody wants you to come.

pagoda *noun* (*plural* **pagodas**) a Buddhist temple with several storeys and upturned roofs, or any building in this style.

paid *verb* past tense and past participle of PAY.

pail *noun* (*plural* **pails**) a bucket.

pain *noun* (*plural* **pains**) **1** an unpleasant feeling in your body caused by injury or illness. **2** emotional distress. **3** *informal* an annoying person or thing; a nuisance. ~ *verb* (**pains, paining, pained**) to upset or annoy somebody.

painful *adjective* causing physical pain or emotional distress. ➤ **painfully** *adverb*.

painkiller *noun* (*plural* **painkillers**) a drug that relieves pain.

painless *adjective* **1** not causing any pain. **2** easy or effortless. ➤ **painlessly** *adverb*.

painstaking *adjective* done with great care, patience, and determination. ➤ **painstakingly** *adverb*.

paint *noun* (*plural* **paints**) a liquid mixture that you brush or spray onto a surface to colour it. ~ *verb* (**paints, painting, painted**) **1** to colour something by putting paint on it. **2** to make pictures with paint.

painter

3 to represent something or somebody in a particular way: *The book paints a romantic picture of village life.*

painter *noun* (*plural* **painters**) **1** an artist who paints pictures. **2** somebody who paints walls and other parts of buildings.

painting *noun* (*plural* **paintings**) **1** a picture that somebody has painted. **2** the art of making pictures using paints. **3** the job of painting walls and other parts of buildings.

paintwork *noun* painted surfaces of buildings or vehicles.

pair *noun* (*plural* **pairs**) **1** a set of two things that go together. **2** a device made up of two connected pieces: *a pair of scissors.* **3** two people who are together. ~ *verb* (**pairs, pairing, paired**) ✻ **pair off** said about people: to organize themselves into groups of two. **pair off/up** to form into a pair or pairs.

pal *noun* (*plural* **pals**) *informal* a friend.

palace *noun* (*plural* **palaces**) **1** the official residence of a monarch or other important person. **2** a large impressive house or public building.

palaeontology /pa li on to lo ji/ *noun* the study of fossils and the geological periods they come from. ➤ **palaeontologist** *noun*.

palatable /pa la ta bl/ *adjective* **1** pleasant to taste. **2** acceptable.

palate /pa lit/ *noun* (*plural* **palates**) **1** the roof of your mouth. **2** your sense of taste.

palatial /pa lay shl/ *adjective* said about a building: impressively large and comfortable. ➤ **palatially** *adverb*.

pale *adjective* **1** with skin that is unusually or unhealthily light in colour. **2** said about a colour: light in shade.

palette /pa lit/ *noun* (*plural* **palettes**) *Art* **1** a thin board on which an artist mixes paints. **2** a range of colours used by an artist or in a painting.

palindrome *noun* (*plural* **palindromes**) a word, phrase, or sentence whose letters are in the same order backwards or forwards, for example *radar, don't nod,* or *no melons, no lemon.*

pall¹ *verb* (**palls, palling, palled**) to stop being interesting or attractive.

pall² *noun* a cloud of thick smoke.

pallet *noun* (*plural* **pallets**) a platform that goods are stacked on for transporting by forklift truck.

palm¹ *noun* (*plural* **palms**) a tall tropical tree with no branches and a crown of long blade-shaped leaves.

palm² *noun* (*plural* **palms**) the inside of your hand between your fingers and your wrist. ~ *verb* (**palms, palming, palmed**) ✻ **palm off** to get rid of something unwanted by persuading somebody to accept it.

Palm Sunday *noun* the Sunday before Easter, when Christians remember the time Jesus rode into Jerusalem before he was crucified.

palpable *adjective* said of the atmosphere in a place: so strong that you feel it easily; obvious. ➤ **palpably** *adverb*.

palpitations *plural noun* unusually fast heartbeats felt by somebody who is ill or nervous.

paltry /pawl tri/ *adjective* (**paltrier, paltriest**) very small or insignificant. ➤ **paltriness** *noun*.

pamper *verb* (**pampers, pampering, pampered**) to give somebody a lot of care and attention, or too much.

pamphlet *noun* (*plural* **pamphlets**) a booklet that gives information or presents a political viewpoint.

pan¹ *noun* (*plural* **pans**) **1** a metal container with a long handle, used for cooking food. **2** the bowl of a toilet. *verb* (**pans, panning, panned**) *informal* to criticize something or somebody harshly.

pan² *verb* (**pans, panning, panned**) to turn a film or television camera horizontally.

panacea /pa na see a/ *noun* (*plural* **panaceas**) a cure for all diseases, or a solution to all problems.

panache /pa nash/ *noun* impressive stylishness in the way you do something.

pancake *noun* (*plural* **pancakes**) **1** a very thin fried round of batter that you eat rolled up with a filling inside. **2** a small round flat cake that you eat with butter and jam.

pancreas /pang kree as/ *noun* an organ near your stomach that releases digestive juices into your intestines. ➤ **pancreatic** *adjective*.

panda *noun* (*plural* **pandas**) (*also* **giant panda**) a large black-and-white mammal from China that looks like a bear.

pandemonium *noun* noisy confusion.

pander *verb* (**panders, pandering, pandered**) (**pander to**) to give somebody everything they ask for, especially when this seems unwise.

pane *noun* (*plural* **panes**) a sheet of glass in a window or door.

panel *noun* (*plural* **panels**) **1** a flat section of a door or other surface. **2** a board with a set of controls or instruments on it. **3** a group of people who judge or discuss something. ➤ **panelled** *adjective*.

pang *noun* (*plural* **pangs**) a sudden strong feeling.

panic *noun* sudden strong feelings of fear or anxiety that cause you to lose self-control. ~ *verb* (**panics, panicking, panicked**) to feel panic. ➤ **panicky** *adjective*.

panoply /pa no pli/ *noun* an impressive display of things.

panorama *noun* (*plural* **panoramas**) an open view of a landscape or area. ➤ **panoramic** *adjective*.

pansy *noun* (*plural* **pansies**) a small garden plant with flowers that have round velvety petals.

pant *verb* (**pants, panting, panted**) to breathe quickly or with difficulty. ➤ **pant** *noun*.

panther *noun* (*plural* **panthers**) **1** a black leopard. **2** *N American* a puma.

panties *plural noun* short underpants for women or girls.

panto *noun* (*plural* **pantos**) *informal* = PANTOMIME.

pantomime *noun* (*plural* **pantomimes**) a comic musical entertainment based on a nursery story.

pantry *noun* (*plural* **pantries**) a room or cupboard for storing food.

pants *plural noun* **1** underpants. **2** *N American* trousers.

papacy /pay pa si/ *noun* (*plural* **papacies**) **1** the position of pope. **2** the period during which somebody is pope.

papal /pay pl/ *adjective* to do with the pope.

paper *noun* (*plural* **papers**) **1** material in the form of thin sheets for writing and printing on or for wrapping things in. **2** a written or printed document. **3** = NEWSPAPER. **4** a set of examination questions. ~ *verb* (**papers, papering, papered**) to cover a wall with wallpaper. ✱ **on paper 1** in writing. **2** in theory.

paperback *noun* (*plural* **paperbacks**) a book with a flexible paper or thin cardboard cover.

paperwork *noun* work that involves dealing with documents.

papier-mâché /pa pyay ma shay *or* pay per ma shay/ *noun* a mixture of shredded paper and glue used to make models.

paprika /pa pri ka *or* pa pree ka/ *noun* a red spice made from sweet peppers.

par *noun* in golf, the number of strokes that is set as the standard for a particular hole. ✱ **below par 1** slightly ill. **2** below the usual or expected standard. **on a par with** equal to.

parable *noun* (*plural* **parables**) a short story that illustrates a moral or religious principle.

parabola /pa ra bo la/ *noun* (*plural* **parabolas**) *Maths* a symmetrical curve of the kind produced when you cut through a cone at an angle parallel to its side.

parachute /pa ra shoot/ *noun* (*plural* **parachutes**) an umbrella-shaped piece of light fabric attached to a person's body by a harness, that slows their descent through the air when they jump out of an aeroplane. ➤ **parachutist** *noun*.

parade *noun* (*plural* **parades**) a public procession. ~ *verb* (**parades, parading, paraded**) **1** to march in a procession. **2** to display something in a way that is designed to make people admire it.

paradise *noun* **1** (*often* **Paradise**) heaven. **2** a very happy, beautiful, or peaceful place or state.

paradox *noun* (*plural* **paradoxes**) a true statement containing parts that seem to contradict each other. ➤ **paradoxical** *adjective*, **paradoxically** *adverb*.

paraffin *noun* a flammable liquid obtained from petroleum and used as a fuel.

paragliding *noun* the sport of travelling through the air hanging from a rectangular parachute. ➤ **paraglider** *noun*.

paragon *noun* (*plural* **paragons**) a person whose behaviour gives a perfect example of a particular quality.

paragraph *noun* (*plural* **paragraphs**) a section of a piece of writing that starts on a new line.

parallel *adjective* said about lines: going in the same direction and staying at the same distance from each other. ~ *noun* (*plural* **parallels**) **1** somebody or something that is equal or similar to another. **2** *Geography* a line representing any of the imaginary circles on the surface of the earth parallel to the equator.

parallelogram *noun* (*plural* **parallelograms**) *Maths* a flat four-sided shape with opposite sides that are parallel and of equal length.

paralyse *verb* (**paralyses, paralysing, paralysed**) to cause somebody to lose the movement or feeling in a part of their body.

paralysis *noun* loss of movement or feeling in a part of the body.

paramedic *noun* (*plural* **paramedics**) a member of a medical team that travels to where people are injured or ill to provide emergency treatment. ➤ **paramedical** *adjective*.

parameter /pa ra mi ter/ *noun* (*plural* **parameters**) *informal* a limit that controls what people can do in a particular situation.

paramilitary *adjective* operating like an army but not part of an official armed force. ~ *noun* (*plural* **paramilitaries**) a member of a paramilitary organization, especially one carrying out terrorist activities.

paramount *adjective* more important than everything else.

paranoia /pa ra noi a/ *noun* a mental disorder that makes somebody believe that other people are trying to harm them. ➤ **paranoid** *adjective and noun*.

paranormal *adjective* said about things that happen: strange and impossible to explain because they break the rules of science; supernatural.

parapet *noun* (*plural* **parapets**) a low wall along the edge of a bridge or roof.

paraphernalia /pa ra fer **nay** li a/ *noun* equipment or belongings.

paraphrase *verb* (**paraphrases, paraphrasing, paraphrased**) to repeat something using different words. ➤ **paraphrase** *noun*.

paraplegic /pa ra **plee** jik/ *adjective* paralysed from the waist down. ➤ **paraplegia** *noun*.

parasite *noun* (*plural* **parasites**) an animal or plant that lives in or on another and gets nourishment from it. ➤ **parasitic** or **parasitical** *adjective*.

parasol *noun* (*plural* **parasols**) a lightweight umbrella that gives shade from the sun.

paratroops *plural noun* soldiers trained to parachute from aircraft. ➤ **paratrooper** *noun*.

parcel *noun* (*plural* **parcels**) an object wrapped in paper for sending by post. ~ *verb* (**parcels, parcelling, parcelled**) to make something up into a parcel.

parched *adjective* **1** said about land: dry from lack of rain. **2** *informal* extremely thirsty.

parchment *noun* thick, high-quality paper.

pardon *interjection* used for saying that you did not hear what somebody said and you would like them to repeat it. ~ *noun* (*plural* **pardons**) **1** forgiveness. **2** a decision by a court, monarch, etc to cancel somebody's punishment. ~ *verb* (**pardons, pardoning, pardoned**) to legally cancel a punishment that somebody was formerly given. ➤ **pardonable** *adjective*.

pare *verb* (**pares, paring, pared**) to cut the skin off a vegetable or piece of fruit. ➤ **parer** *noun*.

parent *noun* (*plural* **parents**) **1** a father or mother. **2** the source from which something develops. ➤ **parental** *adjective*, **parenthood** *noun*.

parentage *noun* somebody's parents, especially their ethnic group or social class.

parenthesis /pa ren **thi** sis/ *noun* (*plural* **parentheses** /pa ren **thi** seez/) **1** a word or phrase inserted as an explanation, which, in writing, is separated from the rest of the sentence by punctuation. **2** (**parentheses**) the curved marks ( ) used in writing and printing to enclose a parenthesis. ➤ **parenthetic** or **parenthetical** *adjective*.

parish *noun* (*plural* **parishes**) **1** an area served by a single church or priest. **2** a unit of local government in rural England.

parishioner *noun* (*plural* **parishioners**) a member of a church parish.

parity *noun formal* the state of being equal.

park *noun* (*plural* **parks**) **1** an area of land designed for recreation. **2** an area maintained in its natural state as a public property. **3** an enclosed area of lawns, woodland, etc attached to a country house. ~ *verb* (**parks, parking, parked**) to leave a vehicle somewhere.

parka *noun* (*plural* **parkas**) a warm jacket with a hood.

Parkinson's disease *noun* a serious disease that causes shaking and weakness of the muscles.

parliament /**pah** la mint/ *noun* (*plural* **parliaments**) an assembly of elected representatives who make the laws of a country. ➤ **parliamentary** *adjective*.

parliamentarian *noun* (*plural* **parliamentarians**) **1** a member of a parliament. **2** (**Parliamentarian**) *History* a supporter of parliament in the English Civil War.

parlour *noun* (*plural* **parlours**) **1** *dated* a sitting room in a private house. **2** a shop or business that offers a particular service.

Parmesan /pah mi **zan**/ *noun* a hard, strongly flavoured Italian cheese.

parochial /pa roh ki al/ *adjective* **1** narrow-mindedly concerned only with local affairs. **2** to do with a church parish. ➤ **parochialism** *noun*.

parody *noun* (*plural* **parodies**) a comic imitation of something, such as the style of a writer or the format of a television programme. ~ *verb* (**parodies, parodying, parodied**) to imitate something for comic effect.

parole *noun* the early release of a prisoner on the condition that they do not break the law again or cause trouble. ~ *verb* (**paroles, paroling, paroled**) to release a prisoner on this condition.

parquet /pah kay/ *noun* flooring made of wooden blocks arranged in patterns.

parrot *noun* (*plural* **parrots**) a large tropical bird with brightly coloured feathers and a hooked beak.

parry *verb* (**parries, parrying, parried**) **1** to avoid answering a question directly. **2** to block a punch or other attacking blow. ➤ **parry** *noun*.

parsley *noun* a herb with flat or curly leaves.

parsnip *noun* (*plural* **parsnips**) a plant of the carrot family that has a root that looks like a whitish carrot and is eaten as a vegetable.

parson *noun* (*plural* **parsons**) a priest in the Church of England; a vicar.

part[1] *noun* (*plural* **parts**) **1** one of the pieces or sections of something. **2** a certain amount of something but not the whole of it. **3** an actor's role in a play. **4** somebody's contribution to something. **5** *Music* the music for a particular voice or instrument in a group. ✻ **take part** to join in with something or be involved in something.

part[2] *verb* (**parts, parting, parted**) **1** to go away from each other. **2** to end a friendship or relationship with somebody. **3** (**part with**) to give something away or sell something. **4** to divide your hair along a line.

partake *verb* (**partakes, partaking, partook, partaken**) *formal* (**partake of/in**) to eat or drink something, or to experience something in some other way.

partial *adjective* **1** not whole or total. **2** favouring one side over another; biased. **3** (**partial to**) very fond of something. ➤ **partially** *adverb*.

participate *verb* (**participates, participating, participated**) to do something that others are also doing; to take part. ➤ **participant** *noun*, **participation** *noun*, **participatory** *adjective*.

participle *noun* (*plural* **participles**) *English* a form of a verb, for example *singing, written,* or *burnt,* that you use with the verbs *be* and *have* to make tenses and that can often be used as an adjective. ➤ **participial** *adjective*.

particle *noun* (*plural* **particles**) **1** a tiny quantity or fragment of something. **2** *Science* a very small unit of matter, especially one smaller than an atom, such as an electron or a proton.

particular *adjective* **1** to do with a single person or thing. **2** special or extra: *nothing of particular importance.* **3** (**particular about**) very concerned about details; fussy. ~ *plural noun* (**particulars**) individual facts or details. ✻ **in particular** specifically or especially.

particularly *adverb* **1** to an unusual degree: *It was particularly hot.* **2** specifically: *I particularly asked you not to touch that.*

parting *noun* (*plural* **partings**) **1** an occasion when people leave each other or end their relationship. **2** the line where the hair is parted.

partisan *noun* (*plural* **partisans**) a member of a band of guerrillas fighting against an army occupying their country. ~ *adjective* supporting one group or view among several.

partition noun (plural **partitions**)
1 a screen or thin wall that divides a room into sections. **2** the dividing of a country into separate territories.
~ verb (**partitions, partitioning, partitioned**) **1** to divide a country into separate territories. **2** to divide a room by means of a partition. ➤ **partitionist** noun.

partly adverb not completely; to some extent or degree.

partner noun (plural **partners**)
1 a person you are doing something with. **2** a person that somebody is married to or has a relationship with. **3** a person that somebody owns a business with. ~ verb (**partners, partnering, partnered**) to be somebody's partner in an activity.

part of speech noun (plural **parts of speech**) *English* any of the classes that words are divided into according to their grammatical function, such as noun, verb, and adjective.

partook verb past tense of PARTAKE.

partridge noun (plural **partridges** or **partridge**) a brownish bird with a round body, often shot for sport and food.

part-time adjective and adverb involving less than the normal working hours. ➤ **part-timer** noun.

party noun (plural **parties**) **1** an informal social gathering with food and drink. **2** a political group that puts up candidates for election.
3 a group of people doing something together. **4** *formal* a person or group involved in a court case or mentioned in a legal agreement. ~ verb (**parties, partying, partied**) *informal* to enjoy yourself at a party.

pascal /pas kal/ noun (plural **pascals**) *Science* a unit used to measure pressure.

pass[1] verb (**passes, passing, passed**)
1 to move past something or somebody. **2** to give or transfer something to somebody. **3** said about time: to go by. **4** to spend time doing something. **5** to be successful in an examination or test. **6** to hit, throw, or kick the ball to another player in a team game.
7 to give official approval to a law or proposal. **8** to pronounce a judgment or sentence on a person convicted of a crime. **9** to go from one quality or state to another. ~ noun (plural **passes**) **1** an act of passing a ball to a teammate. **2** a ticket that allows you free travel or admission. **3** success in an examination or test. * **pass as/for** to be accepted as something: *She looked too young to pass for sixteen.* **pass away** to die. **pass off 1** to make false claims about somebody or something in order to deceive people: *He passed himself off as a doctor.* **2** to take place successfully: *The event passed off pretty well.* **pass out** to become unconscious.

pass[2] noun (plural **passes**) a narrow route through mountains.

passable adjective **1** acceptable but not particularly good; tolerable. **2** said about a road in bad weather conditions: capable of being travelled on. ➤ **passably** adverb.

passage noun (plural **passages**)
1 a corridor. **2** a section of a text or piece of music. **3** a journey by sea or air.

passé /pa say/ adjective no longer fashionable.

passenger noun (plural **passengers**) a person travelling in a vehicle that somebody else is driving.

passer-by noun (plural **passers-by**) a person who is walking past when something happens.

passing adjective lasting only a short time.

passion noun (plural **passions**) **1** very strong emotion, especially love or sexual desire. **2** a strong liking or

passionate

interest. **3 (the Passion)** the sufferings and death of Jesus.

passionate *adjective* **1** expressing or feeling strong emotion, especially love or sexual desire. **2** extremely enthusiastic. ➤ **passionately** *adverb*.

passive *adjective* **1** tending to allow other people to make decisions or take the initiative. **2** not resisting or fighting back; submissive. **3** *English* said about a verb: having as its subject the person or thing that is affected by the action of the verb, for example 'was hit' in *The ball was hit*. ~ *noun (plural* **passives**) *English* the passive form of verbs, or a verb in the passive form. ➤ **passively** *adverb*, **passivity** *noun*.

passive smoking *noun* the breathing in of tobacco smoke from other people's cigarettes.

Passover *noun (often* **the Passover**) the Jewish festival that celebrates the time when the Israelites were freed from slavery in Egypt.

passport *noun (plural* **passports**) an official document that proves somebody's identity and nationality and allows them to travel abroad.

password *noun (plural* **passwords**) **1** *ICT* a word or phrase that you have to key in to get access to a computer program. **2** a word or phrase that you have to say in order to be allowed into a place.

past *adjective* **1** which happened or existed earlier: *the past few months*. **2** finished or ended: *Winter is past*. ~ *preposition* **1** at or to the farther side of something: *We drove past the school; The post office is just past the cinema*. **2** beyond a particular hour: *ten past five*. ~ *adverb* so as to pass by something or somebody: *She walked past without speaking*. ~ *noun (plural* **pasts**) **1** time gone by. **2** a person's earlier life.

pasta *noun* dough formed into various shapes and boiled in water.

paste *noun (plural* **pastes**) **1** any soft, slightly sticky, thick, liquid substance. **2** a type of glue made from starch and water. **3** a type of bright glass used to make imitation jewels. ~ *verb* (**pastes, pasting, pasted**) **1** to stick something with paste. **2** *ICT* to insert something into a document.

pastel /pastil/ *noun (plural* **pastels**) **1** a crayon made from a paste of powdered pigment mixed with gum. **2** a drawing done in pastels. ~ *adjective* pale in colour.

pasteurized *or* **pasteurised** *adjective* heated to remove bacteria. ➤ **pasteurization** *or* **pasteurisation** *noun*.

pastille *or* **pastil** /pastil/ *noun (plural* **pastilles** *or* **pastils**) a sweet that you suck or chew.

pastime *noun (plural* **pastimes**) an activity that you do for enjoyment.

pastor *noun (plural* **pastors**) a priest or church minister.

pastoral *adjective* **1** to do with the countryside, especially representing country life as peaceful and enjoyable. **2** providing care or guidance, for example to students or members of a church congregation.

past participle *noun (plural* **past participles**) *English* a form of a verb, such as *taken*, used with the verbs *have* and *be* to form perfect tenses and passives.

pastry *noun (plural* **pastries**) **1** dough used to make pies, flans, and tarts. **2** a sweet tart or small cake.

past tense *noun (plural* **past tenses**) *English* the verb tense that expresses an action or state in a time that has gone by, for example *I went* or *she was*.

pasture *noun* fields of grass for cattle or sheep to graze on.

pasty[1] /pasti/ *noun (plural* **pasties**) a small savoury pastry case with a filling.

pasty² /**pay**sti/ *adjective* (**pastier, pastiest**) said about somebody's skin or appearance: unhealthily pale.

pat *verb* (**pats, patting, patted**) to hit something very lightly with your open hand. ~ *noun* (*plural* **pats**) a light tap with your open hand. ✷ **a pat on the back** a compliment.

patch *noun* (*plural* **patches**) **1** a piece of material used to cover a hole. **2** a shield worn over an injured eye. **3** a small area that is different from its surroundings: *damp patches on the walls*. **4** a small piece of land used for growing vegetables or fruit: *a cabbage patch*. ~ *verb* (**patches, patching, patched**) **1** to cover a hole with a patch. **2** to mend something hastily or temporarily. ✷ **not a patch on** *informal* not nearly as good as something or somebody.

patchwork *noun* pieces of coloured cloth sewn together.

patchy *adjective* (**patchier, patchiest**) **1** good only in some parts. **2** occurring in some areas and not others. ▶ **patchily** *adverb*.

pâté /**pa**tay/ *noun* a thick savoury paste made from meat or fish.

patent *noun* (*plural* **patents**) an official licence that gives somebody the exclusive right to make, use, or sell something. ~ *adjective* obvious. ~ *verb* (**patents, patenting, patented**) to get a patent for something you have invented. ▶ **patently** *adverb*.

paternal *adjective* **1** typical of a father; fatherly. **2** to do with your father: *my paternal grandmother*. ▶ **paternally** *adverb*.

paternity *noun* **1** the fact that a man is the father of a particular child. **2** the state of being a father; fatherhood.

path *noun* (*plural* **paths**) **1** a track for walking on. **2** a route.

pathetic *adjective* **1** contemptibly bad or useless. **2** causing you to feel pity. ▶ **pathetically** *adverb*.

pathological *adjective* **1** to do with disease. **2** *informal* irrational and uncontrollable: *a pathological fear of publicity*. ▶ **pathologically** *adverb*.

pathology *noun* the study of the causes and nature of diseases. ▶ **pathologist** *noun*.

pathos /**pay**thos/ *noun* a quality that causes you to feel pity or compassion.

pathway *noun* (*plural* **pathways**) a path or course.

patience *noun* **1** the ability to deal with problems and delays in a calm and uncomplaining way. **2** any of various card games designed to be played by one person.

patient *adjective* having or showing patience. ~ *noun* (*plural* **patients**) a person who is receiving medical care. ▶ **patiently** *adverb*.

patio *noun* (*plural* **patios**) a paved area adjoining a house.

patriarch /**pay**triahk/ *noun* (*plural* **patriarchs**) **1** a man who is the head of a family or social group. **2** a bishop in the Orthodox and Eastern churches. ▶ **patriarchal** *adjective*.

patrician *adjective* belonging to, or typical of, the aristocracy. ▶ **patrician** *noun*.

patriot /**pa**triot *or* **pay**triot/ *noun* (*plural* **patriots**) somebody who loves their county and feels very loyal to it. ▶ **patriotic** *adjective*, **patriotism** *noun*.

patrol *verb* (**patrols, patrolling, patrolled**) to walk round an area and check that there is no trouble. ~ *noun* (*plural* **patrols**) a group of people who patrol an area.

patron /**pay**tron/ *noun* (*plural* **patrons**) **1** a person who gives money or other support to an institution. **2** a customer of a hotel, restaurant, etc.

patronage /**pa**tronij/ *noun* **1** money or

patronize

other support given by a patron. **2** the power that a senior politician has to appoint people to political positions.

patronize *or* **patronise** (**patronizes, patronizing, patronized** *or* **patronises**, etc) *verb* **1** to treat somebody in a way that shows you think you are more important or intelligent than them. **2** to be a regular customer of a hotel, restaurant, etc. ➤ **patronizing** *or* **patronising** *adjective*.

patron saint *noun* (*plural* **patron saints**) a saint regarded as protecting a particular place or group of people.

patter[1] *noun* a quick succession of taps or pats. ~ *verb* (**patters, pattering, pattered**) to make gentle tapping sounds on a surface.

patter[2] *noun* fast confident talk, especially a salesperson's persuasive talk or a comedian's banter.

pattern *noun* (*plural* **patterns**) **1** a design in the form of a regular series of shapes. **2** a regular way in which something happens or is arranged: *There's a pattern to these crimes.* **3** a set of instructions for making a piece of clothing. ➤ **patterned** *adjective*.

paunch *noun* (*plural* **paunches**) a large stomach that sticks out. ➤ **paunchy** *adjective*.

pauper *noun* (*plural* **paupers**) *dated* a very poor person.

pause *verb* (**pauses, pausing, paused**) to stop doing something briefly. ~ *noun* (*plural* **pauses**) a brief temporary stop in a process or activity.

pave *verb* (**paves, paving, paved**) to cover a piece of ground with slabs of concrete or stone. ➤ **paving** *noun*.

pavement *noun* (*plural* **pavements**) **1** a raised area at the side of a road for pedestrians to walk on. **2** *N American* the covered surface of a road; tarmac.

pavilion *noun* (*plural* **pavilions**) **1** a building on a sports ground containing changing rooms and other facilities. **2** a small elaborate building or shelter in a garden or park.

paw *noun* (*plural* **paws**) the foot of an animal that has claws. ~ *verb* (**paws, pawing, pawed**) said about an animal: to touch or scratch something or somebody with a paw.

pawn[1] *noun* (*plural* **pawns**) in chess, the piece that has the least value.

pawn[2] *verb* (**pawns, pawning, pawned**) to give something to a pawnbroker as security for the money you are borrowing.

pawnbroker *noun* (*plural* **pawnbrokers**) a person who lends small amounts of money to people who give a valuable object as security for the loan, on the understanding that the pawnbroker can sell the object to somebody else if the money is not repaid.

pay *verb* (**pays, paying, paid**) **1** to give money to somebody in return for goods or services. **2** to give money that is required or owed. **3** to give your attention to something. **4** to make a visit to somebody or something. **5** to express a compliment to somebody. **6** to be worthwhile or wise: *It pays to think carefully before making a decision.* **7** to be punished. ~ *noun* money that somebody receives as a salary or wage. ✳ **pay back 1** to repay money that you owed. **2** to get revenge on somebody. ➤ **payable** *adjective*.

PAYE *abbreviation* = *pay as you earn*, a system by which an employer deducts income tax from an employee's pay.

payee *noun* (*plural* **payees**) a person who receives a payment.

payment *noun* (*plural* **payments**) **1** a sum of money that you pay. **2** the act of paying money.

payroll *noun* (*plural* **payrolls**) a list of employees and the amounts of money they are paid for their work.

PC *abbreviation* **1** personal computer. **2** police constable. **3** politically correct or political correctness.

PE *abbreviation* = physical education, a school subject in which you play sports and do physical exercise.

pea *noun* (*plural* **peas**) a small round green vegetable that is the seed of a climbing plant.

peace *noun* **1** a quiet state in which you are not bothered or disturbed by anything. **2** a situation in which there is no war.

peaceable *adjective* tending to avoid arguments or fights. ➤ **peaceably** *adverb*.

peaceful *adjective* **1** free of noise or disturbance of any kind: *a peaceful afternoon in the garden*. **2** involving no anger, violence, or force: *a peaceful demonstration*.

peach *noun* (*plural* **peaches**) **1** a fruit with downy orange skin and sweet yellow flesh. **2** a light yellowish pink colour.

peacock *noun* (*plural* **peacocks**) a large bird with a small head and brightly coloured tail feathers that it can spread out in a fan.

peahen *noun* (*plural* **peahens**) a female peacock.

peak *noun* (*plural* **peaks**) **1** a mountain or its pointed top. **2** a shade that sticks out on the front of a cap. **3** the highest level or greatest degree of something: *at the peak of his career*. ~ *verb* (**peaks, peaking, peaked**) to reach a maximum or high point. ➤ **peaked** *adjective*.

peal *noun* (*plural* **peals**) **1** the loud and musical ringing of a set of bells. **2** a loud prolonged sound of thunder or laughter. ~ *verb* (**peals, pealing, pealed**) to ring or sound loudly.

peanut *noun* (*plural* **peanuts**) a small oval nut that grows in a pod in the ground.

peanut butter *noun* a spread made from ground roasted peanuts.

pear *noun* (*plural* **pears**) a yellowish brown fruit with a round shape that narrows towards the stalk.

pearl *noun* (*plural* **pearls**) a hard, round, milky-white ball that forms in the shell of an oyster and is used in jewellery. ➤ **pearly** *adjective*.

peasant *noun* (*plural* **peasants**) **1** a farm worker in a poor country. **2** *History* in the feudal system, a member of a class of poor farm workers who gave their labour and often military service to a lord in return for a house and food; a vassal. ➤ **peasantry** *noun*.

peat *noun* a type of soil formed when plants rot in water in boggy areas, often cut into blocks and dried for use as fuel for fires. ➤ **peaty** *adjective*.

pebble *noun* (*plural* **pebbles**) a small round stone. ➤ **pebbly** *adjective*.

peck *verb* (**pecks, pecking, pecked**) **1** said about a bird: to bite at something with its beak. **2** to kiss somebody gently. ~ *noun* (*plural* **pecks**) **1** a bird's biting movement. **2** a light kiss.

peckish *adjective informal* slightly hungry.

pectoral *adjective formal* to do with your chest.

peculiar *adjective* **1** strange. **2** (**peculiar to**) belonging to a particular person or thing: *a style of architecture peculiar to this period*. ➤ **peculiarly** *adverb*.

peculiarity *noun* (*plural* **peculiarities**) **1** a characteristic of a particular person or thing. **2** strangeness.

pedal *noun* (*plural* **pedals**) a lever that you operate with your foot, for example on a bicycle or in a car. ~ *verb* (**pedals, pedalling, pedalled**) to work the pedals of a bicycle.

pedant /ˈpedant/ *noun* (*plural* **pedants**)

peddle

somebody who is too concerned about small details, or too concerned about following rules strictly. ➤ **pedantic** *adjective*, **pedantry** *noun*.

peddle *verb* (**peddles, peddling, peddled**) **1** to sell something, especially door to door. **2** *derogatory* to spread ideas or opinions.

pedestal *noun* (*plural* **pedestals**) **1** a base that supports a column or statue. **2** the supporting column of a washbasin or a toilet.

pedestrian *noun* (*plural* **pedestrians**) a person who is walking, as opposed to somebody in a vehicle. ~ *adjective* not very exciting, interesting, or good.

pedigree *noun* (*plural* **pedigrees**) **1** (*used before a noun*) said of an animal: of a single breed and from parents whose origins are recorded on official documents. **2** a person's ancestry.

pedlar *noun* (*plural* **pedlars**) a person who travels about selling small things.

peek *verb* (**peeks, peeking, peeked**) to take a brief look at something. ➤ **peek** *noun*.

peel *verb* (**peels, peeling, peeled**) **1** to strip the skin off a fruit or vegetable. **2** to come off a surface in thin layers or strips. ~ *noun* the skin of a fruit or vegetable.

peep¹ *verb* (**peeps, peeping, peeped**) **1** to look cautiously or slyly at something. **2** (**peep out**) to appear briefly or partially from behind something. ➤ **peep** *noun*.

peep² *verb* (**peeps, peeping, peeped**) to make a short high sound. ➤ **peep** *noun*.

peer¹ *verb* (**peers, peering, peered**) to look hard at something, for example because you are very curious or because you cannot see very well.

peer² *noun* (*plural* **peers**) **1** a person of the same age or social group as you. **2** a member of the nobility. **3** a member of the House of Lords.

peerage *noun* (*plural* **peerages**) **1** the rank or title of a peer. **2** (**the peerage**) peers as a group.

peer group *noun* (*plural* **peer groups**) people of about the same age or social status as you.

peeved *adjective informal* annoyed.

peg *noun* (*plural* **pegs**) **1** a small pointed or tapered piece of hard material used to hang things on or hold things down. **2** a clip for holding washing on a line for drying. ~ *verb* (**pegs, pegging, pegged**) **1** to fix something with pegs. **2** to keep something, such as prices, at a certain level.

pejorative /pi jo ra tiv/ *adjective* expressing criticism; disparaging. ➤ **pejoratively** *adverb*.

Pekinese *noun* (*plural* **Pekineses**) a small dog with a flat nose and a thick soft coat.

pelican *noun* (*plural* **pelicans**) a large bird with a pouch hanging from its bill for catching and keeping fish.

pellet *noun* (*plural* **pellets**) **1** a piece of ammunition in the form of a tiny ball of lead, fired from an airgun or shotgun. **2** a small round hard piece of a substance.

pelt¹ *verb* (**pelts, pelting, pelted**) **1** to throw things at somebody. **2** said about rain: to fall heavily. **3** to run fast. ✱ **at full pelt** very fast.

pelt² *noun* (*plural* **pelts**) an animal skin with its hair, wool, or fur still on.

pelvis *noun* (*plural* **pelvises**) a basin-shaped set of bones at the base of your spine. ➤ **pelvic** *adjective*.

pen¹ *noun* (*plural* **pens**) a device for writing or drawing with ink. ~ *verb* (**pens, penning, penned**) to write something.

pen² *noun* (*plural* **pens**) a small enclosure for farm animals. ~ *verb* (**pens, penning, penned**) to shut farm animals in a pen.

pen³ *noun* (*plural* **pens**) a female swan.

penal *adjective* to do with the punishment of criminals.

penalize *or* **penalise** *verb* (**penalizes, penalizing, penalized** *or* **penalises,** etc) **1** to give somebody a punishment for breaking a rule or doing something wrong. **2** to put somebody at a disadvantage.

penalty *noun* (*plural* **penalties**) **1** a punishment imposed for breaking a rule or doing something wrong. **2** in football and rugby, a free kick at goal.

penance *noun* something unpleasant that you agree to do as a punishment for a sin that you have committed.

pence *noun* a plural of PENNY.

penchant /pong shong/ *noun* (*plural* **penchants**) a liking for something.

pencil *noun* (*plural* **pencils**) a device for writing or drawing, consisting of a thin stick of graphite inside a thin wooden cylinder. ~ *verb* (**pencils, pencilling, pencilled**) to draw or write something with a pencil.

pendant *noun* (*plural* **pendants**) a piece of jewellery consisting of an ornament hanging from a chain, which you wear round your neck.

pending *preposition* while waiting for something to happen; until. ~ *adjective* not yet decided or dealt with.

pendulum *noun* (*plural* **pendulums**) a weight that hangs from a fixed point and swings freely, used to regulate the mechanism of a clock.

penetrate *verb* (**penetrates, penetrating, penetrated**) to get into or through something. ➤ **penetration** *noun*.

penetrating *adjective* **1** unpleasantly loud: *a penetrating voice*. **2** showing that you know what somebody is thinking or is going to say: *a penetrating stare*.

pen-friend *noun* (*plural* **pen-friends**) a person with whom you make or continue a friendship by writing letters to them.

penguin *noun* (*plural* **penguins**) a large black-and-white sea bird with wings that look like flippers and which cannot fly but swims very well.

penicillin *noun* an antibiotic originally obtained from moulds.

peninsula *noun* (*plural* **peninsulas**) a narrow strip of land almost surrounded by water. ➤ **peninsular** *adjective*.

penis *noun* (*plural* **penises**) the part of a man's body that he uses for urinating and having sex.

penitent *adjective* feeling sorry for the bad things you have done. ➤ **penitence** *noun*, **penitential** *adjective*.

penknife *noun* (*plural* **penknives**) a small knife with a blade that folds into the handle.

pennant *noun* (*plural* **pennants**) a flag that tapers to a point or divides into two points.

penniless *adjective* having no money.

penny *noun* (*plural* **pennies** *or* **pence**) **1** a unit of currency worth 100th of a pound. **2** formerly in Britain, a bronze coin worth 240th of a pound or 12th of a shilling.

pension *noun* (*plural* **pensions**) a regular income that somebody receives after they have retired, from the government, from a previous employer, or from a private pension policy.

pensioner *noun* (*plural* **pensioners**) a person who is old enough to receive a government pension.

pensive *adjective* deeply thoughtful. ➤ **pensively** *adverb*.

pentagon *noun* (*plural* **pentagons**) *Maths* a flat figure with five angles and five straight sides. ➤ **pentagonal** *adjective*.

pentameter /pen ta mi ter/ *noun* (*plural*

pentameters) *English* a line of poetry that consists of five feet.

pentathlon /pen tath lon/ *noun* (*plural* **pentathlons**) an athletics event consisting of five events, especially the modern pentathlon, in which athletes compete in swimming, cross-country running, steeplechase, fencing, and pistol shooting.

Pentecost *noun* **1** a Christian festival that commemorates the time when the Holy Spirit came down on Jesus's disciples, celebrated on the seventh Sunday after Easter. **2** a Jewish harvest festival that is celebrated fifty days after Passover.

penthouse *noun* (*plural* **penthouses**) an apartment on the roof or top floor of a building.

pent up *adjective* held back or confined, not released: *pent-up emotions*.

penultimate *adjective* last but one.

penury /pe new ri/ *noun* severe poverty.

peony /pee o ni/ *noun* (*plural* **peonies**) a garden plant with large flowers that look a little like roses.

people *plural noun* **1** human beings in general. **2** (**the people**) the citizens of a country. ~ *noun* (*plural* **peoples**) all the persons who form a race or nation: *the French-speaking peoples of the world*. ~ *verb* (**peoples, peopling, peopled**) said about people: to fill a place or live in a place.

pepper *noun* (*plural* **peppers**) **1** a hot-tasting black or white spice consisting of ground peppercorns. **2** a hollow red, green, or yellow vegetable that is the fruit of a tropical plant. ~ *verb* (**peppers, peppering, peppered**) to put things in all parts of an area: *hillsides peppered with cottages*. ➤ **peppery** *adjective*.

peppercorn *noun* (*plural* **peppercorns**) the dried berry of a tropical climbing plant, ground to make pepper.

peppermint *noun* (*plural* **peppermints**) **1** a mint plant with dark-green leaves and small pink flowers. **2** a sweet flavoured with peppermint oil.

pepperoni /pe pi roh ni/ *noun* a spicy Italian beef and pork sausage.

per *preposition* for each: *a cost of £30 per person*.

per annum *adverb* for each year.

perceive *verb* (**perceives, perceiving, perceived**) **1** to become aware of something. **2** to regard somebody or something in a particular way: *She is perceived as being tough*. ➤ **perceivable** *adjective*.

per cent *adverb* for each hundred. ~ *noun* (*plural* **per cent**) one part in a hundred: *an increase of half a per cent*.

percentage *noun* (*plural* **percentages**) a proportion expressed as a number in each hundred.

perceptible *adjective* able to be perceived; noticeable. ➤ **perceptibly** *adverb*.

perception *noun* (*plural* **perceptions**) **1** an awareness of your surroundings that you get through your senses. **2** something that you notice; an observation. **3** what you consider somebody or something to be like; an impression: *the public's perception of the royal family*.

perceptive *adjective* tending to notice things or understand situations; observant or discerning. ➤ **perceptively** *adverb*.

perch¹ *verb* (**perches, perching, perched**) **1** said about a bird: to land on something and settle there briefly. **2** to put something in a high or precarious spot: *a hotel perched on the cliff top*. ~ *noun* (*plural* **perches**) a bar or branch for a bird to perch on.

perch² *noun* (*plural* **perches** or **perch**) a freshwater fish with vertical stripes and spiny fins.

perchance *adverb archaic* perhaps.

percolate *verb* (**percolates, percolating, percolated**) said about a liquid or gas: to pass through the tiny holes in a porous substance. ➤ **percolation** *noun*.

percolator *noun* (*plural* **percolators**) a coffee pot in which boiling water passes through a perforated basket containing ground coffee beans.

percussion *noun Music* musical instruments such as drums and tambourines that you play by hitting or shaking them. ➤ **percussionist** *noun*.

peremptory /pɪˈrɛmptəri/ *adjective* giving orders or insisting on something in a forceful way. ➤ **peremptorily** *adverb*.

perennial *adjective* continuing all the time, or happening frequently. ~ *noun* (*plural* **perennials**) a plant that lives for many years. ➤ **perennially** *adverb*.

perfect /ˈpɜːfɪkt/ *adjective* **1** with no mistakes or faults at all. **2** exactly what you want or need: *the perfect house for us.* **3** absolute or utter: *a perfect idiot.* ~ /pəˈfɛkt/ *verb* (**perfects, perfecting, perfected**) to make something perfect. ➤ **perfectible** *adjective*, **perfectly** *adverb*.

perfection *noun* **1** the act of making something perfect. **2** something that is perfect: *This cake is absolute perfection.*

perfectionist *noun* (*plural* **perfectionists**) somebody who likes things to be done perfectly. ➤ **perfectionism** *noun*.

perfect tense *noun English* a verb tense expressing an action or state that is complete, for example 'has gone' in *She has gone* and 'will have finished' in *We will have finished by 5 o'clock.*

perforated *adjective* with tiny holes in.

perforation *noun* (*plural* **perforations**) a tiny hole in something, especially one of a line of holes that allow something to be torn easily.

perform *verb* (**performs, performing, performed**) **1** *Drama* to do something such as sing or act as an entertainment for an audience. **2** to do something: *You have duties to perform.* ➤ **performer** *noun*.

performance *noun* (*plural* **performances**) **1** *Drama* a play, piece of music, or other entertainment presented to an audience. **2** how well somebody does something or how successful something is: *the company's poor performance this year.* **3** the act of doing something: *the performance of your duties.*

perfume *noun* (*plural* **perfumes**) **1** a pleasant-smelling liquid that women put on their skin. **2** a pleasant smell. ➤ **perfumed** *adjective*.

perfunctory *adjective* done without much care, interest, or thought. ➤ **perfunctorily** *adverb*.

perhaps *adverb* possibly but not certainly; maybe.

peril *noun* (*plural* **perils**) **1** danger. **2** a dangerous aspect of something. ➤ **perilous** *adjective*, **perilously** *adverb*.

perimeter /pəˈrɪmɪtə/ *noun* (*plural* **perimeters**) the outer edge of an area, or the distance around the edge.

period *noun* (*plural* **periods**) **1** a length of time. **2** *History* a stage of history: *the Victorian period.* **3** (*used before a noun*) to do with a particular historical time: *period costume.* **4** any of the parts that the school day is divided into. **5** a time when a woman is menstruating. **6** *chiefly N American* a full stop.

periodic *adjective* happening at regular intervals. ➤ **periodically** *adverb*.

periodical *noun* (*plural* **periodicals**) a magazine.

periodic table *noun Science* a list of all the chemical elements, arranged in groups according to their atomic

peripheral

numbers (= the number of protons in the nucleus).

peripheral /pəˈrifirəl/ *adjective* **1** not very important. **2** on the edge of an area. ~ *noun* (*plural* **peripherals**) *ICT* a printer or other device connected to a computer. ➤ **peripherally** *adverb*.

periphery *noun* (*plural* **peripheries**) the edge of an area.

periscope *noun* (*plural* **periscopes**) a device that allows you to see things that are behind or above obstacles, by means of a series of mirrors or prisms.

perish *verb* (**perishes, perishing, perished**) **1** to die. **2** to deteriorate or rot.

perishable *adjective* said about food: liable to rot or decay.

perjury /ˈpərjoori/ *noun* the crime of telling a lie while you are under oath in a court of law.

perk *noun* (*plural* **perks**) *informal* an extra privilege or benefit. ~ *verb* (**perks, perking, perked**) ✱ **perk up** to become more lively or cheerful.

perky *adjective* (**perkier, perkiest**) lively and cheerful.

perm *noun* (*plural* **perms**) a long-lasting curly hairstyle done using chemicals. ~ *verb* (**perms, perming, permed**) to give hair a perm.

permafrost *noun* *Geography* a layer of permanently frozen ground in cold regions.

permanent *adjective* lasting for ever. ➤ **permanence** *noun*, **permanently** *adverb*.

permeable /ˈpərmiəbl/ *adjective* having tiny holes that allow liquids or gases to pass through.

permeate /ˈpərmiayt/ *verb* (**permeates, permeating, permeated**) to spread throughout something.

permissible *adjective* allowed.

permission *noun* the right to do something, given to you by somebody in authority.

permissive *adjective* allowing behaviour, especially sexual behaviour, that some people might disapprove of. ➤ **permissiveness** *noun*.

permit /pərˈmit/ *verb* (**permits, permitting, permitted**) **1** to allow something to happen, or say that somebody can do something. ~ /ˈpərmit/ *noun* (*plural* **permits**) an official document that allows somebody to do something.

permutation *noun* (*plural* **permutations**) one of the various possible ways in which things can be arranged.

pernicious *adjective* very harmful or destructive.

peroxide *noun* (*plural* **peroxides**) **1** *Science* an oxide that contains a high proportion of oxygen. **2** a chemical used for bleaching hair.

perpendicular *adjective* **1** at right angles to the ground; vertical. **2** at right angles to any surface or line. ~ *noun* (*plural* **perpendiculars**) a perpendicular line or surface.

perpetrate *verb* (**perpetrates, perpetrating, perpetrated**) to commit a crime or something wrong. ➤ **perpetration** *noun*, **perpetrator** *noun*.

perpetual *adjective* **1** continuing for ever. **2** repeated or constant. ➤ **perpetually** *adverb*.

perpetuate *verb* (**perpetuates, perpetuating, perpetuated**) to cause something to continue for a long time. ➤ **perpetuation** *noun*.

perplex *verb* (**perplexes, perplexing, perplexed**) to puzzle or confuse somebody. ➤ **perplexity** *noun*.

persecute *verb* (**persecutes, persecuting, persecuted**) to treat somebody cruelly because of their religion, race, political beliefs, etc. ➤ **persecution** *noun*, **persecutor** *noun*.

persevere verb (**perseveres, persevering, persevered**) to carry on trying or doing something in spite of difficulties. ➤ **perseverance** noun.

persist verb (**persists, persisting, persisted**) 1 to continue to do something in a determined or obstinate way, in spite of difficulties or opposition. 2 to continue to exist.

persistent adjective 1 continuing to do something in spite of difficulties or opposition. 2 continuing or recurring: *persistent back pain*. ➤ **persistence** noun, **persistently** adverb.

person noun (plural **people** or formal **persons**) 1 a human being. 2 *English* any of three forms of a verb or pronoun, the *first person* referring to yourself as the speaker, or to yourself and other people; the *second person* referring to the person you are speaking to, or to that person and other people; and the *third person* referring to the person, people, thing, or things you are speaking about. ✷ **in person** actually present yourself.

personable adjective having a very pleasant personality. ➤ **personably** adverb.

personal adjective 1 to do with a particular person: *personal affairs*. 2 done in person, rather than by somebody else on your behalf: *I'll give it my personal attention*. 3 to do with your body: *personal hygiene*. 4 relating to private matters: *a personal chat*. 5 referring offensively to somebody's character, appearance, or private affairs: *That comment was rather personal*.

personal computer noun (plural **personal computers**) *ICT* a small computer designed for one person to use.

personality noun (plural **personalities**) 1 a person's character or typical way of behaving. 2 a famous person.

personally adverb 1 in person: *I haven't experienced it personally*. 2 used to introduce a personal opinion: *Personally, I didn't enjoy the film*.

personal stereo noun (plural **personal stereos**) a small cassette player or CD player used with earphones or headphones.

personification noun 1 *English* in literature, references to objects as if they have human qualities. 2 somebody who is an excellent example of a particular quality: *He was the personification of honour*.

personify verb (**personifies, personifying, personified**) 1 (*often as a past participle*) said about a person: to be an excellent example of a particular quality: *He is kindness personified*. 2 to describe an object as having human qualities.

personnel noun the people employed by an organization.

perspective noun (plural **perspectives**) 1 a point of view. 2 *Art* the impression of distance between objects in a drawing or painting.

Perspex noun *trademark* a transparent plastic.

perspiration noun sweat.

perspire verb (**perspires, perspiring, perspired**) to sweat.

persuade verb (**persuades, persuading, persuaded**) to make somebody believe or do something by reasoning or pleading with them.

persuasion noun (plural **persuasions**) 1 the process of persuading somebody to believe or do something. 2 a particular belief or attitude: *people of every political persuasion*.

persuasive adjective convincing people to believe or do something. ➤ **persuasively** adverb.

pertain verb (**pertains, pertaining, pertained**) *formal* to relate to something or be about something.

pertinent *adjective* relevant. ➤ **pertinence** *noun*, **pertinently** *adverb*.

perturb *verb* (**perturbs, perturbing, perturbed**) to worry or upset somebody. ➤ **perturbation** *noun*.

peruse *verb* (**peruses, perusing, perused**) *formal* to look at or read something in detail. ➤ **perusal** *noun*.

pervade *verb* (**pervades, pervading, pervaded**) to exist in every part of a place or thing. ➤ **pervasive** *adjective*.

perverse *adjective* obstinately doing the opposite of what is reasonable or what people want. ➤ **perversely** *adverb*, **perversity** *noun*.

perversion *noun* (*plural* **perversions**) an example of abnormal sexual behaviour.

pervert /per vert/ *verb* **1** to cause somebody to behave in a way that is not morally right. **2** to affect something in such a way that it does not happen correctly or fairly: *pervert the course of justice.* ~ /per vert/ *noun* (*plural* **perverts**) a person who indulges in sexual behaviour that most people find disgusting or morally wrong.

perverted *adjective* sexually abnormal.

pessimism *noun* a tendency to stress the worst aspects of something or to expect the worst outcome. ➤ **pessimist** *noun*, **pessimistic** *adjective*, **pessimistically** *adverb*.

pest *noun* (*plural* **pests**) **1** an animal or insect that causes damage or carries disease. **2** an annoying person. **3** a nuisance.

pester *verb* (**pesters, pestering, pestered**) to keep annoying somebody.

pesticide *noun* (*plural* **pesticides**) a chemical used to kill insects and other pests.

pet *noun* (*plural* **pets**) an animal, bird, etc that somebody keeps for pleasure. ~ *adjective* favourite. ~ *verb* (**pets, petting, petted**) to stroke an animal affectionately.

petal *noun* (*plural* **petals**) any of the outer parts that form a flower.

peter *verb* (**peters, petering, petered**) (**peter out**) to diminish gradually and come to an end.

petite /pi teet/ *adjective* said about a woman: small and slim.

petition *noun* (*plural* **petitions**) a document asking somebody in authority to take action, signed by a large number of people. ~ *verb* (**petitions, petitioning, petitioned**) to present a petition to somebody in authority. ➤ **petitioner** *noun*.

petri dish *or* **Petri dish** /pee tri/ *noun* (*plural* **petri dishes** *or* **Petri dishes**) *Science* a small shallow glass or plastic dish with a loose cover, used in laboratories.

petrified *adjective* extremely frightened.

petrochemical *noun* (*plural* **petrochemicals**) a chemical obtained from petroleum or natural gas. ➤ **petrochemical** *adjective*.

petrol *noun* a mixture refined from petroleum and used as a fuel for vehicle engines.

petroleum *noun* a thick black liquid found naturally underground, from which petrol, paraffin, and other fuels are obtained.

petticoat *noun* (*plural* **petticoats**) an item of women's underwear that looks like a thin skirt or dress.

petty *adjective* (**pettier, pettiest**) **1** unimportant. **2** doing unkind or selfish things for childish, silly reasons. ➤ **pettiness** *noun*.

petty cash *noun* an amount of cash kept by a shop or other business for small expenses.

petulant *adjective* childishly bad-tempered, impatient, or cruel. ➤ **petulance** *noun*, **petulantly** *adverb*.

petunia *noun* (*plural* **petunias**) a

garden plant with large brightly coloured funnel-shaped flowers.

pew *noun* (*plural* **pews**) one of several rows of fixed benches in a church.

pewter *noun* a dull grey metal that was formerly an alloy of tin and lead but is now a mixture of tin, copper, and antimony (a silvery-white metallic element).

pH *noun Science* a figure used to show how acid or alkaline a solution is.

phalanx *noun* (*plural* **phalanxes**) *History* in ancient Greece, a unit of soldiers attacking in close formation behind a wall of shields.

phallus *noun* (*plural* **phalluses**) an erect penis, or a carving or other representation of one. ➤ **phallic** *adjective*

phantom *noun* (*plural* **phantoms**) a ghost. ~ *adjective* imagined or non-existent.

pharaoh /fair oh/ *noun* (*plural* **pharaohs**) a ruler of ancient Egypt.

pharmaceutical /fah ma sooh ti kl/ *adjective* relating to medicinal drugs. ~ *noun* (*plural* **pharmaceuticals**) a medicinal drug.

pharmacist *noun* (*plural* **pharmacists**) somebody who is trained to prepare and sell medicines.

pharmacy *noun* (*plural* **pharmacies**) a shop, or a department of a hospital, where medicines are prepared and dispensed.

phase *noun* (*plural* **phases**) a stage in a process or activity. ~ *verb* (**phases, phasing, phased**) ✳ **phase in/out** to introduce (or end) something in gradual stages.

pheasant *noun* (*plural* **pheasants** or **pheasant**) a large, brown, long-tailed bird that is often shot for sport and food.

phenomenal *adjective* extremely good or large; remarkable. ➤ **phenomenally** *adverb*.

phenomenon *noun* (*plural* **phenomena**) **1** a fact or happening that people notice or study. **2** an exceptional person, thing, or event.

Usage Note Phenomenon is a singular noun. Phenomena is the plural. It is not correct to talk of 'a phenomena'.

philanthropist /fi lan throh pist/ *noun* (*plural* **philanthropists**) somebody who spends a lot of their own money on projects that benefit the public. ➤ **philanthropic** *adjective*, **philanthropy** *noun*.

philately /fi la ti li/ *noun* the study and collection of postage stamps. ➤ **philatelist** *noun*.

philistine /fi li stien/ *noun* (*plural* **philistines**) a person who has no interest in art, literature, music, or other cultural activities. ➤ **philistinism** *noun*.

philosophical *adjective* **1** to do with philosophy. **2** not angry, worried, or disappointed when bad things happen. ➤ **philosophically** *adverb*.

philosophy *noun* (*plural* **philosophies**) **1** the study of the nature of knowledge and existence. **2** a set of beliefs or principles. ➤ **philosopher** *noun*.

phlegm /flem/ *noun* thick mucus in your nose and throat.

phlegmatic /fleg ma tik/ *adjective* having a calm temperament. ➤ **phlegmatically** *adverb*.

phobia *noun* (*plural* **phobias**) a very strong fear of something. ➤ **phobic** *adjective and noun*.

phoenix /fee niks/ *noun* (*plural* **phoenixes**) a mythical bird that burns itself and then is born again from the ashes.

phone *noun* (*plural* **phones**) = TELEPHONE. ~ *verb* (**phones, phoning, phoned**) to make a telephone call.

phonetic *adjective* **1** to do with spoken language or speech sounds. **2** using

phonetics

symbols to represent speech sounds. ➤ **phonetically** adverb.

phonetics noun the study and classification of speech sounds.

phoney or **phony** adjective (**phonier, phoniest**) informal not real, genuine, or sincere. ~ noun (plural **phoneys** or **phonies**) a phoney person or thing.

phosphorescent /fosfəresnt/ adjective producing a glowing light; luminous. ➤ **phosphorescence** noun.

phosphorus noun Science a non-metallic chemical element that burns very easily.

photo noun (plural **photos**) a photograph.

photocopier noun (plural **photocopiers**) a machine that produces a copy of a document by photographing it.

photocopy noun (plural **photocopies**) a copy of a document made on a photocopier. ~ verb (**photocopies, photocopying, photocopied**) to make a photocopy of a document.

photogenic adjective looking attractive in photographs.

photograph noun (plural **photographs**) a picture that you take with a camera. ~ verb (**photographs, photographing, photographed**) to take a photograph of something or somebody. ➤ **photographer** noun, **photographic** adjective, **photography** noun.

photosynthesis noun Science the process by which plants use sunlight to turn carbon dioxide from the atmosphere into nutrients that keep the plant alive, giving off oxygen as a result.

phrasal verb noun (plural **phrasal verbs**) English a combination of a verb and an adverb or preposition (or both) that together have a special meaning, such as 'blow up' in Bomb disposal experts blew up the package or 'put up with' in I don't know how you put up with it.

phrase noun (plural **phrases**) 1 English a group of words that go together in a sentence but do not form a clause. 2 Music in music, a group of notes that form a unit of melody. ~ verb (**phrases, phrasing, phrased**) to express something using particular words. ➤ **phrasal** adjective.

phrase book noun (plural **phrase books**) a book that contains words and phrases in a foreign language, with their translation.

physical adjective 1 to do with your body: physical exercises. 2 involving a lot of bodily contact: a physical sport. 3 Science involving physics: physical chemistry. 4 involving things that you can touch or see, as opposed to things that you think or feel, or to spiritual things: the physical universe. ➤ **physicality** noun, **physically** adverb.

physical education noun sports that pupils do at school.

physician noun (plural **physicians**) a doctor.

physics noun the branch of science that deals with matter and with electricity, heat, light, and other forms of energy. ➤ **physicist** noun.

physiology noun the branch of biology that deals with how the human body and the bodies of animals work. ➤ **physiological** adjective, **physiologist** noun.

physiotherapy noun treatments for injury that involve physical exercises and massage. ➤ **physiotherapist** noun.

physique /fizeek/ noun (plural **physiques**) the shape and size of a person's body.

pi /pie/ noun Maths the mathematical symbol (π), used to represent the number $^{22}/_{7}$ or 3.142, which is the ratio of the circumference of a circle to its diameter.

piano noun (plural **pianos**) a large keyboard instrument with strings inside that are struck by hammers when you press the keys. ➤ **pianist** *noun*.

piccolo *noun* (*plural* **piccolos**) a small high-pitched flute.

pick[1] *verb* (**picks, picking, picked**) **1** to choose something or somebody. **2** to remove a fruit or flower from its plant. **3** to steal from a person's pocket. **4** to begin a quarrel or fight. **5** to open a lock using a device other than the key. ~ *noun* **1** a choice: *You can have first pick.* **2** the best person or thing in a group: *the pick of the crop.* ✻ **pick on 1** to unfairly criticize somebody who is no worse than others. **2** to bully somebody. **pick out** to select one person or thing from a group. **pick up 1** to take hold of something and lift it. **2** to collect somebody in a vehicle: *I'll pick you up at the airport.* **3** to collect something from a place. **4** to acquire a skill or quality without deliberately trying: *She's already picked up the local accent.* **5** to receive a radio signal. **6** to recover or improve: *The economy is picking up.*

pick[2] *or* **pickaxe** *noun* (*plural* **picks** *or* **pickaxes**) a heavy tool for breaking up concrete or stone, consisting of a long wooden handle and a curved and pointed metal head.

picket *noun* (*plural* **pickets**) **1** a group of striking workers who stand outside their place of work and try to persuade other workers to strike, or a member of such a group. **2** one of many pointed posts that together form a fence. ~ *verb* (**pickets, picketing, picketed**) to be a picket outside a place of work.

pickle *noun* a spicy mixture of chopped vegetables preserved in vinegar or salt water, eaten cold with meat, cheese, or salad. ~ *verb* (**pickles, pickling, pickled**) to preserve food in vinegar or salt water.

pickpocket *noun* (*plural* **pickpockets**) somebody who steals from people's pockets or bags.

pickup *noun* (*plural* **pickups**) a small truck that has an uncovered back section with sides that can drop down for easy loading.

picnic *noun* (*plural* **picnics**) an informal meal that you eat outdoors. ~ *verb* (**picnics, picnicking, picnicked**) to have a picnic. ➤ **picnicker** *noun*.

Pict *noun* (*plural* **Picts**) a member of a Celtic people that lived in northern Britain in Roman times.

pictorial *adjective* consisting of pictures or illustrated by pictures. ➤ **pictorially** *adverb*.

picture *noun* (*plural* **pictures**) **1** a representation of something made by painting, drawing, or photography. **2** a vivid description. **3** an image on a television screen. **4** (**the pictures**) *informal* the cinema. ~ *verb* (**pictures, picturing, pictured**) **1** to show something or somebody in a picture. **2** to form a mental image of something or somebody.

picturesque *adjective* said about a place: quaintly or charmingly attractive.

pidgin *noun* (*plural* **pidgins**) an informal language that combines words and phrases from two or more languages, used as a means of communication between people who speak different languages. ~ *adjective* spoken badly and including many words and phrases from the speaker's native language: *pidgin French*.

pie *noun* (*plural* **pies**) a baked dish with a sweet or savoury filling covered by pastry.

piece *noun* (*plural* **pieces**) **1** a part or fragment of something. **2** a distinct bit or item of something: *a piece of paper*. **3** something that has been produced, such as a musical work or

piecemeal

an antique object. **4** a coin of a specified value: *a ten-pence piece*. **5** a small object used in playing a board game. ~ *verb* (**pieces, piecing, pieced**) ✱ **piece together** to join things to form a whole.

piecemeal *adjective and adverb* done gradually or one piece at a time, often in a rather disorganized way.

piecework *noun* work in which a worker receives a fixed amount of money for each item they produce.

pie chart *noun* (*plural* **pie charts**) *Maths* a chart that shows proportions of a whole as sections of a circle.

pier *noun* (*plural* **piers**) **1** a platform that goes out from the land into a sea or lake, for boats to stop at or for people to walk on. **2** a support for a bridge.

pierce *verb* (**pierces, piercing, pierced**) to go through a surface, making a hole.

piercing *adjective* **1** said about a sound: unpleasantly loud and high-pitched. **2** said about a wind: so cold that it gets through your clothes. **3** said of somebody's eyes: very bright and seeming to be able to see right into or though things.

piety *noun* the behaviour or attitude of somebody who has very strong religious feelings.

pig *noun* (*plural* **pigs**) **1** a farm animal with thick bristly skin, short legs, and a long snout. **2** *informal* a dirty, greedy, or unpleasant person.

pigeon *noun* (*plural* **pigeons**) a large grey bird that you often see in towns.

pigeonhole *noun* (*plural* **pigeonholes**) a small open compartment for letters or documents. ~ *verb* (**pigeonholes, pigeonholing, pigeonholed**) to make a hasty judgment about what type of person somebody is and continue to think of them as that type only.

piggyback *noun* (*plural* **piggybacks**) a ride on somebody's back and shoulders.

pigheaded *adjective* obstinate or stubborn.

piglet *noun* (*plural* **piglets**) a young pig.

pigment *noun* (*plural* **pigments**) **1** *Art* a powdered coloured substance that is mixed with a liquid to make paint or ink. **2** any natural substance that gives something its colour. ➤ **pigmentation** *noun*.

pigsty *noun* (*plural* **pigsties**) **1** an enclosure for pigs. **2** a dirty or untidy place.

pigtail *noun* (*plural* **pigtails**) a tight plait of hair, especially one of a pair worn at the sides of the head. ➤ **pigtailed** *adjective*.

pike[1] *noun* (*plural* **pikes** or **pike**) a large freshwater fish with big teeth.

pike[2] *noun* (*plural* **pikes**) *History* a weapon consisting of a long steel blade on the end of a long wooden shaft, formerly used by soldiers on foot.

pilchard *noun* (*plural* **pilchards**) a small fish of the herring family.

pile[1] *noun* (*plural* **piles**) **1** a quantity of things heaped together. **2** *informal* a large quantity or amount: *I've got a pile of homework to do*. ~ *verb* (**piles, piling, piled**) **1** to place things in a pile. **2** (**pile into** or **out of**) to get into or out of a vehicle in a confused rush. ✱ **pile up** to become a large amount; to accumulate.

pile[2] *noun* the soft raised surface on a carpet or fabric, consisting of cut threads or loops.

pile[3] *noun* (*plural* **piles**) a metal or concrete post driven into the ground to support a building.

piles *plural noun* = HAEMORRHOIDS.

pile-up *noun* (*plural* **pile-ups**) *informal* a collision involving several vehicles.

pilfer *verb* (**pilfers, pilfering,**

pilfered) to steal things of little value.

pilgrim *noun* (*plural* **pilgrims**) a person who is travelling to a holy place as a religious duty.

pilgrimage *noun* (*plural* **pilgrimages**) a journey to a holy place, made for religious reasons.

pill *noun* (*plural* **pills**) **1** a small solid mass of medicine to be swallowed whole. **2** (**the Pill**) a contraceptive in tablet form.

pillage *verb* (**pillages, pillaging, pillaged**) said about an army: to use violence to steal things from a place after occupying it. ➤ **pillage** *noun*.

pillar *noun* (*plural* **pillars**) **1** a thick strong post that supports something. **2** an important member of an organization whose work makes it successful.

pillar box *noun* (*plural* **pillar boxes**) a traditional red postbox in the shape of an upright cylinder.

pillory *verb* (**pillories, pillorying, pilloried**) to publicly ridicule or criticize somebody. ~ *noun* (*plural* **pillories**) *History* a device used in the past for publicly punishing offenders, consisting of a wooden frame with holes to hold the head and hands.

pillow *noun* (*plural* **pillows**) a support for your head when you are in bed, consisting of a cloth container filled with soft material.

pillowcase *noun* (*plural* **pillowcases**) a removable cloth cover for a pillow.

pilot *noun* (*plural* **pilots**) **1** a person who flies an aircraft. **2** an official at a port who goes onto a ship to steer it into or out of the harbour. **3** a trial of something, such as a new product or television programme, to test public opinion. ~ *verb* (**pilots, piloting, piloted**) **1** to fly an aircraft. **2** to steer a ship into or out of a harbour. **3** to test public opinion on something by means of a pilot.

pilot light *noun* (*plural* **pilot lights**) a small permanent flame used to ignite gas in a cooker or boiler.

pimp *noun* (*plural* **pimps**) a man who gets customers for a prostitute and controls the money they earn.

pimple *noun* (*plural* **pimples**) a small raised spot on somebody's skin.
➤ **pimply** *adjective*.

PIN or **PIN number** *noun* (**PINs** or **PIN numbers**) = *personal identification number*, a four-digit security code used with a bank card.

pin *noun* (*plural* **pins**) **1** a small thin pointed piece of metal with a head, used for fastening cloth, paper, etc. **2** a thin piece of wood or metal used for fastening, as a safety catch, or as a support. ~ *verb* (**pins, pinning, pinned**) **1** to fix or fasten something with a pin. **2** to hold somebody firmly against something so they cannot move. ✷ **pin down 1** to force somebody to give a clear opinion or make a decision. **2** to trap an enemy or fugitive by surrounding them or firing on them. **pin something on somebody** to blame them for it.

pinafore *noun* (*plural* **pinafores**) a sleeveless dress worn over a blouse or sweater.

pinball *noun* a game in which you shoot a small metal ball across a sloping surface and score points by hitting obstacles called pins.

pincer *noun* (*plural* **pincers**)
1 (**pincers**) a tool with two strong jaws for gripping things. **2** either of the pair of large claws of a lobster, crab, etc.

pinch *verb* (**pinches, pinching, pinched**) **1** to squeeze something tightly between your finger and thumb. **2** *informal* to steal something. ~ *noun* (*plural* **pinches**) a small amount of a powdered substance that you pick up between your finger and thumb.

pine¹ *noun* (*plural* **pines**) an evergreen

tree with cones and leaves in the form of long thin needles.

pine² *verb* (**pines, pining, pined**) (**pine for**) to have a strong desire to have something or be with somebody; to yearn.

pineapple *noun* (*plural* **pineapples**) a large oval prickly fruit with succulent yellow flesh.

ping *verb* (**pings, pinging, pinged**) to make a sharp ringing sound. ➤ **ping** *noun*.

Ping-Pong *noun trademark* table tennis.

pink *adjective* of a colour midway between red and white. ~ *noun* (*plural* **pinks**) a pink colour.

pinnacle *noun* (*plural* **pinnacles**) 1 the most successful point in an activity: *the pinnacle of her career*. 2 the very top of a mountain or tall rock.

pinpoint *verb* (**pinpoints, pinpointing, pinpointed**) to find or show exactly where something is. ~ *adjective* extremely precise.

pinstripe *noun* (*plural* **pinstripes**) a very thin stripe on fabric. ➤ **pinstriped** *adjective*.

pint *noun* (*plural* **pints**) 1 a unit of capacity equal to one eighth of a gallon (0.568 of a litre). 2 *informal* a pint of beer.

pin-up *noun* (*plural* **pin-ups**) a poster of a sexually attractive person.

pioneer *noun* (*plural* **pioneers**) 1 any of the first people to settle or travel in a territory. 2 a person or company that is the first to do something. ~ *verb* (**pioneers, pioneering, pioneered**) to be the first person or company to do something.

pious *adjective* 1 having or showing deep religious feelings. 2 showing or pretending that your behaviour or attitude is morally superior to other people's. ➤ **piously** *adverb*.

pip *noun* (*plural* **pips**) a small seed of a fruit.

pipe *noun* (*plural* **pipes**) 1 a long tube that liquid or gas flows through. 2 a device for smoking tobacco, consisting of a tube of wood or clay with a mouthpiece at one end and a small bowl for the burning tobacco at the other end. 3 one of a set of tubes that produce the sound on various musical instruments. ~ *verb* (**pipes, piping, piped**) to send liquid or gas somewhere through pipes. ✱ **pipe down** *informal* to stop talking or making noise. **pipe up** to say something after being quiet.

pipeline *noun* (*plural* **pipelines**) a line of pipe for carrying liquid or gas over a long distance. ✱ **in the pipeline** being planned or developed.

piper *noun* (*plural* **pipers**) somebody who plays a pipe or the bagpipes.

pipette /pi pet/ *noun* (*plural* **pipettes**) *Science* a tube-like device used in laboratories for transferring small amounts of liquid from one container to another.

piping *noun* 1 a system of pipes. 2 thin cord used to decorate the edges of something. 3 a thin line of icing or cream used to decorate cakes.

piquant /pee kant/ *adjective* having a pleasantly sharp taste. ➤ **piquancy** *noun*, **piquantly** *adverb*.

piranha /pi rah na/ *noun* (*plural* **piranhas**) a small tropical freshwater fish with sharp teeth that can eat animals much larger than itself.

pirate *noun* (*plural* **pirates**) 1 somebody on a ship who attacks other ships and steals things from them. 2 (*used before a noun*) copied and sold without the permission of the person who has the copyright: *pirate DVDs*. ~ *verb* (**pirates, pirating, pirated**) to make pirate copies of copyright material such as CDs or DVDs.

pirouette /pi roo et/ *noun* (*plural* **pirouettes**) in ballet, a move in which you spin your body round very fast while on one foot. ~ *verb* (**pirouettes, pirouetting, pirouetted**) to perform a pirouette.

Pisces *noun* the twelfth sign of the zodiac (the Fish).

pistachio *noun* (*plural* **pistachios**) a pale-green edible nut.

pistil *noun* (*plural* **pistils**) *Science* the female parts of a flowering plant, comprising the ovary, style, and stigma.

pistol *noun* (*plural* **pistols**) a gun for holding and firing in one hand.

piston *noun* (*plural* **pistons**) in a vehicle engine, the part that is pushed up and down inside a cylinder when the fuel burns, creating the movement that is then transferred to the wheels.

pit *noun* (*plural* **pits**) **1** a hole or shaft in the ground. **2** a hollow in a surface. **3** a coal mine. **4** (**the pits**) an area at the side of a motor-racing track for servicing and refuelling during a race. **5** (**the pits**) *informal* something very bad or of very poor quality. ~ *verb* (**pits, pitting, pitted**) **1** to make small holes in the surface of something. **2** (**pit against**) to set a person or yourself in competition with another person.

pitch¹ *noun* (*plural* **pitches**) **1** a piece of ground marked out for playing a team sport. **2** *Music* how high or low a sound is.

pitch² *verb* (**pitches, pitching, pitched**) **1** to throw something in a rough or casual way. **2** to express or adapt something for a particular audience. **3** to put up a tent.

pitch³ *noun* a thick black substance made from tar and used to seal things.

pitch-black *adjective* completely black or dark.

pitcher *noun* (*plural* **pitchers**) a large jug.

pitchfork *noun* (*plural* **pitchforks**) a farm tool for lifting hay, consisting of a long handle with two long curved metal prongs.

pitfall *noun* (*plural* **pitfalls**) a hidden danger or difficulty.

pith *noun* a white substance between the skin and flesh of a citrus fruit.

pithy *adjective* (**pithier, pithiest**) expressed clearly using no unnecessary words. ➤ **pithily** *adverb*.

pitiful *adjective* **1** causing you to feel pity. **2** of ridiculously poor quality. ➤ **pitifully** *adverb*.

pitiless *adjective* cruel; showing no pity. ➤ **pitilessly** *adverb*.

pitta *noun* (*plural* **pittas**) a type of flat bread that can be split open to hold a filling.

pittance *noun* a very small amount of money.

pity *noun* (*plural* **pities**) **1** sorrow that you feel when bad things happen to other people. **2** something that you regret. ~ *verb* (**pities, pitying, pitied**) to feel pity for somebody.

pivot *noun* (*plural* **pivots**) a pin or point that something turns on. ~ *verb* (**pivots, pivoting, pivoted**) **1** to turn on a pivot. **2** to turn quickly on the spot.

pivotal *adjective* vitally important.

pixel *noun* (*plural* **pixels**) *ICT* each of thousands of tiny spots on a computer screen that together form an image.

pixie *or* **pixy** *noun* (*plural* **pixies**) in fairy stories, a little person depicted as being like a small human with pointed ears.

pizza *noun* (*plural* **pizzas**) a round base of baked dough with a topping of tomatoes, cheese, and other savoury foods.

pizzeria /pee tsa ree a/ *noun* (*plural* **pizzerias**) a restaurant that specializes in pizzas.

placard *noun* (*plural* **placards**) a sign

placate

that somebody carries at a public demonstration.

placate *verb* (**placates, placating, placated**) to make somebody less angry or less hostile to something by offering to do or give them something they want. ➤ **placatory** *adjective*.

place *noun* (*plural* **places**) **1** a position or point in space. **2** a city, town, or other geographical location. **3** a restaurant, theatre, or other establishment. **4** a seat at a table, in a theatre, on a train, etc: *I've saved you a place*. **5** a position in a sequence, for example of winners in a competition or race. **6** a position as a member of an institution, organization, team, etc: *They've offered him a place to study medicine*. **7** a right to do something, or an appropriate occasion to do it: *It's not my place to give you advice*; *This isn't the place for an argument*. *~ verb* (**places, placing, placed**) **1** to put something in a position or condition. **2** to submit a bet, order, etc. ✴ **in place of** as a substitute for something or somebody. **take place** to happen.

placebo /pla see boh/ *noun* (*plural* **placebos**) a medication that has no physical effect, given to a patient for the psychological benefit the patient will feel, or given as a dummy in an experiment.

placement *noun* (*plural* **placements**) **1** the act of putting something in a place. **2** a temporary spell of work that gives somebody practical experience.

placenta *noun* an organ that develops in a woman's womb while she is pregnant and provides the foetus with oxygen and nourishment.

placid *adjective* not easily upset or excited. ➤ **placidly** *adverb*.

plagiarize *or* **plagiarise** /play ja riez/ *verb* (**plagiarizes, plagiarizing, plagiarized** *or* **plagiarises,** etc) to use somebody else's ideas or words in something you write and pretend that they are your own. ➤ **plagiarism** *noun*, **plagiarist** *noun*.

plague /playg/ *noun* (*plural* **plagues**) **1** a highly infectious disease caused by a bacterium carried by rat fleas and transmitted to humans via their bite. **2** a large destructive influx of insects or animals that causes widespread damage. *~ verb* (**plagues, plaguing, plagued**) to annoy or worry somebody constantly.

plaice *noun* (*plural* **plaice**) a large fish with a flat body and brown skin with orange flecks.

plaid /plad/ *noun* woollen fabric with a tartan pattern.

plain *adjective* **1** of simple design, with no pattern or decoration. **2** easy to notice or understand; obvious. **3** expressing opinions or facts in a direct way; candid. **4** said about a person: rather unattractive. *~ noun* (*plural* **plains**) a large area of flat land with few trees. *~ adverb* utterly: *plain silly*. ➤ **plainly** *adverb*, **plainness** *noun*.

plain clothes *plural noun* ordinary civilian clothes, as opposed to a uniform.

plaintiff *noun* (*plural* **plaintiffs**) in a civil court case, the person who is making the accusation and has started the case.

plait /plat/ *noun* (*plural* **plaits**) a length of interwoven strands of hair. *~ verb* (**plaits, plaiting, plaited**) to weave hair into a plait.

plan *noun* (*plural* **plans**) **1** a detailed proposal of how something can be done. **2** (*also in plural*) something that you are intending to do: *What are your plans for the weekend?* **3** a detailed diagram of something that is to be built or made. *~ verb* (**plans, planning, planned**) **1** to decide in advance how you are going to do something. **2** to intend to do something. ➤ **planner** *noun*.

plane¹ noun (plural **planes**) **1** a flat or level surface. **2** informal an aeroplane. **3** Maths an imaginary flat surface that a point is on. ~ adjective flat or level.

plane² noun (plural **planes**) a cutting tool for smoothing a wooden surface by removing thin shavings. ~ verb (**planes, planing, planed**) to smooth a wooden surface with a plane.

plane³ noun (plural **planes**) a large tree with thin bark that comes off in flakes.

planet noun (plural **planets**) a vast object that moves round a star, as the Earth, Mars, Venus, etc go round the Sun. ➤ **planetary** adjective.

planetarium /planɪtairɪum/ noun (plural **planetariums** or **planetaria**) a building or room with a domed ceiling onto which pictures of the stars and planets are projected.

plank noun (plural **planks**) a long flat piece of sawn wood.

plankton noun tiny animals and plants that float near the surface of seas and lakes.

plant noun (plural **plants**) **1** a living organism such as a tree or flower, with roots that absorb water and leaves that make nutrients from sunlight. **2** a factory. **3** machinery and other large industrial equipment. ~ verb (**plants, planting, planted**) **1** to put a seed or plant in the ground for it to grow. **2** to put something firmly in a specified place.

plantation noun (plural **plantations**) **1** a large estate where commercial crops, such as coffee, bananas, and rubber, are grown. **2** an area where trees are grown.

plaque /plak/ noun (plural **plaques**) **1** a small sign fixed to a wall, usually giving historical information about the place. **2** a film of mucus on teeth where bacteria multiply.

plasma noun **1** the liquid part of blood. **2** a gas that contains equal numbers of positive ions and electrons, used in electrical equipment.

plaster noun (plural **plasters**) **1** a substance used as the surface of interior walls, consisting of a mixture of lime, water, and sand, that hardens when it dries. **2** an adhesive strip used for covering and protecting small cuts. **3** a rigid dressing made from plaster of Paris and used for setting a broken bone. ~ verb (**plasters, plastering, plastered**) **1** to coat a wall with plaster. **2** to cover a surface with a thick layer of something. ➤ **plasterer** noun.

plaster of Paris noun a white powder that is mixed with water to form a quick-hardening paste used for setting broken bones and in sculpture.

plastic noun (plural **plastics**) **1** a synthetic substance that can be moulded into any shape and can be rigid or slightly elastic. **2** informal credit cards. ~ adjective made of plastic. ➤ **plasticity** noun.

plastic surgery noun surgical operations carried out to improve somebody's appearance or to repair areas of damaged skin.

plate noun (plural **plates**) **1** a flat dish from which food is eaten or served. **2** a flat piece of metal that is part of a machine or other device. **3** Geography any of the moving blocks that form the earth's crust. ~ verb (**plates, plating, plated**) to coat a metal with a thin layer of gold, silver, tin, etc.

plateau /platoh/ noun (plural **plateaus** or **plateaux**) a flat area of high ground.

platform noun (plural **platforms**) **1** a raised area by the track at a railway station, where passengers stand. **2** a raised area where a speaker or performer can be seen by the audience. **3** a declared political policy.

platinum noun Science a greyish white precious metallic element.

platitude

platitude *noun* (*plural* **platitudes**) a remark that seems boring or insincere because it is the kind of thing people always say in a particular situation.

platonic *adjective* said about a relationship: close but not sexual. ➤ **platonically** *adverb*.

platoon *noun* (*plural* **platoons**) a group of soldiers that is a subdivision of a company.

platter *noun* (*plural* **platters**) a large plate for serving food.

platypus /pla ti pus/ *noun* (*plural* **platypuses**) an Australian mammal that lays eggs and has a furry body, a bill like a duck's, and a broad flat tail.

plaudits *plural noun* comments that express admiration.

plausible *adjective* reasonable enough to be true, although you are not sure that it is. ➤ **plausibility** *noun*, **plausibly** *adverb*.

play *verb* (**plays, playing, played**) **1** to take part in activities for enjoyment or recreation. **2** to take part in a sport or game. **3** to perform music on a musical instrument. **4** to make audio equipment produce music or sounds. **5** to perform a role in a drama or film. ~ *noun* (*plural* **plays**) **1** a piece of dramatic literature for acting on stage or broadcast on television or radio. **2** activity that is done for recreation or amusement: *children at play*. ✳ **play about** to behave in a silly or irresponsible way. **play down** to make something seem less severe or extreme than it really is. **play up 1** to make something seem more severe or extreme than it really is. **2** to cause trouble. **3** *informal* to not be working properly.

player *noun* (*plural* **players**) a person who takes part in a sport or game.

playful *adjective* **1** full of fun. **2** not to be taken seriously; done or said for fun. ➤ **playfully** *adverb*.

playground *noun* (*plural* **playgrounds**) a piece of land for children to play on.

playgroup *noun* (*plural* **playgroups**) a supervised play activity for children below school age.

playing card *noun* (*plural* **playing cards**) each of a set of small cards with numbers and symbols on them, used in playing games.

playing field *noun* (*plural* **playing fields**) a grassy area for playing sports.

play-off *noun* (*plural* **play-offs**) an extra match played between teams who are tied.

playwright *noun* (*plural* **playwrights**) *Drama* somebody who writes plays.

plaza /plah za/ *noun* (*plural* **plazas**) a public square in a city or town.

plc *or* **PLC** *abbreviation* public limited company.

plea *noun* (*plural* **pleas**) **1** a serious or emotional request for something. **2** an accused person's formal statement telling a court whether they are guilty or not guilty of the crime they have been charged with.

plead *verb* (**pleads, pleading, pleaded**) **1** to make a serious or emotional request for something. **2** said about an accused person: to say formally whether you are guilty or not guilty of the crime you have been charged with.

pleasant *adjective* **1** giving pleasure; enjoyable. **2** likable and friendly. ➤ **pleasantly** *adverb*.

pleasantry *noun* (*plural* **pleasantries**) a polite but trivial remark.

please *adverb* used in a polite request or an urgent appeal. ~ *verb* (**pleases, pleasing, pleased**) to give somebody a feeling of satisfaction or pleasure. ✳ **please yourself** to do what you want to do. ➤ **pleasing** *adjective*.

pleased *adjective* **1** satisfied or contented. **2** glad or willing to do something.

pleasurable *adjective* pleasant or enjoyable. ➤ **pleasurably** *adverb*.

pleasure *noun* (*plural* **pleasures**) **1** a feeling of satisfaction or contentment. **2** something that you enjoy.

pleat *noun* (*plural* **pleats**) a fold in cloth made by folding a part over on itself and stitching or pressing it in place. ➤ **pleated** *adjective*.

plectrum *noun* (*plural* **plectrums** or **plectra**) *Music* a thin flat piece of plastic that you hold between your finger and thumb and use to pluck the strings of a guitar.

pledge *noun* (*plural* **pledges**) **1** a solemn promise. **2** something that you give somebody as security for a loan. ~ *verb* (**pledges, pledging, pledged**) **1** to promise something solemnly. **2** to give something as security for a loan.

plentiful *adjective* existing in large quantities. ➤ **plentifully** *adverb*.

plenty *noun* enough or more than you need.

plethora /ple tho ra/ *noun* a very large quantity or number.

pleurisy /ploor i si/ *noun* a serious illness in which your lungs become swollen and breathing becomes very painful.

pliable *adjective* **1** easy to bend. **2** said about a person: easy to influence or persuade. ➤ **pliability** *noun*.

pliers *plural noun* a hand tool for gripping small objects or for bending and cutting wire.

plight *noun* (*plural* **plights**) a difficult situation.

plinth *noun* (*plural* **plinths**) a flat base that something such as a column or statue rests on.

plod *verb* (**plods, plodding, plodded**) **1** to walk with slow or heavy steps. **2** to keep working slowly but hard at something boring.

plonk *verb* (**plonks, plonking, plonked**) to put something down heavily or carelessly.

plop *verb* (**plops, plopping, plopped**) to drop suddenly with a sound like something dropping into water. ➤ **plop** *noun*.

plot *noun* (*plural* **plots**) **1** a secret plan to do something illegal or harmful. **2** the main sequence of events in a book, film, etc. **3** a small piece of land marked out for a specific purpose. ~ *verb* (**plots, plotting, plotted**) **1** to plan to do something illegal or harmful. **2** to mark something on a map or chart.

plough /plow/ *noun* (*plural* **ploughs**) a device that cuts and turns over soil in a field, pulled behind a tractor or horse. ~ *verb* (**ploughs, ploughing, ploughed**) **1** to turn soil over with a plough. **2** (**plough into**) to hit something with a very forceful impact. **3** (**plough into**) to invest a lot of money in something.

plover /plu ver/ *noun* (*plural* **plovers** or **plover**) a small to medium-sized wading bird.

ploy *noun* (*plural* **ploys**) a cunningly devised plan for achieving something.

pluck *verb* (**plucks, plucking, plucked**) **1** to take a firm hold of something and remove it. **2** to pick a flower, fruit, etc. **3** to remove the feathers from a bird's carcass. **4** to produce sounds from a stringed instrument using your fingers or a plectrum. ~ *noun* courage. ✱ **pluck up** to find the necessary courage to do something difficult or frightening.

plucky *adjective* (**pluckier, pluckiest**) showing courage and determination. ➤ **pluckily** *adverb*.

plug *noun* (*plural* **plugs**) **1** a device that connects an appliance to an electricity supply at a socket. **2** a device that seals a hole, for example in a sink or bath. **3** *informal* mentioning something as a way of advertising it. ~ *verb*

plughole

(**plugs, plugging, plugged**)
1 to block or close a hole or gap.
2 *informal* to publicize something, especially by casually mentioning it.
✳ **plug in** to connect an electrical appliance to a power point.

plughole *noun* (*plural* **plugholes**) a hole in a sink or bath through which the water drains away.

plum *noun* (*plural* **plums**) an oval fruit with yellow, purple, red, or green skin and a large oblong seed.

plumage *noun* a bird's feathers.

plumb *adjective* exactly vertical, straight, or level. ~ *adverb informal* exactly.

plumber *noun* (*plural* **plumbers**) a person who installs and repairs water piping and fittings.

plumbing *noun* **1** a plumber's work. **2** the system of pipes, tanks, and fixtures installed for a water supply and heating in a building.

plume *noun* (*plural* **plumes**) **1** a long, brightly coloured feather. **2** a tall thin cloud of smoke or vapour. ➤ **plumed** *adjective*.

plummet *verb* (**plummets, plummeting, plummeted**) to fall sharply and rapidly.

plump¹ *adjective* slightly fat.

plump² *verb* (**plumps, plumping, plumped**) (**plump for**) to choose something.

plunder *verb* (**plunders, plundering, plundered**) to use force to steal things from a place. ~ *noun* things taken by plundering.

plunge *verb* (**plunges, plunging, plunged**) **1** to fall rapidly. **2** to jump or dive into water. **3** to dip something into a liquid. **4** to put something or somebody into an unpleasant state. ~ *noun* (*plural* **plunges**) **1** a rapid fall. **2** a sudden decline in value. ✳ **take the plunge** *informal* to decide to do something after thinking about it.

plural *adjective English* in grammar, referring to more than one. ➤ **plural** *noun*, **plurally** *adverb*.

pluralism *noun* the existence in a society of different social, ethnic, or religious groups. ➤ **pluralist** *adjective and noun*.

plus *preposition* **1** with the addition of: *Four plus five equals nine.* **2** and also: *You need experience plus patience for this job.* ~ *noun* (*plural* **pluses** or **plusses**) **1** a positive factor or quality. **2** (*also* **plus sign**) a sign (+) that indicates addition or shows a positive value. ~ *adjective* **1** said about a number: having a positive value. **2** said about a grade: slightly higher than the grade specified: *B plus*.

plush *adjective* very comfortable and expensive.

plutonium *noun Science* a radioactive metallic element used in weapons and as a fuel for atomic reactors.

ply *noun* (*plural* **plies**) **1** one of several strands in yarn, wool, etc. **2** one of several layers of wood or other material stuck together. ~ *verb* (**plies, plying, plied**) **1** to keep giving somebody something. **2** to keep asking somebody questions. **3** to travel over a specified route regularly.

plywood *noun* board made from thin sheets of wood glued together.

p.m. *abbreviation* = (Latin) *post meridiem* after midday.

pneumatic /new ma tik/ *adjective* operated by or filled with air under pressure. ➤ **pneumatically** *adverb*.

pneumonia /new moh ni a/ *noun* a serious illness in which your lungs become swollen and filled with fluid.

poach¹ *verb* (**poaches, poaching, poached**) to cook food gently in a simmering liquid.

poach² *verb* (**poaches, poaching, poached**) to take birds, fish, or other animals illegally by hunting or fishing without permission. ➤ **poacher** *noun*.

pocket noun (plural **pockets**) **1** a small bag-shaped part of a piece of clothing, for putting things in. **2** any pouch-like compartment for storage. **3** the amount of money that somebody can afford to pay. **4** a small isolated area or group. ~ verb (**pockets, pocketing, pocketed**) to put something in your pocket. ✱ **out of pocket** having lost money. ➤ **pocketful** noun (plural **pocketfuls**).

pocket money noun money that a parent regularly gives to a child.

pod noun (plural **pods**) a long seed case of a pea or bean.

podgy adjective (**podgier, podgiest**) short and plump.

podium noun (plural **podiums** or **podia**) a small raised platform that somebody stands on to give a speech or conduct an orchestra.

poem noun (plural **poems**) a piece of writing in which the words are chosen mainly for the rhythm of their sounds, usually with short lines arranged one below the other.

poet noun (plural **poets**) a person who writes poetry.

poetic adjective **1** to do with poets or poetry. **2** beautiful or pleasing. ➤ **poetically** adverb.

poetic licence noun English a writer's decision to break the usual rules about the meaning or order of words in order to create a particular literary effect.

poetry noun **1** writing in the form of poems. **2** a quality of beauty and grace.

pogrom /ˈpogrom/ noun (plural **pogroms**) an organized massacre of people from a particular ethnic group, especially formerly of Jews in eastern Europe and Russia.

poignant /ˈpoynyant/ adjective causing you to feel very strong emotions, often sadness or pity. ➤ **poignancy** noun, **poignantly** adverb.

point noun (plural **points**) **1** the sharp, tapering end of something. **2** a dot or full stop. **3** an exact position. **4** an exact moment in time or in a sequence. **5** purpose or benefit: *There's no point crying about it.* **6** (often **the point**) the most important element of a discussion or matter. **7** a unit of scoring. **8** each of the 32 main compass directions. **9** (**points**) a device with movable rails that joins two railway lines. ~ verb (**points, pointing, pointed**) **1** to use a finger to show the position or direction of something. **2** to face a particular direction. **3** (**point to**) to indicate that something is probably the case: *The evidence pointed to accidental death.* ✱ **beside the point** irrelevant. **make a point of doing something** to take particular care to do something. **point out** to mention something so that people will realize or consider it. **up to a point** to a certain extent.

pointed adjective **1** having a sharp, tapering end, or several such ends. **2** said about a remark: aimed in criticism at a particular person or group.

pointer noun (plural **pointers**) **1** a needle that indicates a reading on a dial or scale. **2** a useful suggestion or hint.

pointless adjective having no purpose or benefit. ➤ **pointlessly** adverb.

point of view noun (plural **points of view**) an opinion or attitude.

poise noun **1** a calm and self-confident manner. **2** a graceful way of walking or moving.

poised adjective ready to take action.

poison noun (plural **poisons**) a substance that can kill you if it gets into your body, for example when you swallow it. ~ verb (**poisons, poisoning, poisoned**) **1** to harm or kill somebody with poison. **2** to have a harmful influence on somebody or something. ➤ **poisonous** adjective.

poke *verb* (**pokes, poking, poked**) **1** to hit something with a stabbing movement of your fingertip or a sharp object. **2** (**poke out**) to protrude: *a pen poking out of his pocket*. **3** (**poke about/around**) to look about or through something. ~ *noun* (*plural* **pokes**) an instance of poking something; a prod or jab.

poker[1] *noun* (*plural* **pokers**) a metal rod for poking a fire to keep it burning.

poker[2] *noun* a card game in which players bet on the value of their hands.

polar *adjective* **1** *Geography* in the region near a geographical pole. **2** *Science* to do with the poles of a magnet.

polar bear *noun* (*plural* **polar bears**) a large white Arctic bear.

polarize *or* **polarise** *verb* (**polarizes, polarizing, polarized** *or* **polarises**, etc) **1** *Science* to cause light waves to vibrate in a definite pattern or direction. **2** to divide people or their opinions into two opposing groups.
➤ **polarization** *or* **polarisation** *noun*.

pole[1] *noun* (*plural* **poles**) a long thin cylindrical piece of wood, metal, etc, used as a support.

pole[2] *noun* (*plural* **poles**) **1** *Geography* either of the two points at the northern and southern ends of the earth's axis. **2** *Science* either of the terminals of an electric cell or battery. **3** *Science* any of two or more parts of a magnetized object where the magnetism is strongest.

polecat *noun* (*plural* **polecats**) an animal that looks like a dark brown weasel and gives off an unpleasant smell.

polemic /po le mik/ *noun* (*plural* **polemics**) a point of view expressed very strongly or aggressively.
➤ **polemical** *adjective*, **polemicist** *noun*.

pole vault *noun* an athletics event consisting of a jump over a high bar using a long flexible pole.

police *noun* an organization of people whose job is maintaining public order and enforcing the law. ~ *verb* (**polices, policing, policed**) to enforce law and order in an area or at an event.

police officer *noun* (*plural* **police officers**) a member of the police.
➤ **policeman** *noun*, **policewoman** *noun*

police state *noun* (*plural* **police states**) a country in which the government controls political and social life very strictly and secret police officers enforce the law.

police station *noun* (*plural* **police stations**) the headquarters of a local police force.

policy[1] *noun* (*plural* **policies**) a set of proposals or plans for organizing something, especially a country's political life.

policy[2] *noun* (*plural* **policies**) a contract of insurance.

polio *or* **poliomyelitis** /poh li oh mie i lie tis/ *noun* an infectious disease in which the nerve cells of the spinal cord become inflamed, causing paralysis.

polish *verb* (**polishes, polishing, polished**) **1** to make something smooth and glossy by rubbing it, or by rubbing a cream or liquid on it. **2** to bring something up to a high standard. ~ *noun* **1** a special cream or liquid rubbed on a surface to give it a shine. **2** a high standard. **3** a refined way of behaving. ✽ **polish off** to eat or drink something, especially a lot of it.

polite *adjective* behaving in a considerate and respectful way; well-mannered. ➤ **politely** *adverb*, **politeness** *noun*.

politic *adjective* wise in the circumstances.

political *adjective* **1** to do with government or public affairs. **2** to do with politics. ➤ **politically** *adverb*.

political correctness *noun* care taken to avoid offending particular groups of people, especially in the language you use to talk about them. ➤ **politically correct** *adjective*.

political prisoner *noun* (*plural* **political prisoners**) a person who has been put in prison because they have political beliefs that their government does not approve of.

politician *noun* (*plural* **politicians**) a person who is involved in politics, especially as an elected representative.

politicize *or* **politicise** *verb* (**politicizes, politicizing, politicized** *or* **politicises**, etc) **1** to change an issue or event so that it starts to involve politics. **2** to tell somebody about politics so that they start to have political opinions. ➤ **politicization** *or* **politicisation** *noun*.

politics *noun* **1** all the activities to do with running a country or local government. **2** the job of somebody who has been elected as a political representative. ~ *plural noun* a person's political opinions.

polka *noun* (*plural* **polkas**) *Music* a lively dance with two beats to the bar.

poll *noun* (*plural* **polls**) **1** a survey of people questioned at random. **2** (*often in plural*) an occasion when people vote; an election. **3** the number of votes cast in an election. ~ *verb* (**polls, polling, polled**) **1** to question people in a poll. **2** to receive a specified number of votes.

pollen *noun* a fine dust released by the male parts of a plant for fertilizing the female parts.

pollen count *noun* a measure of the amount of pollen in the air.

pollinate *verb* (**pollinates, pollinating, pollinated**) to fertilize a plant by putting pollen on the female parts. ➤ **pollination** *noun*.

poll tax /pohl taks/ *noun* (*plural* **poll taxes**) any tax in which each adult pays the same fixed amount.

pollute *verb* (**pollutes, polluting, polluted**) to make something such as air or water impure by releasing harmful substances into it.

pollutant *noun* (*plural* **pollutants**) a harmful substance that pollutes something.

pollution *noun* **1** substances that pollute something. **2** the fact that something has been polluted.

polo *noun* a team game played on horseback using long mallets to hit a wooden ball into the opponents' goal.

polo neck *noun* (*plural* **polo necks**) a high round folded-over collar on a jumper.

poltergeist /pohl ter giest/ *noun* (*plural* **poltergeists**) a ghost that is supposed to make loud noises and throw objects about.

polyester *noun* an artificial fabric used to make clothes.

polygamy /po li ga mi/ *noun* being married to more than one person at a time. ➤ **polygamist** *noun*, **polygamous** *adjective*.

polygon *noun* (*plural* **polygons**) *Maths* a flat shape with three or more straight sides. ➤ **polygonal** *adjective*.

polyhedron /po li hee dron/ *noun* (*plural* **polyhedrons** *or* **polyhedra**) *Maths* a solid shape with four or more faces.

polymer *noun* (*plural* **polymers**) *Science* a chemical compound that has very large molecules made up of groups of smaller molecules. ➤ **polymeric** *adjective*.

polyp /po lip/ *noun* (*plural* **polyps**) **1** a small sea creature with a hollow cylindrical body attached to a rock at

polystyrene

one end. **2** a small abnormal growth on a mucous membrane in the body.

polystyrene *noun* a type of light brittle plastic used to make packaging and insulating materials.

polysyllabic *adjective* English having two or more syllables.

polytheism *noun* the worship of more than one god. ➤ **polytheistic** *adjective*.

polythene *noun* a tough lightweight plastic often used to make bags.

polyunsaturated *adjective* said about a fat or oil in food: having a chemical structure that causes only a small amount of cholesterol to form in your body.

pomegranate /po mi gra nat/ *noun* (*plural* **pomegranates**) a thick-skinned reddish fruit with bright red flesh that contains many seeds.

pommel *noun* (*plural* **pommels**) the raised part at the front and top of a saddle.

pomp *noun* elaborate costumes and ceremonies used on formal occasions.

pompous *adjective* behaving in a way that shows you think you and your opinions are extremely important. ➤ **pomposity** *noun*, **pompously** *adverb*.

pond *noun* (*plural* **ponds**) a small area of still water.

ponder *verb* (**ponders, pondering, pondered**) to think about something carefully.

ponderous *adjective* very slow or uninteresting. ➤ **ponderously** *adverb*.

pong *verb* (**pongs, ponging, ponged**) *informal* to give off a strong unpleasant smell. ➤ **pong** *noun*.

pontiff *noun* (*plural* **pontiffs**) a pope.

pontifical *adjective* to do with a pope; papal.

pontificate /pon ti fi kayt/ *verb* (**pontificates, pontificating, pontificated**) to express opinions in a pompous or forceful way. ~ /pon ti fi kit/ *noun* (*plural* **pontificates**) the position of pope, or the time during which somebody is pope.

pontoon[1] *noun* (*plural* **pontoons**) **1** a huge portable float that is part of a temporary bridge. **2** a floating jetty in a marina.

pontoon[2] *noun* a card game in which players try to achieve a score as close as possible to 21.

pony *noun* (*plural* **ponies**) a small horse.

ponytail *noun* (*plural* **ponytails**) a hairstyle in which the hair is pulled back tightly and tied so that it hangs down at the back of the head.

poodle *noun* (*plural* **poodles**) a dog with a thick curly coat that is often clipped and shaved.

pool[1] *noun* (*plural* **pools**) **1** a small area of still water that is usually bigger than a pond but smaller than a lake. **2** = SWIMMING POOL.

pool[2] *noun* (*plural* **pools**) **1** an indoor game, similar to snooker, in which you use a long wooden stick called a cue to hit coloured balls into holes at the edges of a cloth-covered table. **2** (**the pools**) a type of gambling in which people guess the results of football matches. **3** a supply of something that anybody in a group can use. ~ *verb* (**pools, pooling, pooled**) said about a group of people: to combine resources in order to achieve a common purpose.

poor *adjective* **1** not having much money. **2** of a low standard or quality. **3** inspiring pity or sympathy: *You poor thing!*

poorly *adverb* in an inferior way; badly: *a poorly designed machine*. ~ *adjective* ill.

pop[1] *verb* (**pops, popping, popped**) **1** to make a short explosive sound. **2** *informal* to go somewhere suddenly or quickly. **3** *informal* to put some-

pop thing somewhere quickly or for a short time. ~ *noun* (*plural* **pops**) **1** a popping sound. **2** a flavoured fizzy soft drink.

pop² *or* **pop music** *noun* modern popular music. ~ *adjective* to do with pop music.

popcorn *noun* maize kernels heated so that they burst and form a white starchy mass.

pope *or* **Pope** *noun* (*plural* **popes** *or* **Popes**) the head of the Roman Catholic Church and bishop of Rome.

poplar *noun* (*plural* **poplars**) a tall thin tree of the willow family.

poppadom *or* **poppadum** *noun* (*plural* **poppadoms** *or* **poppadums**) in Indian cookery, a crisp wafer-thin pancake of deep-fried dough.

poppy *noun* (*plural* **poppies**) a plant with bright, usually red flowers and a large seed case.

populace *noun* (**the populace**) the general public.

popular *adjective* **1** liked or admired by many people. **2** designed to suit the needs or tastes of ordinary people rather than experts or rich people: *popular science*. ➤ **popularity** *noun*, **popularly** *adverb*.

popularize *or* **popularise** *verb* (**popularizes, popularizing, popularized** *or* **popularises,** etc) to cause many people to begin to like, appreciate, or understand something. ➤ **popularization** *or* **popularisation** *noun*.

populate *verb* (**populates, populating, populated**) to live in a place.

population *noun* the people living in a place, or their total number.

populist *adjective* designed to appeal to as many people as possible, and often not very sensible or worthwhile for that reason. ➤ **populism** *noun*, **populist** *noun*.

porcelain *noun* a hard translucent white ceramic material used to make plates, cups, etc.

porch *noun* (*plural* **porches**) **1** a covered entrance to a building. **2** *N American* a veranda.

porcupine *noun* (*plural* **porcupines**) a large rodent with stiff protective bristles on its body.

pore¹ *noun* (*plural* **pores**) each of many tiny openings that moisture can pass through on your skin or on the surface of a plant.

pore² *verb* (**pores, poring, pored**) (**pore over/through**) to look at or read something closely.

pork *noun* the flesh of a pig used as food.

porn *noun informal* = PORNOGRAPHY.

pornography *noun* books, photographs, and films intended to cause sexual excitement. ➤ **pornographic** *adjective*.

porous *adjective* allowing liquids and gases to pass through. ➤ **porosity** *noun*.

porpoise *noun* (*plural* **porpoises** *or* **porpoise**) a small whale with a blunt snout, related to a dolphin.

porridge *noun* a soft food made by boiling oatmeal in milk or water.

port¹ *noun* (*plural* **ports**) **1** a town or city with a large harbour or docks. **2** a large harbour or docks.

port² *noun* the left side of a ship or aircraft looking forward.

port³ *noun* a strong sweet wine made in Portugal.

port⁴ *noun* (*plural* **ports**) **1** *ICT* a socket in a computer for connecting a device to it. **2** an opening through which goods are loaded and unloaded, or through which guns are fired.

portable *adjective* small and light enough to be carried about. ➤ **portability** *noun*.

portal *noun* (*plural* **portals**) a grand door or gateway.

portcullis *noun* (*plural* **portcullises**) a heavy iron gate that can be lowered to prevent people getting into a castle.

portent *noun* (*plural* **portents**) a sign that something unpleasant will happen.

portentous /paw ten tus/ *adjective* indicating that something unpleasant will happen; ominous. ➤ **portentously** *adverb*.

porter[1] *noun* (*plural* **porters**) **1** somebody employed to move patients or equipment in a hospital. **2** somebody employed to carry people's luggage in a hotel or railway station.

porter[2] *noun* (*plural* **porters**) an official in charge of the entrance to a large building.

portfolio *noun* (*plural* **portfolios**) **1** a flexible case for carrying loose papers, pictures, etc. **2** a set of drawings, photographs, etc presented as evidence of artistic talent. **3** the position or responsibilities of a government minister.

porthole *noun* (*plural* **portholes**) a small window in the side of a ship.

portico *noun* (*plural* **porticoes** or **porticos**) a large stone porch at the entrance to a grand building.

portion *noun* (*plural* **portions**) **1** a part or share of something. **2** a helping of food.

portly *adjective* (**portlier, portliest**) rather fat.

portrait *noun* (*plural* **portraits**) **1** a painting or drawing of a person. **2** a description of a person in a novel, film, etc. ➤ **portraiture** *noun*.

portray *verb* (**portrays, portraying, portrayed**) **1** to represent or describe somebody or something in a particular way. **2** to paint or draw a picture of somebody. ➤ **portrayal** *noun*.

pose *verb* (**poses, posing, posed**) **1** to stand or sit in a certain position in order to be painted or photographed. **2** to be a problem or threat. **3** to ask a question. **4** (**pose as**) to pretend to be something. ~ *noun* (*plural* **poses**) **1** a position that you stand or sit in in order to be painted or photographed. **2** an affected way of behaving intended to impress others.

poser *noun* (*plural* **posers**) **1** somebody whose clothes, behaviour, or other qualities are deliberately chosen to impress others. **2** a puzzling or baffling question.

posh *adjective informal* **1** exclusive or luxurious: *a posh hotel*. **2** belonging to or suggesting a high social class: *his posh family*.

position *noun* (*plural* **positions**) **1** the place where somebody or something is. **2** the way in which you are sitting, standing, or lying, or the way in which something is arranged. **3** a situation: *You've put me in an awkward position*. **4** a post, job, or rank. ~ *verb* (**positions, positioning, positioned**) to put something in a particular position.

positive *adjective* **1** concentrating on what is good; optimistic. **2** expressing approval or agreement: *a positive response*. **3** showing the presence of something: *The test was positive*. **4** confident or certain: *I'm positive I locked the door*. **5** *Maths* said about a number: greater than zero. **6** *Science* said about a terminal in a battery: having the higher electric potential and forming the part from which current flows to an external circuit. **7** said about a photographic image: having light and dark parts that correspond to those of the object that was photographed. **8** *English* describing the simple form of an adjective of adverb as opposed to a comparative or superlative, for example *quick* or *well*. ~ *noun* (*plural*

positives) **1** a positive number or value. **2** a good quality or aspect. **3** a positive photograph or a print. **4** *English* the positive form of an adjective or adverb. ➤ **positively** *adverb*.

possess *verb* (**possesses, possessing, possessed**) **1** to own something. **2** to have something as a quality or skill. **3** to influence somebody's behaviour: *What possessed you to lie?* ➤ **possessor** *noun*.

possession *noun* (*plural* **possessions**) **1** something that you own or are carrying with you. **2** the fact that you have or own something.

possessive *adjective* **1** jealously demanding all or most of somebody's attention and affection. **2** reluctant to share or give up possessions. **3** *English* in grammar, showing that something belongs or relates to somebody: *the possessive determiner 'my'*. ~ *noun* (*plural* **possessives**) *English* a possessive word. ➤ **possessively** *adverb*.

possibility *noun* (*plural* **possibilities**) **1** something that might happen or might be the case. **2** the fact that something is possible. **3** (**possibilities**) good qualities that could be developed; potential.

possible *adjective* able to happen or able to be the case.

possibly *adverb* **1** it is possible; maybe: *'Do you think he missed the train?' 'Possibly.'* **2** used to add force to *can* or *could*: *I'll do everything I possibly can.*

post[1] *noun* (*plural* **posts**) **1** an upright piece of wood or metal that forms a support. **2** a pole that marks the start or finish of a race. ~ *verb* (**posts, posting, posted**) to put a notice up in a public place.

post[2] *noun* **1** the system for sending and delivering letters and parcels. **2** a single delivery of letters and parcels. **3** letters and parcels sent or received. ~ *verb* (**posts, posting, posted**) to send something by post.

post[3] *noun* (*plural* **posts**) **1** a job or position. **2** the place where a soldier or police officer is stationed. ~ *verb* (**posts, posting, posted**) **1** to send somebody to work in a different place. **2** to station a soldier or police officer somewhere.

postage *noun* the charge for sending something by post.

postal *adjective* to do with the system of sending and delivering letters and parcels.

postal order *noun* (*plural* **postal orders**) a document that is a safe way of sending money, bought at a post office and able to be exchanged for money at another post office.

postbox *noun* (*plural* **postboxes**) **1** a public box where people put letters that they are sending by post. **2** a box at a post office that an organization can hire and have its mail delivered to.

postcard *noun* (*plural* **postcards**) a card for sending a message by post without an envelope.

postcode *noun* (*plural* **postcodes**) a combination of letters and numbers that identifies a postal address.

postcode lottery *noun* a situation in which people receive good or bad service depending on which part of the country they live in.

poster *noun* (*plural* **posters**) a large picture or sign put up as an advertisement or for decoration.

posterior *noun* (*plural* **posteriors**) *informal* the buttocks.

posterity *noun* future generations.

postgraduate *noun* (*plural* **postgraduates**) a student who is continuing in higher education after completing a first degree.

posthumous *adjective* done, given, or

postman *noun* (*plural* **postmen**) a man who delivers the post.

postmark *noun* (*plural* **postmarks**) a mark stamped on a letter or parcel to show the date and place of posting. ~ *verb* (**postmarks, postmarking, postmarked**) to stamp a letter or parcel with a postmark.

postmortem *noun* (*plural* **postmortems**) an examination of a dead body carried out to find out the cause of death.

post office *noun* (*plural* **post offices**) **1** a national organization that runs a postal system. **2** a local office where you can post letters and parcels and use various other services.

postpone *verb* (**postpones, postponing, postponed**) to change an arrangement so that something happens at a later time or date. ➤ **postponement** *noun*.

postscript *noun* (*plural* **postscripts**) a note added at the end of a letter, after the signature.

posture *noun* (*plural* **postures**) **1** a position of your body. **2** an attitude. ➤ **postural** *adjective*.

posy *noun* (*plural* **posies**) a small bouquet of flowers.

pot[1] *noun* (*plural* **pots**) **1** a round container for holding liquids or solids. **2** a container used for cooking food. **3** the total of the bets taken in a gambling game. ~ *verb* (**pots, potting, potted**) **1** to plant something in a flowerpot. **2** in games such as snooker and pool, to send a ball into a pocket. * **go to pot** *informal* to deteriorate or collapse. ➤ **potful** *noun* (*plural* **potfuls**).

pot[2] *noun informal* cannabis.

potassium *noun* Science a silver-white metallic chemical element.

potato *noun* (*plural* **potatoes**) a rounded, usually light-coloured vegetable cooked and eaten as food.

potent *adjective* powerful. ➤ **potency** *noun*.

potential *adjective* capable of becoming or turning out to be a specified thing: *potential benefits*. ~ *noun* qualities that could be successfully developed. ➤ **potentially** *adverb*.

pothole *noun* (*plural* **potholes**) **1** a hole in a road surface. **2** a natural cave or passage underground. ➤ **potholed** *adjective*.

potion *noun* (*plural* **potions**) **1** in stories, a liquid that has a magical effect on the person who drinks it. **2** a liquid medicine or poison.

pot-luck *noun* whatever happens to be available.

potted *adjective* **1** said about food: preserved in a tin or pot. **2** brief and with only the main details given: *a potted biography*.

potter[1] *verb* (**potters, pottering, pottered**) to spend time doing enjoyable but fairly unimportant things.

potter[2] *noun* (*plural* **potters**) somebody who makes pottery.

pottery *noun* (*plural* **potteries**) **1** articles made of baked clay. **2** the craft of making pottery. **3** a place where pottery is made.

potty[1] *noun* (*plural* **potties**) a bowl-shaped container used as a toilet by a small child.

potty[2] *adjective* (**pottier, pottiest**) *informal* **1** slightly crazy. **2** foolish or silly. **3** (**potty about**) very fond of or enthusiastic about something or somebody.

pouch *noun* (*plural* **pouches**) **1** a small bag made of soft flexible material. **2** a pocket of skin in the abdomen of marsupials for carrying their young.

poultice *noun* (*plural* **poultices**) a

medical treatment for an injured or swollen part of the body, in the form of cloth bag or pad containing a medicinal mixture that you press onto the affected part.

poultry *noun* chickens, ducks, and other domestic birds kept for their eggs or meat.

pounce *verb* (**pounces, pouncing, pounced**) **1** to spring forwards in order to grab something or somebody. **2** (**pounce on**) to be quick to criticize a mistake. ➤ **pounce** *noun*.

pound[1] *noun* (*plural* **pounds** *or* **pound**) **1** a unit of weight equal to 16 ounces (about 0.454 of a kilogram). **2** the basic unit of money in the UK and various other countries.

pound[2] *verb* (**pounds, pounding, pounded**) **1** to beat or crush a substance into a powder or pulp. **2** to hit something or somebody heavily and repeatedly. **3** said about somebody's heart or head: to beat with a heavy rhythm.

pound[3] *noun* (*plural* **pounds**) a place where stray animals are kept.

pour *verb* (**pours, pouring, poured**) **1** to make a liquid flow into or out of something in a stream, for example by tipping the container it is in. **2** to flow in large quantities: *Blood poured from his nose.* **3** to rain hard.

pout *verb* (**pouts, pouting, pouted**) to push your lips out in a sulking or sexually provocative way. ➤ **pout** *noun*, **pouty** *adjective*.

poverty *noun* the condition of being poor.

powder *noun* **1** a substance in the form of tiny dry loose particles. **2** a cosmetic or medicine in the form of fine particles. ~ *verb* (**powders, powdering, powdered**) **1** to sprinkle something with powder. **2** to crush something to powder. ➤ **powdery** *adjective*.

power *noun* (*plural* **powers**) **1** the ability to do something. **2** legal authority or political control. **3** a country that has military strength and international influence. **4** physical strength. **5** electricity or another form of energy. **6** the energy or driving force generated by a motor. **7** *Science* in physics, the amount of work done or energy given off, measured in watts. **8** *Maths* the number of times a given number is to be multiplied by itself. ~ *verb* (**powers, powering, powered**) to make a machine or device work by supplying it with power.

powerboat *noun* (*plural* **powerboats**) a powerful motorboat.

power cut *noun* (*plural* **power cuts**) a failure in the supply of electricity to an area.

powerful *adjective* **1** having great power or influence: *powerful nations*. **2** physically very strong: *powerful arms*. **3** extremely effective or persuasive: *a powerful argument*. ➤ **powerfully** *adverb*.

powerhouse *noun* (*plural* **powerhouses**) *informal* a person or thing that has great strength or energy.

powerless *adjective* lacking the authority, strength, or opportunity to take action.

power station *noun* (*plural* **power stations**) a building where electricity is generated.

pp *abbreviation* **1** pages. **2** = (Latin) *per procurationem*, used to indicate that a person is signing a letter on behalf of somebody else.

PR *abbreviation* **1** proportional representation. **2** public relations.

practicable *adjective* capable of being done. ➤ **practicability** *noun*, **practicably** *adverb*.

practical *adjective* **1** involving really doing things, rather than just thinking or learning about them: *practical experience*. **2** suitable for a particular

practical use: *practical clothes to go hiking in*. **3** realistic in dealing with problems or situations. **4** good at carrying out manual tasks. ~ *noun* (*plural* **practicals**) an examination or lesson that involves really doing something, rather than just writing or talking about it.

practicalities *plural noun* the practical aspects of a situation.

practical joke *noun* (*plural* **practical jokes**) a trick played on somebody to make them look foolish.

practically *adverb* **1** almost; nearly. **2** in a practical manner.

practice *noun* (*plural* **practices**) **1** regular exercises done in order to acquire or improve a skill. **2** the actual carrying out of tasks as opposed to theory: *How will this work in practice?* **3** the usual way something is done. **4** professional work, or the premises of a professional person. * **out of practice** no longer good at something because you have not done it for a while.

Usage Note Notice that *practice* is the correct spelling for the noun and *practise* for the verb.

practise *verb* (**practises, practising, practised**) **1** to do something regularly in order to become skilled in it. **2** to do something as part of your normal way of behaving or living: *He should practise a little politeness.* **3** to do professional work: *She's been practising law for twenty years.*

practitioner *noun* (*plural* **practitioners**) somebody who practises a profession or art.

pragmatic *adjective* making sensible, realistic decisions based on the realities of a situation, rather than on theory or on how the situation ought to be. ➤ **pragmatically** *adverb*.

pragmatism *noun* a practical approach to problems and situations. ➤ **pragmatist** *noun*.

prairie *noun* (*plural* **prairies**) a large area of treeless grassland in North America.

praise *verb* (**praises, praising, praised**) to say that you think something or somebody is very good. ~ *noun* words that express admiration.

praline /prah leen/ *noun* a sweet substance made from almonds heated in boiling sugar, used as a filling for chocolates.

pram *noun* (*plural* **prams**) a four-wheeled carriage for a baby, pushed by a person on foot.

prance *verb* (**prances, prancing, pranced**) to walk in a silly and affected way.

prank *noun* (*plural* **pranks**) a mischievous trick.

prattle *verb* (**prattles, prattling, prattled**) to talk a lot or very fast about silly or unimportant things. ➤ **prattle** *noun*.

prawn *noun* (*plural* **prawns**) an edible shellfish that looks like a large shrimp.

pray *verb* (**prays, praying, prayed**) **1** to say a prayer. **2** (**pray for**) to dearly hope that something happens.

prayer /prair/ *noun* (*plural* **prayers**) **1** a personal request or expression of praise or thanksgiving addressed to God or a god. **2** an earnest hope that something happens.

preach *verb* (**preaches, preaching, preached**) **1** to deliver a sermon. **2** to give advice or warnings in an annoyingly moral or superior way. ➤ **preacher** *noun*.

preamble /pree am bl/ *noun* (*plural* **preambles**) a short statement introducing or explaining what is to follow.

prearranged *adjective* arranged beforehand.

precarious *adjective* **1** likely to fall or collapse. **2** likely to become unpleasant or dangerous at any time. ➤ **precariously** *adverb*.

precaution *noun* (*plural* **precautions**) something you do to help prevent unpleasant things happening. ➤ **precautionary** *adjective*.

precede *verb* (**precedes, preceding, preceded**) **1** to happen before something else. **2** to walk ahead of somebody.

precedence /pre si dins/ *noun* the fact that something is more important and should be dealt with first.

precedent /pre si dint/ *noun* (*plural* **precedents**) something similar that happened before and can be used to help decide how to deal with the present situation.

precept /pree sept/ *noun* (*plural* **precepts**) a rule or instruction.

precinct *noun* (*plural* **precincts**) **1** an area of a town closed to traffic. **2** (**precincts**) the area immediately surrounding a place.

precious *adjective* **1** of great value or high price. **2** loved or cherished.

precious stone *noun* (*plural* **precious stones**) a stone, such as a diamond or ruby, that has great value and is used in jewellery.

precipice /pre si pis/ *noun* (*plural* **precipices**) a steep cliff or sheer wall of rock.

precipitate /pri si pi tayt/ *verb* (**precipitates, precipitating, precipitated**) to cause something to happen very quickly or suddenly. ~ /pri si pi tit/ *adjective* done quickly or hurriedly. *noun* (*plural* **precipitates**) *Science* a solid substance that has been chemically separated from a solution. ➤ **precipitately** *adverb*.

precipitation *noun formal* rain, snow, or hail.

precipitous *adjective* dangerously steep or high.

precis or **précis** /pray see/ *noun* (*plural* **precis** or **précis** /pray seez/) a summary.

precise *adjective* **1** done with great attention to accuracy: *a precise calculation*. **2** this and no other; particular: *at that precise moment*. ➤ **precisely** *adverb*. ➤ **precision** *noun*

preclude *verb* (**precludes, precluding, precluded**) to make something impossible in advance. ➤ **preclusion** *noun*.

precocious *adjective* said about a child: very advanced or mature for their age, perhaps worryingly or irritatingly so. ➤ **precociously** *adverb*, **precocity** *noun*.

preconceived *adjective* said about an opinion or judgment: reached without actual knowledge or experience and therefore likely to be inaccurate or unfair.

preconception *noun* (*plural* **preconceptions**) a preconceived opinion or judgment.

precondition *noun* (*plural* **preconditions**) something that must happen or exist to enable something else to happen or exist.

precursor *noun* (*plural* **precursors**) something in the past that was an earlier version of something that developed later.

predator /pre da ter/ *noun* (*plural* **predators**) an animal that lives by hunting and killing other animals.

predatory *adjective* **1** said about an animal: hunting and killing other animals. **2** taking advantage of other people.

predecessor *noun* (*plural* **predecessors**) somebody who had a job or position before the person who has it now.

predetermined *adjective* decided or arranged beforehand.

predeterminer *noun* (*plural* **predeterminers**) *English* in grammar, an adjective or adverb that can come before a determiner, such as 'both' in *both her hands*.

predicament *noun* (*plural* **predicaments**) a difficult situation.

predicate /ˈpredikət/ *noun* (*plural* **predicates**) *English* the part of a sentence or clause that is not the subject, that contains the verb, and that says something about the subject, such as 'swung open' in *The door swung open*.

predicative *adjective English* said about an adjective: contained in the predicate of a sentence, rather than appearing before the noun it is modifying, for example 'red' in *The dress is red*. ➤ **predicatively** *adverb*.

predict *verb* (**predicts, predicting, predicted**) to state that a particular thing will happen in the future.

predictable *adjective* **1** said about an event: which you knew would happen. **2** said about a person: always behaving in the same way in a particular situation, usually annoyingly so. ➤ **predictability** *noun*, **predictably** *adverb*.

prediction *noun* (*plural* **predictions**) a statement that a particular thing will happen in the future. ➤ **predictive** *adjective*.

predispose *verb* (**predisposes, predisposing, predisposed**) to make somebody likely or willing to do something. ➤ **predisposition** *noun*.

predominant *adjective* **1** existing in larger numbers or quantities than anything else: *Gulls are the predominant birds on the island*. **2** having greater strength or influence than all others in a group. ➤ **predominance** *noun*, **predominantly** *adverb*.

predominate *verb* (**predominates, predominating, predominated**) **1** to exist in larger numbers or quantities than anything else. **2** to have a controlling power over all others in a group. ➤ **predomination** *noun*.

pre-eminent /priːˈeminənt/ *adjective* more influential or important than all others. ➤ **pre-eminence** *noun*, **pre-eminently** *adverb*.

pre-empt /priːˈempt/ *verb* (**pre-empts, pre-empting, pre-empted**) to take action to prevent something from happening. ➤ **pre-emption** *noun*, **pre-emptive** *adjective*.

preen *verb* (**preens, preening, preened**) **1** said about a bird: to clean and smooth its feathers with its beak. **2** to make yourself look smart or attractive.

prefab *noun* (*plural* **prefabs**) a prefabricated building.

prefabricated *adjective* said about a building: made in sections designed to be put together where the building is to be.

preface /ˈprefəs/ *noun* (*plural* **prefaces**) an introduction printed at the beginning of a book. ~ *verb* (**prefaces, prefacing, prefaced**) (**preface by/with**) to say or write something as a way of introducing or explaining what follows.

prefect *noun* (*plural* **prefects**) **1** a senior pupil in a secondary school who has some authority over other pupils. **2** in some countries, the chief administrative officer of a region.

prefer *verb* (**prefers, preferring, preferred**) **1** to like something or somebody better than others. **2** *formal* to bring a charge against somebody.

preferable /ˈprefərəbl/ *adjective* more desirable or suitable. ➤ **preferably** *adverb*.

preference *noun* (*plural* **preferences**) **1** greater liking for one thing over another. **2** a person or thing that you prefer.

preferential *adjective* showing that you favour one person or group above others. ➤ **preferentially** *adverb*.

prefix *noun* (*plural* **prefixes**) *English* a group of letters placed at the beginning of a word and affecting its meaning, e.g. *un-* in *unhappy*.

pregnancy *noun* (*plural* **pregnancies**) the state or period of being pregnant.

pregnant *adjective* said about a woman: having a baby developing in the womb.

prehensile *adjective* said about an animal's tail: able to grab things.

prehistoric *adjective* to do with periods of time in the very distant past, before modern humans had developed and before history was written down.

prejudice /pre joo dis/ *noun* (*plural* **prejudices**) **1** a negative opinion of somebody or something formed for no good reason. **2** biased judgments generally. ➤ **prejudiced** *adjective*.

preliminary *adjective* preparing for an event that is to follow, or taking place in the first stages. ~ *noun* (*plural* **preliminaries**) a preliminary event or action.

prelude /pre lewd/ *noun* (*plural* **preludes**) **1** an introductory performance, action, or event. **2** *Music* an introductory piece of music.

premature *adjective* happening before the proper or usual time. ➤ **prematurely** *adverb*.

premeditated *adjective* considered and planned beforehand. ➤ **premeditation** *noun*.

premier /pre mi er/ *adjective* best or most important. ~ *noun* (*plural* **premiers**) a prime minister, president, or other head of government. ➤ **premiership** *noun*.

premiere /pre mi air/ *noun* (*plural* **premieres**) the first public showing of a film or the first public performance of a play.

premise *or* **premiss** *noun* (*plural* **premises** *or* **premisses**) a statement or idea used as a basis for an argument.

premises *plural noun* the building used by an organization.

premium /pree mi um/ *noun* (*plural* **premiums**) **1** the money you pay for insurance. **2** (*used before a noun*) of excellent quality. ✱ **at a premium** valuable because it is rare or difficult to obtain.

premonition /pre mo ni shn/ *noun* (*plural* **premonitions**) a strong feeling that something unpleasant is going to happen. ➤ **premonitory** *adjective*.

preoccupation *noun* (*plural* **preoccupations**) something that you are constantly thinking about or dealing with.

preoccupied *adjective* concentrating on or thinking about something so much that you do not notice or deal with other things.

preparation *noun* (*plural* **preparations**) **1** things that you do to prepare for something. **2** a medicine or other prepared substance.

preparatory /pri pa ra to ri/ *adjective* done as preparation for something.

preparatory school *noun* (*plural* **preparatory schools**) a private school for pupils from the age of seven to eleven.

prepare *verb* (**prepares, preparing, prepared**) **1** to make something ready for some purpose or activity. **2** to put yourself or somebody else into a suitable frame of mind for something. **3** to put something together from various ingredients. ✱ **be prepared to** to be willing to do something.

preposition *noun* (*plural* **prepositions**) *English* a word used to show a relationship between other words, such as 'with' in *We're pleased with your progress* and 'to' in *They've gone to school*. ➤ **prepositional** *adjective*.

preposterous *adjective* ridiculous and absurd. ➤ **preposterously** *adverb*.

prep school *noun* (*plural* **prep schools**) = PREPARATORY SCHOOL.

prerequisite /pree re kwi zit/ *noun* (*plural* **prerequisites**) something that must be done or must exist before something else can happen or exist.

prerogative /pri ro ga tiv/ *noun* (*plural* **prerogatives**) a special right to do something.

Presbyterian /prez bi teer i an/ *adjective* said about a branch of the Christian Church: governed by committees that include both ministers and certain senior members of congregations. ➤ **Presbyterianism** *noun*.

prescribe *verb* (**prescribes, prescribing, prescribed**) **1** to state what medicine or treatment a patient should be given. **2** to recommend something.

prescription *noun* (*plural* **prescriptions**) a doctor's written instruction for a medicine to be given to a patient.

prescriptive *adjective* giving instructions or laying down rules.

presence *noun* **1** the fact that something or somebody is in a place. **2** the fact that you are with somebody: *They seemed nervous in his presence.* **3** impressive personal qualities that make other people notice and admire you. ✶ **presence of mind** the ability to make calm, sensible decisions in difficult circumstances.

present¹ /pre znt/ *noun* (*plural* **presents**) something that you give somebody; a gift. ~ /pri zent/ *verb* (**presents, presenting, presented**) **1** to give somebody something formally or ceremonially. **2** to introduce one person to another formally. **3** to introduce a television or radio programme. **4** to give something to somebody to consider. **5** to be a problem or difficulty. ➤ **presenter** *noun*.

present² /pre znt/ *adjective* **1** in or at a place: *He wasn't present at the meeting.* **2** existing in something: *Was alcohol present in his blood?* **3** now existing or in progress: *the present year.* ~ *noun* (**the present**) the time now in progress. ✶ **at present** now.

presentable *adjective* smartly dressed enough to appear in company.

presentation *noun* (*plural* **presentations**) **1** an informative talk. **2** the way in which something is presented. **3** the act of presenting something.

presently *adverb* **1** before long; soon. **2** now.

present participle *noun* (*plural* **present participles**) *English* a participle such as *dancing* or *going* that is used with the verb *be* to talk or write about things happening now.

present tense *noun* (*plural* **present tenses**) *English* a verb tense used for talking or writing about things that are happening now.

preservative *noun* (*plural* **preservatives**) a substance added to processed food to make it stay fresh for longer.

preserve *verb* (**preserves, preserving, preserved**) **1** to keep something in its original condition. **2** to treat food in such a way that it can be stored for long periods of time. ~ *noun* (*plural* **preserves**) **1** a jam, jelly, or other food preserved by cooking with sugar. **2** something that is reserved for certain people: *Good wine is no longer the preserve of the rich.* ➤ **preservation** *noun*.

preside *verb* (**presides, presiding, presided**) to be in charge of a formal meeting.

presidency *noun* (*plural* **presidencies**) **1** the position of president. **2** the period during which somebody is president.

president *noun* (*plural* **presidents**) **1** the elected head of state in a republic. **2** the most senior person in a business, club, organization, etc. ➤ **presidential** *adjective*.

press *verb* (**presses, pressing, pressed**) **1** to push firmly and steadily against something. **2** to iron clothes.

3 to try to persuade somebody to do something. **4 (press for)** to make strong demands or claims for something. ~ *noun* (*plural* **presses**) **1 (the press)** newspapers and magazines collectively. **2** a device that makes or extracts something by pressing. **3** a printing press. **4** a publishing house or printing firm. ✻ **be pressed for time** to have little time available.

press conference *noun* (*plural* **press conferences**) a meeting at which somebody answers questions from journalists.

press gang *noun* (*plural* **press gangs**) *History* a group of men who forced people to join the navy or army.

pressing *adjective* needing to be dealt with immediately.

press release *noun* (*plural* **press releases**) a printed statement given to journalists.

press-up *noun* (*plural* **press-ups**) an exercise in which you lie face down and raise and lower your body by pushing against the floor with your hands.

pressure *noun* (*plural* **pressures**) **1** the force created when you push on something. **2** the anxiety you feel because of the need to take action or make a decision, created by the demands of a situation or of other people. **3** *Science* in physics, the force or thrust exerted over a surface divided by its area. ~ *verb* (**pressures, pressuring, pressured**) to try to persuade or force somebody to do something.

pressure group *noun* (*plural* **pressure groups**) a group organized to influence government policy or public opinion on a particular issue.

pressurize *or* **pressurise** *verb* (**pressurizes, pressurizing, pressurized** *or* **pressurises,** etc) to try to persuade or force somebody to do something.

prestige /preˈsteezh/ *noun* the fact that many people think somebody or something is very good.

prestigious /preˈstijus/ *adjective* admired by many people.

presto *adjective and adverb Music* said about a piece of music: played at a fast tempo.

presumably *adverb* as you may reasonably assume.

presume *verb* (**presumes, presuming, presumed**) **1** to think that something is probably the case, based on what you know. **2** to do something that might offend somebody because it shows too much familiarity or a lack of respect: *I wouldn't presume to tell you how to do your job.*

presumption *noun* (*plural* **presumptions**) **1** an attitude or belief based on reasonable grounds. **2** overfamiliar or disrespectful behaviour.

presumptuous *adjective* overfamiliar or disrespectful. ➤ **presumptuously** *adverb*.

pretence /priˈtens/ *noun* (*plural* **pretences**) an example of insincere or deceitful behaviour.

pretend *verb* (**pretends, pretending, pretended**) to behave as if something were the case when it is not.

pretender *noun* (*plural* **pretenders**) somebody who claims they should have a title or position held by somebody else.

pretension *noun* (*plural* **pretensions**) an example of pretentious behaviour.

pretentious *adjective* trying to impress people by a false display of importance or some other quality. ➤ **pretentiousness** *noun*.

pretext *noun* (*plural* **pretexts**) a false reason or excuse.

pretty *adjective* (**prettier, prettiest**) **1** said about a woman or girl: attractive. **2** nice to look at; picturesque: *pretty seaside towns.* ~ *adverb* **1** to some degree; quite: *The food was pretty*

pretzel

good. **2** very. ✱ **pretty much/nearly/well** *informal* almost; very nearly. ➤ **prettily** *adverb*, **prettiness** *noun*.

pretzel *noun* (*plural* **pretzels**) a brittle savoury biscuit in the shape of a knot.

prevail *verb* (**prevails, prevailing, prevailed**) **1** to be the most frequent or widespread: *The west wind prevails in this area.* **2** to defeat somebody. **3** (**prevail on/upon**) to persuade somebody to do something.

prevalent *adjective* widely occurring or existing. ➤ **prevalence** *noun*.

prevaricate *verb* (**prevaricates, prevaricating, prevaricated**) to say or do something that deliberately avoids dealing with a situation. ➤ **prevarication** *noun*.

prevent *verb* (**prevents, preventing, prevented**) **1** to stop something from happening or existing. **2** (**prevent from**) to stop somebody from doing something. ➤ **preventable** *adjective*, **prevention** *noun*.

preventive or **preventative** *adjective* intended to prevent something.

preview *noun* (*plural* **previews**) **1** a brief description of upcoming events. **2** an advance showing of a film or exhibition. **3** *ICT* in a word-processing program, a facility that allows you to see a document as it will appear when it is printed. ~ *verb* (**previews, previewing, previewed**) **1** to give information on upcoming events. **2** to show a film or exhibition before its official public presentation.

previous *adjective* **1** going before in time or order. **2** *informal* acting too soon; premature. ✱ **previous to** before; prior to. ➤ **previously** *adverb*.

prey *noun* an animal killed by another animal for food. ~ *verb* (**preys, preying, preyed**) **1** (**prey on/upon**) said of an animal: to kill particular animals for food. **2** (**prey on/upon**) to target particular people as victims. **3** (**prey on/upon**) to occupy your mind and cause anxiety.

price *noun* (*plural* **prices**) **1** the amount of money for which something is bought or sold. **2** something unpleasant that you suffer in order to achieve something else. ~ *verb* (**prices, pricing, priced**) to set a price for something you are selling.

priceless *adjective* so valuable it cannot be priced.

pricey or **pricy** *adjective* (**pricier, priciest**) *informal* expensive.

prick *verb* (**pricks, pricking, pricked**) **1** to pierce something lightly with a sharp point. **2** to injure yourself slightly with something that has a sharp point. ~ *noun* (*plural* **pricks**) the act of pricking something, or the sensation of being pricked.

prickle *noun* (*plural* **prickles**) **1** a small sharp pointed spike on a plant or animal. **2** a pricking or tingling sensation. ~ *verb* (**prickles, prickling, prickled**) to feel a prickle.

prickly *adjective* (**pricklier, prickliest**) **1** covered with prickles. **2** causing a prickling sensation. **3** easily irritated.

pricy *adjective* see PRICEY.

pride *noun* (*plural* **prides**) **1** a feeling of satisfaction that you get because of your achievements or possessions. **2** an awareness of your own worth and dignity. **3** too great a sense of your own importance. **4** a group of lions. ~ *verb* (**prides, priding, prided**) ✱ **pride yourself on** to be particularly proud of something.

priest *noun* (*plural* **priests**) **1** a member of the clergy in a Christian church, especially in the Roman Catholic Church, the Orthodox churches, or the Church of England. **2** a person authorized to perform the sacred rites of a religion. ➤ **priesthood** *noun*, **priestly** *adjective*.

prim *adjective* (**primmer, primmest**) **1** tending to behave in a formal way.

2 disapproving of, or easily shocked by, vulgar behaviour. ➤ **primly** *adverb*.

primaeval *adjective* see PRIMEVAL.

primarily *adverb* **1** for the most part; chiefly. **2** in the first place; originally.

primary *adjective* **1** more important than anything else. **2** relating to the education of children from five to eleven.

primary colours *plural noun Art* red, yellow, and blue, which are mixed to produce all other colours.

primary school *noun* (*plural* **primary schools**) a school for children aged between five and eleven.

primate *noun* (*plural* **primates**) **1** an animal of the order that includes human beings, apes, and monkeys. **2** an archbishop.

prime¹ *adjective* **1** first in importance: *our prime concern*. **2** of the highest grade or quality: *prime beef*. **3** *Maths* said about a number: that can only be divided by itself and 1. ~ *noun* the most active stage of your life. ➤ **primely** *adverb*, **primeness** *noun*.

prime² *verb* (**primes, priming, primed**) **1** to make something ready to be used or activated. **2** to give somebody information or instructions beforehand.

prime minister *noun* (*plural* **prime ministers**) the most senior minister of a government.

primer *noun* (*plural* **primers**) **1** a book that gives basic information on a subject. **2** a type of paint used as a first coat on some surfaces.

primeval *or* **primaeval** /prie mee vl/ *adjective* relating to the earliest period in the history of the world.

primitive *adjective* **1** to do with societies or cultures that are undeveloped in comparison to western civilizations and in which people live very simple lives. **2** said about accommodation or facilities: of a low or basic standard. ➤ **primitively** *adverb*.

primrose *noun* (*plural* **primroses**) a small plant with pale yellow flowers.

prince *noun* (*plural* **princes**) **1** a son or grandson of a king or queen. **2** a ruler of a principality.

princess *noun* (*plural* **princesses**) **1** a daughter or granddaughter of a king or queen. **2** the wife or widow of a prince.

principal *adjective* most important or influential. ~ *noun* (*plural* **principals**) the head of some schools and colleges. ➤ **principally** *adverb*.

Usage Note Do not confuse this word with *principle*.

principal clause *noun* (*plural* **principal clauses**) *English* (also **main clause**) a clause that can stand alone as a sentence or be the chief clause in a sentence which also has a subordinate clause.

principality *noun* (*plural* **principalities**) a country that is ruled by a prince.

principle *noun* (*plural* **principles**) **1** a rule that you follow in your behaviour. **2** a law or fact that underlies a subject: *the principles of physics*. ✱ **in principle** in theory. **on principle** because of your beliefs or your moral code.

Usage Note Do not confuse this word with *principal*.

principled *adjective* following rules of good behaviour or fairness.

print *verb* (**prints, printing, printed**) **1** to put words or pictures onto paper using a machine. **2** to stamp a mark or design onto something. **3** to publish something, such as a book or newspaper. **4** to make a positive image from a photographic negative. ~ *noun* (*plural* **prints**) **1** printed words or text. **2** a copy of something, such as a painting, made by printing. ✱ **in** *or* **out of print** said about a book: still

printer

available (or no longer available) from the publisher. ➤ **printable** *adjective*.

printer *noun* (*plural* **printers**) **1** a machine that prints material from a computer onto paper. **2** a person who prints books, leaflets, etc.

printout *noun* (*plural* **printouts**) a printed copy of information from a computer or other device.

prior[1] *adjective* done or arranged earlier. ✱ **prior to** before something in time.

prior[2] *noun* (*plural* **priors**) the deputy head of a monastery, ranking below an abbot.

prioritize *or* **prioritise** *verb* (**prioritizes, prioritizing, prioritized** *or* **prioritises**, etc) **1** to deal with something first, because it is more important than other things. **2** to arrange things in order of priority. ➤ **prioritization** *or* **prioritisation** *noun*.

priority *noun* (*plural* **priorities**) **1** something that you deal with first because it is more important than other things. **2** the fact that something is more important than other things. **3** the right to go first, e.g. before other drivers.

prise *or* **prize** *verb* (**prises, prising, prised** *or* **prizes**, etc) to force something open or force it apart from something else, usually with a levering movement.

prism *noun* (*plural* **prisms**) **1** a solid shape with ends that are equal and parallel and sides that are parallelograms. **2** a piece of glass that has this shape and triangular ends, used to deflect or disperse light.

prison *noun* (*plural* **prisons**) a building in which criminals are kept as a punishment.

prisoner *noun* (*plural* **prisoners**) somebody in a prison.

prisoner of war *noun* (*plural* **prisoners of war**) an enemy captured and kept prisoner during a war.

pristine *adjective* spotlessly clean and in excellent condition.

privacy /pri va si/ *noun* freedom from the unwanted company of other people who would otherwise disturb you or watch what you are doing.

private *adjective* **1** intended for the use of a particular person or group. **2** owned or run by an independent individual or company, rather than by the government. **3** not intended to be known by others: *a private chat*. **4** said about a place: where you are likely to be alone or undisturbed. ~ *noun* (*plural* **privates**) a soldier of the lowest rank in the army.

private detective *noun* (*plural* **private detectives**) a detective who acts on behalf of clients and is not a member of a police force.

private school *noun* (*plural* **private schools**) a school that gets its funding in the form of fees that parents pay for their children to attend, rather than from the government.

private sector *noun* the part of the economy that is not controlled by the government.

privation *noun* lack of the basic necessities of life.

privatize *or* **privatise** *verb* (**privatizes, privatizing, privatized** *or* **privatises**, etc) to transfer a state-run business or industry to private ownership. ➤ **privatization** *or* **privatisation** *noun*.

privet /pri vit/ *noun* (*plural* **privets**) an evergreen bush that is widely used in hedges.

privilege *noun* (*plural* **privileges**) a special right or advantage given to a particular person or group. ➤ **privileged** *adjective*.

privy *adjective* (**privy to**) sharing in the knowledge of something secret.

Privy Council *noun* (**the Privy**

Council) a group of senior politicians chosen to give advice to the queen or king.

prize[1] *noun* (*plural* **prizes**) **1** something given as a reward for success or achievement. **2** (*used before a noun*) considered very precious or valuable: *prize possessions*. ~ *verb* (**prizes, prizing, prized**) to value something very highly.

prize[2] *verb* see PRISE.

pro[1] *noun* (*plural* **pros**) *informal* a professional. ~ *adjective* professional.

pro[2] *noun* (*plural* **pros**) ✻ **pros and cons** the arguments for and against something.

probability *noun* (*plural* **probabilities**) **1** the fact that something is probable. **2** something that is probable.

probable *adjective* very likely to happen or be the case, but not certain. ➤ **probably** *adverb*.

probate *noun* the legal process of declaring a will to be valid.

probation *noun* **1** a method of dealing with offenders by which they are allowed to stay out of prison provided that they show good behaviour throughout a specified period. **2** a period during which a new recruit's performance in a job is monitored before a decision is taken to make their employment more permanent. ➤ **probationary** *adjective*, **probationer** *noun*.

probe *noun* (*plural* **probes**) **1** a surgical instrument used to examine a bodily cavity. **2** a device inserted in something to be monitored or measured. **3** an unmanned spacecraft used for exploring. **4** a thorough investigation. ~ *verb* (**probes, probing, probed**) **1** to examine something with a probe. **2** to investigate something thoroughly or question somebody thoroughly. ➤ **probing** *adjective*.

probity *noun formal* honesty and integrity.

problem *noun* (*plural* **problems**) **1** something that causes trouble or is difficult to deal with. **2** a question set for you to solve.

problematic or **problematical** *adjective* presenting a problem.

proboscis /pro bo sis/ *noun* (*plural* **proboscises**) *Science* **1** an animal's long flexible snout, such as the trunk of an elephant. **2** a long sucking tube extending from the mouth of some insects.

procedure *noun* (*plural* **procedures**) **1** a particular or established way of doing something. **2** a series of ordered steps. ➤ **procedural** *adjective*.

proceed *verb* (**proceeds, proceeding, proceeded**) **1** to continue to happen or develop: *My career was proceeding nicely*. **2** to do something that continues for a while: *She proceeded to tell us all about it*. **3** to move or travel in a particular direction.

proceedings *plural noun* **1** a series of events. **2** a legal case. **3** an official record of things said or done at a meeting.

proceeds *plural noun* money earned or obtained.

process *noun* (*plural* **processes**) **1** a series of actions designed to achieve something. **2** a natural series of changes: *the growth process*. ~ *verb* (**processes, processing, processed**) to deal with something that undergoes several stages of treatment: *We're processing your application*.

procession *noun* (*plural* **processions**) a group of people or vehicles moving in a line, for example as part of a ceremony or festival.

processor *noun* (*plural* **processors**) *ICT* the set of microchips in a computer that controls its operations.

proclaim *verb* (**proclaims, proclaiming, proclaimed**) to state something publicly and officially. ➤ **proclamation** *noun*.

procrastinate *verb* (**procrastinates, procrastinating, procrastinated**) *formal* to put off doing something until a later time. ➤ **procrastination** *noun*.

procure *verb* (**procures, procuring, procured**) to obtain something, especially by special care and effort. ➤ **procurement** *noun*.

prod *verb* (**prods, prodding, prodded**) to jab something with your finger or a pointed instrument. ~ *noun* (*plural* **prods**) a prodding action; a jab.

prodigious /pro di jus/ *adjective* remarkable in size or achievement. ➤ **prodigiously** *adverb*.

prodigy *noun* (*plural* **prodigies**) an exceptionally talented child.

produce /pro dews/ *verb* (**produces, producing, produced**) **1** to make or manufacture something. **2** to make something happen or exist: *My suggestion produced a violent response.* **3** to let people see something: *He produced the letter.* **4** to make the arrangements and raise the money for the making of a film, play, piece of recorded music, etc. ~ /pro dews/ *noun* fruit, vegetables, and other foods grown to be sold. ➤ **producer** *noun*.

product *noun* (*plural* **products**) **1** a commodity that is made or grown to be sold. **2** *Maths* the result of multiplying numbers together.

production *noun* (*plural* **productions**) **1** the act of producing something. **2** the total amount of goods produced in an industry or by a company. **3** a play, film, or television or radio programme.

productive *adjective* **1** producing large quantities of something. **2** having good results or benefits. ➤ **productively** *adverb*.

productivity *noun* how much of a commodity an industry or company produces; output.

profane *adjective* treating something religious or holy with a shocking lack of respect. *verb* (**profanes, profaning, profaned**) to treat something religious or holy with a shocking lack of respect. ➤ **profanation** *noun*.

profanity *noun* (*plural* **profanities**) **1** profane language. **2** a swear word.

profess *verb* (**professes, professing, professed**) **1** to state something openly. **2** to claim something that is not true.

profession *noun* (*plural* **professions**) **1** a job that requires special training and qualifications. **2** people who have such a job: *the medical profession*.

professional *adjective* **1** to do with a profession. **2** doing an activity as a job, or done as a job: *a professional musician*. **3** done to a high standard, or to the high standards you expect from people who are paid for their work: *a professional piece of work*. ~ *noun* (*plural* **professionals**) **1** a person who does an activity as their job. **2** a conscientious person who does their work to a high standard. ➤ **professionally** *adverb*.

professionalism *noun* the organized methods and high standard of work that you associate with professional people.

professor *noun* (*plural* **professors**) **1** a university teacher of the highest rank. **2** *N American* a university teacher of any rank. ➤ **professorial** *adjective*, **professorship** *noun*.

proficient *adjective* good at something; skilled. ➤ **proficiency** *noun*.

profile *noun* (*plural* **profiles**) **1** a side view of somebody's face. **2** a brief description of somebody's career or life. **3** a brief description of somebody's character. **4** the amount of public attention that somebody or something gets. ✴ **keep a low profile** to avoid attracting attention.

profit *noun* (*plural* **profits**) **1** the

amount of money that somebody gains when they sell something for more money than it cost to buy or produce. **2** a gain or benefit of any kind. ~ *verb* (**profits, profiting, profited**) to get a benefit of some sort. ➤ **profitless** *adjective*.

profitable *adjective* producing a profit. ➤ **profitability** *noun*, **profitably** *adverb*.

profligate *adjective* wasting a lot of something. ➤ **profligacy** *noun*.

profound *adjective* **1** showing great intelligence or understanding. **2** said about a feeling: strongly felt. ➤ **profoundly** *adverb*, **profundity** *noun*.

profuse /proh**fews**/ *adjective* large in number or amount. ➤ **profusely** *adverb*, **profusion** *noun*.

progeny *noun formal* descendants or children.

prognosis /prog**noh**sis/ *noun* (*plural* **prognoses** /prog**noh**seez/) a doctor's assessment of how an illness is likely to develop.

program *noun* (*plural* **programs**) a set of instructions that make a computer perform a particular activity, or an activity that you use a computer for. ~ *verb* (**programs, programming, programmed**) to give a computer instructions that make it perform a particular activity. ➤ **programmer** *noun*.

programme *noun* (*plural* **programmes**) **1** a radio or television broadcast. **2** a booklet or leaflet that gives information about a play or show. **3** a set of activities designed to achieve something: *the government's road-building programme*. ~ *verb* (**programs, programming, programmed**) to teach or force somebody to behave in a particular way.

progress /**proh**gres/ *noun* **1** things you do that make a goal nearer to being achieved. **2** forward movement towards a place you are heading for. ~ /proh**gres**/ *verb* (**progresses, progressing, progressed**) **1** to develop in a way that makes a goal nearer to being achieved. **2** to move forward.

progression *noun* the act of advancing or developing.

progressive *adjective* **1** moving towards a better state, often through the use of new ideas or methods. **2** developing gradually or in stages. ➤ **progressively** *adverb*.

prohibit *verb* (**prohibits, prohibiting, prohibited**) **1** to say formally that something must not be done. **2** to prevent something from happening. ➤ **prohibition** *noun*.

prohibitive *adjective* said about a cost: so high that you cannot afford it. ➤ **prohibitively** *adverb*.

project /**pro**jekt/ *noun* (*plural* **projects**) **1** a specific plan or design; a scheme. **2** a long piece of work done by a pupil or group over a period of time. ~ /proh**jekt**/ *verb* (**projects, projecting, projected**) **1** to calculate or estimate something using information you have. **2** to cause light or an image to fall on a surface. **3** to stick out beyond an edge or surface.

projectile *noun* (*plural* **projectiles**) something that is fired or thrown at a target.

projector *noun* (*plural* **projectors**) a device for projecting films or slides onto a surface.

proletariat /proh li**tair**i it/ *noun* working-class people.

proliferate *verb* (**proliferates, proliferating, proliferated**) to increase rapidly in number or amount. ➤ **proliferation** *noun*.

prolific *adjective* producing a lot of something. ➤ **prolifically** *adverb*.

prologue *noun* (*plural* **prologues**) **1** an introductory speech at the beginning of a play. **2** an introduction to a book.

prolong *verb* (**prolongs, prolonging, prolonged**) to make something continue for a longer time. ▶ **prolongation** *noun*, **prolonged** *adjective*.

prom *noun* (*plural* **proms**) **1** = PROMENADE CONCERT. **2** = PROMENADE. **3** a formal dance at a high school or college.

promenade *noun* (*plural* **promenades**) a paved walkway by the sea.

promenade concert *noun* (*plural* **promenade concerts**) a concert of classical music at which some of the audience stand.

prominence *noun* the quality of being prominent.

prominent *adjective* **1** famous and well respected. **2** easy to notice. **3** sticking out. ▶ **prominently** *adverb*.

promiscuous *adjective* having many casual sexual relationships. ▶ **promiscuity** *noun*.

promise *noun* (*plural* **promises**) **1** a statement assuring somebody that you will or will not do something. **2** qualities that make you expect something will be successful or excellent. ~ *verb* (**promises, promising, promised**) to assure somebody that you will or will not do something.

promising *adjective* showing signs of future success or excellence. ▶ **promisingly** *adverb*.

promontory *noun* (*plural* **promontories**) a piece of high land that sticks out into the sea.

promote *verb* (**promotes, promoting, promoted**) **1** to give somebody a higher position or rank. **2** to advertise or publicize something. ▶ **promoter** *noun*.

promotion *noun* (*plural* **promotions**) **1** a higher rank or position that somebody is given. **2** the advertising and marketing of a product. **3** a reduction in price or other special offer intended to make people buy a new product or buy more of an existing product. ▶ **promotional** *adjective*.

prompt[1] *verb* (**prompts, prompting, prompted**) **1** to make somebody decide to do something. **2** to remind an actor of the next words they should speak. ~ *noun* (*plural* **prompts**) a reminder for an actor of the next words they should speak.

prompt[2] *adjective* **1** done quickly or immediately. **2** happening or arriving on time. ~ *adverb informal* exactly; punctually: *six o'clock prompt*. ▶ **promptly** *adverb*, **promptness** *noun*.

prone *adjective* **1** (**prone to**) tending to be affected by something or tending to do something. **2** lying flat or face down.

prong *noun* (*plural* **prongs**) each of the pointed parts of a fork.

pronoun *noun* (*plural* **pronouns**) *English* a word used as a substitute for a noun, for example *I, he, these*.

pronounce *verb* (**pronounces, pronouncing, pronounced**) **1** to say the sounds of a word. **2** to declare something officially or publicly. ▶ **pronounceable** *adjective*, **pronouncement** *noun*.

pronounced *adjective* very noticeable; conspicuous.

pronunciation *noun* (*plural* **pronunciations**) the way you pronounce a word.

proof *noun* (*plural* **proofs**) **1** evidence that establishes a truth or fact. **2** a sample of a piece of text printed so that people can check it before it is published. **3** the alcoholic content of a drink. ~ *adjective* preventing something from passing through: *soundproof*.

prop[1] *noun* (*plural* **props**) a pole or other rigid vertical support. ~ *verb* (**props, propping, propped**) **1** (**prop up**) to support something with a prop.

2 to lean something against a vertical surface for support.

prop² *noun* (*plural* **props**) an object used in a play or film, other than painted scenery or costumes.

prop³ *noun* (*plural* **props**) *informal* = PROPELLER.

propaganda *noun* false information that a government or organization spreads in order to make people support or oppose something.

propagate *verb* (**propagates, propagating, propagated**) **1** to grow a plant from a part taken from another plant. **2** to spread information, especially false information. ➤ **propagation** *noun*.

propane *noun* a gas found in petroleum and natural gas and used as a fuel.

propel *verb* (**propels, propelling, propelled**) to make something go in a particular direction.

propellant *noun* (*plural* **propellants**) a gas released under pressure to create a force that makes something, such as a rocket, move.

propeller *noun* (*plural* **propellers**) a device with a circular arrangement of blades that spins round to create the force that makes an aircraft or ship move.

propensity *noun* (*plural* **propensities**) *formal* a tendency.

proper *adjective* **1** correct or appropriate: *not the proper way to behave*. **2** behaving in a formally polite way; genteel.

proper fraction *noun* (*plural* **proper fractions**) *Maths* a fraction in which the number above the line is less than the number below the line.

proper noun *noun* (*plural* **proper nouns**) *English* a noun that is the name of a particular person, place, or festival, and begins with a capital letter, for example *John*, *Taj Mahal*, and *Yom Kippur*.

property *noun* (*plural* **properties**) **1** a piece of land and the buildings on it. **2** something that you own. **3** a quality or attribute.

prophecy /profisi/ *noun* (*plural* **prophecies**) a prediction of what will happen.

Usage Note Notice that *prophecy* with a *c* is a noun and *prophesy* with an *s* is a verb.

prophesy /profisie/ *verb* (**prophesies, prophesying, prophesied**) to predict that something will happen at a certain time.

prophet *noun* (*plural* **prophets**) **1** somebody who claims to be bringing a message from God. **2** somebody who foretells future events. **3** (**the Prophet**) a name used by Muslims for Muhammad, the founder of Islam.

prophetic *adjective* foretelling events that eventually happen.

proponent *noun* (*plural* **proponents**) somebody who argues in favour of something.

proportion *noun* (*plural* **proportions**) **1** a part, fraction, or percentage of an amount or number of things. **2** a ration. **3** the fact that different things or parts are the correct size in relation to each other, for example in a drawing. **4** (**proportions**) the size of something. ✲ **sense of proportion** an ability to tell what is important and what is not.

proportional *adjective* staying the same size in relation to each other. ➤ **proportionally** *adverb*.

proportional representation *noun* an electoral system in which political groups gain seats in proportion to the number of votes they receive.

proportionate *adjective* **1** = PROPORTIONAL. **2** of a suitable level or size in

proposal

the circumstances: *a proportionate response.* ➤ **proportionately** *adverb*.

proposal *noun* (*plural* **proposals**) **1** an idea or plan of action that somebody suggests. **2** a request to marry somebody.

propose *verb* (**proposes, proposing, proposed**) **1** to suggest something for people to consider. **2** to intend to do something. **3** to ask somebody to marry you. ➤ **proposer** *noun*.

proposition *noun* (*plural* **propositions**) **1** something that somebody offers or suggests. **2** *Maths* a formal mathematical statement to be proved. ➤ **propositional** *adjective*.

proprietor *noun* (*plural* **proprietors**) the owner of something such as a hotel or restaurant. ➤ **proprietorial** *adjective*.

propriety /proh prie i ti/ *noun* polite behaviour that does not offend or upset people.

propulsion *noun* the action of propelling something. ➤ **propulsive** *adjective*.

prosaic /proh zay ik/ *adjective* ordinary and uninteresting; dull. ➤ **prosaically** *adverb*.

proscenium arch *noun* (*plural* **proscenium arches**) *Drama* the arch around the stage in a conventional theatre.

proscribe *verb* (**proscribes, proscribing, proscribed**) to say that something is forbidden. ➤ **proscription** *noun*.

prose *noun* English ordinary language, as distinct from poetry.

prosecute *verb* (**prosecutes, prosecuting, prosecuted**) to charge somebody with a crime.

prosecution *noun* **1** the act of charging somebody with a crime. **2** in a court case, the side that argues that somebody has committed a crime.

prosody *noun* English patterns of rhythm in poetry.

prospect /pro spekt/ *noun* (*plural* **prospects**) **1** the possibility of something happening. **2** (**prospects**) chances of getting a good job or a high position in society in the future. ~ /pro spekt/ *verb* (**prospects, prospecting, prospected**) to look for gold or other minerals in an area. ➤ **prospector** *noun*.

prospective *adjective* likely to be a particular thing in the future. ➤ **prospectively** *adverb*.

prospectus *noun* (*plural* **prospectuses**) a printed brochure that gives details of the courses you can do at a college or university.

prosper *verb* (**prospers, prospering, prospered**) to be successful or do well.

prosperous *adjective* rich. ➤ **prosperity** *noun*.

prostate *noun* (*plural* **prostates**) a gland round the neck of the bladder of boys and men.

prostitute *noun* (*plural* **prostitutes**) a person who has sex with people who pay her or him. ➤ **prostitution** *noun*.

prostrate *adjective* lying full-length face down.

protagonist *noun* (*plural* **protagonists**) one of the main characters in a play or film.

protect *verb* (**protects, protecting, protected**) **1** to shield something so that it does not get damaged or injured. **2** to prevent somebody from being harmed or upset. ➤ **protector** *noun*.

protection *noun* **1** the act of protecting something or somebody. **2** something that protects.

protective *adjective* providing protection.

protectorate *noun* (*plural* **protectorates**) a state that is partly controlled by another and is dependent on it for protection.

protégé or **protégée** /pro tizhay/ *noun* (*plural* **protégés** or **protégées**) a young person who is taught, encouraged, and guided by a more experienced person.

Usage Note The spelling *protégé* is used when you are talking about a boy or young man, and *protégée* when you are talking about a girl or young woman.

protein *noun* (*plural* **proteins**) a naturally occurring chemical compound that is an important part of the human diet.

protest /prohtest/ *verb* (**protests, protesting, protested**) **1** to express strong disagreement or objection. **2** to take part in a public demonstration of disapproval. **3** to state something formally: *He protested his innocence.* ~ /prohtest/ *noun* (*plural* **protests**) **1** a formal declaration of disapproval or objection. **2** a public demonstration of disapproval.
➤ **protester** or **protestor** *noun*.

Protestant *noun* (*plural* **Protestants**) a member of any of the western Christian churches that separated from the Roman Catholic church in the sixteenth century. ➤ **Protestant** *adjective*, **Protestantism** *noun*.

protestation *noun* (*plural* **protestations**) a statement that shows you strongly disapprove or disagree.

protocol *noun* (*plural* **protocols**) **1** a required way of behaving on formal or official occasions. **2** a signed record of agreement made at a diplomatic conference.

proton *noun* (*plural* **protons**) *Science* an elementary particle that carries a single positive electrical charge.

prototype *noun* (*plural* **prototypes**) an original model from which later versions are developed.

protozoan or **protozoon** *noun* (*plural* **protozoans** or **protozoa**) *Science* a minute single-celled animal.

protracted *adjective* lasting a long time.

protractor *noun* (*plural* **protractors**) *Maths* a flat semicircular instrument marked with degrees, used for measuring angles.

protrude *verb* (**protrudes, protruding, protruded**) to stick out beyond a surface or edge. ➤ **protrusion** *noun*.

protuberance /protewbrans/ *noun* (*plural* **protuberances**) a swollen or bulging part. ➤ **protuberant** *adjective*.

proud *adjective* **1** pleased about something you have achieved or something you own. **2** making you feel proud: *a proud moment.* **3** having a lot of self-respect: *too proud to accept help.*
➤ **proudly** *adverb*.

prove *verb* (**proves, proving, proved, proved** or **proven**) **1** to show that something is definitely true. **2** to show that you have the required qualities. **3** to turn out to be something.
➤ **provable** *adjective*.

proverb *noun* (*plural* **proverbs**) a short saying that describes a general fact or truth about life.

proverbial *adjective* **1** mentioned in a proverb. **2** well-known. ➤ **proverbially** *adverb*.

provide *verb* (**provides, providing, provided**) **1** to give something or make something available. **2** (**provide for**) to give somebody the things they need to live.

provided or **providing** *conjunction* on condition that.

providence or **Providence** *noun* God, nature, or fate thought of as the power that controls what happens to people.

providential *adjective* happening by

province

good fortune; lucky. ➤ **providentially** *adverb*.

province *noun* (*plural* **provinces**) **1** an administrative district or division of a country. **2** (**the provinces**) all parts of a country outside the capital. **3** something that a person has special knowledge of or special responsibility for: *Cooking is my province.*

provincial *adjective* **1** to do with a province or the provinces. **2** having tastes or attitudes that show a lack of education or experience. ➤ **provincialism** *noun*.

provision *noun* (*plural* **provisions**) **1** the act of providing something. **2** (**provisions**) a stock of food or other supplies.

provisional *adjective* temporary; used for the time being, but likely to be changed or abandoned later. ➤ **provisionally** *adverb*.

proviso /pro vie zoh/ *noun* (*plural* **provisos**) a condition in an agreement.

provocation *noun* something that makes somebody angry.

provocative *adjective* **1** tending or intended to make somebody angry. **2** making people feel sexual desire. ➤ **provocatively** *adverb*.

provoke *verb* (**provokes, provoking, provoked**) **1** to make somebody angry. **2** to cause somebody to behave in a specified way.

provost *noun* (*plural* **provosts**) **1** the head of certain university colleges and public schools. **2** the head of certain Scottish district councils.

prow *noun* (*plural* **prows**) the front part of a ship or boat

prowess *noun* outstanding ability.

prowl *verb* (**prowls, prowling, prowled**) to move about in a stealthy way, waiting to attack somebody or trying to find out something. ➤ **prowler** *noun*.

proximity *noun* nearness.

proxy *noun* (*plural* **proxies**) a person who does something on behalf of somebody else.

prude *noun* (*plural* **prudes**) a person who is easily shocked by nudity or things to do with sex. ➤ **prudish** *adjective*.

prudent *adjective* sensibly cautious. ➤ **prudence** *noun*.

prune[1] *noun* (*plural* **prunes**) a dried plum.

prune[2] *verb* (**prunes, pruning, pruned**) to cut off parts of a plant in order to control its size or encourage flowers or fruit to grow.

pry *verb* (**pries, prying, pried**) to be too interested in other people's affairs.

PS *abbreviation* postscript.

psalm /sahm/ *noun* (*plural* **psalms**) a song or poem from the Book of Psalms in the Bible.

pseudonym /sew doh nim/ *noun* (*plural* **pseudonyms**) a fictitious name used by an author.

psyche /sie ki/ *noun* (*plural* **psyches**) the soul, mind, or spirit.

psychedelic /sie ki de lik/ *adjective* having bright colours and strange swirling patterns. ➤ **psychedelically** *adverb*.

psychiatry *noun* a branch of medicine that deals with mental disorders. ➤ **psychiatric** *adjective*, **psychiatrist** *noun*.

psychic *adjective* sensitive to supernatural forces or influences. ➤ **psychically** *adverb*.

psychoanalysis *noun* analysis of a person's unconscious feelings in order to treat their mental disorders. ➤ **psychoanalyst** *noun*, **psychoanalytic** *adjective*.

psychological *adjective* **1** to do with psychology. **2** to do with your mind. ➤ **psychologically** *adverb*.

psychology *noun* the study of the mind. ➤ **psychologist** *noun*.

psychopath *noun* (*plural* **psychopaths**) a person suffering from a mental disorder that causes violent antisocial behaviour. ➤ **psychopathic** *adjective*.

psychosis *noun* (*plural* **psychoses** /sie koh seez/) a mental disorder that causes a loss of contact with reality. ➤ **psychotic** *adjective*.

PT *abbreviation* physical training.

PTA *abbreviation* Parent-Teacher Association.

pterodactyl /te roh dak til/ *noun* (*plural* **pterodactyls**) a flying dinosaur with teeth and a long neck.

PTO *abbreviation* please turn over.

pub *noun* (*plural* **pubs**) a place where people can buy alcoholic drinks and sit and drink them.

puberty /pew ber ti/ *noun* the period during which young people become sexually mature.

pubic /pew bik/ *adjective* in the area around a person's genitals.

public *adjective* **1** involving people in general: *a public debate*. **2** available for everybody in a community to use: *public parks*. **3** owned by the government or the people of a country: *public money*. ~ *noun* (**the public**) people in general. ✳ **in public** in the presence of strangers. ➤ **publicly** *adverb*.

publican *noun* (*plural* **publicans**) a person who owns or runs a pub.

publication *noun* (*plural* **publications**) **1** the act or process of publishing something. **2** a book, magazine, or other published work.

public company *noun* (*plural* **public companies**) a company whose shares can be traded on the stock exchange.

public house *noun* (*plural* **public houses**) *formal* a pub.

publicity *noun* **1** information or events designed to make people aware of something and make them want to do or buy it. **2** public attention.

publicize *or* **publicise** *verb* (**publicizes, publicizing, publicized** *or* **publicises,** etc) to make people aware of something.

public limited company *noun* (*plural* **public limited companies**) a company whose shareholders have only a limited liability for any debts or losses created by the company.

public relations *noun* the business of informing the public about an organization in order to get their support or goodwill.

public school *noun* (*plural* **public schools**) a famous private school that charges very high fees.

public sector *noun* the part of the economy owned or controlled by the state.

publish *verb* (**publishes, publishing, published**) **1** to produce a book, newspaper, etc for sale. **2** to print information in a book, newspaper, etc.

publisher *noun* (*plural* **publishers**) a company that produces books.

puce *noun* a brownish purple colour.

puck *noun* (*plural* **pucks**) a hard rubber disc used in ice hockey.

pudding *noun* (*plural* **puddings**) **1** a sweet dish eaten at the end of a meal. **2** a sweet or savoury dish made from flour, suet, etc.

puddle *noun* (*plural* **puddles**) a small pool of liquid, especially of rainwater on the ground.

pudgy *adjective* (**pudgier, pudgiest**) short and rather fat.

puerile /pew a riel/ *adjective* childishly silly.

puff *verb* (**puffs, puffing, puffed**) **1** to blow out smoke. **2** to breathe hard and quickly. **3** (**puff out/up**) to make something bigger by sticking it out or filling it with air. ~ *noun* (*plural*

puffs) 1 a small cloud of smoke. **2** a draw on a pipe or cigarette. ✱ **out of puff** *informal* out of breath.

puffin *noun* (*plural* **puffins**) a black-and-white seabird with a short neck and a large, brightly coloured bill.

puffy *adjective* (**puffier, puffiest**) said especially about your eyes or cheeks: swollen.

pug *noun* (*plural* **pugs**) a small sturdy dog with a broad wrinkled face.

pugnacious *adjective* tending to argue or fight. ➤ **pugnacity** *noun*.

puja /pooja/ *noun* Hindu daily worship.

puke *informal verb* (**pukes, puking, puked**) to vomit. ~ *noun* vomit.

pukka *adjective informal* **1** genuine; authentic. **2** excellent.

pull *verb* (**pulls, pulling, pulled**) **1** to take hold of something or somebody and make them move towards you. **2** to remove or detach something with a sharp forceful movement towards you. **3** to make something that is attached behind travel in the same direction: *a tractor pulling a plough*. **4** to strain a muscle, tendon, etc. **5** to move steadily: *The train pulled into the station.* ~ *noun* (*plural* **pulls**) **1** the act of pulling. **2** a force that attracts people. ✱ **pull a face** to grimace. **pull down** to demolish a building. **pull in** said about a vehicle: to stop by the side of the road. **pull off** to achieve something difficult. **pull out 1** said about a vehicle: to move out into a stream of traffic. **2** to decide not to take part in something that you had earlier agreed to take part in; to withdraw. **pull somebody's leg** to deceive or tease somebody. **pull strings** to use your influence to achieve something. **pull up** said about a vehicle: to come to a stop. **pull yourself together** to become calm after being angry or upset.

pulley *noun* (*plural* **pulleys**) a wheel that a rope or chain passes round to lift heavy loads.

pullover *noun* (*plural* **pullovers**) a sweater that you put on by pulling it over your head.

pulmonary *adjective formal* to do with your lungs.

pulp *noun* **1** the soft fleshy part of a fruit or vegetable. **2** a soft shapeless mass produced when you crush or beat something. **3** (*used before a noun*) cheap and sensational: *pulp fiction*. ➤ **pulpy** *adjective*.

pulpit *noun* (*plural* **pulpits**) a raised platform in a church, from which sermons are preached.

pulsate *verb* (**pulsates, pulsating, pulsated**) to beat or throb with a strong pulse. ➤ **pulsation** *noun*.

pulse[1] *noun* the regular pumping movement of blood through your arteries, caused by the contractions of your heart. ~ *verb* (**pulses, pulsing, pulsed**) = PULSATE.

pulse[2] *noun* (*plural* **pulses**) the edible seed of various crops, such as peas, beans, and lentils.

pulverize *or* **pulverise** *verb* (**pulverizes, pulverizing, pulverized** *or* **pulverises**, etc) to crush something into very small particles.

puma *noun* (*plural* **pumas** *or* **puma**) a large American wild cat with a tawny coat.

pumice *noun* a light volcanic rock with a rough surface, used for smoothing things, such as hard skin.

pummel *verb* (**pummels, pummelling, pummelled**) to hit something hard and repeatedly with your fists.

pump *noun* (*plural* **pumps**) a device that makes a liquid or gas flow in a particular direction using suction and pressure. ~ *verb* (**pumps, pumping, pumped**) **1** to make a liquid or gas

pumpkin *noun* (*plural* **pumpkins**) a very large round vegetable with orange skin and yellow flesh.

pumps *plural noun* lightweight canvas sports shoes.

pun *noun* (*plural* **puns**) a humorous use of a word with more than one meaning.

punch[1] *verb* (**punches, punching, punched**) **1** to hit somebody or something with your fist. **2** to push a button or key. ~ *noun* (*plural* **punches**) a blow with your fist.

punch[2] *noun* (*plural* **punches**) a device for cutting holes in paper. ~ *verb* (**punches, punching, punched**) to make a hole in paper.

punch[3] *noun* a drink made from wine or spirits mixed with fruit, spices, and water.

punchline *noun* (*plural* **punchlines**) a sentence or phrase that is the climax to a joke or story.

punctual *adjective* arriving or happening at the exact or agreed time. ➤ **punctuality** *noun*, **punctually** *adverb*.

punctuate *verb* (**punctuates, punctuating, punctuated**) **1** to mark a piece of text with punctuation marks. **2** to occur at intervals during something.

punctuation *noun* English **1** the use of marks such as commas, colons, and full stops to clarify a piece of writing. **2** the marks used for this purpose.

puncture *noun* (*plural* **punctures**) a hole made by piercing something with a pointed object. ~ *verb* (**punctures, puncturing, punctured**) to pierce something with a pointed object.

pundit *noun* (*plural* **pundits**) a person who gives their opinions on something, especially on the likely outcome of an election or other political issue.

pungent *adjective* having a strong sharp smell or taste. ➤ **pungency** *noun*.

punish *verb* (**punishes, punishing, punished**) to make somebody suffer something unpleasant because they have broken a law or rule. ➤ **punishable** *adjective*.

punishment *noun* (*plural* **punishments**) something unpleasant that somebody must suffer because they have broken a law or a rule.

punitive /pewˈnitiv/ *adjective* intended as a punishment.

punk *noun* (*plural* **punks**) **1** (also **punk rock**) a loud aggressive style of rock music typically with abusive or anti-establishment lyrics. **2** somebody who listens to punk or wears the outlandish clothes and hairstyles associated with punk. **3** N American, informal a worthless person.

punt[1] *noun* (*plural* **punts**) a long narrow flat-bottomed boat that you push through the water using a long pole. ~ *verb* (**punts, punting, punted**) to travel in a punt.

punt[2] *verb* to kick a ball with the end of your foot, or after dropping it onto your foot. ~ *noun* (*plural* **punts**) an act of punting a ball.

punt[3] *noun* (*plural* **punts**) *informal* a bet. ~ *verb* (**punts, punting, punted**) *informal* to bet.

punter *noun* (*plural* **punters**) *informal* **1** a person who bets. **2** a customer.

puny *adjective* (**punier, puniest**) small and weak.

pup *noun* (*plural* **pups**) **1** a young dog. **2** a young seal, rat, or other animal.

pupa *noun* (*plural* **pupae** /ˈpewpee/) Science an insect at the stage between a larva and an adult. ➤ **pupal** *adjective*.

pupate *verb* (**pupates, pupating,**

pupated) *Science* said about an insect: to become a pupa. ➤ **pupation** *noun*.

pupil[1] *noun* (*plural* **pupils**) a child or young person who is being taught.

pupil[2] *noun* (*plural* **pupils**) the round dark opening in the centre of the iris of the eye.

puppet *noun* (*plural* **puppets**) **1** a toy figure that you move by strings, wires, or rods, or by movements of your hand and fingers inside the body. **2** a person controlled by somebody else. ➤ **puppeteer** *noun*, **puppetry** *noun*.

puppy *noun* (*plural* **puppies**) a young dog.

purchase *verb* (**purchases, purchasing, purchased**) to buy something. ~ *noun* (*plural* **purchases**) **1** something you buy. **2** the act of buying. **3** a firm grip or contact. ➤ **purchaser** *noun*.

purdah *noun* in some Muslim and Hindu communities, the custom of keeping women away from public view.

pure *adjective* (**purer, purest**) **1** not mixed with any other substance. **2** free from anything that could dirty or spoil it. **3** free from sin; innocent. **4** absolute: *pure cheek*.

puree *or* **purée** /pew ray/ *noun* (*plural* **purees** *or* **purées**) a thick pulp of fruit or vegetables produced by blending or crushing.

purely *adverb* only: *purely for pleasure*.

purgatory *noun* in Roman Catholic belief, a place where the souls of sinners are punished and where they try to become good enough to go to heaven.

purge *verb* (**purges, purging, purged**) to get rid of unwanted things or people. ~ *noun* (*plural* **purges**) an occasion when you get rid of unwanted things or people.

purify *verb* (**purifies, purifying, purified**) to make something pure. ➤ **purification** *noun*.

purist *noun* (*plural* **purists**) a person who thinks people should follow strict rules about how things are done, especially in language. ➤ **purism** *noun*.

puritan *noun* (*plural* **puritans**) **1** (**Puritan**) *History* a member of the group within the Church of England in the 16th and 17th centuries who wanted to get rid of elaborate forms of worship. **2** a person who lives their life according to strict religious and moral rules. ➤ **puritanical** *adjective*.

purity *noun* the state of being pure.

purloin *verb* (**purloins, purloining, purloined**) *formal* to steal something.

purple *adjective* of a colour between red and blue. ~ *noun* (*plural* **purples**) a purple colour.

purport *verb* (**purports, purporting, purported**) to claim to be something. ➤ **purportedly** *adverb*.

purpose *noun* (*plural* **purposes**) **1** the aim of something that you do, or the function that something has. **2** a determined attitude. ✶ **on purpose** intentionally. ➤ **purposeless** *adjective*.

purposeful *adjective* full of determination. ➤ **purposefully** *adverb*.

purposely *adverb* for a particular purpose; deliberately.

purr *verb* (**purrs, purring, purred**) **1** said about a cat: to make a low vibratory murmur of pleasure. **2** said about an engine: to run smoothly. ➤ **purr** *noun*.

purse *noun* (*plural* **purses**) **1** a small bag for holding money. **2** *N American* a handbag. ~ *verb* (**purses, pursing, pursed**) to draw your lips together, for example to express disapproval.

purser *noun* (*plural* **pursers**) an officer on a ship who is in charge of documents and accounts.

pursue *verb* (**pursues, pursuing, pursued**) **1** to follow somebody in order to overtake or capture them. **2** to try to accomplish a goal. **3** to carry something out or continue with something. ➤ **pursuer** *noun*.

pursuit *noun* (*plural* **pursuits**) **1** an activity or pastime. **2** the act of pursuing somebody or something.

purveyor *noun* (*plural* **purveyors**) *formal* a person or company that sells a particular product: *purveyors of fine foods*.

pus *noun* thick yellowish or greenish liquid that forms in an infected part of the body.

push *verb* (**pushes, pushing, pushed**) **1** to make something move away from you with a movement of your hands or body. **2** to urge or force somebody to do something. **3** *informal* to sell illegal drugs. ~ *noun* (*plural* **pushes**) **1** a pushing movement or impact. **2** a determined effort. ✻ **at a push** *informal* if really necessary. **be pushed** *informal* to have too little time. **push for** to demand something strongly. **push in** to unfairly force your way into a queue ahead of others. **push off** *informal* to leave.

pushchair *noun* (*plural* **pushchairs**) a light folding chair on wheels in which a young child can be pushed.

pusher *noun* (*plural* **pushers**) somebody who sells illegal drugs.

pushover *noun informal* **1** a person who is easily defeated or persuaded. **2** something that you accomplish easily.

pushy *adjective* (**pushier, pushiest**) determined in a self-important or aggressive way. ➤ **pushiness** *noun*.

pussy *noun* (*plural* **pussies**) *informal* a cat.

pussyfoot *verb* (**pussyfoots, pussyfooting, pussyfooted**) to talk or act in such a cautious or timid way that you achieve nothing.

pustule *noun* (*plural* **pustules**) a raised, pus-filled spot on the skin.

put *verb* (**puts, putting, put**) **1** to place something in a specified position. **2** to bring something or somebody into a specified condition: *He tried to put us at ease*. **3** to express something in words: *Let me put it another way*. **4** to estimate something: *I'd put the value at around £2 million*. **5** to present an idea or proposal for people to consider. **6** to ask a question for people to answer. **7** to throw a heavy metal ball in the athletics event of putting the shot. ✻ **put down 1** to kill a sick or injured animal painlessly. **2** to pay a sum of money as a deposit. **3** to criticize somebody openly and in a way that makes them lose confidence or appear foolish. **put off 1** to discourage somebody from doing or having something. **2** to postpone something till a later time than originally planned. **put on 1** to pretend to have an attitude or feeling. **2** to increase in weight by a specified amount. **3** to present a performance. **put out 1** to irritate somebody. **2** to inconvenience somebody. **put up 1** to build or erect something. **2** to accommodate somebody for a short time. **put up with** to tolerate something.

putative /pew ta tiv/ *adjective formal* supposed.

putrid /pew trid/ *adjective* decaying or rotten and foul-smelling.

putt *verb* (**putts, putting, putted**) to hit a golf ball gently from somewhere on a green towards the hole. ~ *noun* (*plural* **putts**) a gentle golf stroke.

putter *noun* (*plural* **putters**) a golf club used for putting.

putty *noun* a soft paste used for fixing a pane of glass into a window frame.

puzzle *noun* (*plural* **puzzles**) **1** a problem, game, or toy that tests your ability to think clearly and solve

PVC

problems. **2** somebody or something that is difficult to understand. *verb* (**puzzles, puzzling, puzzled**) **1** to be difficult for somebody to understand. **2** to think hard about something that you do not understand or cannot decide about. ➤ **puzzlement** *noun*, **puzzling** *adjective*.

PVC *abbreviation* = *polyvinyl chloride*, a type of plastic.

pygmy or **pigmy** *noun* (*plural* **pygmies** or **pigmies**) **1** a member of any of several peoples who are short in height. **2** (*used before a noun*) being a small variety of something.

pyjamas *plural noun* a loose top and trousers for sleeping in.

pylon *noun* (*plural* **pylons**) a tower that supports electricity power cables.

pyramid *noun* (*plural* **pyramids**) **1** a shape with a square base and four triangular sides that meet at the top in a point. **2** a massive Egyptian stone tomb that has this shape. ➤ **pyramidal** *adjective*.

pyre *noun* (*plural* **pyres**) a tall fire on which a dead body is ritually burned in some religions.

pyrotechnics *plural noun* an impressive firework display. ➤ **pyrotechnic** *adjective*.

python *noun* (*plural* **pythons**) a large snake that kills its prey by crushing it.

quack[1] *verb* (**quacks, quacking, quacked**) to make the cry of a duck. ➤ **quack** *noun*.

quack[2] *noun* (*plural* **quacks**) **1** somebody who pretends to have medical skills or qualifications. **2** *informal* a doctor. ➤ **quackery** *noun*.

quad *noun* (*plural* **quads**) **1** = QUADRANGLE. **2** = QUADRUPLET.

quad bike *noun* (*plural* **quad bikes**) a vehicle that looks like a motorcycle with four large wheels, use for driving over rough country rather than on roads.

quadrangle *noun* (*plural* **quadrangles**) a courtyard with buildings on all four sides.

quadrant *noun* (*plural* **quadrants**) *Maths* a shape that is a quarter of a circle.

quadratic equation *noun* (*plural* **quadratic equations**) *Maths* an equation in which none of the quantities is raised above the power of two.

quadrilateral *noun* (*plural* **quadrilaterals**) *Maths* any flat shape with four straight sides. ~ *adjective* having four straight sides.

quadruped *noun* (*plural* **quadrupeds**) *Science* an animal that walks on four legs.

quadruple *adjective* **1** being four times as much or as many. **2** having four parts. ~ *verb* (**quadruples, quadrupling, quadrupled**) to become, or make something, four times as much or as many.

quadruplet *noun* (*plural* **quadruplets**) any of four children born at the same time to the same mother.

quaff /kwof/ *verb* (**quaffs, quaffing, quaffed**) *literary* to drink something.

quagmire /kwag mier *or* kwog mier/ *noun* (*plural* **quagmires**) **1** an area of soft boggy land. **2** an awkward and complicated situation.

quail[1] *noun* (*plural* **quails** *or* **quail**) a small bird with a round body and short tail, similar to a partridge.

quail[2] *verb* (**quails, quailing, quailed**) to tremble, or move away, because you are frightened.

quaint *adjective* old-fashioned or unusual in an attractive way. ➤ **quaintly** *adverb*.

quake *verb* (**quakes, quaking, quaked**) **1** to shake or vibrate. **2** to tremble because you are frightened. ~ *noun* (*plural* **quakes**) *informal* an earthquake.

Quaker *noun* (*plural* **Quakers**) a member of a Christian group, called the Religious Society of Friends, that has no priests or ministers and whose members have a strong belief in non-violence. ➤ **Quakerism** *noun*.

Word History The name *Quaker* was perhaps given to the group because their founder, George Fox, told his followers that they should 'tremble at the word of the Lord'.

---

qualification *noun* (*plural* **qualifications**) **1** the fact that somebody has

qualifier

passed an examination or completed a course of study. **2** a quality or skill that makes somebody suitable for a particular job. **3** an extra comment that slightly changes the meaning of a statement.

qualifier *noun* (*plural* **qualifiers**) **1** a player or team that qualifies in a tournament. **2** a preliminary heat in a tournament. **3** *English* = MODIFIER.

qualify *verb* (**qualifies, qualifying, qualified**) **1** to win a place in a tournament, or in a later round of a tournament. **2** to make somebody suitable for or entitled to something, or to be suitable for or entitled to something: *What qualifies you to give advice?*; *He qualifies for the job because of his vast experience.* **3** to get a qualification: *My brother has just qualified as a lawyer.* **4** to slightly change the meaning of a statement.

quality *noun* (*plural* **qualities**) **1** how good something is. **2** a characteristic or individual feature.

qualm /kwahm/ *noun* (*plural* **qualms**) a feeling that something you do is not morally right or fair.

quandary *noun* (*plural* **quandaries**) a feeling of uncertainty about which choice to make.

quango /kwang goh/ *noun* (*plural* **quangos**) an organization set up by the government to do a public job, but not controlled by the government.

quantity *noun* (*plural* **quantities**) **1** an amount or number. **2** (*also* **quantities**) a large amount or number.

quantum leap *noun* (*plural* **quantum leaps**) a sudden large increase or major advance.

quarantine *noun* a state or period of isolation for animals or people, designed to prevent the spread of disease. ~ *verb* (**quarantines, quarantining, quarantined**) to put an animal or person into quarantine.

quarrel *noun* (*plural* **quarrels**) an angry disagreement. ~ *verb* (**quarrels, quarrelling, quarrelled**) to have a quarrel.

quarry[1] *noun* (*plural* **quarries**) a place where a substance such as stone or sand has been dug out of the ground. ~ *verb* (**quarries, quarrying, quarried**) to dig a substance out of the ground.

quarry[2] *noun* (*plural* **quarries**) **1** an animal that is being hunted by another animal. **2** somebody who is being chased by another person.

quart *noun* (*plural* **quarts**) a unit of liquid capacity equal to 2 pints (1.136 litres), a quarter of a gallon.

quarter *noun* (*plural* **quarters**) **1** any of four equal parts into which something is divided. **2** a quarter of a pound in weight. **3** a point of time 15 minutes before or after the hour. **4** a coin worth a quarter of a US or Canadian dollar. **5** a district of a town or city. **6** (**quarters**) living accommodation or lodgings. ~ *verb* (**quarters, quartering, quartered**) to cut or divide something into four equal parts.

quarterfinal *noun* (*plural* **quarterfinals**) any of four matches in the round that is second from last in a competition.

quarterly *adverb and adjective* at three-monthly intervals. ~ *noun* (*plural* **quarterlies**) a periodical published once every three months.

quartet *noun* (*plural* **quartets**) *Music* a group of four instruments, voices, or performers, or a piece of music for such a group.

quartz *noun* a mineral consisting of silicon dioxide, found in granite and sandstone.

quash *verb* (**quashes, quashing, quashed**) **1** to cancel a decision made by a court of law. **2** to stop something, such as a rumour or rebellion.

quaver *verb* (**quavers, quavering, quavered**) said about somebody's voice: to tremble. ~ *noun* (*plural* **quavers**) *Music* a musical note with the time value of half a crotchet.
➤ **quavery** *adjective*.

quay /kee/ *noun* (*plural* **quays**) a place where boats or ships are loaded and unloaded.

quayside *noun* the part of a quay that is right next to the water.

queasy *adjective* (**queasier, queasiest**) feeling sick. ➤ **queasiness** *noun*.

queen *noun* (*plural* **queens**) **1** a female monarch. **2** the wife or widow of a king. **3** in chess, the most powerful piece, allowed to move any number of squares in any direction. **4** a playing card marked with a picture of a queen, ranking above a jack and below a king. ➤ **queenly** *adjective*.

queen mother *noun* (*plural* **queen mothers**) a woman who is the widow of a king and the mother of the reigning sovereign.

Queen's Counsel *noun* (*plural* **Queen's Counsels**) a senior barrister.

queer *adjective* **1** strange. **2** *informal* slightly ill.

quell *verb* (**quells, quelling, quelled**) **1** to stop a rebellion. **2** to force yourself to stop having a feeling.

quench *verb* (**quenches, quenching, quenched**) **1** to satisfy your thirst by drinking something. **2** to put out a fire.

query /kwee ri/ *noun* (*plural* **queries**) a question, especially one expressing doubt or uncertainty. ~ *verb* (**queries, querying, queried**) **1** to suggest that something is not correct or accurate. **2** to express doubt about something.

quest *noun* (*plural* **quests**) a long and difficult search for something.

question *noun* (*plural* **questions**) **1** a phrase or sentence that asks for information. **2** a subject that people are discussing. **3** a thing that something else depends on: *It's simply a question of availability.* **4** doubt or objection: *There's no question about her ability.* ~ *verb* (**questions, questioning, questioned**) **1** to ask somebody a question or a series of questions. **2** to doubt or dispute something: *The teacher questioned my honesty.* ✳ **in question** being discussed. **out of the question** not possible or not worth considering.
➤ **questioner** *noun*.

questionable *adjective* very possibly not true or honest. ➤ **questionably** *adverb*.

question mark *noun* (*plural* **question marks**) a punctuation mark (?) used at the end of a sentence to indicate that it is a direct question.

questionnaire *noun* (*plural* **questionnaires**) a set of questions designed to find out people's opinions about something.

queue *noun* (*plural* **queues**) a line of people or vehicles waiting. ~ *verb* (**queues, queuing** *or* **queueing, queued**) to wait in a queue.

quibble *noun* (*plural* **quibbles**) a minor objection or criticism. ~ *verb* (**quibbles, quibbling, quibbled**) to make minor objections or criticisms.

quiche /keesh/ *noun* (*plural* **quiches**) a savoury tart with an egg-based filling.

quick *adjective* **1** lasting a short time only: *a quick look at the newspaper*. **2** done with no delay; prompt: *quick delivery*. **3** doing things with great speed: *a quick worker*. **4** doing things without delaying or without thinking carefully: *She's quick to find fault*. **5** fast in understanding, thinking, or learning. ~ *adverb informal* fast; soon: *Come quick!* ➤ **quickly** *adverb*, **quickness** *noun*.

quicken *verb* (**quickens, quickening, quickened**) to become more rapid, or increase the pace of something.

quicksand *noun* a deep mass of loose wet sand that heavy objects sink into easily.

quid *noun* (*plural* **quid**) *informal* a pound sterling.

quiet *adjective* **1** making little or no noise. **2** peaceful; free from noise, activity, or excitement: *a quiet afternoon in the garden*. **3** private or discreet: *a quiet chat with the teacher*. **4** involving only a small number of people: *a quiet wedding*. ~ *noun* silence or peacefulness. ➤ **quietly** *adverb*, **quietness** *noun*.

quieten *verb* (**quietens, quietening, quietened**) to become quiet, or make something or somebody quiet.

quiff *noun* (*plural* **quiffs**) hair made to stand up over your forehead.

quill *noun* (*plural* **quills**) **1** a pen made from a feather. **2** any of the large stiff feathers of a bird's wing or tail. **3** any of the sharp spines on the body of a porcupine, hedgehog, etc.

quilt *noun* (*plural* **quilts**) a thick warm cover for a bed.

quilted *adjective* made of thick padded fabric.

quin *noun* (*plural* **quins**) = QUINTUPLET.

quince *noun* (*plural* **quinces**) a yellow round or pear-shaped fruit, used for making jam.

quintessential *adjective* representing a perfect example of something. ➤ **quintessentially** *adverb*.

quintet *noun* (*plural* **quintets**) *Music* a group of five instruments, voices, or performers, or a piece of music for such a group.

quintuplet *noun* (*plural* **quintuplets**) any of five children born at the same time to the same mother.

quip *noun* (*plural* **quips**) a clever, witty, or sarcastic remark. ~ *verb* (**quips, quipping, quipped**) to make a quip.

quirk *noun* (*plural* **quirks**) a strange aspect of somebody's behaviour. ➤ **quirky** *adjective*.

quit *verb* (**quits, quitting, quit** or **quitted**) **1** to stop doing a job or activity. **2** *informal* to stop trying and admit defeat. ➤ **quitter** *noun*.

quite *adverb* **1** wholly or completely: *not quite finished*. **2** to some degree, but not very: *quite good*. **3** more than usually: *It took quite a while*. **4** very: *You can stroke the dog. He's quite friendly*. ~ *interjection* used to express agreement.

quits *adjective* on even terms after repaying a debt or retaliating: *Now we're quits*.

quiver *verb* (**quivers, quivering, quivered**) to shake with a trembling motion. ➤ **quiver** *noun*.

quixotic *adjective* tending to have ideas that will clearly never work. ➤ **quixotically** *adverb*.

Word History Don *Quixote* is the hero of the novel *Don Quixote de la Mancha* by the 16th-century Spanish writer Cervantes. In the book, Don Quixote is portrayed as a simple-minded, middle-aged gentleman who, obsessed with the stories of knights and chivalry that he has read, sets out to right the wrongs of the world in an idealistic but absurd and naïve way.

quiz *noun* (*plural* **quizzes**) a game in the form of a test of knowledge. ~ *verb* (**quizzes, quizzing, quizzed**) to question somebody repeatedly or in a hostile way.

quizzical *adjective* showing that you are puzzled by something. ➤ **quizzically** *adverb*.

quoit /koit/ *noun* (*plural* **quoits**) **1** a ring used in a throwing game. **2** (**quoits**) a game in which quoits are thrown at an upright pin.

quorate *adjective* having a quorum.

quorum *noun* (*plural* **quorums**) the minimum number of members of an organization that must be present at a meeting in order for decisions taken at the meeting to be valid.

quota *noun* (*plural* **quotas**) **1** a share of something that each person is given. **2** a maximum number of things or people allowed.

quotation *noun* (*plural* **quotations**) **1** something said or written by somebody that is later repeated by somebody else. **2** a statement of how much a company will charge for doing work.

quotation marks *plural noun* a pair of punctuation marks (" " or ' ') used to indicate the beginning and end of a direct quotation or to enclose a word or phrase, such as a title.

quote *verb* (**quotes, quoting, quoted**) **1** to repeat something that somebody else said or wrote earlier. **2** to give a quotation for work to be done. ~ *noun* (*plural* **quotes**) *informal* **1** = QUOTATION. **2** = QUOTATION MARK.

quotient *noun* (*plural* **quotients**) *Maths* the number produced when you divide one number by another.

Qur'an *noun* see KORAN.

q.v. *abbreviation* = (Latin) *quod vide* 'which see', used to indicate a cross-reference.

qwerty /kwerti/ *adjective ICT* said about a computer keyboard: having the conventional arrangement of keys for English, with *q, w, e, r, t, y* on the left side of the top row of letters.

rabbi /ra bie/ *noun* (*plural* **rabbis**) the official leader of a Jewish congregation.

rabbit *noun* (*plural* **rabbits**) a small long-eared mammal that lives in a burrow.

rabble *noun* a disorderly crowd of people.

rabid /ra bid *or* ray bid/ *adjective* **1** fanatical. **2** affected with rabies. ➤ **rabidly** *adverb*.

rabies /ray beez/ *noun* a very serious disease that is transmitted when an affected animal bites another animal or a human and that makes animals and people go mad and usually die.

raccoon *or* **racoon** *noun* (*plural* **raccoons** *or* **racoons**) a small North American animal that has a bushy ringed tail and lives in trees.

race¹ *noun* (*plural* **races**) **1** a contest to see who can reach a finishing point first or do something fastest. **2** a contest for a prize or position: *the race for the Tory leadership*. **3** a rush: *It was a race to get the book completed on time*. **4** a strong or rapid current of water. ~ *verb* (**races, racing, raced**) **1** to compete in a race. **2** to have a race with somebody. **3** to go or move at top speed. ➤ **racer** *noun*.

race² *noun* (*plural* **races**) **1** one of the major divisions of human beings, made up of people who share particular physical characteristics such as skin colour or the shape of their eyes or noses. **2** a person's ethnic origin.

racecourse *noun* (*plural* **racecourses**) a place or track where races, especially horse races, are held.

racehorse *noun* (*plural* **racehorses**) a horse bred or kept for racing.

race relations *plural noun* relations between members of a country's different racial communities.

racetrack *noun* (*plural* **racetracks**) a track on which races, for example between cars or runners, are held.

racial /ray shl/ *adjective* to do with race, or based on distinctions of race. ➤ **racially** *adverb*.

racialism *noun* = RACISM. ➤ **racialist** *noun and adjective*.

racism /ray si zm/ *noun* hostility towards, or discrimination against, people who belong to a different race from you. ➤ **racist** *noun and adjective*.

rack *noun* (*plural* **racks**) **1** a framework or stand with hooks or spaces to hold things. **2** (**the rack**) *History* an instrument of torture used to stretch the victim's body. ~ *verb* (also **wrack**) (**racks, racking, racked** *or* **wracks**, etc) to cause somebody great pain or anguish. ✳ **rack/wrack and ruin** a state of destruction or extreme neglect. **rack/wrack your brains** to make a great mental effort.

racket¹ *or* **racquet** *noun* (*plural* **rackets** *or* **racquets**) a lightweight bat with strings stretched across an open frame, used in tennis, squash, badminton, etc.

racket² *noun* (*plural* **rackets**) **1** a loud

and confused noise. **2** *informal* a dishonest or illegal scheme for making a profit.

racketeer *noun* (*plural* **racketeers**) a person who makes money through dishonest schemes. ➤ **racketeering** *noun*.

racoon *noun* see RACCOON.

racquet *noun* see RACKET¹.

radar *noun* (*plural* **radars**) an electronic system or piece of equipment that detects ships, aircraft, etc by sending out radio waves and analysing them when they are reflected back from objects they strike.

radiant *adjective* **1** vividly bright and shining. **2** expressing love, happiness, health, etc. **3** *Science* transmitted by radiation. ➤ **radiance** *noun*, **radiantly** *adverb*.

radiate *verb* (**radiates, radiating, radiated**) **1** *Science* to send out energy in rays or waves. **2** to show a quality or feeling clearly. **3** to move outwards in straight lines from a central point.

radiation *noun* **1** the process of radiating. **2** *Science* energy radiated in the form of waves or particles.

radiator *noun* (*plural* **radiators**) **1** a room heater through which hot water circulates as part of a central heating system. **2** a device for cooling an internal-combustion engine.

radical *adjective* **1** affecting or changing the basic nature of something: *radical changes*. **2** in politics, wanting to make great changes in existing conditions or institutions. ~ *noun* (*plural* **radicals**) **1** a person who holds radical views. **2** *Science* in chemistry, a group of atoms that is capable of remaining unchanged during reactions. ➤ **radicalism** *noun*, **radically** *adverb*.

radii *noun* a plural of RADIUS.

radio *noun* (*plural* **radios**) **1** the transmission and reception of sound signals by means of electromagnetic waves. **2** a device designed to receive sound broadcasts. **3** the radio broadcasting industry. ~ *verb* (**radios, radioing, radioed**) to send a message to somebody by radio.

radioactive *adjective Science* said of a chemical element: sending out harmful rays or particles as the nuclei of its atoms break up. ➤ **radioactivity** *noun*.

radiography *noun Science* the use of X-rays to create images, especially of the inside of the human body. ➤ **radiographer** *noun*.

radiology *noun Science* the use of radioactive substances and X-rays in the diagnosis and treatment of disease. ➤ **radiologist** *noun*.

radio telescope *noun* (*plural* **radio telescopes**) a radio receiver, usually connected to a large dish-shaped aerial, for detecting radio waves from outer space.

radiotherapy *noun* the treatment of disease, such as cancer, by means of X-rays.

radish *noun* (*plural* **radishes**) the dark red root of a plant of the mustard family, eaten as a salad vegetable.

radium *noun Science* a very radioactive metallic element.

radius *noun* (*plural* **radii** /ˈreɪdiˌiː/ or **radiuses**) **1** *Maths* a straight line extending from the centre of a circle or sphere to its circumference, or the length of this line. **2** a circular area around a particular point with a radius of a stated length: *All police cars within a two-mile radius of the house were alerted*. **3** *Science* the bone on the thumb side of the human forearm.

RAF *abbreviation* Royal Air Force.

raffia *noun* fibre from the leaves of a palm tree, used for making baskets, etc.

raffle *noun* (*plural* **raffles**) a lottery in which the prizes are usually goods.

raft

verb (**raffles, raffling, raffled**) to offer something as a prize in a raffle.

raft[1] *noun* (*plural* **rafts**) **1** a flat, usually wooden, floating structure used as a platform or boat. **2** an inflatable boat or mat.

raft[2] *noun* (*plural* **rafts**) a large collection or quantity.

rafter *noun* (*plural* **rafters**) a parallel beam forming the framework of a roof.

rag[1] *noun* (*plural* **rags**) **1** a piece of old worn cloth. **2** (**rags**) clothes that are in poor or ragged condition. **3** *informal* a newspaper.

rag[2] *noun* (*plural* **rags**) a series of processions and stunts organized by students to raise money for charity.

rag[3] *verb* (**rags, ragging, ragged**) to tease somebody.

ragbag *noun* (*plural* **ragbags**) a collection of all sorts of different, low-quality objects.

rage *noun* (*plural* **rages**) violent and uncontrolled anger. ~ *verb* (**rages, raging, raged**) **1** to be very angry. **2** said about a battle or storm: to continue noisily and violently.

ragged /ˈragid/ *adjective* **1** badly torn or frayed. **2** wearing tattered clothes. **3** having an irregular edge or outline; jagged. **4** performed in an irregular or uneven manner. ▸ **raggedly** *adverb*.

ragtime *noun Music* music with a strongly syncopated rhythm, developed in America in about 1900 and usually played on the piano.

raid *noun* (*plural* **raids**) **1** a surprise attack or invasion by a small force. **2** a sudden invasion by the police, for example in search of criminals, drugs, or stolen goods. **3** a robbery. ~ *verb* (**raids, raiding, raided**) **1** to make a raid on a place. **2** to take or steal things from a place. ▸ **raider** *noun*.

rail *noun* (*plural* **rails**) **1** a fixed horizontal bar, used for example as a barrier or to hang things from. **2** a length of steel forming part of the track for trains, trams, etc. **3** the railway. ~ *verb* (**rails, railing, railed**) to put a rail on or around something. ✳ **go off the rails** *informal* **1** to behave strangely or become mentally unbalanced. **2** to be misguided or mistaken.

railing *noun* (*plural* **railings**) a fence made of rails.

railroad *noun* (*plural* **railroads**) *N American* = RAILWAY.

railway *noun* (*plural* **railways**) **1** a track with two parallel rails on which trains run. **2** a railway network, or an organization that runs trains.

raiment *noun archaic or literary* clothing.

rain *noun* **1** water falling in drops from clouds. **2** rainy weather. **3** a dense flow or fall of something. ~ *verb* (**rains, raining, rained**) **1** to have water falling in drops from the clouds. **2** to fall in large quantities, or to throw down or give things in large quantities: *The defenders rained missiles on the attackers.* ✳ **be rained off** to be prevented or interrupted by rain.

rainbow *noun* (*plural* **rainbows**) a multicoloured arch in the sky formed when the sun's rays shine through raindrops, spray, etc.

raincoat *noun* (*plural* **raincoats**) a coat made from waterproof material.

rainfall *noun* the amount of rain that falls.

rainforest *noun* (*plural* **rainforests**) a dense tropical forest with a heavy annual rainfall.

rainy *adjective* (**rainier, rainiest**) characterized by heavy rainfall. ✳ **a rainy day** a future time when money or other things may be in short supply.

raise *verb* (**raises, raising, raised**) **1** to lift something to a higher position. **2** to bring something to an upright position. **3** to increase the amount, level, strength, etc of something. **4** to bring up a subject for discussion. **5** to express a doubt or objection. **6** to collect money for some purpose. **7** to cause something to occur or appear. **8** to rear a child or an animal. **9** *Maths* to multiply a quantity by itself a number of times.

raisin *noun* (*plural* **raisins**) a dried grape.

raison d'être /ray zong de tra/ *noun* (*plural* **raisons d'être** /ray zong de tra/) the main reason that something or somebody exists.

Raj *noun* (**the Raj**) *History* the period of British rule in India before 1947.

rajah or **raja** *noun* (*plural* **rajahs** or **rajas**) an Indian or Malayan prince or chief.

rake[1] *noun* (*plural* **rakes**) a long-handled garden tool with a row of prongs on the head for gathering grass, leaves, etc, or levelling the ground. ~ *verb* (**rakes, raking, raked**) **1** to level or smooth the ground with a rake. **2** (*also* **rake up**) to gather leaves, etc with a rake. ✻ **rake in** *informal* to earn or gain money rapidly or in large amounts. **rake up** to remind people about something bad that happened long ago and had been forgotten.

rake[2] *noun* a sloping angle.

rake[3] *noun* (*plural* **rakes**) *dated* a man who lives a wild, immoral life of drinking, gambling, etc.

rakish *adjective* **1** smart and stylish. **2** lively but rather disreputable.

rally *noun* (*plural* **rallies**) **1** a mass meeting of people to support a cause. **2** a motor race over public roads or country tracks, designed to test driving and navigational skills. **3** a recovery of strength, courage, value, etc. **4** in tennis, etc, a series of strokes exchanged between players. ~ *verb* (**rallies, rallying, rallied**) **1** to come together, or bring people together, to support a cause or renew an effort. **2** to recover after an illness, a fall in value, etc. **3** to drive in a rally. ✻ **rally round** to give practical or emotional support to somebody.

ram *noun* (*plural* **rams**) **1** a male sheep. **2** something used to ram something. ~ *verb* (**rams, ramming, rammed**) **1** to force something down or in by driving or pushing it. **2** to strike against a vehicle, boat, etc or an obstacle violently and usually head-on.

Ramadan /ra ma dahn/ *noun* the ninth month of the Muslim year, during which Muslims fast daily from dawn to sunset.

ramble *verb* (**rambles, rambling, rambled**) **1** to walk for pleasure in the countryside. **2** to talk or write in a disconnected long-winded fashion. ~ *noun* (*plural* **rambles**) a leisurely walk taken for pleasure in the countryside. ➤ **rambler** *noun*, **rambling** *adjective and noun*.

ramifications *plural noun* wide-reaching and complex consequences.

ramp *noun* (*plural* **ramps**) **1** a slope leading from one level to another. **2** a point where roadworks cause a rise or fall in the level of the road.

rampage *verb* (**rampages, rampaging, rampaged**) to rush about wildly or violently. ✻ **on the rampage** behaving in a wild or violent way.

rampant *adjective* **1** spreading or growing unchecked. **2** said about an animal on a coat of arms: rearing up on one hind leg with its forelegs extended.

rampart *noun* (*plural* **ramparts**) a broad embankment or wall built as a fortification.

ram raid *noun* (*plural* **ram raids**) a robbery in which the robbers enter a

ramrod

building by driving a vehicle through its front window. ➤ **ram-raider** noun.

ramrod noun (plural **ramrods**) History a rod for ramming the charge down the barrel of a gun.

ramshackle adjective badly constructed or needing repair.

ran verb past tense of RUN.

ranch noun (plural **ranches**) a large farm for raising livestock, especially in North America. ➤ **rancher** noun.

rancid adjective said about food: smelling or tasting unpleasantly sour.

rancour noun deeply felt ill will or hatred. ➤ **rancorous** adjective.

random adjective occurring or selected by chance. ∗ **at random** without a plan or pattern. ➤ **randomly** adverb, **randomness** noun.

rang verb past tense of RING².

range noun (plural **ranges**)
1 a sequence or series of numbers or amounts between an upper and a lower limit: *in the age range 15–25*.
2 a number of different objects or products of a similar type: *a range of garden furniture*. **3** the maximum distance that something can travel. **4** the distance between a weapon and its target, a camera and the subject, etc. **5** a large connected group of mountains. **6** an open area over which livestock may roam and feed, especially in North America. **7** a place where something, especially shooting, is practised. **8** a large cooking stove.
~ verb (**ranges, ranging, ranged**)
1 to be within particular limits: *Their ages range from 5 to 65*. **2** to travel or roam freely over an area. **3** to include a large number of topics: *Her interests range from ancient religions to modern pop music*. **4** to set things in a particular order or position.

ranger noun (plural **rangers**) a keeper of a park or forest.

rank¹ noun (plural **ranks**) **1** a position in an order that defines how much authority or seniority a person possesses: *the rank of captain*. **2** a line of soldiers standing side by side.
3 (**the ranks**) the ordinary members of an armed force, as opposed to the officers. verb (**ranks, ranking, ranked**) **1** to have a position in relation to others. **2** to decide the relative position or value of somebody or something.

rank² adjective **1** smelling or tasting bad. **2** said about vegetation: growing thickly. **3** said about something bad: absolute or complete: *rank stupidity*.

rank and file noun (**the rank and file**) the ordinary members of an organization, etc as opposed to the leaders.

rankle verb (**rankles, rankling, rankled**) to cause continuing anger or bitterness.

ransack verb (**ransacks, ransacking, ransacked**) **1** to go through a place stealing things and causing chaos. **2** to search something thoroughly.

ransom noun (plural **ransoms**) a price paid or demanded for the release of a captured or kidnapped person. verb (**ransoms, ransoming, ransomed**) to free somebody from captivity by paying a ransom. ∗ **hold to ransom**
1 to kidnap somebody and demand money for their release. **2** to try to make somebody do something by threatening to cause harm.

rant verb (**rants, ranting, ranted**) to talk in a loud, wild, and threatening manner.

rap¹ noun (plural **raps**) **1** a sharp blow or knock, or the sound made by it.
2 (**the rap**) informal the responsibility for an action. ~ verb (**raps, rapping, rapped**) **1** to strike something with a sharp blow. **2** informal to criticize or reprimand somebody sharply.

rap² noun (plural **raps**) Music a type of pop music in which the lyrics are chanted rapidly over an accompaniment with a heavy beat. ➤ **rapper** noun.

rapacious /ra pay shus/ adjective ferociously taking anything you want. ➤ **rapaciously** adverb, **rapacity** noun.

rape[1] noun **1** the crime of forcing somebody to have sexual intercourse against their will. **2** the act of spoiling and damaging something: *the rape of the countryside*. ~ verb (**rapes, raping, raped**) to force somebody to have sexual intercourse. ➤ **rapist** noun.

rape[2] noun a plant with bright yellow flowers and seeds from which oil is obtained.

rapid adjective fast. ➤ **rapidity** noun, **rapidly** adverb.

rapids plural noun a part of a river where the water flows quickly over a rocky slope.

rapier /ray pi er/ noun (plural **rapiers**) a straight sword with a narrow pointed blade.

rapport /ra paw/ noun a sympathetic or harmonious relationship.

rapt adjective completely engrossed.

rapture noun (plural **raptures**) **1** great joy; ecstasy. **2** an expression of extreme happiness or enthusiasm. ➤ **rapturous** adjective, **rapturously** adverb.

rare[1] adjective (**rarer, rarest**) **1** seldom occurring or found; uncommon. **2** unusually good or attractive. ➤ **rarely** adverb, **rareness** noun.

rare[2] adjective (**rarer, rarest**) said about red meat: cooked lightly so that the meat inside is still red.

rarefied /rair i fied/ adjective **1** said about the air or atmosphere: thin; of lower than normal density. **2** distant from ordinary reality and practical matters.

raring adjective *informal* full of enthusiasm or eagerness to do something.

rarity noun (plural **rarities**) **1** the state of being rare. **2** a rare person or thing.

rascal noun (plural **rascals**) **1** a mischievous person. **2** an unprincipled or dishonest person. ➤ **rascally** adjective.

rash[1] adjective acting or done hastily and without considering the risks involved. ➤ **rashly** adverb, **rashness** noun.

rash[2] noun (plural **rashes**) **1** an outbreak of red spots or patches on your body. **2** a large number of occurrences of something bad during a short period: *a rash of burglaries*.

rasher noun (plural **rashers**) a thin slice of bacon.

rasp noun (plural **rasps**) **1** a file with large cutting surfaces. **2** a grating sound. ~ verb (**rasps, rasping, rasped**) **1** to say something in a harsh tone. **2** to make a grating sound.

raspberry noun (plural **raspberries**) **1** a reddish pink edible berry. **2** *informal* a rude sound made by sticking the tongue out and blowing noisily.

Rastafarian noun (plural **Rastafarians**) a member of a religious and political movement that originated among black West Indians and venerates the former Emperor of Ethiopia, Haile Selassie, as God. ➤ **Rastafarianism** noun.

rat noun (plural **rats**) **1** a rodent similar to a mouse but considerably larger. **2** *informal* somebody who betrays or deserts their friends.

ratchet noun (plural **ratchets**) a mechanism consisting of a bar or wheel with angled teeth and a piece of metal that slides over the teeth when moving in one direction but drops between them and stops all movement in the other direction.

rate noun (plural **rates**) **1** the amount or frequency of something measured per unit of something else: *a rate of 5 litres an hour*. **2** speed of movement

rather

or change. **3** a fixed charge, payment, or price. **4** (*also* **rates**) a tax based on the value of the land and buildings owned by a business, charged by a local authority. ~ *verb* (**rates, rating, rated**) **1** to consider something or somebody to be of a particular standard. **2** to be worthy of something. **3** *informal* to think highly of somebody or something.

rather *adverb* **1** more readily or willingly: *I'd rather stay here.* **2** to some extent; quite: *It's rather warm today.* **3** more accurately: *He is my father, or rather, my stepfather.* **4** on the contrary; instead: *The situation did not improve, but rather grew worse.*

ratify *verb* (**ratifies, ratifying, ratified**) to give official approval to a treaty, so that it can come into force. ➤ **ratification** *noun*.

rating *noun* (*plural* **ratings**) **1** a classification based on the standard reached by somebody or something. **2** (**ratings**) a list of television programmes, etc in order of their popularity. **3** an ordinary seaman in the navy.

ratio /ray shi oh/ *noun* (*plural* **ratios**) *Maths* a pair of numbers that show how much bigger one thing is than another, for example six to one or 6:1.

ration *noun* (*plural* **rations**) **1** a share or amount of something that somebody is allowed for their personal use. **2** (**rations**) regular supplies of food given to troops. ~ *verb* (**rations, rationing, rationed**) **1** to limit the amount of something that a person is allowed to have. **2** to limit a person to a fixed amount of something.

rational *adjective* **1** based on reason; reasonable. **2** able to think logically. ➤ **rationality** *noun*, **rationally** *adverb*.

rationale /ra sha nahl/ *noun* a logical basis or reason for doing or believing something.

rationalize *or* **rationalise** *verb* (**rationalizes, rationalizing, rationalized** *or* **rationalises**, etc) **1** to explain unreasonable or harmful actions by saying that they were done for good reasons or with good intentions. **2** to make an industry, etc more efficient by reorganizing it. ➤ **rationalization** *or* **rationalisation** *noun*.

rat race *noun* (**the rat race**) *informal* the fiercely competitive struggle between all the people who want to do well in their careers and in life.

rattle *verb* (**rattles, rattling, rattled**) **1** to make short sharp knocking or jangling sounds when shaken. **2** *informal* to make somebody anxious. ~ *noun* (*plural* **rattles**) **1** a rattling sound. **2** a toy or device that makes a rattling sound. ✻ **rattle off** to say or recite something briskly.

rattlesnake *noun* (*plural* **rattlesnakes**) a poisonous American snake with horny joints at the end of its tail that rattle when shaken.

ratty *adjective* (**rattier, rattiest**) *informal* **1** irritable. **2** shabby.

raucous /raw kus/ *adjective* disagreeably loud and harsh. ➤ **raucously** *adverb*.

ravage *verb* (**ravages, ravaging, ravaged**) to cause serious damage or harm to something.

ravages *plural noun* serious damage or harm done by something.

rave *verb* (**raves, raving, raved**) **1** to talk wildly or madly. **2** to talk or write very enthusiastically. ~ *noun* (*plural* **raves**) *informal* **1** a very large party with dancing to loud electronic music. **2** (*also* **rave review**) a very enthusiastic review of a book, film, etc.

raven *noun* (*plural* **ravens**) a very large black bird of the crow family.

ravenous *adjective* extremely hungry. ➤ **ravenously** *adverb*.

ravine /ra veen/ *noun* (*plural* **ravines**) *Geography* a narrow steep-sided valley.

raving *adjective* mad.

ravings *plural noun* mad or nonsensical speech.

ravioli /ra vi oh li/ *noun* pasta in the form of little cases containing meat, cheese, etc.

ravishing *adjective* extremely beautiful.

raw *adjective* **1** not cooked. **2** not processed or purified; still in its natural state. **3** *ICT* said about data: not analysed or modified. **4** with the skin damaged or rubbed away. **5** lacking experience or training: *raw recruits*. **6** disagreeably damp or cold. * **get a raw deal** to be badly or unfairly treated. ➤ **rawness** *noun*.

raw material *noun* (*plural* **raw materials**) a natural substance that can be converted into a useful product.

ray[1] *noun* (*plural* **rays**) **1** a narrow beam of light or energy. **2** a slight trace of something: *a ray of hope*.

ray[2] *noun* (*plural* **rays**) a fish with a flat body, wing-like fins, and a long narrow tail.

rayon *noun* a fabric made from cellulose.

raze *verb* (**razes, razing, razed**) to destroy a town or building completely.

razor *noun* (*plural* **razors**) a sharp-edged cutting tool for shaving hair.

RC *abbreviation* Roman Catholic.

reach *verb* (**reaches, reaching, reached**) **1** to stretch out your hand and arm. **2** to touch or grasp something by extending part of your body. **3** to extend as far as a place or level: *a skirt that reaches to the ground*. **4** to arrive at a place: *We reached the campsite just before nightfall*. **5** to achieve something, such as a speed or standard. **6** to contact or communicate with somebody. ~ *noun* (*plural* **reaches**) **1** the distance that somebody can stretch out their arm. **2** a straight portion of a river. * **out of reach** in a place that is too high, far, etc for a person to reach. **within reach** able to be reached. ➤ **reachable** *adjective*.

react *verb* (**reacts, reacting, reacted**) **1** to respond to something in a particular way. **2** *Science* to undergo chemical reaction or physical change.

reaction *noun* (*plural* **reactions**) **1** an action or feeling produced by something that happens to you. **2** (**reactions**) the body's ability to move quickly when something happens. **3** *Science* a chemical transformation that takes place when atoms, molecules, etc act on each other and form new substances.

reactionary *adjective* opposing social or political change. ➤ **reactionary** *noun*.

reactor *noun* (*plural* **reactors**) an apparatus in which a controlled chain reaction takes place to produce nuclear power.

read *verb* (**reads, reading, read**) **1** to look at and understand words or symbols. **2** to speak printed or written words aloud. **3** to be worded or phrased in a particular way. **4** said about a measuring device: to indicate a specified measurement. **5** to study a subject at university. * **read between the lines** to work out what somebody wants to suggest but has not stated directly. **take something as read** to accept something as agreed without discussing it.

reader *noun* (*plural* **readers**) **1** a person who reads. **2** a book that teaches reading. **3** a senior university teacher.

readership *noun* the readers of a particular publication or author.

readily *adverb* **1** without hesitating; willingly. **2** easily.

reading *noun* (*plural* **readings**) **1** an event at which something is read

ready

to an audience. **2** books or other material for a particular interpretation of something. **4** the value indicated by an instrument.

ready *adjective* (**readier, readiest**) **1** in a position to do or deal with something straight away: *I'm ready to go.* **2** fully prepared or finished: *Dinner is ready.* **3** available to be used immediately: *ready money.* **4** willing. **5** likely or about to do something. ➤ **readiness** *noun*.

ready-made *adjective* made beforehand and able to be used immediately.

reagent *noun* (*plural* **reagents**) *Science* a substance that takes part in a particular chemical reaction and can be used to detect the presence of other substances that react with it.

real *adjective* **1** actual, genuine, or authentic. **2** significant. **3** used chiefly for emphasis: complete or great: *Her visit was a real surprise.*

real estate *noun chiefly N American* property in the form of buildings and land.

realism *noun* **1** an attitude that concentrates on facts and realities and rejects impractical ideas. **2** *Art, English* the description or representation of things in a way that is true to nature or real life. ➤ **realist** *adjective and noun*.

realistic *adjective* **1** based on, or basing your ideas on, known facts or reasonable expectations. **2** *Art, English* describing or representing things in a way that seems real. ➤ **realistically** *adverb*.

reality *noun* (*plural* **realities**) **1** something that really exists. **2** the state of being real. **3** all real things and events.

reality TV *or* **reality television** *noun* television programmes that show how a group of real people act when placed in a particular situation.

realize *or* **realise** *verb* (**realizes, real-** izing, realized *or* realises, etc) **1** to be or become fully aware of something. **2** to make something a reality: *to realize an ambition.* **3** to convert property, assets, etc into actual money. **4** to earn a particular sum of money: *The sale of the paintings realized £600,000.* ➤ **realization** *or* **realisation** *noun*.

really *adverb* **1** in reality; actually. **2** very; very much.

realm /relm/ *noun* (*plural* **realms**) **1** a kingdom. **2** an area of activity, interest, or knowledge.

ream *noun* (*plural* **reams**) **1** 500 sheets of paper. **2** (**reams**) a great amount of something written or printed.

reap *verb* (**reaps, reaping, reaped**) **1** to cut or harvest a crop. **2** to obtain or win something, especially as a reward for effort. ➤ **reaper** *noun*.

reappear *verb* (**reappears, reappearing, reappeared**) to appear again. ➤ **reappearance** *noun*.

reappraisal *noun* (*plural* **reappraisals**) a reconsideration of something or a new assessment of its value.

rear¹ *adjective* at the back. ~ *noun* **1** the back part of something. **2** *informal* the buttocks. ✱ **bring up the rear** to be the last in a group, series, etc.

rear² *verb* (**rears, rearing, reared**) **1** to breed an animal for use or sale. **2** to bring up a child. **3** said about a horse: to rise up on its hind legs.

rear guard *noun* a military unit guarding the rear of a main force.

rearrange *verb* (**rearranges, rearranging, rearranged**) to arrange something differently. ➤ **rearrangement** *noun*.

reason *noun* (*plural* **reasons**) **1** an explanation or justification of something. **2** a cause. **3** the ability to think, especially in an orderly logical way. **4** sanity. **5** sensible or logical thinking. ~ *verb* (**reasons, reasoning,**

reasoned) 1 to use reason to arrive at conclusions. **2 (reason with)** to talk or argue with somebody so as to persuade them to act sensibly. ✱ **within reason** within reasonable limits. ➤ **reasoning** noun.

reasonable adjective **1** moderate or fair; not extreme or excessive. **2** logical or sensible. **3** quite good. ➤ **reasonably** adverb.

reassure verb (**reassures, reassuring, reassured**) to make somebody feel less worried or anxious. ➤ **reassurance** noun, **reassuring** adjective.

rebate noun (plural **rebates**) **1** a return of part of a payment. **2** a deduction from a sum before payment.

rebel /ˈrebl/ noun (plural **rebels**) **1** somebody who fights against or refuses to obey a government or authority. **2** somebody who rejects accepted ideas or values. ~ /rɪˈbel/ verb (**rebels, rebelling, rebelled**) to be a rebel or start a rebellion.

rebellion noun (plural **rebellions**) an armed campaign against an established government.

rebellious adjective **1** refusing to obey or conform. **2** engaged in a rebellion. ➤ **rebelliously** adverb.

rebound verb (**rebounds, rebounding, rebounded**) to spring back after hitting something. ➤ **rebound** noun.

rebuff verb (**rebuffs, rebuffing, rebuffed**) to reject something or somebody sharply. ➤ **rebuff** noun.

rebuild verb (**rebuilds, rebuilding, rebuilt**) to build something again, especially after it has been damaged or destroyed.

rebuke verb (**rebukes, rebuking, rebuked**) to criticize somebody severely for doing wrong. ➤ **rebuke** noun.

rebut verb (**rebuts, rebutting, rebutted**) to show that a claim or statement is false. ➤ **rebuttal** noun.

Usage Note Refute, rebut or deny? See the note at **refute**.

recalcitrant /rɪˈkalsɪtrənt/ adjective defiant or uncooperative. ➤ **recalcitrance** noun.

recall /rɪˈkawl/ verb (**recalls, recalling, recalled**) **1** to remember something or somebody. **2** to officially ask somebody to come back. **3** said about a manufacturer: to ask for a faulty product to be returned. ~ noun **1** /ˈreekawl/ an official request for somebody to come back or for faulty products to be returned. **2** memory or ability to remember.

recant verb (**recants, recanting, recanted**) to say publicly that something you previously said or believed is wrong. ➤ **recantation** noun.

recap verb (**recaps, recapping, recapped**) informal = RECAPITULATE. ~ noun (plural **recaps**) informal = RECAPITULATATION.

recapitulate verb (**recapitulates, recapitulating, recapitulated**) to repeat the main points of an argument, speech, etc. ➤ **recapitulation** noun.

recapture verb (**recaptures, recapturing, recaptured**) **1** to capture somebody or something again. **2** to recreate something or experience it again. ➤ **recapture** noun.

recast verb (**recasts, recasting, recast**) to make something different, for example to rearrange or change the words in a sentence.

recede verb (**recedes, receding, receded**) **1** to move back or away. **2** to slant backwards: *a receding chin*. **3** said about hair: to stop growing around the temples and above the forehead. **4** to diminish.

receipt noun (plural **receipts**)

receive

1 a written statement confirming that you have received goods or money. **2** the act of receiving. **3** (**receipts**) money received.

receive *verb* (**receives, receiving, received**) **1** to be given something or get something that is sent to you. **2** to suffer or be forced to experience: *She received a severe shock.* **3** to greet or entertain guests formally. ✳ **be received** to produce a particular kind of reaction from people: *The news was received with sighs of relief.*

receiver *noun* (*plural* **receivers**) **1** a radio or television set, or other part of a communications system that receives the signal. **2** the part of a telephone that contains the mouthpiece and earpiece. **3** a person who takes charge of the affairs of a business that is being wound up. **4** a person who buys and sells stolen goods. ➤ **receivership** *noun*.

recent *adjective* **1** happening not long ago. **2** having come into existence only lately. ➤ **recently** *adverb*.

receptacle *noun* (*plural* **receptacles**) an object into which things can be put.

reception *noun* (*plural* **receptions**) **1** the act of receiving. **2** a formal social gathering. **3** an office or desk where visitors or clients go to register or receive help when they arrive. **4** a response or reaction. **5** the quality of the radio or television signal received. **6** the first class for infants in a primary school.

receptionist *noun* (*plural* **receptionists**) somebody whose job is to greet and help callers or clients, for example at an office or hotel.

receptive *adjective* open and responsive to ideas, impressions, or suggestions. ➤ **receptivity** *noun*.

recess /ree ses/ *noun* (*plural* **recesses**) **1** an alcove or niche. **2** (**recesses**) hidden, secret, or secluded places. **3** /ri ses/ a period during which a parliament or court stops working.

recession *noun* (*plural* **recessions**) a period when a country's economy is not producing very much and people have less wealth than usual.

recharge *verb* (**recharges, recharging, recharged**) to put a fresh supply of electricity into a battery so that it works again. ➤ **rechargeable** *adjective*.

recipe /re si pi/ *noun* (*plural* **recipes**) **1** a list of ingredients and instructions for making a food dish. **2** a course of action that is likely to produce something: *a recipe for success.*

recipient /re si pi int/ *noun* (*plural* **recipients**) somebody who receives something.

reciprocal /re si pro kl/ *adjective* **1** felt or shown by both sides; mutual. **2** given or done in return. ➤ **reciprocally** *adverb*.

reciprocate /re si pro kayt/ *verb* (**reciprocates, reciprocating, reciprocated**) to give back the same kind of thing, feeling, or treatment, to somebody that they have given to you. ➤ **reciprocation** *noun*.

recital *noun* (*plural* **recitals**) a concert given by a musician or a small group of musicians.

recite *verb* (**recites, reciting, recited**) to repeat something from memory or read it aloud. ➤ **recitation** *noun*.

reckless *adjective* showing a lack of proper caution; ignoring risks. ➤ **recklessly** *adverb*, **recklessness** *noun*.

reckon *verb* (**reckons, reckoning, reckoned**) **1** to estimate or calculate something. **2** to consider or think of something in a specified way. **3** *informal* to suppose or think. ✳ **reckon with 1** to take something into account. **2** to face opposition from somebody: *If he tries that again, he'll have me to reckon with.*

reckoning noun the act of calculating or estimating. * **into** or **out of the reckoning** included (or not included) among the things or people to be considered.

reclaim verb (**reclaims, reclaiming, reclaimed**) 1 to get something back, especially after losing it. 2 to make something, such as submerged or waste land, available for human use. ➤ **reclamation** noun.

recline verb (**reclines, reclining, reclined**) 1 to lean backwards. 2 to be in a relaxed position.

recluse noun (plural **recluses**) somebody who deliberately avoids company and leads a solitary life. ➤ **reclusive** adjective.

recognition noun 1 the act of recognizing. 2 acknowledgment or reward for your efforts, talents, etc.

recognize or **recognise** verb (**recognizes, recognizing, recognized** or **recognises,** etc) 1 to know something or somebody because you have seen or known them before. 2 to realize or accept something as true. 3 to accept a state, government, trade union, etc as independent, lawful, official, etc. 4 to praise or reward something, such as somebody's talent or achievements. ➤ **recognizable** adjective.

recoil verb (**recoils, recoiled, recoiled**) 1 to shrink back in horror, fear, or disgust. 2 said about a firearm: to move backwards sharply when fired. ➤ **recoil** noun.

recollect /re ko lekt/ verb (**recollects, recollecting, recollected**) to remember something or somebody. ➤ **recollection** noun.

recommend verb (**recommends, recommending, recommended**) 1 to declare something or somebody to be suitable, competent, etc or worth trying. 2 to advise a course of action. * **have a lot** or **nothing to recommend it** to have many (or no) good qualities. ➤ **recommendation** noun.

recompense verb (**recompenses, recompensing, recompensed**) 1 to pay or reward somebody for something they have done for you. 2 to compensate somebody for damage they have suffered. ➤ **recompense** noun.

reconcile verb (**reconciles, reconciling, reconciled**) 1 to make people who have been enemies friends again. 2 to find a way to make something consistent or compatible with something else. * **reconcile to** to persuade somebody or yourself to accept something, even though it is not what they or you want. ➤ **reconciliation** noun.

recondition verb (**reconditions, reconditioning, reconditioned**) to bring something, such as an engine or a tyre, back to a good working condition.

reconnaissance /ri ko ni sins/ noun the work of gathering information about where things are in an area, especially for military purposes.

reconnoitre /re ko noi ter/ verb (**reconnoitres, reconnoitring, reconnoitred**) to make a reconnaissance of an enemy position or a region of land.

reconsider verb (**reconsiders, reconsidering, reconsidered**) to consider something again, especially when thinking of changing a previous decision. ➤ **reconsideration** noun.

reconstruct verb (**reconstructs, reconstructing, reconstructed**) 1 to rebuild something. 2 to build up a mental picture of how something, such as a crime or a battle, happened, or to re-enact it. ➤ **reconstruction** noun.

record /ri kawd/ verb 1 to put something into writing or some other permanent form. 2 to store sounds or pictures on a tape, film, CD, etc so that you can play or show them again

recorder

~ /ˈrekawd/ *noun* (*plural* **records**)
1 a permanent account of something that serves as evidence of it. **2** a list of the offences of which a person has been found guilty. **3** the best recorded performance in a competitive sport, or the fact of being the biggest, smallest, fastest, etc example of something. **4** a flat plastic disc from which sounds can be reproduced. ✻ **put the record straight** to correct a mistake or misunderstanding.

recorder *noun* (*plural* **recorders**)
1 a machine for recording sound or pictures. **2** *Music* a simple woodwind instrument consisting of a tube with finger holes and a mouthpiece.

recording *noun* (*plural* **recordings**) something, such as a sound or a television programme, that has been recorded.

recount[1] /riˈkownt/ *verb* (**recounts, recounting, recounted**) to tell the story of something.

recount[2] /reeˈkownt/ *verb* (**recounts, recounting, recounted**) to count something again, especially votes. ➤ **recount** *noun*.

recoup /riˈkoop/ *verb* (**recoups, recouping, recouped**) to get back money you have spent or lost on something.

recourse *noun* the use of somebody or something for help or protection: *without recourse to cheating*.

recover *verb* (**recovers, recovering, recovered**) **1** to regain possession or the use of something. **2** to get well again after being ill. ➤ **recovery** *noun*.

recreate *verb* (**recreates, recreating, recreated**) to bring something back into existence or copy it exactly.

recreation /rekriˈayshn/ *noun* enjoyable activity you do for relaxation.

recriminations *plural noun* accusations of wrongdoing made against somebody who has made a similar accusation.

recruit *noun* (*plural* **recruits**) a person who has just joined an organization, especially the armed forces. ~ *verb* (**recruits, recruiting, recruited**) to take somebody on as a new member of the armed forces or a workforce. ➤ **recruitment** *noun*.

recta *noun* a plural of RECTUM.

rectangle *noun* (*plural* **rectangles**) *Maths* a shape with four right angles and four sides, especially an oblong. ➤ **rectangular** *adjective*.

rectify *verb* (**rectifies, rectifying, rectified**) to put something right; to remedy or correct it. ➤ **rectification** *noun*.

rectitude *noun formal* moral integrity.

rector *noun* (*plural* **rectors**) **1** a priest in charge of a parish in the Church of England. **2** the head of a university or college.

rectum *noun* (*plural* **rectums** or **recta**) the last part of the intestine, ending at the anus.

recumbent *adjective* lying down or reclining.

recuperate *verb* (**recuperates, recuperating, recuperated**) to get better after an illness. ➤ **recuperation** *noun*.

recur *verb* (**recurs, recurring, recurred**) to happen again, especially repeatedly or after an interval. ➤ **recurrence** *noun*.

recurrent *adjective* happening repeatedly or periodically.

recycle *verb* (**recycles, recycling, recycled**) **1** to convert sewage, waste paper, glass, etc back into a useful product. **2** to reuse something.

red *adjective* (**redder, reddest**) **1** coloured like blood or a ruby. **2** said about hair or fur: between orange and brown. **3** said about somebody's face: flushed, especially with anger or embarrassment. **4** *informal* communist or socialist. ~ *noun* (*plural* **reds**)

1 a red colour. **2** *informal* a communist or socialist. * **in the red** owing money. **see red** *informal* to become angry suddenly. ➤ **reddish** *adjective*, **redness** *noun*.

red card *noun* (*plural* **red cards**) a red card held up by a football referee to indicate the sending-off of a player.

redcurrant *noun* (*plural* **redcurrants**) a small red edible berry.

redden *verb* (**reddens, reddening, reddened**) to become red or make something red.

redeem *verb* (**redeems, redeeming, redeemed**) **1** to make up for the bad effect of something, such as a mistake or error of judgment. **2** in Christianity, to save somebody from damnation. **3** to get or buy something back by repaying a loan or debt. * **redeem yourself** to make up for an earlier poor performance or wrongdoing. ➤ **redeemer** *noun*, **redemption** *noun*.

red-faced *adjective* embarrassed.

red-handed *adverb* in the act of committing a crime or misdeed.

redhead *noun* (*plural* **redheads**) a person with red hair.

red herring *noun* (*plural* **red herrings**) something irrelevant that distracts attention from the real issue.

red-hot *adjective* **1** glowing red with heat. **2** very intense, exciting, or popular.

Red Indian *noun* (*plural* **Red Indians**) *dated, offensive* a Native American, especially of North America.

red-letter day *noun* (*plural* **red-letter days**) a particularly happy occasion.

> **Word History** The term *red-letter day* comes from the practice of marking holy days in red letters on church calendars. Hence, 'red-letter day' came to mean a day of special significance, and from that an especially happy day.

redoubtable *adjective* arousing fear or respect.

redress *verb* (**redresses, redressing, redressed**) to put right a wrong that somebody has suffered. ~ *noun* action or payment to compensate somebody for a wrong or loss. * **redress the balance** to make a situation fair and equal again by giving something to the side that was at a disadvantage.

red tape *noun* official rules and procedures that result in difficulty or delay.

reduce *verb* (**reduces, reducing, reduced**) **1** to become less or make something less. **2** to lower the price of something. **3** (**reduce to**) to bring somebody into a worse state, or force them to do something that they do not want to do: *They were reduced to begging from their friends.* ➤ **reduction** *noun*.

redundant *adjective* **1** no longer useful or necessary. **2** no longer required for a job. ➤ **redundancy** *noun*.

reed *noun* (*plural* **reeds**) **1** a tall grass that grows in wet or marshy areas. **2** *Music* a thin piece of cane, metal, or plastic, fastened over an air opening in an instrument such as an oboe or a clarinet, which produces a sound by vibration.

reedy *adjective* (**reedier, reediest**) **1** full of reeds. **2** said about a voice: thin and high.

reef[1] *noun* (*plural* **reefs**) a ridge of rocks, sand, or coral near the surface of water.

reef[2] *verb* (**reefs, reefing, reefed**) to reduce the area of a sail that is exposed to the wind by rolling up a portion of it. ➤ **reef** *noun*.

reef knot *noun* (*plural* **reef knots**) a secure knot made by tying two ends of rope left over right and then right over left.

reek *verb* (**reeks, reeking, reeked**) **1** to have a strong or offensive smell.

2 (reek of) to give a strong impression of some undesirable quality: *The whole business reeks of corruption.*
➤ **reek** *noun*.

reel¹ *noun* (*plural* **reels**) **1** a round object on which thread, film, tape, cable, etc can be wound. **2** a quantity of something wound on a reel. ~ *verb* (**reels, reeling, reeled**) ✲ **reel in** to draw something towards you by turning a reel. **reel off** to recite or repeat something quickly and without pausing.

reel² *verb* (**reels, reeling, reeled**) **1** to be giddy or bewildered. **2** to walk or move unsteadily.

reel³ *noun* (*plural* **reels**) a lively Scottish or Irish dance.

re-enact *verb* (**re-enacts, re-enacting, re-enacted**) to perform a scene or event from the past, such as a battle.

re-entry *noun* (*plural* **re-entries**) **1** the return to the earth's atmosphere by a space vehicle. **2** entry back into a country.

refectory *noun* (*plural* **refectories**) a dining hall in a monastery or college.

refer *verb* (**refers, referring, referred**) **1** (**refer to**) to mention something or somebody. **2** (**refer to**) to describe or relate to something. **3** (**refer to**) to look in something, such as a book, for information. **4** (**refer to**) to send somebody to another person who will give them treatment, help, information, etc.

referee *noun* (*plural* **referees**) **1** an official who supervises a game or contest and makes sure that people taking part obey the rules. **2** a person who provides a report on somebody's abilities or character for an employer. ~ *verb* (**referees, refereeing, refereed**) to act as a referee for a game or person.

reference *noun* (*plural* **references**) **1** the act of referring to or consulting something or somebody. **2** bearing on or connection with a subject. **3** a mention of somebody or something. **4** a note in an essay, book, etc giving details of a book, article, website, etc where you can find further information. **5** a report on the character, ability, or qualifications of a person who is looking for a job.

referendum *noun* (*plural* **referendums** *or* **referenda**) a vote by all the people in a country on a single question.

referral *noun* (*plural* **referrals**) the act of sending somebody to get help or treatment from another person, especially a medical specialist.

refine *verb* (**refines, refining, refined**) **1** to free a raw material from impurities. **2** to improve something by making small adjustments.

refined *adjective* **1** showing good taste and good manners. **2** purified.

refinement *noun* (*plural* **refinements**) **1** the act of refining. **2** good taste and good manners. **3** a small improvement.

refinery *noun* (*plural* **refineries**) a place where raw materials, such as oil or sugar, are refined.

reflect *verb* (**reflects, reflecting, reflected**) **1** to send light, sound, etc back from a surface. **2** to show the image of somebody or something, as a mirror does. **3** to be evidence of something. **4** to think quietly and calmly. ➤ **reflection** *noun*, **reflector** *noun*.

reflective *adjective* **1** capable of reflecting light, etc. **2** thoughtful. ➤ **reflectively** *adverb*.

reflex /ree fleks/ *noun* (*plural* **reflexes**) an action that takes place automatically and involves no conscious thought.

reflex angle *noun* (*plural* **reflex angles**) *Maths* an angle greater than 180° but less than 360°.

reflexive *adjective* *English* **1** said about

a pronoun: referring back to the subject of a clause or sentence, such as 'herself' in *she blames herself*. **2** said about a verb: formed with a reflexive pronoun, such as 'cut yourself' and 'switch itself off'.

reform *verb* (**reforms, reforming, reformed**) **1** to change something for the better. **2** to cause somebody to adopt a more virtuous, healthier, etc way of life. ~ *noun* (*plural* **reforms**) **1** the act of reforming. **2** a change that improves something. ➤ **reformer** *noun*.

Reformation *noun History* (**the Reformation**) a religious movement that began in the 16th century when some people wished to reform the teaching and practices of the Roman Catholic church and led to the establishment of the Protestant churches.

refract *verb* (**refracts, refracting, refracted**) *Science* to deflect light from a straight path when it enters water or glass at an angle. ➤ **refraction** *noun*.

refrain[1] *verb* (**refrains, refraining, refrained**) (**refrain from**) to keep yourself from doing, feeling, or indulging in something.

refrain[2] *noun* (*plural* **refrains**) words repeated at the end of each verse of a poem or song.

refresh *verb* (**refreshes, refreshing, refreshed**) **1** to make somebody feel strong and vigorous or cool and fresh again. **2** *ICT* to update the data in a file, web page, etc. ✱ **refresh somebody's memory** to remind somebody of something they have forgotten.

refresher course *noun* (*plural* **refresher courses**) a course of training designed to keep you up to date with developments in your subject.

refreshing *adjective* **1** making you feel less tired or less hot. **2** good because it is unusual or different. ➤ **refreshingly** *adverb*.

refreshment *noun* (*plural* **refreshments**) **1** the act of refreshing. **2** something that refreshes you, such as food or drink. **3** (**refreshments**) assorted food and drink, especially for a light snack.

refrigerate *verb* (**refrigerates, refrigerating, refrigerated**) to make or keep something cold or cool, especially food. ➤ **refrigeration** *noun*.

refrigerator *noun* (*plural* **refrigerators**) an insulated cabinet for keeping food, drink, etc cool.

refuel *verb* (**refuels, refuelling, refuelled**) to take on more fuel, or to put more fuel into a vehicle, ship, or aircraft.

refuge *noun* (*plural* **refuges**) a place that provides protection. ✱ **take refuge** to go somewhere you are safe.

refugee *noun* (*plural* **refugees**) somebody who flees to a foreign country to escape danger or persecution.

refund /rɪˈfʌnd/ *verb* (**refunds, refunding, refunded**) to return money to somebody. ~ /ˈreefund/ *noun* (*plural* **refunds**) **1** the act of refunding. **2** a sum refunded. ➤ **refundable** *adjective*.

refurbish *verb* (**refurbishes, refurbishing, refurbished**) to repair and redecorate a house, office, etc. ➤ **refurbishment** *noun*.

refuse[1] /rɪˈfewz/ *verb* (**refuses, refusing, refused**) **1** to be unwilling to accept or do something. **2** to be unwilling to allow or grant something to somebody.

refuse[2] /ˈrefews/ *noun* rubbish.

refute *verb* (**refutes, refuting, refuted**) to use arguments or evidence to prove that something or somebody is wrong. ➤ **refutation** noun.

Usage Note Refute is not simply another word for 'deny'. If you *say* that a statement or accusation is wrong, you are *denying* it. To *refute* a statement or accusation, you must not simply say that it is wrong, you must *show* that it is wrong. *Rebut* means the same as *refute*; it also involves *proving* something wrong.

regain *verb* (**regains, regaining, regained**) **1** to get something back. **2** to reach a place again.

regal *adjective* **1** to do with a king or queen. **2** stately or splendid. ➤ **regally** *adverb*.

regalia /ri gay li a/ *plural noun* the special clothes and symbolic objects that show that somebody is royal or has an official position.

regard *noun* (*plural* **regards**) **1** attention, consideration, or care for something or somebody. **2** appreciation and respect. **3** (**regards**) friendly greetings. **4** an aspect or respect: *We were fortunate in that regard.* **5** a gaze or look. ~ *verb* (**regards, regarding, regarded**) **1** to think of or feel about somebody or something in a specified way: *I regard him as a very close friend.* **2** to look steadily at somebody or something. ✶ **as regards something** as far as something is concerned. **in/with regard to** concerning.

regarding *preposition* about; on the subject of.

regardless *adverb* despite everything. ✶ **regardless of** without considering or worrying about.

regatta /ri ga ta/ *noun* (*plural* **regattas**) a sports event consisting of a series of boat races.

regency *noun* (*plural* **regencies**) **1** a period when a regent rules a country. **2** (**the Regency**) *History* the period (1811–1820) when George, Prince of Wales (later George IV), was regent of Great Britain.

regenerate *verb* (**regenerates, regenerating, regenerated**) **1** to replace part of the body with new growth. **2** to make an area that is in decline busy, lively, and prosperous again. ➤ **regeneration** *noun*.

regent *noun* (*plural* **regents**) somebody who governs a kingdom when the king or queen is too young, ill, etc to rule.

reggae /re gay/ *noun* Music popular music in a West Indian style with a strong beat.

regime /ray zheem/ *noun* (*plural* **regimes**) **1** a system of government. **2** a government in power.

regiment *noun* (*plural* **regiments**) a large unit of soldiers commanded by a colonel and usually divided into companies or battalions. ➤ **regimental** *adjective*.

regimented *adjective* strictly organized or controlled. ➤ **regimentation** *noun*.

region *noun* **1** a fairly large area of a country or the world. **2** an area surrounding a part of the body. ✶ **in the region of** approximately. ➤ **regional** *adjective*, **regionally** *adverb*.

register *noun* (*plural* **registers**) **1** an official written record of items or names. **2** a book in which a teacher records which pupils are present in class. **3** *Music* part of the range of a human voice or musical instrument. ~ *verb* (**registers, registering, registered**) **1** to enter information officially in a register. **2** to put your name in a register. **3** to record or indicate something, such as temperature or pressure, on an instrument. **4** to show an emotion through facial expression or body language. **5** to become aware of something.

register office *noun* (*plural* **register offices**) a place where births, marriages, and deaths are recorded and civil marriages are conducted.

registrar *noun* (*plural* **registrars**) **1** an official keeper of records. **2** a senior hospital doctor.

registration *noun* (*plural* **registrations**) **1** the act of registering. **2** (*also* **registration number**) the letters and numbers on a vehicle's numberplate.

registry *noun* (*plural* **registries**) a place where registers are kept.

registry office *noun* (*plural* **registry offices**) = REGISTER OFFICE.

regress *verb* (**regresses, regressing, regressed**) to return to an earlier or less advanced state. ➤ **regression** *noun*, **regressive** *adjective*.

regret *verb* (**regrets, regretting, regretted**) to be very sorry about something. *noun* (*plural* **regrets**) **1** sadness mixed with disappointment, longing, or remorse. **2** (**regrets**) an expression of disappointment or apology. ➤ **regretful** *adjective*.

regrettable *adjective* unfortunate; unwelcome. ➤ **regrettably** *adverb*.

regular *adjective* **1** done or happening always at the same time or with equal spaces in between: *at regular intervals*. **2** arranged evenly or in a pattern. **3** doing something or going somewhere often: *a regular visitor*. **4** in accordance with established rules. **5** *Maths* said about a polygon: with sides of equal length and angles of equal size. **6** belonging to a permanent army. ~ *noun* (*plural* **regulars**) somebody who is usually present or usually takes part. ➤ **regularity** *noun*, **regularly** *adverb*.

regulate *verb* (**regulates, regulating, regulated**) **1** to control or direct something by rules. **2** to fix or adjust something, such as the speed of an engine or the flow of water along a pipe. ➤ **regulator** *noun*, **regulatory** *adjective*.

regulation *noun* (*plural* **regulations**) **1** the act of regulating. **2** a rule or law.

regurgitate *verb* (**regurgitates, regurgitating, regurgitated**) **1** to bring food back from the stomach to the mouth. **2** to reproduce information with little or no alteration. ➤ **regurgitation** *noun*.

rehabilitate *verb* (**rehabilitates, rehabilitating, rehabilitated**) to enable somebody to live a normal useful life, for example after illness or imprisonment. ➤ **rehabilitation** *noun*.

rehash *verb* (**rehashes, rehashing, rehashed**) to use ideas, written work, etc again without changing or improving them very much. ➤ **rehash** *noun*.

rehearse *verb* (**rehearses, rehearsing, rehearsed**) *Drama* to hold a practice session or practice sessions before a play, piece of music, etc is performed in public. ➤ **rehearsal** *noun*.

reign *verb* (**reigns, reigning, reigned**) **1** to rule as king or queen. **2** to be the dominant feature in a situation at a particular time: *Chaos reigned in the classroom*. **3** to be the current holder of a trophy or title: *the reigning champion*. ~ *noun* (*plural* **reigns**) the time during which somebody or something reigns.

reimburse *verb* (**reimburses, reimbursing, reimbursed**) to pay back money to somebody. ➤ **reimbursement** *noun*.

rein *noun* (*plural* **reins**) **1** a long strap by which a rider or driver controls an animal. **2** (**reins**) controlling or guiding power.

reincarnation *noun* being reborn in another body after death.

reindeer *noun* (*plural* **reindeers** *or* **reindeer**) a deer with large antlers that lives in cold northern regions.

reinforce *verb* (**reinforces, reinforcing, reinforced**) **1** to strengthen

reinforcement

something with additional material or support. **2** to strengthen an army, etc with additional forces.

reinforcement *noun* (*plural* **reinforcements**) **1** the act of reinforcing. **2** (**reinforcements**) additional soldiers sent to strengthen an existing force.

reinstate *verb* (**reinstates, reinstating, reinstated**) to give somebody back the position or status they had before. ➤ **reinstatement** *noun*.

reiterate *verb* (**reiterates, reiterating, reiterated**) to say something again or repeatedly. ➤ **reiteration** *noun*.

reject /rɪˈjekt/ *verb* (**rejects, rejecting, rejected**) **1** to refuse to accept or consider something. **2** to refuse love or care to somebody. ~ /ˈreejekt/ *noun* (*plural* **rejects**) a rejected person or thing. ➤ **rejection** *noun*.

rejoice *verb* (**rejoices, rejoicing, rejoiced**) to feel or express joy or great delight.

rejoin *verb* (**rejoins, rejoining, rejoined**) to return to be with a person, group, etc again.

rejoinder *noun* (*plural* **rejoinders**) a sharp or critical answer.

rejuvenate *verb* (**rejuvenates, rejuvenating, rejuvenated**) to make somebody feel or look young again. ➤ **rejuvenation** *noun*.

relapse *verb* (**relapses, relapsing, relapsed**) to return to a former worse state after a temporary improvement. ➤ **relapse** *noun*.

relate *verb* (**relates, relating, related**) **1** to tell the story of something. **2** to show that there is a connection between two or more things. ✱ **be related to** to be a relation of somebody. **relate to 1** to be connected with, or have to do with something. **2** to feel sympathy or understanding for something or somebody.

relation *noun* (*plural* **relations**) **1** a person who is a member of the same family as you. **2** the way in which people or things are related. **3** (**relations**) the attitude or behaviour which people or groups show towards one another. ✱ **in/with relation to** concerning.

relationship *noun* (*plural* **relationships**) **1** = RELATION (sense 2). **2** the relations between people, groups, organizations, etc. **3** a close friendship or love affair.

relative *noun* (*plural* **relations**) = RELATION (sense 1). ~ *adjective* **1** considered in comparison with something else: *the relative isolation of life in a country village*. **2** *English* said about a pronoun, adverb, etc: introducing a subordinate clause that relates to a word used earlier in the sentence, such as 'that' in *the man that I was talking to* or 'where' in *the place where I was born*. **3** *English* said about a clause: introduced by a relative pronoun, adverb, etc.

relatively *adverb* **1** in comparison with other things. **2** quite; fairly.

relativity *noun* *Science* in physics, a theory worked out by Albert Einstein, which states that mass, dimension, and time will change as velocity increases.

relax *verb* (**relaxes, relaxing, relaxed**) **1** to stop working and rest or enjoy a leisure activity. **2** to make a rule less strict. **3** to make a muscle, etc less tense or rigid. ➤ **relaxation** *noun*.

relay *noun* (*plural* **relays**) **1** a group of people or animals that take over from others to do the same work. **2** a race between teams in which each team member covers a part of the course and then is replaced by another. **3** a device that receives a signal and then transmits it to another device.

release *verb* (**releases, releasing, released**) **1** to set somebody or something free from something, especially imprisonment. **2** to allow something, such as a gas or liquid, to come or flow out. **3** to make something available to be read or bought by the public. **4** to move a handle or catch in order to allow a mechanism to move. ~ *noun* (*plural* **releases**) **1** the act of releasing. **2** a newly issued film, CD, document, etc.

relegate *verb* (**relegates, relegating, relegated**) **1** to remove somebody or something to a less important position. **2** to demote a team to a lower division of a sporting competition. ➤ **relegation** *noun*.

relent *verb* (**relents, relenting, relented**) to decide to be less severe with somebody than you at first intended.

relentless *adjective* showing no sign of stopping or becoming less determined, severe, or intense. ➤ **relentlessly** *adverb*.

relevant *adjective* connected with the subject that is being discussed. ➤ **relevance** *noun*.

reliable *adjective* able to be trusted. ➤ **reliability** *noun*, **reliably** *adverb*.

reliance *noun* the act of relying on somebody or something; dependence or trust. ➤ **reliant** *adjective*.

relic *noun* (*plural* **relics**) an object left behind from an earlier time.

relief *noun* (*plural* **reliefs**) **1** the removal of something oppressive, painful, or distressing. **2** a feeling of happiness or comfort caused by the removal of something that was distressing you. **3** something that makes something else less boring or tiring. **4** aid given to people in need. **5** somebody who takes over a duty from somebody else. **6** *Art* a method of sculpture in which shapes stand out from a flat surface.

relief map *noun* (*plural* **relief maps**) *Geography* a map showing the differences in height of a land surface by colour, etc.

relieve *verb* (**relieves, relieving, relieved**) **1** to give somebody relief. **2** to remove or lessen pain. **3** to release somebody from duty by taking their place. ✱ **be relieved** to stop feeling anxious or distressed. **relieve of** to take something away from somebody. **relieve yourself** to urinate or defecate.

religion *noun* (*plural* **religions**) **1** organized belief in and worship of a god or gods. **2** a particular system of religious beliefs.

religious *adjective* **1** to do with religion. **2** pious or devout. ➤ **religiously** *adverb*.

relinquish *verb* (**relinquishes, relinquishing, relinquished**) **1** to give something up. **2** to release your hold on something or give up your right to something.

relish *noun* (*plural* **relishes**) **1** enjoyment of or delight in something. **2** a spicy sauce or pickle, eaten with plainer food. ~ *verb* (**relishes, relishing, relished**) to enjoy something very much.

relive *verb* (**relives, reliving, relived**) to experience something again in your imagination.

relocate *verb* (**relocates, relocating, relocated**) to establish your home or business in a new place. ➤ **relocation** *noun*.

reluctant *adjective* unwilling or not eager to do something. ➤ **reluctance** *noun*, **reluctantly** *adverb*.

rely *verb* (**relies, relying, relied**) (**rely on/upon**) **1** to have confidence in or trust somebody or something. **2** to be dependent on somebody or something.

remain *verb* (**remains, remaining, remained**) **1** to stay in the same place. **2** to continue to be as before. **3** to be left over.

remainder

remainder *noun* (*plural* **remainders**) **1** the part or number that is left over. **2** *Maths* the number left after division or subtraction.

remains *plural noun* **1** a part remaining after something has been ruined or destroyed. **2** a dead body.

remand *verb* (**remands, remanding, remanded**) to place a defendant or prisoner in custody or on bail until they appear again in court. ✱ **on remand** in custody awaiting trial.

remark *noun* (*plural* **remarks**) something you say; a comment. ~ *verb* (**remarks, remarking, remarked**) **1** to make a remark. **2** *formal* to notice something or somebody.

remarkable *adjective* striking or extraordinary. ➤ **remarkably** *adverb*.

remedial *adjective* **1** intended as a remedy. **2** designed to help people with learning difficulties.

remedy *noun* (*plural* **remedies**) **1** a medicine or treatment that relieves or cures a disease. **2** something that solves a problem or puts a situation right. ~ *verb* (**remedies, remedying, remedied**) to cure something or put it right.

remember *verb* (**remembers, remembering, remembered**) **1** to bring something back into your mind or think of it again. **2** to keep something in your memory. **3** not to fail or forget to do something: *I remembered to switch off all the lights.*

remind *verb* (**reminds, reminding, reminded**) **1** to cause somebody to remember something. **2** to appear to somebody to be like somebody or something else: *She reminds me of my mother.*

reminder *noun* (*plural* **reminders**) a thing that helps somebody to remember something.

reminisce /re mi nis/ *verb* (**reminisces, reminiscing, reminisced**) to talk or write about events or people from your past. ➤ **reminiscence** *noun*.

reminiscent *adjective* (**reminiscent of**) reminding you of something you have seen or known before.

remiss *adjective* forgetful or careless about doing your work or duty.

remission *noun* **1** the act of remitting. **2** a period during which the effects of a disease are less severe. **3** a reduction of a prison sentence.

remit /ri mit/ *verb* (**remits, remitting, remitted**) **1** to cancel a debt or punishment. **2** to send money to somebody. **3** to become less violent or intense. ~ /ree mit/ *noun* the area of responsibility of a person or organization.

remittance *noun* (*plural* **remittances**) **1** a sum of money remitted. **2** the act of remitting money.

remnant *noun* (*plural* **remnants**) a small left-over part of something.

remonstrate *verb* (**remonstrates, remonstrating, remonstrated**) (**remonstrate with**) to protest angrily to somebody about their behaviour, opinions, etc. ➤ **remonstration** *noun*.

remorse *noun* deep distress arising from a sense of guilt for past wrongdoing. ➤ **remorseful** *adjective*, **remorsefully** *adverb*.

remorseless *adjective* relentless; continuing without letting up. ➤ **remorselessly** *adverb*.

remote *adjective* **1** a long way away in space or time. **2** far away from the main centres of activity or population. **3** not belonging to your close family. **4** small; slight: *a remote chance.* ~ *noun* (*plural* **remotes**) *informal* = REMOTE CONTROL. ➤ **remotely** *adverb*, **remoteness** *noun*.

remote control *noun* (*plural* **remote controls**) **1** control over a machine or weapon from a distance, for example by means of an electrical circuit or radio waves. **2** a device by means of which this is carried out. ➤ **remote-controlled** *adjective*.

removal *noun* (*plural* **removals**) **1** the act of removing. **2** the moving of household furniture, etc to a person's new home.

remove *verb* (**removes, removing, removed**) **1** to take something away or off. **2** to get rid of something. ➤ **removable** *adjective*, **remover** *noun*.

remunerate /ri mew ni rayt/ *verb* (**remunerates, remunerating, remunerated**) to pay somebody for work done. ➤ **remuneration** *noun*.

Renaissance /ri nay sans/ *noun* (**the Renaissance**) *History* the period in European history between the 14th and 17th centuries when people rediscovered the art and learning of ancient Greece and Rome and began to think scientifically.

renal /ree nl/ *adjective* to do with the kidneys.

rename *verb* (**renames, renaming, renamed**) to give a different name to somebody or something.

rend *verb* (**rends, rending, rent**) to pull or tear something apart or into pieces.

render *verb* (**renders, rendering, rendered**) **1** to cause somebody or something to be or become something: *Her attitude rendered me completely speechless.* **2** to give assistance, etc to somebody.

rendezvous /ron di vooh/ *noun* (*plural* **rendezvous** /ron di voohz/) **1** a meeting at an agreed place and time. **2** a place where people agree to meet.

rendition *noun* (*plural* **renditions**) a performance or interpretation of an artistic work.

renegade /re ni gayd/ *noun* (*plural* **renegades**) somebody who deserts one faith, cause, or group and joins another.

renew *verb* (**renews, renewing, renewed**) **1** to begin something again. **2** to bring something back to a fresh and new state. **3** to extend the time for which a subscription, licence, etc is valid. ➤ **renewal** *noun*.

renewable resource *noun* (*plural* **renewable resources**) a source of power, such as the wind or sun, that can never be used up.

renounce *verb* (**renounces, renouncing, renounced**) **1** to make a declaration saying that you are giving up something. **2** to break off your connection with somebody.

renovate *verb* (**renovates, renovating, renovated**) to put something into a better state, for example by cleaning, repairing, or rebuilding it. ➤ **renovation** *noun*.

renown *noun* fame.

renowned *adjective* famous.

rent¹ *noun* a regular payment made for the use of something, especially a house or flat, owned by somebody else. ~ *verb* (**rents, renting, rented**) **1** to use property or equipment that you pay rent for. **2** to allow somebody to use property or equipment in exchange for rent.

rent² *noun* (*plural* **rents**) a split or tear.

rent³ *verb* past tense of REND.

rental *noun* **1** an amount paid or collected as rent. **2** the act of renting.

renunciation *noun* the act of renouncing.

reorganize *or* **reorganise** *verb* (**reorganizes, reorganizing, reorganized** *or* **reorganises**, etc) to organize something again or in a different way. ➤ **reorganization** *or* **reorganisation** *noun*.

repaid *verb* past tense of REPAY.

repair *verb* (**repairs, repairing, repaired**) to make something that is damaged or not working fit for use again. ~ *noun* (*plural* **repairs**) **1** the

reparation

act of repairing. **2** a piece of work done to repair something or a place where something has been repaired. ✻ **in good/bad repair** in good (or bad) condition. ➤ **repairable** *adjective*, **repairer** *noun*.

reparation *noun* (*plural* **reparations**) **1** the act of making amends for a wrong or injury. **2** (**reparations**) compensation payable by a defeated nation for war damage.

repartee *noun* the exchange of amusing and witty remarks.

repatriate *verb* (**repatriates, repatriating, repatriated**) to send somebody or something back to their country of origin. ➤ **repatriation** *noun*.

repay *verb* (**repays, repaying, repaid**) **1** to pay back something to somebody. **2** to do something in return for a previous kindness or injury. **3** to be worthy of investigation, attention, etc. ➤ **repayment** *noun*.

repeal *verb* (**repeals, repealing, repealed**) to cancel a law. ➤ **repeal** *noun*.

repeat *verb* (**repeats, repeating, repeated**) **1** to say or do something again. **2** to tell something that has been told to you to somebody else. ~ *noun* (*plural* **repeats**) something repeated, for example a television or radio programme that has been broadcast before. ✻ **repeat yourself** to say something again in the same words. ➤ **repeated** *adjective*, **repeatedly** *adverb*.

repel *verb* (**repels, repelling, repelled**) **1** to drive somebody back or away. **2** to disgust somebody. **3** *Science* said about a magnetic pole: to force another magnet away. **4** said about a substance or material: to prevent substances from sticking to it or mixing with it.

repellent *adjective* repulsive. ~ *noun* (*plural* **repellents**) a chemical substance that repels other substances or drives away insects, etc.

repent *verb* (**repents, repenting, repented**) to feel regret for something bad that you have done. ➤ **repentance** *noun*, **repentant** *adjective*.

repercussions *plural noun* the effects or results of an action or event.

repertoire /ˈre pertwah/ *noun* (*plural* **repertoires**) **1** a list of works or parts that a company or person is able to perform. **2** a range of skills, techniques, etc.

repertory *noun* (*plural* **repertories**) **1** *Drama* the presentation of several different plays in one season at a theatre. **2** = REPERTOIRE.

repetition *noun* (*plural* **repetitions**) **1** the act of repeating. **2** a repeat or copy.

repetitious *adjective* boring because of containing many repetitions. ➤ **repetitiously** *adverb*.

repetitive *adjective* **1** done, uttered, etc repeatedly. **2** = REPETITIOUS. ➤ **repetitively** *adverb*.

replace *verb* (**replaces, replacing, replaced**) **1** to put something back in its former place or position. **2** to take the place of somebody or something. **3** to put something new in the place of something. ➤ **replaceable** *adjective*.

replacement *noun* (*plural* **replacements**) **1** the act of replacing. **2** something or somebody that replaces something or somebody else.

replay /ree play/ *verb* (**replays, replaying, replayed**) to play something again. ~ /ˈree play/ *noun* (*plural* **replays**) **1** a recording of an incident in a sports event that has just taken place. **2** a match played because an earlier match ended in a draw.

replenish *verb* (**replenishes, replenishing, replenished**) to stock or fill something up again. ➤ **replenishment** *noun*.

replica *noun* (*plural* **replicas**) an accurate reproduction, copy, or model.

reply *verb* (**replies, replying, replied**) 1 to answer in words or writing. 2 to do something in response. ~ *noun* (*plural* **replies**) something said, written, or done as an answer.

report *noun* (*plural* **reports**) 1 a detailed account or description of something. 2 a statement of a pupil's performance at school. 3 a loud explosive noise. ~ *verb* (**reports, reporting, reported**) 1 to write or deliver a report. 2 to give news of or information about something. 3 to make a formal complaint about somebody. 4 to present yourself to somebody, especially when you arrive somewhere.

reported speech *noun* English words that express what somebody else said but without quoting them exactly, such as 'he was coming' in *He said he was coming*.

reporter *noun* (*plural* **reporters**) a journalist who reports news for the newspapers, radio, or television.

repose *noun* the state of resting.

repository *noun* (*plural* **repositories**) a place or container where something is stored.

repossess *verb* (**repossesses, repossessing, repossessed**) to take back goods when the buyer does not keep up payments on them. ➤ **repossession** *noun*.

reprehensible *adjective* deserving blame; bad.

represent *verb* (**represents, representing, represented**) 1 to act for or in the place of somebody or something. 2 to be a specimen, example, or instance of something. 3 to be a sign or symbol of something. 4 to portray a person or thing in art. 5 to describe a person or thing as having a particular character or identity.

representation *noun* (*plural* **representations**) 1 a likeness or image. 2 the act of representing. 3 (**representations**) statements made to influence opinion or express a protest.

representative *adjective* 1 serving as a typical example of something. 2 containing typical examples. 3 based on representation of the people in government or lawmaking: *representative democracy*. ~ *noun* (*plural* **representatives**) 1 somebody who represents another person or a group. 2 a typical example of a group or class of things.

repress *verb* (**represses, repressing, repressed**) 1 to use force to control people and limit their freedom. 2 to prevent the natural or normal expression of an emotion. ➤ **repressed** *adjective*.

repressive *adjective* unjustly restricting people's freedom.

reprieve *verb* (**reprieves, reprieving, reprieved**) to delay or cancel the punishment of a condemned prisoner. ➤ **reprieve** *noun*.

reprimand *noun* (*plural* **reprimands**) a formal expression of disapproval of somebody's behaviour. ~ *verb* (**reprimands, reprimanding, reprimanded**) to give somebody a reprimand.

reprisal /ri prie zl/ *noun* (*plural* **reprisals**) a harmful action directed against somebody who has harmed you.

reproach *verb* (**reproaches, reproaching, reproached**) to express disappointment and displeasure with somebody. ➤ **reproach** *noun*, **reproachful** *adjective*, **reproachfully** *adverb*.

reproduce *verb* (**reproduces, reproducing, reproduced**) 1 to repeat or copy something. 2 to enable recorded sound or pictures to be heard or seen again. 3 *Science* to produce offspring.

reproduction *noun* (*plural* **reproductions**) **1** the process by which plants and animals produce offspring. **2** a copy, especially of a work of art.
➤ **reproductive** *adjective*.

reptile *noun* (*plural* **reptiles**) a member of a class of cold-blooded vertebrate animals with scaly skin, including crocodiles, lizards, snakes, and extinct animals such as dinosaurs.
➤ **reptilian** *adjective*.

republic *noun* (*plural* **republics**) a state in which the people have supreme power and whose head is a president, not a monarch. ➤ **republican** *adjective and noun*.

Republican *adjective* **1** supporting a political party in the USA favouring a restricted role for government in social and economic life. **2** in Northern Ireland, supporting the union of Northern Ireland with the Irish Republic. ➤ **Republican** *noun*.

repudiate /ri pew di ayt/ *verb* (**repudiates, repudiating, repudiated**) **1** to refuse to have anything to do with somebody or something. **2** to reject something as untrue or unjust. ➤ **repudiation** *noun*.

repugnance *noun* strong dislike or disgust. ➤ **repugnant** *adjective*.

repulse *verb* (**repulses, repulsing, repulsed**) **1** to drive attackers back. **2** to reject or rebuff something. **3** to cause repulsion in somebody.

repulsion *noun* **1** a strong feeling of dislike or disgust. **2** *Science* in physics, a force that drive things apart.

repulsive *adjective* very ugly; causing feelings of dislike or disgust.

reputable /re pew ta bl/ *adjective* considered to be honest and good.

reputation *noun* (*plural* **reputations**) the quality or character of a person or organization as seen or judged by others.

repute *noun* = REPUTATION.

reputed *adjective* believed or considered to be something.

request *noun* (*plural* **requests**) **1** an act of asking for something, especially politely or formally. **2** something asked for. ~ *verb* (**requests, requesting, requested**) **1** to ask somebody to do something. **2** to ask for something, especially politely or formally.

requiem /re kwee im/ *noun* (*plural* **requiems**) **1** a mass for the dead. **2** *Music* a musical setting of the mass for the dead.

require *verb* (**requires, requiring, required**) **1** to have to have something because it is necessary. **2** to make or command somebody to do something.

requirement *noun* (*plural* **requirements**) something wanted or needed.

requisite /re kwi zit/ *adjective* necessary. ~ *noun* (*plural* **requisites**) **1** something that is necessary. **2** an article of the specified sort: *toilet requisites*.

requisition *verb* (**requisitions, requisitioning, requisitioned**) to demand the use or supply of something officially.

resat *verb* past tense of RESIT.

rescue *verb* (**rescues, rescuing, rescued**) to save somebody or something from danger or captivity.
➤ **rescue** *noun*, **rescuer** *noun*.

research *noun* (*plural* **researches**) study, investigations, experiments, etc aimed at making discoveries or establishing facts. ~ *verb* (**researches, researching, researched**) to engage in research on a subject or for a book, television programme, etc. ➤ **researcher** *noun*.

resemblance *noun* (*plural* **resemblances**) **1** the state of resembling somebody or something else. **2** a point on which two people or things are similar.

resemble verb (**resembles, resembling, resembled**) to be similar to somebody or something, especially in appearance.

resent verb (**resents, resenting, resented**) to feel bitter and angry about something considered wrong or unfair. ➤ **resentful** adjective, **resentfully** adverb, **resentment** noun.

reservation noun (plural **reservations**) **1** the act of reserving something, such as a seat or hotel room, or a record of this. **2** a doubt or objection with regard to something. **3** an area of land set aside for a special purpose, especially for the use of Native Americans.

reserve verb (**reserves, reserving, reserved**) **1** to keep something back for future use. **2** to arrange that a seat, hotel room, etc is kept for your own or somebody else's use. **3** to postpone making a judgment until later. ~ noun (plural **reserves**) **1** a supply of something kept for future use or need. **2** in sport, a player selected to replace another if necessary. **3** an area of land set apart for the conservation of natural resources or rare plants and animals. **4** caution or lack of openness in your words and actions. ✳ **in reserve** kept back ready for use if needed.

reserved adjective quiet and shy in speech and behaviour.

reservoir /re zer vwah/ noun (plural **reservoirs**) a place where liquid is stored, especially a natural or artificial lake where water is collected for use by a community.

reshuffle verb (**reshuffles, reshuffling, reshuffled**) to reorganize a group of government ministers by giving them different jobs. ➤ **reshuffle** noun.

reside verb (**resides, residing, resided**) to live in a place that is your permanent home.

residence noun (plural **residence**) **1** the fact of living in a place. **2** a dwelling, especially a large and impressive house or an important person's official home.

resident adjective living in a place. ~ noun (plural **residents**) somebody who lives in a place.

residential adjective **1** involving residence in a place: *a residential course*. **2** containing private housing rather industrial or commercial buildings: *a residential area*.

residue noun (plural **residues**) what is left over after the main part of something has been taken away or used up. ➤ **residual** adjective.

resign verb (**resigns, resigning, resigned**) to give up your job or position. ✳ **be resigned to** or **resign yourself to** to accept that you cannot stop something unpleasant from happening to you.

resignation noun (plural **resignations**) **1** the act of resigning. **2** a formal letter saying that you are resigning. **3** the state of being resigned to something.

resilient adjective **1** able to withstand shocks or return to shape after bending, stretching, etc. **2** said about a person: able to cope with misfortune or change. ➤ **resilience** noun.

resin noun (plural **resins**) a sticky substance from plants that is used in making varnishes, inks, and plastics.

resist verb (**resists, resisting, resisted**) **1** to withstand the force or effect of something. **2** to struggle against or oppose something.

resistance noun **1** the act of resisting. **2** the ability to resist infection, the effects of drugs, etc. **3** *Science* in physics, the power of something to resist the flow of an electric current through it. **4** (*often* **Resistance**) a secret organization fighting against occupying forces in a country or against a government.

resit verb (**resits, resitting, resat**) to

resolute

take an examination again after failing it.

resolute *adjective* firmly resolved to do something. ➤ **resolutely** *adverb*.

resolution *noun* (*plural* **resolutions**) **1** the process of resolving a problem or dispute. **2** courageous determination. **3** a solemn or official decision to do something, taken by a person or a group at a meeting. **4** *ICT* the ability of a television or computer screen to produce a clear image.

resolve *verb* (**resolves, resolving, resolved**) **1** to find a solution to a problem. **2** to reach a firm decision to do something. ~ *noun* **1** the state of being determined to do something. **2** a firm decision.

resonant *adjective* **1** said about a sound: rich or echoing. **2** said about a space, object, etc: intensifying and enriching sound.

resonate *verb* (**resonates, resonating, resonated**) to produce a rich echoing sound.

resort *noun* (*plural* **resorts**) **1** a frequently visited place that provides accommodation and recreation, especially for holidaymakers. **2** somebody or something turned to for help or protection. **3** recourse. ~ *verb* (**resorts, resorting, resorted**) (**resort to**) to turn to somebody or something in order to achieve something.

resound *verb* (**resounds, resounding, resounded**) **1** to become filled with sound. **2** to resonate.

resounding *adjective* clear; unqualified: *a resounding success*.

resource *noun* (*plural* **resources**) **1** (*often* **resources**) something, such as money or minerals, that you can use when you need it. **2** the ability to deal with a difficult situation.

resourceful *adjective* good at finding ways of dealing with problems or difficult situations. ➤ **resourcefully** *adverb*, **resourcefulness** *noun*.

respect *noun* (*plural* **respects**) **1** admiration for the good qualities of somebody or something. **2** politeness or consideration. **3** an aspect or detail. ~ *verb* (**respects, respecting, respected**) **1** to consider somebody or something worthy of respect. **2** to refrain from violating or interfering with somebody's privacy or rights. ✱ **with respect to** in relation to; concerning.

respectable *adjective* **1** behaving in a way that is considered morally right and acceptable in society. **2** acceptable; fairly good. ➤ **respectability** *noun*, **respectably** *adverb*.

respectful *adjective* showing respect. ➤ **respectfully** *adverb*.

respecting *preposition* with regard to; concerning.

respective *adjective* belonging or relating to each: *They went their respective ways*.

respectively *adverb* in the same order as the people or things previously mentioned: *Mary and Anne were 12 and 16 years old respectively*.

respiration *noun* the act of breathing.

respirator *noun* (*plural* **respirators**) **1** a device worn over the mouth or nose to prevent the breathing in of poisonous gases, etc. **2** a device that pumps air into the lungs of a person who cannot breathe normally.

respiratory /ri spi ra to ri/ *adjective* to do with breathing.

respire *verb* (**respires, respiring, respired**) *formal* to breathe.

respite /re spiet/ *noun* (*plural* **respites**) a period of rest or relief.

resplendent *adjective* shining brilliantly; splendid.

respond *verb* (**responds, responding, responded**) to speak, write, or act as a result of something said, written, or done to you.

respondent *noun* (*plural* **respondents**) **1** a defendant, especially in an appeal or divorce case. **2** a person who replies to a survey, advertisement, etc.

response *noun* (*plural* **responses**) a reply or reaction.

responsibility *noun* (*plural* **responsibilities**) **1** the state of being responsible. **2** something or somebody for which you are responsible. **3** the opportunity to act, take decisions, etc independently.

responsible *adjective* **1** having a duty to deal with something and likely to be blamed if it goes wrong. **2** being the cause of something. **3** involving important duties and decision-making: *a responsible job*. **4** trustworthy, reliable, or sensible. ✱ **responsible for 1** having control or care of something or somebody. **2** causing. ➤ **responsibly** *adverb*.

responsive *adjective* quick to respond appropriately or sympathetically.

rest[1] *noun* (*plural* **rests**) **1** freedom or a break from activity or work. **2** a state of motionlessness or inactivity. **3** repose, relaxation, or sleep. **4** *Music* a silence of a specified duration. **5** something used for support. ~ *verb* (**rests, resting, rested**) **1** to relax, for example by sitting or lying down or sleeping. **2** to stop working or exerting yourself. **3** to lie supported on something. **4** to place something on a support. **5** to remain as specified.

rest[2] *noun* (**the rest**) **1** the part, amount, or number that remains. **2** the other people or things.

restaurant *noun* (*plural* **restaurants**) a place where you can buy a meal and eat it.

restaurateur /re sto ra ter/ *noun* (*plural* **restaurateurs**) the manager or owner of a restaurant.

restful *adjective* quiet, peaceful, or soothing.

restitution *noun* **1** the returning of something, such as property, to its rightful owner. **2** compensation given for an injury or wrong.

restive *adjective* **1** resisting authority or control. **2** restless and uneasy.

restless *adjective* **1** unable to rest. **2** continuously moving or active. ➤ **restlessly** *adverb*.

restore *verb* (**restores, restoring, restored**) **1** to bring something that has decayed or been damaged back to its former good condition. **2** to bring somebody back to a former position of power. **3** to bring something back into existence, force, or use. **4** *formal* to give something back. ➤ **restoration** *noun*, **restorer** *noun*.

restrain *verb* (**restrains, restraining, restrained**) **1** to keep somebody or something under control. **2** to hold onto a person or animal and physically prevent them from moving.

restrained *adjective* calm and controlled; moderate.

restraint *noun* (*plural* **restraints**) **1** moderation and self-control. **2** the act of restraining. **3** a restraining force or influence. **4** a device that prevents freedom of movement.

restrict *verb* (**restricts, restricting, restricted**) **1** to prevent somebody or something from moving or acting freely. **2** to limit something. ➤ **restricted** *adjective*, **restriction** *noun*.

restrictive *adjective* limiting freedom of action or movement.

result *noun* (*plural* **results**) **1** something that exists or happens because a previous action has produced or caused it. **2** the number obtained by doing a calculation. **3** the outcome or final score in a contest or examination. ~ *verb* (**results, resulting, resulted**) **1** to exist or happen as a result of something. **2** (**result in**) to have something as a result.

resume *verb* (**resumes, resuming, resumed**) **1** to continue or begin again after an interruption. **2** to take a position again. ➤ **resumption** *noun*.

résumé /re zew may/ *noun* (*plural* **résumés**) a summary.

resurgence *noun* the reappearance or revival of something. ➤ **resurgent** *adjective*.

resurrect *verb* (**resurrects, resurrecting, resurrected**) to bring something back into use.

resurrection *noun* **1** (**the Resurrection**) in Christian belief, Jesus's coming alive again after his crucifixion. **2** a revival or restoration.

resuscitate /ri su si tayt/ *verb* (**resuscitates, resuscitating, resuscitated**) to revive somebody from unconsciousness or apparent death. ➤ **resuscitation** *noun*.

retail *verb* (**retails, retailing, retailed**) **1** to sell goods in small quantities to customers who will not resell them. **2** to be sold at a specified price. ➤ **retail** *noun*, **retailer** *noun*.

retain *verb* (**retains, retaining, retained**) **1** to continue to have something. **2** to keep something in your mind or memory.

retainer *noun* (*plural* **retainers**) **1** a fee paid to a lawyer so that they will work for you whenever required. **2** a domestic servant, especially an old and trusted one.

retake *verb* (**retakes, retaking, retook, retaken**) **1** to recapture a place. **2** to sit a test or examination again.

retaliate *verb* (**retaliates, retaliating, retaliated**) to take action that repays somebody for some wrong they have done to you. ➤ **retaliation** *noun*.

retard *verb* (**retards, retarding, retarded**) to delay something. ➤ **retardation** *noun*.

retarded *adjective* slow in intellectual or emotional development.

retch *verb* (**retches, retching, retched**) to feel as if you are vomiting, without actually vomiting anything. ➤ **retch** *noun*.

retention *noun* the act of retaining.

retentive *adjective* able to retain something, especially knowledge.

reticent *adjective* unwilling to speak openly about things. ➤ **reticence** *noun*.

retina *noun* (*plural* **retinas**) a membrane at the back of the eye that is sensitive to light.

retinue *noun* (*plural* **retinues**) a group of attendants accompanying an important person.

retire *verb* (**retires, retiring, retired**) **1** to give up your position or occupation permanently, especially at the end of your working life. **2** *formal* to withdraw or retreat from a place. **3** *formal* to go to bed. ➤ **retired** *adjective*, **retirement** *noun*.

retiring *adjective* tending to avoid contact with other people; shy.

retook *verb* past tense of RETAKE.

retort *verb* (**retorts, retorting, retorted**) to answer back sharply. ➤ **retort** *noun*.

retrace *verb* (**retraces, retracing, retraced**) to go over a route again, often in the opposite direction.

retract *verb* (**retracts, retracting, retracted**) **1** to draw something back or in. **2** to withdraw something said or written. ➤ **retractable** *adjective*, **retraction** *noun*.

retreat *noun* **1** the forced withdrawal of troops from a place, especially after losing a battle. **2** an act of moving back and away from something. **3** a place of peace, privacy, or safety.

~ *verb* (**retreats, retreating, retreated**) to make a retreat.

retribution *noun* punishment or retaliation for an insult or injury.

retrieve *verb* (**retrieves, retrieving, retrieved**) 1 to get something back again. 2 to rescue or save something. 3 said about a dog: to find and bring in killed or wounded game. 4 *ICT* to recover data from a computer memory. ➤ **retrieval** *noun*.

retriever *noun* (*plural* **retrievers**) a dog of a breed used to retrieve game.

retrospect * **in retrospect** when considering the past or a past event.

retrospective *adjective* 1 to do with or affecting things in the past. 2 *Art* said about an exhibition: showing how an artist's work has developed over a period. ➤ **retrospectively** *adverb*.

return *verb* (**returns, returning, returned**) 1 to go back or come back. 2 (**return to**) to go back to something that you were doing, discussing, etc before. 3 to put something back in a former place or state. 4 to give or send something back, especially to its owner. 5 to elect a candidate. 6 to announce a verdict. *noun* (*plural* **returns**) 1 the act of returning. 2 a ticket bought for a trip to a place and back again. 3 the profit from work, investment, or business. * **in return** in compensation or repayment.

reunion *noun* (*plural* **reunions**) 1 a gathering of people who have not seen each other for a long time. 2 the act of reuniting.

reunite *verb* (**reunites, reuniting, reunited**) to come together again or bring people or things together again.

reuse *verb* (**reuses, reusing, reused**) to use something again. ➤ **reusable** *adjective*, **reuse** *noun*.

Rev. *abbreviation* Reverend.

reveal *verb* (**reveals, revealing, revealed**) to show or make known something secret or hidden.

revealing *adjective* 1 exposing something, especially part of the body, that is usually hidden. 2 providing important or interesting information.

revel *verb* (**revels, revelling, revelled**) 1 (**revel in**) to get great pleasure from something. 2 to enjoy yourself in a noisy and exuberant way. ➤ **reveller** *noun*, **revelry** *noun*.

revelation *noun* (*plural* **revelations**) 1 the act of revealing something. 2 something revealed, especially a startling fact or something that was being kept secret.

revenge *noun* the act of retaliating in order to get even for a wrong or injury. ~ *verb* (**revenges, revenging, revenged**) 1 to retaliate for an insult, injury, etc. 2 to take revenge on behalf of yourself or somebody else.

revenue *noun* (*plural* **revenues**) the total income produced by a particular source or received by a business, government, etc.

reverberate *verb* (**reverberates, reverberating, reverberated**) said about a sound: to continue in a series of echoes. ➤ **reverberation** *noun*.

revere *verb* (**reveres, revering, revered**) to regard somebody or something with deep and devoted respect.

reverence *noun* profound respect, especially for something sacred.

Reverend *adjective* used as a title for a member of the clergy.

reverent *adjective* showing reverence. ➤ **reverently** *adverb*.

reverie /ˈrevəri/ *noun* (*plural* **reveries**) a daydream.

reverse *adjective* 1 opposite to a previous condition or direction. 2 causing backward movement. ~ *verb* (**reverses, reversing, reversed**) 1 to go or drive backward. 2 to change to an opposite position or direction.

revert

3 to turn upside down or inside out. 4 to change a judgment, decision, etc to its opposite. ~ *noun* (*plural* **reverses**) 1 the opposite of something. 2 the side of a coin, medal, etc that does not bear the principal design and lettering. 3 a gear that causes a vehicle to move backward. 4 a setback. * **in reverse 1** backward. **2** in the opposite direction or order. ➤ **reversal** *noun*.

revert *verb* (**reverts, reverting, reverted**) to return to a former state, practice, belief, etc. ➤ **reversion** *noun*

review *noun* (*plural* **reviews**) 1 an inspection or survey of something, especially in order to decide if changes need to be made. 2 a critical assessment of a book, play, etc. 3 a magazine or newspaper, or part of one, devoted chiefly to critical articles. 4 = REVUE. ~ *verb* (**reviews, reviewing, reviewed**) 1 to carry out, write, etc a review of something. 2 to reconsider something. ➤ **reviewer** *noun*.

revile *verb* (**reviles, reviling, reviled**) to criticize somebody or something very harshly or abusively.

revise *verb* (**revises, revising, revised**) 1 to change and correct or improve something. 2 to refresh your knowledge of a subject, especially before an examination. ➤ **revision** *noun*.

revitalize *or* **revitalise** *verb* (**revitalizes, revitalizing, revitalized** *or* **revitalises,** etc) to give new life or vigour to something or somebody. ➤ **revitalization** *or* **revitalisation** *noun*.

revival *noun* 1 a return or bringing back to life, vigour, popularity, etc. 2 *Drama* a new presentation or production of a play.

revive *verb* (**revives, reviving, revived**) 1 to come back, or bring somebody back, to a state of consciousness, health, or strength. 2 to bring back into an active state or current use.

revoke *verb* (**revokes, revoking, revoked**) to declare that a law is no longer valid. ➤ **revocation** *noun*.

revolt *verb* (**revolts, revolting, revolted**) 1 to rebel. 2 to disgust somebody. ~ *noun* (*plural* **revolts**) a rebellion.

revolting *adjective* extremely horrible; disgusting.

revolution *noun* (*plural* **revolutions**) 1 the overthrow of one government and its replacement by another. 2 a sudden or far-reaching change. 3 *Science* one complete turn of an object round a central point or axis.

revolutionary *adjective* 1 completely new and different. 2 supporting or engaging in revolution. ~ *noun* (*plural* **revolutionaries**) somebody who takes part in a revolution.

revolutionize *or* **revolutionise** *verb* (**revolutionizes, revolutionizing, revolutionized** *or* **revolutionises,** etc) to change something fundamentally or completely.

revolve *verb* (**revolves, revolving, revolved**) 1 to move in a circular course or round a central point or axis. 2 (**revolve around**) to have something as its main concern.

revolver *noun* (*plural* **revolvers**) a handgun with revolving chambers each holding one cartridge.

revue *noun* (*plural* **revues**) *Drama* a theatrical production consisting of brief often satirical sketches, songs, and dances.

revulsion *noun* a feeling of great distaste.

reward *noun* (*plural* **rewards**) 1 something offered or given for service, effort, or achievement. 2 a sum of money offered for the capture of a criminal or the recovery of lost or stolen property. ~ *verb* (**rewards, rewarding, rewarded**) to give a reward to somebody or for something.

rewarding *adjective* personally satisfying.

rewind *verb* (**rewinds, rewinding, rewound**) to wind film, tape, etc back to the beginning or to an earlier point.

rhapsody /rap so di/ *noun* (*plural* **rhapsodies**) 1 an expression of great enthusiasm. 2 *Music* a composition in one continuous movement.

rhetoric *noun* 1 the art of effective public speaking. 2 impressive language that may be insincere or exaggerated. ➤ **rhetorical** *adjective*, **rhetorically** *adverb*.

rhetorical question *noun* (*plural* **rhetorical questions**) *English* a question to which no answer is expected, used to make a statement with dramatic effect.

rheumatism /roo ma tizm/ *noun* a condition characterized by inflammation and pain in muscles and joints. ➤ **rheumatic** *adjective*.

rhino *noun* (*plural* **rhinos** or **rhino**) *informal* = RHINOCEROS.

rhinoceros *noun* (*plural* **rhinoceroses** or **rhinoceros**) a large plant-eating animal with a very thick skin and either one or two horns on its snout.

rhododendron *noun* (*plural* **rhododendrons**) a shrub with clusters of showy red, pink, purple, or white flowers and leathery evergreen leaves.

rhombus *noun* (*plural* **rhombuses** or **rhombi**) *Maths* a parallelogram with equal sides but unequal angles; a diamond-shaped figure.

rhubarb *noun* a plant with large fleshy leaves and edible stalks that are cooked and eaten as a dessert.

rhyme *noun* (*plural* **rhymes**) *English* 1 having the same sound or sounds at the ends of words, as in for example *father* and *rather* or *smiled* and *child*. 2 a word that rhymes with another word. 3 rhyming verse or a rhyming poem. ~ *verb* (**rhymes, rhyming, rhymed**) *English* 1 said about words: to have the same final sound or sounds. 2 (**rhyme with**) said about a word: to have the same final sound or sounds as another word. 3 said about verse: to have lines ending with words that rhyme.

rhythm *noun* (*plural* **rhythms**) a repeated pattern in the flow of sound, for example in music or poetry, or in movement. ➤ **rhythmic** *adjective*, **rhythmically** *adverb*.

rib *noun* (*plural* **ribs**) 1 any of the paired curved bones that protect the heart, lungs, etc in humans and most vertebrate animals. 2 a curved supporting part in the framework of a ship, etc. 3 a rod supporting the fabric of an umbrella.

ribald /ri bld *or* rie bawld/ *adjective* crudely or obscenely humorous. ➤ **ribaldry** *noun*.

riband *noun* (*plural* **ribands**) a ribbon.

ribbon *noun* (*plural* **ribbons**) 1 a narrow band of fabric used for decorative effect or as a fastening. 2 a long narrow strip. 3 a strip of inked material used in a typewriter or computer printer. 4 (**ribbons**) tatters or shreds.

ribcage *noun* (*plural* **ribcages**) the enclosing wall of the chest consisting chiefly of the ribs and their connecting tissue.

rice *noun* 1 a cereal grass widely cultivated in warm climates. 2 the grains of this plant used as food.

rich *adjective* 1 having a great deal of money and possessions. 2 said about a country or area: having many natural resources, successful industries, a strong economy, etc. 3 having high worth, value, or quality. 4 vivid and deep in colour. 5 full and mellow in tone or quality. 6 said about food:

riches

fatty, oily, or sweet. **7** (**rich in**) containing a lot of something.

riches *plural noun* great wealth.

richly *adverb* **1** in a rich manner. **2** fully: *richly deserved*.

Richter scale *noun* (**the Richter scale**) a scale showing the strength of earthquakes.

rick[1] *noun* (*plural* **ricks**) a stack of hay, corn, etc in the open air.

rick[2] *verb* (**ricks, ricking, ricked**) to wrench or sprain your neck, etc.

rickets *noun* a disease that especially affects children, characterized by softening and deformation of bones.

rickety *adjective* likely to collapse.

rickshaw *noun* (*plural* **rickshaws**) a small covered two-wheeled vehicle pulled by one or more people.

ricochet /ri ko shay/ *verb* (**ricochets, ricocheting, ricocheted**) said about a bullet: to rebound off a surface. ➤ **ricochet** *noun*.

rid *verb* (**rids, ridding, rid** *or* **ridded**) to free a person or place of something unwanted. ✳ **get rid of** to free yourself from or throw away something you do not want.

riddance ✳ **good riddance** an expression of relief at becoming free of something or somebody you do not want.

riddle[1] *noun* (*plural* **riddles**) **1** a short and humorous verbal puzzle. **2** something or somebody that is difficult to understand.

riddle[2] *noun* (*plural* **riddles**) a large coarse sieve. ~ *verb* (**riddles, riddling, riddled**) to pierce many holes in something. ✳ **be riddled with** to have something undesirable spread throughout itself.

ride *verb* (**rides, riding, rode, ridden**) **1** to travel on an animal, bicycle, etc. **2** to travel in a vehicle. **3** to be borne up or supported by something. ~ *noun* (*plural* **rides**) **1** a trip on horseback or by vehicle. **2** a mechanical device, for riding on, for example at a funfair. **3** a path used for riding. ✳ **ride high** to be successful. **take for a ride** *informal* to deceive or trick somebody.

rider *noun* (*plural* **riders**) **1** somebody who rides a horse, a bicycle, or a motorcycle. **2** a clause added to a legal document.

ridge *noun* (*plural* **ridges**) **1** a long narrow stretch of high land. **2** the top of a roof where the two sloping sides meet. **3** an elongated part raised above a surrounding surface. ➤ **ridged** *adjective*.

ridicule *verb* (**ridicules, ridiculing, ridiculed**) to say scornful or contemptuous things about something or somebody. ➤ **ridicule** *noun*.

ridiculous *adjective* silly or absurd. ➤ **ridiculously** *adverb*.

rife *adjective* occurring everywhere or very frequently.

riffraff *noun* disreputable or worthless people.

rifle[1] *noun* (*plural* **rifles**) a firearm with a long barrel with spiral grooves cut inside it.

rifle[2] *verb* (**rifles, rifling, rifled**) to search through and steal things from a drawer, safe, etc.

rift *noun* (*plural* **rifts**) **1** a split or crack. **2** a disruption of friendly relations.

rig *verb* (**rigs, rigging, rigged**) **1** to fit out a ship with rigging, sails, etc. **2** (*often* **rig up**) to assemble or erect something. **3** to use dishonest methods to arrange the result of a game or election in advance. ~ *noun* (*plural* **rigs**) **1** a structure supporting the machinery used to drill for and extract oil or gas. **2** an outfit of clothing. ✳ **rig out** to supply somebody with clothes or equipment.

rigging *noun* the ropes and chains for controlling sails and supporting masts on a ship.

right *adjective* **1** in accordance with what is morally good, just, or proper. **2** correct or true. **3** suitable or appropriate. **4** in a correct, proper, or healthy state. **5** on or towards the side of somebody or something that is nearer the east when the front faces north. **6** *informal* real or utter. ~ *noun* (*plural* **rights**) **1** qualities that are morally good. **2** a power, privilege, etc to which you are entitled. **3** the part, direction, etc on the right side. **4** (**the right**) in politics, people with conservative or reactionary views. ~ *adverb* **1** on or towards the right. **2** in a proper or correct manner. **3** exactly: *right now*. **4** in a direct line; straight: *Go right on*. **5** all the way; completely: *right in*. ~ *verb* (**rights, righting, righted**) **1** to correct something. **2** to return a boat, cart, etc to an upright position. **3** to compensate for or avenge a wrong, an injustice, etc. ✶ **by rights** rightfully or justly. **in the right** correct; right. **in your own right** on the basis of your own qualifications or abilities. **to rights** into proper order. ➢ **rightly** *adverb*.

right angle *noun* (*plural* **right angles**) an angle of 90°, for example at the corner of a square. ➢ **right-angled** *adjective*.

righteous *adjective* morally right or justified. ➢ **righteously** *adverb*, **righteousness** *noun*.

rightful *adjective* having a just and legal claim to be or have something. ➢ **rightfully** *adverb*.

right-handed *adjective* usually using the right hand to write with or hold things.

right of way *noun* (*plural* **rights of way**) **1** a legal right to pass over another person's property. **2** the right of one vehicle, ship, etc to enter an area before another.

rigid *adjective* **1** unable to bend or be bent; stiff. **2** unable to be changed; strict. ➢ **rigidity** *noun*, **rigidly** *adverb*.

rigmarole *noun* (*plural* **rigmaroles**) **1** an absurdly long and complex procedure. **2** a nonsensical account or explanation.

rigor mortis /ˌrɪ gər ˈmɔː tɪs/ *noun* the temporary rigidity of muscles after death.

rigorous *adjective* **1** very strict. **2** harsh or severe. **3** scrupulously accurate; precise. ➢ **rigorously** *adverb*.

rigour *noun* (*plural* **rigours**) **1** strictness. **2** (**rigours**) conditions that make life difficult or unpleasant.

rile *verb* (**riles, riling, riled**) to make somebody angry or resentful.

rim *noun* (*plural* **rims**) an outer edge of something circular.

rime *noun* a thin coating of frost.

rimmed *adjective* edged with or bordered by something.

rind *noun* (*plural* **rinds**) a tough outer layer of fruit, cheese, bacon, etc.

ring¹ *noun* (*plural* **rings**) **1** a circular band of precious metal, worn on your finger. **2** a circular line, figure, arrangement, or object. **3** a circular space where a circus performs. **4** a square enclosure in which boxing or wrestling matches are held. ~ *verb* (**rings, ringing, ringed**) to place, form, or draw a ring round something or somebody. ➢ **ringed** *adjective*.

ring² *verb* (**rings, ringing, rang, rung**) **1** to make, or cause something to make, a sound like a bell. **2** (*often* **ring with**) to be filled with the sound of something. **3** (*often* **ring up**) to telephone somebody. ~ *noun* **1** a ringing sound. **2** the act of ringing. **3** *informal* a telephone call. ✶ **ring a bell** to sound familiar. **ring the changes** to vary the manner of doing or arranging something. **ring true** to appear to be true or authentic.

ringleader *noun* (*plural* **ringleaders**) a

ringlet

leader of a group engaged in illegal or objectionable activities.

ringlet noun (plural **ringlets**) a lock of hair curled in a spiral.

ringmaster noun (plural **ringmasters**) the person in charge of a circus performance.

ring road noun (plural **ring roads**) a road round a town or town centre designed to relieve traffic congestion.

ringworm noun a fungal disease in which itchy ring-shaped patches form on the skin.

rink noun (plural **rinks**) 1 a surface of ice for ice-skating, ice hockey, or curling. 2 an enclosure for roller-skating.

rinse verb (**rinses, rinsing, rinsed**) 1 to remove soap from washed clothing with clean water. 2 to remove dirt, etc from something by washing lightly. ~ noun (plural **rinses**) 1 an act of rinsing. 2 a liquid that temporarily colours the hair.

riot noun (plural **riots**) 1 a violent public disturbance caused by a large crowd of people. 2 informal somebody or something wildly funny. ~ verb (**riots, rioting, rioted**) to participate in a riot. * **run riot** to act wildly or without restraint. ➤ **rioter** noun, **riotous** adjective.

RIP abbreviation rest in peace.

rip verb (**rips, ripping, ripped**) 1 to tear something, or to become torn. 2 (**rip out/off**) to remove something by force. ~ noun (plural **rips**) a tear or torn split. * **let rip** informal to do something without restraint. **rip off** 1 to rob or defraud somebody. 2 to steal something.

ripe adjective (**riper, ripest**) 1 said about fruit or grain: fully developed and ready for harvesting or eating. 2 (**ripe for**) ready or suitable for something. * **a ripe old age** a very great age. ➤ **ripeness** noun.

ripen verb (**ripens, ripening, ripened**) to become ripe or make something ripe.

rip-off noun (plural **rip-offs**) informal a swindle.

ripple noun (plural **ripples**) a small wave or a succession of small waves. ~ verb (**ripples, rippling, rippled**) 1 to stir up small waves on water. 2 to flow in small waves.

rise verb (**rises, rising, rose, risen**) 1 to move upwards. 2 to slope upwards. 3 to get into an upright position from lying, kneeling, or sitting. 4 to get up from sleep or from your bed. 5 said about the sun, moon, etc: to appear above the horizon. 6 to increase. 7 said of dough: to swell up. 8 to be promoted to a higher position. 9 to rebel. 10 said about a river: to have its source. ~ noun (plural **rises**) 1 a movement upwards. 2 an upward slope. 3 an increase. * **give rise to** to be the origin or cause of something.

rising noun (plural **risings**) a rebellion or uprising.

risk noun (plural **risks**) a possibility of loss, injury, or damage. ~ verb (**risks, risking, risked**) 1 to put something, such as your life, in danger. 2 to take the chance that something unpleasant will happen. * **at risk** in danger. **at your own risk** with you accepting responsibility for any harm or loss to happens to you.

risky adjective (**riskier, riskiest**) involving danger or the possibility of loss or failure. ➤ **riskily** adverb, **riskiness** noun.

rite noun (plural **rites**) a religious act or ceremony.

ritual noun (plural **rituals**) 1 a solemn or religious ceremony involving a series of actions carried out in a set order. 2 an action always carried out in the same way.

rival noun (plural **rivals**) a person who wants the same thing as you and is competing with you for it. ~ *verb* (**rivals, rivalling, rivalled**) to be as good, or almost as good as something or somebody else. ➤ **rivalry** *noun*.

river *noun* (*plural* **rivers**) a large natural stream of water.

rivet *noun* (*plural* **rivets**) a headed metal pin used to join two metal plates. ~ *verb* (**rivets, riveting, riveted**) 1 to fasten something with rivets. 2 to attract and hold somebody's attention completely. ➤ **riveting** *adjective*.

RN *abbreviation* Royal Navy.

road *noun* (*plural* **roads**) 1 a long open strip of ground with a hard surface for vehicles and people to travel along. 2 a route or path: *the road to ruin*.

roadblock *noun* (*plural* **roadblocks**) a road barricade set up by an army, the police, etc.

road rage *noun* violent and aggressive behaviour by a motorist towards another road user.

roadway *noun* the part of a road used by vehicles.

roadworks *plural noun* work done to repair or construct roads.

roadworthy *adjective* in a fit condition to be used on the roads.

roam *verb* (**roams, roaming, roamed**) to wander.

roar *noun* (*plural* **roars**) 1 the deep prolonged cry of a wild animal, e.g. a lion. 2 a loud cry of pain, anger, or laughter. 3 a loud continuous confused sound. ~ *verb* (**roars, roaring, roared**) 1 to give a roar. 2 to laugh loudly. 3 said about a fire: to burn fiercely and noisily.

roast *verb* (**roasts, roasting, roasted**) 1 to cook something, especially meat, by exposing it to dry heat, for example in an oven. 2 to be excessively hot. ~ *noun* (*plural* **roasts**) a piece of meat roasted or suitable for roasting. ~ *adjective* said about meat: roasted: *roast beef*.

rob *verb* (**robs, robbing, robbed**) to steal something from a person or place. * **rob of** to deprive somebody of something. ➤ **robber** *noun*, **robbery** *noun*.

robe *noun* (*plural* **robes**) 1 a long flowing outer garment, especially one used for ceremonial occasions. 2 *N American* a dressing gown. ~ *verb* (**robes, robing, robed**) to clothe somebody with a robe.

robin *noun* (*plural* **robins**) a small brownish bird with an orange-red throat and breast.

robot *noun* (*plural* **robots**) 1 a machine programmed to carry out a sequence of actions automatically. 2 in science fiction, a machine that looks or acts like a human. ➤ **robotic** *adjective*.

robust *adjective* 1 vigorous and healthy. 2 strongly formed or constructed. ➤ **robustly** *adverb*.

rock[1] *noun* (*plural* **rocks**) 1 hard solid mineral matter forming the earth's crust. 2 a particular form of this, such as granite or limestone. 3 a boulder. 4 a sweet in the form of a hard and brittle cylindrical stick. * **on the rocks** *informal* in difficulties.

rock[2] *verb* (**rocks, rocking, rocked**) 1 to move gently back and forth or from side to side. 2 to sway, or to shake something, rapidly or violently. 3 to dance to or play rock music. ~ *noun* a style of popular music played on electronically amplified instruments and with a persistent, heavily accented beat.

rock and roll *noun* see ROCK 'N' ROLL.

rock bottom *noun* the lowest level.

rocker *noun* (*plural* **rockers**) a curved piece of wood or metal on which an object, such as a cradle, rocks. * **off your rocker** *informal* crazy.

rockery *noun* (*plural* **rockeries**) a bank

rocket

of rocks and earth where small plants are grown.

rocket *noun* (*plural* **rockets**) **1** a firework that shoots high into the air before bursting. **2** a spacecraft, missile, etc propelled by a jet engine that does not use oxygen from the air. **3** *informal* a sharp reprimand. ~ *verb* (**rockets, rocketing, rocketed**) **1** said about prices, etc: to increase rapidly or spectacularly. **2** to travel with the speed of a rocket.

rocking chair *noun* (*plural* **rocking chairs**) a chair mounted on rockers.

rocking horse *noun* (*plural* **rocking horses**) a toy horse mounted on rockers.

rock 'n' roll *or* **rock and roll** *noun Music* a style of popular music, originating in the 1950s, characterized by a heavy beat and simple melodies.

rocky[1] *adjective* (**rockier, rockiest**) **1** full of or consisting of rocks. **2** filled with obstacles; difficult.

rocky[2] *adjective* (**rockier, rockiest**) unsteady.

rod *noun* (*plural* **rods**) **1** a slender bar of wood, metal, etc. **2** a pole with a line for fishing.

rode *verb* past tense of RIDE.

rodent *noun* (*plural* **rodents**) a member of an order of mammals with large front teeth for gnawing that includes mice, rats, squirrels, and beavers.

rodeo *noun* (*plural* **rodeos**) a public performance featuring the riding skills of cowboys.

roe *noun* the eggs or sperm of a fish.

roe deer *noun* (*plural* **roe deer**) a small graceful deer with erect cylindrical antlers.

rogue *noun* (*plural* **rogues**) **1** a dishonest person. **2** a mischievous person. **3** an animal roaming alone that is vicious and destructive.

roguish *adjective* mischievous.

role *noun* (*plural* **roles**) **1** *Drama* a part played by an actor. **2** the function or purpose of a person or thing.

role model *noun* (*plural* **role models**) somebody who serves as an example to others of how to behave.

roll *verb* (**rolls, rolling, rolled**) **1** to move along by turning over and over. **2** to move steadily onward or pass one after the other. **3** said about a ship, aircraft, etc: to rock from side to side as it moves forward. **4** (*often* **roll up**) to wrap something round itself to form a cylinder or ball. **5** to shape or flatten something by rolling it or rolling something over it. ~ *noun* (*plural* **rolls**) **1** something rolled up to resemble a cylinder. **2** a small round or cylindrical loaf of bread. **3** an official list of people's names. **4** a rolling or swaying movement. **5** *Music* a sound produced by rapid strokes on a drum. **6** a long reverberating sound of thunder. ✱ **be rolling in it/money** *informal* to be very wealthy. **on a roll** *informal* having a period of success.

roll call *noun* (*plural* **roll calls**) the calling out of a list of names, for example to check attendance.

roller *noun* (*plural* **rollers**) **1** a revolving cylinder used to move, press, shape, or apply something. **2** a hair curler. **3** a long heavy wave.

Rollerblade *noun* (*plural* **Rollerblades**) *trademark* a roller skate with a single central line of wheels.

roller coaster *noun* (*plural* **roller coasters**) a sort of railway in a funfair, constructed high off the ground with steep slopes and sharp curves.

roller skate *noun* (*plural* **roller skates**) a boot with four small wheels attached to the sole for gliding over hard surfaces. ➤ **roller skater** *noun*, **roller skating** *noun*.

rolling pin *noun* (*plural* **rolling pins**) a long cylinder for rolling out dough.

rolling stock *noun* the vehicles owned and used by a railway.

roly-poly *noun* (*plural* **roly-polies**) a pudding consisting of suet pastry spread with jam, rolled, and baked or steamed.

ROM *abbreviation* ICT read-only memory, a type of computer storage that contains data that can be read but not changed.

Roman *noun* (*plural* **Romans**) a person from ancient or modern Rome. ~ *adjective* to do with Rome or the Romans.

Roman alphabet *noun* the alphabet used for writing most European languages, including English.

Roman candle *noun* (*plural* **Roman candles**) a cylindrical firework that shoots up balls of fire at intervals.

Roman Catholic *noun* (*plural* **Roman Catholics**) a member of the Roman Catholic church, a Christian church headed by the Pope and having a service of worship centred on the Mass. ➤ **Roman Catholic** *adjective*, **Roman Catholicism** *noun*.

romance *noun* (*plural* **romances**) **1** romantic love, or the feelings and behaviour usually associated with it. **2** a love affair. **3** a story or film about romantic love. **4** a romantic quality or atmosphere.

Roman numeral *noun* (*plural* **Roman numerals**) a numeral used in ancient Rome and still sometimes today, using the symbols I, V, X, L, C, D, and M.

romantic *adjective* **1** involving sexual attraction accompanied by tender, loving feelings and elaborate courtship. **2** impractical or very idealistic. **3** (*often* **Romantic**) to do with romanticism. ➤ **romantically** *adverb*.

romanticism *noun* (*also* **Romanticism**) English, Art a late 18th- and early 19th-century literary and artistic movement that emphasized individual aspirations, nature, and the emotions.

romanticize *or* **romanticise** *verb* (**romanticizes, romanticizing, romanticized** *or* **romanticises**, etc) to present a person or incident in a misleadingly romantic way.

Romany *noun* (*plural* **Romanies**) **1** the language of the gypsies. **2** a gypsy.

romp *verb* (**romps, romping, romped**) to play in a boisterous manner. ✱ **romp home** *informal* to win easily. ➤ **romp** *noun*.

rompers *plural noun* a child's one-piece garment.

rondo *noun* (*plural* **rondos**) Music an instrumental composition with an opening section that is repeated between the other sections.

roof *noun* (*plural* **roofs**) **1** the upper rigid cover of a building, vehicle, etc. **2** the top covering part of the mouth, skull, etc. ~ *verb* (**roofs, roofing, roofed**) to cover something with a roof. ➤ **roofed** *adjective*, **roofing** *noun*.

rook[1] *noun* (*plural* **rooks**) a common bird with black plumage, similar to a crow but nesting in colonies.

rook[2] *noun* (*plural* **rooks**) in chess, a castle-shaped piece that can move in a straight line across any number of squares.

rookery *noun* (*plural* **rookeries**) **1** the nests of a colony of rooks, usually built in the upper branches of trees. **2** a breeding ground of a colony of penguins, seals, etc.

rookie *noun* (*plural* **rookies**) *informal* a new recruit.

room *noun* (*plural* **rooms**) **1** a partitioned part of the inside of a building. **2** an extent of space sufficient or available for something.

roomy *adjective* (**roomier, roomiest**) having ample room; spacious.

roost *verb* (**roosts, roosting, roosted**) said about a bird: to settle down for

rooster

rest or sleep. ~ *noun* (*plural* **roosts**) a support or place where birds roost.

rooster *noun* (*plural* **roosters**) = COCK¹.

root¹ *noun* (*plural* **roots**) **1** the underground part of a plant that anchors it and absorbs food. **2** the part of a tooth, hair, the tongue, etc that attaches it to the body. **3** an underlying cause or basis. **4** (**roots**) family background or origin. **5** *Maths* a number which produces a given number when multiplied by itself an indicated number of times. ~ *verb* (**roots, rooting, rooted**) **1** to develop roots, or to enable a plant to develop roots. **2** to fix or implant something firmly. ✵ **root out** to get rid of or destroy something completely. **take root 1** to develop roots. **2** to become fixed or established. ➤ **rooted** *adjective*.

root² *verb* (**roots, rooting, rooted**) **1** said about a pig: to dig with its snout. **2** (*often* **root about**) to search unsystematically.

root vegetable *noun* (*plural* **root vegetables**) the root of a plant, such as a carrot or turnip, that is eaten as a vegetable.

rope *noun* (*plural* **ropes**) **1** a strong thick cord composed of strands of fibres or wire twisted together. **2** (**the ropes**) the sides of a boxing ring. ~ *verb* (**ropes, roping, roped**) **1** to fasten or tie something or somebody with a rope. **2** to enclose or separate off an area with a rope. ✵ **rope in** to persuade somebody to join in or help with an activity. **show somebody the ropes** to show somebody the way things are done.

ropy *or* **ropey** *adjective* (**ropier, ropiest**) *informal*. **1** of poor quality; shoddy. **2** slightly unwell.

rosary *noun* (*plural* **rosaries**) a string of beads used in counting prayers while they are being recited.

rose¹ *noun* (*plural* **roses**) **1** a prickly shrub with large flowers that have a fragrant smell. **2** a perforated outlet for water from a shower or watering can. **3** a pale to dark pinkish colour.

rose² *verb* past tense of RISE¹.

rosemary *noun* a shrubby plant with fragrant leaves that are used as a cooking herb.

rosette *noun* (*plural* **rosettes**) an ornament made of material gathered to look slightly like a flattened rose and worn as a badge, trophy, or trimming.

Rosh Hashanah *or* **Rosh Hashana** ~ /rosh ha**shah**na/ *noun* the Jewish New Year.

roster *noun* (*plural* **rosters**) a list giving the order in which members of staff are to perform a duty, go on leave, etc.

rostrum *noun* (*plural* **rostra** *or* **rostrums**) a raised platform, especially for somebody making a speech.

rosy *adjective* (**rosier, rosiest**) **1** rose-pink. **2** encouraging optimism; promising.

rot *verb* (**rots, rotting, rotted**) to turn brown, soft, and smelly by the effects of bacteria or fungi; to decay. ~ *noun* **1** the state of being rotten. **2** *informal* nonsense or rubbish.

rota *noun* (*plural* **rotas**) a list specifying the order in which people do jobs or jobs are done.

rotate *verb* (**rotates, rotating, rotated**) **1** to turn round on an axis or a centre. **2** to take turns at performing an act or operation. **3** to exchange individuals or units with others. ➤ **rotary** *adjective*, **rotation** *noun*, **rotatory** *adjective*.

rote ✵ **by rote** repeating something over and over again until you have learned it.

rotor *noun* (*plural* **rotors**) a part that revolves, especially the hub and horizontal blades that enable a helicopter to fly.

rotten *adjective* **1** having rotted. **2** morally corrupt. **3** *informal* extremely unpleasant. **4** *informal* unhappy; ashamed. **5** *informal* inferior; useless.

Rottweiler *noun* (*plural* **Rottweilers**) a tall, strongly built, black-and-tan dog with short hair.

rotund *adjective* **1** plump. **2** rounded.

rouble *noun* (*plural* **roubles**) the main unit of money used in Russia.

rough *adjective* **1** having an irregular or uneven surface; not smooth. **2** not gentle; harsh or violent. **3** said about the sea: moving violently, with large waves. **4** said about the weather: stormy. **5** crudely or hastily made. **6** not thoroughly worked out; approximate. **7** said about a voice: harsh-sounding. **8** *informal* difficult or unpleasant. ~ *adverb* uncomfortably and in the open air: *sleep rough*. ~ *verb* (**roughs, roughing, roughed**) ✽ **rough it** *informal* to live in uncomfortable or primitive conditions. **rough out** to shape or plan something roughly. **rough up** *informal* to beat somebody up. ➤ **roughly** *adverb*.

roughage *noun* coarse bulky food, such as bran, that is relatively high in fibre.

roughen *verb* (**roughens, roughening, roughened**) to make something rough.

roulette /roo let/ *noun* a gambling game in which players bet on which compartment of a revolving wheel a small ball will come to rest in.

round *adjective* **1** circular. **2** cylindrical. **3** spherical. **4** shaped in a smooth curve. **5** said about a number: expressed as the nearest large unit. ~ *adverb* **1** in a circular or curved path. **2** with rotating motion. **3** in or to the other direction: *turn round*. **4** to every part or person: *hand round*. **5** to a particular person or place: *invite somebody round*. ~ *preposition* **1** so as to revolve about or encircle something. **2** to every part or every person. **3** so as to avoid or get past something. **4** in a position on the other side of something: *round the corner*. **5** near to something: *somewhere round here*. ~ *noun* (*plural* **rounds**) **1** a route regularly travelled, for example by a person making deliveries. **2** an event or series of events forming a single stage in a competition. **3** *Music* an unaccompanied song for three or more voices or groups in which each voice or group sings the same tune but starting one after the other. **4** a set of drinks served to each person in a group. **5** a unit of ammunition enabling a gun to fire one shot. **6** a slice of bread, or a sandwich made with two whole slices. ~ *verb* (**rounds, rounding, rounded**) **1** to go round a bend or corner. **2** (**round off/up/down**) to express a figure as a round number. **3** (*often* **round off**) to make round or rounded. ✽ **round about 1** approximately. **2** on all sides of. **round off** to complete something. **round on** to attack or scold somebody suddenly. **round up** to bring people or things together from different places. ➤ **roundness** *noun*.

roundabout *noun* (*plural* **roundabouts**) **1** a road junction with a central island around which traffic moves in a circle. **2** a merry-go-round. ~ *adjective* circuitous; not direct.

rounded *adjective* **1** smoothly curved. **2** fully developed in all respects.

rounders *noun* a team game played with a bat and a ball, in which players hit the ball and then try to score by running round the four sides of the pitch.

Roundhead *noun* (*plural* **Roundheads**) *History* a supporter of Parliament in the English Civil War.

round-the-clock *adjective* lasting or continuing 24 hours a day; constant.

round trip

round trip *noun* (*plural* **round trips**) a trip to somewhere and back.

rouse *verb* (**rouses, rousing, roused**) **1** to wake somebody up. **2** to stimulate your interest, curiosity, etc.

rousing *adjective* loud and exciting.

rout *verb* (**routs, routing, routed**) to defeat an army, team, etc decisively or disastrously. ➤ **rout** *noun*.

route *noun* (*plural* **routes**) a course planned or taken to get you from a starting point to a destination.

routine *noun* (*plural* **routines**) **1** a sequence of actions performed regularly in the same order. **2** *ICT* a sequence of computer instructions for carrying out a given task. ~ *adjective* **1** done regularly. **2** ordinary and rather boring. ➤ **routinely** *adverb*.

rove *verb* (**roves, roving, roved**) to wander. ➤ **rover** *noun*.

row[1] /roh/ *noun* (*plural* **rows**) a number of objects or people arranged in a straight line. ✶ **in a row** *informal* one after another.

row[2] /roh/ *verb* (**rows, rowing, rowed**) to move a boat with oars. ➤ **rower** *noun*.

row[3] /row/ *noun* (*plural* **rows**) *informal* **1** a noisy quarrel. **2** a loud and unpleasant noise. ~ *verb* (**rows, rowing, rowed**) *informal* to quarrel.

rowan /roh an *or* row an/ *noun* (*plural* **rowans**) a small tree with white flowers and red or orange berries.

rowdy *adjective* (**rowdier, rowdiest**) rough or boisterous.

rowlock /ro lok/ *noun* (*plural* **rowlocks**) a device on the side of a boat for holding an oar in place.

royal *adjective* to do with or suitable for a king or queen. ~ *noun* (*plural* **royals**) *informal* a member of a royal family. ➤ **royally** *adverb*.

royalist *noun* (*plural* **royalists**) a supporter of a king or queen or of monarchical government. ➤ **royalist** *adjective*.

royalty *noun* (*plural* **royalties**) **1** people belong to a royal family. **2** a payment made to an author or composer each time a work of theirs is performed or a copy of it is sold.

RSVP *abbreviation* = (French) *répondez s'il vous plaît* please reply.

rub *verb* (**rubs, rubbing, rubbed**) **1** to move back and forth over the surface of something while pressing down on it. **2** to apply a substance to a surface by rubbing. ✶ **rub out** to remove something, or be removable, with a rubber. **rub up the wrong way** to irritate or displease somebody. ➤ **rub** *noun*.

rubber *noun* (*plural* **rubbers**) **1** an elastic substance obtained from the juice of a tropical tree and used in car tyres, waterproof materials, etc. **2** a small piece of rubber or plastic used for rubbing out pencil marks. ➤ **rubbery** *adjective*.

rubber band *noun* (*plural* **rubber bands**) a loop of rubber used for holding small objects together.

rubber-stamp *verb* (**rubber-stamps, rubber-stamping, rubber-stamped**) to approve a plan, etc without properly considering it or because you are told to by somebody else.

rubbish *noun* **1** worthless or rejected articles. **2** nonsense. ➤ **rubbishy** *adjective*.

rubble *noun* broken fragments of building material, such as brick or stone.

rubella /rooh be la/ *noun* a virus disease similar to measles but milder.

rubric /rooh brik/ *noun* (*plural* **rubrics**) a heading or set of instructions at the top of an official document.

ruby *noun* (*plural* **rubies**) a red precious stone.

ruby wedding noun (plural **ruby weddings**) a fortieth wedding anniversary.

rucksack noun (plural **rucksacks**) a lightweight bag carried on the back by shoulder straps.

ructions plural noun informal an angry disturbance or protest.

rudder noun (plural **rudders**) a flat hinged piece attached vertically to a ship's stern or the tail of an aircraft and used for steering.

ruddy adjective (**ruddier, ruddiest**) 1 said about a complexion: having a healthy reddish colour. 2 red or reddish.

rude adjective 1 impolite. 2 vulgar; indecent. 3 sudden and unpleasant. 4 robust; vigorous. ➤ **rudely** adverb, **rudeness** noun.

rudiments /rooh di mints/ plural noun basic principles or skills.

rudimentary adjective 1 basic and simple. 2 only partly developed.

rueful adjective expressing regret. ➤ **ruefully** adverb.

ruff noun (plural **ruffs**) 1 History a broad starched collar of pleated linen or muslin. 2 a fringe of long hairs or feathers growing round the neck of a bird or animal.

ruffian noun (plural **ruffians**) a brutal and lawless person.

ruffle verb (**ruffles, ruffling, ruffled**) 1 to disturb the smoothness of something. 2 to trouble or disconcert somebody. ~ noun (plural **ruffles**) a strip of fabric gathered or pleated on one edge. ➤ **ruffled** adjective.

rug noun (plural **rugs**) 1 a small carpet. 2 a woollen blanket used as a wrap.

rugby or **Rugby** noun a team game played with an oval ball, which features kicking, hand-to-hand passing, and tackling.

rugged /ru gid/ adjective 1 said about terrain: having a rough uneven surface or outline. 2 strongly built; sturdy. 3 said about a man: having attractively strong masculine features. ➤ **ruggedly** adverb, **ruggedness** noun.

rugger noun informal = RUGBY.

ruin noun (plural **ruins**) 1 destruction or severe damage. 2 the remains of a building that has fallen down or been destroyed. 3 a person's downfall, or the cause of it. 4 the total loss of your money and other assets. ~ verb (**ruins, ruining, ruined**) 1 to damage something irreparably. 2 to reduce somebody to financial ruin. 3 to completely spoil a person's enjoyment, a party, etc.

ruinous adjective 1 causing ruin. 2 ruined. ➤ **ruinously** adverb.

rule noun (plural **rules**) 1 a statement setting out correct behaviour that people are expected to obey. 2 the fact of ruling a country, etc, or the period during which a particular ruler or government rules. 3 (**the rule**) what happens normally or customarily. 4 = RULER (sense 2). ~ verb 1 to have supreme authority over a nation or people. 2 to keep something or somebody under control. 3 said about a judge or referee: to make a decision. 4 to draw a line with a ruler. 5 to mark paper with parallel lines. ✶ **as a rule** generally; for the most part. **rule out** 1 to exclude something or somebody. 2 to make or consider something impossible.

ruler noun (plural **rulers**) 1 somebody who rules a country, etc. 2 a smooth-edged strip of wood, plastic, etc used for drawing straight lines or measuring.

ruling noun (plural **rulings**) an official or authoritative decision.

rum noun a strong alcoholic drink.

rumble verb (**rumbles, rumbling, rumbled**) 1 to make a low heavy rolling sound. 2 informal to discover

ruminant

the true character of somebody or something. ➤ **rumble** noun.

ruminant /rooh mi nant/ noun (plural **ruminants**) a mammal that chews the cud, such as a cow, sheep, or camel.

ruminate verb (**ruminates, ruminating, ruminated**) **1** to think deeply. **2** said about an animal: to chew the cud.

rummage verb (**rummages, rummaging, rummaged**) to engage in a haphazard search.

rummy noun a card game in which each player tries to put together combinations of related cards.

rumour noun (plural **rumours**) a statement or statements about something or somebody spread from person to person but not confirmed as true. ✱ **be rumoured** to be said to be, according to rumour.

rump noun (plural **rumps**) the rear part of a mammal, bird, etc.

rumple verb (**rumples, rumpling, rumpled**) to make something wrinkled, crumpled, or dishevelled. ➤ **rumpled** adjective.

rumpus noun (plural **rumpuses**) a noisy commotion.

run verb (**runs, running, ran, run**) **1** to go at a speed faster than a walk, with only one foot on the ground at any time. **2** to cause something to move lightly or freely: *She ran a comb through her hair.* **3** said about a bus or train: to operate on a regular route. **4** to transport somebody a short distance in a vehicle. **5** to take part in a race. **6** to be a candidate in an election: *run for president.* **7** to manage or be in charge of a business, enterprise, etc. **8** to operate a vehicle, machine, etc. **9** said about a machine: to function. **10** to continue or extend over a specified period or length. **11** to flow, or cause water, etc, to flow. **12** said about a colour: to spread or dissolve when wet. **13** to be at a specified level: *Inflation is running at 4 per cent.* ~ noun (plural **runs**) **1** an act of running. **2** a journey or excursion in a car. **3** a regularly travelled course or route. **4** a sloping course for skiing, etc. **5** a continuous period or sequence: *a run of bad luck.* **6** an enclosure for domestic animals. **7** a unit of scoring in cricket or baseball. **8** a ladder in tights or a stocking. ✱ **on the run** trying to avoid arrest or capture, especially after escaping from custody. **run along** informal to leave. **run away** to flee or escape. **run down 1** to knock somebody down with a vehicle. **2** to make critical or insulting comments about somebody or something. **3** to reduce something in size or strength. **run into 1** to meet somebody by chance. **2** to collide with something. **run out 1** to become used up. **2** to come to an end; to expire. **3** in cricket: to dismiss a batsman by breaking the wicket while the batsman is making a run. **run over 1** to injure or kill somebody with a motor vehicle. **2** to read through something quickly. **run up 1** to accumulate debts. **2** to make or erect something quickly. **run up against** to experience an unexpected difficulty.

runaway noun (plural **runaways**) somebody who has fled or escaped. ~ adjective **1** that is out of control. **2** said about a victory, success, etc: decisive.

run-down adjective **1** in a state of disrepair. **2** in poor health.

rung[1] noun (plural **rungs**) a crosspiece of a ladder.

rung[2] verb past participle of RING[3].

runner noun (plural **runners**) **1** a person who runs in a race or for exercise. **2** a groove or bar on which something, such as a drawer, a sledge, or an ice skate, slides. **3** a horizontal stem from the base of a plant that has buds to produce new plants. **4** a long narrow carpet or cloth.

runner bean *noun* (*plural* **runner beans**) the long green pod of a climbing bean, used as a vegetable.

runner-up *noun* (*plural* **runners-up**) a competitor or team that comes second in a contest.

running *adjective* **1** said about water: flowing in a stream, etc or available through pipes. **2** said about a sore: producing pus. **3** made while something is going on: *a running commentary*. ~ *adverb* in succession. ✴ **in or out of the running** having a good (or poor) chance of winning.

runny *adjective* (**runnier, runniest**) **1** thinner or more liquid than usual. **2** said about the nose and eyes: continuously producing mucus or tears.

run-of-the-mill *adjective* average; ordinary.

run-up *noun* (*plural* **run-ups**) **1** a period immediately preceding an event. **2** a run that provides momentum for a jump or throw.

runway *noun* (*plural* **runways**) a strip of ground on which aircraft land and take off.

rupee /rooh pee/ *noun* (*plural* **rupees**) the basic unit of money in India, Pakistan, and Sri Lanka.

rupture *verb* (**ruptures, rupturing, ruptured**) to break or burst something. ➤ **rupture** *noun*.

rural *adjective* to do with the countryside. ➤ **rurally** *adverb*.

ruse *noun* (*plural* **ruses**) a wily scheme or trick.

rush[1] *verb* (**rushes, rushing, rushed**) **1** to move forward or act quickly or eagerly or without preparation. **2** to perform or finish something in a shorter time than usual. **3** to make somebody hurry. **4** to attack somebody or something with a sudden charge. ~ *noun* (*plural* **rushes**) **1** a rapid and violent forward motion; a hurry. **2** a sudden demand for something. **3** a great movement of people, especially in search of wealth. **4** (**rushes**) the unedited print of a film scene.

rush[2] *noun* (*plural* **rushes**) a marsh plant with leaves used to make the seats of chairs, mats, etc.

rush hour *noun* (*plural* **rush hours**) a period of the day when traffic is busiest.

rusk *noun* (*plural* **rusks**) a dry and crisp piece of twice-baked bread, or a light dry biscuit.

russet *noun* a reddish brown colour.

rust *noun* **1** a reddish coating formed on iron by contact with moist air. **2** a reddish brown to orange colour. ~ *verb* (**rusts, rusting, rusted**) to become, or make something, rusty.

rustic *adjective* characteristic of the countryside, especially in being simple or unsophisticated. ➤ **rusticity** *noun*.

rustle *verb* (**rustles, rustling, rustled**) **1** to make light crackling sounds. **2** to steal cattle or horses. ✴ **rustle up** *informal* to produce something, especially food, at short notice. ➤ **rustle** *noun*, **rustler** *noun*.

rusty *adjective* (**rustier, rustiest**) **1** affected by rust. **2** coloured like rust. **3** slow or lacking skill because of lack of practice.

rut *noun* (*plural* **ruts**) a groove in a track worn by a wheel. ✴ **in a rut** doing the same thing continually. ➤ **rutted** *adjective*.

ruthless *adjective* showing no pity or compassion. ➤ **ruthlessly** *adverb*, **ruthlessness** *noun*.

rye *noun* a cereal grass grown for grain that is used to make bread, whiskey, etc.

S *abbreviation* South or Southern.

sabbath *noun* (**the Sabbath**) a special day in the week for rest and worship, Saturday for Jews and Sunday for most Christians.

sabbatical /sa ba ti kl/ *noun* (*plural* **sabbaticals**) a period of paid leave granted to university teachers for study or travel.

sable /say bl/ *noun* (*plural* **sables** or **sable**) **1** an Asian animal of the weasel family with valuable dark brown fur. **2** sable fur or a garment made from it. ~ *adjective literary* black.

sabotage /sa bo tahzh/ *verb* (**sabotages, sabotaging sabotaged**) **1** to damage military or industrial equipment deliberately. **2** to spoil a plan or project deliberately.
➤ **sabotage** *noun*.

saboteur /sa bo ter/ *noun* (*plural* **saboteurs**) somebody who commits sabotage.

sabre /say ber/ *noun* (*plural* **sabres**) **1** a heavy sword with a curved blade. **2** a light fencing sword with a tapering blade.

sac *noun* (*plural* **sacs**) a pouch, often filled with fluid, in an animal or plant.

saccharin /sa ka rin/ *noun* a sweet-tasting compound used as a substitute for sugar.

sachet /sa shay/ *noun* (*plural* **sachets**) a small sealed bag or packet containing a small amount of something.

sack[1] *noun* (*plural* **sacks**) **1** a large bag made of thick material or plastic. **2** (**the sack**) *informal* dismissal from a job. ~ *verb* (**sacks, sacking, sacked**) *informal* to dismiss somebody from a job.

sack[2] *verb* (**sacks, sacking, sacked**) to plunder and destroy a place after capturing it. ➤ **sack** *noun*.

sacrament *noun* (*plural* **sacraments**) **1** an important religious ceremony such as baptism or communion. **2** (**the Sacrament**) in Christianity, the bread and wine used in the communion service.

sacred *adjective* **1** to do with the worship of God or a god. **2** dedicated as a memorial. **3** holy.

sacrifice *verb* (**sacrifices, sacrificing, sacrificed**) **1** to give up or lose something deliberately, for example for a noble cause or to achieve something greater. **2** to kill an animal on an altar, or give away something, as an offering to God or a god. ~ *noun* (*plural* **sacrifices**) **1** something that you sacrifice. **2** the act of sacrificing. ➤ **sacrificial** *adjective*.

sacrilege /sa kri lij/ *noun* damage done or disrespect shown to a sacred object or place. ➤ **sacrilegious** *adjective*.

sacrosanct *adjective* treated with the greatest respect and not allowed to be harmed or changed.

sad *adjective* (**sadder, saddest**) **1** unhappy. **2** causing unhappiness. **3** *informal* pathetic or contemptible.
➤ **sadly** *adverb*, **sadness** *noun*.

sadden *verb* (**saddens, saddening, saddened**) to make somebody sad.

saddle noun (plural **saddles**) **1** a seat fixed on the back of a horse for the rider to sit on. **2** a seat on a bicycle or motorcycle. ~ verb (**saddles, saddling, saddled**) to put a saddle on a horse. ✳ **saddle with** to give somebody a task or responsibility that they do not want.

sadist /say dist/ noun (plural **sadists**) somebody who enjoys causing other people physical pain. ➤ **sadism** noun, **sadistic** adjective.

safari noun (plural **safaris**) an expedition to observe wild animals in their natural habitat or to hunt them.

safari park noun (plural **safari parks**) a large area of land where wild animals are kept for visitors to look at as they drive through.

safe (**safer, safest**) adjective **1** not, or no longer, in danger. **2** not dangerous. **3** unlikely to upset or offend people. **4** trustworthy; reliable. ~ noun (plural **safes**) a specially strengthened cabinet or room for keeping money and valuables in. ➤ **safely** adverb.

safeguard noun (plural **safeguards**) something designed to give protection, for example to ensure that a law or contract cannot be used to harm people. ~ verb (**safeguards, safeguarding, safeguarded**) to protect somebody or something.

safekeeping noun protection, or the state of being kept safe.

safe sex noun sexual activity in which precautions are taken to prevent the transmission of diseases.

safety noun the state of being safe.

safety belt noun (plural **safety belts**) a seat belt in a vehicle.

safety net noun (plural **safety nets**) **1** a net designed to protect acrobats by catching them if they fall. **2** a protective measure.

safety pin noun (plural **safety pins**) an oval clasp with a guard that covers its point when fastened.

saffron noun **1** a yellow spice made from the dried stigmas of a type of crocus. **2** an orange-yellow colour.

sag verb (**sags, sagging, sagged**) to hang down in the middle when it should be taut.

saga noun (plural **sagas**) **1** a medieval story dealing with legendary adventures. **2** a long and complicated story with many different characters and events.

sage[1] noun (plural **sages**) a person famous for great wisdom. ~ adjective wise. ➤ **sagely** adverb.

sage[2] noun a plant of the mint family whose leaves are used as a herb.

Sagittarius noun the ninth sign of the zodiac (the Archer).

sago /say goh/ noun a white powder made from the pith of a palm, used in puddings.

said verb past tense of SAY.

sail noun (plural **sails**) **1** a large piece of fabric spread to catch the wind and propel a ship or boat. **2** a flat board forming an arm of a windmill. **3** a voyage by ship or boat. ~ verb (**sails, sailing, sailed**) **1** to travel in a boat or ship. **2** to control a boat or ship. **3** to begin a journey by water. **4** to move easily and smoothly. ✳ **sail through** to succeed in something easily.

sailboard noun (plural **sailboards**) a flat board with a mast and a sail, used in windsurfing.

sailing boat noun (plural **sailing boats**) a boat propelled by sails.

sailor noun (plural **sailors**) a member of a ship's crew.

saint noun (plural **saints**) **1** a person officially recognized by the Christian church as having lived an exceptionally good and holy life. **2** an outstandingly good or patient person. ➤ **sainthood** noun, **saintly** adjective.

sake

sake *noun* (*plural* **sakes**) benefit, purpose, or interest. ✱ **for the sake of 1** in order to help or please somebody. **2** in order to gain or achieve something: *I gave in for the sake of a little peace and quiet.*

salad *noun* (*plural* **salads**) a dish of mixed raw vegetables.

salamander *noun* (*plural* **salamanders**) **1** an amphibian like a lizard but with a soft moist skin. **2** a mythical animal that can live in fire.

salami /sa lah mi/ *noun* (*plural* **salamis**) a type of large spicy sausage, eaten cold in slices.

salary *noun* (*plural* **salaries**) a fixed monthly payment made to an employee. ➤ **salaried** *adjective*.

sale *noun* (*plural* **sales**) **1** the act of selling something. **2** an event at which goods are sold or auctioned. **3** a period in which goods are sold at reduced prices. ✱ **for/on sale** available to be bought.

salesmanship *noun* skill at selling.

salesperson *noun* (*plural* **salespersons** *or* **salespeople**) a person employed to sell goods. ➤ **salesman** *noun*, **saleswoman** *noun*.

salient /say li int/ *adjective* very noticeable or important. ~ *noun* (*plural* **salients**) a piece of land that juts out, especially into enemy territory.

saline /say lien/ *adjective* containing salt. ➤ **salinity** *noun*.

saliva /sa lie va/ *noun* a liquid secreted into the mouth by glands to help with chewing and digesting food. ➤ **salivary** *adjective*.

salivate /sa li vayt/ *verb* (**salivates, salivating, salivated**) to have a flow of saliva in the mouth. ➤ **salivation** *noun*.

sallow *adjective* sickly yellowish in colour.

salmon /sa mon/ *noun* (*plural* **salmons** *or* **salmon**) a large food fish with pink flesh.

salmonella /sal mo ne la/ *noun* (*plural* **salmonellae** /sal mo ne lee/) a bacterium that causes food poisoning.

salon *noun* (*plural* **salons**) **1** a place where hairdressers, beauticians, fashion designers, etc work. **2** an elegant reception room or living room.

saloon *noun* (*plural* **saloons**) **1** a comfortable bar in a pub. **2** *N American* a bar. **3** a car with a hard roof and a separate boot.

salsa *noun* **1** *Music* a style of lively Latin American popular music or dancing. **2** a spicy Mexican sauce.

salt *noun* (*plural* **salts**) **1** sodium chloride occurring naturally, and used in the form of white powder or crystals for seasoning or preserving food. **2** *Science* a chemical compound that results when the hydrogen atoms in an acid are replaced by an atom of a metal. ✱ **take something with a pinch/grain of salt** to be cautious about believing something to be true. ➤ **salty** *adjective*.

saltcellar *noun* (*plural* **saltcellars**) a small open dish or shaker for salt.

salutary /sal ew ta ri/ *adjective* said about a bad experience: offering an opportunity to learn from it or improve yourself.

salutation *noun* (*plural* **salutations**) a greeting.

salute *verb* (**salutes, saluting, saluted**) **1** to raise your hand to the side of your head as a sign of respect to a superior. **2** *formal* to greet somebody. **3** to praise or admire somebody or something. ~ *noun* **1** an act of saluting somebody. **2** a ceremonial firing of guns into the air.

salvage *noun* **1** the act of rescuing a ship or its cargo from loss at sea. **2** property saved or rescued from a wreck or fire. ~ *verb* (**salvages,**

salvaging, salvaged) **1** to rescue a ship or its cargo. **2** to save something from a building, etc that has been destroyed or from a failure or disaster. ➤ **salvageable** *adjective*.

salvation *noun* **1** being saved from danger or trouble. **2** somebody or something that saves somebody. **3** in Christianity, being saved from sin and damnation.

salvo *noun* (*plural* **salvos** *or* **salvoes**) **1** a firing of a number of large guns all at the same time. **2** a burst of criticism or applause.

same *adjective* **1** being one single thing, person, or group: *We were all sitting at the same table.* **2** identical in appearance, quantity, type, etc: *They were both wearing the same dress.* ~ *adverb* (**the same**) in the same way: *two words spelt the same.* ✳ **all/just the same** nevertheless.

sample *noun* (*plural* **samples**) a part, single item, or small number of things that shows what a larger whole or group is like. ~ *verb* (**samples, sampling, sampled**) **1** to try a sample of something to see what it is like. **2** to take part of something as a sample.

samurai /sa moo rie *or* sa mew rie/ *noun* (*plural* **samurai**) a member of the warrior class in ancient Japan.

sanatorium *noun* (*plural* **sanatoriums** *or* **sanatoria**) a clinic for treating people with long-term illnesses.

sanctify *verb* (**sanctifies, sanctifying, sanctified**) to make something sacred or holy. ➤ **sanctification** *noun*.

sanctimonious *adjective* showing that you consider yourself to be good or pious, often by criticizing other people.

sanction *noun* (*plural* **sanctions**) **1** official permission. **2** a penalty attached to an offence. **3** (**sanctions**) economic or military measures taken to force a nation to comply with international law. ~ *verb* (**sanctions, sanctioning, sanctioned**) to give approval for, or consent to, something.

sanctity *noun* the quality or state of being holy.

sanctuary *noun* (*plural* **sanctuaries**) **1** a place where a person can find refuge and protection. **2** a place where wildlife is protected. **3** the part of a church where the altar stands.

sand *noun* **1** tiny particles formed when rock disintegrates, found mainly on beaches and the beds of seas and rivers. **2** (*also* **sands**) an area of sand. ~ *verb* (**sands, sanding, sanded**) to smooth a surface by rubbing it with sandpaper.

sandal *noun* (*plural* **sandals**) a light shoe consisting of a sole held on the foot by straps. ➤ **sandalled** *adjective*.

sandbag *noun* (*plural* **sandbags**) a bag filled with sand and used to form a barrier.

sandbank *noun* (*plural* **sandbanks**) a large deposit of sand that becomes visible at low tide.

sandcastle *noun* (*plural* **sandcastles**) a model of a castle made from sand.

sander *noun* (*plural* **sanders**) a power tool used for smoothing a surface.

sandpaper *noun* paper with a thin layer of sand glued to it, used for smoothing wood. ~ *verb* (**sandpapers, sandpapering, sandpapered**) to rub or smooth a surface with sandpaper.

sandpit *noun* (*plural* **sandpits**) an enclosure containing sand for children to play in.

sandstone *noun* a rock consisting of compressed sand grains.

sandstorm *noun* (*plural* **sandstorms**) a strong wind driving clouds of sand in a desert.

sandwich *noun* (*plural* **sandwiches**) **1** two slices of bread with a filling between. **2** a sponge cake with jam or

sandwich course

cream between its layers. ~ *verb* (**sandwiches, sandwiching, sandwiched**) to put something between two things of a different kind of thing.

sandwich course *noun* (*plural* **sandwich courses**) a course in which periods of study alternate with periods of practical work experience.

sandy *adjective* (**sandier, sandiest**) **1** consisting of or sprinkled with sand. **2** yellowish red.

sane *adjective* (**saner, sanest**) **1** mentally sound; not mad. **2** sensible or rational.

sang *verb* past tense of SING.

sangfroid /songfrwah/ *noun* a tendency not to get excited or emotional in difficult situations; composure.

sanguinary /sanggwinari/ *adjective formal* bloodthirsty or murderous.

sanguine /sanggwin/ *adjective* cheerfully confident and optimistic.

sanitary *adjective* **1** to do with keeping people healthy. **2** hygienic.

sanitary towel *noun* (*plural* **sanitary towels**) a pad worn by a woman during her period to absorb the flow of blood.

sanitation *noun* facilities that promote hygiene and prevent disease, such as the disposal of sewage and collection of rubbish.

sanitize or **sanitise** *verb* (**sanitizes, sanitizing, sanitized** or **sanitises**, etc) **1** to make something hygienic. **2** to make something unpleasant more acceptable. ➤ **sanitization** or **sanitisation** *noun*.

sanity *noun* the state of being sane.

sank *verb* past tense of SINK.

Sanskrit *noun* an ancient language of the people of India.

sap *noun* a watery fluid that circulates through a plant, taking food to its various parts. ~ *verb* (**saps, sapping, sapped**) to weaken something or somebody gradually.

sapling *noun* (*plural* **saplings**) a young tree.

sapphire /safier/ *noun* (*plural* **sapphires**) a blue gemstone.

Saracen *noun* (*plural* **Saracens**) *History* a Muslim at the time of the Crusades.

sarcasm *noun* ironic language used to express contempt or bitterness. ➤ **sarcastic** *adjective*, **sarcastically** *adverb*.

sarcophagus /sahkofagus/ *noun* (*plural* **sarcophagi** /sahkofagie/) a large decorated stone coffin.

Word History Sarcophagus comes from a Greek word meaning 'flesh-eating'. It was once believed that the stone used to make coffins actually destroyed the flesh of the dead bodies in them.

sardine *noun* (*plural* **sardines**) a small fish of the herring family.

sardonic *adjective* grimly making fun of something or somebody; mocking. ➤ **sardonically** *adverb*.

sari or **saree** /sahri/ *noun* (*plural* **saris** or **sarees**) a length of cloth draped over the body, worn as a dress by women from India.

sarong /sarong/ *noun* (*plural* **sarongs**) a long strip of cloth wrapped around the lower part of the body, worn by men and women in parts of southeast Asia.

sash[1] *noun* (*plural* **sashes**) a band of cloth worn round the waist or over one shoulder.

sash[2] *noun* (*plural* **sashes**) a frame holding a pane of glass in a window.

sash window *noun* (*plural* **sash windows**) a window with two sashes that slide up and down.

SAT *abbreviation* standard assessment task.

sat *verb* past tense of SIT.

Satan *noun* the Devil. ➤ **satanic** *adjective*.

satanism *noun* the worship of Satan. ➤ **satanist** *noun and adjective*.

satchel *noun* (*plural* **satchels**) a bag with a shoulder strap.

satellite *noun* (*plural* **satellites**) **1** an object in space, especially a moon, orbiting another larger object. **2** a spacecraft orbiting the earth or another planet, used for collecting scientific information or in communications.

satellite dish *noun* (*plural* **satellite dishes**) a dish-shaped aerial used to transmit and receive signals for satellite television and other satellite communications.

satellite television *noun* television broadcasting using satellites to transmit and receive signals.

satiate /say shi ayt/ *verb* (**satiates, satiating, satiated**) to give somebody as much as or more than they want. ➤ **satiation** *noun*.

satin *noun* (*plural* **satins**) a smooth silky fabric. ➤ **satiny** *adjective*.

satire *noun* (*plural* **satires**) *English* **1** the use of wit, irony, or sarcasm to make fun of foolishness or wickedness. **2** a literary work that uses satire. ➤ **satirical** *adjective*, **satirically** *adverb*, **satirist** *noun*.

satirize *or* **satirise** *verb* (**satirizes, satirizing, satirized** *or* **satirises**, etc) to criticize or ridicule something or somebody with satire.

satisfaction *noun* **1** the act of satisfying somebody or something. **2** a good feeling arising from doing something well or seeing that something has been well done.

satisfactory *adjective* good enough; acceptable. ➤ **satisfactorily** *adverb*.

satisfy *verb* (**satisfies, satisfying, satisfied**) **1** to give somebody enough, or do enough for somebody, to make them feel pleased. **2** to fulfil or comply with requirements. **3** to convince somebody that something is the case: *I'm satisfied that she was telling truth.*

satsuma *noun* (*plural* **satsumas**) a sweet type of tangerine with a loose skin.

saturate /sa choo rayt/ *verb* (**saturates, saturating, saturated**) **1** *Science* to fill a substance with so much of another substance that no more of it can be absorbed. **2** to make something or somebody thoroughly wet. ➤ **saturated** *adjective*, **saturation** *noun*.

Saturday *noun* (*plural* **Saturdays**) the seventh day of the week; the day following Friday.

sauce *noun* (*plural* **sauces**) **1** a thick liquid used to give an extra taste to food. **2** *informal* cheek or impudence.

sauce boat *noun* (*plural* **sauce boats**) a shallow jug for serving sauce, gravy, etc.

saucepan *noun* (*plural* **saucepans**) a deep cooking pan with a long handle and a lid.

saucer *noun* (*plural* **saucers**) a small shallow dish on which a cup is placed.

saucy *adjective* (**saucier, sauciest**) *informal* **1** cheeky. **2** sexually suggestive. ➤ **saucily** *adverb*.

sauerkraut /sow er krowt/ *noun* finely chopped pickled cabbage.

sauna *noun* (*plural* **saunas**) a small room filled with hot dry air or steam, used to clean and refresh the body.

saunter *verb* (**saunters, sauntering, sauntered**) to walk about in a lazy or casual manner. ➤ **saunter** *noun*.

sausage *noun* (*plural* **sausages**) **1** a food consisting of a tubular skin filled with finely chopped meat, eaten grilled or fried. **2** a food made from cooked or cured meat and spices, eaten cold in thin slices.

sauté /soh tay/ *verb* (**sautés, sautéing, sautéed** *or* **sautéd**) to fry something quickly in oil or fat.

savage *adjective* **1** brutal; cruel and violent. **2** very severe. ~ *noun* (*plural* **savages**) **1** a member of a people

savanna

regarded as lacking a developed culture. **2** a brutal person. ~ *verb* (**savages, savaging, savaged**) **1** to attack or treat somebody brutally or ferociously. **2** to criticize somebody or something ruthlessly. ➤ **savagely** *adverb*, **savagery** *noun*.

savanna *or* **savannah** *noun* (*plural* **savannas** *or* **savannahs**) *Geography* a wide area of tropical grassland with scattered trees.

save¹ *verb* (**saves, saving, saved**) **1** to prevent somebody or something from being harmed or dying or being lost. **2** in Christianity, to preserve a soul from damnation. **3** to put something, such as money, aside so that it can be used in future. **4** to avoid wasting a resource. **5** *ICT* to preserve data by storing it in the computer's memory. **6** to prevent an opponent from scoring or winning a goal or point. ➤ **save** *noun*.

save² *preposition and conjunction* except or other than.

saving *noun* (*plural* **savings**) **1** an amount of money, time, etc saved. **2** (**savings**) money that has been put aside for future use.

saviour *noun* (*plural* **saviours**) **1** a person who saves somebody or something from danger or harm. **2** (**the Saviour**) in Christian belief, Jesus Christ.

savour *verb* (**savours, savouring, savoured**) to enjoy and appreciate something to the full. ~ *noun* (*plural* **savours**) a characteristic taste or smell.

savoury *adjective* said about food: having a salty or spicy flavour. ~ *noun* (*plural* **savouries**) a savoury snack or dish.

saw¹ *verb* past tense of SEE¹.

saw² *noun* (*plural* **saws**) a tool with a long toothed blade, used for cutting wood, etc. ~ *verb* (**saws, sawing, sawed, sawn**) to cut something with a saw.

sawdust *noun* wood powder produced in sawing.

sawmill *noun* (*plural* **sawmills**) a factory where wood is cut into logs or planks.

Saxon *noun* (*plural* **Saxons**) a member of a Germanic people that settled in southern England in the fifth and sixth centuries. ➤ **Saxon** *adjective*.

saxophone *noun* (*plural* **saxophones**) *Music* a brass instrument with a single reed like a clarinet and a pipe that is usually curved at the top and bottom. ➤ **saxophonist** *noun*.

say *verb* (**says, saying, said**) **1** to state something in spoken words. **2** to utter a sound, word, sentence, etc. **3** to recite or repeat something. **4** said about a clock or dial: to indicate or show something. **5** to report or allege something. **6** to assume something for the purposes of discussion: *Say she is telling the truth, what then?* ✲ **have a/no say in something** to have an influence (or no influence) on what is decided.

saying *noun* (*plural* **sayings**) a well-known phrase or proverb.

scab *noun* (*plural* **scabs**) **1** a crust of hardened blood that forms over a wound. **2** *informal, offensive* a person who refuses to take part in a strike. ~ *verb* (**scabs, scabbing, scabbed**) to become covered with a scab. ➤ **scabby** *adjective*.

scabbard *noun* (*plural* **scabbards**) a sheath for a sword or dagger.

scaffold *noun* (*plural* **scaffolds**) *History* a raised platform formerly used for executions.

scaffolding *noun* **1** a temporary structure of poles and planks, erected on the outside of a building that is being built or repaired. **2** the poles and planks used for this.

scald *verb* (**scalds, scalding, scalded**)

to injure or burn somebody with hot liquid or steam. ➤ **scald** *noun*.

scale[1] *noun* (*plural* **scales**) **1** one of the overlapping plates that cover and protect the skin of fish and reptiles. **2** a dry flake of dead skin. **3** a white deposit of lime formed on the inside of a kettle or pipe caused by hard water. **4** a hard deposit on the teeth.

scale[2] *noun* **1** (*usually* **scales**) an instrument for weighing. **2** either pan or tray of a balance. ✱ **tip the scales** to be a deciding factor.

scale[3] *noun* **1** a range of values used in measuring something: *the Richter scale*. **2** the size or extent of something: *She spends money on a grand scale*. **3** the ratio of the size of an object to a model, map, etc representing it: *a scale of one centimetre to one kilometre*. **4** *Music* a series of regularly rising or falling notes. ~ *verb* (**scales, scaling, scaled**) to climb up or over something high. ✱ **scale down/up** to decrease (or increase) something. **to scale** drawn or made in exact proportion to the original.

scalene /skayleen/ *adjective* *Maths* said about a triangle: having sides of equal length.

scallop *noun* (*plural* **scallops**) **1** an edible shellfish with a shell consisting of two fan-shaped halves with wavy edges. **2** each of a series of rounded projections forming a border. ➤ **scalloped** *adjective*.

scalp *noun* (*plural* **scalps**) **1** the skin at the top and back of the human head. **2** a part of this with the hair attached, formerly cut from an enemy as a battle trophy by Native American warriors. ~ *verb* (**scalps, scalping, scalped**) to remove the scalp of an enemy.

scalpel *noun* (*plural* **scalpels**) a small sharp knife with a thin blade, used in surgery.

scaly *adjective* (**scalier, scaliest**) **1** covered with scales. **2** dry and flaky.

scam *noun* (*plural* **scams**) *informal* a dishonest scheme for obtaining money.

scamp *noun* (*plural* **scamps**) a mischievous child.

scamper *verb* (**scampers, scampering, scampered**) to run quickly, lightly, and playfully. ➤ **scamper** *noun*.

scampi *plural noun* large prawns prepared and cooked.

scan *verb* (**scans, scanning, scanned**) **1** to glance at something hastily. **2** to look at or through something carefully searching for something or somebody. **3** to examine, record, or search something using an electronic device that sends out radiation and receives it back. **4** *ICT* to convert data into a digital format so that it can be processed by a computer. **5** *English* said about verse: to conform to a metrical pattern. ~ *noun* (*plural* **scans**) **1** the act of scanning. **2** a medical examination using a scanner. **3** an image produced by a scanner.

scandal *noun* (*plural* **scandals**) **1** an act or event that causes great public indignation. **2** gossip about people and their bad actions. ➤ **scandalous** *adjective*, **scandalously** *adverb*.

scandalize *or* **scandalise** *verb* (**scandalizes, scandalizing, scandalized** *or* **scandalises**, etc) to shock or offend somebody by immoral or disgraceful behaviour.

scanner *noun* (*plural* **scanners**) **1** a device used to scan the human body with X-rays, ultrasonic waves, etc. **2** a device that converts pictures or text into a form that can be processed by a computer.

scansion *noun* *English* the analysis of verse to show its metre.

scant *adjective* barely sufficient; inadequate.

scanty *adjective* (**scantier, scantiest**) small or insufficient in quantity. ➤ **scantily** *adverb*.

scapegoat *noun* (*plural* **scapegoats**) a person who is blamed for the wrongdoing of somebody else.

scapula *noun* (*plural* **scapulae** /ska pew lee/ *or* **scapulas**) *Science* the shoulder blade.

scar *noun* (*plural* **scars**) **1** a mark left on the skin or body tissue by a healed injury. **2** a psychological ill effect caused by trauma. ~ *verb* (**scars, scarring, scarred**) to form a scar, or mark something with a scar.

scarce (**scarcer, scarcest**) *adjective* **1** not plentiful or not sufficient to meet demand. **2** few in number. ➤ **scarcity** *noun*.

scarcely *adverb* **1** only just. **2** almost not. **3** certainly or probably not.

scare *verb* (**scares, scaring, scared**) **1** to frighten somebody suddenly. **2** (**scare off/away**) to drive a person or animal away by frightening them. **3** to become afraid. ~ *noun* (*plural* **scares**) **1** a sudden fright. **2** a widespread state of alarm caused by something: *a bomb scare*.

scarecrow *noun* (*plural* **scarecrows**) an object made to look like a person, set up to frighten birds away from crops.

scarf *noun* (*plural* **scarves** *or* **scarfs**) a strip or square of cloth worn round the neck or head.

scarlet *noun* a vivid red colour.

scarlet fever *noun* an infectious disease causing a fever and a red rash.

scarp *noun* (*plural* **scarps**) *Geography* a steep slope.

scarper *verb* (**scarpers, scarpering, scarpered**) *informal* to run away.

scarves *noun* plural of SCARF.

scary *adjective* (**scarier, scariest**) *informal* causing fear or alarm. ➤ **scarily** *adverb*.

scathing /skay *th*ing/ *adjective* bitterly severe; scornful. ➤ **scathingly** *adverb*.

scatter *verb* (**scatters, scattering, scattered**) **1** to throw things in all directions or at random. **2** to separate and go quickly in various directions.

scatterbrained *adjective* disorganized or unable to concentrate.

scattered *adjective* found in various places over an area.

scavenge *verb* (**scavenges, scavenging, scavenged**) **1** to search for something useful among discarded items. **2** said about animals: to search for and feed on decaying flesh or refuse. ➤ **scavenger** *noun*.

scenario /si nah ri oh/ *noun* (*plural* **scenarios**) **1** *Drama* an outline of a dramatic work, novel, or film. **2** a description of how something could or might happen.

scene *noun* (*plural* **scenes**) **1** a setting in which something real or imaginary happens. **2** a landscape or view. **3** *Drama* a separate incident or passage of dialogue in a play, film, etc, especially a subdivision of an act of a play. **4** a public display of strong feeling that is embarrassing for other people. **5** an area of activity: *the drug scene*. ✻ **behind the scenes** where nobody can see.

scenery *noun* **1** the natural features of a landscape. **2** *Drama* the painted surfaces or hangings used on a theatre stage or film set.

scenic *adjective* having, or to do with, attractive natural scenery. ➤ **scenically** *adverb*.

scent *noun* (*plural* **scents**) **1** a pleasant smell. **2** a light perfume worn on the skin. **3** a smell left by an animal, by which it can be traced. ~ *verb* (**scents, scenting, scented**) **1** to give a pleasant smell to. **2** to find something by smell. ➤ **scented** *adjective*.

sceptic /skep tik/ *noun* (*plural* **sceptics**) a person who doubts accepted opinions or beliefs. ➤ **sceptical** *adjective*, **scepticism** *noun*.

sceptre /septer/ *noun* (*plural* **sceptres**) a staff carried by a ruler as a symbol of sovereignty. ➤ **sceptred** *adjective*.

schedule /she dewl/ *noun* (*plural* **schedules**) 1 a plan of things to be done and the order in which to do them. 2 a timetable. ~ *verb* (**schedules, scheduling, scheduled**) 1 to plan for something to happen at a fixed time. 2 to include something in a schedule. ✶ **on schedule** at the planned time.

scheduled *adjective* said about a flight: operating as part of a regular timetable, not chartered.

schematic /skee ma tik/ *adjective* representing something in a simplified way, for example as a diagram or chart. ➤ **schematically** *adverb*.

scheme *noun* (*plural* **schemes**) 1 a plan for putting something into effect. 2 a systematic arrangement or design: *a colour scheme*. 3 a secret or dishonest plan. ~ *verb* (**schemes, scheming, schemed**) to make a dishonest plan. ➤ **schemer** *noun*, **scheming** *adjective*.

scherzo /skair tsoh/ *noun* (*plural* **scherzos** *or* **scherzi** /skair tsee/) *Music* a lively instrumental piece of music.

schism *noun* (*plural* **schisms**) a fundamental disagreement or split between parts of an institution or organization.

schizophrenia /skit soh free ni a/ *noun* a mental disorder characterized by loss of contact with reality and changes in personality. ➤ **schizophrenic** *adjective and noun*.

scholar *noun* (*plural* **scholars**) 1 a person who has studied a particular academic subject deeply. 2 a student holding a scholarship.

scholarly *adjective* characteristic of scholars or suitable for advanced academic study.

scholarship *noun* (*plural* **scholarships**) 1 academic learning and work. 2 a grant of money awarded to a student to pay for their education and upkeep.

school[1] *noun* (*plural* **schools**) 1 a building or organization for educating children. 2 an establishment that teaches a particular subject or skill. 3 a department or faculty in a university. 4 a group of philosophers, artists, etc, who share the same approach to a subject. ~ *verb* (**schools, schooling, schooled**) to train somebody in a subject or skill.

school[2] *noun* (*plural* **schools**) a large number of fish or sea animals swimming together.

schooling *noun* education received in school.

schooner *noun* (*plural* **schooners**) 1 a sailing ship with two or more masts. 2 a large sherry glass.

sciatica /sie a ti ka/ *noun* pain in the back of the thigh and lower back caused by pressure on a large nerve that runs through this area of the body.

science *noun* (*plural* **sciences**) 1 the study of the physical and natural world, especially by observation and experiments. 2 a particular branch of this study.

science fiction *noun* stories set in the future, in which the writers imagine scientific developments such as travelling through space or time and life on other planets.

scientific *adjective* 1 to do with or based on science. 2 systematic. ➤ **scientifically** *adverb*.

scientist *noun* (*plural* **scientists**) a person who studies a science or is an expert in one of the sciences.

sci-fi /sie fie/ *noun informal* science fiction.

scimitar /si mi ter/ *noun* (*plural* **scimitars**) a short sword with a curved blade.

scintillating /sin ti lay ting/ *adjective* **1** shining or sparkling. **2** lively or witty.

scissors *plural noun* a cutting instrument with two blades pivoted so that their cutting edges slide past each other.

scoff[1] *verb* (**scoffs, scoffing, scoffed**) to speak contemptuously about something.

scoff[2] *verb* (**scoffs, scoffing, scoffed**) *informal* to eat something greedily or rapidly.

scold *verb* (**scolds, scolding, scolded**) to speak angrily to somebody about their behaviour; to tell somebody off.

scone *noun* (*plural* **scones**) a small lightly sweetened cake made from dough or batter.

scoop *noun* (*plural* **scoops**) **1** a large ladle with a deep bowl. **2** a utensil for spooning out ice cream. **3** a deep bucket forming part of a mechanical digger. **4** *informal* a news item published by a newspaper ahead of its competitors. ~ *verb* (**scoops, scooping, scooped**) **1** to take something out or up with a scoop. **2** (*often* **scoop out**) to make a hollow in something. **3** to pick something up quickly. **4** *informal* to report a news item before another newspaper.

scoot *verb* (**scoots, scooting, scooted**) *informal* to go or run suddenly and swiftly.

scooter *noun* (*plural* **scooters**) **1** a child's toy consisting of a narrow board with a wheel at each end and an upright steering handle, propelled by pushing one foot against the ground while standing on the board with the other. **2** a light motorcycle with small wheels.

scope *noun* **1** space or opportunity for action, thought, or development. **2** the extent or range of an activity or responsibility.

scorch *verb* (**scorches, scorching, scorched**) to burn something slightly so that its surface turns brown. ➤ **scorch** *noun*.

scorching *adjective informal* very hot.

score *noun* (*plural* **scores**) **1** the number of points, goals, etc a team or individual makes in a game. **2** (*plural* **score**) a group of twenty people or things. **3** (*often* **scores**) an unspecified large quantity. **4** *Music* the written or printed music of a composition. ~ *verb* (**scores, scoring, scored**) **1** to gain points, etc in a game. **2** to keep the score in a game or contest. **3** to mark a surface with lines or scratches. **4** *Music* to arrange music for a certain combination of instruments. ➤ **scorer** *noun*.

scorn *noun* strong contempt or disdain. ~ *verb* (**scorns, scorning, scorned**) **1** to treat somebody with angry contempt. **2** to refuse or reject something contemptuously. ➤ **scornful** *adjective*, **scornfully** *adverb*.

Scorpio *noun* the eighth sign of the zodiac (the Scorpion).

scorpion *noun* (*plural* **scorpions**) a land animal that looks like a small lobster with a curved-up tail that has a poisonous sting at its tip.

Scotch *noun* (*also* **Scotch whisky**) whisky made in Scotland.

scotch *verb* (**scotches, scotching, scotched**) to put an end to something.

scot-free *adjective* without any penalty or injury.

scoundrel *noun* (*plural* **scoundrels**) an unscrupulous or dishonest person.

scour *verb* (**scours, scouring, scoured**) **1** to clean something by rubbing it with an abrasive. **2** to search e.g. an area thoroughly.

scourge *noun* (*plural* **scourges**) **1** something that causes serious trouble or distress. **2** a whip.

scout *noun* (*plural* **scouts**) **1** a person

sent ahead to collect information about an area or an enemy's position or strength. **2** (**Scout**) a member of the Scout Association, a worldwide movement for young people. ~ *verb* (**scouts, scouting, scouted**) **1** to go ahead of a main group collecting information. **2** (*often* **scout around**) to go around looking for something.

scowl *verb* (**scowls, scowling, scowled**) to frown in an angry or displeased way. ➤ **scowl** *noun*.

scrabble *verb* (**scrabbles, scrabbling, scrabbled**) **1** to scratch or scrape about to find or catch hold of something. **2** to scramble or clamber.

scraggy *adjective* (**scraggier, scraggiest**) unpleasantly thin and bony.

scram *verb* (**scrams, scramming, scrammed**) *informal* to leave hurriedly.

scramble *verb* (**scrambles, scrambling, scrambled**) **1** to move or climb using your hands and feet. **2** to compete to get something in a disorganized way. **3** to muddle something. **4** said about a fighter aircraft: to take off quickly in response to an alert. **5** to beat eggs and cook them in a pan. **6** to put a message into a form that needs decoding. ~ *noun* (*plural* **scrambles**) **1** an act of scrambling. **2** a motorcycle race over rough ground.

scrap¹ *noun* (*plural* **scraps**) **1** a small detached fragment of something. **2** (**scraps**) discarded or leftover food. **3** discarded metal suitable for processing and reuse. ~ *verb* (**scraps, scrapping, scrapped**) **1** to discard or get rid of something. **2** to convert something into scrap.

scrap² *verb* (**scraps, scrapping, scrapped**) *informal* to fight or quarrel. ➤ **scrap** *noun*.

scrapbook *noun* (*plural* **scrapbooks**) a blank book for pasting pictures or cuttings in.

scrape *verb* (**scrapes, scraping, scraped**) **1** to damage or injure something by rubbing it against a rough surface. **2** to remove material from a surface with an edged tool. **3** to make a harsh grating sound. **4** to achieve an exam grade or a pass by a narrow margin. ~ *noun* (*plural* **scrapes**) **1** an act or sound of scraping. **2** an injury or mark caused by scraping. **3** *informal* an awkward situation. ✶ **scrape through** to succeed with difficulty or by a narrow margin. **scrape together** to collect an amount of money, etc with difficulty. ➤ **scraper** *noun*.

scrappy *adjective* (**scrappier, scrappiest**) **1** made up of separate bits that do not form a proper whole; disjointed. **2** careless. ➤ **scrappily** *adverb*.

scrapyard *noun* (*plural* **scrapyards**) a yard where scrap metal is collected.

scratch *verb* (**scratches, scratching, scratched**) **1** to make a surface mark or cut in something with a sharp object. **2** to scrape or rub part of your body to relieve itching. **3** to withdraw from a competition. ~ *noun* (*plural* **scratches**) **1** a mark or injury produced by scratching. **2** *informal* a slight wound. **3** an act of scratching. ~ *adjective* put together haphazardly or hastily. ✶ **from scratch** from the very beginning. **up to scratch** satisfactory or adequate.

scratchcard *noun* (*plural* **scratchcards**) a small card with a coated section to be scratched off to reveal whether you have won a prize.

scrawl *verb* (**scrawls, scrawling, scrawled**) to write or draw something awkwardly or hastily. ~ *noun* an untidy piece of writing or drawing.

scrawny *adjective* (**scrawnier, scrawniest**) thin and bony.

scream *verb* (**screams, screaming, screamed**) to make a loud piercing

scree

cry in fear or pain. ~ *noun* (*plural* **screams**) **1** a loud shrill cry or noise. **2** *informal* a highly amusing person or thing.

scree *noun* *Geography* a mass of loose stones on a hillside or mountain slope.

screech *verb* (**screeches, screeching, screeched**) to make a shrill piercing cry or sound. ➤ **screech** *noun*.

screed *noun* (*plural* **screeds**) a long speech or piece of writing.

screen *noun* (*plural* **screens**) **1** *ICT* the part of a television set or computer monitor on which images are displayed. **2** a blank surface on which photographs or films can be projected. **3** (**the screen**) films or television. **4** a partition or curtain used to divide a room or provide privacy. **5** something that protects or conceals. ~ *verb* (**screens, screening, screened**) **1** to shelter or protect somebody or something with a screen. **2** (*also* **screen off**) to separate or enclose something, for example part of a room, with a screen. **3** to show a film or TV programme. **4** to carry out a test on somebody to check whether they have a disease. **5** to check up on people to see if they are suitable for a job, etc.

screenplay *noun* (*plural* **screenplays**) the script of a film.

screen test *noun* (*plural* **screen tests**) an audition to assess an actor's suitability for a film role.

screw *noun* (*plural* **screws**) **1** a metal pin with a spiral thread running round it and a slotted head, used to fasten parts together. **2** the propeller of a ship or aircraft. ~ *verb* (**screws, screwing, screwed**) **1** to fasten, close, or tighten something by twisting a part with a thread onto another part with a matching thread. **2** to join or assemble something with screws.
∗ **screw up 1** to crush or crumple a piece of paper, etc. **2** *informal* to make a mess of something.

screwdriver *noun* (*plural* **screwdrivers**) a tool with a tip that fits into the head of a screw to turn it.

scribble *verb* (**scribbles, scribbling, scribbled**) to write or draw something hurriedly or carelessly. ➤ **scribble** *noun*.

scribe *noun* (*plural* **scribes**) *History* a person who copies manuscripts.

scrimp *verb* (**scrimps, scrimping, scrimped**) to spend as little money as possible because you do not have much money or you want to save money.

script *noun* (*plural* **scripts**) **1** *Drama* the written text of a stage play, film, or broadcast. **2** written characters; handwriting.

scripture *noun* (*plural* **scriptures**) **1** the sacred writings of a religion. **2** (*often* **Scripture** *or* **the scriptures**) the sacred writings of Christianity as contained in the Bible. ➤ **scriptural** *adjective*.

scroll *noun* (*plural* **scrolls**) a roll of parchment with writing or drawing on it. ~ *verb* (**scrolls, scrolling, scrolled**) *ICT* to move text on a computer screen up and down to view different parts of it.

scrotum *noun* (*plural* **scrota** *or* **scrotums**) the pouch of skin that contains the testicles.

scrounge *verb* (**scrounges, scrounging, scrounged**) *informal* to try to get something from somebody without paying for it. ➤ **scrounger** *noun*.

scrub[1] *verb* (**scrubs, scrubbing, scrubbed**) **1** to clean something by hard rubbing. **2** *informal* to cancel or abandon something. ~ *noun* an act of scrubbing.

scrub[2] *noun* **1** vegetation consisting chiefly of small trees or shrubs.

2 an area covered with such vegetation. ➤ **scrubby** adjective.

scruff noun (plural **scruffs**) the back of the neck.

scruffy adjective (**scruffier**, **scruffiest**) careless and untidy in your personal appearance. ➤ **scruffily** adverb.

scrum noun (plural **scrums**) **1** in rugby, a set piece in which the forwards of each side crouch in a tight formation and push against each other as the ball is thrown in between them. **2** informal a disorderly crowd.

scrumptious adjective informal delicious or delightful.

scrunch verb (**scrunches**, **scrunching**, **scrunched**) to crunch or crush something.

scruple noun (plural **scruples**) a feeling of doubt about the morality of an action. ~ verb (**scruples**, **scrupling**, **scrupled**) to hesitate to do something because you feel it is wrong.

scrupulous adjective **1** very careful and conscientious. **2** eager to avoid doing anything wrong or immoral. ➤ **scrupulously** adverb.

scrutinize or **scrutinise** verb (**scrutinizes**, **scrutinizing**, **scrutinized** or **scrutinises**, etc) to examine something or look at somebody very carefully.

scrutiny noun a careful study or inspection.

scuba-diving noun swimming underwater with a tank of air to breathe from. ➤ **scuba-diver** noun.

scud verb (**scuds**, **scudding**, **scudded**) to move or run swiftly.

scuff verb (**scuffs**, **scuffing**, **scuffed**) **1** to scrape or damage the surface of a shoe or other object. **2** to drag or shuffle your feet while walking. ➤ **scuff** noun.

scuffle noun (plural **scuffles**) a brief confused fight.

scull noun (plural **sculls**) a light oar used by a single rower. ~ verb (**sculls**, **sculling**, **sculled**) to row a boat with sculls.

scullery noun (plural **sculleries**) a small kitchen used mainly for washing dishes.

sculpt verb (**sculpts**, **sculpting**, **sculpted**) **1** Art to make sculptures. **2** to give something a particular shape.

sculptor noun (plural **sculptors**) Art an artist who makes sculptures.

sculpture noun (plural **sculptures**) Art **1** the art of making three-dimensional works by carving or modelling. **2** a piece of work produced in this way. ➤ **sculptural** adjective.

scum noun **1** impurities that have collected on the surface of a liquid. **2** informal a despicable person or group of people. ➤ **scummy** adjective.

scupper verb (**scuppers**, **scuppering**, **scuppered**) **1** informal to prevent something from happening, or to ruin it: *The bad weather scuppered our plans for a picnic.* **2** to sink a ship deliberately.

scurf noun thin dry flakes of skin. ➤ **scurfy** adjective.

scurrilous adjective offensive and defamatory.

scurry verb (**scurries**, **scurrying**, **scurried**) to move with short hurried steps.

scurvy noun a disease caused by a lack of vitamin C.

scuttle[1] noun (plural **scuttles**) a container for storing coal indoors.

scuttle[2] verb (**scuttles**, **scuttling**, **scuttled**) to run hurriedly or furtively.

scuttle[3] verb (**scuttles**, **scuttling**, **scuttled**) **1** to sink your own ship deliberately. **2** to destroy or wreck a plan.

scythe noun (plural **scythes**) a tool with a long curving blade for cutting grass or corn.

SE

SE *abbreviation* Southeast or Southeastern.

sea *noun* (*plural* **seas**) **1** the salt water that covers much of the earth. **2** a large area of salt water. **3** something vast or overwhelming. ✷ **at sea 1** on the sea. **2** lost or confused.

sea anemone /see a ne mo ni/ *noun* (*plural* **sea anemones**) a brightly coloured sea creature with a cluster of tentacles resembling a flower.

seaboard *noun* (*plural* **seaboards**) an area beside or near the sea.

sea change *noun* (*plural* **sea changes**) a complete transformation.

seafaring *noun* travel by sea. ➤ **seafarer** *noun*.

seafood *noun* edible sea fish, shellfish, etc.

seafront *noun* (*plural* **seafronts**) the part of a seaside town facing the sea.

seagoing *adjective* designed for travel on the sea.

seagull *noun* (*plural* **seagulls**) = GULL.

sea horse *noun* (*plural* **sea horses**) a small upright fish with a head like that of a horse.

seal[1] *noun* (*plural* **seals**) **1** a closure that has to be broken before you can open something. **2** a tight closure that prevents air, water, etc getting into something. **3** an emblem or word stamped in wax on a document to show that the document is genuine. ~ *verb* (**seals, sealing, sealed**) **1** to fasten or close something tightly. **2** to close a container in a way that prevents unauthorized opening. **3** to confirm an arrangement or make it secure. **4** to put an authenticating seal on a document. ✷ **seal off** to close an area to prevent people going in or out.

seal[2] *noun* (*plural* **seals**) a sea animal with webbed flippers for swimming.

sea legs *plural noun* the ability to walk steadily and avoid being seasick when on a ship.

sea level *noun* the average level of the sea's surface midway between high and low tides.

sea lion *noun* (*plural* **sea lions**) a large seal with short coarse fur and large flippers.

seam *noun* (*plural* **seams**) **1** a line of stitching joining two pieces of fabric. **2** a line or ridge where two edges meet. **3** a layer of coal or rock.

seaman *noun* (*plural* **seamen**) a sailor. ➤ **seamanship** *noun*.

seamless *adjective* **1** without seams. **2** without breaks or gaps; continuous. ➤ **seamlessly** *adverb*.

seamy *adjective* (**seamier, seamiest**) ✷ **the seamy side** the unpleasant or sordid aspects of something.

Seanad Éireann /sha nad air an *or* sha nath air an/ *noun* (**the Seanad**) the upper house of parliament in the Republic of Ireland.

seance /say ongs/ *noun* (*plural* **seances**) a meeting at which people attempt to communicate with the dead.

seaplane *noun* (*plural* **seaplanes**) an aeroplane designed to take off and land on water.

sear *verb* (**sears, searing, seared**) to burn or scorch something with a sudden intense heat.

search *verb* (**searches, searching, searched**) **1** to look or enquire carefully in order to try and find something. **2** to examine a place thoroughly while looking for something. **3** to examine a person for concealed articles. ➤ **search** *noun*, **searcher** *noun*.

searching *adjective* seeking to obtain detailed or personal information.

searchlight *noun* (*plural* **searchlights**) an apparatus for projecting a strong movable beam of light.

search party *noun* (*plural* **search**

parties) a group of people organized to search for a missing person.

search warrant *noun* (*plural* **search warrants**) a legal document authorizing police to search a building.

seascape *noun* (*plural* **seascapes**) a picture of a view of the sea.

seashell *noun* (*plural* **seashells**) the empty shell of a sea creature.

seashore *noun* sandy or stony land next to the sea.

seasick *adjective* suffering from sickness caused by the motion of a ship. ➤ **seasickness** *noun*.

seaside *noun* (**the seaside**) land bordering the sea, especially a holiday resort or beach.

season[1] *noun* (*plural* **seasons**) **1** one of the four parts (spring, summer, autumn, and winter) into which the year is divided. **2** a period characterized by a particular kind of weather or activity: *the dry season; the holiday season.* ✱ **in season 1** said about food: available or ready for eating at a particular time. **2** said about a female animal: ready to mate.

season[2] *verb* (**seasons, seasoning, seasoned**) **1** to add spices or flavouring to food. **2** to allow timber to dry out so that it is ready for use.

seasonable *adjective* suitable to the season or circumstances.

seasonal *adjective* occurring or produced during a particular season: *seasonal jobs.* ➤ **seasonally** *adverb*.

seasoned *adjective* fit or expert from experience.

seasoning *noun* (*plural* **seasonings**) salt, pepper, or spices added to food to give it flavour.

season ticket *noun* (*plural* **season tickets**) a ticket that gives you the right to travel on something or attend something as often as you want over a fixed period.

seat *noun* (*plural* **seats**) **1** a piece of furniture for sitting on. **2** the part of a chair on which you sit. **3** the buttocks, or the part of a piece of clothing that covers them. **4** a place for sitting, for example in a vehicle or theatre, or the right to sit there. **5** the right to sit in parliament for a particular constituency or on an elected committee. **6** a place where something is established or practised: *a seat of learning.* **7** a large country mansion. ~ *verb* (**seats, seating, seated**) **1** to provide a seat or seats for somebody. **2** to have sitting accommodation for a certain number of people. ➤ **seated** *adjective*.

seat belt *noun* (*plural* **seat belts**) a belt for securing a person in a seat in a vehicle or aircraft.

seating *noun* the number of seats in a place or the way these are arranged.

sea urchin *noun* (*plural* **sea urchins**) a sea creature with a thin shell covered with spines.

seaweed *noun* thick slimy plants that grow in the sea.

seaworthy *adjective* said about a ship: fit or safe for travel at sea. ➤ **seaworthiness** *noun*.

secateurs /se ka terz/ *plural noun* small shears used for pruning plants.

secede /si seed/ *verb* (**secedes, seceding, seceded**) to withdraw from an organization or federation. ➤ **secession** *noun*.

secluded *adjective* quiet and sheltered.

seclusion *noun* the state of being private or secluded.

second[1] /se kond/ *adjective* **1** having a position in a sequence corresponding to the number two. **2** below the first in value, quality, or degree. **3** another. **4** one in every two; alternate: *every second year.* ~ *noun* (*plural* **seconds**) **1** somebody or something that is second. **2** an assistant to somebody boxing or fighting a duel. **3** a slightly flawed or inferior article for sale. **4** (**seconds**) *informal* a second helping of food. ~ *verb* (**seconds, seconding, seconded**) **1** to give support or encouragement to somebody. **2** to support a motion or nomination proposed by somebody else. * **have second thoughts** to reconsider a previous decision. ➤ **seconder** *noun*, **secondly** *adverb*.

second² /se kond/ *noun* (*plural* **seconds**) **1** the 60th part of a minute. **2** a brief moment.

second³ /si kond/ *verb* (**seconds, seconding, seconded**) to send an employee to work temporarily somewhere else. ➤ **secondment** *noun*.

secondary *adjective* **1** not main; less important. **2** said about a level of education: following primary. ➤ **secondarily** *adverb*.

secondary colours *plural noun Art* colours produced by mixing primary colours.

secondary school *noun* (*plural* **secondary schools**) a school for pupils aged from about 11 to about 18.

second cousin *noun* (*plural* **second cousins**) a child of a cousin of your parents.

secondhand *adjective* **1** acquired after being owned by somebody else. **2** dealing in secondhand goods. **3** said about information: passed on to you by somebody else.

second nature *noun* an action or ability that has become instinctive.

second person *noun English* in grammar, the term used to refer to the person or people addressed by a speaker, represented by the pronoun *you*.

second-rate *adjective* not very good; inferior.

second sight *noun* the ability to see future events.

secrecy *noun* the fact of being secret or keeping something secret.

secret *adjective* **1** kept from being seen or known about by other people. **2** done or working in secrecy. ~ *noun* **1** something kept secret, especially a piece of information that should not be revealed to other people. **2** a special way of achieving something: *the secret of success*. ➤ **secretly** *adverb*.

secret agent *noun* (*plural* **secret agents**) a spy.

secretariat /se kri tair i at/ *noun* (*plural* **secretariats**) the administrative department of a large organization.

secretary *noun* (*plural* **secretaries**) **1** a person whose job is to deal with letters and telephone calls and to do administrative work. **2** = SECRETARY OF STATE. ➤ **secretarial** *adjective*.

secretary of state *noun* (*plural* **secretaries of state**) **1** in Britain, a government minister who is the head of a department. **2** in the USA, the government minister responsible for foreign affairs.

secrete¹ /si kreet/ *verb* (**secretes, secreting, secreted**) *Science* to form and give off a substance. ➤ **secretion** *noun*.

secrete² /si kreet/ *verb* (**secretes, secreting, secreted**) to put something in a secret place.

secretive *adjective* inclined to say little and hide your feelings. ➤ **secretively** *adverb*.

secret police *noun* a police organization operating secretly for the political purposes of a government.

secret service *noun* a government agency concerned with national security and intelligence.

sect *noun* (*plural* **sects**) a small group within a religious or political organization that differs in its beliefs from the main body.

sectarian /sek tair i an/ *adjective* **1** to do with a sect. **2** to do with relations between different religious groups: *sectarian violence*. ➤ **sectarianism** *noun*.

section *noun* (*plural* **sections**) **1** a separate part or division of something. **2** the act of cutting or separating in surgery. **3** a cross-section.

sector *noun* (*plural* **sectors**) **1** a part of a larger area. **2** *Maths* a part of a circle between two lines joining the centre to the circumference. **3** a large section of an economy, society, etc: *the education sector*.

secular *adjective* to do with this world; not spiritual or connected with religion. ➤ **secularism** *noun*.

secure *adjective* **1** free from danger or risk of loss. **2** firmly fixed or fastened. **3** assured or certain. ~ *verb* (**secures, securing, secured**) **1** to fix or fasten something firmly. **2** to make something safe from risk or danger. **3** to obtain something by effort. ➤ **securely** *adverb*.

security *noun* (*plural* **securities**) **1** freedom from danger, fear, or anxiety. **2** precautions to ensure that a state or organization is safe from attack or crime. **3** something provided as a guarantee, for example that a loan will be repaid.

sedan chair *noun* (*plural* **sedan chairs**) *History* a portable enclosed chair carried on poles by two people.

sedate *adjective* calm and even-tempered. ~ *verb* (**sedates, sedating, sedated**) to give a sedative to somebody. ➤ **sedately** *adverb*, **sedation** *noun*.

sedative *adjective* tending to calm or tranquillize a person. ~ *noun* (*plural* **sedatives**) a sedative drug.

sedentary /ˈsedɪntəri/ *adjective* doing or involving a lot of sitting.

sediment *noun* (*plural* **sediments**) **1** material that settles at the bottom of a liquid. **2** material deposited by water, wind, or glaciers. ➤ **sedimentary** *adjective*.

seduce *verb* (**seduces, seducing, seduced**) **1** to persuade somebody to have sexual intercourse with you. **2** to persuade somebody to do wrong or be disloyal. ➤ **seduction** *noun*.

seductive *adjective* **1** attractive and sexy. **2** tempting. ➤ **seductively** *adverb*.

see[1] *verb* (**sees, seeing, saw, seen**) **1** to be aware of something or somebody by using your eyes. **2** to realize or understand something: *I see what you mean*. **3** to imagine or envisage something; *I can't see him objecting*. **4** to find out something: *I'll see what can be done*. **5** to make sure that something is done: *See that she leaves at once*. **6** to call on, visit, or meet somebody. **7** to escort somebody to a place: *I'll see you home*. ✱ **see about** to deal with or consider something. **see through** to be aware of a deception. **see to** to attend to, or take care of, something or somebody.

see[2] *noun* (*plural* **sees**) the area over which a bishop has authority.

seed *noun* (*plural* **seeds** *or* **seed**) **1** a small fertilized part of a flowering plant that can produce a new plant. **2** a source from which something develops. **3** a competitor who has been seeded in a tournament. ~ *verb* (**seeds, seeding, seeded**) **1** said about a plant: to produce or shed seeds. **2** to plant seeds in a field, etc. **3** to select the best players in a tournament and arrange for them not to play one another in early rounds.

seedling *noun* (*plural* **seedlings**) a young plant grown from seed.

seedy *adjective* (**seedier, seediest**) **1** shabby or grubby. **2** disreputable or run-down. ➤ **seediness** *noun*.

seeing *conjunction* (*often* **seeing that**) because; since.

seek *verb* (**seeks, seeking, sought**) **1** to go in search of something or somebody. **2** to try to acquire or gain something. **3** to ask for advice, etc.

seem

4 to make an effort to do something. ► **seeker** noun.

seem verb (**seems, seeming, seemed**) to give the impression of being or doing something.

seen verb past participle of SEE¹.

seep verb (**seeps, seeping, seeped**) to pass slowly through small openings. ► **seepage** noun.

seer noun (plural **seers**) a person who predicts future events; a prophet.

seesaw noun (plural **seesaws**) a plank balanced in the middle so that one end goes up as the other goes down, used for a children's game.

seethe verb (**seethes, seething, seethed**) **1** to feel suppressed anger. **2** to bubble and froth like boiling water.

segment noun (plural **segments**) **1** one of the parts into which something, such as an orange, is naturally divided. **2** a marked-off section of something. ► **segmented** adjective.

segregate verb (**segregates, segregating, segregated**) **1** to keep somebody or something separate from others. **2** to prevent different racial groups, religions, or sexes from sharing the same facilities.

segue /se gway/ verb (**segues, segueing, segued**) Music to pass directly from one musical number or theme to another.

seismic /siez mik/ adjective **1** to do with or caused by an earthquake. **2** having a very great effect.

seismology /siez mo lo ji/ noun the study of earthquakes. ► **seismological** adjective, **seismologist** noun.

seize verb (**seizes, seizing, seized**) **1** to take hold of something or somebody abruptly or forcefully. **2** to confiscate something by legal authority. **3** to use or take advantage of something eagerly. **4** (often **seize up**) said about machinery: to become jammed and stop working.

Usage Note Notice that **seize** is spelt *-ei-*. It does not obey the general rule of 'I before E except after C' for words that are pronounced /ee/.

seizure /see zher/ noun (plural **seizures**) **1** the act of seizing. **2** a sudden fit or attack of an illness.

seldom adverb rarely or infrequently.

select verb (**selects, selecting, selected**) to pick out or choose somebody or something carefully. ~ *adjective* **1** picked in preference to others. **2** of special value or quality. **3** socially exclusive.

selection noun (plural **selections**) **1** the act of selecting. **2** somebody or something selected. **3** a collection of selected items. **4** a range of things from which to choose.

selective adjective **1** using or involving selection. **2** tending to choose carefully. **3** affecting only some in a group. ► **selectively** adverb, **selectivity** noun.

self noun (plural **selves**) **1** a person's individual character. **2** personal interest or advantage: *with no thought of self*.

self-absorbed adjective preoccupied with your own thoughts or activities. ► **self-absorption** noun.

self-addressed adjective said about an envelope: with your own name and address written on it.

self-assured adjective confident in yourself. ► **self-assurance** noun.

self-catering adjective said about holiday accommodation: allowing you to prepare your own meals.

self-centred adjective preoccupied with your own wishes or needs.

self-confident adjective confident in yourself and your abilities. ► **self-confidence** noun.

self-conscious adjective nervous and

embarrassed because you are an object of other people's attention. ➤ **self-consciously** *adverb*.

self-contained *adjective* complete in itself.

self-control *noun* the ability to control your own impulses or emotions. ➤ **self-controlled** *adjective*.

self-defence *noun* the act of defending or justifying yourself.

self-denial *noun* deliberately not allowing yourself to have things you want or enjoy.

self-destruct *verb* (**self-destructs, self-destructing, self-destructed**) to destroy itself automatically. ➤ **self-destructive** *adjective*.

self-determination *noun* the right of a person or country to manage their affairs without interference.

self-discipline *noun* the ability to control your thoughts and actions. ➤ **self-disciplined** *adjective*.

self-employed *adjective* working for yourself and not an employer. ➤ **self-employment** *noun*.

self-esteem *noun* self-respect.

self-evident *adjective* requiring no proof; obvious.

self-explanatory *adjective* capable of being understood without explanation.

self-expression *noun* the expression of your own thoughts and feelings, for example in painting, music, or poetry.

self-help *noun* dependence on your own efforts.

self-importance *noun* an exaggerated sense of your own importance. ➤ **self-important** *adjective*.

self-indulgent *adjective* allowing yourself to have too many of the things you want. ➤ **self-indulgence** *noun*.

self-interest *noun* a concern for your own advantage and well-being. ➤ **self-interested** *adjective*.

selfish *adjective* concerned chiefly with your own advantage or needs. ➤ **selfishly** *adverb*, **selfishness** *noun*.

selfless *adjective* having more concern for others than for yourself. ➤ **selflessly** *adverb*.

self-made *adjective* having achieved success by your own efforts.

self-pity *noun* a self-indulgent concern with your own misfortunes. ➤ **self-pitying** *adjective*.

self-portrait *noun* (*plural* **self-portraits**) *Art* a portrait in which the artist is the subject.

self-possessed *adjective* calm. ➤ **self-possession** *noun*.

self-preservation *noun* an instinctive tendency to protect yourself.

self-raising flour *noun* flour with baking powder mixed into it to make cakes, etc rise.

self-reliance *noun* reliance on your own efforts and resources. ➤ **self-reliant** *adjective*.

self-respect *noun* confidence in and respect for yourself. ➤ **self-respecting** *adjective*.

self-righteous *adjective* sure that you are right or morally superior. ➤ **self-righteously** *adverb*, **self-righteousness** *noun*.

self-sacrifice *noun* sacrifice of yourself or your well-being for the sake of others. ➤ **self-sacrificing** *adjective*.

selfsame *adjective* precisely the same.

self-satisfied *adjective* unduly pleased with yourself or your achievements. ➤ **self-satisfaction** *noun*.

self-service *adjective* said about a shop, cafeteria, etc: where customers collect what they want and pay a cashier for it.

self-sufficient *adjective* able to provide for your own needs without outside help. ➤ **self-sufficiency** *noun*.

sell *verb* (**sells, selling, sold**) **1** to give goods or property to somebody in exchange for money. **2** to have

Sellotape

something available for people to buy. **3** to be sold or achieve sales: *Her books sell in millions.* **4** to persuade somebody of the worth of an idea, etc. ✷ **be sold out 1** said about an item: to be unavailable because all have been sold. **2** said about a shop: to have none of an item left to sell. **sell out** *informal* to betray or be disloyal to somebody. ➤ **seller** *noun*.

Sellotape *noun trademark* a transparent adhesive tape.

sell-out *noun* (*plural* **sell-outs**) **1** an event for which all tickets or seats are sold. **2** *informal* a betrayal.

selves *noun* plural of SELF.

semaphore *noun* a system of signalling using the arms or a pair of flags held one in each hand.

semblance *noun* an appearance of something or similarity to something, which may be deceptive.

semen /see min/ *noun* a fluid containing sperm, produced by the male reproductive glands.

semibreve *noun* (*plural* **semibreves**) *Music* a note with the time value of two minims or four crotchets.

semicircle *noun* (*plural* **semicircles**) a half circle. ➤ **semicircular** *adjective*.

semicolon *noun* (*plural* **semicolons**) *English* a punctuation mark (;) used to indicate a break that is stronger than one indicated by a comma but less than that marked by a full stop.

semiconscious *adjective* conscious but not fully aware of what is happening.

semiconductor *noun* (*plural* **semiconductors**) *Science* a substance, used in electronic equipment, that conducts more or less electricity depending on temperature or the presence of certain impurities.

semidetached *adjective* said about a house: joined to another house by a common wall.

semifinal *noun* (*plural* **semifinals**) a match or round that is next to the last in a knockout competition. ➤ **semifinalist** *noun*.

seminar *noun* (*plural* **seminars**) a meeting of a small group to discuss ideas or learn about something, for example a group of university students and a teacher.

seminary *noun* (*plural* **seminaries**) an institution for training clergy.

semiquaver *noun* (*plural* **semiquavers**) *Music* a note with the time value of half a quaver.

semiskimmed *adjective* said about milk: with some of its cream removed.

semitone *noun* (*plural* **semitones**) *Music* a difference in pitch equal to half a tone.

semolina /se mo lee na/ *noun* the hard parts left after milling wheat, used to make pasta and puddings.

senate *noun* (*plural* **senates**) **1** the upper house in the parliaments of countries such as the USA, France, and Ireland. **2** *History* the governing council of ancient Rome.

senator *noun* (*plural* **senators**) a member of a senate. ➤ **senatorial** *adjective*.

send *verb* (**sends, sending, sent**) **1** to cause somebody or something to go somewhere. **2** to cause something to move quickly or violently. **3** (*often* **send out**) to emit or discharge gas or liquid. **4** to cause somebody to be in a specified state; *The remark sent him into a rage.* ✷ **send for** to order somebody or something to come or be brought to you. **send up** to imitate somebody or something mockingly. ➤ **sender** *noun*.

send-off *noun* (*plural* **send-offs**) a gathering of people to say goodbye to somebody starting a journey.

senile *adjective* losing mental or physical faculties through old age. ➤ **senility** *noun*.

senior *adjective* **1** higher in standing or rank. **2** older. **3** for older school students. ~ *noun* (*plural* **seniors**) **1** a person who is older than another person by a specified amount: *He is my senior by ten years.* **2** a person who has a higher rank than you. **3** a student in the upper years of secondary school. ➤ **seniority** *noun*.

senior citizen *noun* (*plural* **senior citizens**) an old age pensioner.

sensation *noun* (*plural* **sensations**) **1** a feeling, especially a physical feeling resulting from stimulation of a sense organ. **2** a surge of interest or excitement, or something that causes great interest or excitement.

sensational *adjective* **1** arousing great interest or excitement. **2** *informal* exceptionally impressive. ➤ **sensationally** *adverb*.

sense *noun* (*plural* **senses**) **1** any of the faculties by which people or animals are aware of things; touch, hearing, sight, smell, or taste. **2** an ability to use the senses for a specified purpose: *a sense of balance.* **3** a vague awareness or impression: *a sense that something was not quite right.* **4** a capacity for appreciating something: *a sense of humour.* **5** (**senses**) soundness of mind; sensible judgment: *came to his senses.* **6** the ability to think and behave sensibly. **7** a meaning conveyed by a word or expression. ~ *verb* (**senses, sensing, sensed**) **1** to be aware of something through the senses. **2** to become vaguely aware of something. **3** to detect something automatically. ✻ **make sense** to be understandable or reasonable. **see sense** to make a sensible decision or behave sensibly.

senseless *adjective* **1** unconscious. **2** foolish or stupid. **3** having no meaning or purpose.

sense organ *noun* (*plural* **sense organs**) *Science* an organ of the body that responds to a stimulus, such as heat or sound waves.

sensibility *noun* (*plural* **sensibilities**) **1** (**sensibilities**) *formal* feelings or ability to feel. **2** sensitivity to emotion in yourself or other people.

sensible *adjective* **1** having or showing good practical judgment or sound reason. **2** plain and practical: *sensible shoes.* ➤ **sensibly** *adverb*.

sensitive *adjective* **1** easily made emotional by things that happen or are said to you. **2** very aware of the feelings of other people. **3** controversial and needing tactful handling. **4** (**sensitive to**) capable of being stimulated by something, such as light or contact. ➤ **sensitively** *adverb*, **sensitivity** *noun*.

sensitize *or* **sensitise** *verb* (**sensitizes, sensitizing, sensitized** *or* **sensitises,** etc) to make somebody sensitive to or aware of something.

sensor *noun* (*plural* **sensors**) a device that responds to heat, light, sound, etc.

sensory *adjective* to do with sensation or the senses.

sensual *adjective* **1** giving physical or sexual pleasure. **2** showing a liking for physical or sexual pleasure. ➤ **sensuality** *noun*, **sensually** *adverb*.

sensuous *adjective* beautiful in a way that appeals to the senses rather than the intellect. ➤ **sensuously** *adverb*.

sent *verb* past tense of SEND.

sentence *noun* (*plural* **sentences**) **1** *English* a group of words that is grammatically complete and expresses a statement, question, command, wish, or exclamation. **2** a punishment pronounced by a court. ~ *verb* (**sentences, sentencing, sentenced**) to impose a sentence on somebody.

sententious *adjective* giving moral advice pompously.

sentient

sentient /sen shnt *or* sen ti int/ *adjective* capable of feeling and perceiving.

sentiment *noun* (*plural* **sentiments**) **1** strong or exaggerated emotion. **2** a view or opinion. **3** a feeling or attitude.

sentimental *adjective* **1** arousing tender or longing feelings. **2** trying to arouse more feeling than is justified by the subject matter. ➤ **sentimentality** *noun*, **sentimentally** *adverb*.

sentinel *noun* (*plural* **sentinels**) a sentry.

sentry *noun* (*plural* **sentries**) a soldier standing guard at a gate, door, etc.

sepal /se pl *or* see pl/ *noun* (*plural* **sepals**) *Science* one of the modified leaves forming the green outer part of a flower.

separate /se pa rayt/ *verb* (**separates, separating, separated**) **1** to move or come apart. **2** to stop living together as husband and wife or as partners. **3** to divide or stand between two or more people or things. **4** to detach something or somebody from a larger group. ~ /se pa rat/ *adjective* **1** set or kept apart; detached. **2** not shared with another. **3** existing independently. **4** different in kind; distinct. ➤ **separable** *adjective*, **separately** *adverb*, **separation** *noun*.

sepia /see pi a/ *noun* a rich dark brown.

September *noun* the ninth month of the year.

septet *noun* (*plural* **septets**) *Music* a group of seven instruments, voices, or performers, or a piece of music for such a group.

septic *adjective* infected with bacteria. ➤ **septically** *adverb*, **septicity** *noun*.

septicaemia /sep ti see mi a/ *noun* blood poisoning caused by micro-organisms.

septuagenarian /sep tew a ji nairi an/ *noun* (*plural* **septuagenarians**) a person between 70 and 79 years old.

sepulchral /si pul kral/ *adjective* **1** to do with a tomb or burial. **2** sombre or dismal. ➤ **sepulchrally** *adverb*.

sepulchre /se pul ker/ *noun* (*plural* **sepulchres**) a tomb.

sequel *noun* (*plural* **sequels**) **1** a play, film, or literary work continuing the story of a previous one. **2** a subsequent development or course of events.

sequence *noun* (*plural* **sequences**) **1** a continuous or connected series. **2** the order in which things, events, etc follow one another.

sequin *noun* (*plural* **sequins**) a small shining disc used on clothing for ornamentation. ➤ **sequinned** *adjective*.

sequoia *noun* (*plural* **sequoias**) a very tall coniferous Californian tree.

seraph *noun* (*plural* **seraphim** *or* **seraphs**) a six-winged angel. ➤ **seraphic** *adjective*.

serenade *noun* (*plural* **serenades**) *Music* **1** a piece of music played outdoors at night by a man for a woman he is courting. **2** a tuneful composition for a small number of instruments.

serendipity *noun* the discovery of pleasing or interesting things by chance. ➤ **serendipitous** *adjective*.

serene *adjective* calm and tranquil. ➤ **serenely** *adverb*, **serenity** *noun*.

serf *noun* (*plural* **serfs**) *History* an agricultural labourer in a feudal society who has to do work for a lord. ➤ **serfdom** *noun*.

serge *noun* a durable woollen fabric.

sergeant *noun* (*plural* **sergeants**) **1** a British police officer ranking below inspector. **2** a non-commissioned officer in the army, ranking above a corporal.

sergeant major *noun* (*plural* **sergeant majors**) a senior non-commissioned officer in the British army or Royal Marines.

serial *noun* (*plural* **serials**) a story

published or broadcast in parts at intervals. ~ *adjective* **1** arranged in a series. **2** appearing in successive instalments. **3** repeating the same offence several times: *a serial rapist*. ➤ **serially** *adverb*.

serialize *or* **serialise** *verb* (**serializes, serializing, serialized** *or* **serialises,** etc) to publish or broadcast a work in the form of a serial. ➤ **serialization** *or* **serialisation** *noun*.

serial number *noun* (*plural* **serial numbers**) a number used as a means of identifying an object.

series *noun* (*plural* **series**) **1** a number of things or events of the same kind following one another. **2** a number of radio or television programmes of the same type or on the same theme.

serious *adjective* **1** requiring careful attention and thought; not funny or light. **2** quiet and thoughtful in behaviour. **3** sincere and in earnest: *I'm serious about this*. **4** having severe or dangerous effects: *a serious accident*. ➤ **seriously** *adverb*, **seriousness** *noun*.

sermon *noun* (*plural* **sermons**) a religious talk forming part of a church service.

serpent *noun* (*plural* **serpents**) *literary* a large snake.

serrated *adjective* having projections like the teeth of a saw. ➤ **serration** *noun*.

serum /seer um/ *noun* (*plural* **serums** *or* **sera**) the fluid constituent of blood.

servant *noun* (*plural* **servants**) a person employed to do work in somebody's house or to help them with ordinary personal tasks.

serve *verb* (**serves, serving, served**) **1** to do work as a servant or employee of somebody or something. **2** to be a member of the armed forces of a country. **3** to be imprisoned for a period of time. **4** to attend to a customer in a shop, bar, etc. **5** to provide somebody with food or drinks. **6** to fulfil a particular purpose: *This box also serves as a window seat*. **7** in tennis and other games, to begin a period of play by hitting the ball or shuttlecock to your opponent. ~ *noun* (*plural* **serves**) the act of serving in tennis, badminton, etc. ✶ **serve somebody right** to be the punishment that somebody deserves.

server *noun* (*plural* **servers**) **1** the player who serves in tennis, etc. **2** *ICT* a computer or program that connects users in a network to a centralized store of data.

service *noun* (*plural* **services**) **1** work carried out for a person, organization, country, etc. **2** a system designed to meet a public need: *a bus service*. **3** the work of attending to customers in a shop, bar, etc. **4** a helpful action or favour. **5** a religious ceremony in a Christian church. **6** a routine inspection and repair of a machine or motor vehicle. **7** a set of matching tableware for serving food. **8** (**services**) a nation's military forces. **9** (**services**) an area where the users of a motorway can park, rest, refuel, etc. **10** a serve in tennis, badminton, etc. ✶ **in** *or* **out of service** currently being (or not being) used or operated. ~ *verb* (**services, servicing, serviced**) **1** to provide a service or services for somebody. **2** to carry out routine repairs and maintenance on a vehicle or machine.

serviceable *adjective* **1** in good working order. **2** reliable and durable.

service industry *noun* (*plural* **service industries**) an industry that provides a service and does not produce goods.

serviceman *or* **servicewoman** *noun* (*plural* **servicemen** *or* **servicewomen**) a member of the armed forces.

service station *noun* (*plural* **service stations**) a roadside garage selling petrol, oil, etc.

serviette *noun* (*plural* **serviettes**) = TABLE NAPKIN.

servile *adjective* too willing to please or satisfy other people. ➤ **servility** *noun*.

serving *noun* (*plural* **servings**) a single portion of food.

servitude *noun* the state of being a slave or completely subject to somebody.

sesame /ˈsesəmi/ *noun* a tropical plant with seeds used as a source of oil and as a flavouring.

session *noun* (*plural* **sessions**) **1** a period devoted to a particular activity. **2** a meeting or series of meetings of a court or council.

set *verb* (**sets, setting, set**) **1** to put something in a particular place or position. **2** to put something or somebody in a specified condition: *The slaves were set free.* **3** to decide on and fix something: *Have you set a date for the wedding?* **4** to give somebody a task to perform. **5** to prepare or adjust a device for use. **6** to prepare a table for use at a meal. **7** to describe an event, story, etc as taking place at a particular place and time. **8** *Music* to write music for a text. **9** to put a broken bone or limb into its normal position for healing. **10** said about jelly, cement, etc: to become solid or hard. **11** said about the sun, moon, etc: to go down below the horizon. ~ *adjective* **1** arranged or fixed in advance. **2** prepared and ready. ~ *noun* (*plural* **sets**) **1** a number of things of the same kind belonging or used together. **2** a radio or television receiver. **3** in tennis and similar sports, a number of games forming a unit for scoring. **4** *Drama* the stage scenery used for a play. ✱ **be set on** determined to do something. **set about** to start doing something. **set back** to delay something or somebody. **set off 1** to start on a journey. **2** to cause something to start happening. **3** to cause a bomb to explode. **set out 1** to start on a journey. **2** to intend to do something. **3** to state or describe something in detail. **set sail** to begin a voyage by sea. **set up 1** to raise something into position. **2** to establish or found something.

setback *noun* (*plural* **setbacks**) a problem or difficulty that causes a delay or interruption.

set piece *noun* (*plural* **set pieces**) **1** a carefully planned and rehearsed action. **2** in football or rugby, a special action such as a corner, free kick, or scrum that restarts play after a stoppage.

set square *noun* (*plural* **set squares**) *Maths* a flat triangular piece of plastic with a right angle, used to mark out angles.

settee *noun* (*plural* **settees**) a long upholstered seat for more than one person.

setting *noun* (*plural* **settings**) **1** the physical or historical background for an object or event. **2** *Music* the music composed for a text. **3** a set of cutlery, glasses, etc for one person at a meal.

settle *verb* (**settles, settling, settled**) **1** to find an answer or solution to a problem or dispute. **2** to place something or somebody firmly or comfortably. **3** to establish a home or a colony in a place. **4** to come to rest. **5** to pay a debt. ~ *noun* (*plural* **settles**) a wooden bench with arms and a high back. ✱ **settle down 1** to become, or to make somebody, calm. **2** to start living a quiet and stable ordered life. **settle in** to become comfortably established in a new place. **settle on** to choose, or decide on, something. **settle up** to pay what you owe.

settlement *noun* (*plural* **settlements**) **1** the process of settling a dispute, etc, or an agreement resulting from this. **2** a place where a new community has been established.

settler *noun* (*plural* **settlers**) somebody

who goes to live in an area that was previously uninhabited.

seven *noun* (*plural* **sevens**) the number 7. ➤ **seventh** *adjective and noun*, **seventhly** *adverb*.

seventeen *adjective and noun* (*plural* **seventeens**) the number 17. ➤ **seventeenth** *adjective and noun*.

seventy *adjective and noun* (*plural* **seventies**) **1** the number 70. **2** (**the seventies**) the numbers 70 to 79. ➤ **seventieth** *adjective and noun*.

sever *verb* (**severs**, **severing**, **severed**) **1** to cut something off or cut through something. **2** to keep people apart.

several *adjective and pronoun* more than a few, but not many.

severe *adjective* **1** strict or harsh in appearance or in dealing with people. **2** having great force or a very harmful effect: *severe injuries*. **3** very plain and simple in design and decoration. ➤ **severely** *adverb*, **severity** *noun*.

sew /soh/ *verb* (**sews**, **sewing**, **sewed**, **sewn** *or* **sewed**) **1** to join or attach something by stitches made with a needle and thread. **2** to make or mend something by sewing.

sewage *noun* waste matter carried off by sewers.

sewer *noun* (*plural* **sewers**) an underground channel or pipe used to carry off waste matter from drains. ➤ **sewerage** *noun*.

sex *noun* (*plural* **sexes**) **1** either of two categories, male or female, into which organisms are divided. **2** the characteristics that distinguish males and females. **3** sexual intercourse or activity.

sex appeal *noun* the quality of being sexually attractive.

sexism *noun* discrimination or prejudice on the basis of a person's sex, especially against women. ➤ **sexist** *adjective and noun*.

sextant *noun* (*plural* **sextants**) an instrument for measuring angles and distances in surveying and navigation.

sextet *noun* (*plural* **sextets**) *Music* a group of six instruments, voices, or performers, or a piece of music for such a group.

sexton *noun* (*plural* **sextons**) an official in charge of a church and churchyard.

sextuplet *noun* (*plural* **sextuplets**) any one of six children born at the same time to the same mother.

sexual *adjective* **1** to do with sex or physical attraction and contact between the sexes and individuals. **2** said about reproduction: involving the fusion of male and female reproductive cells. ➤ **sexually** *adverb*.

sexual intercourse *noun* sexual activity in which the man's erect penis is inserted into the woman's vagina.

sexuality *noun* (*plural* **sexualities**) the factor that decides whether a person is sexually attracted to males or females.

sexy *adjective* (**sexier**, **sexiest**) **1** sexually attractive or stimulating. **2** *informal* interesting or fashionable. ➤ **sexily** *adverb*, **sexiness** *noun*.

shabby *adjective* (**shabbier**, **shabbiest**) **1** worn or threadbare. **2** shameful or despicable. ➤ **shabbily** *adverb*.

shack *noun* (*plural* **shacks**) a small crudely built hut or shelter.

shackle *noun* (*plural* **shackles**) a pair of metal rings joined by a chain used to fasten a prisoner's hands or legs. ~ *verb* (**shackles**, **shackling**, **shackled**) **1** to chain or fasten somebody with shackles. **2** to restrain or handicap somebody.

shade *noun* (*plural* **shades**) **1** partial darkness caused when sunlight is obstructed. **2** an area sheltered from the rays of the sun. **3** a lampshade. **4** (**shades**) *informal* sunglasses. **5** a particular variety of a colour. **6** a small amount. ~ *verb* (**shades**,

shading, shaded) 1 to shelter or screen something from light or heat. **2** to cover or darken something such as a light with a shade. **3** to mark a picture or drawing with darker colour. **4** to change gradually into a different state. * **a shade** slightly; somewhat.

shading *noun* lines, dots, or colour used to represent degrees of light and dark.

shadow *noun* (*plural* **shadows**) **1** a dark shape made on a surface by an object that is between it and a source of light. **2** partial darkness caused when light is interrupted. **3** the slightest trace: *not a shadow of doubt.* ~ *verb* (**shadows, shadowing, shadowed**) to follow somebody closely or keep them under surveillance.

shadow cabinet *noun* (**the shadow cabinet**) the leading members of the opposition in parliament who act as spokespersons on matters that are dealt with by government ministers.

shady *adjective* (**shadier, shadiest**) **1** producing or giving shade. **2** sheltered from the sun. **3** *informal* not completely legal or honest.

shaft *noun* (*plural* **shafts**) **1** the long narrow part of a spear, arrow, or tool. **2** a rotating cylindrical bar that transmits power or motion in a machine. **3** a deep narrow opening leading down to a mine, well, etc or running through the floors of a building. **4** a beam of light. **5** either of two poles between which a horse is hitched to a vehicle.

shaggy *adjective* (**shaggier, shaggiest**) **1** having long, coarse, or matted hair or fur. **2** said about hair: long and untidy.

shake *verb* (**shakes, shaking, shook, shaken**) **1** to move back and forth or up and down with short rapid movements. **2** to tremble. **3** to shock or upset somebody. **4** to weaken somebody's confidence or beliefs. ~ *noun* (*plural* **shakes**) **1** an act of shaking. **2** = MILKSHAKE. * **shake hands** to clasp hands in greeting or agreement.

shake your head to move your head from side to side to express refusal or disagreement. ➤ **shaky** *adjective*.

shaker *noun* (*plural* **shakers**) a small container used to sprinkle a powder over something.

Shakespearean *or* **Shakespearian** *adjective* English to do with the English dramatist and poet William Shakespeare (1564 -1616).

shall *verb* (**shall, should**) **1** used in the first person to express a future action or state: *We shall try to be there.* **2** used to express determination or insistence: *They shall not stop us.* **3** used to express a polite request or suggestion: *Shall I leave?*

Usage Note Traditionally *shall* is used to form the future tense after *I* or *we*, and *will* is used after *you, he, she, it*, and *they*, but *will* is increasingly used in all these cases.

shallot *noun* (*plural* **shallots**) a type of small onion.

shallow *adjective* **1** having little depth. **2** not having deep thoughts or sincere and powerful feelings. ➤ **shallowly** *adverb*.

shallows *plural noun* a shallow area in a body of water.

sham *noun* (*plural* **shams**) something or somebody that is not genuine or what they seem to be. ~ *adjective* **1** not genuine; imitation. **2** pretended or feigned. ~ *verb* (**shams, shamming, shammed**) to pretend.

shamble *verb* (**shambles, shambling, shambled**) to walk awkwardly with dragging feet.

shambles *noun* (*plural* **shambles**) a state of complete chaos or confusion. ➤ **shambolic** *adjective*.

shame *noun* **1** an unpleasant feeling

caused by awareness of having done something wrong or foolish. **2** disgrace or dishonour. **3** a cause of regret. ~ *verb* (**shames, shaming, shamed**) to cause somebody to feel shame. ✳ **put to shame** to show obvious superiority over something or somebody. ➤ **shameful** *adjective*, **shamefully** *adverb*.

shamefaced *adjective* showing shame. ➤ **shamefacedly** *adverb*.

shameless *adjective* not feeling any shame about what other people think is your bad behaviour. ➤ **shamelessly** *adverb*.

shampoo *noun* (*plural* **shampoos**) **1** a liquid soap for washing the hair. **2** a cleaning agent used on a carpet, car, etc. **3** an act of washing with shampoo. ~ *verb* (**shampoos, shampooed, shampooing**) to wash or clean something with shampoo.

shamrock *noun* (*plural* **shamrocks**) a type of clover with three small rounded leaves on each stem, the national emblem of Ireland.

shandy *noun* (*plural* **shandies**) a drink of beer mixed with lemonade or ginger beer.

shan't *contraction* shall not.

shanty[1] *noun* (*plural* **shanties**) a small crudely built hut or shelter.

shanty[2] *noun* (*plural* **shanties**) a song sung by sailors in rhythm with their work.

shantytown *noun* (*plural* **shantytowns**) a poor area of a town consisting mainly of shanties.

shape *noun* (*plural* **shapes**) **1** the form of something created by its outline and outer surface. **2** a circle, square, or other standard geometrical form. **3** the structure or plan of something. **4** the health or fitness of a person, or the condition of a thing at a particular time. ~ *verb* (**shapes, shaping, shaped**) **1** to give a particular shape to something. **2** to decide the nature or course of. **3** (*often* **shape up**) to develop or progress. ✳ **in shape** physically fit. **out of shape 1** damaged, twisted, etc so that it does not have its proper shape. **2** not fit. ➤ **shaper** *noun*.

shapeless *adjective* having no definite shape.

shapely *adjective* (**shapelier, shapeliest**) having a pleasing shape.

shard *noun* (*plural* **shards**) a piece or broken glass or pottery.

share *noun* (*plural* **shares**) **1** a portion of something put together by a number of people that belongs to, or is contributed by, one individual. **2** any of the equal portions into which the invested capital of a company is divided. ~ *verb* (**shares, sharing, shared**) **1** to use or experience something together with others. **2** to allow other people to have, use, etc something you have. **3** (*often* **share out**) to divide and distribute something in shares.

shareholder *noun* (*plural* **shareholders**) an owner of shares in a company. ➤ **shareholding** *noun*.

shark[1] *noun* (*plural* **sharks**) a large sea fish with a tall fin on its back and its mouth on the under part of its body.

shark[2] *noun* (*plural* **sharks**) a person who gets money dishonestly from other people.

sharp *adjective* **1** having a thin edge or fine point for cutting or piercing easily. **2** involving an abrupt change in direction: *a sharp turn*. **3** clear or distinct. **4** sudden and forceful or intense. **5** able to perceive things clearly or understand quickly. **6** sour or acid in flavour. **7** *Music* said about a note: raised one semitone in pitch. ~ *adverb* **1** in an abrupt manner. **2** exactly or precisely. ~ *noun* (*plural* **sharps**) *Music* **1** a note one semitone higher than the natural note. **2** the

sharpen

symbol (#) that indicates such a note. ➤ **sharply** *adverb*, **sharpness** *noun*.

sharpen *verb* (**sharpens, sharpening, sharpened**) to make something sharp. ➤ **sharpener** *noun*.

shatter *verb* (**shatters, shattering, shattered**) 1 to break apart, or to break something into pieces, suddenly and violently. 2 to damage or destroy: *All our dreams were shattered.* ✽ **be shattered** 1 to be shocked and upset. 2 to be completely exhausted. ➤ **shattering** *adjective*.

shave¹ *verb* (**shaves, shaving, shaved**) 1 to cut off hair close to the skin with a razor. 2 (*often* **shave off**) to remove thin layers or slices of something. 3 to touch against something while passing it. ~ *noun* (*plural* **shaves**) the act of shaving. ➤ **shaver** *noun*.

shaven *adjective* shaved.

shaving *noun* (*plural* **shavings**) a thin slice or shred shaved off.

shawl *noun* (*plural* **shawls**) a piece of fabric worn over the head or shoulders.

she *pronoun* 1 used to refer to a female person or animal. 2 used to refer to something regarded as female, such as a vehicle or ship.

sheaf *noun* (*plural* **sheaves**) 1 a bundle of ripe corn after it has been cut. 2 a collection of papers.

shear *verb* (**shears, shearing, sheared, sheared** *or* **shorn**) 1 to cut off the wool from a sheep. 2 (*often* **shear off**) to cut or break off something else. ➤ **shearer** *noun*.

shears *plural noun* a cutting tool like a large pair of scissors.

sheath *noun* (*plural* **sheaths**) 1 a cover for the blade of a knife or sword. 2 a close-fitting casing or covering. 3 a condom.

sheathe *verb* (**sheathes, sheathing, sheathed**) 1 to put a knife or sword into a sheath. 2 to enclose something in a protective covering.

shed¹ *verb* (**sheds, shedding, shed**) 1 to allow leaves, hair, skin, etc to drop off. 2 to take off a piece of clothing. 3 to drop a load accidentally. 4 to get rid of something. 5 to spread light. ✽ **shed tears** to cry.

shed² *noun* (*plural* **sheds**) 1 a simple garden building for storage. 2 a large building for storing or repairing vehicles, machinery, etc.

she'd *contraction* 1 she had. 2 she would.

sheen *noun* a shine on the surface of something.

sheep *noun* (*plural* **sheep**) an animal with a thick woolly coat, kept for its meat and wool.

sheepdog *noun* (*plural* **sheepdogs**) a dog used for guarding and driving sheep.

sheepish *adjective* embarrassed by shame or shyness. ➤ **sheepishly** *adverb*.

sheer *adjective* 1 absolute or utter. 2 said about a cliff, etc: so steep that it is almost vertical. 3 said about fabric: very thin, almost transparent.

sheet *noun* (*plural* **sheets**) 1 a broad piece of cotton or other fabric used as a covering on a bed. 2 a rectangular piece of paper. 3 a piece of thin flat material such as glass or metal. 4 a broad flat expanse of ice, water, etc.

sheikh *or* **sheik** /shayk *or* sheek/ *noun* (*plural* **sheikhs** *or* **sheiks**) an Arab or Muslim leader. ➤ **sheikhdom** *noun*.

shelf *noun* (*plural* **shelves**) 1 a long flat piece of wood or metal fixed horizontally to a wall or inside a frame to hold objects. 2 a flat projecting layer of rock.

shelf-life *noun* (*plural* **shelf-lives**) the length of time for which an item for sale can be kept in a shop.

shell *noun* (*plural* **shells**) **1** a hard protective covering grown by an animal, such as a shellfish or turtle. **2** the hard outer covering of an egg, nut, or seed. **3** the exterior walls or framework of a building. **4** a projectile filled with explosive fired from a large gun. ~ *verb* (**shells, shelling, shelled**) **1** to take an egg, etc out of its shell. **2** to fire shells at something.

she'll *contraction* **1** she will. **2** she shall.

shellfish *noun* (*plural* **shellfish**) a water animal with a shell.

shelter *noun* (*plural* **shelters**) **1** a structure providing cover or protection. **2** the state of being protected. ~ *verb* (**shelters, sheltering, sheltered**) **1** to give cover and protection to somebody or something. **2** to keep somebody who is being hunted safe or concealed. **3** to take cover or find refuge.

sheltered *adjective* **1** protected from hardship or unpleasantness. **2** said about accommodation: designed for elderly or disabled people to live in, with a warden also living there to help them.

shelve *verb* (**shelves, shelving, shelved**) **1** to put something on a shelf. **2** to postpone something or decide not to go ahead with it. **3** said about ground: to slope gently.

shelves *noun* plural of SHELF.

shepherd *noun* (*plural* **shepherds**) somebody who looks after sheep. ~ *verb* (**shepherds, shepherding, shepherded**) to guide or lead people somewhere.

shepherd's pie *noun* a dish of minced meat covered with mashed potato.

sherbet *noun* **1** a sweet fizzy powder, eaten dry or used to make fizzy drinks. **2** a Middle Eastern cold drink of sweetened diluted fruit juice.

sheriff *noun* (*plural* **sheriffs**) **1** an official in an English or Welsh county, with mainly judicial and ceremonial duties. **2** the chief judge of a Scottish county or district. **3** a county law enforcement officer in the USA.

Sherpa *noun* (*plural* **Sherpa** or **Sherpas**) a member of a Tibetan people living on the southern slopes of the Himalayas.

sherry *noun* (*plural* **sherries**) a specially strengthened type of wine from southern Spain.

she's *contraction* **1** she is. **2** she has.

shield *noun* (*plural* **shields**) **1** *History* a large flat piece of wood, metal, etc carried by soldiers to protect themselves against spears, arrows, or swords. **2** something or somebody that protects or defends you. **3** a sports trophy in the form of a small mounted shield. ~ *verb* (**shields, shielding, shielded**) to protect or conceal something or somebody.

shift *verb* (**shifts, shifting, shifted**) **1** to move, or make something move, from a place or position. **2** to change slightly. **3** to remove a stain by hard cleaning. ~ *noun* (*plural* **shifts**) **1** a slight change. **2** a group of people who work for a number of hours during the day and are then replaced by another group doing the same work. **3** the period during which such a group works. **4** a loose dress or slip.

shiftless *adjective* lacking ambition; lazy.

shifty *adjective* (**shiftier, shiftiest**) appearing to be dishonest or untrustworthy. ▸ **shiftily** *adverb*.

Shiite /shee iet/ *noun* (*plural* **Shiites**) a member of one of the main branches of Islam, which considers Ali, Muhammad's son-in-law, as Muhammad's true successor.

shilling *noun* (*plural* **shillings**) a former British coin, worth one 20th of a pound, or twelve old pence.

shilly-shally verb (**shilly-shallies, shilly-shallying, shilly-shallied**) to be indecisive.

shimmer verb (**shimmers, shimmering, shimmered**) to shine with a softly wavering light. ➤ **shimmer** noun.

shin noun (plural **shins**) the front part of the leg of below the knee. ~ verb (**shins, shinning, shinned**) to climb up or down something by gripping it with your arms and legs.

shine verb (**shines, shining, shone**) **1** to give out or reflect light. **2** to be outstanding or distinguished. **3** to direct the light of a lamp or torch. **4** (past tense and past participle **shined**) to polish something. ~ noun **1** brightness from light. **2** brilliance or splendour. **3** an act of polishing. ➤ **shiny** adjective.

shingle noun a mass of small rounded pebbles on the seashore. ➤ **shingly** adjective.

shingles noun a viral disease causing a rash of painful blisters.

ship noun (plural **ships**) a large boat for travelling by sea. ~ verb (**ships, shipping, shipped**) to transport goods by ship or by other means.

shipment noun (plural **shipments**) **1** the process of transporting goods. **2** a quantity of goods transported.

shipping noun **1** ships. **2** the business of transporting goods.

shipshape adjective neat and tidy.

shipwreck noun (plural **shipwrecks**) **1** the destruction or loss of a ship at sea. **2** a wrecked ship or its remains. ➤ **shipwrecked** adjective.

shipyard noun (plural **shipyards**) a place where ships are built or repaired.

shire noun (plural **shires**) an English county.

shire horse noun (plural **shire horses**) a large powerful horse used for pulling loads.

shirk verb (**shirks, shirking, shirked**) to be lazy and avoid carrying out a duty or responsibility. ➤ **shirker** noun.

shirt noun (plural **shirts**) a piece of clothing for the upper part of the body, with sleeves, a collar, and buttons down the front. ✷ **in shirtsleeves** wearing a shirt without a jacket.

shirty adjective (**shirtier, shirtiest**) informal bad-tempered.

shiver verb (**shivers, shivering, shivered**) to tremble with cold or fever. ➤ **shiver** noun, **shivery** adjective.

shoal[1] noun (plural **shoals**) **1** an underwater sandbank exposed at low tide. **2** an area of shallow water.

shoal[2] noun (plural **shoals**) a large group of fish.

shock[1] noun (plural **shocks**) **1** an unexpected experience that upsets or surprises you greatly. **2** a state in which your body temporarily stops functioning as normal, caused by severe injury or trauma. **3** painful convulsions caused by electricity passing through your body. **4** a violent impact or collision. ~ verb (**shocks, shocking, shocked**) **1** to surprise or alarm somebody. **2** to make somebody feel offended or indignant. ➤ **shockproof** adjective.

shock[2] noun (plural **shocks**) a thick bushy mass of hair.

shocking adjective **1** causing shock or indignation. **2** informal very bad. ➤ **shockingly** adverb.

shock wave noun (plural **shock waves**) a high-pressure wave formed by an explosion or when something travels faster than sound.

shod verb past tense of SHOE.

shoddy adjective (**shoddier, shoddiest**) **1** hastily or poorly made or done. **2** discreditable or despicable. ➤ **shoddily** adverb.

shoe noun (plural **shoes**) **1** an outer covering for the foot with a stiff sole. **2** a horseshoe. ~ verb (**shoes, shoeing, shoed** or **shod**) to fit a horse with a shoe. ✴ **be in somebody's shoes** to be in their position.

shoelace noun (plural **shoelaces**) a lace or string for fastening a shoe.

shoestring ✴ **on a shoestring** informal using very little money.

shogun /shoh gun/ noun (plural **shoguns**) History a Japanese military governor.

shone verb past tense of SHINE.

shook verb past tense of SHAKE.

shoot verb (**shoots, shooting, shot**) **1** to wound or kill a person or animal with a bullet or arrow. **2** to fire a gun or release an arrow from a bow. **3** to move suddenly or rapidly. **4** to kick, throw, or hit a ball towards a goal, basket, etc. **5** to direct a sudden glance or question at somebody. **6** to photograph or film a person or scene. **7** to push or slide a bolt into or out of a fastening. ~ noun (plural **shoots**) **1** a new stem or branch of a plant. **2** a shooting trip or party. **3** a session of photography or filming.

shooting star noun (plural **shooting stars**) a meteor appearing as a temporary streak of light in the sky.

shop noun (plural **shops**) **1** a building or room where goods are sold. **2** a place where things are manufactured or repaired. ~ verb (**shops, shopping, shopped**) to visit a shop to buy something. ✴ **shop around** to look around for the best price for what you want to buy. ➤ **shopper** noun, **shopping** noun.

shopfloor noun **1** the area of a factory where people work machinery to make things. **2** workers as distinct from management.

shopkeeper noun (plural **shopkeepers**) somebody who runs a shop.

shoplift verb (**shoplifts, shoplifting, shoplifted**) to steal from a shop. ➤ **shoplifter** noun, **shoplifting** noun.

shopping noun **1** the buying of goods from a shop. **2** things bought from a shop.

shopsoiled adjective dirty or worn because of being handled or displayed in a shop.

shop steward noun (plural **shop stewards**) a union member elected to represent workers in dealings with the management.

shore¹ noun (plural **shores**) the land bordering the sea or a lake.

shore² verb (**shores, shoring, shored**) ✴ **shore up** to support something with a prop to prevent it from sinking or sagging.

shorn verb past participle of SHEAR.

short adjective **1** not tall. **2** not lasting a long time; brief. **3** not enough to meet requirements: *in short supply*. **4** not reaching far enough. **5** abrupt or curt. **6** said about pastry: crisp and crumbly because it contains a high proportion of fat. ~ adverb **1** abruptly or suddenly. **2** not as far as intended or required. ~ noun (plural **shorts**) **1** informal a drink of spirits. **2** a brief film. **3** a short circuit. ✴ **for short** as an abbreviation. **in short** briefly. **short for** abbreviated from a longer word. **short of/on** not having enough of something.

shortage noun (plural **shortages**) not enough of something; a lack or deficit.

shortbread or **shortcake** noun a thick crumbly biscuit made from flour, sugar, and fat.

short circuit noun (plural **short circuits**) a fault in an electric circuit, where the current takes a shorter route than usual and becomes too strong to be safe.

short-circuit verb (**short-circuits, short-circuiting, short-circuited**) to have a short circuit, or to cause a short circuit in something.

shortcoming noun (plural **shortcomings**) a deficiency or defect.

shortcut noun (plural **shortcuts**) a route or procedure that is more direct than the usual one.

shorten verb (**shortens, shortening, shortened**) to become, or to make something, shorter.

shortfall noun (plural **shortfalls**) the amount by which a which a quantity is less than it ought to be.

shorthand noun a method of rapidly writing down what somebody is saying using special symbols and abbreviations.

shorthanded adjective not having enough staff or help.

short list noun (plural **short lists**) a list of selected candidates from which a final choice is made.

short-list verb (**short-lists, short-listing, short-listed**) to place somebody or something on a short list.

short-lived adjective not living or lasting long.

shortly adverb **1** in a short time; soon. **2** abruptly or curtly.

shorts plural noun knee-length or thigh-length trousers.

short shrift noun unsympathetic treatment.

short-sighted adjective **1** unable to see distant objects clearly. **2** not taking likely consequences into account.

short-staffed adjective not having enough staff.

short-tempered adjective quickly or easily made angry.

shot[1] noun (plural **shots**) **1** the act of firing a gun or other weapon. **2** somebody who shoots, especially with regard to their ability: *She's a good shot.* **3** a stroke, throw, or kick in a game when attempting to score. **4** *informal* an attempt or try. **5** (plural **shot**) a small pellet fired from a shotgun. **7** a heavy metal ball thrown as an athletic field event. **8** a single photograph. **9** a single sequence of a film taken by one camera. **10** an injection of a drug or vaccine. ✻ **like a shot** *informal* very rapidly. **a shot in the arm** *informal* a boost.

shot[2] verb past tense of SHOOT.

shotgun noun (plural **shotguns**) a gun for firing metal shot at short range.

shot put noun a sports event involving throwing a heavy metal ball. ➤ **shot-putter** noun.

should verb the past tense of SHALL, used: **1** to introduce a possibility or probability: *I should be surprised if he came; I should think that's very unlikely to happen.* **2** to express obligation or recommendation: *You should apologize to him; You shouldn't have gone there alone.* **3** to express probability: *They should be here soon; They should have got there by now.* **4** to express what ought to be the case: *They should have been here hours ago.* **5** to express a polite form of suggestion or intention: *I should try if I were you; I should like to thank you all for coming.* **6** in some clauses beginning with *if*: *If you should ever need me, just give me a call.* **7** in some statements: *It's only natural that she should want to go.*

Usage Note should or **would**? *Should* and *would* were in the past used in reported speech where *shall* and *will* were used in direct speech: *I shall be there* and *I said I should be there; She will be there* and *She told me she would be there.* This distinction is now rarely made, and *would* is generally used instead of *should.* Note, however, that only *should*, not *would*, is used with the meaning of 'ought to': *I should go, and so should she.*

---

shoulder noun (plural **shoulders**) the joint linking the upper arm to the body. ~ verb (**shoulders, shouldering, shouldered**) **1** to carry something on your shoulders. **2** to assume the burden or responsibility of something. **3** to push or thrust somebody with your shoulder. ✶ **shoulder to shoulder 1** side by side. **2** united.

shoulder blade *noun* (*plural* **shoulder blades**) either of the two flat triangular bones at the top of the back.

shouldn't *contraction* should not.

shout *verb* (**shouts, shouting, shouted**) **1** to utter a sudden loud cry. **2** to say something in a loud voice. ~ *noun* (*plural* **shouts**) a loud cry or call.

shove *verb* (**shoves, shoving, shoved**) **1** to push somebody or something. **2** to put something somewhere roughly or carelessly. ➤ **shove** *noun*.

shovel *noun* (*plural* **shovels**) an implement like a spade with a broad blade with turned-up sides. ~ *verb* (**shovels, shovelling, shovelled**) **1** to dig or clear something with a shovel. **2** to move something hastily or clumsily in a mass: *shovelling food into his mouth.*

show *verb* (**shows, showing, showed, shown** *or* **showed**) **1** to cause or allow something to be seen. **2** to be visible. **3** to put something on display in an exhibition. **4** to present a film or broadcast for people to watch. **5** to display a feeling or reaction. **6** to demonstrate to somebody how something should be done. **7** to explain or prove something. **8** to lead somebody to a specified place: *Show our guests to their bedrooms, please.* ~ *noun* (*plural* **shows**) **1** an entertainment in a theatre. **2** a light radio or television programme. **3** a large display or exhibition. **4** a competitive exhibition of animals, plants, etc. **5** a pretence. ✶ **for show** just to impress or attract attention. **on show** being displayed.

show off 1 to behave boastfully. **2** to display something proudly. **show up 1** to be, or to make something, clearly visible. **2** *informal* to arrive.

show business *noun* the entertainment industry, including the theatre, films, pop music, and broadcasting.

showcase *noun* (*plural* **showcases**) **1** a case with a glass front or top used for displaying articles. **2** a setting for exhibiting something to best advantage.

showdown *noun* (*plural* **showdowns**) a final confrontation to settle a disagreement.

shower *noun* (*plural* **showers**) **1** a brief fall of rain, snow, etc. **2** a large number of things arriving or presented together. **3** an apparatus that sprays water over the body for washing. **4** an act of washing yourself in this way. ~ *verb* (**showers, showering, showered**) **1** to fall, or to cause things to fall, in a shower. **2** to wash in a shower. **3** to present somebody with a lot of things at once.

showjumping *noun* the competitive sport of riding horses over a course of obstacles.

shown *verb* past participle of SHOW.

show-off *noun* (*plural* **show-offs**) somebody who shows off.

showpiece *noun* (*plural* **showpieces**) an outstanding example used for exhibition.

showroom *noun* (*plural* **showrooms**) a room where goods for sale are displayed.

showy *adjective* (**showier, showiest**) **1** making an attractive show. **2** bright and colourful.

shrank *verb* past tense of SHRINK[1].

shrapnel *noun* fragments of metal thrown out when a bomb or shell explodes.

shred *noun* (*plural* **shreds**) **1** a narrow strip cut or torn off something. **2** a fragment or scrap. ~ *verb* (**shreds,**

shredding, shredded) to cut or tear something into shreds. ➤ **shredder** *noun*.

shrew *noun* (*plural* **shrews**) **1** a small mammal with a long pointed snout and small eyes. **2** *archaic* a bad-tempered nagging woman.

shrewd *adjective* showing good judgment; clever and knowledgeable. ➤ **shrewdly** *adverb*, **shrewdness** *noun*.

shriek *verb* (**shrieks, shrieking, shrieked**) to make a shrill piercing cry. ➤ **shriek** *noun*.

shrift *noun* see SHORT SHRIFT.

shrill *adjective* making a high-pitched sound; piercing. ➤ **shrilly** *adverb*.

shrimp *noun* (*plural* **shrimps** or **shrimp**) **1** a small edible shellfish with a long slender body. **2** *informal* a very small person.

shrine *noun* (*plural* **shrines**) **1** a place where people pray to a saint or god. **2** a place for sacred images or relics.

shrink[1] *verb* (**shrinks, shrinking, shrank, shrunk**) **1** to become, or make something, smaller or shorter. **2** to move back or away in fear or revulsion. **3** (**shrink from**) to be reluctant to accept or do something. ➤ **shrinkage** *noun*.

shrink[2] *noun* (*plural* **shrinks**) *informal* a psychiatrist.

shrivel *verb* (**shrivels, shrivelling, shrivelled**) to shrink and become wrinkled through loss of moisture.

shroud *noun* (*plural* **shrouds**) **1** a piece of cloth for wrapping a corpse for burial. **2** something that covers or conceals. **3** any of the ropes supporting a ship's mast. ~ *verb* (**shrouds, shrouding, shrouded**) to conceal or disguise something.

shrub *noun* (*plural* **shrubs**) a woody plant with several stems, smaller than a tree; a bush. ➤ **shrubby** *adjective*.

shrubbery *noun* (*plural* **shrubberies**) an area planted with shrubs.

shrug *verb* (**shrugs, shrugging, shrugged**) to raise then drop your shoulders to express uncertainty or lack of concern. ✱ **shrug off** to disregard something. ➤ **shrug** *noun*.

shrunk *verb* past participle of SHRINK[1].

shrunken *adjective* having shrunk, or seeming to have shrunk.

shudder *verb* (**shudders, shuddering, shuddered**) to make sudden jerky movements, like shivering or trembling but stronger. ➤ **shudder** *noun*.

shuffle *verb* (**shuffles, shuffling, shuffled**) **1** to walk by moving the feet without lifting them. **2** to rearrange playing cards to produce a random order. ➤ **shuffle** *noun*.

shun *verb* (**shuns, shunning, shunned**) to avoid something or somebody deliberately.

shunt *verb* (**shunts, shunting, shunted**) **1** to move railway vehicles to different positions. **2** to move something or somebody to a less important position. ➤ **shunter** *noun*.

shut *verb* (**shuts, shutting, shut**) **1** to move a door, window, lid, etc into a position to close an opening. **2** to bring parts together to make something no longer open: *Shut your eyes.* **3** to stop doing work or business in a shop, office, etc. ~ *adjective* **1** in the closed position. **2** not open for business. ✱ **shut down** to stop working, operating, or doing business. **shut in/out** to stop somebody or something leaving (or entering) a place. **shut up 1** to lock something securely. **2** to confine somebody or something. **3** *informal* to stop talking.

shutter *noun* (*plural* **shutters**) **1** each of a pair of hinged outside covers for a window. **2** a device that opens and closes the lens aperture of a camera.

shuttle *noun* (*plural* **shuttles**)

1 a device used in weaving that passes the thread of the weft between the threads of the warp. **2** a public-transport vehicle that travels back and forth over a regular route. **3** a space vehicle that travels from and back to earth. ~ *verb* (**shuttles, shuttling, shuttled**) to travel, or transport something, back and forth on a regular route.

shuttlecock *noun* (*plural* **shuttlecocks**) a rounded piece of plastic with a projecting feathery top, struck with rackets in badminton.

shy[1] *adjective* (**shyer, shyest**) nervous about meeting or talking to people; timid. ~ *verb* (**shies, shying, shied**) said about a horse: to start in fright. ✳ **shy away from** to avoid something through nervousness. ➤ **shyly** *adverb*, **shyness** *noun*.

shy[2] *verb* (**shies, shying, shied**) to throw something.

Siamese cat *noun* (*plural* **Siamese cats**) a cat with blue eyes and short pale fur with a darker face.

Siamese twins *plural noun* twins who are born with some part of their bodies joined.

sibilant *adjective English* producing a hissing sound. ~ *noun* (*plural* **sibilants**) a sibilant speech sound, such as s.

sibling *noun* (*plural* **siblings**) a brother or sister.

sick *adjective* **1** affected by a disease; ill. **2** likely or about to vomit. **3** disgusted. **4** said about humour: dealing with things that most people find gruesome. ✳ **be sick 1** to be ill. **2** to vomit. **make somebody sick** to make somebody feel disgusted. **sick of** fed up with. ➤ **sickness** *noun*.

sicken *verb* (**sickens, sickening, sickened**) **1** to become ill. **2** to make somebody feel disgusted.

sickle *noun* (*plural* **sickles**) a tool with a curved blade, for cutting plants or hedges.

sick leave *noun* absence from work because of illness.

sickly *adjective* (**sicklier, sickliest**) **1** weak and often unwell. **2** very unpleasant or making people feel sick.

side *noun* (*plural* **sides**) **1** a surface forming a face of an object, usually not the front, back, top, or bottom. **2** either surface of a thin object. **3** a boundary line of a square or triangle or other figure. **4** a position to the right or left of a person, object, or point. **5** an area or direction considered in relation to a line dividing something. **6** the right or left part of the body. **7** a sports team. **8** a person or group in competition or dispute with another. **9** an aspect or part of something or somebody. **10** *informal* a television channel. ~ *adjective* **1** positioned on a side. **2** additional or subordinate: *a side issue*. ~ *verb* (**sides, siding, sided**) (**side with/against**) to support (or oppose) somebody in a dispute. ✳ **on the side** in addition to a principal occupation. **take sides** to support one or other of the people involved in a dispute.

sideboard *noun* (*plural* **sideboards**) **1** a piece of furniture with cupboards and drawers for storing crockery, cutlery, etc. **2** (**sideboards**) = SIDEBURNS.

sideburns *plural noun* a strip of hair on each side of a man's face in front of his ears.

Word History *Sideburns* is an alteration of *burnsides*, an earlier form of the word. *Burnsides* were named after Ambrose Burnside, a 19th-century American general who had notable sideburns.

---

sidecar *noun* (*plural* **sidecars**) a small vehicle with a single wheel, attached

side effect *noun* (*plural* **side effects**) an additional and often unpleasant effect that a drug has on you besides the effect it is supposed to have.

sidelight *noun* (*plural* **sidelights**) a small extra light beside the headlight on a motor vehicle.

sideline *noun* (*plural* **sidelines**) **1** a business or activity additional to your main occupation. **2** a line marking a side of a court or playing field.

sidelong *adjective and adverb* directed to or from one side.

sidereal /sie**deer**i al/ *adjective Science* to do with the stars.

sideshow *noun* (*plural* **sideshows**) a small show or stall at a circus or fairground.

sidestep *verb* (**sidesteps, sidestepping, sidestepped**) to avoid dealing with an issue or question.

side street *or* **side road** *noun* (*plural* **side streets** *or* **side roads**) a minor street or road branching off a main road.

sidetrack *verb* (**sidetracks, sidetracking, sidetracked**) to make somebody think or talk about something that is not relevant to what they are mainly concerned with.

sidewalk *noun* (*plural* **sidewalks**) *N American* a pavement.

sideways *adverb and adjective* **1** to or from the side. **2** with one side forward.

siding *noun* (*plural* **sidings**) a short length of railway track connected to a main track.

sidle *verb* (**sidles, sidling, sidled**) to walk timidly or furtively.

siege *noun* (*plural* **sieges**) an operation in which a city, castle, etc is surrounded until the people inside it are forced to surrender.

siesta /see**e**sta/ *noun* (*plural* **siestas**) an afternoon nap or rest.

sieve /siv/ *noun* (*plural* **sieves**) a device with a mesh for straining liquids or separating the larger or harder parts of something from smaller or softer parts. ~ *verb* (**sieves, sieving, sieved**) to filter something with a sieve.

sift *verb* (**sifts, sifting, sifted**) **1** to put something through a sieve. **2** to study or examine something, such as evidence, thoroughly.

sigh *noun* (*plural* **sighs**) a deep audible breath that expresses relief, weariness, or grief. ~ *verb* (**sighs, sighing, sighed**) to make a sigh.

sight *noun* (*plural* **sights**) **1** the process of seeing or ability to see. **2** a view or glimpse of somebody or something. **3** something interesting to be seen. **4** (**sights**) the things regarded as worth seeing in a particular place. **5** *informal* something ridiculous or displeasing in appearance. **6** the aiming device on a gun. ~ *verb* (**sights, sighting, sighted**) to see or have a glimpse of something or somebody. ✻ **at first sight 1** when you first see something or somebody. **2** when you first think about something. **in sight** visible. **out of sight** hidden or not visible.

sighted *adjective* able to see.

sightless *adjective* unable to see; blind.

sight-read *verb* (**sight-reads, sight-reading, sight-read**) *Music* to read and perform a piece without studying it beforehand.

sightseeing *noun* touring around a place looking at interesting sights.
➤ **sightseer** *noun*.

sign *noun* (*plural* **signs**) **1** something that indicates the presence or existence of something. **2** a board or notice giving information, directions, etc. **3** a motion or gesture by which you indicate to somebody what you think or want. **4** any of the twelve divisions of the zodiac. ~ *verb* (**signs, signing, signed**) **1** to put a signature on a letter, cheque, etc. **2** (*also* **sign up**) to hire somebody with a contract of employment. **3** to use sign language to express something. ✵ **sign on 1** (*also* **sign up**) to commit yourself to a job by signing a contract of employment. **2** to register as unemployed. ➤ **signer** *noun*.

signal *noun* (*plural* **signals**) **1** an action, gesture, sound, or word that causes somebody to do something, makes an event take place, or gives information or a warning. **2** a set of coloured lights controlling the flow of road or rail traffic. **3** the sound or image conveyed by telephone, radio, radar, or television. ~ *verb* (**signals, signalling, signalled**) **1** to make or send a signal. **2** to warn or order somebody to do something by a signal. **3** to be a sign of something. ~ *adjective* conspicuous or outstanding. ➤ **signaller** *noun*, **signally** *adverb*.

signal box *noun* (*plural* **signal boxes**) a building by a railway line from which signals and points are worked.

signatory *noun* (*plural* **signatories**) somebody who has signed a document.

signature *noun* (*plural* **signatures**) **1** a person's name written by them in a distinctive way to serve as an identification or authorization. **2** the act of signing your name.

signature tune *noun* (*plural* **signature tunes**) an identifying tune used at the beginning of a television or radio programme.

signet ring *noun* (*plural* **signet rings**) a ring engraved with a seal or a person's initials.

significance *noun* **1** meaning. **2** importance.

significant *adjective* **1** having meaning. **2** important. **3** considerable or substantial: *a significant increase*. ➤ **significantly** *adverb*.

signify *verb* (**signifies, signified**) **1** to mean something. **2** to indicate or imply something. **3** to be important; to matter.

signing *noun* (*plural* **signings**) **1** somebody who has recently signed a contract with a sports team. **2** the use of sign language.

sign language *noun* a system of hand gestures and other signs used by deaf people.

signpost *noun* (*plural* **signposts**) a post by the road with signs on it to direct travellers.

Sikh /seek/ *noun* (*plural* **Sikhs**) a person who belongs to an Indian religion that combines aspects of Hinduism and Islam. ➤ **Sikhism** *noun*.

silence *noun* (*plural* **silences**) **1** absence of sound or noise, or a period when there is no sound or noise. **2** inability or unwillingness to speak. ~ *verb* (**silences, silencing, silenced**) **1** to make something silent or much quieter. **2** to prevent somebody from speaking or expressing an opinion.

silencer *noun* (*plural* **silencers**) a device for muffling the noise made by a gun or vehicle exhaust.

silent *adjective* **1** free from sound or noise. **2** saying nothing. **3** said about a film: without spoken dialogue. ➤ **silently** *adverb*.

silhouette /si loo et/ *noun* (*plural* **silhouettes**) the shape or outline of somebody or something, appearing as a dark shadow against a lighter background.

silicon *noun* Science a non-metallic element that is used in alloys, as a semiconductor, and in the manufacture of glass.

silk *noun* **1** a tough shiny fibre produced by silkworms and used for textiles. **2** thread or fabric made from

silkworm noun (plural **silkworms**) the larva of a silk moth, which spins silk in making its cocoon.

sill noun (plural **sills**) a narrow shelf projecting from the base of a window frame or doorway.

silly adjective (**sillier**, **silliest**) 1 lacking common sense or sound judgment. 2 trifling or frivolous. ➤ **silliness** noun.

silt noun a deposit of sediment at the bottom of a river. ~ verb (**silts**, **silting**, **silted**) ✻ **silt up** to become clogged or blocked with silt.

silver noun 1 Science, Art a chemical element that is a soft white metal used in jewellery, ornaments, etc. 2 coins made of silver or a similar metal. 3 a shiny grey colour. ~ adjective 1 made of silver. 2 coloured silver. 3 marking a twenty-fifth anniversary: *silver jubilee*. ➤ **silvery** adjective.

silverfish noun (plural **silverfishes** or **silverfish**) a small silvery wingless insect found in houses.

silver medal noun (plural **silver medals**) a medal of silver awarded for second place in a competition or race.

silver wedding noun (plural **silver weddings**) a twenty-fifth wedding anniversary.

similar adjective generally like something else but not identical to it. ➤ **similarity** noun, **similarly** adverb.

simile /si mi li/ noun (plural **similes**) English a figure of speech comparing two different things, for example *as quick as lightning*.

simmer verb (**simmers**, **simmering**, **simmered**) 1 said about a liquid: to bubble gently just below boiling point. 2 to cook something in a simmering liquid. ✻ **simmer down** to become less excited. ➤ **simmer** noun.

simper verb (**simpers**, **simpering**, **simpered**) to smile in a foolish self-conscious manner. ➤ **simper** noun.

simple adjective 1 easily understood or done. 2 basic or plain. 3 free from showiness; unpretentious. 4 lacking intelligence. 5 of humble birth or position. ➤ **simplicity** noun.

simple-minded noun lacking common sense or intelligence.

simplify verb (**simplifies**, **simplifying**, **simplified**) to make something simple or simpler. ➤ **simplification** noun.

simply adverb 1 in a simple way; clearly. 2 without ornamentation. 3 solely or merely. 4 without any question.

simulate verb (**simulates**, **simulating**, **simulating**) 1 to imitate something. 2 to reproduce what happens when you do something such as flying a plane. ➤ **simulation** noun, **simulator** noun.

sin noun (plural **sins**) 1 an offence against moral or religious law. 2 an action considered to be wrong. ~ verb (**sins**, **sinning**, **sinned**) to commit a sin. ➤ **sinner** noun.

since adverb 1 between a time in the past and now: *He has since reconsidered his decision*. 2 ago: *three years since*. ~ preposition in the period between a time in the past and now: *The situation has changed since last Wednesday*. ~ conjunction 1 in or during the time after. 2 because.

sincere adjective honestly meaning what you say or what is said. ➤ **sincerely** adverb, **sincerity** noun.

sine noun (plural **sines**) Maths the ratio in a right-angled triangle between the side opposite a particular angle and the hypotenuse.

sinecure /si ni kewr/ or /sie ni kewr/ noun (plural **sinecures**) a paid job that involves little or no work.

sinew noun (plural **sinews**) a piece of tissue that connects a muscle with a bone.

sinful *adjective* **1** committing sins. **2** wicked or very bad. ➤ **sinfully** *adverb*, **sinfulness** *noun*.

sing *verb* (**sings, singing, sang, sung**) **1** to produce musical sounds with your voice. **2** to perform a song. ➤ **singer** *noun*.

singe *verb* (**singes, singeing, singed**) to burn something slightly.

single *adjective* **1** not accompanied by others. **2** individual or distinct: *every single one*. **3** suitable for or involving only one person. **4** consisting of or having only one part. **5** not married. **6** said about a ticket: valid for a journey to a place but not back again. ~ *noun* (*plural* **singles**) **1** a CD or record with one short track or a small amount of music. **2** a single ticket. **3** (**singles**) people who are unmarried or do not have a regular partner. ~ *verb* (**singles, singling, singled**) ✱ **single out** to select somebody or something specially from a group. ➤ **singly** *adverb*.

single file *noun* a line of people moving one behind the other.

single-handed *adjective* done by one person alone or without help. ➤ **single-handedly** *adverb*.

single-minded *adjective* having one single purpose that you are determined to carry out. ➤ **single-mindedly** *adverb*.

single parent *noun* (*plural* **single parents**) a person bringing up a child without a partner.

singles *noun* (*plural* **singles**) a tennis, badminton, or squash match between two players.

singlet *noun* (*plural* **singlets**) a vest or a similar garment without sleeves.

singsong *noun* (*plural* **singsongs**) **1** a monotonous way of speaking like the rhythm of song. **2** an informal gathering for singing.

singular *adjective* **1** *English in* grammar, referring to one person or thing. **2** very unusual or strange. ➤ **singular** *noun*, **singularly** *adverb*.

sinister *adjective* seeming likely to be evil or harmful. ➤ **sinisterly** *adverb*.

sink *verb* (**sinks, sinking, sank, sunk**) **1** to go down below the surface of liquid or to the bottom of the sea, a container, etc. **2** to penetrate, or make something such as your teeth penetrate, the surface of something soft. **3** to dig or bore a well or shaft. **4** to fall or drop to a lower place or level: *He sank to his knees*. **5** to invest money in something. ~ *noun* (*plural* **sinks**) a basin connected to a drain and a water supply. ✱ **sink in** to be understood.

sinuous *adjective* having a wavy form; winding. ➤ **sinuously** *adverb*.

sinus /sie nus/ *noun* (*plural* **sinuses**) a cavity in the bones of the skull that connects with the nostrils.

sinusitis *noun* inflammation of a nasal sinus.

sip *verb* (**sips, sipping, sipped**) to drink something delicately or a little at a time. ➤ **sip** *noun*.

siphon *or* **syphon** *noun* (*plural* **siphons** *or* **syphons**) **1** a tube for transferring liquid up over the side of a container and down to a lower level by atmospheric pressure. **2** a bottle for holding and squirting out a fizzy liquid. ~ *verb* (**siphons, siphoning, siphoned** *or* **syphons**, etc) to draw off liquid with a siphon. ✱ **siphon off** to take money in small amounts.

sir *noun* **1** a respectful word used to address a man. **2** (**Sir**) used as a title of a knight or baronet.

sire *noun* (*plural* **sires**) **1** the male parent of an animal. **2** *History* a form of address to a king.

siren *noun* (*plural* **sirens**) **1** a device that makes a loud wailing sound as a warning. **2** (**Siren**) in Greek mythology, one of a group of winged women who lured sailors to destruc-

sirloin

tion by their singing. **3** a dangerously seductive woman.

sirloin *noun* a cut of beef from the upper part of the loin.

sissy *noun* (*plural* **sissies**) *informal* a cowardly or effeminate man.

sister *noun* (*plural* **sisters**) **1** a woman or girl who has the same parents as another person. **2** a female colleague. **3** a female member of a religious order. **4** a senior female nurse. ➤ **sisterly** *adjective*.

sisterhood *noun* (*plural* **sisterhoods**) **1** the state of being sisters. **2** a religious community of women. **3** a group of women bound by a common interest.

sister-in-law *noun* (*plural* **sisters-in-law**) **1** the sister of your husband or wife. **2** the wife of your brother.

sit *verb* (**sits, sitting, sat**) **1** to rest in a position supported by the buttocks and with your back upright. **2** to have enough seats for a certain number of people. **3** said about a court or parliament: to be in session for official business. **4** to lie or stand in a particular position. **5** said about a bird: to cover eggs until they hatch. **6** *Art* to pose as a model for an artist or photographer. **7** to be a candidate in an examination.

sitar *noun* (*plural* **sitars**) *Music* an Indian lute with a long neck. ➤ **sitarist** *noun*.

site *noun* (*plural* **sites**) **1** an area of ground occupied by a building, town, etc. **2** a scene of a specified activity. **3** *ICT* = WEBSITE. ~ *verb* (**sites, siting, sited**) to place or build something in a particular position.

sit-in *noun* (*plural* **sit-ins**) the occupation of a building by a number of people as a protest.

sitter *noun* (*plural* **sitters**) **1** *Art* somebody who sits as an artist's model. **2** = BABYSITTER. **3** = SITTING DUCK.

sitting *noun* (*plural* **sittings**) **1** *Art* a period of posing for a portrait. **2** a period when a group of people are served a meal. **3** a session of an official body.

sitting duck *noun* (*plural* **sittings ducks**) *informal* an easy target.

sitting room *noun* (*plural* **sitting rooms**) a room for sitting and relaxing in.

situated *adjective* in a particular place or situation.

situation *noun* (*plural* **situations**) **1** the conditions and circumstances at a particular time or place. **2** the position of something in relation to its surroundings. **3** a job or post. ➤ **situational** *adjective*.

six *noun* (*plural* **sixes**) **1** the number 6. **2** a shot in cricket that crosses the boundary before it bounces and scores six runs. ✶ **at sixes and sevens** in confusion or disorder. **knock for six** *informal* to overwhelm or astonish somebody. ➤ **sixth** *adjective and noun*, **sixthly** *adverb*.

sixteen *adjective and noun* (*plural* **sixteens**) the number 16. ➤ **sixteenth** *adjective and noun*.

sixth sense *noun* an instinctive ability to know what is going to happen that does not rely on information from your five physical senses.

sixty *adjective and noun* (*plural* **sixties**) **1** the number 60. **2** (**the sixties**) the numbers 60 to 69. ➤ **sixtieth** *adjective and noun*.

sizable *or* **sizeable** *adjective* fairly large.

size *noun* (*plural* **sizes**) **1** the overall dimensions or measurements of something. **2** each of a series of measurements in which things, especially items of clothing, are made. ~ *verb* (**sizes, sizing, sized**) to arrange or grade things according to their size. ✶ **size up** to form an opinion or estimate of somebody or something.

sizeable *adjective* see SIZABLE.

sizzle *verb* (**sizzles, sizzling, sizzled**) **1** to make the hissing sound of frying food. **2** *informal* to be very hot. ➤ **sizzling** *adjective*.

skate[1] *noun* (*plural* **skates**) an ice skate or a roller skate. ~ *verb* (**skates, skating, skated**) to glide along on skates. ➤ **skater** *noun*.

skate[2] *noun* (*plural* **skates** *or* **skate**) a food fish of the ray family.

skateboard *noun* (*plural* **skateboards**) a narrow board mounted on small wheels for riding on. ➤ **skateboarder** *noun*, **skateboarding** *noun*.

skeleton *noun* (*plural* **skeletons**) **1** the framework of bones in the body of a human or animal. **2** basic framework.

sketch *noun* (*plural* **sketches**) **1** a rough drawing. **2** a brief description or outline. **3** *Drama* a very short comic play. ~ *verb* (**sketches, sketching, sketched**) **1** to make a sketch of something or somebody. **2** to describe something briefly.

sketchbook *noun* (*plural* **sketchbooks**) a pad of plain paper for sketching.

sketchy *adjective* (**sketchier, sketchiest**) lacking detail; done roughly and with gaps in it. ➤ **sketchily** *adverb*.

skew *adjective* slanting; not straight or level. ~ *verb* (**skews, skewing, skewed**) **1** to make something skew. **2** to present something in a biased way.

skewer *noun* (*plural* **skewers**) a long wooden or metal pin for holding food together while cooking.

ski *noun* (*plural* **skis**) one of a pair of long narrow strips of wood, metal, or plastic attached to your feet for gliding over snow. ~ *verb* (**skis, skiing, skied**) to travel on skis. ➤ **skier** *noun*.

skid *verb* (**skidded, skidding, skidded**) **1** said about a vehicle: to slide out of control. **2** to slip or slide. ~ *noun* (*plural* **skids**) **1** an act of skidding. **2** a runner used as part of the landing gear of an aircraft.

ski jump *noun* (*plural* **ski jumps**) a steep ramp that skiers jump off onto a slope below.

skilful *adjective* having or showing skill; expert. ➤ **skilfully** *adverb*.

Usage Note Notice that there is only one *l* before the *-ful* ending.

ski lift *noun* (*plural* **ski lifts**) a series of seats suspended from an overhead cable, used for transporting skiers up and down a mountainside.

skill *noun* (*plural* **skills**) **1** the ability to do things, or one particular thing, well. **2** a special ability you have or that you need for a job.

skilled *adjective* **1** having skill. **2** requiring trained workers.

skim *verb* (**skims, skimming, skimmed**) **1** to remove floating fat or scum from the surface of a liquid. **2** to pass swiftly or lightly over something. **3** to read something over quickly.

skimmed milk *noun* milk with the cream removed.

skimp *verb* (**skimps, skimping, skimped**) (**skimp on**) to use too little of something to do a job properly.

skimpy *adjective* (**skimpier, skimpiest**) inadequate in quality, size, etc; scanty. ➤ **skimpily** *adverb*.

skin *noun* (*plural* **skins**) **1** the external covering of the body of a person or animal. **2** an outer covering, such as the peel or rind of a fruit or vegetable. **3** the skin and fur of an animal, prepared and used e.g. for clothing. **4** a film that forms on the surface of a liquid. ~ *verb* (**skins, skinning, skinned**) to remove the skin of an animal. ✳ **by the skin of your teeth** only just; barely.

skin diving *noun* swimming under water with flippers and an aqualung.

skinflint *noun* (*plural* **skinflints**) *informal* a very mean person.

skinhead *noun* (*plural* **skinheads**) a member of a group of young people with extremely short hair.

skinny *adjective* (**skinnier, skinniest**) *informal* very thin. ➤ **skinniness** *noun*.

skint *adjective informal* having no money.

skintight *adjective* said about clothing: fitting close to your body.

skip¹ *verb* (**skips, skipping, skipped**) **1** to move with light leaps, or by hopping on alternate feet. **2** to jump repeatedly over a rope swung over your head and under your feet. **3** to pass over or omit something. **4** to fail to attend a class, appointment, etc. ~ *noun* (*plural* **skips**) a skipping movement.

skip² *noun* (*plural* **skips**) a large open container for waste or rubble.

skipper *noun* (*plural* **skippers**) *informal* the captain of a ship, aircraft, or sports team.

skirmish *noun* (*plural* **skirmishes**) a brief clash or fight.

skirt *noun* (*plural* **skirts**) a women's and girls' piece of clothing that hangs from the waist. ~ *verb* (**skirts, skirting, skirted**) **1** to go or extend along the edge of something. **2** (*also* **skirt round**) to avoid dealing with a difficulty.

skirting *or* **skirting board** *noun* (*plural* **skirtings** *or* **skirting boards**) a strip of board fixed along the base of an inside wall.

skit *noun* (*plural* **skits**) a satirical sketch.

skittish *adjective* **1** said of an animal: nervous and easily frightened. **2** lively or frisky. ➤ **skittishly** *adverb*.

skittle *noun* (*plural* **skittles**) **1** (**skittles**) a game played by rolling a wooden ball at a group of pins in order to knock them over. **2** a pin used in skittles.

skive *verb* (**skives, skiving, skived**) *informal* to avoid work or duty. ➤ **skiver** *noun*.

skulk *verb* (**skulks, skulking, skulked**) to move stealthily or furtively.

skull *noun* (*plural* **skulls**) a bony case forming the skeleton of the head and enclosing the brain.

skullcap *noun* (*plural* **skullcaps**) a close-fitting cap without a peak.

skunk *noun* (*plural* **skunks**) a black-and-white American animal that can spray a foul-smelling liquid in self-defence.

sky *noun* (*plural* **skies**) the upper atmosphere seen from the earth as a blue covering during daylight.

sky blue *noun* a light blue colour.

skydiving *noun* the sport of jumping from an aircraft and performing body manoeuvres in the air before opening a parachute. ➤ **skydiver** *noun*.

skylark *noun* (*plural* **skylarks**) a lark that rises almost vertically in flight and sings as it flies.

skylight *noun* (*plural* **skylights**) a window in a roof or ceiling.

skyline *noun* (*plural* **skylines**) an outline of buildings or landscape seen against the sky.

skyscraper *noun* (*plural* **skyscrapers**) a very tall building with many storeys.

slab *noun* (*plural* **slabs**) a large thick flat piece of something, especially stone.

slack *adjective* **1** not taut; loose. **2** lazy or lax. **3** not busy. ~ *noun* (*plural* **slacks**) **1** the part of a rope or string that is not held taut. **2** (**slacks**) casual trousers. ~ *verb* (**slacks, slacking, slacked**) **1** to be lazy or work carelessly. **2** to slacken. ➤ **slacker** *noun*, **slackly** *adverb*, **slackness** *noun*.

slacken *verb* (**slackens, slackening, slackened**) **1** to become, or make something, less taut. **2** to become, or make something, less active, rapid, or intense.

slag[1] *noun* waste matter left over from when metal ores are smelted. **2** waste material from coal mining.

slag[2] *verb* (**slags, slagging, slagged**) ✴ **slag off** *informal* to criticize somebody abusively.

slagheap *noun* (*plural* **slagheaps**) a mound of waste material from a mine.

slain *verb* past participle of SLAY.

slake *verb* (**slakes, slaking, slaked**) to satisfy or quench a thirst or desire.

slalom *noun* (*plural* **slaloms**) a skiing or canoeing race on winding course between obstacles.

slam *verb* (**slams, slamming, slammed**) **1** to shut something noisily. **2** to put or throw something down noisily. **3** (**slam into**) to crash into something violently. **4** *informal* to criticize somebody or something harshly. ➤ **slam** *noun*.

slander *noun* (*plural* **slanders**) **1** the crime of saying untrue things that damage a person's reputation. **2** something said that is untrue and damaging to a person's reputation. ~ *verb* (**slanders, slandering, slandered**) to say untrue things about somebody that damage their reputation. ➤ **slanderer** *noun*, **slanderous** *adjective*.

slang *noun* informal spoken words and phrases, often of a kind associated with a particular group of people. ➤ **slangy** *adjective*.

slant *verb* (**slants, slanting, slanted**) **1** to lean or slope. **2** to present information from a particular point of view. ~ *noun* (*plural* **slants**) **1** a slanting direction or position. **2** a particular point of view or emphasis.

slap *noun* (*plural* **slaps**) **1** a sharp blow with the open hand. **2** a noise that suggests a slap. ~ *verb* (**slaps, slapping, slapped**) **1** to give somebody a slap. **2** to hit something with the sound of a slap. **3** to put paint or makeup on hastily or carelessly.

slapdash *adjective and adverb* done in a haphazard or slipshod manner.

slapstick *noun* comedy characterized by farce and horseplay.

slap-up *adjective informal* said about a meal: lavish or extravagant.

slash *verb* (**slashes, slashing, slashed**) **1** to cut with violent sweeping strokes. **2** to cut slits in something. **3** *informal* to reduce a price drastically. ~ *noun* (*plural* **slashes**) **1** a slashing cut. **2** *English* a small diagonal line (/) used in writing to show alternatives.

slat *noun* (*plural* **slats**) a thin narrow strip of wood, metal, or plastic, usually one of a number arranged side by side and overlapping each other. ➤ **slatted** *adjective*.

slate[1] *noun* (*plural* **slates**) **1** a fine-grained rock that is easily split into thin layers. **2** a flat piece of this used as roofing material or for writing on.

slate[2] *verb* (**slates, slating, slated**) *informal* to criticize somebody severely.

slaughter *noun* **1** the killing of livestock for food. **2** the violent killing of many people. ~ *verb* (**slaughters, slaughtering, slaughtered**) **1** to kill animals for food. **2** to kill people violently or in large numbers.

slaughterhouse *noun* (*plural* **slaughterhouses**) a place where animals are killed for food.

slave *noun* (*plural* **slaves**) **1** a person held as the property of another person and bound to obey them. **2** a person who is dominated by a specified thing: *a slave to fashion*. ~ *verb* (**slaves, slaving, slaved**) to work very hard.

slave driver noun (plural **slave drivers**) informal somebody who makes other people work very hard.

slaver /slaver or slayver/ verb (**slavers, slavering, slavered**) to have saliva dripping from your mouth.

slavery noun **1** the state of being a slave. **2** the practice of owning slaves.

slavish adjective **1** showing no originality. **2** servile. ➤ **slavishly** adverb.

slay verb (**slays, slaying, slew, slain**) archaic to kill somebody violently or with great bloodshed.

sleaze noun informal corrupt or immoral behaviour.

sleazy adjective (**sleazier, sleaziest**) **1** said about a place: squalid and disreputable. **2** said about behaviour: corrupt or immoral.

sled noun (plural **sleds**) N American = SLEDGE.

sledge noun (plural **sledges**) **1** a vehicle with runners for travelling over snow or ice. **2** a toboggan.

sledgehammer noun (plural **sledgehammers**) a large heavy hammer.

sleek adjective smooth and glossy.

sleep noun **1** a natural period of unconsciousness with the eyes closed and the body relaxed. **2** a period spent sleeping. ~ verb (**sleeps, sleeping, slept**) **1** to rest in a state of sleep. **2** informal (**sleep with/together**) to have sexual intercourse with somebody. **3** to provide sleeping accommodation for a specified number of people. ✵ **go to sleep 1** to fall asleep. **2** to become numb. **put to sleep** to kill an animal humanely.

sleeper noun (plural **sleepers**) **1** a sleeping car. **2** a ring or stud worn in a pierced ear to keep the hole open. **3** one of the wooden or concrete supports on which railway rails are laid.

sleeping bag noun (plural **sleeping bags**) a padded bag for sleeping in when camping.

sleeping pill noun (plural **sleeping pills**) a tablet taken to help a person sleep.

sleepwalk verb (**sleepwalks, sleepwalking, sleepwalked**) to walk about while you are asleep. ➤ **sleepwalker** noun.

sleepy adjective (**sleepier, sleepiest**) **1** ready to fall asleep. **2** said about a place: quiet and inactive. ➤ **sleepily** adverb, **sleepiness** noun.

sleet noun partly frozen falling rain, or snow and rain falling together.

sleeve noun (plural **sleeves**) **1** the part of a piece of clothing covering the arm. **2** a covering for a record. ✵ **up your sleeve** kept hidden for future use. ➤ **sleeveless** adjective.

sleigh /slay/ noun (plural **sleighs**) a large sledge pulled by horses or reindeer.

sleight of hand /sliet ov hand/ noun skilful use of the hands in conjuring or juggling.

slender adjective **1** gracefully slim. **2** flimsy or meagre.

slept verb past tense and past participle of SLEEP.

sleuth /slooth/ noun (plural **sleuths**) informal a detective.

slew[1] verb (**slews, slewing, slewed**) to slide or swing about out of control.

slew[2] verb past tense of SLAY.

slice noun (plural **slices**) **1** a thin, broad, flat piece cut from something. **2** a portion or share. **3** a tool with a broad blade for lifting food. ~ verb (**slices, slicing, sliced**) **1** to cut something into slices. **2** to cut through something. **3** to cut something off something else.

slick adjective **1** done quickly and skilfully. **2** superficially impressive but not sincere. **3** smooth and slippery.

~ *noun* (*plural* **slicks**) a film of oil floating on water. ➤ **slickly** *adverb*.

slide *verb* (**slides, sliding, slid**) **1** to move, or move something, over or along a smooth surface. **2** to go, or put something somewhere, quietly and unobtrusively. **3** to get worse. ~ *noun* (*plural* **slides**) **1** a structure with a smooth sloping surface down which children slide in play. **2** a sliding movement. **3** a clip for the hair. **4** a flat piece of glass on which an object is examined under a microscope. **5** a transparent photograph that is viewed with a projector.

slight[1] *adjective* **1** small. **2** having a slim or frail body. **3** not serious; minor or unimportant. ➤ **slightly** *adverb*.

slight[2] *verb* (**slights, slighting, slighted**) to treat somebody with disrespect or indifference. ➤ **slight** *noun*.

slim *adjective* (**slimmer, slimmest**) **1** attractively thin. **2** small in width in relation to length or height. **3** slight: *a slim chance*. ~ *verb* (**slims, slimming, slimmed**) **1** to make yourself thinner, for example by dieting. **2** (*often* **slim down**) to make something smaller. ➤ **slimmer** *noun*.

slime *noun* an unpleasantly thick and slippery substance.

slimy *adjective* (**slimier, slimiest**) **1** like slime, or covered with slime. **2** *informal* trying insincerely to be pleasant or friendly.

sling *noun* (*plural* **slings**) **1** a looped piece of material used to raise or support something. **2** a bandage suspended from the neck to support an injured arm. **3** a short strap used as a simple weapon for throwing stones. ~ *verb* (**slings, slinging, slung**) **1** to throw something carelessly. **2** to raise or carry something in a sling.

slink *verb* (**slinks, slinking, slunk**) to move quietly or stealthily.

slinky *adjective* (**slinkier, slinkiest**) *informal* sleek and sexy in movement or appearance.

slip[1] *verb* (**slips, slipping, slipped**) **1** to slide out of place. **2** to slide accidentally on a slippery surface. **3** to decline from a standard. **4** to go quietly and quickly: *We'll slip out the back way*. **5** to move, place, or pass something quickly and easily: *I slipped the note into the drawer*. **6** to get free from a restraint: *The dog slipped his collar*. ~ *noun* (*plural* **slips**) **1** an instance of slipping. **2** a minor mistake. **3** a woman's short undergarment. **4** in cricket, a fielding position close behind the batsman on the off side. ✳ **give somebody the slip** *informal* to escape from somebody who is chasing you. **let slip 1** to say something casually or accidentally. **2** to fail to take a chance. **slip up** to make a careless mistake. **slip your mind/memory** to be forgotten or overlooked. ➤ **slippage** *noun*.

slip[2] *noun* (*plural* **slips**) **1** a small piece of paper. **2** a small, slim young person: *a slip of a girl*. **3** a shoot cut for planting or grafting.

slipper *noun* (*plural* **slippers**) a flat comfortable shoe for wearing indoors.

slippery *adjective* (**slipperier, slipperiest**) **1** causing people or things to sliding because of being icy, greasy, wet, or polished. **2** said about a person: not to be trusted.

slip road *noun* (*plural* **slip roads**) a short road by which you get onto or off a major road or motorway.

slipshod *adjective* careless or slovenly.

slipstream *noun* (*plural* **slipstreams**) **1** a stream of air or water driven backward by a propeller. **2** an area of reduced air pressure immediately behind a moving vehicle.

slip-up noun (plural **slip-ups**) informal a small mistake or oversight.

slipway noun (plural **slipways**) a ramp sloping down into water, for launching ships or boats.

slit verb (**slits, slitting, slit**) to make a narrow cut in something. ~ noun (plural **slits**) a long narrow cut or opening.

slither verb (**slithers, slithering, slithered**) 1 to move across a surface with a sliding or twisting motion. 2 to slide unsteadily on a slippery surface. ➤ **slither** noun, **slithery** adjective.

sliver /sli vǝr/ noun (plural **slivers**) a small slender piece cut or broken off something.

slob noun (plural **slobs**) informal a lazy slovenly person.

slobber verb (**slobbers, slobbering, slobbered**) to let saliva dribble from your mouth.

slog verb (**slogs, slogging, slogged**) 1 to move slowly and laboriously. 2 to work hard and continuously. 3 to hit something hard and wildly.

slogan noun (plural **slogans**) a brief catchy phrase used in advertising or to sum up a particular point of view.

sloop noun (plural **sloops**) a sailing ship with one mast.

slop verb (**slops, slopping, slopped**) 1 said about a liquid: to spill over the side of a container. 2 to serve or apply something messily.

slope verb (**slopes, slopping, sloped**) 1 to be at a angle. 2 to place something at an angle. ~ noun (plural **slopes**) 1 a strip or area that is lower at one end than the other. 2 the side of a mountain or hill. ➤ **sloping** adjective.

sloppy adjective (**sloppier, sloppiest**) 1 slovenly or careless. 2 excessively sentimental. ➤ **sloppily** adverb, **sloppiness** noun.

slops plural noun 1 fairly liquid waste food fed to animals. 2 liquid household waste.

slosh verb (**sloshes, sloshing, sloshed**) 1 said about liquid: to move with a splashing motion or sound. 2 to splash through water, mud, etc. 3 informal to hit somebody hard.

slot noun (plural **slots**) 1 a narrow opening that you insert something into. 2 a place in a timetable or scheme. ~ verb (**slots, slotting, slotted**) * **slot in/into** to fit something between other things. ➤ **slotted** adjective.

sloth /slohth/ noun (plural **sloths**) 1 laziness. 2 a slow-moving mammal that hangs from the branches of trees. ➤ **slothful** adjective.

slot machine noun (plural **slot machines**) a machine operated by inserting a coin in a slot.

slouch verb (**slouches, slouching, slouched**) to sit, stand, or walk limply or lazily. ➤ **slouch** noun.

slovenly /slu vn li/ adjective 1 untidy or dirty. 2 lazy and careless. ➤ **slovenliness** noun.

slow adjective 1 moving or only able to move at a low speed. 2 requiring or taking a long time. 3 said about a clock or watch: showing a time earlier than the actual time. 4 not able to learn or understand things easily. 5 lacking in activity. ~ adverb slowly. ~ verb (**slows, slowing, slowed**) to become, or to make something, slow or slower. ➤ **slowly** adverb, **slowness** noun.

slow motion noun the effect of running a film or video at less than the standard speed, so that movement is slowed down.

slowworm noun (plural **slowworms**)

a small lizard with a snake-like body.

sludge noun soft wet mud or a slimy substance. ➤ **sludgy** adjective.

slug[1] noun (plural **slugs**) a small slimy animal like a snail with no shell.

slug[2] noun (plural **slugs**) informal a bullet.

sluggard noun (plural **sluggards**) a lazy person.

sluggish adjective **1** slow in movement or action. **2** lacking energy or activity. ➤ **sluggishly** adverb.

sluice /sloos/ noun (plural **sluices**) **1** (also **sluice gate**) a gate or other device for controlling the flow of water. **2** a channel for carrying off surplus water. ~ verb (**sluices, sluicing, sluiced**) to wash something in running water.

slum noun (plural **slums**) **1** a poor run-down area in a city. **2** a squalid place to live. ➤ **slummy** adjective.

slumber verb (**slumbers, slumbering, slumbering**) literary to sleep. ➤ **slumber** noun.

slump verb (**slumps, slumping, slumped**) **1** to sit or drop down heavily. **2** to decline rapidly. ~ noun (plural **slumps**) a period when the economy of a country is in a bad state and little business is being done.

slung verb past tense and past participle of SLING.

slunk verb past tense and past participle of SLINK.

slur[1] verb (**slurs, slurring, slurred**) **1** to pronounce words or sounds unclearly. **2** Music to perform notes of different pitch in a smooth or connected manner. ~ noun (plural **slurs**) Music a curved line connecting notes to be slurred.

slur[2] verb (**slurs, slurring, slurred**) to make unfair and insulting comments about somebody. ➤ **slur** noun.

slurp verb (**slurps, slurping, slurped**) to eat or drink something with a loud sucking sound. ➤ **slurp** noun.

slush noun **1** partly melted or watery snow. **2** informal excessively sentimental language. ➤ **slushy** adjective.

sly adjective (**slyer, slyest**) **1** cunning and furtive. **2** humorously mischievous; roguish. ➤ **slyly** adverb.

smack[1] noun (plural **smacks**) **1** a sharp blow with the open hand. **2** the sound of such a blow. **3** a loud kiss. ~ verb (**smacks, smacking, smacked**) **1** to give somebody a smack. **2** to strike or collide with something sharply. **3** to open your lips with a sudden sharp sound. ~ adverb informal exactly or directly.

smack[2] verb (**smacks, smacking, smacked**) (**smack of**) to have a trace of something undesirable.

small[1] adjective **1** of less than normal size. **2** young or immature. **3** not great in quantity, value, importance, etc. ✻ **the small of the back** the narrowest part of your back. ➤ **smallness** noun.

smallholding noun (plural **smallholdings**) a small farm mainly growing vegetables. ➤ **smallholder** noun.

small hours plural noun (**the small hours**) the hours just after midnight.

smallpox noun an infectious disease with fever and pustules that form scabs, usually leaving permanent scars.

small print noun (**the small print**) a part of a document printed in small type, often setting out unattractive conditions for something.

small talk noun light or casual conversation.

smarmy adjective (**smarmier, smarmiest**) informal insincerely friendly or polite.

smart

smart¹ *adjective* **1** neat or elegant in dress or appearance. **2** clever. **3** brisk. ➤ **smartly** *adverb*, **smartness** *noun*.

smart² *verb* (**smarts, smarting, smarted**) **1** to be the source or place of a sharp stinging pain. **2** to feel upset or angry.

smart card *noun* (*plural* **smart cards**) a plastic card with a memory chip that holds information.

smarten *verb* (**smartens, smartening, smartened**) (*often* **smarten up**) to become, or make somebody, smarter.

smash *verb* (**smashes, smashing, smashed**) **1** to break, or break something, violently into pieces. **2** to drive, throw, or hit something violently. **3** in tennis, to hit a ball downward forcefully. **4** to destroy or defeat something. ~ *noun* (*plural* **smashes**) **1** the action or sound of smashing. **2** a violent blow or collision. **3** *informal* a smash hit.

smash hit *noun* (*plural* **smash hits**) *informal* a very successful song, show, etc.

smashing *adjective informal* excellent.

smattering *noun* a slight knowledge of a subject or a foreign language.

smear *verb* (**smears, smearing, smeared**) **1** to rub or spread a sticky or greasy substance onto something. **2** to damage the reputation of somebody. ~ *noun* (*plural* **smears**) **1** a sticky or greasy mark. **2** an untrue accusation. **3** material smeared on a slide for examination under a microscope. ➤ **smeary** *adjective*.

smell *noun* (*plural* **smells**) **1** the sense which uses sensitive areas in the nose to detect a kind of flavour given off by things. **2** the quality given off by something and detected by this sense; an odour. **3** an unpleasant odour. **4** an act of smelling. ~ *verb* (**smells, smelling, smelt** *or* **smelled**) **1** to detect the smell of something. **2** to sniff something in order to detect its smell. **3** to have a specified smell, especially an unpleasant one. ✻ **smell a rat** *informal* to suspect that something is wrong. ➤ **smelly** *adjective*.

smelt¹ *verb* (**smelts, smelting, smelted**) to melt ore to separate out the metal. ➤ **smelter** *noun*.

smelt² *verb* past tense and past participle of SMELL.

smile *verb* (**smiles, smiling, smiled**) to make the corners of your mouth curve up to express amusement, friendliness, pleasure, etc. ➤ **smile** *noun*.

smirk *verb* (**smirks, smirking, smirked**) to smile in a smug manner. ➤ **smirk** *noun*.

smite *verb* (**smites, smiting, smote, smitten**) *archaic* to strike somebody or something sharply or heavily. ✻ **be smitten by/with** to be attracted to something or somebody.

smith *noun* (*plural* **smiths**) a person who works with metal, especially a blacksmith.

smithereens *plural noun* small fragments.

smitten *verb* past participle of SMITE.

smock *noun* (*plural* **smocks**) a garment like a long loose shirt often worn over other clothes to protect them.

smog *noun* (*plural* **smogs**) a fog made heavier and darker by smoke. ➤ **smoggy** *adjective*.

smoke *noun* **1** the visible mixture of gases and particles produced by burning. **2** an act of smoking tobacco. ~ *verb* (**smokes, smoking, smoked**) **1** to emit smoke. **2** to inhale and exhale the smoke of a cigarette, pipe, etc. **3** to preserve meat or fish by exposing it to smoke. ➤ **smoked** *adjective*, **smoker** *noun*, **smoky** *adjective*.

smokeless *adjective* **1** producing little or no smoke. **2** where smoke is not permitted.

smokescreen *noun* (*plural* **smokescreens**) **1** a screen of smoke used to conceal a military position or activity. **2** something said or done to confuse people or conceal what is really happening.

smooth *adjective* **1** having a continuous even surface. **2** even and uninterrupted in movement or flow. **3** free from difficulties or obstructions. **4** free from lumps. ~ *verb* (**smoothes, smoothing, smoothed**) **1** to make something smooth or flat. **2** to remove obstructions or difficulties from somebody's way forward. ➤ **smoothly** *adverb*, **smoothness** *noun*.

smorgasbord /smaw gas bawd/ *noun* a variety of foods and dishes, such as hot and cold meat or fish, cheeses, salads, etc.

smote *verb* past tense of SMITE.

smother *verb* (**smothers, smothering, smothered**) **1** to suffocate somebody by covering their nose and mouth. **2** to extinguish a fire by covering it with something to exclude oxygen. **3** to prevent something, such as an emotion, from being visible or expressed. **4** to cover something thickly with something.

smoulder *verb* (**smoulders, smouldering, smouldered**) **1** to burn with smoke but no flame. **2** to show suppressed anger, hate, jealousy, etc.

smudge *noun* (*plural* **smudges**) a blurry mark or streak. ~ *verb* (**smudges, smudging, smudged**) **1** to make a smudge on something. **2** to make something indistinct.

smug *adjective* (**smugger, smuggest**) excessively pleased with yourself; self-satisfied. ➤ **smugly** *adverb*, **smugness** *noun*.

smuggle *verb* (**smuggles, smuggling, smuggled**) **1** to import or export goods illegally without paying duties. **2** to bring somebody or something into or out of a place secretly. ➤ **smuggler** *noun*.

smut *noun* (*plural* **smuts**) **1** a particle of soot or dirt. **2** indecent language, writing, or pictures. ➤ **smutty** *adjective*.

snack *noun* (*plural* **snacks**) a light meal eaten between regular meals.

snag *noun* (*plural* **snags**) **1** a hidden or unexpected difficulty. **2** a sharp or jagged projecting part. ~ *verb* (**snags, snagging, snagged**) to catch or tear something on a snag.

snail *noun* (*plural* **snails**) a small slow-moving animal with a soft body and a hard shell.

snake *noun* (*plural* **snakes**) a reptile with a long tapering body and no legs.

snakes and ladders *noun* a board game in which players move counters along squares, advancing up a ladder towards the finishing point or going back down a snake towards the starting point.

snap *verb* (**snaps, snapping, snapped**) **1** to break with a sharp cracking sound. **2** to bite or close your jaws with force. **3** to close or fit in place with a sharp sound. **4** to reply irritably. **5** to lose your self-control suddenly. **6** to take a snapshot of something or somebody. ~ *noun* (*plural* **snaps**) **1** the sound of snapping. **2** a sudden spell of harsh weather. **3** = SNAPSHOT. **4** a card game in which players try to be the first to shout 'snap' when two identical cards are laid down. ~ *adjective* done suddenly or unexpectedly: *a snap decision*. ✱ **snap up** to take or buy something suddenly or eagerly.

snapdragon *noun* (*plural* **snapdragons**) a plant with bright white, red, or yellow two-lipped flowers.

snappy *adjective* (**snappier, snappiest**) curt and irritable. ✱ **make it**

snappy *informal* be quick. ➤ **snappily** *adverb*.

snapshot *noun* (*plural* **snapshots**) a photograph taken quickly.

snare *noun* (*plural* **snares**) **1** a trap for catching small animals with a noose that is pulled tight. **2** something that traps or deceives people. ~ *verb* (**snares, snaring, snared**) to catch something in a snare.

snarl[1] *verb* (**snarls, snarling, snarled**) **1** to growl with bared teeth. **2** to speak in an aggressive or bad-tempered manner. ➤ **snarl** *noun*.

snarl[2] *verb* (**snarls, snarling, snarled**) (*often* **snarl up**) to become, or make something, tangled.

snatch *verb* (**snatches, snatching, snatched**) **1** to seize, grab, or take something suddenly and forcibly. ~ *noun* (*plural* **snatches**) **1** an act of snatching. **2** a brief period of time or activity. **3** a fragment of music or conversation.

snazzy *adjective* (**snazzier, snazziest**) *informal* attractive and stylish.

sneak *verb* (**sneaks, sneaking, sneaked**) **1** to go stealthily or furtively. **2** (**sneak on**) *informal* to tell somebody in authority about somebody else's misbehaviour. **3** to put, bring, or take something somewhere in a furtive manner. ~ *noun* (*plural* **sneaks**) *informal* somebody who sneaks on others. ~ *adjective* done secretly or unofficially: *a sneak preview*. ➤ **sneaky** *adjective*.

sneer *verb* (**sneers, sneering, sneered**) to smile or speak in a scornfully jeering manner. ➤ **sneer** *noun*.

sneeze *verb* (**sneezes, sneezing, sneezed**) to blow air suddenly out of the nose and mouth, because of irritation in the nasal passages. ✱ **not to be sneezed at** not to be underestimated or despised. ➤ **sneeze** *noun*.

snide *adjective* slyly disdainful or insulting.

sniff *verb* (**sniffs, sniffing, sniffed**) **1** to draw air audibly up your nose. **2** to smell something. ➤ **sniff** *noun*.

snigger *verb* (**sniggers, sniggering, sniggered**) to laugh in a partly suppressed or derisive manner. ➤ **snigger** *noun*.

snip *verb* (**snips, snipping, snipped**) to cut something with shears or scissors using short rapid strokes. ~ *noun* (*plural* **snips**) **1** a cut made by snipping. **2** *informal* a bargain.

snipe *noun* (*plural* **snipes** *or* **snipe**) a wading bird with a long straight bill. ~ *verb* (**snipes, sniping, sniped**) **1** to shoot at people from a hiding place at long range. **2** (**snipe at**) to criticize somebody in a sly or bad-tempered manner. ➤ **sniper** *noun*.

snippet *noun* (*plural* **snippets**) a small piece from writing or conversation.

snivel *verb* (**snivels, snivelling, snivelled**) to complain in a whining way. ➤ **snivel** *noun*.

snob *noun* (*plural* **snobs**) somebody who feels superior and looks down on others who are less wealthy, important, or cultured. ➤ **snobbery** *noun*, **snobbish** *adjective*, **snobby** *adjective*.

> **Word History** The word *snob* originally meant a shoemaker. Later it came to mean any member of the lower classes, and from there the meaning changed to denote somebody who despises their own social class and who would like to belong to a higher one.

snog *verb* (**snogs, snogging, snogged**) *informal* to kiss and cuddle.

snooker *noun* a game played on a billiard table with cues, a white ball, and 21 coloured balls.

snoop *verb* (**snoops, snooping, snooped**) to look around a place trying to find out about somebody. ➤ **snooper** *noun*.

snooty *adjective* (**snootier, snootiest**) *informal* snobbish; haughty.

snooze *verb* (**snoozes, snoozing, snoozed**) *informal* to sleep lightly for a short time. ➤ **snooze** *noun*.

snore *verb* (**snores, snoring, snored**) to breathe with a hoarse noise during sleep. ➤ **snore** *noun*.

snorkel *noun* (*plural* **snorkels**) a tube allowing a swimmer to breathe while under water. ➤ **snorkelling** *noun*.

snort *verb* (**snorts, snorting, snorted**) to force air through the nose with a r harsh sound. ➤ **snort** *noun*.

snot *noun informal* mucus from the nose.

snout *noun* (*plural* **snouts**) the projecting nose of a pig or other animal.

snow *noun* ice crystals formed in the atmosphere and falling as light white flakes. ~ *verb* (**snows, snowing, snowed**) to fall as snow. ✷ **be snowed under** to have a lot of work to do.

snowball¹ *noun* (*plural* **snowballs**) a round mass of compressed snow. ~ *verb* (**snowballs, snowballing, snowballed**) to increase or expand rapidly.

snowboard *noun* (*plural* **snowboards**) a board resembling a short wide ski, used to slide down mountains over snow. ➤ **snowboarder** *noun*, **snowboarding** *noun*.

snowdrift *noun* (*plural* **snowdrifts**) a deep bank of snow formed by the wind.

snowdrop *noun* (*plural* **snowdrops**) a plant that produces white flowers in late winter.

snowman *noun* (*plural* **snowmen**) a pile of snow shaped to resemble a human figure.

snowplough *noun* (*plural* **snowploughs**) a vehicle or device for clearing snow from roads, etc.

snowshoe *noun* (*plural* **snowshoes**) a flat frame attached to a boot or shoe for walking over soft snow.

snowy *adjective* (**snowier, snowiest**) **1** with snow falling. **2** covered with snow. **3** white like snow.

snub *verb* (**snubs, snubbing, snubbed**) to ignore somebody or be unfriendly to them as a way of showing that you disapprove of them. ➤ **snub** *noun*.

snub nose *noun* (*plural* **snub noses**) a short and slightly turned-up nose.

snuff¹ *verb* (**snuffs, snuffing, snuffed**) to extinguish a flame or candle. ✷ **snuff it** *informal* to die.

snuff² *noun* powdered tobacco inhaled through your nose.

snuffle *verb* (**snuffles, snuffling, snuffled**) to sniff noisily and repeatedly. ➤ **snuffle** *noun*.

snug *adjective* (**snugger, snuggest**) **1** warm and comfortable. **2** fitting closely. ➤ **snugly** *adverb*.

snuggle *verb* (**snuggles, snuggling, snuggled**) **1** to curl up comfortably. **2** to get close to somebody for comfort or in affection.

so *adverb* **1** to such an extreme degree: *Why are you so upset?* **2** also: *I worked hard and so did she.* **3** used as a substitute for a word or phrase used before: *'It'll come out right in the end.' 'Do you really think so?'* **4** in this or the same way: *Hold the racket so.* ~ *conjunction* **1** with the result that. **2** in order that. **3** for that reason. ✷ **and so on/forth** and other things like that. **or so** approximately. **so as to** *or* **so that** having as a purpose or result.

soak *verb* (**soaks, soaking, soaked**) **1** to leave something covered in liquid. **2** to make something or somebody thoroughly wet. **3** said about a liquid: to spread over or pass through something completely. ✷ **soak up** to absorb a liquid, information, etc. ➤ **soak** *noun*.

so-and-so *noun* (*plural* **so-and-sos**)

soap

1 an unnamed or unspecified person or thing. **2** an unpleasant person.

soap *noun* (*plural* **soaps**) **1** a substance used with water to produce a lather for washing or cleaning. **2** = SOAP OPERA. ➤ **soapy** *adjective*.

soapbox *noun* (*plural* **soapboxes**) an improvised platform for a speaker to stand on outdoors.

soap opera *noun* (*plural* **soap operas**) a radio or television serial dealing with the lives of a group of characters.

Word History Soap operas got their name from the fact that, in the USA, programmes of this type were formerly sponsored by soap manufacturers.

soar *verb* (**soars, soaring, soared**) **1** to fly or rise high into the air. **2** to increase rapidly.

sob *verb* (**sobs, sobbing, sobbed**) to cry with short noisy gasps. ➤ **sob** *noun*.

sober *adjective* **1** not drunk. **2** serious. **3** subdued in tone or colour. ~ *verb* (**sobers, sobering, sobered**) (*also* **sober up**) to become, or to make somebody, sober or serious. ➤ **soberly** *adverb*.

sobriety /soh brie ti/ *noun* the state of being sober.

so-called *adjective* commonly or wrongly named.

soccer *noun* a football game with a round ball that must not be handled during play except by the goalkeepers.

sociable *adjective* eager to be with people and enjoying companionship. ➤ **sociability** *noun*, **sociably** *adverb*.

social *adjective* **1** to do with human society and people's place in it. **2** involving friendly relations with other people: *social life*. **3** said about animals: living and breeding in organized communities. ~ *noun* (*plural* **socials**) a social gathering or party. ➤ **socially** *adverb*.

socialism *noun* a political theory that supports state ownership of the main industries of a country and equality in the distribution of goods. ➤ **socialist** *adjective and noun*.

socialize *or* **socialise** *verb* (**socializes, socializing, socialized** *or* **socialises,** etc) to mix with other people in a friendly way.

social security *noun* a system of financial benefits provided by the state for those in need.

social services *plural noun* public services provided by the state, especially welfare services offered by social workers.

social worker *noun* (*plural* **social workers**) a state employee whose job is to help the poor, elderly, disadvantaged, etc. ➤ **social work** *noun*.

society *noun* (*plural* **societies**) **1** a community of people with common traditions, institutions, and interests. **2** wealthy or privileged people regarded as setting standards in fashion or behaviour. **3** an organized group with a shared interest, aim, etc: *an amateur dramatic society*. **4** companionship or association with others. ➤ **societal** *adjective*.

sociology *noun* the study of social institutions and relations. ➤ **sociological** *adjective*, **sociologist** *noun*.

sock[1] *noun* (*plural* **socks**) a knitted covering for the foot extending above the ankle. ✳ **pull your socks up** *informal* to make an effort to do better.

sock[2] *verb* (**socks, socking, socked**) *informal* to hit somebody forcefully.

socket *noun* (*plural* **sockets**) **1** an opening or hollow into which something fits. **2** an electrical device into which a plug, bulb, etc can be fitted.

sod *noun* (*plural* **sods**) a clump of grass together with roots and soil.

soda *noun* **1** a chemical compound containing sodium. **2** = SODA WATER.

soda water *noun* water made fizzy with carbon dioxide.

sodden *adjective* very wet; saturated.

sodium *noun Science* a soft silver-white metallic element.

sodium bicarbonate *noun* a white chemical compound used in baking powder and medicine.

sodium chloride *noun* the scientific name for ordinary salt.

sofa *noun* (*plural* **sofas**) a long upholstered seat with a back and arms or raised ends.

soft *adjective* **1** yielding to physical pressure; easily shaped or spread; not hard. **2** said about a sound: quiet and not harsh. **3** smooth and comfortable to the touch: *soft fabrics*. **4** said about light or colour: not bright or glaring. **5** said about a drink: not containing alcohol. **6** said about water: free from chemical compounds that cause scaling and prevent lathering. **7** said about a drug: not of the most addictive or harmful kind. **8** kind or lenient. **9** *informal* silly or foolish. ✻ **have a soft spot for** to be fond of somebody. **soft on** not strict in dealing with something. **soft touch** *informal* a person who is easily taken advantage of. ➤ **softly** *adverb*, **softness** *noun*.

soften /sofn/ *verb* (**softens, softening, softened**) **1** to become, or to make something, soft or softer. ✻ **soften up** to reduce the strength or resistance of somebody or something.

soft-boiled *adjective* said about an egg: boiled until the white is solid but not the yolk.

soft-hearted *adjective* kind and understanding.

softly-softly *adjective* patient and cautious.

software *noun ICT* the programs used by a computer to process data.

softwood *noun* the wood of a coniferous tree.

soggy *adjective* (**soggier, soggiest**) **1** waterlogged. **2** heavy and damp.

soil¹ *noun* **1** the loose upper layer of the surface of the earth, in which plants grow. **2** a nation's territory or land.

soil² *verb* (**soils, soiling soiled**) to make something dirty.

sojourn /sojern/ *verb* (**sojourns, sojourning, sojourned**) *formal* to stay in a place temporarily. ➤ **sojourn** *noun*.

solace *noun* consolation or comfort in grief or difficulty.

solar *adjective* to do with the sun or its light or heat.

solar cell *noun* (*plural* **solar cells**) a device that converts sunlight into electrical energy.

solar panel *noun* (*plural* **solar panels**) a panel full of solar cells.

solar plexus *noun* a network of nerves in the abdomen behind the stomach.

solar system *noun* (**the solar system**) the sun together with the planets and other bodies that revolve round it.

sold *verb* past tense and past participle of SELL.

solder *noun* a soft alloy that melts easily and is used to join metal surfaces. ~ *verb* (**solders, soldering, soldered**) to join metal surfaces with solder.

soldering iron *noun* (*plural* **soldering irons**) an electrical device for melting and applying solder.

soldier *noun* (*plural* **soldiers**) a person serving in an army.

sole¹ *noun* (*plural* **soles**) the underside of your foot, or of a shoe, boot, etc. ~ *verb* (**soles, soling, soled**) to put a sole on a shoe.

sole² *noun* (*plural* **soles** *or* **sole**) a sea flatfish used for food.

sole³ *adjective* only. ➤ **solely** *adverb*.

solemn *adjective* **1** done in a formal and ceremonious way. **2** serious and sombre; not cheerful. ➤ **solemnity** *noun*, **solemnly** *adverb*.

solemnize *or* **solemnise** *verb* (**solemnizes, solemnizing, solemnized** *or* **solemnises**, etc) to perform a marriage with ceremony.

solenoid /so li noyd/ *noun* (*plural* **solenoids**) a coil of wire that produces a magnetic field when an electric current passes through it.

solicit *verb* (**solicits, soliciting, solicited**) **1** to try to obtain something by asking for it. **2** said about a prostitute: to try to get clients. ➤ **solicitation** *noun*.

solicitor *noun* (*plural* **solicitors**) a qualified lawyer who advises clients, prepares legal documents, etc.

solicitous *adjective* showing care or concern about somebody. ➤ **solicitously** *adverb*, **solicitude** *noun*.

solid *adjective* **1** without a cavity inside; not hollow. **2** hard, dense, or compact, and able to retain its shape; not liquid or gaseous. **3** consisting entirely of a single substance: *solid gold*. **4** *Maths* three-dimensional. **5** without break or interruption: *for three solid hours*. **6** well constructed; firm and not likely to break. ~ *noun* (*plural* **solids**) **1** a solid substance. **2** (**solids**) solid food. **3** *Maths* a three-dimensional figure. ➤ **solidity** *noun*, **solidly** *adverb*.

solidarity *noun* unity based on shared aims and support for one another's actions.

solidify *verb* (**solidifies, solidifying, solidified**) to become, or to make something, solid. ➤ **solidification** *noun*.

soliloquy *noun* (*plural* **soliloquies**) *English* a speech expressing a character's thoughts aloud while alone, especially on stage.

solitaire *noun* (*plural* **solitaires**) **1** a game for one person in which pieces are removed from a board by jumping one over another until only one piece remains. **2** a single gem set alone in a ring.

solitary *adjective* **1** liking to be alone. **2** lonely. **3** single; sole.

solitary confinement *noun* a punishment in which a prisoner is kept alone in a cell and not allowed contact with other prisoners.

solitude *noun* the state of being alone.

solo *noun* (*plural* **solos**) **1** a musical composition, song, or dance for one performer. **2** a flight by one person alone in an aircraft. ~ *adjective and adverb* done or performed by one person. ➤ **soloist** *noun*.

so long *interjection informal* goodbye.

solstice *noun* (*plural* **solstices**) either of the two occasions each year when the sun is highest (in midsummer) or lowest (in midwinter) in the sky at noon.

soluble *adjective* **1** *Science* able to be dissolved in liquid. **2** capable of being solved. ➤ **solubility** *noun*.

solution *noun* (*plural* **solutions**) **1** an answer to a problem. **2** a means of solving a problem. **3** *Science* a mixture formed when a substance is dissolved in a solvent.

solve *verb* (**solves, solving, solved**) to find an answer to, or explanation for, a problem, mystery, etc.

solvent *adjective* **1** having enough money to pay all your debts. **2** *Science* able to dissolve other substances. ~ *noun* (*plural* **solvents**) *Science* a liquid that can dissolve other substances. ➤ **solvency** *noun*.

sombre *adjective* **1** dark and gloomy. **2** of a dull or dark colour. **3** serious or grave. ➤ **sombrely** *adverb*.

sombrero /som brair oh/ *noun* (*plural* **sombreros**) a Mexican-style hat with a wide brim.

some *adjective* **1** quite small in number or amount: *some grapes; some water.* **2** unknown or unspecified: *Some fool left the door unlocked!* **3** an unspecified number of things of a particular kind: *Some birds cannot fly.* ~ *pronoun* an unspecified part, amount, or number but not all. ~ *adverb* approximately; about: *some eighty houses.* ✳ **some day** at some future time. **some time** quite a long time.

somebody *pronoun* some person.

somehow *adverb* **1** by some unknown means. **2** no matter how. **3** for some unknown reason.

someone *pronoun* some person.

somersault /suˈmersawlt/ *noun* (*plural* **somersaults**) a movement in which a person turns head over heels forwards or backwards. ~ *verb* (**somersaults, somersaulting, somersaulted**) to perform a somersault.

something *pronoun* **1** some unspecified or unknown thing. **2** a certain amount. ~ *adverb* in some degree; somewhat.

sometime *adverb* at some unknown or unspecified time. ~ *adjective* former.

sometimes *adverb* at intervals; occasionally.

somewhat *adverb* to some degree.

somewhere *adverb* **1** in or to some unspecified place. **2** at an unspecified point.

somnambulist *noun* (*plural* **somnambulists**) somebody who walks in their sleep. ➤ **somnambulism** *noun*.

somnolent *adjective* sleepy; drowsy. ➤ **somnolence** *noun*.

son *noun* (*plural* **sons**) **1** a male child. **2** a male descendent.

sonata *noun* (*plural* **sonatas**) *Music* a composition for one instrument, often with piano accompaniment, usually in several movements.

song *noun* (*plural* **songs**) **1** *Music* a set of words sung to a musical tune. **2** the act of singing: *burst into song.* **3** the tuneful sounds made by birds and some other animals. ✳ **for a song** for very little money. **a song and dance** *informal* a fuss or commotion.

songbird *noun* (*plural* **songbirds**) a bird that sings tunefully.

sonic *adjective* to do with sound waves. ➤ **sonically** *adverb*.

sonic boom *noun* (*plural* **sonic booms**) an explosive sound produced by an aircraft travelling at supersonic speed.

son-in-law *noun* (*plural* **sons-in-law**) the husband of your daughter.

sonnet *noun* (*plural* **sonnets**) *English* a poem of 14 lines having a fixed rhyme scheme.

sonorous *adjective* pleasantly rich or deep in sound. ➤ **sonority** *noun*, **sonorously** *adverb*.

soon *adverb* **1** after a short time. **2** promptly. **3** in comparisons: rather: *I'd sooner stay here.* ✳ **sooner or later** eventually.

soot *noun* a fine black powder formed by the incomplete burning of coal, wood, etc.

soothe *verb* (**soothes, soothing, soothed**) **1** to calm somebody by comforting them. **2** to relieve pain. ➤ **soothing** *adjective*.

sophisticated *adjective* **1** highly developed or complex. **2** having refined tastes; cultured. **3** intellectually subtle or refined. ➤ **sophistication** *noun*.

sophistry *noun* (*plural* **sophistries**) persuasive but invalid reasoning.

soporific *adjective* tending to cause sleep.

sopping *adjective* wet through; soaking.

soppy *adjective* (**soppier, soppiest**) *informal* **1** weakly sentimental. **2** *informal* feeble or silly. ➤ **soppily** *adverb*, **soppiness** *noun*.

soprano *noun* (*plural* **sopranos**) *Music*

a female singer with the highest singing voice.

sorcerer *noun* (*plural* **sorcerers**) a person who uses magic. ➤ **sorceress** *noun*, **sorcery** *noun*.

sordid *adjective* 1 dirty or squalid. 2 dishonest or immoral. ➤ **sordidly** *adverb*.

sore *adjective* (**sorer**, **sorest**) 1 painful or tender. 2 severe; urgent: *in sore distress*. 3 angry or upset. ~ *noun* (*plural* **sores**) a painful area on the body. ✱ a **sore point** a cause of irritation or distress. ➤ **soreness** *noun*.

sorely *adverb* much; extremely.

sorrow *noun* (*plural* **sorrows**) 1 deep distress caused by a loss or failure. 2 a cause of sorrow. ~ *verb* (**sorrows**, **sorrowing**, **sorrowed**) to feel or express sorrow. ➤ **sorrowful** *adjective*, **sorrowfully** *adverb*.

sorry *adjective* (**sorrier**, **sorriest**) 1 feeling regret. 2 feeling sympathy or pity. 3 bad or regrettable.

sort *noun* (*plural* **sorts**) 1 a class, kind, or type. 2 *informal* a person: *a cheerful sort*. ~ *verb* (**sorts**, **sorting**, **sorted**) to arrange things in order or in groups. ✱ **out of sorts** slightly unwell. **sort of** *informal* somewhat; in a way. **sort out** 1 to deal with a difficulty effectively. 2 to separate something from a mass or group. 3 to clear up or tidy up something.

sortie *noun* (*plural* **sorties**) 1 a sudden attack by troops from a defensive position. 2 a mission or attack by one aircraft.

SOS *noun* 1 an internationally recognized signal of distress. 2 a call for help.

so-so *adjective* neither very good nor very bad.

soufflé /sooh flay/ *noun* (*plural* **soufflés**) a light fluffy baked dish made with eggs.

sought *verb* past tense and past participle of SEEK.

sought-after *adjective* much in demand.

soul *noun* (*plural* **souls**) 1 the spiritual part of a human being, believed by some to live on after a person dies. 2 emotional sensitivity or depth. 3 a person: *a dear old soul*. 4 *Music* a kind of music originating in black American gospel singing, characterized by intensity of feeling.

soul-destroying *adjective* very dull and uninteresting.

soulful *adjective* expressing intense feeling. ➤ **soulfully** *adverb*.

soul mate *noun* (*plural* **soul mates**) a very close friend whose thoughts, feelings, and character correspond very much with yours.

soul-searching *noun* close examination of your feelings and motives.

sound[1] *noun* (*plural* **sounds**) 1 the sensation perceived by the sense of hearing, caused by vibrations travelling through the air. 2 something heard; a noise or tone. 3 an impression conveyed by being heard. 4 recorded sounds or radio broadcasting. ~ *verb* (**sounds**, **sounding**, **sounded**) 1 to make, or cause something to make, a sound. 2 to give a specified impression; to seem: *It sounds too good to be true*.

sound[2] *adjective* 1 healthy or in good condition. 2 correct and sensible or reasonable. 3 financially secure. 4 said about sleep: deep and undisturbed. 5 thorough or severe. ➤ **soundly** *adverb*, **soundness** *noun*.

sound[3] *noun* (*plural* **sounds**) a long passage of water connecting two seas or separating a mainland and an island.

sound[4] *verb* (**sounds**, **sounding**, **sounded**) to measure the depth of water. ✱ **sound out** to find out the views or intentions of somebody.

sound barrier noun (**the sound barrier**) an increase in the resistance of the air as an aircraft nears the speed of sound.

sound bite noun (plural **sound bites**) a short excerpt from a speech or statement that contains its main point and is intended to be broadcast.

sound effects plural noun sounds other than speech or music used to create an effect in a play, film, etc.

sound track noun (plural **sound tracks**) the music, or all the sound, accompanying a film.

soup noun (plural **soups**) a liquid food made from stock and usually containing pieces of solid food such as meat and vegetables. ✳ **in the soup** informal in an awkward situation.

sour adjective **1** having an acid taste like vinegar or lemons. **2** rancid or rotten. **3** bad-tempered or embittered. ~ verb (**sours, souring, soured**) to become, or make a relationship, bitter or unfriendly. ➤ **sourly** adverb, **sourness** noun.

source noun (plural **sources**) **1** a place, person, or thing from which something is obtained. **2** an origin or cause. **3** the point of origin of a river or stream. **4** a person, publication, etc that supplies information.

sour grapes plural noun a pretence that something you are unable to have or achieve yourself is not worth having or achieving at all.

south noun **1** the direction exactly opposite to north. **2** regions or countries lying towards the south. ~ adjective and adverb **1** at or towards the south. **2** said about the wind: blowing from the south.

southeast noun **1** the direction midway between south and east. **2** regions or areas lying towards the southeast. ~ adjective and adverb **1** at or towards the southeast. **2** said about the wind: blowing from the southeast. ➤ **southeasterly** adjective and adverb, **southeastern** adjective.

southerly adjective and adverb **1** in a southern position or direction. **2** said about a wind: blowing from the south.

southern adjective in or towards the south.

southerner noun (plural **southerners**) a person from the southern part of a country.

southward adjective and adverb towards the south; in a direction going south. ➤ **southwards** adverb.

southwest noun **1** the direction midway between south and west. **2** regions and areas in the southwest. ~ adjective and adverb **1** at or towards from the southwest. **2** said about the wind: blowing from the southwest. ➤ **southwesterly** adjective and adverb, **southwestern** adjective.

souvenir noun (plural **souvenirs**) something kept as a reminder of a person, place, or event.

sou'wester noun (plural **sou'westers**) a waterproof hat with a brim extended at the back.

sovereign /sovrin/ noun (plural **sovereigns**) **1** somebody possessing supreme power, especially a king or queen. **2** a former gold coin worth one pound. ~ adjective **1** possessing supreme power. **2** said about a country: politically independent. ➤ **sovereignty** noun.

sow[1] /sow/ noun (plural **sows**) an adult female pig.

sow[2] /soh/ verb (**sows, sowing, sowed, sown** or **sowed**) **1** to put seed in the ground to grow into plants. **2** to put some unwelcome feeling or idea into people's minds: *to sow suspicion*. ➤ **sower** noun.

soya bean noun (plural **soya beans**) a bean that is high in protein, obtained from an Asian plant.

soy sauce *noun* a sauce made from fermented soya beans.

spa *noun* (*plural* **spas**) **1** a spring of mineral water. **2** a resort with springs of mineral water.

space *noun* (*plural* **spaces**) **1** unoccupied area or volume. **2** the region beyond the earth's atmosphere. **3** an amount of room set apart or available for something. **4** a period of time. **5** a blank area separating words or lines on a page. ~ *verb* (**spaces, spacing, spaced**) to place two or more things with spaces between them.

spacecraft *noun* (*plural* **spacecraft**) a vehicle for travelling beyond the earth's atmosphere.

spaceman or **spacewoman** *noun* (*plural* **spacemen** or **spacewomen**) a man or woman who travels in space.

spaceship *noun* (*plural* **spaceships**) a manned spacecraft.

space shuttle *noun* (*plural* **space shuttles**) a vehicle for making repeated journeys into space and back to earth.

space station *noun* (*plural* **space stations**) a manned artificial satellite serving as a base for travel in space.

space suit *noun* (*plural* **space suits**) a suit equipped to make life in space possible for an astronaut.

spacious *adjective* containing lots of space; roomy.

spade *noun* (*plural* **spades**) **1** a digging implement with a flat metal blade and a long handle. **2** (**spades**) the suit in a pack of playing cards that is marked with black heart-shaped figures. * **call a spade a spade** to speak frankly and plainly.

spadework *noun* hard or routine preparatory work.

spaghetti *noun* pasta in thin solid strings.

spam *noun* *ICT* unwanted email messages.

span *noun* (*plural* **spans**) **1** an extent or distance from one side to the other. **2** a length of time. **3** the part of a bridge between supports. ~ *verb* (**spans, spanning, spanned**) to extend across something.

spangle *noun* (*plural* **spangles**) a small glittering object or particle.
➤ **spangly** *adjective*.

spaniel *noun* (*plural* **spaniels**) a dog of with short legs, long wavy hair, and large drooping ears.

spank *verb* (**spanks, spanking, spanked**) to slap somebody on the buttocks with the open hand or something flat. ➤ **spank** *noun*.

spanner *noun* (*plural* **spanners**) a tool shaped for turning nuts or bolts.

spar¹ *noun* (*plural* **spars**) a thick bar or pole used to support the sail of a ship.

spar² *verb* (**spars, sparring, sparred**) **1** to box without putting full force into the blows. **2** to argue or wrangle.

spare *adjective* **1** not in use, but kept to replace something that becomes unusable. **2** more than what is required; surplus. **3** healthily lean or thin. ~ *verb* (**spares, sparing, spared**) **1** to make something available for use by other people: *Can you spare a pint of milk?* **2** to refrain from killing or harming somebody. **3** to avoid making somebody experience something unpleasant: *I thought I'd spare you the trouble of going yourself.* ~ *noun* (*plural* **spares**) **1** a spare or duplicate item or part, for example for a machine or vehicle. **2** = SPARE TYRE.
* **to spare** over and above what is needed.

spare tyre *noun* (*plural* **spare tyres**) **1** an extra tyre carried by a motor vehicle. **2** *informal* a roll of fat round your waist.

sparing *adjective* not wasteful; frugal.
➤ **sparingly** *adverb*.

spark noun (plural **sparks**) **1** a small burning particle thrown out by something on fire. **2** a flash caused by an electrical discharge. **3** a trace of something. ~ verb (**sparks, sparking, sparked**) to give off sparks. * **spark off** to cause something.

sparking plug noun (plural **sparking plugs**) = SPARK PLUG.

sparkle verb (**sparkles, sparkling, sparkled**) **1** to give off or reflect glittering points of light. **2** to be very lively or witty. ➤ **sparkle** noun, **sparkly** adjective.

sparkler noun (plural **sparklers**) a firework you hold in your hand and that gives out sparks.

spark plug noun (plural **spark plugs**) a device that produces the electric spark to ignite the fuel in an internal-combustion engine.

sparrow noun (plural **sparrows**) a small brownish bird.

sparse adjective few and scattered. ➤ **sparsely** adverb, **sparseness** noun.

spartan adjective lacking things that make life comfortable or pleasant; austere.

spasm noun (plural **spasms**) **1** a sudden involuntary contraction of a muscle. **2** a sudden strong effort or emotion.

spasmodic adjective occurring unpredictably at intervals. ➤ **spasmodically** adverb.

spastic noun (plural **spastics**) dated, sometimes offensive somebody who has cerebral palsy or has frequent muscle spasms which they cannot control.

spat[1] verb past tense and past participle of SPIT[1].

spat[2] noun (plural **spats**) informal a petty quarrel or disagreement.

spate noun **1** a large number or amount of things arriving in a short space of time. **2** a state of flood.

spatial adjective to do with space. ➤ **spatially** adverb.

spatter verb (**spatters, spattering, spattered**) **1** to splash or sprinkle with drops of liquid. **2** to scatter liquid in drops.

spatula noun (plural **spatulas**) an implement with a thin flat blade, used for spreading, mixing, etc.

spawn verb (**spawns, spawning, spawned**) **1** said about a water animal: to produce or deposit eggs. **2** to produce large quantities of something. ~ noun eggs produced by frogs, oysters, fish, etc.

spay verb (**spays, spaying, spayed**) to remove the ovaries of a female animal.

speak verb (**speaks, speaking, spoke, spoken**) **1** to utter words with your voice. **2** to make a speech. **3** to use or be able to use a language. * **speak out** to state your opinion boldly. **speak up 1** to speak more loudly. **2** = SPEAK OUT. **speak up for** to speak in defence of somebody or something.

speaker noun (plural **speakers**) **1** somebody who is speaking. **2** somebody who makes a speech. **3** somebody who speaks a particular language. **4** an official who acts as chairperson for debates in a parliament. **5** = LOUDSPEAKER.

spear noun (plural **spears**) a weapon with a long shaft and pointed head, for thrusting or throwing. ~ verb (**spears, spearing, speared**) to pierce somebody or something with a spear or pointed object.

spearhead verb (**spearheads, spearheading, spearheaded**) to lead an attack or initiative.

spearmint noun a common mint used in cooking and to flavour chewing gum.

special adjective **1** better or more important than others; not ordinary. **2** meant for a particular purpose or need: *special permission*.

special effects plural noun unusual visual or sound effects introduced into a film or television recording by special processing.

specialist *noun* (*plural* **specialists**) somebody who specializes in a particular subject.

speciality *noun* (*plural* **specialities**) **1** a special skill. **2** a particular subject in which somebody is an expert. **3** a product, service, etc that a person or place specializes in.

specialize *or* **specialise** *verb* (**specializes, specializing, specialized** *or* **specialises,** etc) to concentrate on a particular activity or field. ➤ **specialization** *or* **specialisation** *noun*.

specialized *or* **specialised** *adjective* designed for a specific purpose or occupation.

specially *adverb* **1** for a particular purpose. **2** in a special way.

special needs *plural noun* in education, special requirements that students with disabilities or learning difficulties have.

species *noun* (*plural* **species**) **1** a class of organisms with common attributes and the same name. **2** a kind or sort.

specific *adjective* **1** that is clearly and individually identified: *in this specific instance*. **2** saying exactly what you are referring to; explicit: *Don't talk in generalities. Be specific.* ➤ **specifically** *adverb*.

specification *noun* (*plural* **specifications**) **1** the act of specifying. **2** a detailed description of the structure and design of something.

specify *verb* (**specifies, specifying, specified**) to describe or list the things you want exactly or in detail.

specimen *noun* (*plural* **specimens**) **1** an item, individual, or part typical of a group or whole. **2** a sample taken for medical examination. **3** *informal* a person of a particular kind: *an unfortunate specimen*.

specious /spee shus/ *adjective* seeming to be persuasive or sound but in fact wrong: *a specious argument*.

speck *noun* (*plural* **specks**) **1** a small spot or blemish. **2** a small particle.

speckle *noun* (*plural* **speckles**) a little speck of colour. ➤ **speckled** *adjective*.

specs *plural noun informal* = SPECTACLES.

spectacle *noun* (*plural* **spectacles**) **1** a striking or dramatic public display or show. **2** (**spectacles**) a pair of glasses.

spectacular *adjective* extremely impressive or exciting. ➤ **spectacularly** *adverb*.

spectator *noun* (*plural* **spectators**) **1** somebody who watches a show or sports event. **2** an onlooker.

spectre *noun* (*plural* **spectres**) a visible ghost. ➤ **spectral** *adjective*.

spectrum *noun* (*plural* **spectra**) **1** the series of colours produced when a beam of white light is dispersed by a prism or in a rainbow. **2** a wide range or related things.

speculate *verb* (**speculates, speculating, speculated**) **1** to form an opinion or theory without definite evidence. **2** to invest in a business venture in the hope of making money. ➤ **speculation** *noun*, **speculative** *adjective*, **speculator** *noun*.

speech *noun* (*plural* **speeches**) **1** the expression of thoughts in spoken words. **2** a public talk or address. **3** a group of lines to be spoken by a character in a play.

speechless *adjective* unable to speak, especially from anger or surprise.

speed *noun* (*plural* **speeds**) **1** quickness. **2** the rate at which something moves or is carried out. ~ *verb* (**speeds, speeding, sped** *or* **speeded**) **1** (*past tense and past participle* **sped**) to move or go quickly. **2** (*past tense and past participle* **speeded**) to travel at an illegal speed. * **speed up** *verb* (*past* *tense and past participle* **speeded**) to move or work faster, or make somebody or something go faster. ➤ **speeding** *noun*.

speedboat *noun* (*plural* **speedboats**) a fast motorboat.

speed limit *noun* (*plural* **speed limits**) the maximum speed at which a vehicle is allowed by law to travel on a particular road.

speedometer *noun* (*plural* **speedometers**) an instrument for showing a vehicle's speed.

speedway *noun* (*plural* **speedways**) **1** an oval racecourse for motorcycles. **2** the sport of racing motorcycles.

speedy *adjective* (**speedier, speediest**) swift or quick. ➤ **speedily** *adverb*, **speediness** *noun*.

spell[1] *noun* (*plural* **spells**) a spoken word or set of words believed to make something happen by magic. ✱ **under the spell of** completely fascinated by somebody or something.

spell[2] *verb* (**spells, spelling, spelt** or **spelled**) **1** to name or write the letters of a word in order. **2** *said about* letters: to form a word. **3** to be likely to result in something: *Another bad summer could spell ruin for farmers.* ✱ **spell out** to explain something clearly and in detail.

spell[3] *noun* (*plural* **spells**) a short period or phase.

spellbound *adjective* completely fascinated. ➤ **spellbinding** *adjective*.

spellchecker *noun* (*plural* **spellcheckers**) *ICT* a computer program that checks the spelling of words in a document.

spelling *noun* (*plural* **spellings**) **1** the forming of words from letters. **2** the sequence of letters that make up a word.

spelt *verb* past tense and past participle of SPELL[2].

spend *verb* (**spends, spending, spent**) **1** to use or pay out money. **2** to use or pass time. ➤ **spender** *noun*.

spendthrift *noun* (*plural* **spendthrifts**) somebody who spends money carelessly or wastefully.

sperm *noun* (*plural* **sperms** or **sperm**) a male cell that can fertilize a female egg.

spew *verb* (**spews, spewing, spewed**) **1** to vomit. **2** to throw out something, especially a liquid, in great quantities.

sphere *noun* (*plural* **spheres**) **1** a perfectly round solid; a globe or ball. **2** an area of knowledge or interest. ➤ **spherical** *adjective*.

sphinx *noun* (*plural* **sphinxes**) an ancient Egyptian image in the form of a lion with a human head.

spice *noun* (*plural* **spices**) **1** a vegetable product, such as pepper, ginger, or nutmeg, used to season or flavour foods. **2** something that adds excitement or enjoyment. ~ *verb* (**spices, spicing, spiced**) to add spice to food. ✱ **spice up** to make something more interesting or lively. ➤ **spicy** *adjective*.

spick-and-span *adjective* spotlessly clean and tidy.

spider *noun* (*plural* **spiders**) a small invertebrate animal with eight legs, which makes webs for trapping its prey.

spike *noun* (*plural* **spikes**) **1** a thin pointed object or projection. **2** (**spikes**) running shoes with spikes on their soles. **3** a cluster of flowers growing directly from a single stem. ~ *verb* (**spikes, spiking, spiked**) **1** to pierce something with a spike. **2** to add strong alcohol or a drug to drink or food.

spill *verb* (**spills, spilling, spilt** or **spilled**) **1** to flow or fall, or to let something flow or fall, over the sides of a container. **2** to cause blood to be shed. **3** to flow or empty out of something. ~ *noun* (*plural* **spills**) **1** a quantity of liquid spilt. **2** a fall

spin

from a horse or vehicle. ✶ **spill the beans** *informal* to divulge information indiscreetly. ➤ **spillage** *noun*.

spin *verb* (**spins, spinning, spun**) **1** to revolve rapidly. **2** to make fibre into yarn or thread by drawing it out and twisting it. **3** said about a spider, silkworm, etc: to form a web or silk by sending out a sticky liquid in threads. **4** to dry clothes in a spin-drier. **5** *informal* to present information, news, etc with spin. ~ *noun* (*plural* **spins**) **1** the act of spinning. **2** *informal* a short excursion. **3** *informal* a way of presenting or interpreting news or information that makes it seem favourable to a particular person, the government, etc. ✶ **spin out** to cause something to last longer.

spinach *noun* a plant with large dark green leaves, used as a vegetable.

spinal *adjective* to do with the backbone.

spinal column *noun* (*plural* **spinal columns**) the long structure of bone running from the head to the lower back and enclosing the spinal cord.

spinal cord *noun* (*plural* **spinal cords**) the cord of nerves within the spinal column that carries messages from the brain to the lower part of the body.

spindle *noun* (*plural* **spindles**) **1** a round stick with tapered ends on which the yarn is twisted in hand spinning. **2** a pin or axis round which something turns.

spindly *adjective* (**spindlier, spindliest**) unnaturally tall or slender.

spin doctor *noun* (*plural* **spin doctors**) *informal* somebody employed to present information in a way that is favourable to a government or political party.

spin-drier or **spin-dryer** *noun* (*plural* **spin-driers** or **spin-dryers**) a machine that dries clothes by spinning them in a drum.

spine *noun* (*plural* **spines**) **1** = SPINAL COLUMN. **2** the back of a book, which holds the pages together. **3** a stiff pointed part of a plant or animal.

spine-chilling *adjective* exciting and terrifying.

spineless *adjective* lacking strength of character; cowardly.

spinney *noun* (*plural* **spinneys**) a small wood with undergrowth.

spinning wheel *noun* (*plural* **spinning wheels**) a machine that uses a wheel to spin yarn or thread onto a spindle.

spin-off *noun* (*plural* **spin-offs**) something that is a further development of some idea or product.

spinster *noun* (*plural* **spinsters**) an unmarried woman. ➤ **spinsterhood** *noun*.

spiral *noun* (*plural* **spirals**) **1** a line that winds round and round a central axis in a continuous curve that often gets wider or narrower as it progresses. **2** a continuous increase or decrease in prices, incomes, etc. ~ *verb* (**spirals, spiralling, spiralled**) **1** to follow a spiral course. **2** to increase or decrease continuously or uncontrollably. ➤ **spiral** *adjective*, **spirally** *adverb*.

spire *noun* (*plural* **spires**) a tall pointed structure on top of a church tower.

spirit *noun* (*plural* **spirits**) **1** the soul. **2** a supernatural being or ghost. **3** (**spirits**) mood or state of mind. **4** liveliness, energy, or courage. **5** the basic character, attitude, or feeling in somebody or something. **6** a strong alcoholic drink, such as whisky or gin. ~ *verb* (**spirits, spiriting, spirited**) (*often* **spirit away**) to carry something or somebody off secretly or mysteriously.

spirited *adjective* full of energy and determination. ➤ **spiritedly** *adverb*.

spirit level *noun* (*plural* **spirit levels**) a device that uses the position of a bubble in a transparent tube of liquid to indicate whether a surface is level.

spiritual *adjective* **1** to do with the soul as distinct from the body. **2** religious. ~ *noun* (*plural* **spirituals**) *Music* an emotional religious song of a kind developed by black Christians in the southern USA. ➤ **spiritually** *adverb*.

spiritualism *noun* a belief that spirits of the dead can communicate with the living through a medium. ➤ **spiritualist** *noun*.

spit[1] *verb* (**spits, spitting, spat**) **1** to send saliva, liquid, or food forcibly out of the mouth. **2** to rain lightly. **3** to sputter. ~ *noun* spittle or saliva. ✷ **spit it out** *informal* to say what is on your mind.

spit[2] *noun* (*plural* **spits**) **1** a thin pointed rod for holding and turning meat over a fire. **2** an elongated strip of sand or shingle extending into the sea.

spite *noun* petty ill will or malice. ~ *verb* (**spites, spiting, spited**) to annoy or hinder somebody out of spite. ✷ **in spite of** regardless of; not being prevented by.

spiteful *adjective* deliberately trying to hurt somebody's feelings. ➤ **spitefully** *adverb*.

spitting image *noun* (**the spitting image**) an exact likeness.

spittle *noun* saliva ejected from the mouth.

splash *verb* (**splashes, splashing, splashed**) **1** to fall into or move through a liquid and make it fly up in drops or large amounts. **2** said about a liquid: to be scattered in drops or large amounts. **3** to make something or somebody wet with drops or large amounts of liquid. **4** to display or print something conspicuously. ~ *noun* (*plural* **splashes**) **1** the act or sound of something dropping into liquid. **2** a spot or daub from splashed liquid. **3** a vivid patch of colour. ✷ **make a splash** to make a vivid impression. **splash down** to land in the sea. **splash out** *informal* to spend a lot of money.

splatter *verb* (**splatters, splattering, splattered**) to splash with heavy drops.

splay *verb* (**splays, splaying, splayed**) to spread apart two thing that are joined at one end.

spleen *noun* (*plural* **spleens**) **1** an organ close to the stomach that destroys old red blood cells, stores blood, and produces white blood cells. **2** bad temper.

splendid *adjective* **1** magnificent or sumptuous. **2** excellent. ➤ **splendidly** *adverb*.

splendour *noun* (*plural* **splendours**) a splendid appearance or quality.

splice *verb* (**splices, splicing, spliced**) **1** to join ropes by interweaving the strands. **2** to join lengths of film or magnetic tape. ➤ **splice** *noun*.

splint *noun* (*plural* **splints**) a support for an injured body part, such as a broken arm.

splinter *noun* (*plural* **splinters**) a sharp thin piece of wood or glass, split or broken off lengthways. ~ *verb* (**splinters, splintering, splintered**) to split into splinters.

splinter group *noun* (*plural* **splinter groups**) a small group that has broken away from the main part of an organization.

split *verb* (**splits, splitting, split**) **1** to divide or separate something lengthways. **2** to break or burst apart. **3** to divide or share something between people. **4** to divide a political party into opposing groups. **5** (*often* **split up**) to end a relationship or connection. ~ *noun* **1** a narrow break made by splitting. **2** a division into opposing groups. **3** (**the splits**) a jump or position with the legs extended at right angles to the trunk.

split second *noun* a very short time. ➤ **split-second** *adjective*.

splodge or **splotch** noun (plural **splodges** or **splotches**) informal a large spot, smear, or blot.

splurge noun (plural **splurges**) informal **1** an extravagantly large amount of something. **2** a time when you spend large amounts of money. ~ verb (**splurges, splurging, splurged**) informal to spend money extravagantly.

splutter verb (**splutters, spluttering, spluttered**) **1** to make a series of noisy spitting sounds. **2** to speak hastily and confusedly. ➤ **splutter** noun.

spoil verb (**spoils, spoiling, spoilt** or **spoiled**) **1** to damage or ruin something. **2** to make something less enjoyable or pleasant. **3** to make somebody, especially a child, selfish by treating them too indulgently. **4** to treat somebody or yourself indulgently. **5** to become unfit for use or eating.

spoils plural noun plunder taken in war or a robbery.

spoilsport noun (plural **spoilsports**) somebody who spoils the enjoyment of others.

spoke[1] verb past tense of SPEAK.

spoke[2] noun (plural **spokes**) each of the bars connecting the hub of a wheel with the rim.

spoken verb past participle of SPEAK.

spokesman or **spokeswoman** or **spokesperson** noun (plural **spokesmen, spokeswomen, spokespersons** or **spokespeople**) a person who speaks on behalf of a group.

sponge noun (plural **sponges**) **1** a sea creature with a soft porous body that absorbs water. **2** a piece of the body of a sponge, or of any porous and absorbent material, used for bathing or cleaning. **3** a light type of cake or pudding. ~ verb (**sponges, sponging, sponged**) **1** to clean or wipe something with a sponge. **2** informal to get money from people by exploiting their natural generosity. ➤ **sponger** noun.

sponsor noun (plural **sponsors**) **1** a person or organization that pays towards the cost of a cultural or sporting event. **2** somebody who contributes to charity by giving money for a participant's efforts in a fund-raising event. **3** somebody who introduces a bill in parliament. ~ verb (**sponsors, sponsoring, sponsored**) to be a sponsor for something. ➤ **sponsorship** noun.

spontaneous adjective **1** done from a natural feeling or sudden impulse, without being prompted or forced by anybody else. **2** developing without any obvious external cause: *spontaneous combustion*. ➤ **spontaneity** noun, **spontaneously** adverb.

spoof noun (plural **spoofs**) informal **1** a humorous parody. **2** a hoax or deception.

spook noun (plural **spooks**) informal **1** a ghost. **2** a spy.

spooky adjective (**spookier, spookiest**) informal sinister and frightening. ➤ **spookily** adverb.

spool noun (plural **spools**) a cylindrical device on which thread, wire, tape, etc is wound.

spoon noun (plural **spoons**) an implement with a small shallow bowl attached to a handle, used for eating or serving food. ~ verb (**spoons, spooning, spooned**) to pick up or transfer something with a spoon. ➤ **spoonful** (plural **spoonfuls**) noun.

spoon-feed verb (**spoon-feeds, spoon-feeding, spoon-fed**) **1** to feed somebody with a spoon. **2** to present information to somebody in a way that makes it very easy for them to understand it.

sporadic adjective happening occasionally and unpredictably. ➤ **sporadically** adverb.

spore noun (plural **spores**) a simple reproductive cell produced by fungi, ferns, and algae.

sporran noun (plural **sporrans**) a leather pouch worn in front of the kilt in traditional Highland dress.

sport noun (plural **sports**) **1** a competitive activity or game requiring physical skill and having a set of rules. **2** these activities collectively. **3** a person who accepts (or doesn't accept) defeat graciously: *a good/bad sport*. ~ verb (**sports, sporting, sported**) **1** to wear something distinctive: *sporting a bright yellow tie*. **2** *literary* to play about happily.

sporting adjective **1** to do with sport. **2** playing fair and being generous to opponents. ✶ **a sporting chance** a reasonable chance of success.

sports car noun (plural **sports cars**) a small fast car.

sports jacket noun (plural **sports jackets**) a man's jacket for informal wear.

sportsman or **sportswoman** noun (plural **sportsmen** or **sportswomen**) a man or woman who takes part in sports.

sportsmanship noun playing fairly and being generous to opponents.

spot noun (plural **spots**) **1** a small round area different in colour or texture from the surrounding surface. **2** a dirty mark or stain. **3** a pimple or small blemish on the skin. **4** *informal* a small amount. **5** a place or area. ~ verb (**spots, spotting, spotted**) **1** to notice or detect something or somebody. **2** to mark something with spots. ✶ **on the spot 1** immediately. **2** at the place of action. **spot on** *informal* absolutely correct or accurate.
➤ **spotted** adjective, **spotter** noun.

spot check noun (plural **spot checks**) a random check made to test quality, accuracy, etc.

spotless adjective absolutely clean.
➤ **spotlessly** adverb.

spotlight noun (plural **spotlights**) **1** a lamp projecting a narrow intense beam of light. **2** (**the spotlight**) full public attention.

spouse noun (plural **spouses**) a husband or wife.

spout noun (plural **spouts**) **1** a projecting tube for pouring liquid from a kettle, pot, etc. **2** a powerful jet of liquid. ~ verb (**spouts, spouting, spouted**) **1** to send out liquid, or to flow out, in a powerful jet. **2** to talk about something in a boring or pompous way for a long time.

sprain verb (**sprains, spraining, sprained**) to twist a joint violently so as to cause swelling and bruising.
➤ **sprain** noun.

sprang verb past tense of SPRING.

sprat noun (plural **sprats**) a small sea fish of the herring family.

sprawl verb (**sprawls, sprawling, sprawled**) **1** to lie or sit with your arms and legs spread out in a careless way. **2** to spread over a landscape, etc.
➤ **sprawl** noun.

spray[1] noun (plural **sprays**) **1** fine drops of water blown or falling through the air. **2** a jet of vapour or liquid in fine drops. **3** an aerosol or other device that sends out liquid in a spray. **4** a substance for spraying. ~ verb (**sprays, spraying, sprayed**) **1** to spread a fluid as a spray. **2** to direct a spray of something onto a surface or throughout a place.
➤ **sprayer** noun.

spray[2] noun (plural **sprays**) **1** a flowering branch or shoot of a plant. **2** a small bouquet of cut flowers.

spread verb (**spreads, spreading, spread**) **1** to open or extend something that was folded up. **2** to expand to cover a wider area. **3** to cover a surface with an even layer of some-

spread-eagled

thing. **4** to communicate something to an increasingly large group of people: *spread the news.* ~ *noun* (*plural* **spreads**) **1** the act of spreading. **2** the area over which something spreads. **3** a food product designed to be spread. **4** *informal* a sumptuous meal.
➤ **spreadable** *adjective*, **spreader** *noun*.

spread-eagled *adjective* stretched out with the arms and legs at an angle to the body.

spreadsheet *noun* (*plural* **spreadsheets**) a computer program in which data can be displayed in rows and columns and rapid calculations can be made.

spree *noun* (*plural* **sprees**) a period when you do something without restraint: *a spending spree.*

sprig *noun* (*plural* **sprigs**) a small shoot or twig.

sprightly *adjective* (**sprightlier, sprightliest**) full of vitality and liveliness. ➤ **sprightliness** *noun*.

spring *verb* (**springs, springing, sprang, sprung**) **1** to move suddenly with a jump. **2** to move something by releasing a spring. **3** to appear suddenly or unexpectedly. **4** to cause something to happen: *sprung a surprise on me.* ~ *noun* (*plural* **springs**) **1** the season of new growth between winter and summer. **2** a piece of bent or coiled metal that goes back to its original shape after being compressed or stretched. **3** springiness. **4** a jump. **5** a source of water that comes up out of the ground. ✳ **spring up** to appear suddenly.

springboard *noun* (*plural* **springboards**) **1** a flexible board on which a diver or gymnast springs to gain extra height. **2** something that enables something else to get started.

spring-clean *verb* (**spring-cleans, spring-cleaning, spring-cleaned**) to give a thorough cleaning to a house or furnishings, especially in spring.
➤ **spring-clean** *noun*.

spring onion *noun* (*plural* **spring onions**) an onion with a small mild-flavoured bulb and long green shoots, eaten raw in salads.

springy *adjective* (**springier, springiest**) elastic or bouncy.
➤ **springiness** *noun*.

sprinkle *verb* (**sprinkles, sprinkling, sprinkled**) to scatter something in fine drops or particles over an object or surface. ➤ **sprinkler** *noun*.

sprinkling *noun* (*plural* **sprinklings**) a small quantity spread randomly over an area.

sprint *verb* (**sprints, sprinting, sprinted**) to run at top speed. ~ *noun* (*plural* **sprints**) **1** a short fast race. **2** a burst of speed. ➤ **sprinter** *noun*.

sprite *noun* (*plural* **sprites**) a fairy or elf.

sprocket *noun* (*plural* **sprockets**) a projection on the rim of a wheel that fits into the links of a chain or the perforations on the edge of a film.

sprout *verb* (**sprouts, sprouting, sprouted**) **1** said about a plant: to send out shoots or new growth. **2** to develop or grow something. ~ *noun* (*plural* **sprouts**) **1** a shoot, such as from a seed or root. **2** = BRUSSELS SPROUT.

spruce[1] *noun* (*plural* **spruces**) a type of fir tree.

spruce[2] *adjective* neat or smart in dress or appearance. ~ *verb* (**spruces, sprucing, spruced**) ✳ **spruce up** to make somebody, something, or yourself neater and smarter.

sprung *verb* past participle of SPRING.

spry *adjective* (**sprier, spriest** or **spryer, spryest**) vigorously active; nimble.

spud *noun* (*plural* **spuds**) *informal* a potato.

spun *verb* past tense and past participle of SPIN.

spur *noun* (*plural* **spurs**) **1** a pointed or wheel-shaped device on the heel of a rider's boot, used to urge a horse on. **2** an incentive. **3** a ridge that extends sideways from a mountain. ~ *verb* (**spurs, spurring, spurred**) **1** to urge a horse on with spurs. **2** (*often* **spur on**) to encourage somebody to make a greater effort. ✶ **on the spur of the moment** suddenly; on impulse.

spurious *adjective* false; fake.

spurn *verb* (**spurns, spurning, spurned**) to reject somebody or something with disdain.

spurt *verb* (**spurts, spurting, spurted**) **1** to gush out in a jet. **2** to increase your speed or your efforts for a short time. ➤ **spurt** *noun*.

sputter *verb* (**sputters, sputtering, sputtered**) to make, or to speak with, explosive popping sounds.

spy *verb* (**spies, spying, spied**) **1** to gather information secretly about an enemy or rival. **2** (**spy on**) to watch somebody secretly. **3** to catch sight of or spot. ~ *noun* (*plural* **spies**) a person who keeps watch or collects information secretly.

squabble *verb* (**squabbles, squabbling, squabbled**) to quarrel noisily. ➤ **squabble** *noun*.

squad *noun* (*plural* **squads**) **1** a small group of people, especially soldiers, carrying out a job together. **2** a group of players from whom a sports team is selected.

squadron *noun* (*plural* **squadrons**) a unit of an air force or navy consisting of a number of aircraft or ships.

squalid *adjective* **1** filthy and degraded from neglect or poverty. **2** sordid; disreputable. ➤ **squalidly** *adverb*.

squall *verb* (**squalls, squalling, squalled**) said about a baby: to cry noisily. ~ *noun* (*plural* **squalls**) a sudden violent wind, often with rain or snow. ➤ **squally** *adjective*.

squalor *noun* a squalid state.

squander *verb* (**squanders, squandering, squandered**) to waste or misuse your money, time, talents, etc.

square *noun* (*plural* **squares**) **1** *Maths* a two-dimensional figure with all four sides equal and four right angles. **2** a four-sided space in a town surrounded by buildings. **3** a square space on a board used for playing games. **4** *Maths* the product of a number when multiplied by itself. ~ *adjective* **1** *Maths* with four equal sides and four right angles. **2** forming a right angle. **3** (*often* **all square**) even or equal, for example as regards a score or settling accounts. **4** denoting units of area equivalent to squares whose sides are of the specified length: *square feet*. **5** said about the size of an area: with sides of the specified length: *ten foot square*. ~ *verb* (**squares, squaring, squared**) **1** (*often* **square off**) to make something square or rectangular. **2** *Maths* to multiply a number by itself. **3** to settle an account. ~ *adverb* squarely. ✶ **back to/at square one** back where you started. **square with** to match or agree with something.

square deal *noun* an honest and fair arrangement or transaction.

squarely *adverb* directly; precisely.

square meal *noun* (*plural* **square meals**) a nutritionally balanced and satisfying meal.

square root *noun* (*plural* **square roots**) *Maths* the number that produces a given number when squared: *The square root of sixteen is four*.

squash¹ *verb* (**squashes, squashing, squashed**) **1** to press or crush something into a flat mass. **2** to squeeze or press something into a space. **3** to suppress a rebellion or rumour forcefully. **4** to humiliate or silence somebody, for example with a cutting remark. ~ *noun* (*plural* **squashes**) **1** a situation where you are squashed, for example in a crowd. **2** an indoor game played with rackets by two people who hit a small rubber ball against the walls of a four-walled court. **3** a soft drink made by diluting sweetened and concentrated fruit juice. ➤ **squashy** *adjective*.

squash² *noun* (*plural* **squashes** or **squash**) a gourd eaten as a vegetable.

squat *verb* (**squats, squatting, squatted**) **1** to lower your body so that your knees are bent and your bottom rests on your heels. **2** to occupy property without the owner's permission. ~ *noun* (*plural* **squats**) **1** a squatting posture. **2** an empty building occupied illegally. ~ *adjective* (**squatter, squattest**) short or low and broad. ➤ **squatter** *noun*.

squaw *noun* (*plural* **squaws**) *offensive* a Native American woman or wife.

squawk *verb* (**squawks, squawking, squawked**) **1** to utter a harsh abrupt scream. **2** *informal* to make a loud or vehement protest. ➤ **squawk** *noun*.

squeak *verb* (**squeaks, squeaking, squeaked**) to make a short shrill cry or noise. ➤ **squeak** *noun*, **squeaky** *adjective*.

squeaky-clean *adjective informal* **1** absolutely clean. **2** with no moral or criminal flaws.

squeal *verb* (**squeals, squealing, squealed**) to make a shrill sharp cry or noise. ➤ **squeal** *noun*.

squeamish *adjective* easily shocked or offended.

squeeze *verb* (**squeezes, squeezing, squeezed**) **1** to press something inwards from the sides. **2** to extract liquid, etc from something by squeezing. **3** to force or cram something into or through a small space. **4** (**squeeze in/into**) to fit a person or task into a tight schedule. ~ *noun* (*plural* **squeezes**) **1** an act of squeezing. **2** a quick hug. **3** a small quantity of liquid squeezed out from something. **4** *informal* a crowded situation. ➤ **squeezer** *noun*.

squelch *verb* (**squelches, squelching, squelched**) to make the sucking sound typical of somebody walking through mud. ➤ **squelch** *noun*.

squib *noun* (*plural* **squibs**) a small firework that burns with a fizz before exploding.

squid *noun* (*plural* **squids** or **squid**) a sea creature like an octopus, with eight arms, two long tentacles, and a long tapered body.

squiggle *noun* (*plural* **squiggles**) a short wavy line. ➤ **squiggly** *adjective*.

squint *verb* (**squints, squinting, squinted**) **1** to have a squint. **2** to look or peer with your eyes partly closed. ~ *noun* (*plural* **squints**) **1** an abnormality of an eye, so that it turns permanently towards or away from the nose. **2** *informal* a quick look.

squire *noun* (*plural* **squires**) *History* **1** a young nobleman acting as a knight's attendant and training for knighthood. **2** the principal landowner of a district.

squirm *verb* (**squirms, squirming, squirmed**) **1** to twist about like a worm; to wriggle. **2** to feel very embarrassed or ashamed.

squirrel *noun* (*plural* **squirrels**) a rodent with a long bushy tail that lives in trees.

squirt *verb* (**squirts, squirting, squirted**) to come out, or to send out liquid, in a jet from a narrow opening. ➤ **squirt** *noun*.

St *abbreviation* **1** Saint. **2** Street.

stab *noun* (*plural* **stabs**) **1** a thrust with a pointed weapon. **2** a sharp pain or feeling. ~ *verb* (**stabs, stabbing, stabbed**) **1** to wound somebody with a pointed weapon. **2** to thrust or jab a pointed object somewhere. ✶ **have/make a stab at** *informal* to make an attempt at something.

stability *noun* the quality of being stable.

stabilize *or* **stabilise** *verb* (**stabilizes, stabilizing, stabilized** *or* **stabilises,** etc) to become, or to make something, stable. ➤ **stabilization** *or* **stabilisation** *noun*.

stable¹ *adjective* **1** well balanced or firmly fixed. **2** not likely to change or come to an end. **3** said about a patient: not likely to get worse suddenly.

stable² *noun* (*plural* **stables**) a building in which horses are kept. ~ *verb* (**stables, stabling, stabled**) to put or keep a horse in a stable.

staccato /sta kah toh/ *adjective and adverb* in a series of short, separate sounds.

stack *noun* (*plural* **stacks**) **1** a neat pile. **2** a shaped pile of hay or straw. **3** a chimney. **4** (*also* **stacks**) *informal* a large quantity or number. ~ *verb* (**stacks, stacking, stacked**) **1** to pile things into a stack. **2** to fill a place with stacks of things.

stadium *noun* (*plural* **stadiums** *or* **stadia**) a sports ground surrounded by tiers of seats for spectators.

staff *noun* (*plural* **staffs**) **1** the people who work for an institution, business, etc. **2** the teachers at a school or university. **3** (*plural* **staves**) a long stick used for support when walking or as a weapon. **4** (*plural* **staves**) *Music* = STAVE¹ (sense 2). ~ *verb* (**staffs, staffing, staffed**) to supply staff for, or be the staff of, an organization.

stag *noun* (*plural* **stags**) an adult male deer.

stage *noun* (*plural* **stages**) **1** *Drama* the raised platform or other area in a theatre where actors perform. **2** (**the stage**) the acting profession. **3** a period or step in the development of something. **4** a section of a journey, race, or rally. ~ *verb* (**stages, staging, staged**) **1** *Drama* to produce and perform a theatrical work. **2** to organize a public event.

stagecoach *noun* (*plural* **stagecoaches**) *History* a horse-drawn passenger and mail coach that ran a regular scheduled route.

stage fright *noun Drama* nervousness felt at appearing before an audience.

stage-manage *verb* (**stage-manages, stage-managing, stage-managed**) **1** *Drama* to be the stage manager of a play, etc. **2** to arrange an event, etc so as to achieve a desired result. ➤ **stage management** *noun*.

stage manager *noun* (*plural* **stage managers**) *Drama* a person who is in charge of the stage, cast, and technical staff during performances of a play.

stagger *verb* (**staggers, staggering, staggered**) **1** to move unsteadily or jerkily as if in danger of falling over. **2** to astonish somebody. **3** to arrange a set of things so that they are not in a straight line or start at different times. ➤ **stagger** *noun*, **staggering** *adjective*.

stagnant *adjective* **1** said about water: not flowing and usually overgrown or foul. **2** dull or inactive.

stagnate *verb* (**stagnates, stagnating, stagnated**) to become stagnant. ➤ **stagnation** *noun*.

staid *adjective* unadventurous and usually old-fashioned in attitude.

stain *noun* (*plural* **stains**) **1** a dirty or discoloured mark. **2** a moral blemish. **3** a coloured liquid used in staining. ~ *verb* (**stains, staining, stained**) **1** to mark, discolour, or dirty something. **2** to colour something using chemicals or dyes.

stained glass *noun* coloured glass used

stainless *adjective* **1** free from stain. **2** resistant to rust.

stainless steel *noun* steel containing chromium that resists rust and corrosion.

stair *noun* (*plural* **stairs**) **1** (**stairs**) a flight of steps for passing from one level to another. **2** any step of a stairway.

staircase *noun* (*plural* **staircases**) a flight of stairs with its supporting framework.

stairway *noun* (*plural* **stairways**) one or more flights of stairs.

stairwell *noun* (*plural* **stairwells**) a vertical shaft in which stairs are located.

stake[1] *noun* (*plural* **stakes**) **1** a pointed wooden or iron post used for driving into the ground as a marker or support. **2** (**the stake**) *History* a post to which a person was formerly bound for execution by burning. ~ *verb* (**stakes, staking, staked**) **1** (*often* **stake off/out**) to mark out an area with stakes. **2** to support a plant with a stake. ✱ **stake your claim** to assert your right to have something.

stake[2] *noun* (*plural* **stakes**) **1** a sum of money that is bet on something. **2** an interest or share in something. ~ *verb* (**stakes, staking, staked**) to bet a sum of money, your reputation, etc on something. ✱ **at stake 1** to be won or lost. **2** at risk.

stalactite *noun* (*plural* **stalactites**) an icicle-like deposit of calcium carbonate hanging from the roof or sides of a cave.

stalagmite *noun* (*plural* **stalagmites**) a spike-like deposit of calcium carbonate growing upward from the floor of a cave.

stale *adjective* (**staler, stalest**) **1** said especially about food: no longer fresh. **2** said about a person: lacking energy or new ideas through having done the same thing too often. ➤ **staleness** *noun*.

stalemate *noun* **1** a position in chess representing a draw, where the king, although not in check, can move only into check. **2** a deadlock.

stalk[1] *verb* (**stalks, stalking, stalked**) **1** to follow stealthily something you are hunting. **2** to follow and watch a person with whom you have become obsessed. **3** to walk in a stiff haughty fashion. ➤ **stalker** *noun*.

stalk[2] *noun* (*plural* **stalks**) **1** the main stem of a plant. **2** the stem of a leaf or fruit.

stall[1] *noun* (*plural* **stalls**) **1** a compartment for a domestic animal in a stable or barn. **2** a stand or counter where articles are on sale, for example in a market. **3** (**stalls**) the seats on the main floor of a theatre or cinema.

stall[2] *verb* (**stalls, stalling, stalled**) **1** said about a vehicle or engine: to lose power suddenly and stop. **2** to delay somebody, or avoid answering a question, to give yourself more time.

stallion *noun* (*plural* **stallions**) a male horse.

stalwart *adjective* **1** strong. **2** dependable.

stamen /stay men/ *noun* (*plural* **stamens**) the organ of a flower that produces the male reproductive cell.

stamina *noun* the strength to continue running, working, etc for a long time.

stammer *verb* (**stammers, stammering, stammered**) to speak with involuntary stops and repetitions. ➤ **stammer** *noun*.

stamp *verb* (**stamps, stamping, stamped**) **1** to bring down your foot forcibly. **2** to walk with loud heavy steps. **3** to imprint words, etc on something. **4** to be characteristic of somebody or something: *a quality that* *stamps all her writings.* **5** to attach a postage stamp to an envelope, etc. ~ *noun* (*plural* **stamps**) **1** a printed adhesive piece of paper used to indicate that postage has been paid. **2** an instrument for stamping a mark, etc on a surface. **3** a mark made by stamping. **4** a characteristic quality. **5** the act or sound of stamping your foot. * **stamp out** to put an end to something.

stampede *noun* (*plural* **stampedes**) a wild rush of frightened animals or people. ~ *verb* (**stampedes, stampeding, stampeded**) to run away in panic, or to cause people or animals to do this.

stance *noun* (*plural* **stances**) **1** a way of standing. **2** an attitude or point of view.

stand *verb* (**stands, standing, stood**) **1** to support yourself on your feet in an upright position. **2** (*also* **stand up**) to rise to this position. **3** to rest upright on the ground or another surface. **4** to be located: *The house stands on a hill.* **5** to remain stationary. **6** to remain valid: *My offer still stands.* **7** to tolerate or like: *I can't stand her husband.* **8** to withstand something. **9** to treat somebody to a meal or drink. **10** to be a candidate in an election. ~ *noun* (*plural* **stands**) **1** a support or frame that holds something. **2** a small outdoor stall selling food, etc: *a hot-dog stand*. **3** a structure with tiers of seats for spectators. **4** a determined effort to fight for or resist something. **5** a definite attitude taken towards something. * **stand by 1** to wait in readiness. **2** to support or remain loyal to somebody or something. **stand down** to resign from an office or position. **stand for 1** to represent something. **2** to permit or tolerate something. **stand in for** to act as substitute for somebody. **stand out** to be especially visible, noteworthy, or good. **stand up for** to defend something or somebody against criticism. **stand up to 1** to resist something or somebody. **2** to withstand wear, etc.

standard *noun* (*plural* **standards**) **1** a level of quality or achievement. **2** something that other things are compared with and judged against. **3** (**standards**) principles of acceptable behaviour. **4** a flag or banner. ~ *adjective* regularly and widely used; accepted as normal.

standard English *noun* English normal correct English as used in the speech and writing of educated people and taught in schools.

standardize *or* **standardise** *verb* (**standardizes, standardizing, standardized** *or* **standardises,** etc) to change things so that they are all the same or all have certain features in common. ➤ **standardization** *or* **standardisation** *noun*.

standard lamp *noun* (*plural* **standard lamps**) a lamp with a tall support that stands on the floor.

standard of living *noun* (*plural* **standards of living**) a measure of how well-off an individual or community is.

standby *noun* (*plural* **standbys**) **1** a person or thing held in reserve in case of necessity. **2** a state of readiness for duty or use. ~ *adjective* **1** held in reserve and ready for use or duty. **2** said about tickets: not reserved and available for sale shortly before a performance, flight, etc.

stand-in *noun* (*plural* **stand-ins**) a substitute.

standing *noun* **1** status, position, or reputation. **2** length of existence or duration: *a committee member of long standing.*

standoffish *adjective* reserved; unfriendly.

standpoint *noun* (*plural* **standpoints**) a point of view.

standstill *noun* a stationary state; a stop; a point where no progress is being made.

stank *verb* past tense of STINK.

stanza *noun* (*plural* **stanzas**) *English* a verse of a poem.

staple[1] *noun* (*plural* **staples**) **1** a small wire clip that can be driven through sheets of paper and bent over to hold them together. **2** a U-shaped nail, driven into a surface to secure something to it.

staple[2] *adjective* main or basic. ~ *noun* (*plural* **staples**) the main thing that people eat, use, or produce.

star *noun* (*plural* **stars**)
1 an astronomical object that radiates energy and is visible as a point of light in the night sky. **2** a figure with five or more points that represents a star. **3** a famous entertainer, performer, or sports personality. **4** the leading or outstanding performer in a group. ~ *verb* (**stars, starring, starred**) **1** said about a film, play, etc: to feature a certain actor in a leading role. **2** to play a leading role in a production. **3** to mark something with a star or asterisk. ➤ **stardom** *noun*, **starry** *adjective*.

starboard *noun* the right side of a ship or aircraft looking forward.

starch *noun* (*plural* **starches**)
1 a carbohydrate that is an important foodstuff, obtained chiefly from cereals and potatoes. **2** a powder or spray used to stiffen fabric. ~ *verb* (**starches, starching, starched**) to stiffen clothes or fabric with starch. ➤ **starchy** *adjective*.

stare *verb* (**stares, staring, stared**) to look fixedly at somebody or something. ✱ **stare somebody in the face** to be very obvious. ➤ **stare** *noun*.

starfish *noun* (*plural* **starfishes** or **starfish**) a sea creature with a roughly circular body and five, or sometimes more than five, equally spaced arms.

stark *adjective* **1** said about a landscape, surroundings, etc: bleak or bare; desolate. **2** harshly clear or plain. **3** sheer; utter. ➤ **starkly** *adverb*.

stark-naked *adjective* completely naked.

starling *noun* (*plural* **starlings**) a bird with glossy greenish black plumage.

starry-eyed *adjective* naively idealistic or over-optimistic.

start *noun* (*plural* **starts**) **1** the first part or moment of a movement, activity, journey, etc. **2** a starting place, for example for a race. **3** a lead or advantage given to a competitor in a race: *I'll give you ten yards start.* **4** a sudden involuntary jerk of your body, for example from surprise or alarm. ~ *verb* (**starts, starting, started**) **1** to come into operation or existence, or to cause something to do this; to begin. **2** to make an engine, vehicle, etc start working. **3** to make a sudden jerk as a result of shock or surprise.

starter *noun* (*plural* **starters**) **1** the person who gives the signal to start a race. **2** a device that makes machinery, especially a vehicle engine, start to work. **3** the first course of a meal.

startle *verb* (**startles, startling, startled**) to make somebody start in alarm, etc. ➤ **startled** *adjective*, **startling** *adjective*.

starve *verb* (**starves, starving, starved**) to suffer severely or die from hunger, or cause a person or animal to do this. ✱ **be starving** *informal* to be very hungry. **starve of** to deprive a person or animal of something that they need: *starved of affection.* ➤ **starvation** *noun*.

stash *verb* (**stashes, stashing, stashed**) *informal* to store something in a secret place for future use. ~ *noun* (*plural* **stashes**) *informal* a secret store of drugs, weapons, etc.

state[1] *noun* (*plural* **states**) **1** the condition or situation of somebody or something. **2** a politically organized community that exists as a separate country. **3** the government of a country. **4** one separate part of a country that has a federal government: *the state of Maryland*. **5** (**the States**) the United States of America. **6** (**a state**) *informal* an upset, confused, or dirty condition. ✴ **state of affairs** *or* **state of things** a situation.

state[2] *verb* (**states, stating, stated**) to declare something formally.

stately *adjective* (**statelier, stateliest**) imposing; dignified.

stately home *noun* (*plural* **stately homes**) a large country residence, usually belonging to an aristocratic family.

statement *noun* (*plural* **statements**) **1** a declaration or account of something given in speech or writing. **2** a summary of a financial account. **3** an account of events given to the police or in court.

state-of-the-art *adjective* using the most advanced technology available.

statesman *or* **stateswoman** *noun* (*plural* **statesmen** *or* **stateswomen**) an experienced and respected political leader.

static *adjective* not moving or changing.

static electricity *noun* Science an electrical charge built up, for example by friction, in a material from which it cannot be conducted away.

station *noun* (*plural* **stations**) **1** a stopping place for trains, or a place where many buses or coaches begin and end their journeys. **2** the place where somebody is standing or has to stand, for example during a battle. **3** rank in society. **4** a place equipped for a certain type of work or activity: *a weather station*. **5** a radio or television channel. ~ *verb* (**stations, stationing, stationed**) to send somebody to a place or put them in a particular position.

stationary *adjective* **1** not moving. **2** neither progressing nor deteriorating.

Usage Note Do not confuse *stationary* and *stationery*. Remember that a p**ar**ked c**ar** is *station**ar**y*.

stationer *noun* (*plural* **stationers**) a shopkeeper who sells stationery.

stationery *noun* paper, envelopes, and other materials used for writing, typing, etc.

Usage Note Do not confuse *stationery* and *stationary*. Remember that *station**er**y* is what you use to write lett**er**s.

statistic *noun* (*plural* **statistics**) a piece of data in the form of a number, for example how many people listen to Radio 2, which can be put together and compared with other similar numbers. ➤ **statistical** *adjective*, **statistically** *adverb*.

statistics *noun* Maths the collection and analysis of masses of data in the form of numbers. ➤ **statistician** *noun*.

statue *noun* (*plural* **statues**) a likeness, for example of a person or animal, made from a solid material.

statuesque *adjective* tall, well-proportioned, and stately.

statuette *noun* (*plural* **statuettes**) a small statue.

stature *noun* **1** the natural height of a person when standing upright. **2** a person's standing or reputation.

status /stay tus/ *noun* (*plural* **statuses**) **1** the legal position of a person, territory, etc. **2** a person's position in

status quo

relation to others in a hierarchy or social structure. **3** prestige.

status quo /stay tus kwoh/ *noun* the existing state of affairs.

status symbol *noun* (*plural* **status symbols**) a possession that is thought to show that a person is wealthy or important.

statute *noun* (*plural* **statutes**) a law made by a parliament. ➤ **statutory** *adjective*.

staunch[1] *verb* (**staunches, staunching, staunched**) to stop the flow of blood, etc.

staunch[2] *adjective* steadfast; unchangingly loyal. ➤ **staunchly** *adverb*, **staunchness** *noun*.

stave[1] *noun* (*plural* **staves**) **1** any of the narrow strips of wood placed edge to edge to form a barrel, bucket, etc. **2** *Music* a set of five horizontal spaced lines on which notes are written.

stave[2] *verb* (**staves, staving, staved** or **stove**) ✶ **stave in** to break a hole in something hard. **stave off** (past tense and past participle **staved**) to prevent something threatening from causing harm, at least temporarily.

stay[1] *verb* (**stays, staying, stayed**) **1** to remain in a place and not move. **2** to remain in a particular state and not change. **3** to spend some time, live, or lodge somewhere: *We're staying at the Grand Hotel*. ~ *noun* (*plural* **stays**) **1** a period spent at a place. **2** a postponement of a legal procedure: *a stay of execution*. ✶ **stay put** to stay where placed or left.

stay[2] *noun* (*plural* **stays**) **1** a prop or support. **2** (**stays**) a corset stiffened with bones.

staying power *noun* stamina.

stead ✶ **in somebody's** or **something's stead** in place of somebody or something else. **stand in good stead** to be an advantage to somebody.

steadfast *adjective* loyal or unwavering. ➤ **steadfastly** *adverb*.

steady *adjective* (**steadier, steadiest**) **1** firmly positioned or balanced; not shaking, rocking, etc. **2** continuing at the same rate or level with little variation: *a steady increase*. ~ *verb* (**steadies, steadying, steadied**) to become, or make something, steady. ➤ **steadily** *adverb*, **steadiness** *noun*.

steak *noun* (*plural* **steaks**) **1** a lean high-quality slice of meat, especially beef, suitable for grilling or frying. **2** a slice of a large fish.

steal *verb* (**steals, stealing, stole, stolen**) **1** to take something without permission or illegally, with no intention of returning it. **2** to take a look, kiss, etc quickly and without permission. **3** to come or go stealthily or unobtrusively.

stealth /stelth/ *noun* action or movement that is quiet and intended to be unnoticed and undetected. ~ *adjective* said about aircraft: designed to be able to avoid detection by radar.

stealthy *adjective* (**stealthier, stealthiest**) characterized by stealth. ➤ **stealthily** *adverb*.

steam *noun* **1** the vapour into which water is converted when boiled. **2** the mist formed when water vapour condenses. **3** energy or power generated by steam under pressure. ~ *verb* (**steams, steaming, steamed**) **1** to give off steam. **2** to move by means of steam power. **3** *informal* to move quickly. **4** to cook food in steam from boiling water. ✶ **get steamed up** *informal* to get angry or agitated. **steam up** to become covered with condensation. **under your own steam** independently.

steam engine *noun* (*plural* **steam engines**) an engine driven by steam.

steamer *noun* (*plural* **steamers**) **1** a ship powered by steam.

2 a saucepan or container for cooking food by steam.

steamroller noun (plural **steamrollers**) a machine equipped with wide heavy rollers for flattening and hardening newly laid road surfaces, etc.

steed noun (plural **steeds**) archaic or literary a horse.

steel noun an alloy of iron with carbon that is particularly strong and hard. ~ verb (**steels, steeling, steeled**) ✳ **steel yourself** to prepare yourself to face something unpleasant.

steel band noun (plural **steel bands**) Music a band that plays instruments made from empty oil drums.

steely adjective (**steelier, steeliest**) **1** resembling steel. **2** unyielding; relentless.

steep¹ adjective **1** sloping sharply, or nearly vertical. **2** said about an increase or decrease: sudden and large. **3** informal said about a price: unreasonably high. ➤ **steeply** adverb.

steep² verb (**steeps, steeping, steeped**) to soak something, or to be soaked, in a liquid. ✳ **be steeped in** to be full of something.

steepen verb (**steepens, steepening, steepened**) to become, or make something, steeper.

steeple noun (plural **steeples**) a church tower with a spire.

steeplechase noun (plural **steeplechases**) **1** a horse race over a racecourse with hedges and ditches for jumping. **2** a middle-distance running race over obstacles. ➤ **steeplechaser** noun, **steeplechasing** noun.

Word History Steeplechases were originally horse races across country, using church steeples as landmarks to guide the riders.

---

steeplejack noun (plural **steeplejacks**) a person who climbs chimneys, towers, etc to paint or repair them.

steer¹ verb (**steers, steering, steered**) **1** to control the direction in which a vehicle or ship moves. **2** to guide somebody or something in a certain direction. ✳ **steer clear of** to keep well away from somebody or something. ➤ **steering** noun.

steer² noun (plural **steers**) a bullock.

steering wheel noun (plural **steering wheels**) a wheel that is turned to steer a motor vehicle, ship, etc.

stellar adjective to do with stars.

stem noun (plural **stems**) **1** the main stalk or trunk of a plant or shrub. **2** the slender stalk of a flower, leaf, or fruit. **3** English the part of a word to which a prefix or suffix has been added, such as 'successful' in *unsuccessful* or 'unsuccessful' in *unsuccessfully*. **4** the slender support for the bowl of a wineglass. **5** the bow of a ship: *from stem to stern*. ~ verb (**stems, stemming, stemmed**) ✳ **stem from** to be caused by something.

stench noun (plural **stenches**) a bad smell.

stencil noun (plural **stencils**) a sheet of paper, card, metal, etc with a design or lettering cut into it through which ink or paint is put onto the surface below. ~ verb (**stencils, stencilling, stencilled**) to produce a design, etc using a stencil.

step noun (plural **steps**) **1** a movement made by raising one foot and bringing it down in front of the other in walking. **2** a short distance. **3** a flat supporting surface for your foot when you are moving to a higher or lower position. **4** (**steps**) = STEPLADDER. **5** a stage in the progress of something. **6** (*often* **steps**) an action or measure to deal with something. ~ verb (**steps, stepping, stepped**) to move by raising one foot and bringing it down in front of the other, or in another position. ✳ **step down** to retire or resign. **step in** to intervene in some-

stepbrother

thing. **step on it** *informal* to hurry up. **step up** to increase something.

stepbrother *noun* (*plural* **stepbrothers**) a son of your stepparent.

stepchild *noun* (*plural* **stepchildren**) a child of your wife or husband by a former marriage.

stepdaughter *noun* (*plural* **stepdaughters**) a daughter of your wife or husband by a former marriage.

stepfather *noun* (*plural* **stepfathers**) the husband of your mother by a later marriage.

stepladder *noun* (*plural* **stepladders**) a hinged ladder with flat rungs and often a platform.

stepmother *noun* (*plural* **stepmothers**) the wife of your father by a subsequent marriage.

stepparent *noun* (*plural* **stepparents**) the husband or wife of your parent by a subsequent marriage.

steppe *noun* (*plural* **steppes**) *Geography* a vast grassy treeless plain, especially in southeastern Europe or Asia.

stepping stone *noun* (*plural* **stepping stones**) **1** a stone on which to step when crossing a stream. **2** something regarded as a means of progress or advancement.

stepsister *noun* (*plural* **stepsisters**) a daughter of your stepparent.

stepson *noun* (*plural* **stepsons**) a son of your wife or husband by a former marriage.

stereo *noun* (*plural* **stereos**)
1 stereophonic sound.
2 a stereophonic record-player, etc.
~ *adjective* stereophonic.

stereophonic *adjective* using two different channels to produce sound from two directions and give a more natural effect.

stereotype *noun* (*plural* **stereotypes**) a simplified and standardized image of a person or thing. ➤ **stereotypical** *adjective*.

sterile *adjective* **1** unable to produce young, seeds, or crops. **2** free from germs. ➤ **sterility** *noun*.

sterilize or **sterilise** *verb* (**sterilizes, sterilizing, sterilized** or **sterilises**, etc) to make something or somebody sterile. ➤ **sterilization** or **sterilisation** *noun*.

sterling¹ *noun* British money.

sterling² *adjective* of genuine worth or quality.

stern¹ *adjective* **1** harsh, strict, or severe. **2** firm; uncompromising.
➤ **sternly** *adverb*.

stern² *noun* (*plural* **sterns**) the rear end of a ship.

steroid /steer oid *or* ste roid/ *noun* (*plural* **steroids**) **1** *Science* a chemical compound, such as a hormone, that has a ring of carbon atoms. **2** a drug containing a steroid, especially one used by athletes to enhance their performance illegally.

stethoscope *noun* (*plural* **stethoscopes**) an instrument used by a doctor to detect and study sounds produced in the body, especially by the heart and lungs.

stew *noun* (*plural* **stews**) **1** a dish of meat, vegetables, or both, cooked in liquid in a closed pan. **2** *informal* an agitated state. ~ *verb* (**stews, stewing, stewed**) to cook meat, fruit, etc in liquid in a closed pan.

steward *noun* (*plural* **stewards**)
1 a person who looks after passengers on an airliner, ship, etc. **2** an official in charge of arrangements or crowd-control at a large public event.

stewardess *noun* (*plural* **stewardesses**) a woman who attends to the needs of passengers on an airliner, ship, etc.

stick¹ *noun* (*plural* **sticks**) **1** a twig or slender branch from a tree or shrub.
2 a club or staff used as a weapon.
3 a walking stick. **4** an implement

used for hitting the ball in hockey. **5** a long, slender piece of something.

stick² *verb* (**sticks, sticking, stuck**) **1** to push something sharp or pointed into something or somebody. **2** to attach one thing to another with adhesive. **3** to become firmly attached to a surface, etc. **4** to become fixed or unable to move. **5** *informal* to put something somewhere, especially temporarily. **6** *informal* to bear or stand somebody or something. ✷ **stick around** *informal* to stay. **stick at** not to give up trying to do something. **stick out 1** to jut out; to project. **2** to be very noticeable. **stick to 1** to remain loyal to somebody. **2** not to move away from or change something. **stick together** to continue to support each other; to remain united. **stick up** to stand upright or on end. **stick up for** to defend somebody against attack or criticism.

sticker *noun* (*plural* **stickers**) an adhesive label or notice.

stick insect *noun* (*plural* **stick insects**) an insect with a long thin body resembling a stick.

stickleback *noun* (*plural* **sticklebacks**) a small fish with spines on its back.

stickler *noun* (*plural* **sticklers**) a person who insists on things being done exactly right.

sticky *adjective* (**stickier, stickiest**) **1** adhesive. **2** thick and gluey. **3** coated with a sticky substance. **4** said about the weather: humid or muggy. **5** difficult; tricky.

stiff *adjective* **1** not easily bent. **2** said about a handle, lock, etc: hard to operate or turn. **3** said about the body or part of it: not moving freely, or painful to move. **4** said about a mixture: thick. **5** not relaxed and friendly. **6** said about an alcoholic drink: strong. **7** said about a punishment: harsh or severe. ➤ **stiffly** *adverb*, **stiffness** *noun*.

stiffen *verb* (**stiffens, stiffening, stiffened**) to become, or to make something stiff. ➤ **stiffener** *noun*.

stifle *verb* (**stifles, stifling, stifled**) **1** to suffocate somebody. **2** to suppress something.

stifling *adjective* uncomfortably hot and stuffy. ➤ **stiflingly** *adverb*.

stigma *noun* (*plural* **stigmas**) **1** a mark of disgrace. **2** *Science* the part of a flower that receives the pollen.

stigmatize *or* **stigmatise** *verb* (**stigmatizes, stigmatizing, stigmatized** *or* **stigmatises**, etc) to describe somebody or something in disapproving terms. ➤ **stigmatization** *or* **stigmatisation** *noun*.

stile *noun* (*plural* **stiles**) a step or set of steps for climbing over a fence or wall.

stiletto *noun* (*plural* **stilettos** *or* **stilettoes**) **1** a dagger with a thin blade. **2** (*also* **stiletto heel**) a very narrow high heel on a woman's shoe.

still¹ *adjective* **1** not moving. **2** calm or tranquil. **3** said about drinks: not fizzy. ~ *noun* (*plural* **stills**) a single frame from a cinema film. ➤ **stillness** *noun*.

still² *adverb* **1** as before: *Drink it while it's still hot.* **2** in spite of that; nevertheless. **3** even; yet.

still³ (*plural* **stills**) *noun* an apparatus for distilling spirits.

stillborn *adjective* said about a baby: dead at birth.

still life *noun* (*plural* **still lifes**) *Art* a picture showing an arrangement of objects such as fruit or flowers.

stilted *adjective* said about writing or speech: formal and unnatural.

stilts *plural noun* **1** two poles with supports for your feet, which enable you to walk along above the ground. **2** a set of posts that support a building off the ground or above water level.

stimulant *noun* (*plural* **stimulants**) something, such as a drug, that stimulates you.

stimulate *verb* (**stimulates, stimulating, stimulated**) **1** *Science* to cause an organ of the body to react or a process in the body to take place. **2** to make somebody or something more active or lively. ➤ **stimulation** *noun*.

stimulus *noun* (*plural* **stimuli** /sti mew lie/) **1** something that causes activity or a reaction in a living organisms. **2** an incentive.

sting *noun* (*plural* **stings**) **1** a sharp organ in certain plants or insects that can wound by piercing your skin and injecting a poisonous or irritating substance. **2** a wound or pain caused by stinging. ~ *verb* (**stings, stinging, stung**) **1** said about a plant or insect: to wound somebody or something with a sting. **2** to cause a sharp pain. **3** to make somebody feel upset or hurt.

stingy /stin ji/ *adjective* (**stingier, stingiest**) *informal* mean; not generous.

stink *noun* (*plural* **stinks**) **1** a strong offensive smell. **2** *informal* a row or scandal. ~ *verb* (**stinks, stinking, stank** or **stunk, stunk**) **1** to give off a strong offensive smell. **2** *informal* to be highly suspect or very bad. ➤ **stinker** *noun*.

stint[1] *verb* (**stints, stinting, stinted**) **1** to restrict somebody, especially yourself, to a small amount of something: *Don't stint yourself. We can afford it.* **2** to limit the amount of something you use or do: *Don't stint on the cream.*

stint[2] *noun* (*plural* **stints**) a period of duty or work.

stipulate *verb* (**stipulates, stipulating, stipulated**) to state definitely that something has to be done. ➤ **stipulation** *noun*.

stir *verb* (**stirs, stirring, stirred**) **1** to move a liquid around by making circular movements with a spoon, etc, usually to blend the ingredients. **2** to make a slight movement. **3** to wake and begin to move. **4** to make somebody feel moved or excited. ~ *noun* **1** the act of stirring. **2** a sensation or commotion. ✶ **stir up** to create trouble or ill-feeling between people.

stir-fry *verb* (**stir-fries, stir-frying, stir-fried**) to cook small pieces of food by stirring them together while frying them rapidly. ➤ **stir-fry** *noun*.

stirring *adjective* rousing; inspiring. ➤ **stirringly** *adverb*.

stirrup *noun* (*plural* **stirrups**) either of a pair of D-shaped metal frames attached to a saddle in which a horse-rider's feet are placed.

stitch *noun* (*plural* **stitches**) **1** a loop of thread or yarn left in material by a single in-and-out movement of the needle. **2** a method of stitching. **3** a sharp and sudden pain in the side brought on by running or exercise. ~ *verb* (**stitches, stitching, stitched**) to sew fabric, a garment, etc. ✶ **in stitches** laughing uncontrollably.

stoat *noun* (*plural* **stoats**) a European weasel with a brown coat that turns white in winter in northern regions.

stock *noun* (*plural* **stocks**) **1** a store or supply of raw materials or finished goods. **2** farm animals. **3** the shares of a particular company or type of company. **4** the liquid in which meat, fish, or vegetables have been simmered. **5** the trunk or main stem of a plant. **6** a plant grown for its sweet-scented flowers. **7** a person's line of descent. **8** (**the stocks**) *History* a wooden frame with holes in which an offender's feet could be locked as a public punishment. ~ *verb* (**stocks, stocking, stocked**) **1** to supply a place with a stock of something. **2** to keep a stock of something. ~ *adjective informal* commonly used;

standard. ✳ **in** *or* **out of stock** available (or not available) for sale or delivery. **stock up** to take in a supply of something. **take stock** to review a situation.

stockade *noun* (*plural* **stockades**) a line of stout posts fixed vertically in the ground to form a defensive barrier.

stockbroker *noun* (*plural* **stockbrokers**) a broker who buys and sells stocks and shares. ➤ **stockbroking** *noun*.

stock exchange *noun* (*plural* **stock exchanges**) a place where people buy and sell stocks and shares.

stocking *noun* (*plural* **stockings**) **1** a woman's closely fitting garment for the foot and leg. **2** a man's long sock. ➤ **stockinged** *adjective*.

stockist *noun* (*plural* **stockists**) a shopkeeper who stocks goods of a particular kind.

stock market *noun* (*plural* **stock markets**) **1** a stock exchange. **2** the business of buying and selling stocks and shares.

stockpile *noun* (*plural* **stockpiles**) a reserve supply of something essential for use during a shortage.

stock-still *adverb* completely motionless.

stocktaking *noun* the process of making a detailed list of all the goods held in a shop, warehouse, etc.

stocky *adjective* (**stockier, stockiest**) short and sturdy.

stodge *noun informal* heavy filling starchy food, such as steamed pudding. ➤ **stodgy** *adjective*.

stoic /stoh ik/ *noun* (*plural* **stoics**) a stoical person.

stoical *adjective* bearing pain, hardship, and sorrow without complaining. ➤ **stoically** *adverb*, **stoicism** *noun*.

stoke *verb* (**stokes, stoking, stoked**) to put fuel onto a fire or into a furnace. ➤ **stoker** *noun*.

stole[1] *verb* past tense of STEAL.

stole[2] *noun* (*plural* **stoles**) a large rectangular scarf or shawl worn by women across their shoulders.

stolen *verb* past participle of STEAL.

stolid *adjective* said about a person: difficult to arouse emotionally or mentally. ➤ **stolidity** *noun*, **stolidly** *adverb*.

stomach *noun* (*plural* **stomachs**) **1** an internal organ in which the first stages of digestion occur. **2** the abdomen. **3** appetite or inclination. ~ *verb* (**stomachs, stomaching, stomached**) to accept or put up with something you dislike.

stomp *verb* (**stomps, stomping, stomped**) *informal* to walk or dance with heavy steps.

stone *noun* (*plural* **stones**) **1** the hard mineral matter of which rock is composed. **2** a piece of rock; a pebble. **3** a gem. **4** a piece of stone used for a particular purpose, for example a gravestone. **5** the hard seed in a peach, cherry, plum, etc. **6** (*plural* **stone**) a unit of weight equal to 14 pounds (about 6.35 kilograms). ~ *verb* (**stones, stoning, stoned**) **1** to throw stones at somebody. **2** to remove the stones or seeds of a fruit. ~ *adverb* completely: *stone deaf*.

Stone Age *noun* (**the Stone Age**) *History* the first known period of prehistoric human culture in which people used stone tools.

stoned *adjective informal* under the influence of alcohol or a drug such as marijuana.

stony *adjective* (**stonier, stoniest**) **1** full of stones. **2** resembling stone. **3** cold or unresponsive. ➤ **stonily** *adverb*.

stood *verb* past tense of STAND.

stool *noun* (*plural* **stools**) **1** a seat

stoop without back or arms. **2** a discharge of faeces.

stoop *verb* (**stoops, stooping, stooped**) **1** to bend your body forward and downward. **2** to lower yourself morally. ➤ **stoop** *noun*.

stop *verb* (**stops, stopping, stopped**) **1** to come to an end, or bring something to an end. **2** to cease moving. **3** said about a bus or train: to call at a place to take on or let off passengers. **4** to prevent somebody or something from doing or continuing something. **5** to prevent something from happening. **6** to stay in a place for a time. ~ *noun* **1** an act of stopping. **2** a place where a train or bus halts to let passengers on or off. **3** *Music* a knob on an organ that brings a particular set of pipes into play. ✻ **pull out all the stops** to do everything possible to achieve something. **put a stop to something** to prevent something from continuing. **stop dead** to come to a sudden halt. **stop off/over** to stop somewhere during a journey somewhere, especially overnight. **stop up** *verb* **1** to block a hole, passage, etc. **2** *informal* to delay going to bed until late.

stopgap *noun* (*plural* **stopgaps**) a temporary substitute.

stoppage *noun* (*plural* **stoppages**) **1** a blockage. **2** a period during which employees stop working as a form of industrial action. **3** a deduction from pay for National Insurance, etc.

stopper *noun* (*plural* **stoppers**) a plug or cork.

stopwatch *noun* (*plural* **stopwatches**) a watch that can be started and stopped at will for exact timing of races, etc.

storage *noun* **1** the act of storing. **2** space available for storing things.

store *verb* (**stores, storing, stored**) **1** to collect or keep a reserve supply of something. **2** to put property or furniture in a warehouse, etc until it is needed. **3** *ICT* to enter data in a computer memory, on a floppy disk, etc, for future access. ~ *noun* (*plural* **stores**) **1** a quantity of things kept for future use. **2** a place where things are stored. **3** (*also* **department store**) a large shop selling a variety of goods. **4** *N American* a shop. ✻ **in store** awaiting you in the future. **set store by** to regard something as important and worthwhile.

storey *noun* (*plural* **storeys**) a separate level of a building.

stork *noun* (*plural* **storks**) a large wading bird with a long stout bill and black and white plumage.

storm *noun* (*plural* **storms**) **1** a period of violent weather marked by high winds and usually rain, thunder, lightning, etc. **2** an outburst. ~ *verb* (**storms, storming, stormed**) **1** to shout angrily; to rage. **2** to rush furiously. **3** said about troops: to make a sudden violent attack on a place to capture it. ✻ **a storm in a teacup** a big fuss about something minor. ➤ **stormy** *adjective*.

story *noun* (*plural* **stories**) **1** an account of real or imaginary events. **2** the plot of a play, novel, etc. **3** a rumour. **4** a lie. **5** a news article or broadcast.

stout[1] *adjective* **1** heavily built; fat. **2** strong and thick. **3** bold and brave. ➤ **stoutly** *adverb*.

stout[2] *noun* (*plural* **stouts**) a dark sweet beer.

stove[1] *noun* (*plural* **stoves**) **1** an appliance that burns fuel for heating. **2** a cooker.

stove[2] *verb* past tense of STAVE[2].

stow *verb* (**stows, stowing, stowed**) to pack something away in an orderly fashion in an enclosed space. ✻ **stow away** to hide on board a ship or aircraft, as a way of travelling without payment.

stowaway noun (plural **stowaways**) a person who stows away.

straddle verb (**straddles, straddling, straddled**) 1 to stand or sit astride something. 2 to be built so that different parts or ends are on either side of something: *The village straddles the frontier.*

straggle verb (**straggles, straggling, straggled**) 1 to lag behind or stray away from a group of people going somewhere together. 2 to grow or spread untidily. ➤ **straggler** noun, **straggly** adjective.

straight adjective 1 extending in one direction without bends or curves. 2 level, upright, or properly positioned. 3 tidy. 4 honest or fair. 5 candid; frank; not evasive: *a straight answer.* 6 *informal* heterosexual. ~ adverb 1 directly; in a straight line. 2 without delay or hesitation. * **go straight** to leave a life of crime and live honestly. **keep a straight face** to refrain from laughing. **straight off/out** without hesitation.

straightaway or **straight away** adverb immediately.

straightforward adjective 1 truthful and direct. 2 presenting no hidden difficulties. ➤ **straightforwardly** adverb.

strain¹ verb (**strains, straining, strained**) 1 to make a great effort, often with a particular part of your body, to do something. 2 to wrench or sprain a part of your body by making it do too much. 3 to make relations between people tense or unfriendly. 4 to pass a liquid through a strainer. ~ noun (plural **strains**) 1 a pulling or stretching force exerted on something. 2 a great demand on your strength, resources, etc. 3 mental or emotional stress. 4 an injury caused by excessive effort. 5 *Music* a tune or passage of music.

strain² noun (plural **strains**) 1 a breed or variety of an animal or plant. 2 an inherited characteristic.

strainer noun (plural **strainers**) a device, such as a sieve, to retain solid pieces while a liquid passes through.

strait noun (plural **straits**) 1 (*also* **straits**) a narrow channel connecting two seas. 2 (**straits**) a situation of difficulty or distress.

straitjacket noun (plural **straitjackets**) 1 an outer garment of strong material used to restrict the movements of a violent prisoner or psychiatric patient. 2 something very restrictive or confining.

straitlaced adjective excessively strict in manners or morals.

strand¹ verb (**strands, stranding, stranded**) 1 to cause a ship, whale, etc to run aground on a beach. 2 to leave a person in a strange place with no way of leaving it.

strand² noun (plural **strands**) 1 one of the threads, strings, or wires twisted together to make a cord, rope, etc. 2 a long, stringy piece. 3 an element of a complex whole, for example one of the stories that make up the plot of a novel.

strange adjective (**stranger, strangest**) 1 unusual or surprising. 2 not known, heard, seen, or visited before. ➤ **strangely** adverb.

stranger noun (plural **strangers**) 1 a person whom you do not know. 2 a person unfamiliar with a place.

strangle verb (**strangles, strangling, strangled**) 1 to choke a person or animal to death by compressing their throat. 2 to hinder the development of something. ➤ **strangler** noun.

strap noun (plural **straps**) a strip of flexible material used for fastening, securing, or carrying something. ~ verb (**straps, strapping, strapped**) to secure or attach something with a strap. ➤ **strapless** adjective.

strapping *adjective* said about a person: big, strong, and sturdy.

stratagem *noun* (*plural* **stratagems**) a scheme for deceiving and outwitting an opponent.

strategic /stra tee jik/ *adjective* to do with achieving an advantage or putting long-term plans into effect. ➤ **strategically** *adverb*.

strategy *noun* (*plural* **strategies**) **1** planning for a large-scale operation, for example a campaign or battle, or for something that will take a long time to achieve. **2** a plan or method for achieving an aim. ➤ **strategist** *noun*.

stratified *adjective* arranged in layers.

stratosphere /stra to sfeer/ *noun* (**the stratosphere**) the layer of the earth's atmosphere that lies at a height of 10 to 50 kilometres. ➤ **stratospheric** *adjective*.

stratum /strah tum *or* stray tum/ *noun* (*plural* **strata**) **1** a horizontal layer of rock. **2** a level of society.

straw *noun* (*plural* **straws**) **1** dry stalks of grain. **2** a single stalk of grain. **3** a tube of paper, plastic, etc for sucking up a drink. **4** a pale yellow colour. ✱ **the last straw** the last of a series of misfortunes, which makes a situation unbearable.

strawberry *noun* (*plural* **strawberries**) a small sweet red fruit covered with seeds.

stray *verb* (**strays, straying, strayed**) to wander away from where you ought to be. ~ *adjective* **1** said about a cat, dog, etc: that has strayed; lost. **2** not in the proper place. **3** happening at random. ~ *noun* (*plural* **strays**) a stray cat or dog.

streak *noun* (*plural* **streaks**) **1** a line or band of a different colour from the background. **2** a quality in somebody's character: *a mean streak*. **3** a series of successes, failures, etc. ~ *verb* (**streaks, streaking, streaked**) **1** to make streaks on or in something. **2** to move swiftly. **3** *informal* to run naked through a public place. ➤ **streaked** *adjective*, **streaker** *noun*, **streaking** *noun*.

stream *noun* (*plural* **streams**) **1** a natural channel containing running water, smaller and narrower than a river. **2** an unbroken flow of gas, traffic, people, etc. **3** a group of schoolchildren of the same age and similar ability. ~ *verb* (**streams, streaming, streamed**) **1** to flow in a stream or in large quantities. **2** to produce streams of liquid. **3** to divide schoolchildren into streams.

streamer *noun* (*plural* **streamers**) a narrow strip of coloured paper or fabric used for decoration.

streamline *verb* (**streamlines, streamlining, streamlined**) **1** to give a vehicle, etc a smooth outline so that it moves easily through air or water. **2** to make an organization simpler or more efficient.

street *noun* (*plural* **streets**) a public road in a city, town, or village.

strength *noun* (*plural* **strengths**) **1** the physical power you have in your body. **2** the ability of something to withstand pressure, prolonged use, etc. **3** the intensity of something. **4** a special skill you have, or a good point in your character.

strengthen *verb* (**strengthens, strengthening, strengthened**) to become, or make something, stronger.

strenuous *adjective* requiring effort or stamina. ➤ **strenuously** *adverb*.

stress *noun* (*plural* **stresses**) **1** pressure on a physical object. **2** a feeling of being unable to cope with all the work or problems you have, or something that causes such a feeling. **3** extra loudness given to a syllable, word, etc as you speak it. **4** relative importance attached to an idea, fact, etc. ~ *verb*

(**stresses, stressing, stressed**)
1 to emphasize a point, syllable etc. **2** to cause somebody emotional or mental strain. ➤ **stressful** *adjective*.

stretch *verb* (**stretches, stretching, stretched**) **1** to pull or extend material till it becomes taut. **2** said about material, garments, etc: to have an elastic quality. **3** said about materials, garments, etc: to become permanently larger. **4** to extend your body or limbs to full length. **5** to extend in space or time. **6** to provide an adequate challenge for a person or their mind. ~ *noun* (*plural* **stretches**) **1** an act of stretching. **2** elasticity. **3** an extent or area. **4** a period of time. ✱ **stretch out** to lie down at full length. ➤ **stretchy** *adjective*.

stretcher *noun* (*plural* **stretchers**) a light portable bed for carrying a sick, injured, or dead person.

strew *verb* (**strews, strewing, strewed, strewn**) to scatter things over an area.

stricken *adjective* badly affected by illness, calamity, emotion, etc: *panic-stricken*.

strict *adjective* **1** determined to enforce discipline and observance of rules. **2** exact or precise. ➤ **strictly** *adverb*, **strictness** *noun*.

stride *verb* (**strides, striding, strode, stridden**) to walk with long steps. ~ *noun* (*plural* **strides**) a long step. ✱ **get into your stride** to begin to do something confidently and well. **take something in your stride** to deal with something difficult or unpleasant calmly.

strident *adjective* **1** loud and unpleasant. **2** expressing opinions, demands, etc loudly or urgently. ➤ **stridency** *noun*, **stridently** *adverb*.

strife *noun* conflict.

strike *verb* (**strikes, striking, struck**) **1** to hit somebody or something with your hand, a weapon, a bat, etc. **2** to collide with something. **3** to carry out an attack. **4** to make a mental impact on somebody. **5** to occur suddenly to somebody. **6** said about a clock: to indicate the time by making a sound. **7** to cause a match to start burning. **8** to discover something, such as oil or gold, by digging or boring. **9** to stop working as a protest against an employer. ~ *noun* (*plural* **strikes**) **1** employees' refusal to work because of a dispute. **2** a discovery of gold, oil, etc. **3** a military attack, especially an air attack. ✱ **on strike** said of a worker: refusing to work because of a dispute, etc. **strike off** to forbid a doctor to continue working as a doctor because of misconduct.
strike out to delete something. **strike up 1** to begin to play. **2** to begin a friendship or conversation.

striker *noun* (*plural* **strikers**) **1** a football player whose main role is to score goals. **2** a worker on strike.

striking *adjective* unusual or impressive. ➤ **strikingly** *adverb*.

string *noun* (*plural* **strings**) **1** a narrow cord used to tie or fasten things. **2** *Music* a length of gut, wire, etc used to produce notes in certain musical instruments, such as the violin, guitar, and piano. **3** (**strings**) *Music* the stringed instruments of an orchestra. **4** a group of objects threaded on a string: *a string of pearls*. **5** a succession or sequence. **6** (**strings**) conditions or obligations attached to something: *a relationship with no strings attached*. ~ *verb* (**strings, stringing, strung**) **1** to thread things on a string. **2** to tie, hang, or fasten something with string. **string along** *informal* to deceive or fool somebody. **string out** to spread things out in a line.

stringed *adjective* *Music* said of musical instruments: with strings that produce sound when touched.

stringent /strinjint/ *adjective* strict.
➤ **stringency** *noun*, **stringently** *adverb*.

stringy *adjective* (**stringier, stringiest**) like string; existing in long thin pieces or made up of fibres.

strip[1] *verb* (**strips, stripping, stripped**) **1** to remove a covering or surface material from something. **2** to take off your clothes, or undress somebody. **3** (**strip of**) to deprive somebody of their possessions, privileges, or rank. ~ *noun* the act of undressing, especially a striptease.

strip[2] *noun* **1** a long narrow piece of material. **2** a long narrow area of land. **3** the distinctive clothes worn by a sports team.

strip cartoon *noun* (*plural* **strip cartoons**) a series of drawings telling a usually humorous story.

stripe *noun* (*plural* **stripes**) **1** a narrow band of colour. **2** a narrow band of coloured material worn on a person's sleeve to indicate their rank.
➤ **striped** *adjective*, **stripy** *adjective*.

stripper *noun* (*plural* **strippers**) **1** somebody who performs a striptease. **2** a tool or solvent for removing paint or varnish.

striptease *noun* an entertainment in which a performer undresses gradually in a sexy manner.

strive *verb* (**strives, striving, strove, striven**) **1** to try hard to do something. **2** to struggle against or for something.

strobe *noun* (*plural* **strobes**) a bright light that flashes on and off, for example at a disco.

strode *verb* past tense of STRIDE.

stroke[1] *verb* (**strokes, stroking, stroked**) to pass your hand over something gently. ➤ **stroke** *noun*.

stroke[2] *noun* (*plural* **strokes**) **1** an act of striking something, especially a ball in a game. **2** an unexpected occurrence: *a stroke of luck.* **3** a sudden disabling illness caused when an artery in the brain is blocked or ruptures. **4** a method of swimming. **5** the sound of a striking clock. **6** a mark made by a single movement of a pen, brush, etc.

stroll *verb* (**strolls, strolling, strolled**) to walk in a leisurely manner. ~ *noun* (*plural* **strolls**) a leisurely walk.

strong *adjective* **1** having great physical power. **2** difficult to break or damage. **3** not easily discouraged or frightened. **4** having great resources of wealth, talent, etc. **5** forceful or intense. **6** having a powerful flavour or smell. **7** having a specified number of members: *an army ten thousand strong.* ➤ **strongly** *adverb*.

stronghold *noun* (*plural* **strongholds**) **1** a fortified place. **2** a place dominated by a specified group.

strong point *noun* (*plural* **strong points**) **1** something you are good at. **2** a good quality that something has.

stroppy *adjective* (**stroppier, stroppiest**) *informal* quarrelsome or angrily uncooperative.

strove *verb* past tense of STRIVE.

struck *verb* past tense and past participle of STRIKE.

structure *noun* (*plural* **structures**) **1** something constructed, such as a building. **2** the way in which something is constructed or organized.
~ *verb* (**structures, structuring, structured**) to construct or organize something in a particular way.
➤ **structural** *adjective*, **structurally** *adverb*.

struggle *verb* (**struggles, struggling, struggled**) **1** to move your body, arms, and legs violently in order to do something, such as get free. **2** to find it difficult to do something. **3** to make determined efforts to do something, to fight against something, etc.
~ *noun* (*plural* **struggles**) **1** a violent

effort or exertion. **2** a determined effort or fight to achieve or prevent something. **3** a difficult task.

strum *verb* (**strums, strumming, strummed**) to play a guitar or banjo by brushing your fingertips or plectrum over the strings.

strung *verb* past tense and past participle of STRING.

strut *verb* (**struts, strutting, strutted**) to walk in a proud or stiff way. ~ *noun* (*plural* **struts**) **1** a piece of wood, metal, etc designed to support or strengthen a framework. **2** a strutting step or walk.

Stuart *adjective* to do with the royal family that ruled Scotland from 1371 to 1603 and Britain from 1603 to 1649 and from 1660 to 1714.

stub *noun* (*plural* **stubs**) **1** a small part of a chequebook page, ticket, etc left when the rest is torn away. **2** a short part of a pencil, cigarette, etc left when the larger part has been used up. ~ *verb* (**stubs, stubbing, stubbed**) to strike your foot or toe against a hard object accidentally. ✱ **stub out** to extinguish a cigarette by crushing the end.

stubble *noun* **1** the short stalks of crops left in the soil after harvest. **2** a rough growth of short bristly hairs on a man's face. ➢ **stubbly** *adjective*.

stubborn *adjective* **1** determined not to change or give way. **2** difficult to get rid of. ➢ **stubbornly** *adverb*, **stubbornness** *noun*.

stuck *verb* past tense and past participle of STICK². ~ *adjective* **1** unable to move. **2** unable to solve a problem, finish a task, etc. ✱ **be stuck with** *informal* to be unable to escape from something or somebody. **get stuck in/into** *informal* to involve yourself wholeheartedly in a task, etc.

stuck-up *adjective informal* self-important or conceited.

stud¹ *noun* (*plural* **studs**) **1** a type of button used to fasten a collar to a shirt. **2** a small piece of jewellery for a pierced ear, etc. **3** a nail with a large head used for ornament or protection. **4** a piece projecting from the sole of a boot or the surface of a tyre to increase grip. ~ *verb* (**studs, studding, studded**) to decorate something with many bright objects.

stud² *noun* (*plural* **studs**) **1** an animal, especially a stallion, or a group of animals kept primarily for breeding. **2** a place where such animals are kept.

student *noun* (*plural* **students**) **1** somebody who studies something, especially at college or university. **2** a pupil at a secondary school.

studied *adjective* carefully considered or prepared.

studio *noun* (*plural* **studios**) **1** *Art* the workroom of a painter, sculptor, or photographer. **2** a place where films are made. **3** a room equipped for broadcasting radio or television programmes.

studious *adjective* **1** studying seriously and with commitment. **2** deliberate and meticulous. ➢ **studiously** *adverb*.

study *noun* (*plural* **studies**) **1** acquiring knowledge by reading, etc. **2** a careful examination or analysis of a subject. **3** a room devoted to study, writing, reading, etc. **4** a literary or artistic work intended as a preparation for another work. ~ *verb* (**studies, studying, studied**) **1** to spend time learning about something. **2** to look at or read something attentively.

stuff¹ *noun* **1** personal property, or things used in an activity. **2** an unspecified substance. **3** a group of miscellaneous objects. ~ *verb* (**stuffs, stuffing, stuffed**) **1** to fill something by packing things or stuffing inside it. **2** to fill yourself with food. **3** to force something into a confined space.

stuffing *noun* **1** material used to stuff

stuffy

upholstered furniture, cushions, soft toys, etc. **2** a seasoned mixture of ingredients used to stuff meat, vegetables, etc.

stuffy *adjective* (**stuffier, stuffiest**) **1** lacking fresh air. **2** said about the nose: blocked or congested. **3** formal and conventional in behaviour.

stumble *verb* (**stumbles, stumbling, stumbled**) **1** to trip in walking or running. **2** to walk unsteadily or clumsily. **3** to speak in a hesitant manner. **4** (**stumble on/across**) to find or discover something unexpectedly or by chance. ➢ **stumble** *noun*.

stumbling block *noun* (*plural* **stumbling blocks**) a problem or obstacle.

stump *noun* (*plural* **stumps**) **1** the part remaining in the ground after a tree has been cut down. **2** in cricket, any of the three upright wooden rods that form the wicket. ~ *verb* (**stumps, stumping, stumped**) **1** *informal* to baffle or bewilder somebody. **2** to walk heavily or noisily.

stumpy *adjective* (**stumpier, stumpiest**) short and thick.

stun *verb* (**stuns, stunning, stunned**) **1** to make somebody dazed or briefly unconscious. **2** to overcome somebody with astonishment or disbelief.

stung *verb* past tense of STING.

stunk *verb* past tense and past participle of STINK.

stunning *adjective informal* strikingly attractive or impressive. ➢ **stunningly** *adverb*.

stunt[1] *verb* (**stunts, stunting, stunted**) to hinder the growth or development of somebody or something. ➢ **stunted** *adjective*.

stunt[2] *noun* (*plural* **stunts**) **1** a difficult feat demanding physical or acrobatic skill. **2** something done purely as a way of attracting attention or publicity.

stuntman *or* **stuntwoman** *noun*

(*plural* **stuntmen** *or* **stuntwomen**) a man or woman employed as a substitute for an actor in scenes involving dangerous activities.

stupefy *verb* (**stupefies, stupefying, stupefied**) **1** to make somebody dazed. **2** to astonish somebody. ➢ **stupefaction** *noun*.

stupendous *adjective* marvellous. ➢ **stupendously** *adverb*.

stupid *adjective* lacking common sense or intelligence. ➢ **stupidity** *noun*, **stupidly** *adverb*.

stupor /stew per/ *noun* a stupefied condition.

sturdy *adjective* (**sturdier, sturdiest**) strongly built or constructed. ➢ **sturdily** *adverb*, **sturdiness** *noun*.

sturgeon *noun* (*plural* **sturgeons**) a large edible fish whose eggs are made into caviar.

stutter *verb* (**stutters, stuttering, stuttered**) to stammer. ➢ **stutter** *noun*.

sty[1] *noun* (*plural* **sties**) = PIGSTY.

sty[2] *or* **stye** *noun* (*plural* **sties** *or* **styes**) an inflamed swelling at the edge of an eyelid.

style *noun* (*plural* **styles**) **1** a distinctive or characteristic manner of doing something, especially something artistic. **2** a particular design or arrangement of something, such as hair. **3** elegance or sophistication in dress, social behaviour, etc. **4** *Science* an extension of a plant ovary with a stigma at the top. ~ *verb* (**styles, styling, styled**) to design or arrange something in a particular style. ➢ **stylist** *noun*, **stylistic** *adjective*.

styli *noun* plural of STYLUS.

stylish *adjective* **1** fashionably elegant. **2** characterized by elegance and skill. ➢ **stylishly** *adverb*, **stylishness** *noun*.

stylus *noun* (*plural* **styli** /stie lie/ *or* **styluses**) a tiny pointed piece of material, such as diamond, used in a gramophone to follow the groove on a record and transmit the sound.

suave /swahv/ *adjective* smoothly charming and polite. ➤ **suavely** *adverb*, **suavity** *noun*.

sub *noun* (*plural* **subs**) *informal* **1** = SUBMARINE. **2** = SUBSCRIPTION. **3** = SUBSTITUTE, especially in a sport.

subarctic *adjective Geography* bordering on the Arctic.

subconscious *noun* (**the subconscious**) the part of the mind in which mental activity takes place that you are not aware of. ➤ **subconscious** *adjective*, **subconsciously** *adverb*.

subcontinent *noun* (*plural* **subcontinents**) a large area of land containing several countries but not as large as a continent.

subdivide *verb* (**subdivides, subdividing, subdivided**) to divide a part of something already divided into more and smaller parts.

subdue *verb* (**subdues, subdued, subduing**) to bring something or somebody under control.

subdued *adjective* **1** less cheerful or lively than normal. **2** not very loud or bright; gentle.

subject /sub jikt/ *noun* (*plural* **subjects**) **1** a branch of knowledge or learning that can be taught or studied. **2** the person or thing that is being discussed, written about, studied, represented, etc. **3** *English* in grammar, a word or phrase denoting the person or thing that performs the action of a verb. **4** somebody owing obedience or allegiance to a ruler. ~ *adjective* **1** ruled over by somebody; not independent. **2** (**subject to**) dependent on something: *The plan is subject to approval by the council.* **3** (**subject to**) liable to undergo something: *an area subject to flooding.* ~ /sub jekt/ *verb* (**subjects, subjecting, subjected**) to make somebody undergo something: *They subjected her to intense questioning.* ➤ **subjection** *noun*.

subjective *adjective* affected by a person's views and feelings, not based solely on facts and reason. ➤ **subjectively** *adverb*, **subjectivity** *noun*.

sub judice /sub jooh di si/ *adverb* currently being considered by a court of law and therefore not open to discussion.

subjugate *verb* (**subjugates, subjugating, subjugated**) to conquer somebody and bring them under your control. ➤ **subjugation** *noun*.

subjunctive *noun* (*plural* **subjunctives**) *English* in grammar, a form of a verb that expresses a possibility or a wish and that, in English, rarely differs from the ordinary form of the verb except in expressions such as *if I were rich, if that be the case,* and *long live the king.*

sublime *adjective* **1** astoundingly beautiful or grand. **2** extreme. ➤ **sublimely** *adverb*.

submarine *noun* (*plural* **submarines**) a ship designed to travel underwater. ~ *adjective* situated or happening under the sea. ➤ **submariner** *noun*.

submerge *verb* (**submerges, submerging, submerged**) **1** to go or put something under water. **2** to cover something over with water.

submission *noun* (*plural* **submissions**) **1** the act of submitting. **2** something submitted for consideration, inspection, etc.

submissive *adjective* willing to obey other people. ➤ **submissively** *adverb*.

submit *verb* (**submits, submitting, submitted**) **1** to give in to the authority or wishes of another person. **2** to subject somebody to something. **3** to send something to another person for them to consider, inspect, or judge it.

subordinate /su baw di nat/ *adjective* having a lower rank or less impor-

subordinate clause

tance. ~ *noun* (*plural* **subordinates**) a person of lower rank than you. ~ /suh b aw di nayt/ *verb* (**subordinates, subordinating, subordinated**) to treat something as less important than something else. ➤ **subordination** *noun*.

subordinate clause *noun* (*plural* **subordinate clauses**) *English* a clause that cannot function as a sentence on its own and simply adds detail to a main clause.

subscribe *verb* (**subscribes, subscribing, subscribed**) 1 to make regular payments to receive something, such as a magazine or a service. 2 to contribute an amount of money to a charity, etc. 3 (**subscribe to**) to support or agree with an opinion, view, etc. ➤ **subscriber** *noun*.

subscription *noun* 1 the act of subscribing to something. 2 a sum of money subscribed. 3 a membership fee paid regularly.

subsequent *adjective* following something else in time or order. ➤ **subsequently** *adverb*.

subservient *adjective* very willing to do what other people want. ➤ **subservience** *noun*.

subside *verb* (**subsides, subsiding, subsided**) 1 to become less forceful or intense. 2 said about ground: to cave in. 3 said about a building: to sink into the ground.

subsidence /sub si dins *or* sub sie dins/ *noun* the slow sinking of an area of land.

subsidiary *adjective* 1 additional to a main thing. 2 of secondary importance. ~ *noun* (*plural* **subsidiaries**) a company that is completely controlled by another company.

subsidize *or* **subsidise** *verb* (**subsidizes, subsidizing, subsidized** *or* **subsidises,** etc) 1 to pay a subsidy to somebody. 2 to pay part of the cost of a product or service, making it cheaper for those who buy or use it. ➤ **subsidization** *or* **subsidisation** *noun*.

subsidy *noun* (*plural* **subsidies**) a grant or gift of money, made for example by a government, towards the cost of running a business or service.

subsistence *noun* the minimum of food, shelter, etc necessary to support life.

substance *noun* (*plural* **substances**) 1 a physical material. 2 the essential part or meaning of something. 3 truth or reality: *There's no substance to the story.*

substantial *adjective* 1 large or important. 2 firmly constructed; solid.

substantially *adverb* 1 for the most part; basically. 2 greatly.

substantiate *verb* (**substantiates, substantiating, substantiated**) to provide proof or evidence to support something.

substitute *noun* (*plural* **substitutes**) a person or thing that takes the place of another. ~ *verb* (**substitutes, substituting, substituted**) to put one person or thing in the place of another: *You could substitute a sweetener for sugar.* ➤ **substitution** *noun*.

subterfuge /sub ter fewj/ *noun* (*plural* **subterfuges**) 1 deception or trickery used to hide what you are really doing or planning. 2 a trick.

subterranean *adjective* existing or occurring under the surface of the earth.

subtitle *noun* (*plural* **subtitles**) 1 a printed text that appears at the bottom of the screen during a film or television broadcast, for example to provide a translation of what is being said. 2 a secondary or explanatory title following the main title of a book, etc.

subtle /su til/ *adjective* 1 pleasantly or tastefully delicate. 2 difficult to understand, analyse, or distinguish. 3 ingenious. ➤ **subtly** *adverb*.

subtract *verb* (**subtracts, subtracting, subtracted**) to take one number away from another in calculating the difference between them. ➤ **subtraction** *noun*.

subtropical *adjective* bordering on the tropics. ➤ **subtropics** *plural noun*.

suburb *noun* (*plural* **suburbs**) a part of a city or large town away from the centre. ➤ **suburban** *adjective*.

suburbia *noun* the suburbs of a city, or their inhabitants.

subversive *adjective* tending to undermine the established system, for example of government. ➤ **subversion** *noun*.

subway *noun* (*plural* **subways**) **1** a passage under a street for pedestrians. **2** *N American* an underground railway.

succeed *verb* (**succeeds, succeeding, succeeded**) **1** to achieve what you wanted or intended to do. **2** to follow after another person or thing in order. **3** (**succeed to**) to inherit the throne, a title, etc.

success *noun* (*plural* **successes**) **1** the achievement of what you wanted or intended. **2** somebody or something that succeeds. ➤ **successful** *adjective*, **successfully** *adverb*.

succession *noun* **1** a number of people or things that follow each other in sequence. **2** the process of inheriting the throne, a title, etc. ✱ **in succession** following one another without interruption.

successive *adjective* following one after the other. ➤ **successively** *adverb*.

successor *noun* (*plural* **successors**) a person who holds a title, office, etc after somebody else.

succinct /suksinkt/ *adjective* clearly expressed in few words. ➤ **succinctly** *adverb*.

succour /sukər/ *noun literary* help in time of difficulty.

succulent *adjective* **1** said about food: full of juice and flavour. **2** said about a plant: having fleshy tissues where water is stored. ~ *noun* (*plural* **succulents**) a succulent plant, such as a cactus. ➤ **succulence** *noun*.

succumb /sukum/ *verb* (**succumbs, succumbing, succumbed**) to give in to something or somebody with greater strength.

such *adjective and adverb* **1** of that or the same sort: *There's no such place.* **2** so extreme or extraordinary: *in such a hurry.* ~ *pronoun* similar people or things: *tin and glass and such.* ✱ **such as 1** for example: *reptiles, such as lizards.* **2** like: *women such as my sister.*

such and such *adjective informal* not named or specified.

suchlike *adjective* of the kind mentioned; similar. ~ *pronoun* similar people or things.

suck *verb* (**sucks, sucking, sucked**) **1** to get liquid, etc into your mouth by drawing it in with your lips and tongue. **2** to draw liquid from something in this way. **3** to eat something such as a sweet by means of sucking movements of the lips and tongue. **4** to draw in or up by suction. ✱ **suck in/into** to draw somebody irresistibly into a group, plot, etc. **suck up to** *informal* to act obsequiously towards somebody. ➤ **suck** *noun*.

sucker *noun* (*plural* **suckers**) **1** a mouth or other animal organ adapted for sucking or clinging. **2** *informal* a gullible person.

suckle *verb* (**suckles, suckling, suckled**) **1** to give milk to a baby or young animal from the breast or udder. **2** to take milk from the breast or udder.

suction *noun Science* a force produced by a partial vacuum in something, which causes it to adhere to a surface or suck other things in.

sudden *adjective* **1** happening or

suds

coming unexpectedly. **2** marked by haste; abrupt. ➤ **suddenly** *adverb*, **suddenness** *noun*.

suds *plural noun* the lather on soapy water.

sue *verb* (**sues, suing, sued**) to bring a legal action against somebody to get money from them as compensation for something.

suede /swayd/ *noun* leather with a velvety surface produced by rubbing the flesh side.

suet *noun* the hard fat round the kidneys and loins of cattle or sheep, used in cooking.

suffer *verb* (**suffers, suffering, suffered**) **1** to experience or undergo something unpleasant: *We've suffered a setback.* **2** to feel pain or distress. **3** to get worse: *When morale is low, the team's performance suffers.* **4** (**suffer from**) to be affected by an illness or condition: *She suffers from asthma.* ➤ **sufferer** *noun*, **suffering** *noun*.

suffice /sufies/ *verb* (**suffices, sufficing, sufficed**) **1** to be enough. **2** to be enough for somebody or something.

sufficient *adjective* enough; adequate. ➤ **sufficiency** *noun*, **sufficiently** *adverb*.

suffix *noun* (*plural* **suffixes**) *English* a letter or group of letters placed at the end of a word to alter its meaning or to make a new word, for example '-ed' in *walked* or '-ness' in *happiness*.

suffocate *verb* (**suffocates, suffocating, suffocated**) to die, or cause somebody to die, from being unable to breathe. ➤ **suffocation** *noun*.

suffrage *noun* the right to vote in political elections.

suffragette *noun* (*plural* **suffragettes**) *History* a woman campaigning for the right to vote to be given to women in Britain in the early 20th century.

suffuse *verb* (**suffuses, suffusing, suffused**) to spread over or through something.

sugar *noun* a sweet substance obtained from the juices of various plants and used to sweeten food.

sugar beet *noun* a variety of beet grown for the sugar in its roots.

suggest *verb* (**suggests, suggesting, suggested**) **1** to put an idea forward as a possibility or for consideration. **2** to call something to mind. **3** to express something indirectly.

suggestion *noun* (*plural* **suggestions**) **1** an idea or plan suggested. **2** the implanting of an idea, attitude, etc in the mind of another person. **3** a slight amount; a trace.

suggestive *adjective* **1** conjuring up the idea of something. **2** rather indecent. ➤ **suggestively** *adverb*.

suicide *noun* (*plural* **suicides**) **1** the act of killing yourself intentionally. **2** the ruining of your own interests. **3** somebody who commits suicide. ➤ **suicidal** *adjective*, **suicidally** *adverb*.

suit *noun* (*plural* **suits**) **1** a jacket and either trousers or a skirt, made of the same material and meant to be worn together. **2** a costume worn for a specified purpose. **3** all the playing cards in a pack bearing the same symbol, i.e. hearts, clubs, diamonds, or spades. **4** a lawsuit. ~ *verb* (**suits, suiting, suited**) **1** to be convenient or good for somebody. **2** to look good on somebody or look right with something. **3** to adapt something to a particular situation. ✽ **suit yourself** to do as you like.

suitable *adjective* right for a particular person, situation, etc. ➤ **suitability** *noun*, **suitably** *adverb*.

suitcase *noun* (*plural* **suitcases**) a rectangular case with a hinged lid and a handle, used for carrying clothes, etc when travelling.

suite /sweet/ *noun* (*plural* **suites**)

1 a group of rooms used together. **2** a set of matching furniture. **3** *Music* a series of instrumental pieces to be performed together.

suitor /sooh ter/ *noun* (*plural* **suitors**) *dated* a man who courts a woman and wants her to marry him.

sulk *verb* (**sulks, sulking, sulked**) to be moody and silent through resentment or disappointment. ➤ **sulk** *noun*, **sulky** *adjective*.

sullen *adjective* silently gloomy or resentful. ➤ **sullenly** *adverb*.

sully *verb* (**sullies, sullying, sullied**) to defile or tarnish something.

sulphur *noun Science* a non-metallic chemical element that occurs naturally as yellow crystals and burns easily.

sultan *noun* (*plural* **sultans**) the sovereign of a Muslim state.

sultana *noun* (*plural* **sultanas**) **1** the light brown seedless raisin. **2** a sultan's wife.

sultry *adjective* (**sultrier, sultriest**) **1** oppressively hot and humid. **2** arousing strong sexual desire.

sum *noun* (*plural* **sums**) **1** an amount of money. **2** the result of adding numbers. **3** a simple arithmetical problem involving addition, subtraction, multiplication, or division.

summarize *or* **summarise** *verb* (**summarizes, summarizing, summarized** *or* **summarises**, etc) to make a summary of something.

summary *noun* (*plural* **summaries**) a brief account covering the main points of something. ~ *adjective* done quickly without delay or formality. ➤ **summarily** *adverb*.

summer *noun* (*plural* **summers**) the warm season between spring and autumn. ➤ **summery** *adjective*.

summerhouse *noun* (*plural* **summerhouses**) a small building in a garden designed to provide a shady place in summer.

summit *noun* (*plural* **summits**) **1** the highest point of a hill or mountain. **2** the topmost level attainable. **3** a conference of heads of government.

summon *verb* (**summons, summoning, summoned**) **1** to order somebody to come. **2** to call people to attend a meeting. ✱ **summon up** to gather your strength, courage, etc to enable you to do something.

summons *noun* (*plural* **summonses**) a written notification ordering somebody to appear in court.

sump *noun* (*plural* **sumps**) a reservoir for oil underneath the engine of a vehicle.

sumptuous *adjective* lavishly rich, costly, or luxurious. ➤ **sumptuously** *adverb*.

sun *noun* (*plural* **suns**) **1** (**the sun** *or* **the Sun**) the star round which the earth and other planets revolve. **2** a star. **3** the heat or light radiated from the sun. ~ *verb* (**suns, sunning, sunned**) ✱ **sun yourself** to sit or lie in the sunshine.

sunbathe *verb* (**sunbathes, sunbathing, sunbathed**) to lie or sit in the sun in order to get a suntan. ➤ **sunbather** *noun*.

sunbeam *noun* (*plural* **sunbeams**) a ray of light from the sun.

sunbed *noun* (*plural* **sunbeds**) a couch that you lie on under a sunlamp.

sunblock *noun* a cream that protects your skin from the ultraviolet rays in sunlight.

sunburn *noun* inflammation of the skin caused by overexposure to sunlight. ➤ **sunburnt** *or* **sunburned** *adjective*.

sundae *noun* (*plural* **sundaes**) a dish of ice cream served with a topping of fruit, nuts, syrup, etc.

Sunday noun (plural **Sundays**) the first day of the week, the day following Saturday.

sunder verb (**sunders, sundering, sundered**) literary to break something apart or in two.

sundial noun (plural **sundials**) an instrument that shows the time of day by the shadow cast by a pointer.

sundries plural noun mixed small articles or items.

sundry adjective of various kinds.

sunflower noun (plural **sunflowers**) a tall plant with large yellow flowers.

sung verb past participle of SING.

sunglasses plural noun tinted glasses worn to protect the eyes from the sun.

sunk verb past participle of SINK.

sunken adjective **1** lying at the bottom of the sea. **2** lying below the surrounding level.

sunlamp noun (plural **sunlamps**) an electric lamp emitting ultraviolet light, used for tanning the skin.

sunlight noun light emitted by the sun; sunshine.

Sunni /sooni/ noun (plural **Sunni** or **Sunnis**) a member of the larger branch of Islam that acknowledges the first four spiritual leaders (caliphs) of Islam as the rightful successors of Muhammad.

sunny adjective (**sunnier, sunniest**) **1** bright with sunshine. **2** cheerful; optimistic. **3** exposed to or warmed by the sun.

sunrise noun (plural **sunrises**) the rising of the sun above the horizon, or the time when this happens.

sunroof noun (plural **sunroofs**) an opening or removable panel in the roof of a car.

sunscreen noun = SUNBLOCK.

sunset noun (plural **sunsets**) the descent of the sun below the horizon, or the time when this happens.

sunshade noun (plural **sunshades**) **1** a parasol. **2** an awning.

sunshine noun the sun's light or direct rays.

sunspot noun (plural **sunspots**) a dark marking on the surface of the sun caused by a relatively cooler area.

sunstroke noun an illness caused by being exposed to the sun for too long.

suntan noun (plural **suntans**) a browning of the skin from exposure to the sun. ➤ **suntanned** adjective.

super adjective informal very good.

superannuated adjective **1** retired on a pension. **2** obsolete.

superb adjective **1** of excellent quality. **2** grand or magnificent. ➤ **superbly** adverb.

supercilious /soohpersilius/ adjective disdainful; haughty.

superficial adjective **1** lying on or affecting only the surface. **2** apparent rather than real. **3** said about a person: not capable of serious thought or deep emotion; shallow. **4** not careful, thorough, or deep. ➤ **superficiality** noun, **superficially** adverb.

superfluous /sooperfloous/ adjective unnecessary.

superglue noun a very strong, quick-setting adhesive.

superhero noun (plural **superheroes**) a character in a cartoon, film, etc with extraordinary powers that they use to fight crime, etc.

superhuman adjective exceeding normal human power or capability.

superimpose verb (**superimposes, superimposing, superimposed**) to place one thing over or above something else. ➤ **superimposition** noun.

superintend verb (**superintends, superintending, superintended**) to be in charge of something.

superintendent noun (plural **superintendents**) **1** a supervisor. **2** a police officer ranking above a chief inspector.

superior *adjective* **1** of higher rank, quality, or importance. **2** excellent of its kind. **3** greater in amount or number. **4** conceited. ~ *noun* (*plural* **superiors**) a person who is above another in rank or office. ➤ **superiority** *noun*.

superlative /soo per la tiv/ *adjective* **1** of the highest degree or quality. **2** *English* said about an adjective or adverb: expressing the highest level of a quality, for example *greatest*, *soonest*, *most beautiful*. ➤ **superlative** *noun*.

supermarket *noun* (*plural* **supermarkets**) a large self-service retail shop selling food and household goods.

supermodel *noun* (*plural* **supermodels**) a very successful fashion model who has become a celebrity.

supernatural *adjective* not subject to the laws of nature; involving a god, spirit, devil, ghost, etc. ~ *noun* (**the supernatural**) supernatural forces or beings.

superpower *noun* (*plural* **superpowers**) any of a very few dominant nations in the world.

supersede *verb* (**supersedes, superseding, superseded**) to take the place of something, especially something outmoded.

Usage Note Notice the spelling of *-sede* with an *s*. This is the only /seed/ word spelt with an *s*. Compare *precede* and *proceed*.

supersonic *adjective* moving at a speed greater than the speed of sound in air.

superstar *noun* (*plural* **superstars**) an extremely popular or successful entertainer or sportsperson.

superstition *noun* (*plural* **superstitions**) **1** irrational belief in the influence of the supernatural or chance on human affairs. **2** a superstitious belief.

superstitious *adjective* **1** believing that certain actions have supernatural consequences and bring good or bad luck. **2** based on superstition. ➤ **superstitiously** *adverb*.

superstore *noun* (*plural* **superstores**) a very large supermarket.

superstructure *noun* **1** the part of a ship above the main deck. **2** the part of a structure built on top of a lower part.

supervise *verb* (**supervises, supervising, supervised**) to be in charge of a task or workers and check that work is done properly. ➤ **supervision** *noun*, **supervisor** *noun*, **supervisory** *adjective*.

supine *adjective* **1** lying on your back. **2** weak and inactive.

supper *noun* (*plural* **suppers**) an evening meal or snack.

supplant *verb* (**supplants, supplanting, supplanted**) to remove somebody or something and take their place.

supple *adjective* (**suppler, supplest**) able to bend or twist with ease and grace. ➤ **suppleness** *noun*.

supplement /su pli mint/ *noun* (*plural* **supplements**) **1** a useful addition to something. **2** an extra part added to a book or newspaper. **3** an extra charge. ~ /su pli ment/ *verb* (**supplements, supplementing, supplemented**) to be a supplement to something. ➤ **supplementary** *adjective*.

supply *verb* (**supplies, supplying, supplied**) to provide somebody with something. ~ *noun* (*plural* **supplies**) **1** an amount of something available to be used. **2** (**supplies**) provisions or stores. **3** the act of supplying something. **4** (*also* **supply teacher**) a teacher who fills temporary vacancies in schools. ➤ **supplier** *noun*.

support *verb* (**supports, supporting,**

supported) **1** to serve as a foundation or prop for something. **2** to help somebody or something, for example by giving money. **3** to approve of, encourage, or defend somebody or something. **4** to provide evidence for something. **5** to be an enthusiastic or loyal follower of a football team, etc. **6** to provide somebody with a home and the means of subsistence. **7** to enable e.g. life to exist. ~ *noun* (*plural* **supports**) **1** the act of supporting. **2** something that holds something up. **3** somebody who offers help and encouragement. ➤ **supporter** *noun*.

supportive *adjective* providing help and encouragement.

suppose *verb* (**supposes, supposing, supposed**) **1** to believe something or think it probable, usually without proof. **2** to assume something to be true. ✱ **be supposed to do something** to be expected to do something. ➤ **supposition** *noun*.

supposed /su pohzd *or* su poh zid/ *adjective* believed or imagined to be such. ➤ **supposedly** *adverb*.

suppress *verb* (**suppresses, suppressing, suppressed**) **1** to put an end to something by force. **2** to stop something being published or revealed. **3** to restrain a feeling, etc. ➤ **suppression** *noun*, **suppressive** *adjective*.

supremacy /soo pre ma si/ *noun* supreme authority, power, or position.

supreme *adjective* **1** highest in rank or authority. **2** greatest, strongest, or most important. ➤ **supremely** *adverb*.

surcharge *noun* (*plural* **surcharges**) an additional charge, tax, or cost.

sure *adjective* (**surer, surest**) **1** not having doubts; confident and certain. **2** bound: *She is sure to win.* **3** true and reliable. **4** (**sure of**) confident that something is true, will happen, etc. ~ *adverb chiefly N American, informal* certainly. ✱ **for sure** as a certainty. ➤ **sureness** *noun*.

surely *adverb* **1** it is to be hoped or expected that. **2** without doubt; certainly.

surf *noun* the foam and swell of waves breaking on the shore. ~ *verb* (**surfs, surfing, surfed**) **1** to stand or lie on a surfboard and ride on the waves towards the shore. **2** to browse through the Internet. ➤ **surfer** *noun*, **surfing** *noun*.

surface *noun* (*plural* **surfaces**) **1** the outer layer or upper level of something. **2** the outward appearance of something or somebody. ~ *verb* (**surfaces, surfacing, surfaced**) **1** to come to the surface, especially of water. **2** to become apparent. **3** to give a surface to a road, etc.

surfboard *noun* (*plural* **surfboards**) a long narrow buoyant board used in surfing.

surfeit /ser fit/ *noun* an excessive amount.

surge *noun* (*plural* **surges**) **1** a powerful rising or onrushing movement. **2** a sudden increase. **3** a sudden experience of an intense emotion. ~ *verb* (**surges, surging, surged**) **1** to move with a surge. **2** to increase suddenly.

surgeon *noun* (*plural* **surgeons**) a medical specialist who practises surgery.

surgery *noun* (*plural* **surgeries**) **1** the branch of medicine that deals with disorders by cutting open the body to repair or remove damaged parts. **2** a surgical operation. **3** a place where a doctor or dentist treats patients. ➤ **surgical** *adjective*, **surgically** *adverb*.

surly *adjective* (**surlier, surliest**) irritably sullen and bad-tempered.

surmise *verb* (**surmises, surmising, surmised**) to suppose or guess something. ➤ **surmise** *noun*.

surmount verb (**surmounts, surmounting, surmounted**) **1** to overcome a difficulty or obstacle. **2** to stand or lie on the top of something.

surname noun (plural **surnames**) the name shared by members of a family.

surpass verb (**surpasses, surpassing, surpassed**) to be better or greater than somebody or something.

surplus noun (plural **surpluses**) an amount remaining after what is needed has been used or spent. ➤ **surplus** adjective.

surprise noun (plural **surprises**) **1** the feeling caused by an unexpected event; astonishment. **2** something unexpected or surprising. ~ verb (**surprises, surprising, surprised**) **1** to fill somebody with surprise. **2** to take somebody unawares or attack them unexpectedly. ✳ **take by surprise 1** to meet or attack somebody without warning. **2** to astonish somebody. ➤ **surprised** adjective.

surreal adjective having a strange dreamlike irrational quality.

surrealism noun Art a movement that uses the strange images formed by the unconscious in its work. ➤ **surrealist** noun and adjective.

surrender verb (**surrenders, surrendering, surrendered**) **1** to admit defeat and submit to an opponent. **2** to hand something over to the control or possession of somebody else. ➤ **surrender** noun.

surreptitious /su rep ti shus/ adjective done by stealth. ➤ **surreptitiously** adverb.

surrogate noun (plural **surrogates**) a substitute. ➤ **surrogacy** noun.

surrogate mother noun (plural **surrogate mothers**) a woman who carries and bears a child for a couple who cannot have children.

surround verb (**surrounds, surrounding, surrounded**) **1** to encircle or enclose somebody or something on all sides. **2** to be associated with something: *the mystery surrounding her disappearance*.

surroundings plural noun the area or circumstances surrounding somebody or something.

surveillance /ser vay lans/ noun close watch kept over somebody, for example by a detective.

survey /ser vay/ verb (**surveys, surveying, surveyed**) **1** to examine something closely. **2** to look at something as a whole. **3** to report on the condition of a house for sale. **4** to conduct a survey on a group of people. ~ /ser vay/ noun (plural **surveys**) **1** an enquiry into the opinions or preferences of a group of people. **2** an act of surveying. ➤ **surveyor** noun.

survival noun (plural **survivals**) **1** the fact of continuing to live or exist. **2** something that survives from an earlier time.

survive verb (**survives, surviving, survived**) **1** to continue to exist or live. **2** to escape alive from an accident or disaster. **3** to remain alive after the death of somebody. ➤ **survivor** noun.

susceptible adjective quite easily affected by something. ➤ **susceptibility** noun.

suspect /su spekt/ verb (**suspects, suspecting, suspected**) **1** to imagine something to be true or probable. **2** to believe somebody to be guilty without conclusive proof. **3** to distrust something. ~ /su spekt/ noun (plural **suspects**) somebody who is suspected of a crime, etc. ~ adjective likely to be false or dangerous.

suspend verb (**suspends, suspending, suspended**) **1** to hang something so that it is unsupported underneath. **2** to cause something to stop temporarily. **3** to postpone something, such

suspender

as a prison sentence or a judgment. **4** to order somebody not to do something temporarily, for example not to attend school.

suspender noun (plural **suspenders**) a strap with a fastening device, attached to a belt or corset to hold up a woman's stocking.

suspense noun a state of excited or anxious uncertainty about a decision or outcome.

suspension noun (plural **suspensions**) **1** the act of suspending, or the state of being suspended. **2** the springs, etc supporting the upper part of a vehicle on the axles. **3** Science a state in which particles are mixed with but not dissolved in a liquid.

suspension bridge noun (plural **suspension bridges**) a type of bridge that has its roadway suspended from cables.

suspicion noun (plural **suspicions**) **1** an idea or feeling that something is the case, especially that somebody has done something wrong. **2** a feeling of mistrust. ✱ **above suspicion** too honest or virtuous to be suspected of doing wrong. **under suspicion** suspected of having done something wrong.

suspicious adjective **1** tending to arouse suspicion. **2** distrustful. ➤ **suspiciously** adverb.

sustain verb (**sustains, sustaining, sustained**) **1** to support the weight of something. **2** to give support or sustenance to somebody. **3** to cause something to continue. **4** to suffer or undergo an injury. ➤ **sustained** adjective.

sustainable adjective said about energy or development: not exhausting natural resources or damaging the environment. ➤ **sustainability** noun.

sustenance noun food or provisions.

svelte adjective slender in an elegant and attractive way.

SW abbreviation Southwest or Southwestern.

swab noun (plural **swabs**) **1** a wad of absorbent material used for applying medication, cleaning wounds, taking specimens, etc. **2** a specimen taken with a swab. ~ verb (**swabs, swabbing, swabbed**) **1** to clean a wound with a swab. **2** (often **swab down**) to clean a surface by washing it, especially with a mop.

swagger verb (**swaggers, swaggering, swaggered**) to walk in a very self-confident or conceited way. ➤ **swaggering** adjective.

swallow[1] noun (plural **swallows**) a small migrant bird with long wings and a forked tail.

swallow[2] verb (**swallows, swallowing, swallowed**) **1** to take food or drink down through your throat. **2** to cover something so that it disappears. **3** to believe something without question. ➤ **swallow** noun.

swam verb past tense of SWIM.

swamp[1] noun (plural **swamps**) an area of wet spongy land; a marsh. ➤ **swampy** adjective.

swamp[2] verb (**swamps, swamping, swamped**) **1** to fill a boat with water until it sinks. **2** to overwhelm somebody with too much of something: *We were swamped with enquiries.*

swan noun (plural **swans**) a large long-necked white aquatic bird.

swank verb (**swanks, swanking, swanked**) informal to show off. ➤ **swank** noun.

swap or **swop** verb (**swaps, swapping, swapped** or **swops**, etc) **1** to exchange things with another person. **2** to exchange one thing for another. ➤ **swap** or **swop** noun.

swarm noun (plural **swarms**) **1** a large mass of flying insects. **2** a large number of honeybees emigrating from a hive with a queen bee to start a new colony elsewhere. **3** a group of people or things massing together. ~ *verb* (**swarms, swarming, swarmed**) to move or assemble in a crowd. ✷ **be swarming with** to be filled or covered with a vast number of something.

swarthy *adjective* (**swarthier, swarthiest**) having a dark complexion.

swastika /swɒˈstiːkə/ *noun* (*plural* **swastikas**) an ancient symbol in the shape of a cross with the ends of the arms bent at right angles, used as the emblem of the German Nazi Party.

swat *verb* (**swats, swatting, swatted**) to hit an insect with a sharp slapping blow.

swathe /sweɪð/ *noun* (*plural* **swathes**) **1** a row of cut grain or grass left by a scythe or mowing machine. **2** a long broad strip. ~ *verb* (**swathes, swathing, swathed**) **1** to wrap something with a bandage or strip of material. **2** to envelop something.

sway *verb* (**sways, swaying, swayed**) **1** to move slowly and rhythmically back and forth or from side to side. **2** to change the opinions of somebody. ~ *noun* **1** a swaying movement. **2** controlling influence or power.

swear *verb* (**swears, swearing, swore, sworn**) **1** to use bad language. **2** to utter or take an oath solemnly. **3** to promise emphatically or earnestly to do something. **4** (**swear by**) to place great confidence in something.

swearword *noun* (*plural* **swearwords**) a blasphemous or obscene word.

sweat *noun* fluid given off through the pores of the skin, for example when you are hot. ~ *verb* (**sweats, sweating, sweated**) to give off sweat.

sweater *noun* (*plural* **sweaters**) a pullover.

sweatshirt *noun* (*plural* **sweatshirts**) a loose collarless pullover of heavy cotton.

sweatshop *noun* (*plural* **sweatshops**) a place of work in which people are employed for long hours at low wages and under poor conditions.

swede *noun* (*plural* **swedes**) a large turnip with yellow flesh, used as a vegetable.

sweep *verb* (**sweeps, sweeping, swept**) **1** to clean a floor, etc by brushing. **2** to remove something with a single forceful action. **3** to carry something or somebody along with irresistible force. **4** to move smoothly, grandly, or purposefully. **5** to search an area systematically. ~ *noun* (*plural* **sweeps**) **1** an act of sweeping. **2** (*also* **chimney sweep**) a person who cleans chimneys. **3** a curving course or line. **4** a broad extent. **5** *informal* = SWEEPSTAKE. ✷ **sweep away** to abolish or destroy something completely. ➤ **sweeper** *noun*.

sweeping *adjective* **1** extensive; wide-ranging: *sweeping changes*. **2** said about a statement: applying to a great many things indiscriminately.

sweepstake *noun* (*plural* **sweepstakes**) a lottery or other form of gambling, for example on a horse race, in which the stakes form the prize or prizes.

sweet *adjective* **1** having a taste similar to sugar. **2** having a pleasant smell or taste. **3** delightful or charming. **4** marked by gentle good humour or kindliness. ~ *noun* (*plural* **sweets**) **1** a small piece of confectionery prepared with sugar or chocolate. **2** a dessert. ➤ **sweetly** *adverb*, **sweetness** *noun*.

sweet corn *noun* maize with kernels that contain a high percentage of sugar, used as a vegetable.

sweeten *verb* (**sweetens, sweetening, sweetened**) to become, or make something, sweet.

sweetener *noun* (*plural* **sweeteners**) a sweet substance used as a replacement for sugar.

sweetheart *noun* (*plural* **sweethearts**) a person that you love.

sweet pea *noun* (*plural* **sweet peas**) a climbing plant with colourful fragrant flowers.

sweet pepper *noun* (*plural* **sweet peppers**) the hollow, mild-tasting, green, yellow, orange, or red fruit of a tropical plant, used as a vegetable.

sweet tooth *noun* a fondness for sweet food.

swell *verb* (**swells, swelling, swelled, swollen** *or* **swelled**) **1** to expand, especially by curving outwards or upwards. **2** to increase the number, volume, or intensity of something. ~ *noun* a surging movement of the sea.

swelling *noun* (*plural* **swellings**) a swollen area.

sweltering *adjective* oppressively hot.

swept *verb* past tense and past participle of SWEEP.

swerve *verb* (**swerves, swerving, swerved**) to turn aside abruptly from a straight course. ➤ **swerve** *noun*.

swift *adjective* **1** moving or capable of moving at great speed. **2** occurring suddenly or lasting a very short time. ~ *noun* (*plural* **swifts**) a dark-coloured migrant bird noted for its fast darting flight. ➤ **swiftly** *adverb*, **swiftness** *noun*.

swig *verb* (**swigs, swigging, swigged**) to drink something in long swallows. ➤ **swig** *noun*.

swill *verb* (**swills, swilling, swilled**) (*often* **swill out**) to wash something by pouring lots of water into or over it. ~ *noun* food for pigs, composed of edible refuse mixed with water or milk.

swim *verb* (**swims, swimming, swam, swum**) **1** to propel your body through water by moving your arms and legs. **2** to be flooded with a liquid. **3** said about your head: to have a floating, whirling, or dizzy sensation. ➤ **swim** *noun*, **swimmer** *noun*.

swimming bath *noun* (*plural* **swimming baths**) an indoor swimming pool.

swimming costume *noun* (*plural* **swimming costumes**) a close-fitting garment worn for swimming.

swimming pool *noun* (*plural* **swimming pools**) an artificial pool for people to swim in.

swimsuit *noun* (*plural* **swimsuits**) = SWIMMING COSTUME.

swindle *verb* (**swindles, swindling, swindled**) to take money or property from somebody by fraud or deceit. ➤ **swindle** *noun*, **swindler** *noun*.

swine *noun* **1** (*plural* **swine**) *formal* a pig. **2** (*plural* **swine** *or* **swines**) *informal* a contemptible person. ➤ **swinish** *adjective*.

swing *verb* (**swings, swinging, swung**) **1** to move freely to and fro when hanging from something. **2** to move in a circle or arc. **3** to change from one opinion, mood, etc to another. **4** to influence something decisively. ~ *noun* (*plural* **swings**) **1** a suspended seat on which a person can swing to and fro. **2** a swinging movement. **3** a change in public opinion or political preference. **4** jazz played with a steady lively rhythm and simple harmony. ✷ **in full swing** at the height of activity.

swingeing /swin jing/ *adjective* severe or drastic.

swipe *verb* (**swipes, swiping, swiped**) **1** to hit something or somebody with a sweeping motion. **2** *informal* to steal something. **3** to pass a plastic card with an identifying magnetic strip on it through a machine that can read the information on the strip. ➤ **swipe** *noun*.

swirl *verb* (**swirls, swirling, swirled**) to move in circles or whirls. ➤ **swirl** *noun*.

swish *verb* (**swishes, swishing, swished**) to move with a hissing or brushing sound. ~ *noun* a hissing or brushing sound. ~ *adjective informal* smart and fashionable.

switch *noun* (*plural* **switches**)
1 a device that makes or breaks an electrical circuit and is used for turning a machine, light, etc on or off.
2 a sudden shift or change. ~ *verb* (**switches, switching, switched**)
1 to change something. **2** to exchange one thing for another. ✶ **switch off/on** to turn a light, television, etc off (or on) by operating an electrical switch.

switchboard *noun* (*plural* **switchboards**) a panel with switching devices that enable telephone calls to be directed to particular numbers.

swivel *noun* (*plural* **swivels**) a device joining two parts so that one part can pivot freely. ~ *verb* (**swivels, swivelling, swivelled**) to turn rapidly and smoothly.

swollen *verb* past participle of SWELL¹.

swoon *verb* (**swoons, swooning, swooned**) to faint. ➤ **swoon** *noun*.

swoop *verb* (**swoops, swooping, swooped**) **1** said about a bird: to descend steeply through the air, especially to seize prey. **2** to make a sudden attack or raid. ➤ **swoop** *noun*.

swop *verb and noun* see SWAP.

sword *noun* (*plural* **swords**) a cutting or thrusting weapon with a long, sharp-pointed and sharp-edged blade.

swordfish *noun* (*plural* **swordfishes** or **swordfish**) a large fish with a swordlike beak.

swore *verb* past tense of SWEAR.

sworn *verb* past participle of SWEAR.
~ *adjective* **1** made under oath.
2 determined to remain as specified: *sworn enemies*.

swot *verb* (**swots, swotting, swotted**) *informal* to study hard. ~ *noun* (*plural* **swots**) somebody who studies hard.

swum *verb* past participle of SWIM.

swung *verb* past tense and past participle of SWING.

sycamore *noun* (*plural* **sycamores**) a tree of the maple family with winged seeds.

syllable *noun* (*plural* **syllables**) *English* a unit of spoken language consisting of one vowel sound with or without an accompanying consonant sound: *The word 'sycamore' has three syllables sy-ca-more.*

syllabus *noun* (*plural* **syllabuses** or **syllabi** /si la bie/) a summary of what students have to study for a course or examination.

symbol *noun* (*plural* **symbols**)
1 an object or sign that represents something: *The lion is a symbol of courage.* **2** a special sign used in writing or printing to represent something.

symbolic *adjective* used as a symbol.
➤ **symbolically** *adverb*.

symbolism *noun* the use of symbols to represent other things.

symbolize or **symbolise** *verb* (**symbolizes, symbolizing, symbolized** or **symbolises,** etc)
1 to serve as a symbol of something.
2 to represent something by means of symbols.

symmetrical or **symmetric** *adjective* having the same proportions, shape, etc on both sides of a central dividing line. ➤ **symmetrically** *adverb*.

symmetry *noun* the quality of being symmetrical or having balanced proportions.

sympathetic *adjective* **1** showing compassion and sensitivity to other people's feelings. **2** favourably inclined. **3** congenial. ➤ **sympathetically** *adverb*.

sympathize or **sympathise** *verb*

sympathy

(**sympathizes, sympathizing, sympathized** or **sympathises**, etc) to show sympathy. ➤ **sympathizer** or **sympathiser** noun.

sympathy noun (plural **sympathies**) **1** the ability to share the feelings or interests of another person. **2** a feeling of compassion and kindness towards people who are hurt or in distress.

symphony noun (plural **symphonies**) *Music* an extended piece for an orchestra, typically in four contrasting movements. ➤ **symphonic** adjective.

symptom noun (plural **symptoms**) **1** something that indicates that a person is suffering from a disease or physical disorder. **2** something that indicates the existence of something undesirable.

synagogue noun (plural **synagogues**) the house of worship and communal centre of a Jewish congregation.

synchronize or **synchronise** verb (**synchronizes, synchronizing, synchronized** or **synchronises**, etc) **1** to cause two or more things to happen at the same time. **2** to make two watches show exactly the same time. ➤ **synchronization** or **synchronisation** noun.

syncopate verb (**syncopates, syncopating, syncopated**) *Music* to modify a rhythm by stressing a weak beat or omitting a strong beat. ➤ **syncopation** noun.

syndicate noun (plural **syndicates**) a group of people or organizations who combine to share the work of something or the profits of something.

syndrome noun (plural **syndromes**) a group of symptoms that occur together and characterize a particular medical disorder.

synod noun (plural **synods**) **1** a governing assembly in the Anglican church. **2** a formal meeting of church leaders.

synonym noun (plural **synonyms**) *English* a word that has the same meaning as another word. ➤ **synonymous** adjective.

synopsis noun (plural **synopses** /si nop seez/) a summary.

syntax noun *English* the way in which words are put together to form phrases, clauses, and sentences.

synthesis noun (plural **syntheses** /sin thi seez/) the combination of different elements into a coherent whole.

synthesize or **synthesise** verb (**synthesizes, synthesizing, synthesized** or **synthesises**, etc) **1** to make by a chemical or electronic process something that also occurs naturally: *attempts to synthesize milk*. **2** to combine things to form a whole.

synthesizer or **synthesiser** noun (plural **synthesizers** or **synthesisers**) *Music* an electronic keyboard musical instrument that produces a sound that can be altered, for example to mimic other instruments.

synthetic adjective **1** produced chemically, especially as an imitation of something natural. **2** not genuine or sincere. ➤ **synthetically** adverb.

syphon noun and verb see SIPHON.

syringe noun (plural **syringes**) a device used to suck up liquid and squirt it out again.

syrup noun (plural **syrups**) a thick sticky solution, especially of sugar and water. ➤ **syrupy** adjective.

system noun (plural **systems**) **1** a group of things, ideas, etc that are organized to work together. **2** an organized method of doing something. **3** (**the system**) society or its rules when regarded as restrictive.

systematic adjective methodical in procedure or plan; thorough. ➤ **systematically** adverb.

tab[1] *noun* (*plural* **tabs**) a flap, loop, or strip of material by which you hold or lift something.

tab[2] *noun* (*plural* **tabs**) *ICT* **1** a key that you press to move the cursor a set distance along a line, used for indenting or arranging data in columns. **2** the distance along a line that the cursor moves when you press the tab key.

tabby *noun* (*plural* **tabbies**) a domestic cat with a brownish or grey coat with darker stripes.

tabernacle /ta ber na kl/ *noun* (*plural* **tabernacles**) **1** (*often* **the Tabernacle**) in Jewish and Christian scripture, a tent that the Israelites used as a sanctuary and shrine on their journey out of Egypt. **2** a Mormon or Nonconformist church.

table *noun* (*plural* **tables**) **1** a piece of furniture consisting of a smooth flat slab of wood, etc fixed on legs or some other support. **2** a systematically arranged list of figures, information, etc. **3** = MULTIPLICATION TABLE. *verb* (**tables, tabling, tabled**) to put an issue on an agenda so that it can be discussed officially.

tablecloth *noun* (*plural* **tablecloths**) a cloth that is spread over a table before it is set for a meal.

tablespoon *noun* (*plural* **tablespoons**) **1** a large spoon used for serving. **2** the amount contained in a tablespoon, used as a measure of ingredients in recipes. ➤ **tablespoonful** (*plural* **tablespoonfuls**) *noun*,

tablet *noun* (*plural* **tablets**) **1** a small solid mass of medicine. **2** a flat piece of stone with words carved into it.

tableware *noun* the dishes, glasses, and cutlery used at a meal.

table tennis *noun* a game played with round wooden bats and a small hollow plastic ball on an indoor table with a low net in the middle.

tabloid *noun* (*plural* **tabloids**) a newspaper with a small page size, especially a newspaper featuring mainly sensational stories illustrated with large photographs.

taboo *adjective* not done or talked about for moral or social reasons. ~ *noun* (*plural* **taboos**) something that is not done or talked about because it is regarded as morally wrong or socially unacceptable.

tabular *adjective* said about information: arranged in a table.

tachograph /ta koh grahf/ *noun* (*plural* **tachographs**) a device in a vehicle that keeps a record of the different speeds that the vehicle travels at.

tacit *adjective* implied or understood but not actually expressed. ➤ **tacitly** *adverb*.

taciturn *adjective* tending not to say much. ➤ **taciturnity** *noun*.

tack[1] *noun* (*plural* **tacks**) **1** a small nail with a broad flat head. **2** a long loose stitch used to hold layers of fabric together temporarily. **3** a course of action. *verb* (**tacks, tacking, tacked**)

tack

1 to nail something with tacks. **2** to sew pieces of fabric together with tacks. **3** (**tack on**) to add something as a supplement.

tack² *noun* equipment used in horse riding.

tackle *noun* (*plural* **tackles**) **1** equipment used in a particular activity. **2** a set of ropes and pulleys used for lifting and pulling heavy things. **3** in football, rugby, etc, an attempt to get the ball from an opposing player. ~ *verb* (**tackles, tackling, tackled**) **1** to attempt to take the ball from an opposing player in football, rugby, etc. **2** to set about dealing with a problem, etc. **3** to speak to somebody about a difficult matter.

tacky¹ *adjective* (**tackier, tackiest**) slightly sticky to the touch.

tacky² *adjective* (**tackier, tackiest**) *informal* cheaply made and showing a lack of good taste; vulgar.

tact *noun* the ability to deal with awkward situations sensitively so as to avoid offending people.

tactful *adjective* showing tact. ➤ **tactfully** *adverb*.

tactic *noun* (*plural* **tactics**) **1** a method for achieving something. **2** (**tactics**) military planning concerned with the organization and movements of forces in combat. **3** (**tactics**) the skill of using available means to accomplish something.

tactical *adjective* **1** done to achieve an aim in the near future. **2** said about nuclear weapons: designed for air attack in close support of ground forces. ➤ **tactically** *adverb*.

tactical voting *noun* voting in favour of the candidate most likely to defeat the candidate you least want to win, rather than in favour of your preferred candidate.

tactile *adjective* **1** relating to the sense of touch. **2** said about a person: in the habit of touching people in a friendly way.

tactless *adjective* insensitive or likely to cause offence. ➤ **tactlessly** *adverb*.

tadpole *noun* (*plural* **tadpoles**) the larva of a frog or toad that lives in water and has a round body, a long tail, and no legs.

tae kwon do /tai kwon doh/ *noun* a martial art similar to karate.

taffeta /taf i ta/ *noun* a crisp shiny fabric.

tag¹ *noun* (*plural* **tags**) **1** a loop on a garment, used for hanging it up. **2** an electronic monitoring device worn around the wrist or ankle by people convicted of a crime but not kept in prison. ~ *verb* (**tags, tagging, tagged**) **1** to put an identifying marker, price label, etc on something. **2** to fit a convicted criminal with an electronic tag. * **tag along** to go with somebody.

tag² *noun* a children's game in which one player chases the others.

tagliatelle /tal ya te li/ *plural noun* pasta in the form of long narrow ribbons.

tail *noun* (*plural* **tails**) **1** a flexible part that sticks out at the back of the body of an animal or bird. **2** the rear part of an aircraft that sticks up and out. **3** (**tails**) the side of a coin that does not have the picture of a head on it. **4** (**tails**) a tailcoat. ~ *verb* (**tails, tailing, tailed**) *informal* to follow somebody in order to know what they do and where they go. * **tail back** to form a long queue. **tail off/away** to diminish gradually in strength, volume, etc.

tailback *noun* (*plural* **tailbacks**) a long queue of vehicles moving very slowly or not at all.

tailcoat *noun* (*plural* **tailcoats**) a man's formal evening jacket with two long tapering points hanging down at the back.

tailor *noun* (*plural* **tailors**) somebody whose job is making or altering men's clothes. ~ *verb* (**tailors, tailoring, tailored**) 1 to make or shape a garment. 2 (**tailor for/to**) to adapt something to suit a special purpose.

tailor-made *adjective* perfect for, or specially designed for, a particular purpose or person.

tailspin *noun* (*plural* **tailspins**) 1 a spiralling dive by an aircraft, especially one out of control. 2 *informal* a state of chaos or panic.

taint *verb* (**taints, tainting, tainted**) to spoil or contaminate something. ~ *noun* (*plural* **taints**) a slight trace of contamination or of something undesirable.

take *verb* (**takes, taking, took, taken**) 1 to hold, carry, or transport something. 2 to get something into your possession, sometimes without permission: *Who's taken my pen?* 3 to do or have something: *take a shower/holiday*. 4 to choose something: *Dad took the beef*. 5 to follow a route or use a means of transport. 6 to be taught a subject of study: *Are you taking Spanish next year?* 7 to affect somebody in a specified way: *The remark took us by surprise*. 8 to bring somebody or something to a particular state or position: *Her ability should take her to the top*. 9 to consume medicine. 10 to have a particular opinion: *The teacher took a different view*. 11 to have enough space to contain or accommodate something: *Our car only takes two people.* 12 to tolerate or endure something: *I can't take this noise much longer!* 13 to accept something in payment: *We don't take credit cards.* 14 to accept or make use of a risk, opportunity, etc: *You didn't take the chance when you had it; I'm not taking the blame for your mistakes.* 15 to subtract one number from another. ~ *noun* (*plural* **takes**) 1 a single piece of continuous filming, or a single filmed version of a short sequence of action. 2 money gained from selling something. 3 *informal* an individual's opinion or understanding of something. ✽ **take after** to resemble an older relative in appearance or character. **take against** to come to dislike somebody. **take apart** 1 to dismantle something. 2 *informal* to criticize somebody. 3 to defeat an opponent comprehensively. **take away** 1 to remove something. 2 to subtract a number from another number. **take away from** to make something seem less good; to detract from something. **take back** 1 to return something to its original place. 2 to return unsatisfactory goods to the shop where you bought them. **take down** 1 to dismantle something. 2 to write something down on paper. **take in** 1 to offer accommodation or shelter to somebody. 2 *informal* to deceive or trick somebody. 3 to include something. 4 to understand or appreciate something. 5 to assume something: *I take it you agree.* **take it out on** to vent your anger or frustration on somebody. **take off** 1 to remove clothes. 2 to deduct an amount. 3 to mimic somebody. 4 said about an aircraft: to leave the ground and go into the air. 5 *informal* to be quickly successful. **take on** 1 to agree to do something. 2 to employ or engage somebody to do a job. 3 to start to have an appearance or quality. **take out** 1 to remove something. 2 to obtain authorization, insurance, etc. 3 to escort somebody on a social occasion, or pay for somebody's entertainment. **take over** to take control or possession of something. **take to** to develop a liking for somebody or something. **take up** 1 to lift something. 2 to become interested and involved in an activity. 3 to occupy space or time. 4 to discuss

takeaway

or pursue a matter further. **what it takes** the qualities or resources needed.

takeaway *noun* (*plural* **takeaways**) **1** a shop or restaurant selling cooked food that you take elsewhere to eat. **2** a meal that you buy from a takeaway.

takeover *noun* (*plural* **takeovers**) control of a business company gained by buying a majority of the shares.

takings *plural noun* the amount of money earned by a business during a specified period.

talcum powder *or* **talc** *noun* perfumed powder used for dusting your body to make it dry.

tale *noun* (*plural* **tales**) **1** a story. **2** a lie.

talent *noun* (*plural* **talents**) ability, especially creative or artistic ability.

talented *adjective* having creative or artistic ability.

talisman *noun* (*plural* **talismans**) an object that is believed to bring good luck or produce magical effects.

talk *verb* (**talks, talking, talked**) **1** to communicate by speaking. **2** (**talk about/of**) to discuss something. **3** to reveal or discuss confidential information. **4** (**talk into** *or* **out of**) to persuade somebody to do (or not do) something. ~ *noun* (*plural* **talks**) **1** a conversation. **2** a formal discussion. **3** a lecture. **4** rumour; gossip. ✱ **talk back** to answer somebody in a disrespectful way. **talk down to** to speak to somebody in a way that shows you think they are not intelligent or important.

talkative *adjective* tending to talking a lot.

tall *adjective* **1** of above average height. **2** of a specified height. ✱ **a tall order** an unreasonably difficult task or requirement.

tallow *noun* solid white fat from cattle and sheep, used in soap and candles.

tall story *or* **tall tale** *noun* (*plural* **tall stories** *or* **tall tales**) a highly exaggerated or untrue account of something.

tally *noun* (*plural* **tallies**) a record of things done or used, or of points scored. ~ *verb* (**tallies, tallying, tallied**) to be the same; to agree or match: *Their stories tallied; Her story tallied with what we had already been told.* **2** to count something.

Talmud /tal mood/ *noun* (**the Talmud**) in Judaism, the writings that contain Jewish laws and traditions.

talon *noun* (*plural* **talons**) a curved claw of a bird of prey.

tambourine *noun* (*plural* **tambourines**) *Music* a percussion instrument in the form of a shallow one-headed drum with loose metallic discs at the sides, which you shake or hit with your hand.

tame *adjective* (**tamer, tamest**) **1** said about an animal: not afraid of or dangerous to people. **2** said about an event or activity: not at all interesting or exciting. ~ *verb* (**tames, taming, tamed**) to make a wild animal tame. ➤ **tamely** *adverb*.

tamper *verb* (**tampers, tampering, tampered**) (**tamper with**) to interfere or meddle with something without permission.

tampon *noun* (*plural* **tampons**) a cylindrical pad of absorbent cotton put into the vagina to absorb menstrual bleeding.

tan *noun* **1** a brown colour that your skin develops after being exposed to sunlight. **2** a light yellowish brown colour. ~ *verb* (**tans, tanning, tanned**) **1** said about skin: to become brown through exposure to sunlight. **2** to convert animal skin into leather.

tandem *noun* (*plural* **tandems**) a bicycle with two seats one behind the other.

tandoori *noun* a North Indian method of cooking meat in a clay oven.

tang *noun* a sharp distinctive flavour or smell.

tangent *noun* (*plural* **tangents**) *Maths* **1** in a right-angled triangle, the ratio between the sides opposite and adjacent to an acute angle. **2** a straight line that touches a curve or surface at only one point. ✱ **fly/go off at a tangent** to change suddenly from one subject or course of action to another.

tangential *adjective* **1** *Maths* in the form of a tangent. **2** not very relevant; incidental.

tangerine *noun* (*plural* **tangerines**) a small loose-skinned orange.

tangible *adjective* **1** which you can feel by touching. **2** large or important enough to notice or be worth mentioning: *no tangible improvement*. ➤ **tangibility** *noun*, **tangibly** *adverb*.

tangle *verb* (**tangles, tangling, tangled**) to intertwine things into a disordered mass. ~ *noun* (*plural* **tangles**) **1** a confused twisted mass. **2** a complicated state. ➤ **tangled** *adjective*.

tango *noun* (*plural* **tangos**) a South American ballroom dance with long pauses and exaggerated body positions. ~ *verb* (**tangoes, tangoing, tangoed**) to dance the tango.

tank *noun* (*plural* **tanks**) **1** a large container for liquids or gas. **2** a container for fuel in a motor vehicle. **3** a large, heavily armoured combat vehicle with a movable gun turret.

tankard *noun* (*plural* **tankards**) a silver or pewter mug for drinking beer.

tanker *noun* (*plural* **tankers**) a ship or truck designed to carry liquid in bulk.

tannin *noun* a substance in tea and wine that gives them their sharp taste, also used in tanning and dyeing.

tantalizing *or* **tantalising** *adjective* said about something you want very much: frustratingly close to being available or being achieved, but not quite available or achieved. ➤ **tantalizingly** *or* **tantalisingly** *adverb*.

tantamount *adjective* equivalent to something else, although not quite the same as it: *an admission that was tantamount to an apology*.

tantrum *noun* (*plural* **tantrums**) a fit of childish bad temper.

tap¹ *noun* (*plural* **taps**) **1** a device with a spout and valve attached to a pipe or container to let out liquid or gas. **2** a device attached to a telephone to allow somebody to listen secretly to conversations. ~ *verb* (**taps, tapping, tapped**) to connect a secret listening device to a telephone wire.

tap² *verb* (**taps, tapping, tapped**) to hit something lightly. ~ *noun* (*plural* **taps**) **1** a light blow, or the sound it makes. **2** = TAP DANCING.

tapas *plural noun* Spanish-style assorted cold foods, served as a starter in a restaurant or as a snack accompaniment to beer or wine in a bar.

tap dancing *noun* a style of dancing in which the steps are made audible by small pieces of metal fitted to the dancer's shoes.

tape *noun* (*plural* **tapes**) **1** a narrow band of woven fabric. **2** a narrow band of sticky material used for various purposes. **3** a narrow band of material on which sound or pictures can be recorded, or a cassette containing this. **4** the string stretched above the finishing line of a race. ~ *verb* (**tapes, taping, taped**) **1** to fasten or wrap something with tape. **2** to record sound or pictures on tape.

tape measure *noun* (*plural* **tape measures**) a narrow strip of tape marked off in units for measuring.

taper *verb* (**tapers, tapering,**

tapered) 1 to decrease gradually in thickness, diameter, or width towards one end. **2** to diminish gradually. ➤ **tapering** *adjective*.

tape recorder *noun* (*plural* **tape recorders**) a device for recording sounds on tape and reproducing them.

tapestry *noun* (*plural* **tapestries**) a piece of heavy fabric decorated with woven or embroidered designs.

tar *noun* **1** a thick black liquid used in road surfaces, obtained from coal or wood. **2** a brown residue present in tobacco smoke.

taramasalata /ta ra ma sa lah ta/ *noun* a pinkish paste made from fish roe, olive oil, and seasoning, usually eaten as a starter.

tarantula /ta ran tew la/ *noun* (*plural* **tarantulas**) a large hairy spider found in tropical and subtropical America.

tardy *adjective* (**tardier, tardiest**) late. ➤ **tardily** *adverb*, **tardiness** *noun*.

target *noun* (*plural* **targets**) **1** an object to fire at in practice or a competition, consisting of a central bull's-eye with a series of circles of increasing size round it. **2** a person or object that is fired at, attacked, or criticized. **3** something that you are aiming to achieve. ~ *verb* (**targets, targeting, targeted**) **1** to attack or criticize somebody or something. **2** to aim to affect or deal with something. **3** (**target on/at**) to aim a bomb or missile at something.

tariff *noun* (*plural* **tariffs**) **1** the rates charged by a business, such as a hotel, or a list of these rates. **2** a tax charged on imported or exported goods.

tarmac *noun* **1** a mixture of tar and stones used for surfacing roads. **2** a runway or other area surfaced with tarmac.

Word History Tarmac is short for *tarmacadam*, which comes from *tar* and the name of John *McAdam*, an 18th- and 19th-century Scottish road engineer.

tarn *noun* (*plural* **tarns**) *Geography* a small mountain lake.

tarnish *verb* (**tarnishes, tarnishing, tarnished**) **1** to stain something or make it less shiny. **2** to spoil somebody's reputation.

tarot /ta roh/ *noun* a set of 22 cards with pictures on them, used for fortune-telling.

tarpaulin *noun* (*plural* **tarpaulins**) a sheet of heavy waterproof canvas.

tarragon *noun* a herb with thin leaves that have a flavour similar to aniseed.

tart[1] *noun* (*plural* **tarts**) a pastry case containing a sweet or savoury filling.

tart[2] *adjective* **1** sharp or acid to the taste. **2** said about a remark: sarcastic or hurtful. ➤ **tartly** *adverb*.

tartan *noun* (*plural* **tartans**) **1** a textile design of Scottish origin consisting of checks and stripes of varying colour, usually designating a particular clan. **2** a fabric with a tartan design.

tartar *noun* a crusty mass of calcium salts that forms on your teeth.

tartare sauce /tah tah saws/ *noun* mayonnaise with chopped pickles, olives, capers, and parsley, served especially with fish.

task *noun* (*plural* **tasks**) a piece of work or a duty that somebody is given.

tassel *noun* (*plural* **tassels**) a bunch of cords or threads of even length fastened at one end, used as an ornament.

taste *verb* (**tastes, tasting, tasted**) **1** to take a little food or drink into your mouth to test its flavour. **2** to recognize a substance or flavour by tasting. **3** (**taste of**) to have a specified flavour. **4** to experience or undergo something: *She had tasted freedom.* ~ *noun* (*plural* **tastes**) **1** the sense which uses sensitive areas of the tongue to detect flavours. **2** the flavour of a substance. **3** a small amount of something that you taste. **4** an experience of something: *his first taste of city life*. **5** a person's liking for things of a particular style: *his taste in clothes*. **6** preferences that somebody admires or agrees with; good taste: *She has no taste in music*.

taste bud *noun* (*plural* **taste buds**) any of the small organs on the surface of your tongue that give you the sensation of taste.

tasteful *adjective* showing good judgment of styles or good knowledge of rules of behaviour. ➤ **tastefully** *adverb*.

tasteless *adjective* **1** lacking flavour. **2** not showing good judgment of styles or good knowledge of the rules of behaviour. ➤ **tastelessly** *adverb*.

tasty *adjective* (**tastier, tastiest**) having an appetizing flavour.

tat *noun informal* low-quality or tasteless goods.

tatters * **in tatters 1** torn to pieces; ragged. **2** in a state of ruin or disarray.

tattered *adjective* old and torn.

tattoo[1] *noun* (*plural* **tattoos**) a permanent design on the skin made by inserting pigments with a needle. ~ *verb* (**tattoos, tattooing, tattooed**) to put a tattoo on the skin. ➤ **tattooist** *noun*.

tattoo[2] *noun* (*plural* **tattoos**) an outdoor military display of marching, music, etc.

tatty *adjective* (**tattier, tattiest**) *informal* shabby; dilapidated.

taught *verb* past tense and past participle of TEACH.

taunt *verb* (**taunts, taunting, taunted**) to mock somebody in a way intended to upset them. ~ *noun* (*plural* **taunts**) a mocking provocation or insult.

Taurus *noun* the second sign of the zodiac (the Bull).

taut *adjective* stretched or pulled tight. ➤ **tautly** *adverb*.

tautology *noun* (*plural* **tautologies**) needlessly saying the same thing twice using different words. ➤ **tautological** *adjective*.

tavern *noun* (*plural* **taverns**) *humorous or archaic* a pub.

tawdry *adjective* (**tawdrier, tawdriest**) **1** brightly coloured in a cheap and tasteless way; gaudy. **2** involving unpleasant or shameful behaviour, especially sexual behaviour. ➤ **tawdriness** *noun*.

tawny *adjective* (**tawnier, tawniest**) of a brownish orange colour.

tax *noun* (*plural* **taxes**) any of various payments that people make to the government to pay for public services. ~ *verb* (**taxes, taxing, taxed**) **1** to charge a tax on income, goods, etc. **2** to make strenuous demands on somebody or something. ➤ **taxable** *adjective*.

taxation *noun* **1** the charging of tax. **2** money that the government gets through taxes.

taxi *noun* (*plural* **taxis**) a car that may be hired, together with its driver, to carry passengers. ~ *verb* (**taxis, taxiing, taxied**) said about an aircraft: to move slowly to or from a runway before take-off or after landing.

taxidermy *noun* the art of preparing, stuffing, and mounting the skins of animals to give a lifelike appearance. ➤ **taxidermist** *noun*.

taxing *adjective* physically, mentally, or emotionally demanding.

TB *abbreviation* tuberculosis.

TD *abbreviation* = (Irish Gaelic) *Teachta Dála* Member of the Dáil.

tea *noun* (*plural* **teas**) **1** the dried leaves and leaf buds of an evergreen Asian shrub. **2** a drink made by steeping such leaves in boiling water. **3** a light

tea bag

meal usually including tea with sandwiches, cakes, or biscuits, served in the late afternoon. **4** the evening meal; dinner or supper.

tea bag *noun* (*plural* **tea bags**) a small closed paper sachet holding enough tea for an individual drink.

teach *verb* (**teaches, teaching, taught**) **1** to give somebody knowledge or information about something: *Mum taught me how to wire a plug.* **2** to give lessons in a subject: *My dad teaches German.* **3** to cause somebody to understand something by experience: *That'll teach you not to tease the dog.* ➤ **teaching** *noun*.

teacher *noun* (*plural* **teachers**) a person whose job is teaching in a school.

teak *noun* the hard yellowish brown wood of a tall tree native to India and Southeast Asia.

team *noun* (*plural* **teams**) **1** a group of players that form one side in a game or sporting contest. **2** a group of people who work together. ~ *verb* (**teams, teaming, teamed**) **1** (**team up**) to come together as a team. **2** (**team with**) to combine something, such as an item of clothing, with another thing for a particular effect.

teammate *noun* (*plural* **teammates**) a member of the same team as you.

teamwork *noun* cooperation between people who are doing something as a group.

teapot *noun* (*plural* **teapots**) a container in which tea is brewed and served, usually with a lid, spout, and handle.

tear[1] /teer/ *noun* (*plural* **tears**) a drop of clear salty fluid that comes out of your eye, especially as a result of sadness, grief, or other emotion. ✳ **in tears** crying; weeping.

tear[2] /tair/ *verb* (**tears, tearing, tore, torn**) **1** to rip something by force. **2** to damage a muscle or ligament with a sudden violent movement. **3** to remove something with a sudden violent movement: *She tore the letter out of my hand.* **4** (**be torn**) to be unable to decide between two alternatives. **5** to move with great speed or haste. *noun* (*plural* **tears**) a hole or rip made by tearing. ✳ **tear down** to demolish something. **tear up** to tear something into pieces.

teardrop *noun* (*plural* **teardrops**) a single tear.

tearful *adjective* crying, or tending to cry a lot. ➤ **tearfully** *adverb*.

tear gas *noun* a gas that causes people's eyes to stream with tears, used by the police to disperse crowds.

tease *verb* (**teases, teasing, teased**) to try, usually playfully, to irritate or embarrass somebody by making fun of them. ~ *noun* (*plural* **teases**) *informal* somebody who often teases people.

teaspoon *noun* (*plural* **teaspoons**) **1** a small spoon used for adding sugar, etc to hot drinks and stirring them. **2** the amount contained in a teaspoon, used as a measure of ingredients in recipes. ➤ **teaspoonful** (*plural* **teaspoonfuls**) *noun*.

teat *noun* (*plural* **teats**) **1** a nipple on a female animal. **2** a rubber or plastic mouthpiece attached to the top of a baby's feeding bottle.

tea towel *noun* (*plural* **tea towels**) a cloth for drying dishes that have been washed.

tech *noun* (*plural* **techs**) *informal* = TECHNICAL COLLEGE.

technical *adjective* **1** involving special and usually practical knowledge, especially of mechanical, industrial, or scientific subjects. **2** relating to or used in a particular subject: *technical terms*.

technical college *noun* (*plural* **technical colleges**) a further education college that offers courses in practical subjects.

technicality noun (plural **technicalities**) a fact or detail that you arrive at by applying a rule very strictly, often a fact or detail that most people would agree is not reasonable under the circumstances.

technically adverb if you apply a rule or definition strictly.

technician noun (plural **technicians**) somebody who does practical work, for example in a laboratory.

technique /tek neek/ noun (plural **techniques**) 1 the way in which an artist, performer, or athlete does something. 2 a way of achieving something.

techno noun a form of fast electronically produced modern dance music.

technology noun (plural **technologies**) 1 mechanical, electrical, or electronic devices that perform a function of some kind: *computer technology*. 2 the study of how scientific methods can be used to perform functions of various kinds. ➤ **technological** adjective, **technologically** adverb.

tectonic adjective Geography relating to the earth's crust.

teddy bear or **teddy** noun (plural **teddy bears** or **teddies**) a child's stuffed toy bear.

tedious adjective boring and seeming to last for a very long time. ➤ **tediously** adverb.

tedium noun the state of being bored; boredom.

tee noun (plural **tees**) 1 the area from which a golf ball is hit at the beginning of play on a hole. 2 a peg that you stick in the ground and put a golf ball on for hitting it at the beginning of play on a hole. ~ verb (**tees, teeing, teed**) ✴ **tee off** to begin a round of golf by playing the first shot.

teem verb (**teems, teeming, teemed**) 1 (**teem with**) to be full of people busily moving around. 2 to rain hard.

teen adjective informal to do with teenagers.

teenage adjective to do with teenagers. ➤ **teenaged** adjective.

teenager noun (plural **teenagers**) a person aged between 13 and 19.

teens plural noun the years 13 to 19 in somebody's lifetime.

teeny or **teensy** adjective (**teenier, teeniest** or **teensier, teensiest**) informal tiny.

tee shirt noun see T-SHIRT.

teeter verb (**teeters, teetering, teetered**) to wobble or move unsteadily, as if about to fall over.

teeth noun plural of TOOTH.

teethe verb (**teethes, teething, teethed**) said about a baby: to have teeth developing in the mouth, usually painfully.

teetotal /tee toh tl/ adjective never drinking alcohol. ➤ **teetotalism** noun.

telecommunications noun the science and technology of communicating with people at a distance by telephone, television, radio, etc.

telegram noun (plural **telegrams**) a message sent by telegraph and delivered as a written or typed note.

telegraph noun (plural **telegraphs**) a system in which messages in the form of electrical or radio signals are sent along a wire. ~ verb (**telegraphs, telegraphing, telegraphed**) to send a message to somebody by telegraph. ➤ **telegraphic** adjective.

telepathy /ti le pa thi/ noun communication that occurs directly from one person's mind to another person's mind, without the use of the speech, hearing, or sight. ➤ **telepathic** adjective.

telephone noun (plural **telephones**) a device that uses electrical wires or radio signals to allow people who are far apart to speak to each other. ~ verb

telephone box

(**telephones, telephoning, telephoned**) to call somebody and speak to them by telephone.

telephone box *noun* (*plural* **telephone boxes**) a booth containing a public telephone.

telescope *noun* (*plural* **telescopes**) a tubular device for viewing distant objects in magnified form by means of a lens or a concave mirror. ➤ **telescopic** *adjective*.

Teletext *noun trademark* an information service provided by a television network.

televise *verb* (**televises, televising, televised**) to broadcast a programme, event, etc by television.

television *noun* (*plural* **televisions**) **1** an electronic system for transmitting images together with sound as electrical signals along a wire or through space to a receiving device that then reproduces them. **2** a device with a screen and sound system for receiving and displaying television signals. **3** the television broadcasting industry. ➤ **televisual** *adjective*.

tell *verb* (**tells, telling, told**) **1** to make something known to somebody by speaking about it. **2** to order somebody to do something. **3** to recognize the difference between things. **4** to have an effect: *The strain was beginning to tell on him.* * **tell off** *informal*) to scold or reprimand somebody. **tell on** *informal* to inform on somebody. **tell the time** to read and understand the information on a clock or watch.

teller *noun* (*plural* **tellers**) a member of a bank's staff who deals directly with customers.

telling *adjective* producing a marked effect; significant. ➤ **tellingly** *adverb*.

telling-off *noun* (*plural* **tellings-off** or **telling-offs**) *informal* a severe reprimand.

telltale *noun* (*plural* **telltales**) a person who informs on somebody. ~ *adjective* revealing, betraying, or indicating something.

telly *noun* (*plural* **tellies**) *informal* = TELEVISION.

temerity /ti me ri ti/ *noun* the attitude of somebody who does something although they know it will offend or upset somebody else; nerve.

temp *noun* (*plural* **temps**) *informal* a person employed in a job temporarily.

temper *noun* (*plural* **tempers**) **1** an uncontrolled display of anger. **2** a person's mood: *in a good temper*. ~ *verb* (**tempers, tempering, tempered**) **1** to make something more moderate: *We must temper justice with mercy.* **2** to bring steel to the right degree of hardness by reheating and cooling it. * **keep your temper** to keep your anger under control. **lose your temper** to show your anger.

tempera *noun Art* a method of painting using pigment mixed with egg yolk and water.

temperament *noun* (*plural* **temperaments**) a person's emotional character and its effect on their behaviour.

temperamental *adjective* **1** easily upset or irritated. **2** behaving or operating in an unpredictable way. ➤ **temperamentally** *adverb*.

temperance *noun* the fact of not drinking alcohol.

temperate *adjective Geography* said about a climate: never extremely hot nor extremely cold. ➤ **temperately** *adverb*.

temperature *noun* (*plural* **temperatures**) **1** degree of hotness or coldness as measured on a scale, for example in degrees Celsius. **2** *informal* an abnormally high body heat because of illness.

tempest *noun* (*plural* **tempests**) a violent storm.

tempestuous *adjective* involving displays of strong emotion.

template noun (plural **templates**) **1** a pattern or stencil used as a guide when making, drawing, cutting out, or drilling something. **2** a thing that serves as a model. **3** *ICT* a computer file that you use for creating multiple files in a particular style.

temple[1] noun (plural **temples**) a building used for worship in some religions.

temple[2] noun (plural **temples**) the flat area on either side of your forehead.

tempo noun (plural **tempos**) **1** *Music* the speed that a piece of music is played at. **2** speed in general.

temporary adjective lasting only for a limited time. ➤ **temporarily** adverb.

tempt verb (**tempts, tempting, tempted**) **1** to make somebody want to do or have something very much. **2** to try to persuade somebody to do something immoral or unwise. ✳ **tempt fate** to do or say something that suggests you have too much confidence and therefore might bring disaster as a punishment. ➤ **tempting** adjective.

temptation noun (plural **temptations**) **1** an urge to do or have something, especially something forbidden or unwise. **2** something tempting.

ten noun (plural **tens**) the number 10.

tenable adjective **1** said about an argument or belief: reasonable. **2** said about a position, award, etc: to be held for a specified period.

tenacious adjective unwilling to give up. ➤ **tenaciously** adverb, **tenacity** noun.

tenancy noun (plural **tenancies**) the position of somebody who is renting a building, or the legal agreement under which they rent it.

tenant noun (plural **tenants**) somebody who is renting a building.

Ten Commandments plural noun (**the Ten Commandments**) in Christianity and Judaism, the ten main rules for living given by God to Moses, recorded in Exodus 20:1–17.

tend[1] verb (**tends, tending, tended**) to be likely to do something, or to have the habit of doing something.

tend[2] verb (**tends, tending, tended**) to look after something.

tendency noun (plural **tendencies**) a way that somebody usually behaves in a particular situation.

tendentious adjective presenting a biased view.

tender[1] adjective **1** showing great gentleness and kindness. **2** showing love or affection. **3** said about meat: easy to cut and chew. **4** said about a part of your body: sensitive or sore. **5** young and vulnerable: *a tender age*. **6** demanding careful and sensitive handling: *tender plants*. ➤ **tenderly** adverb, **tenderness** noun.

tender[2] noun (plural **tenders**) a formal offer or bid. ~ verb (**tenders, tendering, tendered**) **1** to give or present something: *He tendered his resignation*. **2** to submit an offer to do work for a particular fee.

tender[3] noun (plural **tenders**) a small truck attached to a steam locomotive for carrying coal and water.

tendon noun (plural **tendons**) a band of strong tissue that connects a muscle with a bone.

tendril noun (plural **tendrils**) a thin part that coils out from the stem of a climbing plant and attaches itself to a support.

tenement noun (plural **tenements**) a large building divided up into separate houses or flats.

tenet noun (plural **tenets**) a principle or belief.

tenner noun (plural **tenners**) *informal* a ten-pound note.

tennis noun a game for two or four players that is played with rackets and

tenon | 682

a ball on a flat court with a low net across the middle.

tenon *noun* (*plural* **tenons**) a part of a piece of wood that has been specially shaped to fit into a matching slot called a mortise, forming a joint.

tenor *noun* (*plural* **tenors**) 1 *Music* a male singer with a high voice. 2 the general meaning of something spoken or written.

tenpin bowling *noun* an indoor bowling game that involves rolling a large heavy ball at ten bottle-shaped pins.

tense[1] *adjective* (**tenser, tensest**) 1 feeling or showing nervousness and anxiety. 2 involving strain or suspense: *a tense moment*. ~ *verb* (**tenses, tensing, tensed**) to become tense. ➤ **tensely** *adverb*.

tense[2] *noun* (*plural* **tenses**) a set of forms of a verb that express action taking place at a particular time.

tensile *adjective* said about a metal: able to be stretched.

tension *noun* 1 feelings of worry and nervousness; stress. 2 a state of latent hostility between individuals or groups: *tension in the Middle East*. 3 a feeling of excited anticipation. 4 voltage: *high-tension cables*. 5 the condition of being stretched tight.

tent *noun* (*plural* **tents**) a light collapsible shelter made of canvas or similar material supported by poles.

tentacle *noun* (*plural* **tentacles**) one of several long flexible parts on the body of an octopus, squid, or similar animal, used for feeling, grasping, and moving.

tentative *adjective* 1 not fully worked out or developed; provisional. 2 hesitant or uncertain. ➤ **tentatively** *adverb*.

tenterhook ✱ **on tenterhooks** in a state of suspense or nervous anticipation.

tenth *adjective and noun* (*plural* **tenths**) 1 at number ten in a series. 2 one of ten equal parts of something.

tenuous *adjective* not strong, certain, or definite and likely to end or fail soon. ➤ **tenuously** *adverb*.

tenure *noun* 1 the period during which somebody has an official position. 2 the right to live in a place.

tepee /**tee**pee/ *noun* (*plural* **tepees**) a Native American conical tent, usually made of animal skins.

tepid *adjective* moderately warm.

tercentenary *noun* (*plural* **tercentenaries**) a 300th anniversary.

term *noun* (*plural* **terms**) 1 a word or expression. 2 any of the periods that a school or college year is divided into. 3 (**terms**) the conditions of an agreement. 4 the time for which something lasts. 5 *Maths* a mathematical expression that forms part of a fraction, equation, ratio, etc. ~ *verb* (**terms, terming, termed**) to describe something using particular words. ✱ **be on good/bad terms with** to have a friendly or unfriendly relationship with somebody. **come to terms with** to accept something sad or unpleasant.

terminal *noun* (*plural* **terminals**) 1 the end of a transport route, with its associated buildings and facilities. 2 a building at an airport with facilities for arriving and departing passengers. 3 a point where a wire can be connected to an electrical apparatus. 4 *ICT* a screen and keyboard, or some other device, used for communicating with a computer. ~ *adjective* 1 said about an illness: certain to cause death. 2 forming an end or boundary. ➤ **terminally** *adverb*.

terminate *verb* (**terminates, terminating, terminated**) 1 to come to an end, or bring something to an end. 2 to deliberately end a pregnancy so that the foetus does not survive.

3 to reach a terminus. ➤ **terminator** noun.

termination noun the ending of something.

terminology noun the words and expressions used in a particular subject. ➤ **terminological** adjective.

terminus noun (plural **terminuses** or **termini** /ter mi nie/) the end of a transport line or travel route.

termite noun (plural **termites**) an insect that lives in colonies and feeds on wood.

tern noun (plural **terns**) a white seabird like a small, slim gull with a forked tail.

ternary adjective Music made up of three parts, the third being a repetition of the first.

terrace noun (plural **terraces**) **1** a paved area adjoining a building. **2** a horizontal ridge cut into a hillside and used for farming. **3** a row of similar houses joined together.

terracotta noun unglazed brownish red pottery.

terrain noun a type of land.

terrapin noun (plural **terrapins**) a small North American freshwater turtle.

terrestrial adjective **1** relating to the planet earth. **2** relating to land as distinct from air or water. **3** said about a television system: not transmitting programmes via satellite.

terrible adjective **1** informal very unpleasant or of very poor quality. **2** causing great fear; terrifying.

terribly adverb informal **1** very. **2** very badly.

terrier noun (plural **terriers**) a small dog of various breeds, originally used to hunt out game from underground dens or burrows.

terrific adjective **1** informal extraordinarily large or intense. **2** informal excellent or very enjoyable. **3** causing great fear; terrifying. ➤ **terrifically** adverb.

terrify verb (**terrifies, terrifying, terrified**) to make somebody extremely frightened. ➤ **terrifying** adjective.

territorial adjective **1** relating to land, especially to the question of who owns it. **2** said about an animal or bird: tending to mark out and defend its own territory.

territory noun (plural **territories**) **1** an area of land that belongs to a country. **2** an area in which somebody or something operates. **3** an area occupied and defended by an animal or group of animals.

terror noun (plural **terrors**) **1** a state of intense fear. **2** something that makes people extremely frightened. **3** acts of terrorism: *the war on terror*.

terrorism noun the systematic use of terror, violence, and intimidation for political ends. ➤ **terrorist** adjective and noun.

terrorize or **terrorise** verb (**terrorizes, terrorizing, terrorized** or **terrorises**, etc) to make somebody extremely frightened, usually by threatening violence.

terse adjective (**terser, tersest**) using few words, and especially seeming unfriendly as a result. ➤ **tersely** adverb.

tertiary /ter sha ri/ adjective **1** of third rank, importance, or value. **2** relating to education in colleges and universities, above secondary level.

test noun (plural **tests**) **1** a series of questions or tasks set as a way of measuring somebody's knowledge, intelligence, or ability. **2** a series of actions performed in order to find something out, for example how well an invention works. **3** = TEST MATCH. ~ verb (**tests, testing, tested**) to subject somebody or something to a test. ➤ **tester** noun.

testament noun (plural **testaments**)

1 (Testament) either of the two main divisions of the Christian bible. **2** something that proves somebody has a particular quality: *a testament to her good intentions.* **3** a will.

test case *noun* (*plural* **test cases**) a legal case whose outcome is used as a basis for judging similar cases.

testicle *noun* (*plural* **testicles**) either of the two oval sperm-producing organs behind a penis. ➤ **testicular** *adjective*.

testify *verb* (**testifies, testifying, testified**) **1** to give evidence under oath as a witness in a court. **2** (**testify to**) to be proof of something.

testimonial *noun* (*plural* **testimonials**) **1** a letter or statement saying how good somebody or something is. **2** a friendly match, especially a football match, played as a tribute to a retiring player, with the player receiving all the money from the sale of tickets.

testimony *noun* (*plural* **testimonies**) the evidence given by a witness in a court.

test match *noun* (*plural* **test matches**) an international cricket or rugby match.

testosterone /te sto sti rohn/ *noun* a hormone that produces male characteristics.

test tube *noun* (*plural* **test tubes**) *Science* a thin glass tube closed at one end and used in chemistry, biology, etc.

tetanus /te ta nus/ *noun* an infectious disease that causes muscle spasms, especially in the jaw.

tether *verb* (**tethers, tethering, tethered**) to fasten an animal somewhere using a rope.

tetrahedron /te tra hee dron/ *noun* (*plural* **tetrahedrons** *or* **tetrahedra**) a solid shape with four flat faces.

Teutonic /tew to nik/ *adjective* characteristic of Germany or German people.

text *noun* (*plural* **texts**) **1** printed or written words. **2** the main written part of a page or book, as opposed to illustrations or notes. **3** a book that is being studied. **4** = TEXT MESSAGE.
~ *verb* (**texts, texting, texted**) to send a text message to somebody.
➤ **texting** *noun*, **textual** *adjective*.

textbook *noun* (*plural* **textbooks**) a book used in the study of a subject.
~ *adjective* being a perfect example of something.

textile *noun* (*plural* **textiles**) a fabric or cloth.

text message *noun* (*plural* **text messages**) a written message sent from one mobile phone to another.
➤ **text-messaging** *noun*.

texture *noun* (*plural* **textures**) the feel of something. ➤ **textural** *adjective*.

than *conjunction* **1** used to introduce the second element in a comparison: *She is older than I am.* **2** used to introduce an alternative or a contrast: *They would starve rather than beg.* **3** used after expressions such as *no sooner* to introduce what happened next.

thank *verb* (**thanks, thanking, thanked**) to tell somebody you are grateful. ✳ **thank you** used for expressing gratitude.

thankful *adjective* glad and grateful that something has happened.
➤ **thankfulness** *noun*.

thankfully *adverb* it is a relief that.

thankless *adjective* bringing no benefit nor appreciation.

thanks *plural noun* **1** an expression of gratitude. **2** thank you. ✳ **thanks to 1** with the help of. **2** because of.

thanksgiving *noun* **1** an expression of gratefulness, especially to God. **2** (**Thanksgiving**) a public holiday in

November in the USA and in October in Canada.

that *pronoun and adjective* (*plural* **those**) **1** the thing or idea just mentioned. **2** a distant person or thing that you point to or mention. ~ *pronoun* used to introduce a relative clause that identifies a particular person or thing: *the man that she married; the book that you want.* ~ *conjunction* used to introduce a clause expressing a purpose, reason, or result: *He said that he'd come; It was so wet that the game was abandoned.* ~ *adverb* **1** to the extent indicated: *a nail about that long.* **2** very: *It's not that expensive.* ✶ **that's that** that concludes the matter.

thatch *noun* straw or reeds used as a roof covering. *verb* (**thatches, thatching, thatched**) to roof a building with thatch. ➤ **thatched** *adjective*, **thatcher** *noun*.

thaw *verb* (**thaws, thawing, thawed**) **1** to go from a frozen to a liquid state, or make something frozen go into a liquid state. **2** to become less numb or stiff from cold. **3** said about relations between people: to become less hostile or reserved. ~ *noun* a period of weather warm enough to thaw ice.

the *definite article* **1** used before nouns when the object or person in question has been previously referred to or is obvious from the circumstances. **2** used to refer to somebody or something that is unique or universally recognized: *the pope.* **3** used before a singular noun to refer to a general type: *a history of the novel.*

theatre *noun* (*plural* **theatres**) **1** *Drama* a building where plays are performed. **2** *Drama* plays in general. **3** (**the theatre**) *Drama* the world of actors, acting, and drama generally. **4** (*also* **operating theatre**) a room where surgical operations are carried out.

theatrical *adjective Drama* to do with the theatre or the presentation of plays. ➤ **theatricality** *noun*, **theatrically** *adverb*.

thee *pronoun archaic or dialect* the form of 'thou' used as the object of a verb or preposition.

theft *noun* (*plural* **thefts**) the act or crime of stealing.

their *adjective* **1** belonging to them. **2** belonging to an indefinite singular person, used instead of 'his or her': *Make sure each child has their coat.*

Usage Note **their**, **there**, *or* **they're**? Do not confuse these three words. They are all pronounced the same, and mixing them up is a common error. *Their* is the possessive form of *they*: *their cars*. *There* is an adverb of place, and is also used in the phrase *there is/are*: *There are some books over there*. *They're* is the shortened form of *they are*: *They're over there on the table*.

theirs *pronoun* the one or ones that belong to them.

them *pronoun* the form of 'they' used as the object of a verb or preposition: *We gave them some money; They took plenty of water with them.*

thematic *adjective* **1** to do with themes, or constituting a theme. **2** classified according to subject. ➤ **thematically** *adverb*.

theme *noun* (*plural* **themes**) **1** *Drama, English, Art* a subject dealt with in a play, novel, painting, etc. **2** a set of features in the design of something that represent an idea. **3** *Music* a group of notes that forms the basis of a piece of music.

theme park *noun* (*plural* **theme parks**) an amusement park sometimes, but not always, based on a specific theme.

themself *pronoun* sometimes used in informal speech and writing instead of THEMSELVES when the subject is an

themselves

indefinite singular pronoun such as *no-one* or *anyone*: *No-one here need blame themself for what happened.*

themselves *pronoun* **1** used instead of 'them' when the people or things that are the subject of a verb are also the object: *They congratulated themselves on doing a good job.* **2** used to emphasize particular people or things: *a problem that they themselves had caused.* **3** used instead of 'himself or herself' to refer to an indefinite singular person: *Each of the players should feel proud of themselves.* ✴ **by themselves** alone.

then *adverb* **1** at that time: *We were living in France then.* **2** soon after that; next: *Then the phone rang.* **3** in that case: *'There's no orange juice.' 'I'll have cola, then.'*

theology /thee o lo ji/ *noun* the study of God and the teachings of organized religions. ➤ **theologian** *noun*, **theological** *adjective*.

theorem *noun* (*plural* **theorems**) a statement in mathematics or logic that can be proved from other more basic statements.

theoretical *adjective* **1** based on theory, not on real activity or practical experience. **2** existing only in theory; hypothetical. ➤ **theoretically** *adverb*.

theory *noun* (*plural* **theories**) **1** a suggested explanation of why something happens. **2** the general principles of a subject. ✴ **in theory** on the basis of general principles or under ideal circumstances, but not necessarily in practice or reality.

therapeutic /the ra pew tik/ *adjective* **1** to do with the treatment of illnesses. **2** having a beneficial effect on a person's physical or mental health. ➤ **therapeutically** *adverb*.

therapy *noun* (*plural* **therapies**) treatments for illnesses or injuries, especially without surgery. ➤ **therapist** *noun*.

there *adverb* **1** in, at, or to that place. **2** on that point or in that particular respect: *I disagree with you there.*
✴ **there is/are** used to introduce a sentence or clause stating that something exists or is true.

Usage Note **there**, **their**, or **they're**? See note at **their**.

thereabouts *adverb* **1** near that place. **2** near that time, quantity, etc.

thereafter *adverb formal* after that.

thereby *adverb* **1** in that way or by that means. **2** as a result of that.

therefore *adverb* because of that.

there's *contraction* **1** there is. **2** there has.

thermal *adjective* **1** to do with heat. **2** said about clothes: designed to prevent body heat from escaping and therefore to keep the wearer warm. ~ *noun* (*plural* **thermals**) **1** a rising current of warm air. **2** (**thermals**) thermal underwear or clothing. ➤ **thermally** *adverb*.

thermodynamics *noun Science* the branch of physics that deals with the relations between heat and other forms of energy. ➤ **thermodynamic** *adjective*.

thermometer *noun* (*plural* **thermometers**) a device that measures and indicates temperature, especially a glass tube containing mercury that rises and falls with changes of temperature.

thermostat *noun* (*plural* **thermostats**) a device that automatically controls temperature. ➤ **thermostatic** *adjective*, **thermostatically** *adverb*.

thesaurus *noun* (*plural* **thesauruses**) a book that lists words and their synonyms and related words, sometimes also including antonyms.

these *pronoun* plural of THIS.

thesis *noun* (*plural* **theses** /thee seez/) **1** a long essay based on original research, especially one submitted for a doctorate. **2** a theory that somebody offers to prove by reasoning.

they *pronoun* **1** used to refer to two or more people or things previously mentioned or being indicated: *Who are they?* **2** used instead of 'he or she' to refer to a single person previously mentioned: *If a student misses a class, they risk failing the course.* **3** people in general: *They say it'll rain tomorrow.*

Usage Note The use of *they* as a singular pronoun meaning 'a person of either sex' is becoming increasingly common, since it is no longer considered appropriate to use *he* for that purpose and the form *he or she* is often awkward to use. It is still best avoided in formal writing, however, and where the clash between singular and plural is very marked. *Everyone should do their best* is acceptable; *A lawyer must respect their clients' confidence* is less so and can easily be reworded as *Lawyers must respect their clients' confidence.*

they'd *contraction* **1** they had. **2** they would.

they'll *contraction* **1** they will. **2** they shall.

they're *contraction* they are.

Usage Note **they're**, **their**, *or* **there**? See note at *their*.

they've *contraction* they have.

thick *adjective* **1** of fairly great width in relation to length. **2** measuring a particular distance from one side to the other: *walls six feet thick*. **3** not flowing or pouring easily: *thick cream*. **4** with parts or particles packed close together; dense: *thick fog; a thick forest*. **5** *informal* stupid. ➤ **thickly** *adverb*.

thicken *verb* (**thickens, thickening, thickened**) to become thick or thicker, or make something thick or thicker.

thicket *noun* (*plural* **thickets**) a dense growth of shrubbery or small trees.

thickness *noun* (*plural* **thicknesses**) **1** the distance from one side of something to the other, as opposed to its length or height. **2** one of several layers of something.

thickset *adjective* heavily built; burly.

thief *noun* (*plural* **thieves**) somebody who steals.

thieve *verb* (**thieves, thieving, thieved**) to be a thief; to steal. ➤ **thieving** *noun and adjective*.

thigh *noun* (*plural* **thighs**) the part of your leg that extends from your hip to your knee.

thighbone *noun* (*plural* **thighbones**) the bone of the thigh; the femur.

thimble *noun* (*plural* **thimbles**) a metal or plastic cap worn on the end of your finger as a protection when sewing.

thin *adjective* (**thinner, thinnest**) **1** of fairly small width in relation to length. **2** without much flesh or fat on your body; slim. **3** flowing or pouring easily: *thin soup*. **4** not dense or closely packed. **5** said about an excuse: unconvincing. **6** said about a voice or sound: feeble and lacking in resonance.
~ *verb* (**thins, thinning, thinned**) to become thin or thinner, or make something thin or thinner. ➤ **thinly** *adverb*, **thinness** *noun*.

thine *pronoun archaic or dialect* yours.

thing *noun* (*plural* **things**) **1** an inanimate object as distinguished from a living being. **2** an object or entity that you do not or cannot name. **3** an event or circumstance: *the next thing that happened*. **4** (**things**) personal possessions.

think *verb* (**thinks, thinking, thought**) **1** to consider something or have something in your mind. **2** to have a particular belief or opinion. **3** to call something to mind; to remember. **4** to intend, plan, or decide to do something: *I think I'll go to bed; She's thinking of taking up golf.* **5** to expect or suspect something: *I* *didn't think he'd agree.* ✻ **think over** to consider something. ➤ **thinker** *noun*.

third *adjective* being number three in a series. ~ *noun* (*plural* **thirds**) one of three equal parts of something.
➤ **thirdly** *adverb*.

third person *noun English* in grammar, the term used to refer to somebody or something other than the speaker or the person spoken to, represented by the pronouns *he, she, it,* or *they.*

Third World *noun* (**the Third World**) the less industrialized nations of the world.

thirst *noun* **1** a desire or need to drink something. **2** a strong wish to have or do something; a craving. ~ *verb* (**thirsts, thirsting, thirsted**) **1** to feel thirsty. **2** to wish strongly to have or do something; to crave.

thirsty *adjective* (**thirstier, thirstiest**) **1** needing or wanting to drink something. **2** causing thirst: *thirsty work*.
➤ **thirstily** *adverb*.

thirteen *adjective and noun* (*plural* **thirteens**) the number 13. ➤ **thirteenth** *adjective and noun*.

thirty *adjective and noun* (*plural* **thirties**) **1** the number 30. **2** (**the thirties**) the numbers 30 to 39. ➤ **thirtieth** *adjective and noun*.

this *pronoun* (*plural* **these**) **1** the thing or idea that has just been mentioned. **2** a nearby person or thing that you point to or mention. ~ *adjective* (*plural* **these**) used to refer to the person or thing that has just been mentioned or is relatively nearby. *adverb* to the extent indicated or specified: *The fish was this big!*

thistle *noun* (*plural* **thistles**) a prickly plant with dense heads of usually purple flowers.

thong *noun* (*plural* **thongs**) a skimpy piece of underwear with thin straps.

thorax *noun* (*plural* **thoraxes** or **thoraces** /thawˈrə seez/) *Science* **1** the part of a mammal's body between the neck and the abdomen. **2** the main section of the body of an insect, spider, etc, carrying the legs and wings.

thorn *noun* (*plural* **thorns**) **1** a short pointed part sticking out of a plant's branch or stem. **2** a woody plant, shrub, or tree with branches covered in thorns.

thorny *adjective* (**thornier, thorniest**) **1** covered in thorns. **2** full of difficulties or controversial points.

thorough /ˈthu ru/ *adjective* **1** showing great care and attention to detail. **2** complete; utter. ➤ **thoroughly** *adverb*, **thoroughness** *noun*.

thoroughbred *noun* (*plural* **thoroughbreds**) an animal that has been bred from the best members of the same breed, strain, etc over many generations. ➤ **thoroughbred** *adjective*.

thoroughfare *noun* (*plural* **thoroughfares**) a road or path.

those *pronoun and adjective* plural of THAT.

thou *pronoun archaic or dialect* you (singular).

though *adverb* however: *It was hard work. I enjoyed it, though.* ~ *conjunction* **1** in spite of the fact that: *Though it rained, we had a good time.* **2** and yet; but: *It works, though not very well.*

thought *verb* past tense of THINK.
~ *noun* (*plural* **thoughts**) **1** the process of thinking. **2** an idea, opinion, or intention.

thoughtful *adjective* **1** thinking about something serious. **2** considering other people's feelings, wishes, or needs. ➤ **thoughtfully** *adverb*, **thoughtfulness** *noun*.

thoughtless *adjective* **1** showing a lack of sensible planning or assessment of risks; rash. **2** showing a lack of consideration for other people's feelings, wishes, or needs. ➤ **thoughtlessly** *adverb*.

thousand *noun* (*plural* **thousands** or

thousand) **1** the number 1000. **2** *informal* (*also in plural*) a very large number. ➢ **thousandth** *adjective and noun*.

thrash *verb* (**thrashes, thrashing, thrashed**) **1** to beat somebody violently with a stick or whip. **2** to defeat somebody convincingly. ✱ **thrash about/around** to move about violently.

thread *noun* (*plural* **threads**) **1** a very thin length of cotton, wool, or other fibre used for sewing, knitting, or weaving. **2** a spiral ridge on a screw, bolt, etc by which parts can be screwed together. **3** a recurring idea or theme in a play, book, etc. ~ *verb* (**threads, threading, threaded**) **1** to pass a thread through the eye of a needle. **2** to pass something somewhere carefully: *Thread the tape through the hem of the sleeve*. **3** to make your way along a winding route, often slowly and between obstacles. **4** to put something on to a thread: *Thread the beads onto the string*.

threadbare *adjective* said about carpet or clothing: with the fabric so worn away so that threads are visible.

threat *noun* (*plural* **threats**) **1** somebody's warning of their intention to harm you if you do not do what they want. **2** a source of possible danger or harm.

threaten *verb* (**threatens, threatening, threatened**) **1** to warn of an intention to harm somebody if something is or is not done. **2** to be a potential source of harm or danger to somebody or something. ➢ **threatening** *adjective*.

three *noun and adjective* (*plural* **threes**) the number 3.

three-dimensional *adjective* solid, with length, breadth, and height.

threesome *noun* (*plural* **threesomes**) a group of three people or things.

threshold /thresh hohld/ *noun* (*plural* **thresholds**) **1** the point or level at which something begins: *on the threshold of a new career*. **2** a doorway, or the stone, plank, etc that forms its bottom surface.

Usage Note Notice that there is only one *h* in the middle of this word although it is pronounced as if there were two.

threw *verb* past tense of THROW.

thrice *adverb archaic or literary* three times.

thrift *noun* careful use of money or other resources. ➢ **thrifty** *adjective*.

thrill *noun* (*plural* **thrills**) **1** a sudden feeling of pleasurable excitement. **2** something that causes such a feeling. ~ *verb* (**thrills, thrilling, thrilled**) to cause somebody to feel pleasurable excitement.

thriller *noun* (*plural* **thrillers**) a novel, film, or drama with an exciting story full of suspense.

thrilling *adjective* intensely exciting or suspenseful. ➢ **thrillingly** *adverb*.

thrive *verb* (**thrives, thriving, thrived**) **1** to be happy and healthy. **2** to be very successful. **3** said about a plant: to grow vigorously. ➢ **thriving** *adjective*.

throat *noun* (*plural* **throats**) **1** the passage through your neck to your stomach and lungs. **2** the front part of your neck. ✱ **at each other's throats** quarrelling violently.

throb *verb* (**throbs, throbbing, throbbed**) **1** said about an injured part of your body: to cause you to feel pain as a strong beat. **2** said about an engine, etc: to make a loud rhythmic noise. ➢ **throbbing** *noun*.

throe ✱ **in the throes of** undergoing the difficult process of doing something.

thrombosis *noun* (*plural* **thromboses** /throm boh seez/) a clot in a blood vessel.

throne *noun* (*plural* **thrones**) **1** the ceremonial chair of a king, queen, or bishop. **2** (**the throne**) the position of king or queen.

throng *noun* (*plural* **throngs**) a large crowd. ~ *verb* (**throngs, thronging, thronged**) to crowd into a place.

throttle *noun* (*plural* **throttles**) a device that controls the speed of an engine. ~ *verb* (**throttles, throttling, throttled**) to strangle or choke somebody. * **throttle back/down** to reduce the speed of an engine.

through *preposition* **1** into something at one side or point and out at the other: *We crawled through a hole in the fence.* **2** during the entire period of: *people who lived through the war.* **3** by means of or because of: *He failed through laziness.* ~ *adverb* **1** from one end or side of something to the other: *The gate opened and we drove through.* **2** from beginning to end: *We watched the film all the way through.* ~ *adjective* **1** allowing a continuous journey to a destination: *the through train.* **2** passing beyond a particular place: *through traffic.* **3** finished: *Are you through with that magazine?* * **through and through** thoroughly; completely.

throughout *adverb and preposition* **1** in or to every part: *This theme runs throughout the film.* **2** from beginning to end: *He remained calm throughout.*

throw *verb* (**throws, throwing, threw, thrown**) **1** to send something through the air with your hand and arm. **2** to put something somewhere roughly or carelessly: *She threw the letter in the bin.* **3** to cause something or somebody to move somewhere violently: *Huge waves threw the little boat around.* **4** to put somebody in a specified condition suddenly: *The news threw us into a panic.* **5** to direct light, a look, etc in a certain direction. **6** to give a party. **7** to have a tantrum or fit. **8** *informal* to confuse or disconcert somebody. ~ *noun* (*plural* **throws**) **1** an act of throwing. **2** a turn at throwing the dice in a board game. * **throw away 1** to get rid of something worthless or unwanted. **2** to use something in a foolish or wasteful manner. **throw out 1** to get rid of something as worthless or unwanted. **2** to order or force somebody to leave a room or building. **3** to dismiss a plan, proposal, etc. **throw up** *informal* to vomit. **throw yourself into** to begin doing something with great energy.

throwback *noun* (*plural* **throwbacks**) somebody or something that has qualities that seem to be from an earlier time.

thrush[1] *noun* (*plural* **thrushes**) a light-brown bird with a spotted breast and a musical song.

thrush[2] *noun* a whitish irritating fungal growth in the mouth or vagina.

thrust *verb* (**thrusts, thrusting, thrust**) to push or drive something with force. ~ *noun* (*plural* **thrusts**) **1** a push or lunge with a pointed weapon. **2** a concerted military attack. **3** the essential meaning of something. **4** the force produced by a propeller, jet engine, etc to give forward motion.

thud *verb* (**thuds, thudding, thudded**) to make a dull heavy sound. ► **thud** *noun*.

thug *noun* (*plural* **thugs**) a violent person, especially a violent criminal. ► **thuggery** *noun*, **thuggish** *adjective*.

thumb *noun* (*plural* **thumbs**) the short thick finger on the side of your hand, separate from your other fingers. ~ *verb* (**thumbs, thumbing, thumbed**) **1** to have a brief look through the pages of a book. **2** to ask for a lift in a passing vehicle by signalling with your thumb. * **under somebody's thumb** under somebody's control.

thump *verb* (**thumps, thumping,**

thumped) 1 to hit somebody with a fist. **2** said about your heart: to beat rapidly. **3** to make the loud dull sound of something heavy hitting a surface. ➤ **thump** noun.

thumping adjective **1** informal impressively large or excellent. **2** throbbing.

thunder noun **1** the low loud sound that usually follows a flash of lightning. **2** a loud reverberating noise; a rumble. ~ verb (**thunders, thundering, thundered**) **1** to move fast and noisily. **2** to make thunder. ➤ **thundery** adjective.

thunderbolt noun (plural **thunderbolts**) a single flash of lightning with the accompanying thunder.

thunderous adjective said about a noise: very loud and deep. ➤ **thunderously** adverb.

thunderstorm noun (plural **thunderstorms**) a storm accompanied by lightning and thunder.

Thursday noun (plural **Thursdays**) the fifth day of the week, the day that follows Wednesday.

thus adverb formal **1** because of this; therefore: *I'll work fewer hours and thus earn less money.* **2** in this way: *Swing your arm thus.*

thwart verb (**thwarts, thwarting, thwarted**) to prevent somebody from doing what they plan or want to do.

thy adjective archaic or dialect your.

thyme /tiem/ noun a herb with small leaves, used to flavour food.

thyroid noun (also **thyroid gland**) a large gland in your neck that produces hormones that influence growth and development.

tiara /tee ah ra/ noun (plural **tiaras**) a jewelled semicircular band that some women wear on their head on formal occasions.

tibia noun (plural **tibias** or **tibiae** /**ti** bi ee/) the inner and usually larger of the two bones between your knee and ankle.

tic noun (plural **tics**) an uncontrollable twitching of a particular muscle, especially in your face.

tick¹ noun (plural **ticks**) **1** a mark (✓) used to label something as correct, to check off an item on a list, etc. **2** one of a series of regular soft high sounds that a clock, watch, or other mechanism makes. ~ verb (**ticks, ticking, ticked**) **1** to mark something with a written tick. **2** said about a clock, watch, etc: to make ticks. ✽ **tick away/by** said about time: to pass, bringing the end of something closer.

tick off 1 to mark an item on a list to show that you have dealt with it. **2** informal to scold somebody.

tick² noun (plural **ticks**) a tiny bloodsucking spider-like creature that often transmits infectious diseases.

ticket noun (plural **tickets**) **1** a printed card or piece of paper that shows you are entitled to something, especially showing that you have paid to travel or gain admission to something. **2** a tag or label.

tickle verb (**tickles, tickling, tickled**) to touch somebody lightly and repeatedly in a way that makes them laugh or feel an uncomfortable tingling sensation. ~ noun (plural **tickles**) **1** a tickling sensation. **2** the act of tickling somebody.

ticklish adjective **1** said about a person: sensitive to tickling. **2** said about a situation: needing to be handled carefully.

tidal adjective to do with tides, or having tides. ➤ **tidally** adverb.

tidal wave noun (plural **tidal waves**) **1** an unusually high sea wave; a tsunami. **2** an unexpected, intense, and often widespread reaction.

tiddlywinks noun a game in which players try to flick small discs into a container.

tide *noun* (*plural* **tides**) **1** the regular rise and fall of the level of the sea. **2** a general trend in events. **3** a powerful surge of feeling.

tidings *plural noun* a piece of news.

tidy *adjective* (**tidier, tidiest**) **1** neat and orderly in your appearance or habits. **2** *informal* fairly large; substantial: *a tidy sum*. *verb* (**tidies, tidying, tidied**) to make something neat and orderly. ➤ **tidily** *adverb*, **tidiness** *noun*.

tie *verb* (**ties, tying, tied**) **1** to fasten something with rope, string, etc. **2** to make a knot or bow in something. **3** to make a bond or connection between people or things. **4** to achieve an equal score in a game or contest. ~ *noun* (*plural* **ties**) **1** something that connects people or things to each other. **2** an item of clothing in the form of a narrow strip of cloth that you tie round your neck and let hang down in front. **3** a match between two teams, players, etc: *a cup tie*. **4** a draw in a game or contest. ✴ **tie up 1** to fasten something securely with rope, string, etc. **2** to bind a person's arms or legs to prevent them moving or escaping. **3** to conclude a matter satisfactorily. **4** to make something unavailable for other purposes or for other people to use.

tie break *or* **tie-breaker** *noun* (*plural* **tie breaks** *or* **tie-breakers**) a point or game used to decide the winner in a contest that has ended with equal scores.

tier /teer/ *noun* (*plural* **tiers**) **1** any of several rows of seating arranged one above and behind the other. **2** any of a series of levels, for example in an administration. ➤ **tiered** *adjective*.

tiff *noun* (*plural* **tiffs**) *informal* a petty quarrel.

tig *noun* = TAG².

tiger *noun* (*plural* **tigers**) a large Asian animal of the cat family that has a tawny coat with black stripes.

tight *adjective* **1** fixed very firmly in place. **2** stretched so as not to be loose or slack. **3** said about clothes: fitting closely or too closely. **4** said about space: difficult to move or manoeuvre in. **5** in short supply; scarce. **6** *informal* ungenerous or unkind. ➤ **tightly** *adverb*, **tightness** *noun*.

tighten *verb* (**tightens, tightening, tightened**) to make something tight, or to become tight.

tightrope *noun* (*plural* **tightropes**) a rope or wire stretched tight for acrobats to perform on.

tights *plural noun* a skintight garment that covers each leg and foot and reaches to your waist.

tigress *noun* (*plural* **tigresses**) a female tiger.

tilde /ˈtɪl də/ *noun* (*plural* **tildes**) a mark ˜ placed over the letter *n* in Spanish when it is pronounced /ny/, and over vowels in Portuguese to indicate that you pronounce them with a nasal sound.

tile *noun* (*plural* **tiles**) a thin slab of fired clay, stone, concrete, cork, etc used to surface roofs, floors, walls, etc. ~ *verb* (**tiles, tiling, tiled**) **1** to cover a surface with tiles. **2** *ICT* to arrange windows on a computer screen so that they are next to each other and do not overlap. ➤ **tiler** *noun*, **tiling** *noun*.

till[1] *preposition and conjunction* until.

till[2] *noun* (*plural* **tills**) a cash register.

till[3] *verb* (**tills, tilling, tilled**) to plough land.

tiller *noun* (*plural* **tillers**) a lever on a boat that turns the rudder.

tilt *verb* (**tilts, tilting, tilted**) to lift something so that its surface slopes or it sits at an angle.

timber *noun* (*plural* **timbers**) **1** wood that has been cut for use in building or carpentry. **2** a large piece of wood that forms part of a building or other structure.

timbre /tamber/ *noun* (*plural* **timbres**) *Music* the tone of a particular singing voice or musical instrument.

time *noun* (*plural* **times**) **1** what exists as the past, the present, and the future, and which we measure in years, weeks, hours, minutes, etc. **2** the point or period when something happens; an occasion: *That was the time we went to France.* **3** a moment in the day as indicated by a clock. **4** the moment when something is due to happen. **5** a person's experience of an event: *Did you have a nice time?* **6** an amount of available time: *Is there time for another game?* **7** *Music* how fast a piece of music is played, or its rhythm measured in the number of beats in each bar. **8** (**times**) *Maths* multiplied by: *Six times eight equals forty-eight.* ~ *verb* (**times, timing, timed**) **1** to measure the time that something takes. **2** to arrange the time that something happens, usually so that it coincides with something else. ✽ **for the time being** for the present. **in no time** very soon; very quickly. **in time 1** sufficiently early. **2** eventually. **on time** at the arranged or expected time. **time off** time spent away from work or relaxing.

timeless *adjective* remaining good, beautiful, stylish, etc no matter how much time passes.

timely *adjective* happening or done at a good time.

timer *noun* (*plural* **timers**) a device or mechanism that starts or stops something at a set time.

time scale *noun* (*plural* **time scales**) the amount of time that something will take, or the time available for something.

timetable *noun* (*plural* **timetables**) a list of times when things are due to happen, for example a list of the times of classes that you have on a particular school day.

time zone *noun* (*plural* **time zones**) *Geography* a region of the earth stretching approximately north and south in which all places are at the same time of day.

timid *adjective* lacking courage or self-confidence. ➤ **timidity** *noun*, **timidly** *adverb*.

timing *noun* **1** the fact that you do something at just the right time. **2** the time when something happens, especially in relation to another event.

timpani *plural noun* a set of two or three kettledrums played by one performer in an orchestra. ➤ **timpanist** *noun*.

tin *noun* (*plural* **tins**) **1** *Science* a silvery metallic element used in alloys. **2** a sealed metal container that food is preserved and sold in. ➤ **tinned** *adjective*.

tinder *noun* any dry substance that burns easily and is used for starting a fire.

tinge *noun* (*plural* **tinges**) **1** a trace of a colour. **2** a quality present in a very small amount. ➤ **tinged** *adjective*.

tingle *verb* (**tingles, tingling, tingled**) to feel a stinging or prickling sensation. ~ *noun* (*plural* **tingles**) a tingling sensation. ➤ **tingly** *adjective*.

tinker[1] *verb* (**tinkers, tinkering, tinkered**) (**tinker with**) to make small repairs or adjustments to something.

tinker[2] *noun* (*plural* **tinkers**) in the past, a person who travelled around mending people's pots, pans, and other metal household items.

tinkle *verb* (**tinkles, tinkling, tinkled**) to make a short light ringing sound. ➤ **tinkle** *noun*.

tinnitus /ti ni tus *or* ti nie tus/ *noun* a ringing or roaring sensation in the ears.

tinny *adjective* (**tinnier, tinniest**)

tinsel

having an unpleasantly thin metallic sound.

tinsel *noun* a glittering Christmas decoration in the form of thin strips of foil threaded on a string.

tint *noun* (*plural* **tints**) a lighter or darker shade of a colour. ~ *verb* (**tints, tinting, tinted**) to alter the colour of something slightly.

tiny *adjective* (**tinier, tiniest**) very small.

tip[1] *noun* (*plural* **tips**) the rounded or pointed end of something. ➤ **tipped** *adjective*.

tip[2] *verb* (**tips, tipping, tipped**) **1** to lift something at one end; to tilt something. **2** to turn a container up or over in order to empty it. ~ *noun* (*plural* **tips**) **1** a place for dumping rubbish. **2** *informal* a messy place.

tip[3] *noun* (*plural* **tips**) an extra sum of money that you give to thank somebody for good service. *verb* (**tips, tipping, tipped**) to give somebody a tip.

tip[4] *noun* (*plural* **tips**) **1** a piece of useful advice. **2** a piece of information from an expert or insider that might bring a profit. ~ *verb* (**tips, tipping, tipped**) to recommend something as a likely success or profitable investment, or somebody as a likely winner.

tipple *noun* (*plural* **tipples**) *informal* an alcoholic drink.

tipsy *adjective* (**tipsier, tipsiest**) slightly drunk. ➤ **tipsily** *adverb*.

tiptoe *verb* (**tiptoes, tiptoeing, tiptoed**) to walk silently or stealthily with your heels off the ground. ✻ **on tiptoe** *or* **on tiptoes** balancing on your toes or the balls of your feet.

tirade /tie **rayd**/ *noun* (*plural* **tirades**) a long speech in which you criticize something angrily.

tire *verb* (**tires, tiring, tired**) **1** to make somebody tired, or to become tired. **2** (**tire of**) to become bored with something.

tired *adjective* **1** needing sleep or rest. **2** (**tired of**) bored or exasperated with something. **3** not original or fresh. ➤ **tiredness** *noun*.

tireless *adjective* continuing without losing energy, enthusiasm, or commitment. ➤ **tirelessly** *adverb*.

tiresome *adjective* annoying or boring. ➤ **tiresomely** *adverb*.

tissue *noun* (*plural* **tissues**) **1** *Science* clusters of cells of a particular type that form animals and plants: *skin tissue; leaf tissue*. **2** a paper handkerchief.

tissue paper *noun* thin gauzy paper.

tit *noun* (*plural* **tits**) a small European bird of various kinds.

titanic *adjective* **1** very big or powerful. **2** involving a lot of energy or effort.

titanium *noun* *Science* a light, strong, grey metallic element used mainly in alloys.

titbit *noun* (*plural* **titbits**) **1** a tasty piece of food. **2** an interesting piece of information.

titillate *verb* (**titillates, titillating, titillated**) to excite somebody, especially sexually. ➤ **titillating** *adjective*, **titillation** *noun*.

title *noun* (*plural* **titles**) **1** the name given to a particular book, film, painting, etc. **2** a word that indicates a person's job, professional rank, or social position. **3** a championship. **4** the status of champion. **5** (**titles**) a list of the people involved in making a film or television programme, shown at the beginning or end.

titled *adjective* having an aristocratic title such as *Lord* or *Lady*.

titration /tie **tray** shn/ *noun* *Science* a method of finding out how much of a substance is contained in a solution by adding measured quantities of another substance that is known to react with it until a reaction occurs.

titter *verb* (**titters, tittering, tittered**) to laugh in an embarrassed or silly way. ➤ **titter** *noun*.

titular *adjective* according to the formal title something or somebody has, but not in reality; nominal: *the titular head of the government.*

TNT *abbreviation* = trinitrotoluene /trie ni e troh **tol** ew een/, a very powerful explosive.

to *preposition* **1** used to indicate a direction or destination: *We walked to school.* **2** before the hour mentioned: *five minutes to five.* **3** used to indicate the person or thing affected by an action: *I gave the book to Phil; She's always nasty to me.* **4** used to indicate addition or connection: *Add another spoonful of flour to the mixture; Connect the red wire to the blue wire.* **5** used to indicate a comparison or ratio: *They won by three goals to one.* **6** used to introduce an infinitive form of a verb: *It's difficult to answer that question.* **7** used to indicate purpose: *He did it to annoy them.* ~ *adverb* into a position of being closed; shut: *Pull the door to.* ✳ **to and fro** from one place to another; back and forth.

toad *noun* (*plural* **toads**) an amphibious creature like a frog but with a shorter squatter body.

toadstool *noun* (*plural* **toadstools**) a poisonous or inedible umbrella-shaped fungus.

toast *noun* (*plural* **toasts**) **1** sliced bread that has been browned on both sides by heat. **2** an act of drinking in honour of somebody or something. ~ *verb* (**toasts, toasting, toasted**) **1** to make bread crisp, hot, and brown by heat. **2** to drink a toast in honour of somebody or something. **3** to warm a part of your body in front of a fire.

toaster *noun* (*plural* **toasters**) an electrical appliance for toasting bread.

tobacco *noun* the dried leaves of an American plant that are smoked in the form of cigarettes or cigars, or in a pipe.

tobacconist *noun* (*plural* **tobacconists**) a person or shop that sells tobacco.

toboggan *noun* (*plural* **toboggans**) a lightweight sledge.

today *adverb* **1** on this day. **2** in the present time or period. ~ *noun* this day.

toddle *verb* (**toddles, toddling, toddled**) **1** said about a very young child: to walk unsteadily. **2** *informal* to go somewhere. ➤ **toddle** *noun*.

toddler *noun* (*plural* **toddlers**) a very young child who is just learning to walk.

to-do *noun* (*plural* **to-dos**) *informal* a situation in which people are complaining, arguing, or fussing.

toe *noun* (*plural* **toes**) any of the movable parts at the end of a human's or animal's foot. ✳ **on your toes** ready to do something; alert. **toe the line** (**toes, toeing, toed**) to follow a rule or order strictly.

toffee *noun* (*plural* **toffees**) a sweet food made by boiling sugar and butter.

tofu /toh foo/ *noun* a soft cheese-like food made from soya-bean milk.

tog *noun* a unit used to measure the warmth of a quilt, a sleeping bag, etc.

toga *noun* (*plural* **togas**) a loose robe worn by citizens of ancient Rome.

together *adverb* **1** in or into one place, mass, or group: *Gather the players together for a team talk.* **2** as a group, not as individuals: *We're working on it together.* **3** in or into contact: *Tie the ends together.* **4** with each other: *They've been together all morning.* ✳ **together with** as well as. ➤ **togetherness** *noun*.

toggle *noun* (*plural* **toggles**) **1** a long

button-like device that fits through a loop to fasten clothes, etc. **2** *ICT* a combination of keys that you press to switch from one screen to another that you also have open. ~ *verb* (**toggles, toggling, toggled**) *ICT* to switch from one screen to another using a toggle.

togs *plural noun informal* clothes.

toil *noun* tiring work. ~ *verb* (**toils, toiling, toiled**) to work hard and long.

toilet *noun* (*plural* **toilets**) **1** a bowl-shaped bathroom fixture that you release urine and faeces into. **2** a room containing a toilet and sometimes a washbasin. **3** *archaic or literary* the act of washing and dressing yourself.

toiletries *plural noun* substances such as soap and shampoo that you use for washing and grooming.

token *noun* (*plural* **tokens**) **1** a voucher used like money. **2** a coin-like disc used instead of money. **3** something that you do or give to show a feeling such as love or affection. ~ *adjective* done or included merely for show, not because you are committed to doing or including it: *the token girl in the team*.

told *verb* past tense of TELL.

tolerable *adjective* **1** not so bad that you cannot tolerate it. **2** fairly good but not excellent. ➤ **tolerably** *adverb*.

tolerance *noun* **1** acceptance of beliefs or ways of living that are different from your own. **2** your body's ability to endure the effects of a drug, virus, radiation, etc.

tolerant *adjective* showing a willingness to accept beliefs or ways of living that are different from your own. ➤ **tolerantly** *adverb*.

tolerate *verb* (**tolerates, tolerating, tolerated**) **1** to accept beliefs or ways of living that are different from your own. **2** to endure something such as the effects of a drug without becoming seriously ill or injured. ➤ **toleration** *noun*.

toll[1] *noun* (*plural* **tolls**) **1** a fee paid for the right to do something, such as crossing a bridge or driving on a road. **2** an amount of loss or damage suffered, such as the number of casualties caused by an accident: *the death toll*.

toll[2] *verb* (**tolls, tolling, tolled**) **1** to ring a bell, or to be rung. **2** to announce something by ringing a bell.

tom *noun* (*plural* **toms**) a male cat.

tomahawk *noun* (*plural* **tomahawks**) a small axe used by Native Americans as a weapon.

tomato *noun* (*plural* **tomatoes**) a round red vegetable with pulpy flesh.

tomb /toom/ *noun* (*plural* **tombs**) a room where a dead body is buried, above or below ground.

tomboy *noun* (*plural* **tomboys**) a girl who enjoys rough physical play and has tastes thought to be more typical of a boy. ➤ **tomboyish** *adjective*.

tombstone *noun* (*plural* **tombstones**) = GRAVESTONE.

tomcat *noun* (*plural* **tomcats**) a male cat.

tome *noun* (*plural* **tomes**) *formal or humorous* a book, especially a large book on a serious subject.

tomorrow *adverb* on the day after today. ~ *noun* the day after today.

ton /tun/ *noun* (*plural* **tons**) **1** a unit of weight equal to 2240 pounds (about 1016 kilograms). **2** (**metric ton**) = TONNE. **3** *informal* (*often in plural*) a large amount or number.

tonal *adjective* **1** *Art* to do with shades or colours. **2** *Music* based on one of the traditional keys. ➤ **tonality** *noun*, **tonally** *adverb*.

tone *noun* (*plural* **tones**) **1** a sound produced by somebody's voice or by a musical instrument. **2** a quality in somebody's voice that expresses their mood or feelings. **3** the main quality of something: *the serious tone of the discussion.* **4** *Music* the difference in pitch between two musical notes such as A and B or C and D. **5** a shade of a colour. ~ *verb* (**tones, toning, toned**) to make your muscles firmer by doing exercise. ✷ **tone down** to soften the brightness, loudness, or impact of something.

tone-deaf *adjective* not very good at hearing the differences between musical notes or at getting the notes right when you sing or play music.

tongs *plural noun* a grasping device consisting of two pieces joined at one end by a pivot or hinged like scissors.

tongue *noun* (*plural* **tongues**) **1** the fleshy organ in your mouth used for tasting food and in speaking. **2** a language. **3** the flap under the laces on the front of a shoe. ✷ **hold your tongue** to say nothing.

tongue-in-cheek *adjective* expressed in a serious way but not intended to be taken seriously.

tonic *noun* (*plural* **tonics**) **1** (*also* **tonic water**) carbonated, slightly bitter mineral water, often drunk with gin. **2** something that makes you feel full of energy or enthusiasm.

tonight *adverb* on this night or this evening. *noun* this night or this evening.

tonne /tun/ *noun* (*plural* **tonnes**) a metric unit of weight equal to 1000 kilograms.

tonsil *noun* (*plural* **tonsils**) either of a pair of small oval masses of tissue that lie one on each side of your throat.

tonsillitis *noun* inflammation of your tonsils.

too *adverb* **1** to a greater degree than is necessary, useful, or allowed; excessively. **2** also.

took *verb* past tense of TAKE.

tool *noun* (*plural* **tools**) **1** an implement, such as a hammer or a knife, used to do a particular type of task. **2** something that is useful or necessary in carrying out a particular activity: *Words are the tools of a writer's trade.*

toot *verb* (**toots, tooting, tooted**) to make a short sound with a horn. ➤ **toot** *noun.*

tooth *noun* (*plural* **teeth**) **1** any of the hard bony parts of your mouth that you use for biting and chewing food. **2** any of the row of parts that stick out on a comb, the blade of a saw, a cogwheel, etc. ➤ **toothed** *adjective*, **toothless** *adjective.*

toothache *noun* pain in a tooth.

toothbrush *noun* (*plural* **toothbrushes**) a brush for cleaning your teeth.

toothpaste *noun* a paste for cleaning your teeth.

top[1] *noun* (*plural* **tops**) **1** the highest part or level of something. **2** the uppermost surface or side of something. **3** a garment that you wear on the upper part of your body. **4** a lid or covering. **4** (**the top**) the highest position in rank or achievement. ~ *adjective* **1** above all others. **2** of the highest quality, standard, etc: *one of the resort's top hotels.* ~ *verb* (**tops, topping, topped**) **1** to be better or greater than something: *Nobody will top that score.* **2** to cover the top of something. ✷ **off the top of your head** without taking time to think about something carefully or get accurate information; impromptu. **top up** **1** to make a partially empty container full. **2** to add an extra amount in order that something reaches a particular level.

top[2] *noun* (*plural* **tops**) a child's toy with a tapering point that you spin it on.

top hat *noun* (*plural* **top hats**) a man's

tall hat with a flat top and vertical sides, worn on very formal occasions.

top-heavy *adjective* unstable or out of proportion because the top part is too heavy for the lower part.

topic *noun* (*plural* **topics**) a subject being discussed or considered.

topical *adjective* to do with things that are happening now. ➤ **topicality** *noun*, **topically** *adverb*.

topography *noun* Geography the shape of a land surface, including its hills and valleys and features such as rivers and roads. ➤ **topographical** *adjective*.

topple *verb* (**topples, toppling, toppled**) 1 to fall down or fall over because of being unsteady or top-heavy. 2 to force a government or leader out of power.

topsy-turvy *adjective and adverb* 1 upside down. 2 in a state of complete confusion or disorder.

top-up fees *plural noun* additional fees charged by universities to bridge the gap between the basic tuition fees they receive and actual tuition costs.

Torah /taw ra/ *noun* (**the Torah**) the first five books of the Jewish Bible.

torch *noun* (*plural* **torches**) 1 a small portable electric lamp powered by batteries. 2 formerly, a stick of wood coated or wrapped with inflammable material and burned to give light.

tore *verb* past tense of TEAR².

torment /taw ment/ *noun* (*plural* **torments**) 1 extreme pain or unhappiness. 2 something that causes extreme pain or unhappiness. ~ /taw ment/ *verb* (**torments, tormenting, tormented**) 1 to cause somebody extreme pain or unhappiness. 2 to tease somebody unkindly. ➤ **tormentor** *noun*.

torn *verb* past participle of TEAR².

tornado *noun* (*plural* **tornadoes**) a violent or destructive whirlwind.

torpedo *noun* (*plural* **torpedoes**) a self-propelling missile launched from a submarine or ship in an attack on another submarine or ship. ~ *verb* (**torpedoes, torpedoing, torpedoed**) to destroy a ship or submarine with torpedoes.

torque /tawk/ *noun* a force that produces rotation, especially in an engine.

torrent *noun* (*plural* **torrents**) 1 a rushing stream of water, lava, etc. 2 a violent outpouring of words: *torrents of abuse*.

torrential *adjective* said about rain: falling very heavily.

torrid *adjective* 1 involving passionate feelings. 2 extremely hot and dry.

torso *noun* (*plural* **torsos**) your trunk, the part of your body between your waist and your neck.

tortilla /taw tee ya/ *noun* (*plural* **tortillas**) 1 in Mexican cooking, a thin maize pancake eaten hot with a filling. 2 in Spanish cooking, a thick omelette containing potato.

tortoise *noun* (*plural* **tortoises**) a reptile with a bony shell that it can withdraw its head, limbs, and tail into.

tortuous *adjective* 1 said about a road or route: full of twists and turns. 2 said about a story, argument, etc: difficult to understand because there are no simple connections between the different parts. ➤ **tortuously** *adverb*.

torture *noun* intense physical or mental suffering inflicted on somebody as a punishment or a way of forcing them to do something. ~ *verb* (**tortures, torturing, tortured**) to subject somebody to torture. ➤ **torturer** *noun*.

Tory *noun* (*plural* **Tories**) a member or supporter of the Conservative Party.

toss *verb* (**tosses, tossing, tossed**) 1 to throw something with a quick, light, or careless motion. 2 to move repeatedly from one position to another: *tossing and turning in bed*. **3** to jerk your head or hair up or back. **4** to flip a coin to decide an issue according to which face lands uppermost. ➤ **toss** *noun*.

toss-up *noun* **1** the tossing of a coin. **2** *informal* an even chance.

tot[1] *noun* (*plural* **tots**) **1** a small child. **2** a small amount of alcoholic spirit.

tot[2] *verb* (**tots, totting, totted**) (**tot up**) to add figures or amounts together.

total *noun* (*plural* **totals**) the amount or number that you get when you add smaller amounts or numbers together. ~ *adjective* **1** forming a total. **2** complete or absolute: *a total idiot*. ~ *verb* (**totals, totalling, totalled**) to be a total amount or figure. ➤ **totally** *adverb*.

totalitarian /toh ta li tair i an/ *adjective* said about a government: strictly controlling all aspects of people's lives and not allowing any political opposition. ➤ **totalitarianism** *noun*.

tote *verb* (**totes, toting, toted**) *informal* to carry something.

totem pole *noun* (*plural* **totem poles**) a tall wooden pole with religious and tribal symbols carved and painted on it, erected by some Native American peoples.

totter *verb* (**totters, tottering, tottered**) to walk in an unsteady way, as if you are about to fall over.

toucan /tooh kan/ *noun* (*plural* **toucans**) a large, brightly coloured tropical American bird with a very large bright beak.

touch *verb* (**touches, touching, touched**) **1** to put your hand, fingers, or other part of your body on or against something. **2** to come into contact with each other. **3** to use or consume something: *I haven't touched my pocket money at all*. **4** *informal* to rival something or somebody in ability or value: *No other player can touch him*. **5** (**touch on/upon**) to mention something or deal with it briefly. ~ *noun* (*plural* **touches**) **1** the sense that you get from physical contact with your hands, fingers, etc. **2** an act of touching something. **3** a detail. **4** (**a touch**) a bit; a little. ✻ **in** *or* **out of touch 1** having (or not having) regular contact with somebody. **2** having (or not having) up-to-date information. **touch up** to improve or perfect something by making small alterations.

touchdown *noun* (*plural* **touchdowns**) a landing by an aircraft.

touching *adjective* causing you to feel sympathy, pity, or sadness. ➤ **touchingly** *adverb*.

touchline *noun* (*plural* **touchlines**) in team games such as rugby and football, either of the lines that mark the sides of the field of play.

touchy *adjective* (**touchier, touchiest**) **1** said about a person: easily offended or made angry. **2** said about a situation: needing to be dealt with sensitively.

tough *adjective* **1** not easily worn out or damaged; hard-wearing. **2** not easily hurt, discouraged, or intimidated; strong. **3** said about food: not easily chewed. **4** said about a situation or activity: requiring great strength of character. **5** aggressive or threatening in behaviour. **6** strict or severe: *tough measures to deal with the problem*. ➤ **toughness** *noun*.

toughen *verb* (**toughens, toughening, toughened**) to make something or somebody tough.

tour *noun* (*plural* **tours**) **1** a journey that involves visits to several places. **2** a visit in which you see around a place and are given information about it. **3** a series of performances given in different places. ~ *verb* (**tours, touring, toured**) to make a tour.

tourism *noun* **1** the activity of visiting places, especially in foreign countries, for pleasure. **2** the work that travel companies do in organizing services for tourists.

tourist *noun* (*plural* **tourists**) somebody who is visiting a place on holiday.

tournament *noun* (*plural* **tournaments**) a championship in which matches are organized in rounds with winners progressing to later rounds.

tourniquet /toor ni kay/ *noun* (*plural* **tourniquets**) a strip of cloth tied tightly around an injured limb to stop bleeding.

tousled *adjective* said about hair: untidy.

tout *verb* (**touts, touting, touted**) to try to sell something. ~ *noun* (**touts**) somebody who offers tickets for an event at excessively high prices.

tow /toh/ *verb* (**tows, towing, towed**) to pull something along behind a vehicle. ✷ **in tow 1** being towed. **2** accompanying somebody.

towards or **toward** *preposition* **1** moving or situated in the direction of: *A man walked towards us; Their house is more towards the school.* **2** in relation to; about: *his attitude towards his work.* **3** leading to the achievement of an aim: *progress towards peace.* **4** as part of the payment of something: *He gave me £50 towards the rent.*

towel *noun* (*plural* **towels**) an absorbent cloth for drying your hands or body after washing.

towelling *noun* absorbent cloth used for making towels.

tower *noun* (*plural* **towers**) a tall narrow building or structure. ~ *verb* (**towers, towering, towered**) to be much taller than somebody or something nearby.

towering *adjective* impressively high or great.

town *noun* (*plural* **towns**) **1** an area with streets, houses, and businesses, larger than a village but smaller than a city. **2** the part of a town where most of the shops and businesses are.

township *noun* (*plural* **townships**) in South Africa, an area of poor housing where mainly non-white citizens live.

towpath *noun* (*plural* **towpaths**) a path along a canal.

toxic *adjective* **1** poisonous. **2** caused by a poison. ➤ **toxicity** *noun*.

toxin *noun* (*plural* **toxins**) a poisonous substance, especially in your body.

toy *noun* (*plural* **toys**) **1** something for a child to play with. **2** something designed for amusement, not for practical use. ~ *adjective* used as a toy. ~ *verb* (**toys, toying, toyed**) **1** (**toy with**) to handle something in an absent-minded way; to fiddle with something. **2** (**toy with**) to consider something as a possibility but without making a firm decision.

trace *noun* (*plural* **traces**) **1** an indication that something or somebody has been in a place. **2** a very small or barely detectable amount. ~ *verb* (**traces, tracing, traced**) **1** to try to find something or somebody by using evidence or remains. **2** to study the development or progress of something by working back towards the source of it. **3** to copy something by following its shape as seen through a sheet of paper laid on top of it. ➤ **traceable** *adjective*.

trace element *noun* (*plural* **trace elements**) *Science* a chemical element present in something in very small quantities.

trachea /tra **kee** a/ *noun* (*plural* **tracheae** /tra **kee** ee/ or **tracheas**) your windpipe, the tube in your throat that takes air into your lungs.

track *noun* (*plural* **tracks**) **1** a rough path or road. **2** a specially laid-out course, especially for racing. **3** the parallel rails of a railway. **4** (also **tracks**) an indication that something has been in a place, for example a line of footprints or the imprint of a tyre. **5** a single song or piece of music on an album. ~ *verb* (**tracks, tracking, tracked**) **1** to find something, especially an animal, by following the tracks it has left behind. **2** to monitor the progress or course of something, for example an item of post or an aircraft. ✻ **keep track of** to remain aware of how something is developing or where it is. **lose track of** to no longer be aware of how something is developing or where it is. **track down** to search for something or somebody until you find them. ➤ **tracker** *noun*.

track record *noun* (*plural* **track records**) a record of the past achievements of a person, organization, team, etc.

tracksuit *noun* (*plural* **tracksuits**) a warm loose-fitting suit worn especially by athletes when training.

tract[1] *noun* (*plural* **tracts**) a pamphlet on a religious or political subject.

tract[2] *noun* (*plural* **tracts**) **1** an area of land. **2** a system of connected body parts: *the digestive tract*.

traction *noun* **1** the friction that stops a moving object from slipping on a surface. **2** in medicine, treatment of fractures or deformities that involves putting tension on them and holding them in place.

tractor *noun* (*plural* **tractors**) a vehicle used for pulling farm machinery.

trade *noun* (*plural* **trades**) **1** the business of buying and selling goods. **2** a type of business. **3** a job that requires manual or mechanical skill, for example joinery or plumbing. ~ *verb* (**trades, trading, traded**) **1** to buy and sell goods. **2** to swap or exchange one thing for another. ➤ **trader** *noun*.

trademark *noun* (*plural* **trademarks**) **1** a legally registered name or distinctive symbol used by a particular company. **2** a feature or way of behaving that is firmly associated with somebody.

tradesman *noun* (*plural* **tradesmen**) a worker in a skilled trade.

trade union *or* **trades union** *noun* (*plural* **trade unions** *or* **trades unions**) an organization of workers formed for the purpose of protecting its members' interests. ➤ **trade unionism** *or* **trades unionism** *noun*, **trade unionist** *or* **trades unionist** *noun*.

tradition *noun* (*plural* **traditions**) **1** a belief, custom, or practice inherited from previous generations. **2** the handing down of information, beliefs, and customs from one generation to another.

traditional *adjective* **1** having existed as a belief, custom, or practice for many years. **2** doing things in the way they have been done for many years. ➤ **traditionalist** *noun and adjective*, **traditionally** *adverb*.

traffic *noun* **1** the vehicles, pedestrians, ships, or aircraft moving along a road or route. **2** the information or signals transmitted over a communications system. **3** trade in illegal merchandise such as drugs. ~ *verb* (**traffics, trafficking, trafficked**) to trade in something illegal or disreputable. ➤ **trafficker** *noun*.

traffic lights *plural noun* an automatically operated signal with coloured lights for controlling traffic.

traffic warden *noun* (*plural* **traffic wardens**) an official who enforces parking regulations.

tragedy *noun* (*plural* **tragedies**) **1** a disastrous or very sad event. **2** *Drama* a serious play in which terrible things happen to the main characters.

tragic *adjective* **1** very sad or disastrous. **2** *Drama* to do with tragedies. ➤ **tragically** *adverb*.

trail *noun* (*plural* **trails**) **1** a mark left by somebody or something that has passed. **2** a marked path through an area: *a nature trail*. ~ *verb* (**trails, trailing, trailed**) **1** to follow the trail of somebody or something in order to find them. **2** to drag, or drag something, along the ground behind you. **3** to walk somewhere heavily or wearily. **4** to do badly in relation to others. * **trail off/away** to become quieter or weaker.

trailer *noun* (*plural* **trailers**) **1** a wheeled vehicle, or part of a vehicle, designed to be towed. **2** a set of short excerpts from a film shown in advance to advertise it.

train¹ *noun* (*plural* **trains**) **1** a connected line of railway carriages or wagons pulled by a locomotive. **2** a moving line of people. **3** a connected series of ideas: *a train of thought*.

train² *verb* (**trains, training, trained**) **1** to teach somebody to do something. **2** to undergo teaching or instruction: *She's training to be a vet.* **3** to make yourself fit by doing physical exercises. **4** (**train on**) to aim something at an object. ➤ **training** *noun*.

trainee *noun* (*plural* **trainees**) somebody who is being trained for a job.

trainer *noun* (*plural* **trainers**) **1** a person who trains people or animals. **2** (**trainers**) sports shoes.

trait *noun* (*plural* **traits**) a quality or characteristic.

traitor *noun* (*plural* **traitors**) **1** somebody who betrays another person's trust. **2** somebody who commits treason. ➤ **traitorous** *adjective*.

trajectory *noun* (*plural* **trajectories**) the curve that a moving object follows through the air.

tram *or* **tramcar** *noun* (*plural* **trams** *or* **tramcars**) a passenger vehicle that runs on rails in streets.

tramp *noun* (*plural* **tramps**) **1** a homeless person who travels around and survives by begging or taking occasional jobs. **2** a long and tiring walk. ~ *verb* (**tramps, tramping, tramped**) to walk or tread heavily.

trample *verb* (**tramples, trampling, trampled**) **1** to crush or damage something by treading on it, or injure somebody by treading on them. **2** (**trample on/over**) to treat somebody in an unfair way that shows you do not care about them.

trampoline *noun* (*plural* **trampolines**) a piece of equipment for bouncing on, consisting of a sheet of strong fabric supported by springs in a frame. ➤ **trampolining** *noun*.

trance *noun* (*plural* **trances**) **1** a state of semiconsciousness, especially brought on by hypnotism. **2** a state of altered consciousness in which somebody experiences religious visions.

tranquil *adjective* calm, quiet, or peaceful. ➤ **tranquillity** *noun*, **tranquilly** *adverb*.

tranquillize *or* **tranquillise** *verb* (**tranquillizes, tranquillizing, tranquillized** *or* **tranquillises**, etc) to make a person or animal calm with drugs.

tranquillizer *or* **tranquilliser** *noun* (*plural* **tranquillizers** *or* **tranquillisers**) a drug used to calm a person or animal.

transaction *noun* (*plural* **transactions**) an instance of buying or selling something.

transatlantic *adjective* **1** crossing the Atlantic Ocean. **2** to do with people or places on the other side of the Atlantic Ocean.

transcend *verb* (**transcends, transcending, transcended**) to go beyond something that limits you or limits something in some way.

transcribe *verb* (**transcribes, transcribing, transcribed**) **1** to make a written copy or version of something. **2** to write something in a different form or language. **3** *Music* to write a tune in musical notation.

transcript *noun* (*plural* **transcripts**) a written or printed copy of something spoken.

transept *noun* (*plural* **transepts**) in a church that is built in the shape of a cross, either of the short sections that go out at the sides of the main long section or nave.

transfer *verb* (**transfers, transferring, transferred**) **1** to take something from one place or situation and put it in another. **2** to move to another job within the same organization. **3** to give somebody ownership or control of something. ~ *noun* (*plural* **transfers**) **1** an act of transferring something or somebody. **2** a picture that you put on a surface by rubbing or pressing it on. ➤ **transferable** *adjective*, **transference** *noun*.

transfixed *adjective* **1** unable to move because you are shocked or scared. **2** staring at something that is holding all your attention. **3** fixed by means of something sharp that has been pushed right through.

transform *verb* (**transforms, transforming, transformed**) to change something so that it has a completely different appearance or character. ➤ **transformation** *noun*.

transfusion *noun* (*plural* **transfusions**) a medical procedure in which a patient who has lost blood is given new blood.

transgression *noun* (*plural* **transgressions**) something bad that somebody has done. ➤ **transgressor** *noun*.

transient *adjective* **1** lasting a short time only. **2** staying or working in a place for a short time only. ➤ **transience** *noun*, **transiently** *adverb*.

transistor *noun* (*plural* **transistors**) *Science* a device that controls a flow of electricity inside a piece of equipment.

transit ✶ **in transit** in the process of travelling or being transported.

transition *noun* (*plural* **transitions**) the process of passing from one state or stage to another. ➤ **transitional** *adjective*.

transitive *adjective* *English* said about a verb: having an object. ➤ **transitivity** *noun*.

transitory *adjective* lasting a short time only.

translate *verb* (**translates, translating, translated**) to say or write a word, phrase, text, etc in another language. ➤ **translator** *noun*.

translation *noun* (*plural* **translations**) **1** a version of a word, phrase, text, etc in another language. **2** the act of producing a version of something in another language.

translucent *adjective* allowing some light to pass through, but not enough for objects beyond to be seen clearly. ➤ **translucence** *noun*.

transmission *noun* (*plural* **transmissions**) **1** a television or radio programme that is broadcast. **2** the act of sending or passing something, such as germs, from one person or place to another. **3** the parts of a vehicle that transmit power from the engine to an axle.

transmit *verb* (**transmits, transmitting, transmitted**) **1** to broadcast a television or radio programme. **2** to send or pass something, such as germs, from one person or place to another.

transmitter *noun* (*plural* **transmitters**) a device that sends out radio or television signals.

transparency *noun* (*plural* **transparen-**

transparent

cies) **1** the quality of being transparent. **2** a photographic slide.

transparent *adjective* **1** able to be seen through and allowing objects on the other side to be seen clearly. **2** easy to understand or realize. ➤ **transparently** *adverb*.

transpire *verb* (**transpires, transpiring, transpired**) **1** to become known. **2** to happen. **3** *Science* said about plants: to give off water vapour from the surfaces of leaves. ➤ **transpiration** *noun*.

transplant /trans plahnt/ *verb* (**transplants, transplanting, transplanted**) **1** to lift a plant from one place and plant it in another. **2** to transfer an organ from one person to another. ~ /trans plahnt/ *noun* (*plural* **transplants**) a surgical operation to transplant an organ. ➤ **transplantation** *noun*.

transport /trans pawt/ *noun* the activity of carrying goods or people from one place to another. ~ /trans pawt/ *verb* (**transports, transporting, transported**) to carry something from one place to another. ➤ **transportation** *noun*.

transpose *verb* (**transposes, transposing, transposed**) **1** to swap two things round so that each is in the position the other was in. **2** *Music* to write or play music in a different key. ➤ **transposition** *noun*.

transvestite *noun* (*plural* **transvestites**) somebody who dresses in clothes of the opposite sex. ➤ **transvestism** *noun*.

trap *noun* (*plural* **traps**) **1** a device for catching animals. **2** a plan or trick designed to catch a person unawares and put them at a disadvantage. **3** a situation from which it is difficult or impossible to escape. ~ *verb* (**traps, trapping, trapped**) **1** to catch an animal in a trap. **2** to put somebody in a position from which it is difficult to escape.

trapdoor *noun* (*plural* **trapdoors**) a lifting or sliding door covering an opening in a floor, ceiling, etc.

trapeze *noun* (*plural* **trapezes**) a swinging apparatus on which circus acrobats perform gymnastic displays.

trapezium *noun* (*plural* **trapeziums** or **trapezia**) *Maths* a flat four-sided shape with only two sides that are parallel.

trappings *noun* impressive things that go with an important position, such as a special uniform or a luxurious office.

trash *noun chiefly N American* **1** worthless things or things you throw away; rubbish. **2** books, paintings, films, etc of very poor quality. **3** a worthless person or worthless people. ~ *verb* (**trashes, trashing, trashed**) *informal* to destroy or vandalize something.

trauma *noun* (*plural* **traumas**) **1** a deeply shocking or upsetting experience. **2** in medicine, an injury or wound.

traumatic *adjective* deeply shocking or upsetting.

travel *verb* (**travels, travelling, travelled**) **1** to go on a journey. **2** to be transmitted from one place to another: *News travels fast.* ~ *noun* (*plural* **travels**) **1** the act of travelling. **2** (**travels**) a long journey, especially to distant or unfamiliar places.

travel agent *noun* (*plural* **travel agents**) a person or business that arranges trips and holidays for people.

traveller *noun* (*plural* **travellers**) **1** somebody who is on a journey. **2** a person who, as part of a group, travels from place to place, setting up a temporary community in each place and usually living an unconventional lifestyle.

traveller's cheque *noun* (*plural* **trav-**

eller's cheques) a cheque that you buy from a bank and exchange abroad for foreign currency.

traverse *verb* (**traverses, traversing, traversed**) *formal* to move or extend from one side of something to the other; to cross something.

travesty *noun* (*plural* **travesties**) a ridiculously bad example of something.

trawl *verb* (**trawls, trawling, trawled**) (**trawl through**) to search through a large number of things.

trawler *noun* (*plural* **trawlers**) a large fishing boat that pulls a huge net along the sea bed to catch fish.

tray *noun* (*plural* **trays**) a flat object used for carrying things on.

treacherous *adjective* **1** involving a betrayal of trust; disloyal. **2** on which it is easy to slip and fall. **3** with hidden dangers or hazards. ➤ **treacherously** *adverb*, **treachery** *noun*.

treacle *noun* thick sweet liquid made from sugar and used in cakes. ➤ **treacly** *adjective*.

tread *verb* (**treads, treading, trod, trodden** *or* **trod**) **1** to walk on something. **2** to press something down by walking on it: *They trod mud into the carpet.* ~ *noun* (*plural* **treads**) **1** the sound of somebody walking. **2** the upper horizontal part of a step. **3** the part of a tyre that makes contact with the road. * **tread water 1** to keep your body upright in water by moving your feet in a treading motion. **2** to stay in the same position without making progress.

treadmill *noun* (*plural* **treadmills**) **1** an exercise machine with a continuous moving belt that you walk or run on. **2** a monotonous routine.

treason *noun* the crime of betraying your country. ➤ **treasonable** *adjective*.

treasure *noun* (*plural* **treasures**) **1** coins, jewels, and other valuable objects from the past, discovered by somebody. **2** something that is extremely valuable. **3** *informal* a very helpful person, or somebody you love very much. ~ *verb* (**treasures, treasuring, treasured**) **1** to consider something to be very valuable or important. **2** to look after something very carefully.

treasurer *noun* (*plural* **treasurers**) the person in charge of the finances of a club or organization.

treasury *noun* (*plural* **treasuries**) **1** a store of money and valuable items. **2** (**the Treasury**) the government department in charge of finance and the economy.

treat *verb* (**treats, treating, treated**) **1** to deal with something or somebody in a certain way: *Prisoners are treated very well here.* **2** to give somebody medical care. **3** to present and discuss a subject. **4** to put a substance on something: *Has this furniture been treated for woodworm?* **5** to pay for something such as food, drink, or entertainment for somebody else to enjoy: *She treated me to a meal in a fancy restaurant.* ~ *noun* (*plural* **treats**) something enjoyable that you do not often do or have. * **my treat** I am paying for this for you.

treatise *noun* (*plural* **treatises**) a book or article on a serious subject.

treatment *noun* (*plural* **treatments**) **1** your behaviour towards somebody or something. **2** the medicine, therapy, or surgery involved in dealing with a patient. **3** the discussion or presentation of a subject: *the book's treatment of war.*

treaty *noun* (*plural* **treaties**) a formal agreement between countries.

treble *verb* (**trebles, trebling, trebled**) to increase, or increase something, to three times the original amount or number. ~ *adjective* **1** three times larger than the usual amount or number: *a treble whisky.* **2** *Music* higher than the usual pitch.

treble clef *noun* (*plural* **treble clefs**) *Music* a clef that shows that the note on the second lowest line is the G above middle C.

tree *noun* (*plural* **trees**) a large plant with a single thick woody stem and branches.

trek *noun* (*plural* **treks**) a long journey, especially on foot. ~ *verb* (**treks, trekking, trekked**) to go somewhere that involves a long tiring walk. ➤ **trekker** *noun*.

trellis *noun* (*plural* **trellises**) a frame of crisscrossing strips of wood used as a support for climbing plants.

tremble *verb* (**trembles, trembling, trembled**) **1** to shake slightly because you are scared, cold, or ill. **2** said about your voice: to have an unsteady quality because you are scared, cold, ill, or upset. ➤ **tremble** *noun*.

tremendous *adjective* **1** very great in size, amount, or intensity: *tremendous heat.* **2** *informal* very good or impressive. ➤ **tremendously** *adverb*.

tremolo /tre mo loh/ *noun* (*plural* **tremolos**) *Music* a trembling effect produced by repeating a note rapidly.

tremor *noun* (*plural* **tremors**) **1** an uncontrolled shaking in a part of your body, for example because you are ill or nervous. **2** *Geography* a movement of the earth that comes before or after an earthquake.

trench *noun* (*plural* **trenches**) a long narrow hole dug in the ground.

trenchant *adjective* expressing opinions in a very direct way. ➤ **trenchancy** *noun*.

trend *noun* (*plural* **trends**) **1** the attitude that most people have, or the way most people do something. **2** a general change in people's attitudes or way of doing something. **3** a current style or taste.

trendy *adjective* (**trendier, trendiest**) *informal* very fashionable.

trepidation *noun* feelings of fear or worry.

trespass *verb* (**trespasses, trespassing, trespassed**) to go onto somebody's property unlawfully or without permission. ~ *noun* the act of trespassing on somebody's property. ➤ **trespasser** *noun*.

tresses *plural noun* long hair.

trestle *noun* (*plural* **trestles**) a framework consisting typically of a horizontal bar with a pair of sloping legs at each end, designed as a support for a table top.

triad /trie ad/ *noun* (*plural* **triads**) **1** *Music* a chord consisting of a note and the third and fifth notes above it. **2** a group of three related people or things. **3** (*often* **Triad**) a Chinese secret society involved in organized crime.

trial *noun* (*plural* **trials**) **1** a legal examination of evidence in a court to decide whether an accused person is guilty of a crime. **2** a test carried out to check how well something, such as a new drug or treatment, performs. ✴ **on trial** undergoing trial in a court of law.

trial and error *noun* a process of trying out a number of methods to find which achieves the desired result.

triangle *noun* (*plural* **triangles**) **1** *Maths* a flat shape with three angles and three straight sides. **2** *Music* a percussion instrument consisting of a steel rod bent into a triangle, which you hit with a small metal rod to make the sound. ➤ **triangular** *adjective*.

triathlon /trie ath lon/ *noun* (*plural* **triathlons**) an athletics event in which athletes compete in long-distance swimming, cycling, and running.

tribe *noun* (*plural* **tribes**) in traditional

societies, a group of people, families, or clans with a common culture, dialect, religion, and ancestry, led by a chief. ➤ **tribal** *adjective*.

tribulation *noun* (*plural* **tribulations**) something bad that happens to somebody.

tribunal *noun* (*plural* **tribunals**) a committee appointed to settle a dispute.

tribune *noun* (*plural* **tribunes**) *History* an official of ancient Rome elected by the common people to protect their interests.

tributary *noun* (*plural* **tributaries**) *Geography* a stream or river that flows into a larger river or a lake.

tribute *noun* (*plural* **tributes**) **1** something that you say or give to show that you admire somebody or are grateful to them. **2** evidence of something good: *This memorial garden is a tribute to the children's hard work.*

trice ∗ **in a trice** very soon or immediately.

triceps /trie seps/ *noun* (*plural* **triceps**) the large muscle along the back of your upper arm.

trick *noun* (*plural* **tricks**) **1** something crafty that is intended to deceive or ridicule somebody. **2** something clever that you do to puzzle or entertain people. **3** a set of cards that you win in a single round of a card game. ~ *verb* (**tricks, tricking, tricked**) to deceive or cheat somebody. ➤ **trickery** *noun*.

trickle *verb* (**trickles, trickling, trickled**) **1** to flow in drops or a thin slow stream. **2** to go gradually or one by one. ➤ **trickle** *noun*.

tricky *adjective* (**trickier, trickiest**) **1** said about a problem or question: difficult to solve or answer. **2** said about a situation: difficult to deal with because of the hazards or sensitivities involved. **3** said about a person: inclined to be sly or deceitful.

tricycle *noun* (*plural* **tricycles**) a three-wheeled vehicle that you pedal.

tried *verb* past tense of TRY.

triennial *adjective* **1** lasting for three years. **2** occurring once every three years.

trifle *noun* (*plural* **trifles**) **1** a type of cold dessert made from layers of sponge cake, fruit, jelly, custard, and whipped cream. **2** something of little value or importance. ~ *verb* (**trifles, trifling, trifled**) (**trifle with**) to behave in a casual or silly way that shows you are not thinking carefully or considerately about something or somebody.

trifling *adjective* small or unimportant.

trigger *noun* (*plural* **triggers**) **1** a small lever that you pull to fire a gun. **2** something that causes an event or reaction. ~ *verb* (**triggers, triggering, triggered**) **1** to activate a mechanism. **2** to make something start to happen or exist.

trigonometry /tri go no me tri/ *noun Maths* the branch of mathematics that deals with the relations between the sides and angles of triangles.

trill *noun* (*plural* **trills**) **1** *Music* a warbling effect that you get when you alternate quickly between a main note and the one above it. **2** a bird's high-pitched warbling sound. ~ *verb* (**trills, trilling, trilled**) said about a bird: to make a warbling sound.

trillion *noun* (*plural* **trillions** *or* **trillion**) a million million (10^{12}) ➤ **trillionth** *adjective and noun*.

trilogy *noun* (*plural* **trilogies**) a set of three related books or films.

trim *verb* (**trims, trimming, trimmed**) **1** to cut bits off something to make it neater, shorter, or smaller. **2** to reduce the size of something, such as a budget. **3** to decorate some-

trimmings

thing with ribbons, lace, etc. ~ *noun* (*plural* **trims**) **1** an act of trimming something. **2** things such as ribbons and pieces of lace used for decorating something. **3** the upholstery and interior of a car. ~ *adjective* (**trimmer, trimmest**) **1** attractively slim. **2** neat and in good condition.

trimmings *plural noun* the traditional garnishes that accompany a dish or meal.

Trimurti /tri moor ti/ *noun* (**the Trimurti**) in Hinduism, the three gods Brahma, Vishnu, and Siva.

Trinity *noun* (**the Trinity**) in Christian belief, the Father, Son, and Holy Spirit, who together are God.

trinket *noun* (*plural* **trinkets**) a small inexpensive ornament or piece of jewellery.

trio *noun* (*plural* **trios**) **1** *Music* a group of three musicians or singers. **2** any group or set of three.

trip *noun* (*plural* **trips**) **1** a journey or outing. **2** the act of stumbling or falling. **3** a device that activates a mechanism. ~ *verb* (**trips, tripping, tripped**) **1** to catch your foot against something and stumble or fall. **2** (**trip up**) to make a mistake. **3** to make a device start or stop working.

tripe *noun* **1** the stomach of a cow or sheep used as food. **2** *informal* rubbish or nonsense.

triple *adjective* **1** consisting of three things or parts. **2** three times larger than the usual amount or number. ~ *verb* (**triples, tripling, tripled**) to increase, or increase something, to three times the original amount or number.

triple jump *noun* an athletics event in which a competitor takes a running start and then performs a hop, a step, and a jump in succession.

triplet *noun* (*plural* **triplets**) one of three babies born at the same time to the same mother.

tripod /trie pod/ *noun* (*plural* **tripods**) a three-legged stand for supporting something, such as a camera.

tripper *noun* (*plural* **trippers**) *informal* somebody who is on holiday or on an outing; a tourist.

trite *adjective* said about a remark: boring or meaningless because it is the kind of thing people usually say in a particular situation.

triumph /trie umf/ *noun* (*plural* **triumphs**) **1** a great success, victory, or achievement. **2** the feeling of happiness or satisfaction that you get when you are successful. *verb* (**triumphs, triumphing, triumphed**) to defeat somebody or something; to win.

triumphant /trie um fant/ *adjective* **1** defeating somebody or something; victorious. **2** expressing great happiness or pride at winning. ➤ **triumphantly** *adverb*.

triumvirate /trie um vi rat/ *noun* (*plural* **triumvirates**) a group of three rulers or powerful people.

trivia *plural noun* unimportant matters, details, or facts.

trivial *adjective* not very important or valuable; insignificant. ➤ **triviality** *noun*, **trivially** *adverb*.

trivialize *or* **trivialise** *verb* (**trivializes, trivializing, trivialized** *or* **trivialises,** etc) to treat something as unimportant or less important than it is. ➤ **trivialization** *or* **trivialisation** *noun*.

trod *verb* past tense and a past participle of TREAD.

trodden *verb* past participle of TREAD.

Trojan *noun* (*plural* **Trojans**) a person from the ancient city of Troy, situated in what is now Turkey.

Trojan Horse *noun* (*plural* **Trojan Horses**) somebody or something that undermines an organization from a position inside it.

Word History In a famous tale of Greek mythology, the Greeks had besieged the city of Troy for ten years but had been unable to capture it. They left a huge wooden horse outside the city, supposedly as a gift to the gods, and pretended to sail away. When the Trojans pulled the horse into the city, Greek soldiers hiding inside the horse jumped out and opened the gates to the Greek army.

troll *noun* (*plural* **trolls**) in Scandinavian folklore, an ugly dwarf or giant.

trolley *noun* (*plural* **trolleys**) **1** a small cart on wheels, used for carrying shopping or luggage. **2** a table on wheels, used for carrying food or drinks.

trombone *noun* (*plural* **trombones**) a brass musical instrument with a sliding part that you move to change the note. ➤ **trombonist** *noun*.

troop *noun* **1** (**troops**) soldiers. **2** a group of people or animals moving together. *verb* (**troops, trooping, trooped**) to go somewhere as a group.

trooper *noun* (*plural* **troopers**) a private in a cavalry or tank regiment.

trophy *noun* (*plural* **trophies**) **1** a cup, medal, plate, etc awarded to the winner of a contest. **2** an object that reminds you of a successful achievement.

tropic *noun* (*plural* **tropics**) *Geography* **1** (**tropic of Cancer**) a line of latitude 23½° north of the equator. **2** (**tropic of Capricorn**) a line of latitude 23½° south of the equator. **3** (**the tropics**) the region between these two lines of latitude.

tropical *adjective* **1** in or from the tropics. **2** said about weather or a climate: very hot and usually humid. ➤ **tropically** *adverb*.

trot *verb* (**trots, trotting, trotted**) **1** said about a horse: to run at a fairly slow speed, slower than a canter, with legs moving in diagonal pairs. **2** to run at a fairly slow pace. ~ *noun* (*plural* **trots**) **1** a trotting pace. **2** a ride at this pace. ✶ **on the trot** *informal* in succession.

trotter *noun* (*plural* **trotters**) the foot of a pig, used as food.

trouble *noun* (*plural* **troubles**) **1** difficulty, problems, or danger. **2** a problem or drawback. **3** angry or violent behaviour: *There was trouble at the football match.* **4** effort that you put into something, or inconvenience you suffer for the sake of something. ~ *verb* (**troubles, troubling, troubled**) **1** to make somebody upset or worried. **2** to disturb or inconvenience somebody. ✶ **ask for trouble** *informal* to do or say something that seems likely to lead to problems or punishment. **in trouble** about to be punished or suffer something unpleasant.

troubled *adjective* **1** worried. **2** involving a lot of problems.

troublemaker *noun* (*plural* **troublemakers**) somebody who deliberately annoys people or creates problems for them.

troubleshooter *noun* (*plural* **troubleshooters**) an experienced person brought in to solve a difficult problem.

troublesome *adjective* causing problems.

trough /trof/ *noun* (*plural* **troughs**) **1** a long shallow container from which farm animals eat or drink. **2** a low area between high areas, for example between waves or ridges.

trounce *verb* (**trounces, trouncing, trounced**) to defeat somebody decisively.

troupe *noun* (*plural* **troupes**) a touring group of actors or other performers.

trousers *plural noun* an outer garment that covers your body from the waist

trout *noun* (*plural* **trouts** *or* **trout**) a fish with a speckled body, related to the salmon.

trowel *noun* (*plural* **trowels**) **1** a small hand tool with a blade curving from side to side, used in gardening. **2** a small hand tool with a flat blade used to mix and handle plaster, cement, etc.

truant *noun* (*plural* **truants**) a pupil who stays away from school without permission. ✷ **play truant** to stay away from school without permission. ➤ **truancy** *noun*.

truce *noun* (*plural* **truces**) an agreement between enemies to stop fighting, often for a set period of time.

truck[1] *noun* (*plural* **trucks**) **1** a large road vehicle for carrying heavy loads; a lorry. **2** a railway wagon for carrying goods.

truck[2] ✷ **have no truck with** to refuse to have anything to do with a person or kind of person, or refuse to accept behaviour of a particular kind.

truculent /tru kew lint/ *adjective* refusing or objecting in an aggressive way. ➤ **truculence** *noun*, **truculently** *adverb*.

trudge *verb* (**trudges, trudging, trudged**) to walk with slow, tired steps. ~ *noun* (*plural* **trudges**) a long tiring walk.

true *adjective* (**truer, truest**) **1** based on fact or reality; not false or made up. **2** properly described as this; genuine: *a true friend; the true leader of our people*. **3** accurate: *a true measurement*. **4** loyal: *Be true to your principles*. ✷ **come true** to happen; to become real. ➤ **truly** *adverb*.

truffle *noun* (*plural* **truffles**) **1** a fungus that grows underground and is considered a great delicacy. **2** a rich chocolate sweet.

truism *noun* (*plural* **truisms**) a statement that is so obviously true that it is not worth making.

trump *noun* (*plural* **trumps**) in card games, a card of the suit that has been chosen to have a higher value than the other three suits. ~ *verb* (**trumps, trumping, trumped**) to defeat a card or player by playing a trump.

trumpet *noun* (*plural* **trumpets**) a brass musical instrument that is flared at the end and has three valves that you press to change the note. ~ *verb* (**trumpets, trumpeting, trumpeted**) **1** said about an elephant: to make its characteristic loud high sound. **2** to announce something impressive publicly. ➤ **trumpeter** *noun*.

truncated /trung kay tid/ *adjective* with a part missing from the end, and therefore shorter than it should be.

truncheon *noun* (*plural* **truncheons**) a short thick stick carried as a weapon by police officers.

trundle *verb* (**trundles, trundling, trundled**) to move slowly on wheels.

trunk *noun* (*plural* **trunks**) **1** the main stem of a tree. **2** the main central part of your body that does not include your head, arms, or legs. **3** the long flexible nose of an elephant. **4** a large box or case with a hinged lid, used for storing or transporting things. **5** (**trunks**) a swimming costume for a man or boy. **6** *N American* the boot of a car.

truss *noun* (*plural* **trusses**) a padded belt that a man wears to support his groin when he has a hernia. ~ *verb* (**trusses, trussing, trussed**) ✷ **truss up** to tie or wrap something up tightly.

trust *verb* (**trusts, trusting, trusted**) **1** to believe that somebody is honest and reliable, or that something is accurate, safe, or reliable. **2** to be confident about allowing somebody to do, have, or look after something: *Would you trust him with your money?* **3** to hope or assume something: *I trust you are well.* ~ *noun* (*plural* **trusts**) **1** confident belief in somebody's honesty or reliability, or in the accuracy, safety, or reliability of something. **2** an arrangement in which money or property is managed by one person on behalf of another. ➤ **trusted** *adjective*.

trustee *noun* (*plural* **trustees**) a person appointed to manage somebody's money or property.

trusting *adjective* showing great trust, often so much that you risk being exploited or hurt. ➤ **trustingly** *adverb*.

trustworthy *adjective* known to be honest, truthful, and reliable. ➤ **trustworthiness** *noun*.

trusty *adjective* (**trustier, trustiest**) *archaic or humorous* reliable; trustworthy.

truth *noun* (*plural* **truths**) **1** (**the truth**) the facts regarding something. **2** the state or quality of being true: *the truth of what you are saying.* **3** something that is true.

truthful *adjective* telling the truth. ➤ **truthfully** *adverb*, **truthfulness** *noun*.

try *verb* (**tries, trying, tried**) **1** to make an attempt to do something. **2** to do or taste something to see if you like it. **3** to test something to see if it is working. **4** to conduct the trial of an accused person. ~ *noun* (*plural* **tries**) **1** an attempt. **2** an experimental test of something. **3** in rugby, a score made by touching the ball down behind the opponent's goal line. ✶ **try on** to put on a piece of clothing to see if it is suitable.

trying *adjective* annoying, unpleasant, or tiring.

tryst /trist/ *noun* (*plural* **trysts**) *literary* a secret meeting between lovers.

tsar *or* **czar** *or* **tzar** /zah *or* tsah/ *noun* (*plural* **tsars** *or* **czars** *or* **tzars**) an emperor of Russia before 1917. ➤ **tsarist** *noun and adjective*.

tsetse fly /tetsi *or* tsetsi/ *noun* (*plural* **tsetse flies**) a blood-sucking African fly whose bite causes a serious illness.

T-shirt *noun* (*plural* **T-shirts**) a collarless short-sleeved casual top.

tsunami /tsoo nah mi/ *noun* (*plural* **tsunamis** *or* **tsunami**) *Geography* a huge sea wave that is produced by an underwater earthquake or volcanic eruption.

tub *noun* (*plural* **tubs**) **1** a large, low, wide container, for example for growing plants in. **2** a small plastic container with a lid, in which food is sold or stored.

tuba /tewba/ *noun* (*plural* **tubas**) a large brass musical instrument.

tubby *adjective* (**tubbier, tubbiest**) *informal* rather fat; podgy.

tuber *noun* (*plural* **tubers**) a fleshy underground stem on some plants, such as the potato.

tuberculosis /tewber kew loh sis/ *noun* a serious infectious disease in which abnormal lumps form in the lungs.

tubular *adjective* cylindrical and hollow like a tube.

TUC *abbreviation* Trades Union Congress, an association of trade unions.

tuck *verb* (**tucks, tucking, tucked**) **1** to push the loose end of something under a surface to hold it in place. **2** to put something into a safe place. **3** (**tuck in/up**) to settle somebody or yourself comfortably in bed with the covers firmly in place. ✶ **tuck away 1** to store or hide in a place that is difficult to find. **2** (**be tucked away**) to be in a quiet secluded place. **tuck in/into** to start eating food with enjoyment.

Tudor *adjective History* to do with the royal family that ruled England from 1485 until 1603.

Tuesday *noun* (*plural* **Tuesdays**) the third day of the week, the day that follows Monday.

tuft *noun* (*plural* **tufts**) a small cluster of long hairs, feathers, blades of grass, etc attached together at the base. ➤ **tufted** *adjective*, **tufty** *adjective*.

tug *verb* (**tugs, tugging, tugged**) to pull hard or suddenly. ~ *noun* (*plural* **tugs**) **1** a hard sudden pull. **2** (*also* **tugboat**) a small powerful boat used for towing larger boats and ships.

tug of war *noun* a sports event in which two teams pulling at opposite ends of a rope try to pull each other across a line in the middle.

tuition *noun* teaching or instruction.

tulip *noun* (*plural* **tulips**) a plant with a brightly coloured cup-shaped flower.

tumble *verb* (**tumbles, tumbling, tumbled**) **1** to fall in a rolling way. **2** said about a price, temperature, etc: to become much lower suddenly. ~ *noun* (*plural* **tumbles**) **1** a fall, especially with a rolling motion. **2** a sudden sharp drop in value or level.

tumbledown *adjective* said about a building, etc: in very bad condition.

tumbler *noun* (*plural* **tumblers**) a wide drinking glass with a flat bottom and straight sides.

tummy *noun* (*plural* **tummies**) *informal* your stomach or abdomen.

tumour *noun* (*plural* **tumours**) an abnormal growth in somebody's body that may be dangerous or harmless.

tumultuous /tew mul chew us/ *adjective* involving great enthusiasm, loud cheering, etc.

tuna *noun* (*plural* **tunas** *or* **tuna**) a large edible fish that lives in warm seas.

tundra *noun* (*plural* **tundras**) *Geography* a vast treeless area in Arctic and subarctic regions, where the soil beneath the surface is permanently frozen.

tune *noun* (*plural* **tunes**) *Music* **1** a series of musical notes; a melody. **2** a song. ~ *verb* (**tunes, tuning, tuned**) **1** to adjust a musical instrument so that it plays the correct notes. **2** to select a particular channel on a television or radio. **3** to adjust an engine so that it runs well. * **in** *or* **out of tune** playing or singing the correct (or wrong) notes. ➤ **tuning** *noun*.

tuneful *adjective* having a pleasant tune. ➤ **tunefully** *adverb*.

tungsten *noun* *Science* a hard grey-white metallic element with a high melting point, used especially for the filaments in light bulbs.

tunic *noun* (*plural* **tunics**) a simple loose sleeveless garment that covers the top part of your body.

tunnel *noun* (*plural* **tunnels**) **1** an underground passage that leads from one side of a hill, river, road, etc to the other. **2** a small underground passage dug by a burrowing animal. ~ *verb* (**tunnels, tunnelling, tunnelled**) to make a tunnel.

turban *noun* (*plural* **turbans**) a head-dress worn especially by Muslim and Sikh men, consisting of a long piece of cloth wound either round a cap or directly round the head.

turbine *noun* (*plural* **turbines**) a machine that produces electricity when a wheel is pushed round by the pressure of wind, water, steam, etc.

turbot *noun* (*plural* **turbots** *or* **turbot**) a large edible fish with a flat body.

turbulence *noun* strong sudden changes in the movement of air or water.

turbulent *adjective* **1** involving many changes, problems, or disagreements, and often involving violence. **2** said about the flow of air or water: involving strong sudden changes in direction. ➤ **turbulently** *adverb*.

tureen /tew reen/ *noun* (*plural* **tureens**) a large bowl with a lid, for serving soup.

turf *noun* (*plural* **turfs** *or* **turves**) **1** grass and the soil that its roots are in, forming a thick mat. **2** a piece of this grass cut from the ground. ~ *verb* (**turfs, turfing, turfed**) to cover an area with turf. * **turf out** to force somebody to leave.

turgid *adjective* said especially about a piece of writing: long and boring.

turkey *noun* (*plural* **turkeys**) a very large bird with a bald head, kept for its meat.

turmeric /ter mi rik/ *noun* a bright yellow spice used especially in Asian cookery.

turmoil *noun* an extremely confused or agitated state.

turn *verb* (**turns, turning, turned**) **1** to move round on a point or axis, as a wheel does. **2** to change position, or change the position of something, so as to be facing in a different direction or the opposite direction: *She turned to look at me.* **3** to go round a corner. **4** to become something: *The weather has turned cold.* ~ *noun* (*plural* **turns**) **1** a single revolution: *a turn of the wheel.* **2** a bend or curve in a path, road, river, etc. **3** an opportunity or obligation to do something: *It's your turn to drive.* * **take turns** *or* **take it in turns** to do something alternately or in sequence with other people.

turn against to become hostile towards somebody or something.

turn back to start to go in the opposite direction, towards where you came from. **turn down 1** to reduce the volume, level, etc of something. **2** not to accept something offered.

turn in 1 to hand something in; to submit work. **2** to hand over somebody, such as a suspected criminal, to the authorities. **turn into 1** to become something different: *The caterpillar turns into a butterfly.* **2** to make something or somebody become something different: *The experience turned him into a bitter person.* **turn off 1** to stop something from working by operating a switch. **2** to leave one road and join another. **turn on 1** to make something start working by operating a switch. **2** to attack somebody suddenly. **turn out 1** to turn off an electric light. **2** to be in the end: *The play turned out to be a success.* **3** to produce something in large numbers: *She turns out five novels a year.* **4** to come out: *The whole village turned out to meet him.* **turn over 1** to put something the other way up. **2** to give something to the proper authority. **turn up 1** to appear unexpectedly, especially after being lost. **2** to arrive. **3** to increase the volume, level, etc of something.

turning *noun* (*plural* **turnings**) a road, path, etc, that branches off another.

turnip *noun* (*plural* **turnips**) a plant with a round white root that is eaten as a vegetable.

turnout *noun* (*plural* **turnouts**) the number of people who attend an event.

turnover *noun* (*plural* **turnovers**) **1** the amount of money taken by a business in a particular period. **2** the rate at which a business loses and replaces its staff. **3** an individual pie made by folding a circle of pastry in half to enclose a filling.

turnstile *noun* (*plural* **turnstiles**) a gate with pivoting arms that turns to let one person in at a time.

turpentine *noun* a clear liquid distilled from the resin of conifer trees, used for cleaning paintbrushes.

turps *noun* *informal* = TURPENTINE.

turquoise /ter kwoyz/ *noun* (*plural* **turquoises**) **1** a light greenish blue colour. **2** a bluish green gemstone.

turret *noun* (*plural* **turrets**) **1** a little

turtle

tower on a building. **2** a revolving structure with a gun mounted on it, on a tank, warship, or aircraft. ➤ **turreted** *adjective*.

turtle *noun* (*plural* **turtles**) a reptile with a bony or leathery shell and flipper-shaped limbs used for swimming.

turves *noun* plural of TURF.

tusk *noun* (*plural* **tusks**) a very long tapering tooth, for example of an elephant, walrus, or boar, that is visible when the animal's mouth is closed.

tussle *noun* (*plural* **tussles**) a rough fight or argument.

tutor *noun* (*plural* **tutors**) **1** a teacher who teaches individuals or small groups privately. **2** a teacher in a university or college. ~ *verb* (**tutors, tutoring, tutored**) to act as a tutor to a person or group.

tutorial *noun* (*plural* **tutorials**) a small class taught at university or college.

tutu *noun* (*plural* **tutus**) a ballerina's short stiff skirt.

TV *noun* (*plural* **TVs**) **1** a television set. **2** the medium of television, or the television industry.

twang *noun* (*plural* **twangs**) **1** a sound like the one made when you pull a piece of elastic then let it go. **2** a nasal quality in the way somebody speaks. ~ *verb* (**twangs, twanging, twanged**) to make a twang.

tweak *verb* (**tweaks, tweaking, tweaked**) **1** to give something a sudden slight jerk or twist. **2** *informal* to make small adjustments to something to improve it. ➤ **tweak** *noun*.

twee *adjective* (**tweer, tweest**) pretty or pleasant in a way that seems slightly artificial or insincere.

tweed *noun* rough woollen fabric used especially for suits and coats.

tweet *verb* (**tweets, tweeting, tweeted**) said about a small bird: to make short high-pitched sounds; to chirp. ➤ **tweet** *noun*.

tweezers *plural noun* a small grabbing device used for plucking out hairs and handling small objects.

twelfth *adjective* having the position in a sequence corresponding to the number twelve. ~ *noun* (*plural* **twelfths**) one of twelve equal parts of something.

twelve *noun and adjective* (*plural* **twelves**) the number 12.

twenty *adjective and noun* (*plural* **twenties**) **1** the number 20. **2** (**the twenties**) the numbers 20 to 29. ➤ **twentieth** *adjective and noun*.

twice *adverb* **1** on two occasions. **2** in double the quantity or degree.

twiddle *verb* (**twiddles, twiddling, twiddled**) to twist or turn something lightly or absent-mindedly. ✳ **twiddle your thumbs** to have nothing to do.

twig *noun* (*plural* **twigs**) a small thin stick or branch.

twilight /twie liet/ *noun* **1** the soft shadowy light between sunset and full darkness. **2** the end of a period of time.

twin *noun* (*plural* **twins**) either of two children born to the same mother at the same time. ~ *adjective* said about two things: functioning as a pair: *twin beds*. ~ *verb* (**twins, twinning, twinned**) (**twin with**) to associate a town in one country officially with a town in another.

twine *noun* strong string.

twinge *noun* (*plural* **twinges**) **1** a sudden sharp stab of pain. **2** a sudden strong unpleasant feeling or thought.

twinkle *verb* (**twinkles, twinkling, twinkled**) said about a star, light, etc: to shine with a flickering or sparkling effect. ➤ **twinkle** *noun*.

twirl *verb* (**twirls, twirling, twirled**) to spin round rapidly. ➤ **twirl** *noun*.

twist verb (**twists, twisting, twisted**) **1** to turn the sides or ends of something in opposite directions, with a rotating motion. **2** to follow a curving or winding path. **3** to bend something out of its normal shape. **4** to injure a joint by turning it too quickly or too far. **5** to understand or repeat something somebody says in a slightly different way for malicious reasons. ~ noun (plural **twists**) **1** a twisting movement. **2** a sharp bend in the shape or course of something. **3** something unexpected that happens in a story.

twit noun (plural **twits**) informal a silly or stupid person.

twitch verb (**twitches, twitching, twitched**) **1** said about a part of your body: to move with a sudden jerky motion that you cannot control. **2** to move with a sudden jerky motion. ➤ **twitch** noun.

twitter verb (**twitters, twittering, twittered**) **1** said about a bird: to make a long series of short high-pitched sounds. **2** to talk quickly in a nervous or giggling way. ➤ **twitter** noun.

two noun and adjective (plural **twos**) the number 2.

two-dimensional adjective existing in only two dimensions rather than three; having only height and width.

two-faced adjective tending to change your opinion or allegiance depending on who you are talking to; insincere.

twosome noun (plural **twosomes**) a pair of people or things.

tycoon noun (plural **tycoons**) a rich and powerful businessperson.

tying verb present participle of TIE.

type noun (plural **types**) **1** a kind or sort. **2** a person or thing with particular characteristics: *He's the quiet type*. **3** printed characters, words, etc, or the style they are printed in: *italic type*. ~ verb (**types, typing, typed**) to write something using a typewriter or computer keyboard. ➤ **typing** noun.

typeface noun (plural **typefaces**) in printing, a particular style of type; a font.

typewriter noun (plural **typewriters**) a machine for writing that prints each letter directly onto paper as you type.

typhoid noun a serious infectious disease with symptoms including fever and severe diarrhoea, caused by bacteria in water or food.

typhoon noun (plural **typhoons**) a violent tropical storm.

typhus noun an infectious disease with symptoms of fever, delirium, and a dark red rash, caused by ticks or lice.

typical adjective **1** having the qualities or characteristics of a type of person or thing: *typical suburban houses*. **2** behaving in the usual annoying way: *It's typical of him to complain*. ➤ **typically** adverb.

typify verb (**typifies, typifying, typified**) to be a typical example of something.

typist noun (plural **typists**) a person whose job is typing letters and documents.

tyrannical adjective controlling people in a very strict and unfair or cruel way. ➤ **tyrannically** adverb.

tyrannosaurus or **tyrannosaurus rex** noun (plural **tyrannosauruses** or **tyrannosaurus rexes**) a very large flesh-eating dinosaur that walked on its hind legs.

tyranny noun (plural **tyrannies**) the very strict and unfair or cruel controlling of people.

tyrant noun (plural **tyrants**) a strict and unfair or cruel ruler.

tyre noun (plural **tyres**) a solid or inflated hollow rubber cushion fitted round a wheel.

tzar noun see TSAR.

ubiquitous /ew bi kwi tus/ *adjective* found everywhere.

udder *noun* (*plural* **udders**) the bag-like part underneath a cow's body that produces milk.

UFO *noun* (*plural* **UFOs**) = *unidentified flying object*, something that might be a spaceship from outer space.

ugly *adjective* (**uglier, ugliest**) unpleasant to see or hear. ➤ **ugliness** *noun*.

UK *abbreviation* United Kingdom.

ukulele /ew ku lay li/ *noun* (*plural* **ukuleles**) *Music* a musical instrument like a small four-stringed guitar.

ulcer *noun* (*plural* **ulcers**) an open sore on your skin or inside your body. ➤ **ulcerous** *adjective*.

ulna /ul na/ *noun* (*plural* **ulnas** *or* **ulnae** /ul nee/) *Science* the bone on the little finger's side of the forearm.

ulterior *adjective* secret and not expressed: *an ulterior motive*.

ultimate *adjective* **1** last in a series; final. **2** greatest. ~ *noun* (**the ultimate**) the most extreme or important of its kind. ➤ **ultimately** *adverb*.

ultimatum /ul ti may tum/ *noun* (*plural* **ultimatums** *or* **ultimata**) a final demand which is made before taking strong action against somebody.

ultramarine *noun* a vivid deep blue.

ultrasonic *adjective Science* said about sound waves: at a higher frequency that humans can hear.

ultrasound *noun* ultrasonic waves or vibrations, used in medical treatments and tests.

ultraviolet *adjective Science* said about light or radiation: beyond the range of colours that humans can see, between violet and X-rays.

umbilical cord /um bi li kl kawd/ *noun* (*plural* **umbilical cords**) a rope-like tube that connects an unborn baby to its mother's body, supplying food and oxygen.

umbrella *noun* (*plural* **umbrellas**) a folding circular object with a long handle in the centre, for holding over yourself when it rains.

umlaut /oom lowt/ *noun* (*plural* **umlauts**) a mark ¨ placed over vowels in German to indicate a change in pronunciation.

umpire *noun* (*plural* **umpires**) a referee in some sports. ~ *verb* (**umpires, umpiring, umpired**) to act as umpire for a game or match.

umpteen *adjective and noun informal* very many. ➤ **umpteenth** *adjective*.

UN *abbreviation* United Nations.

unable *adjective* not able; incapable.

unacceptable *adjective* **1** bad; not satisfactory. **2** not allowed. ➤ **unacceptably** *adverb*.

unaccustomed *adjective* **1** not usual. **2** (**unaccustomed to**) not used to something.

unadulterated /un a dul ti ray tid/ *adjective* not mixed with anything bad; pure.

unaided *adjective* without help.

unanimous /ew na ni mus/ *adjective*

with the agreement of everyone. ➤ **unanimity** *noun*, **unanimously** *adverb*.

unapproachable *adjective* unfriendly or difficult to talk to.

unarmed *adjective* carrying no weapons.

unassuming *adjective* modest; not looking for attention.

unattached *adjective* not married or in a relationship with somebody.

unattended *adjective* not being looked after or watched.

unauthorized *or* **unauthorised** *adjective* done without official permission.

unavoidable *adjective* impossible to prevent. ➤ **unavoidably** *adverb*.

unaware *adjective* not aware of something: *He was unaware of the danger*.

unawares *adverb* unexpectedly.

unbalanced *adjective* **1** mentally ill. **2** not fair or balanced.

unbearable *adjective* too unpleasant or painful to bear. ➤ **unbearably** *adverb*.

unbeatable *adjective* impossible to beat; better than any others.

unbecoming *adjective* not attractive or flattering.

unbeknown *adjective* (**unbeknown to**) without a particular person knowing.

unbelievable *adjective* **1** impossible to believe. **2** extraordinary. ➤ **unbelievably** *adverb*.

unbiased *adjective* fair; not one-sided.

unborn *adjective* not yet born.

unbridled *adjective* uncontrolled.

unbridgeable *adjective* said about a difference of opinions, etc: very great and unlikely to be resolved.

unbroken *adjective* not broken or interrupted.

unburden *verb* (**unburdens, unburdening, unburdened**) to free yourself of your fears or worries by telling somebody else about them.

uncalled-for *adjective* not necessary or pleasant.

uncanny *adjective* (**uncannier, uncanniest**) strange or mysterious. ➤ **uncannily** *adverb*.

uncertain *adjective* **1** not definitely known or trusted. **2** not confident or sure. * **in no uncertain terms** strongly and clearly. ➤ **uncertainly** *adverb*, **uncertainty** *noun*.

uncle *noun* (*plural* **uncles**) the brother of your father or mother, or the husband of your aunt.

uncomfortable *adjective* not comfortable or not making you feel comfortable. ➤ **uncomfortably** *adverb*.

uncommon *adjective* unusual or remarkable. ➤ **uncommonly** *adverb*.

uncompromising *adjective* not willing to compromise. ➤ **uncompromisingly** *adverb*.

unconcerned *adjective* not interested or concerned.

unconditional *adjective* without any conditions or without asking for anything in return. ➤ **unconditionally** *adverb*.

unconscious *adjective* **1** without knowing or being aware. **2** having lost consciousness. ➤ **unconsciously** *adverb*, **unconsciousness** *noun*.

uncontrollable *adjective* not able to be controlled. ➤ **uncontrollably** *adverb*.

unconventional *adjective* different from the behaviour or ideas of most people. ➤ **unconventionally** *adverb*.

uncouth *adjective* not polite in speech or behaviour.

uncover *verb* (**uncovers, uncovering, uncovered**) **1** to take the cover off something. **2** to discover something.

undaunted *adjective* not put off or worried by danger or difficulty.

undecided *adjective* **1** not having decided. **2** not yet decided; without a result.

undeniable *adjective* obviously true. ➤ **undeniably** *adverb*.

under *adverb* below or beneath something. ~ *preposition* **1** lower than. **2** less than. **3** controlled, run or ruled by. **4** undergoing a particular action or process: *under repair*. **5** in the group or category of: *under this heading*. **6** covered or protected by.

under-age *adjective* below the legal age for doing something.

underarm *adjective and adverb* keeping the hand below shoulder level.

undercarriage *noun* (*plural* **undercarriages**) the part of an aircraft that includes the wheels and supports it on the ground.

underclass *noun* (*plural* **underclasses**) the poorest people at the bottom of society.

undercoat *noun* (*plural* **undercoats**) a first coat of paint you put on something before you put on the final coat.

underclothes *plural noun* = UNDERWEAR.

undercover *adjective and adverb* working secretly to get information for the police or government.

undercurrent *noun* (*plural* **undercurrents**) **1** a hidden feeling or tendency. **2** a current underneath the surface of the sea, etc.

undercut *verb* (**undercuts, undercutting, undercut**) to charge less for a product than somebody else.

underdeveloped *adjective* said about a region: with little modern industry or technology.

underdog *noun* (*plural* **underdogs**) a competitor who is expected to lose in a contest.

underdone *adjective* not fully cooked.

underestimate /un der e sti mayt/ *verb* (**underestimates, underestimating, underestimated**) **1** to estimate a size or amount to be less than it actually is. **2** to imagine somebody to be less capable or powerful than they actually are. ~ /un der e sti mat/ *noun* (*plural* **underestimates**) an estimate that is too low.

underfoot *adverb* **1** on the ground. **2** in somebody's way.

undergo *verb* (**undergoes, undergoing, underwent, undergone**) to experience something, or to suffer something unpleasant.

undergraduate *noun* (*plural* **undergraduates**) a student studying for their first degree at a college or university.

underground *adjective and adverb* **1** below the ground. **2** in hiding or in secret. ~ *noun* (**the underground**) **1** a secret group fighting against the government of their country or an enemy occupying it. **2** an underground railway.

undergrowth *noun* plants growing on the ground under trees.

underhand *adjective* done secretly or by tricking people.

underlie *verb* (**underlies, underlying, underlay, underlain**) to be the hidden cause or source of something.

underline *verb* (**underlines, underlining, underlined**) **1** to put a line underneath a word or words. **2** to emphasize something.

underling *noun* (*plural* **underlings**) somebody who works for another person and is less important than them.

undermine *verb* (**undermines, undermining, undermined**) to weaken or wear something away gradually.

underneath *preposition and adverb* **1** below or under. **2** in a hidden way. ~ *noun* the bottom part or surface of something.

underpants *plural noun* a piece of underwear covering your bottom and hips.

underpass noun (plural **underpasses**) a tunnel or road that goes under a road or railway.

underpin verb (**underpins, underpinning, underpinned**) to strengthen and support something.

underprivileged adjective without the advantages, money, and opportunities that most people have.

underrate verb (**underrates, underrating, underrated**) to undervalue or underestimate something or somebody.

undersigned noun (**the undersigned**) the person or people who have signed their names at the end of a document.

understand verb (**understands, understanding, understood**) **1** to realize or know the meaning of something or things about it. **2** to assume something. **3** to sympathize with somebody or accept their feelings.

understandable adjective **1** normal and reasonable. **2** capable of being understood. ➤ **understandably** adverb.

understanding noun **1** knowledge. **2** the ability to understand things. **3** an informal agreement between people. **4** tolerance or sympathy. adjective tolerant or sympathetic.

understatement noun (plural **understatements**) a way of describing something which is not as strong or extreme as the full truth.

understood verb past tense of UNDERSTAND.

understudy noun (plural **understudies**) Drama an actor who learns another actor's part and can play that part if necessary.

undertake verb (**undertakes, undertaking, undertook, undertaken**) **1** to accept or carry out a task or responsibility. **2** to promise to do something.

undertaker noun (plural **undertakers**) somebody who prepares dead bodies for burial or cremation and organizes funerals.

undertaking noun (plural **undertakings**) **1** a serious task or project. **2** a promise.

undertone noun (plural **undertones**) **1** a low, quiet voice. **2** a quality or feeling you can sense although it is not obvious.

underwater adjective and adverb situated or used below the surface of the water.

underwear noun clothing that you wear under your other clothes, next to your skin.

underweight adjective weighing less than the proper or normal weight.

underwent verb past tense of UNDERGO.

undesirable adjective unwanted or unpleasant.

undistinguished adjective not especially good or unusual.

undivided adjective complete; total.

undo verb (**undoes, undoing, undid, undone**) **1** to unfasten or open something. **2** to reverse something that has been done.

undoing noun an action, event, or characteristic that brings somebody ruin or disgrace: *His arrogance was his undoing.*

undoubted adjective certain or genuine. ➤ **undoubtedly** adverb.

undress verb (**undresses, undressing, undressed**) to take off your clothes, or to remove another person's clothes.

undue adjective too much; more than necessary.

undulate verb (**undulates, undulating, undulated**) to rise and fall in waves. ➤ **undulation** noun.

unduly adverb too much.

undying adjective eternal; never-ending.

unearth *verb* (**unearths, unearthing, unearthed**) **1** to dig something up from the ground. **2** to find something after searching for it.

unearthly *adjective* **1** weird or mysterious. **2** *informal* outrageous: *at an unearthly hour.*

uneasy *adjective* (**uneasier, uneasiest**) nervous, worried, or awkward. ➤ **uneasily** *adverb.*

unemployed *adjective* not having a paid job.

unemployment *noun* the state of being unemployed, or the number of people who are unemployed.

unending *adjective* never ending, or seeming never to end.

unequal *adjective* **1** not equal. **2** not balanced or fair. ➤ **unequally** *adverb.*

unequalled *adjective* better than any other.

unequivocal /un i kwi vo kl/ *adjective* clear; not ambiguous. ➤ **unequivocally** *adverb.*

uneven *adjective* **1** not level or smooth. **2** not regular or consistent. ➤ **unevenly** *adverb,* **unevenness** *noun.*

uneventful *adjective* without anything important or interesting happening. ➤ **uneventfully** *adverb.*

unexceptional *adjective* ordinary. ➤ **unexceptionally** *adverb.*

unexpected *adjective* not expected. ➤ **unexpectedly** *adverb.*

unfailing *adjective* constant or continuous. ➤ **unfailingly** *adverb.*

unfair *adjective* not fair or just. ➤ **unfairly** *adverb,* **unfairness** *noun.*

unfaithful *adjective* **1** not loyal. **2** not sexually faithful to your husband, wife, or partner. ➤ **unfaithfully** *adverb.*

unfamiliar *adjective* strange; not well known.

unfasten *verb* (**unfastens, unfastening, unfastened**) to untie something.

unfavourable *adjective* not good or promising. ➤ **unfavourably** *adverb.*

unfeeling *adjective* unkind, unsympathetic, or cruel.

unfit *adjective* **1** unsuitable. **2** not physically fit.

unfold *verb* (**unfolds, unfolding, unfolded**) **1** to open and spread out something that is folded, such as a map. **2** to become known, or to make something known to people, gradually: *Were you surprised at how the story unfolded?*

unforeseen *adjective* not predicted or expected.

unforgettable *adjective* too good or bad to be forgotten. ➤ **unforgettably** *adverb.*

unforgivable *adjective* too bad to be forgiven. ➤ **unforgivably** *adverb.*

unfortunate *adjective* **1** unlucky. **2** not suitable or appropriate. ➤ **unfortunately** *adverb.*

unfounded *adjective* untrue, or without any evidence.

unfriendly *adjective* not friendly.

unfurl *verb* (**unfurls, unfurling, unfurled**) to unroll or open something.

ungainly *adjective* (**ungainlier, ungainliest**) clumsy or awkward. ➤ **ungainliness** *noun.*

ungodly *adjective* (**ungodlier, ungodliest**) **1** not religious. **2** *informal* unreasonable or inconvenient. ➤ **ungodliness** *noun.*

ungracious *adjective* rude or impolite. ➤ **ungraciously** *adverb.*

ungrateful *adjective* not grateful. ➤ **ungratefully** *adverb.*

unhappy *adjective* (**unhappier, unhappiest**) **1** not happy; sad. **2** unfortunate. **3** unsuitable: *It was perhaps an unhappy choice of expression.* ➤ **unhappily** *adverb,* **unhappiness** *noun.*

unhealthy *adjective* (**unhealthier,**

unhealthiest) **1** not in good health. **2** likely to damage your health. ➤ **unhealthily** adverb.

unheard-of adjective not known before; extraordinary.

unhelpful adjective not helpful; uncooperative. ➤ **unhelpfully** adverb.

unhinged adjective mentally ill; crazy.

unhygienic adjective not hygienic.

unicorn noun (plural **unicorns**) a mythical white horse with a horn on its forehead.

unidentified adjective not known or identified.

uniform noun (plural **uniforms**) clothes of the same design which all the members of a school, army, or other group wear. ~ adjective all the same in character or appearance. ➤ **uniformity** noun, **uniformly** adverb.

unify verb (**unifies, unifying, unified**) to make several things into a single thing.

unilateral adjective done or agreed to by only one person or group. ➤ **unilaterally** adverb.

unimportant adjective with little or no importance.

uninhabited adjective with no inhabitants.

unintelligible adjective impossible to understand. ➤ **unintelligibly** adverb.

unintentional adjective not done deliberately. ➤ **unintentionally** adverb.

uninterested adjective not interested or concerned.

Usage Note Do not confuse *uninterested* with *disinterested*, which means 'not biased'.

uninterrupted adjective continuous.

union noun (plural **unions**) **1** the act of joining two or more things into one. **2** = TRADE UNION.

Union Jack noun (plural **Union Jacks**) the national flag of the United Kingdom.

unique /ew neek/ adjective **1** being the only one, with nothing else like it. **2** (**unique to**) found in only one person, place, etc. ➤ **uniquely** adverb.

Usage Note If something is *unique*, it is the only one of its kind. It cannot therefore be 'rather unique', 'very unique', or 'more unique' than something else. It is either unique or it isn't.

unisex adjective suitable for either sex.

unison /ew ni son/ noun Music several parts being performed in harmony at the same time. ✳ **in unison** all together.

unit noun (plural **units**) **1** a single thing or group that is also part of a larger whole thing. **2** a machine, group, or department with one particular function: *an air-conditioning unit; an intensive care unit*. **3** Maths a whole number less than 10. **4** a fixed amount used as a standard of measurement.

unite verb (**unites, uniting, united**) to join together, or make people or things join together, into a single unit or group. ➤ **united** adjective.

unity noun (plural **unities**) the state of being joined together as one thing. **2** agreement.

universal adjective including, from, for, or to do with everybody or everything in the world or in a particular group. ➤ **universally** adverb.

universe noun (plural **universes**) the stars, planets, space, and everything that exists.

university noun (plural **universities**) a place where students work for degrees or higher qualifications, and where academic research is done.

unjust adjective not just or fair. ➤ **unjustly** adverb.

unkempt adjective untidy or scruffy.

unkind adjective not kind. ➤ **unkindly** adverb, **unkindness** noun.

unknown

unknown *adjective* **1** not known. **2** not famous.

unladylike *adjective* said about a woman or girl: not polite or dignified.

unlawful *adjective* against the law. ➤ **unlawfully** *adverb*.

unleaded *adjective* said about petrol: not containing lead, and so causing less pollution.

unleash *verb* (**unleashes, unleashing, unleashed**) to release something that was previously controlled or tied up.

unleavened /un le vind/ *adjective* said about bread: not containing yeast or any substance to make it rise.

unless *conjunction* if not; except when.

unlike *preposition* **1** different from or contrasting with. **2** not typical of. *adjective* not similar; different.

unlikely *adjective* (**unlikelier, unlikeliest**) not likely to exist, to happen, or to be true. ➤ **unlikelihood** *noun*.

unlimited *adjective* not limited; as much or as many as you like.

unload *verb* (**unloads, unloading, unloaded**) to remove cargo from a vehicle, ship, or aircraft.

unlock *verb* (**unlocks, unlocking, unlocked**) to open the lock of a door or container.

unlucky *adjective* (**unluckier, unluckiest**) having or causing bad luck. ➤ **unluckily** *adverb*.

unmanageable *adjective* difficult or impossible to control.

unmarried *adjective* not married; single.

unmask *verb* (**unmasks, unmasking, unmasked**) to reveal what somebody or something is really like.

unmentionable *adjective* not fit to be mentioned; very bad or rude.

unmissable *adjective* too easy or too good to miss.

unmistakable *adjective* clear or obvious; that cannot be mistaken. ➤ **unmistakably** *adverb*.

unmitigated *adjective* complete and absolute.

unmoved *adjective* not affected emotionally by something.

unnatural *adjective* not natural or normal. ➤ **unnaturally** *adverb*.

unnecessary *adjective* not necessary. ➤ **unnecessarily** *adverb*.

unnerve *verb* (**unnerves, unnerving, unnerved**) to make somebody feel uncertain or frightened.

unobtrusive *adjective* not too noticeable or obvious. ➤ **unobtrusively** *adverb*.

unoccupied *adjective* **1** not lived in. **2** not busy.

unofficial *adjective* not authorized or official. ➤ **unofficially** *adverb*.

unorthodox *adjective* not conventional in the things you do or believe.

unpack *verb* (**unpacks, unpacking, unpacked**) to remove the contents of a suitcase, car, etc.

unpaid *adjective* **1** not yet paid. **2** not receiving or involving payment.

unpalatable *adjective* **1** unpleasant to taste. **2** unpleasant to accept.

unparalleled *adjective* greater, better, or worse than any other; unique.

unpleasant *adjective* not pleasant or agreeable. ➤ **unpleasantly** *adverb*, **unpleasantness** *noun*.

unplug *verb* (**unplugs, unplugging, unplugged**) to disconnect an electrical device by taking its plug out of the socket.

unpopular *adjective* not generally liked or approved of.

unprecedented /un pre si den tid/ *adjective* never done or experienced before.

unpredictable *adjective* not predictable; changeable. ➤ **unpredictably** *adverb*.

unprepared *adjective* not ready or prepared.

unpretentious *adjective* not pretentious; modest.

unprintable *adjective* too controversial or offensive to be printed.

unprofessional *adjective* not professional or of a professional standard. ➤ **unprofessionally** *adverb*.

unprofitable *adjective* not producing a profit.

unprovoked *adjective* done to somebody who is doing or has done nothing to cause it: *an unprovoked attack*.

unqualified *adjective* **1** without qualifications or the necessary qualifications. **2** complete: *an unqualified success*.

unravel *verb* (**unravels, unravelling, unravelled**) **1** to undo something knitted or tangled into one long thread, or to come undone in this way. **2** to solve a problem or mystery.

unreal *adjective* **1** not real. **2** strange or dream-like.

unrealistic *adjective* not practical, or not considering things as they really are. ➤ **unrealistically** *adverb*.

unreasonable *adjective* **1** not reasonable or fair. **2** excessive. ➤ **unreasonably** *adverb*.

unreliable *adjective* not able to be relied on. ➤ **unreliability** *noun*, **unreliably** *adverb*.

unremitting *adjective* constant; never stopping or lessening.

unrepeatable *adjective* too shocking or offensive to repeat.

unrequited *adjective* said about love: not felt and shown in return.

unreserved *adjective* **1** complete; without any doubt. **2** not reserved. ➤ **unreservedly** *adverb*.

unrest *noun* riots, protests, or angry disobedient behaviour.

unrivalled *adjective* better than all others.

unroll *verb* (**unrolls, unrolling, unrolled**) to open out something that is rolled up.

unruly *adjective* (**unrulier, unruliest**) difficult to control or manage. ➤ **unruliness** *noun*.

unsatisfactory *adjective* not good enough.

unsaturated *adjective* Science said about a fat in food: containing substances (fatty acids) that do not create unhealthy cholesterol in your body.

unscathed *adjective* not harmed or injured.

unscrew *verb* (**unscrews, unscrewing, unscrewed**) to remove something by twisting it or by taking out screws.

unscrupulous *adjective* not worried about whether what you do is morally right or legal. ➤ **unscrupulously** *adverb*.

unseemly *adjective* said about somebody's behaviour or taste: not proper or suitable.

unseen *adjective* not seen or noticed.

unsettle *verb* (**unsettles, unsettling, unsettled**) to disturb or upset somebody or something.

unsettled *adjective* **1** anxious or restless. **2** said about the weather: changeable. **3** not decided or solved.

unshakeable *adjective* said about a belief: that cannot be changed. ➤ **unshakeably** *adverb*.

unshaven *adjective* not having shaved.

unsightly *adjective* (**unsightlier, unsightliest**) ugly.

unskilled *adjective* not having or needing a special skill.

unsociable *adjective* not keen on meeting and spending time with other people. ➤ **unsociably** *adverb*.

unsocial *adjective* **1** unsociable. **2** said about working hours: involving work when most people are not working.

unsolicited /un so li si tid/ *adjective* not ordered or asked for.

unsound *adjective* **1** not strong or fixed. **2** not valid or true.

unspeakable *adjective* too bad or shocking to describe. ➤ **unspeakably** *adverb*.

unspoilt *adjective* said about a place: not spoilt by modern development.

unstable *adjective* **1** not firmly fixed. **2** likely to change suddenly and dangerously.

unsteady *adjective* (**unsteadier, unsteadiest**) not steady. ➤ **unsteadily** *adverb*.

unstick *verb* (**unsticks, unsticking, unstuck**) to loosen or separate something that is stuck. * **come unstuck** to go wrong.

unsuccessful *adjective* not successful. ➤ **unsuccessfully** *adverb*.

unsuitable *adjective* not suitable or appropriate. ➤ **unsuitability** *noun*, **unsuitably** *adverb*.

unsung *adjective* not praised or famous: *an unsung hero*.

unsure *adjective* not certain or confident.

unsuspecting *adjective* unaware of something that is happening or about to happen.

untangle *verb* (**untangles, untangling, untangled**) **1** to remove the tangles from something. **2** to make something less confusing.

untenable *adjective* said about an opinion or situation: impossible to defend or support.

unthinkable *adjective* impossible to imagine or to consider seriously.

untidy *adjective* (**untidier, untidiest**) not neat; messy or disordered. ➤ **untidily** *adverb*, **untidiness** *noun*.

untie *verb* (**unties, untied, untying**) to undo something that is tied.

until *preposition and conjunction* up to a specific time or event.

untimely *adjective* happening before the natural or proper time.

unto *preposition archaic* to a place or person.

untold *adjective* too much or many to list or to describe.

untouchable *adjective* **1** impossible to beat or equal. **2** not suitable or possible to touch. ~ *noun* (*plural* **untouchables**) a member of the lowest Hindu caste.

untouched *adjective* not influenced or affected by something.

untoward *adjective* unexpected and unhelpful.

untrue *adjective* **1** false. **2** not loyal.

untrustworthy *adjective* unable to be trusted.

unused *adjective* **1** not used; new. **2** (**unused to**) not familiar with or used to something.

unusual *adjective* uncommon or rare; not ordinary. ➤ **unusually** *adverb*.

unveil *verb* (**unveils, unveiling, unveiled**) to remove a covering from something or reveal it to the public.

unwanted *adjective* not wanted or needed.

unwarranted *adjective* not necessary or deserved.

unwary *adjective* not careful or aware of danger. ➤ **unwarily** *adverb*.

unwelcome *adjective* not welcome or wanted.

unwell *adjective* ill.

unwieldy *adjective* (**unwieldier, unwieldiest**) large and awkward to move or deal with.

unwilling *adjective* not willing; reluctant. ➤ **unwillingly** *adverb*.

unwind *verb* (**unwinds, unwinding, unwound**) **1** to undo something that is wound up. **2** to relax.

unwise *adjective* not wise or sensible. ➤ **unwisely** *adverb*.

unwitting *adjective* **1** not intended. **2** unaware. ➤ **unwittingly** *adverb*.

unworkable *adjective* not practical.

unwound *verb* past tense and past participle of UNWIND.

unwrap *verb* (**unwraps, unwrapping, unwrapped**) to take the wrapping off something.

unwritten *adjective* said about a rule: generally followed and accepted, but not official.

unzip *verb* (**unzips, unzipping, unzipped**) 1 to undo something that is zipped up. 2 *ICT* to return a compressed computer file to its full size ready to use.

up *adverb and preposition* 1 at or towards a higher position, level, number, price, or amount. 2 to or at the top. ~ *adverb* 1 out of bed: *get up*. 2 higher or into an upright position: *stand up*. 3 to a better position: *He's certainly going up in the world.* 4 into existence or public notice: *They set up their own business.* ~ *adjective* 1 going on; happening: *What's up?* 2 at an end: *Time's up.* 3 ready: *Tea's up.* 4 *ICT* said about a computer system: functioning normally. * **up against 1** touching. 2 having to face or deal with. **up to 1** until. 2 good enough for or capable of doing something. 3 the responsibility or choice of somebody.

up-and-coming *adjective* likely to succeed.

upbringing *noun* the way you are brought up by your parents when you are a child.

update *verb* (**updates, updating, updated**) to give somebody the latest information on something, or to make something up-to-date. ~ *noun* (*plural* **updates**) a piece of new information.

up-front *adverb* in advance or at the beginning. ~ *adjective* honest and open.

upgrade /up grayd/ *verb* (**upgrades, upgrading, upgraded**) to improve the standard or quality of something, or to raise somebody's grade or level.

~ /up grayd/ *noun* (*plural* **upgrades**) the act or process of upgrading something, or an upgraded version of something.

upheaval *noun* (*plural* **upheavals**) a very big disturbance or change.

uphill *adverb* up a hill or slope. *adjective* 1 going up. 2 difficult; needing a lot of effort: *an uphill task*.

uphold *verb* (**upholds, upholding, upheld**) to support, maintain, or defend a belief or principle.

upholster *verb* (**upholsters, upholstering, upholstered**) to cover a chair or sofa with fabric, padding, and springs. ➤ **upholsterer** *noun*, **upholstery** *noun*.

upkeep *noun* the process or cost of keeping something in good condition.

upland *noun* (*plural* **uplands**) an area of high land.

uplifting *adjective* making you feel more hopeful or optimistic.

upload *verb* (**uploads, uploading, uploaded**) *ICT* to transfer programs or data from a smaller to a larger or more central computer. ~ *noun* (*plural* **uploads**) *ICT* the act or process of uploading a program or file, or a program or file that has been uploaded.

up-market *adjective and adverb* designed to appeal to people who are richer and more sophisticated than most customers.

upon *preposition formal* on or on top of.

upper *adjective* higher in position, rank, or order. ~ *noun* (*plural* **uppers**) the upper part of a shoe, not the sole. * **have/get the upper hand** to have or get control or an advantage.

upper case *noun* capital letters. ➤ **upper-case** *adjective*.

upper class *noun* (**the upper class**) the people belonging to the highest class in society. ▶ **upper-class** *adjective*.

uppermost *adjective and adverb* in or into the highest or most important position.

upright *adjective* **1** vertical; straight up. **2** honest or honourable. ~ *adverb* in or into a vertical position. ~ *noun* (*plural* **uprights**) a vertical post or support.

uprising *noun* (*plural* **uprisings**) a rebellion.

uproar *noun* a noisy or violent disturbance or protest.

uproarious *adjective* very noisy and energetic. ▶ **uproariously** *adverb*.

uproot *verb* (**uproots, uprooting, uprooted**) to pull a whole plant up including its roots. **2** to move somebody away from their home or country.

upset *verb* (**upsets, upsetting, upset**) **1** to make somebody unhappy, disappointed, or worried. **2** to knock something over. **3** to spoil or disorganize something. ~ *noun* (*plural* **upsets**) **1** an unexpected defeat. **2** a slight illness: *a stomach upset*. ~ *adjective* **1** unhappy, disappointed, or worried.

upshot *noun* the final result or outcome.

Word History Upshot originally referred to the final shot in an archery contest.

upside down *adverb and adjective* **1** with the top where the bottom should be. **2** in total confusion.

upstage *verb* (**upstages, upstaging, upstaged**) to take attention away from somebody else by doing something better or more exciting.

upstairs *adverb and adjective* on or to a higher floor.

upstart *noun* (*plural* **upstarts**) somebody who behaves arrogantly after being given or reaching a position of authority.

upstream *adverb and adjective* in the opposite direction to the flow of a stream or river.

uptake *noun* the process of starting to use something. ✱ **quick/slow on the uptake** *informal* quick (or slow) to understand things.

uptight *adjective informal* tense and angry.

up to date *adjective* **1** having the latest information. **2** modern.

up to the minute *adjective* completely up to date.

upturn *noun* (*plural* **upturns**) an improvement.

upward *adjective* moving or extending upwards.

upwards *adverb* to a higher place or level.

upwind *adverb and adjective* in or to a position where the wind is blowing something, such as smoke or a smell, away from you.

uranium /ew ray ni um/ *noun Science* a radioactive metallic element used to produce nuclear energy.

urban *adjective* of or to do with a city or town.

urbane /er bayn/ *adjective* with polite, sophisticated manners.

urchin *noun* (*plural* **urchins**) a poor young child in dirty clothes.

Urdu /oor dooh/ *noun* the language of Pakistan, Bangladesh, and parts of India.

urge *verb* (**urges, urging, urged**) to try hard to persuade somebody to do something. ~ *noun* (*plural* **urges**) a strong wish to have or do something.

urgent *adjective* needing attention immediately. ▶ **urgency** *noun*, **urgently** *adverb*.

urinal /ew rie nl/ *noun* (*plural* **urinals**) a type of toilet fixed on a wall in a public toilet, for men to urinate into.

urinate /ewrinayt/ *verb* (**urinates, urinating, urinated**) to let urine out of your body.

urine /ewrin/ *noun* the yellowish liquid waste that collects in your bladder until you go to the toilet. ➤ **urinary** *adjective*.

URL *abbreviation* ICT = *uniform resource locator*, the address of a page on the Internet.

urn *noun* (*plural* **urns**) **1** a container for the ashes of a dead person. **2** a large container with a tap, for tea or coffee. **3** a large ornamental vase.

US *abbreviation* United States.

us *pronoun* used for 'we' when it is the object of a verb, or after a preposition: *Write to us or phone us*.

USA *abbreviation* United States of America.

usable *adjective* capable of being used.

usage /ewsij/ *noun* the way in which a word or something else is used.

use /ewz/ *verb* (**uses, using, used**) **1** to put something into action or do a particular job with it. **2** to spend or reduce something. **3** to treat somebody selfishly. ~ *noun* /ews/ (*plural* **uses**) **1** a way or act of using something. **2** the ability, right, or benefit of using something. **3** practical value. ✳ **be used to** to be familiar with or accustomed to something. **make use of** to use or take advantage of something. **used to** referring to something that happened regularly in the past: *I used to play golf*. **use up** to use something until it is all gone.

used *adjective* secondhand.

useful *adjective* having a practical purpose or value. ➤ **usefully** *adverb*, **usefulness** *noun*.

useless *adjective* having no use or purpose. ➤ **uselessly** *adverb*.

user *noun* (*plural* **users**) somebody who uses something.

user-friendly *adjective* easy to use or understand.

usher *noun* (*plural* **ushers**) somebody who shows you to your seat in a theatre, cinema, or church. ~ *verb* (**ushers, ushering, ushered**) to show you where you should go or sit.

USSR *abbreviation* formerly, the Union of Soviet Socialist Republics.

usual *adjective* commonly done or used; normal or ordinary. ➤ **usually** *adverb*.

usurp /ewzerp/ *verb* (**usurps, usurping, usurped**) to take a position of power from somebody else, wrongly or illegally. ➤ **usurper** *noun*.

utensil /ewtensil/ *noun* (*plural* **utensils**) a tool used for eating or cooking with.

uterus /ewtirus/ *noun* (*plural* **uteruses**) a woman's womb.

utilitarian /ewtilitairian/ *adjective* practical and useful rather than attractive.

utility *noun* (*plural* **utilities**) **1** a public service such as gas, electricity, or water. **2** usefulness.

utilize *or* **utilise** *verb* (**utilizes, utilizing, utilized** *or* **utilises,** etc) to make practical use of something. ➤ **utilization** *or* **utilisation** *noun*.

utmost *adjective* greatest or most extreme. ~ *noun* the greatest possible amount or extent.

Utopia /ewtohpia/ *noun* an imaginary place where everything is perfect. ➤ **utopian** *adjective*.

utter[1] *adjective* absolute. ➤ **utterly** *adverb*.

utter[2] *verb* (**utters, uttering, uttered**) to speak or make a spoken sound. ➤ **utterance** *noun*.

uttermost *adjective and noun* = UTMOST.

U-turn *noun* (*plural* **U-turns**) **1** the act of turning a vehicle to face the opposite direction. **2** a total change of plan.

vacancy *noun* (*plural* **vacancies**) **1** a job or position that needs somebody to be appointed to it. **2** an unoccupied room in a hotel or guesthouse.

vacant *adjective* **1** said about a job or position: waiting to be filled. **2** said about a room or building: not occupied or lived in. **3** said about somebody's face: showing no expression. ➤ **vacantly** *adverb*.

vacate *verb* (**vacates, vacating, vacated**) **1** to move out of a room or building. **2** to leave a job or position.

vacation *noun* (*plural* **vacations**) **1** a period of the year during which an institution, especially a university, is closed. **2** *N American* a holiday.

vaccinate /vak si nayt/ *verb* (**vaccinates, vaccinating, vaccinated**) to inject a person or animal with a vaccine. ➤ **vaccination** *noun*.

vaccine /vak seen/ *noun* (*plural* **vaccines**) a substance injected into a person's body to give them immunity to a particular disease.

vacillate *verb* (**vacillates, vacillating, vacillated**) to hesitate or waver about something. ➤ **vacillation** *noun*.

vacuous *adjective* having or showing no intelligence; stupid. ➤ **vacuity** *noun*.

vacuum /va kewm/ *noun* (*plural* **vacuums**) **1** *Science* a space from which all the air has been removed. **2** *Science* a space that is completely empty of matter. **3** a state in which an important person or thing is missing and has not been replaced. ~ *verb* (**vacuums, vacuuming, vacuumed**) *informal* to clean somewhere using a vacuum cleaner.

vacuum cleaner *noun* (*plural* **vacuum cleaners**) an electrical appliance that removes dust and dirt by means of suction.

vacuum flask *noun* (*plural* **vacuum flasks**) a container for keeping liquids hot or cold, with a vacuum between an inner and an outer wall.

vacuum tube *noun* (*plural* **vacuum tubes**) *Science* an electronic device that generates a beam of electrons and in which there is a vacuum.

vagabond *noun* (*plural* **vagabonds**) a homeless person who travels around; a vagrant.

vagary /vay ga ri/ *noun* (*plural* **vagaries**) an unexpected happening or unpredictable change.

vagina /va jie na/ *noun* (*plural* **vaginas**) the passage that connects a woman's outer sex organs to her womb. ➤ **vaginal** *adjective*.

vagrant *noun* (*plural* **vagrants**) a homeless person who travels around. ~ *adjective* living as a vagrant. ➤ **vagrancy** *noun*.

vague *adjective* (**vaguer, vaguest**) **1** not clearly expressed or defined: *The rules are rather vague.* **2** not thinking clearly or expressing your thoughts clearly: *She was vague about the details.* **3** not sharply outlined; hazy.
➤ **vaguely** *adverb*, **vagueness** *noun*.

vain *adjective* **1** having or showing excessive pride in your appearance or abilities. **2** said about an attempt: unsuccessful or ineffectual. ✳ **in vain** without success. ➤ **vainly** *adverb*.

Vaisakhi *noun* see BAISAKHI.

valance /va lans/ *noun* (*plural* **valances**) a piece of fabric like a short curtain, hung as a border along the edge of something.

vale *noun* (*plural* **vales**) *literary* a valley.

valedictory /va li dik to ri/ *adjective formal* expressing a farewell.

valency /vay lin si/ *noun* (*plural* **valencies**) *Science* a measure of the ability of a chemical element to combine with other elements, expressed as the number of atoms of hydrogen it will combine with.

valentine *noun* (*plural* **valentines**) **1** a lover or sweetheart chosen on St Valentine's Day, 14 February. **2** a greeting card given to such a person.

> *Word History* Although *St Valentine's Day* is the feast day of two saints of that name, the custom of sending cards to sweethearts has nothing to do with either of them. It is more likely to be a remnant of Lupercalia, the Roman festival of fertility held on 15 February, and also influenced by a former belief that birds chose their mates around this time.

valet /va lay *or* va lit/ *noun* (*plural* **valets**) **1** a hotel employee who attends to the day-to-day needs of guests. **2** the personal male servant of an upper-class man. ~ *verb* (**valets, valeting, valeted**) to clean the inside of a car as a service.

valiant *adjective* showing great courage. ➤ **valiantly** *adverb*.

valid *adjective* **1** having legal force or value: *a valid driving licence*. **2** well-grounded or justifiable: *valid reasons*. ➤ **validity** *noun*.

validate *verb* (**validates, validating, validated**) to make something seem reasonable or correct. ➤ **validation** *noun*.

valley *noun* (*plural* **valleys**) an area of low land between hills or mountains.

valour *noun* personal bravery in the face of danger.

valuable *adjective* **1** having a high value in terms of money: *valuable jewellery*. **2** of great use or worth: *valuable advice*. ➤ **valuably** *adverb*.

valuables *plural noun* valuable personal possessions.

valuation *noun* (*plural* **valuations**) an estimate of the value of something.

value *noun* (*plural* **values**) **1** the amount of money that something is worth. **2** the usefulness or importance of something: *The experience was of great value*. **3** (**values**) moral principles or standards of behaviour. **4** *Maths* a numerical quantity; a number. **5** *Science* the magnitude of a physical quantity. **6** *Music* the length of a musical note. ~ *verb* (**values, valuing, valued**) **1** to estimate the value of something. **2** to judge the usefulness or importance of something. **3** to consider something to be very useful or important: *if you value your life*.

value-added tax *noun* = VAT.

valve *noun* (*plural* **valves**) **1** a mechanical device that controls the flow of liquid or gas in a pipe. **2** a part of your heart that restricts the flow of blood to one direction only.

vampire *noun* (*plural* **vampires**) **1** a dead person believed to come from the grave at night and suck the blood of sleeping people. **2** (*also* **vampire bat**) a South American bat that feeds on blood. ➤ **vampirism** *noun*.

van *noun* (*plural* **vans**) a motor vehicle used for transporting goods.

vandal *noun* (*plural* **vandals**) a person

vandalize

who deliberately destroys or damages property. ➤ **vandalism** noun.

vandalize or **vandalise** verb (**vandalizes, vandalizing, vandalized** or **vandalises**, etc) to destroy or damage property deliberately.

vane noun (plural **vanes**) **1** a blade-like part of a mechanism that is turned by wind or water to produce power. **2** = WEATHER VANE.

vanguard noun the group of people who are leading an action or movement.

vanilla noun a flavouring obtained from the pod of a tropical American orchid.

vanish verb (**vanishes, vanishing, vanished**) **1** to pass quickly from sight; to disappear. **2** to cease to exist.

vanity noun (plural **vanities**) excessive pride in your appearance or abilities; conceit.

vanquish verb (**vanquishes, vanquishing, vanquished**) literary to defeat somebody or overcome something.

vantage point noun (plural **vantage points**) a place from which you have a clear view of something.

vaporize or **vaporise** verb (**vaporizes, vaporizing, vaporized** or **vaporises**, etc) to change a liquid into a vapour, or to become a vapour from a liquid state. ➤ **vaporization** or **vaporisation** noun.

vapour noun a substance such as fog or cloud that consists of droplets of liquid suspended in air.

variable adjective able to vary, or tending to vary. ~ noun (plural **variables**) **1** something that can vary. **2** Maths a quantity that can have any value, or a symbol that represents it. ➤ **variability** noun, **variably** adverb.

variance ✲ **at variance with** not agreeing with something, not matching it, or conflicting with it.

variant noun (plural **variants**) a form of something that is different from the form it usually has. ~ adjective existing in a form that is different from the usual form.

variation noun (plural **variations**) **1** differences in something, especially in amounts or levels. **2** a different version of something.

varicose /va ri kohs/ adjective said about a vein: abnormally and painfully swollen.

varied adjective existing in different forms or types.

variegated /vair i a gay tid/ adjective with patches of different colour. ➤ **variegation** noun.

variety noun (plural **varieties**) **1** the fact that different types of thing exist; diversity. **2** an assortment of different things of the same general type. **3** Science a group of plants or animals that ranks below a species. **4** theatrical entertainment consisting of performances of different types, for example songs, sketches, and acrobatics.

various adjective **1** of different types; assorted. **2** more than one; several. ➤ **variously** adverb.

varnish noun (plural **varnishes**) a clear liquid that you paint onto a surface, usually wood, to give a hard finish. ~ verb (**varnishes, varnishing, varnished**) to paint varnish onto the surface of something.

vary verb (**varies, varying, varied**) **1** to be something different in different situations or at different times; to change. **2** to make changes in something, usually in order to make it interesting.

vascular adjective Science **1** to do with blood vessels. **2** to do with the tubes that carry water, sap, etc around a plant.

vase *noun* (*plural* **vases**) a decorative container for cut flowers.

vasectomy *noun* (*plural* **vasectomies**) a surgical operation that makes a man sterile, involving cutting the tube that carries sperm to the penis.

vassal *noun* (*plural* **vassals**) *History* in a feudal society, a man who promised to be loyal to a lord, especially to fight in an army, in return for protection and a small area of land to farm.

vast *adjective* very great in amount, degree, or intensity. ➤ **vastly** *adverb*, **vastness** *noun*.

VAT *noun* = *value-added tax*, a tax charged on many goods and services that people buy.

Vatican *noun* (**the Vatican**) the official residence of the pope in Rome.

vault[1] *noun* (*plural* **vaults**) **1** an underground room, store, or burial chamber. **2** an arch or series of arches forming a ceiling. ➤ **vaulted** *adjective*.

vault[2] *verb* (**vaults, vaulting, vaulted**) to leap over something using your hands or a pole. ➤ **vault** *noun*.

vaunt *verb* (**vaunts, vaunting, vaunted**) to boast about something.

VCR *noun* (*plural* **VCRs**) = *videocassette recorder*, a machine for playing videotapes and for recording television programmes on videotape.

VDU *noun* (*plural* **VDUs**) *ICT* = *visual display unit*, a device that displays computer data on a screen.

veal *noun* the meat of a calf.

vector *noun* (*plural* **vectors**) *Science* **1** a quantity, for example velocity or force, that has both magnitude and direction. **2** an organism that transmits a disease but is not harmed itself, for example a tick or mosquito.

Veda /**vay**da *or* **vee**da/ *noun* (*plural* **Vedas**) a collection of Hindu sacred writings.

veer *verb* (**veers, veering, veered**) to change direction suddenly; to swerve.

vegan /**vee**gan/ *noun* (*plural* **vegans**) a vegetarian who avoids all food products derived from animals, including, for example, cheese and eggs.

vegetable *noun* (*plural* **vegetables**) an edible part of a plant that has a savoury taste and is usually eaten as part of the main course of a meal.

vegetarian *noun* (*plural* **vegetarians**) a person who does not eat meat. ➤ **vegetarian** *adjective*, **vegetarianism** *noun*.

vegetate *verb* (**vegetates, vegetating, vegetated**) to lead a dull inactive existence.

vegetation *noun* plants.

vehement /**vee**i mint/ *adjective* expressing feelings or opinions strongly. ➤ **vehemence** *noun*, **vehemently** *adverb*.

vehicle /**vee**i kl/ *noun* (*plural* **vehicles**) **1** an object with wheels and an engine, and used to carry people or goods, for example a car, bus, or lorry. **2** a means of expressing, displaying, or communicating something: *This film is the perfect vehicle for his comic talents.* ➤ **vehicular** *adjective*.

veil *noun* (*plural* **veils**) **1** a length of cloth worn by women as a covering for the head or face. **2** something that hides or obscures something.

veiled *adjective* not stated explicitly, but understood: *a veiled threat*.

vein *noun* (*plural* **veins**) **1** any of the tubes that carry blood towards the heart. **2** a streak of a different colour in wood, marble, cheese, etc. **3** any of the ribs forming the framework of a leaf or a wing of an insect. **4** a deposit of ore, coal, etc in rock. **5** a particular mood conveyed by words. ➤ **veined** *adjective*.

Velcro *noun trademark* a fastening device consisting of two strips of fabric that stick to each other.

veld or **veldt** /velt or felt/ noun open grassland in southern Africa.

velocity noun (plural **velocities**) Science speed in a given direction.

velour /vi**loor**/ noun fabric with a surface that resembles velvet.

velvet noun luxurious fabric with a short soft pile. ➤ **velvety** adjective.

vendetta noun (plural **vendettas**) a long-standing quarrel between people who hate each other and try repeatedly to harm each other.

vending machine noun (plural **vending machines**) a coin-operated machine for selling small items.

vendor noun (plural **vendors**) **1** a person who sells small items in the street. **2** in law, a person or company that sells something.

veneer noun (plural **veneers**) **1** a thin layer of wood, plastic, etc that covers the surface of a cheaper material, for example in furniture. **2** a superficial attractive appearance. ➤ **veneered** adjective.

venerable adjective respected because of age, character, and achievements.

venerate verb (**venerates, venerating, venerated**) to respect somebody or something greatly. ➤ **veneration** noun.

venetian blind noun (plural **venetian blinds**) a window blind made of horizontal slats that can be adjusted to allow more or less light in.

vengeance noun punishment inflicted in revenge. ✶ **with a vengeance** with great force or intensity.

venison noun the meat of a deer.

Venn diagram noun (plural **Venn diagrams**) Maths a diagram that uses circles to represent sets, the circles overlapping to show common elements.

venom noun **1** poison secreted by the bites of snakes, scorpions, etc. **2** deep hatred.

venomous adjective **1** poisonous. **2** expressing deep hatred; malevolent. ➤ **venomously** adverb.

venous /**vee**nus/ adjective to do with veins.

vent noun (plural **vents**) an opening that allows gas or liquid to escape. verb (**vents, venting, vented**) **1** to release gas or liquid through a vent. **2** to express feelings forcefully. ✶ **give vent to** to express feelings forcefully.

ventilate verb (**ventilates, ventilating, ventilated**) to cause air to circulate through a room or building. ➤ **ventilation** noun.

ventilator noun (plural **ventilators**) **1** a device or opening for circulating fresh air. **2** an apparatus for providing artificial respiration for a patient who cannot breathe normally.

ventral adjective on the front of something, often on an animal's chest or abdomen.

ventriloquist /ven tri loh kwist/ noun (plural **ventriloquists**) an entertainer who projects his or her voice so that it seems to come from a dummy. ➤ **ventriloquism** noun.

venture verb (**ventures, venturing, ventured**) **1** to go somewhere in spite of dangers or difficulties. **2** to give an opinion, often a controversial one. ~ noun (plural **ventures**) a project that involves risk.

venue noun (plural **venues**) the place where an event happens.

veracious adjective formal truthful; honest. ➤ **veracity** noun.

veranda or **verandah** noun (plural **verandas** or **verandahs**) a roofed and open-sided platform along the outside of a building at ground level, for sitting on.

verb noun (plural **verbs**) a word that expresses an action or state, for example run, give, and be.

verbal *adjective* **1** spoken rather than written. **2** to do with verbs. ➤ **verbally** *adverb*.

verbatim /ver bay tim/ *adverb and adjective* in the exact words used.

verbose *adjective* using more words than necessary. ➤ **verbosity** *noun*.

verdict *noun* (*plural* **verdicts**) **1** the decision of a jury about the guilt or innocence of an accused person. **2** an opinion.

verge *noun* (*plural* **verges**) a strip of grass at the side of a road. ~ *verb* (**verges, verging, verged**) (**verge on**) to resemble something or come near to being something. ✳ **on the verge of** about to do or experience something.

verify *verb* (**verifies, verifying, verified**) to check that something is true or accurate. ➤ **verifiable** *adjective*, **verification** *noun*.

veritable *adjective* used in a description for emphasis; absolute; complete: *a veritable mountain of paperwork*. ➤ **veritably** *adverb*.

vermin *plural noun* small animals and insects that carry disease or cause damage.

vernacular *noun* (*plural* **vernaculars**) informal language, the language of ordinary conversation, or the language of uneducated people.

vernal *adjective* *formal* to do with spring.

verruca /vi rooh ka/ *noun* (*plural* **verrucas**) a wart on the underside of the foot.

versatile *adjective* **1** useful for various purposes. **2** good at various things. ➤ **versatility** *noun*.

verse *noun* (*plural* **verses**) **1** a short section of a poem, song, or hymn. **2** writing that has a regular pattern of sounds, stresses, or syllables; poetry. **3** each of the short divisions of a chapter of the Bible.

versed *adjective* (**versed in**) having knowledge of or skill in something.

version *noun* (*plural* **versions**) **1** one of several forms of something that exist now or have been produced at different times. **2** a person's account of something that happened.

versus *preposition* **1** against in a contest: *Manchester United versus Arsenal*. **2** in contrast to: *free trade versus fair trade*.

vertebra *noun* (*plural* **vertebrae** /vert i bree/ or **vertebras**) each of the bony segments that form the spinal column. ➤ **vertebral** *adjective*.

vertebrate *noun* (*plural* **vertebrates**) an animal that has a backbone, for example a mammal, bird, or fish.

vertex *noun* (*plural* **vertices** /ver ti seez/ or **vertexes**) *Maths* the point where lines or curves meet or cross each other.

vertical *adjective* going up or down at right angles to a horizontal line or surface. ~ *noun* (*plural* **verticals**) a vertical line or surface. ➤ **vertically** *adverb*.

vertiginous /ver ti ji nus/ *adjective* extremely high or steep.

vertigo /ver ti goh/ *noun* a state of imbalance and dizziness caused by looking down from a high position.

verve *noun* energy or enthusiasm.

very *adverb* **1** to a high degree; a lot. **2** used for emphasis: *the very best*. *adjective* **1** actual; same: *the very man*. **2** mere: *the very thought of it*.

Vesak /we sak/ *noun* a Buddhist festival held in May.

vessel *noun* (*plural* **vessels**) **1** a ship or boat. **2** a container for liquid, for example a jug, cup, or bowl. **3** a tube in which fluid is carried in the body or in a plant: *blood vessels*.

vest *noun* (*plural* **vests**) a sleeveless undergarment for the upper body.

vested interest *noun* (*plural* **vested**

vestibule

interests) the fact that somebody is involved in something and cannot therefore make an impartial decision or judgment about it.

vestibule *noun* (*plural* **vestibules**) a small room between the outer door and the interior of a building.

vestige *noun* (*plural* **vestiges**) 1 a trace left by something that has disappeared. 2 a minute amount. ➤ **vestigial** *adjective*.

vestry *noun* (*plural* **vestries**) a room in a church where the members of the clergy put on their robes.

vet *noun* (*plural* **vets**) a person who is qualified to treat diseases and injuries of animals. ~ *verb* (**vets, vetting, vetted**) to check somebody or something to see if they are suitable before accepting them for a job, etc.

veteran *noun* (*plural* **veterans**) 1 a person who has had long experience of something. 2 *N American* a former member of the armed forces.

veterinary *adjective* relating to the medical care of animals.

veterinary surgeon *noun* (*plural* **veterinary surgeons**) = VET.

veto *noun* (*plural* **vetoes**) 1 the right to reject a decision or proposal. 2 an occasion when somebody exercises this right. ~ *verb* (**vetoes, vetoing, vetoed**) to use a veto to reject a decision or proposal.

vexed *adjective* annoyed or upset.

vexed question *noun* (*plural* **vexed questions**) a controversial issue.

VHF *abbreviation* very high frequency.

via *preposition* 1 passing through or calling at a place on the way. 2 by means of.

viable *adjective* capable of working or being successful. ➤ **viability** *noun*.

viaduct *noun* (*plural* **viaducts**) a long bridge that carries a road or railway over a deep valley.

vibrant *adjective* 1 very lively and exciting. 2 said about a colour: very bright. ➤ **vibrancy** *noun*, **vibrantly** *adverb*.

vibrate *verb* (**vibrates, vibrating, vibrated**) to move a very short distance backwards and forwards rapidly. ➤ **vibration** *noun*.

vicar *noun* (*plural* **vicars**) a priest in the Church of England

vicarage *noun* (*plural* **vicarages**) a vicar's house.

vicarious *adjective* experienced indirectly through another person, for example by hearing them talk of their experiences. ➤ **vicariously** *adverb*.

vice[1] *noun* (*plural* **vices**) 1 immoral behaviour. 2 criminal activities involving prostitution and drugs. 3 a serious moral fault. 4 a bad habit.

vice[2] *noun* (*plural* **vices**) a tool with adjustable jaws that hold an object tightly while you are working on it.

vice versa /vies ver sa/ *adverb* with the opposite also being true.

vicinity *noun* (*plural* **vicinities**) a surrounding area or district.

vicious *adjective* 1 cruel and violent. 2 fierce and dangerous. ➤ **viciously** *adverb*, **viciousness** *noun*.

vicious circle *noun* (*plural* **vicious circles**) a situation in which dealing with one difficulty creates a new difficulty that makes the original difficulty worse.

victim *noun* (*plural* **victims**) a person who is killed, injured, deceived, or mistreated.

victimize *or* **victimise** *verb* (**victimizes, victimizing, victimized** *or* **victimises**, etc) to treat one person in a group particularly badly for no good reason. ➤ **victimization** *or* **victimisation** *noun*.

victor *noun* (*plural* **victors**) the person, team, country, etc that defeats an enemy or opponent.

Victorian *adjective* happening or

existing during Queen Victoria's reign, from 1837–1901.

victorious *adjective* winning or successful. ➤ **victoriously** *adverb*.

victory *noun* (*plural* **victories**) the act of defeating an enemy or opponent; a win.

video *noun* (*plural* **videos**) **1** pictures and sound recorded on magnetic tape. **2** a videotape. **3** a video recorder. ~ *verb* (**videos** *or* **videoes, videoing, videoed**) to make a video recording of something.

video recorder *noun* (*plural* **video recorders**) a machine that plays videotapes and records television programmes on videotape.

videotape *noun* (*plural* **videotapes**) **1** magnetic tape used for recording images and sounds. **2** a cassette of this magnetic tape.

vie *verb* (**vies, vying, vied**) to compete with others for something.

view *noun* (*plural* **views**) **1** the things you can see from a particular position. **2** an attitude or opinion. *verb* (**views, viewing, viewed**) **1** to watch something. **2** to think of something or somebody in a specified way. ✻ **in view of** because of; considering. **with a view to** intending to.

viewer *noun* (*plural* **viewers**) a person who watches a television programme.

viewfinder *noun* (*plural* **viewfinders**) the part of a camera that shows you what will appear in the photograph.

viewpoint *noun* (*plural* **viewpoints**) **1** an opinion about something; a point of view. **2** a place from which you get a good view of something.

vigil *noun* (*plural* **vigils**) a period during which people stay awake during the night, to keep watch or to pray.

vigilant *adjective* watching and listening so that you are ready to spot trouble or danger. ➤ **vigilance** *noun*, **vigilantly** *adverb*.

vigilante /vi ji lan ti/ *noun* (*plural* **vigilantes**) a member of an unofficial group of people that try to protect their community from crime, often using violent tactics. ➤ **vigilantism** *noun*.

vigorous *adjective* **1** done with great energy or determination: *a vigorous defence of his actions.* **2** showing great physical strength or health: *vigorous plant growth.* ➤ **vigorously** *adverb*.

vigour *noun* **1** great physical strength or health. **2** great energy and determination.

Viking *noun* (*plural* **Vikings**) a warrior from Norway, Sweden, or Denmark who invaded parts of northern Europe between the eighth and tenth centuries.

vile *adjective* **1** morally despicable. **2** very unpleasant.

vilify /vi li fie/ *verb* (**vilifies, vilifying, vilified**) to say very unpleasant things about somebody or something. ➤ **vilification** *noun*.

villa *noun* (*plural* **villas**) **1** a holiday house in a foreign country. **2** *History* a large private house in ancient Rome.

village *noun* (*plural* **villages**) a small group of streets and houses in the country. ➤ **villager** *noun*.

villain *noun* (*plural* **villains**) **1** a bad character in a story or play. **2** somebody who behaves in a dishonest or criminal way. ➤ **villainous** *adjective*, **villainy** *noun*.

villein /vi lan *or* vi layn/ *noun* (*plural* **villeins**) in a feudal society, a peasant who worked on land owned by a lord and was allowed to keep a small amount of the produce from it.

vindicate *verb* (**vindicates, vindicating, vindicated**) to show that somebody was right to do what they did, or right to have the opinion or

vindictive

attitude they had. ➤ **vindication** *noun*.

vindictive *adjective* eager to take revenge. ➤ **vindictively** *adverb*, **vindictiveness** *noun*.

vine *noun* (*plural* **vines**) a climbing plant, especially one on which grapes grow.

vinegar /vi ni gah/ *noun* a sour liquid made from old wine, cider, or beer, used as a seasoning or preservative. ➤ **vinegary** *adjective*.

vineyard /vin yahd/ *noun* (*plural* **vineyards**) a plantation of grapevines used in making wine.

vintage *noun* (*plural* **vintages**) **1** all the grapes grown in a vineyard in a particular year. **2** a wine made in a particular year, especially a particularly good wine made several years ago. **3** the harvesting of grapes, or the time when this is done. ~ *adjective* **1** said about wine: from a particular year that is marked on the label, and usually of particularly high quality. **2** of the best and most typical of its kind; classic: *a vintage episode of this well-loved programme*.

vinyl *noun* a strong tough type of plastic.

viola *noun* (*plural* **violas**) *Music* a stringed instrument of the violin family, between the violin and cello in size.

violate *verb* (**violates, violating, violated**) **1** to break a rule or law. **2** to treat something holy with great disrespect. ➤ **violation** *noun*, **violator** *noun*.

violence *noun* **1** the use of great physical force to injure somebody or damage something. **2** intense force: *the violence of the storm*.

violent *adjective* **1** using violence or involving violence. **2** extremely powerful: *violent storms*. ➤ **violently** *adverb*.

violet *noun* (*plural* **violets**) **1** a plant with sweet-scented purple or blue flowers. **2** a bluish purple colour.

violin *noun* (*plural* **violins**) *Music* a stringed musical instrument that you hold with one end under your chin and play with a bow. ➤ **violinist** *noun*.

VIP *noun* (*plural* **VIPs**) a very important person.

viper *noun* (*plural* **vipers**) a poisonous snake of the adder family.

viral *adjective* caused by a virus, or to do with viruses.

virgin *noun* (*plural* **virgins**) **1** a person who has never had sex. **2** (**the Virgin**) a name that some Christians use for Mary, the mother of Jesus. ~ *adjective* never used or touched and therefore still fresh, clean, or unspoilt: *virgin snow*. ➤ **virginal** *adjective*, **virginity** *noun*.

Virgo *noun* in astrology, the sixth sign of the zodiac (the Virgin).

virile *adjective* said about a man: having the qualities that people think are typical of a man, especially great physical strength or a strong sexual appetite. ➤ **virility** *noun*.

virtual *adjective* nearly as described, though not actually so: *Traffic is at a virtual standstill*.

virtual reality *noun ICT* a computer environment in which images are produced that have the appearance of reality and can be manipulated electronically as if they were real.

virtue *noun* (*plural* **virtues**) **1** thoughts and behaviour that conform to a high moral standard. **2** a good moral quality. **3** a good feature or quality: *This furniture has the virtue of being easy to assemble*. ✱ **by virtue of** because of.

virtuoso /ver tew oh soh/ *noun* (*plural* **virtuosos** *or* **virtuosi** /ver tew oh see/) *Music* an extremely talented musician. ➤ **virtuosity** *noun*.

virtuous *adjective* morally good. ➢ **virtuously** *adverb*.

virulent /**vi** roo lint *or* vir ew lint/ *adjective* said about a disease: severe and developing rapidly. ➢ **virulence** *noun*.

virus *noun* (*plural* **viruses**) **1** a micro-organism that lives as a parasite in the body and causes disease. **2** *informal* a disease caused by a virus. **3** *ICT* a piece of computer code deliberately put into a system to destroy programs and data.

visa *noun* (*plural* **visas**) an official mark stamped on a passport that allows somebody to enter a particular country.

viscosity *noun* how viscous a liquid is.

viscount /vie kownt/ *noun* (*plural* **viscounts**) a male member of the aristocracy who ranks below an earl or count.

viscountess *noun* (*plural* **viscountesses**) **1** the wife or widow of a viscount. **2** a woman who has the same rank as a viscount.

viscous *adjective* said about a liquid: thick, slow to pour, and often rather sticky.

visibility *noun* **1** the fact that something is visible. **2** how well you can see things in the distance, depending on whether there is fog, mist, or haze.

visible *adjective* **1** able to be seen. **2** able to be noticed: *a visible improvement.* ➢ **visibly** *adverb*.

vision *noun* (*plural* **visions**) **1** the power of seeing. **2** a beautiful person or sight. **3** something that you imagine or see in a dream or trance.

visionary *adjective* showing foresight or imagination. ~ *noun* (*plural* **visionaries**) a person with great foresight or imagination.

visit *verb* (**visits, visiting, visited**) to go to see a person, or see or stay in a place, for a time. ~ *noun* (*plural* **visits**) a trip to see a person or place. ➢ **visitor** *noun*.

visor /vie zaw/ *noun* (*plural* **visors**) a movable part of a helmet that covers your face.

vista *noun* (*plural* **vistas**) an impressive view into the distance.

visual *adjective* to do with what you can see: *make visual contact with the aircraft.* ~ *noun* (*plural* **visuals**) a photograph, computer image, illustration etc. ➢ **visually** *adverb*.

visual display unit *noun* (*plural* **visual display units**) a device that displays computer data on a screen.

visualize *or* **visualise** *verb* (**visualizes, visualizing, visualized** *or* **visualises**, etc) to form a mental image of something or somebody. ➢ **visualization** *or* **visualisation** *noun*.

vital *adjective* **1** of the greatest importance; essential. **2** to do with keeping people or animals alive: *vital organs.* ➢ **vitally** *adverb*.

vitality *noun* the quality of being lively and energetic.

vitamin *noun* (*plural* **vitamins**) any of various substances that are naturally present in foods and are essential for keeping you healthy.

vitriol *noun* **1** hatred, or severe and angry criticism. **2** concentrated sulphuric acid. ➢ **vitriolic** *adjective*.

vivacious *adjective* pleasantly lively. ➢ **vivaciously** *adverb*, **vivacity** *noun*.

vivid *adjective* **1** producing strong feelings or strong mental pictures: *a vivid description.* **2** said about light or colour: clear and bright. ➢ **vividly** *adverb*, **vividness** *noun*.

viviparous /vi vi pa rus/ *adjective* *Science* said about an animal: giving birth to live young, rather than laying eggs.

vivisection *noun* medical operations done on living animals for scientific purposes.

vixen *noun* (*plural* **vixens**) a female fox.

viz. *adverb* an abbreviation of the Latin word *videlicet*, which means 'namely', used in a book to introduce an example of something just mentioned.

vocabulary *noun* (*plural* **vocabularies**) **1** the words used in a language or activity, or by an individual or group. **2** a list of words with definitions or translations.

vocal *adjective* **1** to do with voices or speech. **2** expressing opinions frankly; outspoken. ➤ **vocally** *adverb*.

vocalist *noun* (*plural* **vocalists**) *Music* a singer.

vocals *plural noun* *Music* the part of a piece of music that is sung.

vocation *noun* (*plural* **vocations**) **1** a strong feeling that you should do a particular job or activity, especially involving religion or helping other people. **2** a person's work or career.

vociferous *adjective* stating opinions in a loud and insistent way. ➤ **vociferously** *adverb*.

vodka *noun* (*plural* **vodkas**) a clear alcoholic spirit made by distilling rye or wheat.

vogue *noun* the current fashion. ✶ **in vogue** in fashion; fashionable.

voice *noun* (*plural* **voices**) **1** sounds that you make by forcing air from your lungs through your throat. **2** the ability to speak. **3** *English* the distinction between the active and passive use of a verb. ~ *verb* (**voices, voicing, voiced**) to express something in words. ➤ **voiceless** *adjective*.

voice mail *noun* a system for storing telephone messages in digital form.

void *adjective* having no legal force: *The marriage was declared void.* ~ *noun* (*plural* **voids**) **1** a dark empty space. **2** an absence of something that makes you feel unhappy.

volatile *adjective* **1** involving sudden and dramatic changes: *a volatile situation*. **2** involving angry arguments or violence: *a volatile relationship*. **3** *Science* said about a liquid: tending to evaporate at low temperatures. **4** said about a substance: explosive. ➤ **volatility** *noun*.

volcano *noun* (*plural* **volcanoes** or **volcanos**) a hill or mountain with an outlet at the top from which molten rock may erupt from the earth's crust. ➤ **volcanic** *adjective*.

vole *noun* (*plural* **voles**) a small rodent with a blunt nose and short ears.

volition *noun* the act of choosing or deciding for yourself.

volley *noun* (*plural* **volleys**) **1** in ball games, a strike of the ball before it touches the ground. **2** a number of arrows, bullets, or other missiles fired at the same time. **3** a rapid sequence of questions or criticisms. ~ *verb* (**volleys, volleying, volleyed**) to hit a ball, for example in tennis, before it touches the ground.

volleyball *noun* a team game in which players hit a ball over a high net using their hands.

volt *noun* (*plural* **volts**) the unit used to measure the strength of the electricity used by an appliance or system.

voltage *noun* (*plural* **voltages**) strength of electricity measured in volts: *high-voltage cables*.

voluble *adjective* talking a lot. ➤ **volubility** *noun*, **volubly** *adverb*.

volume *noun* (*plural* **volumes**) **1** a book, especially one of several that form a large work. **2** *Science* the amount of space something occupies, measured in cubic units. **3** the degree of loudness of a sound. **4** the amount of something: *a huge volume of traffic*.

voluminous /vo looh mi nus/ *adjective* **1** containing a large quantity; very large. **2** said about clothes: very big or baggy.

voluntary *adjective* **1** done by choice. **2** done without payment. ➤ **voluntarily** *adverb*.

volunteer *noun* (*plural* **volunteers**) **1** a person who offers to do something. **2** a person who chooses to join the armed forces during a war. ~ *verb* (**volunteers, volunteering, volunteered**) to offer to do something.

voluptuous *adjective* said about a woman: having a curved figure that is sexually attractive. ➤ **voluptuously** *adverb*.

vomit *verb* (**vomits, vomiting, vomited**) to release food from your stomach out through your mouth; to be sick. *noun* vomited food.

voodoo *noun* a type of magic that involves communicating with the spirits of dead people, practised in the Caribbean.

voracious *adjective* **1** having a huge appetite; ravenous. **2** very keen; insatiable: *a voracious reader*. ➤ **voraciously** *adverb*, **voracity** *noun*.

vortex *noun* (*plural* **vortices** /vawti seez/ or **vortexes**) a mass of whirling water or air.

vote *noun* (*plural* **votes**) **1** the formal process of making a choice between several candidates or several courses of action; an election. **2** a choice that you make in an election. **3** (**the vote**) the right to take part in an election. ~ *verb* (**votes, voting, voted**) to cast your vote in an election. ➤ **voter** *noun*.

vouch *verb* (**vouches, vouching, vouched**) (**vouch for**) to tell somebody you are sure that something is true, or that somebody is good or trustworthy.

voucher *noun* (*plural* **vouchers**) a ticket that you can exchange for specific goods or services.

vow *noun* (*plural* **vows**) a solemn promise. *verb* (**vows, vowing, vowed**) to promise something solemnly.

vowel *noun* (*plural* **vowels**) *English* a speech sound, such as /ee/ or /oh/, that you make without stopping your breath with your tongue or teeth, or a letter representing such a sound, such as *a*, *e*, *i*, *o*, and *u*.

voyage *noun* (*plural* **voyages**) a long journey by sea or air. ➤ **voyager** *noun*.

vulgar *adjective* showing a lack of good manners or good taste. ➤ **vulgarity** *noun*, **vulgarly** *adverb*.

vulgar fraction *noun* (*plural* **vulgar fractions**) *Maths* a fraction expressed by numbers above and below a line.

vulnerable *adjective* in a position or situation where you could be attacked or harmed. ➤ **vulnerability** *noun*, **vulnerably** *adverb*.

vulture *noun* (*plural* **vultures**) a very large bird of prey that feeds on dead animals.

vulva *noun* (*plural* **vulvas**) the external part of the female genital organs.

vying *verb* present participle of VIE.

W *abbreviation* West or Western.

wacky *adjective* (**wackier, wackiest**) *informal* odd, strange, or silly.

wad /wod/ *noun* (*plural* **wads**)
1 a bunch or lump of soft material.
2 a thick roll of paper or banknotes.
verb (**wads, wadding, wadded**) to stuff or pad something with soft material.

waddle *verb* (**waddles, waddling, waddled**) to walk slowly with short steps, swinging from side to side. ~ *noun* an awkward waddling type of walk.

wade *verb* (**wades, wading, waded**)
1 to walk slowly through water or mud. 2 (**wade through**) to read something long and dull, with great effort.

wader *noun* (*plural* **waders**)
1 (**waders**) waterproof boots that go up to your thighs. 2 (*also* **wading bird**) a bird with long legs that wades in water looking for food.

wafer *noun* (*plural* **wafers**) a thin crisp biscuit.

waffle[1] /wofl/ *noun* (*plural* **waffles**) a type of thick square pancake with a dimpled surface.

waffle[2] /wofl/ *verb* (**waffles, waffling, waffled**) to talk or write for a long time about nothing important. ~ *noun* unimportant or meaningless talk.

waft /woft/ *verb* (**wafts, wafting, wafted**) to be carried along lightly by the air. ~ *noun* (*plural* **wafts**) a wafting breeze or scent.

wag *verb* (**wags, wagging, wagged**) to move quickly from side to side.

wage *noun* (*plural* **wages**) a regular payment for work, such as manual work. ~ *verb* (**wages, waging, waged**) to carry on a war or other organized fight or action.

wager *noun* (*plural* **wagers**) a bet. ~ *verb* (**wagers, wagering, wagered**) to bet: *wager money on a horse*.

waggle *verb* (**waggles, waggling, waggled**) to move repeatedly from side to side or up and down.

wagon *noun* (*plural* **wads**)
1 a four-wheeled cart for moving things around in, pulled by animals.
2 a railway truck for transporting goods.

waif *noun* (*plural* **waifs**) a homeless, neglected child or animal.

wail *noun* (*plural* **wails**) a long, loud, high-pitched cry of pain or sadness, or a similar sound. ~ *verb* (**wails, wailing, wailed**) to make a wail.

waist *noun* (*plural* **waists**) the part of your body above your hips and below your ribs.

waistcoat *noun* (*plural* **waistcoats**) a sleeveless top with buttons down the front, often worn under a man's jacket or as part of a suit.

waistline *noun* (*plural* **waistlines**) the measurement around your waist.

wait *verb* (**waits, waiting, waited**)
1 to stay somewhere or avoid starting an activity until something happens, or until somebody or something comes: *I'm waiting for the rain to stop*;

Hey – wait for me! **2** to be delayed: *Lunch will have to wait.* **3** to work as a waiter or waitress. ~ *noun* (*plural* **waits**) the act or a period of waiting. ✱ **in wait** hiding, ready to attack.

wait on/upon to serve somebody or do things for them.

waiter *noun* (*plural* **waiters**) a man who works in a restaurant serving food and drink to people.

waiting list *noun* (*plural* **waiting lists**) a list of the people who are waiting until they can join or receive something.

waitress *noun* (*plural* **waitresses**) a woman who works in a restaurant serving food and drink to people.

waive *verb* (**waives, waiving, waived**) not to demand or carry out something which you are entitled to.

wake[1] *verb* (**wakes, waking, woke, woken**) to stop sleeping, or to make somebody stop sleeping: *The noise woke us up; Sorry, did I wake you?* ✱ **wake up** to pay attention to or become aware of what is happening.

wake[2] *noun* (*plural* **wakes**) a party or gathering held when somebody has died.

wake[3] *noun* (*plural* **wakes**) the track left by a ship or some other object moving across water. ✱ **in the wake of** after something and as a result of it.

wakeful *adjective* awake or unable to sleep. ➤ **wakefulness** *noun*.

waken *verb* (**wakens, wakening, wakened**) = WAKE[1].

walk *verb* (**walks, walking, walked**) **1** to move along by putting first one foot on the ground and then the other. **2** to take an animal for a walk. ~ *noun* (*plural* **walks**) **1** a journey or outing on foot. **2** a way of walking. **3** a route or path for walking. ✱ **walk away/off with** *informal* **1** to steal something. **2** to win a prize. **walk out** to leave suddenly or as a protest. **walk out on** to abandon somebody. ➤ **walker** *noun*.

walking stick *noun* (*plural* **walking sticks**) a stick used to support you when you walk.

Walkman *noun* (*plural* **Walkmen** or **Walkmans**) *trademark* a small portable cassette or CD player with earphones.

walk of life *noun* (*plural* **walks of life**) somebody's job or position in society.

walkover *noun* (*plural* **walkovers**) a contest that is very easy to win.

walkway *noun* (*plural* **walkways**) a path or platform for walking along.

wall *noun* (*plural* **walls**) **1** a solid upright structure forming one side of a room, building, or enclosed area, or acting as a barrier. **2** a lining or membrane surrounding a part of the body: *the chest wall.* ~ *verb* (**walls, walling, walled**) to surround or close something with a wall: *The chamber was walled off/up.*

wallaby *noun* (*plural* **wallabies** or **wallaby**) an animal closely related to the kangaroo but smaller.

wallet *noun* (*plural* **wallets**) a flat folded object with pockets for keeping paper money and cards in.

wallop *verb* (**wallops, walloping, walloped**) *informal* to hit something or somebody hard. ~ *noun* (*plural* **wallops**) *informal* a powerful blow.

wallow *verb* (**wallows, wallowing, wallowed**) **1** to roll or lie around lazily. **2** (**wallow in**) to spend too much time thinking about something or feeling an emotion.

wallpaper *noun* (*plural* **wallpapers**) **1** decorative paper for the walls of a room. **2** *ICT* a decorative background on a computer monitor. ~ *verb* (**wallpapers, wallpapering, wallpapered**) to cover the walls of a room with wallpaper.

walnut *noun* (*plural* **walnuts**) a nut

walrus

with a wrinkled surface and a round shell.

Word History The word *walnut* comes from two Old English words: *wealh* meaning 'foreigner' and *hnutu* meaning 'nut'. Walnuts were called 'foreign nuts' because they were introduced to Britain from abroad, probably by the Romans.

walrus *noun* (*plural* **walruses** or **walrus**) a large sea animal with tusks, related to the seal.

waltz *noun* (*plural* **waltzes**) *Music* a dance with three beats to the bar. ~ *verb* (**waltzes, waltzing, waltzed**) **1** to dance a waltz. **2** to arrive somewhere very casually and confidently: *He waltzed in half an hour late.*

wan /won/ *adjective* (**wanner, wannest**) **1** pale and unhealthy in appearance. **2** said about light: dim or faint. ➤ **wanly** *adverb*.

wand *noun* (*plural* **wands**) a thin rod that a magician uses during tricks.

wander *verb* (**wanders, wandering, wandered**) **1** to walk or travel around vaguely without any fixed route. **2** to drift away from the subject you were meant to be talking or thinking about. ~ *noun* (*plural* **wanders**) a walk or journey with no fixed route. ➤ **wanderer** *noun*.

wane *verb* (**wanes, waning, waned**) **1** said about the moon: to become smaller or less bright. **2** to get smaller or weaker. ✷ **on the wane** getting smaller or weaker.

wangle *verb* (**wangles, wangling, wangled**) *informal* to make something happen or get something in a clever and sneaky way.

want *verb* (**wants, wanting, wanted**) **1** to have a wish or desire for something. **2** to be asking somebody to come to you: *Mum wants you.* **3** (**be wanted**) to be hunted by the police. **4** *formal* to need something: *He wants for nothing.* ~ *noun* **1** lack of something. **2** extreme poverty.

wanting *adjective* not up to the necessary standard; lacking something.

wanton *adjective* pointless and unnecessary. ➤ **wantonly** *adverb*.

WAP /wop/ *abbreviation ICT* = *Wireless Application Protocol*, the technology that allows mobile phone users to send emails and connect to the Internet.

war *noun* (*plural* **wars**) **1** violent fighting between groups or nations. **2** a fierce struggle to achieve something or to beat an opponent. ~ *verb* (**wars, warring, warred**) to fight a war: *warring nations.*

warble *verb* (**warbles, warbling, warbled**) to sing in clear, repeated, rising and falling notes.

warbler *noun* (*plural* **warblers**) a type of songbird.

ward *noun* (*plural* **wards**) **1** a room in a hospital containing beds for a number of patients. **2** one of the parts a city, town, or area is divided into for voting, etc. **3** somebody with a legal guardian responsible for them.

warden *noun* (*plural* **wardens**) an official responsible for supervising a particular place or enforcing specific laws or regulations.

warder *noun* (*plural* **warders**) a prison guard.

wardrobe *noun* (*plural* **wardrobes**) **1** a large cupboard to hang clothes in. **2** a collection of clothes belonging to one person or group.

ware *noun* (*plural* **wares**) **1** a particular type or make of manufactured objects: *tinware.* **2** (**wares**) goods for sale.

warehouse *noun* (*plural* **warehouses**) a building or room to store goods in before they are sold.

warfare *noun* war; armed fighting.

warhead *noun* (*plural* **warheads**) the

other benefits to people who need them.

well[1] *adverb* (**better, best**) **1** in a good, proper, or skilful way. **2** in a kind or friendly way. **3** thoroughly or fully. **4** very probably. ~ *adjective* (**better, best**) **1** healthy; cured or recovered. **2** satisfactory or pleasing. ✴ **as well** also.

> *Usage Note* Adjectives such as *well-known*, *well-behaved*, etc should always be spelt with a hyphen when used before a noun: *a well-known story* The hyphen is not necessary when the adjective is used after a verb: *The facts are well known to most of you.*

well[2] *interjection* **1** used to express surprise, anger, or acceptance of something disappointing. **2** used as a pause or hesitation when you start to talk.

well[3] *noun* (*plural* **wells**) **1** a deep hole in the ground made in order to reach a supply of water, oil, or gas. **2** a large vertical space in a building, for stairs or a lift.

well[4] *verb* (**wells, welling, welled**) (*often* **well up**) to rise up to the surface of something: *Water welled up through the drain; Tears welled in her eyes.*

we'll *contraction* **1** we will. **2** we shall.

well-behaved *adjective* showing proper manners or behaviour.

well-being *noun* the state of being healthy and contented.

well done *interjection* used to congratulate somebody.

well-done *adjective* said about meat or other food: cooked thoroughly.

wellington boots *or* **wellingtons** *plural noun* long waterproof rubber boots.

> *Word History* Wellingtons are named after Arthur Wellesley, the first Duke of *Wellington*, a 19th-century British general and statesman who wore a kind of knee-length leather boot.

well-meaning *adjective* kind or helpful, often.

well-off *adjective* **1** rich. **2** comfortable situation.

well-wisher *noun* (*plural* **well-wishers**) somebody who supports an idea or individual and wishes them success.

wellies *plural noun*, *informal* = WELLINGTON BOOTS.

welt *noun* (*plural* **welts**) **1** a strong strip or band. **2** a weal.

welter *noun* a chaotic mass or jumble.

wench *noun* (*plural* **wenches**) *archaic or humorous* a young woman.

wend *verb* (**wends, wending, wended**) to travel along, usually slowly.

went *verb* past tense of GO.

wept *verb* past tense of WEEP.

were *verb* past tense of BE.

we're *contraction* we are.

weren't *contraction* were not.

werewolf /'wairwoolf *or* 'weerwoolf/ *noun* (*plural* **werewolves**) in horror stories, a person who sometimes turns into a wolf.

west *noun* **1** the direction in which the sun sets, directly opposite east. **2** areas lying towards the west. **3** (**the West**) Europe and North America. ~ *adjective and adverb* **1** at or towards the west. **2** said about wind: blowing from the west.

westerly *adjective and adverb* **1** towards the west. **2** said about wind: blowing from the west.

western *adjective* **1** in or towards the west. **2** (**Western**) to do with Europe or North America. ~ *noun* (*plural* **westerns**) a film or book about cowboys and life in the western USA in the late 19th century.

westward *adverb and adjective* towards the west or going west. ➤ **westwards** *adverb*.

wet *adjective* (**wetter, wettest**) **1** covered or soaked with liquid.

Wet suit

rainy. **3** not yet dry or set. ~ *noun* **1** moisture or wetness. **2** (**the wet**) rainy weather. ~ *verb* (**wets, wetting, wet** or **wetted**) **1** to make something wet. **2** to urinate in or on something by accident.

wet suit *noun* (*plural* **wet suits**) a tight rubber suit for wearing in cold water to stop your body heat from escaping.

we've *contraction* we have.

whack *verb* (**whacks, whacking, whacked**) *informal* to hit something or somebody loudly or hard. ~ *noun* (*plural* **whacks**) *informal* a loud hard blow.

whale *noun* (*plural* **whales** or **whale**) a very large mammal that lives in the sea. ✳ **have a whale of a time** to have a very enjoyable time.

whaler *noun* (*plural* **whalers**) a ship used for whaling.

whaling *noun* catching and killing whales for oil, food, etc.

wharf /wawf/ *noun* (*plural* **wharves** or **wharfs**) a platform built beside the sea or a large river, where ships can load and unload.

what *pronoun and adjective* **1** used to ask for information that identifies or describes something or somebody: *What is that tune?* **2** used to refer to an unnamed thing or things: *I know what you mean.* **3** used to express surprise or excitement. **3** whatever. ✳ **what about** used to make suggestions. **what if** what will or would happen if.

whatever *pronoun and adjective* **1** anything or everything that. **2** no matter what. **3** used for emphasis in questions, instead of *what.* **4** at all.

whatsoever *pronoun and adjective* at all.

wheat *noun* a plant whose grain is used to make flour.

wheedle *verb* (**wheedles, wheedling, wheedled**) to persuade somebody by talking to them in a gentle or flattering way.

wheel *noun* (*plural* **wheels**) **1** a circular object that is fixed at or through its centre so that it rotates. **2** (**the wheel**) the wheel used to steer a vehicle or ship. ~ *verb* (**wheels, wheeling, wheeled**) **1** to turn round to face the opposite direction: *He suddenly wheeled round to look at us.* **2** to move something or somebody in a wheeled object, or to move an object along on its wheels.

wheelbarrow *noun* (*plural* **wheelbarrows**) a container with handles at one end and a wheel under the other, for moving things in the garden.

wheelchair *noun* (*plural* **wheelchairs**) a chair that has wheels under it, used by people unable to walk.

wheeze *verb* (**wheezes, wheezing, wheezed**) to breathe with difficulty, with a rough whistling sound. ~ *noun* (*plural* **wheezes**) a wheezing sound. ➤ **wheezy** *adjective*.

whelk *noun* (*plural* **whelks**) a type of small edible shellfish.

when *adverb* **1** at what time? **2** at or during which time. ~ *conjunction* **1** at or during the time that. **2** if or since. **3** although.

whence *adverb and conjunction* *archaic or formal* **1** from where. **2** to the place from which.

whenever *conjunction* at every or any time.

where *adverb and conjunction* **1** at, in, from, or to what place. **2** at, in, or to what point, or in what way.

whereabouts *adverb and conjunction* in what place or general area. ~ *plural noun* the place or general area where somebody or something is.

whereas *conjunction* while in a contrasting way.

whereby *conjunction* *formal* by which.

whereupon *adverb and conjunction* immediately after which.

wherever *conjunction* at, in, or to every or any place. ~ *adverb* used in questions instead of *where*, for emphasis: *Wherever have you been?*

whet *verb* (**whets, whetting, whetted**) **1** to sharpen a blade. **2** to stimulate your appetite.

whether *conjunction* if; as or referring to one of two alternatives.

whey *noun* the watery part of milk, separated from the curd.

which *adjective* used to ask for information that identifies one or more out of a larger group of things or people. ~ *pronoun* **1** which thing or person. **2** used to refer to, or to introduce some extra information about, something you have just mentioned.

whichever *pronoun and adjective* **1** any one or ones out of a group. **2** no matter which.

whiff *noun* (*plural* **whiffs**) **1** a brief or slight smell. **2** *informal* an unpleasant smell. **3** a slight trace or sign.

Whig *noun* (*plural* **Whigs**) *History* a member of a British political party of the 18th and early 19th centuries which wanted to increase the power of parliament.

while *noun* (**a while**) a period of time, often quite a long period of time: *Stay here for a little while; It's been a while since I saw him.* *conjunction* **1** at the time as, or as long as. **2** but; whereas. **3** although. ~ *verb* (**whiles, whiling, whiled**) (**while away**) to spend time in a relaxed way. ✽ **a while** for some time. **worth your while** useful or helpful to you.

whilst *conjunction* = WHILE.

whim *noun* (*plural* **whims**) a sudden idea or wish.

whimper *verb* (**whimpers, whimpering, whimpered**) to make low sad whining sounds. ➤ **whimper** *noun*.

whimsical *adjective* hu... unusual. ➤ **whimsically** a...

whine *verb* (**whines, whining, whined**) **1** to make a long, high-pitched, unhappy sound. **2** to complain in a miserable, annoying way. ~ *noun* (*plural* **whines**) a whining sound. ➤ **whiny** *adjective*.

whinge *verb* (**whinges, whingeing, whinged**) *informal* to complain or moan. ➤ **whinger** *noun*.

whinny *verb* (**whinnies, whinnying, whinnied**) to neigh softly. ➤ **whinny** *noun*.

whip *noun* (*plural* **whips**) **1** a leather strip or cord attached to a handle, used to drive animals along or to hit people with as a punishment. **2** a dessert made by whipping some of the ingredients. ~ *verb* (**whips, whipping, whipped**) **1** to hit a person or an animal with a whip. **2** to beat eggs or cream into a thick froth. **3** to thrash about like a whip. **4** to take or move something away very quickly. ✽ **whip up 1** to stir up or stimulate something. **2** to make something in a hurry.

whippet *noun* (*plural* **whippets**) a dog that looks like a small greyhound.

whip-round *noun* (*plural* **whip-rounds**) *informal* a collection of money made for a particular purpose.

whirl *verb* (**whirls, whirling, whirled**) **1** to spin round suddenly or quickly. **2** said about your head: to feel dizzy. ~ *noun* (*plural* **whirls**) **1** a fast spinning movement. **2** lots of events or parties one after another. **3** a *informal* a try.

whirlpool *noun* (*plural* **whirlpools**) **1** a fast-flowing circular current of water. **2** a type of bath that makes whirling currents of hot water.

whirlwind *noun* (*plural* **whirlwinds**) a small rapidly rotating windstorm. ~ *adjective* happening very quickly and suddenly: *a whirlwind romance*.

whirr or **whir** *verb* (**whirrs** or **whirs, whirring, whirred**) to revolve or move with a continuous buzzing sound. ~ *noun* (*plural* **whirrs** or **whirs**) a whirring sound.

whisk *noun* (*plural* **whisks**) a kitchen utensil for beating food until it is frothy. ~ *verb* (**whisks, whisking, whisked**) **1** to beat a substance with a whisk. **2** to take something away quickly.

whisker *noun* (*plural* **whiskers**) a long stiff hair that sticks out from the area around an animal's mouth. ➤ **whiskery** *adjective*.

whisky *noun* (*plural* **whiskies**) a strong golden-brown alcoholic drink.

Word History The word *whisky* comes from Scottish Gaelic *uisge beatha*, which means 'water of life'.

whisper *verb* (**whispers, whispering, whispered**) to speak very softly and quietly. ~ *noun* (*plural* **whispers**) **1** a very soft whispering voice or whispered words. **2** a rumour.

whist *noun* a card game in which players try to win tricks.

whistle *noun* (*plural* **whistles**) **1** a short tube with a slit in it that makes a loud high-pitched sound when you blow or force air through it. **2** a high clear sound made by blowing through pursed lips or a whistle. ~ *verb* (**whistles, whistling, whistled**) **1** to make a high clear sound by blowing through pursed lips or a whistle. **2** to make a soft whistling sound.

whit * **not a whit** not a bit.

white *noun* (*plural* **whites**) **1** a colour like that of new snow or milk. **2** the clear substance around the yolk of an egg, that goes white when cooked. **3** the white part of your eye. **4** a light-skinned person. ~ *adjective* **1** of the colour white. **2** very pale. **3** said about wine: light yellow or amber. **4** said about coffee or tea: containing milk or cream. **5** to do with people with pale skin. ➤ **whiteness** *noun*, **whitish** *adjective*.

white lie *noun* (*plural* **white lies**) a harmless lie, often told to avoid hurting somebody's feelings.

whiten *verb* (**whitens, whitening, whitened**) to make something white, or to become white. ➤ **whitener** *noun*.

white spirit *noun* a clear flammable liquid made from petrol, used as a solvent.

whitewash *noun* (*plural* **whitewashes**) **1** a liquid mixture used to whiten walls. **2** a deliberate concealment of a mistake. ~ *verb* (**whitewashes, whitewashing, whitewashed**) **1** to cover something with whitewash. **2** to cover up or disguise a mistake.

whither *adverb and conjunction*, *archaic* to or towards what place.

whiting *noun* (*plural* **whiting**) a sea fish related to the cod.

Whitsun *noun* Whit Sunday and the week that follows it.

Whit Sunday *noun* the seventh Sunday after Easter, when Christians remember the coming of the Holy Spirit to the apostles at Pentecost.

whittle *verb* (**whittles, whittling, whittled**) **1** to shape wood by chipping pieces from its surface. **2** (**whittle down/away**) to reduce or remove something gradually.

whizz *verb* (**whizzes, whizzing, whizzed**) **1** to speed through the air with a buzzing or whirring sound. **2** *informal* to go somewhere quickly.

whizzkid *noun* (*plural* **whizzkids**) a very clever or successful young person.

who *pronoun* **1** used to ask what or which person. **2** used to refer to a particular person or people.

Usage Note **who** or **whom**? Grammatically, *who* and *whom* are the subject and object forms respectively of the same word: *Who hit you?*; *Whom did you hit?* In modern English, however, *whom* is increasingly restricted to very formal use, except after prepositions: *Who did you give the packet to?* but *To whom did you give the package?*

whoa /woh/ *interjection* used as a command to a horse to stand still.

who'd *contraction* **1** who would. **2** who had.

whoever *pronoun* **1** whatever person. **2** no matter who. **3** used in questions in place of *who*, for emphasis.

whole *adjective* **1** all of: *the whole group; the whole cake.* **2** not broken or hurt. ~ *adverb* in an undivided piece or state. ~ *noun* (*plural* **wholes**) something that is complete and undivided. ✳ **as a whole** considered all together or in general. **on the whole** generally. ➤ **wholeness** *noun*.

wholehearted *adjective* sincere and enthusiastic. ➤ **wholeheartedly** *adverb*.

wholemeal *adjective* said about bread or flour: made from entire wheat kernels, ground up.

whole milk *noun* milk from which nothing, such as fat, has been removed.

wholesale *noun* selling products in large quantities, usually to shops and businesses. ~ *adjective and adverb* **1** selling or sold by wholesale. **2** on a large scale. ➤ **wholesaler** *noun*.

wholesome *adjective* good for your health.

wholly /hoh li/ *adverb* completely.

whom *pronoun* the form of *who* that may be used as the object of a verb or preposition.

Usage Note **whom** or **who**? See note at **who**.

whoop *noun* (*plural* **whoops**) a loud happy or excited shout. ~ *verb* (**whoops, whooping, whooped**) to make a whoop. ✳ **whoop it up** to celebrate wildly.

whoopee *interjection, informal* used to express joy, enthusiasm, or sarcastic enthusiasm.

whooping cough *noun* an infectious disease that causes spasms of bad coughing with very noisy breathing sounds.

whopper *noun* (*plural* **whoppers**) *informal* **1** something unusually large. **2** a blatant lie.

whopping *adjective, informal* extremely big.

whore *noun* (*plural* **whores**) *offensive* a prostitute.

whorl /werl/ *noun* (*plural* **whorls**) a spiral pattern or movement.

who's *contraction* **1** who is. **2** who has.

Usage Note **who's** *or* **whose**? These two words are pronounced the same, and it is important not to confuse them, especially in questions. *Who's* is the shortened form of *who is* or *who has*: *Who's that?*; *Who's taken my book?* *Whose* is the possessive form of *who*: *Whose is that?*; *Whose book is missing?*

whose *adjective and pronoun* **1** used to ask to whom or to which person something belongs. **2** belonging or referring to the person just mentioned.

Usage Note **whose** *or* **who's**? See note at **who's**.

why *adverb* for what reason or purpose? ~ *conjunction* the reason or purpose for which. ~ *interjection* expressing mild surprise, disapproval, or anger. ✳ **why not** used in making a suggestion.

wick *noun* (*plural* **wicks**) a piece of cord which runs down through the centre of a candle, oil lamp, etc and which you light at the top end.

wicked *adjective* **1** morally bad; evil.

wicker noun twigs, reeds, or canes woven through each other, used to make baskets and furniture. ➤ **wickerwork** noun.

wicket noun (plural **wickets**) **1** either of the two sets of stumps which you bowl the ball at in cricket. **2** the area between the wickets on a cricket pitch.

wicketkeeper noun (plural **wicketkeepers**) in cricket, the fielder who stands behind the wicket.

wide adjective (**wider, widest**) **1** broad. **2** having a particular width. **3** fully opened. **4** including or covering a large range. **5** missing the target. ~ adverb **1** over or separated by a large distance horizontally. **2** to the fullest extent. **3** so as to miss the target. ➤ **widely** adverb.

wide awake adjective fully awake.

widen verb (**widens, widening, widened**) to make something wider or get wider.

widespread adjective found or spread over a large area.

widow noun (plural **widows**) a woman whose husband has died and who has not remarried. ✶ **be widowed** to become a widow or widower.

widower noun (plural **widowers**) a man whose wife has died and who has not remarried.

width noun the measurement across horizontally, from side to side. ➤ **widthways** adverb.

wield verb (**wields, wielding, wielded**) **1** to carry and use a tool or weapon. **2** to use power or influence.

wife noun (plural **wives**) the woman a man is married to.

wig noun (plural **wigs**) an artificial covering of hair to wear on your head.

wiggle verb (**wiggles, wiggling,** **wiggled**) to make short jerky movements from side to side or up and down, or to move something in this way. ~ noun (plural **wiggles**) a wiggling movement. ➤ **wiggly** adjective.

wigwam noun (plural **wigwams**) a Native American hut made by covering a dome-shaped framework with skins, mats, or bark.

wild adjective **1** living or growing in a natural state. **2** uncontrolled. **3** very angry or excited. **4** not sensible; crazy or desperate. ~ noun (plural **wilds**) **1** (**the wild**) a wild or natural state. **2** (**the wilds**) remote country. ➤ **wildly** adverb, **wildness** noun.

wild card noun (plural **wild cards**) **1** a playing card that can represent any card. **2** ICT a character that you can use, in a search, to represent any character or string of characters.

wildebeest /wil di beest/ noun (plural **wildebeest**) = GNU.

wilderness noun (plural **wildernesses**) an uncultivated and uninhabited area.

wildfire ✶ **spread like wildfire** to spread very quickly.

wild goose chase noun (plural **wild goose chases**) a hopeless search or expedition.

wildlife noun the wild animals, birds, and insects of an area.

wiles plural noun deceitful plans and tricks.

wilful adjective **1** determined to have your own way; obstinate. **2** deliberate. ➤ **wilfully** adverb, **wilfulness** noun.

Usage Note Notice that there is only one *l* before the *-ful* ending.

will[1] verb (**will, would**) **1** used about actions or events in the future: *Do you think it will rain?* **2** used in questions and invitations: *Will you come to my party?* **3** used to show intention, willingness, consent, or capability: *I will* *ask him; Will your Dad let you come?; This will remove most stains.*

Usage Note will or **shall**? See note at **shall**.

will² *noun* (*plural* **wills**) **1** the mental power you use to control your wishes, choices, intentions, or actions; determination or willpower. **2** a wish or intention. **3** a legal document stating what you want to happen to your property when you die. ~ *verb* (**wills, willing, willed**) **1** to make something happen, or try to make something happen, using your determination or willpower. **2** to give something to somebody in your will. * **at will** as or when you want.

willing *adjective* ready, pleased, or eager to do something. ➤ **willingly** *adverb*, **willingness** *noun*.

willow *noun* (*plural* **willows**) a tree with long trailing flexible branches.

willy-nilly *adverb* whether you want to or not.

wilt *verb* (**wilts, wilting, wilted**) to lose freshness and become limp.

wily /wie li/ *adjective* (**wilier, wiliest**) crafty.

wimp *noun* (*plural* **wimps**) *informal* a weak or cowardly person.

win *verb* (**wins, winning, won**) **1** to beat your opponent in a battle, contest, or argument. **2** to receive a prize in a contest or competition. **3** to get something through effort or skill. **4** (**win over/round**) to get somebody to like you or do something you want. ~ *noun* (*plural* **wins**) a victory in a game or contest. ➤ **winnable** *adjective*.

wince *verb* (**winces, wincing, winced**) to tense your muscles and face suddenly and noticeably when something is painful or unpleasant.

winch *noun* (*plural* **winches**) a machine with a rope or chain wound round a rotating drum, used for lifting or pulling things. ~ *verb* (**winches, winching, winched**) to lift or pull something with a winch.

wind¹ /wind/ *noun* (*plural* **winds**) **1** a fast natural movement of air across land or sea. **2** gas in your stomach or intestines. **3** the ability to breathe. **4** *Music* wind instruments as a group. ~ *verb* (**winds, winding, winded**) to make somebody short of breath. * **get wind of** to hear a rumour about something. **put the wind up somebody** *informal* to frighten somebody. ➤ **windy** *adjective*.

wind² /wiend/ *verb* (**winds, winding, wound**) **1** to make a twisting movement or follow a twisting path. **2** to wrap something repeatedly around an object or cylinder. **3** to turn a key or knob several times on a clock, etc to make it work. * **wind down** to become gradually slower or more relaxed. **2** to bring something to an end gradually. **wind up 1** to close or end something. **2** *informal* to tease somebody. **3** *informal* to be in a particular place, situation, or condition at the end of something. ➤ **winding** *adjective*.

windfall *noun* (*plural* **windfalls**) **1** a sum of money or other benefit that you receive unexpectedly. **2** a fruit blown down by the wind.

wind instrument *noun* (*plural* **wind instruments**) *Music* a musical instrument that you blow into to make a sound.

windmill *noun* (*plural* **windmills**) a mill operated by long sails that turn round in the wind, or a similar structure or device that uses wind power.

window *noun* (*plural* **windows**) **1** an opening or a section of glass in the side a building or vehicle, to let in light and air. **2** *ICT* a rectangular area on the computer screen which displays a separate file.

windowpane *noun* (*plural* **windowpanes**) a panel of glass in a window.

window-shop *verb* (**window-shops, window-shopping, window-shopped**) to look in shop windows without intending to buy anything. ➤ **window-shopping** *noun*.

windowsill *noun* (*plural* **windowsills**) the shelf along the bottom of a window.

windpipe *noun* (*plural* **windpipes**) the tube that goes from your mouth to your lungs.

windscreen *noun* (*plural* **windscreens**) a transparent screen at the front of a motor vehicle.

windstorm *noun* (*plural* **windstorms**) a storm with high winds but little or no rain, snow, etc.

windsurfing *noun* the sport of riding across water on a sailboard. ➤ **windsurfer** *noun*.

windswept *adjective* exposed to, or blown about by, strong winds.

windward *adjective and adverb* in the direction from which the wind is blowing.

wine *noun* (*plural* **wines**) an alcoholic drink usually made from grapes.

wing *noun* (*plural* **wings**) **1** one of the two movable parts of a bird, bat, or insect, which it uses for flying. **2** either of the horizontal pieces on each side of an aircraft. **3** a part of a building that sticks out from the central part. **4** a smaller group within a political party or other organization. **5** (**wings**) *Drama* the area at the sides of a stage out of sight of the audience. **6** the area near one of the sidelines on a football or hockey pitch. ✻ **under your wing** in your care. ➤ **winged** *adjective*.

wink *verb* (**winks, winking, winked**) **1** to shut one eye briefly as a signal or to show that you are teasing. **2** to flash every now and then. ~ *noun* (*plural* **winks**) an act of winking. ✻ **not sleep a wink** to get no sleep.

winkle *noun* (*plural* **winkles**) a small edible sea snail with a spiral shell.

winner *noun* (*plural* **winners**) a person, team, etc that wins or has won something.

winning *adjective* **1** that wins or has won something. **2** that results in victory. **3** endearing: *a winning smile*.

winnings *plural noun* money that you have won.

winter *noun* (*plural* **winters**) the coldest season, between autumn and spring. ~ *verb* (**winters, wintering, wintered**) to spend the winter somewhere.

wintry *adjective* (**wintrier, wintriest**) said about the weather: like winter; cold.

wipe *verb* (**wipes, wiping, wiped**) **1** to clean, dry, or remove something by rubbing lightly or quickly. **2** *ICT* to erase data or a recording completely. ~ *noun* (*plural* **wipes**) **1** an act of wiping. **2** a disposable moist cloth. ✻ **wipe out** *informal* to destroy something or somebody completely. ➤ **wiper** *noun*.

wire *noun* (*plural* **wires**) **1** metal in the form of a flexible thread. **2** a line of wire for conducting electrical current or telephone signals. ~ *verb* (**wires, wiring, wired**) **1** to provide something with wiring. **2** to connect or fasten something with wire.

wireless *noun* (*plural* **wirelesses**) *dated* a radio.

wiring *noun* a system of wires that supplies electric current in a building or device.

wiry *adjective* (**wirier, wiriest**) **1** resembling wire. **2** thin and strong.

wisdom *noun* **1** good sense or judgment. **2** knowledge and experience.

wisdom tooth *noun* (*plural* **wisdom teeth**) any of the four large teeth that push up at the back of your jaw when you are an adult.

wise *adjective* **1** showing good sense and judgment. **2** knowledgeable and experienced. ➤ **wisely** *adverb*.

wish *verb* (**wishes, wishing, wished**) **1** to feel or say that you want something. **2** to hope that somebody will have or get something: *I wish him luck*. *noun* (*plural* **wishes**) something you want or hope for. ✱ **best/good wishes** a greeting people use conventionally to wish people health and happiness.

wishbone *noun* (*plural* **wishbones**) a V-shaped bone from the front of a chicken or other bird.

Word History The *wishbone* gets its name from the superstition that when two people pull the bone apart, the one who gets the longer piece can make a wish and it will be granted.

wishful *adjective* to do with wishes rather than reality: *wishful thinking*. ➤ **wishfully** *adverb*.

wishy-washy *adjective* **1** weak and watery. **2** feeble or vague.

wisp *noun* (*plural* **wisps**) a thin strand of something. ➤ **wispy** *adjective*.

wistful *adjective* sad and full of longing. ➤ **wistfully** *adverb*.

wit *noun* (*plural* **wits**) **1** sense or intelligence. **2** (**wits**) sanity. **3** the ability to use words or ideas in a humorous way. **4** a witty person. ✱ **be at your wits' end** to be extremely worried or desperate. **have/keep your wits about you** to be alert.

witch *noun* (*plural* **witches**) a woman with supernatural powers or who uses black magic.

witchcraft *noun* the magic used by witches.

witch doctor *noun* (*plural* **witch doctors**) a tribal healer who uses magic to treat people.

witch-hunt *noun* (*plural* **witch-hunts**) a campaign to blame and punish a particular group of people for something unfairly.

with *preposition* **1** used to show people or things being together or in a group: *Come with me*. **2** having or including: *tea with sugar*. **3** using: *Stir it with a spoon*. **4** because of: *He's shaking with cold*. **5** used to describe how to do something: *Treat it with care*. **6** against: *Don't fight with your sister*. **7** relating to; to do with: *Something's wrong with my watch*.

withdraw *verb* (**withdraws, withdrawing, withdrew, withdrawn**) **1** to remove something or take it back. **2** to leave or retreat from a place.

withdrawal *noun* (*plural* **withdrawals**) **1** the act of withdrawing something, or something that you withdraw. **2** the process of giving up using a drug, often with unpleasant side effects.

withdrawn *adjective* shy and uncommunicative.

wither *verb* (**withers, withering, withered**) to become dry, shrivelled, and weak, or to make something do so.

withering *adjective* sarcastic; making you feel stupid or bad.

withhold *verb* (**withholds, withholding, withheld**) not to give somebody something they expected or wanted.

within *preposition and adverb* **1** inside. **2** not beyond. **3** during or before the end of a specific period of time.

without *preposition* used to say that something is absent, missing, or unavailable, or that something does not happen.

withstand *verb* (**withstands, withstanding, withstood**) to be unharmed by something or resist it successfully.

witness *noun* (*plural* **witnesses**) **1** somebody who sees an event take

witticism

place. **2** somebody who gives evidence in a court of law. **3** somebody who watches you sign a document and signs their own name to prove that you did. ~ *verb* (**witnesses, witnessing, witnessed**) **1** to see something happen personally. **2** to act as legal witness to something: *Would you witness my signature?* **4** (**witness to**) to say that something is true.

witticism *noun* (*plural* **witticisms**) a witty remark.

witty *adjective* (**wittier, wittiest**) funny in a clever way; showing wit. ➤ **wittily** *adverb*.

wives *noun* plural of WIFE.

wizard *noun* (*plural* **wizards**) **1** a man with supernatural or magical powers. **2** a very clever or skilful person. **3** *ICT* a computer program that helps you to do something in a step-by-step process. ➤ **wizardry** *noun*.

wizened *adjective* dry, shrunken, and wrinkled because of being old.

wobble *verb* (**wobbles, wobbling, wobbled**) to rock unsteadily from side to side. ➤ **wobble** *noun*, **wobbly** *adjective*.

woe *noun* (*plural* **woes**) **1** *literary* great sorrow or suffering. **2** (**woes**) troubles or hardships. ➤ **woeful** *adjective*.

wok *noun* (*plural* **woks**) a large bowl-shaped cooking pan used in Chinese cookery.

woke *verb* past tense of WAKE[1].

woken *verb* past participle of WAKE[1].

wolf *noun* (*plural* **wolves**) a wild animal related to the dog, which hunts in packs. ~ *verb* (**wolfs, wolfing, wolfed**) to eat food very quickly and greedily.

woman *noun* (*plural* **women**) an adult female human being.

womankind *noun* women as a whole, as opposed to men.

womb /woohm/ *noun* (*plural* **wombs**) the organ in a woman's body inside which a baby grows until it is born.

wombat *noun* (*plural* **wombats**) a plant-eating Australian animal that looks like a small bear.

won *verb* past tense of WIN.

wonder *noun* (*plural* **wonders**) **1** a feeling of admiration and astonishment. **2** something that gives you a feeling of wonder. ~ *verb* (**wonders, wondering, wondered**) **1** to feel curiosity or doubt about something: *I wonder where she is.* **2** to be astonished and impressed: *We wondered at the speed and skill of the riders.* ✱ **no wonder** it is no surprise.

wonderful *adjective* very good; excellent. ➤ **wonderfully** *adverb*.

wondrous *adjective literary* wonderful.

wonky *adjective* (**wonkier, wonkiest**) *informal* crooked.

wont /wohnt/ *noun formal* habit: *I had a nap after lunch, as is my wont.*

won't *contraction* will not.

woo *verb* (**woos, wooing, wooed**) **1** to try over time to make a woman love and marry you. **2** to try to get somebody's support or approval.

wood *noun* (*plural* **woods**) **1** the hard material that forms the stems and branches of trees or shrubs. **2** a dense group of trees. ➤ **woody** *adjective*.

wooded *adjective* said about land: covered with trees.

wooden *adjective* **1** made of wood. **2** awkwardly stiff.

woodland or **woodlands** *noun* land covered with trees.

woodlouse *noun* (*plural* **woodlice**) a small grey creature with a segmented body and many legs, which lives in damp places such as under stones and in rotting vegetation.

woodpecker *noun* (*plural* **woodpeckers**) a bird that drills holes in trees with its beak to find insects to eat.

woodwind *noun* wind instruments made of wood, etc and not brass, such as the clarinet, flute, and oboe.

woodworm *noun* a type of beetle larva that makes holes in dead wood.

woof *noun* (*plural* **woofs**) the low gruff sound that a dog makes. ~ *verb* (**woofs, woofing, woofed**) to make a woof.

wool *noun* (*plural* **wools**) **1** the soft fibre that a sheep's coat is made of. **2** yarn made by spinning wool.

woollen *adjective* made of wool. ~ *noun* (**woollens**) woollen clothing.

woolly *adjective* (**woollier, woolliest**) **1** made of wool, or like wool. **2** vague or confusing. ➤ **woolliness** *noun*.

word *noun* (*plural* **words**) **1** a group of letters that make up a single piece of language with a meaning, or a sound or group of sounds representing one of these. **2** a short remark or conversation. **3** (**the word**) an order or command. **4** a promise: *You have my word.* **5** news or information. ~ *verb* (**words, wording, worded**) to use or choose particular words to say something. ✱ **from the word go** from the beginning. **in other words** expressing the same thing in a different way. **word for word** in the exact words used.

wording *noun* the words used in a piece of writing or to say something.

word processor *noun* (*plural* **word processors**) *ICT* a computer or program used to write, store, and print text. ➤ **word processing** *noun*.

wordy *adjective* (**wordier, wordiest**) using too many words.

wore *verb* past tense of WEAR.

work *noun* (*plural* **works**) **1** activity in which you do or produce something using physical or mental effort. **2** your job. **3** something produced by a particular person or method, or from a particular material. **4** (**works**) a factory. **5** (**works**) the working or moving parts of a mechanism. ~ *verb* (**works, working, worked**) **1** to do some kind of work or your job. **2** to operate or function, or to make a machine operate or function. **3** to succeed or be effective. **4** to use effort or persistence to get something into a particular state: *He worked the stone loose.* **5** to carry out farming, mining, etc in a place. **6** to bring about an effect or result. ✱ **have your work cut out** to have a difficult task. **out of work** unemployed. **work out 1** to calculate or think of the answer to a question or problem. **2** to be successful in the end. **3** to do physical exercises. **work up 1** (**get worked up**) to become angry, upset, or excited. **2** (**work up to**) to prepare for something in gradual stages.

workable *adjective* said about a plan: practical or possible to do.

worker *noun* (*plural* **workers**) **1** somebody who works. **2** a member of the working class.

workforce *noun* (*plural* **workforces**) the people who work for a particular company, or in a particular industry, area, or country.

workhouse *noun* (*plural* **workhouses**) *History* in Britain in the past, a public institution where very poor people lived and worked.

working *adjective* **1** that functions or performs work. **2** having paid work. **3** during which you work: *the working day.* **4** to do with work: *working conditions.* **5** useful to base further work or ideas on.

working class *noun* (**the working class**) people who work for wages, especially those doing manual work. ➤ **working-class** *adjective*.

workload *noun* (*plural* **workloads**) the amount of work that somebody has to do.

workman *noun* (*plural* **workmen**) a manual worker.

workmanlike *adjective* skilful or competent.

workmanship *noun* the amount of skill shown in a product or by a worker.

workout *noun* (*plural* **workouts**) a session of energetic physical exercise.

workshop *noun* (*plural* **workshops**) **1** a place where things are made or repaired. **2** a meeting to learn, discuss, and work on something as a group.

workstation *noun* (*plural* **workstations**) *ICT* an individual VDU and keyboard connected to an office or school network.

worktop *noun* (*plural* **worktops**) a flat surface for working on in a kitchen.

world *noun* (*plural* **worlds**) **1** (**the world**) the earth with everybody and everything on it. **2** the life, work, or environment of one group, person, region, or area of activity: *the Muslim/medical world*. **3** a very great number or amount. **4** a planet. ✶ **the best of both worlds** the best things about two different situations. **think the world of** to love or admire somebody very much.

worldly *adjective* (**worldier, worldiest**) **1** to do with the things in this world and not religious or spiritual matters. **2** knowing or understanding a lot about people and life.

world war *noun* (*plural* **world wars**) a war involving many or most of the main nations of the world.

worldwide *adjective and adverb* throughout or involving the entire world.

World Wide Web *noun ICT* (**the World Wide Web**) a huge system of interconnected sites and files containing information that people can access through the Internet.

worm *noun* (*plural* **worms**) **1** a small soft animal with a long body and no limbs or backbone. **2** (**worms**) the condition of having parasitic worms living in your body. ~ *verb* (**worms, worming, wormed**) **1** to move along by winding or wriggling. **2** to clear an animal's body of parasitic worms. **3** (**worm out of**) to get information from somebody cleverly or gradually. ✶ **worm your way into** to get into a good situation in a sneaky dishonest way.

worn *verb* past participle of WEAR.

worn-out *adjective* **1** exhausted. **2** damaged and not fit to use any more.

worried *adjective* anxious; feeling or showing worry. ▶ **worriedly** *adverb*.

worry *verb* (**worries, worrying, worried**) **1** to feel, or make somebody feel, anxious about something that has happened or might happen. **2** to bother somebody. **3** said about an animal: to keep biting and shaking something. ~ *noun* (**worries**) **1** an anxious, unhappy, uneasy feeling. **2** a difficulty or something that makes you worry. ▶ **worrier** *noun*, **worrying** *adjective*.

worse *adjective* **1** of a lower quality. **2** more unhealthy. **3** more serious or severe. ~ *adverb* **1** less well. *noun* something worse. ✶ **the worse for** harmed or affected badly by. **worse off** poorer or in worse circumstances.

worsen *verb* (**worsens, worsening, worsened**) to get worse or make something worse.

worship *noun* **1** praise, prayer, and thanksgiving to God or a god, or religious practices generally. **2** extreme admiration or devotion. **3** (**Your/His/Her Worship**) a title used for some officials. ~ *verb* (**worships, worshipping, worshipped**) **1** to offer prayer and praise to God or a god. **2** to admire somebody or something very much or too much. ▶ **worshipper** *noun*.

worst *adjective* **1** of the lowest quality. **2** least suitable or sensible. **3** most severe or serious. ~ *adverb* least well. *noun* the worst thing. ✳ **at worst** *or* **at the worst** *or* **if the worst comes to the worst** in the worst situation, or if the worst thing happens.

worth *adjective and preposition* **1** equal in value to. **2** deserving; good enough for. ~ *noun* **1** financial value. **2** the amount you can buy for a particular price: *twenty pounds' worth of petrol.* **3** usefulness or goodness. ✳ **worth it** worth the time or effort spent.

worthless *adjective* **1** valueless. **2** useless.

worthwhile *adjective* worth the time or effort spent.

worthy *adjective* (**worthier, worthiest**) **1** (**worthy of**) good or important enough for. **2** deserving respect, support, or a particular position or title. ➤ **worthily** *adverb*, **worthiness** *noun*.

would *auxiliary verb* **1** the past tense of WILL[1], used for example in reported speech: *You said you would phone.* **2** used when you think or suppose something might happen: *I thought you would phone.* **3** used in questions and invitations: *Would you close the door, please?* **4** used when you would prefer or like something: *We would like coffee.*

Usage Note **would** or **should**? See note at **should**.

wouldn't *contraction* would not.

wound[1] /woohnd/ *noun* (*plural* **wounds**) **1** an injury in which you tear, cut, or break the skin. **2** an injury to your feelings. ~ *verb* (**wounds, wounding, wounded**) to give somebody or something a wound.
➤ **wounded** *adjective*, **wounding** *adjective*.

wound[2] /wownd/ *verb* past tense of WIND[2].

wove *verb* past tense of WEAVE.

woven *verb* past participle of WEAVE.

wrack *verb* see RACK.

wrangle *noun* (*plural* **wrangles**) a long unpleasant quarrel. ~ *verb* (**wrangles, wrangling, wrangled**) to quarrel angrily or for a long time.

wrap *verb* (**wraps, wrapping, wrapped**) **1** to cover or enclose something in paper or fabric. **2** to wind something flexible round somebody or something. ~ *noun* (*plural* **wraps**) **1** a shawl. **2** material used for wrapping. ✳ **wrap up 1** to put on warm clothes. **2** (**be wrapped up in**) to be concentrating completely on something. ➤ **wrapping** *noun*.

wrath /roth/ *noun* strong anger.

wreak /reek/ *verb* (**wreaks, wreaking, wreaked**) to inflict or cause something very bad: *wreak havoc.*

wreath /reeth/ *noun* (*plural* **wreaths**) flowers or leaves twisted or formed into a circular shape: *a holly wreath.*

wreathe /reeth/ *verb* (**wreathes, wreathing, wreathed**) (**be wreathed in**) to be surrounded, wrapped, or decorated with something.

wreck *noun* (*plural* **wrecks**) **1** a shipwreck. **2** the broken remains of something. **3** somebody in a very bad state. ~ *verb* (**wrecks, wrecking, wrecked**) **1** to ruin or destroy something. **2** (**be wrecked**) said about a ship: to sink or be destroyed.

wreckage *noun* broken parts of something that has been wrecked.

wren *noun* (*plural* **wrens**) a very small brown bird with a short tail.

wrench *verb* (**wrenches, wrenching, wrenched**) to pull or twist something violently. ~ *noun* (*plural* **wrenches**) **1** a sudden violent twist or sideways pull. **2** an emotionally painful separation from somebody or something. **3** a spanner.

wrest *verb* (**wrests, wresting, wrested**) to take or get something by

wrestle

pulling and twisting violently, or by force: *wresting the letter from my hand*.

wrestle *verb* (**wrestles, wrestling, wrestled**) 1 to fight somebody using your hands, by pushing, pulling, and holding them against the ground. 2 to struggle hard with something. ➤ **wrestler** *noun*.

wretch *noun* (*plural* **wretches**) 1 a very unhappy person you feel sorry for. 2 *informal* a horrible person.

wretched *adjective* 1 very unfortunate and unhappy. 2 nasty or horrible.

wriggle *verb* (**wriggles, wriggling, wriggled**) 1 to move with short, quick twisting and turning movements. 2 to escape cleverly from a difficult situation or task: *He wriggled out of making a speech*. ~ *noun* (*plural* **wriggles**) a wriggling movement. ➤ **wriggly** *adjective*.

wring *verb* (**wrings, wringing, wrung**) 1 to twist something tightly when it is wet in order to squeeze water out of it. 2 to get something from somebody with great effort or force: *I wrung the truth out of her*. 3 to twist something hard or repeatedly. ✽ **wringing wet** said about clothing or hair: so wet that water is dripping from it.

wrinkle *noun* (*plural* **wrinkles**) a small crease in skin or fabric. ~ *verb* (**wrinkles, wrinkling, wrinkled**) to make wrinkles in something, or to develop wrinkles. ➤ **wrinkly** *adjective*.

wrist *noun* (*plural* **wrists**) the joint where your hand joins onto your arm.

wristwatch *noun* (*plural* **wristwatches**) a watch that you wear round your wrist.

writ *noun* (*plural* **writs**) a formal document from a court, ordering or forbidding something.

write *verb* (**writes, writing, wrote, written**) 1 to use a pen, pencil, etc to form words or symbols on a surface. 2 to be the author or composer of something: *write a poem*. 3 to compose and send a letter: *He wrote to me*. 4 to complete or fill in a cheque. ✽ **write down** to record information in writing. **write off** to consider or treat something as being completely lost, useless, or not worth repairing. **write up** to write an account of something, or produce it in a finished written form. ➤ **writer** *noun*.

write-off *noun* (*plural* **write-offs**) something that has been written off.

write-up *noun* (*plural* **write-ups**) a written account or review of something.

writhe *verb* (**writhes, writhing, writhed**) to squirm in pain or embarrassment.

writing *noun* (*plural* **writings**) 1 written letters or words; handwriting. 2 the act or occupation of writing books, poetry, plays, etc. 3 (**writings**) an author's written work. ✽ **the writing on the wall** a sign that something is going to go wrong or end badly.

wrong *adjective* 1 not correct or true. 2 mistaken. 3 bad, immoral, or unfair. 4 not working correctly. ~ *adverb* incorrectly or wrongly. ~ *noun* (*plural* **wrongs**) an unfair or bad act. ~ *verb* (**wrongs, wronging, wronged**) *formal* to treat somebody unjustly or unfairly. ✽ **be in the wrong** to be mistaken or incorrect. **get the wrong end of the stick** to misunderstand something. **go wrong** to stop working correctly. ➤ **wrongly** *adverb*.

wrongful *adjective formal* wrong, unfair, or against the law. ➤ **wrongfully** *adverb*.

wrote *verb* past tense of WRITE.

wrought /rawt/ *adjective* said about metal: beaten into shape by tools.

wrought iron *noun* a tough pure form of iron that is easy to shape.

wrung *verb* past tense of WRING.

wry *adjective* (**wryer, wryest**) mocking

or showing disapproval but in a mild way: *wry humour; a wry smile.* ➤ **wryly** *adverb*.

WWI *abbreviation* World War I.

WWII *abbreviation* World War II.

www *or* **WWW** *abbreviation ICT* World Wide Web.

WYSIWYG /wɪzɪwɪg/ *adjective ICT* = *What You See Is What You Get*, used to describe text or images which look exactly the same on the computer screen as they do when you print them out, or to systems that produce text or images of this sort.

xenophobia /ze no foh bi a/ *noun* a strong fear or dislike of foreigners.
➤ **xenophobic** *adjective*.

Xerox /zeer oks/ *noun* (*plural* **Xeroxes**) *trademark* **1** a photocopier. **2** a photocopy.

Xmas /kris mus/ *noun* (*plural* **Xmases**) *informal* = CHRISTMAS.

X-ray *noun* (*plural* **X-rays**) **1** a kind of radiation of very short wavelength that can pass through certain solids and act like light to expose photographic films or plates.
2 a photograph of a person's insides made using X-rays, used by doctors to examine patients. ~ *verb* (**X-rays, X-raying, X-rayed**) to examine a patient using an X-ray.

xylophone /zie lo fohn/ *noun* (*plural* **xylophones**) a musical instrument consisting of a series of wooden bars that are struck with two small hammers.

yacht /yot/ noun (plural **yachts**) a sailing boat used for pleasure cruising or racing. ➤ **yachting** noun, **yachtsman** noun, **yachtswoman** noun.

yak[1] noun (plural **yaks** or **yak**) a large long-haired ox of Tibet.

yak[2] or **yack** verb (**yaks, yakking, yakked** or **yacks, yacking, yacked**) informal to chatter.

yam noun (plural **yams**) a starchy root vegetable grown in tropical countries.

yank verb (**yanks, yanking, yanked**) informal to pull with a quick vigorous movement. ➤ **yank** noun.

yap verb (**yaps, yapping, yapped**) to bark in a high-pitched way. ➤ **yap** noun, **yappy** adjective.

yard[1] noun (plural **yards**) a unit of length equal to three feet (about 0.914 of a metre).

yard[2] noun (plural **yards**) 1 a small walled and paved area beside a building. 2 an area with buildings set aside for a specified business or activity: *a builder's yard*.

yardstick noun (plural **yardsticks**) a standard used for comparison: *a yardstick for sporting achievement*.

yarmulke or **yarmulka** /yah mul ka/ noun (plural **yarmulkes** or **yarmulkas**) a skullcap worn by Jewish males.

yarn noun (plural **yarns**) 1 thread prepared and used for weaving, knitting, or sewing. 2 informal a story of adventures, especially one that is unlikely to be true.

yashmak noun (plural **yashmaks**) a veil worn over the face by some Muslim women, so that only the eyes show.

yawn verb (**yawns, yawning, yawned**) to open your mouth wide and breathe in, usually because you are tired or bored. ➤ **yawn** noun.

yawning adjective said about a gap or hole: wide, deep, and open.

ye pronoun archaic an old word for YOU.

year noun (plural **years**) 1 the period of about 365¼ days required for the earth to revolve round the sun. 2 a period of 365 or 366 days, divided into twelve months, beginning on 1 January and ending on 31 December. 3 a period of time equal to this but beginning at a different time. 4 a period of time during which a school or college is in session. ➤ **yearly** adjective and adverb.

yearling noun (plural **yearlings**) an animal in its second year.

yearn verb (**yearns, yearning, yearned**) to long sadly for something or somebody. ➤ **yearning** noun and adjective.

yeast noun a fungus used to ferment alcohol and to make bread rise.

yell verb (**yells, yelling, yelled**) to make a sharp loud cry. ➤ **yell** noun.

yellow adjective 1 of the colour of egg yolk or lemons. 2 informal cowardly. ~ noun (plural **yellows**) a yellow colour. ~ verb (**yellows, yellowing, yellowed**) to become yellow or make something yellow. ➤ **yellowish** adjective, **yellowness** noun.

yellow card *noun* (*plural* **yellow cards**) a yellow card held up by a football referee when taking a player's name for breaking a rule.

yellow fever *noun* a serious infectious disease found in hot countries, marked by fever, jaundice, and bleeding.

yelp *verb* (**yelps, yelping, yelped**) to make a quick shrill cry or bark. ➤ **yelp** *noun*.

yen¹ *noun* (*plural* **yen**) the main unit of currency in Japan.

yen² *noun* *informal* a strong desire or inclination for something.

yes *interjection* used to express agreement, willingness, or pleasure. ~ *noun* (*plural* **yeses** or **yesses**) a positive reply or vote.

yesterday *adverb* on the day before today. ~ *noun* (*plural* **yesterdays**) **1** the day before today. **2** time not long past: *all our yesterdays*.

yet *adverb* **1** up to this or that time: *I haven't had breakfast yet.* **2** only having done so much or got so far: *We can't stop yet.* **3** as of now; still: *We have yet to learn the truth.* **4** at some future time and despite present appearances: *It may yet happen.* **5** in addition: *yet another example.* **6** used to indicate a still greater degree; even: *at a yet higher speed.* **7** nevertheless: *a small, and yet powerful, bomb.* ~ *conjunction* but nevertheless: *I don't want to go, yet I can't think of any way out of it.* ✳ **yet again** once more.

yeti /ˈyeti/ *noun* (*plural* **yetis**) = ABOMINABLE SNOWMAN.

yew *noun* (*plural* **yews**) an evergreen tree with poisonous red fruit.

Y-fronts *plural noun* *trademark* men's underpants in which the front seams take the form of an upside-down Y.

yield *verb* (**yields, yielding, yielded**) **1** to produce something: *Cows yield milk.* **2** to give up something to somebody else. **3** to give way to somebody or something. **4** to give way under physical force. ~ *noun* something yielded, or the amount of it.

yob *noun* (*plural* **yobs**) *slang* a boy or young man who causes trouble in public.

yodel /ˈyohdl/ *verb* (**yodels, yodelling, yodelled**) to sing or call by suddenly changing from a natural voice to a very high voice and back. ~ *noun* (*plural* **yodels**) a yodelled song or call. ➤ **yodeller** *noun*.

yoga /ˈyohga/ *noun* a Hindu system of exercises for achieving bodily or mental control and well-being.

yogurt *or* **yoghurt** *or* **yoghourt** /ˈyogert/ *noun* (*plural* **yogurts** *or* **yoghurts** *or* **yoghourts**) a slightly sour food made of milk with bacteria added, and more solid than milk.

yoke *noun* (*plural* **yokes**) **1** a bar or frame by which two animals, for example oxen, are joined at the necks for working together. **2** a shaped piece at the top of a garment from which the rest hangs.

yokel /ˈyohkl/ *noun* (*plural* **yokels**) an unsophisticated country person.

yolk /yohk/ *noun* (*plural* **yolks**) the yellow round mass that forms the inner portion of an egg.

Yom Kippur /yom kiˈpoor/ *noun* a Jewish festival observed with fasting and prayer on the tenth day of the Jewish year.

yonder *adjective and adverb* *literary* over there.

yonks *plural noun* *informal* a long time; ages.

yore ✳ **of yore** *literary* long ago.

Yorkshire pudding *noun* (*plural* **Yorkshire puddings**) a savoury baked pudding made from batter, usually eaten with roast beef.

you *pronoun* (*plural* **you**) **1** the person or people being addressed. **2** a person; anyone: *You need flour to make bread.*

young *adjective* **1** in an early stage of life, growth, or development. **2** suitable for or typical of young people. ~ *plural noun* **1** an animal's babies. **2** (**the young**) young people.

youngster *noun* (*plural* **youngsters**) a young person, especially a child.

your *adjective* **1** belonging to or associated with the person or people being addressed. **2** belonging to or associated with people in general.

Usage Note **your** *or* **you're**? *Your* is the possessive form of *you* (*It's your turn now*) and should not be confused with *you're*, the shortened form of *you are* (*You're not as young as you were*).

you're *contraction* you are.

yours *pronoun* the one or ones that belong to or are associated with you.

Usage Note Notice that there is no apostrophe in *yours*.

yourself *pronoun* (*plural* **yourselves**) **1** used to refer back to the person or people being addressed: *You'll hurt yourself/yourselves*. **2** used to emphasize 'you': *You yourself knew what to expect*. **3** = ONESELF. ✸ **by yourself** alone.

youth *noun* (*plural* **youths**) **1** the time of life when you are young. **2** a boy, especially a teenager. **3** young people. **4** the state of being youthful.

youth club *noun* (*plural* **youth clubs**) a local organization providing leisure activities for young people.

youthful *adjective* **1** relating to or typical of youth. **2** not yet mature or old; young. ➤ **youthfully** *adverb*, **youthfulness** *noun*.

youth hostel *noun* (*plural* **youth hostels**) a place providing low-cost bed and breakfast accommodation, especially for young travellers or hikers.

yo-yo *noun* (*plural* **yo-yos**) *trademark* a toy consisting of two joined discs that is made to fall and rise when held by a string attached and wound between the discs.

Yule *or* **Yuletide** *noun dated* an old name for CHRISTMAS.

yummy *adjective* (**yummier, yummiest**) *informal* delicious.

yuppie *or* **yuppy** *noun* (*plural* **yuppies**) *informal* a young person in a professional job with a high salary and a fashionable lifestyle.

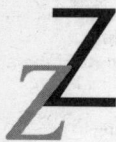

zany /zay ni/ *adjective* (**zanier, zaniest**) absurdly comical.

zap *verb* (**zaps, zapping, zapped**) *informal* **1** to kill somebody. **2** to move somewhere quickly. **3** to switch quickly from channel to channel on a television set using a remote control.

zeal *noun* extreme enthusiasm.

zealot /ze lot/ *noun* (*plural* **zealots**) an extremely enthusiastic person, especially a fanatical follower of a religious or political movement.

zealous /ze lus/ *adjective* extremely enthusiastic. ➤ **zealously** *adverb*.

zebra *noun* (*plural* **zebras** *or* **zebra**) an African mammal with black and white stripes that is related to the horse.

zebra crossing *noun* (*plural* **zebra crossings**) a road crossing with broad black and white stripes where vehicles must stop so that pedestrians may cross safely.

Zen *noun* a Japanese form of Buddhism that aims for spiritual awareness through meditation.

zenith /ze nith/ *noun* (*plural* **zeniths**) the highest or most successful point of something.

zero *noun* (*plural* **zeros** *or* **zeroes**) **1** the symbol 0; nought. **2** a temperature of 0° Celsius, the freezing point of water. ~ *verb* (**zeroes, zeroing, zeroed**) ✴ **zero in on** to focus attention on something.

zero hour *noun* the time at which an event, especially a military attack, is scheduled to begin.

zest *noun* **1** enthusiastic enjoyment. **2** an exciting or stimulating quality. **3** the outer peel of a citrus fruit used as flavouring. ➤ **zestful** *adjective*.

zigzag *noun* (*plural* **zigzags**) a line or course consisting of a series of sharp turns in opposite directions. ~ *adjective and adverb* forming or going in a zigzag. ~ *verb* (**zigzags, zigzagging, zigzagged**) to move along a zigzag course.

zillion *noun* (*plural* **zillions** *or* **zillion**) *informal* an indefinitely large number.

Zimmer frame *noun* (*plural* **Zimmer frames**) *trademark* a metal frame with four legs, designed to help people who have difficulty in walking.

zinc *noun* *Science* a bluish white metallic element, used as a protective coating for iron and steel.

zing *noun* *informal* energy or vitality.

zip *noun* (*plural* **zips**) a fastener that joins two edges by means of two rows of teeth brought together by a sliding clip. ~ *verb* (**zips, zipping, zipped**) **1** to close or open a garment with a zip. **2** *ICT* to compress a computer file.

zodiac /zoh di ak/ *noun* a band in the sky, through which the paths of the sun, the moon, and most of the main planets pass and which is divided into twelve signs for astrological purposes.

zombie *noun* (*plural* **zombies**) **1** in voodoo, a human being who is believed to have died and been brought back to life. **2** *informal* a person who seems lifeless.

zone *noun* (*plural* **zones**) an area.

zoo *noun* (*plural* **zoos**) a place where a collection of living animals is kept and exhibited to the public.

zoology /zooh o lo ji/ *noun* the branch of biology that deals with animals.
➤ **zoological** *adjective*, **zoologist** *noun*.

zoom *verb* (**zooms, zooming, zoomed**) to move quickly.

Prefixes and Suffixes

a- *prefix* meaning **1** in the specified state or manner: *ablaze*; *aloud*. **2** not; without: *asexual*; *atheist*.

ab- *prefix* meaning from, away, or off: *abduct*; *aberration*.

-ability or **-ibility** *suffix* meaning ability to be or suitability for: *manageability*; *possibility*.

-able or **-ible** *suffix* meaning **1** able to be: *adjustable*; *breakable*; *negligible*; *visible*. **2** providing or possessing: *comfortable*; *knowledgeable*. ➤ **-ably** *suffix*, **-ibly** *suffix*.
Usage Note Note also *soluble*.

-ac *suffix* meaning a person affected with a particular condition: *haemophiliac*; *maniac*.

ad- *prefix* meaning movement, especially to or towards: *admit*; *advance*.
Usage Note The prefix *ad-* often changes its form to match the letter that follows it. For example, *ad-* becomes *ac-* before *c* (*accelerate*), *ag-* before *g* (*aggression*), and *an-* before *n* (*annotate*).

aer- or **aero-** *prefix* meaning **1** to do with air: *aerate*; *aerodynamic*. **2** to do with gas: *aerosol*. **3** to do with aircraft: *aerodrome*.

-age *suffix* meaning **1** an action or result: *shrinkage*. **2** cost: *postage*.

ambi- *prefix* meaning both or two: *ambidextrous*; *ambiguous*.

amphi- *prefix* meaning **1** of both kinds: *amphibious*. **2** all around: *amphitheatre*.

an- *prefix* meaning not or without: *anaesthetic*.

-an or **-ean** or **-ian** *suffix* meaning belonging to, coming from, or connected with: *American*, *Shakespearean*, *Christian*.

Anglo- *prefix* meaning to do with England, the English, or the United Kingdom: *Anglo-American*.

-ant or **-ent** *suffix* meaning **1** somebody or something that carries out a particular action: *deodorant*; *entrant*; *regent*. **2** being in a specified condition: *repentant*; *dependent*. ➤ **-ance** *suffix*, **-ancy** *suffix*, **-ence** *suffix*, **-ency** *suffix*.

ante- *prefix* meaning before: *antenatal*.

anti- *prefix* meaning **1** opposing or against: *antiseptic*. **2** opposite to: *anticlockwise*.

aqu- or **aqua-** or **aque-** or **aqui-** *prefix* meaning to do with water: *aquarium*; *aqualung*; *aqueduct*.

-ar *suffix* meaning a person who does something: *burglar*; *liar*.

arch- *prefix* meaning chief or principal: *archbishop*.

-arian *suffix* meaning **1** a person who believes in or supports a philosophy or way of life: *vegetarian*. **2** a person with a particular interest or job: *librarian*. **3** a person of a specified age: *octogenarian*.

-ary *suffix* meaning **1** connected with something: *budgetary*; *military*. **2** a place for something: *aviary*; *library*. **3** a person engaged in an activity: *missionary*.

-ate *suffix* meaning **1** characterized by something, or in a particular state: *passionate*; *inanimate*. **2** to act on somebody or something in a particular way: *assassinate*; *insulate*. **3** a person or people with a specific function: *magistrate*; *electorate*. **4** *Chemistry* a salt of an acid whose name ends in -ic: *sulphate*.

-ation *suffix* see -ION.

aut- or **auto-** *prefix* meaning relating to yourself: *autobiography*.

be- *prefix* meaning **1** to do something

all over or all round something: *beset*. **2** to so something thoroughly or intensively: *bewail*. **3** to treat as something: *belittle*.

bene- *prefix* meaning good or well: *benefit*; *benevolent*.

bi- *prefix* meaning two: *bicycle*; *bilingual*.

bio- *prefix* meaning to do with life or living things: *biography*; *biology*.

cata- *prefix* meaning **1** complete: *cataclysm*; *catastrophe*. **2** downward: *cataract*.

centi- *prefix* meaning **1** hundred: *centipede*. **2** one hundredth of: *centimetre*.

-cide *suffix* meaning a person or thing that kills: *insecticide*; *suicide*. ➤ **-cidal** *suffix*.

circum- *prefix* meaning around: *circumference*.

co- *prefix* meaning with or together: *coexist*; *co-pilot*.

con- *prefix* meaning with, together, or jointly: *concert*; *consensus*.
  Usage Note The prefix *con-* often changes its form to match the letter that follows it. For example, *con-* becomes *col-* before *l* (*collect*), *com-* before *b*, *m*, and *p* (*combine*; *community*; *companion*), and *cor-* before *r* (*correspond*).

contra- *prefix* meaning against or contrary: *contraception*; *contradict*.

counter- *prefix* meaning **1** acting to oppose or retaliate for something: *counterbalance*; *counterattack*. **2** corresponding: *counterpart*. **3** duplicating or substituting for something: *counterfeit*; *counterfoil*.

-cracy *suffix* meaning rule by: *democracy*.

-crat *suffix* meaning **1** a member of a ruling class: *aristocrat*. **2** a supporter of a particular form of government: *democrat*.

cross- *prefix* meaning **1** movement or position across something: *crossbar*. **2** being shaped like a cross: *crossroads*. **3** using two or more things and relating them to one another: *crosscheck*.

-cy *suffix* meaning **1** a quality or state: *accuracy*; *bankruptcy*. **2** an activity: *piracy*.

de- *prefix* meaning to remove something or reverse an action: *decapitate*; *deactivate*.

deca- *prefix* meaning ten: *decathlon*.

deci- *prefix* meaning one tenth of: *decimate*.

demi- *prefix* meaning half or partly: *demigod*.

di- *prefix* *Chemistry* meaning two: *dioxide*.

dis- *prefix* meaning **1** the opposite of: *disarm*; *disappearance*; *dishonest*. **2** the removal of: *dislodge*.

-dom *suffix* meaning **1** a state or condition: *boredom*; *freedom*. **2** a rank: *dukedom*. **3** a territory ruled by somebody: *kingdom*.

dys- *prefix* meaning abnormality, or difficulty in doing something: *dyslexia*.
  Usage Note Do not confuse *dys-* and *dis-*.

e- *prefix* meaning **1** out of: *evict*. **2** electronic: *email*.

-ean *suffix* see -AN.

-ed *suffix* forming the past tense and past participle of most verbs in English: *ended*; *fortified*.

-ee *suffix* meaning **1** a person to whom something is done: *employee*; *trainee*. **2** a person who does something: *absentee*; *escapee*.

-eer *suffix* meaning a person involved in some activity: *mountaineer*.

electr- or **electro-** *prefix* meaning electric or caused by electricity: *electrocute*.

en- *prefix* meaning **1** to put into or onto: *enthrone*. **2** to cause to be: *enslave*. **3** to provide with: *entitle*.

Usage Note The prefix *en-* becomes *em-* before *b* and *p* (*embed*; *empower*).

-en *suffix* forming the past participle of some verbs: *spoken*; *written*.

equi- *prefix* meaning equal or equally: *equilibrium*; *equinox*.

-ent *suffix* see -ANT.

-er¹ *suffix* forming the comparative of many adjectives and some adverbs: *easier*; *faster*; *quieter*.

-er² *suffix* meaning **1** a person or thing that does something: *reader*; *scraper*. **2** a person who lives or belongs somewhere: *foreigner*; *Londoner*.

-es *suffix* see -S.

-ess *suffix* meaning female: *actress*; *manageress*.

-est *suffix* forming the superlative of many adjectives: *easiest*; *fastest*; *quietest*.

-ette *suffix* meaning **1** small: *cigarette*. **2** female: *suffragette*.

eu- *prefix* meaning good, well, or nicely: *eulogy*.

ex- *prefix* meaning **1** out of or outside: *exclude*; *express*. **2** former: *ex-wife*.

extra- *prefix* meaning outside or beyond: *extraordinary*.

-ferous *suffix* meaning bearing or containing: *coniferous*.

-fold *suffix* meaning multiplied a stated number of times: *twofold*.

for- *prefix* meaning to prohibit, omit, or refrain from something: *forbid*; *forget*; *forgo*.

fore- *prefix* meaning **1** in advance: *forecast*; *foresee*. **2** situated in front: *forecourt*; *forefoot*.

-ful *suffix* meaning **1** full of or characterized by: *colourful*; *delightful*. **2** the amount contained in something: *roomful*; *teaspoonful*.

-fy *suffix* meaning **1** to cause to be: *liquefy*; *purify*. **2** to fill with: *horrify*.

geo- *prefix* meaning to do with the earth: *geography*; *geology*.

-gon *suffix* *Maths* meaning having a certain number of angles: *octagon*; *polygon*.

-gram *suffix* meaning something drawn or written: *diagram*; *telegram*.

-graph *suffix* meaning **1** something written, drawn, printed, etc: *autograph*; *photograph*. **2** a device that records or transmits: *telegraph*.

haem- or **haemo-** *prefix* meaning to do with blood: *haemophilia*.

hepta- *prefix* meaning seven: *heptagon*.

hetero- *prefix* meaning other or different: *heterosexual*.

hexa- *prefix* meaning six: *hexagon*.

hom- or **homo-** *prefix* meaning the same or similar: *homogeneous*; *homosexual*.

-hood *suffix* meaning a particular state or condition, group, or time: *childhood*; *brotherhood*; *manhood*.

hydr- or **hydro-** *prefix* meaning water or liquid: *hydraulic*.

hyper- *prefix* meaning too much or very much: *hyperactive*.

hypo- *prefix* meaning **1** under: *hypodermic*. **2** too little: *hypothermia*.

-ian *suffix* see -AN.

-ibility *suffix* see -ABILITY.

-ible *suffix* see -ABLE.

-ic *suffix* **1** (*also* **-ical**) meaning having the nature or characteristics of: *ironic*; *fanatical*. **2** *Chemistry* having a higher valency: *mercuric*. ➤ **-ically** *suffix*.

-ician *suffix* meaning somebody who is a specialist in a particular trade or activity: *electrician*; *magician*.

-ics *suffix* meaning **1** a subject area or branch of knowledge: *economics*; *mathematics*. **2** actions of the specified kind: *acrobatics*; *hysterics*.

-ide *suffix* *Chemistry* meaning a chemical compound of two elements: *chloride*.

-ie *suffix* see -Y.

in- *prefix* meaning **1** not or lacking in: *inedible*. **2** in or into: *influx*.

Usage Note The prefix *in-* often

changes its form to match the letter that follows it. For example, *in-* becomes *il-* before *l* (*illegible*), *im-* before *b*, *m*, and *p* (*imbalance*; *immerse*; *impossible*), and *ir-* before *r* (*irresponsibility*).

-ing *suffix* forming the present participles and gerunds of verbs: *going*; *waiting*.

-ion or **-ation** or **-tion** *suffix* meaning **1** the act or result of doing something: *calculation*; *succession*. **2** a state resulting from a particular condition: *agitation*; *jubilation*.

-ise *suffix* see -IZE.

-ish *suffix* meaning **1** slightly: *coolish*. **2** approximately: *eightish*.

-ism *suffix* meaning **1** a belief or philosophy: *Buddhism*; *Marxism*. **2** prejudice on the grounds of something: *racism*; *sexism*. **3** a practice: *cannibalism*. **4** a state or condition: *magnetism*.

-ist *suffix* meaning **1** a person who performs an activity: *botanist*; *cyclist*. **2** a believer in something: *Buddhist*; *Marxist*. **3** *Music* a player of an instrument: *harpist*; *organist*. **4** a person who is prejudiced: *sexist*.

-ite *suffix* *Chemistry* a salt of an acid whose name ends in *-ous*: *sulphite*.

-itis *suffix* meaning inflammation of part of the body: *appendicitis*.

-ity *suffix* meaning a state or condition: *formality*.

-ive *suffix* meaning **1** doing something: *descriptive*. **2** being in a certain condition: *defective*. **3** a person or thing that does something: *detective*.

-ize or **-ise** *suffix* meaning **1** to become or cause something to be: *crystallize*; *liquidize*. **2** to subject to something: *criticize*.

kilo- *prefix* meaning one thousand: *kilometre*.

-kin *suffix* meaning a small something, or a thing that resembles a small version of something: *lambkin*; *catkin*.

-less *suffix* meaning **1** not having: *childless*. **2** free from: *painless*.

-logy or **-ology** *suffix* meaning a science or area of study: *biology*; *geology*.
➤ **-logical** *suffix*, **-logist** *suffix*.

-ly *suffix* meaning **1** having the characteristics of: *fatherly*. **2** recurring at intervals of: *hourly*. **3** in such a manner: *slowly*.

mal- *prefix* meaning bad or abnormal: *malfunction*.

mega- *prefix* meaning one million: *megahertz*.

-ment *suffix* meaning an action or its result: *development*; *harassment*.

micro- *prefix* meaning very small: *microchip*; *microscopic*.

mid- *prefix* meaning in the middle of: *the mid-1970s*; *in mid-sentence*.

milli- *prefix* meaning one thousandth of: *millimetre*.

mini- *prefix* meaning small: *minibus*.

mis- *prefix* meaning **1** bad or badly, or wrong or wrongly: *misfortune*; *misbehave*. **2** not: *mistrust*.

mono- *prefix* meaning one or single: *monologue*; *monorail*.

multi- *prefix* meaning several or many: *multicoloured*; *multilateral*.

-ness *suffix* meaning a state or quality: *goodness*; *happiness*.

non- *prefix* meaning **1** not: *nonalcoholic*. **2** the opposite of the thing specified: *nonconformity*.

nona- *prefix* meaning nine: *nonagenarian*.

ob- *prefix* meaning **1** against or opposing: *object*. **2** in the way: *obstruct*.

Usage Note The prefix *ob-* often changes its form to match the letter that follows it. For example, *ob-* becomes *of-* before *f* (*offend*) and *op-* before *p* (*oppose*).

oct- or **octa-** or **octo-** *prefix* meaning eight: *octet*; *octagon*; *octopus*.

-ology *suffix* see -LOGY.

omni- *prefix* meaning all or universally: *omniscient*.

-or *suffix* meaning somebody or something that performs an action: *vendor*.

ortho- *prefix* meaning right, correct, or straight: *orthodox*.

-ous *suffix* meaning **1** full of or characterized by: *envious*. **2** *Chemistry* having a lower valency: *mercurous*. ➤ **-ously** *suffix*.

out- *suffix* meaning **1** towards or on the outside: *outbreak*. **2** result: *outcome*. **3** doing something better than somebody else: *outsmart*.

over- *prefix* meaning **1** outer or covering: *overcoat*. **2** excessive or excessively: *overactive*. **3** above: *overarm*.

pan- *prefix* meaning all or completely: *panorama*.

para- *prefix* meaning **1** protecting against: *parachute; parasol*. **2** alongside: *parallel*. **3** helping: *paramedical*. **4** beyond: *paranormal*.

-pathy *suffix* meaning **1** feeling: *sympathy*. **2** a branch of medicine: *osteopathy*.

penta- *prefix* meaning five: *pentameter*.

per- *prefix* meaning **1** through or throughout: *percolate; pervade*. **2** thoroughly: *perfect*. **3** with bad effects: *pervert*.

peri- *prefix* meaning around or surrounding: *perimeter*.

phil- or **philo-** *prefix* meaning love of: *philanthropy; philosophy*.

-phile *suffix* meaning somebody who has a love of or attraction to something: *paedophile*. ➤ **-philia** *suffix*.

-phobia *suffix* meaning fear: *claustrophobia*. ➤ **-phobic** *suffix*.

physio- *prefix* meaning to do with the body: *physiotherapy*.

poly- *prefix* meaning many or much: *polygon*.

post- *prefix* meaning after or later: *postdate; postscript*.

pre- *prefix* meaning earlier than: *prehistoric*.

pro- *prefix* meaning **1** before in time order: *prologue*. **2** favouring or supporting: *pro-European*. **3** forwards or onwards: *proceed; progress*. **4** substituting for: *pronoun*.

pseudo- *prefix* meaning false: *pseudonym*.

psych- or **psycho-** *prefix* meaning to do with the mind or brain: *psychology*.

quadr- *prefix* meaning four: *quadrilateral*.

radio- *prefix* meaning involving rays or radiation: *radiology*.

re- *prefix* meaning **1** again: *reprint*. **2** back or to a previous state: *recede; restore*.

retro- *prefix* meaning backwards: *retrospective*.

-s or **-es** *suffix* forming **1** the plural form of most nouns: *ships; boxes*. **2** the third person singular of the present tense of verbs: *walks; fetches*.

self- *prefix* meaning affecting or involving yourself or itself: *self-confident; self-defence; self-destruct*.

semi- *prefix* meaning **1** half: *semicircle; semitone*. **2** partly: *semiliquid*.

-ship *suffix* meaning **1** a state or condition: *friendship; membership*. **2** skill: *scholarship*. **3** a position or rank: *chairmanship*.

sub- *prefix* meaning **1** under or below: *submarine*. **2** lower in rank: *subordinate*.

Usage Note The prefix *sub-* often changes its form to match the letter that follows it. For example, *sub-* becomes *suc-* before *c* (*succeed*), *suf-* before *f* (*suffix*), *sug-* before *g* (*suggestion*), and *sup-* before *p* (*supply*).

super- *prefix* meaning **1** higher, greater, or larger than: *supersonic; superstore*. **2** placed above something: *superimpose*.

syn- *prefix* meaning **1** together with:

syndicate. **2** similar or the same: *synthesize.*

Usage Note The prefix *syn-* often changes its form to match the letter that follows it. For example, *syn-* becomes *syl-* before *l* (*syllable*) and *sym-* before *b*, *m*, and *p* (*symbol*; *symmetry*; *sympathy*).

-t *suffix* forming the past participle of some verbs: *kept*; *leant.*

tele- *prefix* meaning involving or across a distance: *telephone; telepathy.*

tetra- *prefix* meaning four: *tetrahedron.*

-th *suffix* **1** meaning a state or condition: *warmth.* **2** indicating an ordinal number or a fraction: *fourth.*

therm- or **thermo-** *prefix* meaning to do with heat: *thermodynamic.*

-tion *suffix* see -ION.

trans- *prefix* meaning **1** across: *transatlantic.* **2** so as to change the form of: *transform.*

tri- *prefix* meaning three: *triangle.*

-tude *suffix* meaning a state or condition: *gratitude.*

ultra- *prefix* meaning beyond: *ultrasonic.*

un- *prefix* meaning **1** not; the opposite of: *unskilled.* **2** the reverse of a particular verb: *undress.*

under- *prefix* meaning **1** below: *underground.* **2** less than normal: *undernourished.*

uni- *prefix* meaning one or single: *unison.*

vice- *prefix* meaning deputy: *vice-president.*

-vore *suffix* meaning an animal that eats a certain kind of food: *carnivore*; *herbivore.* ➤ **-vorous** *suffix*.

-ward or **-wards** *suffix* meaning in the direction of: *backward; eastward; upwards.*

-ways or **-wise** *suffix* meaning in the manner or direction indicated: *lengthways; clockwise.*

-y *suffix* meaning **1** covered with: *dirty; hairy.* **2** like or having the quality of: *icy; sticky.* **3** a state or condition: *jealousy.* **4** (*also* **-ie**) a person you are fond of: *daddy; auntie.* **5** (*also* **-ie**) somebody associated with a particular kind of thing: *hippy; junkie.*

Nationalities and Languages

Afghan *noun* (*plural* **Afghans**) a person from Afghanistan. ➤ **Afghan** *adjective*.

Albanian *noun* (*plural* **Albanians**) **1** a person from Albania. **2** the language spoken by the people of Albania. ➤ **Albanian** *adjective*.

Algerian *noun* (*plural* **Algerians**) a person from Algeria. ➤ **Algerian** *adjective*.

American *noun* (*plural* **Americans**) **1** a person from the USA. **2** a person from any country in North, South, or Central America. ➤ **American** *adjective*.

Andorran *noun* (*plural* **Andorrans**) a person from Andorra. ➤ **Andorran** *adjective*.

Angolan *noun* (*plural* **Angolans**) a person from Angola. ➤ **Angolan** *adjective*.

Antiguan /an tee gan/ *noun* (*plural* **Antiguans**) a person from Antigua. ➤ **Antiguan** *adjective*.

Argentinian *noun* (*plural* **Argentinians**) a person from Argentina. ➤ **Argentinian** *adjective*.

Armenian *noun* (*plural* **Armenians**) **1** a person from Armenia. **2** the language spoken by the people of Armenia. ➤ **Armenian** *adjective*.

Australian *noun* (*plural* **Australians**) a person from Australia. ➤ **Australian** *adjective*.

Austrian *noun* (*plural* **Austrians**) a person from Austria. ➤ **Austrian** *adjective*.

Azerbaijani /a zer bie jah nee/ *noun* (*plural* **Azerbaijanis**) **1** a person from Azerbaijan. **2** (*also* **Azeri** /a zair i/) the language spoken by the people of Azerbaijan. ➤ **Azerbaijani** *adjective*, **Azeri** *adjective*.

Bahamian /ba hay mi an/ *noun* (*plural* **Bahamians**) a person from the Bahamas. ➤ **Bahamian** *adjective*.

Bahraini /bah ray ni/ *noun* (*plural* **Bahrainis**) a person from Bahrain. ➤ **Bahraini** *adjective*.

Bangladeshi *noun* (*plural* **Bangladeshis**) a person from Bangladesh. ➤ **Bangladeshi** *adjective*.

Barbadian *noun* (*plural* **Barbadians**) a person from Barbados. ➤ **Barbadian** *adjective*.

Belizian /be lee zi an/ *noun* (*plural* **Belizians**) a person from Belize. ➤ **Belizian** *adjective*.

Belorussian *noun* (*plural* **Belorussians**) **1** a person from Belarus. **2** the language spoken by the people of Belarus. ➤ **Belorussian** *adjective*.

Beninese *noun* (*plural* **Beninese**) a person from Benin. ➤ **Beninese** *adjective*.

Bermudan *noun* (*plural* **Bermudans**) a person from Bermuda. ➤ **Bermudan** *adjective*.

Bhutanese /booh ta neez/ *noun* (*plural* **Bhutanese**) a person from Bhutan. ➤ **Bhutanese** *adjective*.

Bolivian *noun* (*plural* **Bolivians**) a person from Bolivia. ➤ **Bolivian** *adjective*.

Bosnian *noun* (*plural* **Bosnians**) a person from Bosnia (or Bosnia-Herzegovina). ➤ **Bosnian** *adjective*.

Botswanan *noun* (*plural* **Botswanans**) a person from Botswana. ➤ **Botswanan** *adjective*.

Brazilian *noun* (*plural* **Brazilians**) a person from Brazil. ➤ **Brazilian** *adjective*.

British *plural noun* (**the British**) the people of Great Britain. ➤ **British** *adjective*.

Nationalities and Languages

Briton *noun* (*plural* **Britons**) a person from Great Britain.

Bulgarian *noun* (*plural* **Bulgarians**) **1** a person from Bulgaria. **2** the language spoken by the people of Bulgaria. ➤ **Bulgarian** *adjective*.

Burkinan /ber kee nan/ *noun* (*plural* **Burkinans**) a person from Burkina Faso. ➤ **Burkinan** *adjective*.

Burmese *noun* (*plural* **Burmese**) **1** a person from Burma, which is also known as Myanmar. **2** the language spoken by the people of Burma. ➤ **Burmese** *adjective*.

Burundian /boo roon di an/ *noun* (*plural* **Burundians**) a person from Burundi. ➤ **Burundian** *adjective*.

Cambodian *noun* (*plural* **Cambodians**) **1** a person from Cambodia. **2** the language spoken by the people of Cambodia, also known as Khmer. ➤ **Cambodian** *adjective*.

Cameroonian *noun* (*plural* **Cameroonians**) a person from Cameroon. ➤ **Cameroonian** *adjective*.

Canadian *noun* (*plural* **Canadians**) a person from Canada. ➤ **Canadian** *adjective*.

Cape Verdean /kayp ver di an/ *noun* (*plural* **Cape Verdeans**) a person from Cape Verde. ➤ **Cape Verdean** *adjective*.

Chadian *noun* (*plural* **Chadians**) a person from Chad. ➤ **Chadian** *adjective*.

Chilean *noun* (*plural* **Chileans**) a person from Chile. ➤ **Chilean** *adjective*.

Chinese *noun* (*plural* **Chinese**) **1** a person from China. **2** the language or languages spoken in China. ➤ **Chinese** *adjective*.

Colombian *noun* (*plural* **Colombians**) a person from Colombia. ➤ **Colombian** *adjective*.

Comorian /ko maw ri an/ or **Comoran** /ko maw ran/ *noun* (*plural* **Comorians** or **Comorans**) a person from the Comoros. ➤ **Comorian** or **Comoran** *adjective*.

Congolese *noun* (*plural* **Congolese**) **1** a person from the Democratic Republic of the Congo. **2** a person from the Republic of the Congo. ➤ **Congolese** *adjective*.

Costa Rican *noun* (*plural* **Costa Ricans**) a person from Costa Rica. ➤ **Costa Rican** *adjective*.

Côte d'Ivoirean /koht di vwah ri an/ *noun* (*plural* **Côte d'Ivoireans**) a person from Côte d'Ivoire, the country that used to be known as the Ivory Coast. ➤ **Côte d'Ivoirean** *adjective*.

Croatian *noun* (*plural* **Croatians**) **1** a person from Croatia. **2** the language spoken by the people of Croatia. ➤ **Croatian** *adjective*.

Cuban *noun* (*plural* **Cubans**) a person from Cuba. ➤ **Cuban** *adjective*.

Cypriot /si pri ot/ *noun* (plural **Cypriots**) **1** a person from Cyprus. **2** the form of Greek spoken by the people of Cyprus. ➤ **Cypriot** *adjective*.

Czech /chek/ *noun* (*plural* **Czechs**) **1** a person from the Czech Republic. **2** the language spoken by the Czechs. ➤ **Czech** *adjective*.

Dane *noun* (*plural* **Danes**) a person from Denmark. ➤ **Danish** *adjective*.

Djiboutian /ji booh ti an/ *noun* (*plural* **Djiboutians**) a person from Djibouti. ➤ **Djiboutian** *adjective*.

Dominican *noun* (*plural* **Dominicans**) **1** /do mi nee kan/ a person from Dominica. **2** /do mi ni kan/ a person from the Dominican Republic. ➤ **Dominican** *adjective*.

Dutch *noun* **1** (**the Dutch**) the people of the Netherlands. **2** the language spoken by the people of the Netherlands. ➤ **Dutch** *adjective*; **Dutchman** *noun*, **Dutchwoman** *noun*.

East Timorese noun (plural **East Timorese**) a person from East Timor. ➤ **East Timorese** adjective.

Ecuadorian noun (plural **Ecuadorians**) a person from Ecuador. ➤ **Ecuadorian** adjective.

Egyptian noun (plural **Egyptians**) a person from Egypt. ➤ **Egyptian** adjective.

English noun **1** (**the English**) the people of England. **2** the language spoken by the people of Great Britain, the United States, Australia, New Zealand, and most of Canada, and spoken in many other countries. ➤ **English** adjective, **Englishman** noun, **Englishwoman** noun.

Equatorial Guinean noun (plural **Equatorial Guineans**) a person from Equatorial Guinea. ➤ **Equatorial Guinean** adjective.

Eritrean /e ri tray an/ noun (plural **Eritreans**) a person from Eritrea. ➤ **Eritrean** adjective.

Estonian noun (plural **Estonians**) a person from Estonia. **2** the language spoken by the people of Estonia. ➤ **Estonian** adjective.

Ethiopian noun (plural **Ethiopians**) a person from Ethiopia. ➤ **Ethiopian** adjective.

Fijian noun (plural **Fijians**) **1** a person from Fiji. **2** the language spoken by the people of Fiji. ➤ **Fijian** adjective.

Filipino /fi li pee noh/ or **Filipina** noun (plural **Filipinos** or **Filipinas**) a man (or woman) from the Philippines. ➤ **Filipino** adjective.

Finn noun (plural **Finns**) a person from Finland. ➤ **Finnish** adjective.

French noun **1** (**the French**) the people of France. **2** the language spoken in France and parts of Belgium, Switzerland, Canada, and Africa. ➤ **French** adjective, **Frenchman** noun, **Frenchwoman** noun.

Gabonese noun (plural **Gabonese**) a person from Gabon. ➤ **Gabonese** adjective.

Gambian noun (plural **Gambians**) a person from the Gambia. ➤ **Gambian** adjective.

Georgian noun (plural **Georgians**) **1** a person from the country of Georgia. **2** the language spoken by the people of Georgia. **3** a person from the state of Georgia in the USA. ➤ **Georgian** adjective.

German noun (plural **Germans**) **1** a person from Germany. **2** the language spoken in Germany, Austria, and parts of Switzerland. ➤ **German** adjective.

Ghanaian /gah nay an/ noun (plural **Ghanaians**) a person from Ghana. ➤ **Ghanaian** adjective.

Greek noun (plural **Greeks**) **1** a person from Greece. **2** the language spoken by the people of Greece. ➤ **Greek** adjective.

Grenadian /gri nay di an/ noun (plural **Grenadians**) a person from Grenada. ➤ **Grenadian** adjective.

Guatemalan /gwah ti mah lan/ (plural **Guatemalans**) a person from Guatemala. ➤ **Guatemalan** adjective.

Guinean noun (plural **Guineans**) a person from Guinea. ➤ **Guinean** adjective.

Guyanan /gie a nan/ noun (plural **Guyanans**) a person from Guyana. ➤ **Guyanan** adjective.

Haitian /hay shn/ noun (plural **Haitians**) a person from Haiti. ➤ **Haitian** adjective.

Honduran noun (plural **Hondurans**) a person from Honduras. ➤ **Honduran** adjective.

Hungarian noun (plural **Hungarians**) **1** a person from Hungary. **2** the language spoken by the people of Hungary. ➤ **Hungarian** *adjective*.

Icelander *noun* (*plural* **Icelanders**) a person from Iceland. ➤ **Icelandic** *adjective*.

Indian *noun* (*plural* **Indians**) a person from India. ➤ **Indian** *adjective*.

Indonesian *noun* (*plural* **Indonesians**) a person from Indonesia. ➤ **Indonesian** *adjective*.

Iranian *noun* (*plural* **Iranians**) 1 a person from Iran. 2 the language spoken by the people of Iran. ➤ **Iranian** *adjective*.

Iraqi *noun* (*plural* **Iraqis**) a person from Iraq. ➤ **Iraqi** *adjective*.

Irish *noun* 1 (**the Irish**) the people of Ireland. 2 the Celtic language spoken in Ireland. ➤ **Irish** *adjective*, **Irishman** *noun*, **Irishwoman** *noun*.

Israeli /iz ray li/ *noun* (*plural* **Israelis**) a person from Israel. ➤ **Israeli** *adjective*.

Italian *noun* (*plural* **Italians**) 1 a person from Italy. 2 the language spoken by the people of Italy. ➤ **Italian** *adjective*.

Jamaican *noun* (*plural* **Jamaicans**) a person from Jamaica. ➤ **Jamaican** *adjective*.

Japanese *noun* (*plural* **Japanese**) 1 a person from Japan. 2 the language spoken by the people of Japan. ➤ **Japanese** *adjective*.

Jordanian *noun* (*plural* **Jordanians**) a person from Jordan. ➤ **Jordanian** *adjective*.

Kazakh /ka zak *or* ka zak/ *noun* (*plural* **Kazakhs**) 1 a person from Kazakhstan. 2 the language spoken by the people of Kazakhstan. ➤ **Kazakh** *adjective*.

Kenyan *noun* (*plural* **Kenyans**) a person from Kenya. ➤ **Kenyan** *adjective*.

Kiribatian /ki ri ba ti an/ *noun* (*plural* **Kiribatians**) a person from Kiribati. ➤ **Kiribatian** *adjective*.

Kuwaiti *noun* (*plural* **Kuwaitis**) a person from Kuwait. ➤ **Kuwaiti** *adjective*.

Kyrgyz /keer giz/ (*plural* **Kyrghiz**) 1 a person from Kyrgyzstan. 2 the language spoken by the Kyrghiz. ➤ **Kyrgyz** *adjective*.

Laotian /low shn/ *noun* (*plural* **Laotians**) 1 a person from Laos. 2 the language spoken by the people of Laos. ➤ **Laotian** *adjective*.

Latvian *noun* (*plural* **Latvians**) 1 a person from Latvia. 2 the language spoken by the people of Latvia. ➤ **Latvian** *adjective*.

Lebanese *noun* (*plural* **Lebanese**) a person from the Lebanon. ➤ **Lebanese** *adjective*.

Liberian *noun* (*plural* **Liberians**) a person from Liberia. ➤ **Liberian** *adjective*.

Libyan *noun* (*plural* **Libyans**) a person from Libya. ➤ **Libyan** *adjective*.

Liechtensteiner /lik tin stie ner/ *noun* (*plural* **Liechtensteiners**) a person from Liechtenstein.

Lithuanian *noun* (*plural* **Lithuanians**) 1 a person from Lithuania. 2 the language spoken by the people of Lithuania. ➤ **Lithuanian** *adjective*.

Luxembourger *noun* (*plural* **Luxembourgers**) a person from Luxembourg.

Macedonian *noun* (*plural* **Macedonians**) 1 a person from Macedonia. 2 the language spoken by the people of Macedonia. ➤ **Macedonian** *adjective*.

Malagasy /ma la ga si/ *noun* (*plural* **Malagasy** *or* **Malagasies**) 1 a person from Madagascar. 2 the language spoken by the people of Madagascar. ➤ **Malagasy** *adjective*.

Nationalities and Languages

Malawian *noun* (*plural* **Malawians**) a person from Malawi. ➤ **Malawian** *adjective*.

Malaysian *noun* (*plural* **Malaysians**) a person from Malaysia. ➤ **Malaysian** *adjective*.

Maldivian /mawl di vi an/ *noun* (*plural* **Maldivians**) a person from the Maldives. ➤ **Maldivian** *adjective*.

Malian *noun* (*plural* **Malians**) a person from Mali. ➤ **Malian** *adjective*.

Maltese *noun* (*plural* **Maltese**) **1** a person from Malta. **2** the language spoken by the people of Malta. ➤ **Maltese** *adjective*.

Mauritanian *noun* (*plural* **Mauritanians**) a person from Mauritania. ➤ **Mauritanian** *adjective*.

Mauritian *noun* (*plural* **Mauritians**) a person from Mauritius. ➤ **Mauritian** *adjective*.

Mexican *noun* (*plural* **Mexicans**) a person from Mexico. ➤ **Mexican** *adjective*.

Moldovan /mol do van/ *noun* (*plural* **Moldovans**) a person from Moldova. ➤ **Moldovan** *adjective*.

Monegasque /mo nay gask/ *noun* (*plural* **Monegasques**) a person from Monaco. ➤ **Monegasque** *adjective*.

Mongolian *noun* (*plural* **Mongolians**) **1** a person from Mongolia. **2** the language spoken by the people of Mongolia. ➤ **Mongolian** *adjective*.

Montenegrin *noun* (*plural* **Montenegrins**) a person from Montenegro. ➤ **Montenegrin** *adjective*.

Moroccan *noun* (*plural* **Moroccans**) a person from Morocco. ➤ **Moroccan** *adjective*.

Mozambican *noun* (*plural* **Mozambicans**) a person from Mozambique. ➤ **Mozambican** *adjective*.

Namibian *noun* (*plural* **Namibians**) a person from Namibia. ➤ **Namibian** *adjective*.

Nauruan /now rooh an/ *noun* (*plural* **Nauruans**) a person from Nauru. ➤ **Nauruan** *adjective*.

Nepalese *noun* (*plural* **Nepalese**) a person from Nepal. ➤ **Nepalese** *adjective*.

Nepali /ni paw li/ *noun* (*plural* **Nepali** or **Nepalis**) **1** a person from Nepal. **2** the language spoken by the people of Nepal. ➤ **Nepali** *adjective*.

New Zealander *noun* (*plural* **New Zealanders**) a person from New Zealand.

Nicaraguan *noun* (*plural* **Nicaraguans**) a person from Nicaragua. ➤ **Nicaraguan** *adjective*.

Nigerian /nie jeer i an/ *noun* (*plural* **Nigerians**) a person from Nigeria. ➤ **Nigerian** *adjective*.

Nigerien /nee zhair i an/ *noun* (*plural* **Nigeriens**) a person from Niger. ➤ **Nigerien** *adjective*.

North Korean *noun* (*plural* **North Koreans**) a person from North Korea. ➤ **North Korean** *adjective*.

Norwegian *noun* (*plural* **Norwegians**) **1** a person from Norway. **2** the language spoken by the people of Norway. ➤ **Norwegian** *adjective*.

Omani /oh mah ni/ *noun* (*plural* **Omanis**) a person from Oman. ➤ **Omani** *adjective*.

Pakistani *noun* (*plural* **Pakistanis**) a person from Pakistan. ➤ **Pakistani** *adjective*.

Palestinian *noun* (*plural* **Palestinians**) a person from the region of Palestine in the Middle East, especially from the Palestinian Administered Territories bordering the state of Israel. ➤ **Palestinian** *adjective*.

Panamanian *noun* (*plural* **Panamanians**) a person from Panama. ➤ **Panamanian** *adjective*.

Paraguayan /pa ra gwie an/ *noun* (*plural*

Paraguayans) a person from Paraguay. ➤ **Paraguayan** *adjective*.

Peruvian *noun* (*plural* **Peruvians**) a person from Peru. ➤ **Peruvian** *adjective*.

Pole *noun* (*plural* **Poles**) a person from Poland. ➤ **Polish** *adjective*.

Portuguese *adjective* (*plural* **Portuguese**) 1 a person from Portugal. 2 the language spoken in Portugal and Brazil. ➤ **Portuguese** *adjective*.

Puerto Rican *noun* (*plural* **Puerto Ricans**) a person from Puerto Rico. ➤ **Puerto Rican** *adjective*.

Qatari /ka tah ri/ *noun* (*plural* **Qataris**) a person from Qatar. ➤ **Qatari** *adjective*.

Romanian *noun* (*plural* **Romanians**) 1 a person from Romania. 2 the language spoken by the people of Romania. ➤ **Romanian** *adjective*.

Russian *noun* (*plural* **Russians**) 1 a person from Russia. 2 the language spoken by the people of Russia. ➤ **Russian** *adjective*.

Rwandan *noun* (*plural* **Rwandans**) a person from Rwanda. ➤ **Rwandan** *adjective*.

Salvadorean *noun* (*plural* **Salvadoreans**) a person from El Salvador. ➤ **Salvadorean** *adjective*.

Samoan *noun* (*plural* **Samoans**) 1 a person from Samoa. 2 the language spoken by the people of Samoa. ➤ **Samoan** *adjective*.

Saudi Arabian or **Saudi** *noun* (*plural* **Saudi Arabians** or **Saudis**) a person from Saudi Arabia. ➤ **Saudi Arabian** or **Saudi** *adjective*.

Scot *noun* (*plural* **Scots**) a person from Scotland. ➤ **Scots** *adjective*, **Scottish** *adjective*, **Scotsman** *noun*, **Scotswoman** *noun*.

Senegalese *noun* (*plural* **Senegalese**) a person from Senegal. ➤ **Senegalese** *adjective*.

Serb or **Serbian** *noun* (*plural* **Serbs** or **Serbians**) 1 a person from Serbia. 2 (**Serbian**) the language spoken by the people of Serbia. ➤ **Serb** or **Serbian** *adjective*.

Seychellois /say shel wah/ *noun* (*plural* **Seychellois** /say shel wah/) a person from the Seychelles. ➤ **Seychellois** *adjective*.

Sierra Leonean /see e ra lee oh ni an/ *noun* (*plural* **Sierra Leoneans**) a person from Sierra Leone. ➤ **Sierra Leonean** *adjective*.

Singaporean *noun* (*plural* **Singaporeans**) a person from Singapore. ➤ **Singaporean** *adjective*.

Slovak /sloh vak/ *noun* (*plural* **Slovaks**) 1 a person from Slovakia. 2 the language spoken by the people of Slovakia. ➤ **Slovak** *adjective*, **Slovakian** *adjective*.

Slovene /sloh veen/ or **Slovenian** *noun* (*plural* **Slovenes** or **Slovenians**) 1 a person from Slovenia. 2 the language spoken by the people of Slovenia. ➤ **Slovene** or **Slovenian** *adjective*.

Somali *noun* (*plural* **Somali** or **Somalis**) a person from Somalia. ➤ **Somali** *adjective*.

South African *noun* (*plural* **South Africans**) a person from South Africa. ➤ **South African** *adjective*.

South Korean *noun* (*plural* **South Koreans**) a person from South Korea. ➤ **South Korean** *adjective*.

Spaniard *noun* (*plural* **Spaniards**) a person from Spain.

Spanish *noun* 1 (**the Spanish**) the people of Spain. 2 the chief language of Spain and many Central and South American countries. ➤ **Spanish** *adjective*.

Sri Lankan *noun* (*plural* **Sri Lankans**) a person from Sri Lanka. ➤ **Sri Lankan** *adjective*.

Sudanese noun (plural **Sudanese**) a person from Sudan. ➤ **Sudanese** adjective.

Surinamese noun (plural **Surinamese**) a person from Suriname. ➤ **Surinamese** adjective.

Swede noun (plural **Swedes**) a person from Sweden. ➤ **Swedish** adjective.

Swiss noun (plural **Swiss**) a person from Switzerland. ➤ **Swiss** adjective.

Syrian noun (plural **Syrians**) a person from Syria. ➤ **Syrian** adjective.

Taiwanese noun (plural **Taiwanese**) a person from Taiwan. ➤ **Taiwanese** adjective.

Tajik /tah jeek/ noun (plural **Tajiks**) **1** a person from Tajikistan. **2** the language spoken by the Tajiks. ➤ **Tajik** adjective.

Tanzanian noun (plural **Tanzanians**) a person from Tanzania. ➤ **Tanzanian** adjective.

Thai /tie/ noun (plural **Thai** or **Thais**) **1** a person from Thailand. **2** the language spoken by the people of Thailand. ➤ **Thai** adjective.

Tibetan noun (plural **Tibetans**) **1** a person from Tibet. **2** the language spoken by the people of Tibet. ➤ **Tibetan** adjective.

Tobagan /toh bay gan/ noun (plural **Tobagans**) a person from Tobago, in Trinidad and Tobago. ➤ **Tobagan** adjective.

Togolese noun (plural **Togolese**) a person from Togo. ➤ **Togolese** adjective.

Tongan noun (plural **Tongans**) **1** a person from Tonga. **2** the language spoken by the people of Tonga. ➤ **Tongan** adjective.

Trinidadian /tri ni day di an/ noun (plural **Trinidadians**) a person from Trinidad, in Trinidad and Tobago. ➤ **Trinidadian** adjective.

Tunisian noun (plural **Tunisians**) a person from Tunisia. ➤ **Tunisian** adjective.

Turk noun (plural **Turks**) a person from Turkey. ➤ **Turkish** adjective.

Turkmen noun (plural **Turkmens** or **Turkmen**) **1** a person from Turkmenistan. **2** the language spoken by the Turkmens. ➤ **Turkmen** adjective.

Tuvaluan /tooh va looh an/ noun (plural **Tuvaluans**) **1** a person from Tuvalu. **2** the language spoken by the people of Tuvalu. ➤ **Tuvaluan** adjective.

Ugandan noun (plural **Ugandans**) a person from Uganda. ➤ **Ugandan** adjective.

Ukrainian noun (plural **Ukrainians**) **1** a person from Ukraine. **2** the language spoken by the people of Ukraine. ➤ **Ukrainian** adjective.

Uruguayan /ew ru gwie an/ noun (plural **Uruguayans**) a person from Uruguay. ➤ **Uruguayan** adjective.

Uzbek /ooz bek/ noun (plural **Uzbeks**) **1** a person from Uzbekistan. **2** the language spoken by the people of Uzbekistan. ➤ **Uzbek** adjective.

Vanuatuan /va nooh ah tooh an/ noun (plural **Vanuatuans**) a person from Vanuatu. ➤ **Vanuatuan** adjective.

Venezuelan /ve ni zway lan/ noun (plural **Venezuelans**) a person from Venezuela. ➤ **Venezuelan** adjective.

Vietnamese noun (plural **Vietnamese**) **1** a person from Vietnam. **2** the language spoken by the people of Vietnam. ➤ **Vietnamese** adjective.

Welsh noun **1** (**the Welsh**) the people of Wales. **2** the Celtic language spoken in Wales. ➤ **Welsh** adjective, **Welshman** noun, **Welshwoman** noun.

Yemeni noun (plural **Yemenis**) a

person from Yemen. ➤ **Yemeni** *adjective*.

Zambian *noun* (*plural* **Zambians**) a person from Zambia. ➤ **Zambian** *adjective*.

Zimbabwean *noun* (*plural* **Zimbabweans**) a person from Zimbabwe. ➤ **Zimbabwean** *adjective*.